DESIGNING
and
DRAWING
for the
THEATRE

Model by David Mitchell
THE SLEEPING BEAUTY
Music by Peter Ilyich Tchaikovsky

Choreographed by Peter Martins
New York City Ballet
New York State Theatre, New York (1991)

LYNN PECKTAL

DESIGNING

and

DRAWING

for the

THEATRE

McGraw-Hill, Inc.
New York   St. Louis   San Francisco
Auckland   Bogotá   Caracas   Lisbon   London
Madrid   Mexico City   Milan   Montreal
New Delhi   San Juan   Singapore
Sydney   Tokyo   Toronto

ABOUT THE AUTHOR

A native of Kingsport, Tennessee, Lynn Pecktal began designing professionally at Robert Porterfield's Barter Theatre of Virginia while attending Emory and Henry College. He then studied scenic design with Donald Oenslager and costumes with Frank Poole Bevan at the Yale Drama School. His early experience included stints as assistant designer to both Jo Mielziner and Eugene Berman.

Mr. Pecktal is the author of two acclaimed books, *Designing and Painting for the Theatre* (Harcourt Brace Jovanovich) and *Costume Design, Techniques of Modern Masters* (Back Stage Books, Watson-Guptill, 1993). *Designing and Painting* became an instant success when it was first published by Holt, Rinehart and Winston in 1975, and has been in print without a break since that time. On its publication Oliver Smith made the following comment in *Theatre Crafts* magazine: "The best contemporary book on scenic design and scenic execution: fascinating, tremendously informative, and indispensable."

Costume Design won USITT's 1994 Golden Pen Award. The award is given by the United States Institute for Theatre Technology for an outstanding book which makes a significant contribution to the body of literature in the performing arts. The award is granted only when a work is deemed to be significant. One of the reviewers wrote that *Costume Design, Techniques of Modern Masters* "surpasses any other treatment of costume design. It is partic-ularly important for its excellent illustrations which are in very well done color." Another praised the author's "remarkable ability to capture the 'voice' of each designer fully illuminating the creative force of each." Mel Gussow of The New York Times gave *Costume Design* a glowing review on WQXR Radio.

He has designed the settings for over 125 legitimate stage productions, including *Don Pasquale* and *Naughty Marietta* for the Cleveland Opera Company, and *The Music Man* at the outdoor Jones Beach Theatre on Long Island, and his costume designs were featured in the world premiere of Tennessee Williams' *Tiger Tail* at the Alliance Theatre in Atlanta.

Mr. Pecktal won a Maharam Award in 1977 for supervising Edward Gorey's scenery for *Dracula* on Broadway, an assignment he repeated in London's West End, in Australia, and for the show's three national touring companies. His other Broadway credits are Paul Giovanni's *The Crucifer of Blood* (which he also did in London and Los Angeles); the Negro Ensemble Company's production of *Home*; John Guare's *Bosoms and Neglect*; *Harold and Maude*; Edward Gorey's *Gorey Stories*; and Howard Sackler's *Semmelweiss* at the Kennedy Center. In addition, he has supervised Robert Wilson's scenery for Heiner Muller's *Hamletmachine* at New York University.

Mr. Pecktal has taught thesis and advanced scenic design at Carnegie-Mellon University and has lectured at theatre conferences and universities around the country.

Designing and Drawing for the Theatre

This book is printed on acid-free paper.

91011 QPK QPK 05432

ISBN 0-07-557232-X

This book was set in Melior by CRWaldman Graphic Communications.
The editors were Judith R. Cornwell and John M. Morriss;
the designer was Karen K. Quigley;
the production supervisor was Friederich W. Schulte.
Project supervision was done by The Total Book.
Arcata Graphics/Kingsport was printer and binder.

Cover
Stage design by Eugene Berman
COSI FAN TUTTE by Wolfgang Amadeus Mozart
Piccola Scala, Milan, Italy
Sketch (1955), premiere (1956)
(Collection of Lynn Pecktal)

Library of Congress Cataloging-in-Publication Data

Pecktal, Lynn.
    Designing and drawing for the theatre / Lynn Pecktal.
        p.   cm.
    Includes index.
    ISBN 0-07-557232-X
    1. Theaters—Stage—setting and scenery.   I. Title.
PN2091.S8P36   1995
792'.025—dc20   94-21038

To
Betty McAlpine
with much love and affection

CONTENTS

INTRODUCTION

I began writing and compiling *Designing and Drawing for the Theatre* over a dozen years ago while teaching design at Carnegie-Mellon University in Pittsburgh. I wanted to do a new book that would present works and approaches of contemporary stage designers, as well as emphasize this period's design processes.

Along with current designers, the book contains designs of some of the twentieth century's best-known earlier artists. Among them are Jo Mielziner, Boris Aronson, Donald Oenslager, Ben Edwards, Oliver Smith, William and Jean Eckart, Robert O'Hearn, Lester Polakov, Rouben Ter-Arutunian, Alvin Colt, Miles White, Raoul Pène du Bois, Pavel Tchelitchew, Motley, James Stewart Morcom, Peter Larkin, Eldon Elder, Eugene Berman, and Oliver Messel. It is a treat to have stage designs of artist and illustrator Edward Gorey.

Stage designers use their talents in many places. Not only do they design for Broadway plays and musicals, but also for ballets, operas, television, films, clubs, commercials, rock groups, pageants, fashion shows, exhibits, industrials, theme parks, circuses, dance theatres, and revues. They design for regional theatres and teach scenic, costume, and lighting design in universities and colleges around the country. They participate in theatre seminars and give lectures.

There are numerous gifted designers and artists creating highly original and spectacular designs in the spoken theatre today. I list their names and productions throughout the book in the captions, contents, acknowledgments, and indexes. Directors, choreographers, and other collaborators are credited as well.

I feel it most important to devote a great portion of this volume to a selection of practical drawings with dimensions. These many detailed drawings are arranged in groups for comparative viewing, and consist of all sorts of scenery, dressing, props, and furniture. A basic sampling of subjects includes wainscoting, drapery, foliage, chandeliers, headers, ground rows, balusters, cut drops, fences, doors, gates, windows, chairs, tables, beds, railings, folding screens, grillwork, and so on. I have made these drawings, positioned them on the pages, and placed them in various parts of the book. They may be used for reference when doing scenic designs, show models, research on specific items, or for building full scale objects to go on stage. Sometimes looking at a layout of several drawings on one page provides inspiration for what is needed to spark your own imagination and to make you create original designs that are exciting and appropriate.

The drawings with dimensions work beautifully in drawing and painting classes when the idea is to go from using the small-scale drawings in the book to making full-scale drawings for scenic pieces and props. Assignments for projects are usually twofold: for doing drawing only or for doing both drawing and painting. For example, you might want to draw a panel of wainscoting in full scale at one time, then paint it at a later date.

Your enlarged drawings will be made on brown paper with charcoal sticks or pencils when doing drawing only, or when making perforated pounces for repeats. Full-scale drawings to be painted are put on stretched muslin, canvas, or other materials, and you may or may not ink the drawing before painting, depending on the effect desired. Even drawing the details on the surface of an already built scenic piece or prop may be part of the assignment.

The subject normally dictates what the appropriate painting technique will be. For instance, on a panel of wainscoting you would paint with the controlled technique of light, shade, and shadow. For foliage you might concentrate on just painting areas of loose textures and patterns. Other techniques may be used for drapery, chandeliers, and furniture.

Overall the book has more than 4600 illustrations. Besides the drawings already mentioned, you will find drafting for shows with many drawings of ground plans, front and side elevations, top views, section drawings, and drawings of details. In addition, the book contains perspective sketches, schematic drawings, computer drawings, prop drawings, drawings of house curtains and auditorium draperies, drawings of geometric shapes and solids, archive drawings, an assembly drawing, a cutaway drawing, and more. I have drawn model furniture in ½-inch scale that may be copied, then cut out and glued together. This is a good exercise in making model furniture.

There are a great many photographs documenting designs in black and white, and in color. A basic list reveals there are pictures of 164 models, 240 scenic designs, 38 costume sketches, 14 costume composite layouts numbering over 184 sketches, and 129 production photographs. Other photographs show scenery and props in the process of execution, as well as pictures of finished designs.

Conversations with designers have become a tradition in my books, since the first one with Jo Mielziner in 1975. I am delighted to present conversations with twelve contemporary designers in this volume. These chats start with Tony Walton and end with John Napier. I hope *Designing and Drawing for the Theatre* will provide the same inspiration and interest to today's readers as *Designing and Painting for the Theatre* did twenty years ago.

ACKNOWLEDGMENTS

Many designers, artists, and other theatrical collaborators have been extremely helpful during the writing of *Designing and Drawing for the Theatre*. They have provided wonderful set and costume designs, models, drawings, photographs, conversations, information, and quotes.

I would like to sincerely thank the following individuals, both past and present, for their work and generous participation: Arnold Abramson, Dale Amlund, Loy Arcenas, John Arnone, Boris Aronson, Lisa Aronson, Randy Barcelo, Gregg Barnes, Nadine Baylis, John Lee Beatty, Eugene Berman, Rolf Beyer, Carlo Galli Bibiena, Maria Björnson, Mariuca Brancoveanu, Zack Brown, Patton Campbell, Robert Chase, Felix E. Cochren, Franco Colavecchia, Alvin Colt, John Conklin, Virginia Dancy, Lindsay W. Davis, Raoul Pène du Bois, Clarke Dunham, Marsha Louis Eck, William and Jean Eckart, Ben Edwards, Karl Eigsti, Eldon Elder, John Falabella, Kenneth Foy, Esteban Francés, Ralph Funicello, Chuck Giles, Edward Gorey, Peter Gould, David Gropman, Peter Harvey, Desmond Heeley, Robert Hungerford, George Izenour, Andrew Jackness, Fred Jacoby, Neil Peter Jampolis, David Jenkins, Rik Kaye, John Keck, Marjorie Bradley Kellogg, Willa Kim, Ray Klausen, Allen Charles Klein, Larry Klein, Heidi Landesman, Hugh Landwehr, Peter Larkin, Ming Cho Lee, Adrianne Lobel, William Ivey Long, Santo Loquasto, Thomas Lynch, Andrew B. Marlay, Charles E. McCarry, Bill Mensching, Oliver Messel, Leo Meyer, Jo Mielziner, David Mitchell, Robert D. Mitchell, James Stewart Morcom, Roger Morgan, Motley, Robert Motley, John Napier, Donald Oenslager, Robert O'Hearn, Stephan Olson, Atkin Pace, Robert Perdziola, David Peterson, Lester Polakov, Jean-Pierre Ponnelle, Leigh Rand, Carrie Robbins, Julia Rogoff, Philip Rosenberg, Pier Luigi Samaritani, Thomas Peter Sarr, John Scheffler, Karen Schulz, Douglas W. Schmidt, Maurice Sendak, Loren Sherman, Eduardo Sicangco, Oliver Smith, Douglas Stein, Tony Straiges, Pavel Tchelitchew, Rouben Ter-Arutunian, George Tsypin, Robert Van Nutt, José Varona, Robin Wagner, Tony Walton, Elmon Webb, Nancy Winters, Miles White, Robert Wilson, John Wulp, Franco Zeffirelli, Darrell Ziegler, and Patricia Zipprodt.

Special appreciation goes to these individuals and organizations for their assistance and support: Lincoln Center Library staff, Mrs. Donald M. Oenslager, Pam Jordan and the Yale Drama School Library, Rita Pew and Brian Pew, Stephanie Wiles and the Pierpont Morgan Library, Arthur and Rozanne Seelen of the Drama Book Shop, Paul Stiga, Joseph Campanella, Hartford Stage Company, Arena Stage, Charlene Loo and Ever Ready Blue Print, HarperCollins, Radio City Music Hall, Metropolitan Opera, New York City Opera, Rose Brand, Rosco Laboratories, Gerriets International, Gilshire Corporation, Roth Wilkofsky, Christopher Rogers, Peter Labella, Neils Aaboe, Mel Haber, Nancy Blaine, Jim Ryan, Elbert Kuhn, and all the publications and photographers credited in the book.

I am indebted to Karen Quigley, designer, for her lovely work, and especially for the beautiful cover of the book.

Many thanks to Fred Schulte, production supervisor, for doing an excellent job throughout on an extremely detailed volume with countless illustrations. I am very pleased with his direction.

Annette Bodzin, project supervisor, has been with the book since it went into production at McGraw-Hill. I have enormous admiration for her perseverance and patience, and I am most appreciative of her talents. Authors are fortunate to have her work on their books.

It has been a great pleasure to work with Judy Cornwell, my sponsoring editor and an old friend from years back. I thank her kindly for her always consistent good work and loyal support. I am most grateful for all.

Lynn Pecktal
New York City

1

THE STAGE DESIGNER
AND DESIGNING

BECOMING A
STAGE DESIGNER

More than anything else, it is probably the excitement of the world of the legitimate theatre that attracts the sensitive artists to become a part of it. In the live theatre original designs can be realized, fame and fortune can be attained by the lucky few, and awesome projects take you to spectacular locales. A stage designer experiences interesting challenges with collaborators old and new, and goes on to the next project with renewed pride, commitment, and enthusiasm.

Talks with a great many successful designers in the commercial theatre have revealed motivating influences that range from ordinary events in their lives to life changing artistic experiences. Some designers exhibited a talent for drawing at a very early age. Others became interested in the spoken theatre as a result of seeing professional productions while they were in grammar school, high school, or even college. A few designers became intrigued early on with the idea of being involved in operas, magic shows, circuses, or church pageants. Still others, after seeing live theatre, began to instinctively create their own puppet and marionette shows.

Whatever the experience, the stage designers discovered that the theatre was most appealing. They found that

Paint elevation by Tony Walton for the show portal and show scrim, THE WILL ROGERS FOLLIES, Palace Theatre, New York (1991).

they really liked the work and the process of production, the collaboration with other creative people, the attention and the applause. They also realized that it might just be possible to make a living doing what they enjoyed most.

Designing for the theatre holds other, less obvious satisfactions. It requires an enormous scope of knowledge. Scenic designers need to know about art and architecture, drawing and painting, upholstery and drapery, lighting and costumes, colors and textures, shapes and proportions, people and places, events and history. Every new production offers a chance to expand your skills and knowledge.

The scenic designer is expected to create work that is always fascinating, appropriate, and/or beautiful. To do this the designer draws upon his or her own store of practical knowledge, aesthetic sense, intellect, intuition, and natural talent.

But in addition to possessing enormous artistic talent, a designer is expected to work quickly, to be on time, to make pleasant appearances, and to be a diplomat when necessary. For example, when a producer calls the designer about a problem with the scenery or with a current running production, the producer only wants to hear the designer say, "We'll get on it first thing in the morning, and it will be fixed before the evening performance." The designer must then communicate with the production carpenter, the production stage manager, and the general manager (also, sometimes

the producer) and figure out when and how the problem may be solved.

Wearing all these hats is a tall order. But to a great degree, those who have chosen stage designing as a career quickly discover that when they become involved in the creativity of the theatrical world, it seems a perfectly natural place for them to be.

WHERE TO STUDY

Deciding where to study, whether for graduate or undergraduate school, can be difficult for a talented artist. When looking for a school, inquire where the leading stage designers of today have studied. Which schools have produced the greatest number and best-known working designers in the commercial theatre? Is the same faculty still teaching at those schools? Are you able to get the theatre courses that you want? Is there an opportunity to work with fellow students who are studying directing?

Write or telephone the school of your choice for information and make an appointment for an interview and a portfolio showing of your designs and other work. The main thing to shoot for is acceptance at the school of your choice. Often, this is a matter of having a great portfolio, a serious intent, and excellent references.

Many designers worry about the high cost of tuition once they are accepted by a school, and that is something that must ultimately be dealt with. But the most important issue is

1

Setting by Tony Walton
FOUR BABOONS ADORING THE SUN by
   John Guare
Directed by Peter Hall
Costumes by Willa Kim
Lighting by Richard Pilbrow
Projections by Wendall K. Harrington
Vivian Beaumont Theatre
New York (1992)
Pictured (left to right): Stockard Channing,
   James Naughton, Eugene Perry.

to get enrolled in the school you want. See if a scholarship is available. By all means, be determined and be relentless. Remember, such perseverance is something you will need in your career later on.

STUDYING SPECIFIC SUBJECTS

Because the theatre encompasses a wide variety of subjects, almost every creative topic in the arts is helpful to study. Whether in undergraduate or graduate school, if you feel you need to pursue a particular course, do it. You may be able to take courses as electives, audit a course, or sometimes enroll in courses at a school where you aren't matriculated. The point is to get the vital information and experience that will help you in your career as a professional stage designer. You may want to take courses in fundamentals of design, drawing and composition, painting, sculpture, drafting, art history, architecture, graphics, calligraphy, or ceramics.

It is extremely important to learn to draft as early as possible, because it will enable you to do your own drafting or to assist an established designer. Even if the only available drafting course is a beginning drafting course in high school or college, the instruction can always be useful. In any drafting course you can learn the fundamentals of basic drawing procedures, such as making plans, front elevations, side or end views, top views, sections, and details. Drafting courses that may be available to you include mechanical drawing, engineering drawing, and descriptive geometry.

If you take a drafting course that is not theatre-oriented, do a theatre project on your own. This simply means that you select a show to design and the theatre you would be designing it to go in. Then draw up your own plans to have the scenic production executed. Keep in mind that you are drawing all of the necessary plans, and that from reading your drafting the show will be built and painted by a professional scenic shop and put on the stage. Doing your own project is one of the best ways to learn how to put your thoughts and ideas together and how to present them so your designs will become fully realized.

ORGANIZING THE JOB

A vital part of a designer's training is learning how to organize the job. Without this skill it could be difficult for a designer to accomplish the work with the most impressive performance possible.

The first task is to figure out how much time should be spent on various aspects of the production. Time should be well managed and tasks accomplished in a logical and practical way. How quickly can you come up with original ideas? How long does it take to identify and discard secondary ideas and keep the best ones? How much time do you need to build a model or do the drafting? How much time can you spend in meetings? in traveling? in bookkeeping?

Organizing the job also means learning how to conserve your energy. To get the most creative output from yourself and others, you must approach each project with a completely positive way of thinking and working. Do not spend a great deal of energy on tiny details. Sort out the trivial things, and concentrate on overview and what the end result of the job is to be. Of course, this can be brought about by totally visualizing the job. Be completely positive about the success of the creative work. Do not for one moment waste energy by thinking of failure or any other negative aspect of the situation. It is good to apply this not only to one particular production, but also every job you work on.

STARTING OUT TO DESIGN IN THE THEATRE

Often the novice scenic designer will wonder where to go, what to do, and how to approach the work situation in general. Many theatre design students are not always sure where to turn when they finish their course of study. While teachers and other faculty may offer advice, it can still be difficult to make a final choice because there seems to be so much at stake.

Whether a designer chooses the commercial theatre, resident theatre, or teaching in a university as a career is of course up to the individual. Each offers valuable and unique opportunities to the talented designer. The right choice for one creative artist may be totally inappropriate for another.

From the very start, a novice scenic designer should always be aware of the creative gamble in the theatre. No school and no book can tell a creative designer how to become a success in the theatre. Having talent and creative gifts is wonderful, but what really counts is how one organizes one's talent and markets it in the business of the theatre. Stamina, patience, and the drive to survive creatively and economically must go hand in hand with talent.

How to go about making a living in the theatre is an urgent consideration. A designer does not give talent away any more than a doctor, lawyer, or any other professional offers knowledge and expertise without a fee. You have to learn how to set a reasonable price for your talent but still make a profit in order to be able to continue on to the next production. This comes with a bit of experience, through trial and error, and sometimes from discussions with respected colleagues, but it must be done. In the commercial theatre, a designer must know how to hire assistants and have assistant fees included as part of the producer's expense rather than come out of the designer's fee. It is not unusual to hear that a well-known designer has spent almost all of his or her fee to pay assistants. Even if this occasionally does happen on a large show, a designer cannot repeat this pattern on every production.

The wise designer plans how to meet expenses and to make some profit on a show no matter what fee has been negotiated. Above all, a designer knows that it is not very pleasant to work in the theatre and just barely survive. Stage designers often take work in a related field to maintain a comfortable standard of living.

When a designer signs on for a show, he or she must know how to get through it successfully and go on to get that second and third job. This is perhaps the most challenging aspect of designing in the theatre, opera, or dance. Simply put it means warranting enough attention in the theatrical industry to keep your name and reputation alive. What is so difficult about this is that there is no way to tell whether a show will be a hit or a miss. The critics and the public are the ones who ultimately decide whether or not a show will run.

Students will also ask experienced

Designed by John Napier
CATS—Music by Andrew Lloyd Webber
Based on *Old Possum's Book of Practical Cats* by T. S. Eliot
Lighting by David Hersey
Associate director and choreographer: Gillian Lynne
Directed by Trevor Nunn
Winter Garden Theatre, New York (1982)
(Photograph © Martha Swope)

4

designers if it is a good idea to try to find an agent when they first come to New York. Often, an agent does not always know how to read a designer's portfolio. It must be realized from the start that an agent has to make a living, and is going to take the standard percentage from the designer's fee. This is usually ten percent or it may be slightly higher, depending on the agent and the designer. While an agent can help negotiate a contract, he or she has no more power than some of the more established designers as far as getting work is concerned.

Raoul Pène du Bois strongly advised that a designer is better off having a good lawyer rather than an agent to handle business matters. Good theatrical lawyers know how to negotiate contracts to get reasonable fees and royalties for designers. But keep in mind that above-scale fees most likely are not negotiable until after a designer has achieved some noted success.

WORKING IN THE COMMERCIAL THEATRE VERSUS UNIVERSITY THEATRE

While one creative person enjoys working in the commercial theatre, an-other gifted individual may prefer a career in the university theatre. University theatre is another opportunity to work as a designer, and can offer a lovely opportunity in which to be creative. A combination of teaching and designing in a university atmosphere is an ideal situation for many talented individuals.

What works so well for many artists who work chiefly in the academic world is that rather than working intermittently as a freelance designer they are employed year-round, and they enjoy both teaching and designing in a university environment. A designer in a university can plan a full year knowing what classes in design and any related field he or she might be teaching, as well as what shows he or she may be designing during that particular school year.

There are also opportunities for a designer in a university situation to take the summer off from teaching and travel abroad to study, to design in another theatre, or just to vacation. A steady job teaching and designing in a university, of course, enables a designer to maintain a balance between artistic work and monetary compensation. This does not exist in the same way anywhere in the commercial theatre, because of the completely differ-ent nature of the work.

Another approach to a career in the theatre is to work in a dual capacity as a freelance designer in the commercial theatre and as a teacher in a university. This combination of designing and teaching can provide a nice balance between creating individual projects and sharing experiences with students. There is also the security of a consistent and dependable income.

DESIGNING FOR THE COMMERCIAL THEATRE

Broadway has not lost its reputation as the pinnacle of success in designing for the professional theatre. However, the only difference between Broadway and stock, regional, or university theatre is the scale of the production in regard to budget and scenery, and perhaps the amount of time available for designing and mounting a show. The quality of the physical production should always be first-rate regardless of the locale or the circumstances.

Not only are you responsible for the finished design—painted sketches and/or painted model(s)—you are also obliged to produce complete drawings for building; for the positioning, storage, and movement of the scenery on

Model by Oliver Messel
THE SLEEPING BEAUTY

Music by Tchaikovsky
Sadler's Wells Ballet

Royal Opera House
Covent Garden, London (1946)

Stage design by William and Jean Eckart
DAMN YANKEES—locker room corridor
Book by George Abbott and Douglass Wallop
Music and lyrics by Richard Adler and Jerry
  Ross

Dances and musical numbers staged by Bob
  Fosse
Directed by George Abbott
Forty-sixth Street Theatre, New York (1955)

stage; and for the masking, furniture, and special props.

Always remember that talent, organization, humor, and practicality are essential. If a producer says, "Lovely, but we cannot afford it," you may then have to get together with the director and revamp or perhaps even rethink the physical design from a completely different point of view. Unfortunately, this is the nature of the business, and nothing is sacred when large sums of money are involved.

In an interview in *After Dark* magazine (July 1978), John Lee Beatty told writer Glenn Loney about how the United Scenic Artists, Local 829 exam prepares the designer for making changes requested by producers in a short period of time: "You go in and design a set in a day. That sounds ridiculous, but it's exactly what I've had to do with *Ain't Misbehavin'* for Broadway. I hadn't met with the producers until I showed them the model, but they gave me one day to redesign it. I began with a concept, of course, but it was suddenly and radically changed. Overnight, I had to redraft the entire show. The union exam makes sure people can deal with professional pressures like this."

No matter how stunning and theat-rical a design is, it is worth little if it cannot be fully realized on the stage. The design must be completely practical. It must also be within the budget of a production. The best producers and general managers might simply say, "I'm sorry, take it back to the drawing board and rework it to fit our budget." Then you are bound professionally and by your contract to comply with management's wishes. Whether you have little experience or a great deal, you are expected to use your imagination and create new designs that are just as devastating and effective as the original ones.

THE DEMANDS OF SCENIC DESIGN

Certain basic requirements of every stage work must be respected by the director and designer in preserving the integrity of the piece. According to the type of work (drama, musical comedy, opera, ballet, for example) and the director's aims, the scenic designer and the director are concerned with these aesthetic and mechanical elements: place and locale, time and period, theme, mood, scenic style, social status of the characters, movement and posi-tion of the actors, and changing of the scenery.

THE ELEMENTS AND PRINCIPLES OF DESIGN

As in all the visual arts, scenic designers use the elements and principles of design as a basis for their work in the theatre. These elements and principles work hand and hand in a composition, and it would be difficult to separate one from the other; experienced designers put them to work without consciously analyzing each one. Their intuition, discrimination, and observation tell them what to do.

When you look at the designs, models, and sketches throughout this book, notice consciously how the elements and principles of design are used in the various productions. This is a good practice for any designer; it will also stimulate ideas of your own and should raise questions in your mind about how you might have designed the same productions.

As cooks use ingredients according to recipes to prepare delicious meals, scenic designers use the *elements of design* (line, shape, color, texture,

Settings by Adrianne Lobel
THE MAGIC FLUTE by Wolfgang Amadeus Mozart

Directed by Peter Sellars
Lighting by James F. Ingalls
Glyndebourne Festival Opera

Glyndebourne, England (1990)
(Photographs by Guy Gravett)

space) as their ingredients in a composition, organizing them according to the *principles of design* (balance, proportion, emphasis, rhythm, unity) to make a design that is appropriate, interesting, and exciting. Imagination and ingenuity blended with a bit of daring make the stage design unique.

Further readings on both "The Demands of Scenic Design" and "The Elements and Principles of Design" may be found in Chapter 1 of *Designing and Painting for the Theatre* (1975) by Lynn Pecktal.

READING A SCRIPT

It is common practice among experienced designers to read a script several times: once for pleasure and to become familiar with content; again to establish mood, time, locale, and flow of action; and a third time (or more) to study position and movement of the actors and how the scenery will change. On the second and third readings, designers often take notes as well as make small rough realization sketches.

While our primary focus is scenery,

the evolving of design ideas or a design concept described here should also apply to costume and lighting design.

Again, the most experienced stage designers do not always consciously analyze every single aspect of a play and write it down. However, novices may want to go through a script several times to organize and write down notes and ideas according to emotional responses, visual effects, and practical necessities.

One of the fascinating things about working on a new and completely original show is that as a designer you may supply ideas that the playwright or composer will use in the actual construction of the script or musical score.

DECIDING ON
A DESIGN CONCEPT

Once you have read the script of a play (or listened to the score of an opera and read the libretto, or listened to the music for a ballet or a musical), and have had some time to think about it, no doubt you will form definite thoughts about a design concept. You might go

ahead and do several small idea sketches to show to the director or choreographer.

On the other hand, the director or choreographer may say, "Let's talk first before you do any actual sketches." In that case, a more spontaneous approach may come about.

Still yet another approach exists. If you as a designer are doing a very simple one-set interior, such as *The Corn Is Green* by Emlyn Williams, the director may say, "Let us follow the script exactly and do what the playwright wants. Make some thumbnail sketches for me to look at." In other words, you are serving the playwright in a traditional manner without having any kind of elaborate design concept in mind. As a matter of fact, if someone in the audience were to ask what the design concept for the production was, you might answer, "There was really no design concept per se. We just did what seemed right and what the playwright asked for."

In any event, you must also know that other factors have a bearing on the concept. These include the position of entrances and exits, the placement of furniture arrangements, the stage space needed for each individual scene, the amount of time available to do the show, the overall budget for the scenery (and costumes and lights, when applicable), the equipment and total area of the stage space, and the number of stagehands and staff members it will take to run the show.

For clarity, we might say that a design concept can go from a simple and basic one, as required by the playwright in the description of the setting, to a nontraditional yet highly original idea.

What is enormously helpful to a designer is to collaborate with a director who has a strong pictorial eye and a good knowledge of history. And of course it is paramount to the success of a production that both the director and the designer fully understand the play.

For purposes of discussion, it might be worthwhile to think in terms of three different groupings for a design concept for a play. These may be:

Production designed by John Napier
MISS SAIGON by Alain Boublil and Claude-Michel Schönberg; Music by Claude-Michel Schönberg; Lyrics by Richard Maltby, Jr., and Alain Boublil; Lighting by David Hersey; Costumes by Andreane Neofitou and Suzy Benzinger; Musical staging by Bob Avian; Directed by Nicholas Hytner; Broadway Theatre, New York (1991) (Photograph by Michael Le Poer Trench/Joan Marcus)

1. *A basic design concept.* This follows the playwright's descriptions and directions as closely as possible, with particular attention to locale, theme, mood, time span, position of furniture and props, entrances, blocking, time of day, and any other pertinent facts the playwright has included.

The original ground plan found in the script, with positions of furniture and entrances and exits, may be followed by both the director and the designer simply because they feel safer with it, as well as thinking that it is quite possibly the most suitable one for the particular play. However, the most imaginative directors and designers will most likely want to do something fresh and new.

Let us assume that you are designing a production of *Ah, Wilderness!* by Eugene O'Neill. The ground plans published with the script are from the original 1933 production designed by Robert Edmond Jones. The play has four different settings: a living room, a dining room, a beach, and a bar. You may or may not find these four different ground plans interesting; or you may want to try a different approach; or the original designs may spark you to go to a library theatre collection to see what the original production photographs look like. Again, you may

want to base your designs on the originals, but add something fresh and inventive of your own in the scale or color, for example.

Where one playwright will give long and detailed instructions and descriptions to the director and designer in a script, another playwright will offer only minimal descriptions, sometimes nothing more than announcing where the scene takes place. This in itself, of course, forces the designer to elaborate, improvise, and be original.

2. *A basic design concept with modifications.* In this case, the playwright's original descriptions may be modified slightly or quite a bit. This basic design concept with modifications made by the director and designer may involve one or more of the descriptions.

There are any number of examples of how a production concept may be modified. Some of these may be:

a. Adding more doors than described in the script

b. Changing the proscenium ground plan(s)

c. Adapting the playwright's instructions for a proscenium production to an open stage or arena production

d. Using a sofa and a chair instead of chairs and a table

3. *A design concept with a completely*

Stage designs by Allen Charles Klein
LULU by Alban Berg
Directed by Wolfgang Weber
Text by the composer from Wedekind's
    Erdgeist and *Die Büchse der Pandora*
Vienna State Opera
Vienna, Austria (1983)

Paris Act: "The gambling table was dropped below stage level on elevators and the gambling was seen reflected in the mirrored ceiling suspended above. The mirror surface was made of polished aluminum.

"This design demonstrates a method of dividing the stage in two playing areas, whereby the action in one area (i.e., the gambling) does not intrude on the intimate conversations of the principal playing area. Note the intense sharp patterns of light which contribute to the pictorial composition."

London Act: "The design is interesting for its use of over 6,000 vacuum-formed, costumed figures in diminishing perspective on a stage over 120 feet deep. The proscenium opening was 42 feet wide by 40 feet high."
—Allen Charles Klein

different approach than the playwright has specified. Here the director and designer use a totally different and radical approach that may be considered original, unusual, exciting, spontaneous, and extremely theatrical. In a radically different approach, the design may be set in another locale and in another time period. This sort of change can spark controversy from critics and audiences alike, but it can also generate enormous publicity and increase box office sales tremendously.

EXAMPLES OF PRODUCTION AND DESIGN CONCEPTS

It should be enlightening and should stimulate your imagination to read about concepts and approaches in some notable productions. What follows are selected commentaries on productions ranging from the interesting to the original to the far-out indeed.

A very innovative design concept was evolved by director A. J. Antoon and designer John Lee Beatty when they teamed together to do a production of *The Taming of the Shrew* (1990) at the Delacorte Theatre in Central Park, New York City. It was decided not to do the play in its original Italian setting of Padua, but instead to have it take place in the American Southwest of the late nineteenth century and have the actors speak the lines of Shakespeare with a western twang.

In an article in *The New York Times*, Marilyn Rothstein elaborated on the concept of this production:

In keeping with the Old West theme, the actors wear leather holsters and tote six-shooters that sometimes twirl on their index fingers. Part of the action takes place in a local saloon. The John Lee Beatty set itself could easily be mistaken for the outside of a stable on the front of which is painted a scene reminiscent of a Frederic Remington painting, complete with roaming wild stallions, a sandy brown desert and a plethora of buttes.

"I tried to find a milieu that would illuminate the play in some way," says Mr. Antoon, the 45-year-old American director who began the marathon [NY Shakespeare Festival's 36-play marathon] a couple of years ago with a "Midsummer Night's Dream" that was set in Bahia, Brazil. . . . "I thought that in the Old West women were a prize because there weren't that many of them on the frontier," he says. "And the very macho feeling that happens in many of the scenes felt really like saloon scenes to me. And I remembered reading about black cow-

Stage design by Zack Brown
SPRING'S AWAKENING by Frank Wedekind
A project (1975)

"Inspired by photographs by Clarence John Laughlin, this finale to Wedekind's play takes place not in a graveyard, as called for, but in a transformation of the 'white box' unit of the production concept into a Victorian memento mori—whitewashed and filled with decayed, dusty artificial floral tributes."

—Zack Brown

boys, and I wanted to work with Morgan Freeman."

By way of research, Mr. Antoon read as much as he could and saw as many movies as he could manage about the American West. "The West was much tougher than it is in this production," he says. "This is something between 'My Darling Clementine' and 'Destry Rides Again.' The comedy of 'Destry' has the exact spirit of this production. Nothing is made serious in terms of killings. It's not like the old John Wayne westerns."

Mr. Antoon says he has one primary goal with this production of "Taming of the Shrew": "allowing an American audience to find it more accessible."

"I want the children, the teenagers, to totally understand it," he says. "I want them to get it from beginning to end. I don't want any lines or any esoteric analogies or puns that were famous or understandable in Shakespeare's time to get in the way of their appreciating the story. Be-

cause if you need an encyclopedia to sit there and watch it, forget it."

Frank Rich in *The New York Times* (January 18, 1990) described Tony Walton's design for the setting for *Grand Hotel* (1989):

Mr. Walton's set for Grand Hotel, *which merges seamlessly with Tommy Tune's staging of that musical, is as interesting for what it leaves out as for what it includes. There are no drops, no heavy*

scenery, no realistic bedrooms. Instead, Mr. Walton creates the ambiance of nearly every public and private room of a grand hotel in Weimar Berlin by relying simply on three chandeliers, a proscenium-wide band platform, several dozen straight-backed chairs, a skeletal revolving door and four ghostly, translucent pillars in which evocative period bric-a-brac floats like the cultural detritus in a Joseph Cornell box. The constantly changing

"Here is the first image in our production of PAL JOEY. After following him through increasingly glamourous settings, we find Joey back at the bus station again at the end, starting again from nothing." —Thomas Lynch

Stage design by Thomas Lynch
PAL JOEY
Music by Richard Rodgers

Lyrics by Lorenz Hart
Book by John O'Hara
Directed by Robert Falls

Goodman Theatre
Chicago, Illinois (1988)

configurations of these simple fixtures is all that is needed to take the action from a bar to a bedroom to the lobby and back again. The audience's eyes fill in what Mr. Walton leaves out.

Still yet another example of a specific design concept effectively enhancing a production is the one director Peter Sellars and his designers created for Mozart's *Zauberflöte* at the Glyndebourne Festival (1990). Critic John Rockwell of *The New York Times* reviewed the English production (which debuted May 21) on June 18, 1990; the article is quoted here in part:

This Zauberflöte has its miscalculations but seems quite the best Mozart Mr. Sellars has done, possibly equaled only by his "Cosi." It is physically very beautiful, always thought-provoking and, at its best, as moving as any of the many Zauberflötes this critic has encountered.

Mr. Sellars, who brought over his core American production team, places the action in contemporary Los Angeles, where he is now based. Adrianne Lobel's settings, brilliantly lighted by James F. Ingalls, consist of a platform with a basement-like chamber underneath and mostly tripartite projections above. The projections are of commercial picture postcards of Los Angeles photographed and reproduced in such a way that the stock scenes take on eerily unnatural colors, like tinted cards from the 1950's.

Dunya Ramicova's costumes evoke Los Angeles as well, from scruffy beach bums (Tamino at the outset) to trendy club denizens (the Queen of the Night and the Three Ladies) to bizarre cult followers (Sarastro, et al.) to a Jesse Jackson lookalike (Monostatos) to mutant skinheads (Monostatos's slaves) to the birdman Papageno, who looks more or less as he usually does, which in this context makes him seem like an amiable transvestite.

The main reason to set the action in Los Angeles (other than, as Mr. Sellars has argued, to give the English something exotic) is to play with the parallels between Sarastro's Freemasonry and Southern California's cults. This is not entirely thought through; does Mr. Sellars approve of cults, disapprove of them, or is his ambivalence founded in the ambivalence of Schikaneder's libretto?

Another controversial decision is the elimination of all the spoken dialogue. This is partly replaced by red-illuminated messages that appear intermittently between the stage's two levels and that function sometimes as supertitles, sometimes as commentary. Mr. Sellars has also freighted nearly all the characters with a curious gestural language, somewhere between deaf signing, Oriental dance and cult ritual.

In *New York* magazine (August 7, 1989), Peter G. David commented on Peter Sellars' designers and his productions of Mozart's operas:

The trilogy of Mozart/DaPonte operas staged by Peter Sellars at PepsiCo's Summerfare festival unsettled almost everyone who attended, and few emerged from the experience without strong opinions.

. . . Sellars, of course, was cast as hero or villain, depending on how one responds to his work. Those who insist that an acceptable opera production must begin with pleasing period sets and by-the-book blocking knew what to expect, and they either stayed away or checked out early. . . . Don Giovanni relocated in New York's Spanish Harlem? Cosi fan Tutte in a tacky roadside diner? The Marriage of Figaro in Manhattan's Trump Tower? Enough said—the very idea is an "outrageous perversion" of Mozart. And it could be, in the hands of a less musically sensitive or ingeniously inventive spirit than Sellars, who takes these operas at their word—in the deepest sense—and invariably kindles a theatrical fire that illuminates the interior landscape of each.

DESIGNING ORIGINAL SHOWS VERSUS REVIVALS

Naturally, it is much more exciting to design an original production than to do one that has been produced many times before. The design concept of the new show that has become very successful will of course be copied over and over by theatre companies and by designers and directors everywhere.

Preliminary model by Boris Aronson
PACIFIC OVERTURES
Book by John Weidman

Music and lyrics by Stephen Sondheim
Directed by Harold Prince
Choreography by Patricia Birch

Winter Garden Theatre
New York (1976)
(Courtesy of Lisa Aronson)

Stage design by John Lee Beatty
OH, HELL by David Mamet
Directed by Gregory Mosher
Mitzi E. Newhouse Theatre
Lincoln Center, New York (1989)

But it can also become an interesting challenge for a designer to do something visually different and unique on a revival. The challenge to find a completely new approach is always there. However, if you are working with a director whose intent is to duplicate the original approach, then there really is not much that you can do. If you create a design that does not effectively convince the audience, or if it is so different that it calls attention to itself away from the performance, then your design concept has not served the theatricality of the script or music.

A unified concept can generate a highly exciting and successful production, whether for a play, opera, musical, or ballet. The idea for a design concept may come from one or more creative collaborators on a production. On many highly successful productions, the director/choreographer and stage designer work together to arrive at an original concept for the theatrical presentation of the script, music, or choreography. Suggestions may also come from the playwright, librettist, composer, and on occasion even the producer. In addition, well-known actors, singers, and dancers committed to a production may have definite opinions of their own to contribute.

A designer with a reputation as a famous artist or a painter can have different thoughts about a design concept than traditional scenic designers. For example, an artist such as Edward Gorey may be selected to design a production because of his unique style, and his stage scenery would automatically be noted as a special and artistic concept. Two examples of easel painters working in the theatre are Salvador Dali and Eugene Berman. I once asked Berman about design concept and he answered, "What concept? I just do what I feel is right for the production."

RESEARCH AND WHERE TO DO IT

For an individual show, the designer may need to research sociological aspects of a historical era, design and color of the period of the play's action, fashion, customs, architecture, furniture, construction, and anything else needed to make a satisfying environment for the characters on stage.

The serious young designer soon learns the importance of research in a theatrical career. Even while still a student, the most aspiring designer builds a personal collection of theatre, art, and architectural books as well as magazine and newspaper clippings and photographs.

An important thing to remember about research is this: Once you have completed it and digested it and absorbed it, wait a while. Then use this newly acquired knowledge as a basis and put your talent and originality to work to create a spontaneous and wonderful design that is all yours and one that is completely right for the show.

Naturally, research for a specific production may extend beyond a designer's personal collection. The following list indicates how extensive a designer's research may be on a project and suggests various subjects and where to do the actual research. (Of course, numerous other examples or subjects would also be correct.)

1. *Architecture libraries.* Study the works of architects such as Philip Johnson, I. M. Pei, Frank Lloyd Wright, and countless others of different periods and discover the best approach on which to base a theatrical design.

2. *Library picture collections.* Find Art Deco items such as wallpaper, furniture, dishes, or other period materials. Also study pictorial socioeconomic and historical details of the era.

3. *Library stage design picture files.* See how an individual theatre piece has been treated as to style, mood, and period. This will help you decide whether to make your production realistic, highly stylized, or totally abstract.

4. *Music archives.* For an opera, listen to the score and use your emotional and spiritual response to help you develop the right feeling in the designs.

5. *Actual locations.* For a production set in the Rockies or the West Indies, travel there to photograph trees, foliage, and rocks with sky at different times of day so the colors, shapes, and textures may be used to establish an authentic locale in the production.

6. *Art museums.* Study paintings of Francesco Guardi, Nicolas Poussin, and Peter Paul Rubens to note their use of color, historic details, and themes.

12

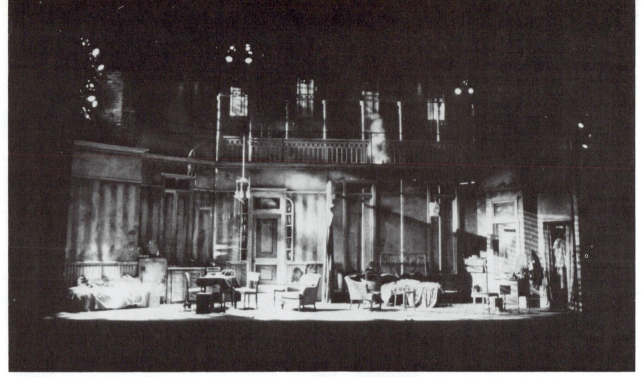

Setting by John Falabella
A STREETCAR NAMED DESIRE by Tennessee
Williams

Directed by Edwin Sherin
Lighting by Marcia Madeira
Hartman Theatre Company

Stamford, Connecticut (1984)
(Photograph by Marcia Madeira)

7. *Art libraries.* Peruse drawings involving perspective designs, graphic techniques, pencil sketches, and textures. Observe the drawing styles of Jacques Callot, Jean Bérain, and Albrecht Dürer.

8. *Film libraries.* Look at slides and microfilms of the work of famous artists and designers, such as Piranesi, to use for details in fireplaces, capitals, arches, or other architectural features.

9. *Video or motion picture collections.* Watch films that portray the particular historical period or locale of the play. When *The Music Man* was produced at the Jones Beach Theatre in 1979, for research the cast and designers looked at the film version that was made following the original stage production. Sometimes stage productions are based on successful films. Examples: *Meet Me in St. Louis, Singin' in the Rain*, and *Seven Brides for Seven Brothers.*

10. *Video files of operas, ballets, and plays.* Videos of past productions are good for looking at colors, patterns, shapes, movement, and flow of action of the production and are a good record of the sets, costumes, and lighting working together.

11. *Experiments with actual materials.* Do a translucent muslin drop (use a small piece of muslin) with aniline dye painting on the front and opaque patterns in silhouette on the back. Also look at painted scenic samples or fabrics under different colored gels.

12. *Fabric houses.* Find fabrics and select samples as to color, texture, pattern, weight, durability, and how they hang so your knowledge of this can be applied to drapery, curtains, upholstery, and costumes. Go to a local fabric house, or in the New York City area you might go to Schumacher's or Stroheim & Roman.

13. *Magazine files.* Search in publications such as *Architectural Digest*

Stage designs by Peter Harvey
A STREETCAR NAMED DESIRE

by Tennessee Williams
Directed by Neal Kenyon

Asolo Theatre, Sarasota, Florida (1976)
Left photograph: revised version.

Model by Ralph Funicello
A STREETCAR NAMED DESIRE

by Tennessee Williams
Directed by John Hirsch

Stratford Shakespeare Festival
Stratford, Ontario, Canada (1984)

to find articles on the sculpture of Louise Nevelson and Isamu Noguchi to use as inspiration for a sculptural design project.

DOING RESEARCH FOR A SPECIFIC PRODUCTION

The amount of research you will do as a designer on a production varies from using what you already have stored up in your head to studying objects, patterns, and historical periods in an extraordinary number of places. For example, Oliver Smith talked with the author in *Designing and Painting for the Theatre* (1975) about not having to do actual research when designing *Hello, Dolly!* (1964). Smith commented: "I had to do something where there was too much scenery to get onto a stage which was too small. It was first a technical solution of the use of space. I would say the scenic elevations were a rather joyous comment on a period and style which I have always enjoyed and liked. Therefore, I used the vocabulary I've been acquiring for probably thirty years. I didn't have to do any research. I could just sit down and draw it very quickly."

As I interviewed John Napier for the conversation in this book, I asked whether he did a lot of research for *Starlight Express* (1987). He replied, "None at all. It's absolutely out of the imagination. I looked at a few details of trains and then forgot about them. It was intended to be a lightweight spectacle, unabashed, with no pretensions and on roller skates. Bizarre! To some extent it caught the popular public imagination."

At the other extreme from Smith's not needing to do research for *Dolly*, other designers may immerse themselves in involved areas of research.

Stage design by Jo Mielziner
A STREETCAR NAMED DESIRE

by Tennessee Williams
Directed by Elia Kazan

Ethel Barrymore Theatre, New York (1947)
(Photograph by Peter A. Juley and Son)

Setting by Tony Walton
CONVERSATIONS WITH MY FATHER by
 Herb Gardner
Directed by Daniel Sullivan

Costumes by Robert Wojewodski
Lighting by Pat Collins
Royale Theatre, New York (1992)

Pictured (left to right): Richard Libertini and
 Judd Hirsch.
(Photograph by Tony Walton)

When David Mitchell designed *Foxfire* (1982), he traveled to the southern state of Georgia, the exact locale of the play, in order to study the area. While there, he took photographs and bought covered shingles and building siding to use for the scenery in the actual show.

Designers sometimes travel a great distance to do research for a production. When costume designer Patricia Zipprodt was creating costumes for *Shōgun* (1990), the musical based on James Clavell's novel, she spent three weeks in Japan, going to costume workrooms of the Kabuki Theatre and film companies to research fabrics used in sixteenth- and seventeenth-century Japanese theatre. In a *New York Times* article dated June 15, 1990, Enid Nemy reported Miss Zipprodt as saying that her designs were inspired by paintings, period wall panels, and museums:

For the first time in her [Miss Zipprodt's] experience (and she believes possibly the first in theatre generally) the 9,000 yards of fabric will be handpainted, silk-screened and tie-dyed here from white fabrics, many of them, like brocades and silk gauze, imported from Japan.

"These designs have nothing to do with the 'Pacific Overtures' and 'Madame But-

terfly' designs," said Miss Zipprodt, who is working with the Martin Izquierdo Studio, one of the leading costume craft houses. *"This is a different period, the Momoyama—much more free, more wild, more sensuous. To get the right fabric, the right weave, the right weight and the right color would be like looking for a needle in a haystack."*

The scenery, costumes, and props for Peter Brook's production of *The Mahabharata* (1987) were designed by Chloé Obolensky, a veteran of several years at Mr. Brook's theatre in Paris. In *The New York Times* (September 30, 1987) Nan Robertson mentioned that Miss Obolensky made several trips to India for inspiration.

THE STAGE SET AS A CHARACTER

Is the stage set to be thought of as a character in a production? Should it be? The following comments from reviewers, designers, and directors provide some insight on this provocative question.

In a *New York Times* article (March 12, 1978) Leticia Kent's topic was "on Broadway the spectacle's the thing."

Among the productions then playing Kent cited Robin Wagner's train set for *On the Twentieth Century*. Comments on that production are quoted here in part:

"The train," said Richard Eder of The New York Times, *". . . is one of the most spectacular achievements of the production."*

"I think of the set as a character," said Robin Wagner. . . . *"As a character it can live. The unit set—a basic set with movable parts—is disappearing. You'll also see fewer doors and windows and fewer naturalistic houses in sets. Films do that better. Contemporary theatre design deals with whole space—including the audience."*

One of the first things Harold Prince, the show's director, suggested to Mr. Wagner was that he wanted the set to take the place of choreography. Mr. Wagner said that he had worked closely with Cy Coleman, the composer of *Twentieth Century*, because the set, besides being thought of as a character, was supposed to complement the score.

Certainly another fine example of a setting's being considered as a character in a play would be Ming Cho Lee's highly original design for *K2* (1983). The production was presented first at Washington's Arena Stage and then at the Brooks Atkinson Theatre in New York. Nan Robertson's discussion of the play and the setting in *The New York Times* is quoted here in part:

When Ming Cho Lee, one of the country's best known—and most dauntless—set designers, opened the script by Patrick Meyers, these were the first words he read: "Place: A ledge, eight feet wide and four feet deep, located on a 600-foot ice wall at 27,000 feet on K2, the world's second-highest mountain."

"I almost had a heart attack," Mr. Lee recalled the other day during rehearsals. "When you read the script, your first impression is that somebody must be absolutely out of their minds to do such a show." . . . Almost a year ago, Mr. Lee told Zelda Fichandler, the producing director of the Arena Stage in Washington, where the play had its premiere in Arena's Kreeger Theatre: "It's going to be a monster. It's an ice cliff near the top of the Himalayas that has to be climbed by a real man in front of a real audience every night. You can't fake it, like a James Bond

movie. There are the safety problems; all the rigging. But we should do it realistically. If the play doesn't have that kind of reality, that danger, it will lose something vital.

. . . All the critics from New York, Washington and Baltimore singled out the set: "not only stunning, but is such an organic part of the action that to begin any review without referring to it would be impossible; the first marvel of this astonishing production is the evocation of this frozen mountain."

In an article entitled "Björnson's Dark Fancies" in *Theatre Crafts* (February 1988), freelance writer Sheryl Flatow reported that "the Paris Opera House played an important role in Maria Björnson's designs for *The Phantom of the Opera*" (1988). Ironically, this production was also directed by Harold Prince. Flatow observed, "While Björnson's sets function on a symbolic level, they also convey a sense of the expansiveness of the opera house. They take us from the rooftop to the subterranean lake, to the majesty of the grand staircase, to the backstage labyrinth. In fact, the Paris Opera House is so crucial to the story of Phan-

tom that it takes on a persona of its own and is, in effect, one of the show's leading characters.

Flatow quoted Björnson: "Hal shared my interest in the psychological aspect of the show, and working with him was very interesting because he has a strong visual sense. . . . He told me he wanted Turkish dark corners and lots of curtains and heaviness, and that one sentence put me on the right track."

REALIZING A TYPICAL STAGE DESIGN IN THE COMMERCIAL THEATRE

The following is an overview of the basic steps involved when designing a production in the commercial theatre.

1. The designer is contacted by a director, producer, or general manager. Contact usually comes about as a result of previous work and association with the director or producer(s) or by a recommendation from a colleague. On rare occasions a designer is engaged as a result of a portfolio showing.

Final model by Boris Aronson
FOLLIES
Book by James Goldman

Music and lyrics by Stephen Sondheim
Directed by Harold Prince and Michael Bennett

Winter Garden Theatre, New York (1971)
(Photograph by Mikio Sekita)
(Courtesy of Lisa Aronson)

16 Models designed by Robin Wagner
CITY OF ANGELS
Book by Larry Gelbart; music by Cy Coleman;
   lyrics by David Zippel
Directed by Michael Blakemore
Film sequence art director: Charles E. McCarry
Film director: Jim Ritchie
Virginia Theatre, New York (1989)

"The musical is set in Hollywood and focuses on a screenwriter and his fictional detective hero. The 'real world' of the screenwriter is designed in color. The 'film world' of the detective is designed in black and white. The two worlds interact throughout, which is much of the fun.

"The 1-inch scale cityscape was built and filmed for use in one number as an old-fashioned matte shot background with live actors in front." —Charles E. McCarry

2. Discusses the production with the director and producers. The designer reads the script, is interested, and agrees to design the scenery.

3. Negotiates with the producer and signs a union contract. This includes a minimum fee, a weekly royalty (AWC: additional weekly compensation) and/or weekly percentage, and appropriate billing. Billing may be covered by a rider specifying the exact wording, size, position, and order of billing.

4. Has meetings back and forth with the director. Also has meetings with the other collaborating designers, the production stage manager, and the production stage carpenter. (The span of time a designer and director work on a production may range from several weeks to a year or two or more until opening night.)

5. The designer re-reads the play (listens to the music and lyrics if a musical) and does research. If a designer has an assistant, the assistant may help in the research.

6. The designer does rough sketches and rough models. Has more meetings. Designer proceeds with ½-inch scale color sketches (or collages or photomontages) and/or ½-inch scale color model. At the same time does drawings for the drafting to get ready for the bid session. Collects fabric samples for draperies, curtains, upholstery, and other materials.

7. Works with the person in charge of props, who may take Polaroid photographs of what has been found to show both designer and director for approval.

8. The designer and management hold

a bid session with scenic studios to see which shop(s) will build and paint the scenery for the show, do any sculpture work, or provide any special machinery. The same scenic shop may also make up the backdrops, draperies, curtains, masking, and other soft goods or upholstery. However, there may also be a separate bid with a drapery house.

9. When the bids come in, the designer may have to rework the scenery to simplify certain ideas in order to reduce the cost in materials and execution, as well as possibly make changes in the design to reduce the number of stagehands needed to run the show. Additional meeting(s) with the director and/or producer.

10. Designer then may have to get new bids on certain items and meet with management to discuss.

11. Once the producer and/or general manager agree to put the show in a specific shop, the designer makes periodic visits to see how the building and painting are progressing.

12. Designer attends rehearsals. Checks with the director and production stage manager to see if any changes are necessary.

13. Prior to load-out of scenery in the shop, the designer may visit almost daily.

14. Designer goes to the theatre where scenery is being set up and light and sound equipment are being positioned. Lights are focused and cued.

15. Attends all technical rehearsals with scenery, costumes, lights, special effects, music, and sound. Makes any adjustments as necessary.

16. Also attends dress rehearsals with

all the visual elements in place, plus actors (singers, dancers, and musicians).

17. When the show runs, the scenic designer makes periodic checkups to see how the scenery, furniture, and props are holding up. Touch-ups are held to paint damaged or worn scenery and also for any building that is necessary.

18. For hit shows, the scenic designer and other collaborators may be involved with preparing other companies of the same show, often as identical as possible, at other times somewhat different. These are touring national companies, bus-and-truck productions, and foreign productions.

ESTABLISHING YOUR REPUTATION AS A DESIGNER

A great part of a stage designer's early career is spent proving over and over that he or she is talented and capable of handling both the visual and practical elements of any stage production. A young designer can become so busy doing this that one of the most important aspects of a career is overlooked, namely, establishing that he or she is a creative person who is easy to work with. It is extremely important for a young talented designer to establish as early as possible that he or she is an amiable collaborator. This sometimes requires extraordinary tact, skill, and patience.

The people who tend to come off best in the theatre are those individuals

who are, of course, extremely talented, possess an extraordinary sense of humor, never gripe or look on the gloomy side of life, and truly enjoy their work and colleagues. A great number of the most successful artists in the theatre are most gracious and never assume anything. The most enduring and deserving artists have impeccable manners, always thank everyone who warrants it, and have respect for their colleagues.

A second, equally important aspect of a designer's reputation is to be known as a very resourceful artist who does not always create designs that are terribly expensive. You don't want people to feel they cannot afford to hire you. This may be a very difficult problem to cope with, especially when you are starting out.

While a designer does not pursue an expensive design without the knowledge and support of the director, a director may not always understand the cost of scenery and scenic effects as well as the designer does. If a director insists on expensive scenery, then be

sure of his or her support when you discuss the cost with management. At the same time, it would be wise to investigate less expensive alternatives. It is a good idea not to let the scenery for a production get expensive without management's being aware of it. General managers and producers can easily shy away from a designer who is labeled as "expensive."

A third aspect of establishing your reputation is not to be too picky about taking shows when they are offered to you. You may be extremely busy, or you may not like the show, but don't close all the doors, because word will get out that you are overly selective. This is one of the biggest mistakes in a designer's career, and very frequently the designer will think he or she is right in being selective at the time. If you happen to be doing a number of plays and feel you can't afford the time to do another one, rethink that decision. Look around and hire one, two, or three assistants to help you with the work and go right on. Most likely you will be offered even more work, because direc-

tors and producers usually want to hire creative artists and designers who are hot properties.

DESIGNING HIT SHOWS

There is no hands-on formula that is guaranteed to make a show a hit. Normally, the same amount of time, talent, effort, and energy goes into a production whether it runs for one night or several years. It is no secret that the critics and the theatregoing public decide what the fate of any production will be. Eagerness, inspiration, hope, and preparation, however, are vital to make the collaboration process work. Unfortunately, there are times when the final result is not well received by the theatregoers.

It is a glorious feeling when a show does become a hit. The critics and the audience let you know immediately when the production is a smash. The news that tickets are selling out at the box office is a sure indication that success is imminent: Word spreads like wildfire to the producer's office, the company, then the industry itself. The producers take on an exuberant air. Suddenly, money is available for publicity in the newspapers, on television, and on radio.

Once the show has been proclaimed a hit by the critics and audience and settles down for a long run, there is talk about other companies. These include national tours (one, two, or more weeks at each stop), bus-and-truck (split weeks, one-nighters, or more), and foreign productions (London, Australia, Paris, and so on). The original designer can be involved in any or all of these new productions.

Fortunately for a designer on a hit

show, there is normally an additional designing fee and a weekly royalty for each of the national, bus-and-truck, and foreign companies. When these duplicate companies are touring while the original Broadway production is still playing, the designer's income is most rewarding. Any designer with a hit show that has several companies will tell you how pleasant it is to have a weekly royalty check from each company.

When a show becomes a hit, it or members of the company may be nominated for and win a Tony Award. This honor brings additional attention and publicity to the show and the collaborators. Not only does the Tony nomi-

nation or award enhance the run of the show, but it can lead to more work for the designers, director, and others. Producers of new shows will then tell backers and investors that they have so-and-so doing the sets and likewise for the costumes and lights. Directors are also hailed for the current smash hit. Success in the theatre tends to breed more success, which is one of the reasons why a designer may be willing to work and rework designs and ideas, and spend a long time evolving the work.

BROADWAY PRODUCERS

If you picked up a *Playbill* and glanced at the top of the show title page, most likely you would find producers' names who are household words in the commercial theatre. These are the people who find the money, the talent, and the plays and put them all together and make it work. They have influence, they have power, and they are usually working on that next big project. It is important that designers, especially novices, be familiar with their work.

The following list includes some of the best-known Broadway producers and coproducers in the latter part of the twentieth century:

Allan Carr	Doris Cole Abrams
Cameron Mackintosh	Zev Bufman
	Maxine Fox
David Merrick	Douglas Urbanski
The Shubert Organization (under the direction of Gerald Schoenfeld, chairman, and Bernard B. Jacobs, president)	Barry Weissler
	Fran Weissler
	Roger S. Berlind
	Ray Larsen
	Maurice Rosenfield
	Lois F. Rosenfield
Harold Prince	David Geffen
Mike Nichols	James B. Freydberg
Terry Allen Kramer	Max Weitzenhoffer
James M. Nederlander	Jerome Minskoff
	Hillard Elkins
Emanuel Azenberg	Arthur Cantor
Michael White	Cynthia Wood
Elizabeth I. McCann	Richard Armitage
Roger Horchow	Roger Peters
Elizabeth Williams	Pierre Cossette
Nick Vanoff	Martin Richards
Charles H. Duggan	Sam Crothers
Gladys Nederlander	Sander Jacobs
Nelle Nugent	Brian Eastman
	James Walsh

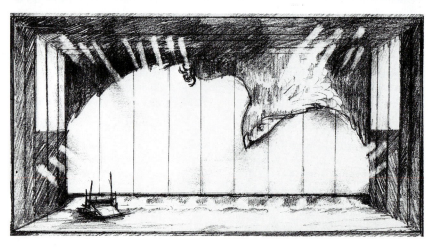

Stage designs by Santo Loquasto
OF BRIGHT AND BLUE BIRDS AND THE GALA SUN
Choreographed by Paul Taylor
City Center Theatre, New York (1990)

Michael Codron
Robert Fryer
Duncan Weldon
Kenneth Waissman
Robert Stigwood
Alexander Cohen
Hildy Parks
Bernard Gersten
Robert Whitehead
Francine Lefrak
Ivan Bloch
Lester Osterman
Rocco Landesman
Heidi Landesman
John Wulp
Edgar Lansbury

Stewart F. Lane
Raymond Katz
Hinks Shimberg
Paul Libin
Marvin Krauss
Kenneth D.
    Greenblatt
Saint Subber
Joseph Harris
Lucille Lortel
Frederick M. Zollo
Elliot Martin
Susan R. Rose
Roger L. Stevens
T. Edward
    Hambleton

DIRECTORS WHO CREATE ON BROADWAY

Like designers, directors do productions on Broadway, Off-Broadway, for national tours, for opera and dance companies, in regional and repertory theatres, in stock shows, and in university theatres. They also direct for films, television, and other commercial projects. In addition, directors teach, conduct seminars, and give lectures.

Directors often work in multiple performing categories. Some may be choreographers, dancers, or actors, and occasionally they may be playwrights, authors, or designers. Directors create original works and do revivals in many places. They are employed nationally and internationally and go where the work is being produced.

While designers are usually selected by the director with the producer's agreement, sometimes it may be the other way around. At any rate, designers should get to know directors well. A truly healthy and creative collaboration on a production is what counts. Besides talent, perseverance, and hard work, a close working relationship with the director is essentially what

Setting by Adrianne Lobel
L'ALLEGRO, IL PENSEROSO ED IL MODERATO
Music by George Frideric Handel; Choreographed by Mark Morris; Costumes by Christine Van Loon; Lighting by James F. Ingalls; Opera National de la Monnaie, Brussels, Belgium (1988); (Photograph by Klaus Lefebvre)

gets the designer more work. Like other creative people, directors like to work with people they enjoy. So an amiable and trusted relationship with the director is what matters as far as getting that next job.

The list of directors and/or choreographers whose work has been seen on Broadway includes the following:

Stage design by Robert Perdziola
CHERUBIN by Massenet—Act I
Directed by Lou Galterio
Manhattan School of Music, New York (1987)

"This French opera was done with satin appliqués on a netted frame with chiffon drapes, flowers, and peacocks."
—Robert Perdziola

19

Act curtain by Edward Gorey
AMPHIGOREY: The Musical
Written and designed by Edward Gorey
Music by Peter Golub

Directed and choreographed by Daniel Levans
Produced by the American Music Theatre
    Festival
Plays and Players Theatre

Philadelphia
Pennsylvania (1992)
(Photograph by Lynn Pecktal)
(Courtesy of Edward Gorey)

Gene Saks
Marshall W. Mason
James Lapine
Harold Prince
Tommy Tune
Tom Moore
Arthur Laurents
Trevor Nunn
John Caird
Mike Nichols
Morton Da Costa
Terry Hands
Michael Rudman
George Abbott
Christopher
    Chadman
Susan Stroman
Bob Avian
Nicholas Hytner
Frank Galati
Ellis Rabb
Arvin Brown
Peter Brook
Douglas Turner
    Ward
Mike Ockrent
Theodore Mann
Vivian Matalon
Tom O'Horgan
Melvin Bernhardt
John Madden
Michael Blakemore
Michael Smuin
Clifford Williams

Jack Hofsiss
Peter Masterson
Michael Cacoyannis
Michael Lindsay-
    Hogg
Carole Rothman
Jerry Zaks
Gordon Davidson
Michael Kahn
Arthur Penn
Frank Corsaro
Geoffrey Holder
Joe Layton
Albert Marre
Martin Scorsese
Steven Schacter
Richard Foreman
Richard Maltby, Jr.
Elizabeth Swados
Philip Rose
Stephen Schwartz
Martin Charnin
Grover Dale
Andrei Serban
Arthur Storch
Lindsay Anderson
Gerald Freedman
Craig Anderson
Alan Ayckbourn
Charles Nelson
    Reilly
Terry Schreiber
Robert Allan
    Ackerman

Herbert Ross
Des McAnuff
Jonathan Miller
Geraldine Fitzgerald
Daniel Sullivan
David Hare
Mark Lamos
Howard Davies
Dan Siretta
Gerald Gutierrez
Liza Gennaro
Peter Martins
Lloyd Richards
José Quintero
Stephen Porter
Vinnette Carroll
Edwin Sherin
Peter Wood
Mel Shapiro

Peter Coe
Stephen Zuckerman
Tony Tanner
Gilbert Cates
Athol Fugard
George Schaeffer
Twyla Tharp
Liviu Ciulei
Dennis Rosa
Jeffrey B. Moss
David Rotenberg
Emily Mann
Maurice Hines
Norman Rene
Brian Murray
Peter Hall
David Trainer
Austin Pendleton
Graciela Daniele

DIRECTORS WORKING WITH DESIGNERS

In the theatre there is no way to predict which director will work with which designer on the next production. Some directors in the commercial theatre collaborate repeatedly with the same designers, while others work with new teams of creative artists. You will also find the same scenic, lighting, and costume designers working as a team but sometimes working for a different director from one show to the next.

One of the best-known examples of a director/choreographer collaborating with the same design team would be the late Michael Bennett's association with Robin Wagner (scenery), Theoni V. Aldredge (costumes), and Tharon Musser (lighting). Their productions with Bennett include the legendary long-running Broadway show *A Chorus Line* (1975), *Ballroom* (1978), and *Dreamgirls* (1981, 1987). Of course, these designers have worked as a threesome with various other directors. For instance, Wagner, Aldredge, and Musser did the musicals *Forty-Second Street* (1980) with the late director/choreographer Gower Champion and *Teddy and Alice* (1987) with director John Driver.

Another highly talented team in the theatre is director Trevor Nunn working with John Napier (scenery and costumes) and David Hersey (lighting). Their very successful collaborations include *Starlight Express* (1987) and *Cats* (1982), and *The Life and Adventures of Nicholas Nickleby* (1981), which was directed by Trevor Nunn and John Caird and designed by John

Napier and Dermot Hayes, with costumes by John Napier, lighting by David Hersey, and the New York production designed in association with Neil Peter Jampolis (sets and costumes) and Beverly Emmons (lighting). In addition, for *Les Misérables* (1987) the credits read: designed by John Napier, lighting by David Hersey, costumes by Andreane Neofitou, directed and adapted by Trevor Nunn and John Caird.

Tony Walton has collaborated on numerous theatrical ventures with Mike Nichols, including *Death and the Maiden* (1992), *Elliot Loves* (1990), *Social Security* (1986), *Hurlyburly* (1984), *The Real Thing* (1984), *Drinks Before Dinner* (1978), and *Streamers* (1977). Twenty-some years earlier, Nichols chose Oliver Smith as his designer for such distinguished hits as *Barefoot in the Park* (1963), *Luv* (1964), *The Odd Couple* (1965), and *Plaza Suite* (1968). Walton has teamed with Jerry Zaks as director and designed sets and costumes for *Anything Goes* (1987) and sets for *The House of Blue Leaves* (1986), *Front Page* (1986), *Lend Me a Tenor* (1989), *Six Degrees of Separation* (1990), *Square One* (1990), and *Guys and Dolls* (1992).

Designer David Mitchell has had the good fortune to have smash hits in both plays and musicals. He has designed the settings for Neil Simon's *Brighton Beach Memoirs* (1983), *Biloxi Blues* (1985), and *Broadway Bound* (1986), all three directed by Gene Saks. Mitchell has also designed the scenery for the musicals *La Cage aux Folles* (1983) with director Arthur Laurents; *Barnum* (1980), directed by Joe Layton; *Annie* (1977) and *Annie II* (1989), directed by Martin Charnin; and *The Gin Game* (1977), with director Mike Nichols.

Undoubtedly, of all Broadway directors, Harold Prince has worked with the most diversified roster of scenic designers. In January of 1988, with the American debut of the megahit *The Phantom of the Opera*, Prince and his designers Maria Björnson (settings and costumes) and Andrew Bridge (lighting) received glowing accolades from the critics and public alike. The show had also been a smash hit in London when it opened there in 1986.

Prince's other scenic design collaborators include Thomas Lynch on *Kiss of the Spider Woman* (1990); Alexander Okun on *Roza* (1987); David Chapman on the revival of *Cabaret* (1987), based on original designs by Boris

Aronson (1900–1980); Clarke Dunham on *Grind* (1985) and *End of the World* (1984); Tony Straiges on *Diamonds* (1984); Timothy O'Brien and Tazeena Firth on *A Doll's Life* (1982) and *Evita* (1979); Eugene Lee on *Merrily We Roll Along* (1981) and *Sweeney Todd* (1979); Robin Wagner on *On the Twentieth Century* (1978); and Robert Randolph on *It's a Bird, It's a Plane, It's Superman* (1966).

As a colleague and collaborator with Harold Prince, Boris Aronson created the scenery for numerous well-known productions. It is interesting to note that of the six productions for which Aronson won Tony Awards, five were collaborations with Harold Prince. These were *Pacific Overtures* (1976); *Company* (1970), with musical numbers staged by Michael Bennett; *Follies* (1971), also directed and choreographed by Michael Bennett; *Zorba* (1968); and *Cabaret* (1966). Other celebrated shows Aronson did with Prince were *Fiddler on the Roof* (1964) and *A Little Night Music* (1973).

Costume designer Florence Klotz has had a long and lasting relationship with Harold Prince. She designed the costumes for *Roza* (1987), *A Little Night Music* (1973), *Follies* (1971), *A*

Model by Rouben Ter-Arutunian
SPHINX

Choreographed by Glen Tetley
American Ballet Theatre

Kennedy Center, Washington, D. C. (1977)
(Photograph © Martha Swope)

22

Doll's Life (1982), *On the Twentieth Century* (1978), *Pacific Overtures* (1976), *Grind* (1985), and *Superman* (1966).

DESIGNERS WHO CREATE BOTH SETS AND COSTUMES

While stage designers in Europe have traditionally created both sets and costumes, it does not always happen that way in America. However, on the contemporary scene there are still outstanding artists who design both sets and costumes for the same production. Among them are the following:

Tony Walton	Peter Harvey
John Napier	Carl Toms
Desmond Heeley	Franco Colavecchia
John Conklin	Peter Wexler
Santo Loquasto	John Falabella
Zack Brown	Steven Rubin
Rouben	William and Jean
Ter-Arutunian	Eckart
Neil Peter Jampolis	Robert O'Hearn
Maria Björnson	Robert Fletcher
Allen Charles Klein	John Scheffler
José Varona	Cletus Anderson
Eduardo Sicangco	Fred Voelpel
Michael Yeargan	Eiko Ishioka
Robert Israel	Robert Perdziola
Felix E. Cochren	Ed Wittstein

Some of the best-known theatrical designers who excelled in designing lovely sets and costumes in the commercial theatre over the years were Oliver Messel (1904–1978), Cecil Beaton (1905–1980), and Raoul Pène du Bois (1914–1985). In the early part of his career Boris Aronson not only designed exciting settings, but also created highly imaginative costumes.

Oliver Messel was a prominent stage designer who exemplified all the qualities essential for a vibrant and successful career. He was a brilliant natural talent with superb taste. His stage and costume designs were always delicate, stylish, and magically theatrical, never tawdry. Oliver Messel's most memorable productions would certainly include *Ring Round the Moon* (1950), *The Lady's Not for Burning* (1949), and *The Dark Is Light Enough* (1954).

After living in Barbados for many years, Oliver Messel returned to New York in 1976 to design sets and costumes for the new American Ballet Theatre production of *The Sleeping Beauty* at the Metropolitan Opera House. John Russell of *The New York Times* (June 14, 1976) talked with Messel about this production and the 1946 *Sleeping Beauty* Messel had designed thirty years earlier for the Royal Ballet.

Mr. Messel first designed for the London stage at a time when no leading lady would have been seen dead with a microphone and every leading man had a cafe au lait Hispano-Suiza with a supply of autographed postcards on the dashboard.

"You didn't learn stage designing at school," he said. "You just did it if you were lucky enough to have someone ask you. Diaghilev asked me to make masks for Zéphyre et Flore, and C. B. Cochran asked me to design for his revues, and there I was."

It didn't seem quite as easy as that to those of us who saw C. B. Cochran's production of Offenbach's Helen of Troy. *Cochran at that time could call on the pick of the European theatre. Max Reinhardt directed. George Robey, the greatest English comic of the first half of this century, made his first appearance in light opera. Leonide Massine did the dances. The reviews averaged three full columns, each of them as broad as the backside of an elephant, and the space given to Mr. Messel's sets and costumes was more than today's papers would give to an entire production.*

"When I began to work, the visual side of the English theatre was abysmal. Even Diaghilev's costumes were very tacky, if you look at them now. There were just a few years in which you could do good things. Now we shall never have quality again, because it costs too much and no one knows how to get it. Well, almost no one. Madame Karinska is perfection, of course. Lucky Balanchine to have her to work for him alone! . . .

"In 1946 Covent Garden had been shut for seven years. When it reopened with The Sleeping Beauty, *the time was right, the place was right and the ballet was right. We'd read about* The Sleeping Beauty, *we knew that it was the ballet for which Diaghilev would gladly have ruined himself, but we'd never dreamed of seeing it. It was a happy ending night."*

Robert Wahls got Oliver Messel to recall his early training and career for an article ("A Designing Man") which appeared in the *Sunday News* in New York City on June 13, 1976;

The stitchers moved their arms like a silent symphony string section in the atelier of sisters Grace Miceli and Maria Brizzi 13 floors up over West 54th St. Among the silks and organdy, Oliver Messel, England's dean of set and costume design, holds a headpiece designed for Carabosse, the Wicked Fairy.

Messel, uncle to Princess Margaret's estranged Lord Snowdon, is watching the execution of his designs for American Ballet Theatre's new production of the Petipa-Tchaikovsky The Sleeping Beauty. *Oliver designed the Carabosse headpiece and made it himself on a base of pipe cleaners. He exudes pleasure:*

"Yes, some of the headpieces I put together myself in my hotel suite. I enjoy putting a finger in the pie. When Oliver Smith and Lucia Chase asked me to design this 'Sleeping Beauty,' well, it couldn't have been a greater compliment. Oliver is the world's great designer.

"I am shy and I felt as though I'd shut myself off on Barbados. I wasn't at all sure I could cope with dressing up in tie and jacket and coming to New York. But you've met the Sicilian sisters, Grace and Maria, and this marvelous crew. I felt at home at once.

"In the tropics, where I've been since 1960, you wear no tie, no shoes and you run around practically like Tarzan."

Oliver Messel says he was 70 on Jan. 13 and he's survived both arthritis and a serious heart attack. Just 30 years ago he staged the Royal Ballet's original Sleeping Beauty.

"That was just after World War II in which I served. And that production really established the Royal Ballet—formerly Sadler's Wells—both at Covent Garden and at the old Met here.

"I still have the rose Margot Fonteyn gave me on opening night. She danced Aurora, but the initial applause was for Moira Shearer who had made the film The Red Shoes. *But after Margot's pas du deux the audience rose and screamed for her."*

Of course Messel's association with ballet design predates the Royal Ballet. It was Serge Diaghilev who gave him his first

Setting, costumes, lighting, and projections by
Clarke Dunham
TALES OF HOFFMAN by Jacques Offenbach
Directed by Dino Yannopoulis
Curtis Institute Opera
Walnut Street Theatre
Philadelphia, Pennsylvania (1975)
(Photograph by Clarke Dunham)

commission to design masks for Zéphyre et Flore.

"I was just 19 and had set out to be a painter but with a friend, Rex Whistler, I played around with masks and mime. A friend knew both my stockbroker father and Diaghilev as well as the producer, Sir Charles Cochran. They saw an exhibit of mine and called me."

For Cochran, Messel designed masks and costumes for Noel Coward's 'Dance Little Lady,' 'This Year of Grace' and a series of London revues. His film assignments, incidentally, range from Douglas Fairbanks in The Loves of Don Juan to Katharine Hepburn and Elizabeth Taylor in Suddenly, Last Summer.

"I also designed costumes for Elizabeth Taylor for 'Cleopatra.' The production was so delayed things became confused. At any rate, my designs appeared in Life Magazine and Elizabeth turned to Irene Sharaff. My lawsuit brought more than the assignment!"

A product of English schools, Messel once was caned by a sadistic master.

"I think it's good not to be too happy as a child. I was so unhappy I used to shut myself in my room in a fantasy world. I believe that helped develop my imagination.

"I was extravagant building my house but it turned into a shop window for my wares and I found a whole new career in architecture, although I've never taken exams or studied."

As for the estrangement between Princess Margaret and Lord Snowdon, Messel takes no sides because "I'm devoted to them both."

After Sleeping Beauty, it'll be back to Barbados and architecture, and at quiet times, painting. His recent portrait of Mick Jagger has been sold to Elton John.

The Theatre Museum of London chose the works of Oliver Messel for its first exhibition, which was mounted in the galleries of the Victoria and Albert Museum in 1983. Oliver Messel's comments on training and creating for the theatre were included in the museum's publication that accompanied its inaugural exhibit.

I never thought of having anything to do with the theatre. I merely trained as a painter at the Slade. The curious thing was that in my time there were no such things as schools for the theatre or design, or anything like that. We just went to study and to paint, and if anyone was given a job to do for the theatre, they did it or didn't. . . . When I'm designing, which is always terribly hard, I wrap a cold towel around my head and I have an awful headache because I think, 'Oh God, I mustn't repeat this! I can't repeat that.' That's the terrible thing about the theatre—you have to be like a chameleon, always changing and trying to think of something that hasn't been done before. . . . With the theatre you're submitted to the author's point of view. You must illustrate what is there and not yourself.

DESIGNERS WHO DESIGN SETS AND LIGHTS

Just as some talented designers do costumes as well as sets on a production, many famous scenic designers in the theatre firmly believe in doing the lighting as well as the sets in order to fulfill what they regard as a total scenic concept. Two of the most notable examples of designers who created their own lighting were Jo Mielziner (1901–1976) and Donald Oenslager (1902–1976). Howard Bay (1912–1986) and William Ritman (1928–1984) also did lighting. Other contemporary designers who may design sets only, both sets and lights, or sets, cos-

Setting by George Tsypin
THE SCREENS by Jean Genet
Directed by JoAnne Akalaitis

Costumes by Eiko Ishioka
Lighting by Jennifer Tipton
Tyrone Guthrie Theatre

Minneapolis
Minnesota (1989)
(Photograph by George Tsypin)

"The synthetic net was stretched over the entire stage and audience. That was 'the land of the dead.' As actors died one by one they reappeared on the net in slow movement, falling, crawling, sinking in that metaphorical 'desert in the sky.'" —George Tsypin

tumes, and lighting include Ben Edwards, William and Jean Eckart, Lester Polakov, Neil Peter Jampolis, Robert Randolph, James Tilton, Clarke Dunham, Eldon Elder, Fred Kolo, Lloyd Burlingame, David Hays, David F. Segal, Paul Wonsek, and Kevin Rigdon.

Jo Mielziner (1901–1976) was a unique talent in the American theatre. He was multitalented in four distinct categories: he could design, paint, draw, and do stage lighting with equal finesse and great theatricality. At an earlier period in his career Mielziner also designed costumes. The following excerpts are from Clive Barnes's tribute to Jo Mielziner in *The New York Times* on March 16, 1976:

It was Mr. Mielziner's ability to see the stage as an environment rather than a setting that gave him his very special place in the American theatre. He moved with the playwrights. At one time theatrical setting was a commonplace profession. Men such as Lee Simonson changed all that, but it was perhaps Mr. Mielziner who first understood that almost cinematic mystery of place that he brought, for example, to his settings for those great plays of that period, Tennessee Williams' The Glass Menagerie *and Arthur Miller's*

Death of a Salesman. *They helped change the face of the American theatre. . . .*

A house would light up showing the interior, or a wood could emerge from a backcloth. Mr. Mielziner was also very aware of the influence of lighting on the settings, and he understood the illuminating lessons of Gordon Craig and Adolphe Appia. But everything he did was himself and was American. . . .

As a person he was modest, fascinating, and with the gentleness that comes from strength. Recently an English critic wrote that the thing that most impressed him about the American theatre was the superiority of American stage design over the rest of the world. Perhaps it was flattery, but not really. And that superiority owes an enormous amount to the scenic imagination and theatrical gesture of Jo Mielziner.

Albin Krebs in *The New York Times* (March 16, 1976) also noted some highlights of Jo Mielziner's life and career:

Mr. Mielziner designed the settings for such dramas as Eugene O'Neill's Strange Interlude, *Elmer Rice's* Street Scene, *Tennessee Williams'* The Glass Menagerie, Summer and Smoke, *and* Cat on a Hot

Tin Roof; *Rudolf Besier's* The Barretts of Wimpole Street *and Mr. Rice's* Dream Girl.

Of such Mielziner designs, the writer Djuna Barnes once said, "Jo has a unique gift to lay age upon his settings, giving them a rich patina of occupancy." . . .

Mr. Mielziner, unlike so many other designers, worked with a very small staff, usually only two assistants. "I could enlarge my office," he said, "and hire 50 men and become a millionaire. But I'd simply sicken myself with grouse and good port, and die of shame."

He said that his greatest headache—"indeed heartache"—was the frenetic haste it took to do his design jobs. The scene designer, he explained, has about three or four days to work out his design, and maybe three weeks to render hundreds of sketches and find dozens of props. He also had to experiment endlessly with lights.

"I like to brood," he said, "and there's no time for brooding. Only 100-hour work weeks in which one minute you're creating magic, the next minute you find

David Mitchell: FOXFIRE (1982); Tony Straiges: SUNDAY IN THE PARK WITH GEORGE (1983), Playwrights Horizons (Photograph by Ney Tait Fraser)

Loren Sherman: SHŌGUN (1990), Lighting: Natasha Katz; Charles E. McCarry: THE COMEDY OF ERRORS (1991)

Peter Larkin: THE RINK (1984); Boris Aronson: THE GENTLE PEOPLE (1939) (Courtesy of Lisa Aronson, Photograph by Tony Holmes)

James Stewart Morcom: MOULIN ROUGE, Radio City Music Hall (1962), Costumes: Frank Spencer. (Photograph by James Stewart Morcom); Peter Harvey: A MIDSUMMER NIGHT'S DREAM (1979)

Randy Barcelo: THE MAGIC OF KATHERINE DUNHAM (1987); Ray Klausen: HAPPY BIRTHDAY, HOLLYWOOD (1987), Lighting: Jeff Engel, *Pictured:* Patti LaBelle

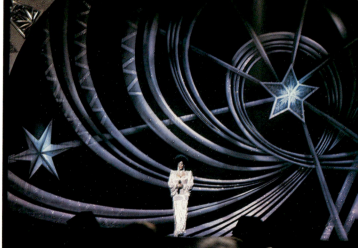

Ming Cho Lee: ATTILA (1980); William and Jean Eckart: FLORA, THE RED MENACE (1965)

Boris Aronson: CABARET (1966); Boris Aronson: THE ROSE TATTOO (1951) (Sketches Courtesy of Lisa Aronson, Photographs by Tony Holmes)

Tony Walton: GUYS AND DOLLS (1992); Tony Walton: THE WILL ROGERS FOLLIES (1991), Costumes: Willa Kim, Lighting: Jules Fisher. *Pictured*: Tommy Tune, Jeff Calhoun, and cast.

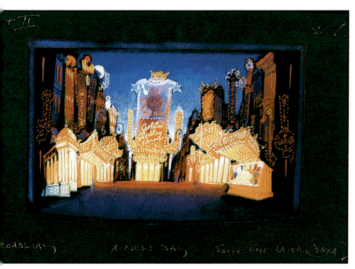

Maria Björnson: THE PHANTOM OF THE OPERA Scenic Detail (1988) (Photograph by Arnold Abramson); David Mitchell: THE SLEEPING BEAUTY (1991)

Costume designs by Willa Kim for Robert Lowell's THE OLD GLORY, Endecott and the Red Cross, American Place Theatre (1976)

Costume designs by Eduardo Sicangco for CARMEN, New York City Opera (1992). *Left:* March of the Toreadors. *Right:* Chorus and Supers for Act 1.

yourself serving as a practical plumber or making a four ton set disappear.''

By 1922 . . . he was most impressed with what was going on in the Berlin theatre world. . . . "The possibilities seemed limitless there," Mr. Mielziner recalled years later, "and everything was breaking away in new directions. In the theatre no one was interested in dramatizing man and his problems; they wanted to examine what this new world was doing to man. They did this even in the classics—Shakespeare, Schiller, Goethe were all treated with great violence. Scenery was strong in color with no attempt at realism. Structural elements were brought right out onto the stage. The lighting was particularly effective—harsh, glaring spots focused directly on the actors. I've never forgotten it.' "

DESIGNERS WHO PREFER DESIGNING SETS ONLY

A number of notable scenic designers usually prefer to design scenery only. Among them are the following:

Ming Cho Lee
David Mitchell
Oliver Smith
Tony Straiges
Robin Wagner
David Jenkins

Rolf Beyer
Ray Klausen
Sandro La Ferla
Bennet Averyt
James D. Sandefur
Ray Recht

Douglas W. Schmidt
Eugene Lee
Peter Larkin
John Lee Beatty
Karl Eigsti
Bob Shaw
Kert Lundell
Robert Darling
Marjorie Bradley Kellogg
Andrew Jackness
Heidi Landesman
Adrianne Lobel
John Wulp
Don Jensen
John Kasarda
Ed Burbridge
John Jenson
Hal Tine
Chris Barreca
Richard Seger
John Ezell
James Leonard Joy
Hugh Landwehr
Stephan Olson
James Morgan
Bob Phillips

Harry Feiner
Holmes Easley
John Shimrock
James Noone
Robert D. Mitchell
Douglas Stein
John Arnone
Thomas Lynch
David Potts
David Gropman
Karen Schulz
Charles E. McCarry
Philipp Jung
Michael Anania
Alexander Okun
John B. Wilson
Edward T. Gianfrancesco
Miguel Romero
Daniel Ettinger
Loren Sherman
Loy Arcenas
Kenneth Foy
Elmon Webb and Virginia Dancy
George Tsypin
Ralph Funicello

Setting by John Falabella
BROADWAY SINGS: THE MUSIC OF JULE STYNE
For "Great Performances," PBS-TV
Scene: "Every Street's a Boulevard."
Directed by Joe Layton
Costumes by Theoni V. Aldredge
Lighting by Ken Billington
St. James Theatre, New York (1987)
Pictured: Chita Rivera and company.
(Photograph by John Falabella)

COSTUME DESIGNERS WHO WORK IN THE COMMERCIAL THEATRE

Like scenic designers, costume designers create work in a wide diversity of places. Besides Broadway and regional theatre, they design for operas, ballets, films, television, ice shows, pageants, and almost any other entertainment where costumes are needed. Some costume designers design only costumes, while others also create scenery. Some of the most popular and best-known costume designers who work on Broadway and on other theatrical productions include:

Florence Klotz
Theoni V. Aldredge
Patricia Zipprodt
Ann Roth
Jane Greenwood
Jennifer von Mayrhauser
Willa Kim
Freddy Wittop
Ruth Morley
Linda Fisher
Andrew Marlay
Randy Barcelo
William Ivey Long
Rita Ryack
Nancy Potts
Julie Weiss
Franne Lee

Sara Brook
David Toser
Nan Cibula
Albert Wolsky
Christina Giannini
Bill Walker
Patricia McGourty
Lowell Detweiler
Judy Dearing
Joseph G. Aulisi
Dunya Ramicova
Donald Brooks
Ann Hould-Ward
Laura Crow
Jess Goldstein
Whitney Blausen
Alvin Colt
Carol Oditz

Jeanne Button
David Murin
Patton Campbell
Pearl Somner
Carrie F. Robbins
Robert Morgan
Lindsay W. Davis
Miles White
Judith Dolan
John David Ridge
Carol Luiken
Robert Wojewodski
David Charles
Sarah Gifft
Geoffrey Holder
Ann Emonts
Dona Granata
Ray Diffen
Sam Kirkpatrick
Robert Mackintosh
Suzanne Mess
Ray Aghayan
Nanzi Adzima
Bernard Johnson

Noel Taylor
Gail Brassard
Sarah Edwards
Candice Donnelly
Walker Hicklin
Costanza Romero
Holly Hynes
Stanley Simmons
Patricia Quinn Stuart
Lewis Brown
Martin Pakledinaz
Gregg Barnes
Hal George
Marianna Elliott
Susan Hilferty
Catherine Zuber
Diedre Clancy
David Loveless
Cynthia O'Neal
Lucinda Ballard
Robert Pusilo
Ramse Mostoller
Toni-Leslie James
Irene Sharaff

Tharon Musser
Richard Nelson
Thomas Skelton
Jules Fisher
Peggy Clark
Roger Morgan
Marc B. Weiss
Paul Gallo
Beverly Emmons
Richard Pilbrow
Martin Aronstein
Dennis Parichy
Ronald Wallace
Pat Collins
Richard Riddell
Peter Kaczorowski
Peggy Eisenhauer
Joan Sullivan
Craig Miller
Andy Phillips
Marcia Madeira
Allen Lee Hughes
Jennifer Tipton
John Gleason
Judy Rasmuson
Jackie Manassee
William Mintzer
Dawn Chiang
Andrew Bridge
Marilyn Rennagel
Barry Arnold

Terry Hands
Natasha Katz
James F. Ingalls
Mary Jo Dondlinger
Mimi Sherin
John Michael
    Deegan
Christopher Akerlind
Frances Aronson
Ralph Holmes
Arden Fingerhut
Jane Reisman
Jeff Davis
Richard Winkler
Nananne Porcher
Todd Lichtenstein
Spencer Mosse
F. Mitchell Dana
Robert Brand
Christina Giannelli
Derek Duarte
Ian Calderon
David Noling
Ruth Roberts
Abe Feder
Pamela Cooper
John McLain
Scott Pinkney
Duane Schuler
Gil Wechsler
Stephen Strawbridge

LIGHTING DESIGNERS WHO WORK IN THE COMMERCIAL THEATRE

While some lighting designers may design sets or costumes on occasion, they usually prefer to do lights only. Included in the roster of lighting designers who have done Broadway, opera, and other theatrical productions are:

David Hersey
Ken Billington

Robby Monk
Shirley Prendergast

Stage design by Donald Oenslager
DON CARLOS by Giuseppe Verdi
Libretto by François Joseph Méry and Camille
    du Locle
The garden—monastery of St. Just
Directed by Tito Capobianco
Hemis Fair '68
Produced by the San Antonio Symphony
San Antonio, Texas (1968)
(Photograph by Peter A. Juley and Son)

It is often interesting to go back in time and read what well-known designers have said about designing. In the April 13, 1968, issue of *Opera News* (vol. 32, no. 24) Jean Rosenthal expressed her feelings about stage lighting:

I have always believed that the use of stage light should be an organic part of the stage effect, and that the audience should not be aware of the beauty of the light effect but of the beauty and appropriateness of the stage atmosphere. The poor, romantic garret in La Bohème *seems to me to be more compelling if the atmosphere of a cold, moonlit night outside and the light of the candle inside provide the contrast of light and shadow, rather than streaking the stage with slashes of cross-light that are momentarily effective, but for the most part, irritating.*

Good lighting, like good anything, does take more time than hasty improvisation. It requires that the director, the set designer and the lighting designer collaborate from the inception of the production. The effects can then be planned so that space is provided for interesting and appropriate positions of the lighting instruments. The patterns of light are dependent on the direction from which they are projected. The leafy, mottled forest light in the new Metropolitan Hansel and Gretel was no happy accident; it was made possible because Nathaniel Merrill, the stage director, and Robert

~THE GARDEN~ MONASTERY OF ST. JUST

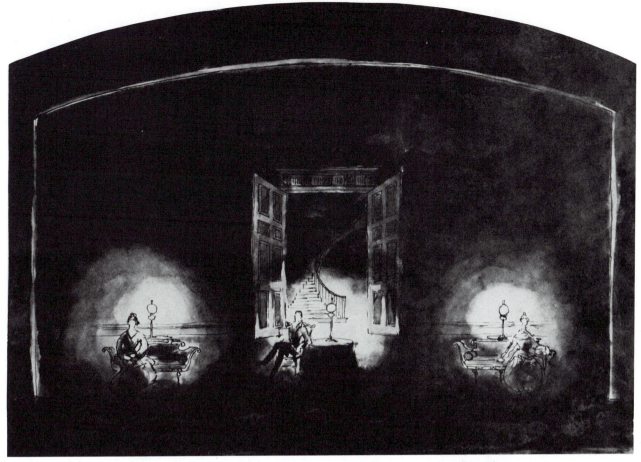

Stage design by Ben Edwards
MORE STATELY MANSIONS
by Eugene O'Neill
Directed by José Quintero
Broadhurst Theatre
New York (1967)

O'Hearn, the scenic designer, helped prepare the effect in advance.

WELL-KNOWN PERSONALITIES WHO HAVE DESIGNED FOR THE THEATRE

Producers and directors have sometimes sought out famous artists to design a cohesive production by doing both sets and costumes. At the same time, the artist's personality and artistic stamp on the show gives it a special look.

This group of talented individuals includes painters, illustrators, fashion designers, and theatrical and film directors. A list of such artists might very well include well-known personalities who also are or have been members of the United Scenic Artists Union. To name only a few: illustrator Maurice Sendak; painter David Hockney, directors and designers Franco Zeffirelli, Pier Luigi Pizzi, and the late Jean-Pierre Ponnelle; fashion and costume designers Oleg Cassini and Bob Mackie; and set, costume, and fashion designer Erté (1892–1990).

The surrealist painter Salvador Dali (1904–1989) was a member of United Scenic Artists Union, Local 829 for forty-five years. His stage work included decor and costumes for *Bacchanale* (1939) and *Labyrinth* (1941), both for Ballet Russe de Monte Carlo; also *Mad Tristan* (1944) and *Sentimental Colloquy* (1944), both for Ballet International. In addition, Dali designed for opera.

The sculptor Isamu Noguchi (1904–1988) created much significant work for the performing arts. He was a union member from 1956 to 1971. Noguchi designed the decor for renowned choreographers such as Martha Graham, George Balanchine, and Merce Cunningham.

Other well-known artists who have designed for the theatre, opera and ballet in years past include Marc Chagall, Joan Miró, Pavel Tchelitchew, Pablo Picasso, Giorgio de Chirico, Henri Matisse, and Marcel Vertès.

Another prominent personality in the arts is illustrator and author Edward Gorey, whose design work has been seen on Broadway, in productions of the Eglevsky Ballet Company, and on PBS Mystery Theatre. Although

Gorey did not produce or direct *Dracula* (1977) at the Martin Beck Theatre in New York City, the production was advertised here and abroad as the "Edward Gorey production of *Dracula*." His original concept and stylish approach made it a delight for all who saw it, as well as for those who worked on the show with him. Howard Kissel of *Women's Wear Daily* had this to say about Gorey's set and costume design for *Dracula*:

But what makes the uptown "Dracula" so entertaining is seeing Gorey's delicious work in three dimensions—he has put bats everywhere: on the wallpaper, on the closures of Renfield's pajamas, on those parts of a heroine's bed canopy usually reserved for cherubs. The vault scene is stunning—it reminds us of the sheer fun of scenic splendor, which our theatre has thought itself "mature" for avoiding. If one goes to see "The Magic Flute" at the Met for Marc Chagall why shouldn't one go to see "Dracula" for Edward Gorey?"

Sometimes a famous clothing designer is asked to create costumes for the theatre. Usually this comes about because he or she is currently a popular

Stage design by José Varona
CINDERELLA by Serge Prokofiev

Choreographed by Valery Panov
Berlin Deutsche Oper

West Berlin
Germany (1976)

personality in the world of high fashion and high society. French designer Christian Lacroix was engaged to design the costumes for the American Ballet Theatre's new *Gaité Parisienne*, which premiered in Tampa, Florida, in January 1988. In "A Ballet by Massine and Colors by Lacroix" (*The New York Times*, January 20, 1988), Michael Gross quotes Lacroix:

"The first creation of this ballet was in 1938, 50 years ago," he said. "Leonide Massine choreographed that production set to music by Jacques Offenbach. Mr. Massine's son, Lorca, has staged the new version.

"The costumes fifty years ago were very romantic and very soft and very pastel things," Mr. Lacroix continued. "For me, 'Gaité Parisienne' is something colorful, not pale. So I proposed to Baryshnikov and Massine doing something stronger, acider, something more modern. I prefer to be inspired by Toulouse Lautrec and the turn of the century and all the bright, very daring French posters, because the music is not sweet. It's very dynamic."

His costume designs include "a lot of primary [and secondary] colors: blue, red and green," Mr. Lacroix said. He has also used graphic mixtures of stripes, spots, and checks. "It's very dynamic to mix," the designer explained. "I wanted some-

thing very readable from far away in the audience. Something shaped, built, constructed."

The neo-romantic painter and designer Eugene Berman (1899–1972) brought his phenomenal talent to the theatre in designing beautiful settings and costumes for the opera and ballet. In 1972, when I had the privilege of assisting Eugene Berman, he commented about his preference for designing both costumes and scenery for a production:

I think that a stage designer has to do everything so as to give complete unity to a production. I think a collaborative situation in which one does scenery and another does the costumes is purely an American phenomenon. It doesn't make any sense. It doesn't work. I firmly disapprove of such a manner of working. I think a man who designs for the theatre has to do the whole production or he shouldn't touch the theatre.

One designer has to conceive of the whole thing together as a unit. If you have very elaborate scenery, you have to have simpler costumes and the other way around. But you have to have everything in your mind and decide what you want. You cannot work with somebody else who is doing his part and wants also to be a star. It doesn't work. I would never

touch a thing if I could not conceive it, the whole thing, from A to Z.

A CHAT WITH EUGENE BERMAN

While I was assisting Eugene Berman, it was my good fortune to talk with him about his career as an opera and ballet designer when he was in New York to design sets and costumes for *Pulcinella* during the Stravinsky Festival at Lincoln Center. I asked him about his career in a taped session on June 12, 1972, at Nolan's Scenery Studio in Brooklyn.

Do you prefer easel painting or do you prefer designing for the theatre and ballet?

I am a painter. Theatre is a sideline, but very much a sideline. There is no comparison, no hesitation. I am also a stage designer because I am a painter and because I paint. The European painters of my generation—not all of them, but some of them—were also interested in the theatre. But it is an avocation. I don't consider designing for the theatre my profession. I like the theatre and I have a sense of the theatre.

I don't want to work any more in the theatre because it is not the important thing in my life. It takes an enormous amount of time and energy. Fundamentally. I prefer staying in my studio and painting and not being beset by all these problems.

You mentioned that in the early part of the century many well-known artists designed for the theatre.

That theatre doesn't exist anymore. It couldn't exist anymore because of the complete change of modern society and of all the conditions of life.

We worked for a completely different theatre. It was like a court theatre. It was done for an elite of society, an elite of intellectuals, of artists. It was run by an extraordinary man—Diaghilev—under completely different conditions than those that exist today. I think because of his own prestige and his personality he could go to Picasso, Braque, Matisse, and all the greatest artists and ask them to work for him, and they would do it for peanuts or for nothing. The artists were interested in collaborating and collaborating with Diaghilev. But they would not work for Mr. [Sol] Hurok or Mr. [Rudolph] Bing or for any of the directors who have

Setting and costumes by Jean-Pierre Ponnelle
IDOMENEO by Wolfgang Amadeus Mozart
Text by Abbe Varesco
Directed by Jean-Pierre Ponnelle
Lighting by Neil Peter Jampolis
Salzburger Festspielhaus
Salzburg, Austria (1983)
(Photograph by Neil Peter Jampolis)

anything to do with the kind of modern theatre. It was like Wagner working for Ludwig of Bavaria. It was the last flourishing of something that doesn't exist anymore. These were people who were not thinking in terms of a commercial theatre, but purely as an artistic theatre.

Now a thing has to be large-scale for a very large public and has to collect that much money! I think with the transfer of all the theatre and of the arts to America because of the Second World War, everything is now on a different basis. It is run on a consumer basis and everything now is commercialized. The consumer spirit of modern American life puts everything that was yesterday into the ash can today. I think they want to have a sort of eternal world—new things, new people whether good or bad, it doesn't matter. I think the cynicism of Americans in treating art values and of proclaiming, of admiring, buying, accepting, discarding, throwing into the ash can, rediscovering, and so on is infantile. It's like a little child who says, "I don't like that toy because I played with it yesterday. I need a new toy from day to day. Let's break up that toy of yesterday and trample it."

"The face of Neptune was executed in fiber glass and sprayed with stone texture to match the stone of the theatre back wall (Felsenreitschule) 'the stone riding school.'"
—Neil Peter Jampolis

Working in the theatre for one reason or another everywhere is warped with difficulties and with timely considerations and habits which are deteriorating. Labor everywhere is costly. Time means money. People who run the theatre have less and less money. Formerly, private people would give much money to certain things. But private people are now sort of so burdened with taxes and so on. To a certain extent the people who run the theatre, on the one hand, have certain excuses for not doing things the way they were done thirty or forty years ago. Conditions now are much more difficult. And also, the people now are much more commercially minded.

When you design an opera or a ballet, you like to paint on your own scenery. Is that your personal way of working or is that the European way?

Not necessarily the European way. It depends on the painter. Many people don't do that, some do. I paint on my backgrounds because I often am not satisfied with the way my scenery is interpreted. If everything is done well, I don't feel the necessity to correct or to interfere. When the scenic artists do their job very, very well and with a real intuition, I am very happy. I know Johnny Keck now, and next time if I have to have anything done, I know I would trust him to the extent that I

would keep away or come at the last minute and maybe do a few corrections.

The sketch is small, and then I see that enormous thing for the stage and I feel it needs addition and it needs developing. You cannot complete everything in a sketch. Also, if you have to do a mural, you have to lay your hands on that mural. You don't just do what you have in the sketch. A mural has to be developed. I think that some of the scenery occasionally has to be developed and filled in. Very often it has to be corrected in the design, in the structure, the colors, the form, the construction, the many details.

If a theatre design student asked what you thought was necessary to prepare for a career in the theatre, what would you say?

I think that a good stage designer should of course be a theatrical man, have a flair for the theatre and be a good painter. And most of the existing stage designers don't paint. They are specialized and they never develop as painters, and therefore they don't develop into [great] stage designers. I think that a stage designer who is not a good painter is not a good stage designer. It doesn't mean that if he is a good painter, he can also be a good stage designer, because I know a lot of good painters who are not interested in the theatre and don't understand the theatre. You have to be a good painter and you have to have a theatrical sense and be interested in the theatre and understand what the theatre is all about. It's all of that. So it goes both ways.

Then you would advise a talented young designer who is just starting out to get a painting and drawing background before anything else?

Surely, but to continue to paint, not give it up as soon as they get established on Broadway or in the theatre and then say, "Now I am a stage designer and I am designing," which most of them do. You know, they paint a little bit in the beginning, and then they sort of give it up and they become specialized stage designers. They don't develop as painters, and they are very primitive painters. They maybe know technically important things to solve, the mechanics of moving things on stage, devising very clever information, and so on, but they are not painters. You have to be a good painter to be a good stage designer. But that's not the American notion of a stage designer. The stage designer is something between an engineer and an—I don't know.

CODESIGNING PRODUCTIONS

Sometimes a stage designer will team up with another to work on various productions in the theatre. Some of these associations are long-term, while others last for only one or two shows. When two designers work together and share billing on a production, they tend to have equal weight in making decisions and similar artistic input to the design process. There are several examples of notable designers, both past and present, in the theatre who have collaborated as a team. These include stage designers William and Jean Eckart (sets, lights, and costumes), Elmon Webb and Virginia Dancy, Michael J. Hotopp and Paul de Pass, Herbert Senn and Helen Pond, Michael Yeargan and Lawrence King, and Timothy O'Brien and Tazeena Firth.

WORKING WITH ASSOCIATE DESIGNERS

Designers also work with colleagues who are designated associate designers, and this position, as the title implies, ranks above the assistant designer. A designer may be offered the job of associate designer after assisting on many collaborations with the head designer, or may be hired as an associate on the very first show the two do together. The success of this arrangement depends on the schedule, the negotiation of a mutually satisfactory compensation, the working out of a compatible working relationship, and the availability of the associate designer.

Some of the most notable examples of the role of associate designers have been with productions that were first presented in London and then brought to New York. American designers have been engaged as associate designers to re-create or adapt designs according to the original production. For Peter Shaffer's play *Amadeus*, directed by Peter Hall (1979), John Bury designed the production for the world premiere in London at the National Theatre. Bury also designed the New York produc-

Stage design by John Lee Beatty
LIPS TOGETHER, TEETH APART

by Terrence McNally
Directed by John Tillinger

Manhattan Theatre Club
New York (1991)

Scenery by Loren Sherman
SHŌGUN: The Musical by James Clavell
Book and lyrics by John Driver
Music by Paul Chihara
Directed and choreographed by Michael
   Smuin
Costumes by Patricia Zipprodt
Lighting by Natasha Katz
Hair and wigs by Patrik D. Moreton
Marquis Theatre, New York (1990)

tion (1980) at the Broadhurst Theatre, for which there were three associate designers: Ursula Belden (scenery), John David Ridge (costumes), and Beverly Emmons (lighting).

When the Royal Shakespeare Company performed *Much Ado About Nothing* and *Cyrano de Bergerac* in a double bill at the Gershwin Theatre in New York (1984), the settings were by Ralph Koltai, costumes by Alexander Reid, and lighting by Terry Hands. Also appearing on the title page of the *Playbill* was the credit line: "American Production Designed in Association with John Kasarda, Settings [and] Jeffrey Beecroft, Lighting." The plays were directed by Terry Hands.

Possibly the largest number of associates working on a production was for the hit musical *The Phantom of the Opera* at the Majestic Theatre in New York (1988) with sets and costumes designed by Maria Björnson, lighting designed by Andrew Bridge, and sound designed by Martin Levan. Credited in the back of the New York *Playbill* were

the U.S. and U.K. design staffs. The U.S. staff included one associate designer each for the categories of scenic, costume, lighting, and sound, with three assistants to the scenic designer and two assistants each to the costume, lighting, and sound designers (thirteen in all). The U.K. design staff listed a production technical consultant, one associate designer each for scenic, costume, lighting, and sound, one automation consultant, one draperies consultant, one sculpture consultant, and one sound consultant (total of eight).

THE SCENERY SUPERVISOR

A supervisory scenic designer's role in the commercial theatre is hard to define and varies with the individual production. The supervisory designer is usually a stage designer who is selected because he or she is adept at getting a production on stage and treats it as if it were his or her own show. The supervisory designer is a colleague of the main designer, and is similar if not identical to an associate designer, but prefers the supervisory title. On Broadway the supervisory designer is a union designer working with the main designer, who may or may not be a member of the union.

The following is a list of possible situations for a scenery supervisor:

1. The scenic designer in the capacity of supervisor may be engaged to duplicate the scenery from a production in London or another city for a commercial production in New York. The scenic supervisor's role usually is to keep the design faithful to the original production.

2. In another capacity, the scenic designer may be hired as a union designer on a Broadway show for which the head designer may be a prominent artist or illustrator who does not know the techniques of mounting a show on the Broadway stage. Or the head designer may be a beginning designer who is not yet a member of the union.

3. In still a third situation in the commercial theatre, the scenery supervisor may be a union designer working with another designer who also belongs to the union but who desires the skill and knowledge of the scenery supervisor.

In all kinds of productions, the title chosen for a designer working in collaboration with another scenic designer varies according to the relationship in the design process. Costume and lighting designers may also work in similar supervisory capacities. One certainly finds an overlap in duties and talent between various titles. One scenic designer will prefer the title of scenic supervisor when working with the

32 scenic designer who is actually credited with designing the show. Another designer will choose the title of associate designer instead of supervisory designer, while a third designer in a lesser capacity will be satisfied to be called an assistant designer.

The billing positions for these various titles may also vary. The scenic designer and supervisory designer normally get billing on the title page of the program, while an associate designer may or may not be given credit on the title page, and an assistant designer is usually listed in the back pages of the program unless a special rider to the contract and understanding exist from the very top. Of course, there may be an exception when an assistant has responded far beyond the call of duty and the head designer and management decide that more credit should be given, but this is a fairly rare occurrence.

DIRECTORS WHO DESIGN

Some directors are multitalented and enjoy taking on the added responsibility of designing the production themselves. Directors who choose to wear two such distinct and diversified hats on a large production must be admired enormously for their extraordinary ambition. To stage a big project involves months of preparation in research, study, and thought, but to design it as well can become a herculean task.

While a director-designer may have plenty of help from a team of very competent assistants, he or she nevertheless must make all the major decisions and ordinarily must do so in rapid succession. When the production is finally mounted, the director may be reviewed by critics in both areas, staging and design.

For the Houston Grand Opera's spectacular opening at the Alice and George Brown Theatre in the Wortham Center in Houston, Italian director and designer Pier Luigi Pizzi was engaged to do Verdi's *Aida*. The production was reviewed by Donal Henahan in *The New York Times* (November 16, 1987). His remarks on the direction and design are quoted here in part:

Pier Luigi Pizzi's uncluttered direction and stark designs bowed to "Aida" tradition, but certainly did not scrape. Yes,

he brought on elephants in the triumphal scene, but not the live kind, thank you. Huge but toylike tuskers with warriors astride were rolled about on wheels in a battle dance (inventively choreographed by Richard Caceres). A children's ballet, against all odds, actually proved palatable.

The sets consisted largely of ceiling-to-floor panels and pillars that slid in and out as scenes shifted. Mr. Pizzi, who likes to contrast brilliant light and Stygian gloom, illuminated the action with dozens of hand-held torches, as if to emphasize the darkly violent side of Egyptian society. The most memorable image, however, was a 25-foot-high bronze death's head of the god Ptah, which dominated the first temple scene (and, less logically, the Nile scene).

Other prominent artists who have been involved in theatrical productions as both director and stage designer include Wilford Leach (1929–1988), Jean-Pierre Ponnelle (1932–1988), Liviu Ciulei, Robert Wilson, and Franco Zeffirelli.

HIRING ASSISTANTS

Scenic, costume, and lighting designers hire assistants from time to time. This has been an established practice in the commercial theatre for many years, and also for opera and dance. Usually, the assistants are designers in their own right and are getting experience and learning the ropes while waiting to get shows on their own. It is both a learning experience and creative participation for a designer to assist another. Some well-known designers expect input from assistants, while others tend to suppress it.

Besides theatre work, assistants may be needed when the designer designs for television productions, feature films and commercials, display firms, restaurants, industrial shows, fashion shows, and nightclubs and discos. Designers may also be theatre consultants or teachers.

The reasons why assistants are needed vary as much with each designer as does the individual production. One or more of the following reasons may exist:

1. Time may be short.
2. The designer may be doing the sce-

nery for more than one production at the same time, or may be doing work in a related field.
3. A designer may be creating both set and costumes or set and lighting, and on occasion may be doing all three.
4. An assistant may be needed to do drafting or to work on models.
5. An assistant may be hired to fill in an area where the designer is not strong.
6. Assistants are needed to do research in libraries, to shop for fabrics, and to search for all kinds of materials.
7. The designer may need an assistant to go to the various scenic and costume shops, as well as to lighting firms.
8. Assistants are called on to go to rehearsals with and without designers.

During their careers, numerous designers have assisted other designers. Examples include Douglas W. Schmidt, David Mitchell, Marjorie Bradley Kellogg, and Leigh Rand assisting Ming Cho Lee; Irene Sharaff assisting Aline Bernstein; John Lee Beatty assisting Douglas W. Schmidt; Ming Cho Lee and Robert D. Mitchell assisting Jo Mielziner and Boris Aronson; Carl Toms, Robert O'Hearn, and William Pitkin assisting Oliver Messel; Florence Klotz assisting Alvin Colt; Robin Wagner and Robert O'Hearn assisting Oliver Smith; Ann Roth assisting Irene Sharaff; Gary Jones assisting Ann Roth; and David Peterson, Charles E. McCarry, Atkin Pace, and Thomas Peter Sarr assisting Robin Wagner.

While scenic designers may have new assistants help them with their productions from time to time, there are designers who are husband and wife and also work with each other. One of the longest designer associations was that of Lisa Jalowetz Aronson assisting her husband Boris Aronson. Another husband-and-wife scenic design team of long standing is David Jenkins and Leigh Rand, who still continue their professional working relationship, with Leigh assisting David. Ming Cho Lee has had the good fortune to have his wife, Betsy Lee, as studio and office manager and model maker to him for many years.

CHANGING DIRECTORS

In the commercial theatre, all sorts of things can happen before a show is finally put together and opens. One situation that can cause problems for the designer is a change in directors. This may happen by mutual agreement between the directors and the producers, but for an original production it may mean that there is a disagreement between the playwright and the director or among the director, the playwright, and the producer. This may happen during rehearsals, during an out-of-town engagement, or during previews in New York just before the show officially opens.

An unexpected change of directors can be frustrating for the scenic designer, because it may take place after decisions have already been made with the first director on the final design, and the sketches, models, and drawings have been completed. In such cases, the design often suffers because the original concept evolved from discussions with the first director while a work was being written. There is often no time to start from scratch with the new director. A director may also leave a production because the leading player or star becomes upset with the direction or the design concept. When this unfortunate situation develops in the commercial theatre, it usually hinders the production and does nothing to enhance the star's reputation.

A change of a director in a production may also mean that the scenic designer stays on and agrees to work with the new director and to make adjustments according to what the new director wants. A wise management and new director usually know that it would be a costly error to scrap all the scenic production and start completely new.

CHANGING THEATRES

A show may be slotted to go into a certain theatre and then for various reasons be moved to a different theatre. The reason for the change could be that another show changes theatres, closes, or extends its tour prior to coming to New York; or the producers want to move the show to a very respected theatre in a great location; or a house with a larger seating capacity suddenly becomes available.

Experienced designers are none too pleased to have to cope with a change of theatre once the models and drawings have been started, because a change of theatre usually means having to rework the drawings to the di-

Stage design by José Varona
PAQUITA by Ludwig Minkus
Choreographed by Natalia Makarova
National Ballet of Canada
Toronto, Ontario
Canada (1991)
Universal Ballet Company
Seoul
Korea (1991)

mensions of the new space. It causes real problems if the show is a big musical. If a designer knows ahead of time that there is a possibility of a production's playing in one of three different theatres, he or she can be thinking of how the set design will work in each. Ground plans and designs may have to be adjusted in a short period of time once the producers give the go-ahead and name the theatre.

CHANGING DESIGNERS

A scenic designer and other designers on a show are sometimes released from their contract, or sometimes a designer prefers to withdraw from a production when there are substantial differences between the director and/or management. This means that another scenic designer is engaged to do the scenery. While artistic differences may be the reason released to the public, a designer may also leave a show because the director who selected him or her has been fired.

WOMEN DESIGNING SCENERY

In the United States, it has long been common knowledge that most of the

Model by Loy Arcenas
DAY TRIPS by Jo Carson
Directed by Michael Engler
Hartford Stage Company
Hartford, Connecticut (1990)

successful scenic designers in the theatre are men. In recent years that has begun to change more and more. For some curious reason, women working in the theatre became more highly recognized artists in costume and lighting design rather than scenic design, although there were many women who had the experience and an excellent background in scenic design. Even though famous veterans Peggy Clark and Jean Rosenthal (1912–1969) designed scenery at some point in their long careers, both became best-known as lighting designers. On the other hand, Aline Bernstein (1880–1955) was an early pioneer in the fields of both scenery and costume design. She designed the sets and costumes for the Theatre Guild and for other prominent productions. Kate Drain Lawson and Emeline Roche also worked as set and costume designers in the commercial theatre. Besides designing costumes for numerous Broadway productions, Lucinda Ballard and Irene Sharaff designed both scenery and costumes for ballets, and designed for films.

In Europe quite a number of respected women scenic designers have been contributing notable works in both scenery and costume categories for a great many years. Among them are Tanya Moiseiwitsch, Sophie Fedorovitch, Doris Zinkeisen, Motley (Elizabeth Montgomery, Margaret Harris, and Sophie Harris), Jocelyn Herbert, and Sally Jacobs (all United Kingdom); Ita Maximowna (Berlin); Alexandra Exter (Russia); and Lila de Nobili (France).

It is encouraging to see more work by talented contemporary American women in the theatre. One of the most outstanding at the present time is Heidi Landesman, who was the first woman to win a Tony Award for her scenic designs, for the hit musical show *Big River* (1985). She was also a producer for that musical and for another smash hit musical, *Into the Woods* (1987). Landesman won another Tony Award for her scenery in *The Secret Garden* (1991) and in addition was a producer on the show. Other prominent women scenic designers are Marjorie Bradley Kellogg, Adrianne Lobel, Karen

Schulz, Kate Edmunds, and Ursula Beldon. These creative artists have worked on Broadway, Off-Broadway, and in regional theatre. While Willa Kim usually does costumes, she also designs scenery, particularly for the ballet.

Veteran stage designer Jean Eckart has teamed with her husband, William Eckart, to design sets, costumes, and lights for numerous Broadway productions. Helen Pond has collaborated for many years with Herbert Senn to design scenery for Broadway and opera productions.

Two notable women designers from abroad, Maria Björnson and Chloé Obolensky, received wide acclaim for their work in New York. Björnson received a Tony Award for her sets and costumes for *The Phantom of the Opera* (1988). Obolensky designed the sets, costumes, and props for *Mahabharata* (1987) and the sets and costumes for *The Cherry Orchard* (1988), both Peter Brook productions at the Brooklyn Academy of Music Majestic Theatre.

REVIVALS

Revivals of famous shows tend to retain the original collaborative team of designers whenever possible. For director/producer Harold Prince's revival of *Cabaret* (1987) at the Imperial Theatre in New York, the scenic design by David Chapman was based on the original designs by Boris Aronson with costumes designed by Patricia Zip-

prodt, who also did them originally. The lighting for the revival was designed by Marc B. Weiss, while Jean Rosenthal designed the lighting in 1966 when the production opened at the Broadhurst Theatre in New York.

THE TIME A DIRECTOR AND DESIGNER SPEND ON A PRODUCTION

In the commercial theatre, the amount of time the theatrical director and the scenic designer spend in meetings is always variable and may differ for each collaboration team and the individual production. Sometimes it only takes several weeks to get a show on, while other creative artists work on the production one year or two or more years. It goes without saying that if a production has been mounted and has had a run, and then moves from a resident company or an Off-Broadway house to Broadway, there are fewer, if any, problems to resolve.

In the foreword of Arnold Aronson's *American Set Design* (1985), Harold Prince remarked on the interval of time he is involved with a scenic designer on a project: "I think probably I was asked to write these words because my dependence on design is pretty well documented. It takes me an average of two years to direct a play or musical and the designer comes into the collaboration almost immediately. Occasionally, he or she is on the project before there's a play, on call as the play is being written."

Many successful designers accept the long period of time that it takes to work on an opera or an original production, and they usually consider this par for the course. On occasion, you will hear that a designer turned down a show because there was not a year or more to work on it. Other designers and artists tend to believe that during a long period of development, a play can be overanalyzed and overresearched and that the visual concepts can lose their spontaneity and freshness.

David Mitchell discussed with Studs Terkel in *New York* magazine (May 15, 1978) how he begins working on a production:

After I've read the script, I begin discussions with the director. How does he want the show to look? Some directors are very specific; some give you their thoughts rather subtly, obliquely. I try to put myself in a frame of mind to make the director's thoughts and feelings work.

Before I draw my pictures, I start out with a little play period where I don't box myself in by thinking, ''Well, we have to have a scene at this particular point.'' Forget about that. Once you start thinking about specific requirements, you restrict yourself. So give your imagination free play; you move around painted bits of cardboard, photos, forms, and shapes, trying to get the feeling that's right for the show. The first thing I do on a job is I go into the locale and take a lot of pictures. . . .

Mr. Mitchell had time to go to Chicago to photograph ''the muscular look, the modern look of Chicago'' that director Stephen Schwartz wanted for the locale of *Working*.

Once the pictures had been assembled, my assistants and I organized them into a slide show, and then we sorted the photos and tacked them up on boards—a storyboard of images throughout the show as we go from one sequence to another. Now, what were our dreams of what we'd like to do, and what were our limitations? We went to look at the space we had to work in. We had a ground plan of the threatre and the storage areas where we had to put the scenery. And then, what were the actors supposed to be doing? Eventually the pictures and the ground plan merged, and then we put the background and the actors together.

In the same article in *New York* magazine (May 15, 1978) David Mitchell talked about the amount of time he spent on designing *Annie* (1977) and how some of the ideas in the show came about by chance:

The most complicated thing is making a ground plan and section of the stage, so you can plan the height of scenery, plan where things will be stored, plan entrances and exits. Some scenery is moved by winches, some is ''flown'' from pipes above the stage, some is on elevators, some is on casters moved by stagehands—all of this has to be figured out. Eventually you work with a carpenter and a scenic shop in doing the working dia-

Model by Loy Arcenas
THREE POST CARDS by Craig Lucas
Directed by Norman Rene
South Coast Repertory
Costa Mesa, California (1987)

gram of the sets—that's the drawing from which the scenery is built. You design the props too—tables, chairs, everything.

The design comes out of the way we work in the studio. For instance, in Annie we went out and did a lot of research on thirties New York in the Bettmann Archive. We were very short on time on that show (about three weeks to design the sets and three to build and install them), so I employed five people immediately to take the research and make photocopies and make little cardboard cutouts of the photos. We had a thirties–New York tabletop that was six feet long. And the wonderful thing about that show was that some things were just accidents. Like the Duesenberg car. That wasn't in the script, but when we had it in cutout, Tom Meehan and Marty Charnin and Mike Nichols instantly realized that this could be Daddy Warbuck's car, and it could be the way to get Annie from the Lower East Side to Fifth Avenue. And so we pasted together a lot of things, and the style of the set evolved that way.

More often than not, in the commercial theatre there never seems to be enough time to mount a production. But there can be a surprisingly pleasant realization once the show is on and running that an unbelievable amount of creative work can be accomplished in a short period of time in the wonderful world of the theatre. When push comes to shove, and the gestation period for a scenic design is extremely short (for whatever the reason), any real professional knows that talent, experience, and intuition are the bottom line in creating a stunning and sensational set. The fact that there is no time to research the candy wrappers and seams in the wallpaper can put a real spark in the designer's imagination. The wisest of stage designers know that, as usual, it is important to do a thoroughly great job, to enjoy it all the way, but that it is not their last show. So they get on with it, and then go to the next project with renewed vigor, excitement, and anticipation.

WORKING WITH THE SAME COLLABORATIVE TEAM

A creative collaborative team that has had a previous smash hit frequently will be selected to do another big show in the future and prove that the same magic formula works again for a new

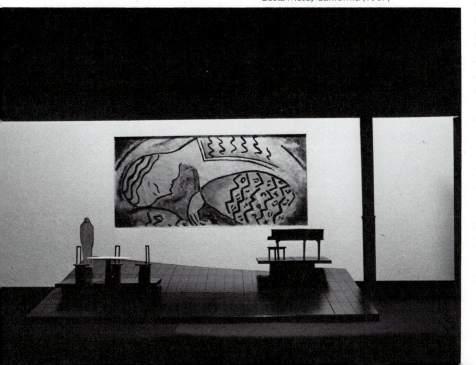

artistic and box office success. *Sunday in the Park with George* at the Booth Theatre in New York (1984) had music and lyrics by Stephen Sondheim and book and direction by James Lapine. The scenery was by Tony Straiges, the costumes by Patricia Zipprodt and Ann Hould-Ward, and the lighting by Richard Nelson. A few seasons later, the credits were identical for the musical *Into the Woods* at the Martin Beck Theatre in New York (1987), except that costumes were by Ann Hould-Ward, based on original concepts by Patricia Zipprodt and Ann Hould-Ward.

GETTING A SHOW IN THE COMMERCIAL THEATRE

It is always possible that a successful repertory production will move to Broadway with the same designers who worked on it originally. Two examples of this involved productions by the Yale Repertory Theatre. *'Master Harold' . . . and the Boys*, written and directed by Athol Fugard, opened at the Lyceum Theatre in New York (1982) with the setting by Jane Clark, costumes by Sheila McLamb, and lighting by David Noling. Another premiere production of the Yale Repertory Theatre, August Wilson's *Fences*, was directed by Lloyd Richards at the Forty-sixth Street Theatre in New York (1987). The set design was by James D.

Sandefur, costume design by Candice Donnelly, and lighting design by Danianne Mizzy.

ACCEPTING A JOB AS A DESIGNER

In the commercial theatre a well-known designer may take every show that he or she is offered, with the rationale that only one in every seven or eight will be a hit, and it is difficult enough to earn a living in the theatre.

A different point of view might be expressed by another name designer. He or she will not be so concerned that a show will be lucrative. For personal satisfaction he or she may only want to design a particular play, musical, dance piece, or opera. The designer may also want to be involved in the creative process of bringing a new play or musical to production and performance by sharing thoughts and ideas with the playwright and director while the show is being written and have the design evolve as part of the original work.

There are any number of reasons why you may be contacted to design the scenery, lighting, or costumes on a production. Among these are:

1. A director who has worked with you tells the producers or general managers that you are the designer he/she wants.
2. The producers or general managers have worked with you on other productions.
3. Your work has been seen by the director or producer and he or she feels that your style is just right for the production.
4. The playwright may insist upon having you create the set design for his or her script.

You may be contacted by telephone to discuss the possibilities of your designing the show. At the initial contact, there are at least three routine questions you should ask the general manager or producer: Who is the director? What is the budget for scenery, costumes, and lighting? When and where does the show open?

Initially it may be wise to say, "I would definitely be interested," rather than "Yes." This does not commit you to do the show before you have all the information to intelligently assess the offer.

The next logical step is to schedule an appointment with the producer or general manager to discuss the important details. This meeting should be amiable and the discussion should explore the budget, schedule, general set requirements, contractual agreements, and any other details you feel are important to your role as the designer of the production. If these points are mutually agreeable, then the answer is definitely "Yes."

Stage design by Jo Mielziner
OUT CRY by Tennessee Williams

Directed by Peter Glenville
Lyceum Theatre

New York (1973)
(Photograph by Peter A. Juley and Son)

Stage design by Lester Polakov   by Carson McCullers   Staged by Harold Clurman
THE MEMBER OF THE WEDDING   Based on her novel   Empire Theatre, New York (1950)

CONTRACT INFORMATION AND JOB DESCRIPTIONS

The following information is quoted from the United Scenic Artists, Local 829 contract information booklet and is generally applicable to Broadway productions.

THE SCENIC DESIGNER (ART DIRECTOR) SHALL:

1. Design the sets for the production;
2. Provide a working model, complete color sketches or color sketch models, story boards, illustrations, continuity sketches and perspectives;
3. Provide necessary working drawings for construction carpenter;
4. Provide contracting painter with color schemes or color sketches, and designation of surface texture;
5. Design, select or approve properties required for the production, including draperies and furniture;
6. Design and/or supervise special scenic effects, including projections, locations and dressing of sets and scenery, matte shots, gobos, and visual transition devices;
7. Supervise the building and painting of sets and the making of properties, con-

sult on lighting of a TV set and compatibility of motion picture sequences in live programs.

THE COSTUME DESIGNER SHALL:

1. Design the costumes;
2. Provide a costume plot listing the costume changes by scene for each character;
3. Provide color sketches of all designed costumes and a visual representation for selected costumes;
4. Provide complete color sketches or outline sketches with color samples, including necessary drawings or descriptions of detail and its application for the contracting shop, including selection of all necessary fabrics and trims;
5. Be responsible for selection and coordination of contemporary costumes, including selection from performer's personal wardrobe;
6. Supervise fittings and alterations of costumes;
7. Design, select and/or approve all accessories: headgear, gloves, footwear, hose, purses, jewelry, umbrellas, canes, fans, bouquets, masks, etc.;
8. Supervise and/or approve makeup and hairstyling, selection of wigs, hairpieces, mustaches and beards.

THE LIGHTING DESIGNER SHALL:

1. Design the lighting;
2. Provide a full equipment list and light plot to scale showing type and position of all necessary instruments;
3. Provide a color plot and necessary information for contract electrician;
4. Provide a control plot;
5. Design, supervise and plot special effects;
6. Supervise the hanging and focusing of lighting equipment and the setting of all light cues;

All Designers and Art Directors discuss estimates for building and painting of sets and properties with contractors, costume designs with costume shops, lighting specifications with lighting contractors.

THE ASSISTANTS TO THE SCENIC, COSTUME AND LIGHTING DESIGNERS are engaged in order to assist the Designers in the work of the Designers. All terms and conditions of agreements under which Designers work apply equally to Assistants.

THE CHARGEMAN SCENIC ARTIST shall be responsible to the Scenic Designer (Art Director) for the accomplishment of work which includes the following:

1. The preparation, painting and/or coloration of all textures, plastering, appliquéing on scenery, sets and properties as necessary;
2. The application of all decorative wall or surface coverings applied by any means;
3. Creative scenic artwork, including projections and enlargements, drawings for profiles and for the carpenter shop;
4. All lettering and sign work, sculpturing, modeling, mold-making, casting, portraits or special artwork (including paintings and murals);
5. Miniature sets and/or models.

THE JOURNEYMAN SCENIC ARTIST is engaged in order to assist in the work of the Chargeman.

SHOPMEN may have the following duties:

1. Make and maintain tools, i.e., drawing sticks, pounce bags, snaplines, floggers, etc.
2. Maintain inventory of all paints, dyes, binders, solvents and supplies, and notify the Chargeman or shop purchasing agent of any immediate shortages;
3. Clean and maintain all brushes and pails used by the Scenic Artist;
4. Prepare glues, sizes, anilines and textural solutions used by the Scenic Artist;
5. Stand by to assist the Scenic Artist in such areas as bringing equipment to work areas, snapping lines, taping and laying paper, moving scenery, laying out and folding up of drops, and in any other way that he or she may be called upon to assist, with the exception of any actual drawing, painting, or application of scenic material;
6. Maintain the cleanliness of work areas;
7. Run any errand which pertains to the work of the Scenic Artist's crew and is requested by the Chargeman.

IN LIVE THEATRE, INCLUDING OPERA AND BALLET:

Designers attend pre-Broadway and Broadway set-ups, technical and dress rehearsals, first public performances and openings out of town and in New York. Scenic Designers conduct the scenic rehearsals, Costume Designers conduct costume rehearsals; Lighting Designers conduct lighting rehearsals. If the Lighting Designer is required by the Producer to be at more than three out-of-town stops prior to Broadway, he shall be paid the daily rate up to four days for each additional stop.

Designers attend public performances from time to time to conduct a normal check of the sets, costumes or lighting.

Assistants to each of the Designers shall be engaged by the Producer at the request of the Designer, with the Producer's approval. Designers' Assistants file separate agreements with the Union.

An individual agreement for each production must be signed by the Producer and all Designers and Assistants. All individual agreements must be signed and filed in triplicate with the Union for approval. The Designer may not work until the signed agreement has been approved in writing by the Union.

RIDERS

Fees are negotiable above minimum, and riders are permitted as long as they do not lessen or abrogate the terms of the contract.

BILLING

Equal for all designers—size and format negotiable above certain minimum standards. Billing is tied to billing of other collaborators.

TITLE

Designs remain the property of the designer but may not be sold for use in another production without the written consent of the original Producer.

ALTERATIONS

No alterations are to be made after opening night without the express consent of the Designer.

RIGHT OF FIRST REFUSAL

The original Designer has the right of first refusal for any subsequent reproduction using the original designs or design concepts—two weeks must be allowed for the decision. If the original Designer declines, the Producer selects a substitute Designer subject to the approval of the original Designer.

TV REUSE

There is a fixed schedule of residual rights, both domestic and foreign for each type of contract.

Do not sign any agreements or make any deals for cable TV without checking first with the Union for appropriate contracts and rates.

EXPENSES

All authorized out-of-pocket expenses and work transportation expenses shall be reimbursed by the Producer.

RESPONSIBILITY

No party is liable for failure to fulfill obligations due to strikes, accidents, fire, etc., or for the failure of the contracting shops to execute the designs.

ARBITRATIONS

All agreements provide arbitration clauses for adjustment of disputes and grievances.

PAYMENT

All payment to members in all areas covered by the Union have payroll taxes withheld by the Employer.

MEMBER/EMPLOYEE BILLINGS

No Member shall submit or be requested to submit a bill for services rendered to the Employer. No Member shall render services to an Employer as an independent contractor by means of the corporate form or otherwise. All members must be paid through the normal employee payroll procedures, with all applicable taxes withheld. Employers must pay all pension and welfare contributions and union dues directly to the funds or Union.

DUES/ASSESSMENTS BILLING PROCEDURE

All members will be billed for dues and assessments at the beginning of each quarter. Remittances should be made by check or money order, and should be made by mail. If a member does not receive a bill because of change of address or any other reason, this does not constitute an excuse for not paying indebtedness on time. Billing is an extra courtesy and reminder: the obligation to pay the total indebtedness on time is the responsibility of each member.

GENERAL NOTES

Please remember that all rates appearing in this booklet are minimums. Designers may work for any amounts above minimum that they can negotiate.

2% of all monies earned under the Union's jurisdiction by contract or letter of agreement, including overscale, overtime, and AWC [additional weekly compensation], is assessed from every member as administration dues.

There is a contract filing fee of $4 on contracts and letters of agreements over $1500, $2 for those less than that.

Rates for Broadway Shows

According to the agreement with the United Scenic Artists, Local 829 and the League of American Theatres and Producers, Inc., the rates of Broadway shows, effective 1992, are as follows.

39

DISPOSING OF SCENERY AFTER A SHOW

Scenery that is no longer needed for a commercial Broadway run can be disposed of in several ways after the show closes. It can be used in a national touring production of the show, given to various individuals or scenic studios for reuse, destroyed if no one wants it, or put in storage for future use.

One very unusual use of scenery after a show closed was reported in an article in *New York* magazine, May 8, 1989, titled "Old Sets Don't Die—They Go to Jersey." The article described the afterlife of a Tony Award–winning stage setting. Developer Sam Lefrak, whose daughter produced the play, *Cafe Crown*, found a new life for the set of the play, which closed in March of 1989 after a short run on Broadway. Lefrak had the scenery saved and shipped to New Jersey, where he plans to build an upscale French restaurant around it. The new restaurant will be called, of course, Cafe Crown. Lefrak was quoted in the article as saying, "The set won accolades from the press during the show's run. There's no reason to let that beautiful set die with the show." The play's scenery was created by Tony-winning set and costume designer Santo Loquasto, who modeled it after a restaurant in the Eiffel Tower. The article appeared before Loquasto won a Tony for this production.

DOING FOREIGN PRODUCTIONS

If you have been fortunate enough to design or supervise the scenery for a show that has become a commercial hit on Broadway, there is a good possibility that the production will be done in London, Paris, or Australia. Foreign producers tend to want the same physical production as the original, including costume and lighting designs. While foreign producers are in touch with the Broadway producers and know the original designer fees and royalties (additional weekly compensation), it is up to you, the designer, to be practical and firm in your business negotiations. For instance, the fact that theatres in another country do not gross as much money as in New York should not induce you to lower your basic design fee or weekly royalty. Re-

SCENIC DESIGN

Dramatic

Single set	Fee	$ 5,383				
	Advance	1,350				
	Total	$ 6,733				
Multiset	Fee	$ 7,837				
	Advance	1,730				
	Total	$ 9,567				
Unit set	Fee	$ 9,794				
	Advance	2,540				
	Total	$12,334				

Musical

Single set	Fee	$ 5,383
	Advance	1,350
	Total	$ 6,733
Unit set	Fee	$ 9,794
	Advance	2,540
	Total	$12,334
Multiset	Fee	$17,642
	Advance	3,760
	Total	$21,402

LIGHTING DESIGN

Dramatic

Single set	Fee	$ 4,037
	Advance	1,013
	Total	$ 5,050
Multiset	Fee	$ 5,878
	Advance	1,298
	Total	$ 7,176
Unit set	Fee	$ 7,345
	Advance	1,905
	Total	$ 9,250

Musical

Single set	Fee	$ 4,037
	Advance	1,013
	Total	$ 5,050
Unit set	Fee	$ 7,345
	Advance	1,905
	Total	$ 9,250
Multiset	Fee	$13,232
	Advance	2,820
	Total	$16,052

COSTUME DESIGN

Dramatic
Characters

1–3	Fee	$ 2,940		21–30	Fee	$ 6,853
	Advance	710			Advance	1,580
	Total	$ 3,650			Total	$ 8,433
4–7	Fee	$ 255		Period	Fee	$ 1,470
	Advance	30		Supplement	Advance	230
	Total	$ 285			Total	$ 1,700
8–15	Fee	$ 4,897		31–35	Fee	$ 255
	Advance	1,270			Advance	30
	Total	$ 6,167			Total	$ 285
Period	Fee	$ 984		36 &	Fee	$ 8,810
Supplement	Advance	150		Over	Advance	1,890
	Total	$ 1,134			Total	$10,700
16–20	Fee	$ 255		Period	Fee	$ 1,956
	Advance	30		Supplement	Advance	310
	Total	$ 285			Total	$ 2,266

Musical
Persons

1–15	Fee	$ 5,881		31–35	Fee	$ 289
	Advance	1,420			Advance	50
	Total	$ 7,301			Total	$ 339
16–20	Fee	$ 289		36 &	Fee	$17,642
	Advance	50		Over	Advance	3,760
	Total	$ 339			Total	$21,402
21–30	Fee	$11,750				
	Advance	2,850				
	Total	$14,600				

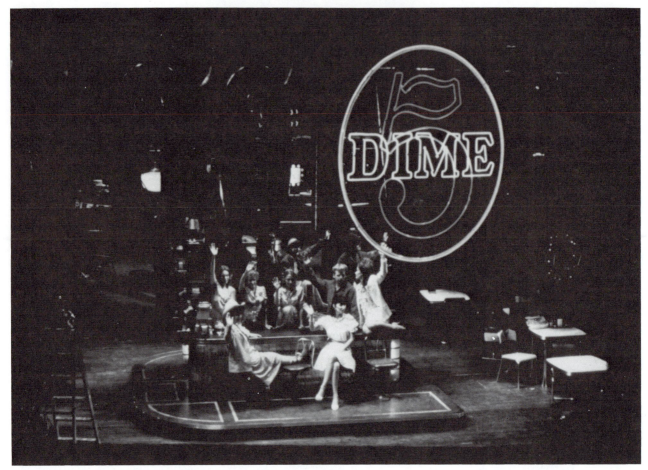

Setting by David Gropman
COME BACK TO THE 5 AND DIME, JIMMY
  DEAN, JIMMY DEAN by Ed Graczyk
Directed by Robert Altman
Costumes by Scott Bushnell
Lighting by Paul Gallo
Martin Beck Theatre
New York (1982)

member, too, that foreign producers do want you because you worked on the original production. This does not mean, however, that you can increase your fees to some out-of-sight figure. Often foreign producers expect to pay at least what you received initially, but this can vary according to the terms of your agreement.

Before you agree to a per diem, check out current costs and make sure that it is sufficient to cover both your meals and hotel. With the constant fluctuations in prices and exchange rates, the best approach is to ask management, friends, travel agents, or contacts in that particular city what the going rate is for hotels and meals.

For foreign productions you should have a letter of agreement that clearly defines all factors related to your responsibility on the production. This agreement or contract should be dated and signed by both parties and should include:

1. The design fee for the production.
2. A weekly royalty for each week the show plays, starting with the first paid performance.

3. Appropriate billing (size and positioning no less than the original) in the playbill and any souvenir program. A copy of your original playbill billing attached to your letter of agreement is always good to have.
4. The use of only an approved biography.
5. The exact number of days you are needed to be in the particular city.
6. The amount of your per diem.
7. Round-trip airfare.
8. Transportation provided while you are there.
9. Design assistant(s) according to need.

GETTING A PRODUCTION ON

Broadway producers and general managers expect the best work from a designer regardless of the time limit for getting a physical production on the boards. They want the best talent possible for the least amount of money. That is why good producers and general managers have gotten where they are. And it is how they manage to stay there. You may have anywhere from ten days to one or two years to get a production mounted. A designer is expected to deliver quality work on time. No excuse for delay is considered acceptable except perhaps a serious illness or death of a close family member. After all, the show must go on!

THE CONTACT SHEET

For the convenience of everyone involved in a production, the producer(s) supply a contact sheet. This is the list of names, addresses, and telephone numbers of the crew, suppliers, production staff, designers, unions, and actors. The purpose of a contact sheet is what its name so simply implies—to provide the information necessary for those working on a production to contact each other. For a play, the following may be included:

Setting and lighting by Neil Peter Jampolis
CARMINA BURANA Part II
Directed by Moses Pendleton
Costumes by Kitty Daly
Pilobolus Touring Company (1986)
(Photographs by Neil Peter Jampolis)

"Negative images were projected from the balcony rail on black scrim upstage. Projectors in wings threw patterns on stock barrels painted gray (with bright color interiors)."
—Neil Peter Jampolis

PRODUCTION STAFF

Producer(s)	Special effects
Coproducer(s)	General manager
Director/Choreographer	Company manager
Playwright/Composer/Lyricist	Advertising agency
	Press representative
Scenic designer and assistant(s)	Production stage manager
Costume designer and assistant(s)	Stage manager(s)
Lighting designer and assistant(s)	Assistant stage manager(s)
Sound designer and assistant(s)	Assistant(s) to the director
Supervisory designers: scenery, costumes, and lights	Graphic artist
	Dialogue coach
	Hair designer
	Magic illusions
Makeup designer	Production carpenter
Properties	Stage crew

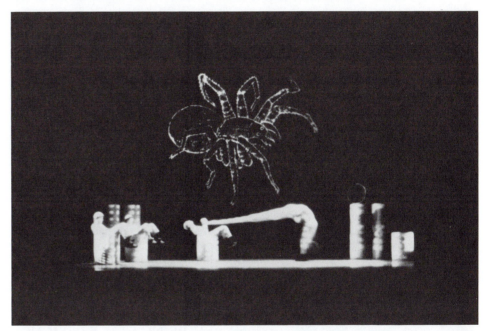

WRITING A RÉSUMÉ

No matter what a stage designer's age or experience is, the publicity department in all theatrical companies expects a résumé to use to write the bio for the theatre program and for basic advertising purposes. Résumés as well as bios also can help you get work.

When putting a résumé together, always try to get it on a single sheet of paper. If you have too many credits to fit on one sheet, then the copy can be reduced to fit on one page, but don't reduce it so small that it is difficult to read. The information should be arranged neatly and with as much eye appeal as possible. Put your name, address, and telephone number at the top of the page. A logo can be an interesting way to make your résumé memorable, and it should be above your name.

List the names and dates of the productions you have done, beginning with the latest show followed by the other productions in descending chronological order. Some designers like to give the name of the director following the title of the show. Produc-

Stage design by Elmon Webb and Virginia Dancy

PETER PAN by J. M. Barrie—Act 3
Directed by John Going

Alliance Theatre, Atlanta, Georgia (1978)
(Photograph by Elmon Webb)

tions may be grouped according to whether they are Broadway, pre-Broadway, international, opera, ballet, Off-Broadway, Off-Off-Broadway, regional, dinner theatre, summer stock, or university, with the latest production always listed first. Also indicate if you designed sets, costumes, or lighting. Although it is customary to give the dates of the productions, if there has been a long hiatus between shows, it may be wiser to omit the dates.

In addition, include any architectural and theatrical consultation, industrial shows, feature films, commercials, and television productions you have designed. Depending on your experience, it is helpful to give the names of any well-known designers you have assisted. Finally, specify any awards, honors, or teaching positions. Brevity and a neat layout are essential in writing a résumé.

It is important to take the time to keep your résumé up-to-date. Theatre designers are freelance artists, and the producers and directors who employ them are always asking for a list of credits. This information is used not only for the bios in the theatre program but in newspaper and magazine articles, and it is often requested by theatre book authors and publishers.

some working designers enjoy having some work ready to show when the demand arises. Original pieces of work are wonderful for indicating just what the design actually is all about, and also for showing different styles of design in productions.

PHOTOGRAPHING A DESIGNER'S WORK

Photographs of your stage designs are an excellent record of your work for your portfolio, for possible future publication, and for posterity. What a loss

SHOWING STAGE DESIGNS

A scenic designer often keeps a portfolio available because people always want to see new designs together with a sprinkling of old ones. While the best-known designers do not always keep a portfolio with current projects in them,

Costume designs by Desmond Heeley
THE MERRY WIDOW Ballet—Two guests—
    Act 3
Production: Sir Robert Helpmann
Choreographed by Ronald Hynd
National Ballet of Canada
O'Keefe Center, Toronto, Canada (1986)

Costume design by Desmond Heeley
THE NUTCRACKER (right)
Choreographed by Ben Stevenson
Houston Ballet
Houston, Texas (1987)

it would be if we did not have a photographic record of the theatrical designs of Jo Mielziner, Robert Edmond Jones, Lee Simonson, Boris Aronson, Oliver Smith, Ben Edwards, Donald Oenslager, and Norman Bel Geddes.

Unfortunately, producers do not usually include good set shots in a photo call, so it is up to the designer to arrange to have photographs made of his or her work on the stage. This can be a tricky situation, since it costs money to have a crew on hand to shift and light individual scenes. For this reason, many designers photograph their own work at dress rehearsal or from the back of the house during performance.

A photograph of a set model is a valuable addition to a portfolio, and may be the best record that one can get of the actual production. Keep in mind that photographs of models are just as important as photographs of the actual stage sets.

Designers take color slides of models and sketches and production shots in the theatre. Slides are inexpensive and easy to duplicate. Black-and-white photographs are also good to have and easy to duplicate. It is simple to have contact sheets made from black-and-white film; be sure to select only the best for prints.

Models by George Tsypin
DEATH IN VENICE by Benjamin Britten
A project (1984)
(Photographs by George Tsypin)

Photograph left and below:
"Plexiglas panels and two-way mirrors enclosed the main character in a reflective, fragile, shimmering world of Venice and in his mind. You never could tell if all the people he met on his journey were just the reflections in the mirror or real. A second-act claustrophobic space of narrow Venice streets is opened up and Ausherbach finds himself on the beach with the other singers popping up out of window-graves in the floor and transparent (vacuum form) facade-cloud hovering above."
—George Tsypin

REVIEWS OF THE DESIGNER'S WORK

The work of the collaborative team of designers, along with that of the director, the playwright, the composer, the lyricist, and others, is frequently mentioned in reviews of the production. Some artists say they never look at reviews, while others admit to devouring them down to the very last word.

Like any creative person's, the designer's career may be boosted a great deal by a sensational review. But reviews can also work in mysterious ways. Sometimes they help a designer enormously. In other situations they mean absolutely nothing to anybody; and on occasion they provide only marvelous humor and choice bits of puzzlement.

CONVERSATIONS WITH DESIGNERS

If you read all the conversations with the creative people in this book, you will find that there is no secret formula for becoming a successful stage designer in the commercial theatre. You may be intrigued and amazed at how these designers become household names in the world of the legitimate theatre.

Interestingly enough, almost all of these designers had a very early association with theatrical productions. They tell what they instinctively and intuitively enjoyed in their early youth and how natural it seemed for them to be involved with artistic endeavors. The designers discuss their ways of working, their likes and dislikes, their favorite shows, and shows they would like to do.

I was indeed fortunate in talking with renowned stage designers in *Designing and Painting for the Theatre* (1975). These conversations started with Jo Mielziner and continued through an enormous range of twentieth-century designers that concluded with Robin Wagner. In between were conversations with Donald Oenslager, Raoul Pène du Bois, Howard Bay, Ben Edwards, Ming Cho Lee, Rouben Ter-Arutunian, Robert Randolph, and Oliver Smith.

In this second work, *Designing and Drawing for the Theatre*, it has been my pleasure to exchange ideas with such wonderful and notable designers as Tony Walton, Douglas W. Schmidt, John Lee Beatty, Robert O'Hearn, David Mitchell, Santo Loquasto, David Jenkins, John Conklin, Tony Straiges, and John Napier. Because of their prominent work and profound influence on American stage design, I have once again talked with scenic designers Robin Wagner and Ming Cho Lee.

Tony Walton talked about theatre and his work in one of Manhattan's historic Upper West Side apartment complexes, in which he lives with his wife Gen and maintains a studio. He was born in 1934 in Walton-on-Thames, Surrey, England, and educated at Radley College, the City of Oxford School of Technology, Art and Commerce, and the Slade School of Fine Art in London. His first assignment in New York was *Conversation Piece* in 1957. Walton has designed operas and ballets in England, Italy, and the United States, and has created settings and costumes for Britain's National Theatre and many principal West End theatres. Among his ballet designs are *Peter and the Wolf* for American Ballet Theatre and seven ballets for the San Francisco Ballet. His numerous production and costume design credits for films include *Mary Poppins, Murder on the Orient Express, The Wiz, Deathtrap, Star 80, Equus, Petulia, Heartburn, The Boyfriend, The Glass Menagerie, The Sea Gull, Death of a Salesman, Prince of the City,* and *All That Jazz.* Tony Walton has also designed for television. His awards include three Tony Awards, four Drama Desk Awards, an Emmy Award, and an Academy Award. Among his theatre design credits are:

Broadway Settings
Conversations with My Father (1992)
Death and the Maiden (1992)
Guys and Dolls (1992)
The Will Rogers Follies (1991)
Grand Hotel (1989)
Lend Me a Tenor (1989)
Linda Ronstadt
   Canciones de Mi Padre (1988)
Social Security (1986)
I'm Not Rappaport (1985)
Leader of the Pack (1985)
Hurlyburly (1984)
Whoopi Goldberg (1984)
The Real Thing (1984)
Sophisticated Ladies (1981)
Woman of the Year (1981)

A Day in Hollywood/A Night in the
   Ukraine (1980)
The Act (1977)
Chicago (1975)
Pippin (1972)

Broadway Settings and Costumes
Jerome Robbins' Broadway (1989)
   ("Comedy Tonight"—S and C)
Little Me (1982)
Bette Midler's Clams on the Half Shell
   Revue (1975)
The Good Doctor (1973)
Shelter (1973)
Uncle Vanya (1973)
The Apple Tree (1966)

Golden Boy (1964)
A Funny Thing Happened on the Way
   to the Forum (1962)

Lincoln Center Theatre Settings
Four Baboons Adoring the Sun (1992)
Six Degrees of Separation (1990)
Waiting for Godot (1988)
   (Newhouse Theatre)
Anything Goes (1987) and C
The Front Page (1986)
The House of Blue Leaves (1986)

Off Broadway Settings
Elliot Loves (1990)
Square One (1990)
Drinks Before Dinner (1978) and C

Model by Tony Walton
GRAND HOTEL: The Musical
Based on Vicki Baum's *Grand Hotel*

Directed and choreographed by Tommy Tune
Book by Luther Davis

Songs by Robert Wright and George Forrest
Martin Beck Theatre, New York (1989)
(Photograph by Tony Walton)

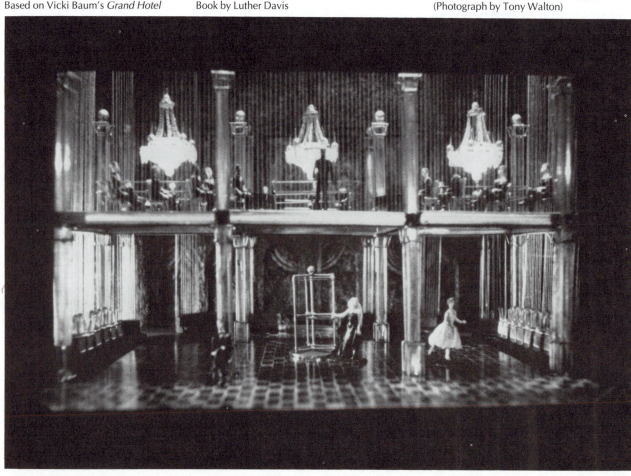

How did you first become interested in designing for the theatre?

It was almost by accident, really. I was doing some marionette productions when I was in college in England. The marionettes were a hobby that became an ever-increasing addiction, and some of the productions were very ambitious. After having done a number of Gilbert and Sullivan productions and then a short Mozart opera, *Bastian et Bastienne*, we tackled *The Magic Flute*. We used the string marionettes and very elaborate lighting. I was designing the sets and the marionettes and the clothes for the marionettes, and supervising the lighting and singing the part of Papageno. I was all over the place. And then John Piper, who is a very distinguished English painter, stained-glass creator, and stage designer, came to see this marionette production of *The Magic Flute* and he said to me, "You should do this." Somewhat baffled, I said, "What is this?" And then he proceeded to tell me what stage design was.

I was totally naive about it at the time. And he offered to have me taken in at the Slade School of Fine Arts in London, where he was a visiting professor and on the board. At this time I was simultaneously studying at the City of Oxford School of Technology, Art and Commerce, which was something of a Ruskinian school.

It was an extraordinary change to go from this nuts-and-boltsy sort of school to the Slade, which was basically a school for painters. But there was a rather strange stage design department run by a painter called Robert Medley, who had designed the sets for the Auden-Isherwood plays, *A Dog Beneath the Skin* and *The Ascent of F6*. His approach was simply to do a painting and pretty much have the scenic shops figure out how it was supposed to be transformed into a stage setting. It was totally idealistic and he felt no need to teach any of us about ground plans. It was a frustrating time except that he was trying to give us a key to our own visual natures or our own visual responses to different material.

It also was very destructive to some students who had come there with a very solid education in theatre design. Some had come from Bristol, for example, and were, I thought, at a very high level. But they would respond to a test situation with rather similar-looking results, as occasionally happens with Yale students. Robert Medley felt very strongly that that wasn't where they should be at that stage in their training, and that they should be trying to find out how they were different from each other rather than how to arrive at similar solutions.

As a fellow student, I was alarmed by this because I could just see those students slowly crumbling. All the things that they had learned to rely on, their props, as it were, were gradually removed. Only one of them survived the process and later became a very wonderful assistant to me, but alas, she didn't continue in design; she became a successful actress.

I was somewhat confused about this very idealistic approach, because I was simultaneously working as an assistant designer with Anthony Purvis at Wimbledon Repertory Theatre, which was like a year-round summer stock. That was mostly a case of knocking the same old bits of scenery into new shapes each week or every other week and slapping some new color on them.

So the two experiences couldn't have been more diametrically opposed. One was totally practical while the other was totally idealistic. And I couldn't relate them. But in retrospect it seems that it was a good kind of contrast to have to deal with: the practical reality in the theatre and the dreaming in the art school.

How long did you stay at the Slade School after assisting Anthony Purvis?

It was more or less concurrent. While I was assisting him, he also gave me two or three shows to design, and we jointly designed a gargantuan Christmas pantomime, which is an English tradition. That was a hair-raising undertaking, because basically you're doing the equivalent of a massive musical with twenty sets or so in the space of a week or two. Soon after that, my fiancée had opened over here in *My Fair Lady*, so I came over to join her briefly and then stayed.

Was that the first time you had been to New York?

No. I was a trainee pilot in Canada during my two years compulsory military service, and I used to escape whenever we were given leave to New York. It was during the height of the Kazan, Williams, Miller, Inge period, and the Rodgers and Hammerstein, Lerner and Loewe musicals. It was an astonishing time. I came over here to stay in 1956, knowing nothing, of course, of the union. I had arrived just after the exam had been taken so I couldn't take it the first year. Before I left England I had been doing some occasional caricatures for the *London Daily Express*, so I showed some of these around, and *Playbill* took me on as their resident caricaturist. I did about a year's work on all the graphics there. It was a wonderful way to get to see shows for free.

Did you take the union exam before you got a show or did you get a show first?

I got a show, actually, indirectly as a result of the exam. I took the exam and was lucky enough to get in the union. Somebody who had been sitting alongside me during the exam had been offered a job by some Yalemates. It was to do the designs for a revival of Noel Coward's *Conversation Piece*. And when he didn't get in the union, he said, "But there was this English person sitting beside me," and he recommended me. So that's how that came about.

You got this without knowing the director?

I had never met anybody connected with it. I had a portfolio of stuff and the producers saw it, and it was satisfactory to them. So that's how I came to be signed on. It was literally this fellow examinee's recommendation that caused it to happen.

You worked with Philip Wiseman, who directed Conversation Piece *in 1957 at the Barbizon Plaza. Did this do things for you careerwise?*

It was very well received on the visual end. It was a delightful production. The part of Melanie was splendidly played by Joan Copeland, Arthur Miller's sister, so we had the excitement of Miller and Marilyn Monroe attending rehearsals as well as Noel Coward. He was over here for *Nude with Violin*, and he was actually deeply involved in *Conversation Piece* because the two shows were concurrent. He spent quite a bit of time getting involved in the casting, and quite a bit of time in coming to rehearsals and previews and so on.

What a wonderful happening at the right time. What came about as a result

I think the next thing that happened wasn't as a result of it. The next show I designed was in England. It was for Sandy Wilson and a relatively new producer at that time called Michael Codron, who is now a great force in the English theatre. He was the original principal supporter of Harold Pinter, and also one of the producers of *The Real Thing* in New York. Anyway, he was planning a production of Sandy Wilson's new, rather esoteric musical based on Ronald Firbank's *Valmouth*. My agent in England introduced me to Michael Codron, as he knew Michael was looking for a designer for the Sandy Wilson show. So along I went to show my wares.

I think the fact that *Conversation Piece* was Regency and that *Valmouth* was turn-of-the-century was helpful. They were both elegant, witty, high-style period pieces. And so I had something to show that had a faint stylistic connection.

You did both sets and costumes?

Yes, I did both the sets and costumes on *Valmouth*. I only did the sets on *Conversation Piece*. But from then on after *Valmouth* for many years I almost always did both sets and costumes. Though there was one instance in London when Balmain did the costumes.

It was a curious thing, I suppose, like an actor getting typecast, but as a result of those productions I tended to be offered high-style, period pieces. And in many instances those were lucky experiences. As an indirect result of *Valmouth*, a very distinguished gallery in St. James offered me a one-man exhibition. It was substantially of stage designs, though it also had a lower gallery that showed my caricatures. I think there were a few watercolors that were not for specific shows, and there may have even been a couple of book illustrations. In that first year in New York, I had done some magazine covers and book covers and illustrations, and there might have been a couple of those. And there was a painting that was for one of two murals I had done for the Seven Arts Center, which was a theatrical complex in New York in the fifties. So it was a mixture, but it was mostly stage design and, surprisingly, most of it sold, so it was very exciting from that point of view.

But I stood there in the midst of it before it was all taken down thinking,

Sketches and model by Tony Walton
A FUNNY THING HAPPENED ON THE WAY TO THE FORUM
Directed by George Abbott
Alvin Theatre, New York (1962)
1. ½-inch scale model for original set (1962).
2. Sketch for FORUM movie setting (design of Senex House and Bakery, etc.).
3. Sketch for Chichester/London "thrust" revival of FORUM. English revival directed by Larry Gelbart, Picadilly Theatre, London.

"I should be thrilled about this, yet somehow I don't really feel present in this room." I was looking around the walls where the stage designs were hanging, and so much of it was all faintly similar. I had a really strange couple of weeks after that thinking, "Am I going to be like a typecast actor? A sort of sub–Cecil Beaton or Ronald Searle or something like that forever?" So I very consciously for a while made choices that were as far away from that style as possible. If it were possible to do sets that looked like Rorschach tests or were totally slab sculptural, I would tend to go that route. And even on book illustrations, I would tend to take those things that would permit me to move away from high style to see if I could stretch and to see what my limitations were.

One of your earliest successes in the musical theatre was A Funny Thing Happened on the Way to the Forum *in 1962. How did that come about?*

Hal Prince had seen *Valmouth* and one or two other things. I think he had seen *The Pleasure of His Company* in London, which I had designed over there. That was the production for which Balmain did the costumes. There were perhaps a couple of other things that Hal saw. There was a play called *Fool's Paradise*, which was also a Michael Codron production.

Prince was producing as opposed to directing on that, wasn't he?

Right. And at the time that he approached me, Jerry Robbins was going to be the director, and my first meeting was with Robbins. It would have been a very different animal if Robbins had been the director throughout. But very soon after that first meeting he had a gargantuan success with *Ballets: U.S.A.* and was asked to undertake a world tour with it, and he devoted himself to that for a while. Then George Abbott became the director and Jack Cole the choreographer.

The show had severe problems out of town. People were somehow really turned off by it. Steve Sondheim asked for Robbins to be brought back in. And he did come in, as you know, and turned it around triumphantly. It is one of the famous instances of a really astonishing input by Robbins. In this case, it totally changed the nature of the beast.

Right up until the time it came into New York, it opened with a sort of soft shoe sung by David Burns called "Love is in the Air." Well, unbeknownst to all of us, it gave a wrong signal for the nature of the evening. And Robbins came in and said, "There's nothing wrong with this. You just have to let them know what they're in for." And Steve, who was being battered at that stage, said, "Give me some specifics." Robbins literally said, "You have to tell them it's a comedy tonight. It's all about lovers and liars and clowns." I think Steve actually took some lines from Robbins and incorporated them skillfully into his finished lyric.

And the moment that number went in, it turned the show completely upside down. It became this uproarious thing received with passion and affection. It was the opening number, "Comedy Tonight," and Robbins also choreographed it, and it was magical and hilarious. It was an astonishing thing to see it happen. He did a lot of other miraculous things throughout the show, too, with minimal resources.

What research did you use for that show?

Well, I switched once it became Abbott's as opposed to Robbins', because I think in the original attack by Robbins we were going in a much more—it's crude to put it this simplistically—a much more stylized, perhaps almost balletic vein. The buildings were to be made of silk and rope. And when it became the Abbott production it became much more deeply rooted in slapstick and baggy pants with a cruder, more vaudevillian type of scenery.

I did an enormous amount of research into the original ancient Roman theatre of Plautus, Terence, and others. And there are strange little relics of that research in the final set, although it would be very hard for somebody who wasn't familiar with the original Roman theatre to recognize it. Then I tried to push that into a sort of cardboard vaudevillian vein, hoping to keep it very crude, very unsophisticated, and hopefully feisty and brightly colored. I tried to sneak in the art surreptitiously, and have the overall impact come more as a kick in the pants than an approach to the intellect.

And this is true also for the costumes, although in some cases there the situation dictated the results—one instance being the baggy tights that the comedians had. Their loosely knitted wool garments. That came about because Zero Mostel, who was playing Pseudolus, couldn't be bare-legged as he should be as a slave. He had a badly damaged leg as the result of being knocked down and dragged by a bus. Well, in the very early and crudest Roman comedy they used to wear sort of long johns with gargantuan phalli attached to them. So because of Zero's badly damaged leg, we realized we could capitalize on something of this sort and that's how that design materialized. Now it's become a kind of signature of the show, and everybody always does it, no matter where it's done. That was one way that the research ultimately and harsh reality dictated the final result. There's no way to know whether we would have gone that way anyway. But the fact is, we were forced to. The options had been narrowed interestingly by Zero's accident.

After this success came Golden Boy *and* Apple Tree?

Well, you can probably recognize now this desperate attempt to be different on each project from those two shows! *Golden Boy* came about partly because Richard Pilbrow, the lighting designer, and I, who were in partnership in a company called Theatre Projects in England, had done a certain amount of quite successful scenic projection. We had designed a production called *Pieces of Eight* produced by Michael Codron. It was a musical revue written by Pinter, N. F. Simpson, and Peter Cook. Because it had been very successful, Michael Codron wanted to do a sequel called *One Over the Eight*. Codron said, "It's going to be essentially the same mixture, the same comedian as star and the same writers. I don't want it to look like a complete rip-off of itself, so I'd love you to come up with some completely different scenic attack."

And so we decided to go the projection route, although up until that time many ambitious projection attempts had tended to be very unfortunate. Mielziner had recently had an unlucky experience with it so we were quite nervous about it. Richard went off to Germany and studied their projection techniques very meticulously. Of course, in Germany they generally do it in the repertory system and they can work it out by trial and error. We had to plan the you-get-in-Sunday-and-open-on-Monday version so everything had to be worked out in theory. There was no time for us to experiment in the theatre or work it out through trial and error.

This was actually well before *Forum* because *Forum* used our projection technique to change the skies fairly radically for the chase or for a soft, romantic, musical moment. It was only surreptitiously used in *Forum* because we didn't want any sense of modern technology in the show. But it was a way of getting some visual variety into a one-set musical.

On *One Over the Eight*, the musical revue for which we devised this projection scheme, we opened at the Shakespeare theatre in Stratford-on-Avon out of season. Two pairs of 5-kilowatt Rieche and Vogel projectors were set up on towers on either side of the stage crisscrossing their beams onto a curved cyclorama. We worked the whole dry tech run-through, and it was very exciting. The projected images were vignetted together and it all worked out just right from having been

Production designed by Tony Walton with
  Philip Rosenberg
ALL THAT JAZZ—final sequence (1979)
Directed by Bob Fosse
Costumes by Albert Wolsky
Cinematography by Guisseppe Rotunno
Pictured (left to right): Ben Vereen, Roy Scheider, Kathy Doby, and Ann Reinking.

mathematically preconceived and distorted.

So we were quite tickled with ourselves when Michael Codron and the director and cast turned up. And then they launched into the opening dance number on stage. The towers started moving maybe only half an inch or a quarter of an inch 24 feet up. But the image on the cyclorama, of course, was moving 6 or 7 feet and hurtling about. It was a nightmare!

To his eternal credit Codron didn't panic, and he said, "OK guys, you've got a couple of hours to figure this out. I'm taking the company to continue rehearsing at the church hall." And Richard Pilbrow and myself retired to the Dirty Duck pub next door, and said, "Oh my god, what are we going to do?"

Had you discovered what the problem was?

It was because the stage floor at Stratford-on-Avon was trapped, and the traps were shifting slightly as the company danced on stage. And that shift was causing the projection towers to rock. Anyway, sitting there in the pub in absolute blind despair, we saw that one of the barmen was making a cork collection, and suddenly thought, "That's it!" We asked the barman if we could use all his corks and we rushed back and sliced them up and put them all in the cracks between the elevator traps on stage. And that worked. Nothing shifted anymore. It was a miracle.

Well, the design style of *Golden Boy* came about because of that show. The projections were seen by a lot of people. Following that I did some operas that involved a lot of projections. One that used it very ambitiously at Covent Garden was Michael Tippet's *Midsummer Marriage.*

At any rate, the director of *Golden Boy*, Peter Coe, had seen this and thought it was a way to approach *Golden Boy* cinematically that might give it a fairly radical updating because they wanted it to have some relationship to the troubled New York nights, and the troubles between the black and white New York residents in the sixties. So this was a way to make it seem of the moment. But the original production was radically altered when Peter Coe was replaced by Arthur Penn. When the Peter Coe version opened out of town, it actually was pretty successful, but Sammy Davis was not getting the personal reviews he had hoped for.

It was radically altered to become a much more intimate drama. In the original production there were a lot of moving screens that traveled and turned, and the images were frequently turning up on moving surfaces. Hardly any of that survived to the Broadway version. But, even so, it was still essentially a very largely projected show.

Were you pleased with the final outcome of that production?

I was sad that it wasn't closer to the technical attack that we had originally taken on it. I was thrilled that it survived six months of out-of-town changes to become mysteriously a success on Broadway. But it seemed to me to be physically a bit of a mishmash by the time it opened. People who hadn't seen what the original intention was, luckily didn't seem to see it as a mishmash. And Tharon Musser's beautifully cohesive lighting may have been largely responsible for that. Anyway, after *Golden Boy*, a lot more invitations came to do projected shows. So then I very consciously tried to avoid them for a while.

Shortly after that you did The Apple Tree *with Mike Nichols. Was this the first show with him?*

Yes, it was our first Broadway show together. We were already friends though. In fact, oddly enough, he was the most helpful person on *A Funny Thing Happened on the Way to the Forum*. When I first met with George Abbott, he was just about to leave for Florida for some ballroom dancing and high times! And he had said, "I like quite a lot of levels and a lot of entrances and exits," or something like that. And I said, "Oh, could I bring you some sketches or models or something down to Florida?" And he said, "No, no, no, you don't have to do that." And I said, "When will you be back?" And he said, "Oh, I'll be back in time for the first day of rehearsal." I said, "I can't just show it to you then!" He said, "Sure, I'll see it when the rest of the cast does and respond to its challenges in the same way that they do."

That is literally what happened. So I felt a little lonely during the design process. And since Nichols was then almost on the verge of switching from being a comedy performer to becoming a director, I asked him if he would mind my using him as a sounding board. And he came by and looked at the model and I said, "Look I've done this dopey thing. What I'd really love to do is make more of an impression. This is only my second Broadway show. And it's ancient Rome, and you could really put the glory of it up there and have the time of your life. But because it's George Abbott, I'm just trying to plug into what it's becoming now that it's his production. But I'm beginning to get cold feet about it, and I'm wondering about taking a more detailed classical approach." And he said, "No, the design doesn't remind me of anything, so it may well be right. Why don't you just stick with it?"

He was a real help. Just extraordinarily helpful in that situation. I think I would have backed off and done something, as it were, flashier, if he hadn't said stick with this.

So his association with you at that point is what started a collaboration that lasted over many shows and a twenty-year period, was it not?

Yes, and he's one of the most remarkable people to work with. *The Apple Tree* was a tough one for both of us. And oddly enough, Robbins was very helpful on that too, not that he actually participated, but he gave a list of suggestions and some of them were extraordinary. One that I remember particularly in *The Apple Tree* was when Eve discovers that she's naked. He said, "When Eve wraps herself in the brown towel, even though brown is a recurring joke in the show, if instead she picked up an orange towel, she'd get a laugh." We were dubious, but we tried it and he was right. And that was very spooky and intriguing. He was filled with these extraordinary little fine-tuning instincts.

What is one of your favorite shows that you have done with Mike Nichols?

Probably the most delightful all-around experience was *The Real Thing*, even though that was a rather daunting prospect going in. One of the givens was that Mike didn't want it to be anything like the London version. They had done a beautifully stylized production there designed by Carl Toms. But Mike wanted to know much more about the inner life of the characters through their environments. For the American audience's sake, he wanted to have a much more realistic series of environments.

There were so many short scenes—I think there are eleven or so scene changes. Mike said we can't have more than a four- or five-second gap between any of the scenes, and most of them required virtually a full stage set. The prospect of achieving that was terrifying! But the process of finding the solution to it was very exciting. He got totally behind it and was able to use it fully in the way he staged the production. And, of course the text itself was wonderful, and it was a remarkable cast.

How did you resolve the many quick scene changes?

There were, in effect, five turning or moving elements in it: a large central turntable with moving parts within it flanked by two periaktoi: erratically configured 3-sided revolving towers that completed the outer edges of each environment and in some instances supplied the entrances.

In this particular instance we weren't using turntables so that the audience would ever be conscious of them. Although ultimately there was one instance where a rehearsal room gradually turned from one side of the stage to the other to complement the mood of the scene. But generally we had hoped to conceal the mechanics, so there was often a gratifying gasp from the audience each time that what appeared to be a full stage set became a completely different one in a matter of seconds. There was never a stage wait from one scene to the next.

It was mechanically complex. And it took me forever to work out. In fact, I used to have to get up at three in the morning, because that was the only time the city was quiet enough that I could figure out the problems of maneuvering from Scene 1 to Scene 11 without someone breaking into a car or some eruption outside to completely distract me and send me back to Scene 1. So it took tremendous concentration to work the principle of it out. The main turntable, by the way, was used again for *Chess*.

This was rented from somewhere?

Well, it was made at Gossard's for *The Real Thing*, but it went back to Showtech when the production closed. The workings of *The Real Thing* are not easy to describe. You really need to diagram it to clarify it, or to see the model from a bird's-eye view to understand it.

You and Mike Nichols did Streamers *at the Long Wharf Theatre in New Haven and then it opened at the Mitzi E. Newhouse at Lincoln Center. Was New Haven a tryout for the show?*

No. Originally it wasn't a show that Joe Papp had wanted to do, although he had done all of Rabe's other work. Nichols and Rabe met in the course of filming different things in Hollywood. And Rabe said he had this piece that he felt strongly about. And when Mike read it, he had a powerful response immediately. At the first reading many people found it a very difficult play. But Nichols was conscious of the power waiting to be unleashed, yet most of us who read it didn't quite recognize that at first.

It was a fascinating thing to work on, because Nichols found a way in his staging to make the audience feel as if they were somehow living in the same tiny space as the folk within the play's action. It was somehow possible for the cast to perform at an almost conversational level until the major eruptions. And it was, perhaps, the first time that we'd really been made aware of the power it was possible to convey in that kind of very, very held-back performance level.

For example, if you had seen a clip of that performance filmed for television, you wouldn't have seen it played as you normally see theatre on television, with the characters bellowing into a void. It was literally performed as we're talking now. And somehow within both those spaces, the Long Wharf and the Mitzi Newhouse, that was possible.

Nichols is very, very canny, mind you, about technology, about being able to imperceptably mike things or even the surreptitious use of follow spots so that the audience is not aware of it at all. But these things can emphasize dramatically something that's being done in a very low-key way.

For example, in the *Uncle Vanya* we did at Circle in the Square, which is my other favorite of the shows we've done together, we had that remarkable cast—George C. Scott, Julie Christie, Nicol Williamson, Elizabeth Wilson, Lillian Gish, Cathleen Nesbitt, Barnard Hughes, and on and on, an amazing team. Well, he had Jules Fisher use hidden follow spots in the grid, an astonishing thing to try at the Circle in the Square. And I had dressed all of the principals, with these remarkable faces, in a very low-key coloration. It was a very restrained palette so that the faces would dominate. Nobody ever believes to this day that there were follow spots in that production. It created a mysteriously magical impression though. I think it must have been very uncomfortable, mind you, for the poor follow spot operators lying jammed up there in the grid!

How many did you have?

I can't remember, this is a while ago now. I just remember the first audience on that. Here was this tightly controlled thing with this highly controlled palette and then the first preview audience came in with their Bloomingdale's bags and their yellow and red galoshes: you just wanted to spray the first two rows.

What kind of space did you have to work in for your Uncle Vanya *at The Circle in the Square?*

The stage at Circle in the Square is like a long tongue which is really more suited to a fashion display or something of that sort. It's a very difficult space for directors and designers. We used a kind of interior/exterior construction at the mouth end of the tongue, as it were, which by the use of a canopy and leaf patterns, benches and garden furniture gave the sense of being the exterior of the house. By throwing a rug or a fur over a bench or a paisley over a table, and by lowering a lamp and losing the canopy and its leaf shadows, a quick sense of interior was achieved.

It was a wonderful production to work on. Jules is always a treat to work with. It was one of those very few instances that you dimly hope might be recognized as a finely tuned and painstaking piece of work. But at the time there were a couple of flashier things that I had worked on which somehow left a stronger impression. That can be slightly frustrating.

It's the same thing with movies. The better you disguise your work, the less you are presumed to have done. And that's the deal. For the movie *Murder*

Movie designs and settings by Tony Walton
THE BOYFRIEND (1971)
Directed by Ken Russell
Costumes by Shirley Russell
Cinematography by David Watkin
  Pictures:
1. Sketch/collage for "Poor Little Pierrette" sequence.
2. Twiggy and company in "Poor Little Pierrette."
3. Sketch/collage, same sequence.
4. Twiggy and company, same sequence.

on the Orient Express, the real train didn't even exist at the time except for bits and pieces in museums. All the interior and some of the exterior train shots were sets filmed in the studio. We even constructed a demented version of the Istanbul railroad station in an engine shed in France, because that's the only place we could find and dress up an appropriate engine and carriages to look like the departure of the Orient Express. Yet it's generally assumed to have been shot in the real train and real stations.

How long did you spend on that film from beginning to end?

Oh, it's hard to remember. It was a Sidney Lumet film and those go very, very fast. So probably eight or nine months on that. The filming period would have been about eight weeks, maybe less.

Are you involved on the set for all of that time?

Yes, also because of being responsible for the costumes.

When you work in film, do you have as much visual control as you would on a play?

It all depends. In the theatre you are really designing the image that's presented to the audience, especially if you're doing costumes as well. It's as if you have selected the frame from the movie that you wish the audience to see. In movies you have next to no control over that. What you are really doing is creating an environment from which the appropriate images can be selected. It can sometimes be very frustrating for that reason. You can try to structure something very specifically with the environments, the costumes, and props and so on. But in the end it's going to be a face or two, perhaps shoulders, and some crucial close-up prop that's going to dominate the visual flavor of a scene. It's one of the reasons that I try whenever possible on movies to do costumes, because it's one of the few ways one has to try to ensure a look. Sometimes the movie doesn't really require that. If it's a real slice of life, for example, *Heartburn*, it's not imperative to it. In fact, it would be almost destructive to that. You want the audience to feel, "Oh Christ, yes, that's just what life is like!"

You mean the film with Meryl Streep and Jack Nicholson?

Yes, and again Mike Nichols was the director. Ann Roth did the costumes on that. The effort on everybody's part was to have a recognition factor going. So there was a conscious effort to create familiar environments and a non-attention-getting visual style and filming style.

Where was that shot?

Here in New York at Camera Mart, the old Fox stage. The Washington apartment where the bulk of the story takes place was built here in that studio. We did a week of mostly exterior shooting in Washington to establish some locations but all the built part of it was in New York. Some New York locations also stood in for Washington locations, both interior and exterior.

If you're offered a movie and a play at the same time, and you want very much to do both, but you know that the movie would probably be more lucrative, how do you work that out?

Well, it tends to be more to do with what the film is and who the director is. It's hard, because I'm sure all theatre designers' accountants say to them as mine does, "If you want to stay with your hobby, the theatre, you'd better also try to work on something else that's going to support it."

Do you prefer the theatre as far as artistic merit is concerned?

Mostly, but it would be wrong to generalize because each individual experience is what counts. You can get involved in a theatrical experience that can be a nightmare for whatever reason. And then you can get involved in a movie experience that can be as delicious as working with Nichols or Lumet almost always is. Lumet does an astounding amount of homework. I've done about seven films with him, and some of those like *The Sea Gull*, *Equus*, *The Wiz*, and *Deathtrap*, stem from plays, so there's an interesting gray area where it stops being theatrical and starts being a movie. There are some instances though where there is a very conscious effort to hang on to theatricality.

Two films I worked on, *The Glass Menagerie* directed by Paul Newman and the Volker Schlondorff *Death of a Salesman* with Dustin Hoffman and John Malkovich, were very conscious efforts to work strictly with the play text and not to make a new screenplay. This was also true of Lumet's film of

The Sea Gull. It's very interesting when you get an instance like any one of those where the job is to try to bring the play to film life without its losing its theatricality. Movies tend to be more about moving images than about long speeches. So it's tricky.

In both *Salesman* and *Glass Menagerie*, in slightly different ways, we were walking a very fine line between theatre and film and trying to come up with, as it were, almost a new medium to embrace both and try to employ the strengths of each. Film is essentially a visual medium, and the fewer words the better, and obviously in both those pieces it's all words, wonderful words. And there's no way to duck that.

For *Salesman*, Volker Schlondorff the director and Michael Ballhaus the cinematographer were the people Arthur Miller and Dustin Hoffman chose to try to find this fresh approach to keep the text intact and still not just let it be a filmed play. They started with the idea that with such a density of dialogue something about the way it's filmed or staged or set should at appropriate moments give the audience a reminder that this is not really a movie in the sense that you normally think of movies. For example, few of the walls were connected at the corners, yet there were details and textures that in a tight frame could become very realistic and persuasive over quite long periods of time. But when the density of dialogue or the theatricality of the moment became too overpoweringly so, the camera could pull back and reveal that it was a very artificial environment to permit the heightened dialogue to seem more appropriate.

We even went so far as to try to avoid any conventional set dressing so that where you would normally fill a

kitchen with kitchen artifacts there were just the barest number of kitchen items. There was virtually nothing that wasn't specifically mentioned in the text by the playwright, one exception being an American flag, which gets very subtly used on a partial living room wall towards the end. But almost everything else we used was called for in the play text. If it was not called for, it's not there. And that was a very interesting challenge, because for movies you often need to do quite a lot of set dressing to keep the texture of the image interesting. So we took another tack in making the wall textures interesting in themselves.

Do you prefer films to television?

I've never been entirely comfortable with television. Partly, I suppose, because there's such a diminution of any strong visual attack you might have. It's enormously diminished both by what is possible to show and by the fact that the line system, at least as of this year, on television, radically over-simplifies and reduces what's there. And it needs much too much light to reveal what's there to the television camera as opposed to the amount of light needed for film. So much of television looks brightly and flatly lit for that reason.

The video version of *Pippin* was taped from a live stage performance, and there were quite a lot of darks and sometimes there were candles involved. The candles were impossible to shoot in the way that Fosse conceived them, because the flame of a candle was such a high contrast to the other elements on the darkened stage that they would leave trails of light across the screen that would then be visible as "ghosts" throughout the next few scenes. In order to even things out,

the overall stage lighting had to be brought up radically so that the candle wouldn't be this little trailing scribble across the screen, and then the mood of the scene was destroyed. If there is something very bright, it actually burns into the cathode ray tube and leaves this visual memory for a while.

How would you rank Pippin *with your theatrical successes?*

The original production was an enormously enjoyable one, because it was one where the expectations, at least on my part and on the part of some others in the creative team, were not particularly high when first we were sent the source material. This is an impolite thing to say, but it was hard to imagine how Fosse was going to make something vital out of this.

But he invited Jules Fisher and myself to watch the first dance number that he had just worked out. It was before "rehearsals proper" started. He was working with two gals and himself, and they did a version of what later became the TV commercial for *Pippin*. It had nothing to do with anything you could recognize in the script or the score. It wasn't even at that time choreographed to any music from the show. It was choreographed, I think, to "Down by the Riverside" and a little piece by Satie. But we sat there with our jaws in our laps saying, "Oh my god, he's going to make something astonishing out of this!"

And from then on the work process with him was remarkable, and very, very exciting. He was a tremendously demanding collaborator both in theatre and in film. He had an absolutely astonishing instinctual command of the medium, and was one of the best possible film directors to work with,

52 though very difficult, because he was a very complex man.

You won an Academy Award working with Fosse on All That Jazz *in 1980.*

I won it with Philip Rosenberg and the set decorators. We worked jointly on that. I tend to get all the credit for the fantasy scenes, but it was much more shared than it is possible to clarify in the film credits.

But a pleasant experience all the way around?

No, actually movie experiences with Fosse never could be described as just pleasant. It always was extraordinarily fascinating, in many cases wonderful, and in many cases hair-raising. He could be very, very hard on his closest collaborators, all of us, and amazingly hard on himself. So that didn't make it easy to work on, but it always was an enormously worthwhile experience. He was able to make use of whatever you were able to provide him with in ways sometimes far beyond your expectations. Whereas with some directors you feel you might have provided something that really had an enormous range of possibilities, and you come away feeling, well none of that got used. You can never quite get that feeling in the theatre because what you do is visible and more often than not survives. In film, it doesn't necessarily survive the cutting room process or the director's visual approach.

Occasionally in film it can be the cinematographer who isn't entirely sympathetic to a design approach. In fact, historically—especially in Europe—art departments and camera departments are often at odds. That's one of the first things you hope to overcome by trying to make some kind of working relationship between the cinematographer and yourself because you're so totally interdependent. I've been very lucky in these relationships.

Ballhaus, for example, who did the *Death of a Salesman* and *The Glass Menagerie*, is a remarkable cinematographer. He is totally involved in the whole design process, fascinated by it, tremendously helpful, supportive, very clear about his own needs. So ahead of time you can do things that can be incorporated into your joint effort. Some cinematographers barely want to even look at the design or the setting or whatever until they walk on to shoot, and then sometimes they

might do something radical that completely destroys what you had conceived. For example, if the cinematographer had in his mind that this scene should be totally backlit and he walks in and he sees there's no source to do that, he might do something quite savage with the designed environment in order to make that possible. And that may be completely at odds with the way that the interior or whatever structure it is that you're photographing has been conceived. So its visual logic can be blown away completely.

But if you have a good working relationship with the film's director and cinematographer it can be the most rewarding thing of all, partly because the actual act of collaboration with the two of them can produce unexpected wonders.

If you do a production in England or London today, how does it differ from the point of view of getting the show into a shop? Is it similar to New York?

It's pretty similar getting it into a shop and it's getting more and more similar getting it out of the shop. But there is an expectation from the U.S. craft shops that a designer has a certain union-approved technical expertise that should permit him to dictate how most of the physical aspects of the production should go together. In the European tradition, that really doesn't come up. I mean there are remarkable exceptions to this—Svoboda and Napier and many others are very knowledgeable technically. But the tradition, at least until recently in Europe and England, is that the designer is, from the scenic shop's point of view, a sort of wonderfully gifted idiot who has these visual gifts, but not necessarily any very intensive technical training.

This is, to some extent, true for me. For example, in my Slade School training it was almost a point of honor not to know how to do a ground plan. I was begging to be taught how, and our teacher there at the time thought it was a very undignified thing to even think about. He said, "Just let the workshops figure it out for you!"

Many scenic shops in Europe work largely from models and sketches, and their expectation tends to be that they should figure out how all this works. Therefore they correctly feel that their participation is every bit as crucial creatively as the designer's. In some instances that's a very productive thing

in that they can bring to it an additional imagination, a new vitality that will keep the design impulse alive all the way from its inception up to the moment it is delivered as a finished piece of work.

There are sometimes instances in the American system where it's very hard to keep the design impulse alive, because it's a beating-your-head-against-a-brick-wall situation every step of the way. "You can't do this because of that or this is too expensive and therefore we'll just do it out of timber instead of steel." Not that that isn't equally true in Europe, but here the designer often has to be the one who says, "All right, then here's what we'll do." And he really has to know how to do it and how to demonstrate the doing of it.

I'm lucky enough now to have had continuing relationships with some of the very best scenic shops here—most recently Showtech—and in some instances they have been able to come in at an early enough stage to guide the technical process.

It's important for you to have them come in before you get the show finished, then.

Yes, but you can't often do that because you have to go to competitive bids. No shop is obliged to come in before that, because there's no guarantee that they are going to end up with the show. So that's a very tricky situation in the American system.

Would it be different in the English system?

Yes, there are strong on-going allegiances between designers and shops and producers and shops. You're still going to be approached as a gifted idiot though. The shop will expect to come up with many of the technical solutions, and possibly to adjust a great deal of the work that you've done to adapt it to practical reality. The European scenic shop expectation is much more that they should be a crucial creative part of the technical input all the way through, really.

There was an example of this a number of years ago with Oliver Messel's design for *Ring Around the Moon*, the Anouilh play which Peter Brook directed. It was one of the most beautiful designs for this one-set play imaginable. He had a model which I think had been worked on by Carl Toms and Fred Nihda that had been made from pipe cleaners and fuse wire and so on. It was this cobwebby evocation of a vaulting winter garden. At that time pretty much everything in theatre construction was based on timber and canvas. And the technicians in the scenic shop said, "How do you expect us to build this, this wonderful thin and fuzzy line?" And he said, "I don't know, but I thought you'd have an idea." And they said, "Well, if we try to make that curve out of timber, it's going to have to be this thick." And you saw Messel suddenly envisioning this big, clunky version of the dream he had, and he dissolved in despair. Then they all rallied around and soothed him and said, "We'll work it out, don't worry, we'll work it out." And they came up with this steel, aluminum or whatever structure which was at that time a completely fresh way of achieving that delicate look theatrically. So it was a very productive piece of ignorance in his case.

You can get that to happen here, but you have to really encourage it. For example, with *Pippin*, it was hard to persuade anybody that making all those drops out of rope and having them fold up under the stage and be dragged almost endlessly upward would ever work. And I couldn't prove it. I had made no previous attempt at anything like this. I only had a gut feeling that it would work.

How did you get it to work out?

I'd been working with Pete Feller's shop for quite a few shows so we had a good working relationship. He was always enormously supportive, and in that instance he had the canny idea of employing another designer, Bob Randolph, as a sort of intermediary to supervise the construction of the rope drops. Pete Feller didn't even use his normal shop men to construct them, but used apprentices and crafts people under Bob Randolph to create these crazy drops. We all had a lot of input on the work, but Bob was sort of the dean of the crafts folk, and he came up with specific notions as to how to organize this unusual operation: But even later, when we sent the designs and drawings, which were by then very explicit, to be duplicated for a production elsewhere, they would often have the same totally panic-stricken reaction, "How could this possibly work?"

The production photographs would

be very helpful in that case, wouldn't they?

Well, one of the frustrations of working in the Broadway system is that it's extremely difficult to get good production photographs. It's so expensive to have a photo call because all the crew members have to be paid. One of the miracles of the wonderful Boris Aronson book is that he almost always managed to get his productions photographed, sometimes privately and paid for by himself. But the norm, sadly, is that a photographer comes in and cracks off a few close-up shots that can be used in the daily press along with the reviews. And the producers say somewhere down the line we'll have a proper photo call, but it never happens, or very seldom.

No, because if it's a hit they say we don't need them, if not we can't afford them.

So in the instance of *Pippin*, I went to the general manager and said, "I have to have photographs to show the Australian technical team that this can work." And they finally worked it out that we could photograph the show between the matinee and evening while the crew restored the show to Scene 1. But the problem with that was that they had to run the scenes backwards in order to properly prepare for Scene 1, and the lighting board only went forwards. So there was only one scene right in the middle of the show that was appropriately lit. Everything else was lit with the lighting from the opposite end of the show. But those crazy photos were all we had to work with for a while. The restaging years later in Canada for the video version gave me an opportunity to photograph it myself. So I finally got some vaguely acceptable photographs. I do, on occasion, try to get my own photographs now, but they're very catch-as-catch-can.

You have designed a number of shows at Lincoln Center, including Anything Goes, *which is a major musical. How did you adjust this production for the budget?*

The Lincoln Center operation is not like a regular commercial management doing a major musical. Productions were not initially planned to be open-ended, so we had to take advantage of whatever conveniences we could to bring it in on a more or less manageable budget for a likely limited run. There

were pieces from about nine shows represented in the set for *Anything Goes*. The staircases are actually the lobby staircases from *The Front Page*, which I had done at the Beaumont prior to *Anything Goes*. The Austrian was used in *The House of Blue Leaves* prior to *The Front Page*, and there are pieces from *Social Security*, which had just closed, the bar for example, and some pieces in the stateroom.

You didn't run into any union problems doing that?

Well it's a not-for-profit theatre, so it was possible to do that, but I don't think it would be encouraged too often!

You've had a successful collaboration with Jerry Zaks on The Front Page, The House of Blue Leaves, *and* Anything Goes. *How did the two of you start working together?*

Well, I think we were put together for *The House of Blue Leaves*. I had worked with Bernard Gersten at the Public, and Greg Mosher at the Goodman. Jerry was new to the thrust stage and perhaps both Greg and Bernie Gersten felt we might be good for each other since I had had experiences working with both of them on thrust stages previously. I'm not sure of this, though. But however it happened, I'm eternally grateful to them for introducing me to Jerry. He's a treat to work with.

Jerry and I started working together on *The House of Blue Leaves*, which was strictly planned for the Mitzi Newhouse, the little theatre downstairs. The Mitzi has no stage depth at all. It has the thrust and then nothing upstage of it. *Blue Leaves* was playing well in this tiny barrel and felt excitingly explosive in there. So it was a startling moment when Greg Mosher and Bernie Gersten said to Jerry and myself, "Go up and take a look at the Beaumont to see if you think the show could work there," Once we all agreed to risk the move to the Beaumont, we were able to take advantage of the depth there to make a little more out of the Queens environment and the views toward Manhattan.

At that time the Beaumont was looked upon as rather a dodo. I suppose it was thought to be usable—if at all—for some kind of epic theatre. It doesn't at all have the compact configuration of the Mitzi. It's a kind of sloppily exploded and expanded version of

54 it. But we hoped that the energy that by then had been generated within the production of *Blue Leaves* would be sufficient for it to galvanize this yawning space. We enlarged the circular forestage somewhat and also some of the key furnishing items, but tried to keep these alterations inconspicuous.

The Beaumont was enormously helped, first of all, by some improvements in the acoustics which Mosher, Gersten, and their team had put in the works, and secondly by adding a secondary grid. The Mielziner lighting positions are miles away from the stage, and very, very hard to tightly control lighting from. And in putting the lower grid in we had a place from which we could hang the Austrian curtain that later turned up in *Anything Goes*, and that was a way of hiding the set for the prologue of *Blue Leaves*, which takes place in a piano bar. Paul Gallo, the lighting designer, and I have been adjusting this lower grid in various ways for each production since. The grid itself, just by the presence of Paul's lighting equipment on it, gives the illusion that the ceiling of the theatre is much lower than it actually is, a little less of an echoing void. Everything has seemed to work better in the Beaumont since this lower grid went in. Paul Gallo, incidentally, has been a won-

Costume sketch by Tony Walton for Ken Howard as Teddy Roosevelt, 1600 PENNSYLVANIA AVENUE (1976).

derful new bonus in my professional life.

When you begin your work on a design, do you make lots of rough sketches?

It very much depends on what it is. I do love to do a lot of doodling, and I love the research process. I do an enormous amount of research, and if it's a musical or an opera, musical research. I was already a Porter fanatic before we started on *Anything Goes*, but I wanted to get my hands on everything of his and just have it be a part of what we were listening to while we were working on it. In addition to Porter we had a great deal of Fred Astaire material to look at and listen to, because one of the principal things we tried for was to have everything seem as effortless as possible in the way that Fred Astaire epitomized. He could take some deft movement and make it look like he was just being Fred Astaire, whereas he had actually just spent perhaps several weeks and lost 15 pounds in rehearsal getting that effect right! And that was a key element in all of our efforts on this show. Actually, the way the show works internally and mechanically and the way some of the sets change via the basement is bizarrely out of the ordinary. But the effort was to hide all that, to get as far away from the *Starlight Express* syndrome as possible.

There were, of course, a number of major physical requirements, not the least of which was that we wanted to have the music front and center by placing the orchestra in the most ideal stage space. The band was to have the best position for sound and all else came after that. It's intriguing looking back on it now, because even some of the people involved in it think of it now as a very simple physical production, which is, of course, what we had hoped it would appear to be.

Now that we're looking at new versions for a Broadway house and a touring company and London it's astonishing to rediscover the amount of research we got together and the tortuous routes we took in arriving at the finished design.

But I love the research, and frequently it infuriates the folk working with me. On a play about Hoagy Carmichael and Bix Beiderbecke I had their music on to the exclusion of anything else for months. And my cohorts finally screamed for a relief from this.

When designing, I like to be so totally immersed in the source material that there's no escape and one can't avoid doing something in the vein of that source material. It's why opera can be so wonderful to work on, because it does three-quarters of the work for you.

Do you like doing opera?

I love it. It's a glory to work on because the music is guiding you on very specific paths. Even on a new musical, the music, perhaps more than anything, is the trigger point for what the visual flavor is.

How did you research Sophisticated Ladies, *and was that show able to tour as you originally designed it for Broadway?*

Well I love anything that forces me to study the work of somebody I admire enormously, and that was one of those instances, just as *Anything Goes* was. I have always been a passionate fan of Cole Porter as I have been of Duke Ellington. It's astounding to have a paying job that forces you to study every aspect of that person's work and their nature and learn everything you can about their lives and try to get as close to what they would do if they had been their own designer. It is the best possible gift to be given. And so I have amassed this staggering library of Ellington records and Porter records and Bix Beiderbecke and Hoagy Carmichael and others because I needed them to work on those shows.

Anyway, the Ellington piece was originally conceived by Donald McKayle as a series of band shows that in a linear style echoed the way Ellington's band had evolved and enlarged over the years. It was complicated by the fact that the ultimate director/choreographer, Michael Smuin, successfully reconceived the show, and wanted to have a band that could expand or contract for the needs of each number. Sometimes it was just the very small group that Ellington started out with, and sometimes it was the very full band that he ended up with, and also, of course, all the variations in between. So the set was made up of a kind of jigsaw puzzle of varied height platforms that could break up and could move apart or slide back together in various configurations. Sometimes it had to be clear that the band was the prominent reason for the whole eve-

Designs and setting by Tony Walton for PIPPIN; Directed by Bob Fosse; Costumes by Patricia Zipprodt; Lighting by Jules Fisher; Imperial Theatre, New York (1972).
1. Opening number: "Magic to Do."
2. Preliminary sketch: start of palace scene
3. Preliminary scene for "pop-up" palace
4. Sketch: Chapel rope portal and backdrop.
5. Chapel scene performance.

ning, and sometimes it would need to recede to become less evident and to allow full dancing and performing space. So it was all those technical needs that dictated the nature of it. Also, the fact that the band needed to travel the whole stage, upstage, downstage, or anywhere in between, meant that there couldn't really be any additional constructed decorative pieces that could fit on stage level. Everything had to hang above it or sneak in amongst it. That was an interesting challenge. And it was why we ended up with so many flying neon elements.

It became doubly intriguing when the road tour—as planned—didn't allow for any setup time at all. This meant the band couldn't be on stage, but had to be in the orchestra pit. So I reconceived the design completely, using more drops and some translucent built pieces.

Now are we talking about a bus-and-truck as opposed to a national tour?

Yes. Well, those definitions are becoming very muddy now. Basically we had to come up with a production that had the band in the pit, and that meant that all of the basic scenic elements had gone, because they all had to do with the band or some aspect of its platforming. And the original production had many suggestions of Ellington's era that were inscribed in neon above the band and around them. None of this could travel at speed. So the new touring production was much more a matter of stylized drops which incorporated images of Ellington and his musicians and some aspects of his life, and these left full dancing space for the whole evening.

One of the few things that had become crucial as a result of the staging of the original production was an illuminated staircase that was like an arcing sculptural piano keyboard that rose up and moved into various configurations, and much of the staging was readjusted by Michael Smuin to make even more capital out of that. So here was a hangover of one production that now had to be integrated fully into this

stylistically completely different production. It was an interesting task. But those kinds of challenges often are what makes doing the new version intriguing.

Where was the staircase built?

That staircase was built at Variety Scenic Studios. The bulk of the original Broadway set was built at Metro. The touring version was built and painted at Gossard's, principally by the guys who eventually banded together with Bill Mensching to form Showtech, one of the few shops that still does their own scenic painting, which is an extraordinary boon to a designer.

Atlas Scenic Studio still does both building and painting. There seem to be too few shops continuing to do that.

Yes. It makes such a difference having everything in one place, otherwise you're continuously nipping from place to place. And the set usually arrives at the scenic painting shop at the last moment and there isn't time for them to do anything but just knock it out. So the poor apologetic scenic artists often have a miserable look because they don't have the time to ask the designer, "Is this what you meant?" They have to hurtle it to some sort of completion, hope for the best, and sling it onto the waiting trucks. It's rough on everybody.

Isn't it still part of the contract that the designer is to see the set erected in the shop before it loads out, or is that a rarity now?

We actually did contract *The Real Thing* that way. It was crucial for that show because everything interacted so dangerously with everything else that we really had to know that it worked. And we had to know that it worked quietly and at a very high speed and that it wouldn't be flying off the stage into the audience. The original version was done at Sam Gossard's, which is now, alas, gone. But the principal folk who worked on it, in addition to Sam, mostly became Showtech, as I mentioned, and they did the touring version out of their own new shop.

But generally in the Broadway structure now, it is almost impossible to see the set assembled in the shop before the load-out because the money isn't secure until the last possible moment. And that may mean that it's not until almost the first day of rehearsals that the checks can actually be signed. You often don't have the luxury of getting the building started until then, which means that with a week to load out of the scenic shop and into the theatre you've got a maximum of three weeks to build it. And the chances of getting it built, painted, and preassembled in the shop within that period of time are, alas, minuscule.

Hurlyburly. *Comment on that production.*

That was fascinating partly because there was nothing in the text whatsoever to indicate the setting. The published script now specifically describes the set that we arrived at. But at the time that Nichols and I got the original text there was literally no physical description of any sort.

So I asked David Rabe if he had anything specific in his head while he was working on this almost stream-of-consciousness piece. And he said, "Well, my favorite theatre is the Shakespearian theatre and whenever I'm writing I somehow have the form of the Globe Theatre in my head. But on the other hand," he said, "I also had, in the case of *Hurlyburly*, the feeling that this was about the walking wounded coming together in some sort of jungle and licking each other's wounds." I said, "Well, the characters are talking about Hollywood. Is this the Hollywood Hills?" He had written it out there and he said, "Yes, well. . ." The nearest we could get to an actual specific was that maybe it was a guesthouse on the estate of a much larger house that had been somewhat abandoned and was now rented out. The furniture didn't really belong to the people who were there, and it had become debased over a period of time.

So, in marrying all those elements in the design, the architectural silhouette of the Globe is there, and the sort of cage in the jungle is there with this enormously overgrown Los Angelean shrubbery enwrapping the whole thing, and crawling over the Malibu lights that Jennifer Tipton used for exterior lighting. Then inside we tried to make something interesting out of various ill-assorted elements, none of which would belong to any specific person there but would perhaps be leftovers from the fifties and early sixties. So it had this dreadful shag rug and table made of polished driftwood and fur lamp shades and so on, but all things that nobody could really love anymore.

Do you prefer to do sketches or models, or both?

It all depends. *Anything Goes* and the Linda Ronstadt tour, *Canciones de Mi Padre*, were almost simultaneous polar opposites in that *Anything Goes* is a hopefully elegant sculptural construct while *Canciones de Mi Padre* was all about somewhat naive loose sketching and painting. I did do little rough doodles for *Anything Goes* to try to get a feel of how we would get from scene to scene and what the basic necessities were in each scene, and then I developed those a little bit. I never did fully painted sketches for that, except for specific details that were needed for the shops. The main design was worked out by making rough models of the things I hoped I could use from the other shows. I wanted to see if I could make a structure that could use them. Once I found that, we then went ahead to a very finished half-inch detailed model with all the furniture. Every set was fully integrated with every other so it needed to be a much more refined, sophisticated model.

Do you do a model for every show?

Yes, pretty much. Sometimes they're much cruder than others. For the Linda Ronstadt show I just did the roughest quarter-inch model because it had a much more two-dimensional approach and it could be done with flat artwork as opposed to a fully modeled form. Her show stems from the songs that her father had taught her, her sister and brothers when they were very young. So she was making the show as a gift for him, and she was tapping into her Mexican roots. She sent me materials that she felt strongly related to all this. And I researched a lot as usual. Sometimes the design would stem from Mexican folk painting on a chest or a tray or a plate or something; sometimes it would be from a piece of pressed tin. I photographed all these things and took them to her and said, "Now, what do you really love and which seem closest to you and to the nature of the material?" She would select her favorites with great conviction, and from that I started drawing a kind of storyboard of the whole show, very specific things, scene by scene.

Is it usual for a touring musical evening like this to be fully designed?

I don't think so, not quite to this extent. This is almost a musical of about the size of *Pippin*. Technically, physically, and scenically it has about the same number of sets and scene changes as that show. Jules Fisher, who also lit *Pippin*, has lit it and he has about 700 lamps. But this show frequently plays one-nighters. So almost all of it goes up on the same grid and the lights are contained in the grid and are focused to match painted marks within the grid itself. Nearly all of the scenery hangs to this same grid, and it all goes up together. So the trucks can arrive at eight o'clock in the morning and at eight o'clock that same night they can play the show. It is all very painty, and an enormous amount of it is soft and is hanging on travelers.

Did you have a good budget?

It was pretty good. I was able to incorporate some things like the crescent moon box and the star drop from Linda's Nelson Riddle show, so we saved a bit of money that way. But it was approached in a very healthy way, actually. And also a very unusual way in that her manager, who is also the show's producer, said to Michael Smuin, the director of the show, and myself, "Just do something splendid, because I don't want to interfere. I don't even want to know what you're doing as long as Linda's happy with it. I just want to turn up when it's on and say, 'Oh, well done!' " And that's how it went. He and his team were almost continuously excited and supportive. It was a delightful experience.

When you do costume sketches, do you do line drawings and paint them fully? What materials do you use for those?

I try to find a different approach and drawing style for the costumes on every show. It's partly a way to keep it interesting for me, but it is also a means for me to fumble my way into the nature of the show itself. In the case of *Anything Goes* I did line drawings on tracing paper and made blueprints of those so they'd be on a blue background. I knew going in that much of the visual palette was going to be white and blue. So it gave me a starting point. And I liked the texture of the blueprint behind it when I started painting them.

Sketch by Tony Walton
MARY POPPINS (1964) the movie
Rooftop sequence at dusk
Directed by Robert Stephenson

Also, it permitted me to print multiple line drawing versions for all interested parties: the costume shops, the wardrobe team, the milliner, the wigmakers, etc.

For something like the Ronstadt musical evening, where everything is in a way plucked out of the darkness, as with much Mexican black enameled work with its highly colored flowers, birds, or whatever, I started working on black paper or black card. And sometimes I do that for ballet design, because so often ballet is relatively light scenically. With designs on black paper it's as if you are pulling out each element and lighting it piece by piece.

Quite often the medium I work in is in response to what the last job was. If the last job was a film which hasn't required a lot of very specific drawing, I quite often feel hungry to just go through the act of drawing or painting again. That sometimes will dictate the choice of what the approach to the work would be. It takes me a while to get back into the swing of it. Sometimes I choose something just as an exercise for myself to get my craft back into action again or get tuned up.

It's also terribly important to one's creative juices, is it not?

Yes. I was very surprised on *Anything Goes* that although, as ever, I did an enormous amount of research, when I actually started drawing the costumes what happened was a kind of sense memory of doing the costumes on *Murder on the Orient Express*, which was set in the same era. After a time I stopped looking at research, and things started flowing back in through the fingers even though the two jobs were years apart. By the time that happened I suppose something had got tuned back up. If you're not tuned up and you're struggling every step of the way to get the drawing to look presentable to the director, you're not leaving yourself accessible to visceral and intuitive responses. So ideally, one should be at a point where one knows that the information is flowing through onto the sketch in the way that it needs to be most helpful to the people who are going to be working from it.

You mean for others to understand from your renderings what you want it to look like even if you are not going to be there in the costume or scenic shop.

Yes, But sometimes even if you *are* around. I mean, one of the best lessons I've had was an experience with Sean Kenny at Stratford-on-Avon. As a pref-

ace to that, let me say that in the kind of training I had had it was pretty much one's obligation to physically do every paint detail or every patch of painting on a costume sketch oneself. Well, a lot of designers don't always do that. They have sketch artists, especially on movies, who do part or even almost all of that for them. And some can work just as effectively that way. But my training had been that sketches and paint details must be all your own handiwork.

I was working on the revue that I mentioned earlier which had the near calamity with projectors, and Sean Kenny, who had designed *Oliver* was designing *The Devils*, and it was being built at Stratford-on-Avon. He was a good friend, so the painters let me know he was coming down and I ran up to say hello to him.

He was a little late. And then he arrived, rushed in with this armful of magazines from the train. And he threw them down and said, "I haven't had a chance yet to do the paint elevation for the show scrim, but you see this?" And it was the back of a magazine with a Michelin tire ad or something in an abstract style. And he said,

"It's sort of like this, a little more romantic. I'd like it to be warmer." And the head scenic artist said, "Well, Jane paints like that, Jane, you should show him your things." And she lived only a couple of streets away and so she went and got her stuff. He said, "Oh, my god, that's exactly the kind of thing. Have you got a piece of acetate?" And he laid this acetate over it and marked off a little rectangle and said, "If you could heat up that and get like a flame coming through, that would be fantastic!" I thought, "This is the most startling thing! It's just so totally at odds with everything we were taught."

And then he was gone, and in the next few days while we were tinkering with our problem-laden show, I would occasionally for relief go up to watch progress on this scrim of Sean's. And they were so deeply involved on this drop. And it was theirs! It was their thing. And if it worked, it was wonderful. It was as much theirs as it was Sean's. And I thought, "What a lesson!" It was such a beautiful piece of work.

Around that time, as a costume designer I had been a little self-conscious about not really knowing enough about cutting and draping and the craft aspects of it. For the first few shows I didn't even know how lucky I was. I was working with these incredible costume makers, one of whom was Barbara Matera, who heads our principal costume shop here now. And they

Setting and costumes by Tony Walton
SHELTER
Book and lyrics by Gretchen Cryer
Music by Nancy Ford
Directed by Austin Pendleton
Lighting by Richard Pilbrow
Golden Theatre, New York (1973)
Setting with multiple projections for the song
    "Mary Margaret's Place in the Country."
(Photograph by Tony Walton)

were not just bailing me out; they were bringing this creative thing to it that I barely even knew was being brought because I was so inexperienced. So then I tried to learn more of the craft and I studied it for a while, and on my next show went to Bermans, which with Nathans was London's biggest costume house.

Well, the next show I designed was the London production of *The Most Happy Fella*, which went fine and was a great success and so on. But I thought I had done the most boring set of costumes ever put on any stage. They were perfectly serviceable, but there was nothing interesting about any of them. I thought, "What on earth happened?" And then right after this, the Sean Kenny episode happened. And I thought, "Well maybe what I've done is I've killed the continuance of the creative process somehow by trying to call all the shots and dominate the costume making process." So for the next show I consciously went back to some of the people who'd built costumes for me before and said, "Hey, you know I barely know anything about cutting and draping and so on. Please help me work all this out." And they did, and the work came alive again.

And, I suppose, I try to do something vaguely similar in less contrived ways with the scenic artists, and certainly with any assistants I may have. It's a way for them to feel that if this works, it's partly because of their involvement. Hopefully, it helps them to be a true participant in the process of getting the original and imaginative impulse from square one to the finished thing on the stage. If you can keep the creative process alive all the way through, I think that's the really crucial thing. It's one of the things that's really hard to teach—how to keep the links

in the chain being not just participatory, but truly involved creatively. Without it the piece won't have the life left in it at the end that it had when you started. If somebody's just delivering your requests respectfully and out of interest in getting paid, then it's very tough to push the original creative energy all the way through the work process to a living completion.

Do you have any feelings about new work you'd like to do in the theatre?

If I'm lucky enough to have a choice about what's next. I tend to try to choose the polar opposite of what I have most recently done. Your own signature is going to erupt sooner or later through your limitations and dictate a certain style whether you want it to or not. So I've been trying to postpone the acknowledgment of the clear signature for as long as possible.

And that's the only thing that occasionally occurs to me as being somewhat different from some of my colleagues. A strong influence on me was Boris Aronson. I was conscious that Boris's gift was such a powerful one that it knitted all his work together somehow, but he started everything from scratch. Each time out it was as if he had never done anything before and was beginning afresh, and somehow you don't see the "Aronson style" slapped all over everything that he did. Of course, there are some people whose personal style is so powerful that it becomes its own merit. Even though it may feel limiting to them, it's delightful to everyone else. I wouldn't want to think "This is what I do," and just do it until I'm bored. I hope to pursue variety for as long as I can, to stretch my capacities a bit. It's a way of keeping excited and fascinated with the whole process.

The productions I'm working on currently are a good example of a very enjoyable range of wildly differing pieces: *Death and the Maiden, Four Baboons Adoring the Sun, Conversations with My Father*, ABT's *Peter and the Wolf* and Jerry Zaks' revival of *Guys and Dolls*. All of these open within a four-week period and none of them have anything in common. Each requires a radically different approach and none of them is remotely like the other productions I still have running: *Grand Hotel* and *The Will Rogers Follies*. So for me, variety really is the spice of life.

2

THEATRES

DESIGNING FOR VARIOUS STAGE SPACES

A seasoned stage designer expects to design settings for a wide variety of stages. Once a designer decides to do a production, the task is to present the appropriate design concept in the producer's preselected theatre space. The range in shape and size of stages found in university, regional, Off-Broadway, Broadway, and other theatres offers a challenge to even the most experienced designer. It would be an unwise limitation on a career for a serious scenic designer to say, "I only work on the proscenium stage," or "I prefer to design for a completely open stage." The experienced designer usually looks forward to working in types of theatres other than the proscenium stage simply because it is another challenge and it is often a pleasant change of pace. If you can get a glance at a designer's résumé, notice the many theatres and companies where he or she has worked. The same designer may create stage scenery for quite different theatres, such as the Metropolitan Opera House in New York City; the Arena Stage in Washington, D. C.; the Tyrone Guthrie Theatre in Minneapolis, Minnesota; the American Repertory Theatre in Boston, Massachusetts; and the Mark Taper Forum in Los Angeles, California to name but a few.

The proscenium theatre has traditionally been one of the most popular types of stages. Many resident theatres around the country have proscenium theatres as their main stage, and some-

times they also have open stages as a second or third space.

Numerous variations are found in the proscenium stage, depending on when a particular theatre was built, its size, its location, and how it is used. For example, one theatre may have a regular apron or an apron extension downstage of the proscenium opening, or an apron and then an orchestra pit. In addition to the apron and/or orchestra pit, sometimes there may be small side stages on either side of the proscenium opening that are valuable areas for additional staging, especially in multiset productions. In other configurations, a proscenium stage may have a thrust stage, ranging from small to large, with various platform shapes and steps extending out in front of the opening arch. Other arrangements of playing areas in front of the proscenium opening include stairs and step units, ramps, and runways, all of which have many designs, and orchestra pits that may be fully or partially covered. Elevators may operate in the stage floor proper or platforms may rise up in the orchestra pit to provide various levels and thus create an even more versatile playing space.

Open stages are often the most challenging spaces in which to work. Open stages can be vastly flexible in design and in the scenery that goes on them. Basic platform shapes or playing areas may be round, square, rectangular or some other shape, with seats surrounding the platform, or placed on two or three sides of the platform. In another open stage space there may be playing

areas on a large platform, with seats only on two sides. Yet another space might have a stage just at one end, with seats in the opposite end. Still another stage might be in the shape of a quarter-circle in the corner of a room, with seats continuing the same arc outward from the playing area.

Types of Stage

The scenic designer today may be called upon to design settings for many kinds of acting spaces, although the proscenium or "picture-frame" stage opening is still most usual. These are the most frequent forms:

Proscenium stage. The audience sees actors perform on a raised stage framed by a decorative arch at one end of the auditorium. Sometimes a proscenium stage has small side stages.

Proscenium stage with extended apron or thrust. This is the same type as above, but with an extended playing area in front of the proscenium arch which brings the action nearer to the audience.

Open stage. These stages have half- or three-quarter-round seating. The stage may be circular, semicircular, square, rectangular, or otherwise angular. There is an intimate relationship between the audience and the actors. Most scenery is usually located at the upstage wall.

Arena stage (theatre-in-the-round). In this the audience completely surrounds the stage. Costumes and props are emphasized more than scenery. Blocking and staging is done for viewing by an audience on all sides. The stage may be circular, square, rectangular, or otherwise angular. This type of stage is common in music tents.

Open-air theatres. These vary from proscenium stages (usually without the horizontal arch) to open stages. Semicircular seating is common.

Mobile street theatres. Here the audience can be positioned anywhere and can view the action from the front, sides, or around the complete stage.

Types of Stage Setting

The architectural qualities of the stage (and sometimes the auditorium) in part determine what kind of physical set will work for an individual production in a specific house. The general categories of stage setting are single sets, multiple (individual) sets, unit sets, and simultaneous scene settings. The

range is nevertheless quite wide, since most of the categories can embrace elements from more than one of the following characteristic setting forms:

Box setting

Wing, border, and backdrop setting

Portal, wing, border, and backdrop setting with profiled or three-dimensional set pieces

Set pieces in front of a cyclorama or backdrop

Drapery settings with props

Projected scenery on backdrops or cycloramas

An arrangement of platforms and levels

A basic rule for productions with completely separate (multiple) sets is that all the settings should be in one scenic style, for overall unity. Even within this limitation the designer has ample opportunity to be versatile, to

create variety in mood within the nuances of the single style. This rule should not be violated without careful thought. It has sometimes been successfully disregarded in designs for works in which the action takes place in numerous locales or covers a great time span, such as when some scenes are flashback, or when certain sets are conceived intentionally in a contrasting style.

PROSCENIUM STAGES

Dimensions of the Proscenium Opening

Dimensions of the proscenium opening vary with the individual theatre. The scenic designer decides on the proscenium opening dimensions that will be appropriate both visually and practically for a specific production.

The Width In the commercial Broadway theatre, a good average proscenium opening width is 40′–0″. One may also consider a workable range of 38′–0″ to 42′–0″. A designer is usually delighted with any of these widths, and would not make alterations, except possibly to make the proscenium opening smaller by closing it in with portals or tormentors. Obviously, if a

Setting by Adrianne Lobel
COSÌ FAN TUTTE by Wolfgang Amadeus Mozart
Libretto by Lorenzo da Ponte
Directed by Peter Sellars
Lighting by James F. Ingalls
PepsiCo Summerfare
Purchase, New York (1986)
(Photograph by Adrianne Lobel)

"In order to bracket Peter Sellars' idea of setting COSÌ in a diner with a strong sense of the eighteenth century, I designed a realistically detailed and dimensional silvery, shimmery diner surrounded by flat painted eighteenth-century trees and soft cloud borders. The diner looked like a space ship dropped onto the stage at Drottingholm." —Adrianne Lobel

Setting by Loren Sherman
THE NEST OF THE WOODGROUSE

by Victor Rosov
Directed by Joseph Papp

Lighting by Arden Fingerhut
Public/Newman Theatre, New York (1984)

particular proscenium opening is not wide enough, and the illusion of a wider proscenium width is desired, then the action of the play may have to be extended to side stages or boxes, or side extensions with platforms and steps may have to be added to the apron. A portal may also be added downstage to give the illusion of a wider proscenium opening; this would, at the same time, make a deeper playing area. However, adding this feature is fairly rare in the commercial theatre. Usually, the scenic designer does not adjust the width dimension of a proscenium opening, but instead is more concerned with selecting an appropriate height dimension that is visually pleasant with a proscenium opening width dimension of 40′−0″.

The Height Most commercial Broadway theatres have a permanently fixed house grand drape and/or valance that does not move up and down for trimming the top of the proscenium opening, and often there is not a house

"The American premiere of a Russian comedy about family life and the friction between generations; a kind of Soviet 'Life With Father' with a political layer. Set in the apartment of a well-off government official, with a dining room on stage right and a library on stage left."

—Loren Sherman

teaser. When a house teaser *is* available, it may be fixed in place and/or have an irregular shaped bottom. It is another matter completely in opera and dance houses or in regional theatres where an adjustable teaser is readily available. Then the height of the proscenium opening can be changed as appropriate for the individual production.

The Proscenium Opening and Specific Items of Dressing

Because the scenic designer has a highly creative and artistic eye and a particular individual style, he or she may be engaged to collaborate with a theatre consultant or architectural firm to design a grand drape, a border, and a house curtain for a legitimate theatre. (A framed valance at the very top of the proscenium opening sometimes works with the grand drape as part of its design.) The scenic designer is hired to create the decor while the theatre consultant or architect works on the practical aspects of rigging, structural con-

Model by Loy Arcenas
THE GLASS MENAGERIE
  by Tennessee Williams
Directed by Tazewell Thompson
Arena Stage (Kreeger)
Washington, D.C. (1989)

Ground Plan of Basic Open Stages with Seats

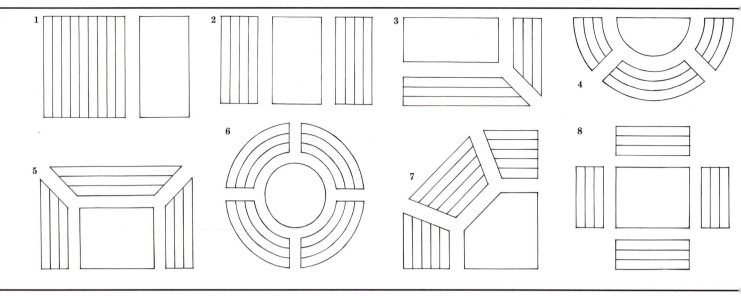

Proscenium Apron Extensions and Orchestra Enclosures (with & without Runways)

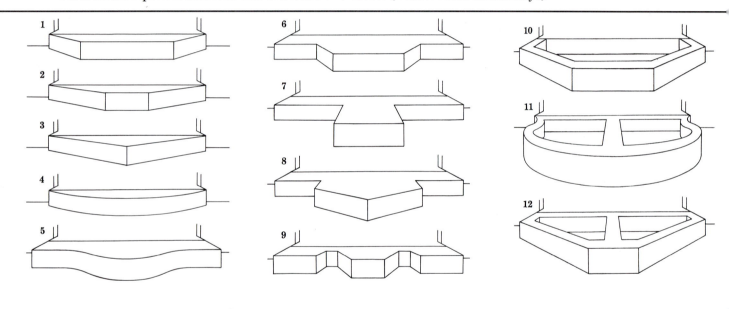

Ground Plan and Elevation of Proscenium Thrust Stages

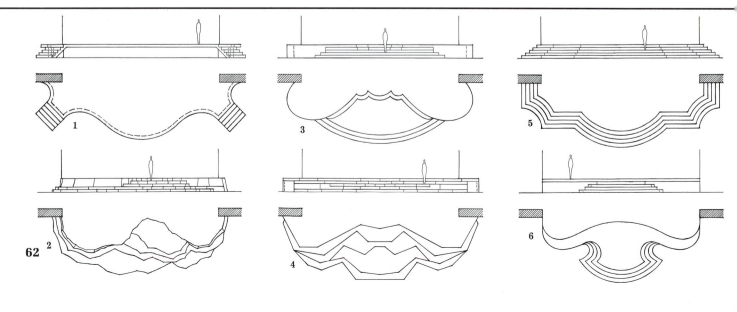

62

Apron Extensions with Platforms, Ramps, and Steps

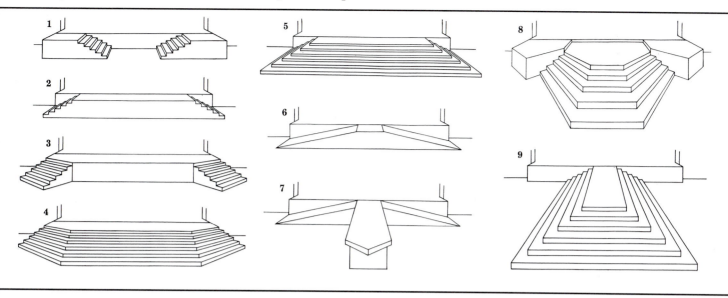

Ground Plan of Runways and Steps Going into the Audience

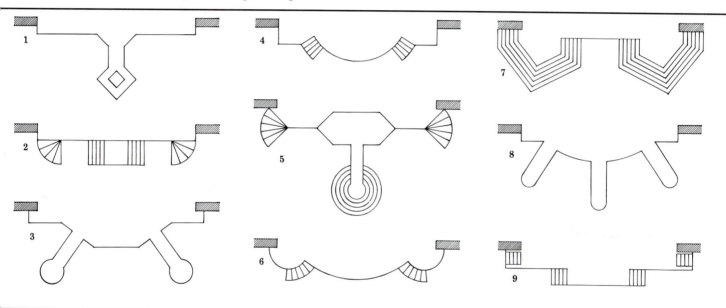

Orchestra Pit Section

1 PO
2 SP

1'-0"
6"
1'-7"
28'-6"
3 HC
9'-8"
6'-10"
1'-7"
4"
3'-9"
7'-0"
4 PIT
2'-0"
3'-8"

Plan of Side Stages

1

2

3

Views of an Open Stage

32'-6"

35'-0"

4'-6"

64 siderations, costs, and other pertinent factors. As a part of this team the scenic designer may work in a new legitimate theatre or on the renovation of an old one. There are also productions where a designer may want to create a special look in the house by completely changing the existing proscenium decor as well as the decoration of the boxes and other visual features in the house.

When you are designing the decorative accessories to be positioned in and back of the proscenium opening of a legitimate theatre, always remember the sequence in which they work together to form an attractive and practical unit. This is important because there is a tradition to be observed in the purpose or function of each component. At the same time, these important proscenium accessories should be visually exciting. Use the following list as a guide for sequence and description of items when designing proscenium decor.

1. *Proscenium opening* (also called proscenium arch or proscenium frame). The surrounding detail on the wall with the opening (proscenium arch) varies greatly from theatre to theatre. It can be highly elaborate in detail and architectural shape or extremely plain.
2. *Grand drape.* Depending on the individual theatre, this drapery at the top

of the proscenium opening is either fixed in place and not adjustable or movable and adjustable. The grand drape can be created in a variety of ways: (1) it can be draped in swags and jabots and positioned on a frame (or without a frame), (2) hung in fullness, or (3) painted on one piece of straight fabric with a profiled bottom edge. The grand drape may also have a decorative framed valance around the top and in front of it. Sometimes the framed valance may have extending decor, such as giant profiled jabots on each of the two vertical sides of the proscenium opening. The jabots may continue partway or all the way down from the valance to the stage floor. Instead of jabots, there may be soft legs of gathered fabric in fullness. However, legs or jabots are not normally found in the commercial Broadway theatre.

When the grand drape does not have a straight line across the bottom or when there is no border whatsoever to move up or down, or when the grand drape is positioned very high, it is then necessary to use the bottom of the house curtain (when flown out) as the top of the proscenium opening and at the same time serve as the front top masking for the scenery.
3. *Smoke pocket with the fire curtain.* The fire curtain can be made of asbestos, or noncarcenogenic fire-resistant

fabric, or steel. A deluge (water) curtain can also be used in lieu of a traditional fire curtain.
4. *House border* (or house teaser). The house border is positioned behind the grand drape, and may be either permanently in place or rigged to move up and down. As a practical feature, the bottom of the border is designed to be straight across, but this may vary. Commercial theatres do not always have a house border; sometimes the grand drape works alone with the house curtain.
5. *House curtain* (act curtain or main rag). A house curtain may be one of the following:
   a. *A drop curtain* that flies vertically in or out, the most common style found in the commercial theatre.
   b. *A tableau curtain* (or tab), which consists of two pieces of fabric in fullness and opens and gathers from the center as each piece is pulled upward toward the two proscenium corners (like an opera curtain), where they hang in large curved drapery swags on the left and right.
   c. *A draw curtain*, which has two pieces of fabric in fullness on traveler tracks opening from the center, with one piece going offstage left and the other offstage right.
6. *House portal.* The house portal is a one-piece unit of framed masking

Covering the Orchestra Pit to Create Entrances and Exits for Actors

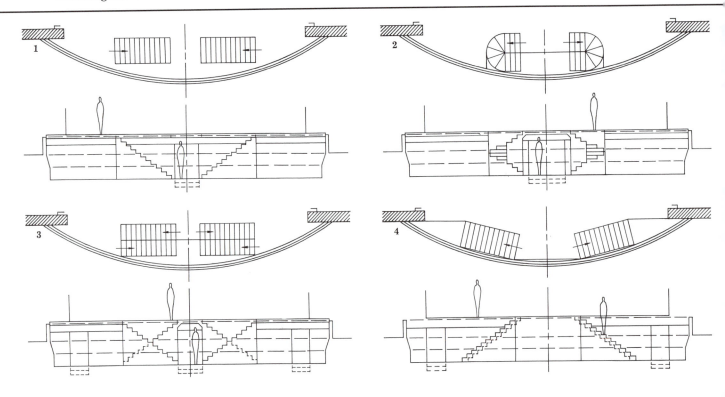

Paint elevations by Rolf Beyer
TWELFTH NIGHT by William Shakespeare
Hopkins Center
Dartmouth College
Hanover, New Hampshire (1968)
(Photograph by Al Olsen)

"Side stages were used and the two-story pavilions were practical. Other units flew in in front of the upstage translucency."
—Rolf Beyer

scenery with two side legs and header (border) at the top, all in the same plane, usually with thickness (the reveal) pieces bordering the three inside sides of the portal opening. The portal thickness going around the inner opening may be perpendicular to the face or beveled on a 45-degree angle.

Instead of a house portal, some theatres may still use two framed legs with thickness left and right. These framed legs are called *tormentors* and are often adjustable, in that they move on and off stage as desired to close in or extend the opening, and have an adjustable teaser (or border) at the top. The *teaser*, which hangs in front of these hard tormenter legs, may be framed or soft, with or without fullness, and can be moved up or down to change the height of the opening.

For touring or economical purposes, a soft one-piece portal that hangs on one lineset and easily folds up may be appropriate. Or a combination of three pieces consisting of two legs and one border can also work well. Of course, not every production utilizes a portal. It is up to the designer to decide whether or not to use one. If a portal is to be used, the best result visually is achieved by a framed portal

that appears to be made as one neat, continuous piece of scenery.

7. *Show curtain* (act, scene curtain, or production curtain). The show curtain is positioned behind the house curtain, and is placed either upstage or downstage of the portal. The choice of where the show curtain is positioned depends on whether the portal should frame the curtain or the curtain should cover the portal, or whether more action space is needed in front of it, or any other similar requirements. Although show curtains tend to be used most often for musicals, operas, operettas, and revues, they can be ideal for plays as well, depending on the approach. It is always best to use cable guides on each end of the show curtain to keep it taut and straight and to guide it when it is being flown in or out.

A show curtain may be soft and may open and close in the same mechanical fashion as the house curtain. It may also consist of a number of other arrangements, such as individual panels of fabric or a single piece of fabric. While the show curtain is usually thought of as a soft and painted piece of scenery, it can be made of various combinations of different materials and still work as a device to introduce the mood or flavor of the show. It can be a configuration of hanging panels, framed flats, or soft fabrics.

8. *Black backup drop.* A black backup drop is needed behind a translucent show curtain when the show curtain is made of sharkstooth scrim, gauze, translucent muslin, or other non-opaque material. The black backup drop masks the upstage lights or work

lights during the show. It usually has the same dimensions as the show curtain, and may be made of velour, Granada cloth, or duvetyne (if opaque enough). Cable guides should be attached on the two offstage ends of the black backup drop.

Designing a Grand Drape and a House Curtain

Besides working as a consultant designing the proscenium accessories for a legitimate theatre, every now and then a designer has an opportunity to design a grand drape and a house curtain to be used as a setting in a motion picture or television production. Whatever the production, there are many possibilities to be aware of in this kind of design project.

Each individual theatre is a unique combination of architectural style, color, period, and size. You are usually expected to work with the physical requirements and conditions of the specific theatre. For instance, if the theatre interior is neutral enough, the idea may be to design a grand drape and house curtain that are totally independent of the style of the architecture. On the other hand, you may be asked to recreate designs in the flavor of the original period of an existing legitimate theatre with the exact original colors of the walls, ceiling, seats, and carpets. In addition, you may be asked to design draperies and curtains for the theatre boxes positioned left and right of the proscenium opening, as well as related interior items such as the curtains and/or decor surrounding the exit doors, and the pleated curtains in front of and

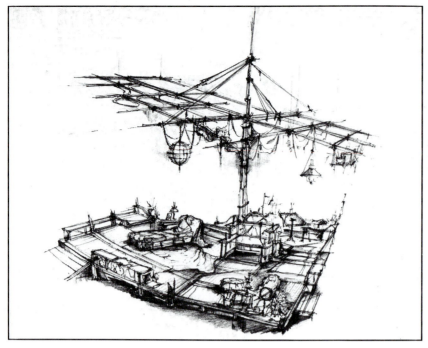

Stage design by Santo Loquasto
HEARTBREAK HOUSE by George Bernard Shaw
Arena Stage, Washington, D.C. (1976)

around the orchestra pit. On still other jobs you may be asked to design new seat covers and select new carpet, not only for the theatre proper but for the floors in the lobbies and lounges.

When designing the decorative accessories for the proscenium opening in a theatre, there are several points to consider. Always keep in mind the order of the position of the pieces, which is: (1) the grand drape (may or may not

Stage design by Santo Loquasto
THE SUICIDE by Nikolai Erdman
ANTA Theatre, New York (1980)

have a decorative framed valance above it); (2) the smoke pocket with the fire curtain; (3) the border (fixed or movable, depending on the design and the effect); and (4) the house curtain. It is a good idea to ask yourself these questions:

1. What is the basic shape and size for which the grand drape is being designed? Is the shape of the top of the proscenium opening straight, curved, or a mixture of the two? Is the grand drape covering an obstruction of

beams, or is it to hang in a completely open space?

2. What kind of house curtain is to be used in the theatre? Does it fly in and out, part in the center and move off and on on traveler tracks, or tab by opening in the center and pull back and up on each of the two sides?

3. Is the design of the bottom of the house curtain to be straight or irregular?

4. Is the house curtain to fly out with the bottom of the curtain to serve as the top trim of the proscenium opening, or does it fly all the way out so the bottom of it is not seen?

5. Is the grand drape to work with a straight bottom teaser hanging upstage of it, with the house curtain hanging upstage of the teaser, or is a teaser not being used?

6. If a decorative teaser is hanging behind the house curtain, is it to be fixed in place or is it to be adjustable so it can move up and down?

7. What kind of fabrics and materials is the house valance made of?

8. Is the grand drape to be with or without fullness?

9. Is there to be a framed decorative valance hanging in front of the grand drape?

The grand drape may be the one feature of the proscenium decor that requires the most study and thought. It is usually a simple matter to create a basic design for a proscenium with a straight top opening, but for discussion let us assume that the grand drape is being designed for a proscenium with a curved shape at the top. The bottom of the grand drape is to be covered with velour stretched out flat. Ornamentation includes fringe, decorative bands, roping, covered rosettes, and tassels.

These steps may serve as a guide for creating a grand drape:

1. Because of fire laws, it is best to always use flameproof materials.
2. Make a scaled drawing in ½-inch scale. Get on-site dimensions in the theatre.
3. For very unusual top opening shapes, make a full-scale drawing on sheets of brown paper so the drawing can be used for the building. Also, while in the theatre check to see how the grand drape being designed can be attached in place once it is built.
4. Use this full-scale drawing to construct a wooden framework to go behind the fabric and the decorative drapery details. This framework may be made similar to the basic construction of a series of stage flats, with hardware for joining and hardware for attaching the grand drape in place in the proscenium opening. The construction of the framework for the grand drape also depends on the design. For instance, if swags and jabots are being used, then their positions would dictate where to have wood to fasten them.
5. Use muslin or black twill for lining behind the fabric.
6. Paint the wooden framing a dark or matching color.
7. For random rosettes or other ornamentation, it may be necessary to have a wire mesh put over the wooden framework before any fabric is attached.
8. Plan on having the fabric and materials executed so they can be easily removed for cleaning. For attachment use Velcro, tie lines, and grommets or other devices to allow easy removal and attachment.

The following specifications for designing a house curtain and a grand drape were evolved by the Roger Morgan Studio, Inc., in New York City for the Salt Lake City Dance Company

Theatre. These details are a good example of what is expected when a designer is creating a house curtain and grand drape in a theatre.

DECORATIVE HOUSE CURTAIN AND CHORUS DRAPERIES

PART I—GENERAL RELATED DOCUMENTS
The General Conditions, and Supplementary General Conditions and Division I, General Requirements, are hereby made a part of this section as fully as if repeated herein.

Scope
A. Work Included
   Provide all labor and materials as required to furnish and install all of the drapery items as described herein.
B. Related Work in Other Sections
   The following items of associated work are included in other sections of these specifications.
   1. Complete stage rigging installation.
   2. Complete stage draperies.

Qualifications
A. This trade contractor shall be one who has been established as a professional scenic painting studio having a bonafide place of business complete with technical field service organization for a period of not less than five (5) years and be of proven technical and creative ability.
B. A list of references consisting of a minimum of five (5) projects of equal size or larger than herein specified, with special emphasis on scenic painting capabilities is a requirement of all bidders.

Bidders are requested to furnish additional background information in the form of color photographs of previously executed scenic painting similar to the work required by this specification.

The information requested must accompany the Bid Proposal in order for the Bid Proposal to receive proper consideration.
C. This trade contractor shall execute all of the scenic painting required by these specifications in his own scenic painting studio and all scenic painting shall be carried out by experienced, professional scenic artists.

This trade contractor shall retain sole responsibility for the manufacture of all drapery items called for in this specification whether executed by his own shop or by a qualified sub-contractor.
D. The names of any sub-contractors utilized for this work along with appropriate references shall be submitted with the Bid Proposal in order for the Bid Proposal to receive proper consideration. All sub-contractors must be approved by the Architect.
E. Installation shall be supervised by the trade contractor's own experienced superintendent having extensive experience in installing work of this kind.

Responsibility for the satisfactory completion of the manufacture and installation of this equipment shall rest solely and exclusively with this trade contractor. The

Stage design by Karl Eigsti
WHEN YOU COMIN' BACK, RED RYDER? by Mark Medoff
Cincinnati Playhouse in the Park, Cincinnati, Ohio (1976)

68 contractor shall not employ any person to do the work of a particular craft unless that person is qualified in that craft. No unskilled laborer shall be permitted to do the work of a craftsman.

Submittals

A. All submittals for this work shall be made directly to the Theatre Consultant. All samples and drawings will be forwarded to the Architect by the Consultant and the Architect will return the submittals to the contractor with the appropriate approval notations.

B. Provide ½ yard minimum size sample of each fabric type and samples of all trim for approval prior to fabrication. Work shall not commence until an approval of the samples has been transmitted to the contractor.

C. Provide a sample of the house curtain fabric, two linear yards in length, fully painted. The sample shall be oriented vertically and include the lower portion of the curtain as well as part of the stenciled damask pattern with overpainting. Painting on the actual curtain shall not be started until this sample has been approved by the Architect.

Painter's Elevations

In addition to the written and graphic information incorporated in this specification, the contractor shall be furnished with large scale fully detailed painter's elevations which will provide specific information regarding the style, techniques and colors required for the work. Large scale drawings of the stencils will also be provided.

Project Conditions

A. All questions requiring clarification or interpretation of the specification should be addressed directly to the Theatre Consultant.

B. All dimensions shall be verified in the field, prior to fabrication by this trade contractor.

No extras will be allowed because of the Contractor's misunderstanding as to the amount of work involved or his lack of knowledge of any of the conditions pertaining to the work based on his neglect or failure to visit or make examination of the site.

C. Substitutions, changes or deletions from these plans and specifications will not be allowed without the prior approval, in writing, of the Theatre Consultant and the Architect.

D. Substitutions for specified equipment or installation methods will not be accepted or approved unless appropriate drawings or other significant data are submitted proving the equivalence or superiority in quality and performance of the proposed substitution(s).

E. The owner reserves the right to waive all formalities, to be the sole judge of quality and equality of the several bid proposals, and reserves the right to reject any or all bids.

Warranty

A. This trade contractor shall assure that this equipment is properly installed, free of defects in materials and workmanship and shall provide a warranty on all equipment and workmanship provided under this contract for a period of one year from the date of final acceptance by the Owner.

B. During the guarantee period, repair or replacement of defective materials and/or repair of faulty workmanship shall be provided, at no cost to the Owner, within 10 days written notification of defect(s).

Omissions

As it is not practical to enumerate all items of equipment, it shall be the responsibility of the Contractor to supply all equipment required to provide a satisfactorily operating system in accordance with the intent of the Drawings and Specifications regardless of whether or not such items are herein specified or indicated.

Delivery and Installation

A. Bid price shall include full freight charges for the complete system to the job site, F.O.B. factory.

B. Manufacturer agrees to assume cost of air freight shipment if required to meet delivery dates.

C. This equipment shall be installed, complete in all respects no later than date specified. It shall be the responsibility of this trade contractor to coordinate all installation dates with the construction manager in order to avoid conflicts with other trades. Do not make any shipment of materials to the job site without the prior approval of the construction manager.

PART II—PRODUCTS

Fabrics

A. Cotton Velour. 54" wide, 100% Cotton. 25 oz. per lin. yd. "Town Hall" as supplied by M. H. Lazarus & Co., N.Y., NY. Color to be selected by Architect from Lazarus Color Line.

B. Twill Lining. Black 54" wide, 100% Cotton "Ranger Twill Lining" as supplied by M. H. Lazarus & Co., N.Y., NY.

C. Jute Webbing. 12 lb., 3½" wide jute webbing.

All fabrics shall be flameproofed and all finished goods shall be supplied to the Owner with proper flameproofing certificates, acceptable to Salt Lake City Fire Department authorities. All fabrics shall be without flaws, with each width of color continuous for the full height of the curtain with no horizontal seams or piecing. The lay of the fabric shall be identical at each width for all velour draperies supplied to avoid stripe effect.

House Curtain Construction

Fabricate a new house curtain and install it on the existing house curtain counterweight set. Curtain shall be made up of velour and painted with an elaborate stenciled damask pattern with painted gold fringe and braid.

Furnish all necessary hardware and equipment required to complete the installation in a satisfactory manner. Adjust the counterweights so that the completed curtain will be easily operated by one man.

A. Dimensions. Completed curtain shall fly as a straight lift curtain made up of two equal sized panels parting at the center. Finished dimensions of each panel shall be as follows: Width—27'-6" Height—32'-0"

B. Fullness. 100%

C. Top. Curtains shall be box pleated at the top and reinforced with 12 lb., 3½" wide jute webbing. Each pleat is to be equipped with a brass grommet and a #4 braided masonry tie line, 33" long.

D. Bottom. Bottom of each curtain to be weighted with a #200 lead tape weight inserted in a 6" hem.

E. Center Edges. Center edges are to be faced back with 1½ widths of velvet.

F. Offstage Edges. Offstage edges of the curtain are to be reinforced with 12 lb., 3½" jute webbing for the entire height of the curtain.

Wire guides as manufactured by J. R. Clancy Co. (#270 Lignum Vitae) are to be installed and furnished with steel straps. Space the guides 2'-0" o.c. and bolt through the fabric and the webbing for the entire height of the curtain.

G. Wire Guide Cables. It shall be the work of this contractor to install the curtain guide cables using ¼" 6 × 19 plow steel cable. Two ¼" cable clips are to be used at each fastening point. The cables shall be installed at each outer perimeter of the curtain and be securely attached to the stage floor and run the full height to the grid.

H. Tailoring. All of the curtains shall be hand tailored so that no machine stitches are visible on the front. This note applies to house curtain, border, grand drape.

I. Lining. Each panel shall be fully lined with black twill lining. Lining shall be sewed into the hem at all edges of each drapery. Do not secure lining with loose tabs.

Border Construction

Fabricate a new house border and install it on the first counterweight line set directly upstage of the smoke pocket. Painting on the border shall be similar to that on the house curtain.

A. Dimensions. Completed border shall fly as a straight lift curtain and will be made up in one piece. Finished dimensions shall be: Width—52'-0" Height—28'-0"

B. Fullness. 100%

C. Top and Bottom. (As noted above.)

D. Offstage Edges. Offstage edges of the border are to be reinforced with 12 lb., 3½" jute webbing for the entire height of the border.

E. Lining. (As noted above.)

Grand Drapery Construction

Fabricate a new grand drape in the form shown on the drawings. This drape will require some painting on it, but will be less elaborate than

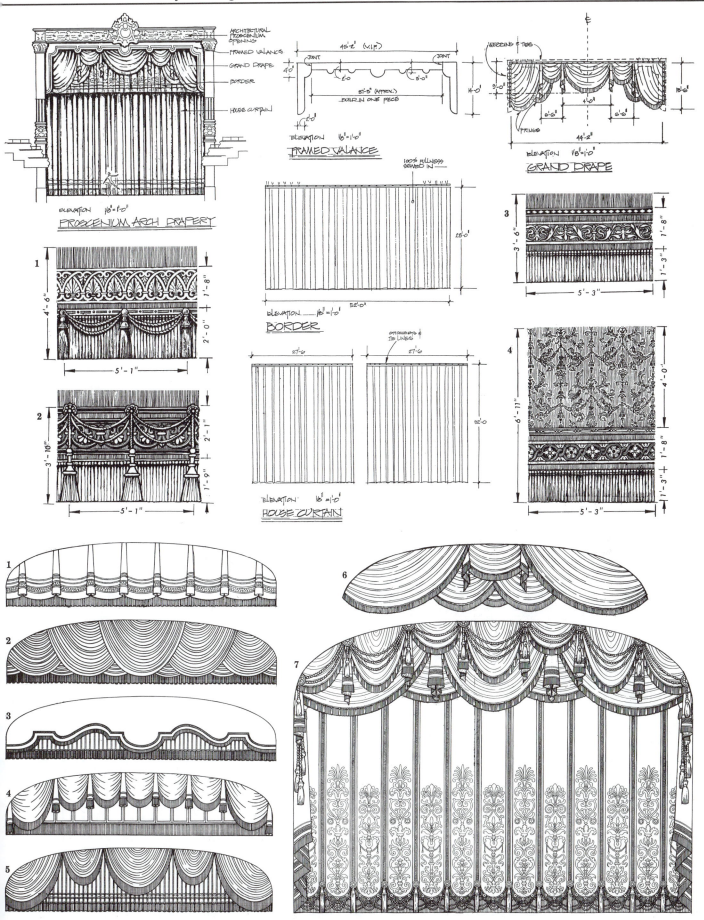

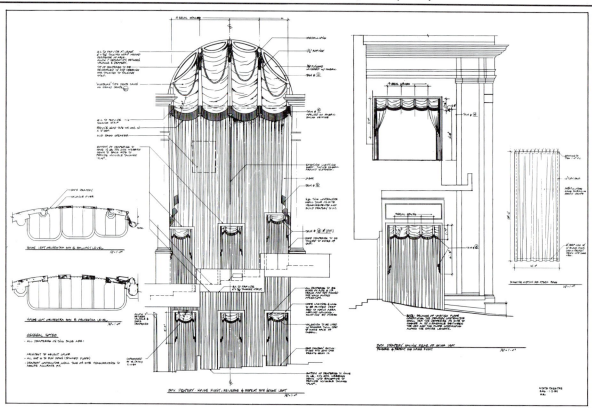

Pantages Theatre, Toronto, Ontario, Canada (1989)

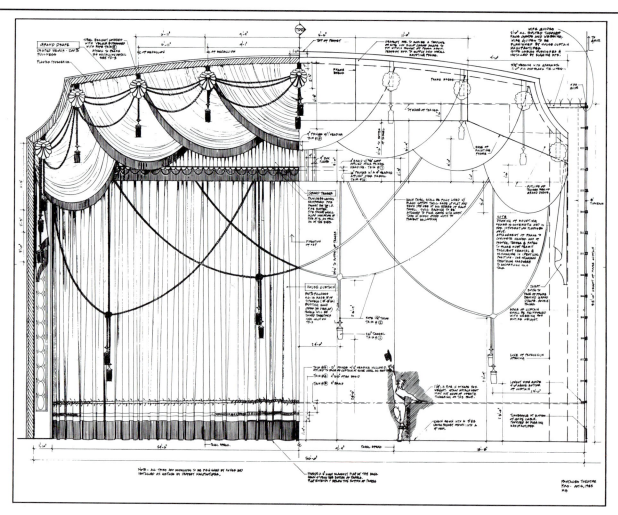

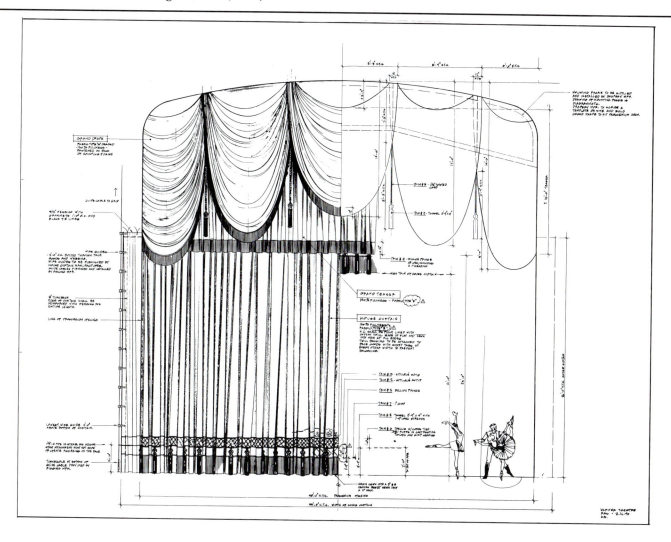

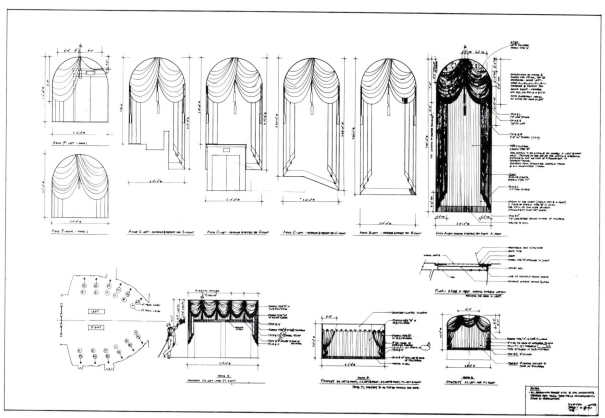

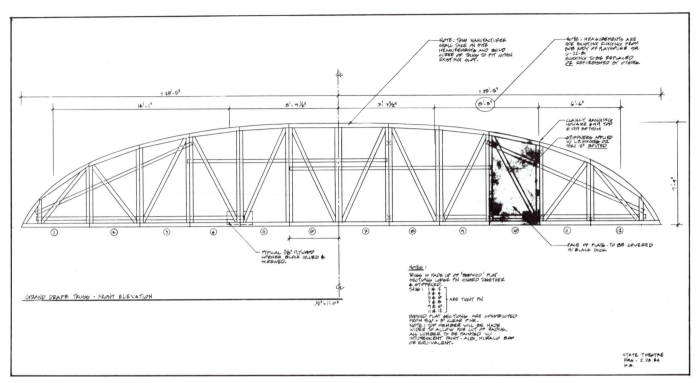

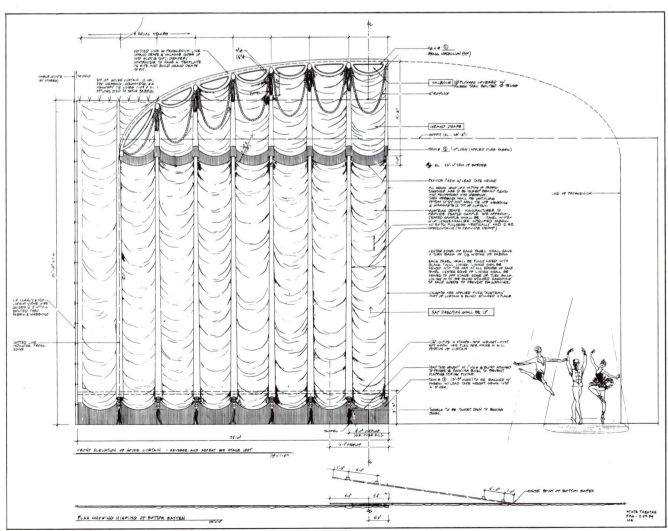

Palace Theatre, Cleveland, Ohio (1987)

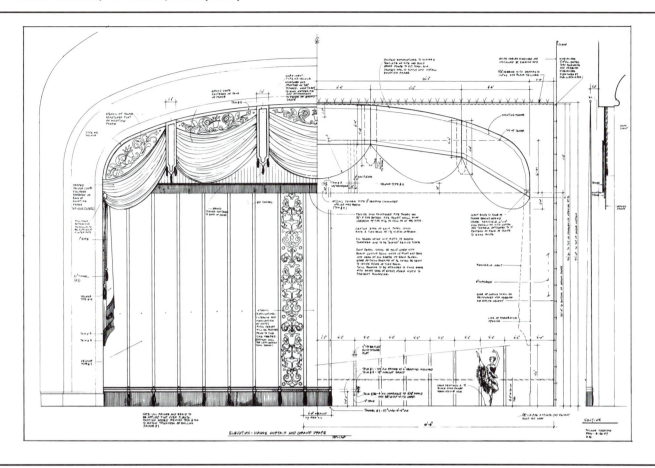

Walter Kerr Theatre, Broadway, New York (1990)

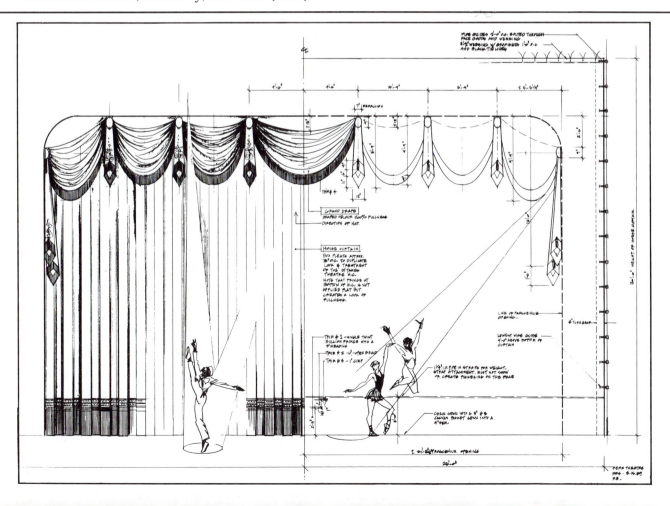

74 the house curtain. Use real gold fringe at the edges.

A. Dimensions. (Refer to drawings.)

B. Fullness. Swags shall be made up with approximately 150% fullness vertically (or as required to create the appearance shown on the drawing. The drape may be made up in two layers which can be tied in to one pipe.

Sew the draping into a strip of vertical 3½" webbing to maintain the shape. Sew the horizontal fullness in to the webbing at the top and provide brass grommets and tie lines. Provide grommeted webbing at extreme left and right sides with fullness sewed into it.

Jabots are to be made up in fullness using the velour faced back 100% and sewed into the webbing at the top.

Trim with fringe.

C. Lining. No lining is required for the grand drape.

D. Installation. The grand drape shall be attached to a pipe installed inside the thickness of the proscenium arch, directly behind the hard valance. The drape must be tied on to the pipe with tie lines in order to permit easy removal if necessary. No attachments with nails or staples are to be made.

Valance

A. Construction. Frame the valance of ⁵⁄₄" × 4" white pine covered with ½" fir plywood (interior AD). Provide a 4-inch thickness at all exposed edges. Provide continuous blocking along the length of the thickness for support.

B. Paint. Before covering the valance, paint the exposed wood front and back with fire retardant (intumescent) paint, "ALBI" or equal, following manufacturer's instructions for method of application.

C. Covering. Cover the valance with the velour. Velour should be stretched, glued, and stapled on the back.

D. Decorative Painting. Valance shall be painted with gold braid and details with same toning.

E. Joining. Valance must be made in sections for transportation. Care must be taken to place the joints in such a way as to conceal them as well as possible.

F. Installation. Use ¼" × 3" × 3" steel clip angles and lag bolt the valance to the 3-inch thick good ground provided in the proscenium area thickness. Conceal all bolts from view.

Verify all dimensions of the proscenium arch in the field prior to constructing the valance.

PART III—CHORUS AREA DRAPERIES
Scope

A. Additional drapery panels are required to hang under the 3-tiered boxes at the extreme edges of the proscenium opening.

B. These panels are to be made up in the same type and color velour as required for the house curtain. Painting on these curtains will be required similar to that on the house curtain. Line each panel with the black twill lining material.

C. When closed, the panels will secure the area behind them so that the area may be used for quick changes by the performers.

D. Panel E will conceal the enclosed area from the eyes of patrons using the stairway from the orchestra level to the boxes. When the draperies are removed from the hanging rods, the area may be occupied by chorus members who will perform with the orchestra for certain pieces.

Construction

A. Panels. An identical set of draperies is required for each side of the stage. Panels A, B, C, D, will require painting on the front, Panel E will not require painting. See schedule for approximate dimensions. Verify all dimensions prior to fabricating the panels.

B. Rods. Constructed of ¾-inch I.D. steel pipe, to be provided and installed so that they may be easily removed. Provide and install sturdy brackets to receive the rods. Make the brackets as inconspicuous as possible.

C. Large Rings may be used to attach the panels to the rods. Provide good quality snap hooks sewed into the webbing of each panel at 9" o.c. so that each panel may be easily removed from the rings. Locate the hooks so that when the panel is installed the hooks, rings and rod will not be visible from the front side.

D. Construction Details. Make up each panel in the finished width shown on the schedule with the fullness sewed into the jute webbing. The velour shall be faced back 18 inches on each side. Line each panel with black twill lining sewed in at all edges.

Provide 8" black duck apron at bottom with separate chain pocket containing sufficient jack chain of appropriate weight to cause the curtain to hang in straight folds. The chain pocket shall hang three (3) inches above the floor.

Panels A, B, C shall each be made up using 3 widths of velour.

Panel D shall be made up of two separate panels sewed together into one piece of webbing at the top. Provide 12" of overlap at the center. Use 2 widths of velour for each individual panel. Total of 4 widths are required.

Panel E shall be made of 5 widths. Panel E may be installed without a pipe. Provide eyes installed in the face of the upper balustrade to which the snap hooks may be attached.

E. Installation. Install these draperies carefully so that when closed, no light will spill out from the enclosed area within the draperies to the seating area. Provide a good seal at the top and bottom. Provide additional clips or ties if required to seal the sides of the columns.

Photographs, across:

1. Rendering for National Theatre of Greece.
2. Setting at Epidaurus (1982). (Photograph by Patrick H. Horrigan)
3. American Indian basket design.
4. Plan drawing indicating location at Epidaurus (1982).
5. & 6. Production photographs showing surface of ground cloth, Olympic Arts Festival, Los Angeles, California (1984). (Photographs by Takis Diamantopoulos)

Side Stages

Side stages are of enormous help in staging large multiset productions. A number of theatres around the country either have side stages in place or have available house space to erect both side stages and extensions of the apron. The use of side stages offers a number of advantages, which include the following:

1. Allows small scenes to be played and lighted independently on the left and right forestage.
2. Creates a panoramic view of the overall production when scenery and actors are lighted on the main stage and the side stages.
3. Permits scenery and props on each side to be positioned without moving them during the show. These items may be cumbersome and heavy pieces of scenery such as trees, rocks, cars and the like. On the other hand, small pieces and props such as profile pieces, platforms, and furniture can be moved as needed.
4. Allows more entrances and exits left and right if doors or openings are available in the proscenium or side walls, including stairs built in or extending from the offstage edges of the side stages.
5. Gives the director an opportunity to use diagonal blocking patterns from the downstage side areas to the main upstage area.
6. Permits scenes to be played on either of the sides while scenery is being changed on the main stage.
7. Establishes specific areas for musicians and instruments, choruses or narrators.

Using a Basic Unit Set for a Proscenium Production

The basic unit set is included in this section rather than elsewhere because a designer might want to create a very

Sketch, drawing, and settings by Robert D.
  Mitchell
OEDIPUS REX by Sophocles
Directed by Minos Volanakis
Costumes by Dionysos Photopoulos
Lighting by Minos Volanakis
Epidaurus Theatre
Athens, Greece (1982)

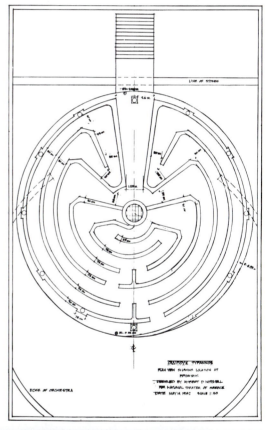

"The set for OEDIPUS was designed specifically for the ancient theatre at Epidaurus. It consisted of a large circular canted playing area. The downstage end of the playing area intersected the *orchestra* of the ancient theatre, and the upstage end rose to the approximate height of the ancient *proskenion*. The action of the play appeared to take place in a sacred forecourt in front of the palace of Thebes. On the stone surface of this forecourt, vestiges of an ancient sacred labyrinth were still visible. At its center, an eternal flame burned beneath the ground, and at its periphery twelve smaller flames glowed in the darkness. The design of the labyrinth was taken from an American Indian basket design.

"This production was constructed for both indoor and outdoor presentation, and employed a ground cloth of sculptured foam rubber covered with fabric. At a distance, this ground cloth looked like stone, but its soft surface permitted the actors to dance upon it in bare feet." —Robert D. Mitchell

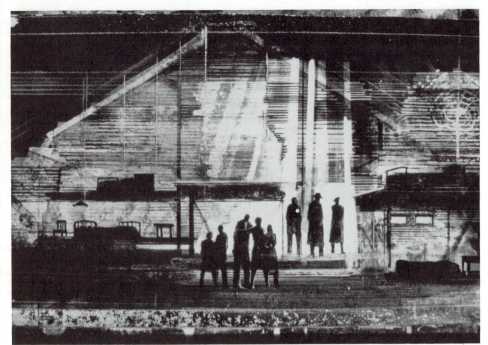

Stage design by Franco Colavecchia
YOURS, ANNE
Libretto by Enid Futterman
Music by Michael Cohen
Directed by Arthur Masella
Playhouse 91, New York (1985)
(Photograph by Phil Jones)

neutral basic set on a proscenium stage and combine it with the use of the two side stages out in the house.

A basic unit set for the proscenium stage that does not move works beautifully when designing a multiscene production. Usually the basic unit set for multiscene productions is designed to have walls with openings for plugs and various other scenic units to change during the course of the play. The walls may be heavy and thick in appearance or be thin and skeletonized in design.

The walls and/or scenic pieces may incorporate an architectural feature from a specific historical period, such as Gothic, modern, medieval, or ancient Egyptian. Or there may be no suggestion of historical period and the setting created may be purely arbitrary. These basic sets work splendidly for classic Greek, Roman, and Shakespearean comedies and tragedies.

Along with ingenious changes in stage lighting, the treatment of the walls and openings, and the staging of the actors, the scenes in a production can have an enormously interesting theatrical flavor. Basic unit sets for proscenium productions may be thought of in two categories: (1) framed hangers with openings and (2) downstage angled walls and upstage center wall with openings.

Framed Hanger with Openings A full-stage framed hanger is usually positioned parallel to the proscenium opening ranging from a bit above the proscenium wall to midstage. It often has three openings (but there may also be two, four, or five) which are used for both the action and scenic plugs to come in and go out. These openings may be circular, square, rectangular, or any other shape or a combination of shapes.

Examples of using plugs to come in or go out of the openings: In the first scene a sky backdrop with artificial foliage hedges masking the bottom of the drop may be seen behind all three arches. For the next scene the left and right openings may be filled from behind with voluptuous Baroque draperies while the center arch is left completely open except for an elaborate chandelier. For the following scene, the center opening may be backed with a large panel of stenciled brocade patterns while a very tall and openwork window unit goes in behind the stage right opening and a double door fills in behind the stage left opening.

Downstage Angled Walls and Upstage Center Wall with Openings This array normally features a large main opening at center stage (sometimes with one or more continuous platforms to raise the level of the playing area from the stage floor) and angled walls downstage left and right. These angled walls may feature both doors and balconies. Various platforms and levels may also be added to the basic platform arrangement as an integral part of the design. A ceiling piece overhead may also tie the three walls together. Of course, more variety in the overall blocking of the actors can be obtained when there is a two-level arrangement of openings instead of one. A design with two-level openings can be achieved very successfully on a stage with a proscenium opening with a width of 40'-0", a height of 25'-0", and a depth of 24'-0". This is not to say that a smaller proscenium opening would not adequately accommodate a two-level design, but the larger proscenium proportions present a more stunning effect for the production.

Model by Tony Walton
Bette Midler's CLAMS ON THE HALF SHELL REVUE
Directed and choreographed by Joe Layton
Minskoff Theatre, New York (1975)

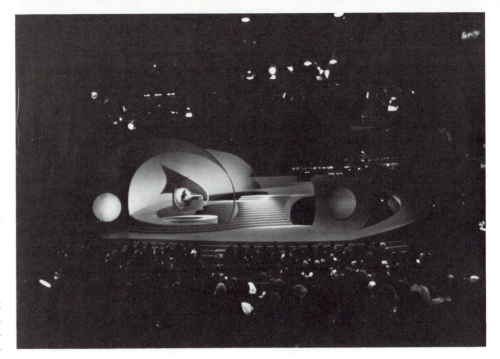

Setting by Ray Klausen
THE AMERICAN MUSIC AWARDS
Directed by Bob Bowker
Lighting by Truck Krone
ABC Stage 59
Hollywood, California (1980)
(Photograph by Ray Klausen)

Moving Units
behind the Openings

Scenic pieces in a basic proscenium unit set may be changed by any of these devices:

1. *Flying items in and out.* Backdrops, panels, banners, signs, and chandeliers can fly in and out.
2. *Flippers.* Hinged flats or openwork scenery may open and close like a door to reveal a new decor on its opposite side or a prop, furniture, or actor upstage of it.
3. *Sliders.* Units behind an opening may slide on and off like doors of a display case to cover or reveal. Sliders may come from left, right, above, and below.
4. *Traveler tracks.* Curtains and draperies may be pulled to show new scenic arrangements or to hide scenery upstage or offstage.
5. *Rolling units on casters.* Units may move mechanically in tracks or be pushed on and off stage manually.
6. *Carrying props on and off.* Depending on the concept, actors and stagehands may be involved in bringing items on or off stage.

APRONS

Putting a Facing on the Apron in the Theatre

On occasion the scenic designer will want to cover the facing of the apron in the theatre so that its shape, color, molding, or texture is not seen. The covering would, in this case, obliterate the detail on the apron, thus putting more emphasis on the stage setting itself. Covering the apron front is also a great way to merge the apron with a partial stage extension (or thrust) that is being added to the stage front.

The choice of covering for an apron depends on the effect desired. Keep in

Stage design by Oliver Smith
A TASTE OF HONEY by Shelah Delaney
Directed by Tony Richardson and George
  Devine
Lyceum Theatre, New York (1960)

mind that a fabric with a nice texture takes lighting well, while a slick painted surface reflects light and can be distracting to the audience. To make the apron front disappear as much as possible, choose a black textured fabric. Black velour with the nap running down works beautifully for this. Other fabrics to use for this include black duck canvas or black duvetyne.

The covering fabric can be mounted over framed flats that have first been covered with ⅛- or ¼-inch plywood. It usually works better when the flats are constructed to fit exactly the contour of the apron front. This is especially important when the front is irregularly curved.

If theatre management permits, the fabric also can be attached with tacks or staples directly onto the apron facing. Soft (unframed) fabric is good to use to cover aprons that have a straight line across the front. The fabric can be started at the front edge of the show

deck or painted ground cloth, or it can begin at the edge of the stage floor and then extend down over the apron until the fabric edge reaches the house floor.

Apron Facings for Touring Companies

For touring companies, a sufficient amount of extra fabric that would cover aprons in both the average and larger-size houses should travel with the show. The best producers and general managers obtain dimensions of all the stages listed on their tour itinerary so it is no problem to estimate how much fabric is needed. However, it is wise for the scenic designer to discuss with the production carpenter the amount of fabric needed for the apron facing. Of course, for touring companies a soft fabric covering is more practical than a framed apron facing because of the variations in apron shapes in the different theatres. The extra apron facing

fabric can be rolled around a rigid cardboard tube and then covered with heavy brown paper or a piece of canvas for traveling.

ORCHESTRA PITS

Alternative Uses for the Orchestra Pit

The orchestra pit can be used to extend the setting beyond the proscenium opening for a drama, comedy, or musical production. For a non-musical production the following may be used:

1. A *hard cover* over the pit so the downstage area may be used as an extension (or thrust) continuing from the apron.
2. A *hard cover* with trapped areas into the pit for actors to make entrances and exits.
3. An *open pit top* so one or more sets of stairways and platforms can provide entrances and exits.
4. An *open pit top* for platforms to raise and lower mechanically with actors and/or props, furniture, or decor.
5. An *open* or *partially open pit* for positioning lighting instruments to light actors or scenery or to create special effects, such as positioning lighting instruments upstage in the pit and placing a mirrored surface downstage on an angle so that projections can be directed on a backdrop or show curtain.
6. An *open pit* to hold a water tank for a pool.

For a musical production, the following may be used:

1. An *open pit* for a full orchestra or a *partially covered top* for a smaller group of musicians.
2. A *closed top* with the orchestra on stage.
3. An *open pit top* with a full orchestra but with a center runway going over the orchestra and out into the audience.
4. An *open pit top* with a full orchestra and a continuous contoured runway at stage height bordering the downstage edges of the orchestra pit.
5. An *open pit top* with a full orchestra with both a center runway and a contoured runway going around the downstage edges of the orchestra pit.

When a runway is used over the orchestra, it is sometimes necessary to stretch an openwork grid of hemp or a net over the entire top of the orchestra pit. In the event of an accident, this hemp grid or net protects the musicians from falling props, furniture, or even actors and dancers. For example, in the Broadway production of *Les Misérables*, a thin net is slung over the orchestra pit to protect the musicians from stray pieces of silverware that are spilled during the wedding scene. The hemp grid also acts as a safety net to catch any actors and dancers should they fall.

Using Facings and Covers in the Orchestra Pit

While an orchestra pit may already have a facing of straight or gathered fabric such as velour or other soft material, or may have a built facing made of wood that is constructed to have a hard cover over the top, sometimes the facing is re-covered with a black fabric (or other color) when the pit itself is not being used for that individual production. Both the cover and the facing surrounding the upper portion of the pit are treated like the front of the apron in a non-musical house. Again, the point is to make the pit area as visually attractive as possible and at the same time make it seem to be a pleasing extension of the stage setting. Often the treatment is to cover a shiny or light-colored facing, neither of which may be desired.

Checklist of Subjects for Apron and Orchestra Pit Facings

When the designer wishes to change the appearance of a facing on an apron or orchestra pit, it may be done by (1) painting the designs on a flat surface, (2) applying three-dimensional materials and textures, or (3) a combination of the two. These designs may be appropriate:

Solid-looking surfaces	Shingles
Painted textures	Foliage
Stenciled designs	Bunting
Rough boards	Paneling
Bricks	Latticework
Stones	Moldings

Entrances and Exits in the Orchestra Pit

The scenic designer always has the opportunity to enhance the director's blocking in a production by providing downstage entrances and exits in the orchestra pit. The drawings of the covered orchestra pits in this chapter show various stairways that can accommodate actors. The following dimensions and information apply to those four drawings. Proscenium opening: 40'-0". Inside pit dimensions: 45'-0" across the front of the proscenium, 6'-6" from the outer edge of the pit to the stage floor, and 7'-0" actual pit depth. All steps: 10-inch treads, 7-inch risers.

1. Covered pit with steps going down from stage right to center and stage left to center. Each unit: 4'-0" wide by 9'-2" long. Distance between units: 5'-0".
2. Covered pit with steps going down from center to stage right and back to center and from center to stage left and back to center. Each unit: 5'-6" wide by 6'-0" deep with 7-inch risers. Distance between units: 8'-0".
3. Covered pit with double stage steps going down from stage right to center and from center to stage right, and from stage left to center and from center to stage left. Each unit: 5'-0" wide (2'-6" and 2'-6") by 9'-2" long. Distance between units: 4'-0".
4. Partially covered pit with center platform extension (downstage face: 11'-0"). Steps going down from center to stage right and from center to stage left. Each unit: 4'-0" wide by 9'-2" long.

Using Runways Going into the Audience

Scenic designers create runways for productions that play in theatres, civic centers, convention halls, shopping centers, sports arenas, gymnasiums, or other places. Single, double, or multiple runways may be needed for singers, actors, dancers, fashion show models, and beauty pageant contestants. Runways are designed to be straight or curved, to go into the audience and back, or they circle out into the house from one side of the stage to the other. They may or may not have steps that go down into the audience. A runway may be designed so that house seats are rearranged along its sides, or the runway may be built over seats that are not used by the audience so that it is above the eye level of the audience seated along the sides.

Runways without details are commonly used as basic walkways to accommodate performers. Runways should be sturdy and wide enough so the performers can use them without being nervous about misjudging the width of the platform in a darkened theatre.

One of the most common features of a runway extending into the house is a border of electric lights on the outer edges. Not only are these lights visually exciting, but they also nicely define the edges of the runway for the performers using them.

The materials for runways may be ¼-inch Masonite on ¾-inch plywood (just as with stage platforms and wagons) with wooden or metal supporting structures underneath.

THE STAGE

Requesting Plans for a Theatre

When you have been engaged to design a production in a specific theatre, always ask for a set of ½-inch scale drawings of the stage. These drawings should include at least a ground plan and a hanging section view. It is also good to have a plan and a section drawing of the auditorium in order to accurately determine sight lines. Some proscenium theatres have both ground plan and section drawings available, whereas others only have a ground plan. On occasion, you may find that a well-known commercial theatre will have just a simple ground plan in ¼-inch scale that may need updating.

Drawings in ½-inch scale not only save time when going from a smaller scale such as ¼-inch, but usually tend to be more accurate. However, this can vary. If there are no drawings available for the proscenium stage other than ones in ¼-inch scale, then you must

work with them. When going from a ¼-inch ground plan to a ½-inch ground plan, using a set of dividers saves a lot of time. Open the dividers to measure a dimension on the ¼-inch plan, and then double it for a ½-inch scale plan by putting the first point of the dividers on the ½-inch drawing and then just pivoting to the right and then to the left to complete the total dimension. With this method, it is not necessary to take every dimension on the ground plan with a scale ruler. Before starting with dividers, always check out the basic overall dimensions of the width and depth of the ground plan as well as the depth and height of the hanging section drawing.

If possible, double-check measurements in the actual theatre to see whether the plan you have been given is accurate. If you find a discrepancy in the drawings and are unable to personally visit the theatre, call the technical director or stage carpenter to check it out and to get accurate information. If you are a great distance away from the theatre, then put a note on the drawing saying to check a particular dimension, or note the specific question you have about that particular theatre.

Using the Bottom of the House Curtain for the Top Trim of the Proscenium Opening

The bottom of the grand drape may be in a straight line across the bottom edge, or it may be curved or irregular in shape. Even if the bottom is straight across, it may be too high for the desired top trim of the proscenium opening. For discussion, let us assume that when the house curtain is flown out the bottom of it will become the desired top opening for the proscenium.

While it is standard procedure to look at the hanging section drawing and the model in progress and then decide what looks best for the top trim of the proscenium opening, the ideal is to leave the drawing board and go to the theatre to check this out. The purpose here is twofold. Not only are you seeing

the house curtain trim you have selected for the production, but you also get a better feeling of how this chosen height looks with the house portal you have designed in the model. Check the overall scale of the actual proscenium to see whether the selected height on your hanging section drawing and model portal opening is too high, too low, or just right.

The choice of the portal opening (width and height) as it relates to the proportion of the proscenium opening (width and height) is of paramount importance because it is basically on view by the audience throughout the performance and therefore should look as attractive as possible. For example, here are two choices: (1) You may decide to make the dimensions for the opening in the house portal the very same as the proscenium opening; or (2) you may wish to come in 2 feet from each side of the proscenium opening, and come in 2 feet from the top at the house curtain trim.

A portal opening (in contrast to the proscenium opening) should never look too low or scrunched, especially in a theatre with a high proscenium opening. Making a portal too low is a common error novice scenic designers and sometimes very experienced craftsmen make. If this ever seems to

HAMLETMACHINE by Heiner Muller
Direction and set design by Robert Wilson
Scenery supervised by Lynn Pecktal
Costume design by William Ivey Long
Lighting design by Jennifer Tipton and Robert Wilson
NYU Undergraduate Drama
Mainstage Two, New York (1986)

(Photograph by Bob Marshak)
(Courtesy of John Wulp)
Fire was a recurring image throughout the play. In the film which was the third section of the performance, the actors were consumed by fire. *Pictured at left:* Brad Friedman; *top to bottom:* Kevin Kuhlke, Jyllian Gunther, Jennifer Gilley, Alana Adena Teichman.

80 be the case, rethink the design. You can do one of several things, according to the individual show:

1. Make the house portal opening higher and add a unit such as an inner portal with a smaller or decreasing opening like a mat on a painting.
2. Use a framed border at the top with or without details.
3. Add a ceiling piece (straight up and down or slanted).
4. Create a profiled border with textured patterns or other appropriate designs.

When you go to the theatre to double-check the house curtain trim and your desired portal opening, sit in various seats throughout the auditorium and study how the portal dimensions will look with the proscenium opening. It is very helpful to have the production carpenter (or a stagehand) available to raise and lower the house curtain to various heights while you sit in the audience and look at the different positions as the curtain goes up and down. So that you are not in doubt about the dimensions, the person operating the house curtain can give you an estimation or can look at the height measurements marked backstage each time the curtain is lowered or raised. If the height measurements of the curtain are not marked anywhere backstage, you can use a steel measuring tape to take dimensions. Simply attach the steel loop on the end of the tape to the bottom of the curtain with a large safety pin, then choose the measurement at the desired height. You may want to first look at the curtain at a height of 18'-0", then 19'-6", 20'-0", and so on. Later on, when the scenery moves into the theatre, the house curtain will be marked according to your selection so it always flies out at the chosen height at each performance.

While you are in the theatre figuring the top trim of the house curtain, also look at the remaining portion of the house curtain at the desired trim and see how this compares in proportion with the decorative grand drape above. This should be a pleasant-looking arrangement.

If you are working in a theatre with a house curtain on a traveler track or with an opera curtain neither of which flies out, you can hang a velour border just upstage of the house curtain to trim the top of the portal unit. A straight border (without any fullness) flatly stretched out usually looks best.

Upstage Obstructions in the Theatre Stage Space

When you are designing scenery and plan to use the full depth of stage space in the theatre, always remember to check out any obstructions upstage and in the offstage left and right spaces. Obstructions are not always shown on the theatre plan and section drawings. The reasons for this may be simply that no one has taken the time to record them; or recent alterations may have added or removed obstructions that would affect the scenic designer's plans; or the alterations did not seem to be significant enough to require updating the theatre plan and section drawings. That is why it is so important for the designer to double-check the possibility of stage obstructions before planning offstage storage space.

While obstructions in theatres vary enormously, these items may be located near the back wall and may prevent the designer from having as much scenery space as might be desired:

1. Radiators on the floor or wall
2. Air-conditioning and heating vents
3. Paint frames
4. Light storage
5. Scenery in storage
6. Jogs or pilasters

Overhead Obstructions in the Theatre Stage Space

There are also numerous items positioned overhead in theatre stage spaces that may hinder the workable stage space. Again, these obstructions depend on what is happening in the individual theatre. Be on the lookout for these objects when positioning scenery on drawings:

1. Overhead beams
2. Hanging motion picture screens
3. Light bridges and equipment
4. Leg and border sets
5. Cyclorama and rigging

Loading Doors

When you check out the backstage loading doors for in-town or touring shows, the following information is important as it relates to the size and shape of the scenic units to be loaded into the theatres.

1. *Maximum height and width.* Are the loading doors single or double doors? Is there more than one set of loading doors? Will the largest piece of scenery go through the door(s) straight up and down while it is being carried in, or can it be tilted on a diagonal to clear?
2. *Location of loading doors.* Are they positioned in the side or upstage wall of the stage house? Or are they located in an opening down a hall from the side or upstage wall? Are there turns the scenery must make to reach the stage?
3. *How the doors open.* What protection is there if the scenery has to be loaded in during bad weather? Do the doors open on a covered, partially covered, or uncovered area? Do the doors open onto a loading platform, ramp, or directly to the back of the truck? Do the doors open level onto an alley or street? Can extra scenery be stored in the alley during performance in case there is not enough space in the offstage areas inside?

"MEDEA was originally designed for the thrust stage of the Circle in the Square Joseph E. Levine Theatre on Fiftieth Street in New York City. The 1/16-inch scale model for this production shows one of the first ideas for the serpent-drawn sun chariot sent to rescue Medea at the end of the play. The actress, Irene Papas, was to appear behind a huge plastic fresnel lens which would rise like a great sun behind the upstage limit of the set. This effect, which proved to be too expensive, was replaced by a dimensional replica of the descending concentric steps leading to Medea's underground abode. In the original and all successive mountings of the production, Medea appeared inside this emblematic mandala either upstage of the playing area or, in outdoor productions, often at some distance, but always above the playing area. As staged in the Roman theatre of Herod Atticus at the base of the Acropolis in 1985, a giant construction crane raised the sun chariot some 50 feet above the Roman architectural *scaenae frons.*

"Despite the fact that this production has most frequently been performed in classic theatres on the Greek mainland, it owes virtually nothing at all to scholarly reconstructions of early Greek dramaturgy. The decision to show Medea as having reverted in her manner of living to sacred, earthbound troglodytic existence grew out of an attempt to put contemporary audiences in closer touch with the world and time of Euripides and with the specific imagery of the play."

—Robert D. Mitchell

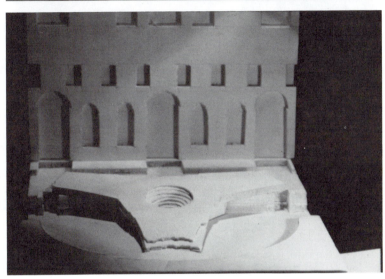

Models, sketch, and settings by Robert D.
  Mitchell
MEDEA by Euripides
Directed by Minos Volanakis

Photographs, across:
1. Model in ¹/₁₆-inch scale for MEDEA, Circle in the Square, New York (1972). (Photograph by Patrick H. Horrigan)
2. Sketch for MEDEA, Mt. Lycabettos Theatre, Athens, Greece (1976). (Photograph by National Theatre of Northern Greece)
3. Dress rehearsal for MEDEA, Salonika, Greece (1976), for the production at Mt. Lycabettos Theatre. *Pictured:* Melina Mercouri and company. (Photograph by Patrick H. Horrigan)
4. Model in ¹/₁₆-inch scale for MEDEA, Herod Atticus Theatre, Athens, Greece (1985).
5. & 6. Building the MEDEA Set, Herod Atticus Theatre (1985). (Photographs by Robert D. Mitchell)

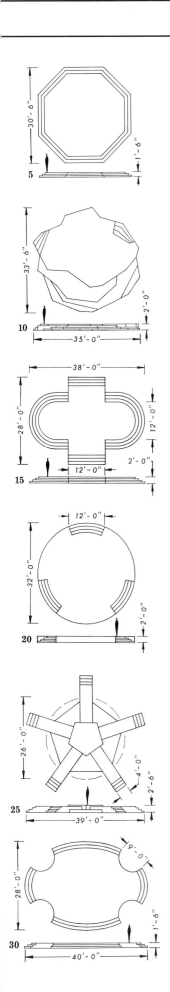

5

10

38'-0"

28'-0"

12'-0"

2'-0"

12'-0"

15

12'-0"

32'-0"

2'-0"

20

26'-0"

4'-0"

2'-6"

25

39'-0"

9'-0"

28'-0"

1'-6"

30

40'-0"

Setting by Andrew Jackness
AN AMERICAN COMEDY by Richard Nelson
Directed by John Madden

Lighting by James F. Ingalls
Mark Taper Forum
Los Angeles, California (1983)

Renovating the Theatre to Accommodate the Scenery

In the 1980s several Broadway theatres underwent all sorts of alterations to accommodate highly successful productions that had proved themselves to be a smash hit elsewhere, most notably London, to play in New York with sim-

ilar design concepts. Such was the case for the British blockbuster musical *The Phantom of the Opera* (1988), with the production designed by Maria Björnson, lighting designed by Andrew Bridge, and direction by Harold Prince. The show, which was still playing in London, had become such a powerful box office draw there that no

Setting by Ralph Funicello
MEASURE FOR MEASURE by William Shakespeare
Directed by Robert Egan
Costumes by Robert Blackman

Lighting by Martin Aronstein
Mark Taper Forum
Los Angeles, California (1985)
(Photograph by Ralph Funicello)

84

expense was spared to accommodate the sumptuous design and special effects at the Majestic Theatre in New York City. *Starlight Express* was another successful show brought over from London while it was playing in the West End. The settings and costumes were designed by John Napier, lighting designed by David Hersey, and the direction was by Trevor Nunn.

As early as September 6, 1987, *The New York Times Magazine* ran a story by Bruce Weber proclaiming the complications involved at the Majestic Theatre, which required extensive physical renovations to the stage so the production could retain its original flavor. The article is reprinted here:

"It's not really a renovation," Frederick Olsson says. "We're altering the house to fit the show." As facilities director for the Shubert Organization, Olsson is overseeing the modifications being made in Broadway's Majestic Theatre to accommodate Andrew Lloyd Webber's "Phantom of the Opera," the hit British musical that opens here in January.

The Majestic has been dark since "42nd Street" played to its final audience there on April 5. Shortly afterwards, Olsson, working with Peter Feller, an outside consultant, and Maxwell Lincer, a structural engineer, began readying the theatre for the elaborate gadgetry of the Webber extravaganza. In addition to forging a number of structural changes in the building, Olsson's crew has dug a pit—30 feet by 15 feet by 7 feet—from which elements of the scenery ("various candelabras, mausoleums and rooftops") will appear to the audience to rise up out of the stage. The roof has been reinforced with steel, better to support the chandelier that is to be suspended above the audience and that the phantom will cause to come crashing down to stage level.

The proscenium opening has been raised in order to augment sightlines and allow the audience to witness the phantom performing on a newly-constructed network of catwalks 31 feet above the stage.

"We'll cut portals in the proscenium plasterwork so that the phantom will have access from backstage to the catwalks," Olsson says. "We still have to figure out how to get him from way up there back down onto the stage, though."

By early October, when the scenery is brought in (the stage itself will be cut out and replaced by a customized one), most of the work on the stage area will be complete. Olsson estimates the cost at more than $1 million. "Not much more," he says, "Not if I want to keep my job."

By the time *Phantom* had opened on January 26, 1988, it had broken all advance box office sales records in the history of the Broadway theatre. In the *New York Post* (January 30, 1988) Stephen M. Silverman reported that the show had a $17 million advance and was sold out until year's end.

The Phantom of the Opera made phenomenal news in all the entertainment media. It has been a big story on television, in newspapers, and in magazines. Patricia Morrisroe in *New York* magazine (January 18, 1988) wrote:

Mackintosh says that it will take Phantom, *which cost $8 million, 65 weeks to break even. The Shubert Organization has spent $1.5 million revamping the Majestic Theatre. It's not as deep as Her Majesty's where* Phantom *is playing in London, so major reconstruction was needed. "They had to dig out under the stage, remove the staircases, clear the wing space, and clear the draining system," says Mackintosh. "We gained four or five working feet. Still, the theatre is about ten feet shallower than Her Majesty's." . . .*

"Phantom is very expensive to run," he [Mackintosh] says. "There are four major set pieces—elaborate grand operas. And the choruses are lavishly dressed. We've got 35 in the cast, plus 60 in the crew. We need several people just to take care of the wigs. We are re-creating a style of theatre that went bankrupt."

Another lavish Broadway musical required an enormous amount of planning and financing in order for the show to go on. According to Leslie Bennetts in *The New York Times* (February 23, 1987), it cost $8 million to transform *Starlight Express* for Broadway:

"Starlight" is "phenomenally complex," Mr. [Trevor] Nunn said, and many of the potential pitfalls are apparent from even a brief look at the $2.5 million set that has transformed the Gershwin Theatre.

The modest little story Mr. Lloyd Webber wrote for his son has now been transposed by the set designer John Napier onto a panorama of all 50 American states, with scenes that range from the Grand Canyon and the Rocky Mountains to the White House and the Brooklyn Bridge—all linked by an intricate array of railroad tracks.

The set construction used 1,000 feet of fluorescent tubing, 7,000 sheets of plywood and 120,000 pounds of steel, along with 22 miles of fiber optics to provide 10,000 points of light. More than 50 miles of cable connect the network of lights to six computers with another four computers coordinating sound and scenery. The set also includes a steel bridge that moves up and down, backward and forward, rotates 360 degrees and tilts while serving as a crucial pathway for the 27-member cast, all of whom zoom around the tracks on roller skates, impersonating railroad trains at full throttle.

"Pretty much every square inch of the set has some hydraulic device of one sort or another, and every part connects up with some other part, and it has to be absolutely precise because human beings are traveling around at great speeds on it," Mr. Nunn explained. "It's not just a matter of something tilting at the right angle and meeting with the right gate, it's the gate opening at the exact moment that five skaters traveling toward it at 30 miles an hour are five feet away."

Preparing the Theatre before the Sets and Lights Come In

A day or so before the scenery and lighting equipment loads into the theatre, a work session for getting the stage ready is often scheduled by the production carpenter. This involves a crew to check out the lines in the grid for hanging scenery, lighting, any special effects, rigging, sound equipment, and so on. All lines must be inspected to see if they are working properly; some lines may have to be moved, some lines may need to be added, while others stay where they are.

Here is a typical example of what might have to be done in the theatre. An individual line may have to be spot-

Setting by Clarke Dunham
A PHANTASMAGORIA HISTORIA OF D. JOHANN FAUSTEN MAGISTER, PHD, MD, DD, DL, ETC.
Directed by Vasek Simek
Costumes by Patricia Quinn Stuart
Lighting by David F. Segal
Truck & Warehouse Theatre
New York (1973)
(Photograph by Clarke Dunham)

ted for rigging an item such as a chandelier or a sign if a regular batten is too long. Loft blocks are positioned as needed on the grid floor and one hemp line supports the item being spotted.

A hanging plot or line plot is prepared in advance by the production carpenter. It may include a list of spot lines as well as the appropriate position for portals, a show curtain, backdrops, a cyclorama, any other flying scenic units, masking legs and borders, electrical pipes and booms, sound speakers, and so on. The plot could also include the position of any winches to be used, such as off left, or off right, upstage, or in the basement.

Every possible detail is planned so that the load-in of the actual physical production will run smoothly and efficiently. This detailed planning avoids unnecessary expense, long hours, confusion, and a tired crew. The wise production carpenter knows only too well that when a load-in schedule is delayed, the hourly rate of a forty-man crew will add an enormous expense to the budget of the show.

The following is a hanging plot and spot line list for a national company of *Dracula*.

HANGING PLOT AND SPOT LINE LIST

First available set behind house curtain

0'-0"	Portal and #1 Masking Legs
1'-0"	#1 Electric: trims at 25'-0" (5 set Crossover)
3'-0"	Show Curtain
3'-6"	Truss
4'-6"	#2 Electric: tails down and trims at 29'-0"
5'-6"	Scaffold
7'-0"	#3 Electric: trims at 30'-6"
7'-6"	Downstage set for Bat Platform
10'-6"	Back set of Bat Platform

12'-6"	#1 Black Border
12'-9"	Center set for Basic Set
14'-6"	#4 Electric: trims at 33'-3"
15'-0"	#4A Electric: trims at 25'-0" and Crossover
18'-0"	#2 Black Border
18'-6"	Back set for Basic Set
18'-9"	Center Bookcase Flat: Works in Slider
19'-6"	Bedroom Flat
21'-6"	#5 Electric: trims at 29'-0"
23'-6"	Sky Drop
24'-0"	Vault Drop

0'-6"	#1 Boom: 18'-6" right and left of center
16'-6"	#2 Boom Right: 25'-0" right of center
11'-6"	#2 Boom Left: 32'-0" left of center
16'-6"	#3 Boom Left: 25'-6" left of center
17'-6"	#2 Masking Legs—4 lines: 25'-6" right and left of center (DS)
23'-6"	#2 Masking Legs—4 lines: 25'-6" right and left of center (US)
3'-0"	2 Lines for Show Curtain for Guide Cables: 20'-6" right and left of center.

Cable pick-ups for all electric pipes on switch board side of stage.

Working on Large Stages

It can be awe-inspiring to observe or read about the most gigantic and best-equipped theatres in the world. One of the most famous proscenium stage spaces is that of Radio City Music Hall in New York City. Since the theatre opened on December 27, 1932, millions of people have seen countless productions on the mammoth stage there. The Radio City Music Hall souvenir booklet, edited by Edward Serlin and Abraham Pokrassa, contains this description of the great stage:

Here is a vast area, 67 feet deep, 114 feet wide, and not unlike the deck of an aircraft carrier. Part of the stage is composed of three hydraulically-operated elevator platforms 70 feet long which can be locked together or raised and lowered separately, from sub-basement level, 27 feet below the stage, to 13 feet above it. Each elevator platform contains a section of an enormous turntable, 43 feet in diameter, which may be raised or lowered while revolving. The speeds of the turntable and elevator platforms may be varied to meet the demands of any scene. The orchestra pit is also equipped with an elevator floor that rises from sub-basement to stage level, where it forms an apron extension to the stage, increasing its depth to 84 feet. On this pit elevator

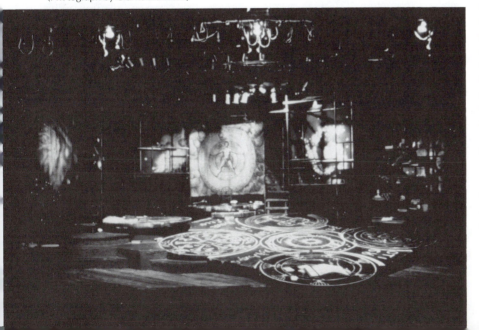

86

rides the "band wagon"—the platform of the Symphony Orchestra which can, upon reaching stage level, travel under its own power back across the footlights to the back of the stage, then rise another 13 feet into the air. The orchestra can also take a subway ride—travel below the stage out of sight and reappear on stage on any one of the three elevators.

The Music Hall Stage is equipped with every imaginable effect. Some of its resources are meteorological: the rain curtain produces a real shower from 75 feet above the footlights, clouds can float lazily over the scenery, fearsome lightning flashes may be summoned to the accompaniment of rolls of thunder. Other effects are astronomical: 500 twinkling stars can appear against the "sky" of the cyclorama backdrop, the moon in all its phases is always on call. Still others are pyrotechnical: electrically-operated fireworks can blaze through the backstage sky, a steam curtain helps create an effect of flame and smoke.

OPEN STAGE PRODUCTIONS

Open stages may range from fixed to movable stages. Common types of open stages are:

1. A square, rectangular, or other shape, with the audience seated on all sides. An average minimum square stage may be 16'-0" by 16'-0".
2. An oval or circular stage with the audience surrounding the stage.
3. A rectangle or square with seats on three sides, with the fourth side joining a wall or having scenery positioned there.
4. A rectangle or square with seats on two sides. The remaining two sides may be walls or scenery.
5. A square or rectangle shape with seats on one end.
6. A corner stage with seats surrounding it. The shape of the stage may be a quarter-circle, triangular, or other.
7. An irregular-shaped stage positioned in a space with the seats mixed in and interspersed around the playing areas.

Open stages may or may not have an open fixed metal pipe grid for positioning lighting instruments.

An intimate open space can enhance a dramatic piece. Two examples of noteworthy open stage productions were presented by New York University's Tisch School of the Arts. One

highly acclaimed event was Robert Wilson's production of Heiner Muller's *Hamletmachine* (1986). Wilson designed and staged the drama in the open space Main Stage Two theatre. The basic stage area was approximately 26'-0" wide by 38'-2" long. The unit for seat risers located at one end of the room was approximately 21'-0" deep by 17'-9" wide by 56" high (seven rows at 3'-0" deep by 8" high, with the first row on the stage floor). The playing area was the flat floor at the opposite end of the rectangle from the audience.

Wilson's scenery in this space included filled scrim backdrops, a corrugated metal ground row, a tree, furniture, and props. Lighting instruments were positioned on a pipe grid approximately 10'-0" from the floor.

Another open-stage production at the Tisch School of the Arts was *Semmelweiss* by Howard Sackler, directed by Larry Arrick (1985), which was mounted in the Main Stage One theatre. The scenery was designed by John Wulp. The dimensions of this theatre are approximately 32'-8" by 63'-6", including audience seating. The height is 16'-0". Audience seating, which is in front of the playing area at the opposite end of the rectangle, is 18'-0" deep by 19'-0" wide by 48" high. The first row of seats is on the floor, while six rows of seats rest on 6-inch risers going up 48 inches. The playing area on the flat floor was 26'-19" by 32'-8". The height from the floor to the lighting grid was 14'-0". What made the physical production work so well for the play was a second-story gallery going around the entire rectangular-shaped room that became an additional playing area for a cast of sixty-three actors. This 6-inch platform was 6'-10" above the floor and was approximately 5'-9" wide on the two long sides and approximately 4'-0" wide on the front and rear. Three existing columns on one side of the room were utilized as part of the scenery, and new matching columns were duplicated on the opposite side. The second-floor platform was positioned between these six columns and the wall. Four stairways rose from the floor to the platform gallery above.

Aside from the elevated gallery, the main scenery for the play was the wall at one end of the room. Center double doors in the wall opened and allowed a castered 6-inch-high wagon to come on and off stage with furniture and

props. Other props were carried on and off stage by the actors.

Designing the Actual Open Stage

Although some theatres may have a specifically built platform for an open stage (on all sides) that cannot be altered drastically, there are companies that have open playing spaces in which the stage can be designed completely from scratch. The former usually allows the scenic designer to modify the stage by adding a certain number of platforms or plugs, combined with furniture, set dressing, and props, to create the overall stage picture. But the completely open playing space provides the designer with the most freedom simply because there is such a nice expanse of floor space in which a great many different platform shapes, levels, and configurations may be considered.

If you are designing the open stage itself in a flexible space and the stage is to be repositioned for upcoming and individual productions, then it is a good idea to design the stage with a group of various-shaped platform modules. These modules, used in various combinations and with steps, are a practical way to create versatile playing areas. The basic modules may be made in the shape of rectangles, squares, and triangles. The sizes for the rectangle modules may be 4'-0" by 8'-0"; for the squares, 4'-0" by 4'-0"; and the triangles may have a 90° angle with two 4'-0" sides. Hexagons, trapezoids, and parallelograms are also interesting shapes for these platform modules. Bolts or clamps can be used to hold the platforms together.

Three examples of height dimensions for basic step and platform units are: (1) 6, 12, 18, and 24 inches; (2) 8, 16, and 24 inches; and (3) 9, 18, and 27 inches.

Materials for the platform tops may be (1) canvas on ¾-inch plywood on wooden supporting structures, or (2) ¼-inch tempered Masonite on ¾-inch plywood on wooden supporting structures. Facings for the platforms are made as separate pieces. Use canvas on ¼-inch plywood, or painted ¼-inch Masonite, or velour on ¼-inch Masonite. To help deaden the sound when actors walk on the platforms, use Ozite rug padding or layers of fiber glass insulation material underneath.

Ground plans by John Lee Beatty
TALLEY'S FOLLY by Lanford Wilson
Directed by Marshall W. Mason
The ground plans for the same play were pro-
duced in three different type theatres. (See
sketches in the color photographs.)

1. Brooks Atkinson Theatre, New York (1980),
   Broadway proscenium theatre.
2. Mark Taper Forum, Los Angeles, California
   (1979), three-quarter thrust stage.
3. Circle Repertory Theatre, New York (1979),
   Off-Broadway black box theatre.

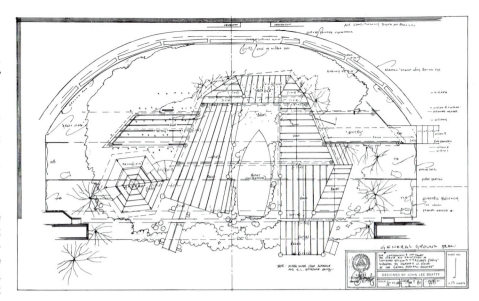

Rather than adding platforms, the
designer and director may wish to just
utilize the basic flat floor for the production. It may be decided to paint the
floor a solid color or to texture it with
paint or to render floor designs in great
detail. Another approach would be to
cover the floor with carpet or to use
area rugs. Still another idea would
be to paint designs on a canvas
ground cloth or on sheets of ¼-inch
Masonite or other comparable or
similar materials.

Arranging Seats in an Open Stage Theatre

There are many types of theatre seats.
The most comfortable is upholstered,
but open stage theatres use folding
metal chairs (with or without padding), bleacher seats, or plastic chairs.
Some full-round theatres have seats
that can be moved and arranged for
each production, while others do not
allow any change in the seating plan.
Flexible seating is usually an added bonus for the designer because it allows
more freedom in the design idea and
because unique seating arrangements
can be developed that will work best
with the open stage design.

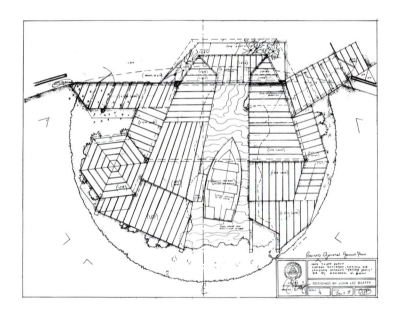

The first one or two rows of seats in
an open stage theatre may be positioned on the actual stage floor, or they
may be placed on tiered platforms
starting at 8 inches high or higher to
separate them from the playing area or
any allotted space such as an aisle between the first rows and the playing
area. The seats continuing after the first
row are usually positioned on raised
levels (or platforms) so that the sight
lines for the audience are good. These
raised units with seats are sometimes
fixed on casters so they can be moved
around easily when the seating arrangements are changed for the next
production. The idea of being able to
change the configuration of both the

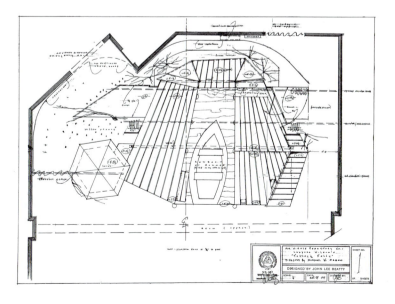

playing area and the seating arrangement can be found in many black box theatres. These theatres allow enormous possibilities for experimentation in productions of new and original plays, as well as the classics and contemporary plays.

For a full-round production, the seats may be arranged to work appropriately with the selected platform design or the flat floor shape of the stage. If the stage is to be a geometric shape, such as a square, rectangle, circle, oval, diamond, or other shape, the seats may be positioned appropriately around it.

Designing Units for Offstage Space

Depending on the play, dance, or opera, and the staging, offstage units may have to be designed to serve the needs of that specific production because no facilities are available or because of the design concept. Such areas may be created to facilitate any of the following:

1. A place for actors to enter and exit
2. A place for scenery, prop, and furniture storage
3. Places to position lighting instruments
4. Places to put sound equipment
5. Quick change rooms
6. A place for costume storage
7. A location for the production stage manager
8. A place for stagehands and technicians to wait between scenes

Because offstage units are part of the visual concept in an open stage production, the scenic designer may want to create them to be either (1) neutral-looking or (2) decorative. Neutral units could be covered in black velour or duvetyne or painted a solid color. Dec-

orative units could be designed to fit the theme of the show. Examples of these designs include shingled walls, stone or brick towers, tall draped tents, metal towers on casters with hangings of erosion cloth and burlap, vertically shaped hedges of artificial leaves and vines, and many other designs.

The number of offstage units that are necessary depends on the requirements for the show. There could be one, two, three, or four units. For example, an 18'-0" square open stage with rows of seats positioned on each of the four sides could have four square offstage units placed nearby at the four corners of the stage. In another instance, an open stage positioned at one end of a rectangular room with seats placed on the opposite end of the stage might have only two offstage units.

Offstage units may have various shapes. Typical shapes of ground plans are square or rectangular, but they may also be circular, hexagonal, or other shapes. The units may be fully or partially enclosed. For example, the unit could be one, two, three, or four large, tall square or rectangular columns positioned on the diagonal in each of the corners of a square open stage. These columns could be made as three-fold flats or four flats fully enclosed, or with a pipe structure overhead for positioning lighting instruments. The bottom section of the columns could appear as solid or be draped. Arches or doorways for entrances and exits could be visible to the audience or hidden from view. The entire unit could be on a castered platform. The height of the ceiling in the playing area dictates the height of the standing units.

Designing for Open Stage Productions

Just as designing for the proscenium stage with its apron, apron extensions, orchestra pit (open or covered), or thrust has definite requirements, designing for the open stage has requirements of another sort. These are some points to consider when designing open stage productions:

1. The playing area is usually smaller than that on a proscenium stage.
2. Details in construction, painting, and sewing should be refined because the scenery, furniture, and props are seen very close up by the audience and often from more than one side.
3. Scenery, furniture, and props must be low enough so they do not obstruct the audience's view. Scenery may also be positioned above the actors but, of course, it must be planned so that it does not block the stage lighting or sight lines from the audience.
4. How the scenery, furniture, and props are moved on and off stage must be carefully planned.
5. Offstage storage for scenery and props is not always available.
6. The entrances and exits for actors need particular planning.
7. Lighting and lighting effects must be imaginative and appropriate.
8. The floor and main playing area become the largest and most significant scenic unit. You may want to create a playing area in which the stage is just a flat floor. Or it may be only one simple 6-inch-high platform. A platform usually defines the playing area better than painted designs on a flat floor. A

Model by Marjorie Bradley Kellogg
REQUIEM FOR A HEAVYWEIGHT by Rod Serling
Directed by Arvin Brown
Martin Beck Theatre, New York (1985)
(Photograph by Diann Duthie)

''Though we needed hotel rooms as well as locker rooms, we wanted the below-the-street quality and grit of seedy arenas and gymnasiums to ride throughout this multiscened teleplay. It seemed important to feel we were at the *bottom*, with the weight of everything—cement, girders, the world—looming above our heads ready to press us back down should we attempt to rise.''
—Marjorie Bradley Kellogg

Model by Marjorie Bradley Kellogg
THE VALUE OF NAMES by Jeffrey Sweet
Directed by Emily Mann
Hartford Stage Company
Hartford, Connecticut (1984)
(Photograph by Diann Duthie)

"The spacious volume of the Hartford stage wanted compressing into an open but intimate arena for three characters to battle out the issues of ethics, blacklisting, and naming names." —Marjorie Bradley Kellogg

series of platforms of different heights and shapes with steps and ramps can be more interesting than a flat floor.

Materials and subject matter for the floor treatment are very similar to those used on the proscenium stage. The floor may be finished as a series of abstract patterns, simple random textures, or realistic designs painted in standard theatrical fashion. You may want to have a combination of both real and simulated materials: boards, tiles, bricks, stones, concrete, patterned rugs and carpets, and others. There is also the opportunity to use all kinds of projected light patterns on the floor, which can be very dramatic and visually exciting.

Checklist of Basic Scenery for Open Stage Productions

In the checklist that follows, scenery and props for an open stage production are listed for hanging items above the actors and for low units standing on the floor. The position of scenery above should always be discussed with the lighting designer so that it does not get in the way of lighting instruments.

SCENERY AND PROPS ABOVE

Leafy foliage
  branches
Chandeliers
Draped garlands
Floating ceiling
  pieces
Painted banners
Opaque and gauze
  draperies
Latticework headers
Hanging flags
Ceiling fans
Painted and electric
  signs
Suspended car-
  touches
Hanging lanterns
Draped canopies
Suggestive cornices
Geometric fabric
  shapes
Hanging street
  lamps
Grillwork patterns

SCENERY AND PROPS BELOW

Metal grillwork
  railing
Shrubs and foliage
Low bookcases
See-through fences
Chaises and sofas
Sections of stone-
  work
Stools and chairs
Tables and desks
Rambling brick
  walls
Rugs and carpets
Platforms, steps,
  ramps
Ottomans and
  pouffes
Benches and boxes
Rocks and stones
Planters of flowers
Garden furniture
Statuary and foun-
  tains
Pillows and spreads

Changing Scenery and Props for Open Stage Productions

Designing a multiscene production that requires a different design idea for each scene is a formidable task on an open stage. But to a designer who approaches every project as a potential learning experience, the challenge is welcome and exciting.

When scenery and properties are changed in an attractive and creative manner, the audience often enjoys being in on the change and looks forward to it. The general rule of thumb is to design scenery that can be changed fairly fast and smoothly.

Interesting scene changes can be accomplished on an open stage by using one or more of these ideas:

1. Objects that seem to come from nowhere by descending from above, flying out of boxes or troughs (with hinged lids), rising up out of trapdoors, or moving on stage on tracks.
2. Objects that reverse and become something else on the other side. These may pivot on casters, or hinge to fold open or to reverse.
3. Objects that combine with other objects to make another item.
4. Objects of soft material that unfold or unroll and stretch out as horizontal or vertical pieces.
5. Objects that lift off, go up, or go down and reveal another item inside. Items may be suspended in soft dark bags with the bottom flap held together with pieces of Velcro.

Planning Pre-Performance and Finale Scenery

One way to give visual variety to an open stage production and to set the mood is to plan scenic arrangements that are in place before the performance. These may be fairly large pieces that are removed just before the action starts. Similar effects can be considered for intermission and for the finale. Listed are a few examples of scenic pieces that can be used in this way.

1. *Folding screens.* A group of decorative folding screens can be placed prominently on the main stage to hide three or four pieces of elegant furniture. When the performance is ready to begin and the lights go down for the opening, the lead actress takes her place and is revealed after the lights come up. Other actors or stagehands could remove the folding screens and make a choreographed exit.
2. *Painted banners.* Colorfully painted banners of chiffon and scrim may be suspended from the grid and fly out at the top of the show. They could also fly in at the end of the performance.
3. *Flags on long poles.* Flags and/or streamers may be attached to long poles with detailed finials or spearheads at the top. These poles, ranging from 7 to 8 feet, then may be placed in appropriately cut holes in the platformed floor so that they tilt slightly

when they are inserted vertically. The poles are self-supporting and can be inserted by actors or stagehands at the top and finish of the show.

4. *Pieces of fabric.* While it is standard practice in open stage theatres for the stage to be seen when the audience enters, there are times when a designer will want to obscure it. This may be done by using pieces of fabric (filled scrim, muslin, duvetyne, or other) on overhead traveler tracks. These pieces may be designed as painted show curtains or solid masking pieces, and the shape of the tracks above may be straight or curved. The curved tracks should not be so extreme that they make the pieces of fabric difficult to move off and on. A piece of hanging lash line may be attached to the first and last carrier so the pieces of fabric can be pulled off and on by hand from the house floor. There must be good available storage space offstage for the gathered fabric so it does not bunch up too close to the playing area and look unattractive.

Changing Scenic Pieces during a Performance

Numerous ideas can be explored for changing scenery during performance in the completely open stage. Moving scenic pieces for the open stage often works best when the pieces are not too large or bulky. The idea is to make a strong visual theatrical statement in a short amount of time. It is always necessary to resolve where the scenery will store, how it will come onstage and play, and then how it will go off and into storage again. For instance, fabric items that are flexible and without framing can be very practical and used in a great many different ways, such as in the following examples.

Flexible Fabric Cylinders Lightweight and openwork fabrics, such as chiffon and sharkstooth scrim, may be shaped into flexible cylinders with hoops attached on the inside of the fabric cylinder so they are positioned horizontally when hanging and are flat when the column is collapsed. These cylinders shaped with fabric work nicely for forming basic columns, trees, giant peppermint candy sticks for children's shows, and other scenic items. Average diameters for these fabric cylinders are 15 inches, 18 inches, and 24 inches. However, these diame-

ters may be varied as necessary for the desired effect.

If you are using the fabric cylinder method for trees, you might want to vary the size of the diameters by making them smaller at the top and also by gathering the fabric a bit instead of stretching it out neatly over the metal hoop. For musicals and revues, the collapsible cylinders may have mirrored discs or sequins glued on the outside. These may be attached in patterns or at random.

The fabric cylinders can hang and then be collapsed into a neatly stacked pile. They may be preset in openings in the stage platform that are covered by a hinged lid, or they may be preset in openings in the actual floor where trapdoor openings are available. The stacked fabric columns can also be brought onstage in boxes or baskets during the action or during blackouts.

Thin cables or nylon lines can be lowered from the flies and attached to the fabric by a stagehand so that the top of the cylinders can fly up into the grid to form the fabric shape. Still another idea is to hold the fabric cylinders in black bags above the stage and out of sight. Then, when they are to be used on stage, the entire bag is lowered in with the line attached, the bag is removed, the fabric cylinders rest on the floor, and then the tops fly up toward the grid to form the shape.

Another effect with the flexible fabric cylinder can also be created. Instead of a completely straight-up-and-down shape, the fabric columns can be squeezed together by hand and then tied together between the horizontal wire hoops. This gives a vertical series of diamond-shaped patterns.

Decorative Net Draperies Painted lightweight net drapery swags (with or without jabots) can look beautiful when lighted appropriately and hung artistically from the grid above an open stage. These draperies can be executed in short pieces and held in place with small lengths of Velcro fastened on the ends. The draperies can then be removed by gently pulling them away from the attached spot. A lovely effect can be achieved by draping the netting in the scenic studio so that all that has to be done in the theatre is to attach the corresponding pieces of Velcro to the grid and then press the Velcro pieces on the drapery pieces into place. While drapery swags are usually the most

popular choice, long net legs may also be used and attached at the top in the same way.

Establishing Aisles

A flexible arrangement of seats in a completely open or full-round theatre lets the designer and director establish the position and number of aisles for a production. The aisles may have these functions:

1. For the audience to enter and leave the theatre at the beginning, intermission(s), and end of the show. This means that the aisle widths must be able to accommodate the size of the audience so they can enter and exit properly. It is usually necessary to have aisles a minimum of 3 feet wide. The aisles of course must be unobstructed for passage in any emergency and to comply with fire laws. Safety precautions include marking with Glo Tape or partially covered tiny lights to emphasize the edge of seating levels, aisle platforms, or ramps.

2. For the actors to use the aisles for entering and leaving the playing area. They may be directed to do this with stage lighting during performance or in blackout between scenes and acts. Again, safety is vital for smooth, continuous moving patterns for egress or ingress. Steps, ramps, and walkways should also be well marked and edges lighted wherever an accident might occur. Actresses in certain period costumes need appropriate space and smooth floor surfaces to enter and exit the stage. For example, a larger width than 3 feet would be necessary for two actresses to pass each other when they are wearing large hoop skirts.

3. For the stagehands (and/or actors) to move stage props, furniture, and any scenery during performance. This also applies to the beginning and end of the performance. Aisles and walkways (both onstage and offstage) must include ample space for moving props and furniture so that objects can easily go through doors, around corners, and up and down levels, ramps, or platforms when they are used onstage and then returned offstage into storage.

It should also be noted that aisles are often used as well in theatres where the seating arrangement is not flexible. A thrust or open stage theatre may have vomitories in which to make entrances and exits to the playing area from under seating areas. These "voms" may be passages or ramped or stepped tunnels.

As with proscenium productions, the planning of the stage lighting and positioning of instruments is of paramount importance and should always be considered at the beginning of the project in collaboration with others involved in the production. While some open stage theatres have overhead metal grids of identical or similar shape as the fixed open stage platform below, others may have a very flexible general structure above so that lighting instruments can be moved as necessary. For this reason, the scenic designer and lighting designer must work together and must have excellent communication when developing both the ground plan and the hanging section drawings or elevations for the open stage production.

Black Box Theatres

The black box theatre is an ideal space in which to design highly individual stage settings for any kind of production. Because this type of theatre is extremely flexible in terms of where the action can be staged and where the audience can be seated in relation to the action, it presents a great challenge to the designer.

Black box theatres may have stage areas flat on the floor or elevated on platforms. The seats can usually be moved into a variety of seating arrangements, in parallel, circular, or angled rows or in a combination of these arrays.

ADVANTAGES

- Extremely flexible for positioning the area for the action of actors.
- Flexible in how the seating can be positioned in relation to the stage (area).
- Motivates the designer(s) to use ingenuity and imagination to create when budget and space are small.
- In very small spaces, scenery may go to the walls and be braced against them, especially when portals are used.

DISADVANTAGES

- Usually has limited seating.
- May not make much money because of the small number of seats.
- Usually not much offstage space.
- May not be able to fly out any scenery.
- Details on scenery, props, and costumes are viewed at a much closer

range than in larger theatres.
- Light instruments may be practically on top of scenery in the small theatres.

Creating a Model Setting for a Black Box Theatre

As a project, design a painted model in ¼-inch scale of a setting for *Salonika* by Louise Page. Make the model for an open stage (or arena) production in a black box theatre. Use a playing area 24'-0" wide by 14'-0" deep with a 16'-0" ceiling. Position a sky drop behind the playing area and follow the playwright's instructions to accommodate five actors: "A beach. Smooth. After a tide. Lying on the sand naked and the same color as the sand, Peter. There are no footmarks to him." Use real sand and indicate how you would contain it. The director would prefer the outer shape of the sand to be anything but a rectangle. Devise your own seating arrangement for 199 patrons and have four different entrances and exits.

Designing the Same Show with Five Different Approaches

During a designer's career, he or she may be engaged to design the scenery for a production that has to be revamped several times to fit the individual physical theatres where it plays.

Deciding how to resolve the physical aspect in multiple ways is an ideal project for both the novice and the experienced designer. Suppose you have been asked to design the scenery for a production of *Burn This* by Lanford Wilson.

The setting: A loft in a converted cast-iron building, lower Manhattan.

ACT 1
Scene 1: Mid-October, late afternoon.
Scene 2: Early December, late at night.
Scene 3: The next morning.

ACT 2
Scene 1: New Year's Eve.
Scene 2: The next morning.
Scene 3: A month later.
Scene 4: Late that night.

The five production situations are listed.

1. *A regular commercial run.* Design the scenery for this one-set drama for a full-size proscenium stage 40'-0" wide by 23'-0" high by 30'-0" deep,

with a grid height of 68'-0". The show becomes a hit and plays at the theatre for a lengthy run.

2. *A repertory company.* The producers would like to do the same production in repertory with two other plays at another theatre. The dimensions at this proscenium theatre are 36'-0" wide by 20'-0" high by 12'-0" deep from the rear of the proscenium wall to the back wall. The grid is 38'-0" high. The theatre has a thrust stage that includes the apron and is 14'-0" deep from the back of the proscenium wall to the front edge of the thrust stage. The overall width is the same as the width of the opening, and the deck height of the thrust is the same as the stage floor: 3'-2"

3. *A national touring company.* Because the play has become increasingly popular, it is now going on tour with a national touring company playing one- and two-week engagements. You have been asked to rework the design and drawings so that the scenery can play on various stages. The smallest proscenium stage is 34'-0" wide by 24'-0" high by 20'-0" deep, with a grid 46'-0" high. The largest proscenium stage is 50'-0" wide by 28'-0" high by 35'-0" deep. The grid height for this theatre is 80'-0".

4. *A bus-and-truck company.* After the national company has been mounted, the producers decide to send out a bus-and-truck company of the same production. It will go to smaller cities and play one or two performances at each stop. Design a set for a proscenium house with these dimensions: 32'-0" wide by 18'-0" high by 17'-0" deep, with the highest grid height being 36'-0". These dimensions were selected so that the set would not be too bulky for putting up and taking down for one- and two-night stands.

5. *A resident company.* A resident theatre would like the same scenic designer to create the setting for their company, but the theatre has a completely open stage in the arena. It is a circle 24'-0" in diameter and 1'-6" high. Around the entire stage is a step unit that is 1'-0" wide by 9" high. Above the stage at a height of 16'-0" is a grid of metal pipes used for lighting instruments and any suspended scenery. It is also in the shape of a circle and is 24'-0" in diameter. There are four aisles in the audience going to the stage for actors to make entrances and exits.

Robert O'Hearn maintains and lives in a studio on lower Broadway in New York City. Born on July 19, 1921, in Elkhart, Indiana, he was educated at Indiana University and the Art Students League. His first Broadway show was designing the settings and costumes for *The Relapse* at the Morosco Theatre in 1950 with direction by Cyril Ritchard. This was followed by *Love's Labour's Lost, A Date with April, Festival, Othello, Henry IV (Part I), Child of Fortune, The Apple Cart,* and *Abraham Cochrane*. He has created the sets and costumes for countless productions for theatre, dance, and opera companies, among them American Ballet Theatre, Ballet West, Pacific Northwest Dance, Los Angeles Ballet, New York City Ballet, American Shakespeare Festival (Stratford, Connecticut), Saratoga Theatre, Olney Theatre, and Brattle Theatre. He currently teaches at the Indiana University School of Music in Bloomington, Indiana. Robert O'Hearn's scenic and costume design credits include:

The Metropolitan Opera
Porgy and Bess (1985)
The Marriage of Figaro (1975)
Boris Godunov [unproduced] (1970)
Parsifal (1970)
Der Rosenkavalier (1969)
Hänsel and Gretel (1967)
Die Frau ohne Schatten (1966)
La Ventana (1966)
Pique-Dame (1965)
Samson et Dalila (1964)
Aïda (1963)

Die Meistersinger von
  Nürnberg (1962)
L'Elisir d'Amore (1960)

Other Opera Companies
Washington Opera Society
San Francisco Opera
Central City Opera
New York City Opera
Karlsruhe Opera
Houston Opera Company
Boston Opera

Canadian Opera Company
Bergenz Festival (Austria)
Miami Opera Company
Chicago Lyric Opera
Opera Colorado
Michigan Opera Theatre
Santa Fe Opera
Hamburg State Opera
Vienna Volksoper
Strasbourg Opera Company
Los Angeles Civic
  Light Opera

Setting and costumes by Robert O'Hearn
DIE MEISTERSINGER VON NÜRNBERG by
  Richard Wagner

Libretto by the composer
Act 2—the street outside the house of Pogner
  and Sachs

Directed by Nathaniel Merrill
The Metropolitan Opera, New York (1962)
(Photograph by Louis Melançon)

Louis Melançon
METROPOLITAN OPERA HOUSE
NEW YORK, N.Y.

How did you first become interested in designing for the stage?

I was very lucky. I had a wonderful high school teacher, James Lewis Casaday, who was a wonderful director and inspiration. And I worked with him for four years in South Bend, Indiana. I really learned more from him than anybody else. In my two years at the University of Indiana I don't think I learned as much in that time in the theatre department as I did working with Mr. Casaday in high school. So I was very lucky because from the age of fifteen, I knew that I wanted to design stage sets.

When I got to New York I took art classes at the Art Students League, and I had also taken art classes in college. I think drawing and painting are so important to a designer. It's pretty hard to get by if you can't draw and paint because it limits you. But as you know, there have been and are some designers who couldn't draw or paint.

Did you do stock or repertory theatre?

I did several summers of summer stock, which was very helpful. But the best thing that happened was in 1948 when I went to Brattle Theatre in Cambridge and stayed there for four years and designed sixty productions. It was a classical repertory company. We did Shakespeare, Shaw, Ibsen, Chekhov. I had met Robert Fletcher previously at a summer theatre, and he was going to do the costumes and also act at the Brattle Theatre, and he asked me to come up and do the scenery. It was a very exciting period. A lot of very well known people came out of that group. There was Nancy Marchand, Jerry Kilty, and Albert Marre, who directed most of the productions. The building is still there, as a matter of fact. It must be 100 years old now.

Sarah Caldwell was just starting out in Boston and she saw the productions at the Brattle Theatre and asked me to do Verdi's *Falstaff* with her. That was the first opera production that she directed and the first opera that I designed. I did about six productions with her in that period.

Nathaniel Merrill was a technical director for her on *The Rake's Progress*, which we did with Stravinsky conducting. And then several years later Nathaniel directed *Ariadne auf Naxos* at the Opera Society in Washington, and he asked me to design it. He was

also working at the Met then, as one of the lowly stage directors. And Mr. Bing happened to be in Washington and came over and saw a dress rehearsal of a *Don Giovanni* that we did, and asked both of us to do *Elixir of Love* at the Met in 1960. Since then I've done a total of twelve productions at the Met. The most recent one was *Porgy and Bess* in 1985.

How many productions do you have in repertory at the Metropolitan Opera?

Let's see, they're still doing *Elixir of Love* this season. *Die Meistersinger* is still used; *Samson et Dalila* they did last season. It's about time they do *Die Frau ohne Schatten* again. *Hänsel and Gretel* is coming back; they still use my *Rosenkavalier*, *Parsifal*, and *Porgy and Bess*. So that's eight that are still in active repertory.

Do you go over to the opera house each time they come back?

Usually, and especially if the sets haven't played there for several seasons. There was a period where they did *Rosenkavalier* once every year for about five years. I didn't go back each time for that. But if an opera hasn't been around for a while, yes, I do go back. They usually call me and ask me to go in. I don't like to force myself on them, because the union requires a very expensive fee.

What do you mean, a fee?

Well, it's a daily fee. I think now it's something like $315 a day. You know, if you go in for three days it adds up. But after all, most of the productions that I did I don't get any royalty for. The royalties are only for productions from 1970 on. I think *Parsifal* and *Porgy and Bess* are the only ones I get royalties on.

That must be hard to understand sometimes when you see how many times they play.

Yes. Look at *Rosenkavalier*. They do it, and they do it, and they do it. But there have been several of them on television and *Hänsel and Gretel* and *L'Elisir d'Amore* are out on laser disk and VHS. I get nice royalties from those.

Do you get a royalty each time that they duplicate it somewhere else other than at the Met?

When they first show it on television, the fee you get gives them an unlimited use for one week, but none of these "Live at the Met" shows have come back.

Have you done costumes for everything that you've done sets for at the Met?

At the Met, yes. Many of the regional companies can't afford to do new costumes, and most of them are rented from Malabar in Toronto, which is about the only place that keeps complete opera costume productions together. Malabar has been doing that for years.

In other words, if you did an out-of-town production, you'd probably do scenery.

Yes. Chances are I'd only do the scenery.

You wouldn't be involved in the costumes at all?

No. I did the costumes for *Pique-Dame* at the San Francisco Opera, and we built all of those costumes. I've done several productions in Europe where I've done both costumes and scenery.

If you aren't doing the costumes yourself, would you know the person who was going to do the costumes and would you get together with that person?

Oh, surely. Suzanne Mess has designed the costumes for most of those productions. We've worked together for twenty-five years now. Certainly, we know each other's color, and there has never really been any problem.

How much would it cost to do a full opera at the Met today with sets and costumes? What kind of budget would be needed?

Well, I know that in 1985 *Porgy and Bess* cost $750,000 for the scenery and the costumes. It was executed in 1984 by Messmore and Damon, which is one of the few remaining full union scenic shops on Manhattan island. Messmore did a fantastic job on that.

Now, it's very amusing that I was not told what the budget was for that until after it was all designed and went out for bids. In a way that's flattering, because they might feel that if they give you a budget it's going to cramp your style, and they'd rather have you do what you want to do and then, if they can't afford it, you may have to cut back on it. But it's a very peculiar feeling if you don't really know what the budget is.

Sometimes the size of productions can present problems.

I saw *Siegfried*, which is a very handsome production, and it has three stagefulls of realistic scenery, with a very incredible forest with more realistic trees than you can imagine. And each set has its own separate rake to it. The first act is a complete built cave with trees up on the top, and on and on and on. There is a big transformation effect in the last scene with fire, and the rock sinks down and Brünnhilde is sleeping there. They did that production in the afternoon and at night they did *Turandot* with about two and a half hours in between. Now, how they did that, I don't know, because *Turandot* is huge! And for *Siegfried*, I think they probably used both side stage and rear stage to put these sets on because there are big chunks of rock and scenery. Meanwhile, where do they have this *Turandot* production which is so enormous?

How long did you spend working on Porgy and Bess?

Well, they wanted the designs a year ahead. I think, on the actual scenery, I probably worked about four months, which would include making the models and the working drawings, the whole thing.

You did all the working drawings yourself?

I did the working drawings myself. I had an assistant to work on models. That was David Harnish, a wonderful model builder. Then I probably spent about six weeks researching and doing the costume sketches. There was a different sketch for every character, because it's not the kind of thing you have repeats in. So I think there are about 190 costume sketches for that, which is a lot of individual sketches.

What is the average number of costumes that you have done for a production at the Met?

Oh, I think even something like *Aïda* might only be eighty sketches for four hundred costumes because you have so many repeats in that opera. Some designers cheat and do just line draw-

ings, and then they stick little fabric swatches on the drawings. I think it's not fair to the costume builders and it's not fair to yourself as a designer because you can't really see how that's going to look. So much has to do with the proportion of the area that the fabric covers and the colors that I think you're going to be much better off if you paint it all on. It helps the people who are building the costumes because then they can really look at it and know where something is, and they don't have to keep asking questions all the time. And a lot of times, the designers aren't around that much because they may be from Europe.

Where did you research Porgy and Bess?

I got a lot of authentic patterns at the Studio Shop on Seventh Avenue. They build costumes there for Off-Broadway shows. Betty Williams, who runs it, has an incredible collection of period patterns, such as Butterick paper patterns that people use for home sewing. So I selected real patterns of the period. The Met made copies of them. In fact, they weren't too keen on doing that because they felt that it wasn't really necessary, but they did it anyway. I wanted it to look like 1932, and I felt that it was important to use those patterns, so that's what we did. Some skirts were made fuller.

Then I went to the Schomburg Center for Research in Black Culture library in Harlem and got a lot of pictures there. The Schomburg library is a branch of the New York City Library, and I Xeroxed things from the picture collection there.

You said you did 190 costume sketches in color. How many people were in the cast? Did that include principals and supernumeraries?

Well, there were about 100 people in the cast. Most of them change costumes for Kittiwah Island, so that's a whole other set of costumes. And the dancers change. So you have two complete sets of clothes. Most of the principals don't have many changes. Bess has four costumes. Porgy wears the same thing all the way through.

How many duplicate costumes would you do for the principals? Or does another department say, "We are going to need this in such-and-such a size because of cast changes?"

Actually, *Porgy and Bess* got a little complicated because Grace Bumbry had her own ideas about what she wanted to wear, and so we ended up doing completely different designs for her. When Roberta Alexander, who has a good figure, did it, we used the original designs for her. So those are really two different sets of clothes for Bess.

Sometimes costumes can be a problem. When women singers get heavy, you can't show their arms and you can't show their back. But it's harder with contemporary costumes or in the thirties. Usually you can hide someone with a big cape or something as you often get in opera, but it's much more difficult in modern clothes.

In the production of *Aïda* that I did at the Met, we probably had four complete sets of Radames' costumes, and there are at least four costume changes for Radames besides different footwear. That's a lot of costumes. And we probably have the same number of different sets of costumes for the Aïdas because you get tall slim women or short heavy women, and they can't fit into the same costume. They adjust the costume for them if possible. There isn't any health rule that says they can't wear someone else's costume. The costumes are very, very expensive, and you can imagine the cost of a number of duplicates.

Who directed this production of Porgy and Bess?

Nathaniel Merrill, the same director I've worked with for most of my productions at the Met. We've done forty productions together. The first one was in 1958. Besides the Met we've worked at the Central City Opera House in Colorado and for the Miami Opera, and I've done some operas with him in Europe. We did *Porgy and Bess* at the Vienna Volksoper and we did it at Bregenz on the big lake stage in Austria, and we did productions together in Strasbourg.

What is your method of working when you are attacking a new opera? After that many productions together, does he trust you to go ahead and to make sketches and show them to him?

Pretty much. We usually have a few words, and sometimes it's only a few words on the telephone. For the Met you may start a couple of years ahead, or at least a year, and the directors don't really have their minds on the

Stage design by Robert O'Hearn
PARSIFAL by Richard Wagner

Libretto by the composer
Act 2—the magic flower garden

Directed by Nathaniel Merrill
The Metropolitan Opera, New York (1970)

production yet. It's very hard to get them talking in a concrete way about it. So usually I would go ahead and do floor plans and some rough sketches so we'd have something to talk about. And then, once the director sees something like that he'll say, "Well, I like this one better," or "Why don't you combine these two?"

I often say that to a great extent I feel that I direct these productions because when you do the floor plan, and the entrances and platforms where the chorus is going to be and enter from, you've already done a lot of the directing. Very often you as the designer decide the look of the production, whether it's going to be real or abstract or in color or no color. So particularly in opera, I think the designer does a lot of the directing.

When you do scenery at the Met, do you still work with David Reppa, the associate designer?

Well, David doesn't have much to do with my productions, because I supply all the information that he and the staff need. I do complete models, and complete working drawings, and paint elevations.

Starting with the first production that you did there?

Yes, I've done it for every show I've ever designed anywhere. American designers do that anyway, particularly with the early productions, because the Met didn't have a design department then. Actually they have two different departments, one a design department and one a technical department, which are different suites of offices with different personnel. They are definitely separate. But the reason that they really have the design department is that the European designers are used to the opera houses in Europe that have their own staffs and they just take in some loose sketches and some loose floor plans and these departments completely develop the productions for them. David can have one, two, or three people drafting and assisting him.

That is particularly what happens to Zeffirelli's designs. David's department does the model, and they do all the drafting based only on scene sketches. Often the sketches are very loose. Zeffirelli would come in occasionally and say, "Make it bigger," or something like that. That's what hap-

pened on his *Tosca* and his *Turandot.* The Met staff did all the work. Schneider-Siemssen sends in very accurate models, but they are drafted by the Metropolitan Opera design department.

When you render something, what is your favorite technique?

I like to suit my medium to the particular production, and what I feel about how it's going to look. I like to change my medium so I don't just keep doing everything the same all the time and so everything doesn't look alike. I get bored with my own style. When you use a different kind of paper, a different kind of medium, it makes you do things differently. I have used oil a lot, and sometimes I use it on illustration board and sometimes I use prepared canvas board.

You're talking about oil just like you use on a fine art painting?

Yes. It's perfectly easy to use. I use oil in tubes, of course. I get a waxed paper palette that comes in pads and I tear off the sheets after I use them.

What do you use to thin the oil paint?

Stage design by Robert O'Hearn
LA BOHÈME by Giacomo Puccini
Libretto by Giuseppe Giacosa and Luigi Illica
Directed by James Lucas
Miami Opera Company
Miami, Florida (1977)

I thin it with turpentine and a few drops of Japan Drier, which makes it dry much faster, so that after a few hours you can do glazes over it. However, I find that I very seldom come back and rework. It has a look to it that's just different somehow. You can do things in oil that you can't do in other media. In a way it's an easier technique because it's comparable to scene paint in that it stays moist longer. You know, the way that a drop on the floor stays wet. Instead of sinking into the board and drying immediately the way acrylic does, oil paint stays wet or moist for hours or for days if you want. And you can blend it so well.

If you are doing a glaze, do you still thin it with turpentine?

Yes. You thin it with turpentine until it becomes almost like watercolor. Sometimes I will first do a thin coating of shellac on the board so that the oil won't sink into the board. But if you don't want the oils to get too shiny, you just don't bother to do that.

The smell of turpentine bothers some people. Does it you?

It doesn't seem to bother me, no. I just take a small old shrimp cocktail glass, pour the turpentine in, and add a few drops of Japan Drier. It doesn't permeate the place really.

You prefer that over using dyes, or would you use dyes depending on the effect?

Well, you can use oil just like watercolors. The sketch I designed for the *My Fair Lady* backdrop for Detroit was done with thin oil paint. I did the sky in several layers, and I did some glazes over it to kind of blend it all together.

One of the best sketches I ever did, which is in your first book, was for *The Elixir of Love*. I wanted it to look like the painter Guardi, and so it was done in oil. I think it has a look that you would have a hard time getting in acrylic.

Again, it depends on the kind of production. In particular if it's a serious or dark sort of thing, I often work on a gray mat board called TV Gray. At least that's what it's called in New York. It's a medium light gray color. I do dark shadows with charcoal and highlights with white pastel, and then I may fix it and reinforce it with acrylic and then add color to it. I developed this technique from looking at Renaissance master drawings. The things that Dürer does, for instance. He does light and dark on middle ground, and it's a way of very quickly getting the quality of light direction and form in a drawing. I'm sure you've seen still lifes done that way and you get an incredible quality very fast. A lot of my sketches are done that way, particularly the roughs. It is a quick way to do roughs and immediately get light and form.

Whenever I teach, I always show this technique, because it seems to help students a lot. As soon as you show light direction in a sketch, it gives you form. And if you don't have a light direction and shadow, the sketch is very flat.

I also like working in Dr. Martin's dyes. It's such fun to bleach things out with Clorox. You need to mix the Clo-rox half with water or it turns the paper brown. The dyes give such a clean look, and then to wet them and bleach out things you can get wonderful effects. Acrylics, certainly, have great advantages, too. They are waterproof and dry quickly. You can keep working over them. Something that I've been doing to a great extent lately is having things Xeroxed on watercolor paper or just ordinary Xerox paper, mounting it, and painting over it with matte medium.

How do you mount it?

With a spray-on adhesive. I found a watercolor paper that is flexible enough that my local Xerox man will print onto it. I dampen and stretch it just like I would any watercolor paper. Spray it with a little fixative because the Xeroxed drawing doesn't stick too well. It has the advantage that if you mess up a sketch, you don't have to redraw the whole thing. You get a very clear black line and you can Xerox just from a drawing on tracing paper. It saves time and tracing. The best surface is a good watercolor paper which is dipped in water and taped to a board with old-fashioned gummed brown tape. It dries tight and flat. As you work, it stays moist longer for blending and always dries flat again.

How many sketches do you usually make? Do you do several or do you have good luck the first time or so?

I usually have good luck. And I usually don't have time to do more than one. A lot of people don't do color sketches anymore. They're very important to me because I want to know what it's going to look like. It's very important to have color sketches. And you can do sketching much faster than a model, and you're not investing the time that you do in making a model. You can work out a lot of your problems in a sketch.

When I do the drawing for a set sketch, I use what I call *the* perspective grid. I'm sure there are several perspective grids around, but I use the one that Christini taught years ago. Christini was the Italian scenic artist and designer who taught for quite a while at

Indiana University. I learned it from a student who graduated from Indiana University about fifteen years ago. I've used it ever since for creating my sketches so they look exactly the way the set is going to look. With this grid you know how high and wide everything is going to be. If something is 18 feet high, you know what it looks like and you can build it that way in your model. It's a wonderful technique.

You take your floor plan, which is on a straight graph grid, and do it in perspective on the grid, and you now know exactly all the dimensions because you're in exact scale around the outside border. You put tracing paper over the grid, and then do your sketch. I've done it for every show that I've done in the last fifteen years. If I add 2 feet of depth or if I think I want a piece to be a little bit wider, I make it wider and track it back through and make it wider in the ground plan. So you can work backwards and forwards with the grid.

We're talking about sets. What do you use for costume sketches?

For costume sketches I usually just do a pencil drawing with watercolor over it. I work from pans or cakes of watercolor because I don't mix up much color at a time for a costume sketch. It's better to have one of these trays with thirty different cakes of color so you can go from one to the other very quickly. I seldom use oil for

costume sketches. That would be much too complicated to get into.

How tall do you make costume figures in a sketch?

The figure is usually about 11 or 12 inches high. If you get them too big, they are too hard to handle. I think you should do one costume sketch to a page or a sheet because if you do several figures together, it's a big nuisance for the shop. They have to keep passing the sketch around.

Even for groups of peasants or something like that?

Really, yes. It looks nice to have a group together, and some designers do that sometimes because they're all in related colors. I think the only time I ever did a group of costume sketches on one sheet was for *Der Rosenkavalier*. It made a very funny sketch to show these six lackeys of the Baron in ill-fitting, secondhand livery.

When you first came to New York, did you assist other designers?

Oh yes, I think that was most important. I assisted Lemuel Ayers for about three years. He was a wonderful designer and a wonderful man. I worked with him on *Camino Real*, and we got along very well so I continued to work for him on *Kismet, Pajama Game,* the New York and road company productions, and I supervised *Kismet* in England when he couldn't go there.

I also assisted Oliver Messel on *House of Flowers, The Dark Is Light Enough*, and *Rashomon*. He was hired to redecorate the Billy Rose Theatre, which is now the Nederlander Theatre, and I worked with him on that project. He didn't draft, but he did very elaborate, completely finished models for everything. As he made a model, he would draw the pieces on quarter-inch graph paper, and that's as far as he got into drafting. In England they were used to this. They would build from the model and from this graph paper drawing, but over here when they did *House of Flowers*, the shops wanted drafting. So I was hired to draft the shows for him. He liked what I did because I still kept the free look of what he had, and didn't tighten it up too much.

How did you get the job of assisting Oliver Messel?

I wrote a letter to him saying that I admired his work so much, and said that I would love to work with him if he needed anyone over here, and told him what I'd been doing. Jean Rosenthal lit *House of Flowers*, and I think she did some asking around, because they were actually looking for someone to draft for him. So I came highly recommended, and just went over and started working.

Then I worked for Oliver Smith on ten or twelve productions. I assisted him on *West Side Story, My Fair Lady, Jamaica, Winesburg, Ohio, Nude with Violin, Time Remembered, The Saturday Night Kid*. I bet you never heard of that one, did you? Shelley Winters? I don't think it lasted very long.

You have done opera in the round. Where was that?

At Boettcher Hall in Denver, which is a round concert hall. Nathaniel Merrill started Opera Colorado there about six years ago now. And I designed *Aïda* and *Don Giovanni* there, and last season I did *Samson et Dalila* and *Manon Lescaut*. They're very exciting in the round, especially *Aïda*, absolutely spectacular. This is completely in the round.

What kind of space are we talking about?

It's a huge stage. It's about 75 feet wide and about 40 feet deep. It's an oval with one side of it chopped off where the orchestra pit is. And there are two big voms, which make it pos-

Stage design by Robert O'Hearn
LA SYLPHIDE, Act 2—a forest
Original choreography by August Bournonville

Choreographed by Harald Lander
American Ballet Theatre
Municipal Auditorium, San Antonio, Texas
(1964)

Stage design by Robert O'Hearn
IDOMENEO by Wolfgang Amadeus Mozart
Libretto by Giovanni Battista Varesco
Directed by Bliss Hebert
Washington Opera Society
Washington, D.C. (1961)

sible to do scenic units of some substance, otherwise you really couldn't do all that much. Because of those you can do big entrances, you can do platforms, and you can have stairways.

How high is the actual stage? It's not on the same level of the front row seats, is it?

No. It's very exciting with the sound coming from the middle, with the audience sitting all around the stage. Acoustically it's wonderful.

Manon Lescaut didn't work as well as some of the other productions, because it has four different sets which tend to be realistic sets and the kind of thing you couldn't do a unit for. If you can do a unit, as you can for *Aïda* or for *Samson et Dalila*, it works much better in that kind of theatre. They had an enormous chorus, by the way, with about 120 members.

You did both sets and costumes?

I did the ballet costumes for *Aïda* and they rented my costumes from the Met for *Samson*. Malabar did *Don Giovanni* and *Manon Lescaut*.

What height were you working with?

The ceiling of the place is about 60 feet up. But there are circular bridges on which the lights are hanging over the stage, and they are 24 to 30 feet high.

What do you feel was the most successful production there?

I think the *Aïda* is the most spectacular I have done, even with its problem of doing the tomb scene and suffocating people at the end of the opera in the round. It was rather a puzzle to figure out. There was a triangular-shaped platform with steps going up, and the whole top of it was actually a big stone that went down into this platform. In the last act we had four huge, twisted ropes that came down and attached to it. And so when Amneris threw herself on this stone, it slowly lifted up about 12 feet in the air, and Radames came up on a lift underneath it, and that was the tomb underneath the stone. The audience got the message immediately. There was a big gasp and applause. It was what you'd call a coup de theatre. No one expected this platform that you looked at through the whole evening to suddenly take off and go up in the air.

How many different sets did you have for this Aïda *in the round?*

Aïda has about seven sets. There was a variety of look in it there.

And you did models for it?

Yes, quarter-inch models. For *Samson et Dalila* I did a half-inch model because I had to work out columns and how they were going to fall down. You must have columns in *Samson et Dalila* because *Samson* has to push columns down. So for the first time, we had some obstructed seats in the audience. The columns were rigged with hydraulics so that as soon as *Samson* started pushing, they threw a switch offstage and the things would start coming over. There were three huge columns that fell down on the stage, and then rubber and stone debris from

bags that were hanging up above the stage. And that looked as if the place was really coming apart. It was happening right in the middle of the audience so it had to be carefully worked out so you didn't kill anyone. But it was fun to do, and it was really quite spectacular.

When you are designing for the Met, do you plan to use their stage equipment as much as possible in your design?

Oh, sure, yes. You base it upon what they have. For instance, there are the rolling wagons, which they have on both sides of the stage, and there is the rear stage, which is a big 60-foot square that moves up and down and has a revolve in it. Sometimes they don't want you to use the side stages because they want to keep them for storage for a production playing in repertory. It's very expensive to completely clear all these stages, so they don't always want you to use them. It's very understandable.

Porgy and Bess used the revolve on the big rear stage, which was brought downstage because the scene shifts have to work fast with specific musical timing. Serena's room and the Hurricane House were behind Catfish Row on the revolve. Kittiwah Island was manually set. *Die Frau ohne Schatten* was even more complicated because we used the understage area, which came up on elevators several times in the production, besides a side stage and the rear stage revolve.

Do you have a favorite design among your many opera productions at the Met, in the United States or elsewhere?

Well, I think *Die Frau ohne Schatten* is *the* production of my career. It was a fantastic thing. I had to completely reinvestigate myself and everything I could think of to create it. And I think it was a truly original creation. No one has ever done anything like it. It was just before what we know as psychodelic, but that is what it was. The drop elevations were done in batik and the research was in microorganisms and crystals. Karl Boehm, the conductor, took my arm at the curtain call the last time it was at the Met and he said, "What you have done, my boy was the best. That was the best I've seen." So that was something! And to create something in your life that is truly unique like that, is a gratifying experience.

3

THEATRICAL DRAWING

SCENIC DRAWING

Scenic drawing in the truest sense of the term is not only drafting and technical drawings, but much, much more. Scenic drawing involves every aspect and process of drawing that is required to mount a production. It includes the drawing required of both the scenic designer and the scenic artist. Design and painting students should always be aware that good drawing is as important as good painting. How can a lovely scenic painting be fully realized if you do not begin with a good drawing? Many colleges and universities and theatre schools around the country teach courses in scenic painting, but they do not always offer courses in scenic drawing. Somehow, the emphasis that should be given to scenic drawing and what it encompasses has been neglected.

One remedy to the neglect of scenic drawing instruction is independent study. Peruse the classic architecture and perspective designs of the Bibiena family (seventeenth and eighteenth centuries), Giacomo Torelli (1608–1678), Gaspare Vigarani (1586–1663), Jean Bérain (1640–1711), Bernardino Galliari (1707–1794), Sebastiano Serlio (1475–1554), and others. These are all superb examples of theatrical drawing on a grand scale. Copy the drawings and compare your work with the perspective rendered by these artists. Study the detail in the drawings. Look at the drawings as a group and note that all of these artists did place as much emphasis on the study of theat-

rical drawing as they did on painting. As we approach the end of the twentieth century, with its technical accomplishments and discoveries, it is interesting to realize that in the theatre we still rely on basic drawing as a constant means of creative communication.

Aspects of Theatrical Drawing

In the commercial theatre the drawing processes in any production are a collective effort involving both the scenic designer and the scenic artist. The drawing for a show starts with the scenic designer's very roughest set sketch, continues with the design process, and goes all the way through the execution of the actual scenery in the scenic studio, where it is drawn and painted by the scenic artist.

Certain drawing processes may vary according to the individual show, but basically, the procedure for the drawing on a production remains the same.

As an overview, the required drawings for a commercial production are listed in the sequence of their execution (as much as possible), but there is always a degree of overlap in the drawing process. The usual places of execution for these drawings are the designer's studio (1 and 3 through 8) the theatre (2), the scenic studio (10 through 16), and the rehearsal hall (9).

1. Making Small Thumbnail Scenic Sketches Simple idea sketches are the first drawings made by the scenic designer. They may be done in pencil or

pen on the back of napkins, envelopes, or place mats, or on a sketch pad. Thumbnail sketches run the gamut from very rough, casual drawings to finished sketches. Normally, thumbnails are not drawn in any particular scale, but some designers prefer to draw them in ⅛-inch or ¼-inch scale. These small sketches often have a pleasant spontaneity that can be lost when they are enlarged to ½-inch scale. Thumbnail sketches are rendered in black and white or in color.

2. Doing Rough Measurement Drawings in the Theatre Both the novice and the established designer go to the theatre to double-check the dimensions of the stage, to see the workable stage space, and to study the sight lines from various seats in the house. Even with plans of the theatre in hand, a designer should go to the theatre with an assistant to take the actual measurements of the stage. The reason for doing this is that theatre plans may not have been updated to show renovations or additions, or ½-inch plans may not have all the dimensions needed by the designer. Rough drawings are made with pencil or pen on something like ordinary 8½ × 11-inch paper or legal pads to record on-the-spot dimensions.

3. Drawing the Presentation Sketch The presentation sketch is drawn to show how the set is intended to look from the audience, usually from the center of the orchestra seats. An interesting project for the novice is to do

100 additional presentation sketches of the set as it would appear when viewed from the center of the mezzanine and also from the balcony seats.

Presentation sketches are rendered in full color, with stage lighting and mood indicated. They may be made of an endless number of subjects, from a show curtain consisting of a collage of musical instruments to a perspective rendering of the interior of a French salon in the afternoon, with light streaming in through the windows, to a perspective view of a battlefield and tents at twilight.

A careful drawing is always the prerequisite to doing an attractive sketch. The drawing may be executed with a light pencil for a charming romantic watercolor sketch or a collage. For some individual styles of rendering, the drawing may be finished with black or sepia ink or other colors. Colored pencils and felt-tip pens are also appropriate for creating sketches.

4. Drawing Scenery for the Model
While the drawing for the presentation sketch is usually done in perspective, the drawing and measuring of the units for the ½-inch scale model is normally done to resolve true dimensions and shapes. Scenic pieces for the model are drawn with drafting tools and also by freehand drawing. Drawings may be done specifically for the model and then copied on the drafting, or vice versa, going from the drawings on the drafting, transferring them to illustration board, cutting them out, gluing and putting them together to make three-dimensional units that make up the model.

Subjects for the model drawings can vary enormously. Just to cite a few possibilities, a drawing or drawings may be needed for a layout of cobblestones to go on a full-stage canvas ground cloth; or for a layout for wooden parquetry or brick paviors on the tops of platforms; or for various inside ceiling shapes; or for outside roofs with several gables; or for curved staircases or cantilevered balconies.

5. Making Drawings for Paint Elevations The drawings for paint elevations may be similar to those done for presentation sketches and models. In the traditional sense, ½-inch scale paint elevations are made to use for painting the flat scenic pieces, such as backdrops and flats, as well as three-dimensional ground rows or other built-up scenic units. However, pieces may be removed from a painted ½-inch scale finished model, when necessary, to function as rendered paint elevations. Unlike presentation sketches, paint elevations are not normally rendered with stage lighting or in perspective unless both of these are intended to be a part of the design.

A variety of simple freehand pencil (or pen) rendering techniques may be utilized in drawing paint elevations, presentation sketches, or models. Sometimes freehand pencil renderings are needed on the drafting to be printed. Freehand rendering may be done with all sorts of dots and lines to create texture, atmosphere, and shading. For example, a style may be created in the drawing as well as kinds of shading with lines such as freehand hatching and crosshatching.

6. Doing the Drafting for the Show
The ½-inch scale drafting is done mechanically with drawing instruments which include the T-square, triangles, compasses, French curves, dividers, scale rulers, and pencils. Freehand drawing is also a part of the drafting whenever foliage, drapery, natural ornamentation, figures, statuary, or portraits go on the drafting.

The basic list of drawings for the ½-inch-scale drafting includes:

1. Master ground plan.
2. Hanging section view.
3. Layout of soft scenery for the masking legs and borders, show curtains, sky drops, cycloramas, and black backup drop, all in ¼-inch scale, or when there is unusual or elaborate detail, ½-inch scale. Details may go to an even larger scale.
4. Front elevations of framed and soft scenery in the order the scenic units play, and also any necessary views to be put on the drawings for clarity in detail and for building. In addition to the front elevation of a particular item, other views of that item may appear on the same drawing. These views may include the ground plan, side view (or end view), top view, rear view, or section views (vertical, horizontal, or other). The drawings of details (which may be done in various scales) should be put along the side of the elevation drawings, if possi-

Right:
Stage designs by David Mitchell
ANNIE
Book by Thomas Meehan, based on "Little Orphan Annie" comic strip
Music by Charles Strouse
Lyrics by Martin Charnin
Choreographed by Peter Gennaro
Directed by Martin Charnin
Alvin Theatre, New York (1977)
(Photographs by David Mitchell)

Photographs, across:
1. Times Square, collage, early model.
2. Pen and ink background.
3. Collage, early model.
4. Moving buildings in "N.Y.C." number.
5. Arrival at the mansion—U.S. sliders.
6. Hooverville, finished model.
7. Collage, early model.
8. ANNIE 2 in Washington, D.C. (1989), Coney Island.

ble. Sometimes informal perspective sketches are made on a drawing to show a particular detail more clearly.

Dimensions are placed on the drawings not only for building the scenery, but also for positioning it on stage. All sorts of notes for building, support, hardware, and specific explanations are shown on the drafting to avoid any error in interpretation by the various people who will use the drawings for their part in the production.

7. Doing Figure Drawing for Costumes Designers draw human figures for male and female characters and also children for costume renderings. Views of costume figures include front, side, back, and costume details. The size of the drawn figures may average from 9 to 12 inches in height for the male, while figures shown in a group on one costume plate may be somewhat smaller.

8. Drawing Light Plots The layout for the light plot and section view is drawn mechanically with straight edges, triangles, pencils, rulers, compasses, and light instrument templates. The position of the lighting instruments and all necessary information are shown on the ½-inch scale drawings.

9. Duplicating the Ground Plan for Rehearsal The production stage manager and an assistant use the scenic designer's ½-inch scale ground plan to mark and tape the outline of the scenery on the floor of the rehearsal hall and to position the rehearsal furniture. If a

Stage design by Charles E. McCarry
A KISS IS JUST A KISS by Paul Foster
Directed by Don Scardino
Manhattan Punch Line Theatre
New York (1983)

ground plan is complicated, the scenic designer is sometimes asked to check to see if the taping is accurate.

10. Making Drawings for the Shop
Once the scenic shops have received complete copies of the designer's drawings in ½-inch scale, they make their own working drawings of the scenery for their carpenters and technicians to use in executing the scenery. The shop drawings specify breaks, hardware, materials, and methods. For example, a shop drawing of a show deck would indicate the 4'-0" by 8'-0" sections with tracking positions for moving units; how a large suspended ceiling piece breaks and where the

stiffeners for bracing are located on the back of it; and the rear view of an interior wall showing the position of stiles, rails, and toggles for hard flats covered with luan and duck.

11. Drawing the Full-Scale Detailed Pounces for One or More Repeats
Once a show is in a scenic shop, the scenic artists make full-scale drawings with charcoal on lengths of brown paper that have been taped together. These drawings are then perforated with a pounce wheel and the design is transferred (by pouncing a bag of powdered charcoal along the outline) onto a surface for painting, for building, or both. A full-scale pounce may be made for a perspective landscape design that goes on a translucent muslin backdrop 48'-0" wide by 28'-0" high, or for a repeat design for painting rosettes on a cornice, or for building and painting

terrace balustrades with statues on pedestals. When a show is a hit, paper pounces are usually kept to use for national and bus-and-truck companies. Drawing a full-scale paper pounce, perforating it, and rubbing the tiny holes with powdered charcoal not only saves time but it keeps from having to square off the lines on the actual muslin. It also minimizes the amount of charcoal that would go on the muslin as compared with using a charcoal stick held by a bamboo holder to draw the lines.

12. Drawing on Actual Scenic Surfaces for Painting All sorts of drawings are made directly on the surface materials because this is the simplest way to execute the design. There is no need to make a full-scale pounce drawing if there are to be no repeats of the particular design.

Drawing for painting may be done in charcoal for opaque hanging panels of street buildings in the 1900s; for laying out painted panels of wainscot designs in a Gothic library; or for marking and snapping lines to paint vertically striped wallpaper in a bedroom set.

13. Creating the Full-Scale Drawings to Go under Scenery Scenic artists in the scenic studio make full-scale drawings on lengths of gray bogus paper taped together (laid out flat on the floor) and then paint design outlines with dark latex or vinyl paint to go under openwork materials. The basic drawing in charcoal (a charcoal stick held in a long bamboo holder) is done on the gray paper after a grid of 2'-0" squares

Stage designs by Karl Eigsti
YENTL by Leah Napolin and
 Isaac Bashevis Singer
Conceived and directed by Robert Kalfin
Eugene O'Neill Theatre
New York (1975)

has been snapped in charcoal (charcoal powder put on a snapline or a charcoal stick rubbed on the line), and a comparable grid on the ½-inch paint sketch is marked off with a wax pencil on clear acetate. This painted drawing on gray paper shows through the openwork material, making it unnecessary to draw on the actual openwork material with charcoal; thus there is no need to worry about drawing in charcoal that could create smudges, dust or excess charcoal marks on the material. Painting is then done according to the details on the paint elevation(s).

Examples of subjects for drawing on gray paper to go under drops might be a design with an assemblage of cumulus clouds in a bright sky; a formal garden of topiary trees and hedges; or a large group of abstract shapes and forms. Gray bogus paper is also excellent for soaking up the water under muslin and gauze backdrops.

Stage design by Charles E. McCarry
HOOTERS by Ted Tally

Directed by Gary Pearle
Playwrights Horizons, New York (1978)

14. Doing Drawings for Scenery to Be Cut Out Sometimes rather than drawing a pounce, perforating it, and then transferring it to a surface with a bag of charcoal, a drawing is done directly on the wood or fabric to be cut out. This is often done during busy times in the scenic studio when carpenters do not always have time to wait for a complete full-scale drawing from the scenic artist. The designer's ½-inch scale drafting or the ½-inch scale paint elevation is used as a guide and reference.

For example, on a cutout set piece that consists of a group of painted rocks, a scenic artist may draw directly on the plywood. The carpenter first builds the framed flat set piece with an extra allowance of ¼-inch plywood on the outer edges, and after the drawing is done on the piece, the carpenter then cuts the excess plywood away. Another example would be when the scenic artist is asked to draw the details of an elaborate railing on a curved staircase that has been constructed of laminated wood. Here the scenic artist also draws directly on the curved laminated wood, and often the drawing is done with a paint brush. Designs such as swirling curlicues may be painted on the new wood, and then the unpainted wood gets cut away by the carpenter.

Still another example would be a piece of fabric on which designs are drawn, and then the excess is trimmed off. This could be a painted muslin cut backdrop of various overscale decorative signs that has the outer edges inked so they can be cut out as a complete unit and glued onto one large piece of scenic 1-inch square netting.

15. Making Full-Scale Drawings for Building Scenery and for Creating Sculpture While shop carpenters use the designer's ½-inch scale drawings to build most of the scenery, a scenic artist will make a full-scale drawing for the carpenters to use when an item is out of the ordinary and requires artistic drawing rather than basic straight and geometric shapes.

Working with the ½-inch scale drafting, the paint elevations, the model, and any additional research material furnished by the designer, plus additional research material from the studio, scenic artists often make complete full-scale drawings for various objects to be made by the shop carpenters working together with the scenic artists. This includes armatures and appropriate views for all sizes of sculpture (cherubs, angels, warriors, and idols), moving vehicles (three-dimensional chariots and surreys and profile cars), ornate metalwork (gates, sign supports, chandeliers, sconces, fences, and grills), and staircases (volutes and balustrades).

Stage design by Kenneth Foy
RAGS—Book by Joseph Stein
Music by Charles Strouse
Lyrics by Stephen Schwartz
Directed by Alan Johnson
A London project (1988)

16. Using a Projector to Make Drawings Occasionally a projector is used in the scenic studio to enlarge a detailed drawing to full scale when it is not too large. This requires adjusting the projector so the enlarged drawing is indeed in the appropriate scale. Drawing may be done with pencil or charcoal on brown paper, muslin, canvas, or other material.

SUPPLIES AND EQUIPMENT

Supplies and Equipment for a Design Studio

There is absolutely no end to the equipment a designer may put into a studio to make it work properly. Most designers tend to combine old equipment with new, especially with drafting tables, stools, and chairs. Ideally, a scenic designer's studio will have duplicate items available in almost all categories. Having more than one of the same item saves enormous time and of course is really useful when an object breaks or gets misplaced.

It is always nice to have a good working space, with room to spread the designs on tables. Space is especially important when doing a big show. Besides basic space, it is vital to have good lighting and ventilation.

Drafting Tables Drafting tables for a stage designer go from very plain traditional wooden models to lavish adjustable tables that operate simply at the touch of a lever. Some designers feel that an elaborate drafting table indicates success, while others could care less.

When buying a drafting table, high on the list of features to look for are a good-sized, adjustable, and sturdy top or board. Good drawing board sizes are 31 × 42 inches, 31 × 48 inches, or 38 × 48 inches. If there is a choice of spending a great deal of money on just one very expensive drafting table, remember that it is better to use the funds to purchase two so that an assistant can use the other one. A large sheet of white illustration board or heavy white paper is also good to use under tracing paper when doing drawings.

Drawing Boards Some designers work on the tops of drafting tables, others draw on drawing boards placed on top of drawing tables, and still others

draw on both. The nice thing about having several drawing boards is that you can work back and forth on different drawings without removing them from the board each time. Drawing boards may be wood, laminated, or hollowcore. Wooden drafting boards may range in size from 12 × 17 inches to 31 × 42 inches. Laminated drawing boards have plastic laminated on both sides and all edges. They come in white and black, and sizes for both start at 24 × 36 inches and go to 38 × 60 inches; size 44 × 72 inches also comes in white. Hollowcore drawing boards are lightweight and are available in sizes 12 × 17 inches to 24 × 36 inches.

A vinyl board cover may be used on the drawing board. The vinyl plastic gives a smooth, even finish to any surface. It comes with ivory on one side and green on the other, or white on one side and green on the other.

T-Squares, Parallel Rule, and Drafting Machine As with drawing boards a designer should have small, medium, and large T-squares. There is nothing more aggravating than having a T-square that does not work with the appropriate drawing board. T-squares with transparent clear plastic edges that are permanently fused to the wood are excellent to use. They come in these sizes: 18-inch, 24-inch, 30-inch, 36-inch, and 42-inch. Other T-squares come in steel and aluminum in various sizes.

A true-edge T-square guide for truing up the edges of drawing tables and boards is very useful to have.

A parallel ruling straight edge attaches to a drawing board for full or partial coverage. The spring-loaded ball bearings allow the blade to float over the working surface. The blade is made of ebony-finish phenolic with clear plastic edges. It is available with braided cable, hardware, and instructions. The parallel ruling straight edge comes in these sizes: 30-inch, 36-inch, 42-inch, 60-inch, and 72-inch.

The drafting machine is a great tool for reading measurements and making lines of any angle at any position on a drawing board or drafting table. The drafting machine is a T-square, triangle, ruler, and protractor all in one unit.

Drafting Papers Like other products, drafting papers vary from store to store.

Designers find drafting papers they like to use just as they do with pencils and sketching boards. Rolls of drafting papers can be purchased in these sizes.

21 in. × 20 yd.	42 in. × 20 yd.
24 in. × 20 yd.	36 in. × 50 yd.
30 in. × 20 yd.	42 in. × 50 yd.
36 in. × 20 yd.	

Papers also can be bought in these pad sizes: 9 × 12-inch, 11 × 14-inch, 14 × 17-inch, 19 × 24-inch, and 24 × 36-inch. When selecting paper to do drafting, you usually come out ahead by buying rolls of paper that are 36 inches wide because you can turn the paper and do a 24 × 36 or 36 × 48-inch drawing with the same roll. It is always good to have extra drafting paper on hand.

The more transparent the paper and the darker the pencil lead plus the heavier the stroke of the pencil, the more contrast you will get when the drafted drawing is printed. But some designers prefer a paper that is not so thin that it tears easily, and feel that it is worth buying good paper to do good drafting on because in the long run it saves time.

The following papers come in rolls and pads and are available at Sam Flax in New York City, Atlanta, and Tampa.

1. *Flax No. 38 Tracing Paper.* Highly transparent, lightweight professional-quality tracing paper. Strong 25-lb. smooth surface is ideal for quick color pencil, crayon, and marker sketches. For rough sketches, preliminary drawings, and overlays.
2. *Flax No. 51 H Parchment Tracing Paper.* Heavyweight, 32 lb. tracing parchment with excellent transparency and finish. Stronger and heavier than regular tracing paper. Smooth finish accepts pencil and ink and erases easily without smudges.
3. *Flax No. 1 Tracing Vellum.* Heavyweight, transparent, natural tracing vellum. Ideal medium for pen-and-ink and pencil drawings. Will accept a light wash of watercolors or liquid dyes. Has excellent erasing qualities, leaving no smudge marks.
4. *Flax Planprint Tracing Vellum.* 100 percent rag tracing vellum for engineering and technical drawings. Planprint, a strong 16 lb. vellum, accepts repeated erasures, leaving no ghost marks. Ideal medium for pencil and

Geometric Shapes

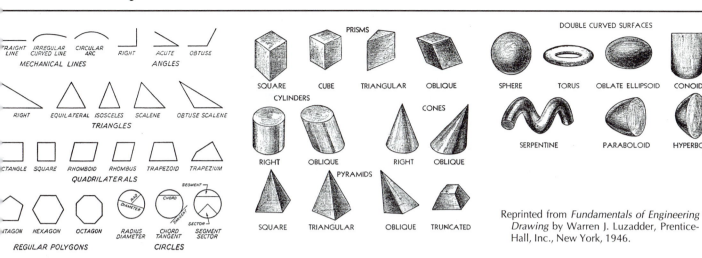

MECHANICAL LINES: STRAIGHT LINE, IRREGULAR CURVED LINE, CIRCULAR ARC

ANGLES: RIGHT, ACUTE, OBTUSE

TRIANGLES: RIGHT, EQUILATERAL, ISOSCELES, SCALENE, OBTUSE SCALENE

QUADRILATERALS: RECTANGLE, SQUARE, RHOMBOID, RHOMBUS, TRAPEZOID, TRAPEZIUM

REGULAR POLYGONS: PENTAGON, HEXAGON, OCTAGON

CIRCLES: RADIUS DIAMETER, CHORD TANGENT, SEGMENT SECTOR

PRISMS: SQUARE, CUBE, TRIANGULAR, OBLIQUE

CYLINDERS: RIGHT, OBLIQUE

CONES: RIGHT, OBLIQUE

PYRAMIDS: SQUARE, TRIANGULAR, OBLIQUE, TRUNCATED

DOUBLE CURVED SURFACES: SPHERE, TORUS, OBLATE ELLIPSOID, CONOID, SERPENTINE, PARABOLOID, HYPERBOLOID

Reprinted from *Fundamentals of Engineering Drawing* by Warren J. Luzadder, Prentice-Hall, Inc., New York, 1946.

Geometric Solids

1. Sphere. 2. Tetrahedron. 3. Cube.
4. Octahedron. 5. Icosahedron.
6. Dodecahedron. 7. Great dodecahedron.

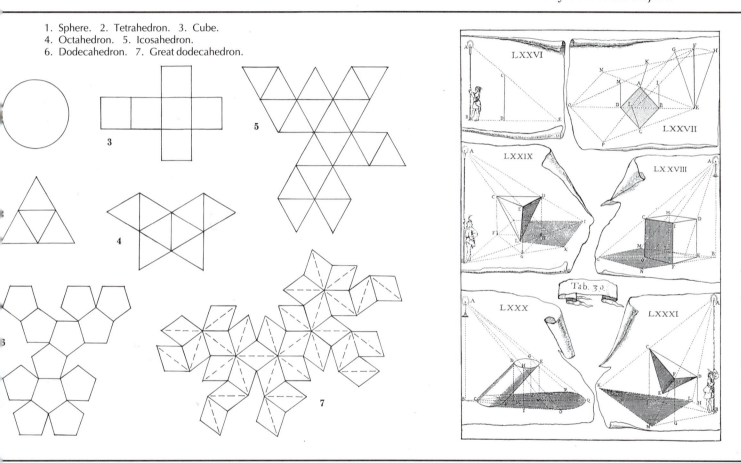

Shadows Made by Geometric Objects

Constructing Often-Used Geometric Shapes: 1. Pentagon; 2. Hexagon; 3. Octagon

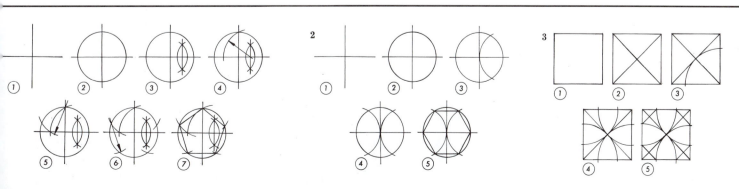

Stage designs by Tony Walton
VALMOUTH by Sandy Wilson
Directed by Vida Hope
Saville Theatre, London (1958)
York Theatre, New York (1960)

Top: Hare Hatch House.
Bottom: village square scene.
Opposite, top: Hare Hatch tea party.
Opposite, bottom: chapel scene.

pen application and will not discolor with age or use.

Other drafting papers, which may be found at Art Brown and Bro., Inc., in New York City, include the following:

1. *Azon Tracing Vellum.* An ultra transparent paper suited for drafting and engineering drawings. Free of oils and odors, and has unusual resilience and durability. Takes pen and ink, washes, and pencil. 100 percent rag, 16-lb. weight.
2. *Superior Tracing Vellum.* A heavyweight, extremely transparent tracing vellum. Finest quality.
3. *Vidalon Tracing Vellum.* An imported vellum paper, fine tooth, no oil or odor, in rolls.
4. *K & E Albanene Prepared Tracing Rolls.* This offers a special surface designed to provide high-quality drawings for clear reproductions.
5. *Madison Tracing Paper.* An architect's sketching and tracing paper. Yellow color, very thin, and extremely transparent.
6. *Lexington Tracing Paper.* Thin, extra-clear transparent paper for all tracing purposes.

Graphite Paper This is a thin transfer paper that is coated with graphite. When doing a rendering, it is good for transferring the drawing for a set design on tracing paper onto illustration board or heavy paper. The graphite lines can be erased as easily as pencil lines.

Pencils for Drafting Drawing pencils used by designers vary considerably. One designer may do drafting with a 2H, 3H, or 4H pencil while another may use a No. 2 or No. 3 standard writing pencil with eraser. The scenic designer learns how to use pencils to vary the weight of the line and to make the line light, medium, or heavy.

The degree of hardness in drawing pencils is indicated by a standard code shown on each pencil. These may be in 17 degrees from 9H (extremely hard) through 6B (very soft). The selection, of course, is determined by the purpose in mind, and the use of drawing pencils varies with every designer. For drawing, a designer may choose graphite drawing pencils such as Venus Drawing Pencils and Turquoise 375 Graphite Pencils, or a lead holder that has leads inserted in it. The best way to find out how any drawing pencil will work on the tracing paper is to try a sample on the paper and then have it printed.

Erasers and Eraser Shields Among the many erasers available are Mars-Plastic drafting eraser, Eberhard Faber erasers, Pentel retractable erasers, battery-operated erasers, gum erasers, and self-sharpening paper wrapped erasers in the shape of a pencil with a sharp point for accuracy.

Eraser shields are standard, thin, flexible stainless steel shields with varied-shaped openings to protect the areas surrounding the desired erasure.

Drawing Instruments Drawing instruments may be purchased individually or in sets. Sometimes items in a set go unused, particularly if the set includes pens for drawing in ink. It may be better to invest in duplicate or different sizes of the same drawing instrument and purchase them separately. Necessary instruments include bow compasses, bow compass combinations, grade school compasses, beam compasses, dividers, and proportional dividers.

Protractors Clear plastic protractors are easy to read and come in both circular (360-degree) and semicircular (180-degree) shapes, in sizes of 4, 6, and 8 inches.

Plastic Drawing Templates Numerous plastic templates are made for drawing with pencil or pen. The sizes of the templates vary. The subjects of the templates include circles, ellipses, squares, diamonds, triangles, furniture, general-purpose, alphabet, lettering guides, and others.

Scale Rules and Rulers The architect's triangular scale rule is constantly needed when drafting, and a flat scale rule is useful. In addition, a designer should also have metric scale rules. Other items to have on hand for measuring are steel rulers in 12-inch, 24-inch, and 36-inch sizes. Aluminum rulers are available in 12, 18, 24, 30, 36, 48, 60, and 72 inches.

Transparent Triangles Various sizes of 30-degree–60-degree and 45-degree transparent plastic triangles are wonderful to have. The most practical sizes range from 6 to 18 inches, but even smaller sizes are good to have on hand. Steel and aluminum triangles can be used as well. An adjustable triangle of transparent plastic is available in which any angle from 0 to 90 degrees can be drawn direct from the base line.

Transparent Drawing Curves There are a number of transparent plastic curves, or French curves, that can be purchased individually or in sets. Other tools for drawing curves include an adjustable ship curve, which is a plastic curve that can be finger-shaped to the exact curve in seconds; and Copenhagen ship curves, which are fifty-six curves in a set. Also available is a C-Thru transparent flexible curve that has one side fully divided in millimeters with the other size graduated in inches.

Tapes and Dispensers Drafting tape is used to hold drawings on the board or table. It comes in widths of ½ inch, ¾ inch, and 1 inch. Masking tape is great for all-purpose paint masking, and it is available in widths of ¼ inch, ½ inch, ¾ inch, 1 inch, 1½ inches, 2 inches, and 3 inches. Scotch Magic Transparent Tape is excellent for repairing tears in drawings and for many other uses in the studio. A wide variety of dispensers is made for these various tapes. In addition, Scotch Double-Coated Tape is good for mounting and when a two-sided adhesive is needed.

Lamps and Lighting Designers have a choice of working in natural light, with incandescent lamps or fluorescent lamps, or with a combination of incandescent and fluorescent lamps. Magnifier lamps with either incandescent or fluorescent lighting are also helpful when doing detail drawing and model work.

Tracing Boxes While it is ideal to have a large table with the top as a tracing box, designers also use portable light tracing boxes that rest on any work space. They are especially practical for copy work, tracing drawings, and looking at color slides. Porta-Trace Portable Light Units are made in these sizes: 11 × 18 inches, 16 × 18 inches, 18 × 24 inches, and 14 × 36 inches.

Drafting Chairs and Stools There is an enormous range of styles in drafting chairs and stools. Usually, an adjustable chair on casters is the most practical. In choosing a drafting chair, look for an attractive one that has a comfortable seat and an adjustable height.

Storing Prints and Drawings Drawings are stored in cardboard tubes and plastic tubes with caps, in five-drawer flat files of wood and metal, and in upright roll files. Available studio space often determines the kind and size of storage.

Tape Measures Tape measures are always needed for measuring small objects, such as furniture and props, and for getting dimensions on stage. It is always good to have a 6-foot tape measure and a longer one of 25 or 50 feet.

Miscellaneous Items The designer is expected to have such items on hand as a stapler and staples, rubber bands, paper clips, designer's stamp, personalized stationery, envelopes, mailing cardboard, address and telephone number list, file folders, file cabinet(s), business cards, and index cards.

DRAFTING

Because so very many visual decisions must be made on the drawing board, every designer should know how to draw and draft his or her own stage designs. It is on the drawing board that the design begins to become a reality. And it is here that the designs development becomes a melding of the artistic and the practical, and the technical aspects of the stage setting are resolved. Drafting involves much more than merely making technical drawings.

While beautiful sketches can sell the visual idea of the show, it is the actual drafting of the sets with scaled dimensions and notations that tells whether or not a show will physically work on stage and whether it will cost too much to build and paint.

When doing the drafting for a show, common sense and basic logic take precedence over any dictatorial drawing rules that you may feel compelled to follow. Remember, if the scenery units are drawn well and clearly and it is explained on the drawings how the units are to be executed, no one is going to say, "But you have not done this according to the standard rules of drafting!" Each individual production is unique unto itself, and different rules apply to each show.

Perhaps the most important aspect of the designing process is proportion. This element of design is dealt with at the drawing board. Proportion of an individual scenic unit pertains to:

1. The overall relationship of the height to the width to the depth.
2. The relationship of one scenic unit to another in the stage space.
3. The relationship of the details—their size and placement—to the overall dimensions of the scenic unit.
4. The relationship of one group of scenic units to another group when they are seen on stage under designed stage lighting.

Deciding What Views to Put on the Drafting

If there is ever any question in your mind whether to include something on a drawing, then it is usually best to go ahead and put it down on paper. It is always better to overdraft and overdimension a bit rather than the reverse. Having a drawing or note repeated on another sheet often makes it easier for the head carpenter in the scenic shop to double-check what you really want. Also, remember that other carpenters in the shop do not always have a full set of drawings available. Even a single sheet of a blueprinted drawing is sometimes cut up in the scenic studio and given to several different carpenters to build from.

When drafting a unit of scenery, it is generally expected that a front elevation, a ground plan, and an end view will always be shown. This makes it clear to everyone who will depend on the drafting to know what the scenic designer wants, and ensures that the scenic designer will not be disappointed in the final result.

In addition, it is frequently necessary to show a section view of certain shapes and units in order to specify how they are to be built, because it is not obvious from looking at the other views. This *section view*, or *section drawing*, of a piece of scenery is made as if by taking a knife and cutting through an object; the drawing indicates what the piece would look like after the knife has sliced through it. This "cutting" of an object may also be done vertically, horizontally, or on angles if necessary. The various section views on a sheet of drafting are differentiated by section lines to show contrast. These are usually parallel lines drawn on 45, 30, or 60 degrees, and the spacing varies as well as the width of the lines.

Section views can be drawn from the exact center of an object, near center, at a quarter or a third of the object, or anywhere it is necessary to show specific building details. Typically, section views are shown for three-dimensional tree trunks or rock formations or statues. Among the most common examples of section drawings on drafting are those for moldings in an interior set.

A word of caution about becoming too elaborate and flamboyant when making section drawings on the drafting: Sometimes when the heads of the scenic shops see involved section drawings, they get the impression that a particular piece of scenery will be expensive to build and therefore costly in time and labor, not to mention materials. When this is the case, a piece of scenery can have an exorbitant price placed on it at the bid session, and then the producer will insist it be cut. Remember, theatrical scenery most often should be devised to create an illusion on stage rather than to duplicate museum pieces.

Besides making a front elevation, a ground plan, an end (or side) view, or a section view, you may also have a drawing of the opposite end, a top view, a back or rear view, and for a special item there may be a view looking from under a scenic object.

Rather than creating a profusion of drawings showing different views of an object, it is often much simpler to do a basic freehand perspective sketch nearby the elevations or plan of an object to show just exactly what is wanted. Sometimes two or three informal perspective sketches are easier to do and are clearer than a section view.

The beginning designer soon learns about the various views to be done in drafting as well as the various widths and heavinesses of lines. While much of basic theatrical drafting is done with good clean medium-weight lines, lines such as outlines of objects and cutting lines are heavier. Broken lines denoting hidden parts may be medium to light in weight, and dimension lines are indicated with very light lines. The new designer should always look at illustrations of different kinds of lines to study what they are used to indicate on a drawing.

Doing a Schematic Drawing of a Multiset Production

A great way for a scenic designer to convey initial ideas about the scenery is to make a schematic layout of the production. The layout is usually made on a single sheet of tracing paper, and has small drawings in ⅛-inch scale of the scenery for the entire show. While this kind of preliminary presentation is not expected from every scenic designer, it is an excellent way for the designer to show just what is happening scenically and to get more concrete ideas about the visual elements, the overall size, the way the show moves, and something of what it will cost.

The schematic drawing contains a series of small drawings of front elevations (⅛-inch), and accompanying these individual elevations are ground plans (⅛-inch) to go with the eleva-

Assembly drawing by Julia Rogoff of the main unit (face and hand) for MIDSUMMER MAR- RIAGE, designed by Robin Don and directed by John Copley for the San Francisco Opera (1983). The face and hand were made of Sty- rofoam. A steel staircase curved around the stage left side of the face.

These notes were on the drawing for the stair assembly procedure.
1. *Erect lower section first.*
   a. Pickup points and cable lengths:
      (1) Between treads 2 and 3 use 25′ cable, doubled.
      (2) Between treads 7 and 8 use 10′ cable.
      (3) Between treads 15 and 16 use 5′ cable.
   b. Raise stair section above trim.
   c. Insert support pipes (trees) with foot pads attached.
   d. Lower onto marked footprints on boxes.
   e. Bolt down (⅜ × 2½ hex bolts), 16 re- quired.
2. *Erect upper section.*
   a. Pickup points and cable lengths:
      (1) Between treads 17 and 18 use 10′ cable.
      (2) Between treads 22 and 23 use 16′ cable, doubled.
      (3) Between treads 28 and 29 use 5′ cable.
   b. Raise stair section to trim and hook up- per plate onto receiver plate.
   c. Align flanges between stair sections and insert bolts; *do not tighten:* (4) ¾ × 3 hex required.
   d. Insert bolts in top end of receiver plate: (3) ½ × 1½ hex; (2) ½ × 3½ hex.
   e. Insert support post (tree trunk).
   f. Tighten all bolts.
3. *Install hand rail posts and rail.*

tions whenever they are needed. Something like a plan of a backdrop would not be necessary to show. All drawings are neatly labeled but are not dimensioned since this is a schematic. However, these drawings are laid out so they look crisp, clean, and clear. Scenic items are named and simply described with short notes as to mate- rials, textures, or effects. Examples: velour, pressed metal, or scrim. Things like practical doors are labeled.

Items are also labeled according to how they move: the fence flies, the small wagon is pushed on by hand, the hanger unit flies, the profiled building is on elevators, the wagon unit is winched, the travelers work manually, the furniture is preset, the walls pivot, and the pallets are winched.

In addition, the schematic layout may include a list of translucent and opaque backdrops and scrims. It may also tell the number of winches in the deck, and the number of hoist winches on the grid, plus any other data.

A schematic drawing may be accom- panied by a preliminary ground plan and a section drawing, both made in ½-inch scale.

Checklist of Drawings to Be Drafted for a Proscenium Production

The drawings to be drafted for a pro- scenium production may be made for (1) one setting, (2) two or more settings, (3) a unit set with a change in plugs,

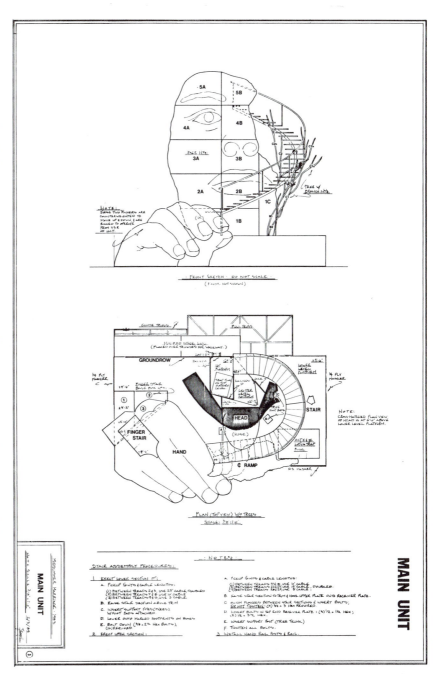

110 draperies, furniture or props, or (4) a simultaneous scene set in which two or more sets are situated on the stage at the same time. The following lists of drawings may be used as a guide when applicable.

One Setting May be an interior box set or exterior garden or other.

1. Master ground plan in ½-inch scale.
2. Hanging section drawing in ½-inch scale.
3. Portal drawing in ½-inch scale with plan and side view or section.
4. Soft scenery in ¼-inch scale; includes all masking, legs, borders, tabs, plain backdrops, and reflector drops.
5. Drawing of ceiling pieces in ½-inch scale as seen when on stage looking up at the ceiling; also side view or sections when needed.
6. Front elevations of all flats in ½-inch scale, with plan and section on same drawing when necessary.
7. Drawing of floor or ground cloth in ½-inch scale.
8. Details of molding, woodwork, cornice, wainscoting, or other in scales of 1 inch, 1½ inches, 3 inches, or full, depending on the subject. Details may also be put on the same sheet.
9. Drawings of detailed backdrops, ground rows or other scenery in ½-inch scale.

Two or More Settings May be two interior or exterior sets, wing and border sets, unit set with changes, or multiset on one stage.

1. Master ground plan in ½-inch scale.
2. Hanging section drawing in ½-inch scale.
3. Individual ground plans of each set with positions of furniture and/or props. Half-inch scale is usually preferred.
4. Portal drawings in ½-inch scale with plan and side view or section.
5. Soft scenery in ¼-inch scale; includes all masking, legs, borders, tabs, plain backdrops, reflector drops, plain scrims, or gauzes. Drawings of all show curtains in ½-inch scale.
6. Front elevations of all flats in ½-inch scale, with plan and section on same drawing when necessary.
7. Front elevations in ½-inch scale of all three-dimensional pieces, including sculptured figures, trees, boats, etc., plus plan and side view or section on same drawing.
8. Drawings of all detailed backdrops in ½-inch scale.
9. Drawing of stage deck layout or of painted ground cloth in ½-inch scale.
10. Drawing of furniture and props in scales of 1-inch, 1½-inch, or 3-inch scale.

Drafting a Single-Set Production

The average single set usually takes less time to draft than a show having two or more sets. The drawings for a one-set show include: (1) the ground plan; (2) the hanging section view; (3) the front elevations of all the scenic units accompanied by plan, side, or end view and when necessary, top view; and (4) any details. All of these drawings are normally done in ½-inch scale, except the drawings of the details. For obvious reasons the detail drawings are usually larger and may range from $1'' = 1'-0''$ to $1½'' = 1'-0''$ to $3'' = 1'-0''$ to full scale for items such as molding samples.

The exception to this rule is a drawing for soft scenery that has very little or no detail work on it. Then it is usually done in ¼-inch scale. Another exception to doing all the drawings in ½-inch scale is when they are all drafted in ¼-inch scale. Quarter-inch scale is used when details are not too heavy and when the drawings are accompanied by a lot of verbal discussion on certain specifics of drawing and building. Doing elevations in ¼-inch scale can be quite risky, to say the least. However, every designer tends to remember doing ground plans and elevations on ¼-inch graph paper for stock (and sometimes regional) productions when there was not much time available to do them. But you certainly would not want to do the drafting in ¼-inch scale for a first-class production where substantial money and time are involved.

When drafting either a single- or multiple-set production, you should put everything on the drafting so that each item can be bid on for executing the scenery and furniture. This is especially vital in the commercial theatre.

The resident, repertory, or stock theatre is another matter, simply because stock items are used over and over again. Nevertheless, they must also be shown on the drafting so that everyone involved with the production knows what is going on. Such stock items include masking legs and borders, portals, cycloramas, ground rows, platforms, and backdrops.

Drafting a Multiple-Set Production

Naturally, the drafting for a production with two or more sets requires more time and drawings than drafting for a single set. Much of the time is always spent organizing the offstage space as well as that onstage. Storage space must be planned for every piece of scenery. On a large show packed with scenery, even more concentrated planning is required. The drawings for scenery on multiple-set shows follow the same pattern as for single-set productions, except there is a great deal more to draft. The necessary drawings for multiple-set shows are: (1) the master ground plan; (2) the hanging section drawing; (3) the front elevations with other necessary views of all the flats, portals, wagons, and any other scenic units in the production; (4) the soft scenery—backdrops, gauzes, legs, borders, and any decorative panels; (5) floor drawings of the ground cloth or deck; and (6) any details or other appropriate drawings to tell how to build the scenery in the scenic shop and also to tell how to position it on stage.

The master ground plan for a multiset show should indicate the individual ground plans for all the sets superimposed, one over the other. The reasons for this are (1) to see whether all of the various sets will fit in the space, and (2) how all the sets will work with the positioning of the lighting instruments. The master ground plan should also indicate visually and practically the contrast and versatility of each plan, so that one differs from the other in respect to position of entrances and exits, walls, overall widths, depths, and so on.

The ground plans for the different sets can be shown by varying the drawn lines as much as possible. The multiple sets can each be drawn with a heavy line, a medium line, or a light line. They can also be indicated by several sizes of broken lines so that the difference from one set to another is completely clear. For example, the pattern for one set may be a long dash, a short dash, and a long dash; for another set, one long dash and two short dashes; for another, two long dashes and two short dashes; and so on. Dots can also be used with long dashes and with short dashes in any number of combinations. Often designers find that it works best to improvise with their own patterns.

Drawing Separate Ground Plans of Individual Sets

Separate drawings should be made of each ground plan in a multiset show if the master ground plan becomes too crowded and there are so many items of furniture and props that it is impossible to see everything clearly on the master plan.

These drawings should be done in the same ½-inch scale as the master ground plan. This is also as a consideration for the lighting designer, who also works in ½-inch scale. The individual drawings need not include as much offstage detail as the master plan unless the scenery, lights, or scenic storage require it. Prints of the separate drawings of the ground plans in ½-inch scale should be stapled between the master ground plan and the hanging section drawing in the set of printed drawings.

Checking Out Scenic Traffic Patterns

Even if the position of the scenery for multiple sets is worked out well on the ground plan, the traffic patterns for moving on and off stage quickly and smoothly must always be checked out. The producers and the production carpenter need to have the assurance that all of the shifting is within workable possibilities. It is up to the scenic designer to resolve the shifts (with the production carpenter) and to place the units offstage on the master plan.

Planning for scenery to hang overhead and fly in and out during the show is one of the best and most efficient methods of changing scenery. The scenery is automatically well organized by the fact that it is designated to fly and remains in that position during the performance.

Scenery on the floor that is tracked off and on also must have its own definitive storage area offstage. Units that are specified to store offstage (left,

right, and upstage) must also be able to move off and on quickly. Such scenic pieces may be staircases, windows, doors, alcoves, backing units, pianos, tables, or sofas. All of these units may be mounted on platforms with swivel or fixed casters or may just have casters on the individual piece. But the point is that all these units must be able to be moved around each other with sufficient space for the stagehands to walk while shifting them.

There are two simple methods for proving to yourself and others that the items stored offstage can move off and on appropriately. The first method is to make small ½-inch scale portable ground plans of the individual scenic pieces cut from heavy paper or illustration board. These cutouts can be easily moved around on the master ground plan. A second method is to use the built three-dimensional pieces from the ½-inch scale model to move around on the master ground plan. Both the cutout pieces and the built model pieces should be marked with the number of the act and scene in which they are to play onstage. Either method clearly indicates to everyone involved in this aspect of the production that all scenic units will fit in the storage space and, at the same time, be easily and quickly moved on and off stage during performance.

Of course, the model is ideal for judging the overall three-dimensional aspects of the moving scenic units. But the pieces of heavy paper are also good when placed on a flat master plan and moved around to see how offstage units are working. For instance, suppose you have three wagon units on swivel casters in various shapes on the ground plan. These may be fairly sizable units in terms of width and depth. Let us say that the average size of a platform is 5'-0" by 7'-0" by 1'-0" high. By placing the heavy paper pieces on the plan, you can tell the order of storage so that a piece does not get locked in and five other items have to be moved around to get it out.

By moving these pieces of paper around on plan you can see the best possibilities for the order of offstage storage. You can also see whether the units will turn corners, move around each other, and go between portal legs, ground rows, and any velour masking legs and still miss each other when they do the reverse move and go back into storage after playing onstage.

When cutting out the pieces of paper to make ground plans of the moving pieces, always remember to calculate and compensate for the space needed above for scenery like the overhang on balconies and on roofs.

If scenic units are too large to work in the offstage areas, then they may have to be made to break in smaller sections to move and store properly. Part of a vertical piece of scenery on a wagon unit may have to be redesigned to fly or fold back, or whatever. The point is to rethink and rework the unit properly so that the visual look and the playing space are not sacrificed just because the scenery storage space is difficult. That is simply a part of the challenge in the designing of a big show.

Still other practical aspects must be considered here. In resolving the final space arrangements on the master plan, always study the offstage walking paths for the actors and staff to see if people can move swiftly and pass each other as they leave the onstage area and go offstage and vice versa during performance. Also make sure that an upstage crossover space is available for everyone to use. And, again, always think of the space that must be kept available for the positioning of lighting instruments.

Of course, if a designer is working in a theatre with a stage having wonderful proportions, then offstage problems may not exist. The Ahmanson Theatre in Los Angeles, for example, has superb working stage facilities and a spacious backstage area.

The exact organization of the units in storage often must be rehearsed two or three times by the stagehands in the theatre to see what works best. In spite of all your work and preplanning, some alterations may have to be made in your storage plans. Do not get uptight about how scenery is arranged backstage to accommodate the crew, because it is they who have to make your scenery work during performance.

Drawing the House Curtain on Plan

When drawing a house curtain on the plan, always follow this sequence: Draw (1) the proscenium opening, (2) the smoke pocket with the safety curtain (not all theatres have this safety curtain), and (3) the house curtain or main curtain. Always try to get an accurate dimension from the back of the proscenium wall to the actual horizontal center line of the house curtain when it is hanging so that it can be shown as accurately as possible on plan. This broken line representing the house curtain on plan is drawn parallel to the proscenium opening and is used to indicate the position of a flat (or stretched-out) house curtain without any fullness to speak of. If the house curtain you are dealing with has a lot of fullness in it, then use the basic straight line on plan as a guide for the center line, but draw and indicate the fullness with a curved zigzag line. In other words, will the actual hanging house curtain need a 9-inch width of space or more running across stage? Naturally, the type of curtain makes a difference when positioning portals or other scenery, because you do not want the back of the house curtain to be so tight that it rubs against the face of the first portal (painted or unpainted) every time the curtain flies in and out. Also, being on the ground plan, the house curtain can be checked out by the production carpenter.

Not Using a House Curtain

Even when the designer and director have decided that the house curtain will not be used in a production, it still should be shown on plan with the space that it takes up because nothing else can work in that space. Usually house curtains are flown out or tracked off or tabbed up and are left in the offstage space. Taking them down is not normally done because of the expense in time and labor. The storage problem and the chance that a curtain may get damaged in the process of being taken down, stored, and put back up make removing it too big a risk.

Sight Lines

While directors are generally aware of good and bad sight lines in the theatre, sometimes you will work with a director who is a sight-line enthusiast, to say the least. Sooner or later you will find a director who does not know how to cope with the subject of sight lines. He or she will want to be able to see every scene from every seat in the house. When you find yourself in this situation, there is nothing you can do but try to be calm and pacify the director by promising to do everything you can

to design scenery that will satisfy him or her. Even though the patrons buying tickets may know that they will miss something in buying poor seats, you must nevertheless support the director as much as possible. Obviously, a designer who can design a set in the commercial theatre where every seated patron can see all the action is creating nothing short of a miracle.

It is the responsibility of the designer as a member of a collaborating team to show as much support toward the director as possible. Making the director feel very secure about the physical production is necessary and is what some theatre artists and craftspeople refer to as "hand-holding."

Even if you have plan and section views of the theatre, it is often easier and simpler to go to the theatre with your colleagues to view sight lines and to decide on sizes, shapes, and positions of scenery and props. To check out the sight lines, sit in the center of the first orchestra row, then the center of the last orchestra row, then various extreme side seats left and right. Next, go to the mezzanine, and the first and second balconies, and look at the stage from the first and last rows center, then the extreme left and right seats. Everyone involved usually concurs on which sight lines are the best.

A good example of collaborative planning was the pre-production for *Dracula* (1977) at the Martin Beck Theatre in New York. When the scenery was being designed, the director, producers, and designers met at the theatre to look at (1) the sight-line positions of the five basic walls of the arch stage setting, (2) the height of the flats (30 feet), and (3) the height of the show portal opening (22 feet). Since there was no show playing in the theatre at the time, the task of looking at various marked positions on an empty stage was simple to accomplish. The height of the show portal opening was simulated by taking out the house curtain so the bottom of it stopped at 22 feet. To do this, a steel tape was attached with a large safety pin to the bottom of the house curtain and then it was flown out to 22 feet.

At another time, the director, producer, and designers went again to the Martin Beck to check the tilted angle of the upstage end of Dracula's coffin lid. Since the moment when the lid was lifted off was a very dramatic moment in the show, it was important that all

of the audience in the orchestra could see Dracula's face. This viewing of the coffin's position was simulated by having two people hold three pieces of 1 × 3-inch board in the measured angles on stage while the director went into the auditorium to check the sight lines from various seats in the orchestra.

Figuring the Masking for a Production

It is standard procedure in the proscenium theatre to mask the outer edges of the main stage setting with units of scenery so the audience does not see where the set ends and also does not see backstage. (Of course, there are productions that avoid masking of any kind.) To figure what masking (secondary scenic units) is necessary and where it is to be positioned, you need to use:

1. Your master gound plan of the show, together with the plan of the stage and a plan of the auditorium
2. Your hanging section drawing of the show, together with a section drawing of the stage and auditorium

Experience will quickly teach you that when figuring masking, you usually are planning horizontal and vertical masking at the same time. In other words, you are concentrating simultaneously on both the sight lines and masking problems.

Figuring the Masking without House Plans

While it is very helpful to have an accurate plan and section drawing of the house, it is not always possible to obtain these drawings. Sometimes management does not have them. The next best thing is to visit the house to look at the stage from a seat in all sections of the theatre. But what can you do if

Setting by Karen Schulz

even this is not possible because the theatre is in a distant city?

Experience, again, is very helpful in figuring out the masking for a theatre where there are no available drawings (ground plan and hanging section) or if distance prevents you from visiting the theatre.

Even though you can figure sight lines and masking fairly well from the stage dimensions alone, there are other sources to draw on so you feel secure about the house conditions. An alternative is to get on the telephone with the right people and ask a lot of specific questions concerning the physical setup of the theatre house. Persons to chat with about this are the house carpenter, the stage manager, the house manager, or the producer in the particular city where the theatre is located. Another alternative is to consult local craftspersons and colleagues in your own city who have worked in that particular theatre. Designers usually are more than happy to share any built-in problems about a particular theatre with you. Fortunately, there are also theatre houses that present no or relatively few problems to deal with in regard to masking.

Basic Ways of Dealing with Masking

The most accepted methods of masking for the proscenium theatre tend to be:

1. Mask for the first row.
2. Mask for the third or fourth row.
3. No masking requirements (open back wall, exposed stage lights, offstage scenery, hanging pipes and cables).

Most producers will accept third- or fourth-row masking. However, it is important to clarify with management what is considered acceptable masking. (Directors do not always get involved in this aspect of the design.) This should be done in the early stages of the designing process rather than waiting until the actual scenery gets on stage.

Even after the masking has been discussed and a verbal agreement has been reached in early meetings, this may often be forgotten along the way. So the idea here is to figure on as much masking as you feel is needed for the production. Remember, you can always cut certain masking pieces after the bid session because of cost. And in this way, if a producer complains about specific masking not being there on stage, you can simply emphasize that it was deleted to cut added cost after the first bid. This kind of incident can happen fairly often, and when it does, you are only protecting yourself as a practical and perceptive designer. A displeased producer can certainly add the cut masking back in the show, and occasionally this does happen.

While some producers insist on first-row masking, others are happy with masking for the third or fourth row. They know that third- or fourth-row masking means that the lighting instruments do not have to be positioned quite so high, and borders do not have to be constructed to be so high. Again, experienced theatregoers who elect to sit in the first three or four rows undoubtedly know that they are going to see certain lighting instruments and offstage pieces of scenery that the rest of the house does not see, but they obviously do not mind this because seeing the actors and staging up close is their most important priority.

Drawings by Karen Schulz
THE INSPECTOR GENERAL by Nikolai Gogol
Directed by Liviu Ciulei
Circle in the Square Theatre, New York (1979)

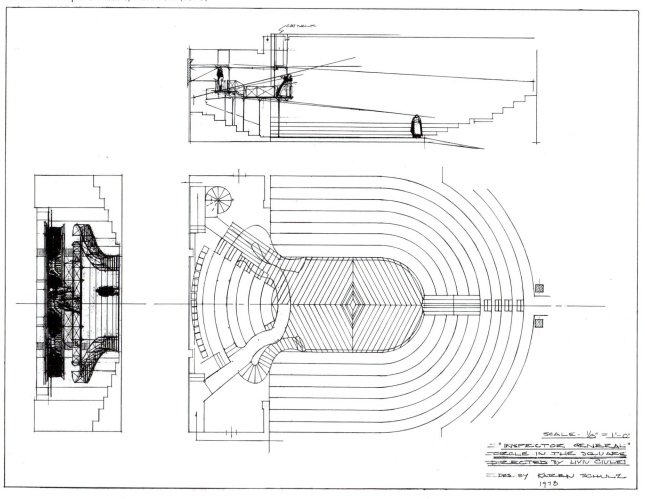

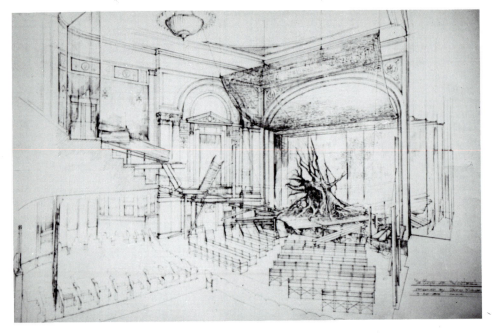

Drawings by David Mitchell
THE BOYS OF WINTER by John Pielmeier
Directed by Michael Lindsay-Hogg
Biltmore Theatre, New York (1985)

Drawings (top to bottom and top to bottom, opposite page):
1. The set with in-house insulation.
2. Section of the set and theatre.
3. Section of in-house insulation.
4.–6. Drawings of the tree.
(Photographs by David Mitchell)

The Center of Lines

While it is necessary to know the lengths of pipes above the stage for hanging scenery in the particular theatre where your production is to be presented, it is also essential for planning that you know the distance from the center of one hanging pipe line to the center of the next. The center of one pipe to the center of the next pipe is commonly 6 inches or 4½ inches, but it may be 1 foot or more. You sometimes hear of scenery on 3-inch centers, but that can be risky. For 4½-inch centers, the dimensions would be 0″, 4½″, 9″, 1′-1½″, 1′-6″, 1′-10½″, and so on. For 6-inch centers the dimensions would be 0″, 6″, 1′-0″, 1′-6″, 2′-0″, and so on.

Information on centers of lines can be found on the two drawings that theatres should furnish: the theatre ground plan and the theatre hanging section drawing. By knowing the distance between centers, you can then plan where the various scenic units will hang. Although you need appropriate clearance space in front and back of all units flying in and out on any production, you need even more for scenery that moves during the show. It is a different matter during an act break when changing units of scenery that are tightly hung, because stagehands can take the time to ease pieces in slowly or pull other pieces back so they don't hit each other.

When you are figuring the overall space for hanging scenery, be sure to add on the extra depth for any scenery hardware, bracing, or stiffeners. Stiffeners on the backs of scenic pieces are normally positioned on edge (either vertically or horizontally), and the average stiffener is 3 or 4 inches in width.

Consider the following items and estimate how much overall space you would need when planning space for each scenic unit and clearance space.

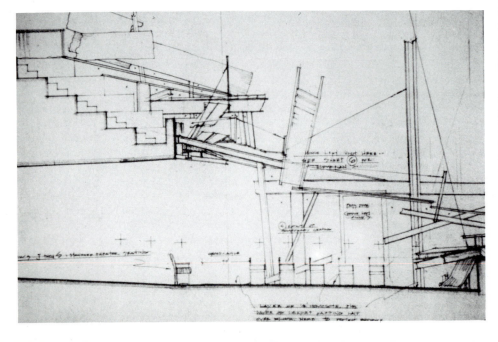

1. *Muslin backdrop* with a sandwich batten at top and bottom.
2. *Sharkstooth scrim* with pipe at top and bottom.
3. *Framed hanger unit* (built like flats) with canvas on ⅛-inch plywood on 1 × 3-inch framing, plus 1 × 3-inch stiffeners on edge on the back of the flats.
4. *Velour curtain* in 100 percent fullness with pipe at top and chain in the bottom.
5. *Light instruments* mounted on the first light pipe with clearance for any scenery upstage of it. For this, use an up-to-date instrument template.

Always have the production carpenter (or technical director) look at your plans before you finalize them, and also discuss with the lighting designer the space needed for lighting instruments.

The Length of Pipes for Hanging Scenery

Before starting with the actual drafting, it is always a good idea to find out the length of the pipes (or battens) for hanging scenery in the theatre where the show will be playing. These pipes are a practical guide for planning the maximum width of backdrops, full-stage framed hangers, and lighting pipes. Of course, there are times when a designer may want to put extensions on a pipe for a particular piece of scenery, but any possibilities should always be checked out before you make definite plans. Knowing the pipe lengths at the outset may also keep you from having to make a lot of changes in your drafting.

Information concerning pipes hanging from the grid may be found on theatre plans and theatre information sheets or obtained from production carpenters, house carpenters, scenic shops, and other designers.

Positioning Scenery on Sets of Lines

When you are designing a show and have been given plans of the specific theatre, you may find that the position of the lines vary. This is especially true if you are supplied with both ½-inch and ¼-inch drawings of the ground plan and hanging sections. Though you may find it frustrating to do so,

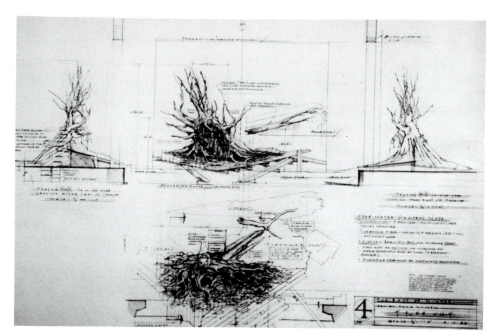

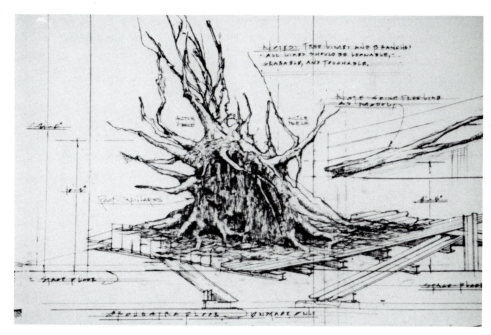

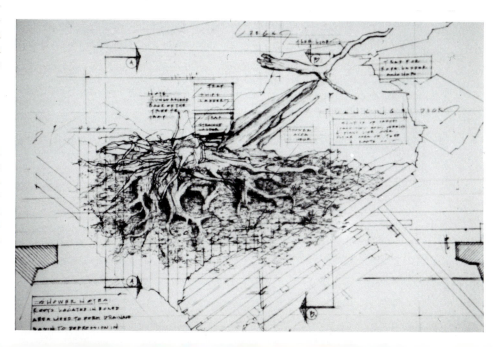

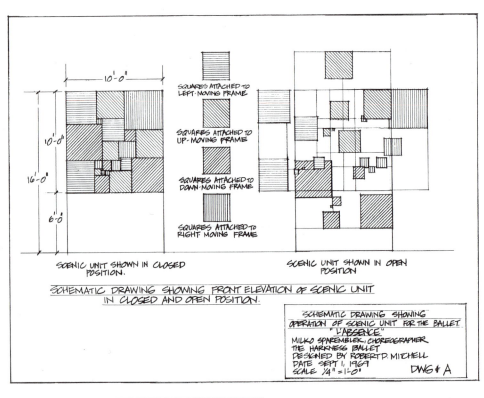

SCHEMATIC DRAWING SHOWING FRONT ELEVATION OF SCENIC UNIT IN CLOSED AND OPEN POSITION.

SCHEMATIC DRAWING SHOWING OPERATION OF SCENIC UNIT FOR THE BALLET. "L'ABSENCE" MILKO SPAREMBLEK, CHOREOGRAPHER THE HARKNESS BALLET DESIGNED BY ROBERT D. MITCHELL DATE SEPT. 1, 1969 SCALE ¼"=1'-0" DWG # A

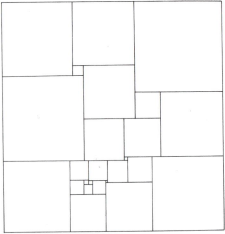

telephoning stage carpenters or management for clarity is always best.

Sets of lines may be spaced on 6-inch centers, 4½-inch centers, 12-inch centers, 9-inch centers, or other dimensions. Lines may also be spaced at random. Even though you may have many available sets of lines to work with, you must always plan to have some extra space for scenery to swing back and forth a bit when it flies out so that everything works smoothly. While equipment like cable guides attached to the sides (working on steel cables) helps, you still must always allow extra space for moving units up and down in the flies to avoid any risk of their becoming hooked, jammed, or cut.

Drawings and model by Robert D. Mitchell
L'ABSENCE Ballet
Choreographed by Milko Sparemblek
Harkness Ballet
Clowes Memorial Hall
Indianapolis, Indiana (1970)
(Photographs by Patrick H. Horrigan)

Drawings, across:

1. Schematic drawing A showing operation of scenic unit.
2. Schematic drawing B showing operation of scenic unit and mirror unit.
3. Drawing of a square composed of twenty-five smaller squares.

"The title of this ballet, which was originally subtitled *Penelope*, refers to the sense of loss experienced by Penelope during the absence of Ulysses. The ballet departed radically, however, from the narrative details of the Ulysses legend and concentrated instead on Penelope's subjective feelings and state of mind. Scenery, music, and dance attempted to evoke this state of mind through primarily abstract means.

"The decors consisted of a scenic unit composed of twenty-five movable, opaque projection screens of differing sizes. These screens faced upstage with their downstage sides painted black. Images were projected on the upstage surfaces of these screens from two offstage projectors, but these images could only be seen by the audience when the screens were moved apart from each other. This was accomplished by means of four movable frames mounted in the scenic unit (drawings 1 and 2). Each frame contained six or seven screens. A mirror unit upstage of the scenic unit allowed the audience to see the projected images in greater and greater detail as the frames moved apart from each other. The intended effect was of a coruscating black square (the closed scenic unit surrounded by an aura of light rays: photograph top right this page) gradually breaking apart to reveal brilliantly colored and patterned images. As the ballet drew to a close, these images recongealed into a floating void (remaining photographs).

"No two of the twenty-five screens were of the same size and each was a perfect square, as was the scenic unit itself when in its closed position. The design of the scenic unit was based on a recent breakthrough in a branch of mathematics called combinatorial analysis, which produced the graphic solution to the problem of assembling such a composite square (drawing 3)."

—Robert D. Mitchell

LENGTHS OF PIPE IN VARIOUS THEATRES

THEATRE	PROSCENIUM WIDTH	LENGTH OF PIPES	CENTERS
Ahmanson Theatre, Los Angeles	39'-9"	50'-0"	4½"
George Gershwin Theatre, New York	42'-0" to 64'-4"	50'-0" extendable to 60'-0"	6"
O'Keefe Theatre, Toronto	59'-10"	60'-0"	6"

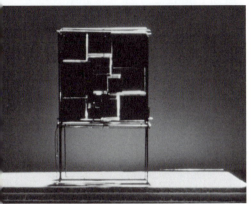

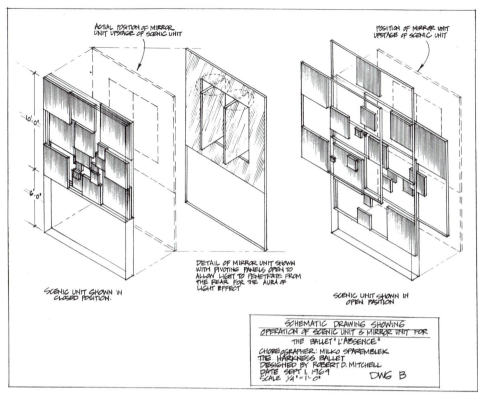

ACTUAL POSITION OF MIRROR UNIT UPSTAGE OF SCENIC UNIT

POSITION OF MIRROR UNIT UPSTAGE OF SCENIC UNIT

DETAIL OF MIRROR UNIT SHOWN WITH PIVOTING PANELS OPEN TO ALLOW LIGHT TO PENETRATE FROM THE REAR FOR THE AURA OF LIGHT EFFECT

SCENIC UNIT SHOWN IN CLOSED POSITION.

SCENIC UNIT SHOWN IN OPEN POSITION

SCHEMATIC DRAWING SHOWING OPERATION OF SCENIC UNIT & MIRROR UNIT FOR THE BALLET "L'ABSENCE"
CHOREOGRAPHER: MILKO SPAREMBLEK
THE HARKNESS BALLET
DESIGNED BY ROBERT D. MITCHELL
DATE SEPT 1, 1969
SCALE ¼"=1'-0"   DWG B

Becoming Familiar with Stage Hardware

Designers, stage carpenters, and technicians are always keeping abreast of the newest kind of stage hardware used in the theatre. Stage hardware can encompass a wide variety of items and materials. It includes items both for the theatre and for the scenery. For instance, objects such as loft blocks, rope locks, and counterweight block sets would be theatre hardware, while casters, pin hinges, brace cleats, hanger irons, and many other pieces of equipment necessary for mounting and maintaining a show would be scenery hardware. While the scenic designer is not always expected to know every detail of stage hardware, he or she must be familiar with such objects in order to design practical and working scenery. Information on stage hardware may be obtained by:

1. Requesting catalogs from scenic manufacturers. These catalogs usually illustrate items with photographs and diagrams and include sizes, shapes, materials, and cost. Catalogs are sometimes free upon request or cost a minimal amount. Mutual Hardware Corporation and Alcone Company, Inc. Paramount Theatrical Supplies are two excellent firms that have illustrated catalogs with descriptions, a

price list, and ordering information. Both firms are located in Long Island City, New York.
2. Consulting an experienced production stage carpenter.
3. Talking with heads of scenic studios.
4. Questioning other designers and stage technicians.
5. Drawing on your own experience in the theatre.

Checklist of Methods of Shifting Scenery

Listed below are useful methods of shifting scenery:

Wagons or wagon stages	Sliding flats in grooves
Flying units in and out	Hinged flats opening and closing
Travelers	Jackknife stage units
Turntables	Scenery moved *a vista* by actors
Revolving stages	Scenery shifted manually by stagehands
Periaktoi	
Elevators or elevator stages	Scenery moved by winches

Common Notes That May Appear on the Drafting

When the drafting for a show in the commercial theatre is being done, certain items, processes, and materials are often strongly emphasized so that there is no question about what is needed

and expected in executing the scenery. Producers always want the best possible deal because they are paying a lot of money for each and every item.

The following notes may be put on the drafting sheets by the designer. They may also be suggested by the production carpenter or the producer or general manager.

1. For estimate only.
2. Discuss breaks of all units for shipping and load-in.
3. Scenery is to meet the requirements of the most stringent federal, state, and local fire and safety codes.
4. Provide all rigging and cables.
5. All hardware to be selected or approved by the production carpenter.
6. Use ⁵/₄-inch construction.
7. Soundproof deck and all platforms.
8. Itemize winches separately.
9. Designer to select all door hardware.
10. Confirm all dimensions on site in the theatre.
11. Any mechanical devices to be tested in the shop and prerigged if possible to save load-in and set-up time.
12. Paint all rigging, cables, and hardware black.
13. Provide jacks as needed.
14. All scenic units (platform, floor, and apron fabric) downstage of smoke pocket are to be constructed of flameproof materials.
15. Load-in date: (give actual date).

DISCUSSING ASSISTANT DESIGNING WITH LEIGH RAND

It is always interesting to talk with a designer who has had a great deal of experience working as an assistant to other designers. New York–based scenic designer Leigh Rand has been an assistant to her husband David Jenkins and her colleague John Conklin for many years. In the following interview we chatted about her career and the various aspects of an assistant designer's work in the West Side design studio she shares with her husband.

When you first came to New York, did you work as an assistant to a designer?

Yes. Soon after I came to New York after graduating from Yale, I worked with Ming Cho Lee nonstop for about two years. I loved working for Ming, and I learned a tremendous amount from him. I really learned to draft when I assisted Ming. I had no theatre background prior to Yale except as a member of a sort of theatre club. Theatre was not a subject that was included in the curriculum at my college. I could always draw pretty well, but I never had any formal training except for one year after I graduated from Wellesley. I didn't get into Yale the first year I applied. So I got a job in Boston and studied with Horace Armistead at Harvard. Harvard only offered theatre courses in their summer school program. And I took some drawing at the Boston Museum of Fine Arts.

I think I can draw pretty well and I wish I could do more of it. I'd like to do illustrating, but I never have a long stretch of time to do it. I can draft for fifteen minutes and stop and then start again. But if I'm trying to do a drawing for a medieval children's story, I lose the flow of what it was I was trying to do if I stop in the middle. It just doesn't work, so I stopped the idea of illustrating altogether.

What made you decide to keep working as an assistant?

When I was working for Ming I realized that I really liked doing assistant work. I like other people fighting the battles while I work out the hows and wheretofores of making a design work. I also wanted to be free to use my creative energy in raising a family, and working as an assistant is perfect for me. It keeps me at home, and it lets me keep up with David's work. I love the theatre. I would never want to be out of the theatre.

I think assistant work is very, very interesting, but I don't think there are many people who want to be an assistant. I know of specific instances when assistants worked for David that they would always be thinking how they would do it if they were the designers. Trying to always make artistic decisions slows them down, and it isn't what David needs them to do.

Do you work as a studio assistant exclusively for John Conklin and your husband David Jenkins?

I work principally for John Conklin. I have done the drafting for him for over fifteen years. We've been friends since Yale. When the apartment across the hall became available, he bought it. And of course, I just have to go across the hall to his studio.

I also assist other theatre and television designers when there is a gap in John's and David's schedules. But so far this year John has designed about fifteen shows, and he's got three more to go. There has been a phenomenal amount of drafting to do for that. I've gone through four or five rolls of 50-yard paper in the past eight months, and you get fifty 24 × 36-inch sheets from each roll.

How many hours a week do you work?

I usually work between twenty and twenty-five hours a week. If it is more than thirty-five hours a week, my home life falls apart. But with John Conklin this year, I've been working almost nonstop.

How does it work when David and John both have productions that have similar deadlines?

I fit it in. John's schedule is a little more flexible than David's because a lot of John's work is for operas that are generally done way in advance. For example, I will start drafting in September for the following summer's production at the Santa Fe Opera, and we did a big production before Christmas that isn't going to open in Munich until late spring. So with that kind of schedule if I squeeze a week forward or backward here or there, it's all right.

David's work is mostly for theatres that have bid sessions. So there is an absolute deadline for the drafting to be finished. There is no way that David can shift that around, so I jump in and do whatever I can do. When I work for David I don't work just as a studio assistant. I may do a little research, and run around doing errands and shopping for wallpaper and things like that. The best fun I ever had assisting David was working on the TV series "The Best of Families." That was great because there were two assistants and we divided up the work that needed to be done. I did the plants, wallpaper, fabrics, and occasional odds and ends. Fred Kolo did all the furniture and big props. I also did all the drafting at the beginning of the project. It was my last full-time job, because I only had one child then.

How long does it take you to draft a one-set show for David?

About two days. I can usually do a ground plan, a section drawing, and maybe three sheets of elevations, if there's not much detail, in two or three days. And that is working eight hours a day. I tend to do the details as I go along. I draft very fast. That is one of the reasons that I've been able to do what I do. I'm fairly accurate. The one thing that lets me draft as fast as I do is the fact that I've been accurate. If I started having to go back over it and check myself a lot, I wouldn't be able to do it as quickly. So far it has been all right.

I am also organized, which I think you have to be. I was very good at math, too, and now I'm able to use a little math, and a little bit of a sort of three-dimensional sense.

You have to figure out the dimensions for units such as stair risers and treads and turns of stairs.

Yes. It is easy mathematics, but if you don't like numbers it's a drag to get bogged down with. I still have trouble with true views of objects that rake in two planes.

Do you do perspective sketches on the drafting to show how a complicated piece is built?

No, I do true views because I think they are much more helpful. I haven't run into anything so complicated that it couldn't be broken down into simpler parts and presented in true views. I did run into one piece that I absolutely could not draft. It was for John Conklin's *Ariodante* for Santa Fe Opera. It was a raking slab that tapered in, and the front and back tapered in, it was leaning in space and it was intersecting with something else that was leaning in. They were all irregular shapes. But in the end, Josie Caruso and I worked it out. She did it in a model, and I did a true view of how it hit the floor and the height and a couple of sections through it. I really never could do an elevation of it. They built it from the model, which is the most sensible way of doing something like that anyway. There is so much now being done with models, and it takes a little pressure off the draftsman.

Do you make models as well?

I do models for David, and I sometimes do model work for John, too. Principally, I do the drafting because I do it better and faster. If John and David have work to do and I don't have any drafting, then I'll do a model for them or whatever else is necessary. Sometimes David hires somebody else to do models, too, if I am working. My loyalty really is to John, simply because I have done more work for him. He also tells me way in advance what he wants me to do. On the other hand, David comes along and says, "I wonder if you wouldn't mind building a model of such and such next week?" But it always works out.

Josie Caruso really does all of the models for John. And, of course, since his studio is across the hall, it works out wonderfully. I work very closely with Josie. I suppose, normally, an assistant does model work and drafting in equal amounts, depending on how busy the designer is. If you do the drafting and the model, then you catch your own mistakes when you build a model through. But I do so little model work for John, Josie catches the things that need to be clarified when she builds the model. Then I will express it better in the drawing, which to me is the most interesting part of doing drafting— organizing it, making it clear, and expressing the ideas that John has so the shop doesn't have any trouble building it.

If you were doing a deck and you know what has to happen with items like wagons and winches, would you just go ahead and put the height on the drawing, or would you get that information from David and John?

David will decide that. For example, he'll say, "What was that deck on such and such? Wasn't that a good angle of rake?" Otherwise, both David and John do basic designing and just give me very rough drawings. David's roughs are much more detailed than John's. But John gets me much more information than I need. David has quite complete rough drawings, but he will sometimes leave out something critical, whereas John will give the angle of the rake, the overall dimensions, and nothing will be square about it. There won't be any straight lines, but I can draw from that information better than I can from David's much more detailed roughs.

Sometimes I draw out the designs before John has even tried the model, and then I give the drawings to Josie and she makes a rough model. And then I go back and do the finished drawings. John pretty much deals with his own masking, too.

John hardly ever makes a mistake, which I do not understand. In fact, the few times that I have found a mistake, I tend to think I have done something wrong, because he so rarely makes mistakes. His ability to concentrate and to remember things is fascinating to me. I guess that's how he can do the volume of work that he does.

After working with David and John over the years, do you know what kind of materials or moldings they would prefer?

David always does his own moldings and I always do moldings for John. Working for John has never been boring. He's never done the same thing twice in fifteen years. He has used design motifs or elements or conceptual themes over again on occasion, but there has never been a repetition of a design. To work for that long with all that variety is a great treat. That's why I continue to enjoy every show I do with John or with David. I look forward to starting new with them because it is always a different idea.

Whom else do you assist?

I like to work for other people, too. I've gotten a number of jobs through Hudson Scenic, which is run by friends of ours. If a young designer says, "Oh my God, I have to get all this drafting done and I don't have the time, do you have anybody in mind who could do it?" Hudson will often call me to do the drafting. I used to worry about being a middle-aged assistant. You know, very few people hire an assistant because of their years of experience. An assistant to a designer is usually younger and less experienced. Then I assisted Linda Hacker, and I liked her and her work so much. The fact that she was twenty years younger than I was made absolutely no difference to me and apparently no difference to her.

I have women designer friends who think that I have abdicated my possibilities as a designer and accuse me of playing second fiddle to David because I don't want to compete with him as a designer. But it is what I wanted to do. It wasn't a sacrifice. It was a positive choice.

These days there are a number of women who are trying to get right up there and fight alongside with men. There are other women who have certain expectations for me as a woman. So I didn't know what it was going to be like to work for a younger woman who didn't have the responsibilities of a husband, children, and home. I have worked for two or three women designers and I have liked them all enormously. And I have gone out of my way to work for women now.

I worked for Alison Yerxa, who did *The Gospel at Colonus*. She is a painter, actually, and not a scenic designer, and so her perspective on a set is all straight front. She will do a combination elevation, then I have to sort out all the railings and do true views. As a painter she doesn't care about true views. She wants to know what it looks like when it's all put together, and that is the information she gives you. But it was great. She is extremely talented and interesting. So I like that. Meeting new people like that is wonderful.

And when I have a gap in work, I do a couple of jobs with an old classmate of mine who designs on the coast and who comes to New York to do television specials. So I do work in television, which is challenging. I enjoy it because it forces me to come out of myself a little bit to confront reality. I do supervision-type work and very little drafting. It's going in and finding a piece of scenery and dealing with the shop, telling them to alter it in such-and-such a way. And I am on hand while they are taping. That usually gives me the heebee-jeebies because I have worked by myself so much.

What study or experience do you think is needed most by someone who wants to be an assistant?

I think you should be a designer. It would be very hard to do what I do without having been trained to be a designer. But then you have to think of the designer you are assisting first and not think of yourself as the designer on that particular work. Once in a while David likes me to give my opinion, but I prefer not to do that. I find that it gets in the way of my being able to present his ideas on paper graphically. I don't want to have to make an aesthetic judgment. Being able to do that is a matter of practice. I've gotten less interesting, but more efficient. I like to sit in the theatre and tell David what I think of his sets.

BASIC SCENIC UNITS

Scenery includes both units standing on the floor and items suspended from the grid, or a combination of both. The kind of set used normally determines how units are built.

When designers are creating scenery for a production, they do not always conscientiously analyze whether individual pieces are hanging items suspended from the grid, standing on the floor, or a combination of both of these. It tends to work best to think about the overall design first and then decide how it is to be executed. Review the following checklist of basic scenic units as often as necessary when designing scenery.

Checklist of Basic Scenic Units

STANDING UNITS	HANGING UNITS
Plain flats	Backdrops and cut drops
Door flats	Cycloramas
Door frames with doors	Neutral legs and borders
Arch flats with thicknesses	Drapery swags and legs
Window flats	Various ceiling pieces
Arches with or without doors	Framed profile pieces
Fireplace flats and mantels	Free-form shapes
Mantelpieces	Chandeliers and lamps
Ground rows and walls	

Rocks and mounds	Projection screens
Steps and staircases	Fragmentary units
Suggestive set pieces	Scrims
Trees and shrubs	Gauzes

COMBINATION STANDING AND HANGING UNITS

Framed portals	Freestanding cutout arches and columns
Upstage framed surround units	
Tree trunks and foliage units	Hard legs and soft borders

The Basic Widths and Heights of Stage Flats

Most designers are trained early in their careers at stock and regional theatres to design flats that can be used over and over again. Designers often continue thinking this way all through their careers simply because it is practical and logical. However, unlike stock and regional theatres, in the commercial theatre all the flats are usually built for each show.

Ground plan drawn by Julia Rogoff for the 1985 San Francisco Opera production of DIE GÖTTERDÄMMERUNG, designed by John Conklin and directed by Nikolaus Lehnoff. The front opening was 47'-0" wide by 28'-0" high. Act 3-1.

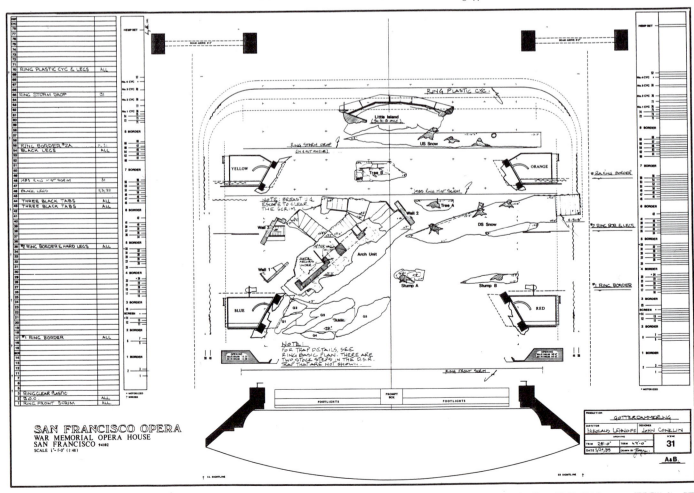

It is easier to figure sizes of flats when there is some kind of boundary to work with. When thinking of the size of flats, you must consider not only the visual aspect but also the practical limitations. The bulkiness and weight of construction in flats as well as whether a set must shift during performance are important factors in designing.

The width of basic flats may vary from 1'-0" to 5'-9". Some designers will think in terms of basic old-fashioned stock flats, which vary in increments of 3 inches, whereas other designers will not think this way at all. The maximum width of 5'-9" has always been a standard width for flats because of the available widths of canvas and muslin. It has also been a good maximum width for handling, for storage, and for travel, as it fits nicely into vehicles for transporting.

Of course, for a very wide expanse of wall, combinations of two and, if necessary, three flats can be used. When appropriate, small jogs can be positioned between a combination of two or three wide flats. A jog less than 1'-0" (such as 9" or 6") is usually made of one solid piece of wood and covered with canvas.

When you have a group of three wide flats, decide whether you want tight

pin hinges countersunk on the face with the flats covered with one piece of fabric, or whether you want loose pin hinges on the rear and the three flats covered individually with fabric, in which case the two cracks between the three flats would not be covered. This often works fine if the sides of the flats are hinged tightly together, and also if the covering on the face or specific paint treatment disguises the cracks.

It has been a standard method in the past to fasten a wide two-fold (like 10'-6") together with tight pin hinges on the face, cover each flat with canvas, and add a dutchman (a 5½-inch strip of canvas glued over the crack between the flats and over the hinges). This arrangement allows the flats to fold face-to-face, thus protecting the painted surface during travel and storage. However, a dutchman of canvas or muslin usually shows, especially when it is painted and is then folded several times during travel and setup. The fold and the knuckles of the hinge beneath become increasingly obvious. Instead of a dutchman, it is always better to use two widths of canvas stitched together beforehand to cover the flats. Sew the canvas face-to-face at the selvage edge. The stitched side is the

"wrong side" of the fabric, the side that is glued onto the flat. A neat seam always looks better than a long vertical patch.

A tumbler is sometimes added in a unit of three or four flats that have to fold. For a three-fold or four-fold unit, a 3- to 4-inch width of canvased wood may be hinged in between the flats so that they can fold for travel and storage. The use of a tumbler should be discouraged because the unit becomes heavy and awkward, the tumbler requires the use of several more hinges, plus on any formal set you can usually tell where the tumbler is—usually an obvious area, because it is dead center in a four-fold flat unit. In any case, when either a two-fold or three-fold flat unit is to be covered with canvas or muslin, always machine stitch the three or two widths of fabric together first so that the unit can be covered with one piece of canvas or muslin.

Ground plan drawn by Julia Rogoff and Larry Klein for LA BOHÈME (1986) at the San Francisco Opera, designed by David Mitchell and directed by Gerald Freedman. The front opening was 50'-0" wide by 30'-0" high. Act 2: A square surrounded by shops. The drawing was computer-generated. The deck began at 6¾" downstage and increased to a height of 54" upstage.

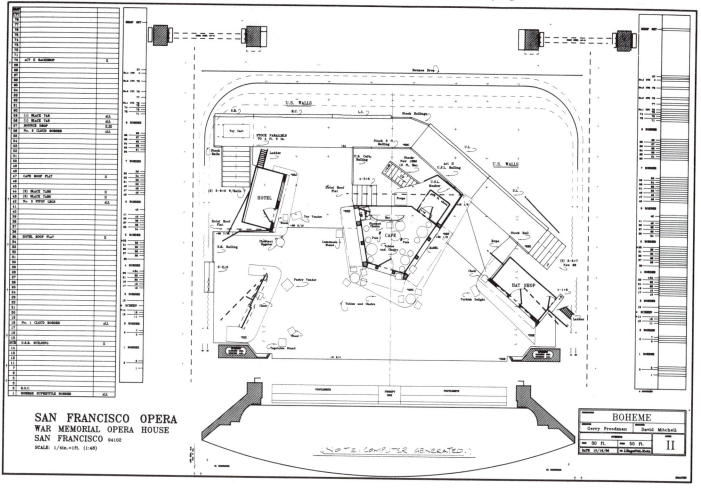

Some designers create sets where the pin hinges go on the rear. This arrangement works well when it produces a very tight, hardly seen crack between the two flats. The cracks can be disguised with painted patterns, such as striped wall-paper, or with real fabric wrapped around the edges. Arrangements of prints and paintings or other set dressing can also be used to hide a great many of the obvious cracks in joins.

The height of flats is most often determined by the size of the stage and by the kind, and locale of the play. As a rule of thumb, a good height for flats for an average-size interior set may be either 14'-0" or 16'-0". (It is usually standard in the theatre for flats to increase in height by increments of 2 feet.) Sets built with tall flats create a visual excitement for most theatrical productions. For this reason alone, it is always good to think high with regard to the height of flats. For very large-scale stages, 18'-0" and 20'-0" are excellent heights. But if the height of a stage will only allow 10'-0" and 12'-0" high flats, then that is the best you can do. Most often, basic interior sets require flats of the same height, although this may vary with sets built in perspective or with profile pieces at the tops of flats. Exterior sets can have flats either with many varying heights or with the same height, again depending on the design.

Showing Flats in Position on the Ground Plan

To show flats in position on the ground plan, it works best to shade in the basic plan of the actual bottoms of the flats. This technique is especially helpful when applied pieces, such as baseboards or woodwork, are to be added to the flats. Once you have drawn the main set with the basic flats on the ½-inch scale plan, do the following:

1. Draw the main set on the ½-inch scale ground plan showing the basic 1-inch-thick flats as they rest on the stage floor. This plan is to be used for both building and positioning on stage and should be extremely clear to all who will use it (scenic shop, production carpenter, lighting designer, crew, and so on).

2. If you have designed an interior set with applied woodwork that rests on the stage floor (such as a ¾-inch-thick

baseboard that goes in front of the flat), it may be indicated as being applied to the face of the flat by a simple, neat, unbroken line. Of course, anything positioned above the floor can be indicated with a broken line, but it is not always necessary to go to the trouble to indicate this on the drawing of the ground plan. For any additional applied piece that does rest on the floor, simply write a note saying "baseboard (or woodwork) added to the basic flats throughout (the set)." Remember, when setting up in the theatre the production carpenter begins by positioning the basic set, and he or she is not really interested in looking at a lot of unnecessarily added lines.

However, there are always exceptions. For the ground plan of flats with numerous detailed built units resting on the floor, such as pilasters and bookcases, you might want to draw not only the basic flats of the set but also the floor woodwork in front that is involved with these units. For a set with a prominent ceiling piece, you might need to indicate with a broken line the position of the cornice pieces above, showing the overall depth of the cornice.

The Joining of Flats

When you are drawing flats on a ground plan to show how they go together in sequence, always indicate this clearly so the production carpenter and scenic shop have no problem in building and positioning them on stage.

Basic flats are usually shown to be 1-inch thick (¾-inch wood plus ¼-inch plywood corner blocks/keystones). In ½-inch scale, the perimeter of the base of the flat is drawn and may or may not be shaded.

If you wish to use a drawing pencil to shade the floor plan of the main set (drawn in ½-inch scale), it is all right to do this, provided that the outline of the 1-inch flats is darker than the shading so that the flats are clearly defined and easy to see. In other words, if the building carpenter puts a scale on your drawing to see the width of a flat, the exact dimension in ½-inch scale should be immediately apparent. Carpenters want to see not only where a flat starts and stops, but exactly how one flat joins the next flat. Do the flats butt end to end, angle to each other, or what? Whether the flats on plan are

shaded or not, the carpenters should be able to tell at once just how the flats join each other.

The basic methods for joining flats are shown:

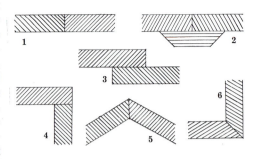

While certain rules for joining flats together have been established over the years, for practical purposes you should also have joins that are visually appropriate. Flats do not always follow the tradition of being lashed together. An outside and prominently placed 90-degree corner should be mitered with each of the two flats on 45-degree angles. It has been a practice in the past not to use this method because flats designed to have edges with 45-degree ends broke and splintered easily and also limited the reuse of basic stock flats.

Checklist of Scenic Units for an Individual Production

One of the most helpful pieces of information on the scenic designer's drawings is a checklist of all the scenery pieces in the production. This list, positioned at the bottom or top of the master ground plan, mentions every item that is to be built or renovated. It includes all framed and soft scenery, deck, ground cloth, masking legs and borders, added apron extension, and so on. In other words, this checklist indicates everything management is paying for. In essence it is a table of contents for the scenery, and it works well for both single-set and multiset shows. Important pieces of furniture and props that are to be built or renovated can also be listed and numbered and placed at the end of the scenic unit list.

Although various methods of labeling scenery have been used in the past, the best and simplest way to do this is to give each individual piece of scenery a number, starting with 1, then continue consecutively with 2, 3, 4, and so on. When items are added after the list has been numbered, they can be labeled 1a, 1b, 1c, and so on. A circle drawn with a circle template around each number makes it stand out and easy to locate in the checklist. When an item is cut from the show, write "delete" or "omit" after the number on the checklist.

The assigned number for each piece of scenery is repeated on every drawing where the item appears and on the built unit. This numbering system avoids confusion and can serve various functions:

1. It allows direct and simple communication with the production staff about an individual piece of scenery. The scenic designer, lighting designer, general manager, and production stage carpenter can discuss separate pieces of scenery in production meetings (or over the telephone) by using the assigned numbers as reference.
2. Management can refer to the numbers when conferring with the scenic studio. The general manager may call the scenic studio and say, "How much is item 19 going to cost?" or inform the studio, "Cut items 13 and 14." Also, when management has asked the scenic studio for an individual cost breakdown, the studios can send in (or telephone) their price quotes for each numbered scenic item.
3. The assigned number of an individual piece of scenery on a drawing can also be used to label the actual scenery (marked on the back) so that when it is being loaded and unloaded in the theatre it is easily identified. The production carpenter and stagehands can check on the plan to see where the numbered piece is to be located on stage.
4. For consistency and clarity, the assigned number can also be used to label the paint elevations and sketches.

Figuring the Weight of Scenery Units

The weight of hanging units of scenery that are to fly in and out during the performance needs to be estimated as accurately as possible. While it is extremely important that the gridiron and counterweight system always be in excellent working order, this is especially true when scenic units are expected to be heavier than usual. If there is any question about the working or-

der and the safety of the grid and counterweight system, then structural engineers and/or architectural consultants should be hired to check out all the conditions in the stage house.

The wise scenic designer should always make sure that the proper materials are selected to be used for scenery so that weights do not get out of hand. The weight of scenic units also may be estimated by the production carpenter and the head carpenter in the scenic studio. And the most reliable production carpenter will tell you when something is just too heavy or if he or she can make it work.

Examples of scenery units which could become too heavy include:

1. Framed hanger units with velour on $\frac{1}{8}$-inch plywood on 1 × 3-inch framing.
2. Flats with erosion cloth glued on $\frac{1}{8}$-inch or $\frac{1}{4}$-inch plywood on wooden framing.
3. Entire sets which are heavier than normal flying units.

Weight List of Flying Scenic Units

A list of flying scenic units indicating the weight of each is essential in order to assure that there will be appropriate weights on hand in the theatre to put in the arbors of the counterweight system to properly balance the scenery. While designers are not always expected to know the specific weight of a unit, if the show is going to be heavy, meet with the carpenter early on to get some estimates. Then, if necessary, you can make changes in your choice of materials.

An excellent example to mention here was the flying scenery used in *The Crucifer of Blood* (1978) at the Helen Hayes Theatre (since demolished) that had to be modified for the Ahmanson Theatre (1980) in Los Angeles. Certain materials used at the Helen Hayes Theatre also had to be modified to reduce the weight of the flying pieces so that they could accommodate the grid structure in the Haymarket Theatre in London (1979). Not only did flying units have to be modified, but also the rolling floor units because of the Haymarket's raked stage.

The following weight list of flying units for *The Crucifer of Blood* at the Ahmanson Theatre, Los Angeles, shows a fairly heavy physical produc-

tion for a play. This list was made after the show was hung.

1.	#1 Framed velour portal	775 lbs.
2.	Scrim show curtain drop	32 lbs.
3.	Black backup drop	128 lbs.
4.	#1 Framed Pondicherry unit	940 lbs.
5.	Framed opium den wall	736 lbs.
6.	#2 Framed velour portal	775 lbs.
7.	#2 Framed Pondicherry unit	1090 lbs.
8.	#3 Framed Pondicherry unit	608 lbs.
9.	#3 Framed velour portal	775 lbs.
10.	#1 Framed Agra gate unit	864 lbs.
11.	Pondicherry scrim drop	32 lbs.
12.	Lightning box	640 lbs.

ORIGINAL DRAWINGS AND PRINTS

Keeping Original Tracings

Original production drawings are kept in the scenic designer's personal collection. All original tracings should be kept organized in the playing sequence of the production because they are usually needed in a hurry. These drawings are needed for: (1) making any revisions on the scenery, such as additional designs or adjustments after the first bid session; (2) for use by national or foreign companies; and (3) for general reference to check shapes, sizes, and positions of units on stage.

Original drawings are best to use for making corrections or adjustments because both the front and the back of the tracing paper can be used for drawing. Normally, original drawings keep their shape, while prints may stretch or shrink, giving inaccurate measurements of lines when using a scale ruler.

Prints of the Designer's Drawings

Printed copies of the designer's original drawings may go to the following:

1. Scenic designer
2. Supervisory or associate scenic designer (when applicable)
3. Assistant scenic designer(s) (when applicable)
4. Lighting designer
5. Director
6. Assistant director (when applicable)
7. Production stage manager
8. Production stage carpenter

Model and Ground Plan by Karen Schulz for THE FOREIGNER (1984) by Larry Shue,
Directed by Jerry Zaks, Astor Place Theatre, New York

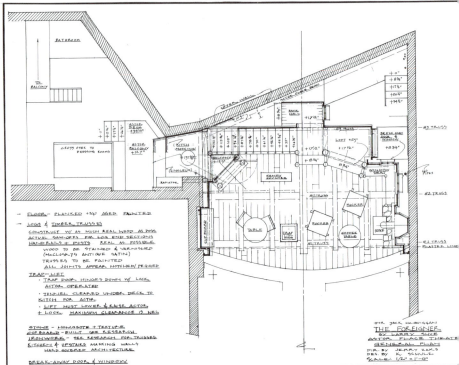

9. Production property person
10. Scenic studio: painting
11. Scenic studio: building
12. Drapery house: backdrops, curtains, upholstery
13. Special effects designer (when applicable)
14. Producer and general manager (office copy)
15. Bid session (as many as needed)
16. Producers

It should be noted that full sets of drawings go to carpenters, scenic shops, and so on. But a director and stage manager may want only plans, and lighting designers may need only a plan and a hanging section, while a drapery house will need only an elevation drawing. However, occasionally they may request other drawings as well.

Sepia Copies from Original Tracings

Transparent sepia copies are sometimes made from the original tracings of the scenery. While sepia copies are more expensive than the usual black-on-white or blue-on-white prints, and some of the fine details in the drawings can be lost, they nevertheless serve a good purpose. They are used by producers to have additional prints made at their convenience. For instance, when a show has become a hit and other companies are being put together, the producer can use his or her set of sepia copies to make prints. This way the designer does not have to be contacted each time copies of drawings are needed.

WORKING WITH THE PRODUCTION CARPENTER

In the commercial theatre, a good production carpenter is the scenic designer's valued colleague and friend who sees to it that the physical production works beautifully on stage. It has often been said that a scenic designer's work is only as good as the reliable assistance and cooperation provided by a talented production carpenter.

The production carpenter may be selected by the producers, the general manager, or even suggested by the scenic designer. The production carpenter stays with the show until everything is under way, which is usually until the show opens, unless there is a preference to stay or if prior commitments do not permit it. The post is then taken over either by the stage carpenter or by an assistant who has normally worked side by side with the production carpenter on the production. Word of a great production carpenter's ability and reputation spreads through the industry like wildfire, and the best ones may work on several shows at one time.

The most conscientious production carpenters are involved with the progress of the scenery even while the designer is drafting it. As a collaborative effort this not only saves time but indicates to both the designer and the production carpenter that things are within reason and are going to work out fine. Before the bid session, the scenic designer again saves time and energy by giving the production carpenter a full set of drawings to look over and to check out everything that has been put on the drawings. It is always best to do this before the many sets of drawings are printed for the bid session so that any corrections can be made.

A production stage carpenter's duties include:

1. Direct communication with the scenic studio about general construction, preferred hardware, positions of breaks, kind of bracing, rigging, jacks, the best casters, materials for sound-proofing platforms, and so on.
2. Communication with management and the scenic studio about schedule dates: loading out of the shop and into the theatre.
3. Deciding on the number of trucks needed, when they leave the studio and arrive at the theatre, and what pieces can be loaded in at a later date.
4. Determining the number of men and women needed to unload and set up.
5. Knowing the number of men and

women needed to run the show.

6. Being in consultation with management and the director: planning the number of hours allotted for rehearsal with scenery, costumes, lights, sound, and special effects.
7. Arranging for the necessary equipment in the theatre: cables, pipes, weights, winches, and many other special items, such as cutting traps and any specific rigging required for special effects.
8. Making up a spot line list, if necessary, for scenery or lighting items, and checking out the call for work in the theatre.

Estimating the Number of Backstage Crew on a Production

When a show is being designed, the scenic designer is expected to think about the number of men and women that will be needed backstage to run the show. During the design process, a designer may confer with the production stage carpenter about certain questions: "Can two men move this castered wagon offstage left?" "Will the head prop man and his assistants have enough time to make the change with the furniture to be taken off manually?" "Do we have enough flymen to take out and bring in the cutdrops and backdrops from Scene 3 to 4?" Ideally a production carpenter is selected early for the show by management. Some management teams in the commercial theatre retain their own carpenter.

Once the scenic designer has designed the scenery for a show—complete with models, drawings, and sketches—a production meeting is held to go over all the movement or technical changes. This session involves the general manager, designer, production stage carpenter, and any special effects person. A production meeting is scheduled for all shows whether for a one-set or a multiset production.

The main point of this meeting is to make any changes and finalize how the physical demands of the show can be handled with the size crew allowed by management. Sometimes the designer

must revamp the scenery many times to make it work with the size of the backstage crew management is willing to hire.

Persons Usually Invited to a Bid Session

Persons who are usually invited to the bid session include:

1. Scenic designer(s)
2. Heads of scenic studios (building and painting)
3. Heads of drapery houses (backdrops, curtains, upholstery), if the scenic studios do not supply these products
4. Producer(s) and general manager(s)
5. Production stage carpenter

SCENERY SPECIFICATIONS

Scenery Specifications for Bidding

Once the scenery drawings have been finished by the designer, it is often the technical director's (or production carpenter's) job to go over the drafting and make his own list of specifications for bidding. This list is attached to the designer's drawings which are submitted to the shops to bid for the show. The list of specifications made by John Cleavelin for the 1984 bus-and-truck production of *Dracula* produced by the Paramount Theatre for the Performing Arts in Austin, Texas, is provided for interested designers and technicians to study.

Dracula *Bus and Truck Company*
  I. Soft goods
   A. Flameproof certificates.
   B. All goods to include webbing, grommets on 1'-0" centers (from

center line), 3'-0" tie lines and pipe pocket
   1. Pipe to be included.
   2. Webbing of all goods shall be marked indicating production, name and number of item, and center line.
  C. All drops and goods to have side hems.
  D. Ground cloth to be #10 duck or approved equivalent.
   1. Webbing to be on all edges.
   2. All seams to have two rows of stitching.
   3. A center line to be marked upstage and downstage.
   4. Corners to be marked as to their respective stage location.

II. *Flown scenery*

    A. *Flown scenery to have one safety bolt in all hardware pieces required.*

    B. *Flown scenery to include all hanging cable and hardware as necessary.*

        1. *Hanging cable to be ⅛" unless otherwise specified.*

        2. *Hanging cables to be premeasured to necessary length and to include chain or other leveling device on either end.*

    C. *All loose pin hinges to be of the Stanley modified variety or equivalent to accept a #20 or #30 bent nail.*

    D. *All stiffeners and jacks to be provided as necessary.*

    E. *Sill irons to be provided as necessary.*

III. *Deck scenery*

    A. *All castered units to have ¾" to 1" clearance.*

        1. *All casters to have a 3" wheel (minimum).*

        2. *All casters to be Darnell or Colson made.*

    B. *Platforming.*

        1. *All lids to be ¾" stock without voids.*

        2. *All lids to be nailed on.*

        3. *All lids and edges to be covered with #10 duck.*

        4. *All joints to be glued.*

    5. *All hinges to have one safety bolt per leaf.*

    C. *All flatage to be constructed as per lines 4 and 5 of section B above.*

        1. *Flatage less than 14'-0" high to be constructed of ¾" stock.*

        2. *Flatage 14'-0" to 20'-0" high to be constructed of 4/4" stock.*

        3. *Flatage over 20'-0" high to be constructed of 5/4" stock.*

        4. *Hinges to not span more than 4'-0".*

        5. *Top and bottom hinges to be no more than 6" from the edge.*

        6. *All units to be labeled and numbered properly.*

Scenery Specifications for an Individual Company

An individual company such as the New York City Opera has definite specifications for scenery construction. Their list of specifications is attached to and becomes a part of all contracts. Any variations must be approved by the technical department.

New York City Opera Scenery Specifications for Shops

    I. *General*

        1. *Provide a notarized flameproof certificate covering all scenery and props.*

        2. *Provide an itemized piece list and inventory listing all pieces.*

        3. *Label each piece with the name of the production, and with "NYCO."*

        4. *Label all units, including jacks and railings, for easy assembly.*

    II. *Framed scenery*

        1. *Maximum size: 8'-0" × 21'-0".*

        2. *Any bolts used in assembly must be ⅜".*

        3. *All rotolocks must turn clockwise to fasten.*

        4. *Lumber shall be C select or better.*

        5. *Use 5/4" for vertical stiffeners.*

        6. *Jacks are to be mounted on stiffeners, never to replace a stiffener.*

        7. *Mount all hinges with one safety bolt per leaf.*

        8. *Round the end of all jacks and vertical stiffeners.*

        9. *Include straight foot irons on all jacks.*

        10. *All pieces must be backpainted with flameproofing paint.*

    III. *Hangers*

        1. *Maximum sizes: Depth—4½"; Weight—750 #.*

Costume sketches by Lindsay W. Davis
PIQUE-DAME (22 by 16 inches)
Act 1 chorus on the promenade
A project: the Metropolitan Opera (1979)

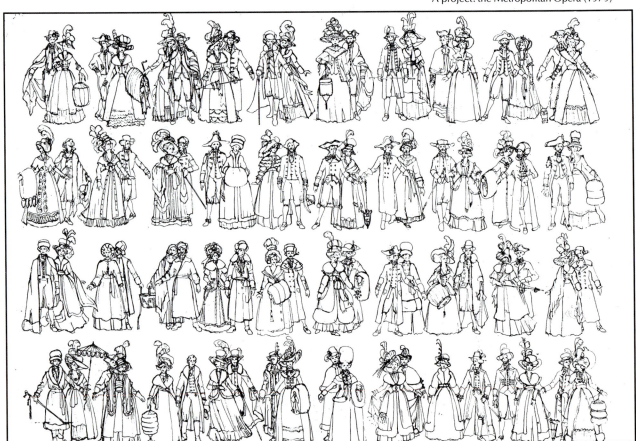

2. *Rig flown scenery, in general, to hang from the top.*

3. *Use ⅛" cable terminating w/2 nicopress sleeves and thimbles, plus 3 ft. of 4/0 passing link welded trim chain, assuming weight does not exceed 250 lbs. × no. of pick-ups.*

4. *Include all rigging hardware and cable for pipes trimmed at 37'-0".*

5. *Aircraft cable should be dipped or painted flat black.*

IV. *Platforms*

1. *Use ⅝" stock for parallels over 4'-0" high.*

2. *Use ¼" fir plywood corner blocks and keystones with glue and nails.*

3. *Parallel tops must be of ¾" AC plywood with 1 × 3 locating battens.*

4. *All platform tops are to be padded unless otherwise agreed.*

V. *Wagons*

1. *Preferred maximum height: + 9'-4".*

2. *¾" minimum caster clearance.*

3. *4" minimum wheel diameter.*

4. *Caster type must be approved by NYCO Production Department.*

5. *Casters must be bolted onto structural members.*

6. *Casters must have hard rubber wheels unless otherwise agreed.*

7. *Swivel casters must be of the heavy duty double bearing sleeve type.*

VI. *Escapes*

1. *Preferred size: Width—4'-0"; Rise—8"; Tread—10".*

2. *Escape steps must be of clip-on type unless otherwise designated.*

3. *Include removable paralleling safety railings of ⁵⁄₄" stock on both sides.*

4. *Escape steps must allow for rapid forward descent (AGMA contract).*

VII. *Soft goods*

1. *Standard drop sizes: Width— 59'-6"; Height—36'-0" or 40'-0"; Thread count—140; Vel. weight—21 oz.*

2. *All fabrics used in scenery fabrication must be flameproofed.*

3. *All goods include webbing, side hems, grommets on 1 ft. centers (measured from center line), 3 ft. tie lines, and pipe pocket with a skirt.*

4. *Ribbon and jute are not acceptable as tie line.*

5. *Run seams horizontally.*

6. *Clearly mark webbing with CL, production name, dimensions, and "NYCO".*

7. *All cut drops must be netted. 1 in. black cotton net preferred.*

VIII. *Ground cloths*

1. *Standard sizes: Width—58'-0"; Depth—38'-6"; Weight—#8; Webbing—4".*

2. *Mark CL clearly on webbing, U. S. and D. S.*

3. *Double the webbing thickness at the corners, and center line.*

4. *Double stitch (welt) seam with opening facing upstage.*

5. *Use heavy thread.*

New York City Opera Design Parameters

These parameters should be of interest to designers, production carpenters, technicians, and stagehands. The design parameters have been compiled by Rik Kaye, Director of Production and Chuck Giles, Technical Director.

New York City Opera design parameters are defined in large part by our rotating repertory schedule, crew work rules, and the stage dimensions of the New York State Theatre.

I. *Schedule*

1. *Time is perhaps the most crucial constraint on our repertory sea-*

Costume designs by Willa Kim
Robert Lowell's THE OLD GLORY
My Kinsman, Major Molineux
American Place Theatre
New York (1976)

128

son. *Regardless of cost or need, it is not expandable. We are often squeezed for every second available. A long Saturday matinee can end as late as 4:45 PM. The crew must break from 5:45–7 PM. The change over for the evening performance should be completed by 7:30 PM.*

2. *It is our goal, therefore, to strike any production in 30 minutes, and set the next in 1 hour. Woven into this time we must clear the stage, strike and set hangers, change ground cloths, set the next production and focus specials. We strike only the elements that conflict and endeavor to avoid conflicts with large flying pieces. We also try to avoid refocus of overheads and instruments that focus on scenery other than the preset. In general, stock masking should not be moved.*

II. *Lighting*

   1. *Specials may be assigned as available from NYCO's repertory light plot in consultation with NYCO Resident Lighting Designer, Jeff Davis.*

   2. *Electric pipes, X-ray pipes, and lighting ladders cannot be moved to other locations. However, feasible additions can be discussed.*

III. *Scenery/Hanging Plan*

   1. *The portal width of 44'-0" (13.4 m) is fixed.*

   2. *Portal height is 26'-0" (7.9 m) and cannot be higher if supertitles are used.*

   3. *40'-0" × 12'-0" (12.2 m × 3.7 m) black legs are spotted on travelers as indicated.*

   4. *Linesets 4–7, and those immediately upstage of the electrics, should be avoided for fast moving pieces, or full stage drops. Linesets 87 and above are usually used for storage and should not be considered available.*

   5. *Standard trims are as follows: Portal border—26'-0" (7.9 m); Bor-*

ders—#1 Border 31'-0" (9.5 m), others are 30'-0" (9.1 m); Electrics—Masked behind borders from extreme seats; Lighting ladders 27'-6" (8.4 m).

   6. *Preferred stock sizes are: Backdrops—59'-6" wide × 36'-0" or 40'-0" high (18.2 m × 11 m – 12.2 m); Ground cloth—58'-0" wide × 38'-6" deep (17.7 m × 11.7 m).*

   7. *Additional notes: Scenery must be built according to NYCO scenery specifications. The freight elevator is 11'-0" w × 21'-0" d × 9'-0" h (3.4 m × 6.4 m × 2.7 m). All scenery must break down easily to fit into the elevator for storage. Linesets are all on 4½" (11.5 cm) centers. Maximum depth of hanging scenery is 4½" (11.5 cm). US area above lineset 87 is used for repertory scenery storage. NYCO stock parallels and escapes are in 8" (20.4 cm) height increments.*

Cutaway Drawing of the Metropolitan Opera House from *Theatre Design* (1977) by George C. Izenour. Reproduced with permission of McGraw-Hill, Inc.

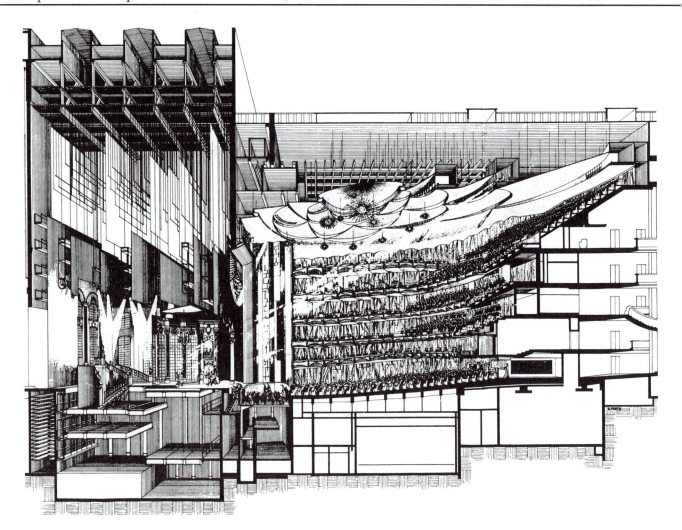

IV. Wardrobe

Costumes must be extremely durable and constructed to allow for numerous refittings as casts change. Costume construction should be approached in the same manner as a costume rental house would execute them. That is, with maximum amount of alteration flexibility as possible. Costume elements which play next to the skin must be washable and removable from the costume for cleaning. Fabrics should contain some percentage of man-made fiber so that ironing may be kept to a minimum.

Technical Requirements for a Touring Company

Because a touring company most often follows the plan of the original show, the exact crew, facilities, and equipment necessary to make the show work properly are known. The list of technical requirements for a touring production of *Evita* is a good example of what needs had to be met in the theatres where the show was to play.

Evita Tour #4 Technical Requirements

Minimum Proscenium Opening: 25'-0" high × 32'-0" wide (20'-0" high possible)

Minimum Stage Depth (measured from 2nd usable pipe to rear wall): 28'-0" normal hang, 23'-0" minimum (20'-0" possible only with backstage crossover)

Minimum Grid Height (from stage floor to grid): 50'-0"

Minimum Backstage Dimensions: 65'-0" wall to wall clear space (32'-6" right and left of center line)

Minimum Height Clearances offstage: 50'-0" clear from floor to grid

Minimum Number of Line Sets: 25 with nothing hanging on them (with 500 lb. arbors)

Minimum Counterweight: 7000 lbs. available *on loading gallery*

In/Out Time (estimated): 6 hours in, 2½ hours out

I. CREW REQUIREMENTS (Yellow Card)

	LOAD-IN	PERFORMANCE	TAKE-OUT
Carpenters	10	7–8	10
Electricians	12	4	12
Props	4	4	6
Projectionist	1	0	1
Wardrobe	4	10*	4
Truck Loaders	5	0	5

*Wardrobe show call: 5 men, 5 women

II. Carpentry Requirements

1. Flying system must be cleared of all scenery, lights, masking, and orchestra shells before arrival of company. Failure to provide cleared flying system (particularly in first ten feet behind proscenium) will result in some scenic elements being left out and delays during the load-in.
2. 7,000 lbs. of counterweight available for our use on the loading dock.
3. Stage area must be cleared of all miscellaneous scenery, chairs, tables, pianos, and swept.
4. Loading dock area must be clear. If load-in is from a street or parking lot, arrangements must be made so that two 45 foot trucks can pull up to the dock without any cars in the way.
5. If the flying system is a hemp system (sandbags and ropes), 25 1½" I.D. pipe battens, 50'-0" long must be available.
6. We hang 25 sets of lighting and scenery and normally play to a depth of 28'-0" (from 2nd usable pipe or last architectural impediment).

III. Projection requirements

1. We utilize front projection. Space must be made in the house for an operator, four carousel slide projectors, and one 16 mm film projector as follows.
2. If it is possible to hang projectors from balcony rail, space must be made available for an operator within 100 feet of projection equipment with a view of the stage. A booth is sufficient for this purpose.
3. If seats on orchestra level are pulled, there must be three rows of four seats each (directly in front of each other). Seats (or booth) at balcony level may or may not be satisfactory, depending on projection angle. Seats at the rear of the orchestra may or may not be satisfactory, depending on balcony overhang.
4. In any case, projection position must be within 125 feet of stage, and in a center section. Projectors can be separated from operator, but must be within 100 feet.

IV. Sound requirements

There must be a position for sound console and operator in the house, preferably on orchestra level. It must not be in an enclosed booth. It must be within 150 feet of the stage. If seats are to be pulled, three rows of six seats (directly in front of one another) are necessary in a section at center or just off center.

V. Wardrobe/hair requirements

1. A threaded faucet and drain for washer to be hooked up to (preferably not in a dressing room).
2. One 6 foot rolling rack, four additional racks (minimum 4'-0" long) or equivalent racks in four star dressing rooms.
3. Three separate 20 amp circuits located in areas to be used as headquarters for wardrobe and hair departments.

VI. Miscellaneous

1. One 4'-0" × 8'-0" × 16-inch riser for piano in pit.
2. Tuned upright piano in pit (A = 440) or if available and pit space permits, tuned baby grand piano.
3. We use eight open flame torches in the show, as well as lit cigarettes and cigars. Please arrange for fire marshall to come by during the load-in to inspect and approve torch device.

Cutting Scenery to Come In on Budget

One of the most important aspects of a bid session is to know exactly where you stand so far as the budget of the show is concerned. If you are way over budget for the scenery on a show, the producers or general manager will simply ask you to take the show back to the drawing board and rethink it. This can mean cutting $5,000, $10,000, $20,000, or more from your design. Most producers stick firmly to their original budget and often this is not a flexible area. Other producers sometimes make a few allowances.

Drawings by Robert D. Mitchell
UNDER THE SUN (Calder Ballet)
Choreographed by Margo Sappington
Pennsylvania Ballet Company
Shubert Theatre
Philadelphia, Pennsylvania (1976)
(Photograph by Lynn Pecktal)

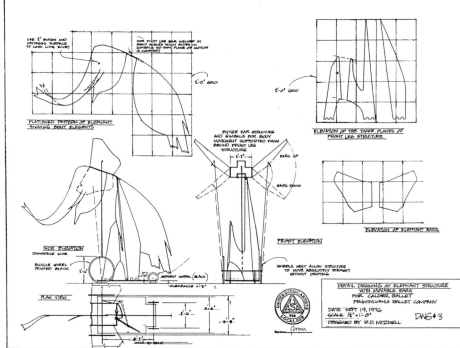

"UNDER THE SUN was produced by the Pennsylvania Ballet to honor a visit to the United States by Alexander Calder in 1976. Taking its inspiration from Calder's own works in all media, the ballet was based largely on a fable invented by the choreographer Margo Sappington involving the earthly existence of many fabulous creatures. Evoking the imaginative world of Calder, however, required the invention of a multitude of special props. The show curtain for the ballet consisted of a gigantic blowup of one of his paintings realized as a scrim with a variety of fabric panels attached to its surface. (See models in color photographs.)

"*Curtain photo:* Front lights beginning to fade on the show curtain while stage lights reveal a planet-strewn vision of outer space into which an enormous Calder sun-creature flies out.

"*Large elephant photo:* The entrance of a large elephant with movable ears loosely based on one of Calder's own toys. Each dancer holds a brightly colored disk attached to an expanding and contracting scissor mechanism which allows him to control all the movements of the disk.

"*Remaining photo:* The last moments of the ballet. Here the combination of scenery, costumes, and props was intended to evoke the experience of watching a Calder mobile. Dancers with hand props suggested the look and movement of brightly colored metal shapes, while the linear mobiles overhead appeared to connect these shapes. These wire mobiles were designed to move slowly but unpredictably above the heads of the dancers."
—Robert D. Mitchell

Reworking the budget, of course, means that you must have another conference with the director. It is in your favor if you and the producer(s) have asked the scenic studios to give you a cost breakdown of each scenic unit, be-

cause you can tell immediately which are the expensive items. This reworking may involve a great deal of hard work in a short amount of time, but it is absolutely necessary and is par for the course in the commercial theatre.

Remember, it is your responsibility to work for the best possible results on the show, no matter whether it is going to be enormously successful or a one-night flop—and this you never know.

Cutting Specific Scenic Items

While you may cut any number of scenic items on a show, this task varies with the individual production and the

designer(s). This of course can often require a great deal of ingenuity in a short amount of time. The main consideration here is to cut portions of scenery without hurting the overall quality or the desired look of the show.

Rather than cutting whole pieces of scenery, consider deleting (1) specific expensive building materials, (2) fabrics, and (3) painting materials and techniques. A simple technique can frequently be used to simulate expensive building materials, or the same effect could be accomplished with another material. For example, duvetyne could substitute for the more expensive velour. Elaborate painted details could be cut. Even after careful, se-

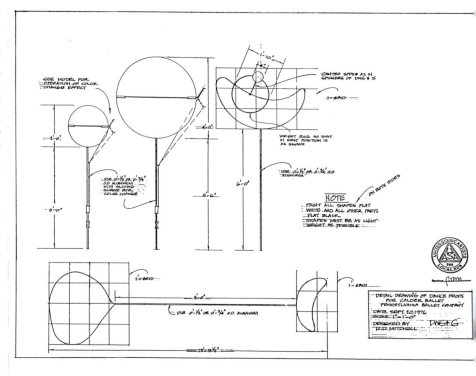

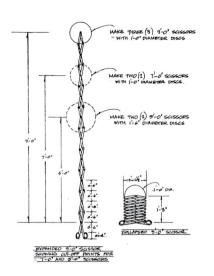

Note on constructing scissor props

MAKE THREE (3) 9'-0" SCISSORS WITH 1'-0" DIAMETER DISCS

MAKE TWO (2) 7'-0" SCISSORS WITH 1'-0" DIAMETER DISCS

MAKE TWO (2) 5'-0" SCISSORS WITH 1'-6" DIAMETER DISCS

COLLAPSED 5'-0" SCISSOR

EXPANDED 9'-0" SCISSOR SHOWING CUT-OFF POINTS FOR 7'-0" AND 5'-0" SCISSORS

DETAIL DRAWING OF SCISSOR DANCE PROPS
FOR CALDER BALLET
PENNSYLVANIA BALLET COMPANY
DATE SEPT. 20 1976
SCALE 1"=1'-0"   DWG # 7
DESIGNED BY R.D. MITCHELL

8. Cut detailed painting. Again, you can delete certain portions of detailed painting instead of cutting the whole unit. You might cut stenciled surfaces and go to blended textures with brush or spraying.

9. Simplify any canvas appliqués on scenic netting.

10. Reduce any plastic items such as Plexiglas or acrylic sheets, and so on.

11. Reduce the detailed painting on a sharkstooth scrim.

12. Cut a sharkstooth scrim.

13. Cut a drop and reuse another with a change of lighting effects and/or projections.

14. Reduce or cut sculptured scenery and shop for a substitute piece of sculpture.

15. Eliminate detailed painting going offstage and fade to solid color painting.

16. Eliminate painting entirely where it doesn't show, such as behind cabinets, bookcases, or the like.

lected replanning, it still may be necessary to cut an individual piece of scenery here and there.

This rehashing process may sound agonizing to the young designer. But experience brings knowledge of what runs up the cost on specific items of scenery and what pieces or materials can easily be cut without jeopardizing the design.

Another way to save costs is to think in terms of how you can dress the set(s) with props or dressing in a way that the audience won't miss some of your intended built and painted effects. The following are somewhat standard deletions and may be considered as examples of how to cut when budget demands.

1. Cut all black velour fabric and replace with black Granada cloth for portals, masking legs and borders, backdrops, or on units to be covered with black velour.

2. Cut a translucent muslin drop and use a muslin drop with seams.

3. Cut three-dimensional molding and use painted molding. Sometimes three-dimensional molding can be reduced to a combination of part three-dimensional and part painted.

4. Cut down part of a platform unit.

5. Cut or simplify any metal scenery.

6. Cut a curved cyc and use a straight backdrop.

7. Cut a filled-scrim backdrop or show curtain and use a muslin drop with seams.

DRAWING PRACTICES AND TECHNIQUES

Drawing with a Consistent Line

For drafting, the scenic designer is taught to draw mechanically with a single consistent pencil line because that is the neatest and most accurate way to show the shape of an object with pencil and paper. Consistency of line is achieved by executing a line with the same width and the same pressure on the pencil. This produces the best contrast with the lines on the printed copies of the drafting after they have been taken to the blue-printers. Naturally, some lines are drawn with heavy weight, some with medium weight, and some with light weight, depending on their purpose. The scenic designer is expected to do just this on all the various sheets of drafting that form the set of drawings for building and executing the show in the studio.

In another example of single-line work the scenic artist in the scenic studio makes a full-scale drawing on brown paper and then with a pounce wheel perforates a single line in the paper so that a bag of powdered charcoal can be rubbed over the tiny holes to transfer the drawing onto a surface for building or painting.

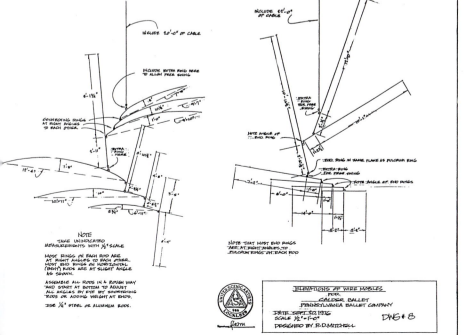

ELEVATIONS OF WIRE MOBILES
FOR CALDER BALLET
PENNSYLVANIA BALLET COMPANY
DATE SEPT. 20, 1976
SCALE 1/2"=1'-0"   DWG # 8
DESIGNED BY R.D. MITCHELL

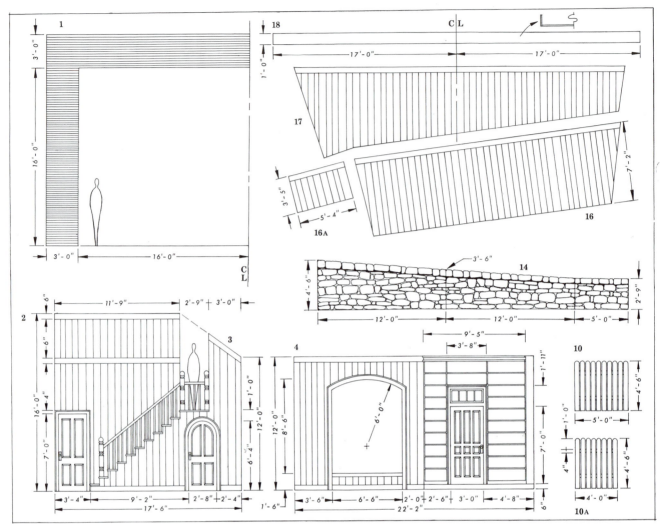

Original drawings were done in ½-inch scale. Not shown are the sky backdrop, molding drawings, and other details. The portal opening was 32'-0" by 16'-0".

Note that the ground plan and section drawing are shown in smaller scales than the front elevations (above).

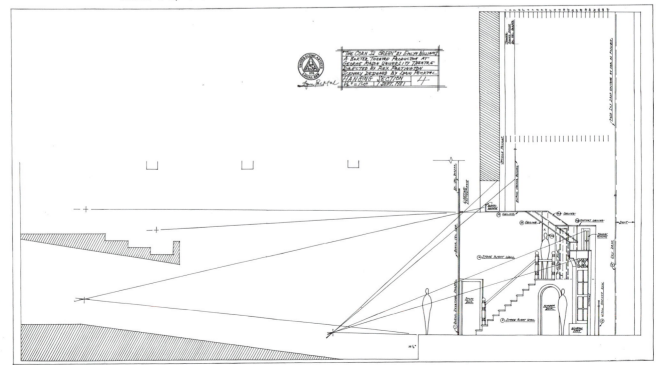

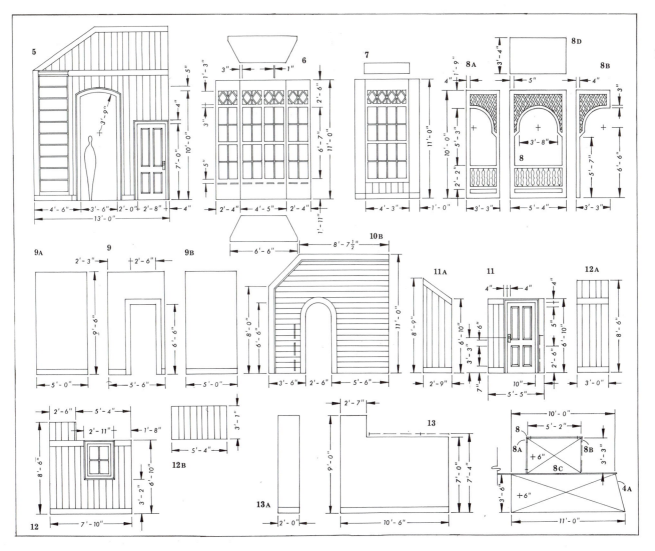

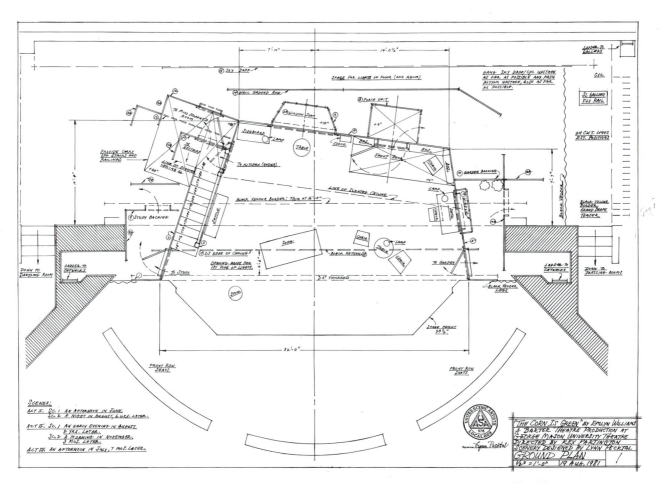

"THE CORN IS GREEN" BY EMLYN WILLIAMS
A BARTER THEATRE PRODUCTION AT
GEORGE MASON UNIVERSITY THEATRE
DIRECTED BY REX PARTINGTON
SCENERY DESIGNED BY LYNN PECKTAL
GROUND PLAN
1/2" = 1'-0"   19 AUG. 1981

Basic Rendering on Elevations with Freehand Lines, Dots, and Shading

While the scenic designer normally does mechanical drawing on drafting with a T-square, triangle, French curves, and compasses, there are some parts of drawings, as well as complete drawings, in which freehand rendering is done for specific reasons.

When doing freehand rendering with a pencil and you want to use various rendering techniques, keep in mind that pencil leads come in various line weights and the quality you get in a drawing depends on the grade of the graphite, the texture of the paper, and the amount of pressure on the pencil. When preparing to execute freehand pencil renderings, consider these points:

1. The width and length of the line. (It may be regular or be made to do something like going from thick to thin or thin to thick.)
2. The weight of the line (the heaviness or lightness).
3. The direction of the line (diagonal, vertical, horizontal, curved, radiating).
4. The space between lines (regular or irregular).
5. The overlapping of lines (slight to solid).

Costume designs by Peter Harvey
FIREBIRD 2006 (idea sketches)
Choreographed by Fernand Nault
Colorado Ballet, Denver, Colorado (1981)

There are numerous ways a pencil can be used to render lines, to shade, and to make dots on elevations of drafting. Sometimes shading is also done on the ground plan. Remember that all sorts of rendering techniques can be employed to simulate a flat or dimensional surface, a reflective or nonreflective surface, a textured surface, or planes that are shadowed. The following are just a few examples of rendering ideas for elevation drawings:

1. Show different planes of stones in a large wall to indicate overlapping the various blocks of stonework. (The most distant stones may be the lightest, the most forward the darkest, with the middle ones in medium shading.)
2. Specify three-dimensional shapes (statues, trees, or draperies) with conventional shading to make them seem shaped naturally by using the technique of light, shade, and shadow in the pencil rendering.
3. Explain on the elevation of a cut drop what portion of the material gets cut out and is then supported by 1-inch scenic netting with one specific example of pencil rendering; or what gets support by another material, such as linen scrim, shown by another different example.
4. Tell what the actual materials are supposed to be (drawn lines to indicate wood graining on doors or timbers, and wavy lines to denote water. The latter may be a series of horizontal wavy lines that are spaced wide at the bottom of the drawing and gradually

closer as it goes upward in elevation.) Other materials, such as stucco and concrete, may be represented with fine dots.

5. Indicate a reflective material such as glass panes in windows (diagonal lines with varied lengths and irregular spacing, or random scattered dots going from light placement to almost solid shading in the upper corners and around the edges).
6. Show the different shapes and intensity of materials (old and varied-shaped bricks) rendered as dark, medium, and light, with unbroken and some broken corners; and antique and aged wooden shingles).
7. Make the position of the portal legs more prominent (by shading them on the 1/2-inch scale master ground plan) and also sometimes the basic outline of a box set (also shaded with pencil, but only when the break of the next adjacent flats can be indicated with a heavier line for clarity).
8. Make 1/2-inch scale drawings of floor details of ground cloths and decks (rendered outlines of cobblestones, brick paviors, wood, or stone paving).

Drawing Half of a Design

This method of drawing half of a design on folded paper is not new. It is commonly used when making a large, symmetrical, full-scale perforated pounce or when drafting a symmetrical design. For a perforated pounce, draw half of the design in charcoal or pencil on brown paper. When ready to run a pounce wheel over the drawing, simply fold the paper at the center line and secure the open edges together with pieces of masking tape. Then prick the outline of the half drawing through both layers of the paper simultaneously, remove the masking tape, and unfold the pounce. The entire design will have been completed for the pounce.

For drafting, draw half of the symmetrical design on tracing paper, fold the paper in half, and trace the drawing to complete the second half of the symmetrical design. When the tracing is completed, unfold the paper that now has the completed design on it. This drawing can be placed under a larger sheet of tracing paper and retraced on the larger sheet. This process can be followed for any number of designs, including bells, finials, chandeliers,

gothic windows, newel posts, and stencils.

Tracing over a Single Drawing

This basically involves making a single drawing (the rough) on a smaller piece of tracing paper and putting it under a larger sheet of tracing paper (the final when finished). This is done (1) to see where the drawing looks best in the design or (2) to trace duplicates of the same design in position on a larger drawing.

Single tracings are used in countless ways. They may be: A tracing of a typical standing 6-foot human figure to be placed next to a piece of scenery; a baluster to be repeated in a balustrade; a section of iron grillwork to be reversed and repeated; a repeat pattern of floral wallpaper; a leaf for an asymmetrical potted plant arrangement—and on and on.

A big advantage of using a single tracing is that it can be moved around on the larger drawing in order to figure out the exact position of an object. This is very helpful when figuring how high a chandelier should be, or if a prominent sign on a clapboard feed store is too large or too small, or whether the proportion of a framed valance on window draperies works well.

Tracing over Multiple Drawings

There are times when tracings of two or more drawings are used under a larger sheet. It is a simple way of relating the proportions of the different shapes to each other. A composite overlay can be part of the finished presentation, or it may be used for exploration in evolving the design to your satisfaction. Listed are just a few examples of multiple drawings used as either underlays or overlays.

1. Multiple settings on a master ground plan
2. The 6-foot figure of an actor standing in front of furniture positioned in front of an interior set
3. Three full exterior sets consisting of irregularly shaped cut legs and borders as they appear in front of a pastoral landscape and sky
4. Drapery treatment over Venetian blinds on window panes with foliage appearing outside

Practicing Freehand Drawing

Every designer and artist should practice freehand drawing whenever possible. Not only does it stimulate one's thinking, but it is rewarding when something interesting appears on the page. As a student designer it is extremely important to learn to discipline oneself to draw the same object several times before settling on the final sketch that is to be painted and rendered in color. Very often, the young artist will draw something too quickly and will begin the painting without taking the time to study the drawing and to think out all the possibilities. The best actor tries reading a line many different ways before getting it right. The designer and the artist do the same thing in making a sketch.

Beginning drawing assignments for the designer should include a series of simple sketches done one after another of the same subject, with about five or ten minutes spent on a sketch. These sketches should be done as a continuous outline of an object, like the drawings in the most basic coloring book. Shading or scratchy or multiple broken lines should not be used. Imagine that the drawing is to be made as a line drawing to be published in a magazine, or possibly it is to be perforated for transferring a design with a bag of powdered charcoal. It is extremely helpful when doing the initial sketch to think of how you will execute the painting for the light, shade, and shadow.

Materials for Sketching

These materials are appropriate for making sketches.

DRAWING

Regular writing pencils	Charcoal pencils or sticks
Wax pencils	Ballpoint pens
Pen and ink	Crayons and pastels

GROUNDS

White or colored papers	Brown Kraft paper
Tracing paper	Gray bogus paper
	Newsprint paper pads

Subjects for Practicing Freehand Drawing

There is an absolute treasure of subject matter from which the stage designer can choose to make basic drawings.

Again, these drawings should consist of simple and continuous lines without any shading. To practice freehand drawing, you might want to choose one of the following subjects:

1. *A still-life arrangement.* This could be anything from simple flowers in a milk carton to a bouquet of red roses arranged in a silver champagne cooler. It could be a still-life of a group of pots and pans from the kitchen, or any interesting objects that you have on hand. Suggested size of the drawing: 14 × 14 inches.
2. *Hanging drapery swags.* Take pieces of fabric and drape them on a wall or on the backs of two straight side chairs to form a nice curved swag with jabots on each end. The size of the draped fabric should be at least 2 feet high by 4 feet wide. A different kind of draped effect can be obtained with the various fabrics that you use. For instance, try any of the following draped on the bias: velour, sharkstooth scrim, muslin, or brocade. See how each piece of fabric drapes.
3. *Trees in nature.* Select an exterior tree growing in its natural surrounding and make sketches of it during the different seasons of the year. Suggested sketch size: 8 ½ × 14 inches.

Freehand Sketching in the Theatre

It is also a good idea to go to the theatre and make sketches of how the scenery will look from a specific location. For instance, if you are designing the setting for an open stage production, make several drawings from various locations. In fact, the custom in an open stage is to do locations like the numbers on the face of a clock. With this in mind, plan to do a freehand sketch of how the set will look from the first row at the six o'clock position, looking straight ahead at twelve o'clock.

Then go to several rows of seats in the middle of the house and do another sketch of what the set is to look like from ten o'clock looking toward four o'clock. As you are sketching, make sure you are drawing continuous single lines as opposed to scribbling or shaded lines. When you have completed the sketch with the drawing done as an outline of the set, props, and furniture or whatever, begin to do any necessary shading or texturing that you may want to do. It makes a sketch more interesting if you include figures of actors in the appropriate costumes as well as indicating stage lighting as much as possible. Think of where the instruments may be positioned and where you would have light, shade, and shadows, and render this with pencil or pen.

When the sketches are finished, copies may be made of each sketch and you can paint one or more renderings of the scene. This is an ideal approach because you can dash them off without having to worry about ruining the only good one.

The same approach to sketching in varying positions may be used in the proscenium theatre. Do one sketch from the customary position in the center of the orchestra. Then execute another sketch from the house left side of the mezzanine, and still yet another from above at the right side of the balcony. Not only is this an excellent opportunity for practicing sketching, but it also indicates how you must think about the different aspects of the set. And of course, making the latter two sketches may demand a great deal of your imagination.

Drawing Faces and Figures for Costume Sketches

The talented costume designer who cannot execute sketches with well-proportioned and handsome faces and figures may find the impact of his or her costume presentation is diminished. Since a beautifully executed sketch of the appropriate character enhances the costume design and gives an added punch to the selling of the idea (whether individually or in a group), it is important for designers who don't draw figures and faces well to find other methods of presentation to show off their costume designs to best advantage.

Using Paper Dolls for Costume Designs

One way to present costume designs is to use paper dolls to display the sketches.

1. Purchase paper dolls in novelty, toy, and specialty shops or have them created by an artist you may know.
2. Whether made from scratch or purchased, the male figure should be 10 to 12 inches high, with the female and children figures in proper proportion.
3. Select paper dolls that have various hairstyles and makeup, since these features vary a great deal according to the characters in a show.
4. Cut out the paper dolls and, if necessary, mount them on a medium-heavy board. Cut tabs to make the figures stand up for presentation.
5. Plan on making one or more costume sketches to fit on the paper doll. It is very simple to attach one cutout painted costume and then change quickly to another.
6. It is also a good idea to finish the backs of the paper dolls so that costumes can be shown from the rear when such a view is necessary for a particular costume.
7. Samples of fabric, trim, and other materials can be attached to the paper costume.

A collection of paper dolls may be used over and over for different presentations. The paper dolls pack nicely in a box for storage or for carrying.

Tracing Costume Figures

As an alternative to using paper or real dolls, a designer who has problems rendering costume figures may find various photographs and drawings suitable to trace for the individual figure in detailed costume plates. Use transfer paper to put the basic figure shapes onto the board for finished drawing and painting. In this way, the basic drawings can be kept on file and can be used repeatedly. The idea here is to create a large collection of figures (male, female, children, and young adults) to have them ready to use when time is short. This idea works well for either straight or angled views of a single figure and when more than one figure is used on a costume plate.

Another method of tracing figures from photographs or drawings is to use a light box. Put the item to be copied on top of the lighted box, and cover it with a sheet of clear acetate. Use a fine-point pen with ink that will take on acetate, and trace the figure. The acetate tracing can be photocopied on 25 percent white rag paper. Mount the photocopies on board for the final rendering. You could also retrace from the acetate drawing on the light box directly on paper suitable for rendering.

Costume designs by William Ivey Long for THE POINTER SISTERS—"Jump," directed and choreographed by Kenny Ortega, national tour 1987–1988.

Or, you could place tracing paper over the acetate drawing on the light box, and with a pencil trace the figure. Once the drawing is on the tracing paper, copies can be made using a blueprint machine.

These figure tracings should be in appropriate proportion to each other, with the basic male figures approximately 10 to 12 inches high. Use a copying machine to reduce or increase the size of a few of the drawings to manage a group of figures.

Sources for tracing costume figures are available in high-fashion magazines, photography magazines, anatomy books, children's books, art books, clothing catalogs, and other publications.

Organizing Research Material

Every designer collects research material of some kind and puts it away for later reference and study. But unless it is kept in some order and stored where it is always accessible, it can often go untouched. Both complete issues and individual pages from all kinds of magazines are invaluable. Magazines and books may include the following:

Architectural Digest
Town and Country
House Beautiful
Travel and Leisure
Colonial Home
Casa Vogue
National
   Geographic
Elle
New York
   Magazine
Art and Antiques
Vogue
Vanity Fair
Interior Design
The World of
   Interiors
Better Homes and
   Gardens
House and Garden
Home
Country Living
Metropolitan Home

Departures
Natural History
Southern Living
Connoisseur
Historic
   Preservation
Casa Vogue
   Antiques
European Travel and
   Life
Southern Accents
La Mia Casa
   Antiques
Laura Ashley Home
   Furnishings
Vogue Decoration
Mirabella
Theatre Crafts
Opera News
Theatre World
Lighting
   Dimensions
Dover books

There are also catalogs and pamphlets of many kind that include art supplies, molding, balusters, wood products, sculpture supplies, lighting equipment, sheet metal ornaments, pressed metal ceilings, paint catalogs, and lettering books. In addition, designers and artists photograph scenes and objects that strike their fancy to use for research.

One of the best ways to keep research materials in an organized manner is to put them in regular metal or wooden file cabinets. Manila or similar folders for every subject on which research is collected help keep materials together. These folders may either sit or hang in the file cabinet drawers. Arrange the subjects in alphabetical order so that the research material can be found quickly when needed.

Another aspect of compiling research material is to avoid letting it accumulate in a large stack and go unfiled. It is tiring and boring to file a great amount of loose research material and place it in individual files at one time. If pages of research are filed immediately after they are found and clipped, then it is easier to keep the collection up-to-date.

The categories and headings for individual research subjects are endless, but this list of subjects may be helpful:

States of the United States	Asian countries
Foliage, trees, and shrubs	Costumes of all periods
Baroque and Rococo designs	Ancient Rome and Egypt
Circuses and theme parks	Chandeliers and lamps
Figure drawings and portraits	Artists and painters
Props and set dressing	Architectural designs
Fountains and gardens	Furniture of all kinds
United States	Theatrical sets
European countries	Rugs and carpets
Statuary and sculpture	Fabrics and materials
	Animals and birds
	Dishes and pottery
	Maps and prints

Costume designs by William Ivey Long for LEND ME A TENOR by Ken Ludwig, directed by Jerry Zaks, Royale Theatre, New York (1989).

Archival drawings are a permanent record of a production's scenic units as they are actually constructed. They are often done for new productions, such as those in large-scale opera companies in which the scenery goes into storage for an extended period of time and then comes back into repertory. These drawings show any changes that have been made in the course of construction and production that do not appear on the designer's original drawings.

To keep track of the process in which new productions actually take shape, a permanent staff member is needed to do the archival drawings. For instance, draftsperson Julia Rogoff spent approximately four years making archival drawings for the San Francisco Opera Company. Rogoff drew ground plans in ¼-inch = 1'-0" scale and elevations, sections, and details in, typically ½-inch = 1'-0" scale, with dimensions and notes. The drawings were then reduced for easy handling and filing. The archival drawings completed by Rogoff have served several purposes:

1. They were used as a guide to assemble and set up the pieces of scenery when the new production returned to the repertory. The drawings clearly indicated to the stage carpenter and stagehands just how to put together each piece of scenery based on the labeling system marked on each unit.

2. They were kept on file to be easily referred to whenever the San Francisco Opera scheduled the production to return to the repertory.

3. They are used for replacing or rebuilding a scenic piece if it is damaged in storage or in performance. The drawings also make it easy to identify any piece of scenery that may be missing from storage.

4. They also provide essential information to another company that is renting the scenery for its own production. The drawings are also helpful for the new company to determine sight lines and new hangings that may be necessary for the scenery to fit its stage.

5. Whether on a new production or a revival, the archival drawings are used for rehearsal information by the opera staff, including the director, scenic and lighting designers, carpenters, and stage manager.

Douglas W. Schmidt talked about theatre and design in his studio located in the heart of Manhattan's theatre district. Born October 4, 1942, he was educated at Boston University. His Broadway debut was *Paris Is Out!* by Richard Seff in 1970. He has designed the scenery for a great number of companies, including the Juilliard Opera Theatre, Guthrie Theatre, Cincinnati Playhouse in the Park, Arena Stage, Music Theatre of Tanglewood, Theatre of the Living Arts, Juilliard Dance Company, Baltimore's Center Stage, Old Globe Theatre, Mark Taper Forum, Ahmanson Theatre, San Francisco Ballet, Manhattan Theatre Club, Studio Arena Theatre, New York City Opera, Chelsea Theatre Center, American Conservatory Theatre, PepsiCo Summerfare, Art Park, San Francisco Opera, American Shakespeare Festival, Saratoga Spa Theatre, and New York Shakespeare Festival. He has also designed for television. He is the recipient of two Drama Desk Awards, a Maharam Award, and an Obie Award. Among his scenic design credits are:

Broadway
Nick and Nora (1991)
Smile (1986)
Dancing in the End Zone (1985)
Porgy and Bess (1983)
   Radio City Music Hall
Frankenstein (1981)
They're Playing Our Song (1979)
Peter Allen: Up in One (1979)
Romantic Comedy (1979)
The Most Happy Fella (1979)
Runaways (1978)
The Robber Bridegroom (1976)
Angel Street (1975)
Over Here! (1974)
Fame (1974)

Veronica's Room (1973)
The Country Girl (1972)
Grease (1972)

San Francisco Opera
Aïda (1981)
Samson et Dalila (1980)
Angle of Repose (1976)

New York Shakespeare Festival
Agamemnon (1977)
   Beaumont Theatre
The Threepenny Opera (1976)
   Beaumont Theatre
Kid Champion (1975)
   Public Theatre

Our Late Night (1975)
   Public Theatre

**Repertory Theatre of Lincoln
   Center, Beaumont Theatre**
A Streetcar Named Desire (1973)
The Plough and the Stars (1973)
Twelfth Night (1972)
Enemies (1971)
Antigone (1971)
Mary Stuart (1971)
An Enemy of the People (1971)
The Good Woman of Setzuan (1970)
Operation Sidewinder (1970)
The Time of Your Life (1969)

Setting by Douglas W. Schmidt
TRUFFLES IN THE SOUP
Author/director: Daniel Sullivan

Costumes by Ann Hould-Ward
Lighting by Pat Collins

Seattle Repertory Theatre
Seattle, Washington (1989)
(Photograph by Chris Bennion)

How did you first become interested in designing for the theatre?

As a kid I was always interested in the theatre. I remember one experience on the stage of the Taft Auditorium in Cincinnati, Ohio, when Harry Blackstone, Sr., the magician, called for volunteers from the audience. I was among the group of children who scrambled onto the stage. I was probably five or six years old then, and after that experience, I became a child magician. I had interests in theatre all through grade school and high school. In high school I wrote, directed, and designed some plays.

I went to Boston University in 1961 as a directing major in the arts program. Horace Armistead was the head of the department and Raymond Sovey was a professor there. I discovered very early on that sheer numbers dictated that design would be a much easier route to follow. As I looked across the room there seemed to be five hundred directing majors and four design majors, and so I said, "I think I want to be over there with the designers." It had been a toss-up between the two anyway. I was at the school for three years, and then I was offered a job with Ming Cho Lee at the New York Shakespeare Festival.

Had Ming seen some of your work, or did you contact him?

In 1963 I sent a résumé out for a summer job, and I got a call from Betsy Lee, who said, "Well, we like your drafting, but you've got to come down right away and interview. This is a summer job, but we start early." School was in session, and there was still snow on the ground in Boston. So I schlepped down to New York on the Night Owl from Boston and showed up at Ming's and interviewed for the job. He called back a couple of days later and said, "The job is yours if you want it, but we start next week." And I remarked, "But I seem to be in the middle of the semester here." He said, "I know it's difficult, but that's the way it's got to be." And so at that point I had to make an important decision about my future.

Did you finish at Boston University?

No, I didn't. I rented a U-Haul and never looked back. Actually, if I had it all to do over again, knowing what I know now, I probably would have finished school. But I think simply that the nature of this business is that you

have to evaluate where your interests lie, and at that moment my interests lay in New York City and the Broadway stage.

I came in very early spring and worked until the end of the summer assisting Ming on his shows for Joe Papp. I worked for Ming over a period of three years. The last year I was sort of in and out, not full-time. I was full-time for about two years. We worked regular hours, which for Ming was from ten o'clock in the morning until seven o'clock at night. Occasionally he would say, "Take a half a day off and come in at noon." It was seven days a week until the end of the summer. While I was working for Ming, I was also doing things on my own. Later during that early period, via Ming's mentorship, I designed for Joe Papp. Joe's career had just begun its stellar rise. I also designed at the Playhouse in the Park in Cincinnati. I did them primarily by mail and would take a week or two off and go out and do a show and then come back to Ming's.

The very first show that I designed in Cincinnati was the Ibsen play *Ghosts*. It was directed by Lloyd Richards, and it was a very gratifying experience. He's a wonderful director. This was before his Yale connection, and when he came back to New York after that season, he had a play that he was going to do Off-Broadway and he called me. It was *The Ox Cart*, and it played at the Greenwich Mews Theatre, which Stella Holt was running. That was the first job that really spun off from another working situation.

Was that production noteworthy?

Yes, it was actually. You might call it Hispanic soap opera. I don't know exactly how to describe it. It was about the Puerto Rican experience of the agricultural tradition giving way to inner-city conflict. A family moves from the countryside into the city, and has to deal with all of the obvious conflicts that arise from that. It had a wonderful cast. Miriam Colon was the ingenue, and a guy named Raul Julia played the older brother. Raul was stupendous, and it was the first time I'd ever seen him. I think it was the first time anybody had ever seen him. He was just great.

What was the budget like?

It was definitely up into the three figures! We might have had $500 if we

were lucky. I know the minimum fee to design a show for Off-Broadway was $125 at that time, and that meant to design the show, paint it, and do all that yourself. *The Ox Cart* was produced by Miriam and her husband, who were just at that point forming the Puerto Rican Traveling Theatre Company. That has now developed into a major company in this town on West Forty-third Street. They do a lot of touring around the boroughs. The costumes were done by Joseph Aulisi, who is now a major film designer, and the lighting designer was James Gore.

Did that show help you to make definite decisions about your career?

No, I already knew what I wanted to do and that seemed like the first step. In those days, you did as much as you physically could do, and you could occasionally get into trouble just by virtue of overextension. But when you're young, you can take a lot of abuse, and you want to progress as rapidly as possible. The only way to do that is to get out there and get the credits, and more importantly to work with the directors because that's how you get jobs. *The Ox Cart*, for example, proves the point of the opportunity to come to New York from the regional theatre. The director asked for me, and I came with him. And really that's how it still happens. It doesn't happen by and large through producers, although occasionally it might. Generally, it's through having worked previously with directors who are comfortable with you.

Comment on how your first Broadway show came about.

For years I thought it something to be best forgotten, but now I realize that it was, in one way, historic and I'm pleased and rather proud of having been associated with the other people who were involved with it. I don't really remember the specifics of how I was contacted, except that I suspect I was recommended by Ming or, as most young designers, by someone else whom I had worked with.

My first Broadway show opened in January of 1970. It was called *Paris Is Out!* It was a comedy written by Richard Seff, who was a big-time agent then. He was part of one of those agencies that eventually became amalgamated with some other big agency. Richard decided to go his own way and to be a playwright, and after that became an actor. He wrote this comedy which I suspect was heavily autobiographical. It had a very sitcom plot about an aging Jewish couple who are taking a cruise for the first time in their lives. From the surface it sounds pretty inane, but you must realize that the mother was played by Molly Picon in one of her last shows and Sam Levene was the father. So there were these two wonderful, crusty, hysterically funny characters on stage. It was really quite enjoyable to watch these pros who had been working together in a performance style of theatre we know less and less about, because it was born of Second Avenue. It had an age-old quality about it that you immediately responded to. It was so warm and endearing.

Describe the scenery.

It was very simple. In fact, it was two box sets that moved on and off. As I was reading the play I thought, "Thank God it's not that complicated since this is my first Broadway show. It's a living room box set." When I got to the last scene, the script said, "Now we're in the cabin on the boat!" So I used a double turntable kind of truck, which worked very well for that very fast scene change.

What happened after this? How did you get your next show?

I was working fairly regularly by then in regional theatre and Off-Broadway. I was doing quite a lot of work for the American Place Theatre and for the opera theatre at Juilliard. When I first came to New York to work for Ming, he was finishing up an opera at Juilliard with the director Christopher West. I remember the very first chore assigned to me was to cut out a million delicate birch trees for Ming's model of Leoš Janáček's opera *Kata Kabanova* for Juilliard. The summer wasn't even geared up yet, as Ming was just beginning to have conceptual meetings with Joe Papp, who was directing *Hamlet*, the first Shakespeare Festival show.

How many shows did you do at Juilliard?

Quite a number. The first one I did was in 1966. It was a production of *La Bohème* with Christopher West directing. I think he directed everything uptown until the very end. He died during the production period of *The Mines of Sulphur*, which we were working on

together, and then John Houseman took over. John Houseman was just in the process of getting his faculty together and organizing the new drama division at Juilliard. *The Mines of Sulphur* was in 1967. It was a Richard Rodney Bennett opera that was premiering in America, and it was very interesting. Between 1966 and 1967 I did *Bohème, The Marriage of Figaro*, and *The Mines of Sulphur* at Juilliard.

Were there good budgets?

Yes, reasonably. You could certainly do far more than you could Off-Broadway. Again, the scenic art was always something the designer ended up either organizing or doing himself. The fees were not great, but you have to remember this was the mid-sixties. The designer's fee was something like $500, and that was better than Off-Broadway. Even to this day you can't make a living doing this kind of work. (Well, it's gotten so to this day that you can't even make a living doing Broadway.) Those opportunities exist for new talent to develop, and it can be looked at as exploitive and some people feel that it is. On the other hand, you've got to get the experience somewhere, and these shows don't even pay the producers a lot of money. So I always felt it a learning experience, and I was always grateful for that opportunity.

Tell how Grease *came about.*

Grease was a musical that was running in Chicago to great acclaim. It was seen by Maxine Fox and Ken Waissman, who were in partnership at the

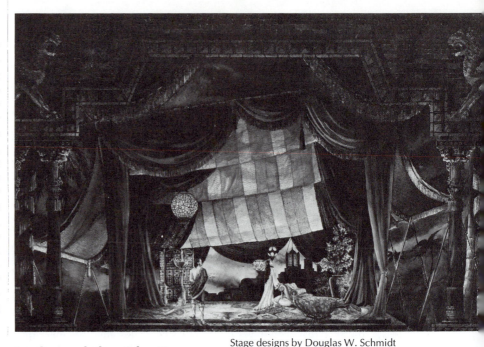

Stage designs by Douglas W. Schmidt
SAMSON ET DALILA by Camille Saint-Saëns
Left: Act 2; *right:* Act 3, Scene 1
Directed by Nicolas Joel
San Francisco Opera
San Francisco, California (1980)

time and looking for something to produce. She and Ken optioned this property to produce Off-Broadway. In their first venture as producers of an Off-Broadway show, they wanted to have people around them whom they liked and trusted, and that's really how Carrie Robbins and I got involved with it. Maxine had been a classmate of mine at Boston University, and Carrie had known Maxine from somewhere else. They hired a director whom we had never heard of, but they had seen some of his work at Yale and liked it very much. This was Tom Moore. And for the choreography they hired Patty Birch, who I believe I had just done something with at Juilliard. So, it was people who knew each other and respected each other and were happy to be working together. Not that there weren't conflicts and bumps along the road, but even in the direst moments of that highly volatile situation of getting a show on, we all at heart had faith in each other.

The playwrights were Jim Jacobs and Warren Casey from the Chicago production, and they had loved and nurtured this baby into being. When Patsy and Tom came aboard as choreographer and director, of course they wanted to stir it up a little bit and do some work on it. That's the nature of the beast. There is always some negotiating during that period of prepro-

duction. But it was a great success downtown at what was then the Eden Theatre. It opened in February of 1972. *Grease* moved to the Broadhurst in June of that year, and then in November it moved to the Royale Theatre. It ran eight years, and closed in April 1980.

How would you describe what you designed for Grease?

I did a classic Elizabethan formal wooden O. It had an above, inner below, and a pair of stairs leading up to the platform in the center. It was as simple and classical as I could make it. It really grew from the director and the choreographer searching for the most straightforward approach that we could come up with. And then it was all decked out with high school pictures and gym lockers and the vernacular of the period to give it the fifties flavor. But basically it was an Elizabethan stage.

Did Grease *bring a lot of attention to your work?*

From 1970-ish through the time that *Grease* opened and through 1974, more or less, was the period that I was working as a resident designer at Lincoln Center for Jules Irving. It is a period of time that I look back on with great fondness. I was very fond of Jules and the people who worked there, and they are friends for life even though the company has long since disappeared. It's such a pleasure to see the people that you thought had talent having fulfilled that promise. I did about eighteen productions during that regime. That

was in the Vivian Beaumont and the Forum theatres.

Do you have a favorite production or two during that time?

My fond remembrances often do not necessarily correspond with the quality of the show. For me, the experience of working in the theatre and designing is the excitement of the chemistry. It's about people with energy and intelligence and enthusiasm coming together and mixing and stirring up, and the process of evolving a production scheme and carrying out a vision with the director. Occasionally that will bear wonderful fruit. I always say that sitting around the table is where we'll have the fun. We get into the theatre and it's pure hell. That's no fun really. It's only fun in the theatre when it finally is together and you can see what you've got. Then you either love it or you hate it. The real fun is where you say, "What if?" and plan, and talk and enjoy each other. Every one of those productions at Lincoln Center has something to say for it in terms of that. *Operation Sidewinder* comes to mind.

It was a play by Sam Shepard. A fantastic surreal vision of the apocalypse which probably was better on the page than on the stage, I don't really know. You get so involved in these things you can't tell. Frankly, I enjoyed it. I thought it was pretty interesting. The set turned the Vivian Beaumont into a painted desert. It was all papier mâché mesas painted Day-Glo. It had a very Pop look, much in the style of the art of the period. But the fun of it was working with Michael Schultz, a direc-

tor who has seemingly forsaken the stage for film, which I think is too bad because I think one of his greatest strengths is his gentleness of approach and his way of communicating with his artistic staff and with his actors.

What were your limitations or your boundaries, or did you have any?

There were always boundaries. The company was always foundering economically.

The interesting thing about the pressure from the economics was that it forced us into using the space in ways that would limit the amount of resources we had to pour into it. It's a vast, vast stage. There is room there to store half the Metropolitan Opera rep if you wanted. The theatre was originally designed as a rep house to have three or four shows in it simultaneously. It never happened because rep is not looked upon with great favor, especially on that scale. In this town there's no way to afford it. Maybe it's not necessary.

Did you utilize both the thrust and the proscenium stage?

Depending on the financial constraints, the proscenium would get smaller and smaller and smaller, and we'd end up on the thrust. Some productions we did completely on the thrust. I remember *Playboy of the Western World* was a little thrust and some furniture and a small back wall with all those great big brown panels brought down to the floor. On other occasions, like *Operation Sidewinder*, we'd use the whole stage right up to the back wall with a whole huge painted cyc and the turntable and anything else that was in the theatre.

What kind of turntable was available?

There is a big turntable built into the stage. It's 40 feet across or something like that. Actually, the turntable itself is about 30 feet across and then there's a ring that goes around it which I would think is about 5 or 6 feet wide. It's a turntable within a turntable, and we used that quite a lot. In fact, we even overused at some points. We had so much stuff on it for *Enemies*, the stagehands had to give it a shove to get it started.

But all in all you enjoyed your experiences there?

Very much. It was a family, and Jules was very much the father figure. We all admired and respected him and we did feel the responsibility that he entrusted us with, which was to get the show on and ensure that the company had a viable following year. Just in terms of artistic satisfaction, I would have to say that it gradually built over the four years that I was there. At the end, we were producing as well as any company in the country at the time, and to critical acclaim. By then it was just too late. The steam had run out and we were history, which is an irony, because that last year we did some of the great productions that that period is remembered for. We did that wonderful production of *A Streetcar Named Desire* with Rosemary Harris and James Farentino, Trish Connelly and Phil Bosco, a great cast. We did a spectacular production of a play called *Enemies* by Gorki. It felt very nice to go out of there with our heads up. *Streetcar* went to Broadway after it closed at Lincoln Center.

It was just one thing after another. For years Jules would have to go out and rustle up money himself. That theatre was an extremely difficult plant to maintain. I was not completely privy to the financial structure, but I knew a bit about it. It was a heavy burden for a company that was not established and that did not have a great following. You were responsible for not only getting the season on, hiring the staff, doing the production, paying the ushers, opening the doors, and heating it, you had to do your share of keeping up the plaza and fixing the leaking fountain and the parking garage underneath it. It was just insane. So much energy went into fulfilling the obligations of being a constituent of Lincoln Center that it's a miracle that any shows got on at all, especially in a time when the live theatre was not something that popular at Lincoln Center. Theatre had been through a lot of rocky years there and never really found a loyal following.

How much time would you say you spent on a production?

You tried to keep ahead. Toward the end of the production period of one play, you tried to be working on the next one. So we would have an opening in January and it would run for two months, and then we would have another opening in the beginning of March, then we'd have another opening the beginning of May.

The hope always was that we would find some big popular success that could be plugged in. Occasionally they did book things in for the summer just so the building would generate some money. It was a very expensive theatre to keep closed. *Man of La Mancha* went in there one summer, and a Ustinov play went in another summer, but those were extracurricular, and they were not part of Vivian Beaumont. That was when it became just a booking house. I went back there for two shows with Joe Papp. I did *Threepenny Opera* and the Serban *Antigone*.

What about The Threepenny Opera? *How did that go?*

That was a wonderful experience for me. The director was Richard Foreman, Pat Collins was the lighting designer, and Theoni Aldredge did the clothes. Richard Foreman is a performance artist whose work I had admired greatly in the seventies and I still do. I got to know him because of Stanley Silverman, who was the musical director at the Vivian Beaumont during the RTLC regime. Stanley was writing these apparently very strange music theatre pieces with Richard. I thought it would be interesting to see a performance, so I went across town to Hunter College to see one of their pieces called *Elephant Steps* and was blown away! I was quite enthralled by the kind of stuff they were doing.

Subsequently I saw some of the things that they produced in the Berkshires by Lyn Austin at a place called Wheatleigh, an estate that abuts Tanglewood. So when Joe Papp announced that Richard was going to do *Threepenny* in a new translation by Ralph Manheim, I was thrilled to be in on it, and also because I think Richard Foreman is one of the most original director-designers working in the theatre today. He never ceases to amaze. I just love his work.

Working for him was unlike my experiences with any other director I had ever worked with before, believe me. He was, and still is, a visionary and has a very particular point of view about music theatre. I found that I was a collaborator in a different way. One is usually a collaborator with a visual predominance in the balance of the director-designer relationships. That was not so with Richard, because he is

Stage designs by Douglas W. Schmidt
FRANKENSTEIN by Victor Gialanella
Directed by Tom Moore
Palace Theatre, New York (1981)
Photographs (from top):
1. The laboratory.
2. Elizabeth's boudoir.
3. The graveyard.

so visually acute and has such a unique theatrical aesthetic that most of it is in his head and the process was simply getting it right and editing it. I became very much a sounding board, I guess you would say, for his ideas.

It was kind of frustrating at first, because I never knew quite where I stood as a designer. Often I would suggest something like, "This should be red." He would say, "Right, let's make it green." I didn't know exactly what to make of it. "Well, green, okay," and this would go on and on. Finally I realized that he was taking anything that you might expect and reversing it, always challenging the audience's assumptions. It was always a surprise, and it really was fascinating.

I loved the show. I thought very seldom have a director, an aesthetic, and a playwright been so perfectly matched. I referred to it as the definitive *Threepenny Opera*. I had seen the production of it that was done in the fifties down at the Theatre de Lys, and I remembered it as being this kind of cute, coy, amiable, funny, quaint, and offbeat little musical comedy. My remembrance of the piece had been so affected by that production that it wasn't until I first started working on it that I realized what a vituperative piece of work it actually is. I remember reading the script and being literally shocked by some of the things Brecht was saying. They're talking about eating excrement and things like that! Our production was a very hard-edged version of the show. I can't say, because not reading German I really don't know, but my sense is that it's far more what the original intent must have been. It was like a whole new ball game. It was not the *Threepenny Opera* that I knew, and that really made it exciting.

Did you enjoy doing the New York Shakespeare Festival's Agamemnon *at the Vivian Beaumont?*

I can't honestly say "enjoy" is a word that I would use to describe it, but I was certainly stimulated by it. Andrei Serban directed it, and he was flush with the success of *The Cherry Orchard*, which he had just done in early 1977. He, at the time, and still does to some degree, had a reputation as a kind of maverick, the hottest thing to come along and very unpredictable. I found all of that to be true in spades, unlike Richard Foreman, whom I knew I could never predict, but that in itself became predictable. I ended up trusting Richard, because I knew that he was searching, and I knew that ultimately we would find the ground, and it was a collaborative process. I didn't feel that way with Andrei, particularly.

With Andrei it was a grab bag. The images were so disparate that I never had a handle on what we were after. It just felt to me so often that the weather or what he had for lunch, or what kind of subway ride he had affected what we would be talking about on any given day. That feeling lasted right up until the opening night. We spent thousands of dollars building scenery, but, literally, the day it was loaded in and was sitting backstage, he walked in and said, "Oh, I think I've changed my mind about that. I don't think we want to use it."

Had you worked with a director in a similar capacity like this before?

Never as seemingly capricious as this. Now I don't deny there might have been some grand master plan that I was never privy to, but the more I worked with him, the more admiration I developed for Santo Loquasto, who had just done *The Cherry Orchard* with Andrei. Santo had actually managed to end up with a show that had a look to it, that didn't somehow get sabotaged along the way or seem bizarrely arbitrary, which is what I kept feeling we were suffering from with *Agamemnon*. Undeniably Andrei achieved some powerful effects onstage. One of the contributions that I count as my own was frankly just so astronomically complicated that he couldn't begin to cut it. So we had to do it. And he loved it.

What was it?

It was dropping the seating elevator and creating a huge hole in the middle of the Beaumont. There was a steel mesh platform over this hole so there was an acting area below in the basement that you could see through the floor, and there was an onstage-level acting area directly over it. I designed it as a show-in-the-round, putting the onstage audience onstage on air casters so that you could move them out of the way during the performance and bring the scenery in. Of course, the scenery we were going to bring in upstage right and left got cut. The thrust area out in the middle of the house became the center of focus like a Greek theatre.

But you still had an audience in the house?

You had five hundred seats on the stage on bleachers to make it a full round configuration. The audience on the stage was on bleachers that were on air casters so you could blow them off the floor a little bit and move them on two great wagons and open the space to make it three-quarter, and then we would bring in scenic pieces or chorus or whatever. However, there ended up being only one scenic piece, although there were originally more.

Andrei had this vision of some African plain dwellers and he brought this picture in and it really was fascinating. There were these mud huts that looked like great domed eggs sitting on stilts. He thought that was a very strong visual image, which it was. We wanted to do some kind of boulder-stream plain as the central setting, and we built these big fiber glass rocks and put them on wheels. They were just immense. We might have tried them once for rehearsal, and then they were loaded right back in the truck. They were gone.

They didn't yell in the office?

Oh, sure. That's part of the act with Andrei. He had just had a big success so they were quite willing to extend that to him. Joe Papp is a great producer. He is one of the great producers of all times. If he has faith in people, even if they falter somewhere along the way, he will back them to the hilt and sometimes further than his resources will allow. I think that is just about the best thing you can say about somebody in this business—to use the strength of their convictions to the point of putting them on the line. Joe Papp (1922–1991), in my book, is the essence of that and he did it for this production.

Was the fact that you had the audience on stage and used the seating elevator considered innovative? Had that been done at the Beaumont prior to this production?

No, that hadn't been done before. The idea of using the pit hole actually had occurred to me years before for a production of an Edward Bond play called *Narrow Road to the Deep North* which I designed in that space. I wanted to do that show like a square Japanese plank platform floating in the mountain mists. The idea was that this would be suspended and hover in this ocean and have a mythic quality to it. We ran afoul of the New York City Buildings Department and the fire laws became a problem. There was a question of exits and the safety in how to get people out in case of an emergency. Because of our two-month period between shows, we just didn't have the time to chase it down with the city. So that idea as an interesting new way to use that space was abandoned for that production, and it had never been done before. I proposed it again for *Agamemnon*, because we were going to emphasize the amphitheatre aspect. I thought this might be a good way to get action on levels. Of course Joe said, "Let's just do it." Whatever problems there might have been, I never heard about them.

Would you say that the period you worked at Lincoln Center played a great part in the creative and artistic growth of your career?

Oh, very much so. Coincidentally with that, I was working right across the street at Juilliard, and I was going back and forth between the two. Often I would be opening an opera for Houseman or somebody in one theatre and doing technical rehearsals in another. I remember one time I was working on *Narrow Road to the Deep North* at the Beaumont, taping scenes with The Acting Company on the Juilliard main stage, and we were shooting a video production of *Antigone* in the lobby spaces of the theatre which Gerry Freedman was directing for PBS. It was crazy. I would do a little something for the TV show, then I'd run to the theatre and act as if I'd been there all day watching and I would take notes, then run across the street to Juilliard to the theatre. It was really a nutty two weeks. It's amusing now, but it wasn't then.

How many assistants do you use when you're working on a project?

Personally, I try to keep the number of assistants as small as possible, not for any other reason than it's easier for me to concentrate on the project if I don't have three people standing around saying, "OK, we need something to do." Then I've got to invent something for them to do or critique something or say, "Change everything." If there's just one person there, I have more time for the design process. Obviously, there are some shows where you need more than one assistant, a big musical for example. For *Smile* I had three, sometimes four people here.

What was the time on Smile?

It seemed like the better part of the decade! You can't stay fresh on something over that long period of time. It's just too depleting to respond almost on a daily basis to the vagaries of the producing process. I have a drawer full of designs for that show, each one different. Each, hopefully, in some way responds to the problems, but for almost

every theatre in New York! The capitalizing process is so involved that from one day to the next you never know who is producing the show, what tour it's going on, where it's going to open out of town, or what theatre they've got lined up. Nine times out of ten you're designing a show that doesn't have a theatre yet, and so you don't know what space you're designing for.

It's very difficult to design a musical that way. It's not so hard for a box set show, because if the theatre isn't deep enough you can chop something off a wall and get it in somehow. But in a musical you have to rely on using every square inch of space. You have to deal with that space in a very clever and involved way in order to get all the things you need on and off the stage. You just can't suddenly switch gears two months into a project and say, "Oh, by the way, we're going into a theatre that's 3 feet shallower and has no wing space off stage left." You can't do that without throwing the whole process back to the beginning. And that's what happened with *Smile*.

How did you cope with that?

I just kept designing. That's what a designer signs on for. This went on for about eighteen months, and then it was canned, and then it came back. It went on forever. I think the workshop process is very valuable, but between the workshop and the final opening on Broadway there are many negotiations, revisions, and changes of venue.

Directors want to go into a workshop situation with a physical production in mind, and so, more often than not, you end up designing with some makeshift, slammed-together platforms. It's important to do that, but the downside of it is that it often ties a director and a choreographer to a style of doing things in the workshop that isn't going to happen on the Broadway stage. The way they have been doing it in workshop can sometimes become much more satisfying to them because they feel in control and comfortable with it, and then they often won't want to muck around with it and change it for the more complicated Broadway stage. So the designer is often saddled with things that come out of the workshop. It's a classic situation. They've been rehearsing with a certain chair for six weeks in a rehearsal hall somewhere, and when they suddenly get on the

stage, it isn't the same chair. The star has a fit so you end up with this awful chair that has nothing to do with the show simply because they've been rehearsing with it.

The workshop is one aspect of how producing has changed. It's no longer standing around a piano and singing a couple of songs in front of a lot of potential backers who are there drinking cocktails. You've got to let them see the show. Sometimes the workshops can be elaborate. The more elaborate, the more concrete ideas there are, and the more work you've got to do in the process to realize that. *Smile* was one of those. I think the workshop for that cost a quarter of a million dollars.

Tell me about They're Playing Our Song.

That musical was done in 1978 at the Ahmanson Theatre in Los Angeles and came into New York from there. It was at a time when Neil Simon was doing tryouts in Los Angeles. It was probably the first show I have done that budgetary considerations did not dictate the design to some degree. Whatever we wanted to do, as long as we justified it and backed it up with hard facts and did our homework on it, it was OK. I am particularly fond of that show because it gave me a chance to work with projected multi-image media on a large scale.

The set itself was a series of moving projection screens which we combined with props and furniture and walls of scenery. There were six projection screens, and they were floor to fly height, I guess about 16 feet. They were on tracks parallel to the footlights and they would move and recombine for the different scenes. There are a lot of scenes in this show, fifteen or sixteen, I think. As with most of Neil's writing, there are real characters, real situations, and real places. The characters are always plopping down on the bed or playing a piano or cooking dinner or doing something that has to be there for the credibility of the scene. So there is a lot of physical stuff in this show.

What we wanted to do was to give it a cinematic fluidity which the script almost demanded. If you read the script, you can't believe that now they're in the car, they're on the freeway, now they've gotten to the beach house and the next thing you know, they're in a recording studio. It has to

Stage design by Douglas W. Schmidt
PORGY AND BESS
Directed by Jack O'Brien
Radio City Music Hall, New York (1983)

be organic in design due to the flow of the show, because there are so many scene changes. If you stopped every time to change the scene, it would be like a car chugging and sputtering trying to get going. We really couldn't afford that, so it all had to be seamless and flow.

It was directed by the late Bob Moore, who was terribly inventive and terribly clever, and a terribly funny fellow whom we all miss a great deal. He had his ideas of what he wanted for the scene work, but he didn't have a clear idea for the look of the show. So in our first meetings we evolved a concept that this would be the first "high tech" musical. High tech was the rage then. So that was our takeoff point.

We used the vernacular of that decorating and architectural movement to frame this story of two Yuppies falling in love. It was a very cute idea, and I think it worked very well. Mostly the "high tech look" came from the graphics which were projected on these moving panels, and we used a lot of photographic effects, neon, and architectural graphics.

The projections were from the front of the house balcony rail position. We had a battery of sixteen 35-millimeter projectors on the front of the rail that were formatted in overlapping segments so that we could do animation. We could move figures in sequential fashion and give it, again, an almost cinematic look. Actually, on this show, I pretty much designed the graphics myself, working with designer Wendall Harrington, who made it all work. She was very experienced in projected media for industrial shows and that sort of thing.

What did you use for the screen panels?

We used a Raven screen product, I don't know who actually makes it, that's who we bought it from. It was a silver-coated plastic that has a concentrated or limited reflection cone so that all the light that is shot at it is reflected back within a narrow cone. This concentrates the light so that it has very high reflective capabilities, much like the material that traffic signs are made of. The extreme seats outside of that cone experience a little bit of fall-off, but not total fall-off. It's a very bright image so it was clearly visible to probably seven-eighths or maybe even more of the house. It's really a great look, and I've used the screen a lot since then. I find it's very valuable for front projection. In fact, we may even use it in this *Around the World in Eighty Days*. Wendall was very helpful, and ultimately it became a collaboration between us. In fact, we codesigned our next media outing, which was a concert for Peter Allen in 1979 that he did at the Biltmore Theatre, and it ran all that summer.

Porgy and Bess *at the Music Hall. Was that an important production in your career?*

It was very important. It was a chance really to pay homage to a major musical achievement of the American theatre, and I enjoyed it immensely. I was working with Jack O'Brien, who directed it. He had done it before and Gilbert Hemsley, who was the lighting designer, had worked on it before. In fact, everybody involved with it except me had done it before. With this revival at Radio City Music Hall they had a chance to do *Porgy and Bess* the way they wanted to do it.

I was very proud to have been the designer of choice. It's a once-in-a-lifetime experience to work in the scale of the stage at Radio City Music Hall. My own personal feeling was that the scale was just a little too big for the opera. If I have any regrets at all, it's that we didn't have a slightly more amiable, a little more friendly venue for it, because musically I think it suffered. But the scale certainly worked visually. Where else, outside of making a movie, would you get the chance to do such an elaborate job? In fact, for a while we were talking about doing a film version. It would be great to do it because I think Jack, more than anybody, has a handle on that piece. There were segments of it that brought me to tears every night.

It goes on to this day. I just got a call about sending some pictures of myself to Europe because they're going to tour it around again. God knows what it could possibly look like by now. I think I'd just as soon not see it.

You have designed operas for the San Francisco Opera Company. How did your association with them come about?

Through a director, Gerry Freedman, who was signed on to direct an opera called *The Angle of Repose*, which was commissioned by the San Francisco Opera for the Bicentennial in 1976. I was suggested by Gerry and met Kurt Adler, who was then the head of the San Francisco Opera, and proceeded from there. I have designed *Aïda, Samson et Dalila,* and *The Angle of Repose* for the main stage, and then a couple for Spring Opera when they were producing at the Curran Theatre.

How do you compare working on a production there and elsewhere?

Well, there's not much you can compare the San Francisco Opera with in this country other than the Met, Chicago Lyric, maybe Houston. Now I have not worked for the Met, nor Houston. I have worked for Chicago. In fact, *Samson et Dalila* was a coproduction with Chicago. I think that the San Francisco Opera has one of, if not the best shops that I've ever had the privilege to work in. It has a spectacular carpenter, a fellow named Pierre Cayard who has been there for a long time. Jay Kotcher is a scenic artist who came from New York, and he's fabulous. They have a lot of good people there. It is a wonderful space, and they have a huge shop and storage shed, a wonderful facility, and I enjoy the people immensely.

How long do you usually spend on an opera there?

You usually get a year.

A good budget?

The pit is not bottomless, but it has been sufficient. John Conklin actually has more recent experience than I. He did a truly stupendous *Ring* cycle for them which is, I believe, a landmark production. It is beautifully executed and wonderfully lit. Tom Munn is the lighting designer there, a very talented fellow. It's great to work in a house like that. Also, opera is another kettle of fish. The costs involved are so astronomical. To get a rehearsal on for an opera, you have to move mountains. Everything is organized, everything is pretty much on time, and they generally make the most of the time they have on stage. You don't end up doing endless technical rehearsals and sitting there all night lighting the scenery. You wish you had more time, but you get a lot more done in the time that you have. They're a great crew.

You design shows on both the East and West Coasts. How do you make that work for you and maintain a studio in both places?

Well, it's hard, no getting around it. You can't make a living in New York, so you've got to get on an airplane anyway. I've had a place to work in San Francisco for about five years, but I continue to be based in New York. I just have to work out the time commitments, that's all. You have to be where the director is. That's the bottom line. I think that any designer you talk to

today will say that they're working as much out of town as they are in town. You go where the projects start. That's the name of the game now.

What do you like least about working in the theatre?

What do I like least? Solving other people's problems, having to be not only responsible for what's happening visually but how that vision is achieved economically. It's becoming more and more the rule that you're at the mercy of productions that are all put together when you get into them. That for me is the hardest thing. I don't know how to deal with it. So you just do it, and you always feel taken advantage of, because it always means much more work for the designer. Yet in the present climate, I don't know that there is an alternative if you want to continue to design, as is the case of our generation that has so much vested interest in this business that it's almost impossible to walk away. If you do, what do you walk away to? If you start thinking, "Oh, maybe I should be doing films," it's like starting all over again. It's like going out of town and making *The Mummy of Louisana* movies. Do you want to really do that? We're stuck between a rock and a hard place. That's why I advise more and more people who interview with me, especially those who have obvious talent and really could do well, to explore all the other venues. It's all work and none of it is easy, so you might as well get paid nicely for it.

What do you like most about working in the theatre?

It's really the interaction. It's meeting people with energy and enthusiasm who can draw you in and make you a part of the process. The theatre is full of the most interesting people in the world who might in civilian life be outcasts for one reason or another. But the theatre permits them their eccentricities, and once that does not become an issue, they can flourish. It's just great. I mean, some people are so whacky and outrageous, you simply can't believe them, let alone having a great time collaborating with them on a work of art. You could never picture them on the board of Cola-Cola or some big business. But somehow the theatre makes their uniqueness of vision into a virtue and it's fun to be in on that. It really is.

Setting by Douglas W. Schmidt
THE TEMPEST by William Shakespeare
Directed by Jack O'Brien
Lighting by David F. Segal
Old Globe Theatre
San Diego, California (1982)

4

CREATING DESIGNS WITH SKETCHES AND MODELS

RENDERINGS AND MODELS AS PART OF THE DESIGN PROCESS

Designing, drawing, and painting go hand in hand to create beautiful, harmonious designs for the theatre. All three of these skills are equally important in evolving a brilliant setting. While ideally a stage designer is equally adept in designing, drawing, and painting, that is not always the case. The process varies tremendously with the artist. Some designers draw well and do not paint well; some paint well and do not draw well. One top designer will do all the sketches and make the major decisions; another well-known designer will expect help from assistants.

The design process on an interesting theatre project is always exciting and challenging. Once the basic ideas and the concept are resolved with the director, then the scenic designer is free to create the finished designs for the production. For presentational purposes, it is up to the designer to make either a painted rendering or a painted model for a particular production. Some designers prefer making painted renderings of the set, with stage lighting and mood indicated in the sketch. Others like to make a three-dimensional painted model so that spatial relationships can be studied and worked out. In the commercial theatre a designer is obligated contractually to do either a painted rendering or a painted model, not both. Of course, it is a lovely gesture when there is time and incli-

nation to do both. Bear in mind that a designer may have made many preliminary sketches and more than one rough model before arriving at the presentation piece.

Creating a Figure for a Model and a Sketch

It is always essential to put a scaled figure in a model or a sketch. This figure (which in ½-inch scale is 3 inches high) represents the height of a 6-foot man, and indicates to anyone looking at the model or sketch how the height of the actor appears with the scale of the scenery. Scaled costumed figures in a model can also show color, mood, texture, shape, blocking, and grouping, and they create a general excitement that would otherwise be lacking. Many designers keep on hand a collection of cutout figures that can be moved around and positioned in various places in the model.

Usually, figures are cut out of heavy paper or illustration board and then mounted on a base of board, wire, or other material so that they stand without falling over yet are easy to move around. Figures for models may:

1. Be cut out of white illustration board, and used as a plain white figure or have details drawn with a normal writing pencil or pen.
2. Be cut out of heavy paper or board and painted in full color, including the edges and sometimes also finished on the back.
3. Be created in three-dimensional form

with foil that is squeezed and pressed together or made with small, flexible wire, papier-mâché, clay, or other materials.
4. Be cut out of board and painted in various periods of dress, including Elizabethan, classical Greek and Roman, Victorian, and other appropriate periods. The figure collection may include both men and women, young adults, and children.

Making Samples of Paints and Materials

When you are working in a design studio or a scenic shop (as a designer in a commercial, regional, or university production), it is always a good idea to make samples to see how paints, dyes, and glues work on the actual materials you plan to use. This is mentioned here because as you get into the rendering and model stages of developing a stage design you are also thinking about the final execution. Making samples of materials and paints help you make intelligent decisions as to what to use and how to use it.

The following suggestions of samples to be made are offered as a guide in both the design and design execution process.

1. For a set rendering in ½-inch scale, try transparent, semitransparent, and opaque colors on a piece of illustration board to see how each looks when dry.
2. For a model of an exterior building set, create a portion of the set with pieces

Setting and Sketch by Tony Walton
I'M NOT RAPPAPORT by Herb Gardner
Directed by Dan Sullivan
Costumes by Robert Morgan
Lighting by Pat Collins
Seattle Repertory Theatre
Seattle, Washington (1985)
Also American Place and Booth Theatres, New
 York

of illustration board, pieces of veneer, balsa wood, and white glue. Apply modeling paste over the walls and woodwork to create heavy textures, then coat it with gesso to prepare the surfaces for the detailed finished painting. Do the painting to see how it works.

3. Make model samples to solve such potential problems as paint warping boards, paint cracking, paint not taking well on the model material, or glues that do not hold well.

4. For a muslin backdrop, try brushing mixed aniline dye colors on a piece of muslin. Are you painting on raw muslin, starched muslin, or muslin laid in with opaque priming applied on it?

5. For samples to discuss with the prop person, dye cheesecloth with a commercial dye; dip white tablecloths in tea or coffee; dye a bright floral sofa print so it does not pick up the stage lights and pop out too much.

6. Try paints and dyes on a piece of sharkstooth scrim. Do they work OK, or does the flameproofing interfere?

7. Use a hot glue gun to attach large sequins to a sharkstooth scrim. Do the sequins hold well?

RENDERINGS

Doing Successful Renderings

Clear thinking and an unhindered imagination coupled with spontaneous execution usually work best to produce a successful first rendering. Sometimes the first painted presentation rendering will turn out to be brilliant. At other times, it just does not happen. The novice designer should realize that more than one attempt may be needed to arrive at a final rendering. When this is the case, it should be accepted as a part of the creative process. Beginning designers should not allow frustration and a sense of failure to overtake them. Even well-known designers frequently do several painted renderings before being satisfied with one for the final presentation.

Renderings may be executed in any medium. Sometimes a designer feels that the mood of a production dictates the medium to be used for the rendering of a setting. It is a good idea for the new designer to give himself or herself the freedom of being able to work in as many different media as possible.

Here is a project for executing a rendering for each of the four acts of *The Three Sisters* in a different medium.

Making Renderings for a Four-Act Production

The Three Sisters by Anton Chekhov is an excellent example of a play in which the scenic designer is expected to resolve both the visual and the technical aspects of a script with equal finesse and aplomb. It is also a wonderful assignment for the lighting designer and the costume designer. This Russian drama in four acts takes place in 1901 and is set in the capital of a Russian province. There are three settings: two interiors and one exterior.

Remember that the text and subtext of a script reveal a great deal about the design. Chekhov conveys the mood and theme, indicates the time of year and weather, describes the climate, physical setting, furniture, and hand props in the stage directions as well as in the dialogue.

The opening lines of the play (Olga's first speech) mention that it is "May fifth." Olga goes on to say, "This clock struck then too." In her second speech she says, "Today it's warm. We can have the windows open wide, but the birches aren't in leaf yet." From this the designer knows that it is spring, the windows must open, the bare birch trees can be seen from the window, and a clock that strikes must be a part of the set dressing. Obviously, this is a drama where furniture and props play an important role. Tuzenbach plays a piano shortly after Act 1 begins. Toward the end of Act 1 Kulygin says, "There are thirteen of us at the table!" From this speech the designer learns that the table must appear large enough to accommodate thirteen people with the appropriate number of chairs and place settings. It is important to notice all of these details in Chekhov's writing because a director staging the play in a realistic style must have the appro-

priate scenery and props to make the staging work with the dialogue.

Assume that you have been engaged to design a proscenium production of *The Three Sisters* on a good-size stage. The director wishes to stage a production in which both interiors appear to have actual walls, ceilings, floors, and windows. The garden set should also appear to be a real exterior, complete with sky, trees, flowers, fence, and house. This production is to be very realistic in regard to scenery, costumes, lighting, and props.

Designing the Settings for *The Three Sisters*

One of the most exciting things about designing scenery for a multiset show is that it stimulates your imagination to create sets that are as versatile as possible, yet at the same time are just right for the production.

The Three Sisters is an excellent production in which to apply the elements and principles of design. When the curtain goes up on the first act and it is midday, you want the audience to react to the realistic environment, perhaps thinking, "Isn't this interesting? It looks just like I imagined a Russian home in the early 1900s would be. It looks so comfortable that I'd love to be in that room myself." When the curtain rises for Act 2 in the same set, it is eight o'clock in the evening. The set is dark and Natalia comes in carrying a candle. The effect at the opening of this act should be in marked contrast to Act 1. This is a wonderful example of how different the same set looks with a change in the stage lighting.

Drawing by Rouben Ter-Arutunian
THE TEMPEST
NBC Television (1959)
(Collection of Peter Harvey)

For Act 3, Olga's and Irina's room, the visual difference in the set should make the audience think, "Yes, I can well imagine this is Olga's room, and it is obvious that it is a part of the same house as the drawing room and dining room in Act 1. What an interesting contrast to the other set."

By the time the curtain rises on the garden setting in Act 4, the audience has seen two interior sets under different stage lighting. Now this exterior set should make the audience feel that the garden is a natural adjunct to the interior architecture. Also, the mood is entirely different and poignant in feeling. In practical terms, this is an exterior set that must have a sky cyclorama or backdrop, which means that through the various setting changes it must be planned that the sky cyclorama can be stretched out tight so that it is totally free of wrinkles.

After reading the script once, reread it and take careful notes concerning the physical requirements in their proper sequence. Your first notes may be similar to the following sample notes, with more detail filled in later or deletions made after discussion with the director.

ACT 1   The Prozorovs' house. A columned drawing room and beyond it, a large dining room. Midday. A sparkling, sunny day outside. The table is being set for lunch in the dining room. OLGA, a teacher in the Girl's High School, is severely dressed; she keeps correcting

150 *school exercises, whether she is standing still or moving about. MASHA, wearing a black dress, sits reading a book, a hat on her knees. IRINA, dressed in white, stands staring dreamily into the distance.*

(Onstage: OLGA, MASHA, and IRINA)

1. OLGA says on opening, "It's May the fifth, your birthday, Irina . . . Today it is warm. We can have the windows wide open, but the birches aren't in leaf yet."
2. The clock strikes twelve.
3. TUZENBACH sits down at the piano and plays softly.
4. The DOCTOR reads a newspaper, makes notes in notebook, gets another newspaper from his pocket.
5. SOLENY takes a flask of eau de cologne from his pocket.
6. MASHA puts on her hat.
7. Enter ANFISA and FERAPONT with a birthday cake.
8. DOCTOR enters, followed by an ORDERLY carrying a silver samovar.
9. VERSHININ says, "You have the forest and the river and then there are the birch trees, the gentle, modest birches—my favorite tree."
10. IRINA says, "Look at the picture frame Andrei gave me today. . . . And he made that frame too—the one over the piano."
11. VERSHININ says, "But what a lot of flowers you have!"
12. KULYGIN says, "The carpets will soon have to be taken up for the summer."

ACT 2 *Same as Act 1. Eight o'clock in the evening. From the street offstage come faint sounds of an accordion. It is dark in the house. Enter NATALIA wearing a dressing gown and carrying a candle; she crosses to the door of ANDREI'S room and stands outside it.*

(Onstage: NATALIA)

1. ANDREI says that it is "quarter past eight" in the evening.
2. Note for Act 3 set NATALIA says, ". . . Irina's room, for instance, would make a perfect nursery . . . she could share Olga's room."
3. FERAPONT to ANDREI: "The Council chairman sends you a book and some papers." Papers in a packet.
4. MAID lights lamp and candles.
5. MASHA says, "Listen to the noise the stove is making."
6. FEDOTIK and RODÉ enter dining

room, sit, start to sing softly, one of them plays a guitar.
7. TUZENBACH says, ". . . Look, it's snowing."
8. DOCTOR reads newspaper and makes notes in notebook.
9. FEDOTIK says, "Look, I was going down Moscow Street and got these colored pencils at Pyzhikov's for you. And this penknife too . . ." "And I bought myself a pocket-knife . . . here, see . . . here's one blade, and here's the second and the third. Then this is for cleaning your ears, here's a pair of scissors, and this is a nail file."
10. Samovar and tea things served from dining room.
11. FEDOTIK uses deck of cards—already on set?
12. TUZENBACH (picking up a box from table) Where's all the candy gone?
13. TUZENBACH carries decanter of brandy and glasses and drinks with SOLENY.
14. SOLENY takes small bottle of eau de cologne from pocket.
15. TUZENBACH plays the piano.
16. NATALIA enters with a candle.

ACT 3 *OLGA'S and IRINA'S room. Left and right, their beds with screens around them. It is between two and three o'clock in the morning. Offstage a fire alarm is ringing—a fire has been burning for some time already. It is obvious that no one in the house has gone to bed yet. MASHA lies on a sofa, dressed as usual in a black dress. Enter OLGA and ANFISA.*

(Onstage: MASHA, OLGA, and ANFISA)

1. OLGA takes clothes from closet "Here, take this gray one . . . and this one . . . and this blouse . . . and take this skirt, Nanny dear. . . . Take this one . . . and this."
2. (Through the open door [bedroom door] a window can be seen; it is red from the glow of the fire. Outside a fire engine is heard going by.)
3. OLGA takes a drink of water.
4. MASHA picks up a pillow.
5. KULYGIN tried to hide in corner behind wardrobe.
6. DOCTOR washes hands at washbasin.
7. DOCTOR picks up porcelain clock and examines it, drops it, and smashes it.
8. SOLENY says about fire, "They say it's dying down." Also takes bottle of

eau de cologne from pocket.
9. TUZENBACH says to IRINA, "You are so pale, so beautiful, so charming—I think your pallor lights up the darkness like a lamp." Then to MASHA, "Oh, are you here? I can't see you." Then in same speech, "It's getting light already. The morning's here."
10. OLGA tidies up around her bedtable.
11. NATALIA enters with a candle.
12. OLGA goes behind screen around her bed.
13. OLGA gives small cupboard key to ANDREI.
14. IRINA goes behind screen around her bed.
15. End of act, stage is empty. OLGA and IRINA talk from behind screen to each other. Fire alarm sounds.

ACT 4 *The old garden of the Prozorovs' house. A long, fir-bordered path leading to the river, of which a stretch can be seen. Beyond the river, a forest. Right, the terrace of the house and there, on a table, champagne glasses and bottles—obviously they have just been drinking champagne. It is midday. From time to time, people cross the garden on their way from the street to the river. Five soldiers go quickly past. The DOCTOR, in a benign mood which he retains throughout the act, sits in an armchair in the garden, waiting to be called. He wears his military cap and has his cane. IRINA, KULYGIN, wearing a medal (he has shaved off his moustache) and TUZENBACH are standing on the terrace. They are seeing off FEDOTIK and RODÉ who, dressed in marching uniform, come down from the terrace into the garden.*

(Onstage: DOCTOR, IRINA, KULYGIN, TUZENBACH, FEDOTIK and RODÉ)

1. FEDOTIK taking photo at top of act.
2. FEDOTIK gives KULYGIN a notebook and pencil, and together leave to go down to the river, can be seen looking back as they go.
3. DOCTOR reading one newspaper and has another in pocket.
4. ANDREI seen pushing a baby carriage.
5. TUZENBACH goes into house.
6. Someone inside house plays "A Maiden's Prayer" on piano.

"The Three Sisters" by Anton Chekhov from *20th Century Russian Drama*, translated by Andrew R. MacAndrew, Bantam, N.Y., 1963.

7. DOCTOR winds his watch and it chimes.
8. FERAPONT enters with papers.
9. SOLENY has eau de cologne bottle in pocket.
10. IRINA sits on swing upstage.
11. MASHA takes drink of water.

After you have read the play and studied it, collected research, and met with the director and exchanged ideas with each other, you are ready to decide how the sets are going to look, how they are going to move, how they are going to store offstage, and where you are going to allow space to position lighting instruments. No doubt there will be one or more meetings with the director before you proceed to finish the work

Research on any play is important, but extremely so on a play such as *The Three Sisters*. Before or after the meeting with the director you may want to do research in libraries, museums, with videos, film clips, or other appropriate sources. You need to do research

to understand the way of life and the socioeconomic conditions and customs of this period in Russian history, so that you can create a mood of authenticity. You need to know the architecture, the furniture, the clothes, the food, the wallpaper patterns. Also, it is vital to analyze the individual characters and do research on any careers, individual tastes, or hobbies that may influence the setting or costumes.

In order to design a completely functional production of *The Three Sisters*, it is necessary to first make scaled ground plans of each of the three sets, indicating where all the furniture is positioned, so you can get back to the director with your ideas. You will also need to make a ½-inch scale section drawing of the stage. It is not very productive to create a group of pretty pictures if they do not work both aesthetically and practically.

Since this is a production with realistic walls and ceilings, you will probably want to have scenery on wagons to move on and off stage, and these sce-

Stage designs by Franco Colavecchia
CAVALLERIA RUSTICANA by Pietro Mascagni
Libretto by Giovanni Targioni-Tozzetti and
    Guido Menasci
Directed by Frank Corsaro
Music Center Opera
Dorothy Chandler Pavilion
Los Angeles, California (1988)
(Photographs by Phil Jones)

"First Version: Three sketches showing only one set—the inside of a ruined barn. The director's idea was to update the opera (1940s) and attempt a neorealism cinematic approach. All the action, including the Easter Parade, was to take place inside a barn, the villagers supposedly having lost their buildings in the war, etc. Second version: A more conventional production of the opera was decided upon after the first approach was dropped."
—Franco Colavecchia

nic pieces may probably have ceilings with chandeliers. These platform units on casters may have to break in sections and move off in different directions in order to properly utilize the backstage storage space.

For your designs, use these theatre dimensions. Make the proscenium

Model by Tony Straiges
GENIUSES by Jonathan Reynolds
Directed by Gary Pearle
Arena Stage
Washington, D.C. (1983)
(Photograph by Ney Tait Fraser)

opening 38'-0" wide by 23'-0" high. The depth from the back of the proscenium opening to the back wall is 30'-0". From the curtain line to the edge of the apron is 4'-0". From the center line to the stage left wall is 36'-0", and from the center line to the stage right wall is 34'-0". The grid height is 62'-0".

You must also plan the positions of the masking and space for lighting equipment. This means you need to discuss your ideas with the lighting designer as well as the director. It is also vital to know the length of intermissions between the acts in order to plan scenery changes in terms of where pieces go to store in sequence, and to

ensure that the changes can be done in the time allotted for the intermission.

Drawing the Four Designs in ½-inch Scale

After reading the play, discussing it with the director, doing research, and resolving the shifts of each act in the ground plan, draw the sketches for the four acts. No doubt you have already made a number of rough sketches up to this point in the design process.

The four drawings, one for each act, should be done accurately, neatly, and with care. Vertical and horizontal lines should be precise so that any columns and chandeliers are straight and vertical. You can always vary the lines slightly when painting the sketch to add a bit of mood and atmosphere.

Initially, all four drawings should be sketched out so that you can be sure

that the four settings will work nicely together as a unit. Even this far in advance, you can usually tell by noting the scale of the sets, the proportions of different units such as archways, windows, and doors, plus the furniture and dressing whether it is all going to look well together as an ensemble piece. If you have any doubts about a particular set, do another tracing of the set to see if the proportions of the room should be changed. Do the proportions need to be increased or decreased? Check to see whether the furniture has to be repositioned. How does the setting look under stage lighting for that scene? Does each of the four drawings appear to be executed in the appropriate perspective and to be drawn looking from the center of the orchestra seats in the theatre?

Make the drawings on white illustration board. You can work directly on the board or do the drawing on tracing paper and then transfer it onto the board. If you choose to use the tracing paper method, the transfer to the board can be accomplished by laying the drawing on the illustration board and exerting enough pressure on the tip of a pencil at strategic points of the drawing so that slight indentations are left on the surface of the board. This method of transferring small points of the drawing onto the board makes it easier and faster to draw the design directly on the board. You can also use transfer paper to do this for the entire drawing. If the drawing is very intricate, it is probably best to draw it on the illustration board in the first place.

Doing the Renderings

Let us assume that the director has asked you to render the set designs to indicate how each of the four sets will look just as the act curtain goes up. Show the stage lighting for each of the sets and include the individual characters that are onstage at the top of each act. The characters should be rendered in an appropriate costume and positioned according to the action of the play. While the four renderings should be drawn in the same style and scale,

Model (¼-inch) by Charles E. McCarry
A WALK IN THE WOODS by Lee Blessing
Directed by Alex Dmitriev
Philadelphia Drama Guild
Zellerbach Theatre
Philadelphia, Pennsylvania (1990)

Exterior Designs

Below:
Stage designs by John Lee Beatty for TALLEY'S FOLLY.
Shown are renderings for the play in three different theatres:
1. Brooks Atkinson Theatre, New York (1980)
2. Mark Taper Forum, Los Angeles, California (1979)
3. Circle Repertory Theatre, New York (1979)

Right:
Setting and lighting by Neil Peter Jampolis for EUGENE ONEGIN (1986), Banff Center, Eric Harvie Theatre, Banff, Canada.
Stage design by Zack Brown for MANON (1991), Washington Opera, Washington, D.C.
Translucent backdrop design by Rolf Beyer for the opera THE MERRY WIVES OF WINDSOR (1977), Hopkins Center, Dartmouth College, Hanover, New Hampshire.
Stage design by José Varona for THE SLEEPING BEAUTY (1977), Paris Opera, Paris, France.

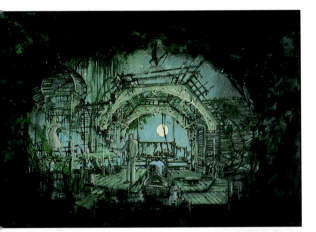

John Conklin: REX (1976); James Stewart Morcom: TIMES SQUARE (1949), Radio City Music Hall;
Ben Edwards: PURLIE VICTORIOUS (1961); Tony Walton: PETER AND THE WOLF (1992)

Costume designs by Eduardo Sicangco for THE 'NOT' MIKADO, Virginia Opera, 1993

Kenneth Foy: OH, KAY! (1990); John Keck: Christmas Show (1976), Music Hall; Ralph Funicello: STREETCAR (1984); Lts: Michael Whitfield; Karen Schulz: HEDDA GABLER (1981), Lts: Timothy J. Hunter

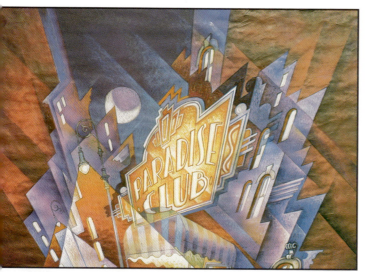

Eduardo Sicangco: BABES IN TOYLAND (1991), Houston Grand Opera (Photographs by Kate Fallon);
William and Jean Eckart: THE MOTHER OF US ALL (1986)

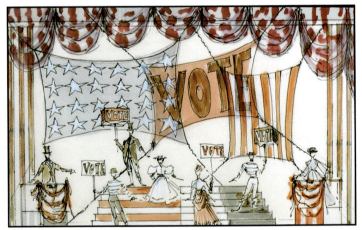

Lester Polakov: THREE SYMPHONIC DANCES (1987); Robert Perdziola: LA FEDELTA PREMIATA (1988);
Robin Wagner: JEROME ROBBINS' BROADWAY (1989); Zack Brown: GAITÉ PARISIENNE (1987)

they nevertheless should have good contrast in color, texture, shape, lighting, and mood.

As a project to enhance your painting techniques and to see what medium you actually prefer to work in, render the ½-inch scale sketches as indicated for each act.

ACT 1
Use: Dr. Martin's Synchromatic Transparent Water Colors and Dr. Martin's Radiant Concentrated Water Colors in bottles. Also needed are water, brushes, jars, and palette for mixing.

ACT 2
Use: Oil paints in tubes. Also needed are turpentine for thinning, drier to put in paints, brushes, cups, palette, and rags.

ACT 3
Use: Acrylic colors in tubes and jars. Also needed are water, brushes, jars, palette, and rags.

ACT 4
Use: Watercolors in tubes and cakes. Also needed are water, brushes, jars, and palette.

Use this project to see which of the various rendering media is the most successful for you, which you like best, which you would like to work in again, and which you need more practice with to improve your technique.

Another objective of this project is to see whether all four sketches hold up as an equally rendered group. Do they each have a unique design? Do they have equal dramatic appeal? Is one weaker than the other three? How is the contrast in coloring, texturing, and rendered lighting? Do the drawn and painted details hold up well for each of the four sketches?

Some designers may question the validity of an assignment dealing with realistic rendering. But there is a saying among artists that if you can paint realistic sketches well, you can usually paint any form or style of stage design.

Using Alternate Methods for Rendering the Same Production

You may find that you prefer to use an alternate method to do these renderings for a production of *The Three Sisters*. Perhaps you feel that one of the following methods is more effective in utilizing your designing and painting talents:

1. Do all four sketches in your favorite medium. Then, as an exercise, repeat one of the sketches in each of the other three mediums as listed.

2. Do the project exactly as assigned, then choose the rendering that you feel is the most successful and do the three other acts in that same medium.

PAINT ELEVATION, COLLAGE, AND PHOTOMONTAGE

The Paint Elevation

The paint elevation is usually a color rendering in ½-inch scale done on white illustration board, but it may be done on almost any kind of board or paper. It is painted just as the unit of scenery is to appear onstage, normally without rendering any stage lighting in it unless that is part of the scenic style. The paint elevation may even be a three-dimensional unit taken out of the ½-inch scale finished model and wrapped with clear acetate to protect it as it is used in the scenic studio.

Basically, the drawing for a paint elevation is taken from the front eleva-

Stage design by William and Jean Eckart
REUBEN, REUBEN—San Genarro
A musical by Marc Blitzstein
Directed by Robert Lewis
Choreography by Hanya Holm
Shubert Theatre
Boston, Massachusetts (1955)

tion of the drafting. An exception to this would be a backdrop, for example, that might not be put in the drafting and that would have to be drawn from scratch.

The Presentation Sketch and Painter's Elevation as One

Sometimes the colored sketch made for the presentational rendering and the painter's elevation can be created as one. For example, the design for a show curtain shown as a straight-on view (without perspective) and the painter's elevation could be classified as one and the same.

A Collage Design

The collage is still one of the best methods of creating an original stage design. It is a fantastic way of making a design come to life either for a presentational rendering or for a paint elevation for a backdrop or a show curtain.

Some designers keep collage materials on file in the design studio. The materials list for collages is never-ending. Materials may include all kinds of papers, fabrics, plastics, felts, metallic wrappers, laces, pictures torn out of magazines and catalogs. (Some of the materials for models listed in the "Models" section of this chapter are also good for collages.)

Collages are normally made in ½-inch scale and the materials may be put on almost any kind of background, such as white or painted illustration board or other colored board. One of the most interesting things about a collage is that you are instantly dealing with various colors, textures, and shapes as you spontaneously juxtapose these different elements to form a fresh and original design.

You should make a basic sketch first before starting to actually put the collage together, even though fresh ideas usually come to mind while you are working. Once the sketch has been drawn, materials may be gathered, cut out, and glued on the board. Besides materials for the collage, it is a good idea to have sharp scissors, X-acto knives, Scotch Spra-Ment Adhesive in an aerosol can, white glue, glue sticks, brushes, and paints.

Things to Use for a Collage Backdrop in a Model

All sorts of different items can be utilized in creating collage backdrops in models. You might start by cutting out photographs or drawings of objects from colorful magazines and catalogs. (This may become an ongoing project.) Subjects that can work beautifully for a collage backdrop in a model include sea shells, flowers, foliage, and over-scale leaves. Textured shapes cut from pictures of tree bark, granite, cement, rippling water, or any number of other textured shapes can be made to appear as if they are floating in space.

You may want to use screen wire stretched on a framework of metal rods or heavy wire as a backing for a collage backdrop in the model. When a see-through fabric, such as linen scrim, sharkstooth scrim, or other gauze, is used for the backing, it is interesting to make opaque cutout objects and glue them on. To make flowers, sea shells, and other objects opaque when they are lighted in the model, glue them on heavy paper, then carefully cut away the excess paper and glue the paper-backed items on the openwork drop.

Stage design and costumes by Zack Brown
ON YOUR TOES—"Slaughter on Tenth Avenue" ballet
Book by Richard Rodgers, Lorenz Hart, and George Abbott; music by Richard Rodgers
Lyrics by Lorenz Hart
Directed by George Balanchine
Virginia Theatre
New York (1983)

"For this revival, Jo Mielziner's set for the New York City Ballet and the 1938 film version of ON YOUR TOES were studied. The intent of the cartoonlike decor remains a mystery to me, but since the choreography existed, so did the floor plan.

"Realizing this number was the finale to the show, musically and dramatically, and that it must be different from the other big ballet and first-act finale, "La Princesse Zenobia" (an ersatz Diaghilev/Bakst oriental fantasia), I headed for as 'modern' (c. 1936) a look as possible. Hence the angular, somewhat sinister 'neo-deco' decor for this wonderful jazz ballet by Richard Rodgers." —Zack Brown

Stage design by Desmond Heeley
MANON LESCAUT by Giacomo Puccini
Act 3
Directed by Gian Carlo Menotti
The Metropolitan Opera
New York (1980)

Not every piece of a collage design need be selected from magazines or catalogs. Drawings can originate on the designer's worktable. Collage designs for a model can be drawn and painted from scratch to create all sorts of effects. For example, a large ornate cartouche can be drawn in ½-inch scale, cut out, and positioned in the center of a gauze drop, and then opaque cutouts of musical instruments and overscale sheets of period music can be added. A design such as this sometimes has garlands of leaves with flowers and draperies. The outer portion around the collage arrangement may be painted and left without any applied collage materials, or the collage materials may form a wide border on the outer edges of the openwork rectangular drop.

Materials such as colored gels, cellophanes, tissue paper, and laces can be overlapped, glazed over with transparent colors, or partially painted with opaque colors to create any number of striking effects.

Designing a Collage Setting

A play that lends itself to a collage setting is Dylan Thomas's *Under Milk Wood.* Assume that the production is a staged reading in which six actors play the parts of the sixty-three characters in the play.

The point of this design project is to evolve a setting with maximum textures. Use these ideas as a basis for your collage setting:

1. An arrangement of levels with steps and platforms. On these levels make seats without backs. The seats are for the actors to sit on and should be simple forms.
2. Two portals to go upstage of the levels. Make each portal 36'-0" wide by 20'-0" high, with an opening in the center of each portal that is 28'-0" wide by 16'-0" high. Space the two portals so they are 4 feet apart.
3. A bobbinet backdrop that is 29'-0" wide by 16'-6" high to go behind and attach to the back of the first portal opening. Add applied textured patterns to go on the face of this bobbinet drop. The total area of applied designs

should be 25 percent or 35 percent of the overall drop.
4. A translucent muslin backdrop the same size as the bobbinet drop to attach directly behind the opening in the second portal. Create abstract painted designs to go on the muslin drop that are a mixture of opaque, semi-opaque, and translucent shapes.
5. A white reflector or bounce drop to hang 4 feet upstage of the second portal.

Creating a Sky Collage

For an abstract sky design, try using three or four different colors of blue paper as the basic material (or create your own combination of colors). Colored tissue papers are wonderful to use because they are translucent, and you can get nice effects by overlapping one color of paper over the other. Tear the paper in long strips before gluing it on a sheet of illustration board. Vary the width and the way you tear the strips of paper. One by one, attach the paper strips to the board. Scotch Spra-Ment or a glue stick can be used for this. Spread out the strips on opened newspapers, then spray or rub the adhesive onto the strips and press them into position using a horizontal placement.

Once the strips of paper are in place, decide whether or not you want to paint over some of the collaged areas with transparent washes of color or to add contrast with pastels, colored pencils, magic markers, or pen and ink.

Making a Photomontage Design

While the collage is a collection of varied materials forming interesting textures, colors, and shapes, the photomontage is simply an assemblage of different pieces of cut-up photographs glued together on a sheet of illustration board or other mounting surface to form an interesting design.

Selections may include color, black-and-white photographs, or black-and-white photographs with transparent washes of color applied over them. The design for the photomontage should always be drawn lightly with a pencil on the mounting board before cutting the photographs with an X-acto knife, razor blade, or scissors. The pieces of photograph may then be attached to the board with a glue stick or Scotch Spra-Ment Adhesive from an aerosol can.

Horizontal Washes on a Sky Drop Rendering

There are several paints you can use to create a striking sky backdrop with horizontal washes. These may be transparent or opaque watercolors, tempera, or Dr. Martin's Synchromatic Transparent Water Colors and Dr. Martin's Radiant Concentrated Water Colors. Use white illustration board or a good white watercolor paper to paint the sky backdrop on.

Suppose the backdrop design you are doing is 48'-0" wide by 30'-0" high. That means the size of the drop in ½-inch scale would be 24 inches wide by 15 inches high. Select a board that is larger than this size by at least another inch or so around the edges. This gives you extra space around the design so you can trim off the side, bottom, or top portion that you like least.

In making a rendering of a backdrop with nice horizontal washes, it is important to be completely organized with the colors, brushes, and materials because the success of the job depends on speed and agility. You should have

Stage designs by John Falabella
HARVEY FIERSTEIN'S SAFE SEX
Directed by Eric Conklin
Lyceum Theatre, New York (1987)
Act 1: "Manny and Jake."
Act 2: "Safe Sex."
Act 3: "On Tidy Endings."

plenty of work space, clean brushes, a container of water, and it also never hurts to have a stack of paper towels handy.

Doing a Smooth Horizontal Blend of Sky Washes One approach to making this type of rendering for a sky drop is to do a smooth horizontal blend of washes. While this is usually a more difficult technique to master than irregular washes, it becomes easier with practice. Mix three transparent colors in containers that are wide and deep enough to take a 1-inch brush. These watercolors should be a dark, a medium, and a light. You may want to mix these three transparent colors in blue or perhaps three different colors, such as blue, green, and gray, or any other suitable combination. Whatever you do, always make samples of the colors you are working with by brushing them on a piece of the same kind of board you are working with to see how they look when they dry.

Assume that you want to begin with the dark color at the top and go to a light color at the bottom. Use a 2½-inch Fitch brush (or similar brush) for wetting the surface of the illustration board before any blending is done. If a paper is being used instead of a board, make sure the edges are well taped-down.

When you are ready, dip the clean Fitch brush into the water and brush the water swiftly and evenly in horizontal strokes across the board to dampen it. Unless it is the effect you want, do not leave any portion of the illustration board dry, so that when the colors are applied they will blend together nicely and produce a good effect as you move gradually from the lightest to the darkest color.

It often works well to turn the board around so the bottom of the drop is at the top of your worktable. In other words, in doing the horizontal washes on the wet board, start with the lightest color at the top and go to the medium and then to the darkest color, which is now on the very bottom. Tilt the board so the bottom edge of the stroke stays wet.

While horizontal sky washes may be executed with a very lovely blend of washes going from dark at the top to light at the bottom, there are times when you may want to do the reverse and have the dark at the bottom in order to give better contrast behind the actors and scenery.

Doing Streaky and Busy Sky Washes
This wash technique may be used not only for quiet, pleasant skies, but also for brooding, turbulent, and erratic skies. The washes of watercolors may be diagonal, wavy, or zigzagged and may vary enormously in strokes, blending, colors, and overall atmosphere. In addition, as part of the sky design you may want to have several light horizontal areas breaking up the sky.

Possibly the best way to create a backdrop design that you like is to do several quick, flamboyant watercolor sketches. You will get many variations and ideas, as no two of these ever turn out exactly the same way.

MODELS

A Model versus a Sketch

Scale models are still highly favored as a means of indicating precisely what the scenic designer plans to put on stage, and very likely they will be for a long time to come.

Experienced scenic designers know the many advantages of doing ½-inch scale models. A model clearly shows the size, shape, color, and texture of the various set pieces. The position of objects on the stage itself, and how one item relates to another, can be seen immediately. By illuminating a model with tiny lights or even regular household light bulbs, certain lighting effects

Drawing by John Arnone
RED AND BLUE by Michael Hurson
Directed by JoAnne Akalaitis
New York Shakespeare Festival
Public Theatre's Other Stage
New York (1982)

"Nine room variations animated and independently illuminated provided the atmosphere for a text performed by unseen actors."
—John Arnone

Setting by Karl Eigsti
SCREENPLAY by Istvan Orkeny
Adapted by Gitta Honegger with Zelda Fichandler
Directed by Zelda Fichandler
Costumes by Marjorie Slaiman
Lighting by Arden Fingerhut
Arena Stage, Washington, D.C. (1983)
(Courtesy of Arena Stage)

can be displayed and the translucency of various materials of the model can be seen.

Another plus of making a model is that the exact size of three-dimensional scenery can be shown. Platforms, walls, backdrops, portals, ground rows, masking legs and borders, and other scenic pieces can be placed in the space comparable to where they will fit on the actual stage. All of these items can be made so that they can be lifted out of the model, looked at individually, moved around, and measured. A model of the stage setting can be a distinct advantage for the director and actors as well as for the technicians, particularly the production carpenter and the staff in the scenic shop.

The model is an excellent device for showing a revolving stage combined with other moving units. A revolve can turn both clockwise and counterclockwise and can even have a smaller revolve in the center that moves in the opposite direction from the larger revolve. Sometimes a floor is built up around a revolve to give the appearance of one flat continuous surface. To show the same identical moves and po-

sitions of a revolve would require making countless numbers of sketches.

All possible scene changes can be looked at and easily studied in a three-dimensional model. The designer and the director may want also to try different approaches to individual pieces. For instance, a platform may be enlarged and placed in the model, a different color for a canopy may be used over a baroque bed, the rake of a ramp can be decreased, a larger center chandelier can be tried, or a different wall pattern and texture might be painted on the backing. It is far simpler to make

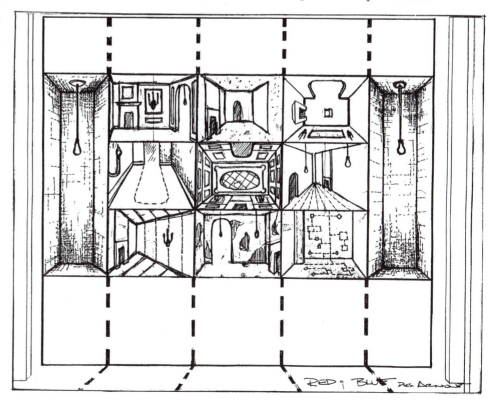

Stage designs by Thomas Lynch
A QUIET PLACE by Leonard Bernstein and
    Stephen Wadsworth
Directed by Stephen Wadsworth
Vienna State Opera
Vienna, Austria (1986)

Top: Act 3. "We were after a realism made lyrical by the overlay of memory. Scenery was built in full detail and then painted with pale photographic images of the same scene."

Bottom: Act 1: "Again memory images take over (both painting and projection) an otherwise straightforward representation of a Westchester funeral home, encroaching on the present reality."   —Thomas Lynch

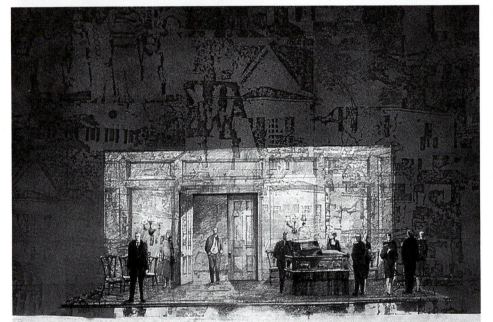

these changes in the ½-inch scale model than to make them after the scenery is in the shop!

A three-dimensional model can also be utilized quite effectively for executing the final drafting. An assistant can lift out the pieces of the model and easily scale the dimensions to go on the drafting by working with dividers and a scale ruler.

Using Parts of the Model as Sketches

Sometimes flat pieces of the set model can be lifted out of a three-dimensional model of the stage, be stacked on top of each other in the order they play on stage, and be used to simulate a kind of presentational sketch in which to show the overall design. Of course, these parts of the model must be items such as a group of flat portals painted on illustration board with cutout inner edges of various shapes, or perhaps a series of cut drops with a backdrop positioned upstage of them. The scene may be a forest in summer, with a sky drop and ground row upstage, or a set of drapery cut drops that form an exotic Egyptian tent.

Naturally, a group of sketches done on pieces of illustration board and stacked together would be thicker than a rendering on a single board, but nevertheless the overall idea is still easy to present to the viewer. This stacked arrangement works very nicely for judging the contrasts between the shapes, colors, and textures, especially for an asymmetrical scenic unit such as the forest or the Egyptian tent. Individually, all of these model pieces function beautifully as finished paint elevations in the scenic shop.

Deciding What Kind of Model to Make

Three-dimensional models of a stage setting may range from a simple preliminary cardboard model to an elaborate, fully detailed model of museum quality. When deciding on the kind of model you want to build, you should consider how much time you have to design a production, how much money is at your disposal to pay however many assistants you need to help execute it, and where the production is being presented. For instance, a model created for Broadway, for the Metropolitan Opera, or for the New York City Opera could be quite different from one built for a regional theatre and different still from a show in summer stock. Often museum-quality work can be found in finished models when the designer has had enough time, money, and assistants to work on it. The quality of the finished model may depend on how ambitious and meticulous the stage designer is and how much effort can be put into a model.

Basic Dimensions for Building a Model for a Commercial Production

These stage dimensions are averages that may be used to make a model for a production in the commercial theatre.

Proscenium width: 40'-0"

Proscenium height: 25'-0"

Model by George Tsypin
IDIOT'S DELIGHT by Robert Sherwood
Directed by Peter Sellars
Eisenhower Theatre
Washington, D.C. (1986)
(Photograph by George Tsypin)

"The action takes place in the lobby of the Italian hotel in the Alps on the eve of World War II. A unified structure, representing the mountains and the interior of the hotel at once, was also a comment on Italian fascist and modern architecture in general. It consisted mainly of a huge reflective wall (black marbelized Plexiglas and steel structure) that tilted forward, serving the notion of 'impending doom,' suspended bridge, and the bar insert in the Mussolini's eagle."
—George Tsypin

Depth (Back of smoke pocket to back wall): 30'-0"

Grid height: 60'-0"

Smoke pocket thickness: 8"

Proscenium thickness: 2'-0"

Apron (Back of smoke pocket to edge of apron): 3'-8"

House curtain (Back of smoke pocket to curtain): 1'-0"

Space stage right (Center line to stage right wall): 35'-0"

Space stage left (Center line to stage left wall): 32'-0"

A Preliminary Cardboard Model

A very rough preliminary model can be made from materials such as cardboard, shirt board, poster board, or Bristol board. The scenic pieces are drawn and scaled on the board, then cut out with scissors or with a paper cutter. The preliminary model can be in ½-inch, ¼-inch, or ⅛-inch scale.

Building a preliminary cardboard model is a quick method of determining the positioning of the ground plan on stage and at the same time creating the actual basic shapes of the front elevations. It is a cut-and-paste approach to indicate to the designer how the first shapes and forms work together in the stage space, where the scenery is positioned, and where the entrances and exits are located. In no way is the preliminary cardboard model meant to be a finished product. Usually it does not have details or furniture indicated; those come at a later stage of the design process.

A ⅛-inch Scale Model

Models made in the very small scale of ⅛ inch are interesting to construct and serve several purposes. A ⅛-inch model can indicate a simple basic design from which the designer can tell whether to go on to build a larger ¼-inch or ½-inch scale model. For a proscenium opening 40'-0" wide by 25'-0" high, the actual size in a ⅛-inch model would really be 5 inches wide by 3⅛ inches high, or about the size of an index card. A stage that is 36'-0" deep would be 4½ inches deep in ⅛-inch scale.

These very small models are excellent for showing early ideas on multiset shows. Let's say that an opera has six sets. It is relatively easy and quick to do two or three different ⅛-inch models. Certainly, these small sizes are not difficult to travel with nor to store. These very small sets can be made with regular stationery or heavy paper. The designs can be drawn lightly with pencil and cut out with a very sharp No. 1 X-acto knife. Small, sharp scissors also work well.

The Simplest White Paper Model

A simple white paper model in ¼-inch scale may be created with heavy white paper. The idea of this model is to show as much of what the designer has in mind as possible in a simple way. It is basically a neat, cutout model without too much, if any, detail, with profile furniture and scenery rather than any three-dimensional forms in the units. It is intended to be quick, easy, and simple. Basic lines are drawn in with pencil or pen.

A Print Model

A print model is built as a check to see if all the drafting will work out when all the pieces are put together. This kind of model is also useful to see the scale, the proportion, and the basic design of the set. It is usually a quicker and less refined model than the typical white model. Like a refined white model, a print model may be in ¼-inch or ½-inch scale.

A print model is exactly what the title implies. It is made from the cut-up prints of the designer's original drafting. Original drawings on tracing paper can be printed as black lines on white or blue lines on white.

The cutout prints may include dimensions and notes or numbers that have been put on the drafting originally. The prints are normally cut out in pieces and glued to heavy paper or board. This makes them easier to han-dle as you work with them. They may be glued to paper or board with a spray adhesive such as Scotch 3M Spra-Ment Adhesive or 3M Super 77 Spray Adhesive. Both come in aerosol cans. Glue sticks are also good to use.

A White Paper Model with Details

A ½-inch white model with details is usually made after the rough preliminary cardboard model has been created. It is done instead of making a print model or a very simple white model in ¼-inch scale because it is ordinarily more presentational and impressive. It can also be done before, during, or after the show has been drafted. It takes quite a bit of time to do a white paper model well, but not as much time as a fully painted model. Of course, the detailed white model normally needs to be accompanied with colored sketches of the front elevations of the scenery.

Basic Steps for Making the White ½-inch Scale Model with Details

The choice of either white illustration board (such as No. 80) or heavy white paper to make the white detailed model is determined by your purpose. For example, if you plan on cutting out a great deal of detail work such as small window panes or latticework with an X-acto knife, then you would choose heavy paper instead of the heavier illustration board. It is a good idea to use heavy board for all the basic walls, and heavy paper for those areas where detailed designs are to be neatly cut out. Sometimes regular typing paper is good for cutting out minute details of model scenery. The variations in the use of heavy paper and illustration board or other material are controlled completely by the design.

Illustration board may be used to support both heavy paper sets and sets made completely out of illustration board. As an example for support on the rear of a model interior set, there

Models by Douglas W. Schmidt
PORGY AND BESS
Music by George Gershwin
Libretto by DuBose Heyward
Lyrics by DuBose Heyward, Ira Gershwin
Directed by Jack O'Brien
Radio City Music Hall, New York (1983)

Costume designs by Allen Charles Klein
TURANDOT by Giacomo Puccini; libretto by
   G. Adami and R. Simoni
Shown: Calaf and Princess Turandot
Directed by Bliss Hebert (1980)
Miami, Dallas, Houston, and San Francisco
   Operas
(Photographs by Scott Pecktal)

may be a flat, continuous horizontal profiled brace on the back going around the very top and the very bottom of the vertical flats. These profiled support pieces may be ½-inch in width and may start at the offstage edges of the downstage returns (left and right) and then go around the entire box set. Also, for support, it is good to have several ½-inch-wide vertical jogs placed on the back of the flats. These may be fitted in between the two flat profiled horizontal bottom and top braces, which are glued on first.

When making a white detailed paper model in ½-inch scale, use these steps:

1. *Do the drafting.* Use the tracings of the original drafting in ½-inch scale.
2. *Have the drafting printed.* Get black line on white background copies of the drafting made when you go to the blueprinters.
3. *Cut up these printed copies.* When the black-on-white prints are made, cut them up and tape or glue them on sheets of 8½ × 11-inch white paper in order to have clean copies made with a copy machine on 25 percent white rag paper. Put as many pieces as you can on each sheet of 8½ × 11-inch white paper, leaving at least ¼ inch of space around each piece. Arranging several pieces on one sheet of paper minimizes the cost of copying

and is an efficient way to keep track of all the pieces. Use a glue stick or small pieces of transparent Scotch tape to fasten the edges of the cutout print pieces to the 8½ × 11-inch white paper. Though 25 percent white rag paper is a bit more expensive than regular copy paper, it is well worth it.

Stage design by Zack Brown
RIGOLETTO by Giuseppe Verdi—Act 3
Libretto by Francesco Maria Piave
Directed by Fabrizio Melano
Washington Opera Company
Opera House, Kennedy Center
Washington, D.C. (1983)

"Solving the actual floor problems inherent in the last act of RIGOLETTO is one thing—creating a stage picture that makes sense is another. Here the attempt was to render the stage action as *believable* as possible with a maximum of atmosphere appropriate to the score."
—Zack Brown

162 Copies made on 25 percent white rag usually duplicate in the same size as the original, take paints nicely, can easily be touched up with pencil or pen, and age well. Photostat copies can also work well, but these are more expensive and the paper is not always as thin as the 25 percent white rag paper used in photocopying machines. Drawings of large set pieces may have to be duplicated on two or three sheets of 8½ × 11-inch paper.

4. *Clean up these prints fastened on sheets of 8½ × 11-inch paper.* In order to get the best possible second prints, the prints now attached on the sheets of 8½ × 11-inch paper may need to be touched up with white paint to eliminate any dimension lines and notes or numbers. Also, lines on the detailed drawings may need to be gone over with a pencil or pen so they are continuous and crisp.

5. *Have neater and better copies made for the actual white paper model pieces.* Take the cleaned-up first prints to the copy machine to make final copies. Be sure to use 25 percent rag paper. At the same time, you may also want to have copies made from drawings of other items that go in the model. These items may be furniture, props, drapery on windows, books in bookcases, pictures on walls, or other scenic elements that are not necessarily included on the drafting. They should be drawn in ½-inch scale and mounted on sheets of 8½ × 11-inch white paper, just as you did for the prints of the drafting.

Make two or more copies of any set details or furniture, because extras may be needed. The cornice detail in an interior set is an example of a drawing that would require a number of

copies to be used for the repeat pattern on the top of flats. It is also nice to have multiple copies of good, consistent line drawings as well as extras in case you make a mess of one. Now clean copies of everything are ready to be glued in place in the model.

6. *Cut up the second copies and glue these on heavy paper or board.* When ready to mount the final clean copies to go in the model, have these materials available:

Medium white paper	Container of water
Heavy white paper	Metal straight edge
White illustration board	Masking tape
White glue (Elmer's)	Razor blade and mat knife
Damp white cotton rag	Scissors and X-acto knife
1-inch stiff bristle brush	Paper cutter
	Wax paper
	Scale

With the scissors, cut out each piece of scenery and furniture from the 8½ × 11-inch copies allowing approximately ¼ inch of space around the perimeter of the drawing. The ¼-inch excess should be trimmed off

Jo Mielziner's backdrop design in ½-inch scale for DEATH OF A SALESMAN (1949) was 45 feet wide by 32 feet high. It was made for a translucent backdrop showing translucent values. It has been covered with clear acetate and marked off in 2-foot squares so it can be drawn in full scale in the scenic studio. The drop has been raised at the bottom. (Photograph by Lynn Pecktal)

once the piece is glued down on the white illustration board.

Prepare pieces of heavy white paper (or board) that are slightly larger than the cutout drawings. It is easier to glue the cutout copies onto slightly larger pieces of heavy white paper (or board) and then trim off the excess than to position them accurately onto a piece the exact size perimeter that is covered with wet glue.

Use a stiff 1-inch-wide bristle brush to apply the white glue. Thin the glue with water in a proportion of approximately 25 percent water to 75 percent glue. Stir it well to obtain a consistent mixture. (Elmer's Glue-All is excellent to use for this.) Then, working with one piece at a time, brush the glue on the board or paper and smooth it out to get rid of any excess glue. It is better to brush on the glue sparsely rather than heavily. Next, starting at the top,

Model design by John Wulp
THE CRUCIFER OF BLOOD by Paul Giovanni
Pondicherry Lodge
Directed by Paul Giovanni
Helen Hayes Theatre
New York (1978)
(Photograph by Brian Pew)

The set consisted of three framed hangers positioned between the portals, with the upstage window unit designed as a box riding on casters. The white paper model (25 percent white rag copies with black line drawings cut up and glued on illustration board) in ½-inch scale is shown in a black box, with outer areas of the framed hangers and portals also painted black.

Stage design by Ben Edwards
THE REMARKABLE MR. PENNYPACKER by
  Liam O'Brien
Directed by Alan Schneider
Coronet Theatre, New York (1953)

lay the cutout drawing on the wet glue-covered board or paper, and let it fall evenly into place.

Smooth out the drawing immediately while the glue is still wet. Place a piece of clean wax paper on top of the freshly glued piece, and with one hand holding the wax paper, use the other hand to rub evenly over the clean wax paper until the drawing is pressed out completely flat. Now remove the wax paper from the drawing. Wet the piece of cotton rag, squeezing out as much water as possible, and use it to wipe away any excess glue.

Applying pressure on the surfaces of glued items while the glue is still wet is an important factor in obtaining smoothed-out surfaces. If necessary stack a pile of magazines or books on top of the glued pieces. Sometimes it is necessary to glue another thickness of the same illustration board on the back of a piece to prevent undesired warping. After completing the individual pieces, put them all together to finish the model.

Setting by Clarke Dunham
THE APPRENTICESHIP OF DUDDY KRAVITZ
Based on the novel by Mordecai Richler
Book by Austin Pendleton and Mordecai
  Richler
Music by Alan Menken;
  lyrics by David Spenser
Directed by Austin Pendleton
Costumes by Ruth Morley
Lighting by Ken Billington
Zellerbach Theatre
Philadelphia, Pennsylvania (1987)
(Photograph by Clarke Dunham)

A Highly Finished Painted Model

Of course, the aim of most ambitious stage designers is to make a beautifully finished model in full color with exquisitely crafted details. For the viewer it should be a gorgeous visual gift, so immaculately realized that it fascinates anyone who studies it.

Some designers in the commercial theatre achieve such brilliantly painted models, usually in ½-inch scale. In the best models nothing has been spared to create theatrical magic. It helps set a model apart from the average to have any mechanical scenery in the model operate flawlessly. It also enhances the quality of the model to have it illuminated with tiny lights.

Models of Difficult Three-Dimensional Pieces

Occasionally a scenic designer will design scenery for which it is difficult to make a drawing that accurately shows the varying shapes and planes so that the carpenters in the scenic shop can build it accordingly. While standard drafting views such as a plan, front, side, rear, top, and sections can be made of the individual piece, the best solution is to make a detailed ½-inch scale model to indicate exactly what is wanted and how it should look so that the scenic shop has no doubt about what you want. The most talented and experienced carpenters can do wonderful things when working with a detailed model.

Some good examples of productions with scenery where it worked well to have a three-dimensional model are Ming Cho Lee's irregular ledge setting for *K2* (1983); Jo Mielziner's varying roof shapes on the revolving house unit for *The Baker's Wife* (1976); the curved metal pipe armatures under the bed and window drapery canopies for the bedroom set designed by Edward Gorey for *Dracula* (1977); and Felix E. Cochren's unit set of leaning posts, angled beams, boards, and walls for the Negro Ensemble Company's production of *Home* (1980).

Painting a Model as One Unit or as Several Units

Plan to paint the various parts of a model when the pieces are removed from the basic model of the stage. This is less tedious and time-consuming than trying to paint the entire model after everything has been glued together in place.

Constructing and painting scenery in a model of an average interior box set, especially one with formal decor that requires much care in painting, is usually a matter of making the pieces, putting them in the stage model, taking them out to work on them, and then trying them in the stage model again and again until you are satisfied with the results. This way it is much easier to manage working with many varieties of paints and materials, including paints in aerosol cans and dyes.

You might want to spray all the portals while they are outside of the model, then put them permanently in the model of the stage once the floor has been painted. On the other hand, if the portals are created with painted designs and the scenic artists need to lift them out of the model to use them individually as paint elevations, then of course, they would not be glued to the floor.

A setting of an atmospheric sculptured cave might be carved out of pieces of Styrofoam that are glued together and shaped as one piece, with small bits of cheesecloth glued over the entire carved surface, then primed with white gesso. The overpainting can be given enormous interest and can be done simply by spraying back and forth, around, and over the surface with different colored paints from aerosol cans. Then the painting can be refined by hand brushing details or by using an airbrush. If you do not have an airbrush, a Preval Spray Pac is good to use for spraying on paints such as caseins, watercolors, and dyes.

Making Large Models in One or More Sections

It is far simpler to build very large models in one or more sections, simply because it makes them easier to travel and store. A ½-inch scale model for a one-set show in a commercial theatre can be 25 inches wide by 16 inches high by 16 inches deep. A ¼-inch scale model could be 13 inches wide by 7 inches high by 8 inches deep. Of course, adding more offstage space in the model of the stage would increase all these dimensions. For example, if a model is

Model designs by Andrew Jackness
SOUTH PACIFIC
Music: Rodgers and Hammerstein
Based on *Tales of the South Pacific*
   by James Michener
Directed by A. J. Antoon
Dorothy Chandler Pavilion
Los Angeles, California (1985)

Model by David Jenkins
HEDDA GABLER by Henrik Ibsen
Directed by Robert Egan
Center Theatre Group, Doolittle Theatre
Los Angeles, California (1986)
(Photographs by David Jenkins)

"Director and design discussions prior to actual production with four design studies of the model for transition of claustrophobic interior to external landscape (Hedda's suicide). Concept was to use rear wall to reveal Hedda's body."
—David Jenkins

being built for a large musical production in a sizable theatre, the apron and orchestra pit, side stages, boxes, and orchestra floor itself may have to be included. In this case, it is practical to think of making the main stage as one section, the orchestra and boxes as another section, and so on; otherwise, a large model like this in ½-inch scale would be difficult to get through average-size doors, not to mention into cars and taxicabs. It would also occupy a large storage space.

Reusing Model Pieces

A scenic designer sometimes reuses pieces from one model in another. When this is possible, it saves an enor-mous amount of time in construction. However, keep in mind that a designer's model can become part of his or her portfolio of design work, and there are times when a collection of a particular designer's models is wanted for an exhibit, or the models are selected to be sold in a gallery or even given to a museum or university collection.

Model pieces may be interchanged even if they are later returned to the model that they were borrowed from. Pieces that do not have to be glued or fastened in place are easier to remove from the model. It is also helpful if the borrowed pieces do not have to be repainted or textured or have accessories changed. But this depends on the designer, the amount of time available, and the style of the piece.

Here are some common items that may be used over and over in a model.

Furniture	Chandeliers and lights
Trees and foliage	Balustrades
Draperies and curtains	Brick and stone walls
Masking pieces	Architectural units
Backdrops	Rugs and ground cloths
Ground rows	Columns and pilasters
	Ceiling pieces

Covering Models with Clear Plexiglas

One of the best ways to protect a finished model from dust, water, and the ravages of time is to have a cover made to fit. A good material to use for the cover is clear Plexiglas. To figure the dimension of the cover, be sure to allow at least ½ inch on the outside dimensions of the width, height, and depth of the model. While these hard plastic covers are ideal for protecting and dressing up the appearance of a model, they must be handled with care so that they do not get scratched, cracked, or broken. Clear hard plastic covers are especially effective to use when the models are on display.

Keeping Models of the Stage for Future Use

Many designers in the commercial theatre have a diverse collection of model stages that have been made for all sorts of different theatres. The models in such a collection may include both ½-inch and ¼-inch scale models and may vary a great deal in shape and

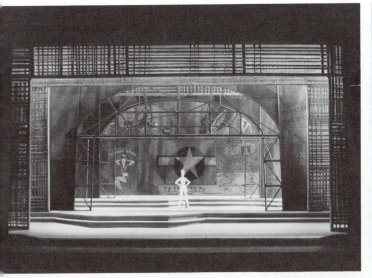

Models by Tony Walton for HURLYBURLY (1984), Chicago and New York versions. (Photograph by Tony Walton)

overall size. They are often revamped according to how they can work for the next production. There are models of stages for straight plays with or without apron extensions, for dramas with thrust stages, for all-purpose productions, for completely open stages, and so on.

Building a Collapsible Model of the Stage

The model of the theatre stage where the setting will play is often cumbersome to store and carry to and from production meetings at various locations. One way to alleviate this problem is to construct a collapsible model of the stage to house the ½-inch scale models of the actual scenery. Having several collapsible stage models on hand for showing different settings simultaneously saves time in model con-

struction. Collapsible models may be black, white, or a combination of colors. The average-size stage model in ½-inch scale may be 25 inches wide by 16 inches high and 17 inches deep, depending on the production and the dimensions of the theatre. But of course for lavish models, where the deck, walls, and set must be glued together permanently and finished as one overall unit, it would not be at all practical to think of using a collapsible model.

One of the best come-apart stage models to build is one that has a raised stage floor. An average height for an apron could be 3′-3″, which in ½-inch scale is 1⅝ inches. For construction purposes, extra support can be added in the space under the stage floor. A raised stage floor is also good to have when the sets going into the model stage are designed to have a raked deck or a deck extending past the apron. Another practical aspect of the raised model floor is that trap openings can be easily cut out and then reclosed as needed for different set models that are to be displayed in the stage model.

Assume you are using the given dimensions, 25 inches wide by 16 inches high by 17 inches deep, for your model. If you are constructing a breakaway model in ½-inch scale and intend to have a raised stage floor showing the apron, then build the bottom portion of the model house so that it measures 25 inches wide by 17 inches deep by 1⅝ inches high (overall height of apron from the floor of the theatre).

This bottom portion of the model can be constructed so that it has a sheet of illustration board on the top and bot-

For a model of the stage, a framework consists of soft wooden strips on ¼-inch Masonite.

tom, with vertical supports (also of illustration board) on edge that are positioned in between. These usually run up and down stage and are spaced 2 to 3 inches apart. It saves weight to make this bottom portion mostly hollow, but it can also be constructed with layers of Styrofoam sandwiched in between the top and bottom sheets of illustration board, with appropriate facings of the same. Lengths of Foamcore board cut to size are also excellent to use. The exact shape of the apron in the theatre in which you are working should be duplicated with accurate dimensions.

Use Elmer's Glue-All (white glue that dries clear) to attach the boards and supports together. It is also helpful to use 1-inch-wide strips of heavy white paper folded down the center to glue various undersections and supports together. Brush glue on one folded side of the white paper strip, press in place, let dry, and then do the same to the other side of the white folded strip. Besides illustration board, ⅛-inch or ¼-inch plywood can be used if desired.

When constructing the four walls (proscenium or front wall, two side walls, and back wall), again use a good illustration or mat board. Plan to support the inside of the walls with ¼ × ¼-inch wooden strips, and let these vertical parts extend approximately 1½ inches on the bottoms so they can fit into square openings cut out in the base of the model.

Make the outsides of the walls line up with the sides of the bottom unit. On the proscenium wall and back wall allow four vertical square posts going into the floor (total of eight), and on each of the side walls allow at least

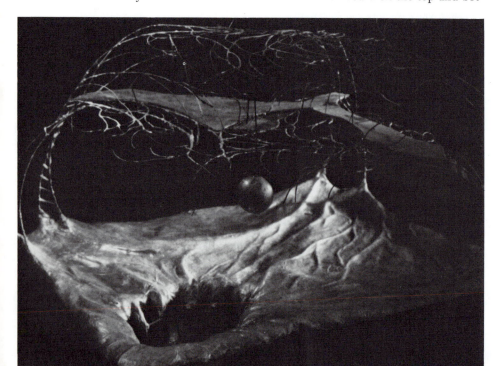

Model by Heidi Landesman
A MIDSUMMER NIGHT'S DREAM by William Shakespeare
Directed by David Chambers
Arena Stage
Washington, D.C. (1981)

Stage design by Heidi Landesman
A MIDSUMMER NIGHT'S DREAM by William
   Shakespeare
Directed by David Chambers
The Acting Company
Public/Newman Theatre, New York (1981)

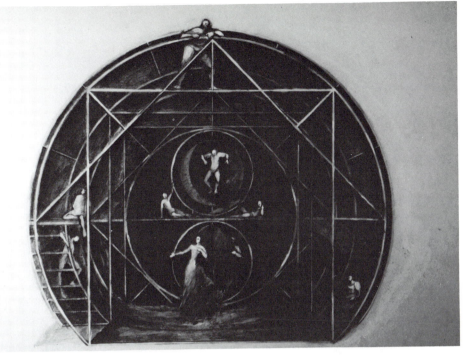

two posts (total of four) doing the same. Make the proscenium wall the full width of the model, and glue on the appropriate measured thickness pieces corresponding to the proscenium opening of the actual theatre.

When the proscenium wall and back wall are built and in place, construct the two side walls to fit in between them. While the four walls have posts extending into the floor, it is necessary to devise some method at the top of the four corners for attaching the walls together. A good method of temporarily fastening the walls is to use pieces of Velcro. (Velcro is available in black or white and comes in rolls of ¾-inch, 1-inch, or 2-inch widths, male hook or female loop. Velcro also comes in colors. Or, instead of Velcro, you may use small metal pins inserted through drilled holes, or any other ideas you might devise.

Model by Karl Eigsti
THE ACCIDENTAL DEATH OF AN
   ANARCHIST by Dario Fo
Adapted by Richard Nelson
Directed by Douglas C. Wager
Belasco Theatre, New York (1984)
(Photograph by Brian Pew)

"An agitprop theatrical interpretation of an interrogation room on the fourth floor of an Italian police station in the suburbs of Milan."
—Karl Eigsti

A model of the stage is constructed to include the apron with its full height, width, and depth when one or more of the following are planned as part of the set design.

1. An extension is to be added to the apron.
2. Platforms, stairs, ramps, or runways are to extend from the apron into the house floor or audience area.
3. A raked stage or platform unit extends past the apron.
4. Practical traps are in the apron stage floor.
5. Decorative elements are to go on the front facing of the apron. These may be a certain kind of painting, sculp-

ture, set dressing, or practical lights.
6. The orchestra pit is open, covered, or partially covered. It may be needed for normal use by musicians and instruments. Or the pit may be designated as another area for making entrances or exits. It may also be used for special effects, for prop storage, and for positioning special lighting instruments.

Constructing a Heavy-Duty Model of the Stage

Materials ¼-inch Masonite or ¼-inch plywood for the base, white pine strips, brads or nails, Elmer's Glue-All, small clamps and wooden blocks, drill and bit, saw, sandpaper, covering ma-

167

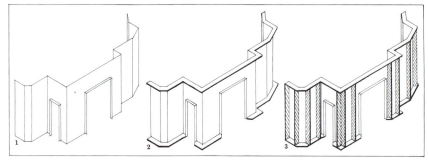

Bracing a model on the rear.

terials, wooden dowels, and any paints that are needed.

The stage designer needs to construct a very strong model of the actual stage in the theatre if this model is going to get a tremendous amount of handling. It must be made of materials that will not bend, warp, or fall apart. When you wish to make a strong model shell of the stage, the best place to buy the building materials is at a local lumber company. The idea is to make a good solid base with an openwork frame of wood, then to cover the walls so they appear solid.

Use this information to make a model of the stage.

1. Select either ¼-inch plywood or ¼-inch Masonite for the floor. Either of these materials can have holes drilled in the corners and have small nails inserted from underneath into the vertical supporting strips (or posts) for the model house walls.

2. Select white pine wood strips. These usually come in standard sizes such as ¼ × ½-inch, ¼ × ¾-inch, ¼ × 1⅛-inch, ⅜ × ⅞-inch, ⁷⁄₁₆ × 1⅜-inch, ½ × ½-inch, ½ × ¾-inch, ⅝ × ⅞-inch and ¾ × ¾-inch.

3. Decide on the overall size of the model. It is best to make a sketch with dimensions and then cut out the floor and white pine strips accordingly. You must figure how the pine strips are going to be positioned, both vertically and horizontally.

4. Figure and saw all of the white pine pieces at the same time. This means having four vertical pieces (one in each corner), two long horizontal pieces at the top front and back (resting on the verticals), and two shorter horizontal pieces at the top of each of the two sides. Once these are in place, add the remaining strips. On the front of the model there should be two vertical strips that form the width of the proscenium opening and that are to go between the plywood base and the top horizontal piece. Between these two verticals and positioned high is the horizontal strip forming the top of the proscenium opening. Finally, for more support, strips of the same thickness should be marked, cut, and positioned horizontally on the bottom (but resting on top of the base) between the two vertical strips—two short on each side of the proscenium opening, two on the sides, and one upstage, for a total of five.

5. Drill holes for the brads or small nails

to go in and also use Elmer's Glue-All to hold the framework together, and then hammer in the nails. When finished, you should have an open rectangular framework.

6. For a very sturdy shell, cover the framework with ⅛-inch plywood, starting with the two side walls, then covering the front and back. Other covering material may be mat board, illustration board, or ³⁄₁₆-inch Foam-core board.

7. When doing a show with hanging scenery, use ¼-inch-diameter wooden dowels that are positioned parallel to the proscenium wall and resting on the tops of the sides of the model. These simulate the hanging pipes in the actual theatre. Smaller-diameter dowels may have to be used if the show is tightly hung with scenery. Even more sophisticated models may have outer walls extending upward to mask these hanging simulated pipes.

8. Mark off positions for sets of lines on top of the sides of the model so that they correspond to the same hanging dimensions in the theatre. This means putting a wooden strip at the top of each side of the model stage to hold the pipes or battens. Define these positions with brads, nails, or slots so the horizontal dowels holding pieces of model scenery can be held in the appropriate positions when showing the scenic pieces. Model scenery may be attached to the dowels with string or wire.

9. Aprons, apron extensions, thrust stages or side stages, ramps and runways into the house of course require additional planning and construction.

Setting by George Tsypin
THE ELECTRIFICATION OF THE SOVIET
  UNION
Directed by Peter Sellars
Costumes by Dunya Ramicova
Lighting by James F. Ingalls
Glyndebourne Festival, England (1987)
(Photograph by George Tsypin)

"For this new opera by English composer Nigel Osborne about conflict between history and individual lives set during the Russian Revolution, I created two levels. On the floor a long white bare Kafkaesque wall, made of layers of flexible light metal and foam, constantly moved, changing configuration. The flexibility and softness of the walls allowed direct interaction of performers and the scenery, creating a terrifying dreamlike effect of the world swirling around the people. Tracks and fragment of the crashed train were suspended above, with memory scenes taking place there cinematically replaying the train crash over and over again."
                                    —George Tsypin

Stage designs by Lester Polakov
COCK-A-DOODLE-DANDY by Sean O'Casey
Directed by Philip Burton
Carnegie Hall Playhouse, New York (1958)

Keeping a Studio Model of the Stage

A scenic designer may have one or more models of stages that stay in the design studio and are used exclusively when scenery is being designed. This model of the stage may be constructed with open walls if needed, because it does not have to be taken to bid sessions or the scenic studio.

The model kept in the studio is extremely practical to have, especially if it has been made as a standard stage

model for an opera or dance company. It could just as easily be a stage model for a resident or university theatre. It can also be more complicated than the usual built model. It may have removable walls, an adjustable proscenium opening, working lights, a complete apron or pit, a revolve in the floor, stock masking legs and borders, plain backdrops, and a cyclorama. The studio model can be highly refined because it does not have to move and therefore weight and bulk are not a problem. Unless there is plenty of viewing space around all sides of the model, it should rest on a table with casters so it can be moved around as needed.

CONSTRUCTING MODELS

Selecting Materials for Making Models

There are no special materials designated exclusively for making models. The best rule of thumb is to use what you can find and what works best for you. Every designer has discovered some new items or materials in the course of making models. Where China silk works for one designer, burlap or rice paper may be ideal for another. Anything that holds its shape, is lightweight, can take paints nicely, and will hold up well for a reasonable amount of time can be used. Sometimes designers invent uses for materials and methods of putting everything together just because they are short on time and do not have on hand the actual items that they would normally use.

The most basic and common materials for simple models tend to be illustration board, mat board, heavy paper, balsa wood, white glue, and various water-base paints. Modeling paste is great for creating heavy textures. Gesso is applied to various surfaces (illustration board, balsa wood, glues, for example) to seal and to prepare the surfaces to take paint well. Gesso can also be used for creating light texturing on

Stage design by David Gropman
PUNTILA by Bertolt Brecht
Directed by Ron Daniels
Yale Repertory Company, New Haven, Connecticut (1977)

Model by Ralph Funicello
MISALLIANCE by George Bernard Shaw, directed by Martin Benson
South Coast Repertory Company
Costa Mesa, California (1988)

Stage design by Robert Perdziola
THE NOSE by Dmitri Shostakovitch
Directed by Lou Galterio
Santa Fe Opera, Santa Fe, New Mexico (1987)

Stage design by Karen Schulz
RED RIVER by Pierre Laville
Directed by Robert Woodruff
Goodman Theatre, Chicago, Illinois (1983)

170 Model by Douglas W. Schmidt
DIAMOND LIL, directed by Paul Blake
American Conservatory Theatre
San Francisco, California (1988)

Stage design by James Stewart Morcom
NATIVE SON by Paul Green and Richard Wright
Directed by Orson Welles
St. James Theatre, New York (1941)

Model by George Tsypin
TANNHÄUSER by Richard Wagner
Directed by Peter Sellars
Chicago Lyric Opera, Chicago, Illinois (1988)

Model by Tony Straiges
THE GREAT MAGOO by Ben Hecht; directed by Mark Lamos
Hartford Stage Company, Hartford, Connecticut (1982)
(Photograph by Ney Tait Fraser)

Stage design by Franco Colavecchia
RASPUTIN by Jay Reise
Directed by Frank Corsaro
New York City Opera (1988)

Model by Heidi Landesman
BIG RIVER—Music and lyrics by Roger Miller
Book by William Hauptman; staged by Des McAnuff
Eugene O'Neill Theatre, New York (1985)

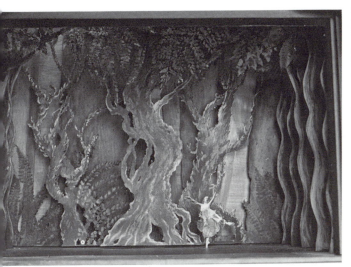

Model by Peter Harvey
A MIDSUMMER NIGHT'S DREAM Ballet—Act I, Scene 1
Choreographed by George Balanchine
Zurich Opera House, Zurich, Switzerland (1979)

Stage design by Thomas Lynch
DON JUAN COMES BACK FROM THE WARS by Von Horvath
Directed by Bruce Siddons
Oregon Contemporary Theatre, Portland, Oregon (1983)

model surfaces. The list of materials for models becomes more specialized depending on the individual designer.

Model Materials and Equipment

Whenever applicable, some of the listed items may also be used for making presentation sketches and paint elevations.

Making a Sample with Materials to Be Used in the Model

If a model, or sketch for that matter, is worth making, it is worth making properly. That is why it is always important to make a sample to test materials that you may not have tried before. The sample does not have to be large. It can be 6 × 6 inches. You may make it by adhering a paper to a board with glue or other adhesive and then painting it. You need to know how the paper is going to hold, if it will stay on when wet, how it will look when it dries, and if you basically like the sample.

A designer automatically learns the best methods through experience. For example, if too much white glue is applied, the board may warp; in time, paper adhered with rubber cement may peel away from the board. To keep illustration or mounting board from warping, you may have to laminate two pieces of board together. Two pieces of illustration board can easily be glued together to form a neat and flat surface. Apply the glue consistently over the surface of one board, then put the second board on the first one and quickly apply weights such as heavy books or magazines on them. Leave them on while the glue dries.

To mount a sketch done on paper, apply Scotch 3M Spra-Ment Adhesive over the face of an illustration board and then place the sketch on the board. Quickly lay a similar-size board on top of the sketch and rub over it in wide, broad strokes so that the sketch is smoothed out and held down nicely. Lift the top board and check the paper sketch to see if there are any areas that need additional smoothing out.

Balsa Wood for Models

Balsa wood is a standard staple to have on hand for making models. It is light, versatile, and comes in assorted sizes. Sizes vary according to the source.

MODEL MATERIALS AND EQUIPMENT

Basic Model Tools

Drills and bits	Coping saws	Butt chisels
Screwdrivers	Punches	Hack saw
Pliers	Measuring and marking tools	Carpenter's square
Hammers	Tweezers	Wire cutters

Materials for Making Stage Models

Mat board	Glues	⅛-inch plywood
Illustration board	Pine strips	¼-inch plywood base
Foamcore board	Nails or brads	¼-inch Masonite base
Balsa wood	Wooden dowels	Upson board

Papers and Boards for Making Models

Marbleized paper	Tracing paper	Watercolor paper
Metallic paper	Fluorescent paper	Gray bogus paper
Miniature wallpaper	Newsprint paper	Brown Kraft paper
Doilies	Construction paper	Illustration board
Charcoal paper	Tissue paper	Mat board

For Cutting and Carving Model Parts

Scissors and shears	Jeweler's saw	Sharp carving knives
Utility mat knives	Sandpaper and sanders	Hot wire loop
Single-edge razor blades	Planes	Manicure scissors
X-acto knives and blades	Various files	Metal straight edges
X-acto razor saw blades	Paper cutter	Dremel hobby tools

For Holding Model Parts While Gluing

Rubber bands	Straight pins	Weights of all kinds
Spring clothespins	Wires	Clamps and vises
Pushpins	Masking tape	String and twine

For Making Textures and Three-Dimensional Shapes

Styrofoam blocks	Liquitex Modeling Paste	Gauze
Sawdust and shavings	Sand and sandpaper	Linen scrim
Aluminum foil	Sculpture clay	Brown paper scraps
Shredded Styrofoam	Wallboard compound	Gray bogus paper
Spackle	Plaster of Paris	Cardboard cartons

For Creating Windows in Models

Clear acetate	Colored gelatins	Gauzes
Glassine paper	Cellophane	Screening

For Painting Models and Making Sketches

Caseins	Liquitex Gesso (white priming)	Watercolors in cakes or tubes
Latexes		Designer's gouache
Acrylics	Regular and colored pencils	Dr. Martin's Synchromatic Transparent Watercolors
Aniline dyes	Art markers	
Oils	Pens and inks	Dr. Martin's Radiant Watercolors
Temperas	Fluorescent watercolors	
Spray paints	Charcoal sticks/pencils	Spray fixatives
Pastels	Metallic paints	

For Mixing Paints

Palettes of porcelain, aluminum, wood, paper, or plastic	Tin cans	Watercolor cups
	Dishes	Jars

For Applying Paints, Dyes, and Inks

Brushes of red sables, white Chinese bristles, camel hair, ox hair, and others	Preval Spray Pac	Sponges
	Pens	Small rollers
	Cotton swabs	Airbrushes

SIZES OF BALSA WOOD (IN INCHES)

36 INCHES LONG

¹⁄₁₆ × ¹⁄₁₆	¹⁄₁₆ × 6	1 × 1
⅛ × ⅛	⅛ × 6	1 × 4
¼ × ¼	¼ × 6	2 × 4
	½ × 3	

18 INCHES LONG

¹⁄₁₆ × ¹⁄₁₆	³⁄₁₆ × ³⁄₁₆	¼ × 3
³⁄₃₂ × ³⁄₃₂	¼ × ¼	¼ × 3
⅛ × ⅛	¹⁄₁₆ × 3	⅜ × 3
	³⁄₃₂ × 3	

12 INCHES LONG

1 × 1	1 × 3	2 × 3
1 × 2	2 × 2	3 × 3
	½ × 3	

Collecting Useful Items for Models

Designers usually find it advantageous to have a great selection of small items and practical materials on hand for making model furniture and props. One of the reasons for creating extremely detailed models is to show as much originality as possible, and having items on hand saves an enormous amount of time. The combination of various objects and materials from a designer's collection often makes very interesting model pieces.

There is an almost endless number of places to find useful model parts. Some of the best are jewelry stores, hobby shops, thrift shops, art stores, lumber companies, hardware stores, and other specialty stores. Listed are some items that may be used for making detailed objects in models.

Cork balls	Plastic/metal discs
Assorted buttons	Ear rings
Sequins	Tiny crystals
Fleurs-de-lis	Strings
Fake pearls	Wood shavings
Rondelles	Tiny pictures
Bracket ends	Small shells
Small half balls	Hard/flexible wires
Bracelet charms	Pebbles
Pipe cleaners	Jump rings
Pieces of felt	Neck chains
Styrofoam blocks	Small sponges
Wooden dowels	Wooden matches
Toothpicks	Small stars
Aluminum foil	Wooden veneers
Small pendants	Clasps
Christmas tree lights	Mirrored discs
Yarns	Jewelry parts

Bell caps	Uncooked rice
Filigree drops	Uncooked lentils
Twigs	Bass woods
Miniature flowers	Nut shells
Various beads	Bottle caps

Gluing ½-inch Scale Model Flats Together on the Back

Assume the model flats in an interior set are being put together. Naturally, you will need to use the ½-inch scale ground plan of the setting for this kind of project.

Flats cut out of cardboard or illustration board can be attached together by gluing strips of paper on the backs of them. When you are preparing to glue one flat to another, plan to work on one vertical side of a flat at a time. Use strips of heavy white paper, such as Flax white opaque ledger bond. To make the strips, cut ½-inch widths of white paper 8 or 10 inches long or longer. Fold each strip in half. Glue the ½-inch strip on the outer vertical edge of the flat, letting it overlap ¼ inch. Of course, this means that you only need to brush glue on half of the strip. Allow each strip to dry, then position the next adjacent flat, brush glue on the remaining half of the strip, press it in place on the second flat, and let it dry.

For cutting smaller widths of paper strips, such as ⅜ inches wide, use a wider piece of paper, such as 1-inch or

Models by Tony Straiges
INTO THE WOODS
Music and lyrics by Stephen Sondheim
Book and direction by James Lapine
Martin Beck Theatre, New York (1987)
(Photographs by Ney Tait Fraser)

so. Fold this strip of paper in half, then place it on the paper cutter so the excess can be trimmed off both sides at once to obtain an approximate overall width of ⅜ inch.

When gluing any paper strips on the back of flats, make the white strips at least ½ inch longer than the height of the actual model pieces. So, if you are gluing a strip on 16-foot flats, then the strips would be 8½ inches long and any excess can be cut off after the glue has dried.

At some point you will need to stand the flats up in their position on the ground plan and add both horizontal and vertical stiffeners on the backs along the edges and wherever necessary. These bracing stiffeners may be made of Foamcore board, thin strips of white pine, balsa wood, or illustration or mounting board. The selection of stiffeners depends on the type of set you have designed and the strength that is needed. Wing and border sets may require one type of bracing; interior sets may have similar or different bracing.

For an interior set, you usually need to brace the back of the set at the very top and the very bottom with a flat ½-inch-wide horizontal piece of illustration board that is contoured to fit according to the individual ground plan. After these two flat bracing pieces are glued in place, several vertical jogs which fit between these top and bottom pieces may be attached on the back.

The order in which you do all the gluing of the basic set and painting depends on the type of set and how the drawing and painting are planned.

174 Usually it is simpler to glue the individual pieces of an aged atmospheric set together and then texture and paint it as one unit, and finally glue it in place in the model stage.

For a set with hand-painted wallpaper flats and very elaborate molding and wainscoting details, it could be much easier to draw all the details and paint the pieces separately while they are laid out flat on the worktable. The painted pieces could be touched up after they have been first glued together and then glued to the already painted stage floor. Something like a ceiling piece should also be painted individually and then glued in place.

MODEL PARTS

Textures on Model Walls, Floors, and Ceilings

Use sandpapers, glues, wallboard compound, spackle, brushes, palette knives, and paints. These textures may be created before painting. You may want rough plaster, stucco, or the like. Use these three methods to create textures on model surfaces.

1. Glue pieces of sandpaper (coarse, medium, or fine) on model walls, floors, or ceilings. Then with water thin the Durabond Wallboard Compound a bit. With a stiff flat brush, apply this mixture to break up the sandpaper surfaces. Paint the surfaces with water paints as desired.
2. Sparsely brush Elmer's Glue-All on the surfaces that are to be textured, and while the glue is still wet add sawdust, shredded Styrofoam, or sand.
3. Dip a putty knife into a container of Dap Spackle and smear the spackle unevenly over the walls, floors, or ceilings where it is needed.

Model Floors

Use ¼-inch Masonite base for durability, illustration board, balsa wood, wooden veneers, drawing and measuring tools, X-acto knives, white glue, paints, and dyes.

Long Boards in Perspective One method is to draw and paint boards directly on the Masonite base before putting the entire model together. Another method is to use actual wood cut out and glued onto the Masonite base. For this, balsa wood or wooden veneers pulled off the surface of old discarded furniture can be used. Draw the boards on the material you choose and cut them out. Then draw a pencil layout for the boards on the Masonite base. Paint the model boards before or after putting them in place and gluing.

Parquet Floors Design, measure, and draw the parquet floor designs on lustration board. Use a straight edge as a guide to ink the patterns. Then paint the entire floor with transparent washes.

An alternate method is to design and draw the layout for the parquet floors on the Masonite base. Use 1/16 × 3-inch or 1/16 × 6-inch pieces of balsa wood and cut individual pieces for the patterns with an X-acto knife or single-edge razor blade. Paint with transparent washes and then glue into place on the Masonite. Finish any additional painting as desired.

Stone Floors Draw various rounded stones with crosshatch patterns in black ink on a sheet of white typing paper. Make the area for these ½-inch-

Settings by John Arnone
ON THE VERGE by Eric Overmyer
Directed by Garland Wright
Costumes by Ann Hould-Ward

Lighting by James F. Ingalls
John Houseman Theatre
New York (1987)
(Photographs by John Arnone)

"A series of self-illuminated vertical and horizontal beams moved in gridlike patterns across the stage to framework the multiple scenes."
—John Arnone

 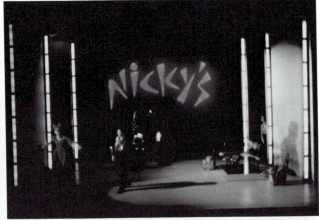

scale stones approximately 7 × 7 inches. Take the finished drawing to a copy machine and make enough copies on 25 percent white rag paper to cover the floor area. Cut out these black-and-white copies with scissors so they can be glued directly on the Masonite. Position and press the cutout paper stones in a random placement or, if preferred, a definite pattern. Paint over the floor with transparent colors.

Flagstone Floors Draw flagstones in the desired pattern on tracing paper. Use graphite transfer paper to copy the shapes on two or three different thicknesses of cardboard. According to the detail, you may also need to transfer the drawing of the flagstone shapes onto the Masonite base for placement of the cutout flagstones. With scissors or an X-acto knife, cut out the flagstones and glue them on the floor of the model. You may want to brush spackle over the stones to give them texture as well as to fill some of the spaces in between the stones. Coat with gesso and paint.

Other Floor Patterns Patterns such as tile, marble, and geometric configurations may be drawn and painted on illustration board and then glued to the Masonite base.

Model Rugs

Use photographs of rugs from magazines, fliers, or newspapers; heavy white paper; glue; brush; and scissors.

Stage design by Peter Harvey
THREE TCHAIKOVSKY BALLETS—*Élégie*
Choreographed by George Balanchine
WNET-TV, "Dance in America"
Opryland Center
Nashville, Tennessee (1978)

Rug Patterns There are numerous rug patterns that can be used in ½-inch scale models. Both color and black-and-white photographs are very useful. Black-and-white rugs can be copied on 25 percent white rag paper and then painted over with transparent watercolors and dyes. Whether color or black-and-white, the rugs should be cut out and glued on a piece of heavy paper before being painted or mounted on the model floor. The heavy paper gives a nice support on the back and makes the piece sturdy enough to be moved around in the model or attached only temporarily in case it has to be moved. It may also be glued down permanently. Patterns for rugs include Oriental rugs, Pakistani rugs, Indo-Persian rugs, Turkish rugs, rag rugs, Dhurries, and many others. Pictures of rugs cut out of magazines can be easily reduced or enlarged on copying machines to the appropriate size to fit into a model.

Model Floors with Turntables

For a model of the stage that is designed to have a turntable, you will probably want to construct a floor that has a smooth moving turntable that can be easily moved by hand. While you can use materials such as a double thick-

ness of illustration board or Foamcore board (³⁄₁₆ inch thick) for the floor, it is just as easy to go with a more durable material, such as a piece of ¼-inch Masonite. Although the Masonite may be heavier, it will not bend and it will hold up better than the other materials mentioned.

A good item to use for the turntable in a model is a revolving disc or lazy Susan made by Rubbermaid and normally used for kitchen objects. This item can be found in most hardware stores or any store that carries household items. The Rubbermaid revolving disc is 10½ inches in diameter and ⅝ inch high. In a ½-inch scale model, this equates to a turntable diameter of 21′–0″. To make a different size turntable using this Rubbermaid turntable, a circle of ¼-inch Masonite from as large as 32′–0″ in diameter (½-inch scale) to as small as 10′–0″ diameter can be positioned on top of this revolving disc.

You will have to build up the deck of the model sufficiently to accommodate the revolving turntable. But that would be fine, because it still would only make the stage floor a little over 1 inch high. And of course the remaining floor surrounding the turntable could also be made of ¼-inch Masonite and have supports under it to elevate it to the same height as the top of the ½-inch Masonite cutout circle on the turntable.

When doing a turntable for a model, always make sure that the Masonite disc is cut out neatly in a clean circle, and that the circular opening in the

176

Model designs by Tony Walton
ANYTHING GOES
Music and lyrics by Cole Porter
Original book by Guy Bolton and P. G. Wode-
  house, and Howard Lindsay and Russel
  Crouse
New book by Timothy Crouse and John Weid-
  man
Directed by Jerry Zaks
Choreographed by Michael Smuin
Beaumont Theatre, Lincoln Center
New York (1987)
(Photographs by Tony Walton)

Model designs: ½-inch scale.
Left: bar—prologue.
Clockwise: Moon's cabin dominating; arrival
in boat; and the beginning of ''Blow, Gabriel.''

floor (also of Masonite) around the turntable is done with care, too.

In addition, model floors may have other indicated or simulated items, such as trapdoors, treadmills, or elevators.

Model Surrounds

Use materials that are soft or hard as well as having plain or textured surfaces. The surround normally positioned upstage may range from a curved cyclorama to a straight back wall with flats on the ends returning downstage. Model surrounds in ½-inch scale may be made of any of these:

1. Stretch jersey as a typical curved cyclorama.
2. Corrugated cardboard with the smooth outer layer torn off at random and used for the front of the surround. In ground plan it may be straight or curved or both.
3. Balsa wood framed panels with spaces between balsa wood slats that are in various designs: diagonal, vertical, and horizontal. The panels may be positioned in a zigzag ground plan.
4. Hanging vertical strips of metallic gold or silver.
5. A full stage unit of cutout geometric patterns with a backdrop upstage showing through the open spaces.
6. Corduroy fabric stretched vertically.
7. A staggered line of thin nonrealistic trees.
8. Screen wire with spackle textures brushed on at random and then painted.
9. Painted designs on muslin: landscapes, seascapes, architectural scenes, abstract designs, and many others.
10. Several hanging panels of thin horizontal rattan roll-up blinds.
11. Plastic bubble packing material made of ⅜-inch circles or bubbles.

Model Show Curtains

Use illustration board, drawing and measuring tools, paints, and dyes. Usually show curtains and backdrops are drawn and painted on illustration board. The design on illustration board may then be attached at the top with string or thin wire to a wooden dowel and hung in the model.

Model Gauze Show Curtains and Gauze Drops

Use linen scrim, cheesecloth, fine bobbinet, organza, or screen wire. If it is necessary to frame the gauze, a frame of metal rods, heavy wire, or wood is also needed.

For unframed fabrics, the edges may be cut neatly and glued back with Sobo glue. Screen wire is especially good for simulating see-through panels in the model because the edges do not have to be glued back.

For a gauze show curtain or a see-through effect with opaque designs glued on the face, use organza or linen scrim stretched on a thin frame made to fit in the ½-inch scale model. Use Sobo to glue on all sorts of decorative items that make up the design. These may include bands of small ribbons, cut-up lace doilies, all sorts of magazine pictures, snowflakes, sequins, laces, string ornaments, tiny flowers, ferns and leaves, plus numerous other objects that may be drawn, painted, and cut out.

Model Hanging Draperies

Use illustration board, fabrics, paints, cutting tools, white glue, masking tape, string, wire, dowels, or other means for attaching in place.

Hanging draperies may include one or more full stage sets of legs and borders; draperies hanging in a framed portal; or free-form shapes hanging in space, in archways, over windows or doors, or as decorative items on stairways and balustrade units.

Painted Draperies Design and draw draperies on illustration board and cut them out with an X-acto knife, mat knife, or razor blade. Paint the draperies, being sure to paint the edges of the board as well. Position and attach the painted draperies in the model.

Sculptured Draperies Draw the draperies on the illustration board and then cut out the basic shape to use as a back silhouette piece. Cut tissue paper into small pieces and roll and glue the paper together in ridges to create three-dimensional curved drapery swags. Then gather and arrange fabric on the face of this sculptured piece and glue it in place. Use little pieces of stretch jersey or other similar fabric cut on the diagonal. To make the fabric hold its shape, it may be brushed with white glue before it is painted. String or heavy-duty sewing thread is good for twisting or plaiting and gluing to make roping and tassels for the sculptured drapery pieces.

Openwork Draperies Various see-through materials, such as fine netting used to decorate women's hats and gowns, can be used to simulate openwork draperies. The material can be gathered and draped without back bracing, but simple back outline supports of flexible wire can be used with the netting. Attach the openwork fabric with threads and thin wires. Decorate or paint as necessary.

Model Beams, Posts, and Boards

Use balsa wood, white pine strips, wooden veneers, sandpaper, white glue, X-acto knives, single-edge razor blades, and hacksaws.

Average Sizes Horizontal beams and vertical posts in ½-inch scale can be made with ¼ × ¼-inch balsa wood, which would make them equal to 6 × 6 inches in the actual model. Model beams and posts with larger dimensions may also be created with balsa

wood or pine strips that measure ¼ × ½ inch, ¼ × ¾ inch, and so on. Sections of open boards may be cut from balsa wood (¹⁄₁₆ × 3-inch or ¹⁄₁₆ × 6-inch) or from wooden veneers. The wooden pieces may be cut out and then glued together with Elmer's Glue-All. Balsa woods can be found in art stores and hobby shops, pine strips and wooden dowels can be found in local lumber stores, and veneer pieces can be salvaged from the surfaces of old furniture.

Model Furniture

Since it is difficult to find furniture and accessories in the appropriate ½-inch scale, model furniture is often made from scratch. Sometimes inexpensive plastic furniture in ½-inch scale can be found and parts of it can be combined with new materials to work in the model. Model furniture may be divided into two main categories: basic, which is white furniture for white pa-

per models; and detailed, which is sculptured and painted furniture for detailed painted models. It is great fun to make model furniture. It can easily become an extremely enjoyable hobby.

Basic Model Furniture in ½-inch Scale

Making folded and glued pieces of white paper furniture calls upon the ingenuity of a designer or model maker. What really counts in making this kind of furniture is how sophisticated you can be in developing your idea.

One of the interesting facets of making basic model furniture is discovering how to create intricate details and precise shapes from heavy white paper. There are many alternatives to choose from when making model furniture. Think back to the familiar childhood experience of cutting out and making small pieces of furniture or other objects that were found on the

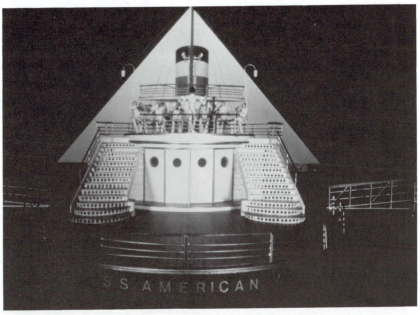

Model by Ben Edwards
MEDEA, adapted from Euripides by Robinson
  Jeffers
Directed by Robert Whitehead
Cort Theatre, New York (1982)

backs of cereal boxes or in books of cut-outs. They were drawn on cardboard and sometimes painted, cut out in one piece, folded along specific lines, and glued together on the cut tabs to make one basic unit. This simple technique is also the basis for making all sorts of white paper furniture.

Imagine how you would design a simple rectangular table to be cut out of one piece of heavy paper. Design a table in ½-inch scale with four straight legs that are each 3 inches square, with a 5-inch band of wood going around the edge of the tabletop. Also design and draw eight small openwork brackets to go in the upper corners on the four different sides of the table. Make the tabletop 48 inches long by 32 inches wide by 30 inches high. Take care to make good consistent drawing lines on all the inner and outer parts of the furniture so it will have strong linear lines.

Now draw a straight horizontal line on the heavy white paper. Using this line as a base, draw stretched-out elevation views in the sequence that the

Model by Loy Arcenas
ONCE ON THIS ISLAND
Book and lyrics by Lynn Ahrens
Music by Stephen Flaherty
Based on the novel My Love, My Love
  by Rosa Guy
Directed and choreographed by Graciela
  Daniele
Booth Theatre, New York (1990)

pieces are to be glued together, that is, one end, the front, another end, and the back. Then draw the top of the table adjacent to the top of the front (or back). Draw four small long, narrow tabs: three around the top of the table and one at the end on the side of a leg. The ends of the tabs should be cut at an angle so that they are easy to fold and tuck in when they are glued. Score the lines where the different pieces are to be folded. Use a sharp X-acto knife, bearing down very lightly. Cut out the table in one piece; then fold and glue it together.

Another simple project to make is a tall straight-back chair. Follow the same method as for making the table and use these measurements for the chair: 18 inches wide by 17 inches deep, with the seat 19 inches high, and 39 inches high from the floor to the top of the back. Draw the elevations in this order: end, front, end, and back. Above

the front elevation of the chair, draw a slightly tapered seat with the tall back of the chair connected to the top of it. You will need to draw four long, narrow tabs for gluing the chair together.

The drawings for both the table and the chair can be prepared in several different ways. They can be done lightly or heavily in pencil, or with pen and ink, or copies can be made with black lines on 25 percent white rag paper from the original drawing. The copies can then be glued onto heavy paper with white glue, painted, cut out, scored slightly at the folds, and glued together at the tabs. This is an ideal way to make duplicates of a piece of model furniture.

Cutting a piece of furniture out of one piece of heavy paper has a number of built-in advantages. All of the different parts are attached so that they do not have to be lined up individually and glued together from scratch. This saves a great deal of time, especially if duplicates are needed. Some other pieces of model furniture that can be cut out as one piece of heavy paper are footstools, ottomans, armoires, chests, and folding screens.

While simple pieces of model furniture can be cut out as one piece, even more effective model furniture and dressing pieces can be made in two, three, or a countless number of parts. For example, one table may have a larger top added to the existing one to make it more realistic and interesting in appearance. For this, it is usually easier to first build a table as described and then add the detail or other modifications.

When you make chairs with curved legs like those of a Queen Anne chair, you can get into all sorts of wonderful possibilities. For instance, curved period furniture can be quite exciting to

Model by Franco Colavecchia
CASANOVA
Libretto and music by Dominick Argento
Directed by Arthur Masella
New York City Opera, New York (1985)
(Photograph by Phil Jones)

build with several different parts cut from the white paper as separate pieces. Curved paper pieces of heavy paper work beautifully for any number of graceful lines found in designs for love seats, chaises, sofas, and the like. With patience and enough time to make model furniture, the possibilities are absolutely endless.

All sorts of paints and textures can be used to create lovely finished effects on white paper model furniture to make it appropriate to be placed in a finished painted ½-inch scale model. However, more elaborate detail is often required for this.

Detailed Model Furniture in ½-inch Scale

Although the initial approach and the designer's thinking process are similar to making white paper furniture, the end result in making very detailed model furniture is highly realistic in all aspects. How far a designer goes to realize model furniture that may appear to be of museum quality depends on the style and the period, the amount of available time, the number of assistants involved, and the budget. There is an enormous amount of pride in great craftsmanship.

Allow enough time for experimentation when making highly detailed furniture for models. In many cases, parts of the furniture are made separately and then assembled. As in making real furniture, it is often easier to carve, shape, sand the body of a sofa, paint it or cover it in actual fabric, and then add the painted carved legs.

Many different materials can go into the creation of a piece of model furniture. For a Hepplewhite wing chair in ½-inch scale, the materials could be as follows:

1. Cardboard for the very bottom base of the seat, with the seat portion above carved in balsa wood.
2. Balsa wood for the straight legs positioned under the cardboard base.
3. Heavy paper for forming the inner and outer arms. The paper can be cut, curved, and glued with inside cardboard sections for support.
4. Heavy paper for making the outer part of the wings and the very rear of the chair back.
5. Tiny pieces of quilting cotton or small cotton balls. These can be used to form the upholstery in and over the back and wings. This stuffing in the chair can be glued to the heavy paper with white glue.

6. Thin muslin, felt, or another material as a final covering. The covered chair may be coated with gesso and painted, or it may be flocked to give a fabric texture.

In making detailed model furniture, the type and style very often determine the approach. A small period love seat might be completely carved from several pieces of balsa wood. To make a contemporary box-type sofa, the entire piece could be carved from Styrofoam, then sanded smoothly, glued together, and covered with a very thin fabric and given a box pleat at the bottom.

Creating Model Furniture
The model furniture in ½-inch scale on the following pages is created to be used in actual models. To do this, take the book to a copy machine and have the pages copied on 25 percent white rag paper in the same size. Cut out the designs, allowing a bit of extra paper around them, and then glue the drawings on heavy white paper. Paint designs of the model furniture and props as desired. Cut out painted designs, score lightly with an X-acto knife, fold, and glue together. Retouch and paint as necessary.

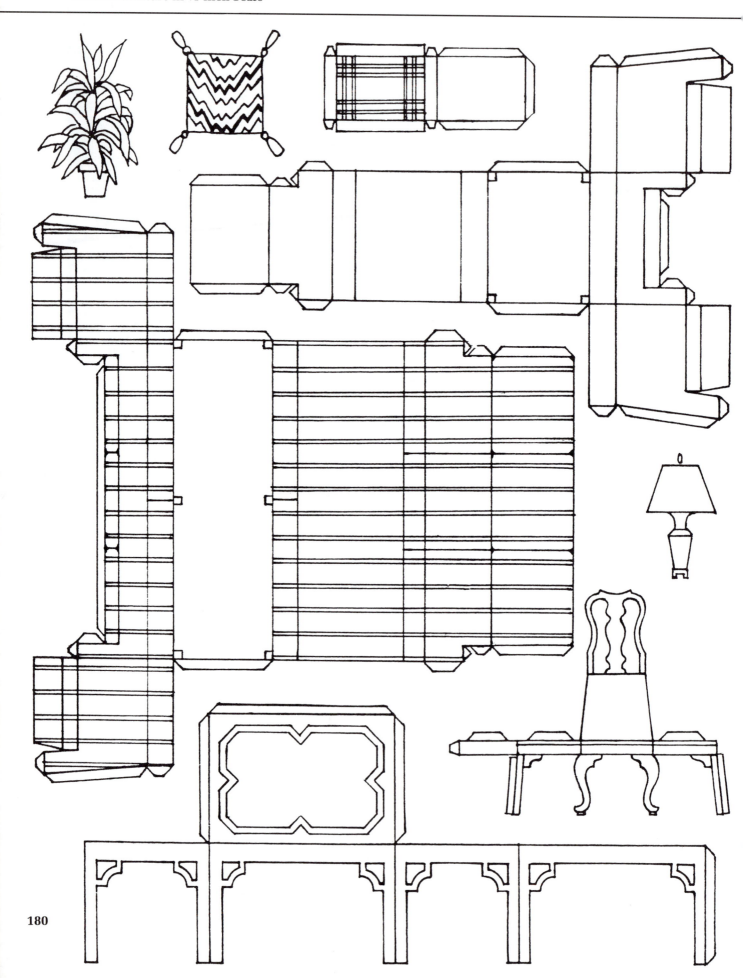

181

182   Model Chandeliers

Model chandeliers may be created in a flat cutout shape or as a three-dimensional design. Of course, the good thing about making them to use on the actual stage is that you can have the selected size, style, finish, and as many matching duplicates as you want.

Assume you are making a three-dimensional brass chandelier that is 35 inches in diameter and 29 inches high. The chandelier has eight ½-inch-diameter arms of curved brass tubing. It has a center brass stem that has a 3-inch ring at the top. Then, working downward, there is a turning that goes down 16½ inches (including the top ring) to a horizontal circular piece 5 inches in diameter by 1 inch high where the eight curved arms attach. Below this 5-inch-diameter piece at 1½-inches is a large 6½-inch brass ball, and just under this ball is a small turned piece with a 2½-inch ring at the very bottom of the stem. The overall width and height of each curved brass arm (including bobeche and candle cup) is 15 inches wide by 9 inches high. Each circular bobeche is 4½ inches diameter by 1 inch high. Each candle cup rests down in the bobeche (total of eight) and is 2 inches high by 1½ inches in diameter. Each candle cover (also total of eight) is 3 inches high by ⅞ inch diameter.

To create a model chandelier of the one just described, use the illustration shown and make a ½-inch scale elevation. This includes the center stem with the large ball and details at the top and bottom, and a left and right arm. Follow these steps when making the model chandelier:

1. Use a small block of balsa wood to carve the center stem. Drill a tiny hole through it lengthwise in which to insert the wire. Then carve the basic shape in the balsa wood with a No. 1 X-acto knife or other carving tool. Sand the center stem with a small strip of sandpaper. Make the small piece under the large ball in the same way.

   An alternate method of making a center stem is to use paper wrapping and gluing. This is a good method to use on turned objects. Use medium-heavy wire for the center stem and with long needle-nose pliers make a tiny loop at the top; then after all the turnings are on, make another loop at the bottom.

2. Use very thin strips of white typing paper cut on the paper cutter to make the turnings on the center stem. These may be cut to be ¼ inch, 3/16 inch, ⅛ inch, and 1/16 inch in width and 11 inches long. The strips are easier to work with when left long and trimmed off later. Brush Elmer's Glue-All on each strip when you are ready to use it. Starting with the widest strip of ¼-inch paper, glue the very beginning edge of the strip, then wrap a few turns to add shape to the wire designated for the center stem. Just a bit below the center of the wrapped ¼-inch paper strip and directly on it, glue the beginning of the ⅛-inch strip and wrap it around the stem. Continue with the other paper strips, using the widths in diminishing succession. The point is to learn how to keep adding wrappings on top of each other so that you can achieve attractive proportions and at the same time make a nice-looking central turning for the chandelier stem. Continue with this paper turning and gluing on the upper portion of the stem.

3. For the 5-inch-diameter horizontal disc (1 inch high) that holds the eight curved arms of the chandelier, use a piece of flat balsa wood. Drill a hole in the center of it for the wire to go through, then slide it onto the bottom so it goes up against the lower part of the center turning.

4. Make the large 6½-inch diameter ball out of balsa wood, or find one the same size and made of wood. Drill a hole in the center of it, insert the wire stem, and slide it under the horizontal disc already in place.

5. Use the ½-inch scale drawing with the two turned arms (opposite each other) to make the curved arms. For this, use thin pieces of wire. Place the wire on the drawing and form the arms according to the shape on the drawing. Use the needle-nose pliers to make the curved arms, letting the wires forming the outer parts of the arms extend long enough to go up through the bobeches, then the candle cups, and

through the candle cover where the light bulbs would attach.

These curved arms should all be shaped at the same time and should be attached to the wooden disc with Duco Cement. These can have heavy-duty sewing thread wrapped around them while they are being glued, or the thread can be arranged neatly to stay on permanently and form part of the overall design.

6. Make the bobeches out of heavy paper. These round members should also each have a tiny hole made in them so they are able to slide over the extended wires on the arms. Then the small candle cups can be made of a tiny strip of white paper wrapped and glued around the wire like the center turning. The candle cover can be made the same way. Clear acetate can be used to simulate profiles of the eight tiny light bulbs. Tiny model candles may also be appropriate; in that case you would not need any of the candle covers, but instead make an 8-inch-high candle for each arm on the chandelier.

7. Spray the chandelier with a metallic brass paint from an aerosol can. Paint the candle cups or candles an off-white.

Model Paintings and Prints

Use very small pictures found in magazines, catalogs, or advertising fliers; white glue; cardboard; scissors; brushes; paints and stains.

It is a good idea to cut out and collect various tiny pictures from magazines or catalogs of framed or unframed portraits, landscapes, seascapes, animals, birds, flowers, or abstract works so they will be on hand to use in models. Use cardboard for backing, and cut it a little larger than the photograph. Brush glue onto the cardboard backing, place the photograph, and press it down in place. Trim off any excess cardboard. If a frame is needed, it can be created with pieces of balsa wood that can be painted or stained. An alternate method would be to paint tiny pictures on heavy paper and either frame them or leave them unframed.

Model Sculpture

Use Bone Ware Clay, Darwi Modeling Paste, wires, modeling tools, damp cloth, and water.

Basic chandelier drawing.

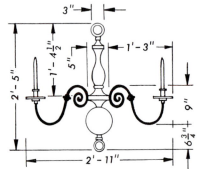

Bone Ware Clay works well for making very small statues, decorative masks, lamp bases, and various ornaments because it comes moist and ready to use, becomes hard when it dries, and then can be painted as desired. It is available in gray and terra cotta in 4-pound packages. Darwi is another material that is good to use for model sculpture. It is a white modeling paste and comes in 1-kilo packages. It is very easy to work with and becomes extremely hard when it dries. Wires with loops and hooks may be put in the sculpture before it is fully shaped so that the sculpture can be hung and attached to a surface or to another item. Other similar clays and modeling materials can be used as well.

Model Shingles, Bricks, Stonework, and Concrete Blocks

Use mounting or illustration board for the supporting surface, pieces of cardboard, a paper cutter, large and small scissors, X-acto knife, cheese cloth, toilet tissue, sandpaper, brush, glue, wheat paste, spackle, gesso, and paints.

Shingles On the mounting or illustration board draw the shapes of the ½-inch scale roofs or walls to be shingled. Cut these shapes out. Draw guide lines on the wall or roof pieces to mark where the shingles are to be glued. Are the shingles to be positioned at random or in an overall consistent pattern? Determine the basic shape and size of the

Stage designs by Lester Polakov
MRS. McTHING by Mary Chase
Directed by Joseph Buloff
Martin Beck Theatre, New York (1952)

pattern for the shingles. Are they straight on the bottom or will they have some other shape? You may want to use two or three different thicknesses of cardboard for the shingles to add variety.

Mark the widths of the shingles on the cardboard in order to cut long strips. Then, with a paper cutter cut a stack of these long strips. Next, slice off lengths of shingles according to the sizes needed. (For this, use the paper cutter or scissors or whatever works best.) If the bottoms of the shingles are curved or are another shape, make a pattern and draw the design with a pencil. Use manicure scissors to cut out the small shapes. While all of this may seem to be a tedious process, it is well worth the effort for creating nice details.

With white glue, put the shingles on the roof or walls in an overlapping fashion. Use an X-acto knife to help arrange the tiny shingles as you glue them. You may want to use a narrow band of shingles to finish off the peaks and valleys of the roofs. When the shingles are glued in place, texture them with spackle and coat the whole area of shingles with gesso. Then paint them either with various transparent glazes or with opaque colors or with a combination of both.

Other varied roof patterns can be created in the model by covering the boards with burlap, corduroy, linen scrim, or wafflecloth.

Bricks This method of creating model bricks includes brickwork for both interior and exterior settings. Contemporary brick sizes can be 8½ × 2½ inches, 8½ × 1¾ inches, 11½ × 2¼ inches, and 11½ × 2¾ inches. To rep-

resent the mortar, the bricks can all have approximately ½ inch of space between them when they are put in place. Mark off the guide lines where the cutout bricks are to be glued on the ½-inch scale walls. Then figure the size brick that is needed. With two different thicknesses of cardboard to give nice contrast, mark the height of the brick, such as 2¾ inches, so that long strips can be cut on the paper cutter. Cut a pile of strips, with the width of the strips being the height of the bricks. Next, take this pile of strips and one by one (or as a group if it goes faster) cut off the individual brick lengths with a paper cutter.

With the X-acto knife, arrange and glue the individual bricks onto the surface that is to get the applied bricks. You will be applying bricks not only to the main ½-inch scale walls, but also to the thicknesses in windows, archways, and doors. You may also be making brick platforms and low brick walls.

Once the bricks have been glued on the individual model part, use a piece of sandpaper to vary the brick edges a bit here and there so they look aged. Then coat the pieces with gesso so they are ready for painting. Often it is easier and faster if the surfaces are laid in with the mortar color and then the colors of the bricks are brushed over the applied bricks.

Stonework Stonework for models may consist of all sorts of random applied stonework, or straight-cut square or rectangular stones. All kinds of stonework can be effective for scenery. These may be natural stones, or you may be creating a flagstone walk with low walls and platforms of the same

Costume designs by Willa Kim
THE TEMPEST Ballet
Choreographed by Michael Smuin
San Francisco Ballet Company
San Francisco Opera House
San Francisco, California (1980)
Trinculo and Caliban

design. It works well to combine various three-dimensional stones with those that are drawn and painted directly on the board. Draw on illustration board the layout for the stones with the proper spaces between them. Then, on cardboard draw the stones that are to be applied. Use small scissors to cut out individual stones. Glue these cutout stones in place, and use bits of toilet tissue glued on with wheat paste to create texturing on the stonework. Add spackle for more texture, then coat with gesso and apply paints.

Concrete Blocks A good size concrete block for the stage is 15½ inches wide × 7½ inches high, with at least a

Stage design by Stephan Olson
WAITING FOR GODOT by Samuel Beckett
A project (1986)
(Photograph by Stephan Olson)

½-inch space in between the blocks. These may be treated in the same manner as bricks.

Model Contours of Land

Use blocks of Styrofoam, brown wrapping paper, gray bogus paper, modeling paste, white tissue paper, glue, sand, sawdust, pieces of gauze or linen scrim, carving tools, sandpaper, gesso, and water paints.

You may be creating a section of land that is outside a house, a strip of beach, a dune, or a barren heath.

A Section of Land Assume you are making a contour section of land with grass and dirt outside a house. Use long blocks of Styrofoam and carve the basic shape with a sharp knife and a piece of

hacksaw blade that has a handle on it. When the rough carving is done, use sandpaper to smooth out the final shaping. When you are satisfied with the overall shape, add irregular textures on the surface with long pieces of brown wrapping paper and gray bogus paper. Tear both papers in long strips and glue these irregular pieces to the Styrofoam surface so they overlap each other here and there. Also, allow some of the Styrofoam to show through occasionally to give contrast. Apply modeling paste where desired, and add more variety in texture with pieces of white tissue paper glued on at random. Coat with gesso and apply paints.

Sandy Beach Assume you are creating a sandy strip of beach, which is basically a smooth finish. Carve the main shape from Styrofoam with a sharp knife and a hacksaw blade. Then sand the rough Styrofoam as smooth as you want it. The portion of beach may be constructed in two or more pieces and then put together. When it is ready, cover the carved Styrofoam with a single piece of linen scrim glued on neatly and without wrinkles. Next, base-coat it with gesso and then paint as desired. Add some real sand where needed.

When making models of beaches or similar pieces that have to be constructed in two or more units, always create the model breaks so they are on angles or in an interesting alignment rather than joining the pieces parallel to each other or straight on to the audience. This should also be emphasized on the drafting as well and is done so the joins are not obvious and it also gives a more interesting line to the design.

Model Rocks and Stones

Use blocks of Styrofoam in various sizes, tools for carving, sandpaper, spackle, plaster of Paris, modeling paste, putty knife, brushes, pieces of linen scrim, gesso, and paints.

Top drawing shows preferred breaks in contoured land strip.

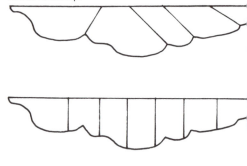

Stage designs by John Scheffler
H.M.S. PINAFORE by Gilbert and Sullivan
Directed by Roger H. Simon
Lehman College Center, Bronx, New York
(1982)
(Photograph by Michael Piotrowski)

Large and Small Rocks It can be most helpful to have research readily available, such as photographs of natural rock formations or even an actual rock or two, when carving model rocks. You should also have a rough ½-inch scale drawing of the rocks and their formation as they are to appear on the stage.

Cut blocks of Styrofoam. Then with a sharp knife use a cutting and sawing motion to carve the basic shaping of each of the individual rocks, varying the shapes as much as possible, yet retaining the appropriate rock shapes. After the basic carving is done, use medium sandpaper to further shape the Styrofoam rocks. To add some contrast in texture, you may want to cover some of the Styrofoam rocks with pieces of linen scrim. Add some random textures by applying Dap spackle or plaster of Paris with a flat bristle brush or a putty knife. Modeling paste may also be used. Paint with water-base paints as desired. Tiny pebbles like those available at pet or garden shops are good to add here and there and in groups.

Jagged Walls of Rock Larger blocks of Styrofoam, such as 2 × 3 × 4 inches, can also be used for creating a unit of tall leaning rocks that form a wall. Use a sharp knife or other cutting tools to carve long irregular, jagged rocks.

These rocks may start out with a wide base and gradually become thinner toward the top. The rocks may be smoothed down with 1-inch strips of coarse sandpaper, and the same treatment used for finishing the large and small rocks may be applied.

Model Trees and Foliage

Use natural and synthetic sponges, twigs, weeds, dried plant materials, wire, wire cutters, transparent tape, Elmer's Glue-All, illustration board, brown Kraft paper, tissue paper, newspaper, scissors, X-acto knife, paints, and brushes.

Trees with Thin Trunks Use twigs and weeds from nature and form thin trunks. For branches, thin flexible wires may be cut in various lengths and

attached at the top of the small trunks with small pieces of transparent tape. Then the tree trunk and the wires should be wrapped with thin strips of tissue paper. Tissue paper may be put on first in layers to add body and shape to the tree before painting. Small cut strips or pieces of newspaper also work well to add texture and irregular shapes to the tree trunk and limbs. For foliage, pinch and pull pieces from sponges and glue them appropriately on the limbs. It is usually easier to paint the trunk and branches separately from the foliage.

Trees with Thick Trunks For large trees, draw the back profile of the trunk on illustration board and cut it out with scissors and an X-acto knife. Also draw and cut out branches and limbs on the board. Use thin flexible wire to

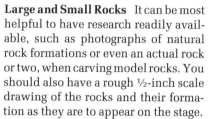

Stage design by John Keck
CHRISTMAS SHOW
"Elves and Bells"
Produced by Peter Gennaro
Radio City Music Hall, New York (1974)
(Photograph by James Stewart Morcom)

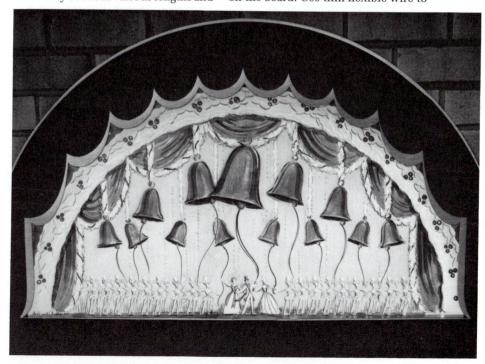

185

Costume designs by Esteban Francés
DON QUIXOTE
New York City Ballet, New York (1965)
(Collection of Peter Harvey)

make the smallest limbs. To build up the thick tree trunk and to give it a nice three-dimensional quality, use pieces of brown Kraft paper and newspaper. Press and squeeze the paper pieces together to make the thick dimensional tree trunk, and shape it according to your design. Wrap tissue-paper strips over the trunk and limbs to give a natural look to the tree. Paint the tree trunk and limbs, then the foliage made of pieces of sponge. Glue the limbs and foliage onto the trunk as desired.

Besides sponges, foliage may be created with dried plant materials. Model trees and foliage may also be purchased at model shops, especially those specializing in model trains and architectural model materials.

Painting an Interior Setting for a Model

Every stage designer works differently when creating a model. The following discussion should be thought of as a guide when putting a model together. When choosing which paints to use for a model or a rendering, consider the results you wish to obtain and what you feel comfortable using. Sometimes you will choose only one medium; at other times you will use a combination of two or more kinds of paint. The point is that a specific medium or combination is used for a specific effect. You should also consider these ques-

tions: Do you want the paints to be opaque, semi-opaque, or transparent? Will you cut around areas to save the clean board to paint in an object rather than doing it as overpainting on an already painted surface? Are the paints to give a matte or a glossy finish? Experiment and do painted sketches more than once to see what works best for the desired result, and at the same time perhaps sharpen your painting technique.

While it is great to try any new method of rendering, normally what you enjoy most is what will give you the best results. You may love to work in oil paints or casein paints, acrylic paints, or magic markers. Many designers find that a combination of paints works beautifully and therefore never plan on using only one medium to work in. Designers often work intuitively to create the best possible painted model or sketch. Usually, the choice of materials is determined in great part by the individual subject of the scenery.

For example, suppose you are planning on painting the model of an interior setting that is made of white illustration board, with the details outlined in pencil. Assume this is a period room that has wallpaper with a red background and stripes are painted over it in brown with an ochre stripe in the center. The woodwork in the room has three-dimensional molding that is light to medium gray. The doors are dark brown. It is a room that has atmosphere and character but is still in good shape.

You have already decided that it will be simpler to paint the model in separate pieces before it is glued together. But before painting, you may want to glue a few basic flats together, such as those forming outside corners. This depends totally on the sizes, shapes, and positions of the pieces in the setting. Before doing any painting on the actual model, make samples of the painting. While doing this, it is always good to think in terms of light, shade, and shadow.

As a project, assume that the wallpaper is to be painted with opaque colors that are later glazed over by thinning down the color with water. Mix two red colors to paint the walls. Use a medium red for the main lay-in color and a lighter red for blending with it. Lay in and blend the walls with the two red colors, making the top portion and the inner corners of the walls darker. Then mix a third red, a darker color,

Costume designs by Willa Kim
LEGS DIAMOND by Harvey Fierstein and
    Charles Suppon
Music and lyrics by Peter Allen
Directed by Robert Allan Ackerman
Mark Hellinger Theatre
New York (1988)

Backdrop by Edward Gorey
AMPHIGOREY: The Musical
Written and designed by Edward Gorey
Music by Peter Golub
Directed and choreographed by Daniel Levans
Produced by the American Music Theatre
  Festival, Plays and Players Theatre
Philadelphia, Pennsylvania (1992)
(Photograph by Lynn Pecktal)
(Courtesy of Edward Gorey)

and thin it with water so it can be used as a transparent color to comb horizontally with the brush over the walls before the stripes are applied.

When you are satisfied with the painting on the walls, mark off the stripes lightly with a pencil. Make the brown stripes 6 inches wide, the red space in between the stripes 8 inches wide to scale. Next, lay in the brown stripes on all the walls. After this, paint 3-inch-wide ochre stripes to scale in the center of the brown stripes. You may want to make a transparent wash to comb over the stripes at the top and fade out about midway down, and also do the same a bit from the bottom up and fade out. This should be done in a controlled pattern.

Go next to the woodwork, which includes wainscoting, the cornice, and the door and window units. It is usually easier to draw, cut out, and paint wainscoting, cornices, and other woodwork as separate pieces, and then glue them on the already painted walls rather than try to cut around evenly with the brush at the bottom and top of the wallpaper. Whatever approach you use, make sure the drawing for the wainscoting, cornice, door, and window units is done with care. Plan on doing these items with transparent washes of color. This means you use a watercolor technique in which the white board is saved and used as a

clean painting surface on which you gradually darken the woodwork areas with a succession of transparent watercolor washes.

For painting the woodwork, mix three transparent gray colors. First mix a medium gray to be used as the darkest color; second, mix a very light gray; and third, mix a gray between the medium and the very light gray. Make these warm or cool grays according to how they look with the wallpaper and the overall desired effect for the interior.

With the two lighter grays, brush washes over the woodwork to serve as the lay-in, to tone it, and to break up solid areas. As you work, you may or may not want to thin these colors down with water to lighten them and to give even more variation in the painting. Then use the medium gray as a shade color to model various moldings and to define the different parts. You may also want to mix and wash a very pale brown over some of the light gray woodwork to give contrast and to make it interesting. Add a transparent shadow color and a thin dark cutting line as needed. Also, you might want to use opaque light or highlight colors in some area.

Plan on painting the doors a dark brown, with the inner panels a darker brown. Then go on to the floors. Paint the parquet patterns on the floor of the

model. Do a brown opaque lay-in, draw out the floor patterns, and use several darker transparent brown colors for painting graining on the floor. Ink the floor patterns with a thin black line.

With the same colors, paint the ceiling dark beige. Do black marbleizing and create a glossy finish on the fireplace. Next, paint a daytime sky backdrop outside the windows. After finishing this, look over the model to see what else you may want to do to refine it.

Glues, Cements, and Adhesives to Use for Putting Model Parts Together

Elmer's Glue-All. Use to bond paper, cloth, wood, polystyrene foam, pottery, and most other porous and semiporous materials. It dries clear and fast and is nontoxic. Use on clean, dry surfaces. For paper, cloth, and porous material, spread the glue thinly, press parts together let dry ten to twenty minutes. For wood, pottery, and semiporous materials, spread glue heavily on both surfaces, weight or clamp, and let dry thirty to forty-five minutes.

Sobo. Sobo is an all-purpose adhesive made by Slomon's Laboratories. It is nonflammable, nontoxic, quick-drying, flexible, and dries neutral. Apply with a brush or any other method you choose. Apply Sobo to one side only and then join the surfaces together while the glue is still moist. Drying time varies according to the porosity of the materials. Fabric treated with Sobo may be dry-cleaned.

Plastic Model Cement. This is the kind of cement used for putting plastic models together.

Pritt Glue Stick. The glue stick is nontoxic and is ideal for lightweight paper products. It is water-soluble.

Duco Cement. Duco Cement is a transparent, flexible, waterproof cement that will mend practically everything except rubber. It dries quickly and permanently and is available in 1 3/4-ounce tubes.

Thermogrip Electric Glue Gun. The heavy-duty glue gun uses hot melt adhesives. A hot glue gun is great for adhering a range of items from small to large, from gathered gauze curtains on a wooden dowel in a model to large sequins on a full-scale show curtain or buckram leaves on a metal framework in the scenic studio.

Settings and costumes by Karl Eigsti
ORPHANS by Kyle Kessler
Directed by Mel Shapiro
Lighting by Kirk Bookman
Pittsburgh Public Theatre
Pittsburgh, Pennsylvania (1987)

Krazy Glue. For plastics, metal, rubber, glass, and ceramics. It comes in a no-drip, no-clog applicator and is available in a 7-ounce size.

Scotch 3M Spra-Ment Adhesive. A fast-drying adhesive in an aerosol can. It gives permanent or temporary bonds, depending on the method of application.

Epoxy Putty by Epoxybond. This two-part epoxy adheres to most metals, wood, ceramics, and glass. It can be molded, drilled, sanded, sawed, filed, and painted. Epoxy is also available in two-part resins.

Speeding Up the Drying of White Glue

Often when using a white glue on models the parts of the paper and board with the glue can be dried quicker when heat is applied. One way to do this is to put the model parts under an incandescent lamp. Another way is to use a hand-held hair dryer.

Sources for Paints and Other Supplies

- *Rosco Laboratories, Inc.,* 36 Bush Avenue, Port Chester, NY 10573, Tel.: (914) 937-1300. (Other locations are in California, Canada, Spain, England, and Portugal.) This is an excellent source for paints, brushes, and many other products for the stage. While all sorts of paints can be purchased from art stores around the country, Rosco also manufactures small quantities of its same scenic paints that are available in large quantities. The small quantities in

a wide range of colors are packaged in kits and can be used for rendering or for experimentation. One advantage to using these kits is that the rendering can be done with the same paints used for the actual scenery. These kits are available for the following paints:

1. Iddings Deep Colors (concentrated casein/fresco paints; dilute with water).
2. Supersaturated Roscopaint (concentrated vinyl acrylic paints; dilute with water).
3. Rosco Off Broadway Scenic Paint (vinyl acrylic latex paints; ready to use).
4. The Rosco Paint Sampler. This is a twenty-four-piece kit that contains 1-ounce samples of Iddings Deep Colors, Supersaturated Roscopaint, Rosco Off Broadway Scenic Paint, Fluorescent Paint, Clear Gloss, Clear Flat, Roscoglo, and Roscoflamex C26.

- *Arthur Brown and Bro., Inc.,* 2 West 46 Street, New York, NY 10036, Tel.: (212) 575-5555. A leading art supply distributor since 1924. Its supplies include watercolors, acrylics, oils, gouaches, art markers, brushes, easels, airbrushes, pastels, chalks, crayons, colored pencils, drafting pencils and papers, boards of all kinds, T-squares, triangles, templates, tapes, spray paints, drawing tables and boards, lamps, clays, sculpture materials, hobby tools, and many other items.

- *Pearl Paint Co., Inc.,* 308 Canal Street, New York, NY 10013, Tel.: (212) 431-7932. This large store carries all sorts of supplies for renderings and models. Supplies include acrylics, caseins, oils, temperas and gouaches, balsa wood, bass wood, wooden dowels, and brass rods. It also carries scenic paints and brushes, fabric paints, and sculpturing products.

"The windows and doors in ORPHANS and ACCIDENTAL DEATH OF AN ANARCHIST seem to be a visual element which constantly reappears in my work. In Pittsburgh, during the run of ORPHANS, the theatre showed my twelve box sculptures in which this visual theme is even more pronounced. The following was the statement from that exhibit:

'I am interested in the way rooms and spaces reflect human behavior. The way an empty room is an echo of an event which has just occurred, or a succession of events like a life is passing.

'In all these rooms, I feel as though an unseen life is taking place behind the translucent windows. At any moment a shadow may cross the window. Someone may come back in through the door.' "

—Karl Eigsti

Model designs by Neil Peter Jampolis/Maurice Sendak
THE CUNNING LITTLE VIXEN
by Leoš Janáček
Text by the composer from R. Tešnohlídek
New York City Opera
New York State Theatre, New York (1981)
(Photographs by Neil Peter Jampolis)
Model in ½-inch scale built by Neil Peter Jampolis and Ray Huessy.

- *Lee's Art Shop*, 220 West 57 Street, New York, NY 10019, Tel.: (212) 247-0110. Lee's is a complete resource of materials for artists, designers, engineers, graphic artists, students, teachers, sculptors, hobbyists, and photographers. It offers papers, boards, Letraset products, art markers, canvas, brushes, acrylic paints, oils, watercolors, modeling paste, glues, cements, spray paints, pencils, pens, templates, drafting supplies, studio supplies, projectors, filing cabinets, X-acto knife sets, hobby tools, sculpture clays, and numerous other items.
- *The Red Caboose*, 16 West 45 Street, 4th Floor, New York, NY 10036, Tel.: (212) 575-0155. While this is really a train store, it stocks many items that are terrific for scenic models. These include trees, shrubs, grass, lamps, searchlights, snow packs, books, paints, stains, and also plastic and brass products (tubes, rods, I-beams, T-shapes, hollow and solid squares, and hollow and solid rectangles).
- *The Train Shop*, 23 West 45 Street, New York, NY 10036, Tel.: (212) 730-0409. Even though it is train-oriented, this shop also has good items for stage models. Among the objects are grass, foliage, turf, trees, and paints. Also available here are balsa wood (soft), bass wood (hard), and lengths of brass, copper, and aluminum.
- *Utrecht Manufacturing Corp.*, 33 Thirty-fifth Street, Brooklyn, NY 11232, Tel.: 800-223-9132. Utrecht has locations in New York City, Chicago, Detroit, Philadelphia, Boston, and Washington, D.C. Utrecht is one of America's major manufacturers of superior professional artist's colors, wood products, and paper converters. It sells acrylic paints, oils, gouaches, watercolors sets, gesso, canvases, brushes, easels, drawing tables and equipment, papers, pads,

boards, and many other design supplies.
- *Hobby Tools.* Dremel is a company that makes popular hobby tools. Included are the Dremel Freewheeler Cordless Moto-Tool Kit No. 850, Dremel Freewheeler Cordless Moto-Tool Kit No. 8500, Dremel Drill Press, Dremel High Speed Router Bit Set, Dremel Cleaning/Polishing Set, Dremel Cutting/Carving Set, Dremel Sanding/Grinding Set, Dremel General Purpose Set, Dremel Moto-Flex Shaft, Dremel 4-inch Table Saw, and Dremel Moto Shop. These tools are available or can be ordered at art and hobby shops.

Health and Safety Factors

Every stage designer, scenic artist, carpenter, and technician should be aware of any potential health hazard when using certain paints, solvents, and thinners in the execution of models, designs, and scenery. As a general rule, it is good to always work in a well-ventilated area or out-of-doors when possible. Also, when selecting paints and solvents be sure to read the printed instructions and precautions on the container. This may even lead you to select safer materials.

Make yourself automatically remember to use certain safety equipment and respect rules when you work with scenic materials. When applicable, this means wearing goggles, gloves, face shields, spray paint respirators, masks, and any other safety devices to protect yourself. Never smoke or permit flames near solvents or other questionable products. Keep containers of paints and solvents closed except when they are being used. With solvents, avoid skin contact, and do not breathe the vapors. Avoid cleaning hands with solvents.

Ming Cho Lee resides in New York City on Manhattan's Upper East Side. I talked with him there about theatre, design, and teaching. Born in Shanghai, China, on October 3, 1930, he was educated at Occidental College and UCLA. His first Broadway show was *The Moon Besieged* in 1962. He was the principal designer for the New York Shakespeare Festival from 1962 to 1973. He has designed the scenery for a multitude of companies, including the Arena Stage, Guthrie Theatre, Mark Taper Forum, Repertory Theatre of Lincoln Center, Seattle Repertory Company, Long Wharf Theatre, American Shakespeare Festival, Metropolitan Opera, New York City Opera, San Francisco Opera, Chicago Lyric Opera, Opera Company of Boston, Indiana Repertory Theatre, Stratford Festival in Ontario, Juilliard Opera Theatre, Houston Grand Opera, Opera Society of Washington, Hamburg State Opera, American Ballet Theatre, Martha Graham Company, Joffrey Ballet, Eliot Feld Ballet, Pacific Northwest Ballet, National Ballet of Canada, and San Francisco Ballet. Ming Cho Lee is Professor of Design and Co-chairman of the Design Department at the Yale School of Drama. Among his awards are a Tony, two Maharams, Drama Desk, Outer Critic's Circle, Peter Zeisler Award, and the New York City Mayor's Award of Honor for Arts and Culture. His scenic design credits include:

Broadway
Execution of Justice (1986)
K2 (1983)
The Glass Menagerie (1983)
The Shadow Box (1977)
For Colored Girls Who Have Considered Suicide/When the Rainbow Is Enuf (1976)
Much Ado About Nothing (1972)
Two Gentlemen of Verona (1971)
Billy (1969)
Little Murders (1967)
A Time for Singing (1966)
Slapstick Tragedy (1966)

New York City Opera
Attila (1981)
Maria Stuarda (1972)
Roberto Devereux (1970)
Faust (1968)
Le Coq d'Or (1967)
Don Rodrigo (1966)

Martha Graham Company
Myth of a Voyage (1973)
The Witch of Endor (1965)
A Look at Lightning (1962)

San Francisco Opera
St. Matthew Passion (1973)
La Favorita (1973)

Metropolitan Opera
Khovanshchina (1985)
I Puritani (1976)
Lohengrin (1976)
Boris Godunov (1974)

New York Shakespeare Festival
Much Ado About Nothing (1972)
Peer Gynt (1969)
Henry IV (1968)
Richard III (1966)
Love's Labour's Lost (1965)
Hamlet (1964)
Electra (1964)

Stage design by Ming Cho Lee
DEATH OF A SALESMAN by Arthur Miller
Directed by Guy Sprung

Avon Theatre
Stratford Festival
Stratford, Ontario, Canada (1983)

When you designed the scenery for the Metropolitan Opera's production of Khovanshchina *you worked with the European director August Everding. Had you worked with him before?*

Yes. He was also the director on *Boris Godunov* and *Lohengrin*. This particular opera, of course, is not a popular one so it has had only one revival since it opened in 1985. If it comes back again, I have a feeling it will not be for some time. It's a very good opera, and yet it's a very imperfect opera. But like all the Mussorgsky operas, it has some terrific passages and is very, very honest in its way.

It was something of an unknown opera, and it's not *Boris Godunov*, it's second-string Mussorgsky. It's a very difficult opera. Long stretches of it are not the most dramatic or theatrical music. It's very much a political-social drama, and if you don't understand Russian, you miss a great deal. Donal Henahan, the *New York Times* critic, is right when he said that this is one opera that should have surtitles. You have whole scenes where you ask, "What the hell are they talking about?" You can read the libretto, you can follow the story, but you still don't know what's going on because during that period Russia went through such complex social upheaval, and the country was fragmented with different groups of extreme fanatics. It was a period of great unrest. Unless you know the background, you would have to read a whole book in order to understand it, and if you don't have surtitles, it can be a very perplexing opera. It's a difficult opera to raise money for. Mrs. Harrington certainly would not support this.

How long did you have to work on this production?

I think maybe a year and a half; it may have been two years. I was very glad to work with John Conklin, who did the clothes. We had a lot of give-and-take, not just about set and costume design, but about how we wanted to approach this piece. We wanted to do something a little bit different from what we had done before, and especially for the Met. Of course, no one was quite ready for it. It's one of the least cluttered productions at the Met today. Everything done there now is so cluttered, and this is a very empty, sparse production even though the scale is very big.

The sparseness is intentional, isn't it?

It is certainly intentional and very difficult to execute because any imperfection just jumps out. Nevertheless, I think we achieved it, although some things are not as clear as they should be, and that creates a kind of perplexity and uncertainty. I would say that I was very proud of the work myself, and I think those who worked on the show were very proud of the production. When we finished putting the show together, everyone was saying, "This is really a good production!" even though it is not a great success.

John and I and August Everding decided to take time to arrive at a production that is severe, hard-edge, and brutal, which reflects the quality of the opera. We tried to get away from the usual operatic literal approach. I actually have a whole set of sketches that are quite literal. I even made a whole group of finished eighth-inch models that we kept tearing down. It's a seven-set show, and I probably have three different versions so there are close to twenty-one little eighth-inch models.

Do you start with an eighth-inch model always and then go to quarter-inch?

I usually start with sketches. Then if there is something that feels good, I go to an eighth-inch model and then blow it up to quarter-inch or half-inch.

The budget for that opera was supposed to be one million and ten, and that included sets, costumes, fees, and traveling. When we were halfway through they said, "We only have $500,000." We said, "For this opera that has an expanded chorus? Impossible!" They insisted, "We simply cannot raise the money. This is an opera that nobody gives money to." We said, "But $500,000! You'd better forget it because it cannot be done." So they offered, "How about $750,000?" We said, "We'll try." And so we made a rough estimate of the cost, but the situation at the Met is more complex now because not all the building and painting is done in the Met shop now. Some of it had to have outside estimates.

This is because they have moved the shop and painting studio from Lincoln Center and cut back on their staff? Do they just do touch-ups now?

They still do some of the work there, but they no longer have the space and facilities. We realized that what I had designed and what John had designed could not possibly be done for $750,000. So I made a major change by combining the sets for Act 1 with Act 2, Scene 2 and Act 3, Scene 2. We thought that the change was to the good anyway, because it really was closer to what we were looking for. All of us were very happy with it.

When we went to bids, it came in rather close. With the costumes and everything added together it was around a million dollars. So we said, "Don't worry. We think we have $250,000 to cut." We got it down to around $800,000 with a sense that we could even get down to $750,000. Then management said, "But a hundred thousand has already been spent on fees, assistants, traveling, and so forth." And we didn't think we could cut another hundred thousand. I mean, there was just no place to cut. By then it got too late to cancel the show, and too late to borrow a show, besides Mr. Everding didn't want to do a borrowed production. John made some adjustments, and I made another major adjustment which cut some of the complexity. We took a whole wooden platform out of it so now it became a white box and a white floor! We finally came to within $50,000 of the target figure. It took a long time to design that production. Essentially the show was designed three times. There were literally three sets of drawings.

But you'd worked on it almost two years?

Yes. The last six or eight months was simply drafting and going to the shop and one thing and another.

You wouldn't do an opera there in less than how much time?

Oh, more than a year. They need six months or more to do the planning and then get it into the shop. Quite often, especially if the opera opens in November, they have a setup and tech and some of the lighting in September or even earlier. So the sets need to be finished. That's at least already two months, then their planning, and going to the shop, and four months in a shop is nothing, especially with the scale of the work.

I know that management plans ahead, but do you feel that you need a year yourself to develop it?

192 Yes, because first of all the scale of the work is bigger and there is an importance to everything you do there. You want to have the chance to throw a whole design out instead of just going with the easiest one. If you get a year, essentially you only have six months to design it. And for the Met it's not enough.

For me, the Met is still the New York institution that I would like to work for in New York, because they do have great respect for the "artist." They treat designers with respect. It's very European in a sense, pleasant and never any problem in terms of expenses. In fact they will call you up and say, "What are your expenses?" It's unlike dealing with Broadway general managers. There is no desire to be insulting at the Met, because they can't do that with the singers. Essentially, the facilities there are yours, and when you go in everyone is courteous and you feel as if you owned the house! It's still *the* place to work in New York. However, you know there is no artistic director or production at the Met. You feel as if you are walking into a place where they are presenters rather than producers.

Now there is no general manager in the sense of a Rudolf Bing or Schuyler Chapin. James Levine has a great deal of musical integrity and I think the orchestra and chorus has become maybe the top. It's really a good sound. There is nothing to be ashamed of musically when they are really with it. But in terms of production, there isn't a company vision. You feel that the criteria tend to be very practical. They don't want to go into a new production unless it is neutral enough that it will last at least ten years. They would not say, "We would like to see this opera done this way so that it will be startling or it will be dangerous." So with the director in Europe, John and I found that while we were designing, we were really also doing the artistic direction.

How did you communicate with a director who is in Europe?

We would communicate by telephone, and then we would send things back and forth. He was here some of the time, but mostly in Europe. There is a certain amount of trust between us. What happened in this particular case was that we all agreed on certain things, but suddenly the money became impossible and we had to

Model designs by Ming Cho Lee
KHOVANSHCHINA by Modest Mussorgsky
Libretto by the composer and V. V. Stassov

Directed by August Everding
The Metropolitan Opera
New York (1985)
Left: Act 1; *right:* Act 2, Scene 2.

change. There was no artistic director so there was no one to say, "We love it so stay with it," or "We hate it, why are you doing it that way?" Nobody, but nobody, expressed an opinion. The only people who expressed an opinion were not in a position to make critical decisions.

What kind of input do you have with the lighting designer at the Met?

Actually, more collaboration than a lot of other times. We got together a great deal, or I would call Gil Wechsler and he would come and take a look and so would John. But neither Jimmy Levine nor Bruce Crawford would come and say we love it or we hate it. At one point we said, "How come it's so difficult?" It's as if you are fighting with yourself, because you have to cut the show, but you also have to make artistic judgments. You have to argue with yourself, "Well, I like it. No, I don't like it," and you also have to cut without a suggestion as to what to cut. Working for the Met in that sense is a very draining experience in that you and the director almost have to function as a producer. That is a very draining thing.

How many days would you say all total that you have to get it all together once it is on the stage?

It all depends whether it is a new

production or a revival. For a new production, they will certainly have a setup and do a certain amount of lighting and technical things. If it's not a late production in the season, quite often you get a week and a half. Now, a week and a half at the Met is not ten days, which is two weeks, and it is not eight hours a day. Because it's a rep house, it's really from 10:00 or 11:00 A.M. until 2:30 or 3:00 P.M. That's only four or five hours every day, because they have to set up in the morning, and you have to focus the lights and then deal with the various things, and at 2:30 P.M. you have to leave, otherwise they won't have an evening show. In the summer, of course, you can work until 5:00 or 6:00 P.M. and then they knock the crew off. For a new production, I think, the director probably has at least two weeks on the stage, if not more.

Well, that's very good.

Very good. But then again, it's only five hours, and then you have to go to the basement on C Level to rehearse. For a new production I think you have one week of piano tech to do light cues and the shifts, etc., and again, it's only about three and a half hours per day, actually 11:00 until 2:30 or up until 3:00, because that's how long the chorus will be available. Then there is at least a week of orchestral dress and orchestral tech and then the final dress.

So in terms of time, the Met is very serious about it although it is never enough time. However, it is unlike City Opera where they throw an opera together very quickly.

Where did you research the opera?

Most of the research was with books and Russian paintings. Betsy and I went to Russia for *Boris Godunov* so we have a lot of pictures of Moscow and other places. Essentially research for *Khovanshchina* was from books.

How long will the opera be in repertory?

It all depends on how often the Met revives the production. And that depends on its popularity and who is available to sing it. They have revived it once, and I have a feeling that they may wait another four years. This is going to stay around, because if they want to do *Khovanshchina*, they won't have the money to make another new production. They don't cancel an old production unless it's a disaster. Usually they are stuck with it unless they get Mrs. Harrington to get Franco Zeffirelli to do a new one.

I'm beginning to wonder if I really want to be tagged as the Russian opera designer in New York! I'm getting a little nervous about that. On the other hand, the opera scene has changed so much. Interestingly enough, there are so few American designers who are doing work at the Met now.

There never has been as many as there possibly should be.

Schuyler Chapin made a real effort to bring American designers into the Met. He felt perhaps we were ready. So quite a few of us have worked at the Met. Then, for a while with John Dexter and others, there was a whole influx of English designers, and they are good. But now it's very much back to pre–Schuyler Chapin's time and it's either the Germans or the Italians.

But of course, that whole era is over because Kurt Herbert Adler has died, and also Carol Fox of the Lyric Opera of Chicago, and Rudolf Bing is in poor health. Those were giants, though. You don't find them now.

You worked with Kurt Herbert Adler.

Oh, yes. He was an odd man, powerful and eccentric. You didn't quite know what he thought all the time. Nevertheless, there was a real vision and he took risks. But today in the entire opera world, you feel they are all sort of functionaries. None of the opera companies really takes either musical or production risks, or has a point of view about opera or music theatre. Nowadays it's all about performance. So it's a curious time. Opera has really changed.

Are we being too analytical about opera productions?

I don't know whether we're being too analytical or not. All I can say is that the climate for doing opera is not easy, and I'm not just talking about designing. I'm talking about directing opera, producing opera. New York is a strange place at this point. On one hand I always feel it's very important to have critics who are not afraid of saying what they like and what they don't like, because if we didn't have criticism, then I think the quality of the work would suffer. We need people who can be honest about what they think and have a right to tell you. Of course, the quality of the critique is also important. In terms of reviews we are essentially talking about *The New York Times*.

At this point, the New York review sets its own kind of approach, its own standard, and it has a very personal preference. That preference, on one hand, is that opera should not be approached in terms of music theatre. It is an opera-oriented viewpoint, and by that I meant that the musical language is sacred, so that everything stems from the integrity of the music. So however theatrical, if the critics feel the directorial approach violates the integrity of the music, they hate it. It's as though they themselves are violated. And yet, at the same time, some of them do have a taste in production that distrusts spectacle. I think the critics probably feel that spectacle violates the musical integrity, so they distrust an enormous amount of clutter, and spectacle for its own sake.

They don't want spectacle? Well, what about Zeffirelli's productions at the Metropolitan Opera?

You should realize that Zeffirelli's *Bohème*, his *Tosca*, his *Turandot* did not get good reviews. The public loved it, but the critics hated it. But at the same time, any production that somehow moves away from the literal approach to the piece makes them very nervous, too. So in terms of critics you have a kind of straitjacket. You are walking a narrow line. You step off one way, and they say, "What are you doing? It's perplexing; I don't understand it." You step off the other way and they say, "Well, a spectacle for its own sake, it's destroying the music." You are walking a very narrow line if you care about reviews at all. And yet, at the same time you have a public that is even more perplexing. Is the audience there because of the singing or to see spectacles?

At the Met or anywhere today.

In New York there is the Met and City Opera. What other opera house do you have? And in New York, I must say, the public seems to be going for the idea that the bigger the production, the

more expensive, the better. And when it's the biggest, the most expensive, there is money to support it.

I'm not sure what City Opera is doing. The few times I've gone recently, I've left early. I can't stand the puniness of the sound. I can't stand the fact that it's obviously underrehearsed; I can't stand the routine way things are being put on. It's routine because there is so little rehearsal time. Quite often I'm not too keen about the physical production, because it looks as if the show just came off the road. And I must say, several times, even for my own shows, I found the lighting so appalling. But worst of all I felt that the people up there are underrehearsed and everyone is reaching for their own gratification and they are performing, rather than doing a work for music theatre where there is a totality that is bigger than just performance.

Meanwhile, Peter Sellars' productions—BAM, PepsiCo at Purchase—those productions are not well received either by New York reviewers. Some other reviewers like it and some don't. In New York reviews, Peter's

Preliminary sketch and ⅛-inch model
  by Ming Cho Lee
TRAVELER IN THE DARK by Marsha Norman
Directed by Gordon Davidson
Mark Taper Forum
Los Angeles
California (1985)

work got dismissed. Peter knows music very well and has a great respect for it. However, his approach, quite often, is through visual imagery.

You have worked with him?

No, I haven't. But my students work with Peter, so I know him very well. Personally, I feel a little bit lost because I now realize that for me the enjoyment of designing in the theatre is the connection between the visual imagery and the text. The text is the content. I get very bored with visual imagery or spectacle for its own sake or when the starting point is the visual imagery and if there is a text, it is made to fit.

You're saying that the text really defines boundary lines, boundary areas.

It's the text that actually provides the content of the piece of the connection in terms of humanistic values. Without text I don't know how you address those humanistic values. The excitement is in using the visual imagery to reveal those values and our connection to them. The transformation from words to visual imagery must keep the connection with the words. When you take the text out, I don't know where I am.

Are we not in a spectacle age again?

Of course, everyone says this is the age for spectacle, everyone is inter-

ested in spectacle. Now I'd like to know why. Why suddenly at this point do we feel that spectacle is a worthwhile experience in the theatre? I am not sure, but it seems as if this is true both in opera and in the theatre. You can hardly get a dramatic show into the commercial theatre. I don't know whether it's the audience that dictates that or whether it's the perception of what audiences like that dictates it, but you keep having megaspectacles. That's very frightening to me.

I thought I went through a kind of middle-age crisis about six years ago. But I thought I came out of it and I was very reassured about my commitment to teaching, my commitment to theatre, my commitment to design for the theatre. I enjoy it. I feel that it's rewarding, if it's meaningful. And I've been going at it reasonably well, except that I'm teaching more and more, and I have found that I am having a harder and harder time doing the amount of work that I used to do. I keep getting late, and when I'm late, I get very nervous and guilt-ridden. And so I decided that given the fact that I'm teaching, perhaps I should be a little bit more careful. I don't take on everything, because I can't handle it. But, also I suddenly feel that I need a little time to assess and not just keep on doing, just to take a look as to what is going on. Who am

I, what are the things that I do enjoy doing, and what's going on around me? And this is the year that I am taking a look at things, just to see where I am or where the world is.

K2 was quite a success for you.
I must tell you that the attention *K2* got was embarrassing for me. It was not a bad play, but the set got too much attention. In fact, it was already into the period of spectacle.

But here the press and the critics could say it was great because the play worked and it was an interesting set design.
No. They didn't say the play worked. Certainly the show had a press representative who got people there and they all looked at the mountain going up. The show didn't get good reviews, but they didn't say that the set overwhelmed it. It would have been very perceptive if they had said that, but they didn't. I was a little bit embarrassed by the attention it got. It was out of proportion with the rest of the kind of work that I do, and it was out of proportion to its accomplishment. In one night I became the set design hero! Then a year later it's something else

now. The only joy I got out of it was I managed to get the Tony Award instead of *Cats*. But still, I was very uncomfortable. It was all about physical spectacles. The show at the Arena Stage in Washington was better, and the set, of course, came from Washington.

Why was it better there?
Well, I thought the New York producer and the playwright made some bad choices. They insisted on getting a superstar to perform. Then everyone dropped out, and they ended up with two people no better known than those who played it in Washington, and they had less time to rehearse. I thought one of the major mistakes the Broadway production made was to have the house curtain in so that when the audience came in they didn't see what was on the stage. I said, "You are making a big mistake because when the house curtain goes up, it is very powerful, and I have a feeling you will have a hard time starting the play." They said, "Well, wouldn't it be dynamite?" My answer was, "No, you don't want that kind of dynamite."
In Washington there was no house curtain. You came in and you saw the

set and you had time to look and say, "My God, is that real?" They turned the air-conditioning a little bit higher than normal and you had people actually sitting down with their coats on. Some people who got into the theatre early went down to the pit and took a closer look at the stage and then went back up to their seats, read the program, so when the show began, everyone knew what the setting was.
But on Broadway, they had the house curtain in. Then the house curtain went up and you got huge applause, and the show didn't start until ten minutes later. This was a big mistake, and I swear I cannot understand how the playwright, the director, the producer can make that kind of a mistake.

You couldn't insist on not having the house curtain in?
No, I could not make them believe me. I even said, "You guys are really stupid. Do you want to ruin your show? I get no joy out of getting that kind of applause. I'd rather have the show run."

Comment on the kind of training needed for theatre designers today.

Let me say what I am doing now with the students at the Yale Drama School. At this point, a great deal of my time with the first-year students is dealing with director-and-designer collaboration. In my first-year class I have second-year directors and first-year designers. I spend as much time with the four directing students as with my design students. Then we put them together on a project. This year they did *King Lear.* Then John Hirsch is coming in, and we are going to do *The Dybbuk.* Quite often I try to put a third-year designer with a second- or first-year director on student shows. I don't believe in the blind leading the blind.

The students, director and designer, are learning the process of talking to each other. What does the designer have to do in order to get meaningful dialogue with the director? In fact, this is the real concentration of the first-year design class. I spend a lot of time saying to first-year design students that you don't work *for* the director, but you are always working *with* the director. Working with the director means that you must have a capacity to think from a director's point of view. If you cannot, then you are lost because the director cannot tell you how to think. The director is not a man of all trades, and he shouldn't be. If the director tells you exactly what you should do, then there is no joy in being a designer. Also, that burden on the director is unfair. I find that a lot of the student designers ask, "Well, what do you want?" I would say, "That's not a fair question. They can tell you what they want, but it's really what all of you want." How do you listen to a director and figure out what is the common vision?

A director can say, "I don't know what I want until I see it." Why *should* a director know what he wants to see if he hasn't seen it? He can say all he wants about how he feels about the play. He may talk about the visual or he may not. He may simply want to talk about people or talk about acting. It's the joy of being a designer to use all those words and emotions and a sense of the play, and be able to transform that into the visual language of sketches, not a finished product, because then the director gets frightened. The designer begins with something very rough yet very expressive to get the dialogue started, and then there is a continuous evolving until the final commitment to do a play a certain way.

And I try to tell the students that if you cannot draw expressively, then the dialogue will not begin. If the dialogue begins based on uncertain drawing, then it's unfair because you are fooling yourself as well as the director. Another thing I try to tell the designers is, "If you don't hear the play, I don't think you can draw the play."

Is drawing a prerequisite for all design students?
Yes, but to draw expressively and quickly.

Must they have a facility in drawing in order to be able to come to the Yale Drama School?
We quite often take students who draw moderately well. There are so few nowadays who can really draw well. That includes even the people from art school. *They* don't know how to draw, and that is frightening.

You will hear, "Well so-and-so doesn't draw well, but he or she makes models," but you still have to draw to make models!
Yes, and when you begin the design process by making models, you make a commitment to a design way too early. What we do now, instead of Donald Oenslager's weekly project for the first-year students, is to do a project every two weeks. That first week, I usually want to see a lot of roughs with ground plans. Drawing without plans is no good. A rough should be a drawing that is clear and reveals a process of thinking. And out of that if there is something that feels good, then most of my students will take the next step and make an eighth-inch model. All the first-year students have stacks and stacks of eighth-inch models.

You insist, you said, that they always do a plan with the roughs.
Yes, thumbnails and plans, and quite often for the second week, not only an eighth-inch model but a whole storyboard of each scene in sequence is required.

When we say scenes, are we talking about mood changes with lighting or are we talking about all acts or just the top of the scenes and the acts—not the progression of light?
No, no. Sometimes it has less to do with lights than just where people are. Quite often the storyboard is almost

like a diagram, a little bit like a lot of Caspar Neher's drawing—just where people are in relation to other people. How do you make the action clear? And with the action clear, how does the spatial design relate to it? This is essentially what I am doing, and it's very exciting.

It seems that at this point the people coming out of Yale work with directors very well. In fact, I think one of the main skills they have is not just to work with a director well, but they *enjoy* working with a director and a director enjoys working with them, because a director doesn't feel as if he is being put on trial, and there are always a lot of options. Also, the directors find that the designers sometimes feed ideas and help them in making choices and making commitments. That, I think, is a little bit of a change even in my previous thinking.

I now find that I do not resent directors who require hand-holding. I feel that a director's job, to be a leader, is very, very hard, and the hands are generally worth holding. What do I have to do to allow the director to see how the physical environment reflects the words or the passion that he has been talking about? It is the designer's job to give a sense of security, too, so that the director is a part of each step in the design process. In each step the director should not feel as if he is being shoved or sales-talked into a certain approach, but rather it's always a process of discovering it together. At this point, with the exception of directors who sometimes have a destructive streak, I find that I enjoy working with most directors. Certainly I enjoy talking with directors much more than going to the shop. In the old days, I enjoyed going to the shop. I feel I knew them, I respected the skill. Now I still respect the skill, but they no longer have time to show their skill.

If I am a student in your class and if I say I can only do a model or I can only sketch, which would you think is more beneficial?
I am going to say better try a sketch first.

And I would have to come up with the model later?
Quite often if someone is having a terrible time sketching and is very good at models, I might say, "All right, just do the model," just to build your con-

fidence up. But when the model becomes a crutch, then I say, "You had better do sketches." When people are having a tough time drawing, I have them do an exercise of sitting at one end of a room and drawing the other end with line only so that I can analyze the line drawing.

How much time do you give them to do this?

Oh, I go there Monday, Wednesday, Saturday and usually I'll have them show me on Wednesday and then Saturday. I would say, "I just want to see the lines. No straight edge, just line drawing and no shading." Then if it's good, I have them go to the other end of that room and draw the opposite

end. Sometimes I then say, "OK, now you go and measure the room and draw a ground plan." I will never allow them not to draw.

Quite often with people who manage to draw reasonably well, the drawing is too flat and the spatial relation is off, then of course they must have an eighth-inch model. It's all very fluid. Back and forth, back and forth. It all depends on where one's strength is, and if the strength becomes a crutch, then I'll try to make sure that the other side is strengthened.

Model by Ming Cho Lee
ELECTRA by Sophocles
Directed by Gerald Freedman
New York Shakespeare Festival
Delacorte Theatre, New York (1964)

Do the design students do figure drawing or portraits?

We now have the money to start a class in life drawing, but we haven't had one. And I'm not confident enough to teach life drawing. I can get by with my own drawing, but I'm not competent to teach it.

That's why you have good scenic artists in the studios where you take research and you say, "Make this realistic," or what have you.

Well, what I have always thought was that the designer had better paint the model or the color elevation well enough, saying that "this is what it is" so that the interpretation is from a solid ground. It's not saying, "But I really don't mean that." It's a big job to make something twenty-four times bigger. If my students' painting is not good enough, I say, "Do you want the scenic artist to reproduce this twenty-four times bigger?" And they say, "Oh, no." And I say, "Well, then what is the scenic artist going to do, design it for you?" And I will not permit that.

Some, though, want the scenic artists to do that, do they not? Then it's not the designer's own work that you're getting.

That doesn't matter. But I think it's unfair to the scenic artist to have to decide at which point it is right. I mean you can't say, "That's what I want," then tell him, "Oh no, no, I said the wrong thing." What kind of nonsense is that? I cannot behave that way. And I don't want my set painted that way.

If you had to choose, what would be your two favorite designs in your career?

I would say I don't know. I don't think I have a favorite. I certainly recognize that there are some designs that are important in the sense that it was a good experience, it was extremely fulfilling, at that time the common vision of the show was realized or somehow came to life. Those are the works that I have very good memories of, and I'm very proud of. Also, I realize that there are some shows that I did, again they were good experiences, that seem to be a breakthrough in terms of American theatre or American design. They changed the perception of many people about what designing is. Some designs that I have done actually were something of a landmark in the prog-

198

Model by Ming Cho Lee
ROMEO AND JULIET by William Shakespeare
Directed by Theodore Mann
Circle in the Square Theatre
New York (1977)

ress of American theatre. I would say that *Electra* in 1964 certainly did that. And then there are some of the operas that I did that certainly have that. But are they my favorites? I can't tell. All I'm saying is that I made certain breakthroughs that are very important. That doesn't mean that they are better design than some of the design I have done later, even though the later ones are less of a breakthrough. A design may be a more personal breakthrough because I am constantly changing.

And would I do *Electra* the same way now? In fact, I would love to do *Electra* and it would be very, very different. I guess I enjoy working with directors much more, and I feel that a really wonderful design tends to be something that a director also has a great deal to do with.

It's very hard for me to talk about favorites, I can only talk about designs that I am not ashamed of, and some of them I am quite proud of. I'm very proud of *Khovanshchina* with all its difficulties, because it's a very different design from all the other designs that are currently at the Met. In some parts of the opera when the chorus is on the stage, the impact is quite remarkable. Even the second time around I was impressed by certain things that I didn't even expect could happen. I was always very proud of *The Glass Menagerie* that I did at the Guthrie.

As opposed to the one that you designed on Broadway?

At Circle in the Square, or four or five years ago on Broadway? I didn't enjoy that. I remember the one at the Guthrie, which was my second, and Emily

Mann was the director. I am very proud of the *Mary Stuart* that I did with John Hirsch at Stratford, Ontario. Even though there were many things wrong with it, I was very proud of the *Death of a Salesman* that I did there. It was very different from Jo Mielziner's design. I always remember the *Hamlet* I did with Liviu Ciulei at Arena Stage. And I'm very fond of the design I did with Gordon Davidson at the Mark Taper for Marsha Norman's play called *Traveler in the Dark.*

Why? What did that have that you liked?

That was very realistic, and it looked like a Wyeth. It's a realistic play, and when you came into the theatre, you thought, "I remember that. I've been there," and it was quite wonderful. The ground was covered with fall leaves and when you walked on it, it made sound and it felt good. So, there are some things I remember with great fondness, but what my favorite is, I have no idea.

What play or opera or production would you love to design as one of your biggest challenges?

You see, everything is challenging, but I think I have passed the concept of "one big challenge," because doing *Boris Godunov* was a challenge; it couldn't be bigger. *Khovanshchina* was a challenge, you know it's a big challenge. I felt that *Lohengrin* was a challenge, which I didn't meet very well. *The Execution of Justice, The Glass Menagerie,* all of them were challenges whether a big show or small. That's not the point anymore. This is part of my current need for reassess-

ment. And I'm also at the stage where doing another show on Broadway is not going to make my résumé better. It's not going to prove anything.

It doesn't have to be Broadway. It could be a small production in regional theatre.

Outside of New York that kind of experience is more possible. If it's a new play, I also like to be involved in the process much earlier. That's what I'm looking forward to. I really would not want to pick up a play or a musical when I didn't like the music or I didn't like the book. I have done that. There is no need for me to do it, and meanwhile I am spending so much time teaching that I don't want to.

What I am actually trying to say is I think if I find myself getting excited about designing again, I will be doing a piece of work that really excites me. It may be a new play or a Shakespeare that I would love to do, and it may be any Shakespeare. Last year I did a *Romeo and Juliet* ballet for the Pacific Northwest Ballet in Seattle. It was a good company, and it was a wonderful experience. We didn't use the Prokofiev music. Kent Stowell decided that he knows the music too well, and that it tends to be too spectacle-oriented rather than narrative-oriented. So he and his music director put together a whole score for *Romeo and Juliet* from unknown Tchaikovsky music. And they put it together so well that you would think Tchaikovsky had actually written it for *Romeo and Juliet.* We had a year to work on it. I needed a year because three or four days a week I'm not in New York. Theoni did the costumes, and there is a "look." It was a great experience. I would say that that kind of experience I would look forward to. There was a certain amount of risk. There was something that was not routine about it. I was excited about the work, not just because of the design possibility, but because the work moved me so that I wanted to do it. It has to do with whom I'm working, the pleasantness of collaboration, the respect for process, and the respect for each other, and whether the work is taken seriously. For me that can take place anywhere.

5

DESIGNING MULTISET PRODUCTIONS

DESIGNING MULTISET PROSCENIUM PRODUCTIONS

Nothing is more thrilling than to see a beautifully designed and mounted multiset production in a proscenium theatre move from scene to scene with extraordinary speed and flow. With spectacular productions in film and on television the norm, audiences have come to expect live stage performances in the proscenium theatre to be as exciting and stunning as possible. The audience does not care or know how a beautiful production evolves, nor should they. The audience's proper concerns are how much they enjoy the production and how exciting it is to see it.

Scenic designers are always looking for new ways to create scenery. While it is appropriate to explore every possibility, it's a good bet that what may be called "old-fashioned painted scenery" is here to stay. Canvas, wood, and paints are not obsolete as materials for creating scenery. An exquisitely painted ballet or opera set under beautiful stage lighting is a feast for the eye, and in opera and especially in dance many productions require a certain kind of painted and painterly scenery. If you as a designer can come up with something more dashing, more abstract, or more significant and the director or choreographer approves, then do it.

Big multiset productions usually offer the greatest challenge to the stage designer. The designer's thoughts, talent, energy, and time are totally involved in the evolution and execution of a big show. Of course, the basic demands a stage designer deals with are the same as for any show. These are (1) time, (2) space, (3) budget, and (4) the director-designer relationship. Every designer wants these factors to be as close to ideal as possible.

1. *Time.* When you are designing a big production with many sets, time is often at a premium. You worry constantly about whether there is going to be enough time in the design studio, in the shop, in the out-of-town theatre, in the theatre for the setup, and whether competent assistants will be available to take over some of the demands of the schedule.
2. *Space.* What kind of space is available on the actual stage? Is there a good depth and off-left and off-right storage space? What about the grid height? If you are doing a big production in a new theatre, you do not want to run the risk of designing an enormous show only to discover too late that it fits into the space too tightly for the necessary scene changes to work.
3. *Budget.* Will the producers be able to pay for the scenery for the show? Have you gone over the budget? Will you have to revamp the scenery and sacrifice some of your better ideas? Will the scenery budget have to be cut in order to allow more money for advertising?
4. *The director-designer relationship.* How the working relationship with the director goes is a big worry for a designer on any show. This is especially true on a first collaboration with a particular director. A single set positioned on stage that does not move during performance is one kind of designing, but a very large moving production is a completely different ball game. Here, accurate decisions must be made quickly, and a clear understanding of the design on the director's part is essential to keep the production moving forward. For instance, often one unit of scenery cannot be moved upstage to gain more playing space because another sizable unit is already there which can't be moved because there is no place to store it. A designer is often on pins and needles, hoping that the new director will comprehend all the visual and technical aspects to be considered in putting the show together, and that their efforts will work to their mutual satisfaction.

This is why a successful designer in the commercial theatre hires good assistants. Assistants can check to make sure that everything works properly on the drafting and in the model as well as in the actual theatre where the show is to play.

Creating "a Vista" Scene Changes

Possibly the most visually exciting productions are those in which the audience watches the scenery move to transform the stage into a new time and place. When the scenic elements (drops, platforms, furniture, and props) are choreographed to move with the lighting and music, the effect can be dazzling. This takes a great deal of preplanning and work before the designs are developed on paper, and the possibilities are dependent upon three main elements: (1) the director's attitude, (2) the size of the budget, and (3) the producer's approval.

You must reach a clear understanding with the director as to what would be an exciting approach to moving the scenery in the changes. You should have at least two or three different alternatives clearly thought out before getting together with the director for a discussion.

Before you begin to think of how wonderful everything can be scenically, consider the personality and professional abilities of the director you are working with. If a director is imaginative, perceptive, understanding, and secure, and expects you to come up with fresh ideas, you will know it immediately. The essence of a productive and satisfying working relationship with a director is a mutual respect for each other's reputation as a professional and a willingness to explore one another's approach to the production.

On the other hand, you may find that the director is completely lost and baffled by what you are trying to do. He or she may not understand or agree with what you have in mind and consequently may want to control every single aspect of the production. When you sense this is happening, it is important that you use common sense and select a simple approach to the scenic production.

Basic Approaches to Designing Multiple-Set Shows

Over the years, designers in the theatre have evolved various ways of paring a show down and containing it on stage. Most of these methods are not new. They have proved to be practical measures over a span of time and continue to do so. When a theatre has good facilities, flying scenery in and out is usually the fastest possible method of scene change. It also keeps the scenery out of the way of other scenery, actors, and crew on the stage floor proper. The challenge, as always, is to design with that unbeatable combination, intelligence and good taste. While certain ideas may overlap from one show to the next, the following are some methods for designing multiple-set productions.

An In-One Playing and Crossing Area Downstage

This is one of the oldest and still one of the most effective methods of dealing with scene changes. The idea is to play a scene in front of a curtain while scenery is being positioned upstage for the next scene. Popular for many years in musicals, revues, burlesque, and music halls, this idea runs the gamut from a simply designed production with all-black velour curtains to a sumptuously designed show with beautiful and ornate motifs appearing throughout. The front curtain may fly in and out or part in the center and open as a traveler (or be one way).

In this in-one situation, upstage masking legs and borders (or framed portals) are standard units. The in-one curtain may also be positioned behind the first portal. Backdrops, panels, and various kinds of other sizable scenery are used to mask the upstage area where the new setup is taking place.

Along these same lines, a secondary area sometimes works well in center stage while another playing area is being set up with scenery farther upstage as the middle scene plays. This in-one playing area may also have a curtain upstage (that flies in or out) so the next scene can be set up upstage of it.

An in-one playing and crossing area is also ideal for dramas with many scenes in which minimal scenery, furniture, and props may be moved on and off with good effect. Minimal scenery, for example, could be hanging light fixtures, carved gates, three-dimensional fireplaces, and trellises with vines.

Soft Legs and Borders with Backdrops

Soft legs and borders with backdrops are standard scenery for ballet and the dance. They range from solid-colored fabric legs and borders to highly designed and painted legs and borders. The inner onstage edges range from straight or simple shapes to elaborate cutout fabrics that need scenic netting or other openwork support behind. Soft legs and borders are appropriate for any number of settings, including forests or pastoral scenes, drapery settings, street scenes, or interiors.

More than one group of legs and borders may be effective for a single production, depending on the design, and also on space and budget. For example, a unit of soft legs and borders can fly in and out in front of a similar leg and border unit. Other soft scenery, such as backdrops of sharkstooth scrim, also work beautifully with this type of setting.

There may be three, four, or five units of legs and borders in an average single setting. The space between units of legs and a border usually ranges from 5 to 6 feet, according to the depth of the stage. This traditional parallel arrangement works beautifully because it allows dancers, singers, or actors to make easy entrances and exits, and it masks lighting instruments and the backstage area and other scenery and equipment. Units of legs and a border are lovely framing devices for backdrops as well as the total picture that includes actors and stage lighting in a scene.

Soft legs and borders pack, store, and travel easily. However, legs that are wrinkled and hang crooked, especially those with painted architecture, neither serve the design and the show nor please the audience. Instead of designing architecture, if possible, design soft legs and borders of drapery or foliage. In this way, if the soft pieces are wrinkled or hang crooked when in the theatre, then the visual results are not quite as disastrous.

Full-stage cut backdrops work well to visually create a feeling of depth on stage. This may be done with two or more cut drops in front of a sky or other painted backdrop. The cut drops can be hung and staggered in between the units of legs and borders according to the spacing that is needed for staging and for a pleasing appearance. The placement and design of the cutout openings in the drops can be used for entrances and exits, depending on the composition, the illusion of perspective, and the overall design.

Ground rows, small set pieces, and furniture may also be a part of this kind of setting for a dance or ballet. The floor treatment may be the regular stage floor, a vinyl dance floor covering, or whatever surface is appropriate for the type of performance. Additional masking pieces are often needed on the offstage edges of painted legs and borders unless the legs are designed wide enough and the borders high enough.

Hard Portals with a Deck and Various Scenic Pieces

For musicals of all sizes, and especially those on a large scale and with many different pieces of scenery, the standard formula of incorporating a series of hard portals (usually appearing as one piece), often on a built deck, is unbeatable. This arrangement also works quite well for dramas and operas when the design concept allows it.

Naturally, framed portals (in one piece) serve the same purpose as arrangements of soft legs and borders. They mask the backstage areas, the lighting instruments, other scenery and equipment, and the actors and stage crew in the wings. But framed portals offer more versatility in a design than do legs and borders. They appear to be solid, stand straight and uniform, do not shake, and can have pieces such as flippers, sliders, and so on attached to them. Portals can also have numerous shapes and do not have to be supported by openwork materials such as scenic netting. The inner and onstage shapes of portals may be made of a basic cutout plywood profile or created with enormous inner three-dimensional applied shapes. An entire portal and the thickness pieces may be

Model designs by Loren Sherman
THE MARRIAGE OF BETTE AND BOO
  by Christopher Durang
Directed by Jerry Zaks
Newman/Public Theatre, New York (1985)
(Photographs by Loren Sherman)

"These are six out of thirty-three scenes ranging in length from fifteen seconds to several minutes. Layers of panels on tracks revealed minimal furniture setups and covered them when they were being changed during other scenes."
                                              —Loren Sherman

painted and marbelized in a grand manner. The possibilities are endless.

Portals may be created with rough crating wood, painted brick patterns, large woven basket patterns, painted concrete or stucco, stenciled wall patterns, printed fabrics, geometric designs, real lights appearing as such, or light boxes illuminating patterns positioned on translucent surfaces in front of them.

The spacing of portals upstage and downstage is similar to the spacing of leg and border units, and for the same reasons, but additional planning is needed when a raised show deck is involved and when units of scenery are designed to track on and off from stage left and stage right.

The spacing between portals has to accommodate the depth of moving units so that they will clear the portals as they move between them. Simple

202 pallets with furniture or other props may also move on and off between portals. The planning of the correct spacing between portals involves the portal (with any thickness) in front, the portal in back, any necessary hardware, and lighting instruments positioned on light booms. The size of moving units and how they move off and on between portals must always be resolved before the drawings are completed.

While the head of the scenic shop can help to work out the mechanics of moving units on and off, the scenic designer is the one who must know the visual requirements, the staging, and the intended effects. The designer must plan to have hanging masking pieces extending past the outer edges of the portal and positioned offstage so that when the unit moves from off to onstage, the audience does not see the backstage area or crew. At the same time, on a tight scenic show, there must be a soft fabric panel usually perpendicularly positioned between the outer ends of the portals to mask the wagon with scenery when it is in storage or not being used. This panel is usually kept soft for safety reasons, and it must be rigged to independently fly out to let the unit roll into position on stage. It is then lowered back into place. The process is repeated when the scene is over and the piece has to go back through the portals into storage.

The scenic designer must also check that enough space has been allotted for the position of the moving scenic unit offstage in storage so that actors have enough room to make exits in costumes or with hand props, and stagehands

can move around the unit. There may be space, but there may also be a wall! You need to work this out so that you do not overdesign or make things too complicated to work with during the actual running of the show. A designer cannot tell a director that actors cannot make any exits downstage or midstage because the wings are full of scenery. You may tell a director, "It's going to be awfully crowded in the wings," but if actors stop dead in their tracks onstage during dress rehearsal and tell their already worried director sitting out in the house that they can't get off stage, you don't want to be around to see what happens.

One way to avoid this is to plan to have only one unit positioned left and only one positioned right, and if possible, to place the sets for the next act of the play on the wagons during intermission. Also, larger wagons can be stored up left and up right to track diagonally and come together downstage to make one larger set. To utilize every bit of space, a narrow but tall center unit of scenery on a platform for a different scene can be stored upstage between the two units. This center unit can track up and down on the center line of the stage. Naturally, these possibilities depend on the space in the theatre and the sizes of the units.

Designing moving units or any unit for the stage is like any artistic endeavor, in that it is the combination of selected ideas that make the statement. The essential thing in designing moving scenery is to figure out the interplay of the various units, how they work with each other on stage while still being attractive and especially how they

function when put together onstage with people—the actors and the stagehands.

Aside from tracked-on units, there may be full-stage backdrops, cut drops, gauze drops, and smaller panels flying in between the portals for various scenes in the production. In addition, there can be full stage framed hangers with cutout arches, windows, or doors that may fly in and out between the portals and the other already-hanging scenic pieces.

A whole setting may be created by flying in two or three framed hangers, with the first one having large cutout arches, the second one a bit smaller and positioned 5 or 6 feet upstage; and behind it a sizable three-dimensional unit on casters with a window and window seat which is manually pushed into place from its storage position upstage.

There are other variations. A full-stage framed hanger with a large cutout opening can be positioned between portals and fly in. Then, upstage of the opening and attached directly to it on the back of the portal opening can be a large three-dimensional room on a castered platform that is rolled manually up to it. This can make a very effective and workable set. The room unit can also be in two pieces, if necessary.

Deciding how to allocate the stage space for all the scenery and all the necessary lighting instruments with actors in costumes and the stage crew backstage is an essential part of the design process. Learning to do it efficiently comes with experience. Some stage designers rely on very trusted assistants to take care of this aspect of their work.

The show deck for a big production with moving units is usually a built-up floor made and put together in sections. Moving units may be castered

Sketches and model by Tony Walton
THE TEMPEST Ballet
Choreographed by Michael Smuin
San Francisco Ballet Company
San Francisco Opera House
San Francisco, California (1980)

Photographs, across: 1. Sketch of ship struck by lightning. 2. ½-inch model of ship in storm. 3. Sketch of ship blasted open—segue into island. 4. Sketch of island with corral.

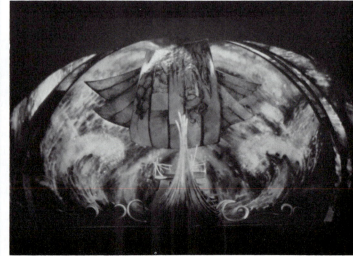

wagons of scenery that move on and off stage with guides in tracks that are positioned in the show deck. These units of scenery may be moved by winches and appear to come on by themselves "a vista." This is always a pleasant sight, especially when several wagons with nicely proportioned scenery come onstage together as a group with scenic pieces flying in, actors and dancers assembling onstage, and stage lights coming up.

The approach to creating scenery for a multiset show is very different when there is enough time to change sets between scenes or during intermissions. Careful planning with respect to facilities, stage space, stage crew, and budget is still necessary, however.

Changing scenery during intermission is still a great method. It allows many opportunities and challenges. Framed portals or leg and border masking may be used as the starting point. For an interior, you might have one large set on a platform with furniture, dressing, ceiling, and a chandelier that tracks up and down stage. The same set may also have to be designed to go on two or three castered platform units that are shifted from various onstage and offstage areas by stagehands.

For another intermission act change, there might be an exterior set that has parts of it flown in from above and other parts positioned on castered platforms that are moved on manually. Occasionally, a portion of an interior set can be cleverly designed on the reverse side of the scenery so that it can be turned around and used for an exterior setting in another scene. This, naturally, saves bracing and space when designed to be on the same platform. (It also presents a lovely view when seen as an "a vista" change.)

For a third-act interior set, a full-stage hanger with a different inner shape may be flown in to work with a sizable three-dimensional wagon designed to play behind it. The framed hanger flies in behind a portal; it may be a stenciled wallpaper pattern and the same design may be continued on the walls of the three-dimensional unit that contains doors, windows, and furniture. This type of set playing behind a framed hanger cuts down the main bulk (width and height) of the interior, and creates a nice intimacy. It can be used for all kinds of productions.

Depending entirely on how the play is written, one of the most interesting ways to save time in scene changes in a multiset show is to have the final set positioned upstage of one or two others. This can be quite a complicated-looking set, and can be dressed within an inch of its life. However, it is often necessary to remove or swing back one or both sides in order to shift the sets.

With all the various ways to change sets that have been discussed in this section, there are regional and university theatres where shows with two or three settings can still be done very simply by opening hinged units and lashing flats together in a very simple "old-fashioned" way. If a method works well, don't knock it just because the idea has been around for a long time.

Unit Sets with Change of Plugs and Other Decor

The unit set not only is one of the most sensible solutions to designing the scenery for a gigantic production, but can be one of the most challenging. In essence, a unit set is one where a large portion of the set stays onstage during all or most of the performance and is altered by adding, subtracting, or changing various scenic pieces during the course of the performance.

The main set or unit set can be a beautiful sculptured arrangement of openwork angular platforms and plastic shapes; a semicircle of arches on a flat floor; or a post-and-beam structure erected on a raked stage. The style of a unit set may be any historical period or place, and of course, the changes of different pieces are always enhanced by imaginative stage lighting.

A unit set is advantageous for interior and exterior sets, or a combination of both. Backdrops and show curtains are nice combinations to vary interest and design. Items such as a sky backdrop, a black velour, and a red-and-gold backdrop can all be used upstage to play behind scenes. The list of items to use in a unit set is endless—lighted chandeliers, ornate portions of grillwork, free-form draperies, horizontal bamboo panels, hanging banners, trees, and foliage are just a few. Sometimes unit sets involve hinged panels or wagon units containing all sorts of practical doors, windows, balconies, stairs, and other units.

Simultaneous Scene Settings

A simultaneous scene setting is one in which multiple settings are positioned onstage at the same time. This setting is usually the interior of a house with two, three, or four rooms juxtaposed on stage and often it is designed with logical architectural decor and furniture. Typical simultaneous scene settings may consist of rooms or areas on only one level, or there may be a second level above, especially for bedroom and hall areas. Other common sets of this type include porches with living rooms, streets with store exteriors and interiors, and so on. However, rooms do not always have to be designed to appear realistic.

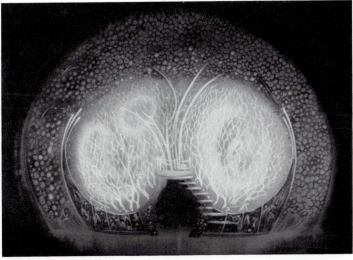

A series of three-dimensional platforms of varied sizes and heights may be positioned together with facings to appear solid, or platform tops can be supported by metal pipes. For areas representing interiors, appropriate furniture and props are positioned according to the needs of the staging. Creative lighting is always crucial to the success of this kind of production. One set or two or more playing areas may be illuminated at the same time.

Simultaneous scene settings can be placed on stage on a large turntable. A built-up show deck is usually needed for positioning turntables and treadmills in it. While we may think of seeing only one set at a time on the turntable, there may be two or more, depending on the positioning of various units on the stage floor and also on whether a second-story set is placed above the deck.

Revolving Stage

A revolving stage can be a wonderful asset to a show when used properly. It can also be a problem if it is inappropriate for a production. Study the list of advantages and disadvantages.

ADVANTAGES

1. Excellent for changing scenery fast.
2. Good for holding large multiset interiors or exteriors.
3. Holds a large amount of furniture, props, and light fixtures.
4. Allows changing one set with at least two others ready to use.
5. Works beautifully for a unit set of arches or for a sculptured abstract assemblage.

DISADVANTAGES

1. Limits having a full stage space.
2. Expensive to construct.
3. Requires constant and appropriate maintenance to work properly.
4. Can be noisy when it moves.
5. Can become visually boring if the same set is viewed more than twice by the audience.
6. Requires building up the whole stage around it unless not to do so is part of the design concept.

Using Periaktoi

Periaktos (singular) is a three-sided revolving unit of scenery. Periaktoi (plural) means two or more of these units. The advantage of using the standard three-sided periaktos is that you have three sides of different designs mounted as one piece of scenery on casters with a center pivot. This allows for a quick change of scenery, either manually or electrically. These variations in periaktoi are possible.

1. A unit has three flat sides with straight-up-and-down outer edges.
2. The center metal pivot remains stationary in the floor. Or the metal pin may be designed to move back and forth in the floor in a track.
3. A unit has three different subjects on each of the three sides (for example, brick wall, banner, and wood panel with molding).
4. One unit is paired with another so the two in combination can form various arrangements.
5. Multiple units are positioned in a straight line similar to the effect of a backdrop, with sufficient space so that the units do not hit each other when they revolve.
6. Units are positioned in a semicircle.
7. Units are positioned in several different configurations, including a random placement.
8. Units have doors or arches for entrances and exits.
9. Units have windows or lighted signs or other special features.
10. One, two, or three of the sides have centers that break and fold back at 120 degrees.
11. One or more vertical outer edges are designed with irregular shapes, such as foliage, drapery, or architecture.
12. Three-dimensional objects such as sculpture or statuary ride on the base of a unit when it has angled or curved sides.
13. When a unit is large enough, a stagehand can work inside the unit to move the unit into various positions.

For *A Chorus Line*, Robin Wagner designed a setting consisting of a periaktos wall. Wagner created eight periaktoi that were positioned upstage in a straight line across the stage. The following information is taken from a drawing (December 21, 1976) for a production of the musical at Her Majesty's Theatre. Each side of a periaktos was 4'-0" wide by 16'-0" high. The face of the wall formed by the eight periaktoi was surrounded on the sides and above with a hard black velour portal-like unit with 4'-0" legs and with trusses behind. Side A (eight panels) was heavy-gauge Mylar mirror, side B (eight panels) was painted appliqué, and side C (eight panels) was black velour (hard). The maximum clearance from the vertical edge of one periaktos to the vertical edge of another was ½ inch. A note on the drawing specified that the base mechanical package should not exceed 4 inches.

Another production utilizing periaktoi was John Wulp's setting for *Semmelweiss* (1978) at the Kennedy Center. Wulp's setting included two large right-angle periaktoi that were turned and moved by the actors. Each of the two units had three faces that were 8'-1", 8'-1", and 11'-3½", and all were 18'-0" high. The diameter required for these two periaktoi to revolve was approximately 12 feet. The units were on tri-swivel casters, and each unit had a center pivot pin that worked in tracks so that the two units could also move on and off stage (in a direction parallel to the apron). Two windows were positioned high in two of the 8'-1" faces of the periaktoi.

Open Stage Scene Changes

The challenge presented by open stage proscenium productions can be wonderfully stimulating and refreshing simply because traditional methods of staging and scenic designing are approached in a more casual and informal manner. Open stage productions may be period dramas done by actors in costume, with furniture; rock concerts with musicians performing on a raked stage with pulsating lights, and special effects; staged readings with actors in modern dress; and dance programs.

Open stage productions often abandon the idea of having any kind of masking. It is intended that the audience see lighting instruments, cable, pipes, trusses, and scenic pieces. However, sometimes certain pieces of scenery are covered or masked backstage just so they will be a surprise when they are unveiled. Scenic pieces may be flown in and out as needed. Furniture and props are brought on and taken off by actors as part of the action, or by stagehands who, on occasion, appear in costume as characters in the show. Creative stage lighting is usually the main carryover from traditional stage presentations that is invaluable from a scenic designer's point of view.

Settings by John Arnone
FRANKENSTEIN by Victor Gialanella
Directed by Michael Maggio
Costumes by Jack Edwards
Lighting by Marcus Dilliard
Tyrone Guthrie Theatre
Minneapolis, Minnesota (1988)

"Performing in eighty theatres in a national tour prior to the Guthrie opening, the set was capable of expanding and contracting to accommodate the physical specifications of the various theatres."
—John Arnone

Designing a Multiset Production without Fly Space

If you are designing a multiset production and there is no real fly space to speak of, you can choose from among several alternatives for changing scenery.

1. Use traveler tracks to move soft scenery (drops, curtains) on and off stage.
2. Use a sky drop upstage that does not move. When it is not needed, cover it by pulling draperies or a drop on a traveler track in the front of it.
3. If there is some kind of overhead space, a soft backdrop can fly out by being tripped. *Tripping* can be achieved by flying out the drop in halves or thirds of the drop's height. The half method requires flying out the top and bottom battens (with lines attached) to form a U in side view. This half method of tripping tends to work better than the thirds method because horizontally sewn webbing and lines do not have to be attached to the actual center fabric of the drop. For tripping in thirds, this strip of webbing (for

the attachment of tie lines to go on a pipe being flow out) that is sewn on the rear of the drop can be obvious under stage lights and can spoil the illusion.

A backdrop can also be designed to be solid on the bottom one-third and soft on the top two-thirds so it can fly out and have the top soft portion fold in half. However, this must be planned carefully so as not to interfere with the visual design of the backdrop.

4. One of the best ways to change scenery when it cannot fly out is to have it move off and on with castered wagons. The wagons may be moved manually or electrically.
5. Sliding panels that move back and forth horizontally can also be effective for fast scene changes.

Using Intermission Time to Good Advantage

For multiset productions, the time during intermission can be put to great use. A three-set play with two intermissions is often ideal because the ten or twelve minutes between acts can be used to change scenery. The playwright who constructs a play with three different sets and two intermissions in between is being extremely considerate and practical for the stagehands changing the scenery. The first set, of course, can be preset at the top of the show.

For heavy multiset shows, such as musicals, scenic units are often planned so they can be set up or dismantled during an intermission. A unit that stores stage left and plays during Act 1 can be taken apart and moved elsewhere so the same storage space can be used in the second act for something else.

Also, a flying unit that works in the first act only can be taken down during intermission and stored elsewhere. Then another scenic unit (in one or more sections) can be put on the same set of lines from the grid and fly in and out during the second act.

The space and timesaving arrangements backstage are extremely important. Scenery movements should always be planned well in advance of going into the theatre. However, the best way for scenic items and props to shift is sometimes learned through the actual experience of using them onstage during the rehearsal and runthroughs.

USING A COMPUTER TO PLOT SCENE CHANGES FOR A MULTISET PRODUCTION: A DISCUSSION WITH ROBERT CHASE

One of the most interesting multiset shows produced in the commercial theatre was the musical Chess at the Imperial Theatre in New York (1988). Robin Wagner designed the scenery and Robert Chase was the computer graphics consultant. Wagner contacted Chase, a scenic construction expert with a background in computer-aided drafting, about having a computer plot the many complex ground plans for the simultaneously moving scenery in the New York production of Chess. I talked with Robert Chase about the advantages of using a computer for the drafting requirements of Chess and how its capabilities may be utilized in the stage designer's studio.

How has the computer been helpful in doing plans for Chess?

When I first met with Robin Wagner we discussed the possibility of animating ground plan views of scenery. He was interested in doing this for Chess because there were many scene changes involving both the turntable and individual units that moved and rotated. It was quite complex trying to track each unit through all the scene changes. The idea was to see if we could generate an animated view in order to analyze where things might run into each other (and what problems we might have) as the turntable rotated and at the same time provide the solutions to those kinds of problems. Unfortunately, the time frame that we were working within was a little compressed in terms of my getting the software from AutoDesk, and at this point the animation software is not really capable of doing exactly what we were interested in doing without a lot of modification.

The first step in attempting to animate the scene changes was, of course, to draft all the different scenes in their various positions. To do that, I began working with David Peterson, Robin's assistant, and we found that in fact the animation was not as necessary as we might have thought. Simply being able to lay scenes over one another and rotate them on the computer enabled us to see where the different pieces were as each scene ended. We could see how and where pieces would have to be moved on the turntable so that when the turntable rotated, they would be in their correct locations for the following scene.

The advantages of using the computer were that (1) we were able to easily overlay one scene on top of another and analyze the beginning and ending positions of the different pieces, and (2) as the show progressed and changes were made, it was very easy for me to manipulate the different units and see what new problems might arise as we changed the relationship of the elements of the show to each other.

As we got more into the technical rehearsals I was able to generate a book of plans so that the stage manager, Alan Hall, could see what changes had been made the day before. The book was a simple 8½ × 11-inch format of every scene in the show, with the position of each unit in that scene and the position that it was moving to for the next scene.

Did you work on the spot in the theatre?

No, I stayed in the studio. David Peterson would give me the changes and I would then make those changes in the drawings and take the new drawings to him. This was a new thing for all of us, and I think that if we had started sooner we would have been able to update the plates and generate new ground plans regularly during the design period. The big problem is when you have five or six different sets of drawings and they have all been altered by different people involved in the show.

In other words, the stage manager would discuss any changes with the stagehands who were running each one of the individual units?

Yes. A stagehand is inside each one of these towers, but they have their own cue sheets, which I have had nothing to do with. The tower operators keep track of their own moves on their own cue sheets. What I was able to do was to give a copy of the entire show to David Peterson and he would then work with the production stage manager, the idea being that everybody had the same information. That is a good foundation for understanding what changes need to be made. If we all have the same information in front of us, then we can make notes on those sheets, combine all the notes, make the changes on the computer, generate new plates, hand them out to everybody, and that way we keep up with everything. You don't end up with everybody having his own set of plates with his own notes all scratched-out and unclear.

The stage manager would use his set to call the cues through the radio head sets?

I am not really sure exactly what the process is. They have position numbers and the stagehands know where they need to be for a particular position. The stage manager might say, "Tower 10 go to position 2," except that these are very complex moves and some of these pieces would run into each other if they all moved at the same time. Inside of each tower the operators have a 360-degree compass with a pivot point in the center where they drop a pin when they reach their position. There is a Velcro strip all the way around the inside of the compass with a little arrow that they stick on it. They preset that arrow so that when they get to their positions and drop their pins, they rotate that arrow to match the line that they just came in on. I think that is how it works. Each cue is broken down into numerous cues. Maybe Towers 9, 10, and 11 would move together first, and then the turntable would move, and then Towers 6 and 7 would move onto the turntable. It becomes a complex series of moves.

On some of these plates the line of movement reaches the edge of the turntable and seems to stop. In fact, elsewhere on the turntable it continues so that if the turntable is rotated into its next orientation, the line of movement will continue to the tower's ending position. What we were able to do on the computer screen was to rotate an entire scene backwards one position in order to mark the locations relative to that previous scene. Any units which stayed on the turntable during a change could be easily placed in their positions before rotation. The ability to overlay scenes and rotate or shift them as they will actually move enabled us to accurately construct starting and ending points for each unit, and probable paths of travel between them.

I think we are really just tapping the surface of what could be accomplished using the computer. It's a fantastic tool for manipulating visual information,

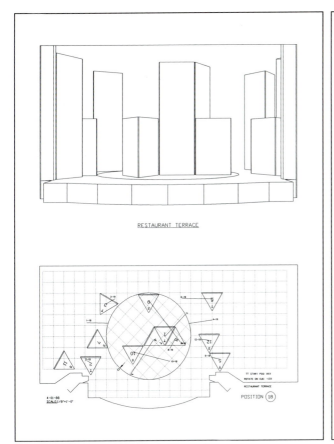

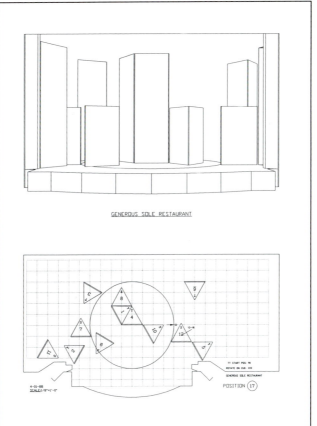

Computer drawings by Robert Chase for CHESS (1988), designed by Robin Wagner, Imperial Theatre, New York.

and essentially what we are doing for drafting and graphics is what word processing did for text editing. It is very easy to move things around and to answer "what if" questions: What if we put this here? What happens? If the turntable rotates only 180 degrees instead of 240 degrees, where does that leave us in terms of where the units need to move to get to the same positions that they would have ended in? In dealing with original designs it is very easy to set up a quick view of what the set will look like in 3-D.

Could you use a computer to great advantage on a three-set ground plan?

Yes. First of all, the full-scale plots that are generated on a plotter are extremely precise. The inked lines are very clear, the text lettering is very clear, and so for technical plates it is wonderful. We used a laser printer for output of drawings in this production because it is fast, quiet, and the 8½ × 11-inch format was appropriate for the application.

The other advantage in AutoCAD is that since you can scale a drawing either up or down and pick out elements of the set to deal with individually, you can coordinate all the different set

pieces and make sure they fit together. You can also break out the individual elements into their own drawings. It's very easy to highlight the elements that are necessary for one person to see in a drawing and to highlight different elements that another person might need to see in the same drawing. For instance, if your idea is to show a rendering of the set, you could change viewpoint, eliminate all of the construction lines and all of the text, and generate a very nice, hidden-line-removed, three-dimensional view. From the very same plate you could go to a plan view with all of the necessary construction information and send it to the shop and have them bid from that plate. So you are really taking a single source of basic visual information and manipulating it to meet whatever particular needs you have to meet for the carpenters on the floor of the shop or for producers who might want an idea of what the thing is to look like.

This can be done for any show. I have been working for two years doing production drawings for shops. There is no question that when you are dealing with construction drawings, it is far more accurate and easier to generate plates that are readable and contain correct information. The computer dimensions drawings automatically. If I have a drawing, I can pick the lower

left and right corners of the flat and the computer automatically puts the dimension in between those two corners set off at the right distance with the right text. It's wonderful! It eliminates the drudgery of drawing and frees you to think more about the layout of the plate, and to get the right information on the plate.

Basically, what you do is go into an empty plate the same as if you put a fresh piece of paper on the drafting table. Normally, we will plan ahead of time what size plate it is going to be. Is this going to be ½-inch scale, a C-size plate, or whatever? We have a set of drawings that have the border, title block, and the text fonts all set up in the computer in the right size for that particular plate. So when you go into the computer, you have an empty sheet that is formulated correctly for the size plate you are planning to draw. Then you go in and simply start drawing.

The way you draw is by using either a mouse or a digitizing tablet. You start at any point that you want to and you can either describe your lines by coordinates or draw them. For instance, I can say, "Go from this point to a point 10 feet straight up and then make a line 5 feet over and then come back down 10 feet and close the rectangle." The computer will automatically do that. When you get into the higher levels of what you can do with the program, I can go in and say, "Give me a flat that is 5 feet by 10 feet tall with toggles every 2 feet on center. Dimension and label it," and the computer automatically does that for me. So for generating construction plates it is fantastic.

These are programs that I have developed specific to theatre. Once the program is written, it is possible for anybody to sit down and type "flat" and then answer the questions prompted by the computer onto the screen, and it will draw a flat. The program is not that difficult to learn. Probably within about two months from start-up a person could effectively draft using AutoCAD. It is only when you really get into the more complex aspects of it that you begin to take full advantage of what it is possible to do with the computer.

What is exciting for me about designing with a computer is that it opens up an entirely different segment of theatre. Construction drawings and production drawings are pretty straightforward. You draw a plate once, dimension it correctly, lay it out nicely, spend a lot of time getting it that way, and that's the end of it. It goes out and gets blueprinted and it gets built. In the design studio, however, you're often dealing with a germinal concept that is constantly going through changes. So here we are taking advantage of another full aspect of what the computer program can do.

I am looking forward to finding what the needs of designers are so that the computer will help designers in the same way that the flat and header and crate programs help shops to make construction drawings. I think there are ways that we could expedite visualizing a design concept so that without too much computer training a designer could sit down at the computer and quickly see what a particular design would look like in a particular theatre. If I had all the Shubert theatres on the computer, we could take whatever design you have and say, "Will this work better in this theatre or that theatre?" or "What do we need to do with it to make it work differently in a different space?" This could be particularly helpful when planning the road show, for instance. It would be wonderful to be able to get the plans and sections of the different theatres that the road show is going to go into and be able to plan ahead of time exactly how you're going to alter the show for each space in order to make it fit and look the best. So I think the potential of computerized design and drafting for the theatre is fantastic.

What software are you using?

The program I'm using is called AutoCAD and CAD stands for computer-aided design and computer-aided drafting. Often you will see CAD and CAM, which is computer-aided design and computer-aided manufacturing. If you want to go one step further with this in the theatre, it is unbelievable what can be done. Right now there are sign shops and other production shops that connect the computer to a router for making signs. You simply type in the text font and the size and the text you want and send it off to the computer-controlled router and it cuts it for you. They also have milling machines that work with a computer to generate three-dimensional forms.

What is this going to do to old-fashioned manpower?

There is no chance that we are going to have an automated flat-building machine. But I think there are some designers who have a negative gut reaction to any kind of computer because it is seen as foreign and cold. The only thing one has to say to these people is that the computer is just another tool. It is like a drafting table, only it frees you from the less enjoyable aspects of drafting so that you really can explore without the time commitment and paper waste that goes on with hand drafting. For instance, one of the things that I think may prove to be quite valuable to scenic designers, now being used by architects, is the computer's ability to generate a perspective rendering. Often a design assistant will do the mechanical drawing of a rendering in perspective from a certain viewpoint and prepare it for the designer to watercolor. It is very easy to use the computer to generate that same wire-frame perspective and you can look at it on the screen and choose exactly the viewpoint that you think highlights the show exactly the way you want it to be seen. Then you can plot it out and apply the artistic overlay to that. With the computer you free yourself from the mundane mechanical processes and give yourself more freedom to explore artistic alternatives. I don't see it as a threat.

David Hersey, the lighting designer for *Chess*, is using an entirely different computer system for his light plots. He uses a computer-aided drafting system also, but on a MacIntosh computer. One of the things that I am working on developing right now with ArtSoft is a program that automates the paperwork associated with the light plot. The one thing that was still a nagging problem with the light plot CAD system is that you still have to extract all the information from the drawing and generate your own information sheet. One of the advantages of AutoCAD is that it is quite easy to embed lots of data associated with any particular block. For instance, each one of those towers that I drew for *Chess* has a number associated with it. It would be easy to assign that number in a way that would not be visible on the drawing but that would be easily abstracted into a data base program. You can assign each rotation in a particular cue, the name of the operator inside, and any other information that is useful or valid. That information can be abstracted automatically and put into a data base file such as D-base.

For *Chess* I generated an outline of all the scene changes, the arrow that the stage manager uses as a cue to start on, the beginning angle of the turntable, whether it's turned clockwise or counterclockwise, how far it turns, the arrow that it turns to, and then the cumulative number of turns that the turntable has made. The turntable has a limited number of turns. It can only turn two and one-half full turns, so we had to solve problems related to that. That is the kind of information you can generate automatically from a drawing by assigning different attributes to particular elements in the drawing.

Right now this kind of computer program is primarily being used by architects and contractors. For instance, an architect is able to take a sixty-story building and regenerate the ground plan for each floor very easily and duplicate anything that is the same on every floor. He can set the electrical on one layer, the plumbing on another layer, and the HVAC on a third layer. A set of plans is sent out to the plumbing contractor that has only the information he needs. Then if you want to see the whole picture, or if you want to see whether there is going to be a conflict with ventilation if the plumber changes the location of a pipe, it's very easy and fast to call up those layers and look at them to see if this pipe will interfere with that particular vent.

Applying that same kind of principle to the theatre would make it very easy to analyze the light plot on the same drawing as the set but on a different layer. It would be quite easy for us to see clearances of scenery as it flies up, or to find the best way to organize the scenery offstage when it moves into the wings. We can work with just those little blocks and move them around. If anything changes, you can change it immediately and not have to go back to the beginning to deal with it.

For *Chess* we had originally planned to do a plate for each scene that would have the ground plan with an elevation next to it. We could find a point in the theatre house and scan the ground plan to get an idea of what the set would look like in that scene, and print it on the same sheet. The computer could do that automatically. It's very easy to insert a line in a program that says, "Change to this viewpoint and freeze three layers." In one drawing I have frozen the text layers and the attributes so that you don't have numbers appearing on top of the towers, and I also removed the hidden lines. Those are all things that you can do very easily in a program. There is nothing difficult in laying out a large sheet. It's just a matter of dealing with the look that you want ultimately. When I plot out the whole show, I leave for two hours and when I come back, all fifty plates are sitting waiting for me.

You could have an endless number of different views.

Infinite. There are different ways you can choose these views, too. I can say, "I'm sitting 30 feet out and I'm 2 feet above the stage level and I'm straight-out center stage," and we can see that viewpoint; or "I want to be 15 degrees off-center looking at the stage from an angle of 15 degrees," and we can look at it that way. If we get the coordinates for the worst seat in the house, we can put those coordinates into the computer and see what the person sitting in that seat sees.

The part I really enjoy is knowing that if something fits in the drawing and it is built as specified, then it is going to fit on stage. I know that may not be a major problem, but it's great when you are dealing with a raked stage and sloped roofs on top of a forced perspective set. Working out those angles can be a nightmare on the drafting table. It's quite simple on the computer. You can go to 3-D and sight down the top of the flat and see the exact angle at which the roof passes over the top of that flat. You can specify that to the shop so that when they build it and put it together it is going to fit.

The computer would be helpful on working out all kinds of problems, like two gables coming together on a roof. You could work that out in a model, but the computer could do it faster.

It's especially valuable when you have pieces like that, where it is not just a roof line that is going to be perpendicular to the ground. You have an abstract forced perspective and you end up with compound miters and complex joints. It's just much easier to solve the problem on the computer. Normally we specify angles to the tenth of a degree. We don't go any closer than that because they don't cut any closer than that. For instance, it would be 1.1 or 2.9. It gives the builder the range that he is shooting for. On dimensions we usually specify with a sixteenth of an inch because tape measures go down to one-sixteenth of an inch.

Are you aware of the computer being used like this on any other stage design project?

As far as I know, aside from maybe some university theatres where there are students using the CAD systems or engineering majors who are involved in the theatre, I don't know of any other

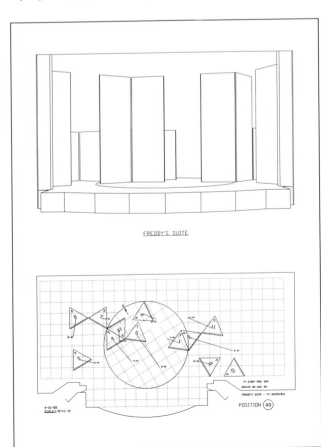

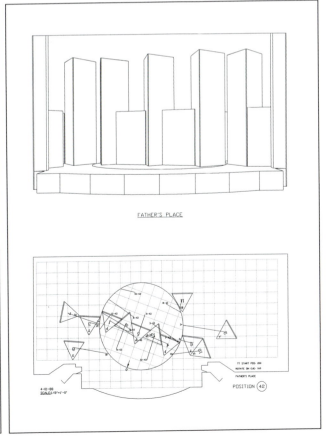

groups who are using CAD in the theatre right now. When you see how quickly it has caught on among architects and contractors and people who generate tremendous volumes of drawings, and as the cost of computer equipment continues to go down, and down, I think there is no question that it's going to be one of the tools that is used in the theatre. It will never replace the drafting table. We will always have drafting tables and there are certain things that are better accomplished on the drafting table. But it is a tool that has a place in the studio and it has a place in the production shop. My job is to show how it can be applied. I'm very excited about exploring new ways it can be used.

The things that seem to be the most important, from my recent experience here in theatre design, are (1) the ability to rapidly generate numerous plan views and quickly adopt changes into them, and (2) the ability to quickly generate axiometric views in order to get an idea of what a piece will actually look like.

There is always going to be room for a model, because the computer cannot replace your interacting with the model as you move around it. A model is always going to convey to people a better sense of the three-dimensional than looking at a computer screen will. Believe it or not, there are 3-D glasses you can plug into computers nowadays, but that's beyond the scope of practicality at this point. However, if you have an idea and you want to change something quickly in the "what if" situation, that can be accomplished very quickly and can be seen on the screen right away. You can quickly sketch something in plan view and

then see what it will look like in three-dimension. So in that sense, if you are in the very preliminary stages of a design and you want to show somebody something, to visualize it quickly, there is no question that the ability of the computer to just rotate it up to the third dimension is extremely valuable.

How would I go about doing something like drapery? I would still have to do it on the drawing board. Let's say I wanted to do a ½-inch scale drapery border with fringe, roping, swags, jabots, and whatever. Could I start from scratch on the computer to draw that?

You could, but I think that what you'd lose is the artistic sense that you would get from a rendering. I think the rendering is always going to be a part of the design. What we could do is the drawing that you are going to give to the shop, which is simply going to indicate that there is a drapery here and the basic size and the layout and how it is supposed to hang. But it's not worth it to get into shading and fringe and all that stuff on the computer, because it's not ever going to do it as well as you will do it by hand.

We could zoom in on a single tassel and draw it very carefully and all I would have to do is repeat that all along the length of that curtain. I could say, "Give me 500 in a row." It's not a question of my having to draw every single one over and over. If I wanted to, I could zoom in very tightly and draw every single strand in the tassel and then simply block it and place it along that curtain at evenly spaced marks, and the computer can do all that quite easily. But the question is, If it is for a drawing like that, then fine, we can do that. If it is for the kind of plan view

and shop drawings that I have been doing in the past, we would never bother to do that. We would simply indicate drape here, red velour, whatever weight it is, and indicate that there is a fringe made up and specify it and that would be the extent of our drafting involvement for that kind of plate. The advantage is that you can do it both ways.

BASIC BUDGETS

While the extravagant costs of commercial productions in the 1990's may imply that the budget for the physical production is exceptionally high for theatre, in general that is not the case. In some regional theatres you can still do a beautiful one-set show for $2,000, $3,000, or less, excluding labor. Granted, you may be asked to incor-

Model and settings by Elmon Webb and
Virginia Dancy
THE PLOUGH AND THE STARS by Sean
O'Casey
Directed by Peter Maloney
Lighting by Lee Watson
Syracuse Stage, Syracuse, New York (1977)
Photographs: Act 1-1; Act 1-2; Act 2-1;
Act 2-2.

"A turntable was used stage right because there
was no storage space for multiset changes.
Stage left had adequate storage space for wagons to be used."

—Elmon Webb and Virginia Dancy

porate some stock items, such as flats
and platforms, into the scenery, but
provided the stock pieces are not too
predominant to work with, that can often be a design challenge.

The idea of using stock pieces usually does not appeal to designers who
have been contracted to do only one
particular show, because it means getting descriptions and photographs or
seeing the items before working them
into the set. If, however, you are in residence, you can easily look at the possibilities of stock scenery, examine its
condition, and get all the appropriate
dimensions. Besides time, you may
also save money: a resident designer's
budget for scenery for a production
may be less than $2,000.

Having the director also in residence
usually makes working together on the
production much easier and simpler.
You can discuss ground plans and
such details as entrances, exits, fireplaces, and windows, and then do a

quick mock-up plan in the rehearsal
facility before putting a plan on paper.
In this space you can go over specifics
with a tape measure and mark them on
the floor to indicate to the director
what you have in mind for the scenery.
With most directors this is much easier
to do in the actual full-scale space than
to demonstrate in a ½-inch scale
model.

It is commonplace in the theatre that
almost any designer can create a sensational set with a lot of money. Most
producers willingly hire a talented and
resourceful designer who can make a
silk purse out of a sow's ear over one
who just wants to spend a lot of money.
It is not unusual for a designer to get
rave reviews for a production in which
the scenery was economical as well as
innovative.

The Sequence of Scenes and Scenic Units

For large multiset shows with plenty of
scenery, the scenic designer is expected to be completely knowledgeable regarding how all the scenery
moves and where it stores. While the
production carpenter can be of invaluable help, it is the designer who must
lead the way with fresh and original
ideas on how the show should move.
This also means that the designer's
ideas reflect collaboration with the
director.

A list showing the sequence of
scenes with the scenic units is a practical necessity. Having this list saves
an incredible amount of time for all
departments in the theatre proper by
showing everyone how the show runs,

Stage design by Franco Colavecchia
THE MAGIC FLUTE by Wolfgang Amadeus
Mozart
Directed by Christoph von Dohnányi
Blossom Theatre
Cleveland, Ohio (1985)
(Photograph by Emilio Bugallo)

212 from the top of Act 1 through each scene and act to the final curtain. This list tells the exact sequence in which each unit plays and how it gets on and off stage. For example, such a list begins with the house curtain in, followed by what is preset in the first scene, house curtain out, the scene plays and ends.

The list of the sequence of scenes with the scenic units is normally put together during a meeting of the director, the designer, the production stage manager, and the production carpenter. Such a list is also an invaluable aid in judging how many stagehands are needed to run the show and whether adjustments must be made to accom-

modate the number of crew, the amount of time needed, and the amount of storage space required. Since a few changes are usually necessary while a show is being put together, the sequence list must be updated and copies distributed to the entire stage crew by the production stage manager.

Sequence of Scenes and Scenic Units for
THE CRUCIFER OF BLOOD (1980), Ahmanson Theatre, Los Angeles, California

Scene 1
Agra

1. House curtain in.
2. Gate unit #6 (With #7 attached) in.
3. All black maskings in place (Except #50A and #51A).
4. House curtain out.
5. Scene plays and ends.

Scene 2
Baker Street

1. Fog show curtain #4 in. Black back-up drop #5 in. (Together, show curtain just slightly ahead).
2. Strike lanterns and chest.
3. Gate unit #6 out.
4. Upstage black panels, #45, #46, #47 out.
5. SR Baker Street unit #18 tracks on.
6. SL Baker Street unit #19 tracks on.
7. Baker Street flippers #9 and #10 on.
8. Get-off platform #21 in place.
9. Get-off platform #20 in place.
10. Upstage black panels #45, #46, #47 in.
11. Black back-up drop #5 out (Bleed through show curtain).
12. Fog show curtain #4 out.
13. Scene plays and ends in front of fog show curtain #4.
14. Fog show curtain #4 in. Black back-up drop #5 in. (Holmes, Irene and Watson finish scene DS of fog show curtain, exit SR.)

Scene 3
Pondicherry Lodge

1. Upstage black panels #45, #46, #47 out.
2. Flippers #9 and #10 off.
4. SL Baker Street unit #19 tracks off.
5. SR Baker Street unit #18 tracks off.
6. Pondicherry units #22, #23, #24 fly in. Set fireplace (SR).
7. Upstage black panels #45, #46, #47 in.
8. Attach Pondicherry window unit #25 to Pondicherry unit.

9. Black scrim #8 in.
10. Lightning box in.
11. Tree unit #25A in.
12. Set table and armchair (SR), screen (SL), wheelchair (C).
13. Scene plays and ends (Two parts to Scene 3).
14. Black back-up drop #5 in.

Second Part of Scene

1. Black back-up drop #5 out.
2. Scene plays and ends.
3. House curtain in.

Intermission
from Pondicherry to
Opium Den

1. Strike all Pondicherry scenery units and props.
2. SR Opium Den unit #26 tracks on.
3. SL Opium Den unit #28 tracks on.
4. Coffin unit #27A and coffin backing unit (Also #27A) on.
5. Opium Den escape stairs #31 on.
6. Opium Den wall #27 flies in.
7. Brazier set (SR).
8. Stool set (In arch).
9. Check position of police launch #35 (L stage starting position).
10. Pull two black travelers #50 and #51 DS, pull two black travelers #50A and #51A US (Ready for large boat to come DS).
11. Set two Opium Den bunks #32 and #33 UC.

Scene 4
Opium Den

1. House curtain out.
2. Scene plays and ends.
3. Pre-strike escape stairs #31 (Before scene has ended).
4. Black back-up drop #5 in.
5. Opium Den units #26 and #28 track off.
6. Coffin masking unit off.
7. Opium Den bunks #32 and #33 off.

8. Coffin unit #27A off.
9. Opium Den wall flies out.
10. Brazier off.
11. Stool off.

Scene 5
Boats

1. Smoke fills stage.
2. Black back-up drop #5 out.
3. Police launch #35 comes on L.
4. Black panel #46 (UC) out (And back in after boat comes on).
5. Large boat #34 tracks on.
6. Scene plays and ends.
7. Fog show curtain #4 in. Black back-up drop #5 in.
8. Black panel #46 (UC) out. (And back in after boat comes off).
9. Large boat #34 tracks off.
10. Police launch #35 off.

Scene 6
Baker Street

1. Black panels #45 and #47 out (Panel #46 also out).
2. SR Baker Street unit #18 tracks on.
3. SL Baker Street unit #19 tracks on.
4. Baker Street flipper #9 and #10 on.
5. Get-off platform #21 in place.
6. Get-off platform #20 in place.
7. Electrics plug up for practicals.
8. Black panels #45, #46, #47 in.
9. Black back-up drop #5 out (Bleed through scrim).
10. Fog show curtain #4 out.
11. Scene plays and ends.
12. Black back-up drop #5 in.

Curtain Calls
Empty Stage

1. Black panels #45, #46, #47 out.
2. Get-off platforms #20 and #21 off.
3. Baker Street flippers #9 and #10 off.
4. SL Baker Street unit #19 tracks off.
5. SR Baker Street unit #18 tracks off.
6. Black panels #45, #46, #47 in.
7. Black back-up drop #5 out.
8. House curtain in.

The Technical Analysis for the Execution of the Scenic Units

One of the best approaches to organizing all of the information for the various scenic units that are to be built and painted in the scenic studio is to make a detailed chart telling what is needed for each unit of scenery and what its function is. The effort this requires is considerable, but it pays off handsomely because the chart contains a wealth of information about the complete group of scenic units.

The chart may be typed with vertical and horizontal lines to form boxes, and it may be reduced on a copy machine in various parts, put together and recopied as a final. Copies are then given out to each person receiving a set of the printed drafting. The following headings should be printed across the top of the chart, with the information for the execution of the scenery below.

1. Number of the Scenic Unit
2. Size
3. Materials
4. Playing Position
5. Method of Change
6. Storage Position
7. Construction Data
8. Hardware
9. Painting Notes
10. Building Bid
11. Painting Bid

Designing Environments for Popular Music Groups

As a working scenic designer in the theatre, you may be asked to design the scenery for all types of productions. You may have been schooled in the art of designing drawing room sets for Restoration comedies and classical Shakespearean backgrounds, but there may come a time when you will create visual environments for musical groups.

This kind of setting can be a complete change of pace, a lot of fun, and very lucrative. In this type of production, the usual style is to have the visual aspects—props, lights, and scenery—move in rhythm or in counterpoint with the music and vibrations of the featured musical group.

The most successful musical groups appear in spaces with a vast seating capacity and a correspondingly vast stage area. This feature alone—working in such a large space—is inviting because it spurs you to imagine designs that can soar beyond the limits of the average proscenium stage production.

The event may take place in a concert hall, stadium, opera house, movie palace, amphitheatre, legitimate theatre, warehouse, gymnasium, sound stage, skating rink, or field. Naturally, the problems when the production is staged indoors are different than when it takes place outdoors. The designer must always be cognizant of the safety, durability, practicality, and cost of the design. For outdoor productions, additional attention must be given to such concerns as waterproofing and the electrical supply.

Designing a rock music production for the most successful groups means not only that the scale of the space and the size of the budget are good, but that there is an enormous imaginative range for all the design collaborations on the production. These include the scenic, lighting, and costume designers; the props, sound, and special effects designers; plus the musicians and other specialists.

Lights and Smoke as Scenery

Of all the visual elements used in a rock music show, perhaps the one the audience most looks forward to seeing is moving lights and smoke combined with the pulsating sounds of the musicians. This seems to have become a standard visual feature for rock music groups.

Metal light grids may move by turning, or may fly in and out with instruments, as lights of various colors go off and on and smoke fills the space from various and sundry locations. The lights and smoke can be synchronized with the music and the choreographed movements of the musicians in spectacular costumes. Since scenery for this type of production tends to be abstract and geometrical, the designer has enormous freedom.

Everyone involved in an event of this kind knows that many preliminary meetings are needed to bring all elements together to work as a unit. Fire laws at various locations must be researched, the position of all special effect items (including smoke) must be worked out, accommodations for the musicians' instruments and cases must be considered, as well as the location of sound speakers and equipment and any other specialty items.

Designs for musical group environments may incorporate one or more of the following: an arrangement of varied platform levels, ramps, runways into the audience, a raked stage, trusses and metal grids of flashing lights, hanging panels of interesting shapes and materials, metallic and mirrored surfaces, rain curtains, cutout overscale logos, unconventional backdrops, and hanging curtains.

SCENIC STUDIOS

Communicating with the Scenic Studio

Once the studio has been selected to build and paint the scenery for a production, it is up to the scenic designer to communicate and keep abreast of the schedule for building and painting it. This may mean a visit to the studio occasionally and in the last week almost daily. If the designer does not go to see how the shop is doing on a particular unit or group of scenic pieces and to approve it, then there is a chance the scenic artists or carpenters will have to revamp the scenery, and that is always costly and causes unpleasant feelings. The same studio will most likely also be doing the touring companies when a show is a big hit.

Going to visit the work in the scenic studio does take a chunk of time out of the designer's day, but that is the way the process works and there is no alternative. Most scenic studios are located some distance from the designer's place of work and take time to get to. The inconvenience is compounded when more than one studio is executing the scenery. One shop may do only building, another only painting, still another may be doing only upholstery and draperies. Of course, the execution process gets even more complicated when more than two shops do a show. This may be the case when time is short, in order to get the scenery done, or if the individual scenic units are bid separately and each goes to the lowest bidder. Some designers prefer to work with scenic shops where all the building and painting is done under one roof.

Actors Going to the Studio

Although detailed drawings and models of scenery and props are available to them, actors often need to make trips to the scenic studio to look at scenic items that they are going to be working with on stage. This is especially true when the stage business is directly related to the scenery and props.

Setting by Eldon Elder
A FAMILY AND A FORTUNE by Julian Mitchell
Adapted from the novel by Ivy Compton-Burnett
Directed by Duncan Ross
Costumes by Janet Christine Warren
Lighting by Richard Nelson
Seattle Repertory Theatre
Seattle, Washington (1974)
Settings/models: the Gaveston home, 1901.

"The play was adapted by Julian Mitchell from a turn-of-the-century English novel. Most of his scriptwriting had been for television; consequently, the play had scenes with no climaxes, transitions, or typical dramatic structure. For example, the play opened with a full English breakfast for eleven people, followed by a scene in the drawing room with high tea for thirteen people. The solution seemed to be to use a 40-foot-diameter revolve that was motor-driven and rotated in both directions. The stage deck was built around it, and it went all the way to the edge of the apron. It was 8 inches deep.

"All of the period structural scenic pieces were appropriate to the period and were fab-ricated from 1-inch square aluminum tubing. The false proscenium was also openwork and constructed of many materials in addition to the 1-inch tubing, such as plastic netting, industrial felt, polystyrene ornaments and flowers, all sprayed silver, and just about anything available to give it the right decorative look."
—Eldon Elder

Photographs, above: 1. & 2. Entrance hall setting and model. 3. & 4. Drawing room and model. 5. & 6. Dining room and model.

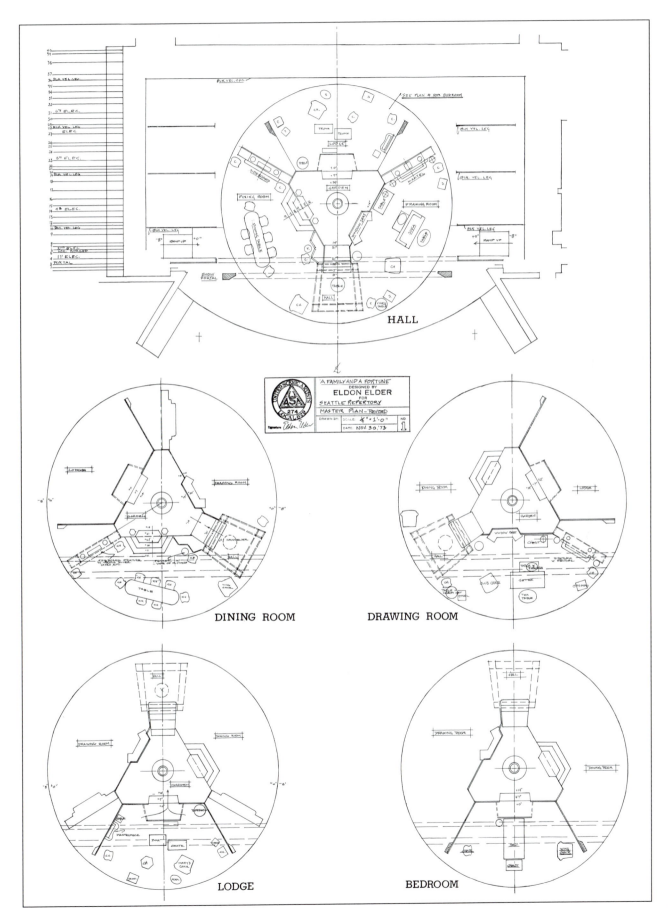

HALL

'A FAMILY AND A FORTUNE'
DESIGNED BY
ELDON ELDER
FOR
SEATTLE REPERTORY
MASTER PLAN—REVISED

DINING ROOM

DRAWING ROOM

LODGE

BEDROOM

David Jenkins' 28'-0"-Diameter Turntable with the Baker Street and Cellar Sets for SHERLOCK'S LAST CASE (1987), Nederlander Theatre, New York.

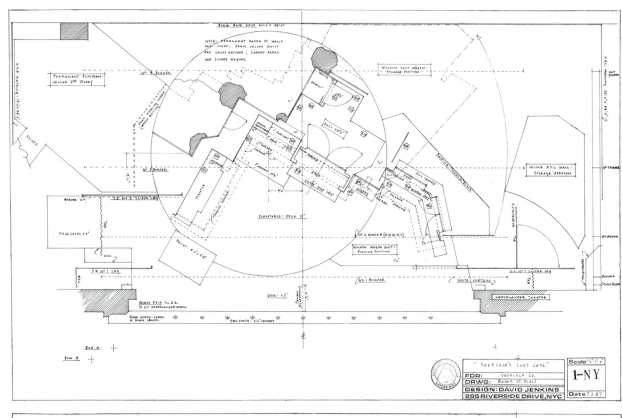

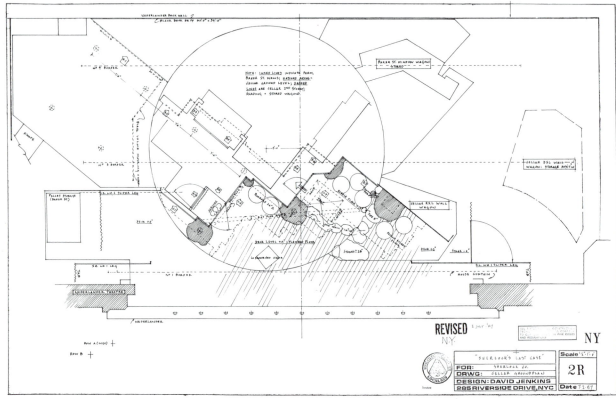

Ground Plans for Periaktoi

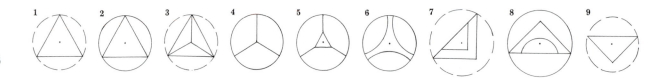

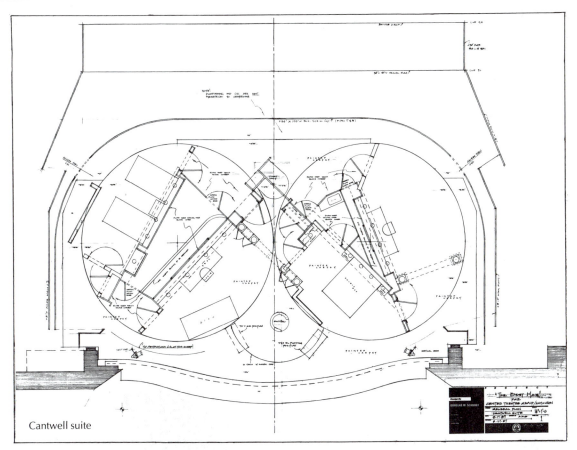

Cantwell suite

"I designed THE BEST MAN for the 1987 revival at the Ahmanson Theatre in Los Angeles. It employed a double turntable scheme (as did the original production) with all stage masking stripped away. All the scene changes took place in silhouette against a huge translucent American flag whose colors gradually decayed as the political corruption of the play revealed itself."

—Douglas W. Schmidt

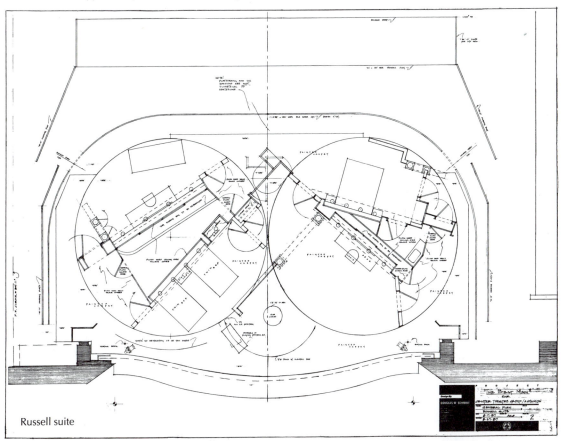

Russell suite

SEMMELWEISS is a drama in twenty scenes, of which plans are shown for twelve. The show deck was 2¼ inches high. The basic set was a curved surround, three castered platforms, and two periaktoi. The surround was 28'-0" high and had three large openings, and ten windows high above. The three large openings allowed the upstage platform and the L and R platforms to come onstage after masking panels flew out. The center platform was 7'-0" × 12'-0" × 6"; L and R were 6'-0" × 12'-0" × 6". The platforms had metal fins (or guides) that worked in ⅜-inch-wide tracks in the deck. The platforms were moved on and off by actors holding 1-inch pipe rails (2'-8" high) attached to the platforms. The pipe rails were like an inverted U shape (one on each end of the center platform, one on the offstage ends of the L and R platforms). The onstage and upstage corners of the L and R platforms had a single metal pole 2'-8" high. Furniture and props rode on the wagons. The two periaktoi were on tri-swivel casters and had pivot pins that worked in a track parallel to the proscenium opening. The two periaktoi were 18'-0" high, with two sides 8'-1" wide and one 11'-3½" wide. There were two windows in each of these units. These were located high above in one of the 8'-1" sides. The actors also turned and moved these units. Curved benches moved around in a circular direction.

Stage design by José Varona
CINDERELLA by Prokofiev

Choreographed by Valery Panov
Berlin Deutsche Oper (1976)

Schematic drawing by David Mitchell
I REMEMBER MAMA
Directed by Cy Feuer
Majestic Theatre, New York (1979)

"It is a large turntable with a smaller turntable off-center that carries the house structure.

There are two furniture pallets (shown by arrows) that nest within the house structure on the smaller turntable. They move by electric winches concealed within the staircase. The house and furniture could assume a nesting position upstage, allowing other scenes to play downstage: a hospital, a farm interior, and a

hotel. When the house was revealed upstage, the correct speed in its counterrevolution to the large table made it move toward the audience in a constant relationship, and the furniture pallets expanding outward to the ends of the smaller table enhanced the effect of this house movement downstage." —David Mitchell

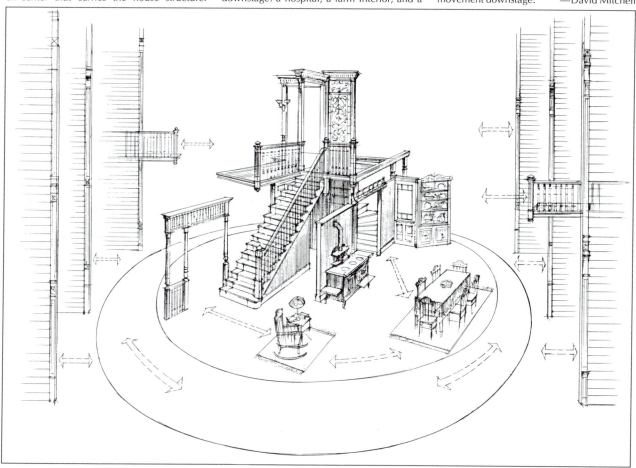

Scenery by John Wulp for THE CRUCIFER OF BLOOD (1978); Scenery Supervised by Lynn Pecktal;
Costumes by Ann Roth; Lighting by Roger Morgan; Directed by Paul Giovanni

THE CRUCIFER OF BLOOD was a good example of a multiset production with basic scenery that worked for all scenes: a 2¼-inch deck both onstage and offstage; three portals; and various soft black masking items—a drop upstage, legs on the offstage edges of the portal legs (or middle of the legs), borders above, and pieces in front of and on the sides of certain scenic units. The scenery for individual scenes moved on and off in several ways: 1. The scrim show curtain and black backup drop flew in and out upstage of portal 1. 2. The framed gate hanger flew in and out upstage of portal 3. 3. The two Baker Street units (forming one when in place) moved on and off by winches (see the two diagonal tracks on the ground plan) under the openings in portals 2 and 3. 4. Three Pondicherry Lodge framed hangers flew in and out (one between portals 1 and 2, two between portals 2 and 3); the castered window unit and pollard lime tree were pushed on and off by stagehands; the scrim drop upstage of the window and the lightning box upstage of the scrim both flew in and out. The fireplace unit was carried on and off by stagehands. 5. The downstage left and right opium den wagon units between portals 1 and 2 moved off and on manually (two tracks parallel to the apron). The main opium den wall was a framed hanger with openings. It hung downstage of portal 2 and flew in and out. The coffin unit and its backing unit on casters were pushed on and off by stagehands, as were the stage left carry-off stairs and the two bunk units upstage of the main opium wall opening. 6. Actors rode in and operated the police launch. The large center boat moved downstage and upstage by winch (track parallel to the center line). 7. Various other pieces of furniture and props were carried on and off by actors and stagehands. *Photographs:* 1. Baker Street. 2. Opium den. 3. Boat. 4. Pondicherry Lodge. (Photographs © Martha Swope) (Glenn Close and cast)

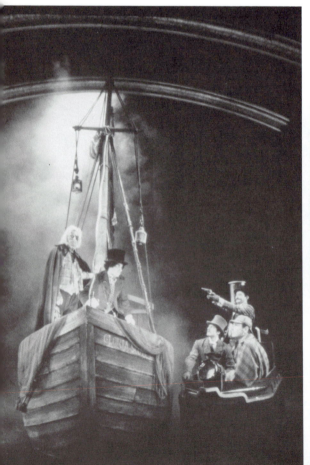

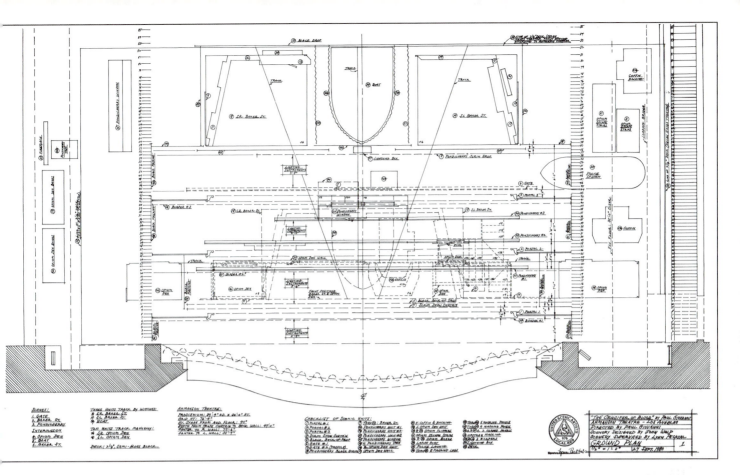

Above: Ground plan for THE CRUCIFER OF BLOOD (1980) at the Ahmanson Theatre in Los Angeles. *Right:* Section drawing looking from center of the stage to stage right shows both hanging scenery and scenery on the floor. The same ground plan was used for the original production at the Helen Hayes Theatre (now demolished) in New York (1978). After the Broadway production ended, the scenery was shipped to Los Angeles. The original plan was also adapted to fit the raked stage at the Haymarket Theatre in London (1979). *Below:* The flattened-out view of the opium den coffin indicating positions of the three-dimensional carved dragons. (Drawings by Lynn Pecktal)

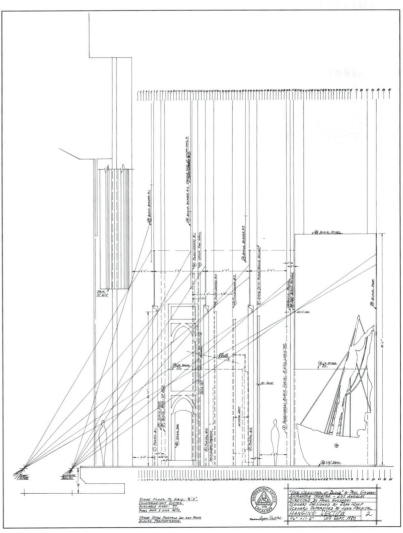

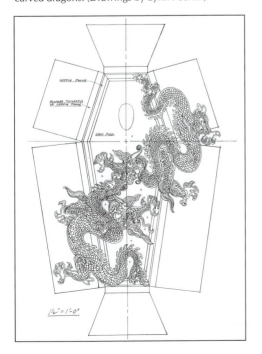

Scenery Designed by Edward Gorey for DRACULA (1977); Scenery Supervised by Lynn Pecktal; Lighting Designed by Roger Morgan; Directed by Dennis Rosa

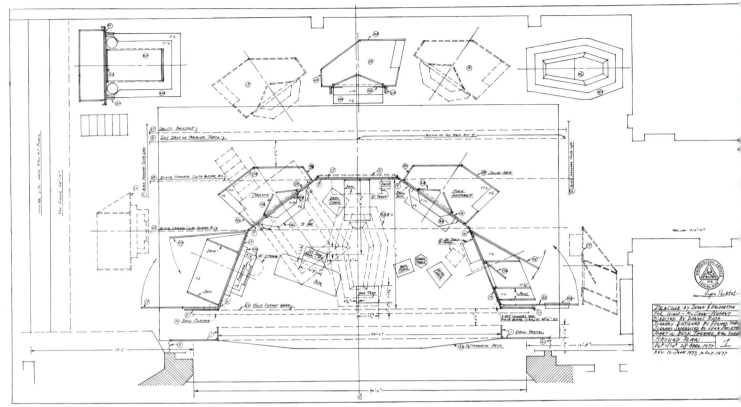

Above: Ground plan, Martin Beck Theatre, New York. *Below:* A vault. *Opposite:* The library and Lucy's boudoir. (Photographs © Martha Swope)

222

The Technical Analysis for the Execution of Scenic Units for DRACULA (1977),
Martin Beck Theatre, New York

NO.	UNIT	SIZE	MATERIALS	PLAYING POSITION	METHOD OF CHANGE	STORAGE POSITION
1.	Show Portal	Opening: 34'-0" W 22'-0" H Overall: 45'-6" W 30'-0" H Reveal: 1'-6"	Canvas on wooden frame. ⅛" ply on reveal (1'-6") all three sides	DS (1'-6" from smoke pocket)	None	None
2.	Black Granada Leg	3'-0" W (or one width) × 30'-0" H	Black Granada Cloth	DS masking (L of Show Portal)	None	None
3.	Black Granada Leg	3'-0" W (or one width) × 30'-0" H	Black Granada Cloth	DS masking (R of Show Portal)	None	None
4.	Show Curtain	40'-0" W × 25'-0" H	Muslin with seams	DS (US of Show Portal)	Flies	Hangs in flies

BASIC SET FOR ALL THREE ACTS—DOES NOT MOVE

NO.	UNIT	SIZE	MATERIALS	PLAYING POSITION	METHOD OF CHANGE	STORAGE POSITION
5.	Right Return	4'-0" W × 30'-0" H × 1⅜" thick	Canvas on ⅛" ply	DR	None	None
6.	Arch Flat #1	10'-0" W × 30'-0" H × 1⅜" thick. Opening: 8'-6" W × 20'-0" H	Canvas on ⅛" ply	DR	None	None
7.	Arch Flat #2	10'-0" W × 30'-0" H × 1⅜" thick. Opening: 8'-6" W × 20'-0" H	Canvas on ⅛" ply	UR	None	None
8.	Arch Flat #3	10'-0" W × 30'-0" H × 1⅜" thick. Opening: 8'-6" W × 20'-0" H	Canvas on ⅛" ply	Center	None	None
9.	Arch Flat #4	10'-0" W × 30'-0" H × 1⅜" thick. Opening: 8'-6" W × 20'-0" H	Canvas on ⅛" ply	UL	None	None
10.	Arch Flat #5	10'-0" W × 30'-0" H × 1⅜" thick. Opening: 8'-6" W × 20'-0" H	Canvas on ⅛" ply	DL	None	None
11.	Left Return	4'-0" W × 30'-0" H × 1⅜" thick	Canvas on ⅛" ply	DL	None	None
12.	Truss Support	42'-0" L × 2'-6" W	1⅛" × 3" wooden framing	DS above basic set	None	None

ACTS I & III-1—LIBRARY: PLUGS & UNITS BEHIND OR IN FRONT OF ARCHES

NO.	UNIT	SIZE	MATERIALS	PLAYING POSITION	METHOD OF CHANGE	STORAGE POSITION
13.	Fireplace Flat (Arch #1)	9'-0" W × 21'-0" H	Canvas on ⅛" ply	DR	6" H wagon on swivel casters	DSR
13a.	Fireplace & Fire Seat Unit	Base of seat: 5'-0" W × 2'-2" D × 4'-4" H (Top: 5'-0" W × 10" D)	Canvas and wood	DR against Fireplace Flat	On swivel casters attached to 13	DSR
14.	French Door Unit (Arch #2)	9'-0" W × 21'-0" H	Canvas on ⅛" ply	UR	Wagon on swivel casters	USR
14a.	French Doors and Overdoor Unit	7'-0" W × 12'-0" H Face: 1" thick. Total: 4" from face to back of doors. Doors: 2'-6" W × 9'-0" H × 1" thick.	Doors: ¾" & ¼" ply with galvanized screening between	UR	Wagon on swivel casters	USR
14b.	Draperies	Approx. 5'-0" W × 9'-0" L (two panels) 100% fullness	Shantung	UR	Wagon on swivel casters	USR

CONSTRUCTION DATA	HARDWARE & OTHER DATA	PAINTING
Provide Stiffeners.	Top: Hardware for hanging. Bottom: Hardware for holding in place.	Details on face (3'-3") and reveal (1'-6") with sides and top going to black. Black flameproofing on back.
Top: Webbing, grommets, tie lines. Bottom: Pocket for chain.	Top: 1'-6" long pipe batten (1¼" I.D.) Bottom: Chain.	None
Top: Webbing, grommets, tie lines. Bottom: Pocket for chain.	Top: 1'-6" long pipe batten (1¼" I.D.) Bottom: Chain.	None
Muslin with seams. Top: Sandwich batten for rolling. Bottom: Skirt & canvas pocket for ¾" I.D. pipe. Sides: No hem.	Mark center line. Top: Sandwich batten 40'-0" L. Loose wooden batten 40'-0" L to roll drop for traveling.	Details on face.
Use actual sketches to draw pounces. Hinge to Arch Flat #1. Bevel onstage edge.	Top: Attach Truss Support. Bottom: Two floor hinges.	Details on face going to black on outer edge (See broken line on drawing.). Black on back.
Unit has 2 breaks & ½" bat appliqué. Provide Stiffeners. Countersink all pin hinges on face. Bevel DS edge.	Top: Hardware for hanging. Bottom: Floor hinges. Heavy strap hinges on flats for all breaks.	Details on face. Black on back.
Countersink all pin hinges on face. Unit has 2 breaks & ½" bat appliqué. Provide Stiffeners. Pin hinge to adjacent Arches.	Top: Hardware for hanging. Bottom: Floor hinges. Heavy strap hinges on flats for all breaks.	Details on face. Black on back.
Countersink all pin hinges on face. Unit has 2 breaks & ½" bat appliqué. Provide Stiffeners. Pin hinge to adjacent Arches.	Top: Hardware for hanging. Bottom: Floor hinges. Heavy strap hinges on flats for all breaks.	Details on face. Black on back.
Countersink all pin hinges on face. Unit has 2 breaks & ½" bat appliqué. Provide Stiffeners. Pin hinge to adjacent Arches.	Top: Hardware for hanging. Bottom: Floor hinges. Heavy strap hinges on flats for all breaks.	Details on face. Black on back.
Countersink all pin hinges on face. Unit has 2 breaks & ½" bat appliqué. Provide Stiffeners. Pin hinge to adjacent Arch & DL Return. Bevel DS edge.	Top: Hardware for hanging. Bottom: Floor hinges. Heavy strap hinges on flats for all breaks.	Details on face. Black on back.
Hinge to Arch #5. Bevel onstage edge.	Top: Attach Truss Support. Bottom: Two floor hinges.	Details on face going to black on outer edge (See broken line on dwg.). Black on back.
Overhead support for Arches extending to offstage edges of Returns.	Provide Stiffeners and appropriate hardware.	Flameproof black.
Provide hardware and equipment to hold unit firmly against Arch #1.		Details on face. Black flameproof on back.
1'-6" H Fire Seat for sitting. Finish top of seat to simulate shape of upholstered unit.		Details on face. Black on back.
Flat bolts to Platform #14c.		
1½" dia. × 6'-0" L wooden drapery rod with supports on face. Finials on rod, rings, & door knobs to be selected. Doors open US. Mullions 1½" wide. Routed on face.	Bolt Door Unit to Flat.	Details on face. Black galvanized screening. Black on back.
Hem all four sides (2" top, 2" sides, 4" bottom). Grommets to attach to rings.	Black rings 2" I.D. Number of rings to be specified.	Details on face.

NO.	UNIT	SIZE	MATERIALS	PLAYING POSITION	METHOD OF CHANGE	STORAGE POSITION
14c.	Platform & Step Unit	Approx. 7'-6" D × 10'-0" W	Canvas on wood	UR	Wagon on swivel casters	USR
14d.	SR Balustrade Unit	3'-0" H (4'-0" overall) × 13'-0" L (three-fold)	Canvas on ¾" ply	UR	Wagon on swivel casters	USR
14e.	Foliage & Jack for support	2'-0" W × 11'-6" H	Canvas on ¼" ply plus Jack	UR	Wagon on swivel casters	USR
15.	Center Bookcase Unit (Arch #3)	9'-0" W × 21'-0" H	Canvas on ⅛" ply	UC	Flies in vertical track	Hangs in flies
16.	Double Door Unit (Arch #4) Main Entrance	9'-0" W × 21'-0" H	Canvas on ⅛" ply	UL	Wagon on swivel casters	USL
16a.	Double Doors & Overdoor Unit	Same as 14a with Solid Doors: 2'-6" W × 9'-0" H × 1" thick	Canvas on wood	UL	Wagon on swivel casters	USL
16b.	Platform & Step Unit	Reverse of 14c	Canvas on wood	UL	Wagon on swivel casters	USL
16c.	Panel Backing	12'-0" W × 12'-0" H	Canvas on ⅛" ply	UL	Wagon on swivel casters	USL
16d.	Ceiling Piece	Approx. 10'-6" L × 5'-6" W	Canvas on ⅛" ply	UL	Wagon on swivel casters	DSL
17.	Study Door Unit (Arch #5)	9'-0" W × 21'-0" H	Canvas on ⅛" ply	DL	6" H wagon on swivel casters	DSL
17a.	Door Unit for 17	Overall: 5'-0" W × 7'-9" H Door: 3'-0" W × 7'-3" H	Canvas on ¾" ply	DL	6" H wagon on swivel casters	DSL
18.	Sky Backdrop	25'-0" W × 25'-0" H	Muslin with seams on wooden battens & stiles	US	Moves on traveler track & also flies	Hangs in flies

ACT II—LUCY'S BEDROOM: PLUGS & UNITS BEHIND OR IN FRONT OF ARCHES

NO.	UNIT	SIZE	MATERIALS	PLAYING POSITION	METHOD OF CHANGE	STORAGE POSITION
19.	SR Bedroom Door Flat	9'-0" W × 21'-0" H	Canvas on ⅛" ply	DR	Hinges DS to Arch #1	DSR
20.	Bed Flat	9'-0" W × 21'-0" H	Canvas on ⅛" ply	UR	Wagon on swivel casters	USR
20a.	Bed & Platform Unit w/Draperies, Cherubs & Mattress	7'-6" W × 9'-0" L × 2'-6" H (Plus Flat & Stiffeners)	Canvas on ⅛" ply	UR	Moves with Bed Unit	USR
20b.	Curtains behind Bed	Approx. 14'-0" W × 17'-6" H	White Chiffon	UR	Moves with Bed Unit	USR
20c.	Drapery for Bed Canopy	Approx. 8'-0" W × 17'-6" H	White Chiffon	Over Bed	Moves with Bed Unit	USR
20d.	White Bedspread	Approx. 7'-10" W × 10'-3" L	White Satin	Bed	Moves with Bed Unit	USR
21.	Center Bedroom Flat	9'-0" W × 21'-0" H	Canvas on ⅛" ply	Center	Flies in & out	Hangs in flies
22.	French Door Bedroom Flat with Windows	Flat: 9'-0" W × 21'-0" H. Doors: 3'-0" W × 7'-0" H	Canvas on ⅛" ply	UL	Wagon on swivel casters	USL
22a.	Platform & Step Unit	Approx. 7'-6" D × 10'-0" W	Canvas on wood	UL	Moves with French Doors	USL
22b.	SL Balustrade Unit	3'-0" H × 12'-0" L (three fold)	Canvas on ¾" ply	UL	Moves with French Doors	USL
22c.	Profile Foliage & Jack for support	5'-0" W × 17'-0" H (part of 22b)	Canvas on ¼" ply plus Jack	UL	Moves with French Doors	USL
22d.	French Door Curtains (Unit 22)	7'-0" H × 6'-0" W	White Chiffon	UL	Moves with French Doors	USL

CONSTRUCTION DATA	HARDWARE & OTHER DATA	PAINTING
Provide Celotex panels under floor to deaden sound.		Details on step facing & tops. 2'-0" edge of platform top going to black on offstage edges. Black flameproofing.
Attaches to Platform #14c. Reinforce with metal or wood for actor to jump over.	Cutout unit	Details on face. Black on back.
Jack unit to support Flat #14.	Provide appropriate hardware.	Details on face. Black on back.
Provide vertical track US of Arch #3 for unit to fly in and out for changes.	Extend width of unit sufficiently to allow Flat #21 to fly in and lash in place for Act II.	Details on face. Black on back.
Bolts to Platform #16b	Canvas bell pull 7'-4" L × 4" W attaches to face (SR side).	Details on face. Black on back.
Doors open US.		Details on face. Black on back.
Provide Celotex panels under floors to deaden sound		Same as #14c.
Three-fold unit bolts to Platform #16b.		Details on face. Black on back.
Pin hinges to #16 & #16c.		
Unit rides on 6" H wagon. Flat #25 used for door masking behind. Provide hardware & equipment to hold unit in place.	Provide hardware to hold unit to Arch #5. Liquor cabinet (2'-6" W × 3'-6" H × 1'-6" D) bolts to face & travels with unit.	Details on face. Black on back.
Provide doorknob & latch. Hinges US and off.		Details on face. Black on back.
Wooden battens at top and bottom. Stretcher frame with ceiling plates. Bracing on two upper corners with middle stile.		Sprayed sky on face.

CONSTRUCTION DATA	HARDWARE & OTHER DATA	PAINTING
Secret Door flush with wall on front. Door hinges US and opens off.		Details on face. Black on back.
Braced with bed. Stiffeners on back. Metal braces (Jacks) in front under draperies.		Details on face. Black on back.
Metal frame for bed canopy (1", 1/2" rods with forming cloth). Small tables ride with unit.		Details on Platforms. Sprayed fabric.
Bottom: 4" hem. Attaches to Flat #20.		Fabric sprayed down.
Attaches to metal framework of 1" dia. & 1/2" dia. metal rods.	Three purchased bat cherubs: 2'-0" L (tall) attach on unit. Two tie-backs: 7" dia. skulls.	Fabric sprayed down.
White bolster: 1'-0" dia. × 3'-10" L with 2 tassels (12" L) in center of each end.	Line Bedspread with white sateen.	None
Platform with Jacks & Stiffeners.		Details on face. Black on back.
Doors open US. Mullions 1 1/2" wide. Routed on face.		Details on face. Black on back.
Provide Celotex panels under floor to deaden sound.		Same as 14c.
Attaches to Platform #22a. Reinforce with metal or wood for actor to jump over.		Details on face. Black on back.
		Details on face. Black on back.
Top: 2" hem. Bottom: 4" hem.	White rings: 2 1/2" dia.	Fabric sprayed down.

NO.	UNIT	SIZE	MATERIALS	PLAYING POSITION	METHOD OF CHANGE	STORAGE POSITION
22e.	Drapery for over French Windows	Approx. 7'-0" W × 17'-0" H	White Chiffon	UL	Moves with French Doors	USL
23	DL Bedroom Unit with Secret Door	Flat: 9'-0" W × 21'-0" H Door: 2'-6" W × 6'-6" H	Canvas on ⅛" ply	DL	Hinges DS to Arch #5	DSL
23a.	Mirror	3'-0" W × 5'-7" H × ¾" thick	¾" ply with edges routed	DL	Moves with 23	DSL

ACT III-2—VAULTS: PLUGS & UNITS BEHIND OR IN FRONT OF ARCHES

NO.	UNIT	SIZE	MATERIALS	PLAYING POSITION	METHOD OF CHANGE	STORAGE POSITION
24.	DR Stone Wall (Arch #1)	9'-0" W × 21'-0" H	Canvas on ⅛" ply	DR	Hinges US to Arch #1	DSR
25.	DL Stone Wall (Arch #5)	9'-0" W × 21'-0" H	Canvas on ⅛" ply	DL	Hinges US to Arch #5	DSL
26.	Coffin	3'-9" W × 7'-9" L × 2'-8" H	Canvas on wood	DC	Platform on swivel casters	Off L
26a.	Platform for Coffin	7'-3" W × 11'-4" L × 1'-6" H	Canvas on wood	DC	Platform on swivel casters	Off L
27.	Vaults Backdrop	31'-0" H × 50'-0" W	Muslin with seams	US	Flies	Hangs in flies

ALL ACTS: SCENIC UNITS & EQUIPMENT

NO.	UNIT	SIZE	MATERIALS	PLAYING POSITION	METHOD OF CHANGE	STORAGE POSITION
28.	Black Granada Masking Border #1	10'-0" H × 50'-0" W	Black Granada Cloth	Midstage	None	Hangs in flies
29.	Black Granada Masking Border #2	13'-0" H × 50'-0" W	Black Granada Cloth	US	None	Hangs in flies
30.	SL Black Granada Leg	8'-6" W (or two widths) × 30'-0" H	Black Granada Cloth	UL	Flies for scenery changes	Hangs from flies
31.	SR Black Granada Leg	8'-6" W (or two widths) × 30'-0" H	Black Granada Cloth	UR	Flies for scenery changes	Hangs from flies
32.	Painted Masonite Deck	28'-0" D × 48'-0" W Total of 42 sheets	¼" Masonite sheets	Full on-stage area	None	None

For example, when *Dracula* (1977) was in production, Frank Langella (who played the title role) was driven to Metro Scenic Studios in Queen's Village, New York, to try out the mechanics of the coffin he would work with in the final scene of the play. Although the coffin was designed and drawn up according to his over-6-foot height, it was important that he be at ease in using it on stage. When Langella climbed into the slanted coffin, the carpenters were able to position the bottom inside block for his feet to rest on and to see where to place the metal handle inside the coffin for his convenience. Any other adjustments were worked out before the scenery and props arrived at the Martin Beck Theatre, thus saving time and labor costs.

For the play *Harold and Maude* (1980), also at the Martin Beck, actress Janet Gaynor, playing the eighty-year-old Maude, had to climb up the back of a tall pine tree during the first scene. The seventy-three-year-old actress motored to Theatre Techniques in Newburgh, New York, to see the tree and to climb up a ladder built into the back of the tree trunk. The limb she would sit on was 7'-3" off the stage floor. During the first attempts at climbing up and down the tree ladder, it was decided by the director Robert Lewis and colleagues that a mechanical lift (small elevator) should be installed to accommodate the business of getting the actress safely and speedily up to the tree limb. This made the actual scene work better onstage and everyone ended up pleased.

Designers in the Scenic Studio

It was my pleasure to work with Oliver Messel (1905–1978) at Nolan Scenery Studios on his last production in 1976. Nolan's was where his scenery for *The Sleeping Beauty* ballet at the Metropolitan Opera was being executed. At that time, the scenic studio was still involved with both building and painting scenery. Arnold Abramson assigned me to assist Messel whenever he visited the studio. To Messel, the studio experience was sheer delight. He loved creating his designs while being with other creative people.

Like Eugene Berman, Messel possessed old-world charm, great style, and a highly individual character. In his impeccable courtesy he was unrivaled by most of his colleagues. He never demanded that something be done. When he asked for a favor, he did so with a gentle, respectful manner that is seldom seen in the theatrical world anymore. Consequently, he got remarkable results from scenic artists and carpenters alike. His pleasant disposition automatically made others want to do things for him.

CONSTRUCTION DATA	HARDWARE & OTHER DATA	PAINTING
Bottom: 4" hem.	Attaches to metal framework. 2'-0" bat cherub at top. Two tie-backs: 7" dia. skulls.	Fabric sprayed down.
Door hinges US. Opens off. Secret Door flush.		Details on face. Black on back.
Mirror rides with Flat #23. Bottom center panel of mirror (glass) is broken during play, each performance.	Provide real glass for breaking; Plexiglas for remaining panels.	Frame painted white with black galvanized screening behind the frame in front of mirror.
Hinges to US of Arch #1. Unit used as bedroom door masking in Act II.		Details on face. Black on back.
Hinges to US of Arch #5. Unit used as library door masking and bedroom door, masking.		Details on face. Black on back.
Top (head) section lifts off (2" thick). The coffin requires special effects.	Lining inside coffin to be selected.	Details on face.
Risers: 9" H	Swivel casters.	Details on face. Black underneath.
Muslin with seams. Top: Sandwich batten for rolling drop. Bottom: Skirt & canvas pocket for ¾" I.D. pipe.	No hems on sides. Loose wooden batten for travel.	Details on face.
Top: Tie lines. Bottom: Hem for ½" I.D. pipe. No fullness.	Trim at 30'-0"	None
Top: Tie lines. Bottom: Hem with chain. No fullness.		None
Top: Tie lines. Bottom: Hem for ½" I.D. pipe. No fullness.	Trim at 30'-0"	None
Top: Tie lines. Bottom: Hem with chain. No fullness		None
Mark ¼" Masonite sheets according to drawing. Paint tops of screws black before putting into Masonite sheets.	Two practical trap doors: one downstage center & one behind sofa.	Stones painted on full stage area going 2'-0" US of Arches, then random stones and into black.

While surveying his scenery as it was being built, he might ask, "How is this coming along? Should we change that some?" In addition, he delighted in sketching statues and ornament in full scale with charcoal sticks on tracing paper for the carpenters and scenic artists to use. Arnold Abramson, chargeman at Nolan Scenery Studios, allowed designers Messel and Berman the privilege of working on their own scenery in a union shop by having scenic artists (employed by Nolan's) standing by for them. This was a special courtesy extended to the greatly respected artists Messel and Berman. One day before leaving the studio he asked if he could have some paper and glue to take back to his hotel so he could make a mask for a chariot. The next day he appeared with a beautifully sculptured mask that he had put together with these simple materials just a few hours earlier.

It was also my good fortune to assist Eugene Berman (1899–1972) when he was in New York to design sets and costumes for New York City Ballet's *Pulcinella* (1972) during the Stravinsky Festival at Lincoln Center. Berman would arrive with a driver at Nolan's in the morning, then in the afternoon he would be taken to Karinska's to oversee the execution of his costumes. In the scenic studio, once Berman got his paints and sketch papers out on the table, there was no time for anything but the work at hand. During the preparation of the scenery for *Pulcinella*, it was agreed that some three-dimensional, full-scale mock-ups of the rolling wagons would be devised so that choreographers Jerome Robbins and George Balanchine could see the actual size and try them out when they visited the scenic studio.

Like Messel, Berman enjoyed creating on the spot when he came to the studio. I soon learned that he wanted finished layouts with dimensions handed directly to him without hesitation or discussion so he could proceed with sketching and painting the details on them. Berman preferred to make multiple sketches, to try numerous possibilities in order to arrive at the most appropriate design. Only after finishing a pile of sketches did he want to discuss his creations in some detail: "Which one is best? Which do you prefer? Don't hesitate to tell me. I am not going to bite your head off," he would plead.

For the *Pulcinella* show curtain, I did manage to say, with a great deal of reluctance, "Why don't you put in some of those famous Berman curtains?" And I was totally flabbergasted when he went to work and did just that. Once again, proof that the greatest designers in the theatre are usually the most humble.

1. DRACULA show curtain being painted on the floor at Nolan Scenery Studios in Brooklyn. The drop was made of muslin with horizontal seams and was painted with waterbase paints. *Pictured:* Robert Motley. After the show became a hit, the show curtain for the national companies and others was made of filled scrim. This material packed and traveled well and allowed any wrinkles to easily stretch out.

2. Overscale tassels and bat cherubs on the Gorey show curtain.

3. The show curtain on the paint frame at the Victor Mara Studio in London.

4. Flats (to go behind the five arches) were laid out horizontally so the detailed painting could be finished and given a transparent gray "bath" of aniline dye, applied with a Hudson spray tank.

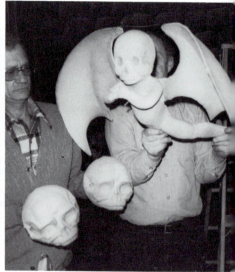

5. & 6. Toy dolls were used to create the bodies for the four three-dimensional bat cherubs over the bed canopy and French door canopy in Lucy's boudoir. Wooden blocks were positioned inside the plastic dolls with extended metal pieces to fasten to the metal framework of the two canopies. Skulls from novelty shops were placed on the dolls for heads. The original bat cherub wings were made with coat hanger wire, newspaper, and wheat paste. These later were created with stronger and more durable materials.

7. Painted profile balustrade unit behind the library terrace.

8. Library radio with the pedestal holding it. The pedestal was painted to appear as marble.

9. Bat balustrade unit behind the bedroom terrace.

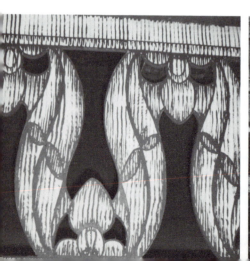

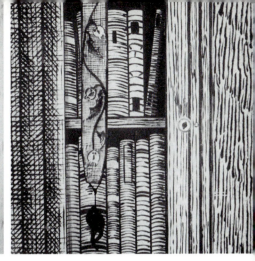

1. Library door panel detail with painted black lines on a white background without any actual three-dimensional molding.
2. Original bedroom fans shown on the center flying panel behind arch no. 3 were painted by Gorey himself. For additional companies of the show, the fans were drawn and painted directly on the flat with bat wallpaper. The bedroom wallpaper was applied by using stencils.
3. The painted library bellpull with a black figure on the bottom. The photograph also shows the different brushwork and details on the column at left, the books, and the door woodwork.
4. The stone floor patterns being touched up by painters at the Shaftesbury Theatre in London.
5. The stage right side of the vault backdrop showing column base, skeleton, and stones. Much of the original line work on

the stones was done at one time with several lining brushes. Three or four lining brushes were clamped together in a straight line with two pieces of thin wood so multiple painted lines could be made with one stroke after the lining brushes were dipped in black paint.
6. The first wing chair for the library set was purchased at the William Doyle Galleries in Manhattan. The woodwork of the chair was painted black and the chair was then upholstered in a painted flamestitch pattern.
7. & 8. Main hand props for the production were placed on the sofa and photographed for future DRACULA productions, including London, Australia, national, bus and truck, regional, and others.
9. Seven three-dimensional painted bats were created for the painted DRACULA portal in London. (Photographs by Lynn Pecktal)

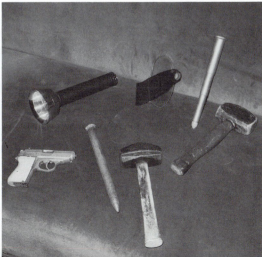
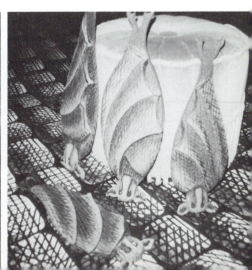

Tony Straiges resides on a picturesque street in Brooklyn Heights. He was born on October 31, 1942, in Minersville, Pennsylvania, and was educated at the Yale School of Drama. His first Broadway assignment was designing scenery for the musical *Timbuktu!* in 1978. He has designed the settings for numerous productions at the Arena Stage, American Repertory Theatre, McCarter Theatre Company, Yale Repertory Theatre, Hartford Stage Company, Guthrie Theatre, Circle Repertory Company, Williamstown Theatre Festival, Baltimore's Center Stage, Hudson Theatre Guild, Hartman Theatre, Virginia Museum Repertory Company, Santa Fe Festival Theatre, Joffrey Ballet, Old Globe Theatre, Juilliard School of Music, American Ballet Theatre, and Manhattan Theatre Club. Among his awards are a Tony, a Drama Desk Award, and an Outer Critic's Circle Award. His scenic design credits include:

Broadway
Shimada (1992)
I Hate Hamlet (1991)
Dangerous Games (1989)
Artist Descending a Staircase (1989)
Rumors (1988)
Into the Woods (1987)
Coastal Disturbances (1987)
Long Day's Journey into Night (1986)
Sunday in the Park with George (1984)
Copperfield (1981)
Harold and Maude (1980)

Richard III (1979)
Icedancing (1978)
A History of the American Film (1978)

Off Broadway
Coastal Disturbances (1986)
Fighting International Fat (1985)
Diamonds (1984)
Messiah (1984)
Sunday in the Park with George (1983)
Summer (1983)
On the Swing Shift (1983)
Talking With (1982)

No End of Blame (1981)
Vikings (1980)
Gertrude Stein Gertrude Stein
   Gertrude Stein (1979)
Just the Immediate Family (1978)

Arena Stage
Women and Water (1985)
Geniuses (1983)
Buried Child (1983)
The Importance of Being Earnest (1983)
Galileo (1980)

Model by Tony Straiges
SUNDAY IN THE PARK WITH GEORGE

Music and lyrics by Stephen Sondheim
Book and direction by James Lapine

Booth Theatre, New York (1984)
(Photograph by Ney Tait Fraser)

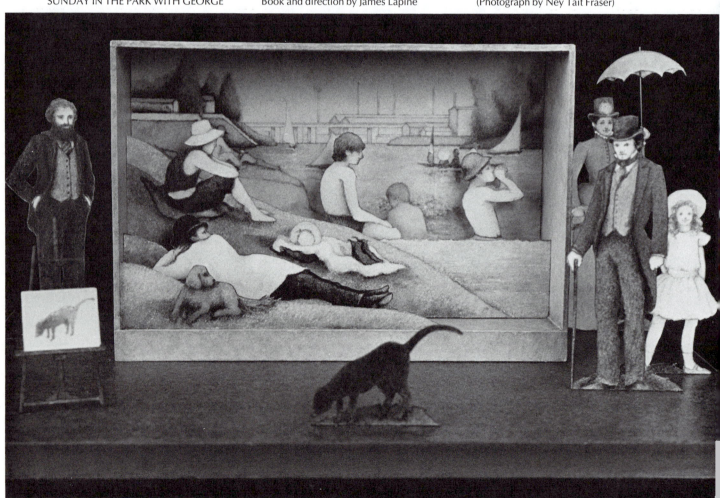

How did you first become interested in designing for the theatre?

When I was a kid in Pennsylvania, I did not know anything about stage design. My family was of Lithuanian descent, and we lived in an Eastern European community; everyone was involved in the church. The Roman Catholic Church brimmed with theatricality. There was the pageantry of the church service, the beautiful garments the priests wore, the ritual, the mystery. Statues were covered with purple cloth during Lent, and then the cloth was unfurled on Easter Sunday like the opening scene in *The Phantom of the Opera.*

The earliest theatre I actually experienced was in grade school. The nuns would put on operettas, and for scenery we had one drop that was used for every show year after year. It was a scene of a park with a gazebo and a lake, trees, and sky, and I thought it was incredible. During those grade school years and into high school I painted scenery whenever shows were put on.

It seems every designer had a puppet theatre. I made a small stage lit by Christmas lights. I would go up in the attic and play records and design scenes to fit the music. I drew an entire circus, cut it all out, and set it up on my bureau. I started drawing early. No one else in my family drew, but they were very encouraging and paid for correspondence art courses. The nuns at school also encouraged my drawing. No one had any idea that I would go into theatre.

Later, when I went to Washington to work for the government, I joined amateur theatrical groups. We painted the scenery in a studio run by John Priest. John built all the opera sets in Washington and rented his studio to our company. He was the first person I met who suggested I study design, and told me about Carnegie-Mellon and Yale. He was one of the most influential people in my life. I still keep in touch with him.

What kind of work were you doing in Washington?

I worked at the Library of Congress in the photo duplication service. The job proved interesting because I became a photographer. I worked with manuscripts, lithographs, and books. Visually the material was rich. But I continued with theatre at night.

Many of the young people working at the library were my age, and also from similar backgrounds. We became friends. After a while we grew restless, and I suggested we create a puppet show. We worked about one year, evenings and weekends, to complete part of the show—scripts, music, portable stage and rigging, and building the puppets. It was very ambitious. We called our enterprise "A Pageant at Christmas," but Christmas came and we were not finished.

We changed the name to "The American Puppet Theatre" and got rid of the Christmas numbers. Then we opened at the House of Representatives as a part of a variety show held every year for the congressmen and their families. It was a big success, and we received invitations from all over Washington, Maryland, and Virginia to play art festivals, hospitals, and the like.

Did you decide to tour the puppet show?

Yes. We moved the show with two trucks, performing in theatres, tents, and gymnasiums. The company had about twenty members, but it only took thirteen people to actually put on the show. We had a great time. The camaraderie of the troupe, the joyful response we received wherever we went, the fun traveling together was wonderful, and I discovered I really liked "show business."

The American Puppet Theatre ran for two years. The operation became more complicated. We had to be careful with copyrights, fire insurance, taxes, and paperwork. I was in charge and became frustrated with all the time and energy it took just to keep it going. I decided to go to one of those schools John Priest had told me about.

Which school did you decide to attend?

I went to Carnegie-Mellon in my home state of Pennsylvania. This turned out to be an unfortunate choice for me. I was an undergraduate in the design department, but received only one hour a week of theatre design. The rest of the time was spent in art classes—drawing, calligraphy, and sculpture. I enjoyed all of these classes, but felt I could draw well enough and wanted more theatre design. After a month at Carnegie, I quit. I took the money I had coming to me from not

finishing the semester and went to Europe. I spent three months just bumming around.

When I came back to the United States I prepared a portfolio of ice show designs and went to California to see if I could get a job with the Ice Capades. I have always wanted to design the Ice Capades or Ice Follies. These ice shows and the Ringling Bros. Circus were the only professional theatrics I saw as a kid. They would play Hershey, Pennsylvania, close to where I lived.

In California the ice show people looked at my portfolio and seemed to like what I was doing, but they certainly would not hire me as a designer, for they had famous designers, and they were already into constructing their new season. But they did say they would like to use me as an assistant for their next season.

Then I went north to San Francisco to visit John Priest, who was now the technical director of the San Francisco Opera. He needed an assistant, and it seemed I arrived at the right time. John taught me to draft. Most of the designers were European, and I would help them with building models. The scenic artists gave me a special card from the union that allowed me to paint the scenery on shows where help was needed. I learned a lot working at the opera house. I also designed small productions for their summer opera season.

I stayed there for two seasons, and then I heard about a theatre design program that Eldon Elder was starting in New York. He received grants from the Rockefeller and Ford Foundations to set up a program at Brooklyn College, though it was not a part of the college curriculum. Eldon was to select four scenic designers, four costume designers, four lighting designers, and four scenic artists from among all the applicants. I became one of the scenic designers, and this was the first time I really studied set design.

How long were you with the program?

I studied with Eldon for two years. Then I decided I wanted to study with Ming Cho Lee. I did not know Ming, but knew his work. He seemed to be the more modern designer of the day. Ming saw my portfolio, and asked me to come to Yale to be part of the graduate program in design. Because I did not have an undergraduate degree, I would be able to receive a master's at Yale in five years. I stayed five years, but did not receive the degree because of incomplete light plots and an incomplete theatre history class.

The degree was not important to me. I loved being there. It was stimulating. I did many shows with Alvin Epstein at the Yale Rep. The Yale Drama School allowed the students to join the Rep Theatre to become members of the American professional theatre. No other school offered that. I think Yale was the place where I discovered what I wanted to do with design.

Design at Yale had a lot to do with Bob Brustein's vision of theatre and the types of plays he chose to produce. Ming responded to that, and we as students took our cue from them. Bob seemed to explore the poetic ideas in a play, and design was "poetic" rather than realistic. My classmates were very talented. Seeing each other's work was worth the price of admission. Also, I came to know that this is what I really wanted to do.

What kind of stage did you have for the Yale Rep productions?

The Yale Repertory Theatre was housed in an old church which offered a bizarre and a difficult space. It did not have a fly area or much wing space. It had a very short frontal stage and a split-level rear. But it is amazing the number of wonderful designs that went up on that stage. When we did *The Rise and Fall of the City of Mahagonny* and *A Midsummer Night's Dream*—both productions with large casts and large orchestras—we moved

back to the Yale Drama School Theatre, which is a beautiful proscenium house. It has ample stage space and a very intimate auditorium. It is one of the best stages around.

How many productions did you design for the Yale Rep and in the Yale Drama School Theatre?

I designed student productions of *The Lower Depths* and *Women Beware Women* and a children's musical based on an Inca legend. At the Rep I did *Mahagonny*, *Midsummer*, *Julius Caesar*, *Troilus and Cressida*, *Victory*, *Shlemiel the First*, *Don Juan*, and *Tales from the Vienna Woods*. For some of these I designed the costumes. Michael Yeargan, an excellent designer, was our resident designer, and I became the associate resident designer. Alvin Epstein directed most of the shows, and Bob Brustein directed *Don Juan*. I worked with some foreign directors, too. *Tales from the Vienna Woods* was directed by Keith Hack, a British director.

What would you say is one of your most memorable productions that you did at the Yale Rep?

There were two of them, but the most memorable would be *A Midsummer Night's Dream*. It is a fantastic play and we had a wonderful collaboration of acting, music, directing, and design. It was like *Les Misérables*, which to me is a great production because all of the elements are united. *Midsummer* was so popular that the waitresses at the Yankee Doodle restaurant in New Haven were talking about it during breakfast. It seemed everyone in town

wanted to see it. We brought it back the next season, and when Bob Brustein moved to Boston, we re-created it there for two seasons.

The other fine memory is *The Rise and Fall of the City of Mahagonny*, another large show. I remember staying up late every night trying to complete designs to show Ming as soon as he arrived at Yale to teach his classes. Alvin decided to set the play in the gold rush period. *McCabe and Mrs. Miller* had just been released and we were all taken by that movie's visual richness. The short life span of those gold rush towns was Brecht's *Mahagonny*. Our city floated away at the end of the show. Alvin did a great job and the score is a knockout.

Did you design at other theatres while you were in New Haven?

During the summers I would do plays with Nikos Psacharopoulos at Williamstown. My first professional show outside of Yale Rep was with the Arena Stage in Washington. The play was *Streamers*, directed by David Chambers, and it began a very long, rewarding relationship with Arena Stage. I started designing two shows every year for them. Arena is my favorite place to work. I like their theatre policies, and they have good artists and craftspeople. They make you part of their family. It's a nice feeling.

Arena has two main operations. One is their arena stage and the other is the Kreeger, which is a sort of proscenium thrust that Robin Wagner designed. It's a bit similar to the Yale Rep.

What would you consider to be one of your successful productions at Arena Stage?

I'm especially fond of three shows. One of them is *The History of the American Film* which we did at the Kreeger and then on Broadway. I thought that a very exciting play. It was clever, and was a good reflection of our times. The design was inspired by Chris Durang's weaving all of those classical films into his play. David Chambers staged it well.

Two shows in the Arena space I am fond of are Tom Stoppard's *On the Raz-*

Model by Tony Straiges
BURIED CHILD by Sam Shepard
Directed by Gilbert Moses
Arena Stage, Washington, D.C. (1983)
(Photograph by Ney Tait Fraser)

zle and John Guare's *Women and Water*. Again, I liked these plays. *Women and Water* is sprawling. It has battlefields, whale ships, steamships, and seascapes. Before I received the script, Doug Wager told me not to be frightened when I read it. Well, it was like a movie. How do you do it? And here lies the beauty of the Arena space. You cannot use doors and walls at the Arena. You cannot be too literal. The space invites the audience's imagination. You rely on your imagination and theirs. An epic like this can only work with a good director. Doug did a bang-up job. He knows how to move people and bridge scenes. If you need one piece of scenery to represent the whole of Atlanta, Doug will help you pinpoint that piece.

When the audience walked in, they saw a gray wooden floor surrounded by a moat. The floor was constructed similar to the way railroad bridges were built during the Civil War in the way the structure supports the tracks. The deck was full of traps. A lovely period song—I think "Beautiful Dreamer"—was sung, and then we went to darkness. An enormous explosion came next, and all the traps sprung open. Men with guns blasting climbed onto the stage and out of the moat. It looked like graves opening with bodies ascending. It happened so fast, it was startling. There was a tremendous feeling of battle.

We used a lot of sound effects. For a steamship scene, two enormous smokestacks lowered in, gently kissing the deck. Moonlight covered the stage and reflected water light lapped against the pylons supporting the deck. Men traveling the ships sat on crates playing cards by the light of lanterns. You could hear the paddle wheels turning water, and the sounds of the engine. It was a quiet night except for the Pamunkee Queen traveling that river, smoke drifting out of her tall smokestacks.

The Arena space challenges the director and designer. When we did *On the Razzle*, Roger L. Stevens, the head of the Kennedy Center, purposely came to see our production because he had seen it in London and he did not

Model by Tony Straiges
THE BEGGAR'S OPERA by John Gay
Directed by Alvin Epstein
Tyrone Guthrie Theatre
Minneapolis, Minnesota (1979)
(Photograph by Ney Tait Fraser)

think the play could be done at the Arena.

Why did he feel the play could not be done on an arena stage?

Well, the script calls for a lot of doors. Neil Simon says you need five doors for farce, and *On the Razzle* at times is like farce. There are many different scenes and there are chases. People hide and disappear, eavesdrop on one another. Doors are out at Arena Stage. We thought and thought and worried about how to do it.

For one of the chase-and-hide scenes we devised a garden made up of hedges. These hedges might have been 4 to 5 feet tall and 8 feet long, and there were lots of them, all propelled by people inside sitting on little seats with wheels attached. To move the piece, they pushed against the floor with their hands—sort of like rowing a boat without oars. The audience did not see these people inside the hedges, but the operators could see out. At one point all of these hedges were choreographed to come traveling on stage, move about, and form various garden shapes. It was hysterical. An actor would be trapped inside a square made by these hedges, then that actor, by ducking or standing, could make himself visible or invisible. Sometimes the hedges would open up to allow an actor to scurry through, then close back up again.

During a restaurant scene, an actor would step behind a folding screen to hide. Two waiters would come over to the screen, fold it flat, and quickly move it to the other side of the stage. It seemed as if the actor had been sand-

wiched into the screen. Meanwhile the actor hiding behind the screen would have gone through a trap. On the other side of the stage, the waiters reopened the screen, and presto! That same actor came out from behind it. He had sprung up from another trap in the floor. This was a dazzling piece of Doug's stage business. He is good at this. Even though we in the production knew how it was being done, it was a marvel to watch each night. And the audience was stumped. They loved it, but had no idea how it happened.

Did you get any other shows from your work at the Yale Rep?

Yes, in fact when I did *A Midsummer Night's Dream*, Carmen de Lavallade was the Titania and Geoffrey Holder, her husband, came up to see it. Geoffrey liked our production very much. He was preparing *Timbuktu!* for Broadway and he asked me to design it. That is how my first Broadway show came about.

I did not know anything about Broadway, and I was timid. I remember at the bid session, there was this one guy who asked me all these questions and made me feel really self-assured and positive about what we were trying to do. I did not know him at the time, but it was Pete Feller. When I became flustered trying to explain the design or would ask, "Can we do this?" Pete was the one who always spoke up and said, "Well, I think you could do it this way" or "that way." I felt a rapport with him immediately. I distinctly remember that. He really wanted to help. He did the show and we formed a solid relationship and are very close friends.

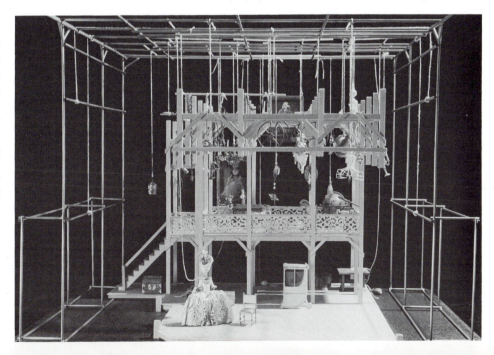

Model by Tony Straiges
THE IMPORTANCE OF BEING EARNEST by
    Oscar Wilde
Directed by Richard Russell Ramos
Arena Stage, Washington, D. C. (1983)
(Photograph by Ney Tait Fraser)

How did Richard III come about?

I received a call from Porter Van Zandt asking me about designing it, with Al Pacino playing the lead, and I thought it was a good idea having Al play Richard. Actually, the production turned out to be successful, and made money because it was after the movie *The Godfather* came out. But it was a bit of a disaster. No one really knew what the set or costumes should be. When we were in Philadelphia they brought in other directors to look at it. One day during rehearsal, Al Pacino was on stage and he just screamed, "Will somebody help me? I don't know what the fuck I'm doing!" I felt sorry for him. The rehearsal process never changed. It was always that atmosphere. I remember the reviews when it came in to New York. They were horrible. But one that really bothered me said it was my fault the background of the scenery showed up Al Pacino's spittle when he spoke. I thought that an odd comment.

The original set I had designed was powerful. When Al and the director came over to look at it, they did not know what to say. It was based on the work of a Japanese sculptor. It was a cold metallic enclosure. It had a searing richness. In one scene religious tapestries flew in front of the steel fortress. Al and the director liked the tapestries and they wanted them for the whole show. I did not understand why these tapestries would remain all evening, but that's what they wanted. They had done the play originally in a church in Boston, and they were still clinging to the church atmosphere. They wanted to have all the platforms and the floor

units support these pipes so Al could lean on the pipes and swing off them. So we placed all the pipes where they wanted them for those pieces of business. It is the only set on Broadway that I felt ashamed of. It didn't make sense.

Al Pacino is a talented actor, but we all needed a strong director. It was like that production of *Macbeth* where the leading lady did not want to use the set and they had to redo it. They ended up having two sets and several directors. I don't know who the director was, but if an actress is saying she is not going to appear on a set, the director must not be very tough. After all, the production mainly comes from the director. He is in charge of the whole thing. As the designer you are really trying to visualize the director's idea—his approach to the play. I think a good production comes from a good director.

How did Sunday in the Park with George *evolve?*

Jim Lapine was a friend of mine when we both were at Yale. He taught a course in graphic arts and he did our posters for the Yale productions. When we both came to New York, he was doing shows Off-Broadway and I was doing my work and we would always go see each other's shows, but we never worked together. Finally, we were going to work on a project, a new play by one of Jim's friends. Then one day a group of us met to go to dinner, and walking up the street Jim said, "Tony, I'm not going to do that play, but I'm going to do a musical and I want you to design it." I said, "What's it about?" And he said, "It's about the painter Georges Seurat." So I asked, "Who's

doing the music, Jim?" He replied, "Steve Sondheim." I said, "Come on, Jim, who's really doing the music?" I thought he was joking. I was floored. So we began work on *Sunday in the Park*. We did it first at the Playwrights Horizons.

What was the space like there?

It's a small space, long and narrow. There is no exit on stage right. We had to cut a hole in the wall on stage left into the lobbies so we could move scrim panels horizontally. You cannot fly large pieces. I remember taking the white model to Steve Sondheim's house. I set it up while Steve saw to the refreshments. Kneeling on the floor, placing all of the figures, making sure the light was right, I realized my knees were shaking, and I wondered if Steve would notice my shaking. When he returned, he asked if he could look and he sat on the floor and peered into the model. So there I was sitting on the floor with Steve Sondheim telling me he liked the design. A great feeling!

How long did the show run at Playwrights Horizons?

About a month. The second act was never completed. The last two or three performances we included the second-act set, which was put together hurriedly and not really designed. Jim had asked for these buildings similar to the buildings in the Broadway version. Jim asked, "Now could they fly out at this point?" I said, "Well, Jim, I never knew they had to fly out. No, they can't. There is no place to fly them out." And so he left them on stage. But these ideas became fully realized in the Broadway version.

Was the anticipation at Playwrights Horizons that the show would be a hit when it went to Broadway?

I think so, because people were really moved by it. I felt we knew we had something special.

Who built and painted it?

Bruce and Bruce built part of the set for the Off-Broadway version, but because there was not enough money, the Playwrights' shop did some of it.

Model by Tony Straiges
JULIUS CAESAR by William Shakespeare
Directed by Alvin Epstein
Yale Repertory Company
New Haven, Connecticut (1976)
(Photograph by Ney Tait Fraser)

The main painters were Dominick Di Rienzi and Jill Biskin. My colleague John Marrett and I spent another two weeks in the theatre painting. Theatre Techniques did the building and Nolan's did the painting for Broadway.

How did the two sets differ?

The main difference is that at Playwrights we were deep and narrow. At the Booth Theatre we were wide and shallow. At the Playwrights' theatre we had limited space. We were restricted to where we could pop up through the floor and to the height of these pop-ups. The under-stage area is not very deep. Loren Sherman devised the pop-up system. It was done with rope and a wooden rig under the stage. An apprentice stayed under the stage to pull the rope, and it worked well.

At the Booth Theater we could "pop up" almost anywhere. We tried not to locate the pop-ups near the beams that support the stage, but between the beams where the traps are laid. The theatre has a tall basement so we had no problem with the tall pop-ups. Pete Feller, Jr., devised the pop-up system. A piston operated the mechanism which ran off a computer.

At Playwrights we had no wing space and no fly space. At the Booth we had both. It was easier to design the show at the Booth Theatre because the theatre is a traditional house built to accommodate and support moving scenery.

Aside from *Midsummer Night's Dream*, *Sunday in the Park* would be my second favorite show. The effort people make to create something is reflected in the script. The set is so integrated into the script and score, as are the costumes and lights. I felt close to the character Georges Seurat. I identified with him. And to be able to design a set for a play about the making of a painting, and that set happens to be the painting, is a rare opportunity.

I enjoyed the relationship and dedicated labor of Pat Zipprodt, Ann Hould-Ward, and Richard Nelson. I admire their talent. I think Jim and Steve wrote a unique and beautiful theatre piece, an everlasting one. It was a unified production.

Did your work on Into the Woods *come about as a result of the success of* Sunday in the Park with George?

I would say so, yes. We did it twice, like *Sunday in the Park*. Our first production opened in San Diego. When I read the script, I had no idea how to do the animals. At one time Jim suggested, "Maybe the animals should be like those bars of soap in the shape of sheep and the like." We finally decided we would do it simply, more like presentational theatre.

It was a big show in San Diego, but it had a simple quality. My problem with the design there was too much of a sameness throughout the forest scenes, which are a major part of the show. I realized I needed to alter the forest more, and when I redesigned it for New York, I utilized three different drops behind the trees, which I think worked. We learned a lot from doing the show in San Diego, not only about the play, but about the design of it. They did a fine job in San Diego, and I know it wasn't easy. For New York everyone wanted more lavishness, and to make it a little more literal.

How would you describe the physical makeup of what you did for Into the Woods?

In San Diego everything tracked off and on from the wings. All the movement was lateral. When we discussed the Broadway show, Jim asked if we could get diagonal movement. So we developed three major units that would turn, travel, and join together to make bridges and form different angles. We made what we call the "Ouija board." Dick Jaris, my talented associate, devised this. It was a dimensional ground plan with tracks. We made these three units in model form, and they function just as the real set does, except you move them by hand. We could turn them around, push them on or off, up and down stage. With this we were able to determine various configurations and learn the limitations. The main unit (the sweep) tracks across stage, and inside it has what is called a "turtle" which enables the unit to go up and downstage. The sweep can also turn around. There is another unit, a small sweep. We call this the "teeter-totter." This moves on and off stage, and can turn around and pivot like a teeter-totter.

At the rear of the stage is the bridge unit. This is a horizontal unit that functions as a bridge for actors—a path. It starts high in the wings and curves low as it heads for the center line. Both sides of the bridge are made up of three units that can telescope into themselves to completely clear the stage or expand to their limits to completely bridge the stage. Both halves of the bridge can work separately or together.

238 Actors usually dart across the bridge or cross the bridge to a point to hop to the main sweep. With these three units we offer a variety of stage movement and stage pictures. At one point near the end of the play most of the forest has cleared off and actors are huddled on the main sweep, an island. The main sweep cracks apart—"no place is safe!" So you have all this variation of these three units, plus trees flying in and out and traveling off and on. There is a lot happening. The show is technically complicated. All the machinery is downstairs. (We call the basement "Pittsburgh.") Upstairs as you watch the show it looks very simple. Pete Feller, Jr., did a beautiful job with these three units.

Are things winched on and off?

Yes. Small units winch on and off, but the main support system for on-and-off travel is the treadmill.

When you get a script, what is your way of preparing the design for a show?

I read the play—think about it, but usually wait until I talk to the director. I listen to him. He can talk about anything he wants to talk about. I take notes. Then I do research. I might make rough sketches and show him the research and sketches. Sometimes the director insists on a fully realized color sketch, but I don't like sketches. I become confused with perspective and I don't trust them. I begin to feel comfortable when I start the white model.

When the white model is done, I take this to the director. We provide figures in scale, and if we need furniture, provide that too. The director likes this period of development because he sees a concrete form of what his vision

might be. We play around, make changes and rip apart. And with this white model I see for myself what I need to do with balance, harmony, discord. After all of this scrutiny, we proceed to a good model. Sometimes if there is no time or money, we rely on the white model alone. By the time the good model is complete, very seldom does the design change from the model to the shop. We have the rough drafting from the first model to base our good drafting on. I try to make most of the decisions with the model, including trims of hanging lamps and hanging pieces. When you are in the theatre, it is always hard to sit in the house and spike pieces, because everyone on stage needs to be on ladders, and you cannot see through this network of carpenters and electricians and ladders.

Do you always do a detailed painted model?

Pretty much, because again that is what I give to the painters. For a drop I will do a paint elevation, but I could not do a paint elevation of a textured brick wall unless I can paint on a textured brick wall model piece.

What do you use primarily to paint your models?

Being influenced by Ming, I gesso them first. I use Windsor and Newton watercolors, but go to acrylics for stronger washes, deeper colors, and deeper glazes. If I am doing a realistic set, I will use latex paints and Minwax stains for wood like they use on the real set.

When we have the time, we make a prop book with furniture details. We decide on the types of furniture we want to use, and place research photos,

dimensions, and color swatches into the book. The book becomes the guide. The prop person and/or I use the book to find similar or exact pieces of furniture. The book is also a way of keeping a record. When we did *Long Day's Journey into Night* in London, they used it for their guide. I remember being impressed with Pat Zipprodt's costume books that she used to keep her records of a show. It takes some time, but in the end it is worth it.

Do you find that it is ever a problem for a producer to pay for an assistant?

Yes, sometimes it is. We try to give an estimate of how much time it is going to take to do a show. If we go over that estimate, and it is our fault, I'll pay the assistant out of my own fee. But if it is because the director has changed his mind, then we ask the producer to pay for that. Sometimes I worry we use too much assistant time. We do detailed models. But they seem to pay off. Many decisions have been made in the model process, and the drafting is pretty accurate because the physical aspects of the set have been worked out by building the model. If the shop is impressed with the model, they will want to do an impressive job. The model and the drafting give the shop much more to go on than drafting and a sketch would. Finally, with a model the director and the producer know what they are going to get.

What do you like most about working in the theatre?

I like the collaboration. I like the excitement of everyone working hard on a project, and when the project goes up and looks good, everyone feels satisfied. I like it when the show is great, when you are moved by it. When I saw *Les Misérables*, the craft of the director and the designers and the actors, I wished I were a part of it.

If you had one design that you would like to be known for, which one would you choose?

I hope I haven't come to that one yet. I hope it is in the future.

Setting by Tony Straiges
A MIDSUMMER NIGHT'S DREAM by William Shakespeare
Directed by Alvin Epstein
Costumes by Zack Brown
Lighting by William B. Warfel
Yale Repertory Theatre
New Haven, Connecticut (1975)

6

INTERIOR AND EXTERIOR SCENERY

FLOORS AND DECKS

The Treatment of Floors

The special treatment of floors in the commercial theatre is traditionally an integral part of the stage design. A stage floor can be treated in a multitude of ways. For example, a stage floor can be painted, have a built deck or a rake, or be covered in carpet, artificial grass, sand, dance flooring, ground cloth, or gym padding.

In his book *The Theatre of Robert Edmond Jones*, Jones put special emphasis on the treatment of the floor for his production of *Lute Song* (1946) at the Plymouth Theatre in New York. Jones made a note on the ground plan (1945) that reads: "Space in front of inner stage, including forestage, to be covered with black linoleum." On a paint sketch for the basic setting, he extended the instruction to say "Polished black linoleum floor." Jones was a master designer of theatrical detail, and for this particular production he designed not only the scenery but also the lighting and costumes. (Mary Martin's costumes were credited to Valentina, however.)

Designing Floors

The design for the floor is always an important design element whether you are working on a proscenium stage or an open stage. Since the floor treatment varies with each show, there are specific questions that need to be an-swered in regard to the particular theatre and the production before you proceed with the design. You might need to consider: What can and cannot be done to the floor in the particular theatre where the show is playing? Can the floor be painted? Does the stage floor have a finish such as a high-gloss gym floor, and can it be altered or does it have to stay as is? Is it a good stage floor that is soft enough to drive nails into, and is it black or a dark color?

Floor designs are created to be interesting, appropriate, and practical. Possible floor treatments may include:

1. Real rough-hewn boards on ³/₄-inch plywood.
2. A flat Masonite floor textured and painted to look like stone, cement, cinder blocks, brick, or tile. Tiles are sometimes done in a checkerboard pattern painted in perspective.
3. Solid or patterned linoleum on ³/₄-inch plywood.
4. Carpet or oriental or figured rugs covering the entire floor.
5. Openings covered with large-scale metal grillwork through which lights may shine.
6. Sections of heavy acrylic plastic sheets with lights shining through in various floor patterns.
7. Varieties of light projections focused on the floor for both proscenium and open stage productions. This can be especially beautiful for opening and closing scenes.
8. All sorts of continuous and overlapping stenciled patterns.
9. Any number of painted geometric shapes.
10. Painted hatching or crosshatching.

Checklist of Typical Materials for Floor Coverings

Regular wood stage floor (or linoleum on wood)
Painted canvas ground cloth on stage floor
Vinyl dance floor covering on stage floor
Painted sheets of ¹/₄-inch tempered Masonite (with smooth side up) on stage floor
Painted sheets of ¹/₄-inch tempered Masonite mounted on ³/₄-inch plywood sheets that are then placed on the stage floor
Painted sheets of ¹/₄-inch tempered Masonite mounted on ³/₄-inch plywood sheets with wooden supporting members beneath to allow space for tracks and equipment

Examples of Floor Treatments

These are various floor treatments that were designed for some Broadway productions.

1. For *Crimes of the Heart* (1981), John Lee Beatty specified that the floor have patterned linoleum mounted on ³/₄-inch plywood with diagonal seams. The patterned floor started at the back of the fire pocket.
2. David Gropman designed a deck with ⁵/₈-inch No. 2 white pine planking attached to ³/₄-inch plywood sheets for *Mass Appeal* (1981).

240

3. In creating the set for *Morning's at Seven* (1980), William Ritman used grass matting over ½-inch Ozite for the two adjacent yards. The grass mats were 12'-0" × 50'-0" (downstage), 7'-0" × 14'-0", and 4'-0" × 16'-0".

4. For the musical *Barnum* (1980), David Mitchell used gymnasium padding on plywood.

5. To help the dancers work better on the wet floor of Santo Loquasto's set for *Singin' in the Rain* (1985), a special paint was used. A fast-drying polyurethane-type enamel (with a little grit put in it) was applied on the floor. The paint has been used by the Coast Guard for its ships and by auto repair shops for their floors.

Making a Separate Drawing of the Floor Details

A separate drawing on the drafting is made when the design for the floor has sufficient detail that must be clearly shown. This single drawing on tracing paper may be made to indicate the requirements for building or painting, or both. It may also be necessary to show details for constructing a flat or raked deck, the cutting and sewing layout for a ground cloth, or the detailed painting that the deck or ground cloth will receive. A separate drawing for the floor is made because the master ground plan usually has so many drawings indicating the positions of portals, wagons, backdrops, and masking, plus other necessary details, that it becomes difficult to see just what applies to the floor treatment only. For instance, if the floor design is made up of hundreds of different stone patterns, then you really need appropriate space to show them properly on a new sheet of tracing paper.

Using a Painted Ground Cloth

A theatre may not permit painting directly on the stage floor. This means that most likely you will want to use a ground cloth, a deck, or sheets of ¼-inch Masonite for the painting surface.

A ground cloth may be designed to have a lot of detailed work, or it may be just painted a simple solid color. A ground cloth works nicely either for a regular run of the play or for a touring company. It can be taken up, folded in a large bundle, and travel in a much smaller space than a built deck constructed of wood and Masonite. A heavy canvas ground cloth with seams running across the stage can be made up in the shape of a rectangle, a square, or any other interesting shape. For strength and support, a ground cloth normally has webbing stitched on the underside around the perimeter so that it does not show when the cloth is in position.

The ground cloth should have grommets in the center of the downstage and upstage edges, in the centers of both sides, and in all four corners. Heavy tacks or nails are put through the grommets to attach the ground cloth in position. Additional tacks or staples are used around the entire perimeter of the ground cloth. When putting a ground cloth down, snap a chalk line on the floor where the downstage edge of the cloth is to go. The order of tacking is (1) at center downstage, (2) at center upstage, and (3) at left and right downstage corners. Fill in with additional tacks or staples across the downstage edge. Then (4) attach the centers of the sides and tack between downstage corners and centers of the sides. Finally, (5) work from the centers of the sides to the upstage corners of the ground cloth and finish tacking where needed.

For touring or repertory productions, a ground cloth is ideal to put spike marks on to indicate the positions of furniture and scenic pieces such as flats, profile cutouts, dimensional trees, and so on.

While a ground cloth is excellent for various purposes, it may not be effec-

Settings by Douglas Stein
THE CHERRY ORCHARD by Anton Chekhov
Directed by Garland Wright
Costumes by Ann Hould-Ward
Lighting by Peter Maradudin
Denver Center Theatre Company
Denver, Colorado (1986)
(Photographs by Douglas Stein)
Left: Act 2; *right:* Act 4; *below right:* Act 1.

tive when heavy castered units must be rolled across the stage for scenic changes or when there is a lot of dancing in the show. The designer should check this out with the choreographer before planning the design for the stage floor. Also, with a ground cloth you cannot get the shiny and glossy surface that you can with smooth, hard sheets of tempered Masonite.

When appropriate, different ground cloths can be used for subsequent acts. For an opera production you may have three or four ground cloths tacked on top of each other. In this case, you would peel back one at a time as each act has played. For a dramatic production you could have a large rug instead of a ground cloth. Unlike ground cloths, which can be folded for travel, a large rug would have to be rolled.

Productions Utilizing Unusual Floor Treatment

Of course, not every production uses a traditional type of stage floor. Every now and then a show comes along where there is the opportunity to design a floor that incorporates natural elements. Two such examples of unusual floor treatments were *The Grapes of Wrath* (1990) at the Cort Theatre in

This is largely visual theatre, and Brook has combined strategies from sundry Eastern theatrical traditions with some of his own, making him the true *macher* of The Mahabharata. *The large circular acting area is covered with reddish sand and has a pool down front and a river upstage, containing genuine water. There are ladders going up a sort of mid-stage proscenium, as well as iron brackets up the back wall. These allow for spectacular gymnastic displays, occasionally with a remote bearing on the action. Luscious carpets and straw matting are intermittently spread on the sand, and a variety of artifacts from chariot wheels (without chariots) to barricade-like screens made of (mahabha) rattan are rolled or brandished about. A band of peripatetic musicians with Oriental instruments pop up in likely and unlikely places to play discreetly disorienting music. Fires, equally ubiquitous, snake across the stage, encircling the actors as if they were so many Brunnhildes.*

Using a Show Deck for a Production

A show deck normally covers the entire stage floor and is needed for large productions where scenic units must move during the course of performance. The moving scenic units may be castered wagons of scenery that move on and off stage with guides in tracks positioned in the top of the show deck. These pieces of scenery may be moved by winches that are operated either manually or electrically. The height of this built-up floor or deck not only allows units to move in tracks, but also allows enough room to house the equipment and hardware underneath the deck. The effect is that from the audience the scenery seems to move effortlessly by itself. Built-up decks are also ideal for making turntables and treadmills work magically and for housing the mechanical apparatus for these as well.

Show decks are often constructed of sheets of 4 × 8-foot Masonite (with the smooth side up) on sheets of 4 × 8-foot plywood with wooden supporting stringers underneath. Occasionally a designer may specify sheets of Benelex instead of ¼-inch tempered Masonite for a deck covering. Although Benelex is more expensive than Masonite, it is a more durable covering and is especially good to use in shows with a lot of dancing and heavy scenic units that

New York, directed by Frank Galati and designed by Kevin Rigdon; and *The Mahabharata* (1987) at the Brooklyn Academy of Music (BAM)'s Majestic Theatre, directed by Peter Brook and designed by Chloé Obolensky.

Glenn Collins reported on a discussion he had with Mr. Galati regarding the physical aspects of *The Grapes of Wrath* in an article for *The New York Times* (April 3, 1990). The article is excerpted here.

In his minimalist paring down of scenery and props, "there were certain elemental things that were vital to the story," Mr. Galati said. Those were the elements: earth, air, fire and water.

"The earth is the dust of the dust bowl— but we also needed dirt to bury Grandpa," [Galati] said of the scene in which actors shovel soil from a trap door to the stage.

Theatrical fog is used "to convey not only moisture, but also the dust of the prairie and the smoke from campfires. . . . The novel is full of campfires." Three fire boxes are set into the stage; they use propane burners to create real fire.

As for water, "not only does there have to be rain, there has to be a flood," Mr. Galati said. The production employs a 12-foot-long, 4-foot-deep tank hidden at the edge of the stage, which serves as both the Colorado River and the flooding stream that threatens the Joads. At one point, in a touch of realism that regularly draws gasps from the audience, two actors leap into the "river" for a cooling swim.

There is also a rain-making pipe above the lighting grid that delivers a sheet of falling water; it can be set to produce anything from a fine mist to a driving deluge. All water used onstage is temperature-controlled, and chemically disinfected, to keep the actors from becoming ill.

John Simon described the floor covering and other scenery for *The Mahabharata* in *New York* magazine (November 2, 1987):

Square (28″ × 28″) and Hexagon (28″ High) Designs to Create Repeating Floor Patterns

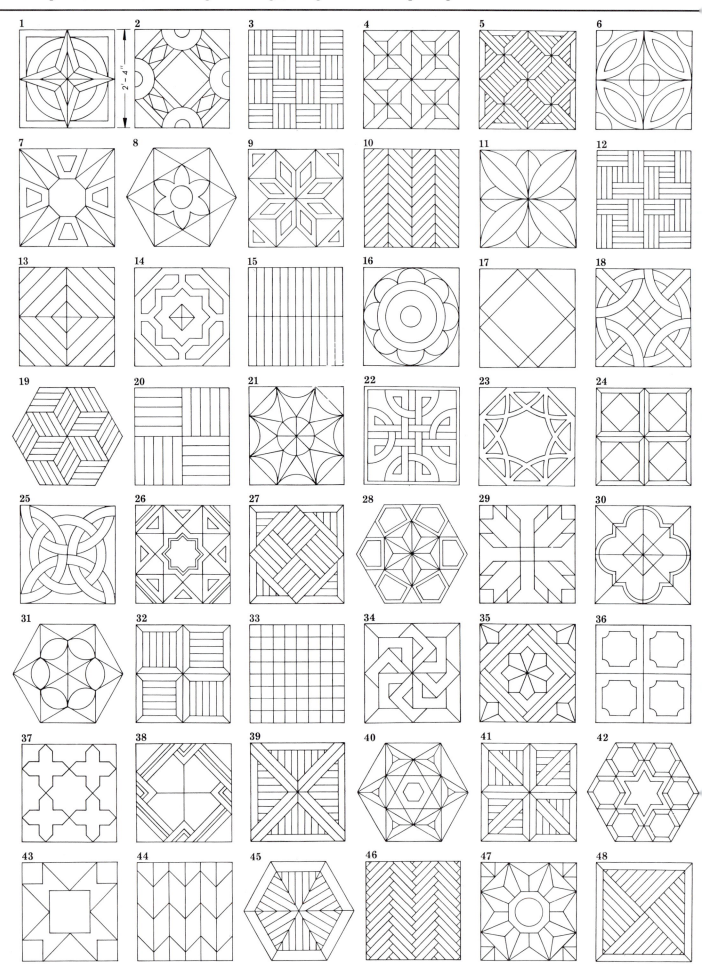

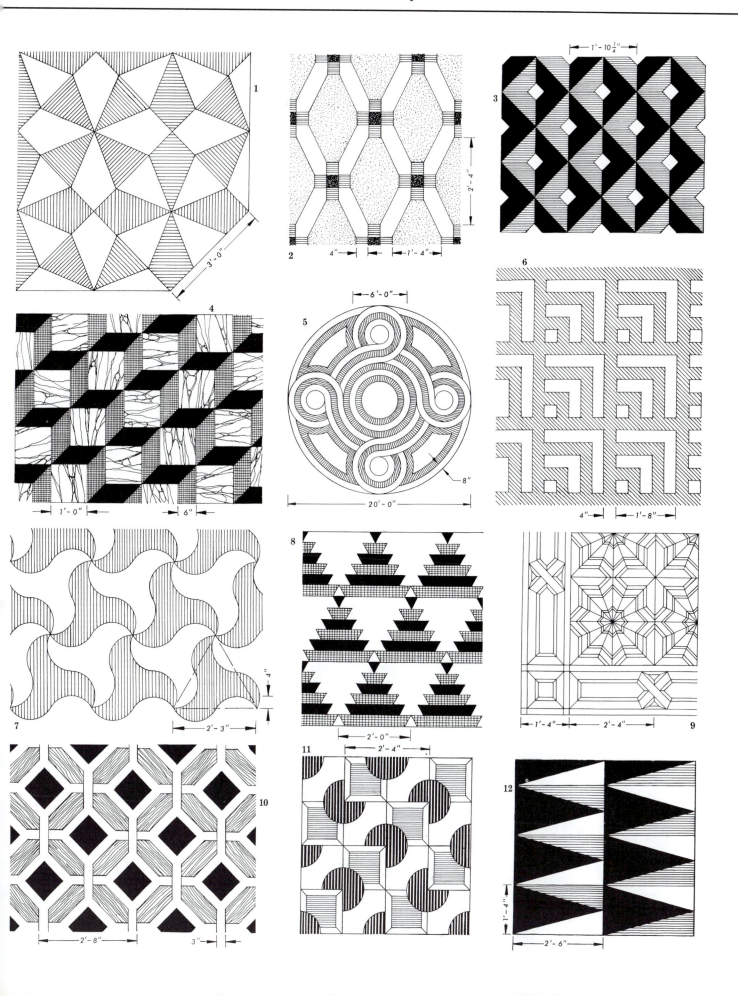

move across the deck. Sometimes a designer and a choreographer may decide to have a floor covering of asphalt tiles for tap dancing.

In order for the surface to be workable and safe, the deck should continue to the offstage walls. There will then be a continuous surface so the scenic units will not roll off the edges of the deck and the actors and stagehands will not have to worry about tripping on or falling off the playing area, especially in the dark. The higher the deck, the more important this becomes. Show decks vary considerably in height. For a simple play, a deck may be created with sheets of 1/4-inch tempered Masonite; for a musical, a deck may be 6½ inches high. The height may be even higher or lower, according to what is involved with the concept and mechanics of the show. For instance, Robin Wagner designed a deck that was 10 inches high with a 28-foot diameter turntable for the musical *Chess* (1988), and to accommodate the treadmills in *Annie* (1977) David Mitchell's deck was also 10 inches high.

Whenever you are working on a production with a show deck, make sure the director understands the ground plan and the amount of space available to play each scene. Once the show deck is built and painted and the tracks and

all the movable units are positioned and ready to play, changes become enormously expensive.

A show deck is built for an individual production and to fit into a specific theatre. If a show that has a deck tours and goes to theatres with different-size stages, additional platforms and plugs must be provided to accommodate the variations in the different stages.

Examples of Deck Details for Specific Shows

The specifications for show decks used in different Broadway productions vary according to the needs of the show and the budget requirements. Some of the following specifications are taken from the notes on the actual production drawings.

For Edward Gorey's *Dracula* (1977), a 1/4-inch Masonite deck 28'-0" by 48'-0" with painted stonework was used in the Wilbur Theatre for the Boston tryout and also for the run at the Martin Beck Theatre in New York. This painted 1/4-inch Masonite deck without 3/4-inch plywood underneath was selected because it was more economical. Later, for the first national company of *Dracula* (1978), the show deck was designed to be more substantial in construction for touring. The 1/4-inch Masonite sheets were mounted on 3/4-inch plywood sheets on strips (1½ inches wide) that were positioned around the edges and on 2-foot centers.

When Tony Straiges designed the scenery for the play *Harold and Maude*

(1980), these notes were put on the ½-inch scale ground plan:

1. *Stage deck is 4 inches high (1/4-inch Masonite on 3/4-inch plywood on supporting structures) and covers the entire stage (on and off), extending DS to front edge of apron with a neat front facing.*
2. *Scenic shop to check out actual existing stage dimensions.*
3. *Provide soundproofing for stage deck.*
4. *Eight units track off and on manually by winches.*
5. *Fixed casters (except small tree).*
6. *Turntable above on stage deck: 26'-0" diameter by 10" high. Movement of turntable: both clockwise and counterclockwise (360 degrees). Turntable moves up and downstage: 7'-6". Bid on the possibility of two different speeds: 1. Fast. 2. Slow. Provide electrical commutators, eight circuits available for practicals and special effects.*

For John Wulp's settings for *The Crucifer of Blood* (1978), the deck was 2¼ inches high. The actual deck was constructed with 1/4-inch Masonite on 3/4-inch plywood on 3/4-inch strips on ½-inch foots. Three units tracked off and on by winches from upstage (the two Baker Street units and the large boat) and the two units downstage were pushed off and on manually (the two opium den units). The tracks in the floor for these units were 3/8 inch wide.

Drawing a Show Deck

Whenever you are planning a show deck for a commercial production, you should consult a scenic shop before you do the drawing and discuss your plans for the scenic units and their movement. It saves time by eliminating a lot of drawing and redrawing if you arrive at a working solution before doing the final drawing for the deck. The overall size of the moving scenic units, where they play onstage, and where they store once they go off are important factors in planning a deck. One of the main questions to resolve about a deck is how high it has to be to accommodate the units of moving scenery and the machinery and equipment to operate it.

Assume for discussion that you are doing a drawing of a simple deck without any tracks in it. This deck is to

Stage design by John Falabella
REMEMBRANCE by Graham Reid
Directed by Munson Hicks
Huntington Theatre Company
Boston, Massachusetts (1987)

cover the entire stage and is to be 1¼ inches high. Castered units are to be manually rolled over it. The main reason for using this particular deck is to give the show a durable painted floor with a glossy finish for a regular run and also to make the deck strong enough for touring. You will need a smooth hard surface for this floor treatment rather than painting on a flexible canvas ground cloth.

For creating a deck of this kind, plan to use units consisting of 4 × 8-foot sheets of ¼-inch tempered Masonite (smooth side up) on 4 × 8-foot sheets of ¾-inch plywood on ¼-inch plywood strips. To make the ½-inch scale drawing for this simple deck, use these steps.

1. Draw a plan of the entire stage, starting at the front of the apron and going all the way to the upstage wall. Continue the drawing to include the extreme left and right walls. The idea is

Stage design by José Varona
COPPÉLIA
Music by Leo Delibes
Choreography by Nicolai Sergeyev
Staged by Petrus Bosman
Act 3 additional choreography by Benjamin Harkarvy
Pennsylvania Ballet
Philadelphia, Pennsylvania (1978)

to do a complete layout of the stage so that the portable deck can be drawn in the stage space.

2. To do the layout of the 4'-0" by 8'-0" units running across stage, start at the back of the smoke pocket and draw a line parallel to the proscenium opening. From this line go upstage as you measure and make a couple of marks (left and right) for each of the lines that will indicate the 4-foot widths of the deck units. Continue doing this until you reach the upstage walls. Then, using these marks as guides, draw in the lines going across stage. Another way to draw this is to place graph paper under the tracing paper that you are working on.

3. Next, begin to make marks for the 8-foot lengths. Start at the center line and make marks left and right so that lines can be drawn through these marks going up and down stage and continue dividing the stage into rectangular shapes for the deck.

4. Measure and mark 4-foot widths downstage from the line in back of the smoke pocket to the front edge of the apron. Then continue drawing the 8-foot lengths so that the same pattern of rectangles continues downstage.

This drawing allows the scenic shop to see how many complete units are

required as well as how many plugs or partial units are needed to finish the offstage edges of the deck. The plugs necessary to fill in the remainder of the deck at the walls may be built on the spot in the theatre, especially if there are obstructions like radiators, pipes, pilasters, jogs, or other irregularities to cut around.

5. Make a note on the drawing to say: "Construct a neat front edge or facing." This facing may be painted or covered with velour. On occasion, the whole facing of the apron is covered all the way from the top of the deck to the floor in the house. Again, there is usually a certain amount of on-the-spot work that must be done to tailor-make a facing in the theatre, especially if the apron has an unusual curve or other irregular shape.

6. Include any other appropriate notes as they may apply on the deck drawing.

For its own purposes a scenic studio will usually do a separate drawing for use by the shop carpenters in building and assembling the deck.

Sources for Floor Coverings

Listed are good sources for obtaining floor coverings.

• *Gerriets International*, R.D. #1, 950 Hutchinson Road, Allentown, NJ 08501. Tel.: (609) 758-9121. A product made by Gerriets is VARIO PVC, which is carpet for dancing. It is double-sided and lightweight. VARIO PVC comes in rolls of 30 or 40 meters approximately 160 centimeters wide. Double-face self-adhesive tape can be purchased here to join the rolls of floor covering, or the company can heat-seal a number of rolls together in any specified size. This double-sided floor covering for dancing comes in the following color combinations: black/white, black/gray, gray/brown, blue/green, and red/tan.

• *Rosco Laboratories, Inc.*, 36 Bush Avenue, Port Chester, NY 10573. Tel. (914) 937-1300. Rosco Dance Floor is a portable, durable, nonreflective vinyl floor ideal for touring companies. This reversible floor features a different color on each side with a nonskid finish designed to provide the controlled slip preferred by dancers. Rosco Dance Floor is flexible and can be rolled and unrolled many times without cracking. The colors available are black/gray (63′ × linear foot), black/white (63′ × linear foot), black/gray (63′ × 131.25′ full roll) and black/white (63′ × 131.25′ full roll). Show Floor is a glossy flooring that can be used to add a glamorous look to any stage, studio, commercial exhibit or special event. Available in a high-gloss white, black, red, blue, and beige. Show Floor is 80 mils thick.

Traps in the Floor for Actors or Scenery

One of the best ways to handle unexpected entrances and exits on stage is to have actors come through trap doors. This works very nicely when the entrance or exit is masked by smoke, folding screens, shrubbery, panels that are flown in, a stack of boxes, an arrangement of furniture, or other scenic objects.

While it is usually actors who enter and exit through a trap, scenery and props may also come on or go off stage this way. Possibly the most unexpected and exciting use of traps is when scenery seems to rise up from the stage floor. Having scenery rise vertically is a lot easier to accomplish when the stage floor has traps or openings already available. Some theatres have a series of available traps, while others have traps randomly placed. The effect is beautiful when a theatre has a long trap running across in the upstage area. Cables or lines can be used to pull up from the trap entire backdrops of painted muslin or large expanses of scenic netting with glued-on designs. One drop on a pipe batten may rise up trailed by another, and as the second one flies upward a third drop may follow if there is enough grid space above the stage.

Designing Raked Decks and Platforms

A raked floor on the proscenium stage often enables the director to block and stage actors more imaginatively than is possible on the regular flat floor. A sloping floor works especially well for a large cast where an open and spacious playing area is desired. Not only do slanted floors allow the director an opportunity to create better composition in the placement of actors within the proscenium frame, but they also permit the scenic designer a chance to make the most of floor designs with color, texture, and shape. A raked deck also enables the lighting designer to show off projected light patterns to a much better advantage than on a plain flat deck. There is the added possibility of having fancy grillwork in openings in the floor with lights placed under them. Heavy translucent plastic sheets with lights under them can also be very effective.

The director and the designer must be aware that a raked deck may not always be suitable for dancing, moving wagons on and off stage, and positioning various pieces of traditional furniture without having them look tilted.

In designing a raked deck, these variations may be considered:

1. A full-stage raked deck with the same slope.
2. A completely raked deck broken up by having various platform shapes positioned at different angles.
3. A flat deck such as the stage floor with the main playing area consisting of a large central raked unit.
4. A flat deck with two or more raked platforms arranged in the stage space with much of the flat floor utilized as well.
5. A combination of several flat and raked platforms overlapping each other.

ADVANTAGES OF A RAKED DECK

• Makes an exciting picture for actors and director to work on.
• Allows more variety for the director in blocking.
• Shows the floor design off to better advantage.

Stage designs by Jo Mielziner
1776—Battlefield and Jefferson's room
Book by Peter Stone
Based on conception by Sherman Edwards
Music and lyrics by Sherman Edwards
Directed by Peter Hunt
Forty-sixth Street Theatre
New York (1969)
(Photographs by Peter A. Juley and Son)

Setting by John Falabella
BROADWAY SINGS: THE MUSIC OF JULE STYNE
Directed by Joe Layton
Costumes by Theoni V. Aldredge
Lighting by Ken Billington
St. James Theatre, New York (1987)
(Photograph by John Falabella)
Pictured: 1920s jazz sequence.

DISADVANTAGES OF A RAKED DECK

- More expensive to construct than a regular stage floor.
- Often requires adjustment on furniture legs (sawing off or adding on).
- Doors and other swinging scenery have to be precisely positioned so they will open properly.
- Units of scenery or props on casters have to be carefully planned so they don't roll downstage.

Raked Decks Extending into the Audience

A raked deck that continues partially or completely out into the audience may have the most dramatic impact. This kind of sloped floor may have all sorts of varied shapes. The front of it may be curved, straight, pointed, or a combination of many symmetrical or asymmetrical shapes. Raked decks are not always designed with one solid plane; they may be broken up into several shapes, and this kind of design can add enormous interest.

Examples of Raked Decks and Platforms

A designer can specify the slope of a raked deck or platform in several ways. Examples of raked platforms for some

Broadway productions include: ⅜″ in 1′-0″ for Ming Cho Lee's *The Glass Menagerie* (1983), O'Neill Theatre; ½″ in 1′-0″ for David Jenkins' *The Elephant Man* (1979), Booth Theatre; 1″ in 1′-0″ for John Bury's *Amadeus* (1980), Broadhurst Theatre; 1 to 15 for Ralph Koltai's floor for the Royal Shakespeare Company (1984), Gershwin Theatre; and 1′-0″ in 16′-0″ for Felix E. Cochern's *Home* (1980), Cort Theatre.

PLATFORMS

Designing Basic Platform Units

When designing platform units, you must decide whether they are to be stationary or movable. For moving platforms, always consider how they are preset at the top of the show, then decide whether they are to move manually or mechanically. Then proceed to work out your design, considering the following ideas, as appropriate:

1. If the platforms move, where do they play and where do they store?
2. Do you have a platform unit with a pivot in the center or on an end?
3. Does a platform unit revolve to reveal a side with new features? Is there a different shape, color, or texture? Are there lights on the upstage side? Is there a material like Mylar, mirrored discs, Glamé (by Rosco), or other materials?
4. Does a platform split in the center and form two platforms?
5. Can a portion of a platform lift up and hinge back to become a practical seat or a table?
6. Can a section of the platform lift out and become an opening for a trap door?

Using Full-Stage Sets on Wagons

If you are designing a show with one or more sets and plan to use a full set of scenery on a rolling wagon, you would be wise to observe these suggestions.

1. Use a 6-inch-high castered platform for the main set. In front of this, plan to have a 6-inch-high stationary platform that runs across the entire width of the front of the stage.

Setting and design by Elmon Webb and
  Virginia Dancy
YOU NEVER CAN TELL by George Bernard
  Shaw
Directed by John Going
Costumes by David Toser
Lighting by Bennet Averyt
Pittsburgh Public Theatre
Pittsburgh, Pennsylvania (1978)

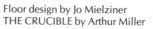

Floor design by Jo Mielziner   Directed by John Berry
THE CRUCIBLE by Arthur Miller   Vivian Beaumont Theatre, New York (1972)

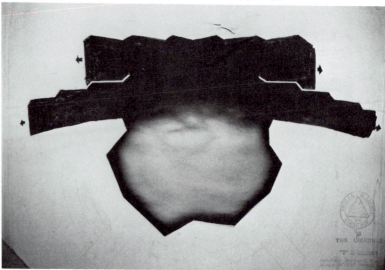

(Photograph by Lynn Pecktal)

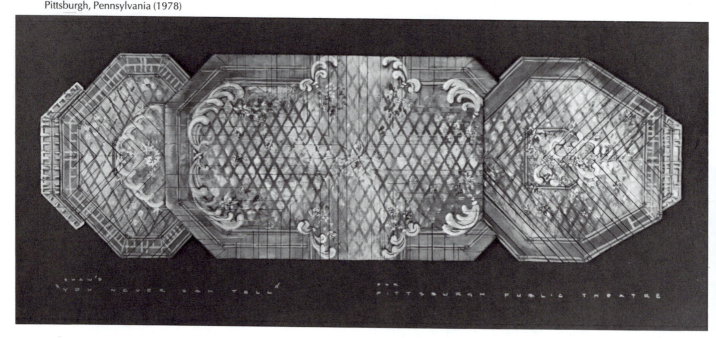

Using a Single Point to Lay Out the Drawing for Boards on Irregular Platforms

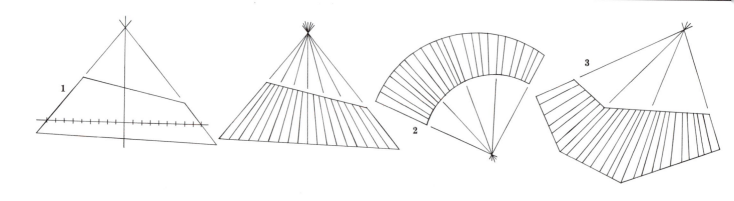

Stage design by Zack Brown
THE CONSUL by Gian Carlo Menotti
Directed by Gian Carlo Menotti
Washington Opera, Eisenhower Theatre
Washington, D.C. (1987)

"Working with Menotti on his own pieces is a challenge. He has staged them himself so often that he has many specific needs, and perhaps fond memories of particularly successful pro-

ductions. He does not, however, force a particular look on the designer. He is very receptive to ideas as long as they meet or enlarge upon his requirements."
—Zack Brown

Setting by Ray Klausen
LYNDA CARTER'S CELEBRATION
Directed by Stan Harris
Costumes by Bob Mackie

Lighting by Truck Krone
ABC Stage 59
Hollywood, California (1981)
(Photograph by Ray Klausen)

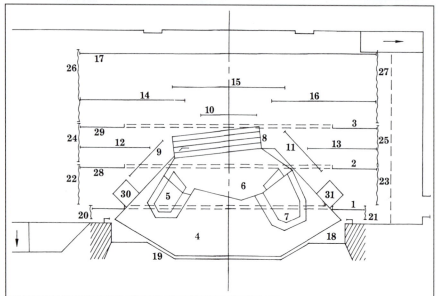

Model and plan by Felix E. Cochren
Scenery supervised by Lynn Pecktal
HOME by Samm-Art Williams
Directed by Douglas Turner Ward
Negro Ensemble Company
Cort Theatre, New York (1980)
(Photographs by Scott Pecktal)

Plan: 1.–3. Black velour portals. 4. Raked platform. 5.–7. Platform units. 8. Steps. 9.–11. Fences. 12.–16. Sharkstooth scrim panels. 17. Black velour drop. 18. Apron. 19. Front facing. 20.–27. Masking panels.

This stationary platform could have a straight front or have the same contour or shape as the theatre apron. Its depth would vary according to the theatre, but it most likely would go from the back of the smoke pocket downstage to the edge of the apron.

The stationary platform may be 3 or 4 feet deep and may be used for each scene. The paint treatment or finish on this front strip of platforms may be the same as or different from the castered platform. It may also be covered with carpet or rugs to match the various sets.

2. Usually a large platform works better if it is divided into two platforms. This makes it easier to move and to store.

3. Make the breaks in the center wall at a logical place. For example, in a box set, the walls could break in the center behind a jog positioned up- and downstage so that the break is not obvious when joined. For an exterior set, the break could be made at the place where an ornate metal fence joins a building.

4. Position a front portal downstage so that the offstage edges of the castered wagons can be masked. The portal does not have to move. It can also mask light instruments that are positioned vertically on the left and right sides as well as horizontally behind the portal header above.

5. To make the overall basic set that is riding on wagons appear wider, add hinged flippers to both the very downstage sides. These hinged flats (positioned perpendicular to the proscenium opening when closed) are opened once the wagons are in place to extend the width of the basic set. The hinged flippers may be painted and treated to match the walls of the basic set on wagons, and may be used as simple returns positioned parallel to the proscenium wall when opened.

6. Design walls so the flats sit on top of the main 6-inch platform. (These flats do not fasten against the outer sides of this platform.) Allow for offstage space on the main platform to attach jacks or other bracing.

7. Use partial ceiling pieces above to brace the units. Plan to have any center joining of the left and right ceiling pieces worked into the basic design so the break is not more obvious than necessary. A ceiling or ceiling pieces may also be flown in from above. However, ceiling pieces are not always an integral part of the design and it may not be necessary to use them.

8. Use archways as openings for entrances and exits instead of actual

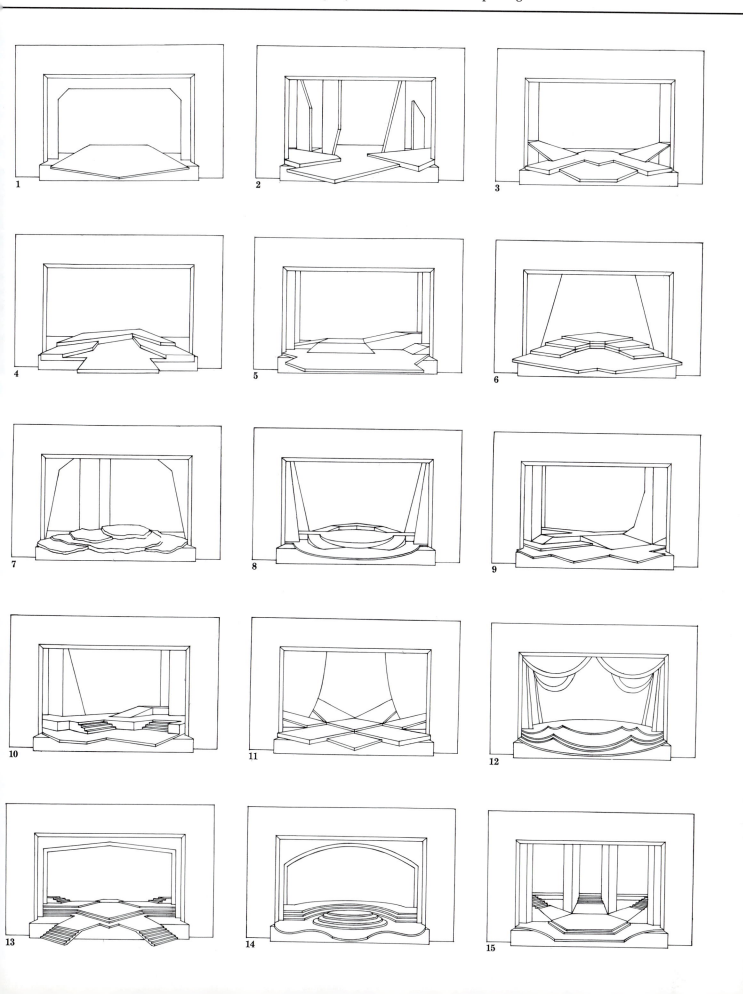

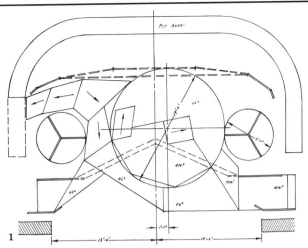

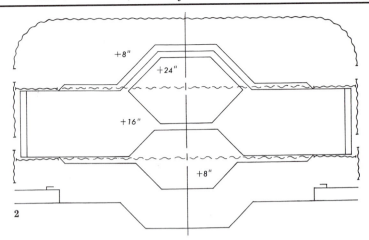

doors. While this is not always possible, it does save additional bracing and cost. Of course, the archways must work with the style and type of play.

9. Plan to have furniture, set dressing, chandeliers, and props ride with the rest of the set on the movable platform. Pictures, chandeliers, fragile bric-a-brac, and so on need to be fastened down so they do not move, sway, or shake as the wagon moves and just after it stops.

10. Have the backing units behind archways and doors work as separate units from the main set. The separate backing units can be easily stored offstage, and sometimes, if doors are closed, can be moved off before the scene ends.

Positioning Platforms Upstage for Large Productions

One of the best places to put a long continuous platform with steps is upstage in front of a backdrop. This platform is positioned parallel to the pro-

scenium opening and works well on a deep set for a ballet or dance production that has a series of wing and border units and a great deal of stage depth. A long platform such as this may be 2'-0" high by 3'-6" wide by 50'-0" long for a proscenium opening 40'-0" wide. It may also have two 8-inch-high steps positioned in front of the platform. This is a nice standard arrangement and works beautifully when used properly. The platform unit can give flexibility to the playing area in these ways:

1. It allows dancers and actors to come on from the wings upstage and make a parallel cross to center stage and then turn and come downstage in their dance.

2. It gives a higher level upstage for blocking a group of actors in contrast to those on the stage floor in the same scene.

3. It allows dancers and actors to come on left and right and then make diagonal crosses to down left and right.

4. It leaves the entire downstage space open for dancing.

5. With lighting instruments positioned upstage on the floor between the platform unit and the backdrop, the platform can serve as a dimensional ground row and mask the lights as they shine up on the backdrop.

6. A cut drop painted with either architecture or draperies can fly in and rest on top of this platform, creating a combined visual unit. The cut drop can have various entrance openings (three, four, or five) through which actors can walk on the platform and come down the two steps to the main stage floor.

7. For other scenes, the long platform positioned upstage parallel to the proscenium opening can be masked and hidden by flying in another drop just downstage of the entire unit.

Designing a Separate Facing for Platforms

There are several advantages to designing the facing for a platform as a separate unit. By designing one long, separate facing, you can cover and disguise the joins or breaks in platforms. To avoid exposing any hardware on the

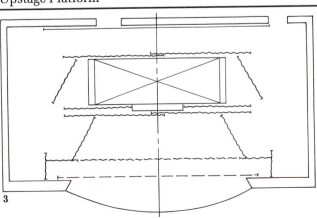

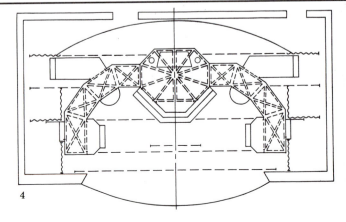

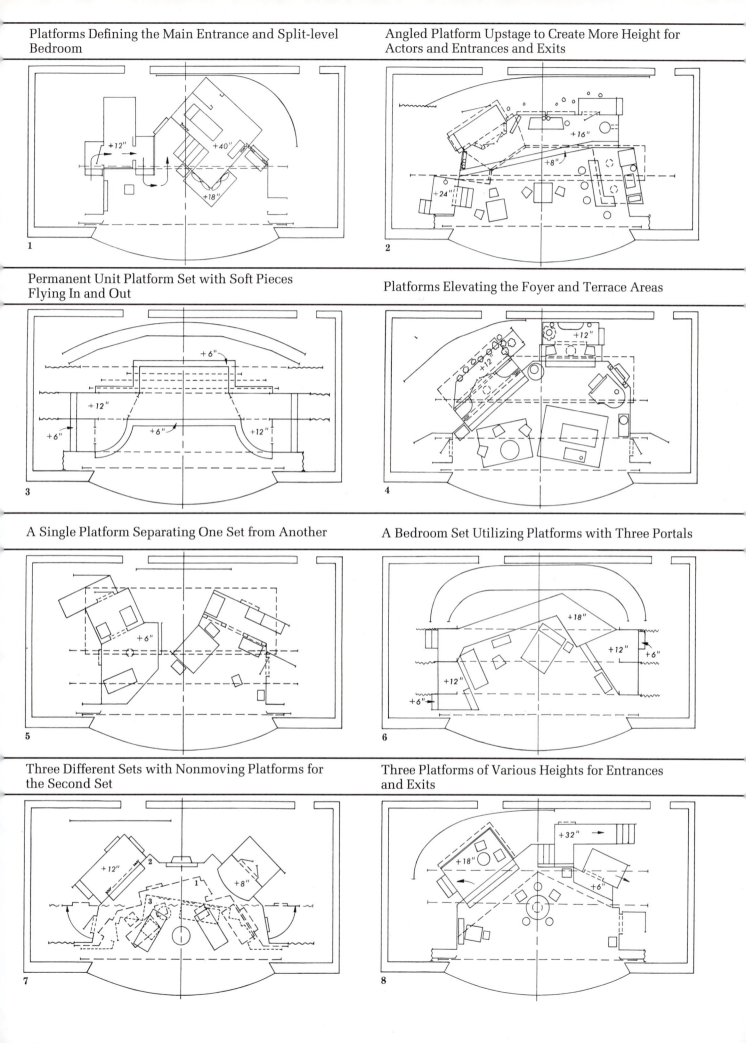

Platforms Defining the Main Entrance and Split-level Bedroom

1

Angled Platform Upstage to Create More Height for Actors and Entrances and Exits

2

Permanent Unit Platform Set with Soft Pieces Flying In and Out

3

Platforms Elevating the Foyer and Terrace Areas

4

A Single Platform Separating One Set from Another

5

A Bedroom Set Utilizing Platforms with Three Portals

6

Three Different Sets with Nonmoving Platforms for the Second Set

7

Three Platforms of Various Heights for Entrances and Exits

8

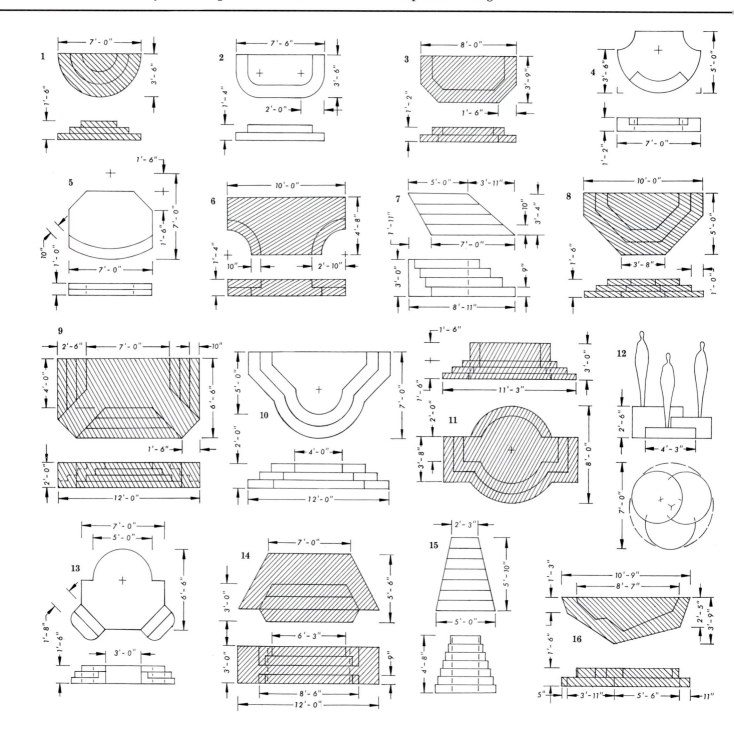

1. Step Unit with Applied Stonework; 2. & 3. Examples of Dimensions for a Platform and a Ramp; and 4. A Perspective Drawing of a Platform Unit

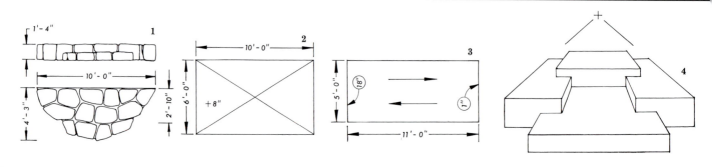

Front and Side Designs for Platforms and Also for Low Walls

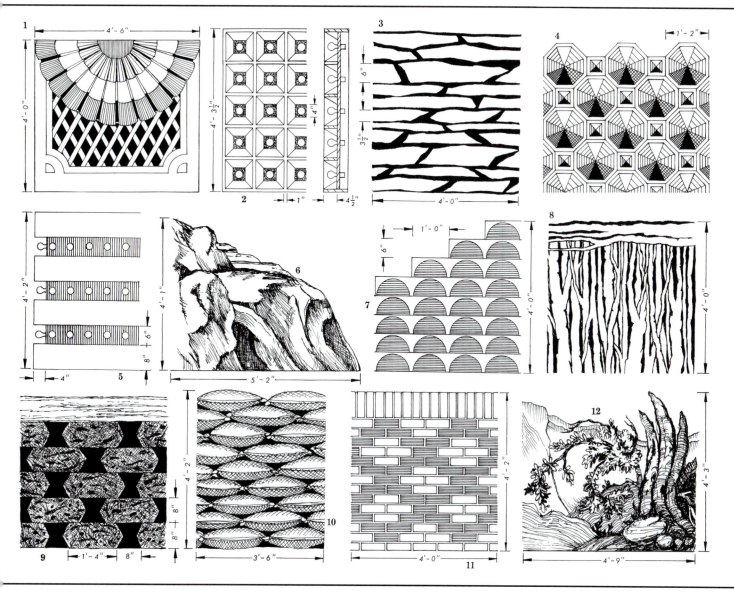

Ground Plan and Front Elevation of Podium Designs for Actors and Musicians

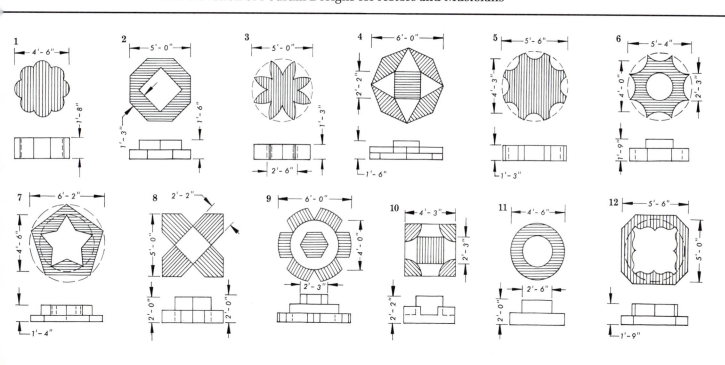

Edward Gorey's floor design for GOREY STORIES (1978), Booth Theatre, New York.

front, attach the rear of the facing unit to the front of the platforms with pin hinges, screws, or bolts. A separate platform facing can easily be covered and wrapped to protect it from getting scratched, nicked, and chipped in travel, loading, and setup. The facing may be made of ¼-inch plywood or two thicknesses of ¼-inch plywood glued together and overlapping the cracks where the lengths of lumber join. A facing may be covered with muslin, canvas, velour, duvetyne, or other appropriate fabric, and can be painted or left as it is.

Deadening the Sound under Platforms

Platforms, raised decks, and raked floors can be undesirably noisy when walked on. To avoid this annoying distraction during a performance, materials are used under these scenic units to deaden the surface noise. The following are considered very good for soundproofing under the top of platforms and raised decks:

1. Layers of Ozite rug padding
2. Sheets of Homosote
3. Thicknesses of fiber glass insulation material

Creating Podiums

Podiums are wonderful small platform units that elevate a performer or orchestra conductor, telling the audience exactly where to look. They are most often designed for singers, actors, and musicians. However, they also work beautifully for fashion shows and beauty pageants.

Podium units consist of one, two, three, or four steps that can be in the shape of all sorts of geometric configurations. They may be covered on the side with mirrored or glittering facings, completely covered in bright carpet, painted in numerous designs, or neutral in shape and color. Podiums may also be made of stained wood with beautiful graining.

INTERIOR AND EXTERIOR DETAILS

Checklist of Wall Treatments

The listed objects and materials may be used for both interior and exterior walls. They are also well suited for either ceilings or roofs. The list includes real materials as well as those that are painted or simulated.

Painted smooth plaster	Fabric coverings
	Clapboards
Woven plastics	Random bricks
Metal grillwork panels	Matchstick boards
	Grass matting
Corrugated aluminum	Vinyl coverings
	Stucco walls
Boards and planks	Glass bricks
Stenciled wallpapers	Wooden shingles
Real wallpapers	Openwork wooden cutouts
Cinder blocks	
Pressed metal designs	Metallized plastics
	Wooden panels
Various tiles	Carved Styrofoam

Patterned bricks	Natural fieldstones
Rough and swirled plaster	Concrete block patterns
Openwork fabrics	Composite stones
Commercially stamped woodwork	Quoin stonework
	Plaster and laths
	Erosion cloth

Painting Individual Wall Patterns

Individual wall patterns may be painted to simulate wallpaper or wall coverings. The number of patterns is endless. Wall pattern designs may be applied on the flats or backdrops by stenciling (floral wallpaper), by painting with a brush and straight edge (stripes), or by using a perforated pounce and inking (scenic wallpaper). Painted wall patterns include:

Stripes	Marbleized panel
Paisleys	Wood graining
Plaids	Damasks
Diamonds	Squares
Florals	Textures
Tiles	Abstracts

Checklist of Architectural and Decorative Wall Features

These basic items and details may be used for walls and ceilings in both interior and exterior scenes:

Columns and pilasters	Bookcases
	Wall niches
Windows with and without trim	Doors with and without trim
Shutters	Stairways
Fireplaces and mantels	Wainscoting
	Railings
Chair rails	Picture moldings
Baseboards	Ceiling beams
Arches with and without trim	Ceiling medallions
	Plate rails

Exterior Building Finishes

Exterior building finishes should be designed to be practical as well as visually appropriate. Some examples of exterior finishes may be real or painted wood, simulated stonework of all kinds, various brick patterns, stucco, cement, marbleizing, tile work, cinder block, or other similar materials. Even a simple design for an exterior building finish can be costly to build, become too heavy, or create problems for storage. There are practical methods of executing an exterior building finish that are equally effective. The desired effect, the durability of the materials for the run of the show, and whether the unit will be reused for another production (depending on where it takes place) are factors that determine the choice of execution.

You may want to use scenic units made of canvas on ⅛-inch plywood on 1 × 3-inch wooden framing, or just canvas on framing without the plywood. Some wonderful effects can be achieved with traditional scenic painting on canvas.

It is up to the designer to figure out how to make the scenery uncomplicated by using imagination and good taste. Remember that good scenic painting, well-designed profiled edges, and some three-dimensional appliqué detail such as molding, rosettes, and other ornaments can work splendidly together, especially when positioned nicely with appropriate props and set dressing and enhanced by attractive lighting.

Setting by Loren Sherman
THE DINING ROOM by A. R. Gurney
Directed by David Trainer
Lighting by Frances Aronson
Astor Place Theatre, New York (1982)
(Photograph by Loren Sherman)

"The play contained seventeen scenes relating to different aspects of the lost elegance of a lifestyle that included cvilized dinners in the family dining room. The set was a 'nonspecific,' though warm, dining room that could serve for all these scenes. The set was a little like a museum exhibit of a dining room from the northeastern United States in the early twentieth century."   —Loren Sherman

Using Abstract Wall Units in an Arbitrary Way

Although we tend to think of wall units in the traditional sense as consisting of flats in an interior or exterior set, three-dimensional walls with various overall sizes and thicknesses can also be created and used in an almost endless number of ways. See page 258. These ideas should be considered.

1. *Shapes.* The walls may be straight, angled, or curved, or a combination of these. Strong angles, gentle curves, or leaning walls work nicely.
2. *Sizes.* Effective thickness of units may be from 2 to 3 feet. Depending on the size of the stage and the design concept, height and width may be fairly large.
3. *Movement.* Units may have fixed or swivel casters. They may move mechanically in a track or be pushed by hand. Also, they may turn by pivoting. When the units are designed large enough, a stagehand can be hidden inside the units and move them on cue. This adds a mysterious quality that can be most successful and delightful.
4. *Storing items.* Units designed to be 3 feet wide can hide furniture and props. Wall units on casters can have hinged doors in the sides, tops, or ends.
5. *Hinged walls.* Wall units may be designed to split in the center to form another wall.
6. *Subjects.* The walls may be used as completely abstract designs, as simple textured surfaces, as shiny surfaces

such as Mylar and mirrored patterns, or as units with various wallpaper motifs.

PILASTERS

Using Pilasters in a Setting

A pilaster is a shallow rectangular element projecting from a wall. This upright unit has a capital and a base and usually imitates the form of a column. Pilasters are ordinarily easier to build than round columns and, of course, look wonderful on stage. One of the great advantages of having pilasters in a stage set is that you can combine them with other woodwork members to create the basic woodwork for archways, windows, and doors. They can also give a nice architectural unity and consistency to the basic woodwork in a set. For instance, if you are designing a set with one large center arch and windows upstage and an entrance left and right, two pilasters holding up a cornice piece can be used for each of the three units. For the stage the pilaster may:

1. Be placed under a cornice, header, or pediment.
2. Go from floor to ceiling or lower.
3. Be part of units such as hallways, doors, windows, or furniture.
4. Be a large unit with four pilasters. The unit may have a cornice at the top with two pilasters resting against a wall on each end and the two cen-

Model by Loren Sherman
MARAT/SADE by Peter Weiss

Directed by Arnold Mittelman
Whole Theatre Company

Montclair, New Jersey (1982)
(Photograph by Loren Sherman)

ter ones positioned in space with an opening to a hall or foyer behind the pilaster unit. The bases of the four pilasters may rest on the floor or on a low wall on either side of an opening at center.

5. Be a doorway unit formed with a cornice at the top and lower down a somewhat smaller horizontal unit positioned in between the two pilasters. A decorative cutout design may be positioned in between the two horizontal members and the pilasters. Often, a single or double door unit (swinging or sliding doors) is positioned below this unit. Draped curtains may also be placed in the opening under the cutouts.

6. Form a large central woodwork unit. It may have only windows or both windows and a window seat behind it. These pieces consisting of pilasters and cornices may also have curved arches with thickness as part of the overall woodwork unit, or other geometric shapes.

7. Be a simple capital at the top and base at the bottom. These may be simple applied blocks of wood with molding going around them, or both the capital and the base may be designed to be more complex. Usually capitals are the most detailed.

8. Have the main vertical units built of wood which may have the natural wood grain show through transpar-

"The set was 40 feet wide and 17 feet deep. Only one entrance—upstairs on stage left to give a 'trapped' feeling. Plumbing elements (showers and baths for treatment of mental patients) were based on eighteenth-century industrial methods as illustrated in Diderot's *Encyclopedia of Trades and Industry*, which was published in 1752. The walls of the set depicted stone in broken condition covered by plaster in broken condition covered by tiles in broken condition." —Loren Sherman

ent stains or washes. The vertical front portions of the pilasters also may be covered first with muslin before molding or any details are applied, and then painted to be opaque.

9. Have details on the face of the pilaster. These may be either painted or

Rolling Wall Units (Interior or Exterior) That Pivot, Turn, and Open and Close

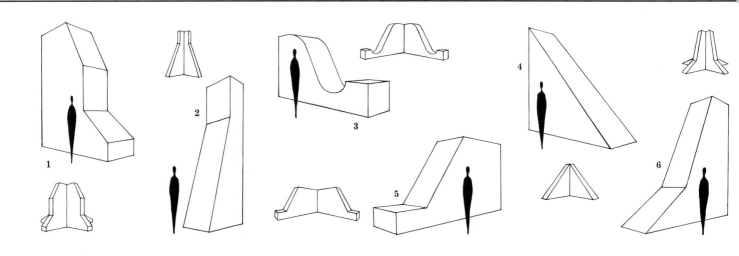

Setting by Heidi Landesman
PAINTING CHURCHES by Tina Howe

Directed by Carole Rothman
Lighting by Frances Aronson

Lamb's Theatre
New York (1983)

Model by Charles E. McCarry
PAINTING CHURCHES by Tina Howe

Directed by Evan Yionoulis
Portland Stage Company

Portland
Maine (1987)

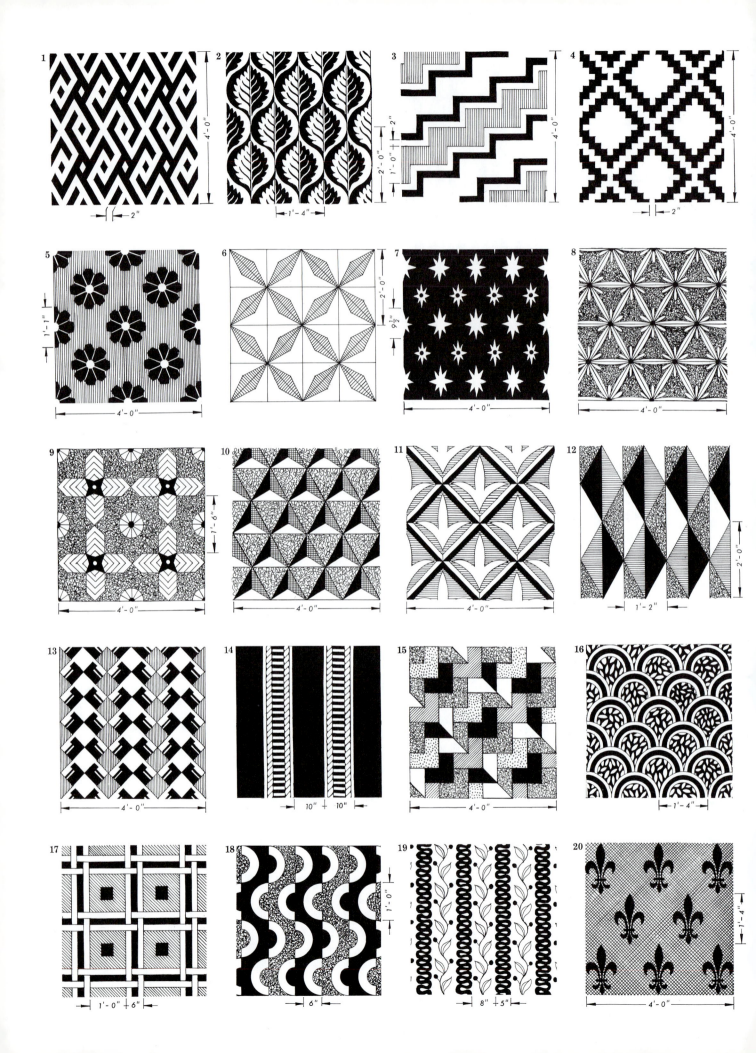

Quilt and Coverlet Patterns for Simulating Bed Covering and Also for Walls

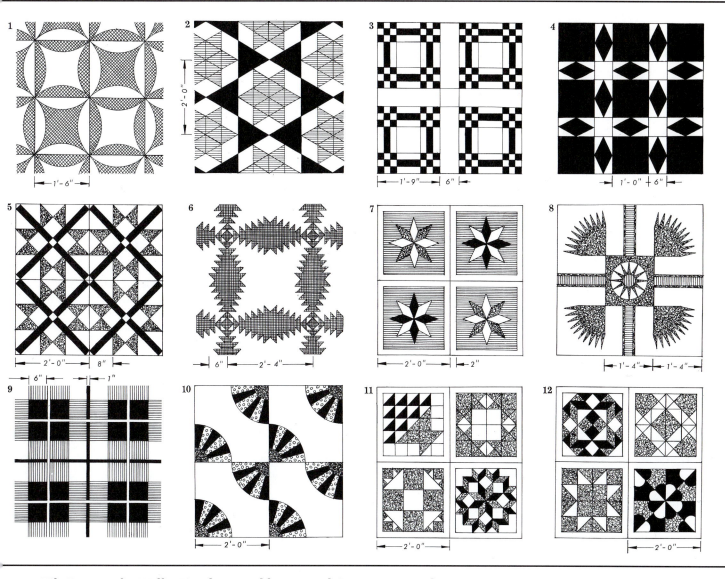

Tile Patterns for Walls, Fireplaces, Tabletops, and Continuous Borders

built designs. The designs may be applied with a stencil or by freehand painting. Also, the designs may be put on by brush after the drawings are transferred with a paper pounce.

10. Panels on the face of a pilaster may be recessed with moldings, be left plain, or have cutout ornaments like rosettes, circles, ovals, or other geometrical shapes applied.

11. Have painted or carved vertical flutes or applied half-round shapes on the face.

The Size of Pilasters

While the measurements of pilasters vary with the design, these dimensions are common:

3 × 6 in.	5 × 12 in.	10 × 28 in.
4 × 8 in.	8 × 18 in.	12 × 36 in.

Making Pilasters

Usually the stage pilaster consists of a face and two sides with an open back; ¾-inch-thick wooden blocks can be positioned inside for support. The sides may be built of ¾-inch wood, with the face made of ¼-inch plywood. When the three sides are put together to form a U shape with the ¾-inch blocks attached inside, the basic pilaster can be covered with one long piece of muslin or canvas. The back of the pilaster may fit flat against the wing, or one side may be wider to form a deeper thickness in the opening of an arch or doorway.

MOLDING, CORNICES, AND WAINSCOTING

Selecting Molding

In selecting molding to use on stage settings, always consider how close the audience will be to the setting. Is the setting to be for a proscenium stage or for in the round? Keep these points in mind when selecting molding.

1. Select molding that reads well from the audience. A combination of basic

molding built in a fairly large scale often works better than what you would purchase for use in a home. Remember that small molding details in ⅛ inch, ³∕₁₆ inch, and even ¼ inch tend to get lost visually when viewed by the theatre audience from 40 feet away. Molding that is seen close up in films and television settings is another matter.

2. Make sure that the molding you select is easy to obtain locally.

3. Select molding that fits within the production budget. Do not be reluctant to make an alternative choice that would save time and money.

Using Simple Pieces of Molding

Instead of using a lot of detailed molding pieces for the stage, it is possible to combine several simple pieces of molding in a multitude of ways to create attractive stage molding that reads well from the audience. Three-dimensional molding may be combined with

Stage design by William and Jean Eckart
MISTER JOHNSON by Norman Rosten

Directed by Robert Lewis
Martin Beck Theatre, New York (1956)

Exterior and Interior Wall and Floor Materials (Photographs by Lynn Pecktal)

Roof Shingles: 1. Painted Shingles on Canvas; 2. Split Shingles; 3. Shingles Made with Rug Padding, Cheesecloth, Scenic Dope, and Paint

Plain Pilasters with Arch   Pilaster Details: Applied and/or Painted

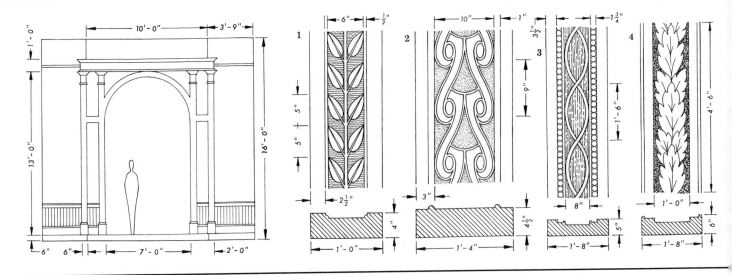

Cornice on Reeded Pilaster   Full-Length Pilasters

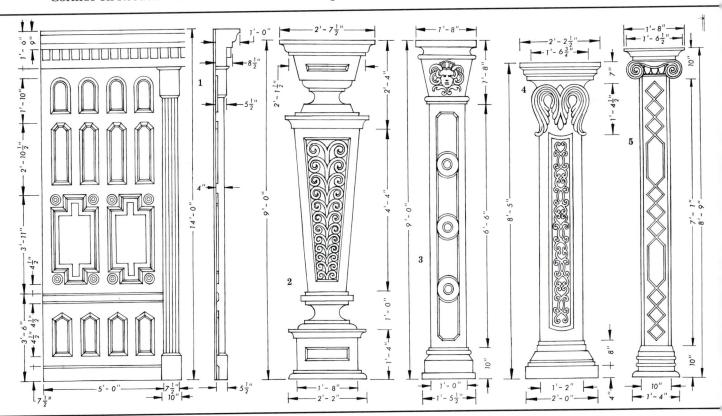

Floor-to-Ceiling Pilasters with Horizontal Members (above and between) Recessed 2 Inches

Stage design by Zack Brown
MANON by Jules Massenet
Libretto by Henri Meilhac and Philippe Gille
Directed by Roman Terleckyj
Washington Opera, Washington, D.C. (1991)

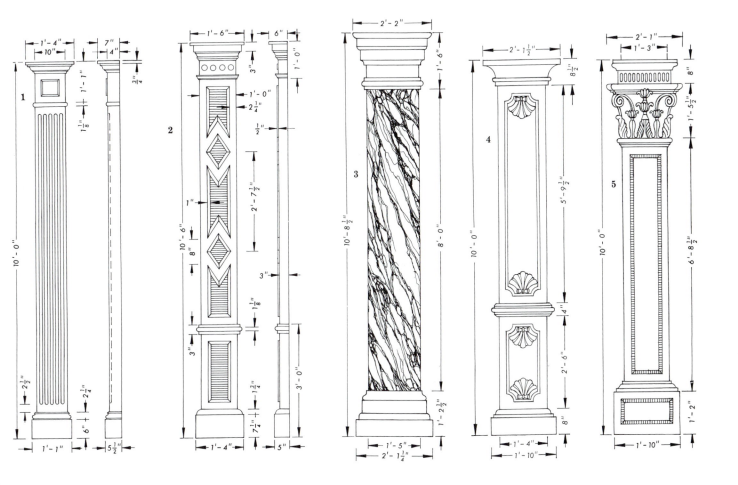

Setting by Elmon Webb and Virginia Dancy
WHAT THE BUTLER SAW by Joe Orton
Directed by Marshall Oglesby
Lighting by James E. Stephens
Syracuse Stage
Syracuse, New York (1977)

painted details of classical stencil patterns such as bands of egg and dart, roping, Greek keys, guilloche, rosettes, and other designs.

Whether used alone or in combination, the molding pieces listed below are great for cornices, wainscoting, door panels, and stair units. These pieces are usually readily available in local lumber stores and often are stock items that are on hand in scenic shops.

Half rounds	Skewbacks
Quarter rounds	Coves
Strips	Nosing and coves
Squares	Pressed moldings

Drawing Molding in Full Scale

Instead of going to the trouble of drawing the details on any complex molding in the small scale of ½ inch, 1 inch, 1½ inches, or even 3 inches, the molding can be drawn in full scale on a separate sheet of tracing paper and included in the group of production prints. The different units of molding for the cornice, picture molding, chair rail, and baseboard can be labeled A,

B, C, D, and so on in the full-scale drawing and then the same labeling can be done on each ½-inch elevation where the molding appears. There are some reasons for doing a full-scale drawing of molding.

1. It clarifies the exact proportions of the molding.
2. It saves time in drawing the molding on each unit of scenery on the designer's ½-inch elevations. You only need to indicate all the lines of the different moldings on one elevation of a flat to show the relationship of proportions. Then on the remaining elevations of flats, only the top and bottom lines of individual molding need be drawn and labeled with the appropriate letters from the full-scale drawing of the molding.
3. It allows the scenic shop to easily build or select molding.
4. It permits the shop to place accessible molding samples directly on the print to see if substitutions or variations can be made when the availability from a local purchasing source is limited.

Molding Dimensions

Listed are frequently used moldings. These standard sizes (in inches) are shown in vertical columns under the headings.

MOLDING DIMENSIONS

HALF ROUNDS	QUARTER ROUNDS
¼ × ½	½ × ½
5/16 × 5/8	3/8 × 3/8
3/8 × 3/4	½ × ½
7/16 × 7/8	5/8 × 5/8
9/16 × 1 1/8	11/16 × 11/16
11/16 × 1 3/8	3/4 × 3/4
11/16 × 1 5/8	1 3/8 × 1 3/8

SQUARES	
½ × ½	1 5/16 × 1 5/16
3/4 × 3/4	1 3/8 × 1 3/8
1 1/16 × 1 1/16	1 9/16 × 1 9/16
1 1/8 × 1 1/8	1 3/4 × 1 3/4

SKEWBACKS	
½ × ½	1 × 1
3/4 × 3/4	1 5/8 × 1 5/8

NOSING AND COVES	
11/16 × 1 1/8	1 1/8 × 1 3/4
3/4 × 1 3/8	1 3/8 × 2 1/4

STRIPS	
3/8 × 7/8	3/4 × 2 1/2
7/16 × 1 1/8	3/4 × 3 1/2
7/16 × 1 3/8	1 1/16 × 1 5/8
½ × 1 5/8	1 1/16 × 2 1/2
½ × 3/4	1 1/16 × 3 1/2
½ × 2 5/8	1 9/16 × 2 1/2
½ × 3 5/8	1 9/16 × 3 1/2
3/4 × 1 5/8	

COVES	
½ × ½	11/16 × 1 1/8
½ × 1 1/2	1 1/8 × 1 3/8
11/16 × 11/16	1 3/8 × 1 3/4

Additional Moldings

If a more extensive list of molding than is shown in the table is necessary for the scenery, a choice may be made from these:

Ogee moldings	Box pilasters
Crown moldings	Sanitary trim and base
Solid crowns	Chair rails
Base moldings	Pressed moldings
Panel moldings	Window and door
Glass moldings	stops

Astragals   Corner guards
Rounds   Picture moldings
Clamshell trim   Shelf edges
Trim and casing

Designing Cornices

A common cornice design has molding pieces at the top and bottom, with a plain unadorned space in the center. Cornice designs may be cut out of wood or other materials and applied on flats or directly on the surface. Designs may include:

Dental   Acanthus
Federal   Plain
Greek key   Egg and dart
Doric   Alternating rosettes
Guilloche   Shell and triglyph
Floral   Fluted

The finished cornice pieces may be attached at the top of the flats by bolts, screws, or hooks shaped to go over the top of the flats.

While cornices can be painted on the top of the actual flats, they tend to look better when they are built as three-dimensional units of projected molding. A cornice in an interior set gives a nice architectural finish to a room. An average size for a cornice in a room 14'-0" high may be 1'-6" high by 6" deep. The same room may also have paneling at the bottom of the walls that is approximately 3 feet high.

Cornices range from simple to elaborate designs. These three-dimensional units at the top of flats at the ceiling line are mitered at the corners to the degree of the angles of the walls. For a good join, it is usually best to erect the set in the shop as it is going to be positioned on stage, and then assemble all the lengths of cornice when all the flats are in place.

For discussion, let us assume that the cornice in side section is 1'-6" high by 6" deep and that this basic shape is designed to be used as a pattern to cut out and build the actual cornice. Of course, this means that the cornice should be fully shown as it appears on the front elevations of the ½-inch scale drawing. However, if the cornice has an unusual shape it may be best to include a side section of the cornice in full scale.

This full-scale drawing can be used to make a pattern to build the actual wooden side sections. These sections can be made of ¾-inch plywood and should have cutout areas where the

horizontal lengths of wood are to run through them. These lengths of wood may be ¾ inch × 1 inch, ¾ inch × 1 ½ inches, ¾ inch × 2 inches, and so on. The point is to create the cornice as lightweight as possible, but at the same time make the framework sturdy enough to hold a covering material to give the cornice a nice smooth exterior surface that will take the paint nicely.

It works well to design a cornice so the basic shape can be made first, then covered with muslin, then have any selected lengths of standard moldings added on top of the muslin. Detailed trims such as ⅛-inch cutouts or three-dimensional rosettes or other items can also be added over the covered muslin.

Instead of gluing on three-dimensional appliqués or details, you might want to paint the detail work with colors mixed to represent light, shade, and shadow. For hand painting work, make a paper pounce out of brown paper, perforate it, and use a bag of powdered charcoal to transfer the designs to the surface. Or you may want to lay in the cornice with a basic color and tone it with paints from Hudson spray tanks.

When building the cornice pieces to attach to the top of the flats, begin with the rear top and rear bottom pieces of wood, which will be the main supports for the cornice pieces. These pieces of

Setting and lighting by Neil Peter Jampolis
WHAT THE BUTLER SAW by Joe Orton
Directed by Michael Bawtree
Costumes by Annie Peacock Warner
Playhouse in the Park
Cincinnati, Ohio (1976)

wood may be ¾ inch by 2 inches and both rest with the flat side against the face of the flat at the top. Cut out a side section from ¾-inch plywood and then notch out a place at the back bottom and top of the section so the two horizontal running pieces fit in neatly and flush. Use this as a practical pattern and cut out more sections. Space them 2 feet apart. This method of building is similar to constructing the framework for a model airplane wing.

Next, continue working on the framework for the face of the cornice. Place lengths of wood across the plywood sections on the front; these pieces may not be as wide as the lengths on the back. Notch out the sections so these lengths of wood fit into the sections. The number of lengths of wood depends on the overall height of the cornice. Use one at the top, then one on the bottom, and one or so in between.

Now you are ready to build the cornice pieces, fitting the inner and outer corners to the angles of the flats on the ground plan. Use a piece of ¼-inch plywood to finish off the ends of each length of cornice.

Several kinds of materials can be used to cover or to fill in the cornice— for example, ⅛-inch plywood, illustration board, sheet metal pieces, and lengths of Styrofoam or Ethafoam. These materials may be put on the cornice framework with glue, staples, or small nails and covered with muslin. Any selected lengths of wooden molding can then be added to the basic shape after it has been covered.

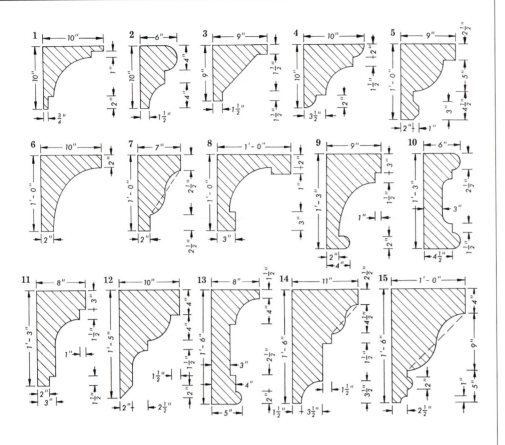

Architectural Designs for Cornices

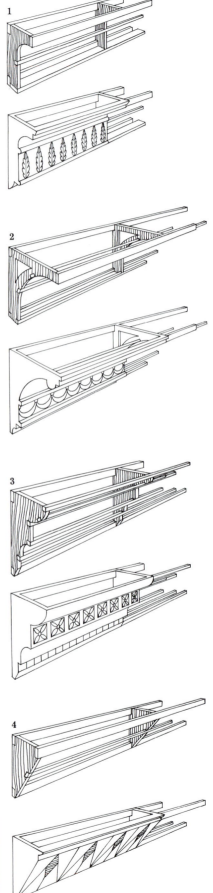

Three-Dimensional Cornices with Painted Details and a Cornice with Dentils

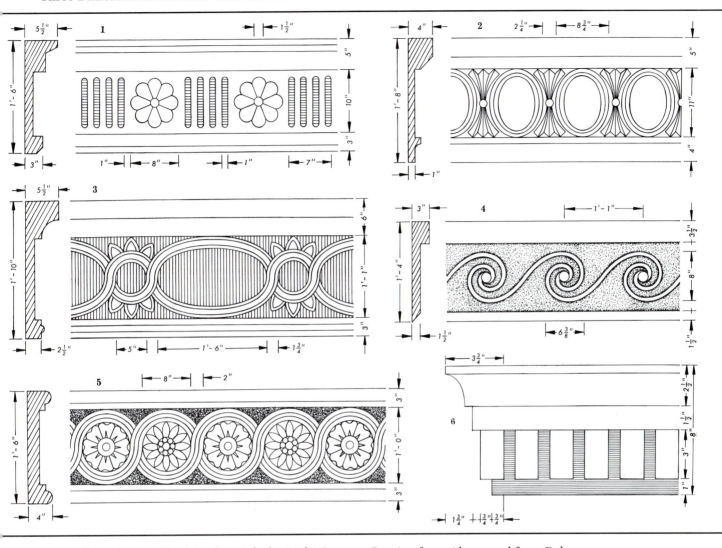

Painted Cornices by Fred Jacoby with the Light Sources Coming from Above and from Below

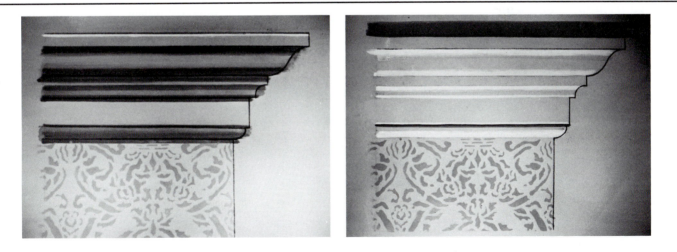

Roman Moldings: 1. Cyma Reversa; 2.–3. Cyma Recta; 4. Ovolo; 5. Scotia; 6.–7. Cavetto

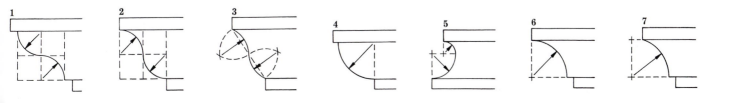

272 Using Picture Molding

Picture molding is an effective architectural member used in various interior settings. It serves three main functions: as an accurate historical feature; as a practical member on which to attach hooks, cords, and wires to suspend pictures, paintings, and mirrors; and as an ideal feature for covering the horizontal cracks where header units join the tops of flats.

Hanging tapestries, bell pulls, masks, decorative rugs, and painted panels may be fastened to the horizontal picture molding running around the interior walls. While simple and inconspicuous hooks may be used, other, more elaborate ornamental objects are also quite appropriate for hanging objects from picture molding. These ornate objects that bring a focus to the detailed elements at the top of hanging pieces may be overscale bows, rosettes, ruffled fabric, or woven medallions and tassels.

The picture molding may also be used as a horizontal dividing line in the wall treatment. For example, it may be positioned where the top of the wallpaper or another design ends and a different pattern or paint treatment begins above the picture molding but below the cornice. Picture molding works nicely to hide any horizontal cracks (joins) of pieces of scenery. Often these pieces are two flats and a header with a cut out arch.

Figuring Proportions of Wainscoting and Cornices in an Interior Set

Use this table of basic proportions for figuring the height dimensions of the wainscoting, picture molding, and cornices in an interior set. Proportions may vary according to the historical period of the production and also the individual style. The sizes of picture molding are suggested as a guide. While you may vary the size a bit, keep the top height of the molding as given.

Designing Wainscoting

This lower portion of woodwork in an interior stage set goes from the floor up to an average height of 2'-6", 3'-0", 3'-6", or 4'-0", depending of course on the scale of the room and the height of the flats (or walls). The historical period of the interior affects the basic design and height of the wainscoting which may include the baseboard at the bottom and the paneling above, with a cap positioned at the top. Sometimes where appropriate, a chair rail is used at the top of the wainscoting instead of a cap.

Wainscoting for a set can be designed to be executed in these ways:

1. *All flat painted woodwork (baseboard, paneling, and cap or chair rail).* Appropriate scenic painting is applied with brushes on canvas or muslin-covered flats (laid flat on the floor) to make the woodwork appear three-dimensional. This task is always easier when the canvas is glued on 1/8-inch plywood that has been mounted on 1 × 3-inch lumber. If there is no backing on the canvas, the impression of the framing of the flat will show through the fabric while you are working on it. This happens when walking and standing on it to execute the drawing and painting.
2. *Partially built woodwork.* This involves using real wood for the baseboard and chair rail. Both should be fastened with screws or bolts onto the face of the canvas flat. Again, it works and looks better when the canvas is backed with 1/8-inch plywood. This method is successful when the center paneling is well painted to appear three-dimensional. Naturally, the real baseboard and chair rail should both have appropriate scenic painting done on them so that they work as a unit with the overall wainscoting.
3. *All-built woodwork.* Built woodwork is possibly the best approach, simply because it pays off in the long run both

visually and practically. While all-built woodwork must have sufficient scenic painting too, this is easier to accomplish on an all-built unit. With the high cost of labor for painting, it is usually more economical to invest in lumber for building and even to minimize painting costs by laying in the color(s), spraying, or dragging graining over with a brush rather than creating all the painting from scratch and getting involved in painting enormous detail. Again, this depends on the historical period of the production. It is another matter when time and budget are plentiful for doing detailed painting. The weight of the additional wood must be taken into consideration so that the woodwork units do not become too heavy. However, the overall all-built and then painted effect is usually well worth the effort involved.

Creating Three-Dimensional Wainscoting

Assume that you are going to make an all-wood three-dimensional wainscoting. This includes the baseboard at the bottom, the cap or the chair rail at the top, and any paneling in between, plus the support backing to hold all of this together as one unit.

For practical and economical purposes, use a sheet of 1/8-inch or 1/4-inch plywood as an overall back support for the wainscoting. The thickness of wood you choose depends on what will hold up best with the applied wood. For instance, if the production is touring, the heavier 1/4-inch plywood would work better as a back support.

This separate base of thin plywood to be attached to the bottom of the flat should be the width of the individual flat (depending on the mitered sides, plus or minus). This means, of course, that the whole basic set must be positioned in the shop exactly as it is to play on stage so that all of the wainscoting pieces can be sawed and fitted according to the angles involved for each and every piece. This positioning of built flats is normally done anyway, because all the units must be fitted together for hardware to be put on. Stylized sets that have single flats positioned and isolated in space are a different matter.

Let us assume that the following discussion of one piece of the plywood back support with molding applies

FLAT HEIGHT	WAINSCOTING HEIGHT	PICTURE MOLDING SIZE AND TOP HEIGHT	CORNICE OVERALL SIZE
10'-0"	2'-6"	1¾" at 7'-6"	1'-0"
12'-0"	2'-9"	2" at 9'-0"	1'-3"
14'-0"	3'-0"	2¼" at 10'-6"	1'-6"
16'-0"	3'-3"	2½" at 12'-0"	1'-9"
18'-0"	3'-6"	2¾" at 13'-6"	2'-0"
20'-0"	3'-9"	3" at 15'-0"	2'-3"

collectively to the whole group of flats. Here we are describing a single average flat.

If we have a flat that is 3'-6" wide and want the applied wainscoting to be anywhere from 2'-6" to 4'-0" high, then the piece of ⅛-inch or ¼-inch plywood would be at least 3 feet 6 inches or wider, depending on the angles of the mitering on the two outside edges.

Cover this rectangular or square sheet of plywood with muslin first, then apply the chair rail (or cap), the baseboard, and any panel molding that may be designed to go in between these two pieces of horizontal woodwork. For some paint treatments, where the center portion of the wainscoting is to have different color(s) or perhaps graining, then the support backing of plywood with muslin glued on the face may be painted before the other wooden members are attached, also on the face. These may be nailed or screwed and/or glued on so that the whole unit of rear support backing with applied woodwork stays together nicely as a unit. This unit can be bolted on the respective flat and taken off or left on for individual painting, depending on the desired effect.

Touch-up paint(s) should always be provided for painting the screw and bolt heads so that they are not obvious when the wainscoting is attached.

Using a Heavier Support on the Rear of the Wainscoting

While ⅛-inch or ¼-inch plywood is a good basic material on which to apply molding that is to be positioned on the bottom front of a flat, there are times when this plywood piece (forming the wainscoting) needs to be made thicker and sturdier. This can be done by framing the plywood (⅛- or ¼-inch) on the back with 1 × 3-inch lumber, as you would a flat, and then positioning it in front of the bottom of the flat. Two reasons for doing this are: (1) the wainscoting piece (made of plywood) needs to be stronger and hold up well in setup and handling, possibly for touring; or (2) the wainscoting is designed to have the center panel(s) recessed a depth of ¾ inch, 1 inch, 1¼ inches, or 1½ inches. Panel molding is usually designed to go in these recessed panels.

At any rate, the bottom of the flat behind the wainscoting (unframed or framed) should not be covered with canvas or plywood, because it is not needed and of course does not show. This means that the horizontal toggle in the flat behind should correspond to the wainscoting top (cap or chair rail) so that the wall covering on the main flat can continue down 3 inches past where the top of the wainscoting attaches. This is built as a separate unit, then attached to the flat by screws and bolts.

Using Natural Wood for the Wainscoting

On productions in which the designer wants to have a natural wood, the effect of graining and texturing can be done with aniline dyes to allow the grain of the wood to show through. Minwax stains may also be used on the natural wood.

An example of this would be a matchstick board with a double groove in the center that runs vertically and is approximately 3½ inches wide by ⅜ inches thick. The boards have tongue-and-groove on the edges and fit together to form an interesting arrangement of vertical boards, with the chair rail at the top and the baseboard at the bottom. The rear support of the matchstick boards may be a lightweight wood; or the chair rail on the face attached at the top and the baseboard attached on the face of the bottom may be strong enough to hold the unit together, especially when it is glued and nailed. But this depends on the overall widths of the wainscoting. Small widths would not always need a support backing. Another interesting aspect of using a simple wood like a matchstick board is that when painted with old graining and texture, it could be used for a set such as a run-down tenement or a Eugene O'Neill bar, but if painted a light opaque color that is neatly applied, it could be used for a formal drawing room set.

Finishing Off the End of Chair Rails

While chair rails may be the top portion of wainscoting in an interior set, they are also sometimes designated to be used on the wall as a separate horizontal running unit. Chair rails may end by:

1. Butting flush with another molding, such as a door casing
2. Returning around an outer corner or a wall and going into the thickness of an opening (right-angle or otherwise)
3. Having the end beveled back 45 degrees (without joining another piece of chair railing)

Using a Plate Rail

In some period sets of a living room, dining room, library, den, bar, or kitchen, the top of the paneling from the floor to a height of 5'-0" or 5'-9" is ideal for positioning a plate rail. This may be a piece of wood (3 to 4 inches wide by ¾ inch high) positioned horizontally at the top of the paneling with a length of molding supporting it from underneath. The plate rail is most appropriate for holding and displaying set dressing such as large platters, plates of various sizes, trays, small pictures, opened hand fans, and framed photographs. Usually it is best if these objects are held in place with wire, brads, or small screws.

In addition to being positioned at the top of paneling, a plate rail may be located above the top of doors, archways, windows, or bookcases. Sometimes an open plate rack is created to hold several plates and platters positioned in a group. This open rack is usually made of wooden, brass, or other metal rods.

STAIRCASE UNITS

Designing Stair Units

There are certain points to keep in mind when designing a stair unit. The stair unit must have the appropriate visual appearance and practicality necessary for it to work well for the production. The stair unit should have pleasant proportions, follow the style of the historical period, and be right for the production.

A frequent error in the design of stair units that is made by both beginning and experienced designers is to design a railing that is too skimpy or lightweight for the spindles or balusters (or other designs below the handrail). The best way to avoid this is to study photographs and drawings of classical architecture that feature stairs and railings. Then work out various proportions and compare them with the photographs until you are satisfied with the result. If spindles and balusters are part of the design, they should be spaced equally and attractively so that their center lines are completely

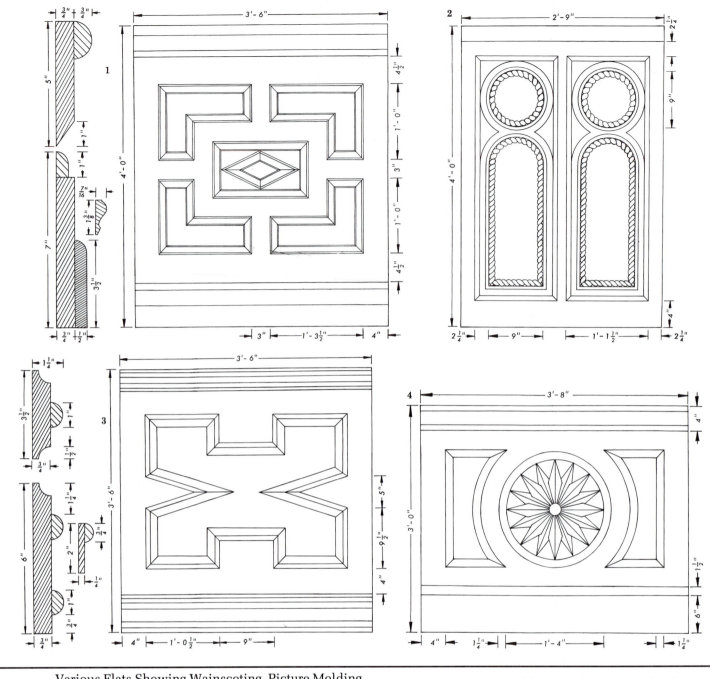

Various Flats Showing Wainscoting, Picture Molding, and Cornice for Each; Picture Molding at Top Left

Molding Panel Above and Below

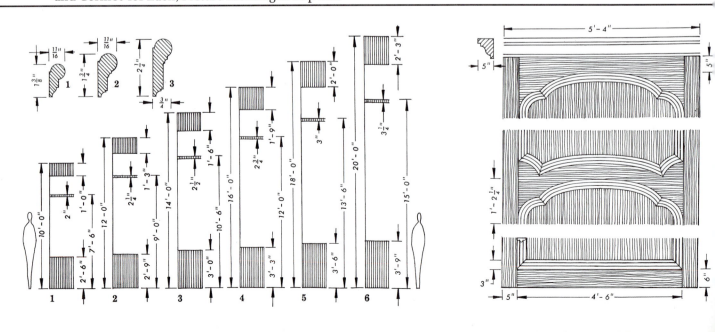

Wainscoting Designs with Alternating Panels and Motifs

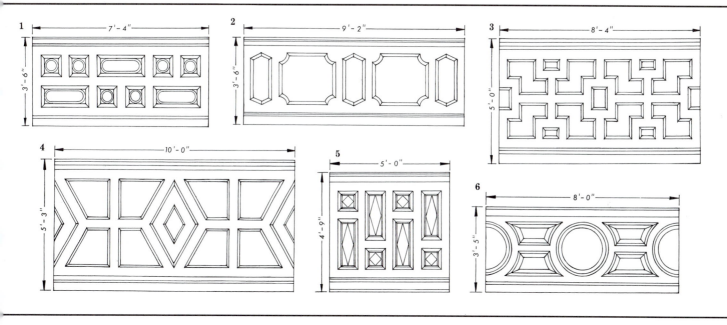

Designs for Upper Wall Details Positioned above the Wainscoting

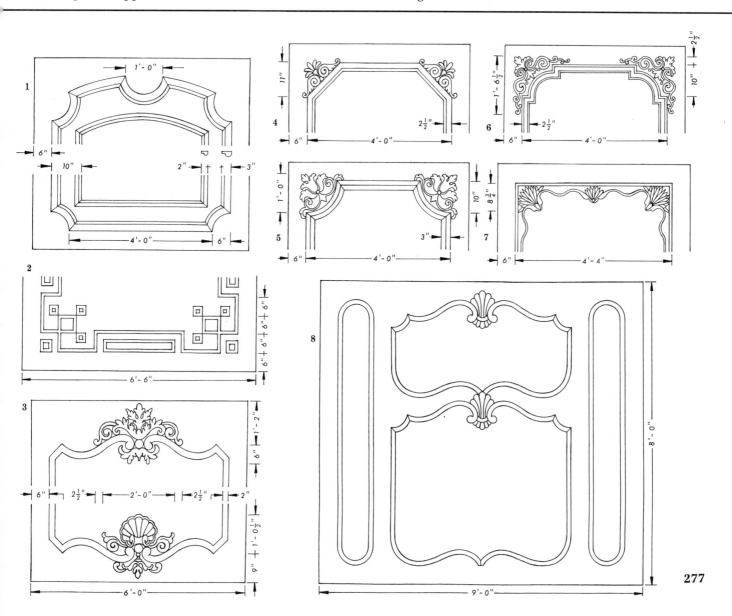

Panel Designs of One Size

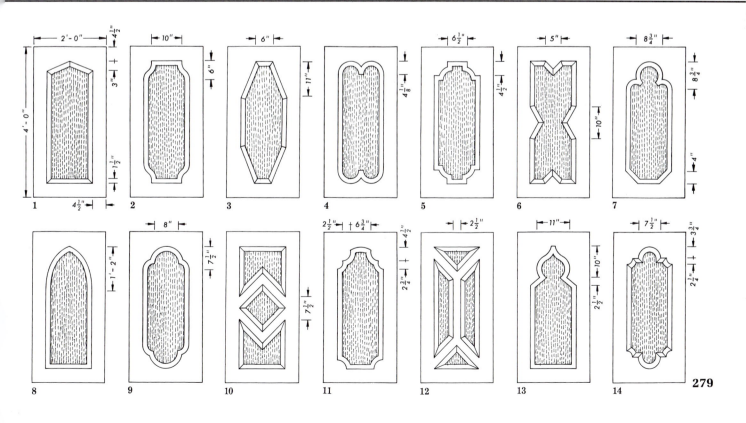

Stair Risers

Stair Edges and Nosings

Stair Handrails

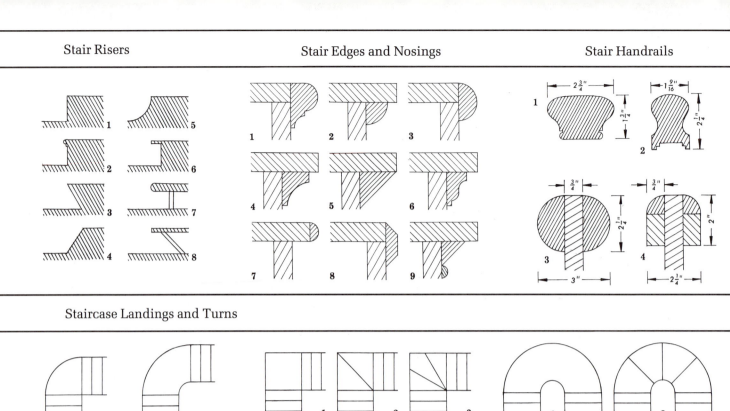

Staircase Landings and Turns

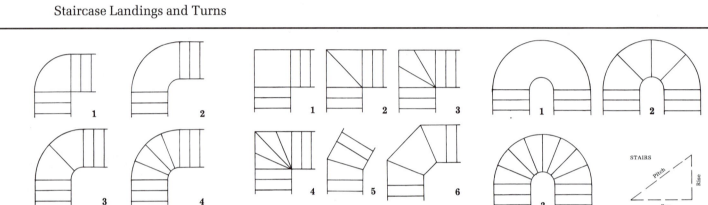

Spindles/Balusters, Newel Posts, and Step Ends

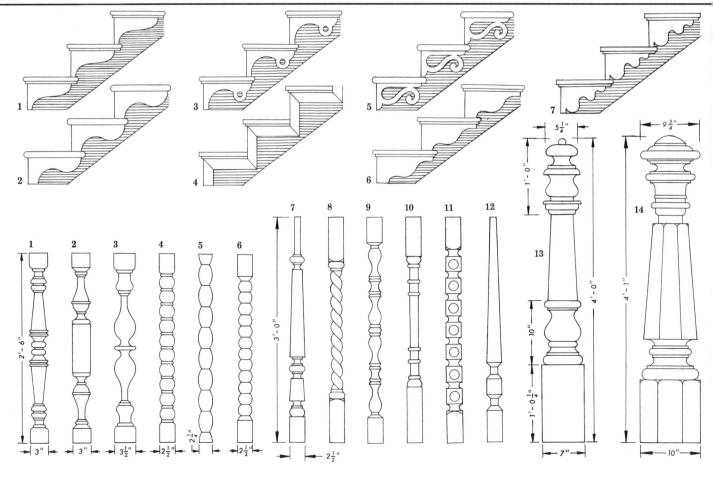

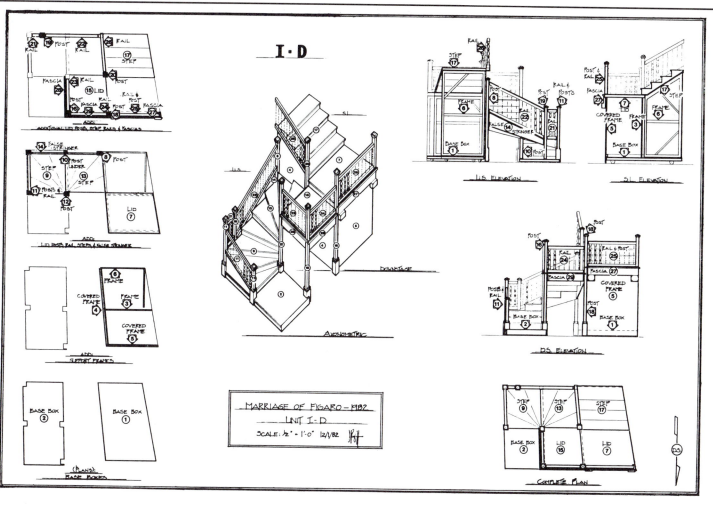

Stage design by José Varona
THE MERRY WIDOW by Franz Lehar

Directed by A. Everding
Deutsche Oper Berlin (1979)

perpendicular to the deck. While this is always the intent, they should be checked because one or two leaning spindles can ruin the appearance of a lovely stair unit.

In terms of practicality, concentrate on making the stair units easy to walk on. The basic considerations are selecting comfortable yet attractive dimensions for the treads and risers, then deciding on the maximum height for the top of the handrail and the dimensions for the newel posts. A stair railing should never shake or lean. Design them with that in mind. Curved or angled stair railings are sturdier than straight ones and, it also helps to have a well-anchored newel post at the base of the stairs. Sometimes a newel post can be designed with an extension at the bottom that goes vertically through two steps, thus giving the stair unit a firmer attachment.

While stairs for the stage consist of parts similar to those in homes and offices, they differ in that they have to be made to travel from the shop to the theatre, and sometimes to the next theatre. Consequently, breaks in the stage stair unit must be considered in the design and construction so it can easily be set up and dismantled.

A theatrical stair unit usually breaks into two main sections: (1) the actual step unit consisting of risers, treads, stringers, and landing platforms; and (2) the masking unit that fits the side of this actual stair unit and that includes the newel post(s), spindles or balusters, handrail, and the bottom framed portion resting on the stage floor, which may be called the *masking piece* or the *facing* or the *cover flat*. This masking piece in front of the step unit may duplicate the exact lines of the vertical risers and the horizontal treads of the basic step unit, or it may be closed with a diagonal piece of wood. The bottom portion of the masking piece is usually covered with muslin or canvas on ⅛-inch plywood on ¾-inch wooden framing, and then is painted according to the desired effect.

When nosing is used on the basic stair step unit, it may continue onto the thickness of the masking unit (when the masking is designed to have the profile of the vertical risers and horizontal treads rather than a closed-in diagonal) and then be mitered on a 90-degree angle and continue around to the face of the masking unit. When appropriate for the design of the set,

step brackets may be added on the end under the nosing to give a nice detail motif.

The overall depth or thickness of the separate masking unit (the unit with newel posts, spindles, and handrail) may be from 3 to 6 inches, but the newel posts, of course, may be even larger, depending on the historical period of the play and the design of the basic step unit. The masking unit is usually attached with pin hinges or bolted to the side of the set of the actual stairs and landing. The masking unit is separately removable to make the entire step unit easier to store, and for travel it can be wrapped well to prevent damage to the painted or stained finish and to be more easily positioned on the truck.

While a decorative railing or balustrade on only one side of the steps tends to be the most common for stage settings, a beautifully designed staircase positioned out from the wall in a spacious room may have elaborate railings with bottom masking pieces on both sides of the step unit. This kind of free-form staircase in the center of a room can incorporate both straight and curved stair units with lavishly designed railings that have handsome and ornate patterns.

Variations in the Stair Unit

While the masking or covering flat on steps for a traditional interior may be constructed in only one piece which includes a triangular flat at the bottom that rests on the stage floor and the open stair railing portion above it, there are exceptions to this. For example, sometimes the masking flat and railing for the stairs are designed and made in two pieces. For a large staircase of stonework against a wall, the masking piece or cover flat for the stairs may be constructed as a separate piece. The wrought-iron railing above the masking piece is positioned so that it is 4 inches from the front of the masking piece and the vertical railing members actually go into holes cut into the treads.

A good method to use for positioning and removing the stair railing from the main step unit is to design the railing with long vertical wooden or metal extensions on the bottom so that they can fit vertically into precut openings in the top of the actual steps. This arrangement can be used for three-

dimensional and ¾-inch-thick profiled railings. It also works nicely for either straight or curved railing units, as well as for both interior and exterior sets. Apart from the traditional staircase units, this method is sometimes devised for quick changes in multiset shows. Railings with long extensions can fit into precut openings in the tops of platforms already positioned onstage for other scenes. In this way, the units can be set up and lifted out quickly for scene changes. (This also works well for attaching other units, such as fence pieces.)

Naturally, not every stair unit has a masking unit. Stairs may be open underneath and may be supported by vertical metal pipes or other open metalwork positioned beneath the treads and risers, and may be with or without a railing. Another design may be a simple stair unit with just four or five steps and a railing constructed with it as one complete piece instead of two separate pieces, which would be more involved and more expensive to construct. Also, some smaller basic units without any railing, such as brick steps, may have the bottom masking piece built directly on the side of the steps as one unit. So the creation of a stair unit depends totally on the kind of design and effect.

Step Unit Styles

During the course of a career, a designer may be called upon to create many different styles of step units. Here are some examples:

1. A castle step unit consisting of large flat square and rectangular stones without a railing set against a wall of similar stone patterns.
2. A traditional colonial step unit in an interior set with appropriate wooden newel posts, spindles, and handrail.
3. A beautifully curved palace staircase with marbleized steps and railings of ornate openwork patterns of gold metal on each side.
4. A rustic staircase of rough-hewn wood with open railings in a large converted barn.
5. A stair unit composed of different sizes and shapes of rocks and stones that one might expect to find in a stage setting for a Greek tragedy.
6. A metal openwork spiral stair unit climbing around a center pole. This is usually bought as a preassembled or ready-to-be-assembled unit, but a set may require a designer to design a

larger or higher spiral unit. Brochures on available preassembled spiral stairs are wonderful to use for research when designing a staircase from scratch.

7. A very large and well-braced staircase unit with upstage carry-off steps, used in lavish musicals. Elaborately costumed show girls seem to rise out of nowhere as they slowly ascend the unseen upstage carry-off steps and appear high above the audience ready to descend the onstage stair unit in choreographed formation.

The Width of Steps

One of the first questions to answer when designing a staircase is, How wide does the actual step unit have to be? The overall size of the stair unit is determined in great part on the available stage space, the style of the production, and the required period detail. The number of actors and actresses who will use the stairs at the same time and the amount of space needed to accommodate period costumes are also important considerations.

An average minimum width for a traditional no-frills step unit (found in a modern interior set) with a railing on one side and a wall on the other is 30 inches from spindles to wall. If stage space is a problem, the width can be narrowed to 24 inches. For settings where the staircase is positioned out in the room away from the wall with an open railing on either side, the overall width, not including the baluster unit, for the actors to walk may be 3'-0", 4'-0", or even wider for a beautifully curved, elegant staircase that flares out at the bottom.

Size of the Treads and Risers

After determining the width of the steps (the actual width where the actors walk up and down), select dimensions for the risers and treads of the stair unit. There are several dimensions for treads (tops) and risers (facings):

6 × 10 in.	7 × 10 in.	8 × 10 in.
6 × 12 in.	7 × 12 in.	8 × 12 in.

While any of these dimensions may work, you may find that 7 × 10 inches or 8 × 10 inches works best. Always try to select a tread and riser dimension that does not include fractions.

Stair Railings

The term *railing* here refers to the overall stair masking unit that includes the spindles or balusters or cutout openwork. (It may or may not include the newel post, since not every stair unit is designed to have a newel post.) Also, for clarity, the *handrail* refers to the topmost part of the railing.

Stair railings may be sloped or straight. For example, the sloped railing goes on the diagonal steps, while the straight railing is positioned on the horizontal stair landings. In the ground plan these railings with the masking piece at the bottom may be straight or curved.

Once you have decided on the dimensions for the treads and the risers of the stairs and have made a side elevation drawing of them, then the slope or pitch of the stairs has been determined. The slope of the top of the handrail above is a line parallel to the slope of the steps below.

To draw the slope of the handrail, use the side elevation of the stairs and starting at the first step, draw a light diagonal line from the very front edge of the tread (the outer corner where the riser and tread meet) upward to include approximately four steps. Then, again starting at the first step, draw a light vertical line continuing up from the front of the first riser, and do the same on the fourth step. From the first vertical line from the tread, measure up 30 inches (a good average height) and make a mark. Measure up 30 inches from the line at the fourth step and make a mark. Through these two marks, draw a line parallel to the light diagonal or pitch line. The line at the top should now be used as the very top of the handrail. Now draw the handrail, as well as the spindles or any cutout work between the handrail and steps forming the details of the entire railing. Then draw in the newel post to see where the top of the handrail is positioned with it. While 30 inches is good for an average dimension to the top of the handrail, 31, 32, or 33 inches may also be used for large-scale staircases.

Stair railing units may be constructed of wood, metal, or a combination of both. A railing may be designed as a three-dimensional unit or as a simple profile piece which is usually cut out of sheets of ¾-inch plywood. For railings designed to be

longer than the sheets of plywood, it works well to glue two ½-inch plywood sheets together to make a 1-inch-thick piece. Stagger the overlap to make one continuous surface on which to cut out the plywood profiles.

A simple flat surface with a well-drawn profile cut from plywood with a three-dimensional handrail can be highly effective by itself when painted. A profile piece can be embellished with molding, wooden ornaments, and/or carved Styrofoam balustrades so that it reads from the audience as a three-dimensional unit.

One of the nice things about using the ¾-inch profile method to build and cut out a stair unit is that it is easy to join all the parts together, and especially to keep the center lines of all the balusters completely parallel with each other and also with the center line of the newel post.

Common Types of Stair Railing and Masking Units

Railing units for stage settings may be constructed in a variety of ways. These units are usually made separately and may be attached to the main step unit with pin hinges, bolts, or screws. These are common types of construction for railing units.

1. All three-dimensional (handrail, spindles, and newel post).
2. All cutout profile pieces, such as those made of plywood in thicknesses of ¾ inch, 1 inch, or 1½ inches.
3. A combination of a three-dimensional and a profiled piece. For example, the handrail and newel post may be three-dimensional, with the railing detail below the handrail cut out of ¾-inch plywood.

Handrails

Handrails (and the rest of the units below them) for the stage may be straight, curved, or a combination of both. They can be created from stock lumber in the shop, made of either wood or metal, or purchased at a lumber company. It is a good idea to study the catalog of moldings and building products and look at the various stairwork fittings that are available. The catalogs also give you an opportunity to see volutes and goosenecks, and how straight and curved stair railings may work together as interesting units.

Stage design by Lester Polakov
MRS. McTHING by Mary Chase
(Rough sketch)
Directed by Joseph Buloff
Martin Beck Theatre
New York (1952)

Left: Stairway unit designed by Marsha Louis Eck for LUCIA DI LAMMERMOOR (1969), New York City Opera. Thick scenic dope was brushed on the ¾-inch plywood cutout to give texture before painting.
(Photograph by Arnold Abramson)

Newel post and stairs designed by Douglas W. Schmidt for DIAMOND LIL (1988), American Conservatory Theatre, San Francisco, California
(Photograph by Ed Raymond)

Setting by Rolf Beyer
THE MISER by Molière
Directed by Rod Alexander

Lighting by Dick Jeter
Hopkins Center
Dartmouth College

Hanover
New Hampshire (1968)
(Photograph by Al Olsen)

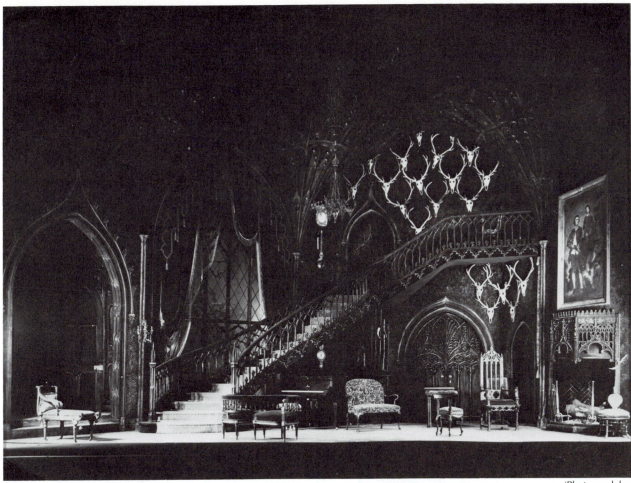

Setting by Ben Edwards
JANE EYRE

Adapted by Huntington Hartford from the
novel by Charlotte Brontë

Directed by Demetrios Vilan
Belasco Theatre, New York (1958)

(Photograph by
Will Rapport)

Model by Tony Walton
CHICAGO—opening scene: "All That Jazz"
Book: Fred Ebb, Bob Fosse
Music by John Kander

Lyrics by Fred Ebb
Based on the play *Chicago* by Maurine Dallas
 Watkins
Directed and choreographed by Bob Fosse

Forty-sixth Street Theatre
New York (1975)
(Photograph by Tony Walton)

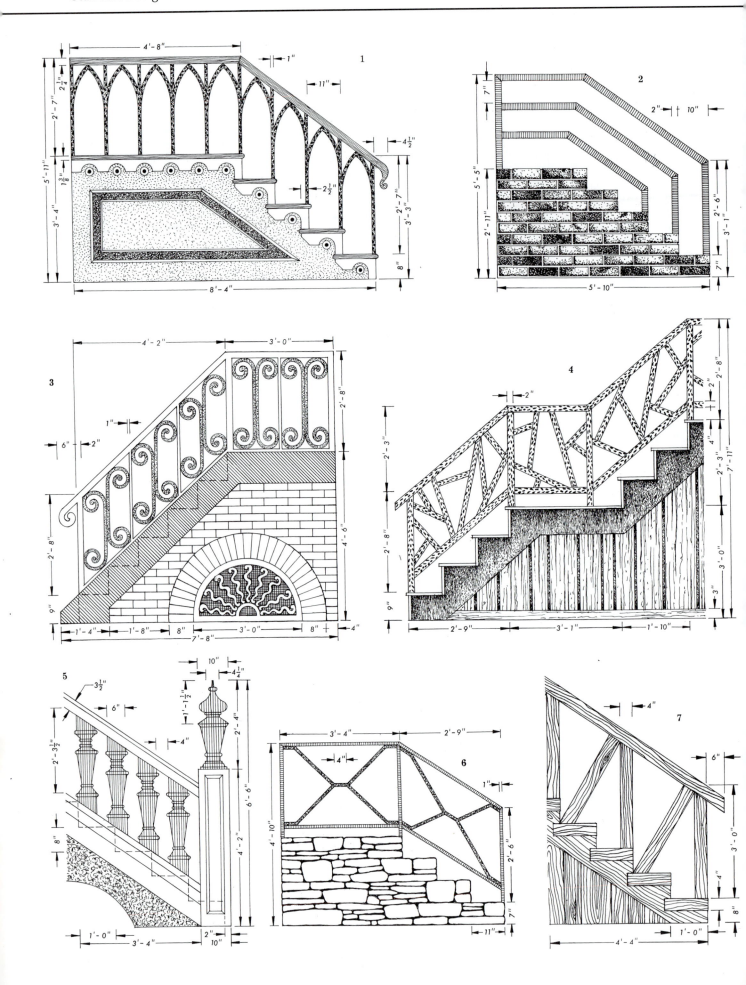

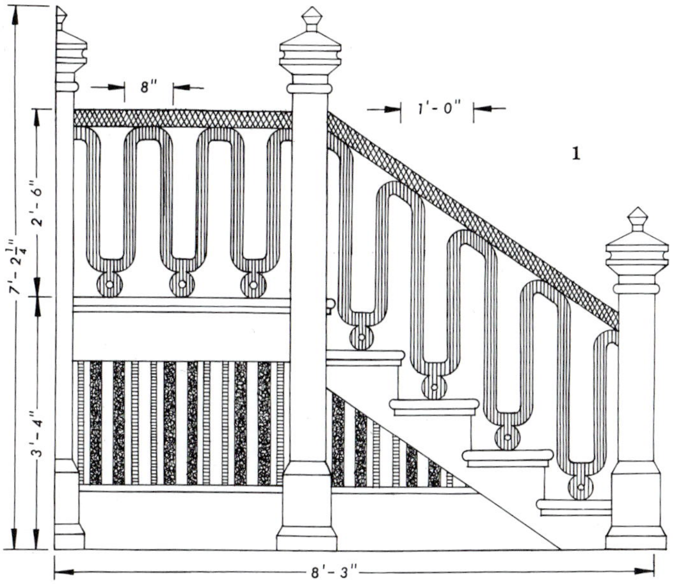

1

8" 1'-0"

7'-2¼" 2'-6" 3'-4"

8'-3"

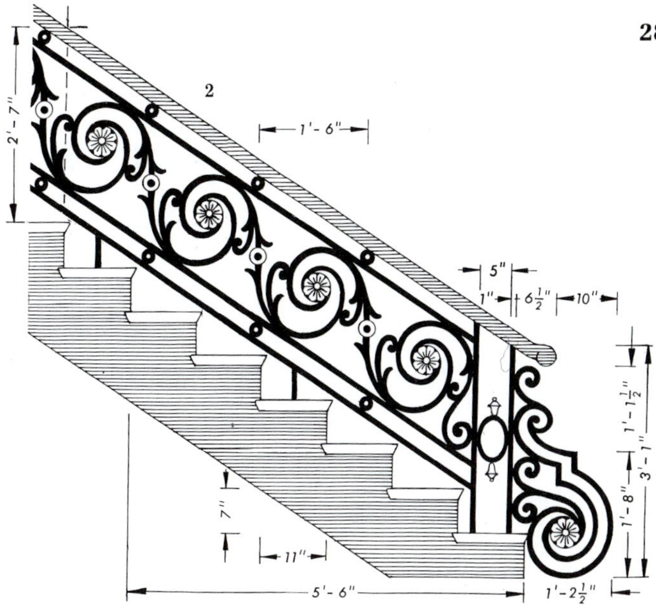

2

2'-7" 1'-6" 5" 1" 6½" 10"

7" 11"

1'-1½" 3'-1" 1'-8"

5'-6" 1'-2½"

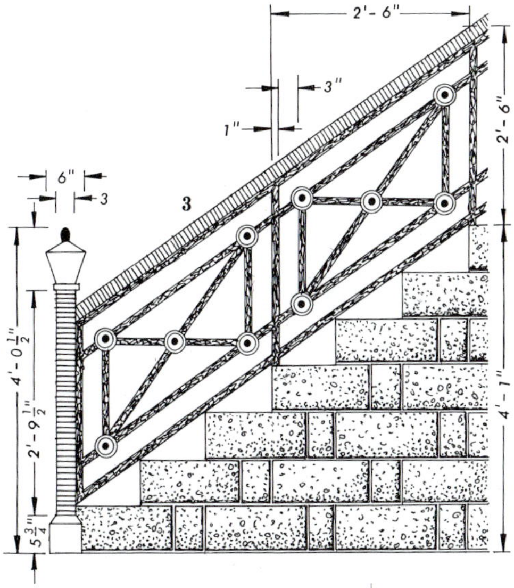

3

2'-6" 3" 1" 6" 3

4'-0½" 2'-9½" 4'-1"

5¾"

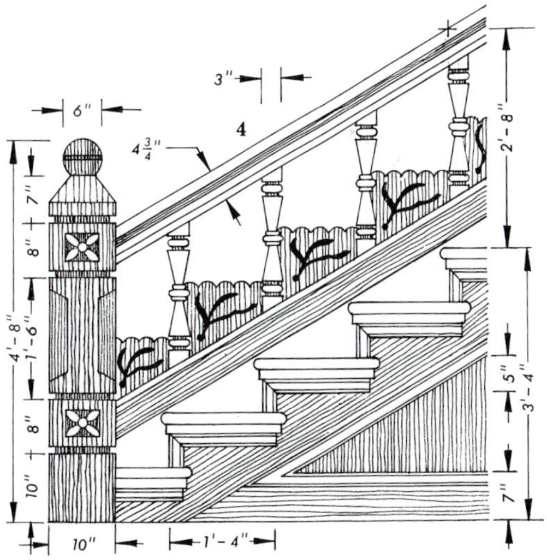

4

3" 6" 4¾" 2'-8"

7" 8" 4'-8" 1'-6"

8" 8" 5" 3'-4" 7"

10" 10" 1'-4"

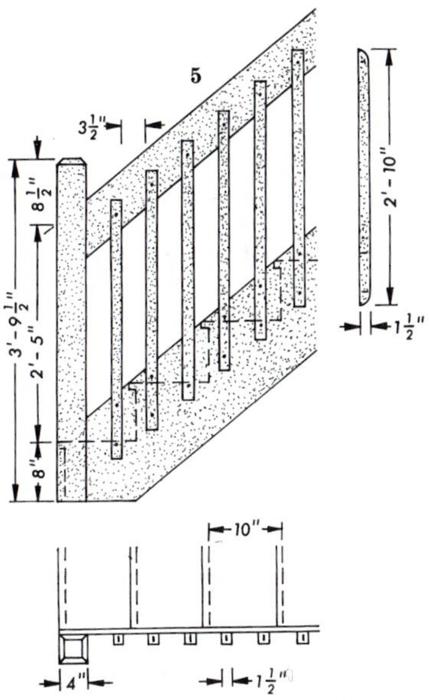

5

3½" 8½" 2'-10" 1½"

3'-9½" 2'-5" 8"

10" 4" 1½"

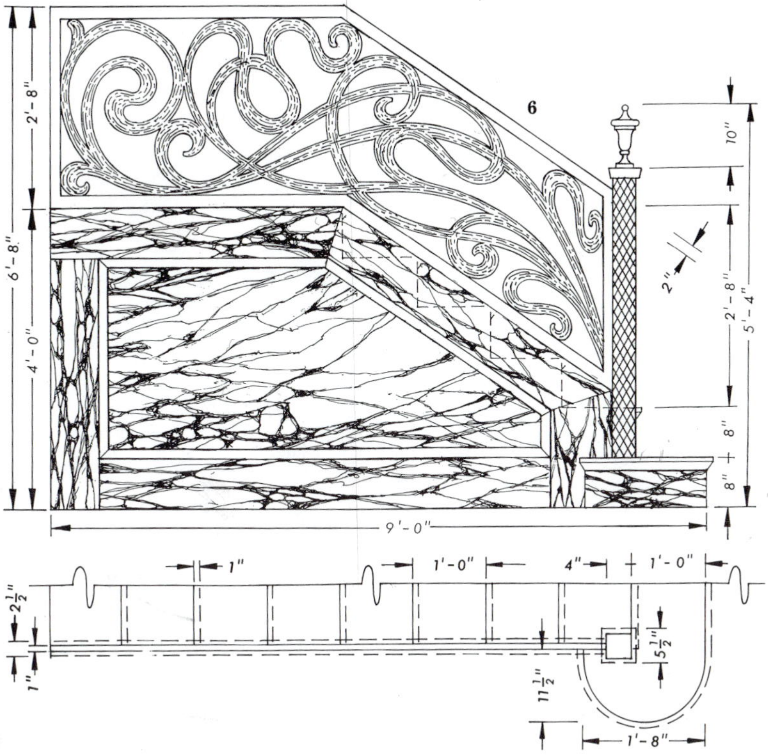

6

2'-8" 10" 2" 2'-8" 5'-4"

6'-8" 4'-0" 8" 8"

9'-0"

2½" 1" 1'-0" 4" 1'-0"

1" 5½" 11½" 1'-8"

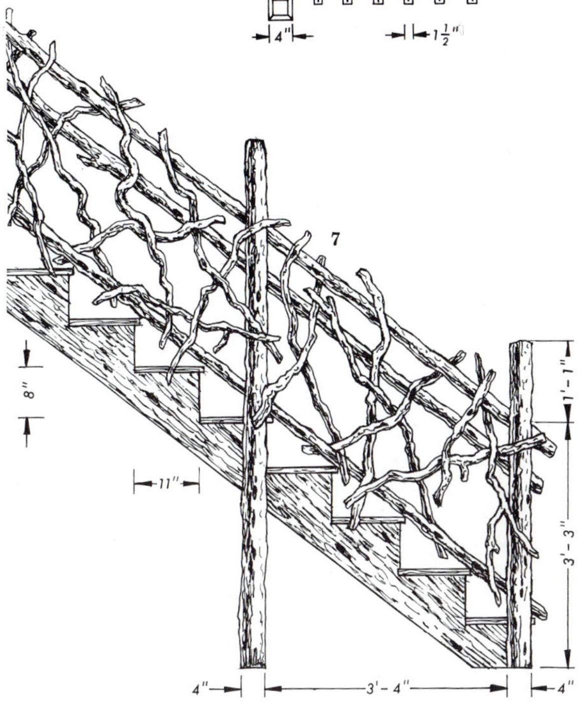

7

8" 1'-1" 3'-3"

11" 4" 3'-4" 4"

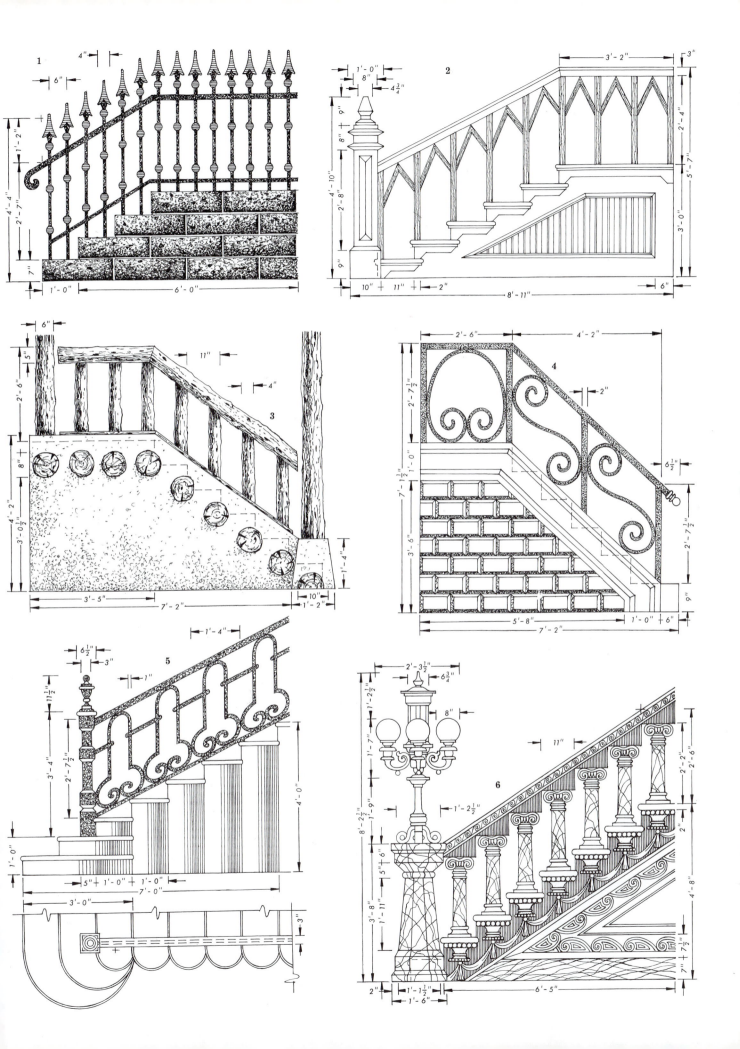

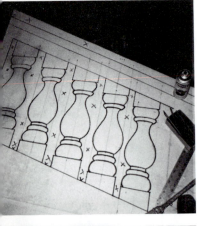

Above: Oliver Messel's profiled balusters for THE SLEEPING BEAUTY.
Below: Turned balusters and London street balusters.
(Photographs by Lynn Pecktal)

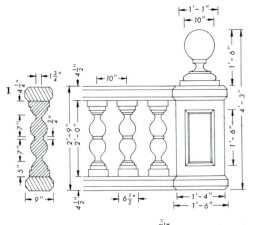

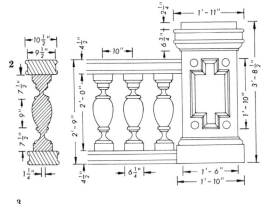

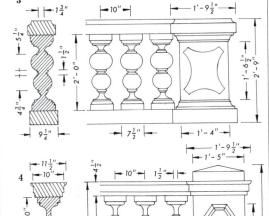

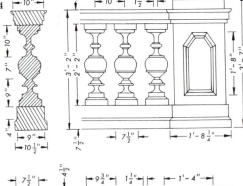

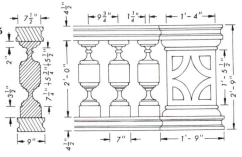

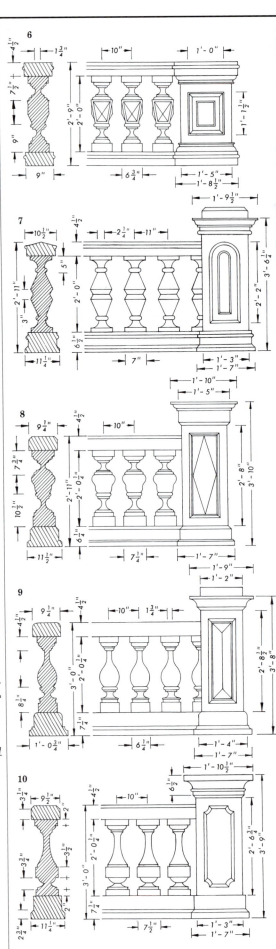

Model by Tony Straiges
SUMMER by Edward Bond

Directed by Douglas Hughes
Manhattan Theatre Club

New York (1983)
(Photograph by Ney Tait Fraser)

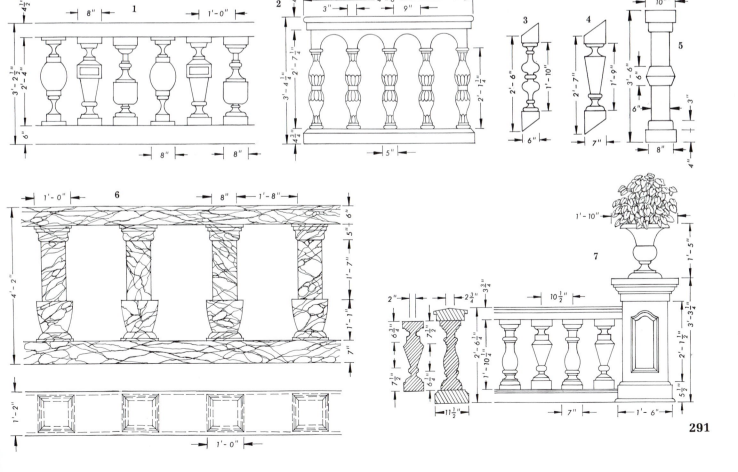

Spindles and Balusters

While some references use the terms "spindle" and "baluster" interchangeably, for clarity let us describe *spindles* as tall and thin members and *balusters* as short and thick members.

The selection of spindles or balusters depends on the design concept and historical period of the stage setting. Each step may have one, two, or three spindles. The number of spindles used per tread also depends on the size of the actual stair tread and the size of the individual spindles. Spindles are usually designed to be of only one specific design, two completely different designs that alternate, or three individual designs that alternate. Alternating spindles can provide pleasant contrast. The same idea of alternating two or three patterns also works nicely for the heavier baluster. When designing railings with either spindles or balusters, always make sure that they are positioned with an appropriate space between them.

Newel Posts

Staircases may have elaborate, modest, or very simple newel posts or, perhaps, none at all. For example, a colonial staircase may have a handrail end at the bottom with a beautiful volute measuring 11½ inches overall in which the vertical spindles spaced under it form a nice curved arrangement. This positioning of the spindles normally falls on the outer extension of the first step, or sometimes includes the second one.

A newel post may match the spindles or may be a totally different design. Newel posts may be round, square, or a composite of shapes. Molding catalogs are an excellent source for examining standard newel posts, such as a starting newel, a landing newel, or an angled newel.

Newel posts in some periods may be topped off with detailed statuary, enormous candelabras, or sumptuous floral arrangements. These additions give a wonderful prominence to the staircase.

Nosing on Stairs

Nosing on the top of the vertical risers and flush with the horizontal treads dresses up the appearance of stair units and enhances period detail. Nosing also protects the edges of the steps.

It may be used for both interior and exterior settings. Large-scale nosing reads well from the stage.

Stair Brackets or Step Ends

Some stair units have brackets with decorative designs at the outer end of each step. Brackets can be built from ¼-inch plywood with cutout ⅛-inch plywood details added. The repeat of these brackets makes an interesting motif on the diagonal side of the stair masking unit.

Carpet on Stairs

Carpet runners may be attached to the stairs to deaden the sound of footsteps as well as to give a pleasant design detail for a particular historical period. Carpet should be fastened well so that there is never any danger of an actor having a fall because of it. Rubberized treads on the individual steps may also be applied to the stair unit.

Carry-Off Steps

Carry-off steps are essential for all stage stair units so that the actors and actresses can make proper entrances and exits on the stage stairs. While carry-off steps are not expected to have the same ample tread and riser dimensions as those on stage, they nevertheless should be sturdy and comfortable enough for the actors to step on without feeling insecure about using them. Carry-off stairs with more than a few steps (three or four) should always have at least one handrail; two are preferable when exits are quick and stairs are long.

Designing a Rolling Stair and Platform Unit

A rolling platform unit with two stair units can work well for musicals, revues, operas, and plays. The idea is to design a basic platform unit with an interesting shape for a ground plan, and with open or skeletal supports for the top or second level. In ground plan the main platform unit can be oval, kidney shaped, a trapezoid, a half circle, or other shapes. A gracefully shaped stair can go up one side of the main platform unit and a second stair can go down the opposite side. Curved stair units are most impressive, but straight and angled stairs can also be very effective.

While not every rolling unit moves during performance, when a unit does move, the effect can be more interesting. If you design a rolling unit to move, the platform must be 4 to 6 inches high on rolling casters so it can move smoothly onstage. You must also decide whether you want the unit to move manually, with stagehands pushing it off and on without following any particular pattern; or with a guide or fin in a track fixed in a show deck on top of the stage floor; or by pivoting from one swinging offstage end, with the other end held by a vertical pin in a hole in the floor.

Uses of a Rolling Stair Platform Unit

Rolling stair units offer a great deal of versatility. If you think of a rolling stair unit as a skeletonized unit braced with round metal pipes and flat metal pieces, you can treat it as a scenic unit for either the proscenium or the open stage. And while the stair and platform unit may be an independent unit when used on an open stage, it may be connected to a wall or be part of a building on the proscenium stage. A nicely proportioned rolling stair unit is great for staging singers and dancers in a big musical number.

CEILINGS

A Full Ceiling

The most common full-stage flat ceiling is used with the typical box set and tends to cover most of it. The ceiling may be hung parallel to the floor so that it appears flat, or at an angle compatible with the top profiles of the flats. Essentially, a full ceiling on a box set gives a sense of completeness. The ceiling usually has a 6- or 12-inch return on its downstage edge to give the appearance of thickness when viewed from the audience. This return may be covered in black velour or similar fabric, or it may be painted to match the ceiling itself. It also may be designed to be a beam or other architectural feature.

A Partial Ceiling

A partial ceiling may also be used for a box set. It can cover just the upstage portion of the setting and be either positioned flat in line with the top of the flats or angled upward. In some cases, a partial ceiling may have a curved inset like a centered dome effect, or a wide front reveal with a curved surface cut into it to allow a space for a chandelier.

Floating Ceilings

Floating ceilings are what the expression implies: ceiling pieces suspended in space so that the outer edges do not rest on any vertical walls. A floating ceiling is hung as an independent unit like an island of scenery suspended above the main setting. A floating ceiling piece may be designed to be the entire stage setting.

Floating ceilings suspended on thin cables may be designed in a variety of shapes. They may have straight, curved, or highly profiled edges. They also may be cut out with openwork, or give the appearance of being solid. For example, you could have a ceiling consisting of an arrangement of angled skylights for the Parisian attic studio in *La Bohème*, an oval latticework ceiling for the garden in *The Importance of Being Earnest*, or a solid, flat ceiling in a slanted position that is outlined in real lights to go above an orchestra positioned on stage.

While most ceiling pieces are framed with wood, a floating ceiling may be made entirely of a soft piece of fabric, such as sharkstooth scrim or filled scrim. Floating ceilings for operas or ballets may be shaped in unconventional ways, such as enormous free-form fabric shapes with curved edges. The fabric edges are hemmed and thin steel cables are stretched through the hem to support the shapes. The ceiling patterns are often on a slant, and one or a group of these pieces may be onstage at the same time.

Floating ceilings may consist of geometric shapes with or without the benefit of being in perspective. Further interest can be added to a floating ceiling by hanging drapery swags and jabots from it, by attaching cutout decorative borders, or by framing it with a well-known performer's name in perspective lettering. Floating ceilings can also serve as baffles for acoustical purposes.

Solid Ceilings and Cutout Ceilings

Whether positioned flat or angled, a ceiling piece is often a combination of solid and cutout areas. There may be painted designs on the solid (opaque) portions with the cutouts left open. Or the openings may be covered from behind with fabrics such as gauze, organza, scrim, or screen wire. All of these materials are extremely effective when lighting instruments are focused down from above or when projected light patterns are used.

Positioning Ceilings on Full-Stage Proscenium Sets

Ceilings on full-stage proscenium settings may be positioned in several different ways:

1. *A flat ceiling*—positioned parallel to the stage floor
2. *An angled ceiling*—positioned on a slant or angle
3. *A combination* of flat and angled ceiling pieces
4. *A vertical ceiling piece* with painted details on a framed header (with legs) or a full-stage or partial-stage ceiling on a drop

In addition, these scenic units may be either a full or partial ceiling on a box set or a floating ceiling isolated and suspended in space.

Creating Ceiling Medallions

Ceiling medallions are ideal designs to use for the embellishment around the position where a chandelier hangs. Medallion designs are typically circular, but they may also be in the shape of an oval, a diamond, free-form ornamental designs, or arbitrary classical motifs such as leaves and vines trailing off from the center. Other designs for ceiling medallions include a series of concentric circles (combined with other shapes, such as acanthus leaves or curled leaves emanating from the center), an art nouveau motif, and a flower with petals.

While ceiling medallions are usually modeled in relief for elegant interiors, this is not always the case for theatrical settings. For the stage, a lovely medallion design can be painted on a flat muslin- or canvas-covered ceiling piece. To read well from the stage, the size of ceiling medallions may average from 1½ to 4 feet in diameter.

A Ceiling Medallion to Be Painted on a Flat Surface For a painted ceiling medallion on a flat surface, do the following:

1. Draw the medallion design on the ½-inch scale drafting and show the size, shape, and exact position of the painted motif. This drawing should be the view of the ceiling as seen when standing on the stage looking up at the ceiling piece.
2. When it applies, put a note on the drawing to say: "Make a full-scale perforated pounce to repeat details of the drawing for painting."
3. Also, if it is appropriate, make a note saying: "Paint very realistically."

A Ceiling Medallion to Be Made in Relief For a ceiling medallion in relief, you also need to do the following:

1. Do a detailed drawing in ½-inch scale on the drafting so that it can be properly enlarged in the scenic studio to create a full-scale perforated drawing on brown paper.
2. Since the ceiling medallion is to be made in relief, specify this with a note saying that it is to be built as a separate piece and then bolted to the ceiling.
3. You may want to give instructions to use ¼-, ⅜-, or ½-inch plywood for the base and have a hole drilled through the center of the medallion for the chain or pipe to go through. You may need to keep a 6-inch-diameter (or whatever) open area where the canopy goes.
4. Specify whether you want the medallion created in relief by shaping details out of materials such as Styrofoam, felt, or Ozite rug padding.
5. Also specify that pieces of linen scrim or lightweight baby flannel dipped in scenic dope should be used to cover the finished design and to give it texture.
6. If applicable, use the same painting technique as that for the flat ceiling medallion.

POSTS, BEAMS, AND TRUSSES

Designing Multisets with Posts, Beams, and Trusses

One exciting way to design a set is to use a series of vertical posts and overhead beams to create an interesting openwork effect. Plan to have supports

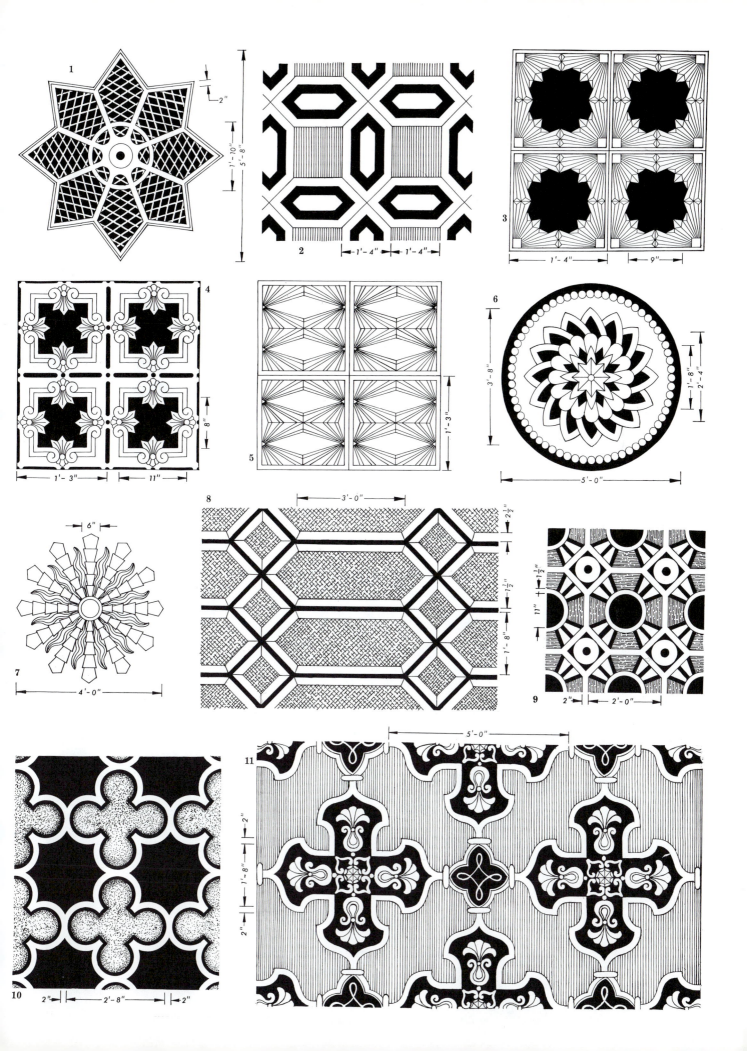

SL Side View of Ceilings: Flats, Slants, Curves, Beams, Headers, and Light Slots

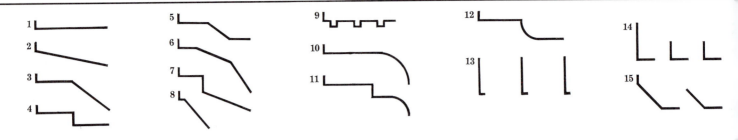

Painted Ceiling Beams and Rustic Exterior Ceiling with Vines and Lanterns

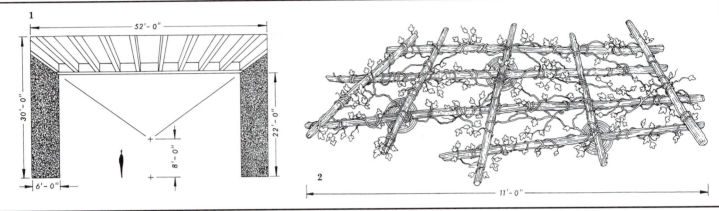

Eldon Elder's Hotel Lobby Design for AMAZING GRACE (1967) by Studs Terkel; Directed by Marcella Cisney; Mendelssohn Theatre, Ann Arbor, Michigan

"At times I wanted the overwhelming large parking garage across the street to be seen; at other times to have a realistic interior with a ceiling. I decided to use a sharks-tooth scrim for the ceiling so when it was lit from above, the ceiling became transparent. When we lit it only from below with sunlight coming through the windows, we had a solid Victorian ceiling and a realistic interior. The only fastening was around the outer ceiling frame; however, we had a hole in the center of the scrim for the chandelier, and the ceiling plate at the top of that also helped support the scrim. The chandelier was suspended on airplane cable."

—Eldon Elder

Solid-Appearing Ceiling Pieces

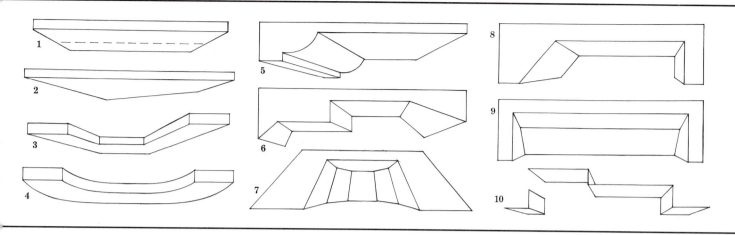

Suspended Ceiling Pieces with and without Draperies

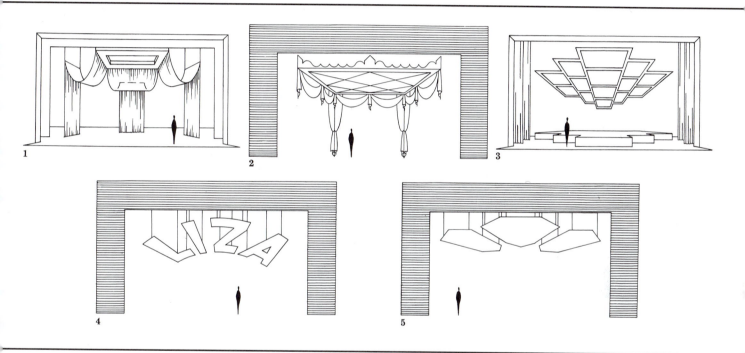

Open and Skeletonized Ceiling Pieces

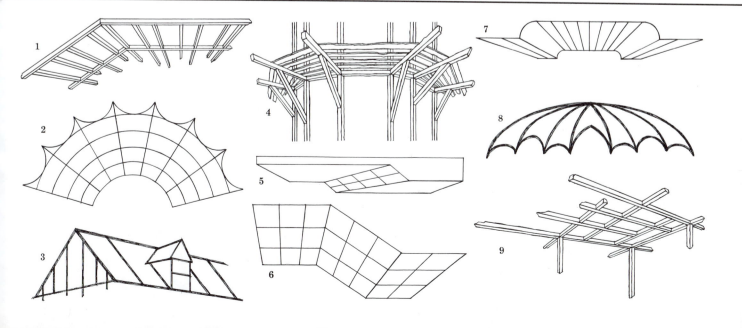

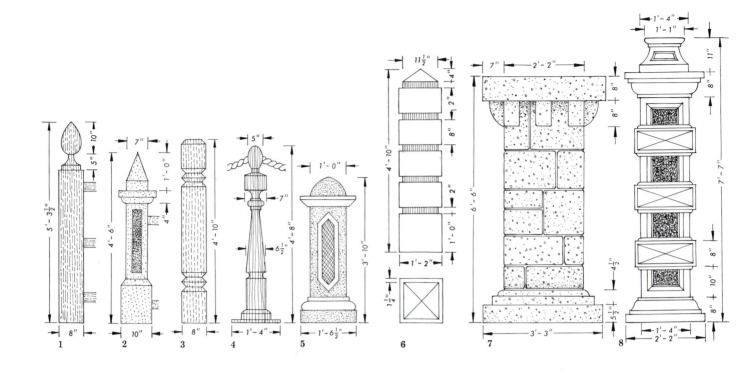

Stage designs by Charles E. McCarry
THE GIRL OF THE GOLDEN WEST
Acts 1, 2, and 3
A project: Yale Drama School (1986)

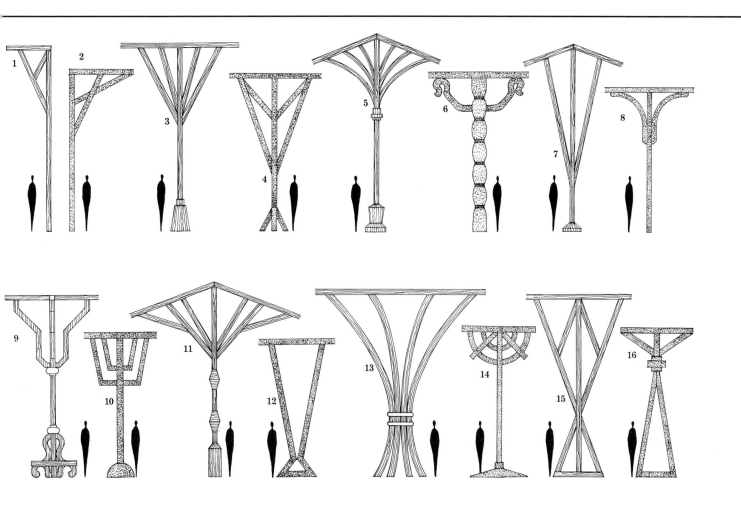

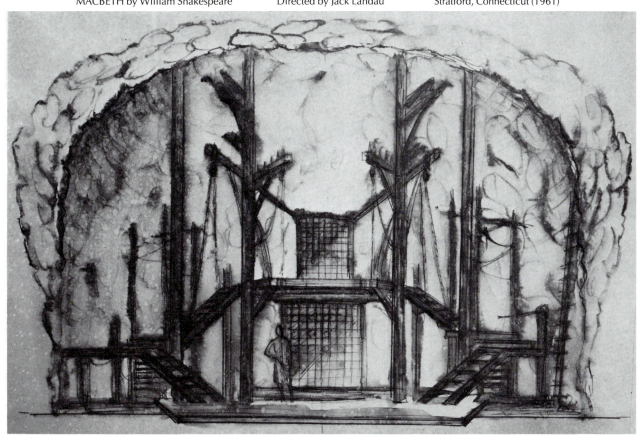

Stage design by Robert O'Hearn
MACBETH by William Shakespeare   Directed by Jack Landau   American Shakespeare Festival
Stratford, Connecticut (1961)

300 at the top of the posts going to the beams above. Decide whether the set is to be a unit set with props, furniture, and plugs coming onstage and offstage with changes in the stage lighting. Does the basic set remain stationary, or does it move on a turntable in both a clockwise or counterclockwise direction? Is the main set to be symmetrical or asymmetrical?

You might want to have a group of platforms and stairs to add visual interest and contrast as well as to make it a more effective set for the actors to work on. For clarity, let us assume that the discussion pertains to a proscenium production.

When creating this kind of openwork post-and-beam setting, begin by arranging three-dimensional model pieces on a scaled ½-inch ground plan. Of course, it is also best if you work in a model with an accurately scaled proscenium opening.

For materials, use small blocks of Styrofoam in various sizes to represent the platforms and ramps. Lengths of balsa wood are good for making vertical posts. Experiment by positioning lengths of balsa at the corners of platform units and stairs as well as in appropriate open areas away from the platforms and stairs. When putting the vertical balsa posts with the platform units, try several different positions and use small pieces of masking tape to hold the units together and in place. Also, try other platforms on angles and platforms with open spaces under them. Once you are pleased with your arrangement, attach the units and record them on the ground plan. At the same time, make rough thumbnail sketches to show any additional design possibilities.

When you are ready, go to the beams overhead. Are the beams to tie in architecturally with the vertical posts on the floor? Are they to be positioned parallel to the deck? Are the horizontal beams above to be positioned parallel to each other, are they to radiate from a distant point, are they to be hung in a random manner, or are they to be placed in some way totally different from any of these possibilities?

If a basic unit set is to serve for more than one scene, you might want to have various pieces fly in and out from above or move off and on from the wings to create other interesting scenic effects. These scenic pieces may move off and on in front of or behind the basic set. They may be drapery swags and jabots, profiled set pieces, chandeliers, foliage, garlands, furniture, upstage drops and scrim panels, or any of several other kinds of scenic items.

For multiset shows you may want to use some of the ideas already mentioned, but instead of having a basic stationary setting or turntable set of posts and beams, have the entire post-and-beam set move offstage for a scenery change. This approach may involve having posts and supports positioned on wagons that move on and off from the wings and also straight or diagonally from upstage. While the wagon units are moving on the deck, beam units may fly in and out from overhead.

Another approach would be not to use post and wagon units on the floor, but instead to use only flying units that move in and out from above. Many kinds of trusses could be a part of the overhead structure. These units may all be the same size or be in a series of decreasing sizes. Overhead Gothic arches with hanging gauze curtains are also highly effective scenic pieces. Other units that could come in and out with the overhead structures might be heavily textured panels of erosion cloth, sculptured figures, open slatted blinds, and detailed tapestries.

Even though the discussion here is for a proscenium production, also think about how your design would work on an open or arena stage.

Try designing a multiset production of *The Weavers*, an 1893 drama in five acts by the German playwright Gerhart Hauptmann. This play portrays the revolt of a German community of weavers against the unbearable conditions imposed by the mill owners and the drama that unfolds. The drama takes place in the 1840s.

Obtain a copy of the play and read it first for enjoyment. Then read it again and concentrate on the scenic demands. You may want to make notes and sketches during this second reading. The settings for the five acts are listed.

ACT I
A large whitewashed room on the ground floor of DREISSIGER'S house at Peterswaldau, where the weavers deliver their finished webs and the fustian is stored.

ACT II
A small room in the house of WILHELM ANSORGE, weaver and houseowner in the village of Kaschbach in the Eulengebirge.

ACT III
The common room of the principal public house in Peterswaldau.

ACT IV
Peterswaldau. Private room of DREISSIGER, the fustian manufacturer—luxuriously furnished in the chilly taste of the first half of this century.

ACT V
Langen-Bielau. OLD WEAVER HILSE'S workroom. On the left a small window, in front of which stands the loom.

Use these suggestions to make ¼-inch scale pencil sketches for each act.

1. Design settings for a full stage (40'-0" wide by 23'-0" high by 30'-0" deep). Use posts and beams that are 4 × 4 inches to 6 × 6 inches. Think in terms of first doing designs that are simply suggestive structural or architectural units to be positioned on stage with furniture in front of an upstage surround. Make two of the stage settings symmetrical and three asymmetrical.
2. Since the first group of sketches are created with posts and beams in an open space, plan on adding 25 percent of the square footage with scenery such as partial or fragmented walls as well as hanging panels, and portions of a ceiling above. To do this, use five pieces of tracing paper laid over the first five ¼-inch scale sketches.
3. As a third possibility, try adding 25 percent square footage of scenery to the first set of designs. These should also be done on tracing paper in ¼-inch scale.

Now decide which group of designs works best for the play. Then, after you have made your decision, enlarge that group of five sketches from ¼-inch scale to ½-inch scale. Render them in color and show stage lighting and mood.

Making Supports, Brackets, and Other Motifs

Depending on the design, it is possible to make supports, brackets, and similar motifs with a variety of materials.

Stage design by John Lee Beatty
CRIMES OF THE HEART by Beth Henley
National Company

Brackets and supports are normally positioned at the top sides of posts and under beams. These corner units may also go at the tops of rectangular arches or in other shapes in architectural openings. Decorative as well as practical, brackets and supports work ideally for porches, barns, taverns, halls, alcoves, and under high platforms. Independent center motifs under beams or in the center of arches are usually completely decorative. Brackets and supports may be designed as Victorian curlicues, as New Orleans grillwork, in fan-shaped patterns, in geometrical shapes, as simple straight wooden beams, or in countless other patterns. Some examples of materials for supports and brackets are listed.

1. A Victorian or Chinese design may be cut out of ¾-inch plywood, sanded neatly, and painted.
2. A 6 × 6-inch beam positioned on a 45-degree angle may be constructed of thin plywood, covered (or not covered) with muslin. Brush the sides with heavy scenic dope to give the appearance of graining and texture. The dope may also be brushed on heavy enough to drag a metal comb through it to give a more defined graining.
3. A bracket pattern to go in an upper corner in a tavern set may be cut out of rough crating lumber and stained with transparent colors to allow the natural graining and texture to show through.
4. An ornament or figure for a top corner may be carved out of Styrofoam; backed with ½-inch (or ¾-inch) plywood; covered with pieces of linen scrim, cheesecloth, or muslin; coated with paint or dope; and painted so the details are modeled with colors representing light, shade, and shadow.
5. A geometrical shape may be made of wood and have the edges routed. The shape may also have stock moldings, wooden dowels, and balls as part of the overall design.
6. A very thin shaped corner or a center design may be made of metalwork.
7. A corner wooden support may have a base cut out of ¾-inch plywood with pieces of plywood in various thicknesses added on top of each other to give a three-dimensional look.

Stage design and costumes by Zack Brown
LA SONNAMBULA by Vincenzo Bellini
Libretto by Felice Romani
Directed by Peter Anastos
Washington Opera, Terrace Theatre
Kennedy Center, Washington, D.C. (1984)

301

Exterior Building Profiles

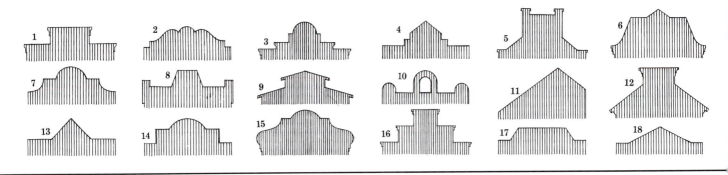

Concrete Block Patterns

Decorative Wooden Clapboards

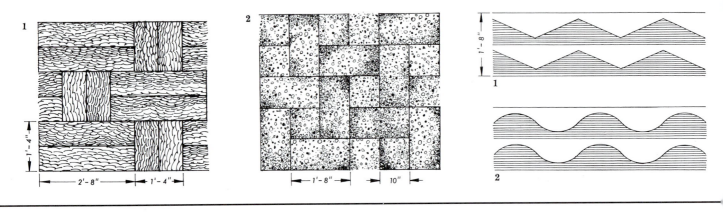

Exterior Facade Patterns: Stonework, Bricks, Concrete, and Marble

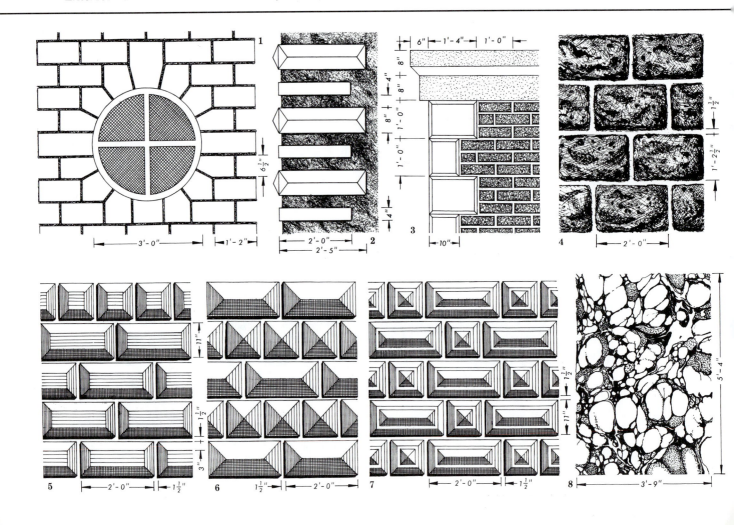

Brick Wall Patterns: 1. Running Bond; 2. Common Bond; 3. English Bond; 4. Flemish Bond; 5. English Cross Bond; 6. End Bricks; 7. Brick Arches

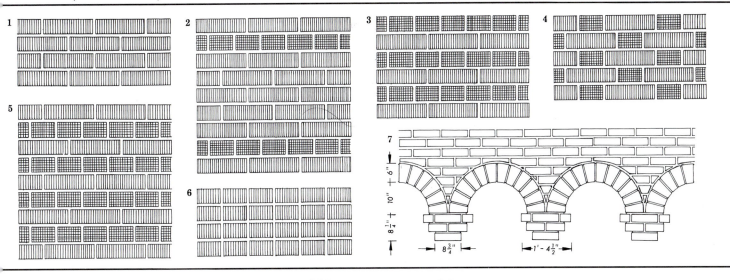

1. Flagstones; 2. Wall of Random Stones; 3. Cobblestones; 4. Squared Stones

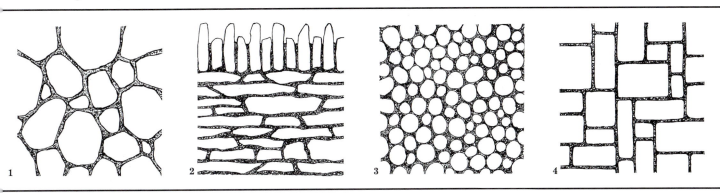

Floor or Wall Bricks: 1. Basketweave; 2. Herringbone; 3. Soldier Courses; 4. Concentric Circles

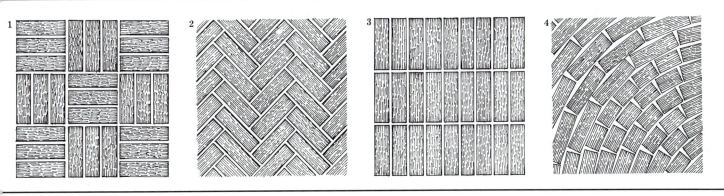

Applied and/or Painted Wooden Siding Shingle Patterns

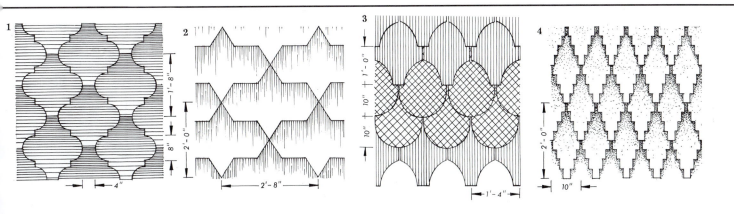

David Mitchell lives and maintains a design studio on Manhattan's upper Central Park West. Born in Honesdale, Pennsylvania, on May 12, 1932, he was educated at Boston University. His first legitimate show on Broadway was *How the Other Half Loves* in 1971. He has created a wide variety of settings for the New York City Ballet, New York City Opera, Paris Opera, Berlin's Deutsche Oper, Washington Opera Society, San Francisco Opera, Santa Fe Opera, Houston Grand Opera, Cincinnati Opera, Goodman Theatre, Studio Arena Theatre, Spoleto Festival, Baltimore's Center Stage, Coconut Grove Playhouse, Pennsylvania Ballet, and Juilliard School of Music. David Mitchell has been the production designer for the films *My Dinner with Andre, One Trick Pony,* and *Rich Kids,* and has also designed for television. Among his awards are two Tony Awards, an Outer Critic's Circle Award, a Drama Desk Award, and a Maharam Award. His design credits include:

Broadway
The High Rollers
  Social and Pleasure Club (1992)
Tru (1989)
Legs Diamond (1988)
Broadway Bound (1986)
The Boys of Winter (1985)
Biloxi Blues (1985)
Harrigan 'N Hart (1985)
Brighton Beach Memoirs (1983)
La Cage aux Folles (1983)
Private Lives (1983)
Dance a Little Closer (1983)
Foxfire (1982)
Can-Can (1981)
Bring Back Birdie (1981)

Barnum (1980)
I Remember Mama (1979)
Working (1978)
Annie (1977)
I Love My Wife (1977)
The Gin Game (1977)
The Incomparable Max (1971)

Off Broadway
Steambath (1970)
Colette (1970)

New York Shakespeare Festival
Mrs. Warren's Profession (1976)
Henry V (1976)
Little Black Sheep (1975)
Trelawney of the ''Wells'' (1975)

Short Eyes (1974)
The Cherry Orchard (1973)
The Basic Training of Pavlo Hummel
  (1971)
Naked Hamlet (1967)
  Public Theatre/Anspacher

New York City Ballet
The Sleeping Beauty (1991)
Ives, Songs (1988)
Brahms-Schoenberg Quartet (1986)
In Memory of (1985)
Liebeslieder Walzer (1984)
The Magic Flute (1982)
The Steadfast Tin Soldier (1976)
  S and C

Model by David Mitchell
CAN-CAN

Music and lyrics by Cole Porter
Book by Abe Burrows

Directed by Abe Burrows
Minskoff Theatre, New York (1981)

How did you become interested in designing for the stage?

I had no real idea about theatre until I was in college, and I didn't have a great deal of knowledge about art until then either. I grew up in a small town, and I was largely self-taught in drawing and painting. I had never even attended the theatre before I went to college, so when I got to Kutztown State Teacher's College (it's now Kutztown University), it was an explosion in interests. I saw some stage plays and I was interested, but I didn't think of it as a livelihood until I was assigned a project in theatre during one of my art classes. I solved the problem that I was given, and did it very easily. My professor said, "You should think about this because I'm amazed at what you came up with." That comment stayed in the back of my mind when I was considering graduate school at Boston University, thinking that I might study art. I knew they had a theatre school, and I thought that I might be able to look into it. I applied for a theatre scholarship in the theatre department and was accepted.

And this was without any experience of designing scenery or any other theatre experience?

Right. I just showed a portfolio and discussed my ideas with Horace Armistead, who was the head of the department, and he assigned me a show. The first show that I designed was *The Time of Your Life* in 1957. It came off quite well. The director, Marvin Starkman, is now an agent in New York, and it was his graduate production.

I stayed at the university for two years, and then I worked in Boston for a while. While I was at Boston University I designed a couple of operas for Sarah Caldwell, *Gianni Schicci* and *Angelique*. Before that I designed the lighting for her production of *Madame Butterfly*. I was with WGBH-TV a short time, and I designed for a dinner theatre on top of the Bradford Roof, and I designed some productions at the Charles Playhouse. I did a *Threepenny Opera* at the Charles Playhouse, when it was first released after its Off-Broadway run.

You decided then to come to New York?

Yes, I guess it was obvious that that's where you had to be, if you were going to pursue a career. Certainly, every student who had any talent was encouraged to leave and go to New York.

Did Horace Armistead tell you what to do when you got to New York? Did you have any idea?

No, not anything specific, and I came in cold. There was not really a big Boston University network when I came here. I knew Ray Sovey from being in the theatre school at Boston University. Ray, of course, had friends and associates that I had met, and there were some friends of Horace's that I had met in Boston. But basically when I came I just had to look around. The producers of the Meadowbrook Dinner Theatre were the same ones who had produced at the Bradford Roof in Boston, so I went over to New Jersey and did dinner theatre there. When I arrived at the Meadowbrook Dinner Theatre, I became one of their rotating designers. Robin Wagner was one of them, and that's where I first met him. He was at that time the busiest of Off-Broadway designers. And I got a couple of Off-Broadway shows on Robin's recommendations.

As a matter of fact, the first Off-Broadway show that I did was *Medea*. Robin couldn't do it, and Judy Marechal produced it at the Martinique Theatre. This was in 1965. That was a nice little theatre in the Martinique, which was then a hotel. But that was years after I first came to New York. I went through the dinner theatre circuit for two years and then finally I just couldn't do it anymore. I just got tired of it. So I did temporary work and kind of put a portfolio together of things that I really wanted to do and began seeing producers and trying to get an agent. I did a production at Equity Library Theatre, and I did shows in church basements and I gradually made a few contacts. Monty Silver became my agent for summer stock, and in 1964 I finally got my first high-paying summer stock job. It was with the Atlanta Theatre Under the Stars, which was an outdoor theatre. The contract there was for the most money I had ever made up to that time. It was a big season and a lot of scenery.

What shows did you do?

It was the first year that *My Fair Lady* was released, and I designed that, and the next was *West Side Story*, and then *The Sound of Music*, *Gypsy*, *Bye Bye Birdie*, and *Tovarich*. The proscenium opening was 60 feet and we had no flies. We had to calculate everything to slide in and out. I did mobile scene changes, which I wanted to do anyway, so we had all these dollies rolling back and forth. There was just miles and miles to paint, and the paint compressor never stopped going. I had a staff of about twenty apprentices.

Just before I went to Atlanta, I got a call from Sid Bennett, whom I had known in Boston. He was at one time the technical director for Sarah Caldwell, and had come to Juilliard as their technical director. Ming Cho Lee was designing an opera for Juilliard, and they were in trouble and needed an extra scenic artist to work on a drop. So I went over and met Ming for the first time, and I did the drop. He was very happy with it, and I stayed on and finished painting the opera for him. Ming asked me to come see him when I came back from Atlanta, and I did.

Then I painted Ming's scenery for the Off-Broadway *Othello*, the one with James Earl Jones. In November I went to work in Ming's studio. I was there for three years. I started in the fall of 1964 and worked there until the spring of 1967, with time out to do a little work here and there. Doug Schmidt was there as the other principal assistant. I went out of town with the first musical that Ming did. It was called *A Time for Singing*. That was in 1966. We worked on Tennessee William's *Slapstick Tragedy* for Broadway and *Don Rodrigo* for New York City Opera. They were exciting times, and for the first time I was doing things that I thought were important. Ming's career was just taking off. In 1965, I was given a school tour production of *Henry V* that Joe Papp directed. Joe was happy with it, and that brought more assignments for the New York Shakespeare Festival. And then Ming was tremendously busy at that time so there was a lot of spin-off from the studio. There were projects and things that he was not interested in or couldn't handle because of his schedule.

How did your first Broadway show come about?

The first legitimate Broadway show was *How the Other Half Loves*. Gene Saks was the director, and I have done six other shows with him over my career.

Everything builds on another. In the sixties during the time I was working

Stage designs by David Mitchell
THE SLEEPING BEAUTY
Music by Peter Ilyich Tchaikovsky
Choreographed by Peter Martins
New York City Ballet, New York (1991)
Photographs: Front curtain projection and
  overgrown chateau (*right*).

for Ming I began designing operas for Tito Capobianco. I did some "mail-ins" for him in South America, which means that I didn't go down there, but I designed the operas and sent them down. Of course, I never had the opportunity to supervise them, but evidently they turned out very well because he then asked me to do *Mefistofele* in 1969. So this was the first big show for me in New York, even though I was doing things for the New York Shakespeare Festival, over the years, from 1967 through 1969.

Mefistofele was for the New York City Opera?

Yes, but this was a big production, and so it was kind of the first big break. It got tremendous reviews and it's been in the repertory ever since. It's one of the most popular shows they've ever done. I designed a kind of light projection show for the beginning of the opera. I haven't seen the production recently, but they've reduced the size of the projectors, and so now it isn't anything like it was when it was first done. But the scenery itself and the drops haven't changed. I got some magnificent painting from the Feller shop when it was in Fort Lee.

And the shop had both building and painting then.

Yes. I had a lot of painting on that set, and there were some great scenic artists who worked on it. I worked all summer on the elevations, and they painted all summer on them. Fortunately, it just happened to be a period

when they weren't busy. They were my first big reviews in New York.

And that success brought more work for you in New York?

That was followed the next spring, in 1970, by two Off-Broadway shows that really did bring about the Broadway show. They were *Steambath* and *Colette*. Both of those shows opened within weeks of each other, and they were totally different in concept. *Colette* had front projections, and it was really props on a platform and a textured wall in back that was painted to receive fragments of projected images. It had bare brick walls around the sides. And then for *Steambath* I had a tremendously realistic set which had real steam. Both of those shows were well reviewed.

Colette was really the first gold-plated hit that I ever had. Unfortunately, it never materialized into any kind of a moneymaker because Zoe Caldwell had to leave four months after opening. They couldn't find a replacement. No one wanted to step in and take over, so it never moved.

You did How the Other Half Loves. *How did that come about?*

Michael Myerberg was the producer of *How the Other Half Loves*, and he was always looking for somebody new and also somebody he could pay less. It's a common practice among producers to find what is many times referred to by producers as "new blood," which is really saying, "We'll get them now before we have to pay them a lot more."

So Michael Myerberg actually did the scouting. He saw those two Off-Broadway shows and he recommended me to Gene Saks, who was directing. I went by and had an interview with Gene. He saw my portfolio and he agreed that I could do it. Gene had seen the two Off-Broadway shows that I had done, and this was also right about the time I did *Trelawny of the "Wells"* for Joe Papp at the Public Theatre. That was in 1970. And so putting the three of them together added up to my getting the job.

Did How the Other Half Loves *help you to get other shows in New York or on Broadway?*

No, not really. That show didn't do a lot for my career, even though it was a tricky Alan Ayckbourn idea with two sets combined in one. The set looked good and, as I recall, got fairly good reviews. It was a mistake to Americanize the play. That's what went wrong. It was really an English class comedy. A lot of it was blurred by Americanizing it. I think American audiences would have liked it much better straight. Sandy Dennis, Phil Silvers, Richard Mulligan, and Bernice Massi were in the cast.

What is your method of working with Gene Saks on a production?

Well, it varies. Gene is easy to work with. We have a discussion, and then I bring sketches to show him and then make a model. It's not particularly different from working with any other director. Sometimes you have less time. Sometimes directors are absent and you have to send them something, but then eventually you have to produce a model. Other directors will give you rough ground plans. Many times you have to work fast. My experience has been no matter what you might have done, what your record may be, everyone wants to have an idea of what you are going to do for them on this particular job before you are hired. Sometimes a director will have other designers in mind as well. So, on occasion, it's important to be able to design a show on somebody's coffee table if you have to.

You have to have an instant vocabulary.

And some very quick ideas. The *Gin Game* was one, however, where I had time. Mike Nichols was the director. The design for *The Gin Game*, with Hume Cronyn and Jessica Tandy, was arrived at with pieces that I had drafted. There were modules of a mansion or a house, wall sections and so on that we pushed back and forth until the right space emerged. That was done in my studio. It was not a sketch but simply a matter of just looking at the space. It was done originally for the Long Wharf production in New Haven, and that set was later adapted for Broadway.

Did Foxfire *come about as a result of working with Hume Cronyn on* The Gin Game?

Not really, no. We all parted good friends and thought someday we would work together again or whatever. But when *Foxfire* was first done, Hume was with other producers and other people, and it was done in Stratford, Ontario, with a Canadian designer. Then they decided they needed more work, and they went to the Guthrie Theatre. This time they had Marshall Mason and John Lee Beatty. John is Marshall Mason's designer and has been over the years. So John Lee designed it at the Guthrie. When they were ready to do it on Broadway they wanted to assemble still another team. Either Marshall Mason wasn't available or they wanted to use someone else. I'm not sure what happened. But the producers gave me a call.

They didn't have a director. They were interviewing directors. Hume said, "I'm going to send the script over to you with some research and I want you to call me back tomorrow morning and tell me what you think." I knew he was not just interested in my opinion of the play but what my ideas for the set were. And so I read it, and that evening I began to think of what I could tell him on the telephone the next day. I made a few rough sketches and called him up and described the set I would design for it, and he liked what he heard. He said, "Now this seems to line up with this director we've been talking to. So I think we'll have to get the two of you together." When I met the director, David Trainer, our ideas meshed quite well, and then we went on from there.

You had a great success with the musical Annie. *How did the initial contact for that come about?*

When *Annie* was done at the Goodspeed Opera Company, the resident designer did it. I think the show got so-so reviews. But Mike Nichols and Lewis Allen saw it, and decided there was something there, so they decided to produce it on Broadway. Marty Charnin was the creator and director. I understand that Tony Walton was approached to design it, but he was busy at the time and couldn't do it, and so then the question came up to Tony, "Well, who do you think can do it?" They knew they wanted a realistic kind of base for it, and Tony Walton recommended me. I had never met Tony, but he had seen my work.

I was not on record for having done a musical, and they weren't even sure who I was. So they called me in, and I was very casual about the interview because I didn't think anything would come of it. I didn't even know that Mike Nichols was involved when I went in for the interview with Lewis Allen and Marty. I didn't even know who Marty was.

I had a lot of slides and projections of my work and a whole presentation that I was using for industrial shows. We talked for a little while, and I had some ideas. When I left, I thought that I probably wouldn't be seeing them again. So I was very surprised when they called me up about a week later and asked me if I was interested in doing the show. At that time I was working for the New York Shakespeare Festival with a retainer, so I turned them down. They said, "Just think about it and maybe you'll change your mind and we'll talk to you next week."

I found out a little bit more about the show and what was involved and I talked to Theoni Aldredge, whom I knew from the New York Shakespeare Festival, and she was doing the costumes for it. Theoni was a friend of Marty's. So when they called me back, I decided to do it, although I knew that I would be endangering my retainer with the New York Shakespeare Festival.

They wouldn't let you do another show while you were there on a retainer?

At that time they didn't. I was on the retainer and I was pretty much committed to doing work at the festival. I had been given permission to do a musical prior to that, which was *I Love My Wife*. That show had money problems and was on hold at the time. That was okay, but not two musicals! But I took the leap and I decided to do *Annie* anyway.

How did you work out the mechanical aspects of Annie?

I had the idea of New York changing and moving in the background so you see different aspects of New York as a kind of permanent background of the show. I always try to visualize some kind of surround for any kind of show that I do, something that most scenes have in common in the show, and design for that. Since this was New York

City, I had it in mind that it would be great to have a shifting backdrop of New York. That was the first idea. Then we got into solving the problems of the individual scenes. I thought that I should start with the biggest number and the one that seemed the toughest. That was "N.Y.C.," which in the original script was a bigger number than it really turned out to be. In the original script, Annie still had Sandy, the dog, with her, and part of the "N.Y.C." number was a walk from upper Fifth Avenue down to Times Square. To me that suggested treadmills. I proposed those, and put the idea of how that could be done into our scheme and model. We had them downstage, side by side so that you could have people and traffic going one way and against Annie, Daddy Warbucks, and the dog.

How high was the total deck?

As soon as you begin talking treadmills, you're 10 inches high. And that's how high the deck became because of that. Using treadmills began to suggest other scenic solutions then. Since we had the treadmills for this number, we began finding other ways to use them. I didn't want the use of the treadmills overworked, and so we added winches and other things that would be sliding in and out with the treadmills to mix it up so you weren't always sure of what you were seeing. That lateral movement became the kind of style or look of the show, with the shifting backdrop in behind and the movement of the units that came in and out. It was somewhat like a movie pan. It was identified by Mike Nichols because when

Models by David Mitchell
ON THE WATERFRONT
A project for music theatre (1990)
Shown: Hold of freighter; Terry releasing the pigeon.

he saw it, he said, "Oh, it's as if you are panning a camera from one side of the stage to the other." And there were flying pieces that worked with it. The combination of sliding and flying and the way the units came in and hit the floor together was a critical aspect of it. You could see the shifts.

I think that when *Annie* came in in 1977 it was a return to an old-fashioned musical, because up to that point most of the musicals being done were big environmental affairs. *A Chorus Line* was something special. That had opened in 1975. But *Chicago* was very much of a structure, with an elevator and the orchestra onstage, and it was very much in the environmental style. *Rockabye Hamlet*, the Gower Champion musical, was done about the same time, too. There was a lot of that style of musical in the seventies. *Annie* looked different because it was, as Clive Barnes said at the time, "a fully groomed old-fashioned musical" with different sets for different scenes, and the movement of the scenery was all in front of the audience's eyes. We closed down the stage only once and the rest of the show was open.

Could you elaborate a bit more on the workings of the treadmills? You said you had a 10-inch deck. What was the overall size of the treadmills?

I think they were about 3 feet wide. Then there was a strip in between of about 6 inches, I think, and there was another treadmill.

What was the total length?

They had to go offstage, so we're really talking about 50 feet. Their lengths were 50 feet. The mechanism for these treadmills had been around since *Oh, Captain* in the early fifties.

That's when they were first used; otherwise the show wouldn't have been able to afford to have them done. They happened to be available, fortunately, but I didn't choose to use them because of that. Theatre Techniques was the shop that had them.

But you inquired about treadmills while you were doing the show?

Yes. There were treadmills available and we could use them. We found out the sizes. Those same treadmill mechanisms were also used earlier for a show called *Subways Are for Sleeping*, which Will Steven Armstrong did in 1962, and then for *Herzl* that Doug Schmidt designed.

Did you change the show much for the national companies?

Well, the moving background of New York became just a backdrop for the national company as opposed to all the buildings that moved. At one point during "N.Y.C." you have the skyscrapers of Central Park South moving with the Chrysler Building and the Empire State Building across the background. That effect we had in New York, but it was just too much to take out on the road with all the travelers and decking.

And you had treadmills in all of the national companies?

The first and second national companies had treadmills. They made new treadmills for them. Then on the third national company, it was decided that we had to have a shorter setup time, and so knowing what we knew from doing the show three times before, we figured out a way to substitute pallets for the treadmills. And that third national worked out quite well. We had a very shallow deck.

Model by David Mitchell
BARNUM
Directed by Joe Layton
St. James Theatre, New York (1980)

What size deck did you have?

We're talking about a 3½-inch deck with everything on pallets on top of it. We did elaborate charts of when everything would be loaded on and off the pallets so the effect of the treadmills would be maintained.

Pallets have been around, but the technology that was in existence was just then being developed where you could accelerate and then decelerate the winches for smooth riding so they wouldn't jolt on a stop or start. My feeling about pallets has always been that they should blend into the floor so that the audience really doesn't have to see them any more than it has to. The pallets in this national company of *Annie* were ¾-inch ply with a Masonite top and metal runners inlaid underneath that. The metal runners in those days would move on a fiber inset inlaid into the stage floor so that was without wheels. We got a very smooth ride and no sound with the pallets. I also used pallets like that in the musical *Working*. We had seven pallets for that show, and some of them moved up and down stage and others moved across stage.

Were they operated by winches?

They were operated by winches, and they moved on a fiber that was very hard and would not wear. It was inlaid into the deck. The pallets themselves had inlaid iron runners that lined up with the fiber strips. The edges of the pallet were beveled so that you didn't have an inch and a half of step-up. You were able to eliminate that by beveling down to a quarter of an inch off the deck. In some instances we used metal edges on it to make it blend in as much as possible. We did that in *Working* and what we finally did in the third national company of *Annie.*

How did you go about designing the production of Barnum?

Basically it was conceived as an in-house environmental, in the auditorium as well as on stage. It was a completely different way of doing a musical because you weren't depending on winches and things tracking on. You were dealing with live bodies bringing all the things on, and that was choreographed as well as the perform-

ers' movements. The performers were given things to work with and move around more than having things move by themselves. Of course, you were flying things in, and so it was also a learning experience for theatre technical people and theatre rigging. You had people on trapezes, and on one occasion in the finale of the show, a performer was flying from one platform to another across the proscenium on a trapeze. There was a lot of construction done in the house as well as on stage to support trapezes. We had circus poles on stage and a high wire as well as a low wire.

Did you have to do research for circus equipment?

Yes, we did. We had the rigger from the Big Apple Circus. The Barnum and Bailey Circus also helped us, and we had quite a few conferences with them and with the people who were going to be doing the rigging. One of the first things we did on the show was to have a meeting with all the performers in a hotel suite at the Algonquin before the rehearsals started. We stayed there all day, and each performer got up and told us everything he or she was able to do as a circus performer.

Then we began to construct ideas for musical numbers with the skills of the performers involved. There was a number called "One Brick at a Time" that was based on the skills of a performer who balanced cigar boxes, and the cigar boxes became bricks and were then used in a juggling act to build up the portal of the museum by throwing bricks around the stage and balancing them.

In other instances, people were going to be using unicycles or walking a slack wire with a violin or whatever, so we were trying to find ways to make all that work on stage. And so a lot of these things become part of the numbers and the way the numbers were done.

There were some specific things that Joe Layton, the director, wanted to do with the rigging up above in terms of tightrope walking and work on rings. When he saw the techniques available, we began finding places for those on the set so that we could use them. So it was really a big playground with as much going on as possible to create the illusion of a three-ring circus.

Talk about how you designed the musical La Cage aux Folles.

Once again, there is always a central problem that needs to be solved. One of the first numbers written was "Mascara." And they wanted that to lead directly from the dressing room set immediately into a number on the club stage. Getting from the apartment dressing room to the stage and then concluding the number on the stage was one of the first requests made in formulating the show. The other was the fact that they wanted to go to a scene backstage. So the scenery on the actual stage of the theatre had to slide smoothly from an apartment to backstage to the club stage. That was another thing that had to be solved. Another problem was how to get into the show and how to suggest both the locale of the club and the club itself.

We decided to start outside the club for the overture and bring the audience in so that the audience would have a feel of the exterior which we would then see later on. We decided on that approach rather than just representing the club, because we felt that the audience had to have a larger picture before the actual theatre stage was turned into the club stage entirely.

That was why we did what we did with the units opening up and revealing the club at the end of the street, supposedly, and then moving the facade of the club downstage toward you, and then having that split as if you'd gone through the doors. Then the house curtains of the club stage expanded and came in on the side to suggest the club stage with the footlights. The trim around the moving show portal lighting up was the final touch.

In order to suggest the more intimate aspects of the club with the stage itself, we had a show portal that slid in and out and lit up to make the space seem like a smaller stage. Then we had the larger opening for the exteriors on the waterfront and so forth.

One of the big challenges was that the apartment had to work so many times, and it had to be fairly complete. You had to have the furniture and you had to represent the dressing room, and you had to represent the front door, and you had to represent the door to the stage, and you had to represent the door to the kitchen. But you had to do it with things that could move in and out very quickly. The apartment was made to work two ways. It could split right down the center and go off into the wings, or it would remain together and then go upstage and something would fly in front of it. We used both changes to give variety. We used one treadmill in *La Cage aux Folles* for bringing some of the furniture on stage. And again, this involved a 10-inch-high deck.

Would you say that this was one of your more mechanical shows?

Well, this had to be, yes. *La Cage* had much more in it in terms of mechanics than *Annie* did, and it all had to fit in the Palace Theatre. We had to do a lot of renovations backstage at the Palace in order to make this show fit. We put in special staircases where the existing ones got in the way on the shallow stage right, and we made special niches on stage left. And then, of course, to make the quick changes that were necessary, we went out into the boxes and

made new walls to create special dressing rooms left and right. They went through the fire wall or where the pass doors are and extended and moved the pass doors back into the auditorium and created two special dressing rooms in the rear of the side boxes. The boxes were partitioned and the lost seats in the boxes were installed in the rear of the orchestra. In the Palace Theatre there was plenty of room at the rear of the orchestra. The dressing rooms were equipped with sinks, mirrors, and everything else needed for elaborate costume changes. There just wasn't enough room backstage to do it.

How many drops did you have?

One of the most successful of those drops was the St. Tropez waterfront. Ordinarily you like to keep your drops upstage to maintain a distance from the audience, and you have to have scrim in front of them. You don't really show a drop without having a scrim in front of it anymore, because any imperfections in the drop are picked up by the incidental lighting. If you have a scrim in front of it, it softens it and fogs it up just enough so that it gives distance.

Just the way the show was working out to do the exterior scenes, I realized I was going to have to bring a drop down in three-quarter-stage. I realized it was going to have to look pretty good. We constructed a truss with lights built in top and bottom. Then a scrim was stretched over the front and that scrim had a muslin ground row applied onto it. The ground row represented beach.

Is this a full-size stage scrim we're talking about?

Yes. So the truss had a scrim and a translucent drop combined with strip lights top and bottom to light the drop. It was about 18 inches deep. That gave us a kind of sparkle and look, particularly in the water, that was required. It was lit by Jules Fisher, and he did a remarkable job.

Would you say that La Cage aux Folles *was a tightly hung show?*

Oh, it was extremely tightly hung. We were 3½ inches apart for the most part.

Did you use cable guides on drops?

Actually, I don't think we had any drops with cable guides. One of the other tricks that we used involved rear-fold travelers. As a drop came on and

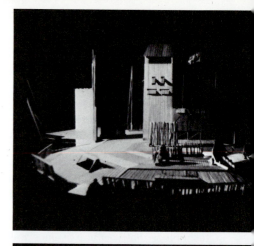

Models by David Mitchell
HENRY V by William Shakespeare
Directed by Joseph Papp
Delacorte Theatre
Central Park, New York (1976)
Photographs: Fortification and tunnels; interior
tower/playhouse; open fields and ships.

went offstage it expanded so it looked as if it was moving across the stage as the next scene was revealed coming in from stage left to stage right. We had curtain sliders that traveled from left to right and you would see a portion of the backstage as well as the onstage. As you moved from offstage to onstage, you had to see the backdrop on stage be revealed and move with the curtain sliders, so the whole stage had to look like it was moving from left to right. That meant that the backdrop had to be on a traveler that folded it up and it would expand when the stage was being revealed and the sliders were moving across. Fred Gallo was the production carpenter.

What was the material for the drops?

The drops were all muslin, and not all of them folded like that. There was just the one drop that worked that way. Basically, we had a decorative drop that was styled after Erté's painting style. We used that for the opening number, and you saw it again during the show. That had this special rear-fold rig, so that it would fold up on itself as it went onstage and then pull out when we wanted to show it again when the stage picture opened up laterally as the curtain sliders were moving across stage to reveal the onstage area. And behind that we had a brick wall that was the backstage. And that was either revealed or covered up by the movement of the curtain back and forth.

And the treadmill, of course, served us very well because people could be standing onstage, and as we wanted to go backstage, then the people who were onstage could appear to be continuing their business in place, but they would be moving away from us as the curtain sliders moved across the stage. Also, the people who were offstage coming onstage, instead of walking into position, were doing their business backstage, but they were standing on the treadmills so their action appeared normal, not just walking into place and then going into the scene. There was really a tremendous amount of pressure on that show. It was a tough one considering the complexity of the show, and the time that we had to do it.

How did your association with George Balanchine and the New York City Ballet come about?

That was pretty roundabout. I didn't really know anything about ballet. I designed a *Trovatore* in 1973 for Tito Capobianco at the Paris Opera, and they had a well-known French designer, Bernard Dayde, as their director of technical services. I got to be friendly with Bernard Dayde and he introduced me to Balanchine, who was there choreographing *Orpheus* for René Claire. This was in 1973, and then in 1976 Dayde was invited to do the set for *Gaspard de la Nuit*, which was one of the productions for the Ravel Festival. Anyway, he felt that he needed an American supervisor, and he asked me to help. I ended up working on several productions while I was there that spring, and became a kind of resident troubleshooter for everything they did on the festival. One of them was a production of the ballet *L'Enfant et le Sortilège*, a Ravel opera that Balanchine turned into a ballet. Kermit Love designed it. I worked on that as well, and then later I did sets and costumes for a little ballet Balanchine did the following summer.

Is this the first time you did costumes?

I had done them on and off, but this is the first time of any significance. There were only two costumes. It was *The Steadfast Tin Soldier*. Later I did the sets and costumes for the *Dance in America* version with Baryshnikov and McBride. And so that began an association on and off with the New York City Ballet.

When Balanchine died, I was working on a new production of *Don Quixote* that he was preparing just before he was taken ill. Soon after, Lincoln Kirstein wanted the *Liebeslieder Walzer* to come back into the repertory and he wanted it designed as Balanchine had

Model by David Mitchell
LEGS DIAMOND by Harvey Fierstein and Charles Suppon
Music and lyrics by Peter Allen
"Times Square"
Directed by Robert Allan Ackerman
Mark Hellinger Theatre, New York (1988)

envisioned a new production, based upon a place that he and Balanchine had seen in Nymphenburg called the Amalienburg Pavilion. It is a small hunting lodge with one of the most beautiful rococo ballrooms in existence. Kirstein and Balanchine visited there when their company was touring Europe, and Balanchine remarked, "This is where *Liebeslieder Walzer* should be." So Kirstein asked me to do it. *Liebeslieder Walzer* was a great success. The revival was something that I was tremendously proud of. And so right after that, he asked me if I could do *Sleeping Beauty*. I did another Balanchine revival, the *Brahms-Schoenberg Quartet* right after that, about a year or two later.

I now have a *Sleeping Beauty* for the New York City Ballet which was commissioned by Kirstein which I've worked on for several years, on and off. We made a ½-inch scale elaborate model with working parts at the cost of over $30,000. It had the scenery for the three acts with rigging so you can pull things up and down and up out of the floor. A slide show was made of the model with Pat Zipprodt's costumes reduced in size so that they all fit in the model. Then the audiovisual production with three projectors and dissolves made the figures move and gave scenic transitions.

The slide show of the model was given as part of Lincoln Kirstein's eightieth birthday at the New York State Theatre. The model, the drawings, and the paintings were on exhibition in the lobby. At the beginning of the event the City Ballet orchestra was on stage playing selections from *The*

ALL FAMOUS AND GIGANTIC JUMBO

A MAMMOTH AMONG ALL THE HUGEST ELEPHANTS · THE LARGEST LIVING QUADRUPED ON EARTH

Stage design by David Mitchell
BARNUM
Directed by Joe Layton
St. James Theatre, New York (1980)
Shown: Jumbo and Tom Thumb in London.

Sleeping Beauty. Peter Martins narrated the slide show, and later presented Lincoln Kirstein with City Ballet's birthday present, which was an announcement of its pending production of *The Sleeping Beauty*.

My understanding is that Balanchine at one point gave up on *Sleeping Beauty* because he didn't feel that the theatre was really practical for what he felt had to happen visually in the ballet. Working traps at the New York State theatre are not really practical, and you're really cramped offstage. There were just too many obstacles to overcome. But Kirstein was determined that it could be done, and he asked me if I would try it. Of course, we tried to include all the things that he had talked with Balanchine about over the years. The vines do overgrow the garden and the chateau. In the last act you have the actual approach to the overgrown chateau, and the vines are pulling back, and you have magical appearances as the chateau comes to life. So there really is a full production trying to approximate, if not in size, at least the spirit of the famous original production at the Maryinsky Theatre in Leningrad.

Balanchine had mentioned *Sleeping Beauty* to me a couple of times, while working on other projects.

Comment on the turntable in I Remember Mama.

On *I Remember Mama* I experimented with a large table with a house structure that was set off-center on a smaller table. It was a section of a house with a suggestion of a kitchen, upstairs,

living room, front hall, back stairs, and back porch. We also had other scenes in a hospital and a farm and so on. You just couldn't be stuck with the house on stage all during the show. So by putting it off center on a large turntable and in its own turntable, we were able to pull the house upstage and then things could fly in front of it. Also, the house could move upstage with the small table keeping it in its same relationship to the audience. The big table would be carrying the house upstage, but the counter-revolve of the smaller table kept the house in the same orientation to the audience.

If you build a painted model, do you do several painted sketches, too?

No, I very seldom do finished sketches, as a matter of fact. There are so many things to work out in a model. I will do rough black-and-white pencil sketches generally on tracing paper for every scene, and they can be printed. That's the way I start. Sometimes I will do a storyboard.

What paints do you like to work with when you do the model and paint elevations?

I use acrylics, but I use a little bit of everything. I like the Dr. Martin's dyes suspended in a matte medium, which keeps the intensity of the dye, for glazes and overlays. It's the same technique as when in scene painting you use dyes and a clear latex. I sometimes paint on canvas because I like the stability of the canvas and I don't have to worry about the board bending. Many times for the model I will turn my

painting elevations into C prints so that we can backlight the elevation and see it like a translucency in the model. A C print is a color reproduction on paper that is translucent, and you can light through it and it will be very much like a translucency on stage. I used painted C prints in almost all models since *Foxfire*.

What do you like most about working in the theatre?

I think each job is different. The freelance quality is adventurous. Theatre is small enough so that you don't feel you're swallowed up. It still has a certain kind of definition when it arrives on stage, whatever your contribution. There's a tremendous kind of pressure and a tremendous involvement of so many people in film that some of your ideas can get lost, and even on the stage, you still have dangers of having things compromised to the point where you're very unhappy. But in the theatre, you have a fighting chance of having your ideas realized. And so I enjoy the challenge of that. And the size of the theatre operation is still something that I feel comfortable with. There's still a chance of doing something special or something that does not have to be as marketable as films have to be.

Would you say that the theatre gives you a better place to create than any other area?

Yes, and you have more variety of things to create. Many things are just excluded in film by the nature of the material. I like the variety of assignments and learning new things. Generally, I like all the aspects of theatre. I like the research and then the manipulation and use of stage space and objects in it because I have a talent for it and I enjoy doing it.

Every show is a new challenge. You reach a certain point when you've had enough experience so that you should be getting better with everything you do. You'll find that even though the job may not be as successful overall, in many ways you've improved. Your talent isn't anything that should be diminished by getting older. You should just be getting better.

312

Motley: A MIDSUMMER NIGHT'S DREAM (c. 1950) (Collection of Peter Harvey); Peter Harvey:
CONCERNING ORACLES (1966) (Costume Photographs by Linda Alaniz)

  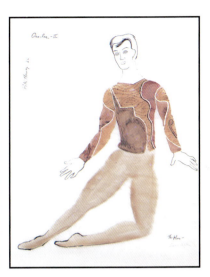

José Varona: CINDERELLA (1976); David Mitchell: THE SLEEPING BEAUTY (1991); José Varona:
CINDERELLA (1976)

Robert O'Hearn: LA TRAVIATA (1968); Zack Brown: THE MERRY WIDOW (1984)

Costume designs by Eduardo Sicangco for AIN'T MISBEHAVIN' (1993), Cincinnati Playhouse

John Keck: ROCKETTES (1978), Costumes: Frank Spencer; John Napier: CATS (Deck) (Photograph by Arnold Abramson); William and Jean Eckart: FIORELLO! (1959) (Two Sketches)

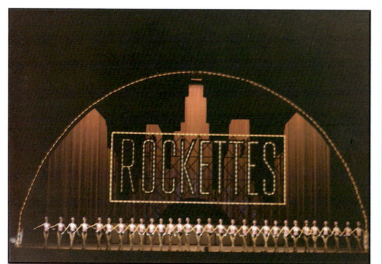

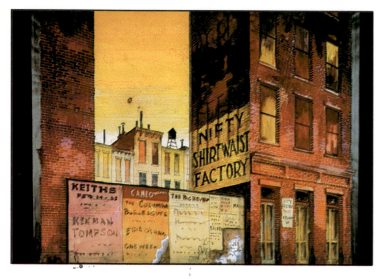

William and Jean Eckart: THE EDUCATION OF HYMAN KAPLAN (1968); Oldsmobile Show (1955); Douglas
W. Schmidt: FRANKENSTEIN (1981); Clarke Dunham: PLAY MEMORY (1984), Lighting: Ken Billington

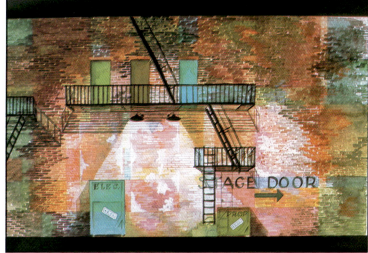

John Scheffler: MACBETH (1979), Lighting: D. Doc Chaves; Lynn Pecktal: THE MUSIC MAN (1979), Jones Beach Theatre

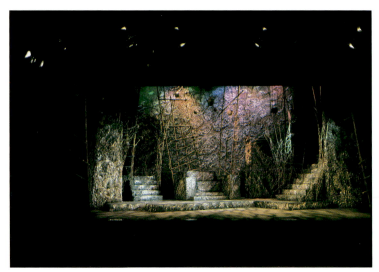

William and Jean Eckart: REUBEN, REUBEN (1955); Tony Straiges: GENIUSES (1983) (Photograph by Ney Tait Fraser)

Franco Colavecchia: CASANOVA (1985) (Photograph by Phil Jones); George Tsypin: THE DEATH OF KLINGHOFFER (1991), Costumes: Dunya Ramicova, Lighting: James F. Ingalls

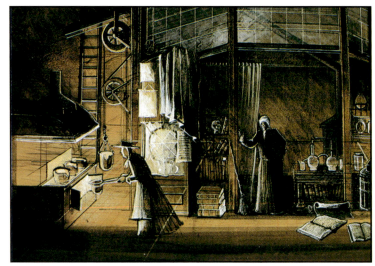

7

PORTALS, FRAMED HANGERS, AND GROUND ROWS

PORTALS, GROUND ROWS, AND OTHER SET PIECES

In this chapter some of the most standard and also some of the most necessary scenery items are discussed. These include such scenic units for the stage as portals, ground rows, and framed hangers. These units are grouped together here in one chapter primarily because they are frequently used scenic pieces, but do not follow any special order or sequence in the designing process.

PORTALS

Designing and Positioning Portals

Portals are units of scenery that frame the basic set(s) or action of a production on a proscenium stage. In a sense, a portal's function is similar to that of a frame on a painting. Portals are designed so that their three onstage edges have an appropriate visual width to make a pleasant proportional composition unit between the house proscenium opening and the set itself.

Portals are normally positioned parallel to and upstage of the house proscenium and are used extensively for all types of proscenium productions, from plays, operas, and musicals to operettas, from ballets to revues.

Occasionally a portal is placed downstage of a proscenium opening when it is necessary to create more depth in the set or to cover the existing

house details and decor on the proscenium opening. Whether for single-set or multiset productions, designers are always looking for designs to create new shapes for portals. When thinking of the portal design, consider these questions: Should the portal be simple or intricate? Should the portal be bright and decorative or dark and subdued? Should it be three-dimensional, painted to look three-dimensional, or a combination of the two? Should it have rows of tracer or nonflashing lights going around the opening?

Functions of the Basic Portals

A basic portal has these functions:

1. Frames the stage setting like a picture frame.
2. Confines the onstage space.
3. Reduces the visual width and height of the stage space.
4. Allows various entrances and exits for actors, dancers, and choruses (left, right, downstage, upstage).
5. Masks the outer edges of the setting(s).
6. Masks lighting instruments left, right, and above.
7. Masks offstage rigging and scenery in storage (also usually needs soft masking added on the outer edges of each leg, and often above, too).
8. Allows scenery to fly in and out.
9. Allows scenery to move on and off from right and left.
10. Allows scenery upstage to move downstage (or vice versa) under the openings.

11. Allows turntables or other units to move and/or play in the center of the stage.

Parts of Portals

The parts of a basic framed portal consist of a framed header at the top and two framed legs on either side. Normally these three pieces are joined together so they are all in the same plane, as though cut out of one piece of illustration board. In essence the shape is like an expanded inverted letter U. In the commercial theatre the framed legs may average from 4 to 6 feet in width and the framed header may have the same dimensions (4 to 6 feet in height) or sometimes be even higher.

When a soft piece is used in place of a framed header, it is usually termed a *border*. A border can function as a decorative scenic piece as well as a masking piece. For masking, the border may be made with or without fullness. The term *teaser* is usually given to this soft piece when it works for masking purposes only. Then it is usually constructed in fullness with pleats at the top.

Shapes of Portals

For proscenium productions, the offstage edges of the legs and headers are generally straight. But the inner profile edges of portals can encompass a multitude of designs and shapes. Inner profile portal shapes may be rectangular, square, semicircular, angular, oval, drapery profiles, foliage shapes, archi-

314   tectural designs, decorative ornaments, or a combination of many more patterns.

Framed (Hard) and Unframed (Soft) Portals in Combination

Several combinations can be considered for creating the effect of a portal. Which combination works best depends on the design, physical bulk, and budget for the production. Some or all can be designed to have adjusted openings so they fit various proscenium openings in theatres. The possible combinations, with examples, are:

1. Hard legs and a hard header (heavy baroque framed ornament bordering all three inner profile edges).
2. Hard legs and a soft border (detailed tree trunks on the sides with leafy foliage overhead).
3. Soft legs and a soft border (pulled-back drapery legs with random drapery swags at the top).
4. Soft legs and a hard header (painted billboards on the legs with actual electric lights in the header above).

Using Framed (Hard) Legs or Unframed (Soft) Legs

HARD LEGS

1. Can have many varied shapes on their profiled edges which do not need to be supported by the benefit of netting, gauze, or wire.
2. Allow a nice even surface for painted details.
3. Often look best under stage lighting since the bottom portion of the legs get the most concentration of light.
4. Do not flutter when actors and dancers go swiftly past them or brush up against them.

SOFT LEGS

1. If edges are profiled, need scenic netting or gauze or other support materials behind to hold them in a neat vertical plane.
2. Do not always become wrinkle-free after storage and travel.
3. Are easy to store, and travel. Usually soft legs are designed without fullness, but they can be for certain drapery effects.
4. Can be folded back and tied that way on the top of the pipe when space is tight.

Model by Heidi Landesman
HOLEVILLE by Jeff Wanshel
Songs and direction by Des McAnuff

Brooklyn Academy of Music
Attic Theatre
Brooklyn, New York (1979)

Using Hard Legs with a Soft Border

Listed are situations in which hard legs with a soft border would be desirable.

1. The onstage profiles may be designed so that scenic netting is required to support them.
2. A practical opening like a window or door may be needed in the hard legs.
3. An architectural unit where a hard and a solid surface is desired and which features columns that have to be straight.
4. A wrinkle-free surface is needed.

Size of Portal Opening Compared with Proscenium Opening

Some commercial theatres have elaborate permanent proscenium treatments, while others have simple lines and minimal detail. In general, if a show is going into a theatre with a sim-

ple proscenium, you might want to make the portal more elaborate; and with a strong ornamental proscenium, you might want to keep the portal simple. Some theatres have proscenium openings with enormous baroque ornamentation and detailed three-dimensional shapes of draperies embellished with swags, jabots, and fringe. This is simply the nature of the architecture in the theatre; it usually works well with the set and should be accepted and taken into consideration as part of the design concept. While the lights are concentrated on the main set, the house proscenium will be lit by the reflected light so the audience watching the action on the stage will see the proscenium framing the picture.

Model by Tony Straiges
COPPERFIELD
Book, music, and lyrics by Al Kasha and Joel Hirschhorn
Direction and choreography by Rob Iscove
ANTA Theatre, New York (1981)
(Photograph by Ney Tait Fraser)

In deciding on the height dimension for a first portal, do not think that 16'-0" to 17'-0" is too high for the trim of the first portal in a commercial theatre. A good height dimension for a first portal in the commercial theatre is 20'-0" high when it has a width of 38'-0" to 40'-0".

Typical first portal opening dimensions may be:

1. The same dimensions as the existing proscenium opening.
2. 1'-0" coming in on each side and top.
3. 2'-0" coming in on each side and top (a good average to use).
4. 3'-0" coming in on each side and top.
5. A combination of the above. For instance, when as much height as possible is needed, the top dimension may be the same as the proscenium top, but the sides may come in 2'-0" or more on each side. Or the top dimensions may be 1'-0" or 1'-6" above the proscenium opening (so lights on the first pipe behind the proscenium opening may get under the portal nicely), with sides the same as the proscenium opening or sides coming in 1'-0" or 2'-0". Portal sizes vary according to individual design and need.

Basic Black Portal

Many repertory and stock companies have basic black portals which are standard units in their theatres. These portals are designed and built according to the existing proscenium openings, and the proportions of the portal openings are usually quite satisfactory. Commercial Broadway houses do not have black portals, so they must be designed for each production going into the individual theatre.

Size of Portals

Basic sizes of portals are determined by

1. The proscenium opening of the theatre in which they are to be positioned, and
2. The particular demands for the individual production.

A designer is always delighted to find a well-proportioned proscenium opening in a theatre. A proscenium opening is seldom too high for a designer's work; on the contrary, many designers have worked in theatres where the height of the proscenium was too low in proportion to the width. (These unbalanced proscenium openings are frequently referred to as "mailbox slots.")

Number of Portals

The number of portals is usually determined by

1. The depth of the stage and
2. The particular demands of the individual production.

You may have only one portal, or two, three, four, or five portals for a production. Usually four is the maximum average, although for productions where a great deal of depth is required, such as an opera or ballet, more may be needed. Remember, too many portals of identical size, shape, and color can become monotonous. On the other hand, if portals are varied in their design with drapery, foliage, or architectural elements breaking up the rectangular opening, then four, five, or even six portals can be worked out nicely and form a pleasing design.

Stage designs by Pavel Tchelitchew
Studies for the Ballet CONCERTO (1942)
The Pierpont Morgan Library, New York, 1982.
   75 : 630
Gift of Mrs. Donald M. Oenslager

Setting by Tony Walton
SOPHISTICATED LADIES
Concept by Donald McKayle

Based on music of Duke Ellington
Directed by Michael Smuin
Costumes by Willa Kim

Lighting by Jennifer Tipton
Lunt-Fontanne Theatre
New York (1981)

Usually a backdrop, cyclorama, or surround is the last piece of scenery positioned upstage. Any of these units should be positioned with sufficient space (visually and practically) upstage of the last portal. For instance, when positioning a backdrop and you have decided on 5'-0" to 6'-0" of space between the last two sets of portals, then you should have a similar space from the last portal to the drop. It works out well if you keep the overall size of the drop consistent with the overall size of the portals. For example, if the outer dimensions of the portals are 52'-0" wide by 36'-0" high, then make the drop the same size.

Spaces between Portals

The spaces between portals are determined according to both the visual and practical aspects of the production. With the visual aspect always in mind, you must consider these points:

1. The movement and storage of the scenery units
2. The space needed for lighting instruments and equipment
3. The space necessary for sound equipment

4. The space necessary for any special effects equipment
5. The space needed for the movement of actors, singers, and dancers

On a production of any complexity, more often than not you will find that the positioning of the portals on the ground plan will be changed several times before complete satisfaction is achieved. If the production is heavy with scenic units on the floor and also in the flies above, you may have to rework things quite a bit. For example, a show which has a full-stage deck with tracked units that have to come on from left and right at various times could also have backdrops and framed set pieces flying in from above. In addition, props and furniture are coming on from various directions. For a multiset show, this process may be repeated several times. Space must also be allotted for lighting and any sound and special effects equipment. All of this has to work in front of, behind, and in between portals.

The two most common ways of positioning basic sets of portals are (1) with equal spacing between, and (2) with decreasing spacing between. While other spacings may be used on

a given production, these two are a good guide for general placement. This effect may vary, especially when the individual portals are designed to be different shapes and colors. Positioning basic portals with decreasing spacing between them as they go upstage visually adds to the feeling of perspective. As previously mentioned, four portals tend to be the standard number used in a show, although five are used for deeper stages or when a special effect of more visual composition is desired. Three portals may work nicely on shallower stages. You must be constantly aware of not only how the placement of portals looks but also how much scenery is to be moved in and out between the portals, as well as how much space is needed for lighting equipment and the general movement of the actors. On a very deep stage with lots of dancing, the space between portals may be as much as 7 to 8 feet.

Decreasing Portals

While the illusion of depth can be obtained from the natural perspective of portals with the same size openings spaced equidistant from each other onstage, an even greater illusion can be gained by making each portal opening 2 or 3 feet smaller as you go upstage. This series of portals (two, three, four, or five) may all be the same color, variations of the same color, or contrasting colors.

This decreasing portal effect is sometimes considered for dance or ballet where an overall open feeling is desired, and at the same time the natural perspective is enhanced.

Decorative Trim on Portals

The decorative trim, built and/or painted, on portals varies widely according to the production. While some portals have no trim, others are designed with lavish detail. The trim on portals may or may not include the thickness around the portal opening. At any rate, the three-dimensional trim is usually built in sections and is bolted or hinged in place so that it can be dismantled and travel separately from the portal. (Even a set that is not being built for a touring company must still travel from the scenic shop to the theatre.) Among the choices for decorative trim to be used on portals are:

1. Painted designs on a flat surface
2. Straight and curved appliqués of various materials
3. Stock molding (wood and/or plastic)
4. Custom-built molding (wood and/or plastic)
5. Stock molding combined with custom molding
6. Plywood cutouts

7. Rows of electric lights
8. Lights behind Plexiglas (or other acrylic sheets) strips
9. Ornate open metalwork (with and/or without gauze)

Thicknesses on Portals

Portals may be designed with or without thicknesses. "Without thicknesses" normally means that the 1-inch edges of the 1 × 3-inch lumber on the edges of the flats are the only thickness seen. In this case, the end of the dressed 1-inch edge is ¾ inch and not a full inch. The back of the thickness is fully blocked in with ¼-inch plywood so that the corner blocks and keystones are not obvious. The strips of ¼-inch plywood are fitted between the corner blocks and keystones.

The most common thickness (return or reveal) around the three sides of the portal opening is the 6-inch return. This is built on a right angle to the back of the portal and the legs. This 6-inch return also serves as a stiffener for the portal.

The next most common thickness is the beveled 45-degree, which may be 6 inches or more. Like three-dimensional trim, the portal thicknesses are built so they can be removed from the

Stage design by Karl Eigsti
EUBIE!
Scene: "I'm Just Wild About Harry"
Conceived and directed by Julianne Boyd
Music by Eubie Blake
Ambassador Theatre
New York (1978)

portal for travel to the theatre, where they are attached with pin hinges.

Masking the Sides and Top of Portals

Soft masking is usually necessary on both sides of the built legs and above the built header at the top of the portal so that the audience does not see backstage and into the flies. When you are resolving the positioning and dimensions of masking, you should always have a drawing of the ground plan and hanging section in front of you.

Assume that you are working with three portals. Naturally, their placement on stage must be resolved before you can decide what masking pieces are needed. Both the overall size of the portal, the width of the legs and header, and exactly where the portal is positioned have everything to do with the masking pieces. While these comments on masking pertain to a proscenium theatre, you may also have portals in a black box theatre where the sides of the legs go right to the walls and the top of the portal header goes up against the ceiling in the room.

Kinds of Portal Masking

Assume for discussion that both the right and left masking legs touching the floor and the border hanging above the portals are all unframed (soft) units. The following information on masking can pertain to framed portals, soft leg and border sets, and other scenic unit

Portal Designs with the Proscenium Opening Indicated by Broken Lines

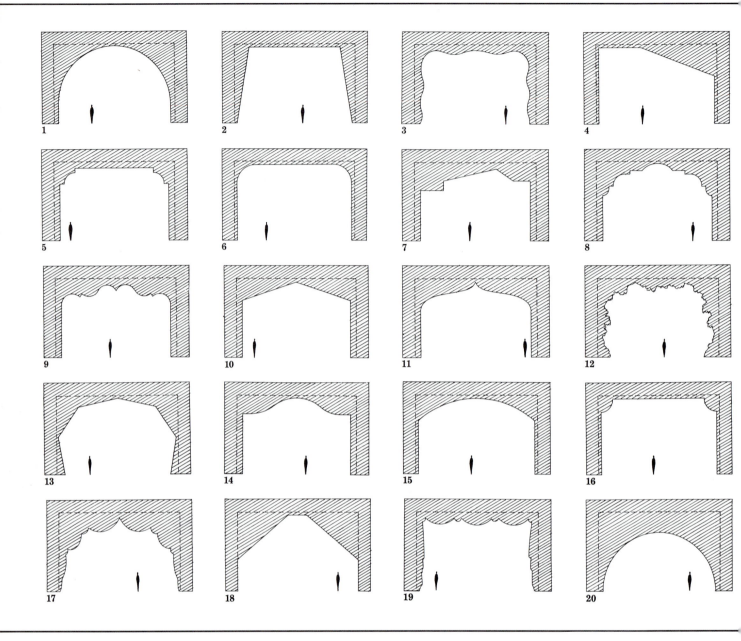

Deciding the Approximate Size of a Portal Opening

Utilizing the Same Width with Different Heights

When the width of a portal opening is known, use this drawing as a guide for selecting the approximate height.

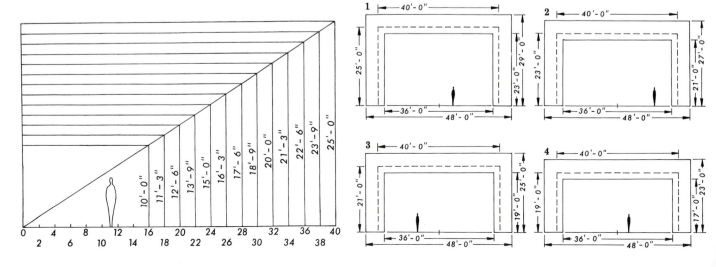

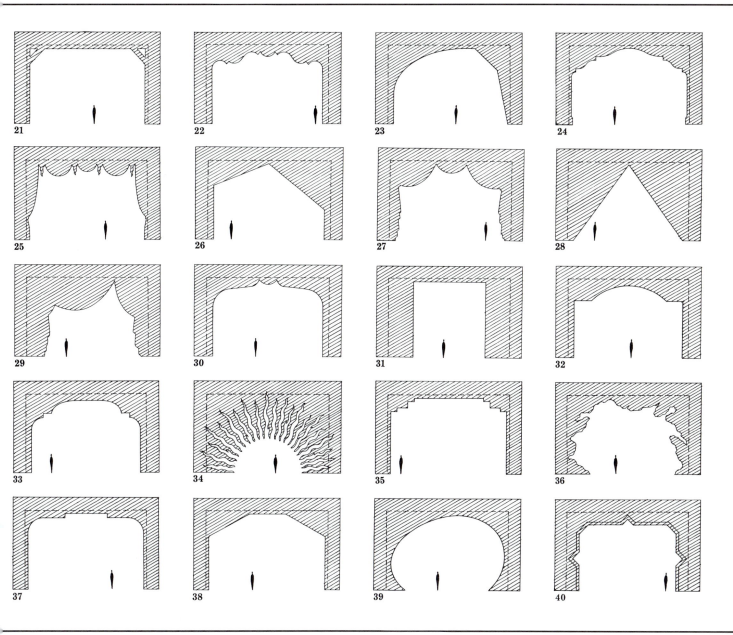

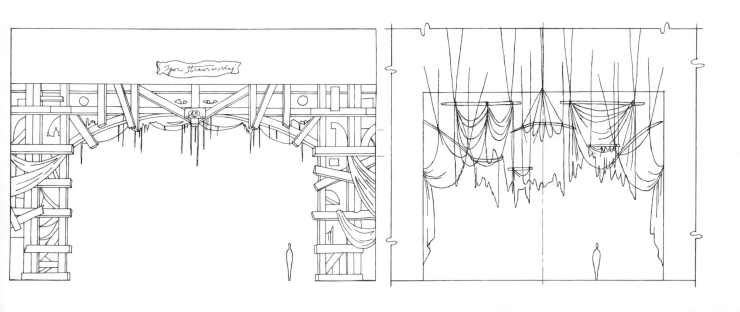

Portal and Drapery (Upstage) by Eugene Berman for PULCINELLA (1972)
(Drawings by Lynn Pecktal)

combinations. Soft masking may be with or without fullness.

Parallel Masking Parallel masking is possibly the best masking to use, and also the easiest to figure out on plan. Here the right and left masking legs are positioned as an extension of the portal and are in a straight line parallel with the proscenium wall. Each soft leg should hang so it overlaps the outer edges of the portal about 4 to 6 inches. Alternatively, the edges of the soft legs can be stapled directly to the outer edges of the hard portal. The height of the masking legs may be the same as the height of the portal top or the same as the height of the top of the masking border hung above the portal top. Parallel masking is usually most useful when there is a lot of offstage space on both the right and left stage. Parallel masking does not need to fly in and out during the performance unless, of course, there is an exceptional requirement for it to do so.

Angled Masking Angled masking normally is used when there is not a great deal of offstage space and when there is not any scenery of any great size that has to come off and on from the wings. However, space is left open for actors and lighting instruments downstage of the angled masking legs. Angled masking is usually positioned so the downstage edge is on a 45-degree angle to the proscenium wall. The height of the angled masking leg works well when it is the same height as the top of the masking border above the top of the framed portal. This is a good rule to follow when drawing masking.

Perpendicular Masking Perpendicular masking is positioned perpendicular to the proscenium wall and is appropriate when the offstage space left and right is very tight. It is especially good to use when scenic units must come off and on (tracked on when possible in very tight situations) or to provide enough space for the cast to make entrances and exits. It is best to have perpendicular masking fly in and out when sizable scenic units must come on and off stage. It is often necessary to rig each piece of perpendicular masking to fly in and out independently of each other. Like angled masking, perpendicular masking should be the same height as the top of the masking border. The soft leg should have a hem for a chain to weigh it down. Metal pipes in the hem can be hazardous to actors and crew, especially for masking that is flying in and out. It is always better to be safe than sorry.

Starting Dimensions from the Edge of the Apron

While it is standard to start dimensions from the back of the smoke pocket or from the back of the proscenium wall when it is consistently straight across the stage, there are exceptions. Sometimes dimensions may be started at the edge of the apron. Such was the case for the national company of the Negro Ensemble Company's *Home* at the Blackstone Theatre in Chicago. The reason for this was to keep the original ramp platform unit downstage as much as possible (starting 6 inches from the edge of the apron). Since the position

Stage designs by John Falabella
NORA by Barry Abbott and Joseph Treviso
A project (1986)
1. Paris street scene.
2. Exterior—Nora's garret in Paris.
3. Interior—Nora's garret in Paris.
4. Paris cafe.
5. Gallery in Kristiania, Norway.
6. Pier in Kristiania.

Model by Loren Sherman
THE CRITIC by Richard Sheridan
A project (1980)

"A project at Yale University. A rehearsal
scene setting point of view from back of stage
looking out at the auditorium."
—Loren Sherman

of the black velour portals and other
scenic elements had to relate exactly to
the main ramp, the edge of the apron
was used as the reference point for
dimensions.

Deciding on the Space from
Back of the Smoke Pocket
to Front of the Portal

Once the plan of the stage has been
drawn in ½-inch scale, you must decide how much space to allow between
the back of the smoke pocket and the
first piece of scenery. The choice of the
first scenic piece depends on the visual
effect, the budget, and the practical
purposes in mind. It may be a framed
portal with painted canvas or a fabric
other than velour. It also may be a return (a flat) or a tormentor on each side
of the stage, or soft hanging legs with a

soft border. In the commercial theatre
this first unit of scenery is often the
framed black velour portal.

The back of the smoke pocket is the
best place to start your dimensions.
This is because the smoke pocket is
normally in a straight line from the left
to the right side of the proscenium. For
theatres that do not have smoke pock-
ets or when it is desired to use the back
of the proscenium, dimensions may
also be started upstage of the proscenium wall when it is definitely known
that both the stage left and the stage
right walls are in a straight line.

Let us assume that the traditional
framed portal is the first piece of downstage scenery. Space must be allowed
for any or all of the following.

1. *The house curtain.* The house curtain,
always located upstage of the smoke
pocket, must have sufficient space to
move in and out. This must be considered whether it is a flying unit or a
traveler rigged to go off and on left and
right. Consider, too, whether the
house curtain has no fullness, some
fullness, or much fullness. The more
fullness, of course, the more space will
be needed.

2. *A light pipe* (or two) *and vertical
booms* left and right. The space for a
horizontal light pipe and instruments
should be at least 30 inches between
the house curtain and the portal. You
may also decide to have the first pipe
positioned just upstage of the first
portal.

3. *A show curtain.* A show curtain may
be positioned between the smoke
pocket and the portal or upstage of the
portal. There is no specific rule as to
where a show curtain should be positioned. It can go where you want and
wherever you can work it in. However, there should be 6 inches of space
in front and in back of the show curtain to allow for clearance as it moves
in and out. It is always best to use cable guides on each end to keep the
curtain in place and pulled taut.

4. *An entrance and exit for actors* between the smoke pocket and portal.
Single-file entrance and exit space for
actors should be at least 3 feet and
more if period costumes demand it for
easy clearance.

5. *An entrance and exit for props.* Any
props of various sizes should be considered if they are to come on downstage in front of the first portal.

1. Framed Portals with Parallel Masking; 2. Framed Portals with Angled Masking; 3. Framed Portals with Perpendicular Masking

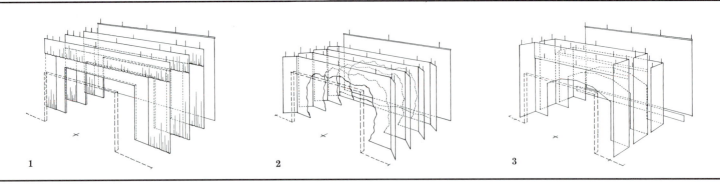

Framed (or Unframed) Hangers with Openings for Scenic Pieces to Be Positioned Behind

1. Legs and Border behind Proscenium; 2. Portal behind Legs and Border; 3. Portal in Front of Legs and Border

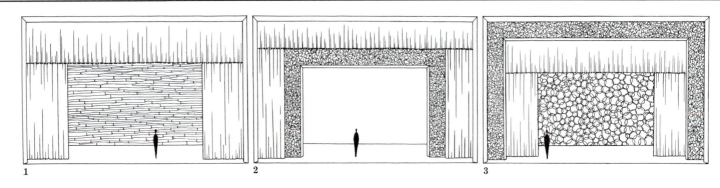

Enclosing the Stage Space with Portals, Drapery, Drops, Flats, and Platforms

1 2 3

4 5 6

7 8 9

10 11 12

Interior Set with Two Framed Portals on a 6-inch Platform with a Three-Dimensional Unit on Casters Positioned Behind

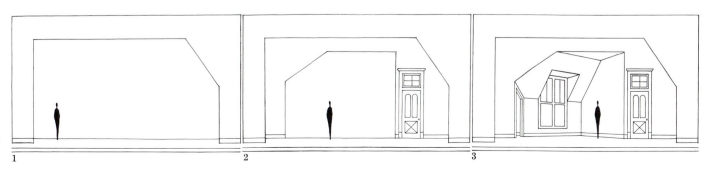

1 2 3

Stage design by William and Jean Eckart
MISTER JOHNSON by Norman Rosten

In Fada, Nigeria
Based on the novel by Joyce Cary

Directed by Robert Lewis
Martin Beck Theatre, New York (1956)

1. Regular Framed Portal with Thickness Pieces; 2. Framed Portal with Beveled Thickness;
3. Framed Header with Framed Legs; 4. Soft Border with Soft Legs

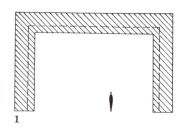
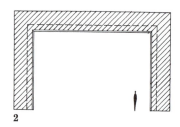
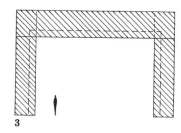
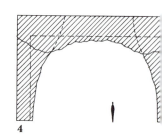

Portal with Applied Stonework

Drapery in a Framed Portal

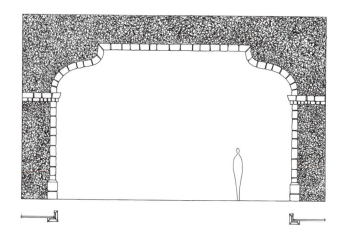
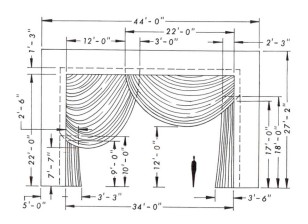

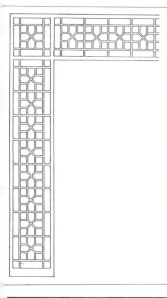

Top: 1. Openwork portal design; 2. & 3. Portal designs for NO, NO, NANETTE (1971) by Raoul Pène du Bois.
Bottom: 4. Painted designs for THE CRUCIFER OF BLOOD (1978) by John Wulp; 5. & 6. Painted framed hanger for ANNIE (1977) by David Mitchell. (Photographs by Lynn Pecktal)

Stage design by Jo Mielziner
I NEVER SANG FOR MY FATHER

by Robert Anderson—Funeral home
Directed by Alan Schneider

Longacre Theatre, New York (1968)
(Photograph by Peter A. Juley and Son)

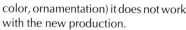

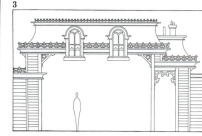

Portal Positioned Downstage of the Proscenium with Unmasked Edges

The kind of production and the physical theatre house determine when a portal is erected downstage of the opening in the proscenium wall of the theatre. A downstage portal may either have the outer edges masked off or have the outer edges showing. A portal may be used downstage of the regular proscenium opening for any of these reasons.

1. To add more overall stage depth for the action and blocking of the production. The existing apron, apron extension, or orchestra pit cover may be used.
2. To add more overall stage depth to accommodate the setting and technical effects required. Also, the apron, an extension of the apron, or a covered pit may be used.
3. To cover the existing house proscenium because for some reason (shape,

color, ornamentation) it does not work with the new production.
4. To enlarge or sometimes decrease the scale (height and width) of the existing proscenium by filling in the larger portal opening with items such as drapery or foliage.
5. To create a black void around the entire setting(s).

Portal Positioned Downstage of the Proscenium with Masked Edges

The masking used on the outer edges of a portal downstage of the proscenium is very similar to the masking

Stage design by Donald Oenslager
DON CARLOS by Giuseppe Verdi
Libretto by François Joseph Méry
and Camille du Locle
Directed by Tito Capobianco
Hemis Fair '68
Produced by the San Antonio Symphony
San Antonio, Texas (1968)
(Photograph by Peter A. Juley and Son)

used upstage of the proscenium. Basically, it is like putting a mat on a painted rendering. A black velour border and legs are common, although these three items may also be other colors and fabrics. How much is needed depends on the area around the proscenium being covered and how far downstage this independent show portal is positioned. While it is standard for the masking pieces to be positioned on the ground plan parallel to the portal, they may also be positioned on angles or on curves.

For small Off-Broadway or regional theatres, the offstage edges of the portals may go to the walls of the house.

Drawing Framed Portals

The typical views needed when making drawings to properly show a portal include a front elevation, a side or section view, and a ground plan, all in ½-inch scale. Besides making individual drawings of the portal, it must then be drawn on the master ground plan

Stage design by James Stewart Morcom
Radio City Music Hall
New York (1961)

and the hanging section drawing. Describe in detail all the information for building, covering, any painting and trim, hanging, and bracing for each portal on these drawings. Do the following, where applicable, on the front elevation, side or section view, and ground plan drawings.

1. Draw the base and center lines.
2. Draw the overall width and put the dimension on the drawing.
3. Draw the overall height and write in the dimension.
4. Draw the inner width of the portal opening and write in the dimension.
5. Draw the inner height of the portal opening and write in the dimension.
6. Draw the total thickness of the portal (side elevation and/or side section drawing) and write in the dimension.
7. For portals that have inner profiles other than straight edges, draw any detail work such as curved lines, ornament, geometrical shapes, and so on.
8. Specify the material(s) to be used to build and cover the portal. For instance, is it velour on a muslin lining on 1 × 3-inch framing; or is it canvas on ⅛-inch plywood on 1 × 3-inch framing? Say whether built (applied dimensional trim) and painted, or just painted.

9. At the top of the elevation, list hardware for hanging and flying.
10. Tell whether the portal remains stationary or flies out during the performance.
11. Put a note at the bottom of the elevation specifying floor hardware (strap hinges or other) for attachment to deck.
12. Specify stiffeners and any other bracing needed on the rear.
13. Draw and show where breaks (header and legs) occur in the portal.
14. Draw and tell specifics of any trim on the portal face or the thickness (reveal). If necessary, draw any trim in larger than ½-inch scale, up to full scale.
15. Say if there are any repeats; if so, tell how many.
16. Make a note for the covering material(s) which apply. These may be ⅛-inch ply on 1 × 3-inch framing or velour on ⅛-inch ply on 1 × 3-inch framing, or other materials.
17. Make a note to say: Provide stiffeners on rear or other supports.
18. Show any hinged flipper flats left and right and give dimensions for them. Indicate on plan how they play, and

also put a note on the drawing that tells how they fold.
19. Indicate the exact position of the portal on the master ground plan.
20. Label number and name on the portal. Say if more than one portal is to be built by the drawing and list all numbers accordingly.

Drawing Unframed Portals

Sometimes a designer will use a soft portal (unframed) for a production. Usually, the main reason for using a soft portal is that it is easier to manage in travel and storage, especially for repertory and touring companies. According to the requirements of a production or theatre, a soft portal can be designed to be one, two, three, or four pieces.

When a portal is designed to be soft (unframed) and in *one piece*, it fits into the category of a cut drop and is labeled as such in the scenic shop because of its execution. However, for the overall set design, it functions as a portal.

A soft portal can also be made in *three pieces* consisting of two legs and a border. The three pieces are designed so that they can be adjusted for various theatres. Both legs are hung on one pipe, while the border is hung on its own pipe in front of the legs. In this way the portal opening can be brought

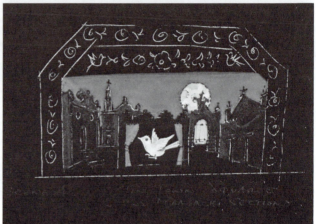

in a few feet (both legs and border) or enlarged.

Another approach is to execute the soft portal in *four pieces*: the border is in two separate pieces which play in front of the two soft legs. The border would be in two pieces when there is to be an overlap of several feet and the designer prefers a center adjustment rather than folding the border back on each end. Again, the two pieces of the border play on one pipe in front of the two legs that are on another pipe.

Another arrangement for a soft portal effect is to make it in *two pieces* which would play on one pipe and be adjustable only for the overall width. More than half of the border and one leg make up one piece. Then the two pieces are hung on one pipe with a center overlap. The adjustment for the width of the portal opening is managed with the positioning of the overlap.

The number of drawing views needed for a soft portal design varies. Usually a soft one-piece portal design only requires a front elevation drawing in ½-inch scale. But for soft portals that are to have the opening adjusted, either smaller or larger, you may want to do three different front elevation draw-

ings to show the normal position of the legs and border as well as the larger and smaller variations. Needless to say, you must always include the soft portal and its position on the master ground plan and on the hanging section drawing.

When making the front elevation drawing(s) for the soft portal, use these steps:

1. Draw the base and center lines.
2. Draw the overall width and height of the soft portal and put dimensions for both on the drawing.
3. Draw the inner width and height and put dimensions for both on the drawing.
4. For soft portals that have inner profiles other than straight edges, draw any detail work such as curved lines, ornament, geometrical shapes, and so on.
5. Specify the material(s) to be used to make the soft portal. Is it muslin, canvas, or linen? Are there cutouts backed by 1-inch scenic netting, sharkstooth scrim, linen scrim, or other see-through material?
6. In a note on the top of the soft portal tell the hanging specifications: web-

Stage designs by Tony Walton
Linda Ronstadt's CANCIONES DE MI PADRE
Directed by Michael Smuin
City Center Theatre, New York (1988), and tour. *Photographs, across:*
1. First dance sequence.
2. Revolutionary sequence.
3. Romantic courtyard sequence.
4. Tin town sequence.

bing, grommets, and tie lines. Many designers prefer black tie lines because they are not as visible as the natural ones.
7. Put a note on the bottom of the soft legs saying one of the following: Pocket for pipe, pocket for chain, or sandwich batten. Also specify if you want a skirt.
8. Make a note on the sides specifying a 2-inch hem.
9. Put a note on the drawing regarding opaquing to prevent light leaks.
10. Indicate if there are repeats to be made. If so, tell how many.

Lining for Hard Portals

Lining is usually needed for portals when an unpainted fabric or thin material is used to cover the face of the portal legs and header. The lining serves several purposes: (1) It prevents any light leaks from behind the portal,

Show portal detail by Tony Straiges for INTO THE WOODS (1987). (Photograph by Ney Tait Fraser)

(2) it reduces the reflected light on a light-colored fabric, and (3) it protects the fabric from behind. Obviously, a lining is not needed when the portal flat is first covered with ⅛-inch plywood.

Velour is one of the most common fabrics that requires a lining when used to cover a portal. Any printed or solid-colored fabrics and any other material that cannot be painted to be opaque may also require a lining. For instance, if you had a material on the face such as watermarked taffeta, it would need to be lined for protection and light leaks.

Materials for Lining Portals

Painted muslin, either new or from old backdrops, is an excellent lining for fabric-covered portals. Other comparable fabrics can also be used for the lining. It is applied just as you would cover a flat by using glue and staples to put it on the portal frame. When the lining fabric is thoroughly dry from the gluing, it should be painted on the back with a dark color to opaque the fabric surface and to stop light reflection.

Setting by Eldon Elder
HIZZONER! by Paul Shyre
Office of the Mayor of New York, 1940s
Directed by John Going
Lighting by John McLain
Longacre Theatre, New York (1989)

When the lining is completely dry from the painting, the velour or other portal covering material can be put on over it.

As an alternative to covering the legs and header with muslin or other fabric first, a dark material can be stapled to the back of the portal(s) in the theatre. However, this is a makeshift method and is usually more expensive in time, labor, and materials, and less successful, than a planned lining.

Movement of Portals during a Performance

As a rule, it is best if framed portals do not have to move during performance, for these reasons:

1. The hardware on the bottom and any bracing on the sides or top must be flexible for flying a portal in and out.
2. A moving framed portal does not always remain straight vertically or rigid in place.
3. If a portal flies, more clearance space must be allowed. For example, a light

pipe with instruments may be positioned tightly just upstage behind a portal, especially if the portal has a 6-inch thickness (reveal) and clearance space has to be allowed for the portal to miss the instruments when it is flying in and out.

"For preshow and intermission effects we used a portal of individual shadow boxes with sepia portrait photographs (all headshots) of Mayor LaGuardia in all his outrageous hats and poses. They were timed to flash in a kind of rhythm with music of the period. The shadow boxes were 4 inches deep. When they were not lit, they had the appearance of a stone arch in the architectural style of City Hall.

"Mayor LaGuardia had his writing table desk built up 4 inches higher than the normal height of 30 inches. The contradiction was that he was a very, very short man, but by having his chair on a platform behind the desk, he appeared to be as tall as the average person, particularly when he stood at this desk. I had his desk reproduced and kept the extra height for the opposite reason. Tony LoBianco, who played Hizzoner, was several inches taller than the Mayor, so Tony looked smaller behind the taller desk."

—Eldon Elder

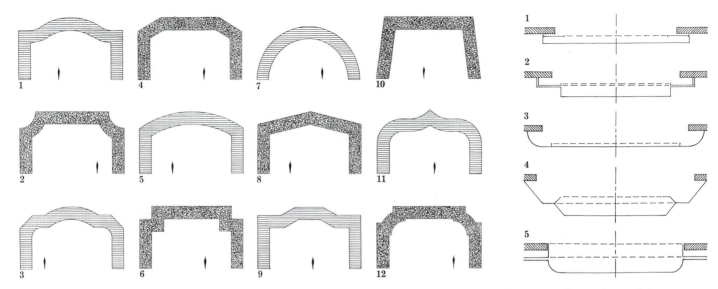

But portals sometimes must be flown in and out during performance. Usually this is done so that a unit or units of scenery such as wagons may track on and off for a particular scene. It may be that only one or two of the last upstage portals are involved. When this is necessary, it is possible to minimize any back-and-forth movement of the flying portal by using cable guides on vertically stretched cable on the two offstage edges of the framed portal.

Riding Strips for Portals

Riding strips are soft wooden pieces nailed temporarily onto the outer edges of scenery to protect it when it leaves the scenic studio and goes to the theatre. Riding strips keep the edges of framed portals and other basic units of

Show portal design by Elmon Webb and Virginia Dancy for PETER PAN (1978), Alliance Theatre, Atlanta, Georgia.

scenery from being scarred, nicked, and scratched on the outer edges. Riding strips may also be added to platforms so the leading edges do not get damaged during loading and unloading.

Protective Covers for Portals When Traveling

Covers are necessary to protect scenery from handling and from changeable weather conditions when loading in and out of the theatre. This protection is especially important when portals have light-colored and delicate surfaces. These covers, wraps, or "skins," as they are called, may be made of canvas, plastic sheeting, polyethylene sheeting, gray bogus paper, or other material. This feature should be noted on the drawings for the scenery so it is not overlooked as an item included in the bids.

Renting Portals and Maskings

Sometimes certain items are rented from scenic shops in order for producers to cut down on costs. Examples of such items include velour-covered portals and velour masking legs, velour drops, and other various soft goods like cycloramas and black backdrops. Black velour items are usually available to rent, and the sizes of these vary considerably. The possibilities of using rentals are discussed by the scenic designer and the producer or general manager. After the decisions about rental items are made, arrangements are carried out by management.

While all sorts of scenic units used in regional, stock, and university theatres may be recycled from production

Edward Gorey's DRACULA show portal in front of the proscenium opening, Shaftesbury Theatre, London (1979).

Stage design by David Mitchell
BARNUM
Directed by Joe Layton
St. James Theatre, New York (1980)

to production, that is not always so in the commercial Broadway theatre. In the commercial theatre stock items such as platforms, cycloramas, portals, backdrops, flats, and decks are not available and must be created from scratch. However, specialty items such as winches, treadmills, sizable traveler tracks, and large turntables are usually rented from scenic shops, firms, or individuals and reused as needed in each show.

Not Using a Portal

Of course, a framed portal is not always necessary for every set. You may not have one in stock for a production, or it may not seem appropriate or practical for the scenery on a show. These scenic items may be used instead.

Setting by Tony Walton
DEATH AND THE MAIDEN by Ariel Dorfman
Directed by Mike Nichols

Costumes by Ann Roth
Lighting by Jules Fisher
Brooks Atkinson Theatre, New York (1992)

Pictured: Richard Dreyfuss, Gene Hackman, and Glenn Close
(Photograph by Tony Walton)

1. *A return (framed flat) left and right.* The return is usually like an ordinary stage flat constructed with a width of 3, 4, or 5 feet. Returns may be framed and covered with velour, duvetyne, painted canvas, or other material. The returns may even be downstage right and left extensions of the set, especially a box set, with the same treatment as the walls, such as painted stenciling and wall paneling. This makes the set look wider and also does not stop the eye on either side of the stage with a contrasting solid color.

2. *A soft border or framed header* hanging above and in front of the two returns. Either of these may hang directly against the returns or from 4 inches, 6 inches, or 1 foot down-stage of them. The border may be black or another color.

3. *Soft legs* with or without fullness on either side. The legs may be black or another color.

4. *A soft border* above and hanging in front of the soft legs. It may hang on the same pipe, against the legs, or inches downstage of it. The border and legs should be the same color.

FRAMED HANGERS

Framed Hanger Units

Although we tend to think of framed hanger units as being large pieces of scenery, the individual units actually can be large, medium, or small. The hanger units are framed when it is desired to make a large flat surface appear solid without wrinkles and to make it sturdy as well as avoiding the joins (cracks) of individual units.

Let us assume for discussion that the pieces of scenery being designed are large framed hanger units to be positioned parallel to the proscenium opening. Although framed hanger units can be hung on an angle to the proscenium opening, this takes up an enormous amount of stage space and requires a great deal of time for rigging and flying in and out. It also cuts down on the space for flying other scenery and for light pipes.

An example of a framed hanger unit is a sky backdrop painted on muslin and stretched over a series of open framed flats filling the full stage width and height. The dimensions of the framing are 25'-0" × 50'-0". This sky drop has a smooth and wrinkle-free surface that will not wave or shake when actors move close to it.

To make a framed hanger unit for the sky backdrop, design a series of open-framed flats to form a wooden structure that is the size mentioned above. Fasten the open flats together on the back with pin hinges and add supporting stiffeners.

Attaching the muslin drop to the flat unit so the drop is taut is essentially like stretching a very large painting canvas. It is not a good idea to attach the muslin drop to the wooden framing

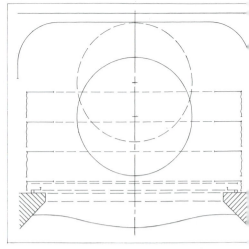

Basic ground plan for HAROLD AND MAUDE showing positions of turntable, four framed portals with masking legs, and cyclorama.

when both are flat on the floor. Instead, first hang the framed unit a few inches off the floor in the theatre. To prevent damage to the painted muslin drop, fly it on a batten just downstage of the hanging framed flats. The muslin drop should have webbing at the top and a 2-inch hem in the bottom and on the sides. Use ladders or a cherry picker to reach the top. First, staple the top center of the drop to the center top of the wooden support structure. Next, staple each end, and then staple across the rest of the top. Do the same procedure at the bottom and sides. Sometimes backdrops are made a few inches larger than the frame when it is desired to fold the four edges of fabric around on the back and staple them.

Comparison of Various Portal Openings and Portal Dimensions

PRODUCTION AND NEW YORK THEATRE	PROSCENIUM OPENING	PORTAL OPENING	PORTAL LEGS	PORTAL HEADER	OVERALL DIMENSIONS	PORTAL THICKNESS	DISTANCE FROM BACK OF PROSC	DISTANCE BETWEEN PORTALS	STATIONARY OR FLIES
THE CRUCIFER OF BLOOD Helen Hayes	40'-0" W by 22'-0" H (House curtain trim)	34'-0" W by 20'-0" H (3 blk vel portals)	7'-0" W	8'-0" H	48'-0" W by 28'-0" H	8½"	4'-2"	7'-0" 6'-0"	Stationary
DRACULA Martin Beck	40'-0" W by 25'-0" H (H. C. trim)	34'-0" W by 22'-0" H (1 painted)	5'-9" W	8'-0" H	45'-6" W by 30'-0" H	1'-6"	2'-6"	Does not apply	Stationary
HOME Cort	37'-4" W by 21'-0" H (H. C. trim)	33'-4" W by 19'-0" H (3 blk vel)	5'-0" W (1st portal)	8'-0" H	43'-4" W by 27'-0" H	6"	2'-0¾"	6'-3" 6'-3"	Stationary
BOSOMS AND NEGLECT Longacre	35'-0" W by 19'-9" H (H. C. trim)	33'-0" W by 18'-9" H (3 blk vel)	5'-0" W	8'-0" H	43'-0" W by 26'-9" H	6"	4'-0"	6'-0" 6'-0"	All fly
HAROLD AND MAUDE Martin Beck	40'-0" W by 26'-0" H (H. C. trim)	36'-0" W by 24'-0" H (1 velour, 3 painted: 26'-0" H)	6'-0" W	1st: 6'-0" H Others: 8'-0" H	48'-0" W by 30'-0" H	1"	2'-6"	6'-6" 6'-6" 6'-6"	Stationary
GOREY STORIES Booth	36'-1½" W by 20'-0" H (H. C. trim)	36'-0" W by 20'-0" H (3 blk vel)	7'-0" W	8'-0" H	50'-0" W by 28'-0" H	6"	3'-6"	7'-6" 7'-6"	3rd Portal flies

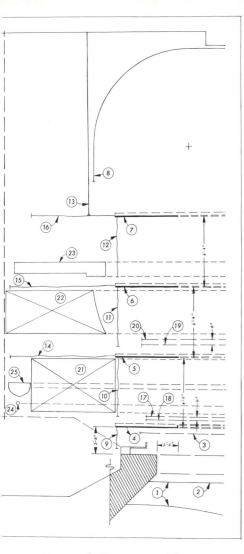

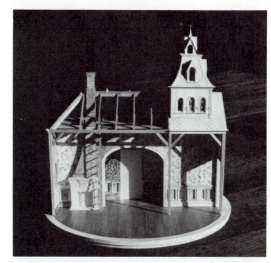

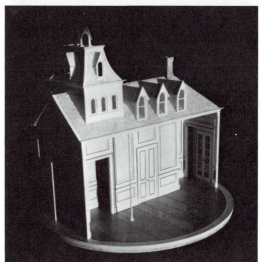

Model of turntable with house unit in ½-inch scale and plan for HAROLD AND MAUDE (1980), designed by Tony Straiges. This is a good example of how scenery is designed to move in and out between fixed framed portals. (The house plans on the turntable are not shown. They were created as one building and moved around on the turntable and under the portal openings.) The stage deck on top of the regular floor was 4″ high. On top of this was the turntable (26'-0″ by 10″ high). Not only did the turntable revolve, but it tracked 7'-6″ up and down stage. The following items are shown on a portion of the stage right ground plan:

1. Orchestra pit. 2. 4″-high stage deck. 3. House curtain. 4.–7. SR legs of framed portals. 8. Filled scrim cyclorama. 9. Masking leg. 10.–12. Masking legs fly in and out. 13–16. Masking legs. 17. & 18. Show curtain and black drop. 19. Beach and forest drop. 20. Black drop. 21. Church and cemetery platform (5″) tracks off and on. 22. Maude's garden platform (5″) tracks off and on. 23. Harold's wall unit tracks off and on. 24. & 25. Small and large trees also move off and on.

Framed Hangers with Special Profile Openings

As mentioned, the size for a framed hanger varies, but let us say it is 50'-0″ wide by 25'-0″ high. The profiled opening in the center of the hanger may be designed to decrease the visual stage space where the action is, as well as to frame the scene. Examples of such profile openings could include an airplane silhouette for a production of *No Time for Sergeants*, a train opening like one used in *Annie Get Your Gun*, or any number of large cutout profiles to frame the action. These flat, framed hanger units are essentially positioned vertically and parallel to the proscenium opening. They usually play behind either a framed hard portal or soft drapery legs masking on the side. A soft, wider masking border is hung at the top. A framed hanger is often designed to be a dark color so there is as little emphasis as possible on the unit except for its silhouette opening. But sometimes it may also have a decorative painted design, such as an overscale picture frame or other designs

around the opening, depending on the show. The opening is frequently backed by a platform at the bottom where the action is to take place, and appropriate backing is placed upstage of that.

Another example of a framed hanger unit playing parallel to the proscenium is a full-stage unit with practical and painted doors that open and close. Hinged jacks that are opened and weighted are used as bracing to help sturdy the framed unit when the doors are opened and closed. Other useful and practical full-stage framed hangers are designed to be windows dressed with draperies, open arches with vertical beaded curtains, and many other structures.

The idea is to conserve up- and downstage hanging space, particularly if the show is a large one. Any number of successful designs can be created by starting out with basic 1-inch-thick flats to make a full-stage piece. Decide where the breaks should come and how deep the thickness pieces on any doors or windows should be. Since the audience will be looking at the unit straight on, the thicknesses may be only 2, 3, or 4 inches deep.

GROUND ROWS

Designing and Drawing Ground Rows

The typical ground row, a long, low piece of scenery, is normally positioned upstage and stretches from one

side of the stage to the other. The ground row conceals the bottom of the backdrop (or cyclorama) while at the same time masking light instruments positioned upstage on the floor. It is usually designed with painted details to give the illusion of depth, with the top profile edge either in full view or silhouetted against a backdrop or cyclorama. However, the ground row may be created as a simple, long, low flat covered with a solid-colored fabric and used mainly to mask the bottom of the drop.

A Single Ground Row Used with Portals

A typical ground row is usually positioned parallel to the proscenium opening, and most frequently it is placed behind the last portal, also positioned parallel to the proscenium opening. Then usually behind the ground row is a backdrop, once again positioned parallel to the ground row. The last portal in a series may be the third, the fourth, or the fifth, depending on the size of the set.

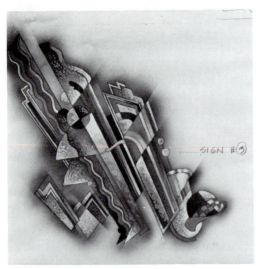

Sign designs by Kenneth Foy for OH, KAY!
(1990), Richard Rodgers Theatre, New York.

Checklist of Subjects
for Ground Rows

Ground rows may be symmetrical or
asymmetrical, in normal scale or overscale, and can be one or more or a combination of these subjects:

Plants and shrubs	Molding panels
Hills	Rooftops
Fields and plains	Tombstones
Oceans	Flowers
Rivers	Airports
Lakes	Snowbanks
Mountains	Stalagmites
Cities and towns	Pipes
Stones	Buildings
Musical instruments	Logs
Abstract patterns	Gardens
Skylines	Piers
Bridges	Balustrades
Beaches	Waves
Dunes	Fences
Trees	Volcanos

Rocks	Docks
Cylinders	Steps
Junkyards	Ruins
Tents	Balloons
Clouds	Bubbles
Craters	Walls

Position and Number
of Ground Rows

While one long ground row positioned
upstage in front of a backdrop or cyclorama is the most common, ground rows
may be positioned anywhere according to the depth of the stage and the
amount of space needed for the action.
Ground rows can be used in a number
of ways including:

1. An open stage with a straight, curved,
   or angular ground row positioned
   downstage of a backdrop or cyc.
2. An open stage with one or more
   ground rows in front of one positioned
   upstage. In this case, the highest
   ground row can be positioned downstage, with those behind diminishing
   in height as they go upstage; or the
   lowest may be downstage, with others
   getting higher as they go upstage.
3. A ground row upstage of a door or
   window unit.
4. A full upstage ground row with partial
   ground rows (quarter-, third-, and half-
   lengths) staggered and parallel downstage in front of the full upstage ground
   row.

Stage design by Donald Oenslager
THE BALLAD OF BABY DOE
Opera by Douglas Moore
Libretto by John Latouche
Directed by Hanya Holm
Central City Opera Association (1956)
(Photograph by Peter A. Juley and Son)

5. Ground rows masking the fronts of
   platforms going across stage, all of
   which may or may not be parallel to
   the apron. The possibilities are numerous. Some examples include a
   water ground row with a moving swan
   or boat upstage of it; a land ground
   row with a tracked covered wagon or
   train going upstage of it; and ground
   rows with docks, fences, shrubs, or
   flowers.

Breaks in Ground Rows

Obviously, breaks are necessary in
long ground rows so that they can
travel and store. These vertical breaks
in flat ground rows are usually hinged
so they fold for moving. But hinges can
make wrinkles and puckers in the fabric that can be disastrous visually, especially when stage lighting highlights
these vertical joins. While it helps to
countersink the hinges at the vertical
breaks, this does not always get rid of
the hinge knuckles.

Listed are the alternatives to using
hinges on the face of the ground row.

1. Make the break where the two pieces
   come together very tight and put the
   pin hinges on the rear. This is especially effective when using a fabric
   such as velour. Wrap the velour fabric
   around the ends of each piece, then
   butt them together and make a tight
   join with the loose pin hinges on the
   back.
2. Use a ¼-inch plywood profile on one
   piece which overlaps the other, particularly in a diagonal, curved, or
   slanted direction so that the vertical
   break is not emphasized. The profile
   may also follow some painted detail

on the face of the ground row, again in one or more places. The same kind of overlapping profile idea can be used for ground rows attached to moving platforms as well as for three-dimensional units. Three-dimensional units, such as a profile of a rock overlapping another similar portion of rock, would have to be built up as three-dimensional rather than being made of ¼-inch plywood.

Two-Dimensional and Three-Dimensional Ground Rows

Ground rows may be thought of as having flat surfaces or three-dimensional shapes. You may have several different combinations. These are some of the possibilities:

1. Flat surfaces with straight top profiles.
2. Flat surfaces with top profiles in irregular shapes.
3. Flat surfaces with top profiles and cutout openings.
4. Flat surfaces with top profiles and cutout openings backed with gauze, scrim, translucent plastic, or other similar materials.
5. Three-dimensional shapes that have straight top profiles.
6. Three-dimensional shapes with top profiles in irregular shapes.
7. Three-dimensional shapes with top profiles and cutout openings.
8. Three-dimensional shapes with top profiles and cutout openings backed with gauze, scrim, translucent plastic, or other similar materials.
9. On the flat-surface and three-dimensional ground rows that are listed, there also may be two-dimensional cutouts or items such as artificial vines and flowers or rows of lights may be added on the top profiles.

Opaque Ground Rows Applied on Scrims or Gauzes

Ground rows painted either with details or in a solid color may be applied effectively on the bottom of scrims or gauzes. The material for the ground row may be glued-on canvas, iron-on fabric, or a similar soft fabric that will fold easily for traveling and storage. The reasons for having an opaque ground row on a scrim or gauze may be:

Stage designs by John Falabella
SULLIVAN AND GILBERT by Ken Ludwig
Directed by Larry Carpenter
Huntington Theatre Company
Boston, Massachusetts (1985)

Photographs, top to bottom:
1. Show curtain.
2. Backstage.
3. Gilbert and Sullivan's dressing room.
4. Mikado rehearsal.
5. Mikado finale.

1. Painted on a scrim to hang in front of a drop or cyc, to create a feeling of depth and changes of color, texture, and pattern with change of lighting and to finish off the bottom of the drop with a realistic landscape or nonobjective design.
2. To save space in depth on the ground plan by eliminating space for jacks and bracing.
3. To eliminate time and manpower in a fast scene change.
4. To mask the bottom of a platform unit upstage which may have a prop tracked on, such as a small boat or a train with lighted windows.
5. To simply create a decorative effect, such as a silhouetted design on the bottom of the scrim.
6. To mask the bottom of a built or painted ground row upstage that is used in another scene.

Ground Rows Painted on the Bottoms of Backdrops and Cycloramas

While a separate built ground row may be positioned in front of a backdrop or cyc, an opaque ground row may also be painted on the bottom of the drop, giving even more illusion of depth. This can work extremely well when the dimensional ground row is positioned a few feet in front of the backdrop and is painted in the middle values, and the ground row on the drop is done in distant tones.

Sizes of Ground Rows

The three dimensions that need to be figured for ground rows are the height, length, and depth.

Height Basic heights of ground rows may be 12, 18, 24, or 30 inches, depending on the desired effect and on how much height is needed to mask the bottom of the upstage drop and any light instruments between the ground

row and drop. These listed height dimensions may be even higher for items such as tents, trees, and buildings.

Length The length of a ground row depends on how far it is to continue offstage. Should it go all the way into the wings or behind the portals, or should the ends be visible to the audience?

Although a long ground row must be divided into sections so that it will travel and store, it is always good to make sections as long as possible. For instance, if a backdrop is 52'-0" wide, it may be desirable to have the ground row to be the same length. This dimension could be divided into three sections of 18'-0" for the center, 17'-0" left, and 17'-0" right, for a total of 52'-0". The row may be a threefold unit with a tumbler hinged at the left or right end of the center section so it will fold up properly. Or the ground row may be three separate pieces and be tightly pin-hinged on the rear when it is put together.

Depth The depth or thickness of an average ground row may be 1 inch to 1¼ inches. The specification on the drafting may call for:

1. Canvas or muslin on ¾-inch framing on ¼-inch plywood corner blocks (1-inch), plus bracing on the rear such as hinged wooden jacks made of 1 × 3-inch lumber or metal braces.
2. Canvas or muslin on ⅛-inch plywood on ¾-inch wood framing on ¼-inch plywood corner blocks (1⅛-inch), plus bracing.
3. Velour on muslin on some framing as above, plus bracing.
4. Burlap or errosion cloth on ⅛-inch plywood on same framing, plus bracing.
5. Rough crating lumber on ¾-inch framing on ¼-inch plywood corner blocks, plus bracing.
6. Corrugated metal on ¾-inch wood framing on ¼-inch plywood corner blocks, plus bracing.

Ground Rows on the Floor Plan

While there are numerous possibilities for positioning a ground row on plan, always remember to allow 30 inches or more of space between the ground row and the face of the backdrop for light instruments. Possible positionings are:

1. A straight ground row in front of a straight backdrop or a curved cyclorama.
2. A curved ground row in front of a straight backdrop or curved cyclorama.
3. A zigzagged ground row in front of a straight backdrop or curved cyclorama.
4. An angled ground row in front of a straight backdrop or curved cyclorama.

Besides being used in front of backdrops and cycloramas, ground rows may be positioned in front of walls, curtains, and draperies. There may be one long ground row in front of a piece of scenery; or two, three, or four ground rows in various sizes, again depending on the production.

Dimensioning Ground Rows on Plan

Although you have given size dimensions on the drafting for building the ground row, it never hurts to repeat the length and position dimensions on the master ground plan. Then everyone connected with the production will have an overall idea of the visual aspect of the ground row as well as the scope of the playing area in front of it. For instance, a straight ground row placed parallel to the proscenium opening (the most common) could be 50'-0" across and labeled as such.

For position dimensions on the ground row, a main center line usually indicates that the ground row is cen-

Model by Douglas W. Schmidt, Proposal for COCA-COLA's 100TH ANNIVERSARY CELEBRATION (1985)

Stage design by José Varona
DON QUIXOTE by Ludwig Minkus
Choreographed by Dalal Achcar
Teatro Municipal
Rio de Janeiro, Brazil (1982)

tered on stage. But you also need to put a dimension on plan indicating how far the ground row is from the piece of scenery in front of it. So from the face of the third portal to the face of the ground row (behind the portal) the distance may be 5'-6".

Include an overall dimension from the back of the smoke pocket (or from the back of the proscenium wall, if it is straight) to the ground row so that the stage carpenter can quickly check the overall distance instead of having to

add up all the spaces between the portals and from the proscenium wall to the first portal, and also from the third portal to the ground row. If there is a total of 19'-6", then the dimensions taken from the plan would read as follows:

From the back of smoke pocket to the face of first portal: 3'-0".

From the face of first portal to the face of second portal: 5'-6".

From the face of second portal to the face of third portal: 5'-6".

From the face of third portal to the face of the ground row: 5'-6".

After putting the long overall dimension on the drawing, make sure you list the distance from the face of the ground row to the face of the backdrop: 3'-0"; and from the face of backdrop to the back wall: 4'-7" (crossover space for actors and technicians). It is also good to give another overall dimension, this time from the back of the smoke pocket to the back wall. In this case, it should be 27'-1".

Stage design by Elmon Webb and Virginia Dancy
PETER PAN by J. M. Barrie—Act 2
Directed by John Going
Alliance Theatre, Atlanta, Georgia (1978)
(Photograph by Elmon Webb)

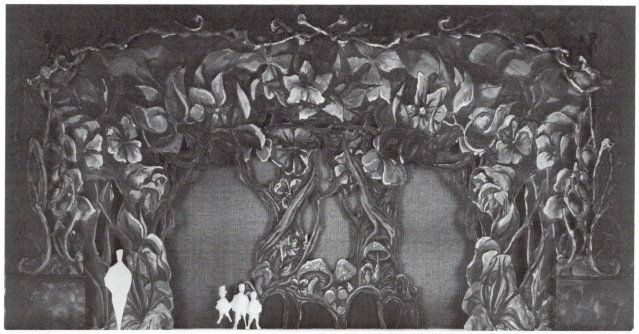

Sides and Sections of Ground Rows

Front Elevations of Ground Rows

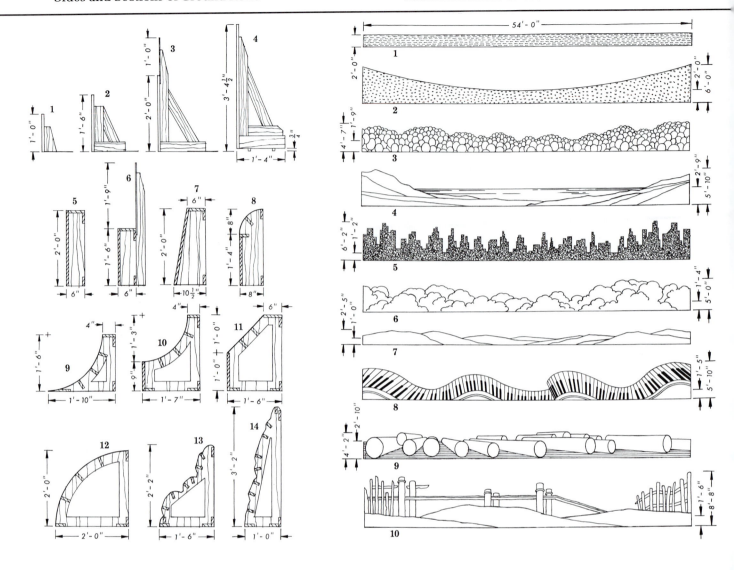

Wave Ground Row, SR 1 and 2 Portal Waves by Elmon Webb and Virginia Dancy for PETER PAN (1978), Alliance Theatre, Atlanta, Georgia

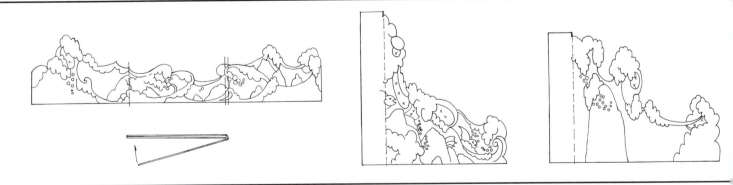

Picket Fence Ground Row with Plexiglas Lamp Globes; Attaching Pieces of a Ground Row by Overlapping

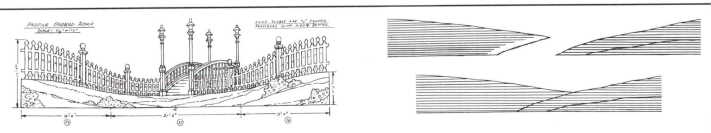

Water Ground Rows: Cut Out of Wood and Painted or Only Painted on Fabric Backdrops

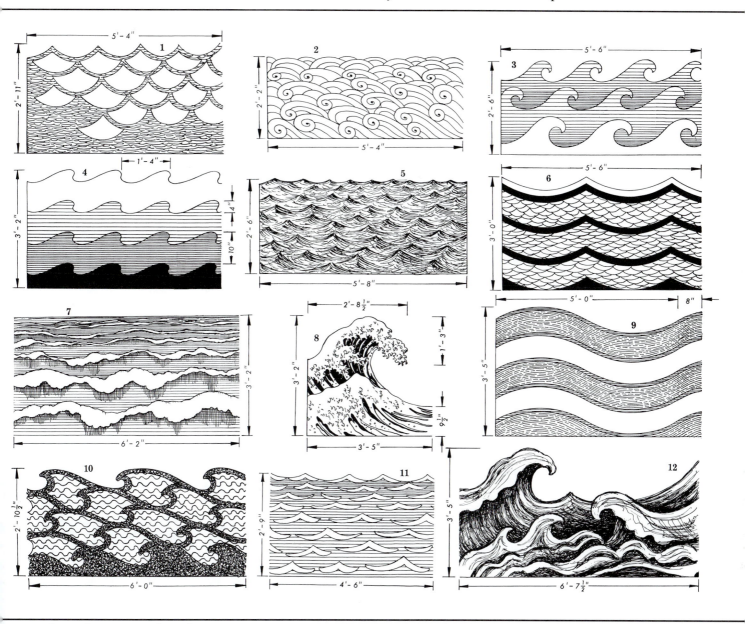

Ground Rows: 1. Edward Gorey, GOREY STORIES (1978); 2. & 3. Hill and Mountain, Atkin Pace, JUST SO (1985); 4. Painted Ground Row on a Drop; 5. Curved Ground Row

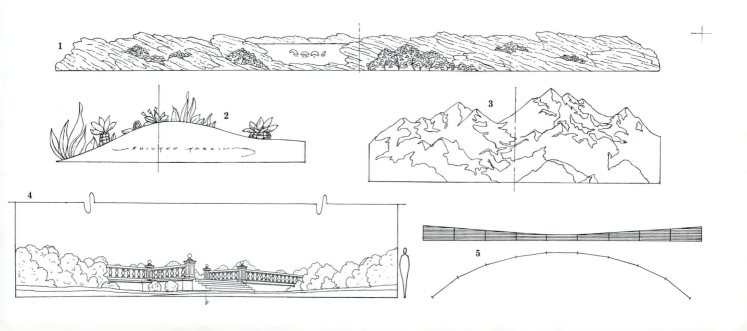

I chatted with Robin Wagner about theatre in his spacious design studio on lower Broadway in Manhattan. Born in 1933 in San Francisco, California, he was educated at the California School of Fine Arts. His first Broadway show was *The Trial of Lee Harvey Oswald* in 1967, followed by the revolutionary production of *Hair* by Ragni and Rado. Since then, he has designed the sets for a large number of successful musical productions in the commercial theatre as well as plays, operas, and the dance. He has also created the scenery for the Arena Stage, Repertory Theatre of Lincoln Center, Hartford Theatre, Fred Miller Theatre, Ensemble Studio Theatre, Theatre of the Living Arts, Actors Workshop, New York Shakespeare Festival, and American Shakespeare Festival at Stratford, Connecticut. He has also designed many productions abroad. Robin Wagner serves on the Theatre Advisory Council to New York City and as a trustee for the New York Shakespeare Festival. He teaches theatre arts at Columbia Graduate School. Among Robin Wagner's awards are the Tony, the Drama Desk, the Outer Critic's Circle, and the Maharam. His design credits include:

Broadway

Crazy for You (1992)
Jelly's Last Jam (1992)
City of Angels (1989)
Jerome Robbins' Broadway (1989)
   Production Scenic Designer
Chess (1988)
Teddy and Alice (1987)
Song and Dance (1985)
Merlin (1983)
Dreamgirls (1981)
42nd Street (1980)
One Night Stand (1980)
Comin' Uptown (1979)

On the Twentieth Century (1978)
Ballroom (1978)
A Chorus Line (1975)
Mack and Mabel (1974)
Full Circle (1973)
Seesaw (1973)
Sugar (1972)
Lysistrata (1972)
Jesus Christ Superstar (1971)
Lenny (1971)
Inner City (1971)
The Great White Hope (1968)
Lovers and Other Strangers (1968)
Promises, Promises (1968)

Beaumont Theatre
Galileo (1967)
The Condemned of Altona (1966)

Ballet Companies
San Francisco Ballet
New York City Ballet
Eliot Feld Ballet

Opera Companies
Metropolitan Opera
Hamburg State Opera
Vienna State Opera
Royal Opera

Model by Robin Wagner
CITY OF ANGELS—Soundstage
Book by Larry Gelbart

Music by Cy Coleman
Lyrics by David Zippel
Directed by Michael Blackmore

Virginia Theatre
New York (1989)
(Photograph by David Peterson)

I talked with Robin Wagner about Chess, *a musical that opened at the Imperial Theatre in New York City (1988).*

How did you first become involved with Chess?

I was working with Michael Bennett, who was the original director. Michael started working with Tim Rice to develop a script from the record album. From that it gradually evolved to the beginnings of what was done in the London production. When we were in production and it was half built, Michael became ill and left the show and Trevor Nunn came in to direct it. By that time we had designed a square revolving stage that included a light Plexiglas deck that could become a chessboard or a single section of a chessboard, or we could use light paths or light the entire thing to make a snowfield in the Alps. In other words, it was a big light box that rose 10 feet, tilted, and revolved in any direction. That became the basic floor for the London production. Along with that there was a bank of sixty-four 30-inch diagonal television sets which were programmed to make either a single picture or sixty-four small pictures. That came in and out and was also a part of the basic set in London. Outside on the proscenium there was another thirty-two television sets on either side which were used for narration, for effects, for ongoing story. It was a media production.

When Trevor came in, he added some furniture and photographic drops that went in behind the graph so that there was a kind of graphic look to the show. It tied the two together, but not fully satisfactorily. In the time that was left, it's a miracle that Trevor was able to put anything at all together. In many ways it was still Michael Bennett's production and yet mostly Trevor Nunn's. So in the process of rehearsal we arrived at the production that played in London.

The London production was a much more presentational entertainment. There really wasn't a book. The numbers were straight-out, and it was much more rock and roll. It was about a series of songs and characters, and it never quite came together the way that a wonderful piece of theatre does, although it certainly has its satisfactions and a lot of people love it.

When it came time to do the New York production of *Chess*, it was agreed that we would start with a clean slate. Trevor had the script rewritten from page one, so the New York production is a totally different production. It is really a book musical, and it is truly a Trevor Nunn production. The set that we've arrived at evolved out of this and in consultation with Trevor.

What exactly did you do as far as the Broadway set is concerned?

What we basically do is start with the wall that lies between the East and the West. It's a large poured concrete wall that re-forms itself to become buildings, interiors, arenas, or parts of the city. In other words, there are twelve basic towers, six of which are 21 feet high and six are half that height. These towers move about re-forming themselves with the aid of a turntable to make up forty-seven different locations in Bangkok and Budapest and all the transitions between. They just keep moving so that they become a cinematic device. That was the premise. We would do it like a film, and it would be continuous. We certainly stop the turntable and we stop the towers, but each time it re-forms, it is a modification of the time before and acts as a transition to the next step, as you do in film. In film you see people leave the room, come out on a street, and walk down the street. It is that kind of attempt to make it truly cinematic. That was the guiding principle or the dynamic.

As far as the set itself goes, it is very simple. It is basically those twelve towers, and there are certain fly pieces that come in to give an indication of location. For instance, there is a "Maximum Clearance" sign that tells you are in a garage, otherwise you may not know that. Anytime there may be any confusion, we try to give an indication of where you are. There is a church in Budapest and we have a rack of votive candles that comes in. When you're in an interior, there is real furniture with lamps, but the walls gave a basic motif for Budapest with a kind of old world paneling. For Bangkok the walls have what I call a "Trump Tower look," with brass facing on them.

There is a third side of the towers that is used for effect on both the low and high towers. We use that third side for the merchandisers on the low walls,

and the tall walls we may or may not use for the ending. That is not clear yet because they're still writing it. We are now in the second week of previews. Last night, for instance, we took out three locations in order to tighten up the show in the second act. We will have to bypass the guidance system when we make changes, so we go into a UV system, which is invisible to the audience but quite visible to the operators. Beyond that, it is a simple turntable show with a lot of catwalks above so that there can be lighting anywhere. There is no masking. The side walls on stage are all ladders that move off and on stage.

How high is the entire deck for this?

The deck itself is a 10-inch deck, and everything works on top of that. There are no traps except for a light trap which is all the way upstage, and it's used for the opening scene where there are a lot of explosions and smoke when we go to Budapest in 1956. For the most part, it is real straightforward.

Was there much research that had to be done in order to get involved with computer ground plans?

The need for almost instantaneous revisions of ground plans became evident as soon as the concept became clear that we were going to have a lot of moving parts. There would be no way to keep up with them manually unless you would have twelve people drafting all day, every day. The basic problems that we had to solve were the changes that went on during rehearsal because the exact sequence was not yet in order. Every time you changed, you had to change your plans and you had to find out where you changed them in order to find the pivot point, because each tower has a pivot point so that it can follow a path to a point and then be precisely on the pivot point and then take a compass turn which puts it precisely where it is supposed to be. Having to draft that would be endless.

So we met initially with Rob Chase about generating the ground plans on a computer so that we could see where they would hit in order to develop traffic patterns. We wanted the computer to tell us the shortest move around something, what was the precise revolution, what was the timing so that another tower could get past it when it went to its narrowest form, and so on.

To do that with accuracy, you literally would have needed twelve draftsmen on the same piece of paper all turning their little compasses. We couldn't even do it in the model. You would need twelve hands and somebody turning the turntable and each one trying to follow their own path. It just became impossible to do it any other way than by computer, which was invaluable in terms of that, plus the record keeping. Whatever change was made could be fed very quickly into the computer, and then you could generate a new set of ground plans with the corrections throughout the rehearsal period. Even though I think the show looks quite simple at this point, it would have been impossible to work out without the computer.

I can lose track of a tower if I don't have a ground plan. I find it very difficult to remember which tower is in certain scenes. I'll know the scene before that Tower 9 is there but because of a 360-degree revolve and the fact that there are three faces on each one it becomes too complicated to keep it all in your head. The computer generates the ground plans in transition, where they started and where they complete their movement each time so you know where you are. If there is something wrong, you can look at it and you can check your computer drawings and you know how to fix it. For instance, you can see that Tower 8 and Tower 9 always hit on a certain cue so you can make a new path or change the timing of the rotation so they don't hit. That can be done quickly with the computer.

Some of them are still hitting, but if you figure there are 550 directional moves and 550 rotates, that is literally 1,100 moves in the show. Some are long, some are short, some cross paths, and they are all broken down in terms of timing. Without the kind of record keeping that we were able to do with the computer, it would have been impossible. It may be that it should be impossible.

How large a crew is required?

There is a flyman, and we have step units and railings that are pushed out. Basically, there are twelve tower operators and two standbys. The principle on these towers is exactly the same, so it's conceivable that any one of those men can operate any tower. At this point we are trying to keep them assigned to a single tower. The actual job done by each operator is the same job, it is just different in degree. In other words, they do rotates and they do movements, and they each have a cue sheet that they follow between sets, and they each have a preset that they follow between sets. They are also on radio with the production manager.

There are three faces on each tower and each face is 7 feet wide. In the third face of each is a set of six small periaktoi which provide three different sides. The other two 7-foot sides are simulated poured concrete. They are simulated; they are extremely light; the tall towers weigh 550 pounds.

What materials did you use to build the towers?

These towers were the product of experimentation. Metro Scenic actually did the experiments to keep the weight down. They are built of an aluminum structure which has been drilled out to lighten it even more. There is a kind of board with a foam base, the outside of which is covered with a flameproof material. They are attached with double-faced tape to the frame. It's a soft material covering that is extremely light so the tape works very well. There are special casters. Each tower has three sets of wheels that are basic triple swivels but with a 4-inch caster, so they are much larger wheels than the usual triple swivel. They move easier once they get going. Then there is a compass inside each one which is the full size of the diameter of the circle that lies between the triangle. There is a break on the compass so they can do their presets.

It's all an evolved process over the course of building the show. You can place the towers all in a line, one end to the other if you like, and you get the sense of a much larger space. When they all go off at the end of the show, they go way upstage and off to the side and you are left with an empty stage, as opposed to the wall which blocks the East and the West at the beginning of the show. It has been interesting, because it's sort of like moving pieces in a chess set, except there are no squares on the board so it's a different set of rules.

Did you want that point brought across in that way?

No, that's not really the point. You have to arrive at that point because they are pieces in the sense that they are being moved and the characters are trapped between them as they become labyrinths. They become many things that stop people from being free, and that is born from the show. There are rules and the structures that these things fit into which don't necessarily have to do with the game of chess, but they do have to do with a kind of cosmic game that people seem to be participating in. That's the premise. We started there. You know, being trapped involves what is essentially between East and West. The Berlin Wall was the initial symbol in our heads, but this is not the Berlin Wall. It is just the wall between the East and the West. The first act ends with the West side of the wall facing the audience as a curtain, whereas the act began with the East wall. There is a subtext to the towers in some way but yet you shouldn't be aware of it. It gave us a premise other than being arbitrary about the use of them.

How many ground plans do you have for the show?

There are forty-seven, without the transitions, and for every ground plan there is a transitional ground plan. I think we'll probably end up with forty-two or forty-three. We originally allowed for fifty. It has been fluctuating.

Using a computer for ground plans is fascinating. Do you think computer ground plans are a thing of the future for the theatre designer?

Since I've become aware of it, I see another potential. With this system that we're using it is possible to generate animated pictures. It is possible that you could design a show, even a more traditional show if you were able to simplify the line, and see how it moves. The real value is that the new scripts, at least the ones that I get, seem to be written like films now. It used to be that you would drop a curtain, change the set upstage, and open the curtain. I haven't seen a production like that for quite a while. Now there are more and more locations, much the same way as the production manager in a film breaks down the locations to set up to film. You go from location to location, and you do your setups and you film. These new musicals seem to be written the same way. Maybe it's just our television sensibilities. We expect to be able to do anything and to go anywhere on the stage. Because the stage is not necessarily a literal place, you don't have to do it in a representational way. In other words, you can just indicate a location and the audience will immediately know what you're talking about.

In a simpler way, this is how we did *Dreamgirls*. We used light towers that moved back and forth across the stage and made up different locations, but they were never literal. While the towers in *Chess* are not literal, the furniture and the behavioral props that the actors touch and use are very real and are meant to be. The scenes are very real and it's naturalistic acting, so that there is a leaning in the cinematic direction with the musical form. I think this might also be true of *Les Miz*. That was cinematic. They just kept moving and you arrive at different locations.

I don't know what the future direction for musicals is, but it does seem as if you are required to do more and more in terms of scenes. We had twenty-eight locations in *Dreamgirls*, and I'm up to forty-seven in this show. God knows what the next one is going to be. Pretty soon we may be back to the one-set shows where the actors do all the locations. I think Shakespeare had those in the Elizabethan theatre, right?

There is nothing that's really new about any of these things. It's pretty straightforward stuff. The only thing that is extremely valuable to me is that the computer has allowed me to record it in such a way that it becomes comprehensible to other people—stage management, the shops. When you have a lot of moving parts to a show, I think the computer is extremely valuable.

Did Dreamgirls *suggest an approach to* Chess?

If I hadn't done *Dreamgirls*, I never would have arrived at the possibility that this would even work for *Chess*. To begin with something that is constantly on the move or re-forming itself was the basic idea for this show. You always work out of your own bag, and my particular one contains a lot of different attempts to make things move in a certain way so there's a linkage. It certainly isn't visual. It doesn't have anything to do with the visual. The working apparatus is even different. These are not motor-operated. It is very different in some ways, but conceptu-

Model by Robin Wagner
DREAMGIRLS
Book and lyrics by Tom Eyen
Music by Henry Krieger
Directed and choreographed by Michael Bennett
Imperial Theatre, New York (1981)
(Photograph by Charles E. McCarry)

ally it's related. *Dreamgirls* was another tricky show to try to get production photographs.

When there is that much movement in a piece you are not building a model that just sits there. We did build ⅛-inch models for each one of these little setups in *Chess*. If you put them in a row to look at them they cover a whole wall. It's really not necessary to do that if you can generate the image on a computer. We did it primarily for the lighting designer because these were sculptural objects and all those models would be very helpful to him. Otherwise, he would be sitting there with one model and moving it each time. Try moving twelve pieces in two locations on one model and it takes you half an hour to set it up.

The lights are ever-changing, too, with all these objects that are moving?

Yes. One of the reasons that we had the catwalks all over the place is that the nature of these moving objects requires that the angle of light can come from any direction. We couldn't use the traditional light rig, as David Hersey calls it. David has access from any place in the grid area and he has access to anywhere in the house area because of the catwalks. He also has lamps that move, refocus, and redirect themselves so that he is able to, in a sense, light forty-seven one-set shows. Every time

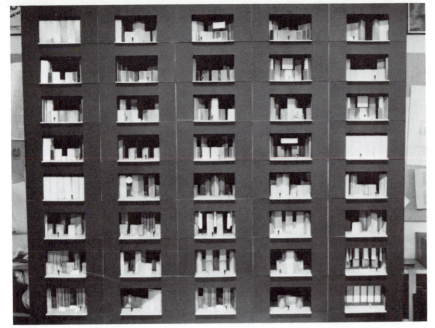

Models by Robin Wagner
CHESS—Scene-to-scene ⅛-inch models
Music: Benny Andersson, Björn Ulvaeus
Lyrics: Tim Rice
Book: Tim Rice and Richard Nelson
Directed by Trevor Nunn
Imperial Theatre, New York (1988)
(Photograph by David Peterson)

a tower moves, he's got a brand-new problem attached to it. The 21-foot towers don't give you a lot of room for ladders or booms. So what we have are flexible walls, and flexible ladders that come on and off stage and the catwalks.

When you say flexible ladders, you are talking about lights, are you not?

Yes, light ladders. They move off the side walls of the backstage so when they are opened up they are 70 feet apart, so you might say it sort of stretches out across the 70-foot space. At other times, there is one point in the show during "Endgame" where every piece of scenery, every actor, and the entire crew is on the 28-foot turntable. In that moment the stage sort of breathes in and all the elements are squeezed together. The set sort of breathes in and out according to the needs of the show.

Is it possible that the reason that more shows aren't being done like this is that you don't often find a director who wants to get involved with this sort of technical movement?

That's a good point. I think that doing this kind of show has to be born from a director who thinks kinetically. In many ways this kind of thing controls what he can do. Once a director is committed to it, as Trevor Nunn in this case, then it becomes so much a part of what they are doing that it's not a problem. That was the way Michael Bennett worked also. It's a way to bring another richness or another level to a show, and that's the same way with lights. You can have 400 lights hanging on a show and there are 400 elements there that

have to be dealt with. But a director who doesn't deal with lights is not going to get the kind of visual look from a show as the director who does deal with lighting. A director who wants to deal with lights and scenery is going to get that much more in terms of different levels.

On the other hand, Peter Brook's production of *The Mahabharata* at the Brooklyn Academy of Music, which I admired greatly, has no moving parts with the exception of the actors. That's another way of doing a show. Why should there be less ways? One of the great things about the theatre is that it has no rules. When you try to impose rules, it becomes a little less theatre. To say there is only one way or that there is a technique that must be followed is to inhibit the life that can flow from a play. The more different approaches there are, the more different elements, the better it can be. I've never seen a Peter Brook play that didn't have music. Tom O'Horgan once said that the removal of music from drama was a twentieth-century hoax. You always had music. So why should you have less in terms of the potential elements of storytelling? If scenery and lights and all the trappings can make up more of the tools by which to tell a story, all the better. If you can do it without such tools, then that's wonderful, too. It certainly shouldn't be there unless it is like a line in the play, unless it means something.

How would you cope with doing a national company of Chess?

I think that would be quite simple now that we've done it. We know we

had twelve pieces, and we know that we had to move them through forty-seven scenes. But now they are fixed. We have arrived at patterns which seem to support the scenes. That means that there is now a map. Now that it has been rehearsed and changed and re-evolved and the problems worked out, there is a plan to follow.

I think it would be quite simple. You would send twelve guys or fourteen in case somebody gets sick. We've discovered many ways of marking the signal device in the floor. We started off with the electrical luminescence and had we been able to fix that, that would have certainly been the best. As it turned out, when we moved to the theatre, adjustments were made from the rehearsal modules to the actual towers that changed the path. A lot of the work that was done in terms of lights in the floor became redundant because new paths had to be made. It would be quite simple to do that at this point. It's much simpler once you've done anything. Once you write the notes on the paper someone else can play them.

Would the computer printouts be self-explanatory to someone who didn't know about the show?

It would be a nice graphic, but I don't know that it would mean anything to anyone who wasn't involved in the show. Unless you know how to read these things, they're sort of like looking at pictographs or hieroglyphics. If you had them in sequence it might give you an idea of how the show works. The problem with showing it is the essence of the need to have it used. We would not have used this device if we could have put it on a page manually. I think the only way you could truly demonstrate or show this would be to put it on videotape. When you see the result in the theatre, it is much simpler. Unless you are really interested and involved with the show, the printouts are not going to mean a lot to you.

Maybe the mystery of the printout makes sense. In other words, I don't know if you call it a departure, but it's different. The printout of the drawings at least shows another viewpoint or another possibility, which is always the thing I am interested in as a designer. What this has got to do with anything traditional I don't know except it may be the most traditional thing of all. Maybe just taking your basic shapes and moving them around a bit, you know. I think designers across the years have always talked about it and it's always seemed impossible, and maybe looking at the computer drawings for *Chess* would generate the possibility of some young designer coming along and figuring out how to really use

Models and backdrop by Robin Wagner
TEDDY AND ALICE
Music by John Philip Sousa
Book by Jerome Alden; lyrics by Hal Hackady
Adaptations and original music: Richard Kapp
Choreography by Donald Saddler
Directed by John Driver
Minskoff Theatre, New York (1987)
Models: White House interior and exterior.
(Photographs by Charles E. McCarry)
Backdrop: across the Potomac.
(Photograph by David Peterson)

it well if it indeed helps to make a play work. I'm talking about just doing some kind of shape that gives you endless variations.

The use of the computer in theatre design is in its infancy. They use a lot of standard and traditional scenic programs in the shops. If someone can get hold of the programming and the system, God only knows what they will come up with. It may be that we will be looking at a new kind of scenery simply because the computer exists.

How do you solve problems that are not objects but events? How do you draw an event as opposed to the objects that make an event, because the essence of this design is its movement? You might as well take a picture of traffic and say, "OK, this is traffic." But that does not describe traffic, it shows cars. It's the same kind of problem. It's one of the reasons that I don't usually exhibit in design shows, because I believe if the design is really innate, if it is really a part of the piece, then on its own it won't mean much.

You feel that the design is a segment pulled out of a whole?

I think if it is successful, it only has a life that can be described in its use in the theatre. If you can hang it on the wall, it is a little less successful than it might have been. It's as much as saying that you cannot have photographs of light cues. You can show a great sunset, but a great stage lighting designer is never going to have an exhibit in a museum. Theatre design is not about painting or sculpture, it's about life, which is the very essence of the theatre. When it's good theatre, it makes you feel something. How do you describe that on a piece of paper? A great novelist can do it on occasion, or a superb poet can make you feel something. Great theatre always makes you feel something. And if what you are doing is basically trying to support that system that helps create that, I don't know if that exists separate in form. It may. Anything that is graphic has its own subjective quality. There are some people who are going to have something to say about that. I mean, how do you show a close-up of great scenic painting? I think in this way you're supposed to see a dynamic. I really don't know what it could mean removed from its context. If twelve pieces are moving 3 feet that are barely perceptible in some instances, how do

you describe the movement of a turntable? You know it goes this way and it goes that way. But if you look at it, if you can look at an animated ground plan where everything is moving in pattern, you begin to understand how it works, where the actors can come from, where the props can come in from, how to light. Computer animation as a communication device is a great tool.

How did you go about getting Robert Chase involved in this as far as your work is concerned?

Rob has been doing computer drafting for a long time. He went to school with my son at Yale some years ago. There is a regular computer network out there of people who are involved with theatre and computers. I don't remember specifically how it happened, but we went to see him downtown where he was working, and it was very clear that computer drafting would be very useful to us. What we were attempting to do at the time was to develop a program whereby all the work would have been done before we got into rehearsal. We could have generated all the different paths and the timings. Everything could have been done. As it was, we only ended up with the first act. The first act is much smoother than the second act because the second act was sort of semi figured out on a computer and semi in rehearsal hall. We did not have the entire second act at the time, so we were still waiting to complete the work. As it turned out, the second part of the value of the system became clear very quickly: generating new paths, new ground plans, where to put the pivot points, how to miss things. I know it has been around for years, but I've never really thought it was sophisticated until recently.

We would still be drawing ground plans if we had not used the computer, and we wouldn't have been able to communicate the information as quickly. By the way, this show was done very quickly, much faster than I am used to working. Most of the shows I worked on with Michael Bennett we would work on for a year. We would do workshops and then we would go back to the drafting board and throw things out and throw things in. We didn't have that luxury with *Chess*. We had an outline Thanksgiving. It went into rehearsal, and the beginning of April we're playing.

Did you feel comfortable with the whole idea when you started out on this as you would on any other show, even knowing the time limitations?

No, no. This has been a frightening experience. Any time that you ever try to do anything different, you get static from the shops, you get static from the crews, you get a lot of things from the unknown. It brings forth everybody's worst fears. What you hear more than anything else is, "It will never work!" Sometimes they are right! When somebody you've known and worked with for years says that, you think about it a lot and that tends to slow you down a bit. It has been a difficult show. In fact, David Hersey said it is the toughest show he has worked on. It certainly is the toughest I've ever worked on. And it is the simplest to look at, with the possible exception of *A Chorus Line*, which was also a very tough show which took almost two years to arrive at. That was a true process of distillation. We were trying to make brandy out of cheap wine, but it turned out that it wasn't cheap wine, it was very fine champagne.

Would you consider your next musical to be an extension of this, or would it have to depend on what it is?

I work from the script. I never know what it is going to be. It is whatever the script is. I don't believe that there is any style to be developed from this. The script always tells you what to do. Whenever you're in trouble, if you really go back to the text and read it carefully, it lets you know what to do. If the text doesn't tell you, the director is going to have some ideas about it. Almost always it is in the words. If a script is a certain way, it has to look the way it has to look in order to live. The great danger is you can overdesign and underdesign. You have to be extremely careful not to snuff out the life of a script visually, because the design is a very powerful instrument. Vision is the strongest sense that a person has and what is there will either support or drown that which has to live in it. There is no way to say the next show would come out of this, although they always relate simply because they are coming through the same channels. In other words, you can only do what you do, I suppose.

When you did Chess *in London, was there any difference in working there on a production than here?*

Sure. I've done seven shows in London. It's very different. There is a whole different attitude toward the work. For one thing, you don't feel enormous pressure that you feel here to have a hit on the stage, because you know that no matter what happens, there's going to be an audience. You're not going to open on Saturday and close on Sunday, which you can do here. The people who work in the crafts that produce the scenery are much more easygoing. They don't feel enormous pressure, either. You don't sense this "You've got to get this show out and get another one on the floor" kind of feeling. There is a kind of pride, if anything, or perhaps it's the same kind of joy you can experience in the process of designing, in doing the work as opposed to seeing it finished and whether or not it's a hit. I think that there is a real pride of craftsmanship that I don't experience as much in this country. But we don't have that in anything here. You get a plumber in and he will leave broken tiles on the floor. We are really more into making money than pride of craftsmanship. In England you would never get rich in the theatre so no one there would ever go into it for that reason. They do very good quality work. You know, most of our traditions come from there and their shops have been doing this stuff several hundred years longer.

The main thrust here is to make the show successful. Here it is very difficult to get the kind of budgets together that will allow you to do any kind of technological work without having done it first in England, because it only costs half as much there. You can't take chances here that you can there.

That's a very good reason why London has become a tryout town in many ways. There are a lot of American dollars over there helping produce these musicals. If you have an assured success there, it invariably will have a much better shot than a show that is grass roots grown. Only the regional theatres are now providing a real kind of birthplace for theatre in this country.

Are new writers, new composers, and new directors not being properly guided by the universities and theatre schools?

Why would anybody in their right mind go into theatre? If you're a really talented writer, you're going to be snapped up by television right away.

And if you are a talented composer, you go into the music business and you're rich overnight. There's not a lot of reason to do musicals or to do theatre unless you really love it, you really want it, and nothing else satisfies you.

I don't know about the training grounds. You can teach technique, but I don't think you can teach people how to think. Much of the great work that has been done in the theatre is well trained, but some is also maverick. It is not the same as that which has come before, which means that the emergence of the uniqueness of an individual in terms of writing or composing or any aspect of the theatre is the major thrust that should be followed in the academic systems. I don't know how you get at it unless if you are really into education. There are great educators who can bring forth really great students who will go out, emerge in the world, and do something wonderful. The real value of education is to know what has been done. How do you provoke people into breaking new ground? What is missing in our system, if that is what you are suggesting, is that we are not breaking new ground here.

I don't believe that's a product of those systems so much as it is a product of our overall political system. We are at a point where we are still fat cats and there are not a lot of walls to tear down. It's sad in a way because in order to do something wonderful you almost always have to have a problem to overcome. We're a very fortunate people and we don't have to overcome those major problems. I believe that the individual with the obstacle is the one who somehow reaches the farthest. Theatre should be born from something deeply felt. How you make a theatre function in ways other than it is now is by helping the young people change it and bring it forth. The older you get, the more interested you are in the status quo. You may not want to be establishment, but you certainly turn into it, and then you are the wall that has to be torn down. So it's the young people who have the energy to do it, and it's very exciting to have that energy. They will relate to it. But how do you get them to go out and say, "It's OK. Tear the walls down if you can."

Do you visit universities?

I've been on panels and I've talked to young people. I have not found that there is a major desire to change any-

Production design by Robin Wagner **347**
JEROME ROBBINS' BROADWAY
Peter Pan—London backdrop elevation
Directed by Jerome Robbins
Imperial Theatre, New York (1989)
(Photograph by Charles E. McCarry)

thing. If anything, this period reminds me a lot of the fifties, with "How do we become successful" as the major question.

I came to New York when the Off-Broadway movement was just being born. Underneath it might have been motivated by some desire for success, but basically you wanted to work. You wanted to just get in there and do something good and different, if possible. I think Off Broadway was sort of born out of that. The greatest desire was to change the world. I don't sense that out there right now. I'm sure it will be along again. The tide comes in and the tide goes out.

What do you like least about the theatre?

That's an interesting question. There is nothing that I don't like about the theatre. There are certain problems that you have to deal with which are again alive with those things that have come before. There are roles and there are ways of doing things that in many ways restrict you, but I can't think of anything that I don't like about the theatre. It has always been very exciting to me and from the time I became aware of it, which was when I was about eighteen years old, I have never been bored with it for a second. I think there may be better ways of life. In many ways you are as good as your last show. But I don't know that I could ever have come across a more satisfying work just in terms of enjoying it and the process of working. Whether the shows are a

success or a failure, the process of trying to make it work, in many ways, is like trying to give birth to something. And when it works, it is a great elation. It is a wonderful thing. Suddenly, there's something on stage that has a life of its own.

Then you suddenly feel yourself being slowly pressed out from it. It doesn't need you anymore. It's like a child growing up and saying, "Leave me alone, Dad." And that's also a kind of good feeling, like the fledgling out of the nest. I don't think there is anything that I have come across that would be more satisfying. I am not sure if it is the right field for someone who wants to make a lot of money, although some people obviously have.

I know a couple of successful architects who just barely eke out a living, and yet they are doing something that they love. I don't think there is anything more satisfying than being creative. If you are really interested in making a lot of money, you should go work on Wall Street or get into real estate, but don't truck around with the theatre because it doesn't make a lot of sense. If you love the big gamble and you want to place your life like a single chip on 1 to 36 and let somebody else spin the wheel, then go into theatre. Maybe you will hit it real big, but for the most part you will walk home. You've got to really want it and love it. It has got to mean a lot to you. There are a lot of cold and dark moments. And when you get your first bad reviews, there are some cold dark segments there, too.

There are lots of questions why I do this. There are a lot of 3 A.M. moments when you say, "Why am I doing this?" But these are all balanced by those moments when you feel really great about having been a part of something. You made the ascent, you're up there for a minute. I believe those moments are worth it.

If you want to be a financially successful designer, do television. There is a real market there and you can sit back and make a lot of money. Who knows, some day it may supersede theatre. It certainly has in the public's eye. Designing for television isn't the same as designing for the live theatre. I think in many ways it is the difference between a handmade boat and a manufactured Fiberglas Chris-Craft.

It's like the actor who wants to be a star. Most of the successful actors, not all of them certainly, have not had success as their thrust but rather to be working actors. To my knowledge, those are the ones who have become the biggest stars of all, because it was process-oriented and not result-oriented. There is a big difference when you are trying to create something. It's like a soufflé. If you open the oven, it's going to be a little flat. The process is where the joy comes from. Once the show is on, you may get royalties, but the real joy is, "It's on, it's live, it's going, and that's exciting."

I love the joy it brings forth. You know when the work is good because it generates its own energy and you are never tired. You know when it's bad because you just can't face the next day. You can always tell. You go around the cast and you can tell when the show is working. They are up, they are excited. There is some strange force at work there when something is working as opposed to when it is not working.

If you had to be remembered for one or two productions, what would you choose?

I don't know. That's too hard. I am very proud of my association with *A Chorus Line*, and probably because it was very hard to do. That would cer-

348 tainly be the only show that would jump right into my head. But they are all team efforts. I don't know how a designer can be separated out from that nucleus of people who make the show. For the most part, you don't know whose work is whose if it is really integrated. That's why it is always sort of interesting to read the reviews to see who did what!

I love to read reviews. I learned a long time ago that if you believe them when they're good, you have to believe them when they're bad. The critics do have a strong power over whether the work will survive, so in that sense they can determine your future in many ways. The basic idea of someone having to have to tear apart someone else's work and reassemble it for a popular audience is a very difficult kind of thing. I've never been able to understand why anyone would want to do that. Those poor guys go in and tear everything apart and know all these people are going to feel awful, and some of them are going to have a very hard time working again, and this man does this for a living! What a rotten job. Yet I admire them as writers, and God knows they've been good to me over the years, although I've had some tough reviews, too. The amazing thing to me is that you can survive for the most part despite reviews. A show can't survive but individuals can no matter how bad the reviews are. There is always someone who loved it.

Do you have any particular production that you would like to do in the future?

I like to do new work as opposed to revivals, so I really can't answer that question because I don't know what is out there. I don't relate to revivals or classics because I believe that they are from another time and another sensibility. I like contemporary work or work that is not yet produced so that I am not in any way having to deal with a prior vision. Although I do opera, I don't enjoy it that much because there are so many traditions that come with each opera that are accepted or expected as part of the production. Unless it is a brand-new piece, working on an opera does not excite me very much. If there is anything that I look forward to doing, it is the things I don't know about yet.

If you hadn't gone into the theatre, what other field would you have gone into?

I started out to be a commercial artist, but I could never draw well enough. I went into the theatre quite by accident. I ran a light board for a contemporary dance company in San Francisco, and when they needed some scenery, I was asked to make it. I was in art school at the time, but when I did these things for theatre I suddenly felt comfortable with something. It was fun and I liked it; otherwise I think I'd have been an anthropologist. I've always been fascinated by mysterious cultural events, like the theatre.

In his long career as a stage designer, Robin Wagner has created some highly effective settings. One of his Tony Award productions that received much praise for its originality and style was *City of Angels* (1989). Frank Rich in *The New York Times* (January 18, 1990) praised Mr. Wagner for *City of Angels* and also for several of his other successful settings. What follows is an excerpt of Rich's article.

But no Broadway musical set of the 1980's was as inspired, and anti-glitz, as the one he [Wagner] created with the director Michael Bennett for "Dreamgirls." While that show-biz saga was ostensibly set in glamorous, realistic locales, from recording studios to Las Vegas showrooms, Mr. Wagner and the lighting designer, Tharon Musser, used only austere, mobile towers of aluminum scaffolding to suggest the many settings. It was an almost completely abstract design—at once an extension of ideas practiced by the designer Boris Aronson in Harold Prince–Michael Bennett musicals of the 1970's ("Company," "Follies") and a prelude to the Walton–Tune conceits of "Grand Hotel."

In "City of Angels," Mr. Wagner not only shows off the logistical genius he brought to "Dreamgirls" and "Jerome Robbins' Broadway" (in which he had the daunting job of melding the classic sets of dozens of designers); he also offers a vivid palette and wit he hasn't before revealed. It's no small achievement to engineer a complex show that is half in black-and-white (for its 1940's detective film-within-the-musical) and half in color. An even higher achievement is the quality of the black-and-white scenery, which has the silken halftones of a pristine Warner Brothers print screened at the Museum of Modern Art.

True man of the theatre that he is, however, Mr. Wagner concludes "City of Angels" not with a cinematic illusion but with a sound-stage set that is in truth little more than a deep theatrical stage from which most scenery has been removed. As that Boston audience of "Golda" discovered, a nearly bare stage is magic. But as Mr. Wagner proves in "A Chorus Line" and in the final coup de theatre of "City of Angels," a brilliant designer can make that magic happen every night.

Models by Robin Wagner
CITY OF ANGELS
Auditorium decor (house left and house right)
Directed by Michael Blakemore
Virginia Theatre
New York (1989)
(Photographs by Charles E. McCarry)

8

THREE-DIMENSIONAL SET DETAILS

DOOR UNITS

A stage setting may be designed to have any number of three-dimensional details, but some appear more frequently than others. These often-used three-dimensional scenic units include doors, windows, arches, fireplaces and mantels, and bookcases. Like the designs of ceilings, cornices, paneling, floors, and other subjects illustrated in the preceding and following chapters, the scaled drawings of the scenic units included in this chapter are intended for actual use in a production, if desired; or an entirely different design may be built around the basic shape and the given dimensions. On the other hand, the drawings may simply serve to inspire new thinking for scenic objects of a similar design.

Positioning a Main Entrance

Since the main entrance is the most important doorway to be designed in a set, you should consider its position first before placing other secondary doorways. While ultimately its placement depends entirely on the play and how it is staged, some directors like a center entrance whether for a comedy, a drama, or a musical. Certainly their reasoning is valid, since the center entrance is where the sight lines in the theatre are the best. Then, too, a dead-center entrance is the classic grand position for a "star" entrance. The center door is often enhanced with a center platform and steps to elevate the star's entrance as he or she stands and waits

for the applause to die down before descending into the room and walking downstage.

Other directors will say in early discussions that they do not care whether the main entrance is center or just off left or right of center. A different-thinking director will like the idea of having the main entrance down left or down right. He or she may say, "I'd like an entrance with a cross that is parallel to the foots in this set," or "I really can use a diagonal cross from up left to down right." It is important to ask a director early on if he or she has any preference for door locations. Once the position of the main door is decided, continue with the other set doors.

An Opening Instead of a Door

There are countless times when a playwright has called for a "door" that in actuality can be a doorway or an archway. Using an opening for an entrance or exit rather than an actual door can save time and money and avoid potential problems with opening and closing a door.

Assume for discussion that we are talking about a living room setting. A large center upstage arch can often solve three or four entrance problems. For example, the main entrance positioned up center can be double doors opening onstage and down. Sharply to stage right there can be a flight of stairs going up. Parallel and downstage to the stairs can be a hall leading to a bedroom. In the opposite direction and across stage to stage left can be a hall

going to the kitchen. Entering through the center archway and going downstage into the main set and to stage left are two other doors with a fireplace unit positioned between them. Upstage left is the door to the dining room, and below the fireplace is the door to the music room. Across to the opposite side of the stage and down right is the door to the library. Just upstage of this door is a bay window. In this interior box set we have a total of seven entrances/exits but only four doors.

When positioning doors on any scenic unit, whether the set is interior or exterior, always think logically about the spacing of the units in relation to each other and in terms of the overall traffic flow of the play. In other words, when you have positioned the doors and windows, the bookcases, and the fireplace in a setting, check out the interrelationships of these units to see if they make sense with each other. Do the proportions for each feature appear appropriate, and do the units seem natural as a group, architecturally speaking—do they work together in the room? Do the architectural features of the room relate logically to the architecture of the total building? Upon close examination of the rough model or sketches, the wall where you have placed the bookcase may need to be wider, the fireplace may have to be more prominent in shape, the architectural motif above the large center arch may need more handsome detail, and so on.

Next, work on the placement of the furniture. See where the sofa and the

349

cocktail table would serve the action best and at the same time where they would visually be the most interesting. Arrange the furniture in groups and islands. Try different arrangements with the wing chair and end tables. Place the desk upstage left under the bookcase that is recessed in the wall. How do all these items relate to each other and to the bay window that is positioned upstage right? Also, check out where you believe each entrance leads to. Do two doors open onto rooms that would have to occupy the same space offstage? Does the view outside a window make it impossible for the door near it to open into another room? Do any exterior walls of the house that are in view relate to the interior you have designed?

Showing a Director the Possibilities

When you have drawn in everything you need on the ground plan, put a sheet of tracing paper over it and with a pencil make a rough traffic map to

Stage design by John Lee Beatty
THE SISTERS ROSENSWEIG by Wendy
   Wasserstein
Directed by Daniel Sullivan
Ethel Barrymore Theatre
New York (1993)

convince yourself that the entrances and exits will work beautifully with each other and also with the positions of the islands of furniture in the room. Draw all the plausible traffic patterns for blocking and staging. Try out these configurations with written stage directions in the script. Select the actual blocking of a scene and see if the set and furniture placement are ideally suited for the action. Make a separate tracing for each of the first few major moves so you know whether you like the plan and whether it makes good sense to you.

For instance, indicate a move with a bold broken line with arrows pointing in the direction of the move. Show how actor A comes onstage, enters through the upstage center doors, walks down center through the archway and goes between the sofa and wing chair, turns

stage right and goes to the library door, pauses, then enters. Actor A then comes out of the library door, makes a diagonal cross upstage behind the sofa to the dining room door, and exits.

When you are ready, go over your ideas with the director. This early exchange of ideas will let you both know if all ideas are compatible and practical or if any changes must be made.

Even though the production stage manager will later do a similar kind of recording of all the blocking with moves, turns, crosses, pauses, and other business in the stage manager's log once everything is determined, it never hurts to expand your creative skills in this area and at the same time show the director how thorough you are.

Solving Door Problems

It is always a good idea for the designer to drop in on rehearsals to see how the blocking is working out in relation to practical stage units such as doors. If

---

Ground Plan with Seven
Entrances (and Exits)

Plans: Archway; Single Door; Sliding Doors; Swinging Door;
Double Doors; Bi-fold Doors; Café Swinging Doors

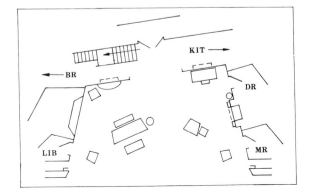

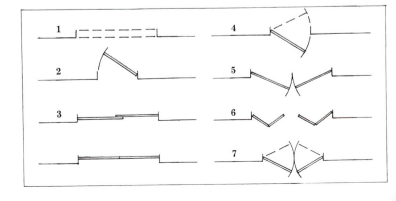

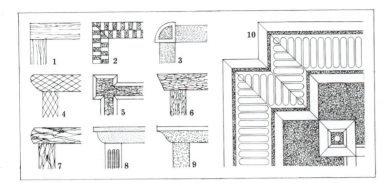

you have designed more than a handful of shows, you know that there is a good chance that one actor will not remember from your plan or from instructions in rehearsal which way a door is supposed to open, especially a fragile set of French double doors. You need to be at rehearsal to remind both the actor and the production stage manager of such matters and, at the same time, to note any additional bracing you may want to add to practical stage units as you watch the action.

The best scenic shops that execute designs for the commercial theatre see to it that stage doors work as they should. This simply means that (1) the door opens and closes properly, (2) the door sounds like a real door when it is closed, and (3) when the door is closed firmly it does not shake the canvas wall, pictures, and other dressing. To prevent the latter, flats may be braced on the back with metal jacks or scaffolding. On occasion the complete door unit can be pushed completely away from the face of the flat by at least ¼ inch to prevent the whole door flat from shaking when the action requires a very forceful door closing. Good shops also add molding to act as a door-

stop without a designer having to put it on the drawing.

Checklist of Door Units

Bar or cafe doors	Louver doors
Sliding doors	Dutch doors
Folding doors	Combination doors
Revolving doors	Double doors
Screen doors	Drawing room doors
Swinging doors	Kitchen doors
French doors	Basement doors
Terrace doors	Dining room doors
Main entrance doors	Church doors

Deciding on a Door

There are several factors to consider when deciding on a door for a set. These include:

1. Kind of door (style)
2. Size of door (width, height, and depth)
3. Shape of door
4. Size of door frame (width, height, and depth)
5. Shape of door frame
6. Position of individual flat or wall
7. Position of door, door wall, and wall onstage
8. Movement of door (slide, swing, fold, revolve)

Designing the Door

Decide what kind of door you want to design for a set. For an interior set, the main front entrance in a home might be made prominent with a carved wood overdoor design or a glass transom. Doors leading to other rooms, such as the dining room, music room, or library, might be double or single doors, with less design emphasis than the main door. In an apartment set, all the doors may be of a similar design, with the main entrance being only larger and positioned in a prominent location.

When designing a door unit and the flat it goes into, it is usually best to start by making a scaled drawing of the basic shape of the door, then of the casing, the molding, and any cutout designs. Or you may want to draw the scaled door with the casing and use pilasters on either side, with a pediment above the door. Perhaps you prefer a casement with a transom, or just a sumptuous arrangement of draperies. Drawing a door (or double door) first and then continuing with the overall design of the door unit and wall usually works well. Because the door must be

Illustrations from *Elements of Interior Design and Decoration* by Sherrill Whiton. Copyright 1951 by Sherrill Whiton. Reprinted by permission of HarperCollins Publishers.

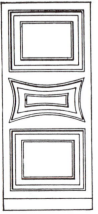

16th Cent. Italian

Spanish

Jacobean

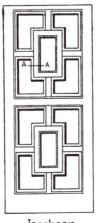

Tudor

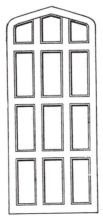

Adam

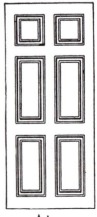

Colonial 1735

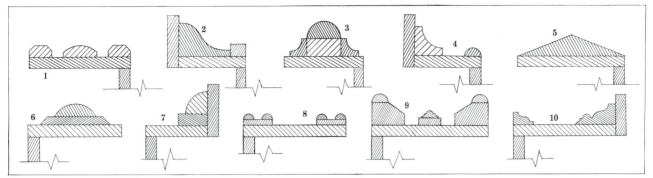

in good proportion with the actors (consider the average height of an actor to be 6 feet), give special attention to the height of the tallest member of the cast. Try some of these common sizes for an average door to see how they work for you: 30″ by 78″ by 1¾″, 33″ by 78″ by 1¾″, 32″ by 80″ by 1¾″, and 34″ by 82″ by 1¾″.

Simple Facts about Designing Stage Doors in an Interior Set

These points should be considered when designing doors.

1. The most prominent door in the stage set is usually the main entrance. It may be larger or more detailed than the other doors in the set.

2. A main entrance door that opens to reveal an exterior backing should hinge with the door opening into the set. The same holds true for French doors. Not only are doors hinged wrong architecturally when they open out to the exterior, but any curtains or draperies on them are supposedly going to get wet in the rain or snow.

3. Secondary doors (bedroom, kitchen, and so on) frequently hinge to open offstage unless the script, you, and the director say otherwise. This saves finishing the offstage side of the door and can also save valuable onstage space. At the same time, a door opening offstage serves as part of the backing. In addition, it allows the thickness to show better, whereas a door hinged to open onstage would decrease this visual feature unless the door is planned to stay back in the thickness and does not have to open onstage more than 90 degrees.

4. In formal interiors, door designs may match each other, may be similar to each other, or be of various designs.

5. The hinging of doors and how they open varies widely. Regular doors may hinge vertically to open in or out or work on overhead tracks so they seem to slide back and forth into the walls. For unusual sets, doors may lower from above and slide down and up, or do the reverse and come up out of the floor, or swing up and down like a drawbridge. For far-out sets, such as science fiction sets, the doors may break into various geometric shapes and open by sliding diagonally up left and right and/or diagonally down left and right. A door may also be opened and closed as folding doors. A full-length swinging door, such as one between a kitchen and dining room, is hinged to swing both ways, as are the shorter and decorative restaurant or bar doors. A Dutch door may have the top portion open with the bottom closed, or the door may be all open. For a hotel set, a salon, or fancy shop, a revolving door works beautifully. An entrance in a side wall of an interior set is hinged upstage to swing offstage so that an actor looks graceful and faces the footlights as he or she exits.

6. An average stage door is hinged into a thickness (two vertical sides, a header above, a sill at bottom) attached perpendicular to the back of a casing (also two vertical sides and a header) which often has molding, cut-out designs, or sculptured motifs. This is an independent door unit in which the thickness fits into the opening of a stage flat and then the back of the casing rests against the face of the canvas flat. The opening in the door flat is made larger than the thickness so it misses any support blocks positioned on the back of the casing as well as on the three sides of the thickness pieces. The door unit may be attached to the flat by bolts, by screws, or by angled strap hinges positioned on each side

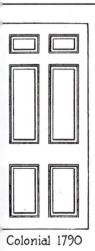

Colonial 1790

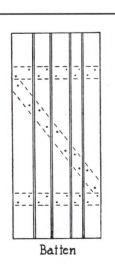

Batten

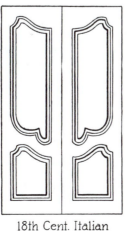

18th Cent. Italian

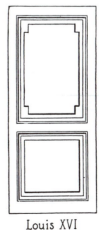

Louis XV

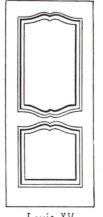

Louis XVI

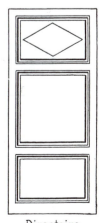

Directoire

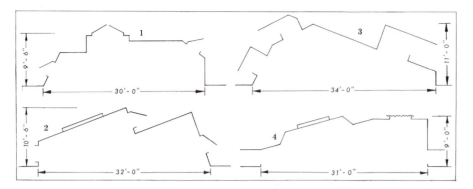

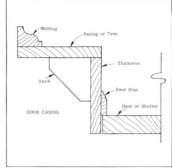

of the two vertical thickness pieces. However, this method does not always work as well as bolts or screws.

An average door thickness may be 6 inches (from the face of the casing to the front of the door), with the casing on the front being 4 to 6 inches in width, depending on the style of architecture and the historical period. Sometimes when the style of the door does not require casing, then the thickness piece unit may be placed perpendicular and flush to the back of the actual flat. This method is also used when the idea is to just paint the casing on the door flat rather than making it as a three-dimensional piece. This approach is occasionally employed to

save space, materials, and weight for a touring set in which the thickness may be decreased from 2½ inches to 4 inches, with a standard door hinged inside the thickness.

Designing a Door in a Framed Hanger

If you have designed a production with a series of regular hard portals with large-size openings, remember that you can have a wall unit containing a

Setting by Andrew Jackness
THE LITTLE FOXES by Lillian Hellman
Directed by Austin Pendleton
Lighting by Paul Gallo
Martin Beck Theatre
New York (1981)

door that opens and closes (actually a framed hanging unit) fly in behind. Both the framed hanger and the door can be braced from behind with jacks so that the entire unit does not move or shake when the door is closed. Sometimes a practical door is also designed and rigged to play with a soft cut drop surrounding it.

Positioning Door Knobs and Handles on Doors

For the average stage door, especially in an interior set, a doorknob or handle is positioned 3'-2" or 3'-3" from the actual floor to the center of the knob. While this is a standard height for actors, the doorknob or handle may be

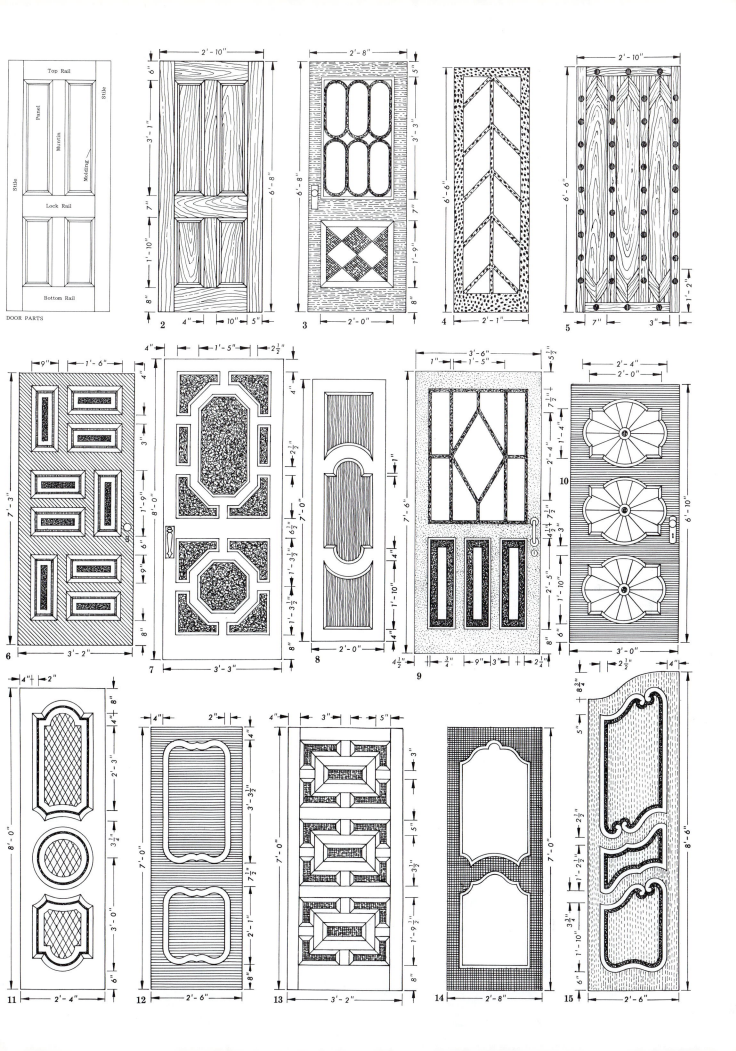

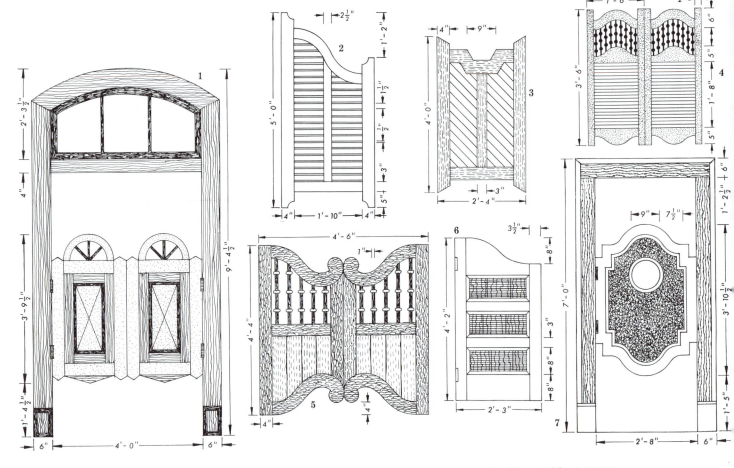

Model by Tony Straiges
JAKE'S WOMEN by Neil Simon

Directed by Jack O'Brien
Old Globe Theatre

San Diego, California (1990)
(Photograph by Ney Tait Fraser)

356

Screen Doors

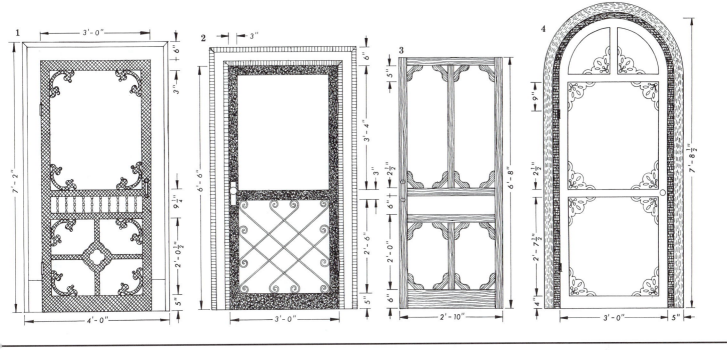

Flush Doors with Small Windows

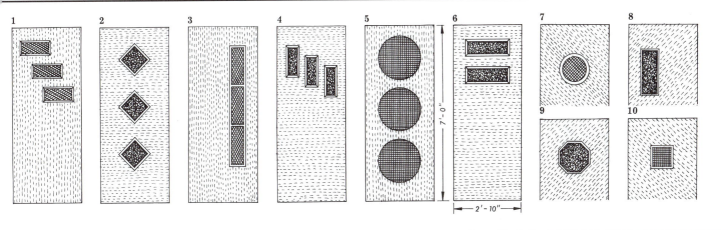

Openwork Doors for Cabinets, Bookcases, and Secretaries

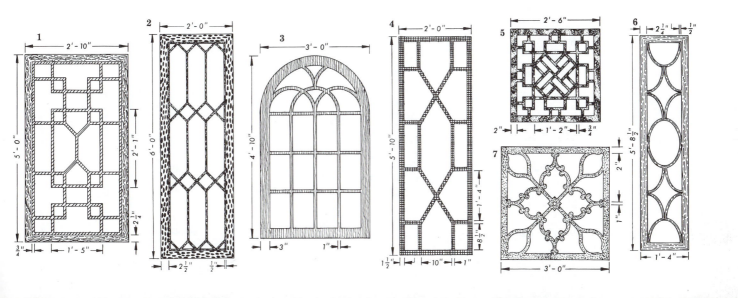

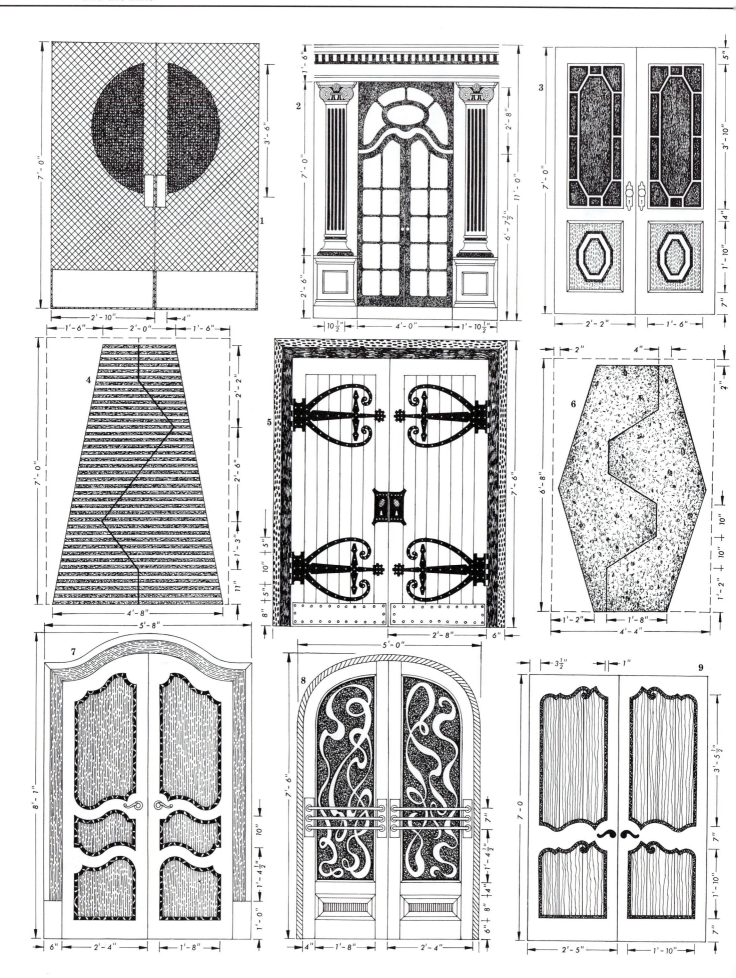

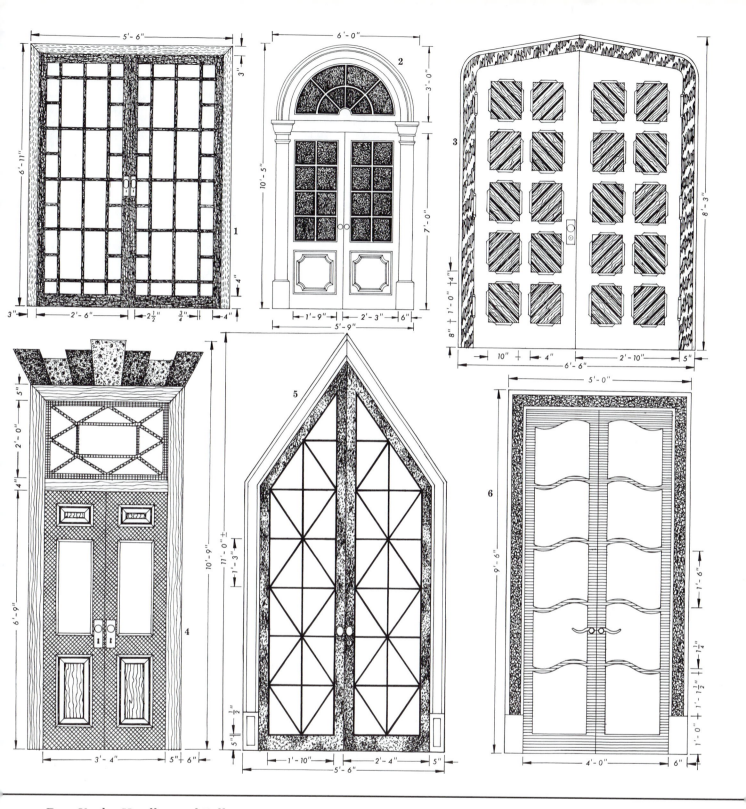

Door Knobs, Handles, and Pulls

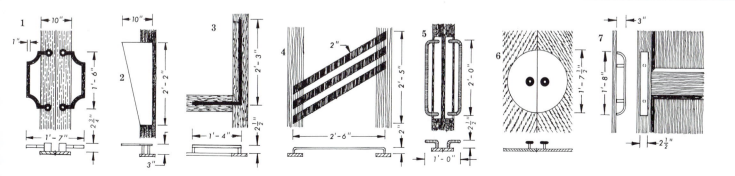

raised higher for very large-scale doors such as those for ancient temples and castles.

Materials for Doors

While basic stage doors are usually constructed of wood, other materials may be used. The choice of material is, of course, determined by the type of door. These are some examples of materials and types of doors.

1. For an interior or exterior stage setting, the standard wooden door, paneled or flush, can be finished with various paint treatments. The door may be stained or coated with a transparent paint to allow the natural graining to show through. Or it may have an opaque painted finish. Or it may be painted with an opaque color with overpainting done with transparent colors to simulate wood graining.
2. For a warehouse set, a corrugated metal or simulated metal door can be used.

Left: Elevator unit with four sliding doors. *Right:* Oliver Smith's painted door for MY FAIR LADY (1976). (Photograph by Lynn Pecktal)

3. For a saloon set, wooden double doors with long panels of glass would be appropriate. The glass may be simulated with clear or frosted Plexiglas, gauze, or screen wire.
4. For a bar setting, the door may be created with tufted vinyl to simulate leather.
5. For a night club or disco, the door may be covered with Mylar or mirrored Plexiglas.

Paint Treatment for Doors

Scenery doors may be painted numerous ways, depending on the desired effect. They may have a flat, semigloss, or gloss finish created by using opaque paints. They may have transparent stains and glazes applied on the wood to allow the natural graining to show through. A transparent graining effect may also be brushed over a painted opaque lay-in which is put on to kill the graining of the wood and to serve as an undercoat for the desired graining and wood color.

Of course, every now and then a vinyl-covered door in a nightclub or bar setting, or a Mylar-covered door in a science fiction setting may be an appropriate finish.

Hardware and Accessories

The hardware on a doorway may vary according to the kind of door in the particular set. A door may be for a home, apartment, hotel, office, church, warehouse, bar, restaurant, or other establishment. The period of the play and the economic status and the taste of the inhabitants may also indicate what the door hardware would be.

The same door hardware that is used on regular doors is usually used on doors on stage. For period doors, the designer may find it necessary to do research for a specific door knob or handle. Door hardware is available in a wide range of sizes and finishes. The designer normally draws the specific door knob or handle on the drafting, and may include a note saying, "Designer to select hardware." This means the designer or an assistant may be looking for a specific type of knob and plate, or the designer may want to see what the scenic shop has available. Basically, the note alerts the scenic shop not to go ahead and put the knob on until the designer has approved.

Besides knobs and handles, the designer is also concerned with the *escutcheon plate* (the metal plate around the knob and keyhole) or the *rose* (the small circular plate where the spindle goes into the door and connects the two knobs with the latch itself). Escutcheon plates for the stage that are very unusual in shape may be cut out of thin plywood or Masonite, painted, and then applied on the door. Or, on occasion, the escutcheon plates are just painted directly on the door. Besides being used as a decorative or protective plate around a keyhole and door handle, an escutcheon plate may also be put on a drawer handle or a light switch. Instead of knobs, simple or plain metal plates are put on dining

Decorative Door Hinges for Castles, Barns, and the Like

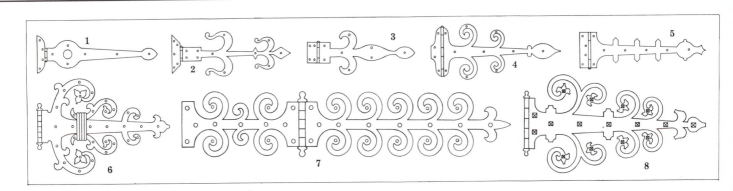

SIZES OF COMMERCIAL DOORS AND SHUTTERS (SIZE IN INCHES)

INTERIOR FLUSH DOORS (1⅜ to 1¾ inch thick)

24 × 80	26 × 80	28 × 80	30 × 80	32 × 80	36 × 80

EXTERIOR CARVED DOORS (1¾ inch thick)

30 × 80	32 × 80	36 × 80

BIFOLD SETS (two-door)

May be Luan, Full Louver, Raised Panel, Colonial Panel, or Mirror

24 × 80	30 × 80	36 × 80	56 × 80	64 × 80
28 × 80	32 × 80	48 × 80	60 × 80	72 × 80

INTERIOR MOVABLE LOUVERED PINE SHUTTERS

6 × 16	7 × 16	8 × 16	9 × 16	10 × 16
6 × 20	7 × 20	8 × 20	9 × 20	10 × 20
6 × 24	7 × 24	8 × 24	9 × 24	10 × 24
6 × 28	7 × 28	8 × 28	9 × 28	10 × 28
6 × 32	7 × 32	8 × 32	9 × 32	10 × 32
6 × 36	7 × 36	8 × 36	9 × 36	10 × 36

EXTERIOR SHUTTERS

15 × 24	15 × 43	15 × 51	15 × 59	15 × 67
15 × 31	15 × 47	15 × 55	15 × 63	15 × 80
15 × 35				

room doors, hospital doors, and similar doors.

A *mortise latch* is the kind of latch set into a mortise in the edge of the door and is used on doors that are seen on both sides. The latch is used without the lock, for obvious reasons. A *rim latch* is attached to the outside of a door that opens offstage and is not seen. Again, the latch is used without a lock. A *tubular latchset*, a simple and inexpensive one for scenery doors, may also be used. The *strike* is the metal pocket put on the door jamb into which the latch catches.

A fanlight door

Once the basic hardware such as knobs, handles, and escutcheon plates has been decided on, the scenic shop usually goes ahead and takes care of the hinges, the clearance around the door, the strike, the doorstop, and the saddle (a raised piece of wood between the jambs of a doorway), which may also be a saddle iron.

Checklist of Hardware and Accessories for a Door

Hinges	Door plates
Knobs, pulls, handles	Doorbells
Latches and locks	Door knockers
Peep holes	Numbers
Mail slots	Safety chains
Name plates	Barrel bolt

Checklist of Signs for Doors

No Exit	Stairway
Staff	No Admittance
Superintendent	Entrance
Men	Push
Women	Pull
Do Not Disturb	Employees Only
Emergency Only	Maintenance
Open Slowly	To Cafeteria

Checklist of Objects Used to Close an Opening Instead of Doors

Draperies	Blinds
Curtains	Louvered shutters
Folding screens	Beaded curtains

Description of a Door on the Drawing

It is important that the designer make very specific notes on the drawings to describe the materials and dimensions of doors. Since doors can be built with numerous materials, a detailed description makes it clear to the carpenter what is involved in the bidding and building of the scenery.

These notes should be placed near the drawing of the door. The overall dimensions of doors should be given, for example, 2'-6" wide by 7'-2" high by 1¾" thick. List the layers of materials in the exact order they are to be put together. This leaves no room for doubt on the part of the builder so that you will get what you want. The following are examples of notes on the designer's drawings for building doors.

1. ¾-inch wood on ¼-inch plywood on ¾-inch wood with back of molding (show full-scale section drawing) resting on the ½-inch plywood on both sides.
2. ½-inch plywood on ¼-inch plywood on ½-inch plywood.
3. ½-inch plywood on screen wire on ½-inch plywood.
4. ¾-inch wood on screen wire on ¼-inch plywood.
5. Canvas on ⅛-inch plywood on 1 × 3-inch framing on ⅛-inch plywood on canvas (both sides of the door are seen).
6. Canvas on ¼-inch plywood on 1 × 3-inch framing.
7. Canvas on 1 × 3-inch framing.

ARCH UNITS

Using Arches for Scenery

Arches are fascinating architectural pieces that can offer the stage designer enormous variety as units for the stage. Arches used on the stage can be designed in any of these ways:

1. Simple and plain, or highly individual in style.
2. Fragmented, skeletonized, or realistic.
3. To be used as entrances, exits, doors, windows, tunnels, or gateways.
4. Dressed with draperies, curtains, chandeliers, louvered shutters, or grillwork.
5. A single arch or two or more.
6. Unspecific as to historical period.

Stage design by William and Jean Eckart
ONCE UPON A MATTRESS—the castle
Book by Jay Thompson, Marshall Barer, Dean Fuller
Music by Mary Rodgers

Lyrics by Marshall Barer
Directed by George Abbott
Musical numbers staged by Joe Layton
Phoenix and Alvin Theatres, New York (1959)

Interior Arch in Front of Double Doors	Skeletonized Arches	Drapery in an Arch; Picture Molding Covering Breaks

  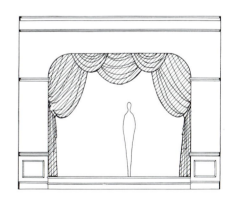

Various Arches with and without Trim

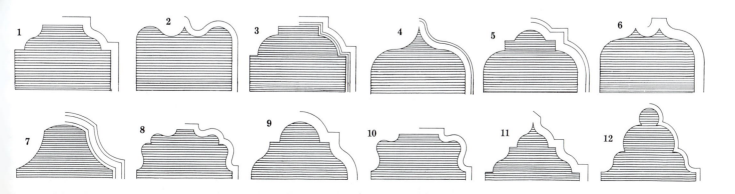

364

7. To be used for both interior and exterior sets.
8. To be placed symmetrically or asymmetrically on the stage.
9. Depending on the production, made of materials such as various woods, stone, metal, brick, plaster, concrete, or natural woven tree branches.
10. Versatile, to be used for both classical dramas and comedies.
11. To be positioned in a permanent plan or move as rolling units.

Arches in an Interior Set

When you read a script, always notice whether or not a real door is necessary, and also check to see if the director needs an actual door for stage business. For instance, you would need a real front door for *Dial M for Murder* and *Burn This*, whereas you would not necessarily need one for *Speed the Plow* or *Kind Sir*.

If you do not have to see and use a real door, you might plan on having entrances and exits positioned just offstage in foyers and hallways behind arch openings. The halls may also have stairs going up and off on one side of the arch, with an exit opposite the stairs leading to another part of the interior or exterior.

Attaching Thicknesses to the Backs of Arches

Sometimes arches are designed without doors and casings, and only thickness pieces are needed. This may happen when the arch opening is supposed to be finished as painted plaster, with stenciled wallpaper, or with real wallpaper and wall coverings when these are put on the main wall

Stage designs by Lynn Pecktal
ROMEO AND JULIET by William Shakespeare
A street and Juliet's bedroom
A project, Yale Drama School (1960)

and the arch thickness is to match it. While the thickness pieces ordinarily are made of wood, they are sometimes built like small jogs when they are as much as 1 foot to 1 foot 6 inches in depth. These thicknesses work best when pin-hinged on the back to butt perpendicularly and flush to the edge of the arch opening in the actual canvas-covered flat.

The size of an arch opening may be so large that it is better to build the two vertical sides and the header thickness above as three separate pieces. This is especially true when there are no doors attached and a wooden sill or thin sill iron is not needed on the bottom of the arch opening. Separate thicknesses work well not only when the arch is very large, but also when the top or two sides of the arch have curved or irregular shapes.

WINDOW UNITS

Designing Window Units

Like door units, windows are usually built to be an independent piece and fit into the window opening in the flats. Certain liberties are often taken with the details on stage windows because they are not always seen as close up as a window in a motion picture or on television. If a window will be partially covered with draperies, curtains, shades, blinds, or a drapery valance, then you would probably want to concentrate on the casing, the inside thickness pieces, and the sashes holding the glass with the thin bars separating the panes of glass.

The design of windows varies enormously, and often the way a window is designed dictates the way it is built. For instance, if you are designing a 12'-0"-tall floor-length window with a decorative profile valance at the top

and draperies in fullness on either side, then it would be easier to design the window unit in three pieces: Use two 1-foot jogs on each side for the thickness pieces and have these butt on edge to a completely open window piece (6'-0" wide by 12'-0") with ¾ × ¾-inch lengths dividing the large piece into rectangular panes positioned vertically.

All sorts of patterns may be used to create interesting windows for the stage. These include a multitude of free-form and architectural patterns, and geometric shapes including circles, diamonds, ovals, octagons, hexagons, and others.

Materials for Window Units

Common window units for the stage may be typical double-hung windows, casement windows, or any number of imaginative designs other than the conventional types found in the home and various dwellings.

Depending on the nature of the design, basic windows for the stage are usually made of soft wood for windows designated to be wood and also for simulating windows to be made of metal. For example, the casing for a double-hung window can be created with a facing or trim of 1 × 4-inch lengths of soft wood and then have a return constructed with 1 × 6-inch pieces of the same wood with a 1 × 6-inch thickness of the same wood. The facing of the casing may also have wooden molding applied around it, and the lower and upper sashes of the double-hung window may be constructed of various pieces of soft wood. Or each of the two sashes may be cut from one piece of ¾-inch plywood.

For windows designed to have a lot of details around the window panes, it works well to make the entire openwork area out of one piece of ¾-inch

4'-0"

6'-0"

1

6" 2"

1½"

1"

2

1'-7"

5'-3"

3

2" 1"

6'-2½"

5'-0½"

7"

1'-8"

4'-10"

4

6"

5'-8"

2"

4'-4"

5

4'-8"

3'-4"

¾

1'-8½"

2'-4"

2"

4'-4"

6

6'-10"

4'-4"

2½" 4" 2"

3'-5"

½"

5"

7

2½"

10" 2'-7" 10"

4'-3"

1½"

3'-0"

3'-11"

4"

2"

8

5'-10"

4½" 2'-9" 2¼"

8"

5'-0"

6" 2"

2'-6½"

4½"

1'-11½"

9

2'-3"

2'-5½"

2"

1½" 3½"

1½" 2" 8" 1½"

5'-1"

3'-6"

1'-8"

10

2"

1"

1"

4'-6½"

5'-2½"

4" 2'-10" 4"

2'-8"

¾

11

2½"

1'-4"

4'-0"

5'-4"

1'-6"

12

6'-0"

3'-8"

13

4'-8"

1'-7"

2"

½"

1'-0½"

14

1'-6"

1½"

1"

5'-7½"

3'-3"

4"

¾

15

5'-5"

1¾"

2'-5"

3'-3"

16

4'-1"

¾"

2" 2'-2" 2"

3'-0"

6¾"

Paint elevation by Eduardo Sicangco
THE NUTCRACKER

Choreographed by Marie Hale
Ballet Florida, West Palm Beach (1992)

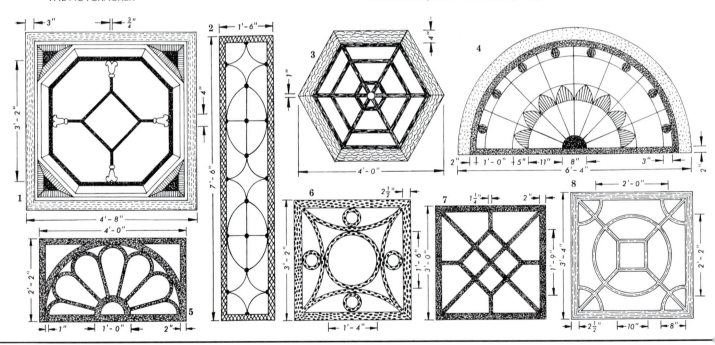

Common Window Types: 1. Double-Hung; 2. Casement;
3. Picture; 4. Sliding; 5. Awning; 6. Jalousie

Window Casing

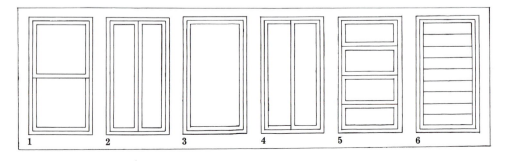

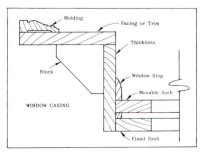

WINDOW CASING

Molding

Facing or Trim

Thickness

Block

Window Stop

Movable Sash

Fixed Sash

plywood. This is especially good for window units that have minute detail work. Such designs include Gothic tracery patterns or a group of thin rectangular bars holding panes of simulated glass. The edges of openwork designs in window units may be finished by shaping them with heavy sanding or by routing. Sometimes thin metalwork is used to create openwork window details. Thin leading designs may be painted on Plexiglas or applied with a mixture of latex paint and pure clear latex.

Clear or frosted Plexiglas or other similar materials may be used to simulate glass, but this can be impractical and can also have an undesirable reflective surface on stage when it is shiny. Wire screening, linen scrim, bobbinet, or other open materials are commonly used instead of real glass. A nice translucent stained glass effect can be created by painting on starched muslin stretched on the back of the open window designs. In this case, aniline dyes are mixed with very heavy starch.

Creating a Mood with Windows

Windows are very important features in a set. They can help establish a mood immediately. Under stage lighting they point up the contrast between an interior and what is happening outside. In ordinary circumstances we know if it is day or night, winter or summer, cheerful or brooding. And through the windows we can see the weather change in front of our eyes—from a calm sky to rain, to lightning, or to snow.

Playwrights' descriptions of windows run the gamut from the casual and vague to the very specific. Among the most memorable designs of Jo Mielziner's career were the enormous center windows for the ghost scene in William Archibald's *The Innocents* (1950). For the scene of the children's pantomine in this play, Mielziner created another sketch showing the windows in darkness.

Planning Windows in a Set

Since doors involve the positions where actors make their entrances and exits on stage, they tend to be thought out and positioned first on the rough ground plan. After doors are positioned, windows usually come next. Sometimes, however, when doors and windows closely relate to each other, they are thought out simultaneously.

While the kind of window selected depends on the historical period, the room it is positioned in, the scale of the set, the use the director plans for it, and the playwright's description, the talented designer puts his or her imagination to work and makes all of the valid requirements blend together beautifully in a visual statement to create a window that is just right.

Windows Used as Entrances and Exits

Every now and then a show will have a window unit that an actor must climb through. In such a case, the window

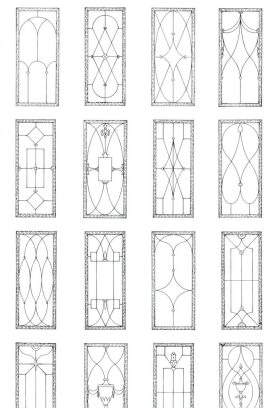

Windows for halls, foyers, and the like

takes on as much importance in its positioning as a door. A classic example of a window used as an important entrance occurred in the Broadway production of *The Crucifer of Blood* by Paul Giovanni. For the Pondicherry

Stage design by Ben Edwards
THE ASPERN PAPERS by Michael Redgrave
Adapted from the story by Henry James
Staged by Margaret Webster
The Playhouse, New York (1962)
(Photograph by Scott Pecktal)

367

Setting by Lynn Pecktal
THE MOUSETRAP by Agatha Christie
Directed by Don Weightman

Costumes by Marianna Elliott
Lighting by Albin Aukerlund
Barter Theatre

Abingdon, Virginia (1958)
Pictured: Ned Beatty, Mitchell Ryan,
and cast.

368

Setting by Adrianne Lobel
THE MARRIAGE OF FIGARO (ACT 3) by
  Wolfgang Amadeus Mozart
Book by Lorenzo Da Ponte
Directed by Peter Sellars
Costumes by Dunya Ramicova
Lighting by James F. Ingalls
PepsiCo Summerfare
Purchase, New York (1988)
(Photograph by Adrianne Lobel)

"Peter Sellars and I decided that a luxury high-rise in New York would be an appropriate setting for Mozart's FIGARO. I borrowed my mother's mink and went 'pretend shopping' for a luxury apartment. I spent several days looking in buildings like City Spire, Olympic Towers, and Trump Tower until I almost started to believe my own story. What struck me as most wonderful was that these towers were built on a feudal system of living. A rich person high above the sordid poverty of New York could be serviced by masseurs, caterers, florists, body builders, chefs, hairdressers, maids, and chauffers without ever having to leave the confines of their glass tinted walls. How much like the aristocracy of prerevolutionary France!"
                                    —Adrianne Lobel

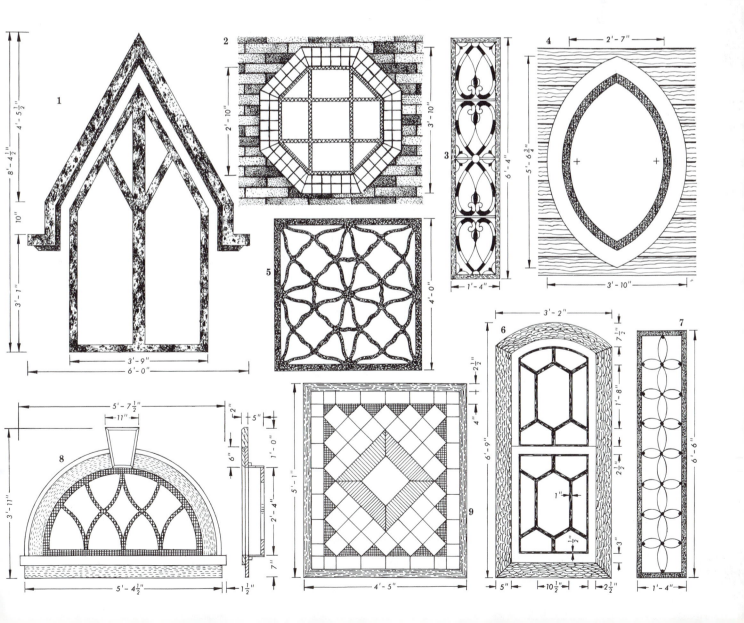

Setting, costumes, and lighting by Neil Peter Jampolis
THE THREEPENNY OPERA by Bertolt

Brecht and Kurt Weill
Directed by Richard Williams
Banff Center

Eric Harvie Theatre
Banff, Alberta, Canada (1980)
(Photograph by Neil Peter Jampolis)

Terrace Doors, Windows, and Seats on a Platform

A: Bay Window Ground Plans; *B:* With a Window Seat; *C:* On a Platform; *D:* With Furniture

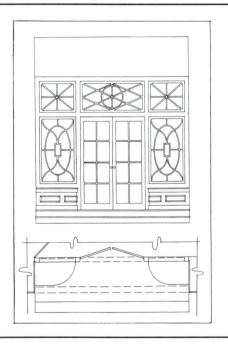

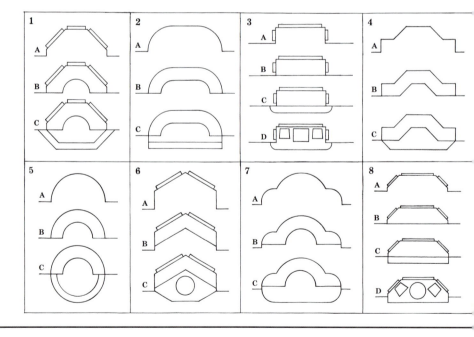

Double-Hung Windows

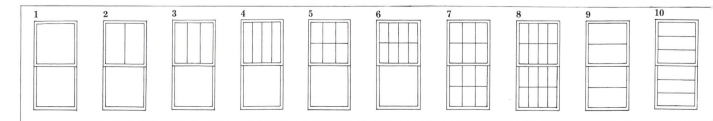

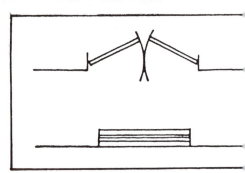

Left: Open window in a lattice flat.

Middle: Three-dimensional window unit designed by John Wulp for THE CRUCIFER OF BLOOD (1978).
(Photograph by Lynn Pecktal)

Above: Ground plans of:
1. Casement window.
2. Double-hung window.

Decorative Window Guards

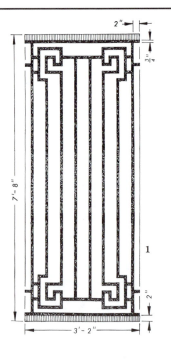

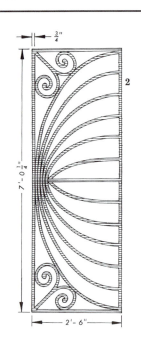

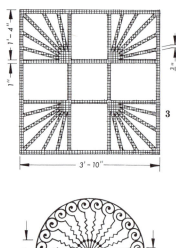

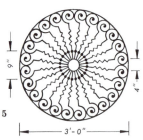

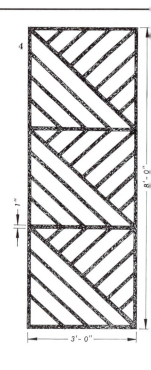

Metal window guards. Window guards for the stage may be constructed of plywood, metal, or a combination of materials.
(Photographs by Brian Pew)

Lodge scene, the window was purposely placed dead center on stage so the actor playing Tonga could be seen by all in the audience as he climbed in the window of a dimly lit set amid lightning and thunder.

Examples of Windows on Stage

Among the many possible examples of window units for stage use are these.

1. A bay window with three sections of windows in an interior brownstone set for the comedy *Bosoms and Neglect* by John Guare.
2. A small window unit positioned high in the dilapidated and realistic basement set in the drama *The Lower Depths* by Gorky.
3. A solarium set for a play designed to be made of virtually tall glass window panes, with only the ceiling designated as a solid area.
4. A New Orleans three-dimensional window unit (6 inches thick) with shutters and curtains mounted on a platform with swivel casters, and the entire unit seen from all sides.

Setting by Tony Walton
THE REAL THING by Tom Stoppard
Directed by Mike Nichols
Costumes by Anthea Sylbert
Lighting by Tharon Musser
Plymouth Theatre, New York (1984)
Pictured: Glenn Close and Jeremy Irons.
(Photograph by Tony Walton)

5. A three-dimensional stained glass window unit suspended center stage 8'-0" off the floor, used as a motif for a religious reading.

Checklist of Window Units

Like doors, there is an unending choice of design for windows. Basic types for the stage include windows to be used in a full realistic set or in one that has only suggestive units. Listed are basic types and variations of window units.

Double-hung windows	Stained glass windows
Casement windows	Picture windows
Sliding windows	Dormer windows
Louvered windows	Curved windows
Awning windows	Oval windows
Bay windows	Hopper windows
Oriel windows	Storm windows
Floor-to-ceiling windows	Fan windows
Combination windows	Leaded windows

MATERIALS TO GO BEHIND WINDOW OPENINGS

Screen wire	Clear sheets of Plexiglas
Cheesecloth	Linen scrim
Sharkstooth scrim	Organza
Bobbinet	Opera net

EXTERIOR ACCESSORIES FOR WINDOWS

Air conditioners	Awnings
Window guards	Window fans
Storm windows	Shutters
Wire screens	Flower boxes

INTERIOR ACCESSORIES FOR WINDOWS

373

Straight curtains	Vertical blinds
Various drapery styles	Venetian blinds
Window shades	Louvered shutters

FIREPLACE UNITS

Using Fireplace and Mantel Units

Fireplace and mantel units can work nicely in an interior setting (and sometimes exterior as well) because they provide a wonderful opportunity to establish an area that has interest, contrast, period, and mood. Also, they give the designer a great chance to create a pleasant composition with set dressing. The choice of a fireplace, of course, depends on the play. You should ask yourself: Does the script demand that the fireplace in the room be neat or messy? Old or new? Interesting or nondescript?

A fireplace and mantel unit can also be a practical area in which the director can devise all sorts of stage business with the actors. Because it has a nice working height and is normally positioned within good sight lines, the mantel shelf can be an excellent place to put such items as books, letters, letter openers, ash trays, and cigarette cases to be used by the actors. It also may be a good location for positioning important props like knives, guns, and daggers.

Setting by Ralph Funicello
TARTUFFE by Molière
Directed by Dan Sullivan
Costumes by Ann Hould-Ward
Lighting by James F. Ingalls
Seattle Repertory Theatre
Seattle, Washington (1988)
(Photograph by Ralph Funicello)

Types of Fireplaces

Interior fireplaces in stage sets include:

1. *Projecting fireplace.* The breast of the fireplace juts out from the wall. May or may not have a mantelpiece.
2. *Flush-face fireplace.* The breast of the fireplace is in the same plane as the wall. May or may not have a mantelpiece.
3. *Freestanding fireplace.* This unit is open all around.
4. *Hooded fireplace.* Projects out above.
5. *Corner fireplace.* In the corner of a room.

As an exercise in research and design, imagine the types of fireplaces you would find in the following settings and choose a different historical period for each:

1. A drawing room in a townhouse
2. A modest apartment in a small town
3. A lavish apartment in a big city
4. A den or family room in suburbia
5. A nice bungalow in a resort area
6. A crude cabin in the mountains
7. An enormous room in a European palace
8. A living room in a crowded tenement
9. A large formal dining room in a castle

Now consider how you would design each of these in (1) a realistic setting, and (2) a stylized or skeletonized setting using minimal scenery, with the main emphasis on props and set dressing.

Materials for Making Fireplace and Mantel Units

The kind and shape of the fireplace unit being designed usually dictate what materials should be used in its construction. The particular period and the social status of the characters in the play influence the choice of materials as well. The mantelpiece and the fireplace unit behind it may be built separately or as one piece.

The most common material for a stage mantel is plain or paneled soft wood that is stained or painted. The soft wood mantel may be constructed to be simple and plain or may have elaborate molding going around it.

For other fireplace units, additional materials may be utilized to create simulated stonework, brick, marble, tiles, or other appropriate finishes. Lightweight materials are always the most practical to use for construction. For example, an old-fashioned fireplace designed to be of rough stonework can have the main outer shape made with ¼-inch plywood nailed over a basic wooden three-dimensional framework. Then irregular stones can be drawn and cut out of sheets of Styrofoam and Homosote. These shapes should be glued and tacked on the plywood. After the final shaping with heavy grinding and sanding, the stones can be covered with pieces of linen scrim that have been dipped in scenic dope. The scenic dope not only protects the carved stones, but also holds the scrim pieces nicely, forms a good undercoating for painting, and gives a textured appearance to the surface. The same materials also work well for fireplaces made entirely of simulated bricks and mortar.

For a marble fireplace, the unit can be made entirely of soft wood which is spackled and then sanded well to make a very smooth surface. It can next be coated with a paint to kill the grain of the wood so it does not show through the overpainting. The overpainting can then be done using a marble painting technique.

All sorts of ornamentations can be applied on a mantelpiece. For example, ready-made and purchased wooden rosettes, metal leaves, or carved Styrofoam details can be added. Patterns may also be cut out of heavy felt and applied to the wood surface. Roping, small wooden balls cut in half, large decorative upholstery nails, and the like can also be applied to add character and decor.

Illustrations from *Elements of Interior Design and Decoration* by Sherrill Whiton.
Copyright 1951 by Sherrill Whiton. Reprinted by permission of HarperCollins Publishers.

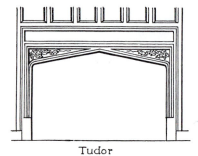

Tudor

Georgian

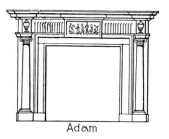

Adam

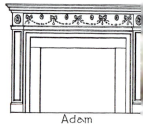

Adam

Stage design by Robert O'Hearn
LA SYLPHIDE—Act 1: interior of a farmhouse
   in Scotland
Original choreography by August Bournon-
   ville
Choreographed by Harald Lander
American Ballet Theatre
Municipal Auditorium, San Antonio, Texas
   (1964)

Using Already-Built Fireplace and Mantel Units

Often, beautiful mantelpieces can be purchased at various locations such as wrecking companies, junk shops, thrift shops, or used furniture stores. These built fireplace units may be in lovely condition and may only need simple repairs and paint to fit in with the rest of the set. In some cases a suitable fireplace may be found and then the wainscoting and paneling can be designed to match the mantelpiece unit.

It is practical for resident, stock, and university companies to collect several types of good fireplace units. Like doors, windows, and balustrade pieces, these scenic units may be reworked, painted, and reused over and over. This can provide enormous savings, both in terms of time spent in shopping or designing and in the cost of materials and labor. When a piece is re-dressed, the audience seldom ever recognizes the same unit unless it is so outlandishly prominent in design that it cannot be disguised properly.

While it is usual to build mantelpieces and fireplaces in the commercial theatre, there may be occasions when a beautiful and appropriate fireplace may be found and worked into the basic set design.

Average Fireplace and Mantel Dimensions

Although fireplace units vary in size with the historical period of the interior and the locale, keep in mind that the fireplace should be nicely proportioned to the scale of the room and to

the actors. A good average height for the mantelpiece is 4'-0"; for larger fireplaces it may go to 4'-6". An average width may go from 4'-6" to 5'-0", while a basic depth may be from 4" to 6", and any details such as pilasters, columns or molding are added on to this depth.

Positioning Fireplace Units

Fireplaces may be positioned on the stage left, right, or center wall. In fact, a fireplace can be placed almost anywhere on stage. An interesting effect can be created by making the fireplace itself completely open so it becomes a see-through unit. The decision of where the fireplace is to go is most often resolved by the director's preference.

Flats Holding Fireplace Units

Often a designer will want to have the flat holding the fireplace unit built so it juts out from the rest of the set. Usually this projected wall has jogs on either side of the fireplace which have a depth of 6, 8, 10, or 12 inches. In this case it is better to have the flat unit holding the fireplace built as one unit and covered with one seamed piece of muslin or canvas.

The two widths of fabric (canvas or muslin) should be stitched together by machine with the seam running vertically. Then the one piece of fabric can be wrapped around the first jog, the main flat, and the second jog. Building this fireplace flat as one item and then covering it with one piece of fabric is simple and makes a better-looking unit that is also easier to paint, especially if toning is being done by spraying the paint on. Also, painting with a stenciled pattern or with stripes on one fireplace flat unit is far simpler than working with three separate pieces.

For very large fireplace units it is better to bevel rather than butt the edges of the jogs and front flat unit at the point where they meet. This eliminates the visibility of the ¾-inch edge, which would require extra care in stenciling and painting. While this is an old method for the joining of the set flats in general, it is essential here to give the fireplace unit a visually finished and smooth appearance. Of course, butting flats where the ¾-inch edge does not show is another matter.

Cornice and picture molding may be built on the fireplace unit as one piece or in separate pieces. However, if the cornice is too large to handle, or if it is easier to paint the parts separately,

Louis XV

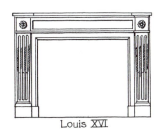

Louis XVI

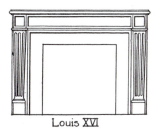

Louis XVI

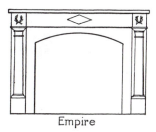

Empire

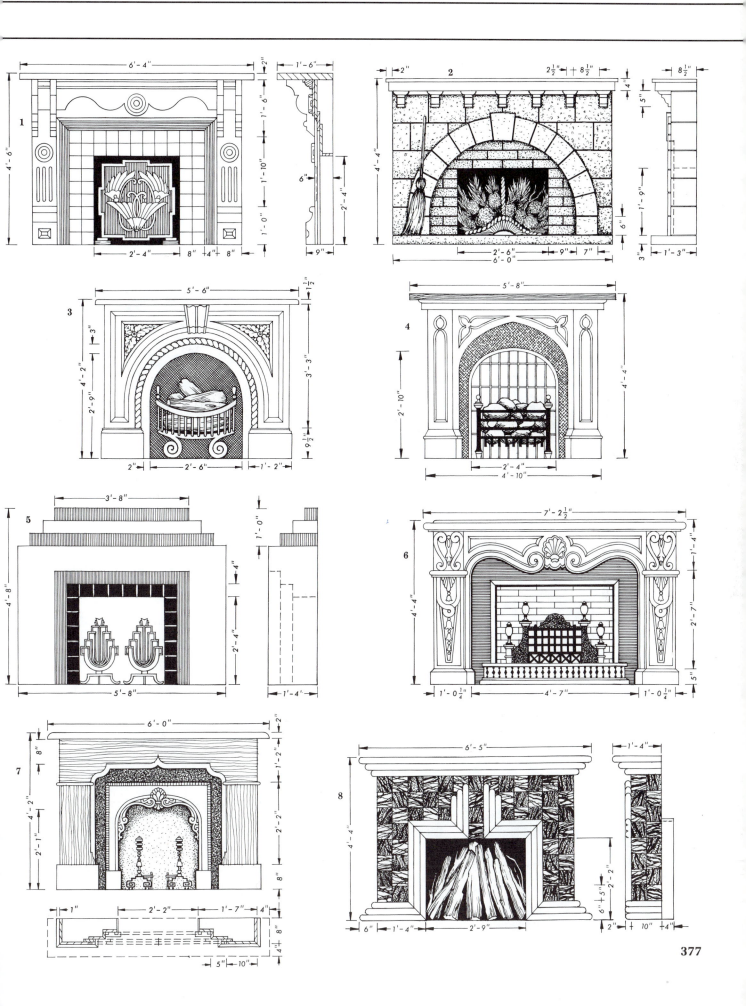

377

Plan and front elevation for Edward Gorey's fireplace unit for DRACULA (1977). Both the fireplace and seat rode on a platform with casters.

Model by Marjorie Bradley Kellogg
EXTREMITIES by William Mastrosimone

Directed by Robert Allan Ackerman
Westside Arts Center

Cheryl Crawford Theatre, New York (1982)
(Photograph by Marjorie Bradley Kellogg)

"Heavily textured interior surfaces, very real but bleached-out, almost hallucinogenic, like the exposure moment of a flash photograph—sort of like seeing a shot of a Louise Nevelson sculpture on the front page of the *National Enquirer*."   —Marjorie Bradley Kellogg

then the fireplace unit may work better built in pieces. Very large fireplace flats behind mantelpiece units may have to be broken in three pieces merely because of size.

Fireplace Backing

In stock and resident repertory companies, several three-fold backings may be kept as standard units. An average-size three-fold fireplace backing may be 4'-0" high with the center 3'-6" wide and the two sides 1'-6" wide. The fireplace backing may be painted black, dark brown, as aged brick in various patterns, as stonework, or as textured cement.

Hearths

Hearths for fireplaces may be painted directly on ground cloths or on ¼-inch plywood. When using plywood, cover it with canvas or muslin. Either of these fabrics can be glued onto the plywood and then painted.

Fireplace Seats

Fireplace seats not only add authenticity to certain period fireplace units, but are another practical place for actors to sit. These also may be built as a bracing feature of the fireplace and may be constructed on casters as a platform to move off and on for scene changes. Materials for fireplace seats include:

- Wood
- Metal
- Combination of wood and metal, real or painted.
- Covered in fabric or in plastic to simulate leather or wood.

Left: Gorey's fireplace had detailed scenic painting on a flat surface. *Below:* Jo Mielziner's fireplace design for THE CRUCIBLE (1972). *Right:* John Wulp's fireplace for THE CRUCIFER OF BLOOD (1978). (Photographs by Lynn Pecktal)

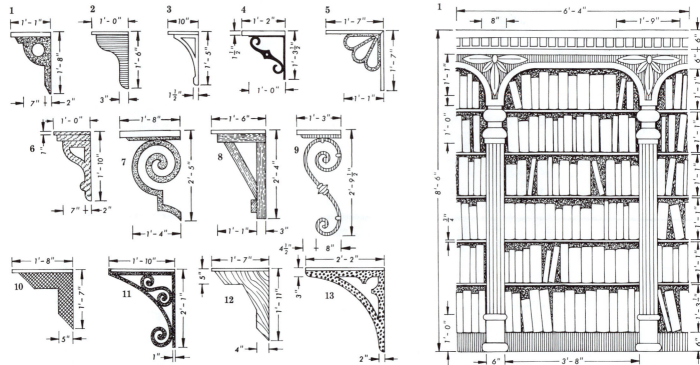

Dressing over Mantels and Fireplaces

Many items may be combined to form attractive arrangements as appropriate set dressing for mantels and fireplaces. In some historical periods, certain items such as mirrors, shelves, and columns are part of the mantel unit. Dressing may include:

Plates and platters	Various mirrors
Ceremonial masks	Framed prints
Plants in cache pots	Clocks and
Antique tapestries	barometers
Assorted paintings	Floral arrangements
Candelabras and	Sconces with shades
candles	Decorative trays
Equestrian panels	Antique mugs

BOOKCASE AND WALL NICHE UNITS

Designing Bookcases

Bookcases can provide a variety of interest to an interior set. They add interest to plain walls, provide an area of business for the actors, and add another element of personalization for the characters who live in the environment. Bookcases can be positioned within the set in any number of areas and can be designed to give an interior a feeling of height. They can hold all sorts of bric-a-brac as well as books,

and the dressing can easily be changed as desired.

Kinds of Bookcases

Like many other scenic units, bookcases vary in design, shape, and size. They may have enclosed or open sides; doors with glass, wire mesh, or other decorative openwork materials; plain straight tops or shaped tops. These are some suggestions to consider when designing bookcases for a setting.

1. Independent bookcases standing on the floor in front of flat walls.
2. Bookcases resting on the floor and fitting into openings in the flat walls.
3. Bookcases made in various shapes to fit into walls above floor level.
4. Bookcases constructed to work as room dividers or built without backs to be positioned out in the floor space as library or bookshop bookcases.
5. Bookcases or shelves hanging on walls or projecting from them.

Size of Bookcases

As in real life, bookcases often look better when they are designed to go from the floor almost to the ceiling rather than extending only halfway up the wall. But of course, this may not necessarily work for the proportions or needs of every stage design.

If you are designing a bookcase unit for an interior set with walls that are 14'-0" high, the bookcase might be 10'-0" or 11'-0" tall and 3'-0" or 4'-0" wide and 10" or 12" deep. Shelves may start practically at the floor. For a bookcase with an 11-foot height, it is a good rule both visually and practically to have a bottom board ¾-inch thick and 6-inches high (when placed horizontally) on the face positioned on the edge and running horizontally on the floor as an actual base of the bookcase. Start the first shelf by placing it directly on top of that ¾-inch edge. This base is the same length as the shelves and after attachment it may be dressed with two pieces of molding, one at the very bottom and the other positioned above on the edge of the shelf, with both continuing around on each of the two sides.

When designing the top of the bookcase, plan on having a similar piece of wood like the arrangement at the bottom. This board may be ¾-inch thick and 4 inches high (when placed horizontally) and the same length as the shelves. It also is positioned horizontally, with the 4-inch face butting in between and flush against the vertical sides of the bookcase. Then the very top of the highest piece of wood is attached directly under and to the bottom ¾-inch thickness of the 4-inch piece (as well as to the vertical sides).

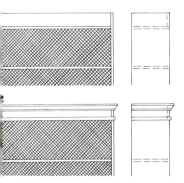

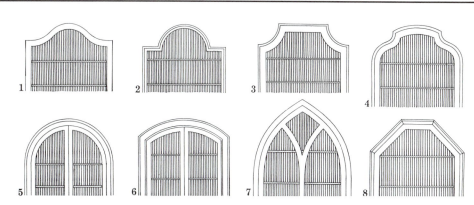

Like the bottom, the top structure may also have a couple of lengths of molding going around it. One may be placed at the very top and the second piece of molding may be positioned at the bottom where the ¾-inch thickness piece of the highest shelf is attached.

In a bookcase of this type it is always good to vary the spacing of the shelves. If the shelves are made to be adjustable, then that is another matter. Start by making the bottom spaces the largest, then decrease from there. For instance, if you are designing a bookcase that is 11'-0" high, the total number of inches you are working with would be 132. Then subtract the 6-inch board at the bottom and the 4-inch one at the top, plus the thicknesses of the two ¾-inch boards attached to them (1½ inches, and these four dimensions would add up to 11½ inches. Subtracting 11½ inches from the total height of 132 inches leaves 120½ inches.

Starting at the bottom, a good idea for spacing would be (in inches): (1) 15, (2) 15, (3) 15, (4) 12, (5) 12, (6) 12, (7) 12, (8) 10¾, and (9) 10¾. These figures add up to 114½ inches. The ¾-inch

Edward Gorey's painted books for DRACULA (1977), New York and London companies. *Pictured:* Clare Hein; Oliver Smith's painted books for MY FAIR LADY (1976). (Photographs by Lynn Pecktal)

thicknesses of the eight shelves in between these spaces would be 6 inches. So the grand total of all the boards, shelves, and spaces would be 11½ plus 114½ plus 6 inches which is 132 inches. This is a typical way of figuring placement of shelves if you want varied spacing between them. For a bookcase with equal spacing between the shelves, the specification is much simpler. Just put an inside height dimension on the bookcase drawing, state the total number of shelves, and say, "Space the given number of ¾-inch shelves equally."

Backings on this type of bookcase may be made of ⅛-inch plywood which may be painted the same color as the shelving or done in a contrasting color or in a pattern. It is usually easier to paint the backings before putting them on.

An alternate design for this type of bookcase is to design the bottom portion to have a set of doors that open and close. This allows actors to use the enclosed area to store props. Also, a bookcase may be created to have a decorative panel on the bottom.

For settings of lofts or libraries, the bookcases may be much higher than for a single-set living room interior, especially if rolling book ladders on tracks are to be positioned with the bookcases in the stage set.

Dressing Bookcases

Obviously, the books to be placed in bookcases must be selected and placed so they are compatible with the characters who live in the set environment. Should the books be in neat and immaculate order? Should they be randomly arranged with other objects so they appear attractive as well as practical? Should the bookcases be dressed with books in a completely unorganized fashion?

For more interest, and to break up the monotony of so many books in a setting, the following may be added to vary colors, textures, shapes, and contrast: porcelain vases, brass urns, straw baskets, ceramic plates, wooden platters, crystal decanters, arrangements of artificial flowers, plaster statuary, Japanese fans, small framed prints, pewter mugs, African masks, and other objects.

Creating Fake Books for Bookcases

Resident and touring companies know the value of having books that are easy to move and store for settings that require books. Sets consisting of drawing rooms, living rooms, studios, and libraries constantly need a good deal of books.

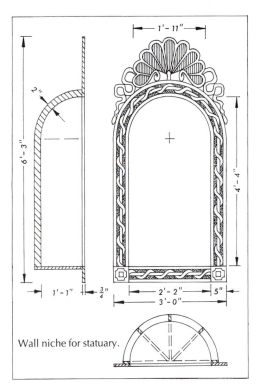

Wall niche for statuary.

This means that lightweight books are always in demand. Some of the best ways to provide them is to use these ideas:

1. *Use book jackets on book shapes made of Styrofoam.* Collect a lot of book jackets, and have available lightweight cardboard, white glue, sheets of Styrofoam, and paint. Cut the cardboard into appropriate pieces to fit the book jackets, then neatly glue the book jackets onto the cardboard pieces. Next, cut rectangular blocks out of the Styrofoam according to the size of each individual book. Sand the top edges of the Styrofoam pieces so they will appear natural when painted and placed in the book jackets and then positioned in the bookcases on stage. Naturally, not all the fake books will be placed standing up in the bookcases, so all three sides need to

be painted only on some of them. Paint the sanded Styrofoam so some books appear to be old and some new. When this is done, glue the simulated hard covers with the dust jackets onto the Styrofoam blocks. This can also work well for sets of books in a series, such as encyclopedias, dramatic works, poetry, architecture, and art. Real hard covers that have been removed from old damaged books can also be used for this process.

2. *Make profile books and paint them.* Another method of creating fake books is to draw profiles of books on plywood, cut them out, and paint them. These may work well in terms of colors, shapes, textures, and sizes, but their successful placement in bookcases depends on the sight lines in the individual theatre. For instance, if there is a balcony the audience may be able to see that the tops of the books do not have any thicknesses, and this would have to be compensated for by using something like painted Styrofoam blocks with the outer backs glued on.

3. *Glue the pages of books together and cut out the insides.* A third approach is to glue pages of books together and then cut out sizable rectangles in them. This technique is very effective for large volumes. They look totally natural when they are closed, and of course these cut books may be used to hide guns, jewelry, money, and other small props in the business of a scene.

Designing Wall Niches

Recessed wall niches are ideal locations for extra-special props. These niches in the walls also provide an interesting design feature and good contrast with hanging pieces of set dressing such as mirrors, paintings, and prints. Niches work beautifully for holding any number of lovely props. These can be all sorts of elegant statuary and busts, urns of exotic floral arrangements such as bird-of-paradise and calla lilies; standing displays of china plates, platters, and other similar objects; pottery collections; African masks and groups of miniature dolls.

Wall niches may be designed in many different shapes and sizes, and may be positioned either horizontally or vertically. The shape of a wall niche, for example, may be an oval, a plain vertical rectangle, or a vertical rectangle with a rounded top or a Gothic shape added.

For scenery designed with average-size flats, wall niches may vary from 3'-6" to 6'-6" in height and 1'-10" to 3'-3" in width. A recessed vertical niche may be positioned 3'-0" or so from the stage floor. Like bookcases and windows, wall niches are usually built as one piece, sometimes with a plain or decorative facing and they fit into an appropriate opening in the flat. The entire niche unit may also be hinged onto the flat from behind the opening.

Niches are built with or without shelves. Shelves for a collection of dishes, for example, may have the front edges profiled and routed to provide more interest, but the rear of the shelves must follow the contour of the backing wall, which may be either straight or curved. Small lights may be mounted inside the niche to add a nice touch of indirect lighting to illuminate the items on display.

Stage design by John Lee Beatty
DUET FOR ONE by Tom Kempinski
Directed by William Friedkin
Royale Theatre, New York (1981)

382

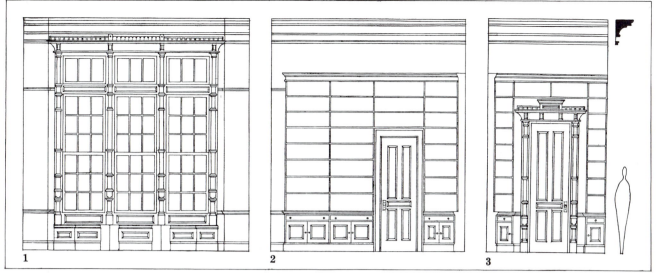

1   2   3

Scenery by John Wulp
Scenery supervised by Lynn Pecktal
BOSOMS AND NEGLECT by John Guare
Directed by Mel Shapiro
Goodman Theatre, Chicago, Illinois
Longacre Theatre, New York (1979)

Shown are presentational drawings and a
model for the living room. The living room,
bedroom, and hospital sets are seen on the
ground plan below. The ground plan indicates
how the three sets shifted on the Goodman
Theatre stage. (Drawings by Lynn Pecktal)

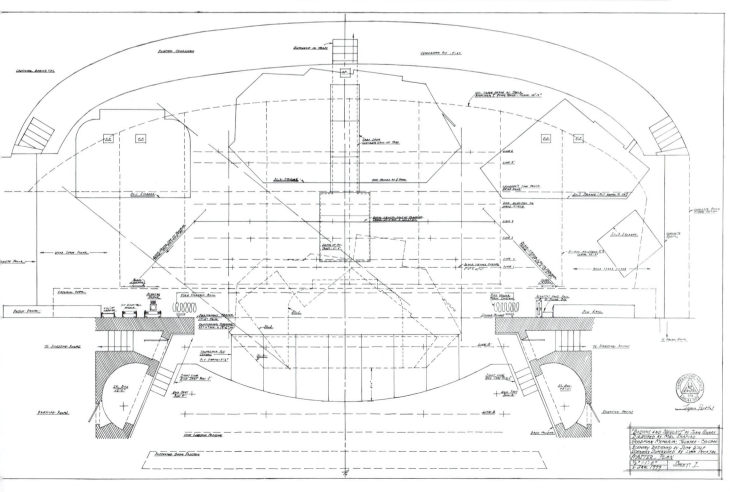

Santo Loquasto lives in a charming old building on upper Riverside Drive in Manhattan. Born in 1944 in Wilkes-Barre, Pennsylvania, he graduated from King's College and the Yale School of Drama. His first Broadway show was *Sticks and Bones* in 1972. He has designed sets and costumes for a great many companies, including the Guthrie Theatre, Hartford Stage Company, Long Wharf Theatre, Williamstown Theatre Festival, Yale Repertory Theatre, New York Shakespeare Festival, Arena Stage, New York Pro Musica, Mark Taper Forum, San Francisco Spring Opera, Michigan Opera Company, Brooklyn Academy of Music, Manhattan Theatre Club, La Mama E.T.C., Playwrights Horizons, Chelsea Theatre Center, and San Diego Opera. Among his production and costume designs for films are *A Midsummer Night's Sex Comedy*, *Falling in Love*, *Stardust Memories*, *Desperately Seeking Susan*, *Zelig*, *Radio Days*, *Another Woman*, *September*, *Big*, *Bright Lights, Big City*, *Alice*, *Crimes and Misdemeanors*, *Shadows and Fog*, and *Husbands and Wives*. He has received Tony, Drama Desk, Maharam, Obie, and Outer Critics Circle awards, and the British Academy Award. His scenery and/or costume design credits include:

Broadway
The Goodbye Girl (1993)
Jake's Women (1992)
Lost in Yonkers (1991)
Grand Hotel (1989)
Cafe Crown
   Brooks Atkinson (1989)
   Public/Newman (1988)
Sweet Sue (1987)
Singin' in the Rain (1985)
The Wake of Jamey Foster (1982)
The Suicide (1980)
Bent (1979)
The Goodbye People (1979)
King of Hearts (1978)
American Buffalo (1977)
Miss Margarida's Way (1977)
Sticks and Bones (1972)

The Secret Affairs of Mildred Wild
   (1972)
That Championship Season (1972)

Beaumont Theatre
The Tenth Man (1989)
The Floating Light Bulb (1981)
The Cherry Orchard (1977)
The Dance of Death (1974)

Newhouse Theatre
A Midsummer Night's Dream (1975)
Macbeth (1974)

Dance Companies
Twyla Tharp Dance
American Ballet Theatre
Joffrey Ballet

New York City Ballet
Paul Taylor Dance Company
The Royal Ballet
Les Grands Ballets Canadiens
National Ballet of Canada
San Francisco Ballet

Public Theatre
Virginia (1985)
Curse of the Starving Class (1978)
Landscape of the Body (1977)

Delacorte Theatre
Richard III (1983)
Hamlet (1975)
The Comedy of Errors (1975)
Pericles (1974)
King Lear (1973)

Scenery by Santo Loquasto
CAFE CROWN by Hy Craft

Directed by Martin Charnin
Lighting by Richard Nelson

Public Theatre/Newman, New York (1988)
(Photograph © Martha Swope)

How did you first become interested in designing for the theatre?

As long as I can remember, the interest was always there. I was stagestruck, essentially, as a very young child. As a five-year-old child I was enrolled in a children's theatre school in Wilkes-Barre, Pennsylvania. It met a couple times a week. My mother thought that it might be a solution to disciplinary problems I encountered in kindergarten. I loved it. And along with loving the performing experience of the theatre, I found that I was very much attracted to the production aspect of it.

As a kid I was always interested in drawing, and it was immediately channeled into design, in the telling of stories or the playing out of stories. That continued in a haphazard way until I was in junior high school. Then I became involved in community theatre, and later, college productions. I was an actor in some of the plays, but I was very much fascinated by scenery and the look of a production. The summer I turned fifteen I went to summer stock as an apprentice in this little non-equity theatre in the Poconos. Of course, I loved it, and the following season I designed two productions.

I don't know what prompts the kind of imagination that needs to explore physical and emotional space. But I do know that it is the theatre that seems to support it. I was always more interested in a three-dimensional full-scale transformation of what I had in mind rather than simply drawing in miniature or drawing in general. I still don't have any patience with the limitations of drawing. Actually, channeling my imagination happened in an atmosphere that was not a particularly artistic one, but nevertheless, it was an environment that allowed me to fantasize about the theatre and about performance.

From the time I was nine I was alone quite a bit because both my parents worked. I would pour over *Theatre Arts* magazines that I would check out of the library over and over again, and I subscribed to Fireside Theatre books. I was fortunate to live near the Poconos, with all those little summer theatres that offered me wonderful experience. It was *Theatre Arts* magazine that brought me into contact with the Williamstown Theatre, and while I was in college I started working there. I still work there when I can.

Where did you go to college?

I went to King's College in Wilkes-Barre, Pennsylvania, where I was an English major. I was active in the theatre there, and I designed and acted and overextended myself in a million ways. The summer before my senior year I worked at Williamstown as an assistant in design. At the end of the summer Nikos Psacharopoulos felt that I was able to take on a show of my own and I designed *Cat on a Hot Tin Roof*. I went back for about ten consecutive seasons, and I returned a couple of years ago to design three plays. I learned so much from the people there and from the experience. That was the most illuminating practical experience I had. I especially learned much from John Conklin. I'm sure it was because of Williamstown and Nikos that I was accepted into Yale. I had a portfolio, but I had his recommendation and at that time he was very well connected with the Drama School.

Were you always interested in doing both sets and costumes?

Yes, I always was. However, I think of myself as a set designer who does costumes. John Conklin, who was very much influenced by the European tradition, encouraged me to do both. Then at Yale along with studying under Mr. Oenslager that first year, I assisted Michael Annals, the English designer. English designers, more than Americans, are of the tradition of doing both the scenery and the costumes.

Did you plan to come to New York and enter the commercial theatre rather than going to a resident theatre or teaching?

I had never thought about teaching. I always knew I wanted to work in New York. From this first childhood dream, it was always in my mind. New York was *the* place. However, I've since learned that often the most interesting work happens outside of New York, in Minneapolis or Hartford or Washington, D.C., for example. But it was always my intention to come here. I didn't come here immediately, however.

What happened after you finished at the Yale Drama School?

What happened was, interestingly enough, linked to my working with John Conklin. While I was in the Drama School, I started working at the Hartford Stage and the Long Wharf. I assisted John on a couple of productions, and when he was not able to do a show, he would say, "Why don't you consider Santo Loquasto?" And so I started designing primarily at the Hartford Stage. Hartford is celebrating an anniversary this year and they wrote an article about several of us. John, of course, holds the marathon record with the number of shows he's designed for them. I was amazed that I was still a contender after all these years.

It was not only great to work there, but it gave me income as a student. To do half a season, which was three plays at Hartford, was terrific. After three years at Yale, I continued working at Hartford as the principal designer, which amounted to six shows a season. Eventually I worked at other places— the Charles Street Playhouse, the Taper, and Arena Stage.

I found myself in a terrific situation. I was being allowed to do work that I probably would not have found in New York. Quite honestly, I'm still very much a person who is responsive to an institutional theatre, whether it's the Public Theatre or Arena Stage or the Guthrie or any of those places. But I also find that after you have worked for a while in New York, you can discover a similar situation. But there is nothing like a talented staff under one roof to create a truly ideal situation.

I put off moving to New York for several reasons. I knew I didn't have many of the technical skills to support myself as a superb assistant. (Now the kids come in with incredible model-making faculties and drafting skills.) I was, however, somewhat confident of my design abilities and my ability to mount productions in a very tangible way. I was, therefore, very happy to stay in New Haven, where I knew I would find design opportunities.

Did you work elsewhere during this time?

I worked one year at the Yale Rep as well. At the time there were young directors from Yale who had moved to New York and who were doing work Off-Broadway and at the Public Theatre. Often they wanted me to design their plays. In addition, the Arena Stage in Washington, D.C., had offered me a contract. I decided to base myself in New York because I wanted to continue designing Off-Broadway as well. So I wasn't simply arriving with my baggage and saying, "Here I am. Now, what do I do?" It was a practical move. The time had come.

Meanwhile, I was trying to gain more experience and meet more directors. I wasn't rabid about it, oddly enough, I was rabid about the work as work which, alas, I still am. It had a lot to do with the love of doing plays such as Giraudoux or Anouilh or O'Neill or whatever I might not get to do in New York. I was and still am a product of that Brustein period at Yale where you really are constantly trying to examine old works and revitalize them. I was attracted to classical rep, I suppose, rather than what I now think of as commercial theatre. I have yet to be associated with what would be called a really commercial hit. Probably the biggest commercial success was *That Championship Season*. The production of *The Cherry Orchard* was certainly a success, but it was not what you would think of as a commercial hit!

How did your first Broadway show come about?

The first Broadway show was David Rabe's *Sticks and Bones*, which I did with Jeff Bleckner, a director with whom I had worked at Yale, Williamstown, and Off Broadway. I was working at Arena Stage and I had been asked to do *Sticks and Bones* at the Public Theatre in the Anspacher Theatre. Joe Papp decided to move the show to Broadway based on its success downtown, and because he felt Broadway audiences should be exposed to the issues explored in the play.

What did you do for the scenery for Sticks and Bones?

The set was quite simple in the Anspacher, as it also was on Broadway. It was a living room and a bedroom unit set, but along with a sense of the house, you had to allow for a ghost figure to appear through the bedroom walls. The young man is haunted by a beautiful woman he had loved in Vietnam. In terms of transferring the production, it was the usual situation where you move from a three-sided theatre into a Broadway proscenium house. You are asked to open up the space without reworking the set. The Broadway theatre introduced sight line problems that had originally been resolved by the elevated seating arrangement at the Anspacher.

Essentially, I just took the same bedroom, wraparound living room with front door, and a floating staircase up to an upper central level into a proscenium theatre. It was not unlike an Elizabethan ground plan, with the bedroom serving as an inner above with corridors to the rest of the house on this second level. Yet the set retained the feeling of a split-level house in the suburbs, and the Oriental details in the decor conjured up a subliminal sense of the East. It was very straightforward, and not a set that made a particularly dazzling debut.

I remember the opening night of *Sticks and Bones* walking out of Barrymore's Bar and looking up at the marquee of the Golden Theatre and thinking how caught unawares I had been by my sudden arrival on Broadway. It was not at all as I had planned it, and it was much sooner than I had ever expected it might happen. I had been propelled by the project and it had swept me along with it. It was not the kind of thing where you take a piece and develop it and move it rather lovingly. It was sudden. It had to move. It was a hit downtown so take it uptown in a terrible rush!

When Sticks and Bones *was running on Broadway, did it get you other work?*

I don't think *Sticks and Bones* did. Jeff Bleckner was becoming a hot property as a director. He had done *Pavlo Hummel* and *Sticks and Bones*. The following fall we did a play called *The Secret Affairs of Mildred Wild*, a very funny Paul Zindel play starring Maureen Stapleton. It was my first experience on Broadway working on a new play from scratch. We took it out of town to New Haven and to Boston, where I met Artie Siccardi and George Green. It changed my life. It was an education. It was also my first show with commercial producers. Georgie referred to me as the "young Boris." I think it had more to do with my rabbinical locks than my talent. Even though the show was a flop, it was great fun to do.

Then *Championship Season*, which I had done the previous spring downtown at the Public, moved uptown. This was an enormous success. There was the national company and the short-lived British production. *Mildred Wild* and *Championship Season* opened weeks apart. That whole situation was sort of amazing.

Did you use assistants on these shows?

I asked people who were more experienced with the New York shops to assist me as far as getting the design into the shop. You have assistants to compensate for areas you're weak in, and also because they provide you with a system of checks and balances where they're always looking to see where you have glided over something or not resolved an element. It is their job to ask you what you really meant here or there. Early on I did do it almost all by myself. You become more trusting when you know that the assistants you are working with are designers and know what you mean by something. What is glorious is to have a real studio of people working with you who are talented and experienced enough to take a rough sketch or an idea and begin to develop it to a point.

Do you work with some of the same assistants you have worked with for a long period of time?

Yes, luckily I do. Most of them now work in films almost exclusively. I've worked with one fellow in particular since 1973, and another one for nine years. None of them work with me exclusively, of course.

How did The Cherry Orchard *come about?*

Starting with *Sticks and Bones* and the *Championship Season* period, I became somewhat attached to the Public Theatre and to Joe Papp. It was at this point that Joe took on the directorship of the Beaumont Theatre, and he essentially asked me to be the staff designer there. My institutional theatre background was especially helpful in dealing with the demands of repertory and in churning out plays without much preparation, which certainly was the situation at the Beaumont, where we often never knew what was coming up next. You had to work very quickly to fill the space.

Other designers, such as David Mitchell, were doing work there as well. Eventually, I felt that because of having to work so quickly and because of the difficulties of the space at the Beaumont perhaps someone else should give it a go. David took on that job for a while. I continued working for Joe, but on a freelance basis. I also felt that I wanted to try other things, many which were actually rather trivial Broadway productions but nonetheless allowed me to meet some people who have remained good friends.

I was still working for the Public from time to time. They had scheduled a production of *The Cherry Orchard* featuring Irene Worth, to be directed by Andrei Serban. I met with Andrei, and he subsequently asked me to design the production. We worked on that for a long period of time.

How did you approach the design for The Cherry Orchard?

Andrei and I talked about it endlessly. I had already done two productions of the play. We largely talked about what Andrei thought about the piece, and decided to pare it down to only those elements that are referred to in the text, but also to find an abstract poetic framework for the piece. This resulted over a period of time. We didn't arrive at that decision immediately. It was about finding a texture or tone or feeling that the entire evening would support. We didn't want to change from act to act. We decided on

Model by Santo Loquasto
PEER GYNT by Henrik Ibsen
Directed by Liviu Ciulei
Tyrone Guthrie Theatre
Minneapolis, Minnesota (1983)

the whiteness of the set, and then within that used the necessary elements that Chekhov referred to as "punctuation." We did that within the sweeping openness of the Beaumont, still trying to keep everything within sight lines.

What we as designers are all trained to do is to meet with the director, read the play, and design the production over a certain period of time (sometimes over a period of minutes), trying to solve the problems of the staging and providing the atmosphere and so on. With someone like Andrei, and with actually quite a few directors I've since discovered, it is still an ongoing process in rehearsals. So what you do with directors like that is you try to give them the kind of physical dynamic that is enormously flexible. Otherwise, you lose your mind. Experience helps you with the budget restraints. I still get quite tense about the kind of haphazardness that this approach can easily lead to. Paradoxically, this approach also allows you to continue to be quite free.

When we were in previews I would see things that were or were not working. Although it could be expensive, I felt I could say, "Now Andrei, you see, I told you the bookcase was too small but you insisted it was perfect. I said it should be enormous. It should sit on that stage like a totem, a symbol. It has

to have enormous physical weight. It's what the characters talk about. It means a million things to these people, about their lives, their youth, history, all that." He would say, "You're right!" And we rebuilt the bookcase.

Then we had terrible trouble in the fourth act. It wasn't working. And I suggested that we undo this framed drop and make it into a huge drop cloth so it was like an enormous dust cover over everything. To do this we would have to have a work call, but this was the luxury that Joe Papp allowed us. Andrei is enormously talented. It's that moment of trying something new that vitalizes him, and makes all of the actors and the designers a little crazy because you never feel that you can set and polish something. It isn't that you want to put it in stone, but you want to feel that you can make it quite beautiful. By "beautiful" I mean simply appropriate. Often Andrei is more than happy to throw it up there to see if it works, and then change it to something else. This method keeps him interested. I think that he finds that it keeps a performance fresh because the cast is still discovering things. It's an interesting process.

Years later I worked with him on an *Uncle Vanya* at La Mama. One of the attractions was that it was for a limited preproduction period. It was a situation that was unlike anything else I

388   have ever done. We would rehearse. We would come to this open space at La Mama. We would build. I would draw little things and say, "Maybe we should have this come out here. Let's build this tonight and we'll see how it looks and works tomorrow." We really did it that way, and it worked. We just kept building, and there were a few things that were changed after they were built. It was platforms and stairs and very simple. We didn't ever go too far. We proceeded slowly and tried something every day. I would never have been that cool about it ten years earlier!

But it was an enjoyable collaboration.

It was amazing. *The Cherry Orchard* was enormously difficult because it was unrelenting for months. It was always a race every day to gather what

Costume designs by Santo Loquasto
THE CATHERINE WHEEL
Choreographed by Twyla Tharp
Winter Garden Theatre
New York (1981)

he wanted to try that night, and attending performances endlessly and battling it out. We did battle it out. This whole process is somewhat erratic. You never feel that it is going in a particular direction. Andrei would just as happily say, "Let's try it all black tonight" after you've been doing it all white! I mean there were moments like that, and I would just say, "Oh, don't be ridiculous."

In a way, that experience ultimately winds up being quite liberating. We all want to be enormously flexible, but the designers have to deal with many practical disadvantages like time and money. It's nuts and bolts when you get down to it.

If you are doing a production in a regional theatre, and you are doing a Broadway production, do you attack designing in the same way?

No, not exactly. You usually find out what a regional theatre is capable of doing or what their strong points are. Often you can do far more elaborately detailed work in a regional theatre than you can afford to do on Broadway. At the same time, you don't talk about winches and turntables, necessarily. Whether it is Broadway or a regional theatre, it all so often has to do with money as well as your preparation time to design and build. There rarely seems to be enough of either.

Many designers seem to be inspired by these limitations. John Conklin and prior to John, Will Steven Armstrong, with whom John also worked, have been unbelievably clever at being able to get mileage out of scenery. Knowing how to take a unit and not only do the obvious sort of thing that flips around and becomes something else, but also knowing how to make a simple idea like putting three boards and a rag on stage and have it look fantastic. Effective scenery doesn't always have to be something that has been slaved over and costs a fortune.

Regional theatres are mostly non-proscenium stages requiring you to be far more sculptural or dimensional in your designs. You are designing for elements that people look at from almost

four sides. This is not to imply that you do cardboard cutouts on Broadway. However, the illusionistic capacity of a Broadway proscenium stage is still far superior to that of a three-sided theatre. In other words, time, money, the actual space and facilities affect how you approach the design.

Does the amount of the budget control how you think about a design?

It has to. I was just asked to do a play at the Second Stage, and the first questions I asked were, "Who's directing it? When is it scheduled? What's the budget? How do you work? Do you have a staff? Is there a technical staff or is the scenery delivered by a shop?" It is immensely important to know the answers to such questions. Off Broadway is not what it was when I first designed there. It used to be that you found a couple of guys and they built the set in the lobby of the theatre, and you set it up, and you painted all night long after rehearsal. I just did a show like that for INTAR, and that's exactly what we did. They rehearsed in the daytime and we would come in at night. Well, it nearly killed me. I'm too old now. But you have to know that. I mean if that's the way it is, and you still go in knowing it, so you're a fool. Nonetheless, there I was.

The money is entirely different out of town. Regional theatres maintain a staff, and the budget is often just for materials. It is usually time that is the enemy in these theatres.

How long do you usually stay out of town when you do a show in a regional theatre?

When I did the scenery and costumes for *Peer Gynt* at the Guthrie, I would fly back and forth. It really meant that I was living in Minneapolis and commuting to New York on occasion! When you do costumes, you have to be there for fittings, and that takes the time. If you do the scenery only, it can be that you deliver the designs, stay a couple of days, go away, and come back. But *Peer Gynt* teched for three weeks. They insisted on that. We would tech in the afternoon, and do a changeover for the evening production. Most regional theatres have a less strenuous routine. They are dark for a week so you do the changeover in a period of a couple of days and then tech it.

You have designed a great deal for the dance. How did you become involved in that?

I suppose it all happened through Jennifer Tipton. I was doing a little opera for the New York Pro Musica in Spoleto, Italy, and while I was there I went to a Jerome Robbins evening for which Jennifer designed the lighting. It was wonderful. Jennifer still thinks it was one of the most perfect programs that she has ever worked on. It was lighting unlike any I had ever seen before. When I returned to New York to do the production of *The Tempest* for Joe Papp at the Newhouse Theatre, I asked if they might entertain the notion of Jennifer Tipton lighting it, and she did. We've been working together since and battling our way through productions for years. There are luxuries in working with the same people over again. I work with Jennifer as often as possible. We know each other—sometimes we probably know each other too well. But on the other hand, I talk to her about what I should provide her and what is not a problem and what is a problem and what shouldn't be a problem.

Anyway, Jennifer invited Twyla Tharp to *The Tempest*. As a result, Twyla asked me to design costumes for a wonderful dance she had created called *Sue's Leg*. That started what has been an ongoing relationship with Twyla. After *Sue's Leg* she did a piece with Baryshnikov which was *Push Comes to Shove*, and she asked me to do the costumes and, of course, Jennifer to light it.

This was my introduction to the American Ballet Theatre, where I've worked for many years with varying degrees of success. Right now I'm working on a piece with Mark Morris and Agnes de Mille. You cannot find more divergent talents. It has been great. Probably designing for the dance is what I enjoy most. It's extremely difficult. I'm often working in extremes: a minimum of detail or an abundance of it. And the scenery is invariably problematic, technically and artistically.

The most difficult aspect of designing for American Ballet Theatre is the touring demands. The problem is—we designers all hate soft scenery, especially legs. Invariably they look terrible. We want the scenery to be framed and neat; we want it crisp. Production still wants soft legs and borders and

Production design by Santo Loquasto
RADIO DAYS
Directed by Woody Allen
Orion Pictures (1987)

drops so that it can all be tossed into a hamper. But it is the touring factor that is important for all dance companies. If you're there at eight in the morning on a snowy day in Chicago watching them set up *Bayadere*, you think, "They do this every day someplace. No wonder they complain. No wonder! It's hard." And you try to design, not only to protect the integrity of the design, but to create a set that will sustain itself performance after performance. When we work with the modern dance companies, I maintain that scenery has to fit into the glove compartment or the station wagon! But it is always interesting.

Bob Joffrey, as a dance historian, was consumed with a passionate concern for recreating historic pieces, whether it was Nijinsky, Cecil Beaton, or Kurt Jooss. He managed to keep his physical productions looking impeccable. They would have hard framed legs. Robert Joffrey was committed and obsessive about maintaining a production in terms of the original interpretation, the dancing, the scenery, the costumes, the lighting.

A consistent polished look to a company must come from the artistic director. The realities of the financial burdens must not be allowed to compromise quality—not excess—quality. When it comes to the tour, they may say, "We just can't do that. We have to simplify it on the road; it's just easier." That's not fair to Cedar Rapids. You start hearing the attitude, "Well, we'll clean it up in New York." The production should be the same everywhere it plays.

How long do you have on a ballet?

The full-length ones take an enormous amount of time, which we rarely have. Let's say it's an abstract dance piece, not a narration. What often happens is that you are called in to see a run-through late in the development of the piece. Then you only have about a month, maybe three weeks, maybe less. Ideally you should have to have about two months to design it and to have it executed—often dealing with complex rehearsal and trucking schedules.

The Informer, the Agnes de Mille piece, had to be ready for trucks to take it to California even though it was just going to lie in the trucks for six weeks. When they called me to do it, there was about a month from the day it started to the load-out. Then they found that there was a truck that was going to go in seven weeks instead of four weeks. We had to make the last truck. The scenery consisted of three drops, legs, borders, and one built piece.

I designed the costumes as well, and there was more time for those. Before you begin designing for dance you usually have to see what the movement is, and you have to hear the music. Ideally, you attend rehearsals as it is developing, and you see what the technical demands are, what the partnering involves. You see the kind of emotion in the story, what you want to evoke. It is necessary to know all that. In dance, there is constant change, and often to the last minute. Jerry Robbins is notorious for this. You do endless mock-ups with different colors and different shapes. Sometimes there is just five minutes left to make the change! I've worked with Jerry on a half dozen things, and the evolution never ceases, even after the premiere. He is completely unpredictable, except that he is always interesting. We make certain provisions for genius, I suppose.

I love designing for dance. It was an unexpected delight to find myself designing as much as I do for dance. When it works, the magic and the honesty of it are really very satisfying for me. I have been extremely lucky in working with a wide range of wonderful and gifted choreographers.

How did you get started in designing for films?

I had been working on a dance production, actually, and I came home to find a message on the machine from Marshall Brickman's office. He had written a film called *Simon* which he would be directing and wanted to know if I would be interested in doing the costumes. As it invariably is with movies, they call you the Wednesday before the Monday they want you to start. I said we should meet and I should read the script and that I would probably love to do it. I thought, "How different can this be?" You find out about blue flaring and things like that. And you meet and talk and talk and talk with them. It was like doing an Off-Broadway show—light on funds, heavy on concept.

Comment on blue flaring.

It's a visual vibration, the flaring of the color blue. There are certain colors that react on film and certain cinematographers really lay out the rules about them. They will tell you that they don't want you to use dead white or they don't want you to use blue, especially a kind of cobalt blue. A blue oxford cloth shirt will register a more intense blue on film than it will to the naked eye. You don't want the shirt to be livelier than the actor's face. There is a whole other set of rules for television, and I think there are more of these kind of problems in video than in film.

So anyway, I did this film of Marshall's, and very shortly after that, Woody Allen's office called me about doing the costumes for *Stardust Memories*. Marshall had been a colleague of Woody Allen's. They wrote *Annie Hall*, *Sleeper*, and *Manhattan* together. Following that, I did several films with Woody Allen as costume designer—*Midsummer Night's Sex Comedy* and *Zelig*. He is great to work with, and they were wonderful projects. Two of them were period films, and *Stardust Memories* was rather theatrical. It was fascinating, and I learned a great deal from working with the wonderful cinematographer Gordon Willis.

What I found, however, was that I missed the theatre. I did *Bent* while I was doing *Stardust Memories*, but it's hard to do both at the same time, although I am constantly trying to. The days are long on films. It's not that you get tired, but you have to be constantly available. You need to be around for things that occur, and you want to be there to make an on-the-spot contribution, if it's appropriate, or if there is a problem, maybe you can help solve it.

Doing films I found myself feeling as though I wasn't using the muscles I had been trained to use. Film is a whole other world. So I went off and did a few plays. Then I was offered a production designer position on a film which allowed me the opportunity to learn about locations and film sets and how to go about all that. Woody then asked me to be the production designer for *Radio Days*, followed by *September*, and then I did *Another Woman*, which we just finished. It will be out next fall. We're shooting a short film right now.

I've worked for other directors as well. I did *Bright Lights, Big City* with a terrific director, Jim Bridges, and again the cinematographer was Gordon Willis. No matter how strong your contribution is as a designer, you are working with and for the cinematographer. You have to make it work for him, because he has to respond to it and make it look as good as he can. That is not a compromise. That is just another fact of life. If the cinematographer is not good at what he does, then it almost doesn't matter what you do as a designer. You learn how to woo the cinematographer to find out what he wants, all of which ultimately results in the film working better.

You were nominated for an Oscar for Radio Days.

I was both surprised and delighted. *Radio Days* was a small period film. It was an intimate comedy and it didn't have the sweep of *The Last Emperor* or *The Empire of the Sun*—films that have had staggering visual impact based on the enormity of the undertaking alone. Of course they were quality films as well. So I was quite surprised to receive the nomination. I was also surprised because *Radio Days* came out at the very beginning of the year, and was already on video. It always seems like a totally remote experience. I was nominated for the costumes for *Zelig* as well. Hollywood is a foreign world to me.

If a student asked what one needed to know or how to go about designing for films primarily, what would you say?

I've learned along the way about what you do in films. What an individual needs to know technically varies

Backdrop design by Santo Loquasto for THE INFORMER (1988), choreographed by Agnes de Mille, American Ballet Theatre.

from person to person. There is a lot of very easily acquired bits of information about what certain cinematographers like and don't like. Right now I'm working with Sven Nykvist, the great Swedish cinematographer. Because he has worked in Europe for years, he can work in very limited situations with very few lights and it will look beautiful, whereas most cinematographers don't want to go into places with low ceilings and cramped working conditions.

In many ways, designing for films is simpler than designing for the theatre. You don't have to deal with sight lines and space limitations. You can practically build a city in full scale. You can also take masking tape and hide something or turn something into an absolutely beautiful visual effect in the most makeshift way. It's shocking how you can cheat. You can hang a piece of lace over a light bulb, and with a very little fan and a little smoke it's just wonderful. When you stand off and look at it, it's a grip stand, clips, and string. That you do learn. On the other hand, you want to build the complete reveal for the outside of the window and not stop short at the window. There are these two extremes where it's the most Mickey Mouse solution and the most fully developed solution.

It's often a gamble as to what will be seen by the camera. And of course you are always being told, "Nobody will notice, nobody will see it." You are always being reminded that there is no dignity in what you're doing, and no matter what you try to do, you're foolish to try to do it.

What do you like least about working in the theatre?

I suppose there are answers such as totally unqualified stagehands and things like that. But I suppose what I love about the theatre is the live performance and what is the most difficult aspect of it is its maintenance. It's the going back and checking on the condition and the placement of the scenery, the furniture, the props, the costumes. With any show that had a lengthy run, I would try to go to the theatre once a week. Even with a simple show like *Sweet Sue* I would go, because I would want to make sure that there were certain little things being kept up for the performance. Stagehands change. I think it's hardest for the lighting designers with light settings and cues. Follow spot operators change, people go on vacation. It's maintaining what you want it to look like, not just simply because things get dirty, things get replaced, things fall apart. It's the cues, keeping the show the way you wanted it to be when you left it in the hands of the stage manager. That's one of the most difficult things about theatre.

Of course, the luxury of a film is that the moment is caught and recaught and recaught until it's what you want. Film is far more easily manipulated.

I love the theatre and I feel quite devoted to it in many ways. You have to stay with it. You can't walk away from a production after it has opened and is running. There are certain ballet repertory productions that I've given up on because no one adequately maintained them. This has occurred in full-length evenings where I've been defeated by the staff, colleagues, and often the other designers involved. It's not that I was better. I may not have really solved the problems, and was unable to remedy the situation which ultimately defeated me. Alas, I've despaired of this on several occasions. I know I thought I would never do that, but I find that if it's a big enough project that drains enormous energy, you find that you—and I'm not feeling sorry for myself—that you are the only one standing there trying to hold it together, then you ultimately feel, "I cannot deal with this any longer."

It's often a combination of finances and lack of standards. Designers are asked to do a ballet or an opera and they think, "How great! I thought I'd never get to do this, and now I'm going to do a *Traviata*." If you have the dreams of a young designer, they are invariably about doing big lavish productions. I have found the simplicity of many productions has been far more satisfying for me. Nevertheless, you think, "Well, I'd love to do an opera, because it has big elements." Then you discover that the company only has $1.98 to spend but they don't care because they just want to get the production on. Reality crashes down around you; it's a big disappointment.

On the more pragmatic level, you may learn how to design around those problems or you may stay away from them. We have all heard stories about the insane demands of certain designers—young and old. But you begin to understand why those designers become madmen. I have heard myself turn into an unbelievably horrible human being in situations where the frustrations have become unbearable!

Also, one of the worst aspects of the theatre is formation of a committee in the face of weak direction. Then you find yourself in a situation where there are many opinions flying and many people in charge. Usually these committees try to respect the choreographer more than a director. Often the choreographer will shrug and have no opinion, or sometimes he may be intimidated by a situation. Usually artistic heads of companies are sensitive to that situation, and will try to pull the information out of the choreographer so that it is ultimately his or her vision

Settings by Santo Loquasto
THE CATHERINE WHEEL
Choreographed by Twyla Tharp
Lighting by Jennifer Tipton
Winter Garden Theatre, New York (1981)
(Photograph by David Byrne)

Stage design by Santo Loquasto
SPEAKING IN TONGUES
Choreographed by Paul Taylor
New York City Center (1989)

of the piece that is expressed. It varies. When it's classical repertory, you find a million points of view about how it was done at the Kirov, or how it was done when so-and-so did it. Suddenly there are a lot of Russian conversations going on in corners of rooms. That kind of situation can be very frustrating.

But you know how to cope with this.
Not always. There comes a point when you don't know who you're trying to please. It is evidently not yourself. There is that whole problem of pleasing people who often have no taste. That is the worst thing. Suddenly you are working with someone, often whom you're very fond of personally, or often whom you think is immensely talented but now is doing something that he or she does not necessarily have a knack for. This is most often the case when close friends and colleagues suddenly want to try something new and they want you to do it with them. When you realize how foreign the ground is and how they are failing, it's often difficult to work or to guide them to a certain point. The director/choreographer has to make it work. Designers do many things and work for many people and learn from all of them.

What do you enjoy most about working in the theatre?
Design on the kind of simplest level, I suppose. Theoretically, the theatre is a controlled situation where you can create a whole picture within a rather specific point of view. It is all there to

be viewed within 40 or 50 feet of space, unlike a film where it is the selective eye of the camera that rules. But more importantly, what I love about the theatre is the performance, the viewing of the whole picture, the contact with the audience, the fact that it's live. The designer contributes to that connection, and with the lighting designer manipulates the audience to respond to the performers. It's how a production marries the elements together. That is what I love. It works when all the people are pulling together. I can't find a clear way of saying this as precisely as I feel it.

Do you really prefer the live theatre as opposed to any other form of entertainment?
It varies. What I like about dance is that it is inherently abstract, and it asks that you draw on your imagination in a way that you are not asked to do in the theatre. It is not so much that naturalism or realism is boring, because as soon as it is placed on the stage it is abstracted since the deception of reality is inherently theatrical.

I did a play called *The Curse of the Starving Class* where the refrigerator had to have more importance than anything else on the stage. You know that in that situation you have to imbue a very fundamental everyday object with unbelievable significance and not make it preposterous or allow it to draw attention to itself. What I am saying in terms of abstraction is that we all want to do things that reflect a pure sense of design culminating from your conversations, the text, the music, the research, and then your hand. You want it to be more of a personal expression somehow. That's why we all

envy David Hockney and Eugene Berman and those artists who could make the scenery look like the way they drew and painted. I don't draw like that, so it doesn't even occur to me. But even the format is very simple with both these men, or Picasso for that matter. It is such a personal expression of their work. Boris Aronson struggled with this. He wanted to redefine what surrounds us, whether it was through his eyes or through someone else's eyes and, of course, ultimately his hand. We all struggle with that as stage designers. We can all do it after the style of whomever, but we know too much about our craft to allow the unsophisticated, spontaneous response to flow out of us. It's a pity, isn't it?

Another thing in terms of students is that they don't observe enough. They look at design only. This is something Liviu Ciulei noted when we went through the Portfolio Review together a few years ago. He said that he expected to see the work of all these young people and that it would be dazzling in its youth and its vision, but not necessarily sophisticated. Instead, it all looked like designs from twenty-five years ago. That's because the students often look more at other designers' works rather than analyzing their instinctive response to the material and trying to capture that.

How does one avoid having someone else's design stick in his or her mind after looking at it?
It's often impossible. There are definitive designs, after all. I look at others' work because they are more esoteric, more adventurous and rigorous, inspirational. They challenge me.

If you had to be remembered for one area or one piece of work at this point in your career, what would it be?
My most enduring work has been in dance, because it has been with people who have vision. Something like *The Cherry Orchard* is still remembered even though it has been many years. I have been fortunate in working with Twyla in particular. The work was often astounding at the time it was performed. We fed each other in a rather spontaneous way. I would think it would be that collaboration that would be best remembered. I wish there were more plays, but I don't think there really are any that I feel that strongly about. It would be in dance.

9

SOFT SCENERY AND DRAPERY

SHOW CURTAINS AND BACKDROPS

Designing a Show Curtain

The design of a show curtain should always be in keeping with the character of the production. It should give the audience a hint of the mood of the play and at the same time stimulate the audience's interest. This is achieved through the theme or subject of the show curtain as well as the choice of colors, textures, and shapes. The overall visual effect created by the scenic designer with the show curtain may be completely realistic, highly stylized, suggestive, or abstract.

When a show curtain is designed for a production, the theatre house curtain may or may not be used. Sometimes the house curtain is kept lowered until twenty or thirty minutes before the performance starts, then it is raised to reveal the show curtain. The house curtain may also come in at the end of the play. Often, instead of using the house curtain, the show curtain is utilized throughout the play, and is raised and lowered at the beginning and end of each act or scene. While a single show curtain is standard for most productions, some productions employ a different show curtain for each act. However, this tends to be rare simply because of space and budget constraints.

Kinds of Show Curtains

We think of the traditional show curtain as a soft scenic piece that flies in

and out, but on more imaginative and theatrical productions that is not always the case. Show curtains may range from simple painted drops to very detailed drops with elaborate painting and/or applied mirrored discs, overscale sequins, three-dimensional fringe, and other decorative motifs. Usually what makes a show curtain simple or complex is the material(s) it is made of and the method used to move it off and on stage. The following examples indicate something of the range of the practical design and basic construction of show curtains.

1. A painted drop of muslin with horizontal seams, made to fly in or out. Top: webbing, grommets, and tie lines. Bottom 2½-inch hem for pipe (with or without skirt in front). Sides: 2-inch hems.
2. A painted sharkstooth scrim (or other gauze) drop made to fly in and out. Top: webbing, grommets, and tie lines. Bottom: 2½-inch hem for pipe. Sides: 2-inch hems.
3. A two-piece curtain of fabric (with or without fullness) moving off left and off right on two traveler tracks and having a 2-foot overlap of fabric when the curtains are closed. Top: webbing, grommets, and tie lines. Bottom: 2½-inch hem for chains. Sides: 2-inch hems.
4. A painted muslin or canvas olio drop which rolls up from the bottom on a horizontal round metal tube. In the theatre the olio drop is used between scenes when a specialty act is performed downstage and the upstage set is being changed. Often this drop has

a painted romantic setting in its main or center portion, and this central design is surrounded by painted old-fashioned advertisements in various styles of lettering. This drop may be suitably used as a show curtain or main curtain.

One of the most reliable ways of creating the effect of a roller drop does not involve using an attached roller, which is often unreliable. Instead, plan on flying the drop out from the bottom with the bottom batten rigged to fly out upstage of the drop's top pipe. To do this, deadtie the backdrop at the top and use a full sandwich batten across the bottom. Rig the bottom sandwich batten to fly out while at the same time having a long unattached roller turning and weighting down on the fabric drop as it flies up via the bottom batten. In side view the backdrop (when the bottom of the backdrop is flying out upstage) looks like a tall U, and the horizontal roller inside appears as a circle in the bottom curve of the U.

5. A one-piece drop of filled scrim going offstage left or right on a one-way traveler track. Top: webbing, grommets, and tie lines. Bottom: 2½-inch hem for chain. Sides: 2-inch hems.
6. A series of hanging panels (three, four, five) which are rigged to fly in and out independently or also together as a unit. These may be soft hanging panels that overlap each other, or they may be framed. Other hanging panels may be slatted structures or lengths of bamboo, arranged horizontally or vertically and backed with scrim or gauze.

Show curtain design by William and Jean
    Eckart
THE GOLDEN APPLE
Written by John Latouche
Music by Jerome Moross
Directed by Norman Lloyd
Choreography and musical numbers staged by
    Hanya Holm
Phoenix and Alvin Theatres, New York (1954)

Scrim front cloth design by Tony Walton
VALMOUTH by Sandy Wilson
Saville Theatre, London (1958)
York Theatre, New York (1960)

Show curtain design by John Scheffler
DRACULA by Hamilton Deane and John L.
    Balderson
Directed by William Prosser
Brooklyn College, Brooklyn, New York (1985)

Show curtain design by Karl Eigsti
AMEN CORNER
Book by Philip Rose and Peter Udell
Based on the play by James Baldwin
Music by Garry Sherman
Lyrics by Peter Udell
Directed by Philip Rose
Nederlander Theatre, New York (1983)

Show curtain design by Clarke Dunham
MADAMA BUTTERFLY by Giacomo Puccini
Libretto by Luigi Illica and Giuseppe Giacosa
Directed by Harold Prince
Lighting by Ken Billington
Lyric Opera of Chicago
Chicago, Illinois (1982)

Show curtain design by Robert O'Hearn
ANNIE GET YOUR GUN
Music and lyrics by Irving Berlin
Book by Dorothy Fields
Directed by Robert Johanson
Paper Mill Playhouse
Millburn, New Jersey (1987)

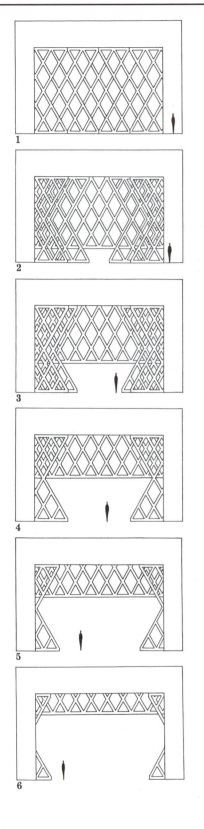

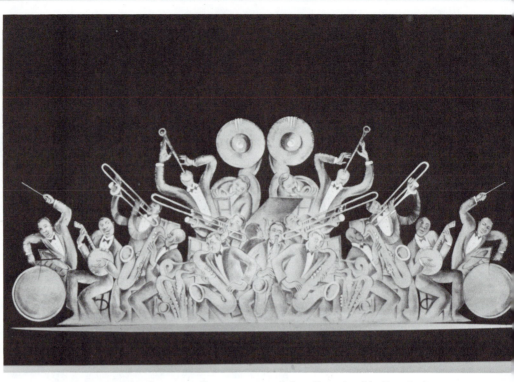

Above: "In-One" drop by Tony Walton
SOPHISTICATED LADIES
Directed by Michael Smuin
National Tour

Below: "Lace drop" by Tony Straiges
INTO THE WOODS
Directed by James Lapine
Martin Beck Theatre, New York (1987)
(Photograph by Ney Tait Fraser)

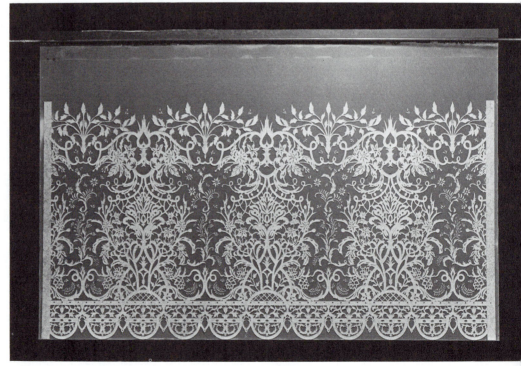

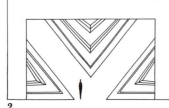

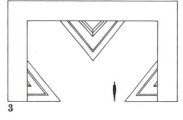

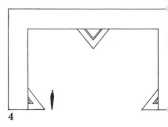

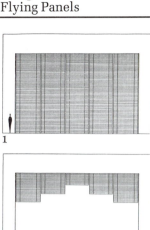

1

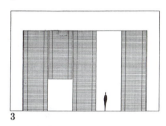

2

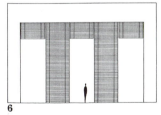

3

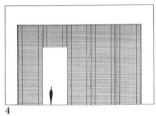

4

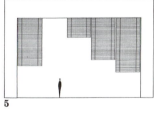

5

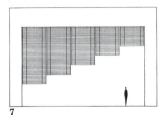

6

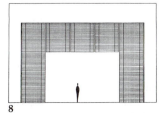

7

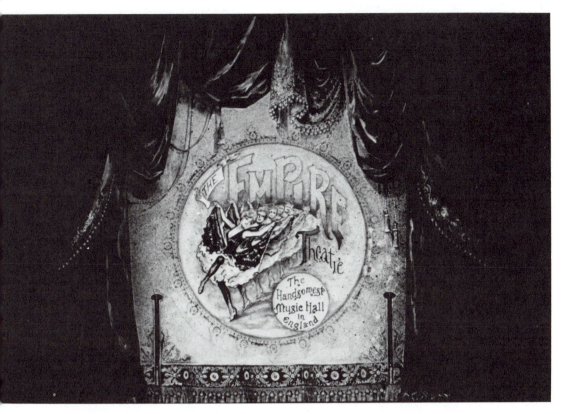

8

Paint elevations by Douglas W. Schmidt
CHAPLIN
Directed by Michael Smuin
Dorothy Chandler Pavilion
Los Angeles, California (1983)

1. Empire Music Hall drop (sharkstooth scrim), 48'–0" wide by 32'–0" high.
2. American vaudeville drop (muslin with sharkstooth scrim panel inset), 48'–0" wide by 32'–0" high.

7. A painted muslin or canvas drop stapled onto a wooden framed unit like a series of regular flats that has practical doors or windows. In essence this is a framed hanger unit. Top: hardware for hanging and flying in and out. Bottom: rubber strips on edges to lessen the noise when flying in. Position jacks on the back of the framed unit with stage weights added for support after flying the framed unit in. Also put stiffeners on the back.

8. A framed unit that breaks away in several parts can also be effective as a show curtain. For example, there may be three flat framed pie-shaped pieces with all three onstage points of each unit positioned on the floor to meet on the center line when it is in place as one unit. When it opens, two pie-shaped framed units track off left and right, with the third pie-shaped framed piece flying out overhead.

Using Pipe in the Bottom of Show Curtains

For show curtains made of sharkstooth scrim, filled scrim, muslin, or other similar materials, a ¾-inch I.D. pipe may be used in a bottom hem. The purpose of the pipe is to give the drop proper weight and to create a long, unbroken line at the bottom of the show curtain. The pipe may go into a 2- or 2½-inch hem. If management is also paying for the pipe, then it should always be listed on the drawing for the show curtain so its cost can be estimated for bids.

The pocket may have a skirt in front which is slightly wider than the finished hem by ½ to ¾ inch. The purpose of this skirt is to cover any space between the bottom of the pipe and the stage due to an irregular stage floor.

Naturally, not every drop need have a skirt. This decision is up to the designer. Often the best visual results are obtained by having only a simple, 2-inch hem (or pocket) lined with canvas or muslin for a pipe to go into. This method, especially if working with a scrim or gauze, will give the least amount of opaque line on the bottom. Some designers do not prefer skirts and would rather have nothing except the hem with pipe.

Checklist of Subjects for Show Curtains

Painted drapery with a grand drape and side curtains	A patchwork quilt
Oversize painting of several main characters	A scrumptious arrangement of Austrian drapery
American, British, French, or other national flag	Logos of the show's title
A picturesque period map	Abstract painting or textures
An English landscape	A framed exterior scene similar to a Currier and Ives
A motif of ancient scrolls and symbols	A collection of French posters
A brooding sky and seascape	Cityscape design of tiny lighted bulbs
An English street in sharp perspective	A flowering jungle or forest design of exotic plants
Overscale faces of playing cards	Many styles of signs outlined in small lights
A collage of musical instruments	Comic cartoon scenes or other zany pictures
A bird's-eye view of a town	Neon signs
Simple, straight panels of fabric	Lacy valentines
Painted facades	A flower collage
	Overscale post cards
	Bamboo panels

Left: Show curtain by Edward Gorey for GOREY STORIES (1978).
Right: A ballet design by Rouben Ter-Arutunian was created by threading gold Mylar strips through black scenic netting.

The Black Backup Drop

The black backup drop is positioned behind a sharkstooth scrim drop, a linen scrim drop, a painted muslin drop, or a backdrop of similar materials, and stops light behind from showing through. The black backup drop may be positioned 6 inches upstage of the backdrop and should be the same size (or close to it) as the backdrop playing in front of it.

A black drop may be made of velour, duvetyne, or any other black fabric heavy enough to be practical. The backup drop usually flies out a few moments before the backdrop in front of it (getting out in time for a light bleed through the scrim or before the front backdrop is to fly out). As a safety precaution to keep the black drop from swinging and hitting a show curtain, it also sometimes has cable guides on each end.

Making a Drawing for a Black Backup Drop

Because of the lack of any detail work, the drawing for a black backup drop may be put on the sheet of drafting with the other pieces of soft scenery. As mentioned in the chapter on drawing, soft scenery is usually drawn in ¼-inch scale. Do the following:

1. Draw the rectangle (or other shape) in ¼-inch scale.
2. Draw a vertical center line.
3. Put on the overall (finished size) dimension of the width.
4. Put on the overall (finished size) height dimension.
5. Tell the kind of material it is to be made of.
6. In either the center of the actual drawing, above, or below the drawing, list these notes:

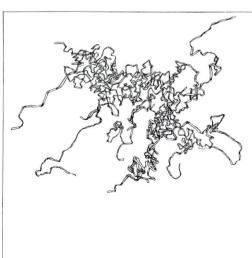

Top: webbing, grommets, and tie lines.

Bottom: 3-inch hem (with skirt) for wooden batten. Or a hem for chain may also be used.

Sides: 2-inch hems. Or webbing may be attached to the sides and have rings attached which work on a stretched cable on each side to guide the drop nicely as it comes in and out and also keep the drop taut. These may be Clancy No. 70 Lignum Vitae guides spaced 24 inches on centers for the entire height. Other guides may also be used.

If you do plan to have a skirt in front of the hem or pocket containing the batten, always make sure that the lining on the back of the black fabric is black and not natural canvas, muslin, or some other light-colored cloth. This is essential because a light lining can be obvious when the skirt flaps while the black backup drop flies in or out. A light lining can simply sabotage the purpose of a black backup drop.

Making a Drawing of a Soft Border

Since the average masking soft border has no painted or other detailed work on it, the drawings are usually done in ¼-inch scale. The drawings for all soft scenery are usually made in this small scale and are grouped on one large

Stage design by Robert Perdziola
LA FEDELTA PREMIATA by Franz Joseph Haydn
Directed by Lou Galterio
Manhattan School of Music, New York (1988)

"This Haydn opera was done with painted cut drops, wings and borders, and in one scene, a pallet of sheep." —Robert Perdziola

sheet labeled "Soft Scenery" in the title block. An example of a border size might be 54'-0" wide by 6'-0" high. In ¼-inch scale, the actual size of the drawing for this border would be 13½ inches wide by 1½ inches high.

When making the drawing for a soft border, use these steps:

1. Draw the perimeter of the finished border.
2. Draw the vertical center line through this horizontal piece of scenery.
3. Draw and label the dimensions for the overall finished length.
4. Do the same for the total height of the border.
5. Tell what kind of fabric it is to be: Granada cloth, velour, canvas, or other.
6. Specify no fullness (unless otherwise desired).
7. Put this information on the drawing, positioning it either in the center of the actual drawing or above or below it:

Top: webbing, grommet, and tie lines.

Bottom: 2-inch hem for ½-inch I.D. pipe. Provide pipe.

Sides: 2-inch hem.

Using a Pipe in the Bottom of a Soft Border

Soft (unframed) borders may be used with or without fullness. More often, however, a flat, stretched-out border with a straight bottom looks best. It is necessary to add weight in the bottom of the border to create a nice straight line. For instance, a black Granada cloth border may have a 2-inch hem in the bottom for putting in a ½-inch I.D. pipe.

Using Filled Scrim for Show Curtains, Backdrops, and Cycloramas

Although filled scrim is considered expensive, it is an excellent fabric for show curtains, backdrops, and cycloramas. Filled scrim takes detailed painting extremely well, hangs beautifully, and takes stage lighting nicely. Wrinkles from folding, storage, and travel stretch out easily.

Because drops are repeatedly taken down and put up when touring, filled scrim is by far the best fabric to use. If muslin or canvas drops are folded and unfolded, the wrinkles seldom all disappear under stage lighting in the theatre. While the problem of folding may be resolved by rolling the canvas or muslin drop on a batten, scenery trucks usually cannot accommodate the very long length.

If a large filled scrim cyclorama has been designed to be of considerable height, say, 40'-0" high, the first piece of fabric may be 28'-0" to 29'-0" high, meaning a part of another width must be added to finish out the top of the cyclorama. While the scenic studio or drapery house may save some money by adding a piece that might be on hand rather than cutting into the same new piece of fabric, this added piece may take the paint differently when using aniline dyes. Therefore, it is wise to specify with a note on the paint elevations, "Make whole cyc out of same piece of filled scrim." It is always better to have a quality cyclorama, even if the price is somewhat higher, than to have an obvious horizontal width across the top that looks different onstage, a problem very little or nothing can be done to resolve. If filled scrim is too expensive, then it would be better to select another fabric and have a quality cyclorama.

OTHER SOFT SCENERY

Supporting Design Motifs with Full-Stage Scenic Netting

Scenic netting in 1-inch squares has long been a favorite choice for a see-through supporting material. It may be used in its natural color or be dyed. All sorts of flat painted designs can be cut out and glued onto the face of the scenic netting. Or actual lengths of other material can be woven in and cut out of the netting. For the ballet, Rouben Ter-Arutunian made beautiful use of lengths of gauze bandage to form patterns through the netting. He has also used strips of Mylar to create interesting patterns against scenic netting. In his production of *The Sleeping Beauty* ballet at the Metropolitan Opera, Oliver Messel specified scenic netting as a background support for the vine hanging drops.

Sewing a Tear in Sharkstooth Scrim

One of the most frustrating things that can happen to scenery is a tear in a sharkstooth scrim. While enormous care should always be taken to keep this from happening, there are times when it cannot be prevented.

The best method of repair depends on the shape of the tear. While tears can be any size or shape, they can be grouped into these general types: (1) straight, (2) angled, and (3) irregular. When repairing any of these, a basic hand stitch should be used.

Assume that an angled tear is being repaired. First temporarily sew the corner of the torn piece in place. Then, with either clear nylon or regular sewing thread, begin at the corner and use a continuous parallel stitch across the tear. This stitch is similar in pattern to a vertical Greek key pattern. The stitches should never be pulled too tight. Keep an even tension so the fabric will not pucker along the stitch line. The basic idea in the repair is to follow the natural weave of the scrim as much as possible.

Attaching Scrim on Frames with Velcro

Sharkstooth scrim can be easily attached to wooden or metal frames with Velcro. This is especially helpful in keeping the scrim fabric from being torn during travel and storage. Also, the same idea can be used during actual performance when a panel or flat is stored and there is time to put the scrim on and take it off. Simply machine sew the Velcro strip (male hook or female loop) onto the outer edges of the scrim after first hemming the edges. Then glue the opposite Velcro strip to a metal or wooden framework. The use of Velcro on scrim pieces is also ideal for banners, signs, and curtains. In addition to scrim, Velcro strips are excellent for attaching other lightweight materials for a quick change during performance or even to hold the material in place during the run of the show.

Repairing a Tear in Canvas

The damage that tends to occur most often to canvas backdrops and flats is straight and angled tears. These tears are usually repaired by one of two methods: (1) hand sewing from the

---

Soft Scenery and Drapery for Small Stages (Opening: 24'–0" Wide by 17'–9" High)

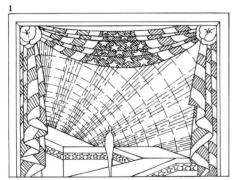
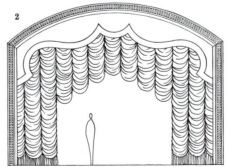

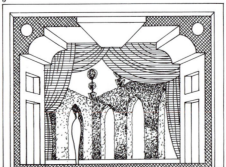
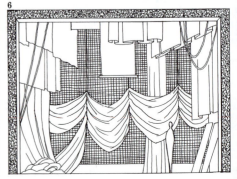

front and back, or (2) gluing a canvas patch on the tear.

Before sewing any tear, the torn piece must be loosely basted to the main piece at reasonable intervals along the break. This is to hold the fabric in place to ensure a well-tailored restoration. For an angled tear, begin by using the needle and thread to tack the torn corner to the main piece of canvas. For a straight tear, begin by tacking along the line of the tear at reasonable intervals. For example, a straight tear that is 2 feet long should be tacked every 3 or 4 inches.

Begin sewing an angled tear at the corner, working away from the tack stitch. For a straight tear, sewing can begin at either end. The best stitch for sewing canvas tears is a swirling figure eight. Move the needle in and out across the tear. Be careful not to sew too tightly so that the fabric stays smooth and flat after the sewing.

A small tear can be readily repaired with a patch glued on the back of the canvas behind the tear. If the edges of the tear are ragged, they may need to be smoothed out before gluing. If the canvas is hanging, hold a block of wood on the opposite side of the patch to steady the surface as you press the patch against it. For the patch, try to find a piece of canvas that is already sized rather than a new piece. If possible, paint the canvas patch with the same color(s) as the main piece before gluing it on.

Ways Perspective Backdrops Are Used

There are several approaches to using perspective backdrops. These may be:

1. *As a scenic unit alone.* Perspective backdrops are often used by themselves on the stage without other scenic pieces except for offstage masking positioned above and on both sides. A backdrop may take the form of a show curtain downstage, in which the subject matter can be one of an almost endless variety, or it may work far upstage and be a perspective motif for a musical, a ballet, or a revue.

2. *As a backdrop outside a box set.* One of the most common uses of the perspective backdrop is to position it outside the doors and windows of a standard box set. Examples of such backdrops might be a view of the Golden Gate Bridge, a row of tenement houses, or a stone wall with trees. For windows it is good to have at least 3 or 4 feet of space between the set and the drop, and even more if it is behind a door where entrances must be made.

3. *As a backdrop behind and above a cutaway set.* A backdrop may be a bird's-eye perspective view of a group of houses or buildings, placed far upstage of an interior or exterior set that is designed to be cut away at the top. It may also be an ordinary view of a city skyline, or something as diverse

as a group of overscale icons or totem poles or masks.

4. *As an extension of a built set.* A backdrop in perspective is wonderful to use upstage of a built set. This is especially effective with a very shallow set like one with 10 to 12 feet of depth, which can be made to appear deeper with the aid of a very well made perspective design. The perspective drop may be drawn and painted as part of the same room or exterior set, or it may be conceived as a different portion of the structure or even another building.

5. *As a backdrop behind cutout units.* A perspective drop can be enhanced by the use of one, two, three, or four full-stage cutout units positioned downstage of it. These pieces of scenery may be about 5 feet or so apart from each other and may be soft cut drops (with or without the benefit of netting or other open materials) or framed cutout hangers. Of course, for smaller stages the depth between the units would be less. Enormous visual variation can be obtained with lighting instruments positioned on the drop and also in between the different units of full-stage scenery.

6. *As a backdrop behind three-dimensional furniture and props.* Often an exciting and original setting can be created by positioning a nice arrangement of furniture on stage and designing an interesting perspective backdrop to hang upstage of it. This can also work quite effectively when the

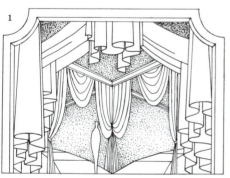

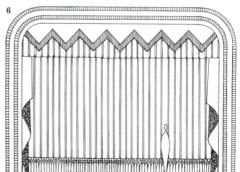

Backdrop Design by James Stewart Morcom for Radio City Music Hall, New York
(Photograph by James Stewart Morcom)

Bass Fiddle Three-Part Drop by Kenneth Foy for OH, KAY! (1990), Richard Rodgers Theatre, New York

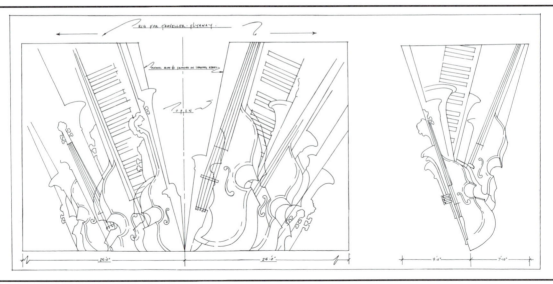

Charles E. McCarry's Act Curtain Painted on Sharkstooth Scrim for GUYS AND DOLLS,
Indiana Repertory Theatre, Indianapolis, Indiana (1989) (Photograph by Charles E. McCarry)

David Mitchell's Backdrop (58'–0″ Wide by 25'–0″ High) for I REMEMBER MAMA (1979), Majestic Theatre, New York (Photograph by David Mitchell)

Oliver Messel's Openwork No. 3 Creeper Drop (60'–0″ Wide by 40'–0″ High) for THE SLEEPING BEAUTY (1976); Three-Dimensional Appliqué on 1-inch Scenic Netting (Photograph by Lynn Pecktal)

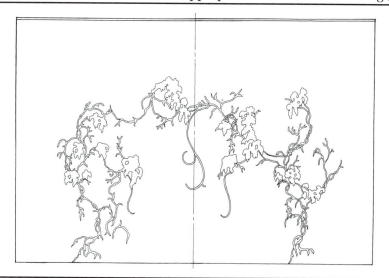

Cut Sky Drop with City Building Silhouettes

New Orleans Backdrop Design with Several Vanishing Points for Creating the Perspective Drawing

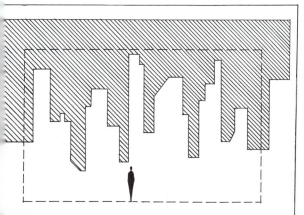

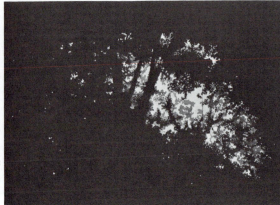

Above: Backdrop design by Ben Edwards
MORE STATELY MANSIONS by Eugene
  O'Neill
Directed by José Quintero
Broadhurst Theatre, New York (1967)

Left: Backdrop design by Ben Edwards
THE TIME OF THE CUCKOO by Arthur
  Laurents
Directed by Harold Clurman
Empire Theatre, New York (1952)

The sketch was cut into two pieces so more
than one scenic artist could work on the backdrop at the same time.
(Photographs by Lynn Pecktal)

Stage design by Lester Polakov
CALL ME MISTER

Music and lyrics by Harold Rome
Directed by Robert H. Gordon
Dances by John Wray

National Theatre, New York (1946)
(Photograph by Lester Polakov)

Backdrop design by Jo Mielziner
THE KING AND I
Music by Richard Rodgers

Book and lyrics by Oscar Hammerstein II
Based on the novel *Anna and the King of Siam*
  by Margaret Landon

Directed by John Van Druten
St. James Theatre, New York (1951)
(Photograph by Peter A. Juley and Son)

Model by George Tsypin
LANDSCAPE OF THE BODY by John Guare

Directed by Robert Falls
Goodman Theatre

Chicago, Illinois (1988)
(Photograph by George Tsypin)

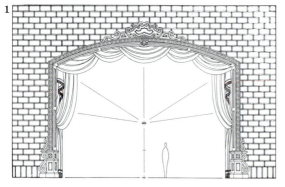

1

2

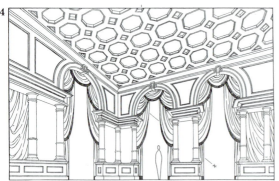

3

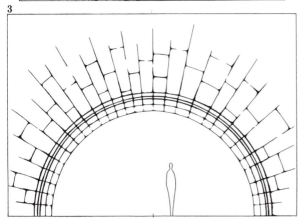

4

5

Above:
Pub cut drop painted on white velour for Oliver Smith, MY FAIR LADY (1976) revival. (Photograph by Lynn Pecktal)

Below:
Oliver Smith's foliage cut leg drop (60'–0" wide by 40'–0" high) for GISELLE (1968), American Ballet Theatre. It was painted on linen with casein paints and aniline dyes. (Photograph by Arnold Abramson)

Sketch and cobweb drawing by Peter Harvey
A MIDSUMMER NIGHT'S DREAM Ballet by
    Mendelssohn

Choreographed by George Balanchine
Zurich Opera House
Zurich, Switzerland (1979)

Bottom, left and right:
Oliver Messel's painted linen cut drop for THE
SLEEPING BEAUTY (1976), shown before cut-
ting and netting. (Photographs by Lynn Pecktal)

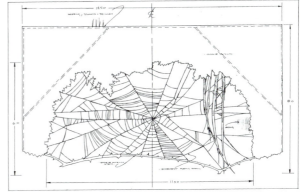

Peter Larkin's Longbourne Header and Legs for FIRST IMPRESSIONS (1959), Alvin Theatre, New York
(Photograph by Lynn Pecktal)

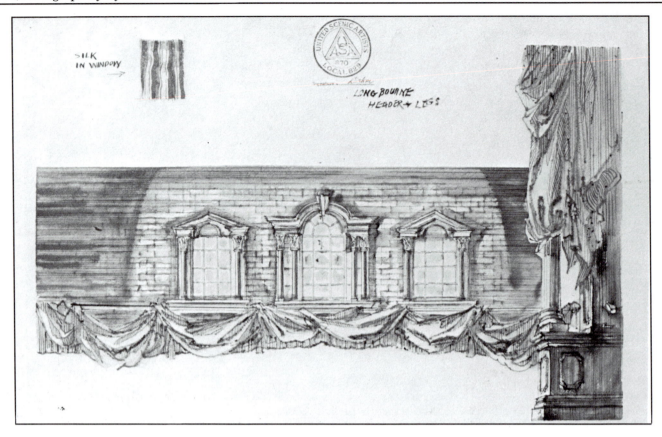

Wings by Charles E. McCarry for GUYS AND
DOLLS (1989), Indiana Repertory Theatre

Boris Aronson's Velour Legs/Border (Details),
THE NUTCRACKER (1976), ABT

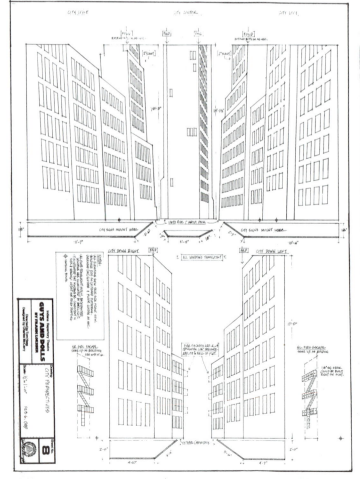

1. Unframed Border with Framed Legs; 2. Unframed Border with Framed Legs; 3. Unframed Border with Unframed Legs

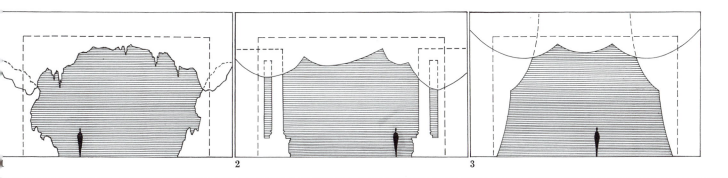

Unframed Canvas Borders with and without 1-inch Scenic Netting behind for Support

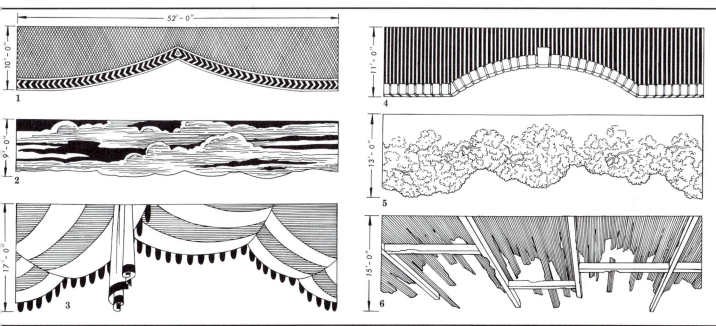

Painted Foliage Border with Scenic Netting behind and Painted Drapery Borders without Netting

Leg for Oliver Messel's THE SLEEPING BEAUTY (1976)

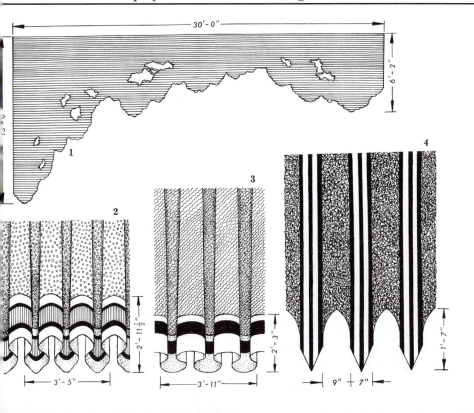

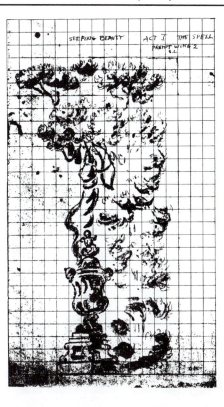

furniture is put on a raked platform which may run partway or entirely across the stage.

Creating a Backdrop of Vertical Streamers

An interesting openwork backdrop can be created by hanging vertical streamers from a suspended batten. This not only is an easy way to add a bit of variety to a show, but is a good practical choice of a scenic unit when actors, dancers, or singers move in and through the open hanging pieces. A backdrop of vertical streamers is especially effective for musical comedies and revues.

The vertical streamers may be cut out of paper, fabric, or plastic. Make them 2 inches wide with a 1- or 2-inch space in between. While these pieces can be stapled directly onto a wooden batten, they should be attached to a length of webbing that has tie lines and grommets, especially if the openwork backdrop is going to be used several times. The streamers may be the same color or alternating colors. One attractive pattern is to have four streamers of one color, then alternate with four streamers of another color, and so on. There are many combinations that can be created. A nice rippling movement can be added to the colorful effect of the streamers onstage by using an electric fan in the wings. When it is desired to keep the bottom of the streamers in place, they can be individually hemmed and have a long thin pipe inserted in the bottom hem of all the streamers.

CUT DROPS

Using a Cut Drop

A cut drop is just what the name implies: a drop that is cut with an opening or openings. It may also have one or more cut outer profile edges rather than straight edges like a regular backdrop.

The main advantages of a cut drop are: (1) The cut drop can cover a large area without any noticeable seams showing, such as in a hard covered unit; (2) it is lightweight; (3) it folds easily for storage and travel, and, of course, (4) it is ideal for touring productions.

Using Multiple Cut Drops

While only one cut drop may be used in a stage setting for one production, in another production an entire setting may consist completely of cut drops. Multiple cut drops positioned in front of one another can give a lovely illusion of a three-dimensional setting. Depending on the depth of the stage and the intended effect, two, three, four, or five cut drops may be positioned parallel to each other (and also parallel to the proscenium opening), with a full-size backdrop placed upstage of the last cut drop. Again, according to the depth of the stage, the cut drops may be 4, 5, 6, or 7 feet apart.

This approach to designing multisets is excellent for ballets, musicals, revues, and all sorts of dance productions because of the open and unobstructed playing space it affords, the easy folding of the cut drops for

storage and travel, and the fast setup in the theatre.

All sorts of subjects are appropriate for cut drop settings. Cut drops are designed to be caverns and caves, rustic beamed structures with randomly placed planks, geometric abstract shapes, tents with varied fabric flaps and panels, jagged oriental trees and foliage, heavy baroque drapery swags and jabots, and architectural structures in a state of ruin and disrepair. When doing cut drops, you might want to design them with straight head-on views, or you might wish to create them to be in very sharp perspective.

Decide early on whether you want the setting of cut drops to be asymmetrical or not. Also determine whether a support background such as 1-inch scenic netting (or other netting) is necessary to hold any cutout edges that fall back or curl backward, so the fabric will remain on a nice vertical plane.

One of the great things about making a series of cut drops in a model is that you can remove and stack each piece on top of the other in order to see the overall visual effect. Looking at a stack of four or five cut drops from the model is an excellent way to see the contrast in shape, color, texture, and detail. You may decide to vary each cut drop considerably in appearance so the designs do not become monotonous or uninteresting.

Cutting Openings in Lightweight Hanging Panels

While hanging panels without openings can work extremely well, even more stylish effects can often be achieved when openings are cut out in the lightweight fabric. Openings may range from random-size circles spaced in a random manner to various shapes such as angled lemon shapes with the curve at the bottom.

The latter tend to distort the basic hanging shape of the lightweight fabric, but that is usually the intent when they are used. Other openings of various sizes may be designed to work well with blowing electric fans. For example, shapes like a large U may be quite

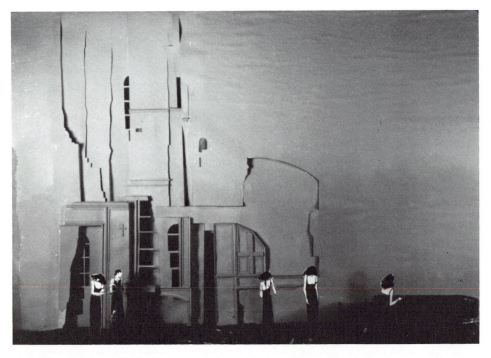

Model by George Tsypin
A SEAGULL by Anton Chekhov
Directed by Peter Sellars
Eisenhower Theatre
Kennedy Center
Washington, D.C. (1985)

Using Lightweight Hanging Fabric Panels

Lightweight fabric panels hanging on a batten and suspended from above make an effective set for dance or ballet. The fabric may be gauze, chiffon, organza, muslin, polyester, or other similar materials. The positioning of the panels is important. In general, two kinds of arrangements are possible.

The first kind is informal, whereby there is space between the panels (which might be from 6 to 8 feet in width), possibly 2 feet between each panel. In addition, the bottom of the panels may be around 1 foot 6 inches to 2 feet off the floor and the same kind of open spacing may be used above the panels, with about 2 feet of space above the top of the batten to the bottom of the header or border.

The second kind of positioning is a more traditional approach, whereby the individual panels overlap each other vertically, with the last panels on each side going off into the masking legs, both on the left and right sides. The tops above may also go out of sight lines and the bottoms of the panels may touch the floor.

Either of these arrangements may be enhanced by using large electric fans on each side of the wings to create movement in the panels. This is especially effective for the first type of arrangement because the bottoms of the panels can be given more movement from the electric fans.

While panels on one hanging pipe can be quite appropriate, interest may be added by positioning one or more pipe battens of hanging panels parallel to and upstage of the first one.

DRAPERY AND DRAPERY ACCESSORIES

Supporting Lightweight Drapery

For lightweight fabrics such as scrim, gauze, chiffon, China silk, and netting, pieces of Velcro (male hook and female loop) are excellent for attaching arrangements of swags, jabots, ruffles, puff or balloon curtains to a surface. For example, you may have:

1. Gathered gauze swags running up a stair railing in a home.
2. Bunting bordering under the ceiling of a saloon.
3. Chiffon curtains gathered over the metal framework of a bed in a castle.
4. China silk swags and jabots on the window valances of a drawing room.
5. Gathered curtains of netting in a disco hanging on arbitrary battens from the ceiling.

Drapery Designs for Windows, Arches, Halls, and Other Settings

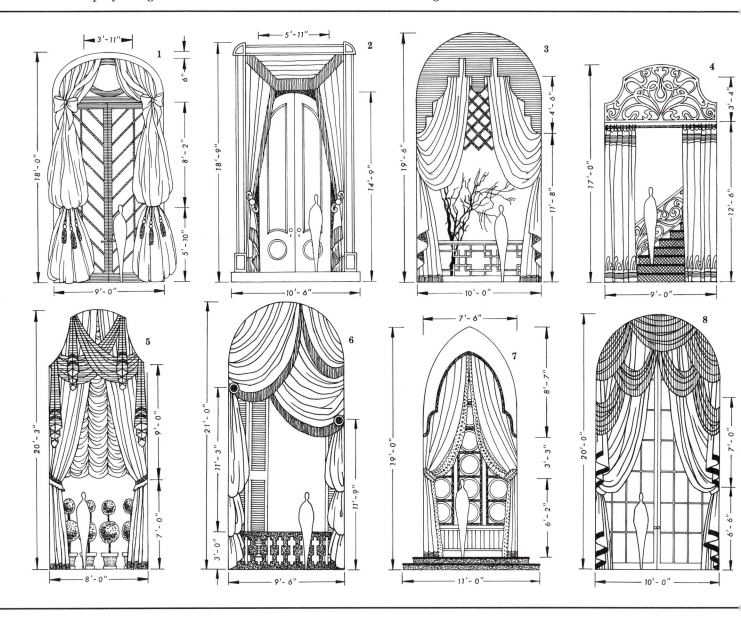

Painted Portal with Painted Draperies

Theatre Box Draperies

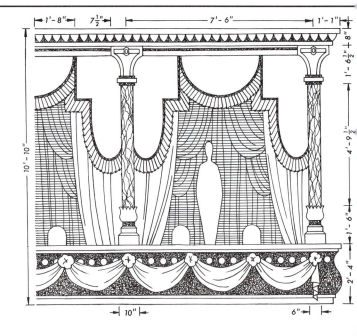

Drapery Jabots, Ends, and Tails

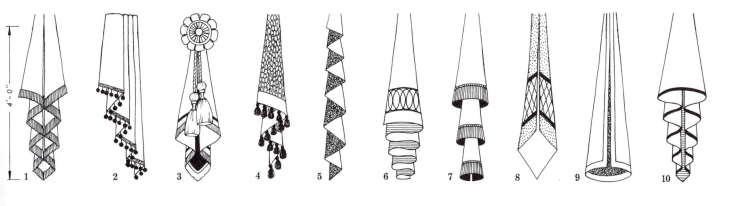

Creating Drapery Swags, Jabots, Ends, and Variations

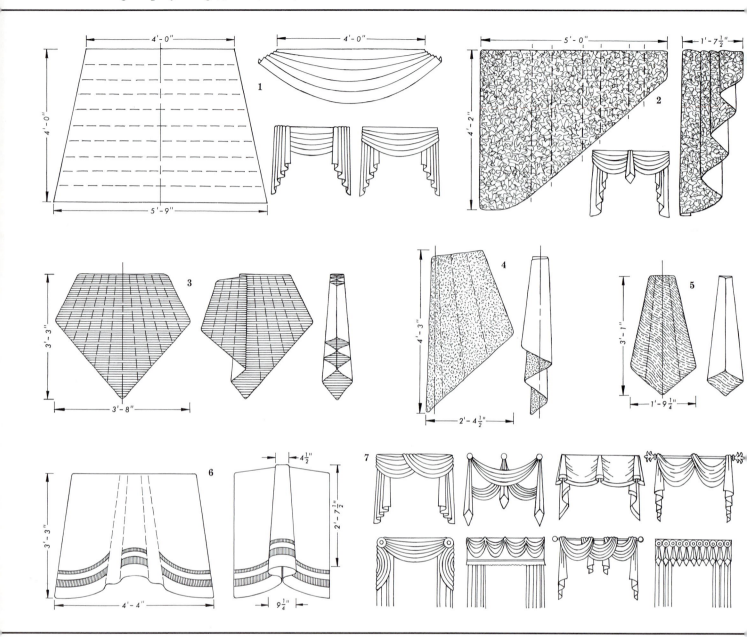

Tassels for Window Draperies and for Full-Stage Drapery Sets

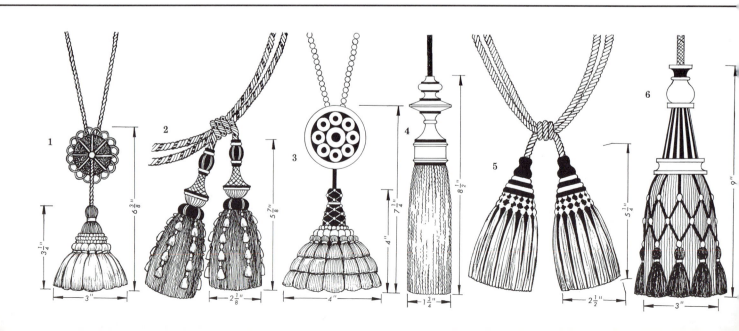

Continuous Fringe and Tassel Trim for Draperies and Show Curtains

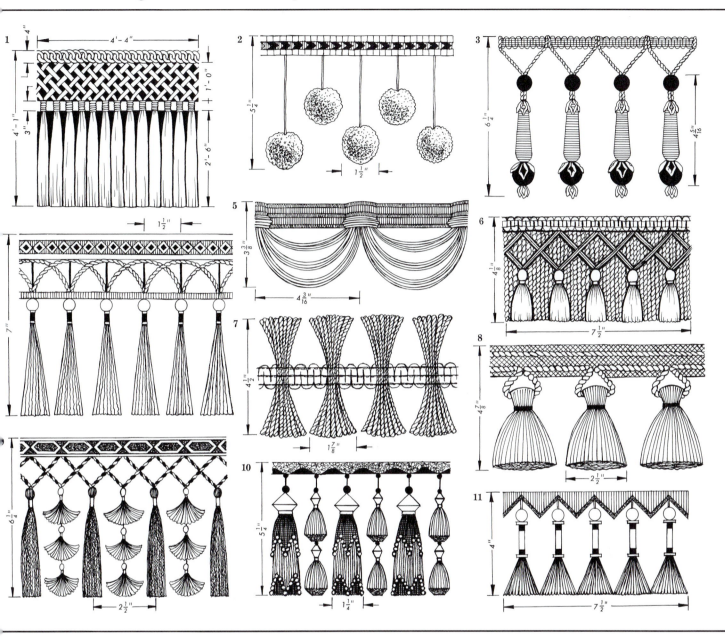

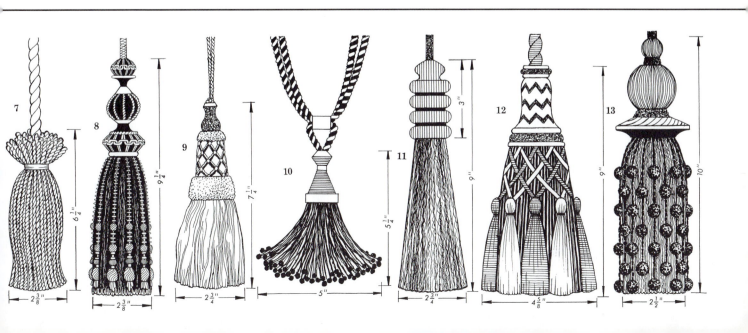

Stage designs by James Stewart Morcom
FIVE KINGS by Orson Welles
An adaptation of Shakespeare's chronicle
  plays
Directed by Orson Welles, Colonial Theatre
Boston, Massachusetts (1939)

As mentioned previously, Velcro is also great to use on items that must come apart during the action or come off and store during a run.

Door or bed canopies may be formed first with metal pipes over which rabbit wire or forming cloth may be attached with lengths of flexible wire to make the lightweight draperies retain their overall shape.

Profile Work on the Outer Edges of the Drapery

While the drawing of the profile of the outer edge of draperies is extremely important, often it is taken for granted and is done without sufficient concentration and skill.

Profile work on painted canvas draperies (borders above and legs on the side) should always be worked out on the ½-inch scale drawings. When there is more than one set in a show, the different sets of legs and borders should be viewed by putting the profile drawings together as a group and looking at them.

This can be accomplished by making the individual drawings on separate sheets of tracing paper and putting them on top of each other for study. Then, when you are satisfied that all the different profiles work together as a unit, record them as such.

Using Small Lights around Drapery Portals

When it is appropriate for the production, a highly theatrical effect can be achieved by using small electric lights along the outer edges of an arrangement of drapery portals. This can pro-

vide a stunning effect for musicals or revues, particularly when the tiny lights are kept unlit until the last few moments of a finale or end of a musical scene.

These tiny lights may be attached around the edges of painted draperies on unframed flat hung fabrics such as muslin, canvas, or linen; around the outside of real gathered draperies; on real fabric draperies positioned inside the opening of a hard portal; or around a series of flat profiled draperies designed to be cut out of ¼-inch plywood covered in muslin, then painted.

Making a Drawing for a Drapery Border and Legs

A drawing should be made of each set of the cut drapery border and cut legs unless, of course, the drawings are to be duplicated for the rest of the units; if that is the case, a note saying this would be enough. You may have to make three, four, or five separate drawings, depending on how many sets of cut borders and legs you have designed.

Suppose you are designing a cut drapery border with two cut drapery legs, all to play onstage behind a portal opening 36'-0" wide by 22'-0" high. Assume that the three cut drapery pieces hang on the same pipe 2'-0" upstage of the portal opening. This means the overall size of the cut border and cut legs should be 44'-0" wide by 26'-0" high.

Front Elevation Using these dimensions and working in ½-inch scale, do the following:

1. Draw the base line in the lower portion of the tracing paper.
2. Next, construct a vertical center line through the base line and extend it upward to the top.
3. Working from each side of the center line, measure off and pencil in the rectangular perimeter so it measures 44'-0" wide by 26'-0" high.
4. Draw the border you have designed at the top and label the overall dimensions: 44'-0" wide by 8'-10" high.
5. Draw the SL leg and label the overall design: 12'-6" wide by 26'-0" high.
6. Do the same for the SR leg: 14'-8" wide by 26'-0" high.
7. Then make a note on the drawing saying what material the border and legs are made of: Border and legs are painted canvas. Canvas to have horizontal seams. Other fabrics, such as muslin, velour, or linen, may be used as well.
8. Put a reference number on each cut drop piece (for example, 28, 29, and 30).
9. Then indicate by notes on the drawing what happens to each edge:

Cut border

Top: Webbing, grommets, and tie lines.

Bottom: Allow 1½ inches of canvas on the bottom of the painted drapery and then cut slits according to the shape of the curve so the fabric can be glued back with white glue.

Sides: 2-inch hems.

Cut legs

Tops: Webbing, grommets, and tie lines.

Bottoms: Hems for chain. (May also be for pipes; may also have canvas skirt in front.)

Onstage edges: Allow 1½ inches of painted drapery and then cut slits the same as the bottom of the border so the edges can be glued back.

Sides: 2-inch hems.

There are variations in design that may involve other notes. For example, in other designs the border and legs might hang on two pipes; the border may be made wider or the legs higher for extending the shapes in different theatres as well as the reverse for compressing the drapery design for smaller theatres.

If you are compressing or expanding the cut border (made in two pieces with a center overlap) with the two side legs that are to vary in height according to the specific theatre, make a drawing to show how the compressed or expanded units are to play. This lets the production carpenter (and others) know the position for lighting, and whether extra pipe, hardware, or whatever is needed. Notes would also be necessary if you need 1-inch scenic netting or gauze to support and ensure that the cut pieces hang OK, if applied trim such as sequins or special finishes is desired, if the backs of the cut pieces are to be opaqued with flexible latex paint, if random twinkle lights are to be added, or if any other items may vary from the norm.

Ornament drawing made with charcoal on brown paper for a sharkstooth scrim show curtain. (Photograph by Arnold Abramson)

Making a Drawing of Real Drapery in a Framed Portal

A drawing should be made for each portal with drapery unless, of course, all the portals are to be treated identically.

Assume for discussion that you are designing a framed canvas portal that is one piece measuring overall 44'-0" wide by 27'-0" high. The portal opening is 34'-0" wide by 22'-0" high with a 6-inch thickness. There are four pieces of drapery in fullness: two large swags, each of varying sizes, and two legs, also of different sizes. The fullness for the drapery is 100 percent. There is no lining. The point is to show on the drawing how these four pieces of drapery are to be constructed to fit behind the portal and to give the necessary dimensions.

Allow the drapery in fullness to extend 1'-3" past all three edges of the portal opening so that the drapery will cover the opening sufficiently.

Front Elevation When doing the front elevation, use these steps to make the drawing:

1. Draw the horizontal base line, then divide the line in half and draw the vertical center line.
2. Draw the complete framed portal and label it with the width and height dimensions.
3. Draw the portal opening and also label the width and height.
4. Draw the stage left top curved swag at the stage left top. The overall width of the top that we see is 22'-0", the low point of the curved drapery is 12'-0", the stage left drapery terminates visually at the portal leg at 17'-0". The actual drapery continues past another 1'-3" where it ends.
5. Draw the stage right top curved swag at the stage right top. The overall width of the top that we see is 15'-0". It overlaps and goes 3'-0" behind the stage left drapery swag. The low point of this curved swag is 7'-6". The stage right drapery terminates visually at the portal leg at 9'-0". The actual end of it goes off another 1'-3".
6. Make a note on the drawing: Both the tops of the left and the right drapery swags tie on the same pipe batten. Allow an extra 1'-3" at the top of both swags so the fabric goes past the top opening and masks sufficiently.

Sew the drapery to webbing (with grommets and tie lines) in fullness according to the drawing.

7. Draw the stage left drapery leg. The leg is actually 18'-0" high. It is 3'-6" at the bottom and 2'-3" at the top. Make a note on the drawing saying: Build wooden (or metal) frame on which to attach drapery in fullness as shown with a slightly curved onstage edge. The top of the frame is to be suspended on cable from the same pipe batten as the two drapery swags. Allow another 1'-3" of drapery in fullness and also 1'-3" for the frame to go offstage left and mask.
8. Also make a note saying: Sew drapery in fullness at top to webbing so it can be tied onto the frame. Provide pieces of Velcro on the fabric so the sides and bottom stay in place on the frame and the whole leg looks like it is falling naturally.
9. Draw the stage right drapery leg. It is 10'-0" high, 3'-3" at the bottom and 2'-6" at the top; plus the additional offstage 1'-3" of draperies in fullness and frame. Make a note to say: Build stage right frame as per stage left frame; provide the same items. It also hangs on cable suspended from the same pipe.
10. Make a note for the framed portal to be covered with canvas: Provide hanging hardware at top; provide stiffeners on the rear.
11. On the same sheet of tracing paper and under the portal and drapery drawing, make a drawing of the ground plan of the portal with the 6 inches of thickness in the opening, and put the dimensions on the drawing. Show the drapery units on the plan as they hang upstage of the portal. Draw them as they appear against the back of the portal opening.

Hanging Draped Swags or Festoons on a Batten

Suppose the design for draped swags is one in which the top of the drapery fabric is masked by a hard portal header or a soft hanging border. Another choice could be a free-form arrangement of hanging draperies in which the tops and sides are not masked but are seen by the audience. Whatever the design, do a drawing in ½-inch scale with the necessary dimensions for creating the swags and jabots. Materials for the draped swags

Drapery Tiebacks, Holders, Rosettes, and Other Embellishments

Drapery and Curtains: 1. Gathered Fabric; 2. Gathered Fabric on a Rod; 3. Gathered Heading Above a Rod; 4. Single and Double Ruffle; 5. Knotted Fabric

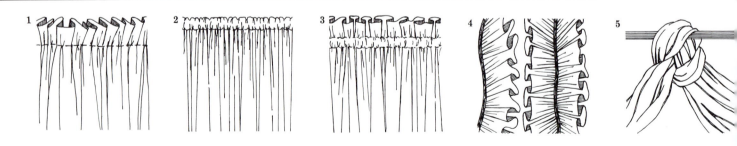

1. French Pleats; 2. Box Pleats; 3. Pinch Pleats; 4. Accordian Pleats; 5. Cartridge Pleats

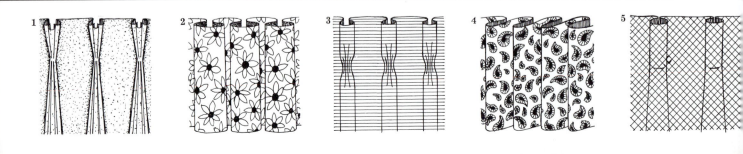

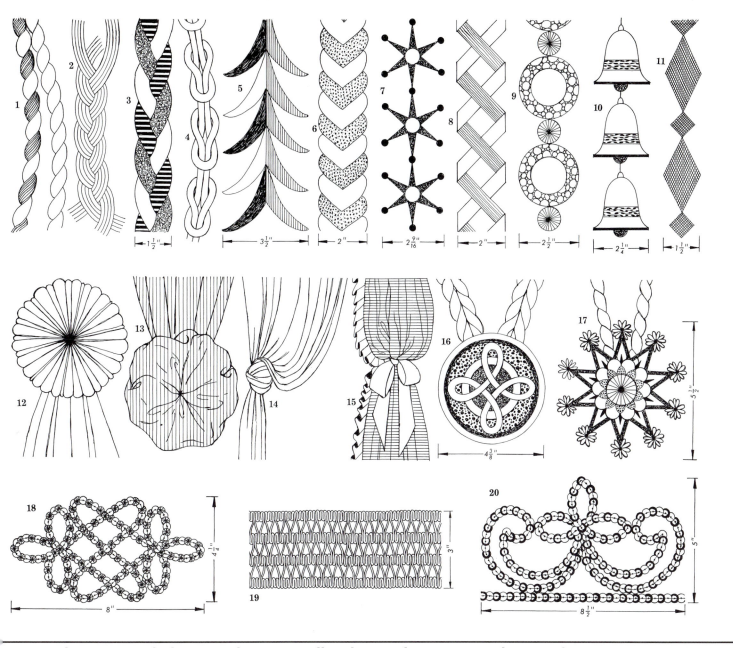

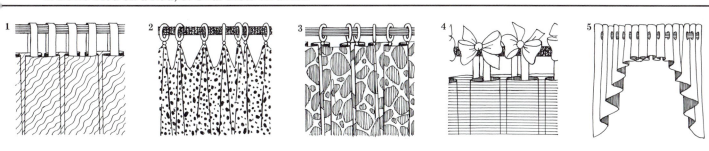

1. Flat Loops Attached to a Straight Top; 2. Scalloped Top with Rings; 3. Straight Top with Rings;
4. Bows Tied on a Rod; 5. Oval Slots on a Rod

1. Pencil Pleats; 2. Austrian Draperies; 3. Overlapping Draperies on a Rod; 4. Gathered and Ruffled
Draperies; 5. Free-Form Draperies Held with a Ring

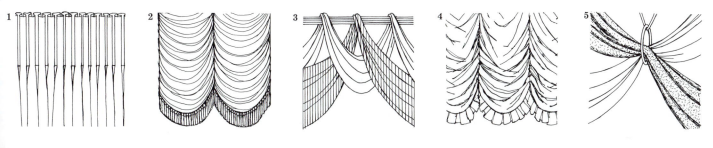

may be velour, duvetyne, sharkstooth scrim, chiffon, or other fabrics.

For discussion let us assume that we are putting draped swags on a pipe batten and the top of the drapery will be masked by a portal header.

When attaching hanging pieces of drapery on a batten to form the swag and jabots, use a length of jute webbing with grommets and tie lines. If you have a portal opening 36'-0" wide with the batten hanging upstage 1'-0" from the portal, and want to have the ends of the drapery masked by the portal, plan on having a piece of webbing at least 40 to 42 feet long.

Center the piece of webbing and tie it on the horizontally hanging pipe batten. Then arrange and pin the draped fabric to the webbing to keep it in place until it is sewed to the webbing. This may be a matter of working back and forth from jabot to swag and so on while adjusting the folds in the fabric so that they hang nicely and look like what is on the drawing. Use heavy pins to hold the fabric on the webbing, and once it is sewn with heavy-duty thread, the excess fabric can be trimmed off.

This entire hanging process may be done in the scenic shop or in the theatre itself when there is extra time and it does not become too costly. If the drapery swags are quite sizable and involve a lot of ladder work and moving back and forth, then it would be best to have the work done in the scenic shop.

Hanging Drapery Swags and Jabots in Curved Arches

The best way to position drapery arrangements in curved arches (or other shapes) is to have a profiled 3-inch wooden batten cut to conform to the curve of the arch with a 1-inch allowance of extra wood. This 4-inch batten can then be attached by screws from the rear and can be used to staple or tack on swags and jabots, and balloon draperies at the top of the arch. Also, for balloon draperies you may need vertical battens along the sides of arches on which to pull back and arrange the long tied-back and bulging draperies, and staple or tack the fabric wherever it is needed so that the desired shapes may be held in place. The side vertical batten can also be screwed to the back of the sides of the arch. Sometimes wooden angled arms are needed on which to staple drapery in fullness. Arms are also good to serve as bases for giant rosettes, leaves, or other decorative motifs that appear to be holding the draperies back. These should be planned in advance as far as size and position and be drawn on the elevation drawings for building. Wooden arms can be prepainted to match the drapery arrangements.

Drapery Trim

For large-scale theatrical-type draperies you need to design trim which is also in a larger scale. Trim for drapery includes decorative woven and openwork bands, gimp, widths of openwork lace, tassels, fringe, covered and painted rosettes, and lengths of roping and cords arranged in interesting clusters. Painted fringes on the bottoms of

Show curtain design by Edward Gorey for DRACULA (1977), Martin Beck Theatre, New York. (Photograph by Lynn Pecktal)

draperies may range from 6 inches to 2 or 3 feet. Painted lengths of gimp, openwork lace, and woven bands may range in combination from 3 to 6 inches, with 9, 12, and 15 inches for the highly decorative lengths.

To save space, cost, and weight yet preserve the lushness and grandiose feeling of opulent theatrical draperies, they can often be designed and painted as canvas borders and legs. The three-dimensional feeling of heavy fullness in the folds of the fabric can be achieved by realistic painting of the onstage cut profile edges of the bottom of the overhead border and side legs.

Drapery Trim Colors

While beautiful theatrical draperies executed in heavy fullness can be any number of colors, perhaps the most familiar and popular are rich red or green draperies. These are often conceived as velvet fabrics, and sometimes cut velvets, as well as damasks and brocades. Other colors, such as pink, blue, and purple, can also be appropriate for theatrical productions.

Gold and silver are common colors for the trim on draperies, especially for the fringe, roping, and tassels.

Draping Patterns of Roping

Open patterns of draped roping hanging on a pipe batten in space can be ideal for a simple suggestion of stage decor.

To really read well, the roping can be 1 inch, 1½ inches, or 2 inches in diameter. The desired draping patterns are retained by attaching them to a length of webbing with grommets and tie lines. Once fastened in place on the webbing, the arrangements of roping may be embellished with large-scale tassels and medallions, as well as other classical ornaments.

Two vertical lengths of roping may be combined with curved open swags to produce interesting effects. The width of the swags can be figured out on the drawing first so the scale of the drapery is bold enough to read well.

Roping on Drapery and Show Curtains

While real roping works well by itself, it is always attractive when combined tastefully with the voluptuous swags and jabots of the old-fashioned stage

Painted curtain by Dale Amlund for the Grand Opera House, Wilmington, Delaware (1976). (Photograph by Lynn Pecktal)

drapery. Real velour drapery with tassels and fringe and roping may be expensive to create for a set, but it makes a beautiful stage design.

Usually the same design can be realized very successfully through the craft of good scenic artists in basically one or more cut drops, depending on the scheme of things. Show curtains and house curtains with all of the above details can also be painted with much success. Skilled painters often create stunning period curtains by using traditional flat painting with shade, shadow, and highlights on velour or other fabric.

Drapery Track and Equipment

A very popular source for drapery track equipment and theatrical fabrics is Rose Brand, 517 West 35th Street, New York, NY 10001, Tel.: (212) 594-7424. This company has track with the necessary accessories. Their list includes:

- Silent Steel[c]—heavy-duty draw track.
- Besteel[c]—standard-duty draw track.
- Rig-I-Flex[c]—aluminum draw track, aluminum walk-a-long track, or black aluminum walk-a-long track with black accessories.
- Specifine[c]—aluminum architectural draw track.

Additional styles of track are available.

The traveler track is sold by the foot with a standard accessory group. This guarantees the lowest price per piece as well as assuring the user that all parts and accessories are included. The standard accessory group for a center-open traveler track includes track channel, single carriers, master carriers (carriers supplied on 12″ or 6″ centers as appropriate), end pulleys, floor pulley, lap clamps, hanging clamps, end stops, and operating cord.

Ordering Traveler Track

Rose Brand requests the following information when you order traveler track so that they can be sure the appropriate track is ordered.

1. The type of track-traveler or walk-along. Specify one-way draw or bi-parting.
2. Use as determined by curtain weight and type and application.
3. Suspension method—direct from chain or cable attached to reinforcing pipe or grid, or flush to ceiling.
4. Length, including overlap and sufficient offstage stacking space.
5. Other accessories, including backpack hardware, pipe clamps, switching devices, trim chain, mule blocks, and so on.

Drapery Fabrics and Materials

For material and trim on drapery, the items below may be the actual thing, painted, or simulated:

Fabric rosettes	Braids
Striped satins	Openwork laces
Brocaded satins	Bullion fringes
Cotton velvets	Thread fringes
Corduroys	Bullion tassels
Cords	Point d'Espagne trimmings
Gimp and galoons	
Tassels	Spangle figures
Sequin trimming	Spangle trimming
Grecian borders	Spangle and bullion balldrops
Crescents	
Stars	Jewel settings
Tiny lights	Decorative buttons
Ruffles	Mirrored discs

Figuring the Fullness of Drapery

Fabric draperies with fullness look lovely onstage and light well. Percentages of fullness vary according to the fabric and the desired effect. For China silk you may need as much as 100 percent to 125 percent fullness. The average percentage of fullness for items like a house curtain and valance is 75 percent, whereas for a cyclorama, masking legs, and borders it would be 50 percent or 60 percent.

When designing draperies, a traveler, backdrop, or curtain to be made in fullness, always add the percentage of fullness you want to the original finished size. The following information tells how much material should be added. For a cloth to be sewn up and finished at an overall width of 50 feet when hanging in the theatre, you would need:

25% fullness: 62½′ wide
50′
+ 12½′ (25% of 50′)
62½′ total

50% fullness: 75′ wide
50′
+ 25′ (50% of 50′)
75′ total

75% fullness: 87½′ wide
50′
+ 37½′ (75% of 50′)
87½′ total

100% fullness: 100′ wide
50′
+ 50′ (100% of 50′)
100′ total

150% fullness: 125′ wide
50′
+ 75′ (150% of 50′)
125′ total

200% fullness: 150′ wide
50′
+ 100′ (200% of 50′)
150′ total

Specifications for Ordering Draperies and Curtains

When ordering draperies and curtains, certain specific information is always needed so nothing is left to chance. This list may also apply to backdrops, cycloramas, or scrims. Give these specifications on the drafting or sketches:

1. Name of the item.
2. Kind of fabric and color(s).
3. Finished height and width dimensions.
4. With or without fullness. If in fullness, give the exact percentage.
5. Kind of lining, if required.
6. Finish at top: webbing, grommets, and tie lines or S-hooks.
7. Finish at bottom: pocket for pipe or hem for chain.
8. Finish for sides: 2-inch hem.
9. Special accessories: sequins, mirrored discs, appliqués, etc.
10. Painting.
11. Fire-retarded.

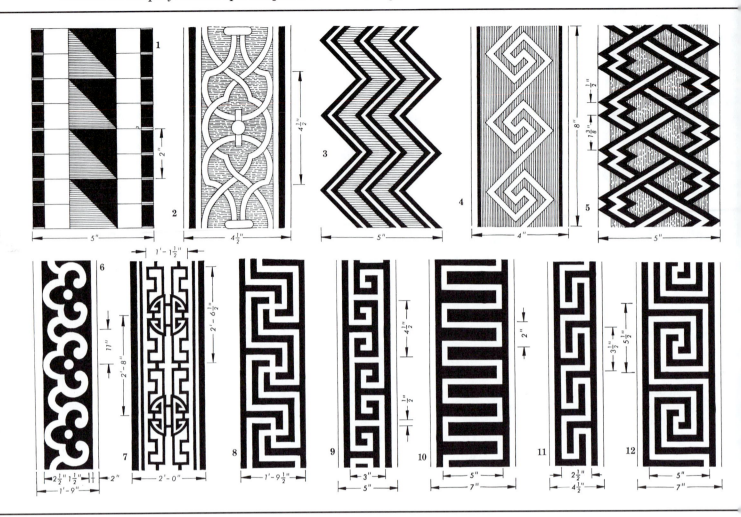

Openwork Drapery and Curtain Trim

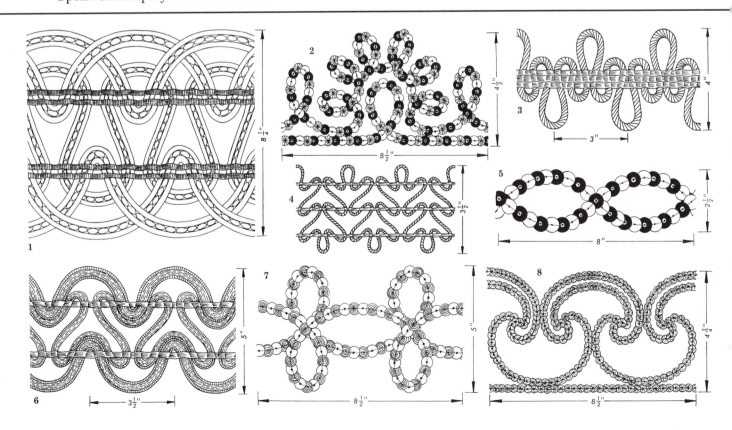

Selecting Theatrical Fabrics and Other Materials

• **Rose Brand**, 517 West 35th Street, New York, NY 10001. Tel.: (212) 594-7424, (800) 223-1624. Space does not permit mentioning every good source for theatrical fabrics around the country, but one of the best-known companies in New York City is Rose Brand. Rose Brand has a wide selection of theatrical fabrics and also provides fabrication, scenic paints and brushes, theatrical tapes, hardware, accessories, and installation services. For some fabrics there is a cutting charge on orders of less than a full bolt, and for certain fabrics there is a yardage minimum. FR means Flame Retardant and NR means Nonflame Retardant. Items and materials from Rose Brand include:

MUSLIN (Approx. 40 to 60 yard bolts)

Width		Width		Width	
45″	Light Weight Muslin (for costumes, lining, patterns)	59″	Heavy Weight Muslin	108″	Heavy Weight Muslin
40″	Medium Weight Muslin	72″	Heavy Weight Muslin	120″	Heavy Weight Muslin
76″	Medium Weight Muslin	80″	Heavy Weight Muslin	142″	Heavy Weight Muslin (11′-10″)
81″	Medium Weight Muslin	90″	Heavy Weight Muslin	197″	Heavy Weight Muslin (16′-5″)
120″	Medium Weight Muslin	96″	Heavy Weight Muslin Bleached White		

EXTRA WIDE SEAMLESS TRANSLUCENT MUSLIN

Width		Width	
14′-5″	Muslin	20′-4″	Blue, Gray, Bleached White Muslin (FR)
14′-5″	Muslin (FR)	32′-9″	Muslin
14′-5″	Blue, Gray, Bleached White Muslin (FR)	32′-9″	Muslin (FR)
20′-4″	Muslin	32′-9″	Blue, Gray, or Bleached White Muslin (FR)
20′-4″	Muslin (FR)		

FLAME RETARDANT SCENERY MUSLIN

Approx. Width		Approx. Width		Approx. Width	
75/76″	Medium Weight Muslin	77/78″	Heavy Weight Muslin	100/102″	Bleached White Muslin
110/112″	Medium Weight Muslin	98/100″	Heavy Weight Muslin	100/102″	Muslin: Sky Blue, Dark Blue, Gray, or Black
68/69″	Heavy Weight Muslin	110/112″	Heavy Weight Muslin		

SCRIMS

Approx. Width		Approx. Width	
15′-6″	Sharkstooth Scrim: White, Black (FR)	31′-0″	Leno Filled Scrim: White, Gray, or Blue (FR)
19′-6″	Sharkstooth Scrim: White, Black (FR)	97″ and 31′-0″	Bobbinette: Black or White (FR)
30′-0″	Sharkstooth Scrim: White, Black, Blue, Gray (FR)	72″	Theatrical Gauze: Natural or White (FR)
35′-0″	Sharkstooth Scrim: White, Black, Blue (FR)	30′-0″	Scenery netting/36 yd. piece: Natural (FR)
36′-0″	Painters Scrim: Natural (NR)	30′-0″	Scenery netting/24 yd. piece: Black (FR)

SCENERY CANVAS

Width		Width	
72″	7 oz. Canvas	68/69″	8 oz. Canvas: Black (FR)
72″, 120″, and 144″	12 oz. Canvas	70/71″	12 oz. Canvas: Natural (FR)
60″	18 oz. Canvas	68/69″	15 oz. Canvas: Black (FR)
68/69″	7 oz. Canvas: Natural (FR)	116″	6 oz. Canvas: Bleached White (FR)

VELOURS (Flame Retardant)

Width		Width	
54″	16 oz. Weight: 10 colors (60–65 yard roll)	54″	25 oz. Weight: 23 colors (50–55 yard roll)
54″	21 oz. Weight: 23 colors (50–55 yard roll)		

DRAPERY FABRICS (Flame Retardant)

Width		Width	
54″	Nassau Chevron Repp: Black, Gray, Beige, Blue	48″	Duval (Opaque Vinyl Bonded Vegas)—Inherently FR
54″	Atlas Oxford Repp: Black, Gray, Beige, Blue	72″	Cyc Cloth: Chroma Key Blue, Chroma Key Green, Light Gray, Dark Gray, Black—Inherently FR
54″	Ranger Lining: Black or Beige		
48″	Vegas/Reno—Inherently FR	59″	Serge: Black Wool, Imported NR

DISPLAY FABRICS

Width		Width	
41″	Exhibition Taffeta, FR: 12 colors	50″	Monks Cloth: Natural
48″	Banjo Cloth, Inherently FR: 14 colors	50″	Bengaline: Assorted colors
60″	Ripstop Nylon, FR: 8 colors	50″	Bengaline Moiré: Assorted colors
60″	Nylon Banner Cloth: Assorted colors (25 yd. min.)	36″	Mylar, 1.4 MIL: Assorted colors (25 yd. roll)
60″	Velcro Fabric: Assorted colors	36″	Bunting: Red, White, Blue stripes
54″	Patent Vinyl: Assorted colors		

MYLAR RAIN CURTAINS (Also called tinsel curtains, slit drapes, or shimmer curtains)

Two Layer Rain Curtain: Standard colors Two Layer Rain Curtain: Iridescent	Two Layer Rain Curtain: Diffraction 24″ Mylar Tassel: Gold, Silver

BALLET NETS

Width		Width	
52″	Ballet Tutu Soft: White, Black	72″	Nylon Netting: Assorted colors (40 yard bolt only)
52″	Ballet Tutu Stiff: White, Black	54″	Nylon Tulle Assorted colors (40 yard bolt only)

CINENET

100% Black Cotton netting used for subtle light reduction in film and television productions.
Single Cinenet for light reduction of ½ stop available in these widths:

Width		Width	
72″	Single Cinenet: Black, Flame Retardant (45 yd. piece)	216″	Single Cinenet: Black, Flame Retardant (40 yd. piece)
144″	Single Cinenet: Black, Flame Retardant (45 yd. piece)	288″	Single Cinenet: Black, Flame Retardant (40 yd. piece)

GAUZE

Width		Width	
36″	Cheesecloth, All Purpose: Bleached White (70 yard box)	36″, 58″	Cotton Scrim (100 yard bolts)
38″, 48″	Chincha Standard (100 yard bolts)	45″	Tropical Net: White—Flame Retardant

COSTUME GOODS

Width		Width		Width	
45″	China Silk: Assorted colors	60″	Spandex: Black, White	45″	Poly Lining: White, Red, Black, Royal
45″	Cotton Back Satin: Assorted colors	46″	Nude Lycra		

NATURAL BURLAP

Width		Width	
48″ and 72″	7½ oz. Burlap	48″	Jute Gauze
48″ and 72″	10 oz. Burlap	48″	Erosion Cloth (75 yard bolt)

COLORED BURLAP

Width	
48″	by roll only (35 yard roll)

DUVETYNE AND COMMANDO CLOTH—Flame Retardant

Width		Width	
54″	Duvetyne: Black	54″	Commando Cloth: Black, Gray, Cranberry, Blueberry, Beige, White
54″	Red Dot Duvetyne: Black		

FELT (Wool/Rayon)

Width	
72″	40 colors, Flame Retardant

BULLION DRAPERY FRINGE AND ROPE

4″, 6″, and 10″	Gold Fringe	6″	Gold Fringe (Design Weight)	1″	Black/Gold Metallic Rope
6″	White Fringe	½″ and 1″	Gold Rope		

CHAINETTE TASSELS

Small Head × 10″	Gold	Large Head × 10″	Gold	(Other colors available. One dozen minimum.)	
Medium Head × 10″	Gold	X-Large Head × 12″	Gold		

METALLICS—(All metallic fabrics can be flameproofed—bolt only.)

Width		Width	
40″	Laminette: Gold, Silver	60″	Metallic Knit Shimmer: Assorted colors
40″	Spongy Lamé: Gold	50″	Metallic Knit Stripe: Assorted colors
40″	Eyelash Cloth; Gold, Silver, Black	40″	Tissue Lamé: Assorted colors
48″	Metallic Knit Bouclé: Assorted colors	40″	Iridescent Laminette: Assorted colors

REAR PROJECTION SCREEN

Width	
55″ and 110″	Gray, Black, Twin White (Flame Retardant)

VELCRO

¾″, 1″, 2″	Male Hook or Female Loop	60″	Velcro Fabric (Assorted Colors)

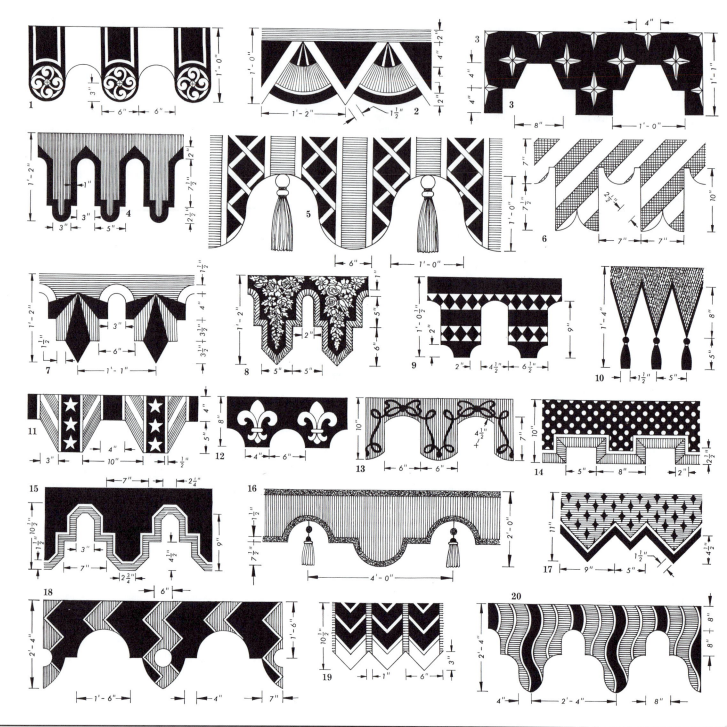

Oliver Messel's Drapery Border (60'–0" × 20'–3") for THE SLEEPING BEAUTY (1976)
(Drawing and Photograph by Lynn Pecktal)

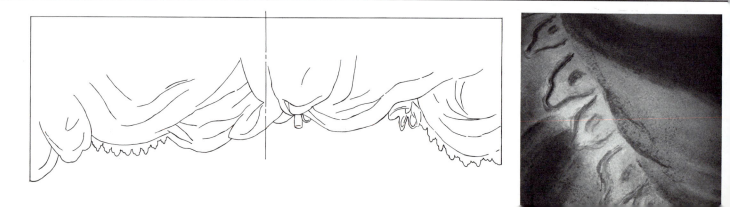

• **Gerriets International**, R.D. #1, 950 Hutchinson Road, Allentown, NJ, 08501, Tel.: (609) 758-9121. There are also offices in California and Great Britain. Gerriets International's products include many imported European scenographic materials and they are ideal to use for creating scenery.

Among Gerriets' products are Vario Dance Floor, stage velours in standard colors and custom colors, and scenic brushes.

(*Note:* Items in capital letters are either inherently nonflammable, self-extinguishing, or have been flame-proofed.) It is invaluable for designers to get a complete list of products and samples of materials.

PROCYC, REAR AND FRONT PROJECTION PLASTICS

Width	Bolt Length		Width	Bolt Length	
55″	71 yd.	REVIEW, TRANSLUCENT	51″	54.6 yd.	GLASSCLEAR PVC FILM
55″	71 yd.	STUDIO, GRAY	51″	54.6 yd.	HIGH GLOSS/MATTE PLASTIC FILM: Black
55″	71 yd.	SHOW, BLACK			
55″	71 yd.	OPERA, CREAMY WHITE	51″	32.8 yd.	HIGH GLOSS/MATTE PLASTIC FILM: Colors or White
55″	71 yd.	OPAQUE, FRONT WHITE			
55″	71 yd.	PROJECTION SCRIM, WHITE	51″	65.5 yd.	HIGH GLOSS/MATTE PLASTIC SHEETING: Black or White
69″	54.6 yd.	ARENA OUTDOOR SCREEN			

UBIQUITOUS TEXTURES

Width	Bolt Length		Width	Bolt Length	
9′-10″	54.6 yd.	CONTRA-H, FINE TEXTURE: BLACK, NATURAL	9′-10″	21.8 yd.	CONTRA-H, SUPER TEXTURE: BLACK, NATURAL
9′-10″	27.3 yd.	CONTRA-H, MEDIUM TEXTURE: BLACK, NATURAL	9′-10″	27.3 yd.	CONTRA-O, CIRCULAR TEXTURE: BLACK, NATURAL

SEAMLESS THEATRICAL GAUZES

Width	Bolt Length		Width	Bolt Length	
14′-5″	65.5 yd.	Translucent Theatrical Gauze	20′-4″	65.5 yd.	TRANSLUCENT THEATRICAL GAUZE
14-5″	65.5 yd.	TRANSLUCENT THEATRICAL GAUZE	32′-9″	65.5 yd.	Translucent Theatrical Gauze
20′-4″	65.5 yd.	Translucent Theatrical Gauze	32′-9″	65.5 yd.	TRANSLUCENT THEATRICAL GAUZE

SEAMLESS WIDE WIDTH COTTON MUSLIN AND CANVAS

Width	Bolt Length		Width	Bolt Length	
10′-4″	65.5 yd.	Super Unbleached Muslin, Raw	32′-9″	65.5 yd.	DAY BLUE MUSLIN
10′-4″	65.5 yd.	SUPER UNBLEACHED MUSLIN	32′-9″	65.5 yd.	NIGHT BLUE MUSLIN
14-3″	65.5 yd.	Super Unbleached Muslin, Raw	9-10″	65.5 yd.	Mannheim Cyclorama Canvas
14′-3″	65.5 yd.	SUPER UNBLEACHED MUSLIN	9-10″	65.5 yd.	MANNHEIM CYCLORAMA CANVAS
14′-3″	65.5 yd.	DAY BLUE MUSLIN	19′-8″	65.5 yd.	SHIRTING BLEACHED MUSLIN
14′-3″	65.5 yd.	CBS GRAY MUSLIN	32′-9″	65.5 yd.	SHIRTING BLEACHED MUSLIN
20′-0″	65.5 yd.	Super Unbleached Muslin, Raw	14′-3″	65.5 yd.	SHIRTING BLEACHED MUSLIN
19′-6″	65.5 yd.	SUPER UNBLEACHED MUSLIN	78″	65.5 yd.	Munster Cyclorama Canvas
19′-6″	65.5 yd.	DAY BLUE MUSLIN	78″	65.5 yd.	MUNSTER CYCLORAMA CANVAS
19′-6″	65.5 yd.	CBS GRAY MUSLIN	13′-9″	65.5 yd.	Eifel Cyclorama Canvas
33′-3″	65.5 yd.	Super Unbleached Muslin, Raw	13′-9″	65.5 yd.	EIFEL CYCLORAMA CANVAS
32′-9″	65.5 yd.	SUPER UNBLEACHED MUSLIN			

STAGE VELOURS (Guaranteed flame retardant for 7 years)

Width	Bolt Length		Width	Bolt Length	
55″	50 yd.	LUXOR PLUS COTTON VELOUR	78″	65.5 yd.	DUVETYNE
54″	44 yd.	CLIVIA 54 COTTON VELOUR	63″	65.5 yd.	CALMUC COTTON FLEECE
55″	49.5 yd.	RENO GOLD/BLACK VELOUR	9′-10″	65.5 yd.	TREVIRA VOILE: WHITE
54″	40 yd.	LIDO PLUS TREVIRA VELOUR	9′-10″	65.5 yd.	TREVIRA VOILE: BLACK

SCENIC FABRICS · CUSTOM-MADE STAGE NETS

Width	Bolt Length		Width	Bolt Length		
51″	65.5 yd.	Dekomolton	65″	65.5 yd.	Waffelcloth	Stage net is custom made by hand to sizes up to 40′-0″ high, with or without flameproofing. 1/4″, 3/8″, 3/4″, and 1″ Square Stage Net
51″	65.5 yd.	DEKOMOLTON	47″	65.5 yd.	Unisatin lining fabric	
47″	65.5 yd.	DELIBLACK	47″	65.5 yd.	UNISATIN	

BURLAP · LINENS

Width	Bolt Length		Width	Bolt Length	
53″	10.9 yd.	Camouflage Foliage	9′-10″	65.5 yd.	Kandel Linen
82″	54.6 yd.	Onionbag Scrim, Jute	78″	65.5 yd.	Rigato Linen
86″	54.6 yd.	Burlap H 425	78″	65.5 yd.	Samos Linen Canvas
51″	32.8 yd.	Burlap H 300	78″	32.8 yd.	Samos Plus Nonskid Cloth
78″	27.3 yd.	Woven Wire Fabric			

SHARKSTOOTH SCRIMS AND BOBBINETS

Width	Bolt Length		Width	Bolt Length	
39'-4"	52.3 yd.	PARSIFAL SEAMLESS BOBBINET: NATURAL (ECRU), BLACK, GRAY	35'-0"	61 yd.	Painter's Sharkstooth Scrim: Raw
55-0"	43.7 yd.	AIDA SEAMLESS BOBBINET: NATURAL (ECRU), BLACK, GRAY	32'-0"	54.6 yd.	ISOLDE SHARKSTOOTH SCRIM, 8 POINT: WHITE, GRAY, BLACK
32'-9"	38.2 yd.	ELECTRA SEAMLESS BOBBINET: NATURAL (ECRU), BLACK, GRAY	98"	43.7 yd.	SCENIC NETTING: NATURAL, BLACK
32'-1"	60 yd.	FALSTAFF SHARKSTOOTH SCRIM, 6 POINT: WHITE, GRAY, BLACK	35'-0"	30 yd.	FIDELIO, 5 POINT SQUARE NET: ECRU, BLACK, GRAY, WHITE

- **Rosco Laboratories** is another well-known company that offers a number of supplies for the set designer, painter, lighting designer, or costume designer. There are locations in New York, California, Canada, Spain, London, and Portugal. Some of Rosco's textiles are available in cut yardage or in finished backdrops. They have a wide variety of materials. Some are listed in the chart below. The toll-free number is 800-431-2338.

ROSCO PRODUCTS INCLUDE:

Rear Projection Screen
Custom-Made Finished Screens
Black Cinefoil
Diffractions
Pearlescents
Flexmirrors
White Cinefoil
Sparklene
Smooths
Metalix
Mirrors
Transparents

SHIMMER SCRIM

Self-extinguishing fabric with a selvage edge for easy sewing. It can be used for scrim effects and has a soft hand for easy draping.

Width	
47"	White-Iridescent/Gold
47"	White-Iridescent/White
47"	Black-Clear/Silver
47"	Black-Clear/Black
47"	Black-Gold/Clear

GLAMÉ (Self-extinguishing)

Width	
48"	Silver, Gold, Silver-Black, Razzle-Dazzle, Diamond Iridescent, Black (10 yd. roll or 110 yd. bolt)

SHOWCLOTH (Self-extinguishing)

Width	
47"	White Gold, Black Gold (10 yd. roll or 110 yd. bolt)

ROSCOMURALS

A computerized painting system for producing expanded images, utilizes new and patented technology to translate standard artwork into large scale images while maintaining the depth, color, and fidelity of the original. Stable, fade-resistant paints are used to produce images on a wide variety of materials for both indoor and outdoor use. This new system also enables original artwork to be manipulated and edited to meet specific project requirements. Images can be produced in seamless panels up to 16' × 62' (4.9 × 19 m) for full-stage drops or TV production backgrounds. Call for complete information.

CASCADE CURTAINS

Flame retardant and faceted ¼-in. strips for spectacular reflection. Heading is the same material and color as curtain with ¾" spacing to hold curtain. Individually packed in clear plastic tube. Each curtain 3'-0" wide.

Length	
2',4',8'	Metallic: Cerise, Blue, Red, Green
16', 24'	Metallic: Silver, Gold
8' only	Luster/Pastel Colors: Blue-Dark (Royal), Blue-Light (Columbia), Pink, Pink-Shocking, Red, White, Yellow (Gold), Black

ROSCOGLITTER

Based on 1 mil. double metalized polyester film cut into ¹⁄₆₄ hexagonal flakes. It can be sprinkled on or mixed directly into clear gloss or flat acrylic for easy application. Colors: Gold, Galaxy Gray, Red, Sky Blue, Royal Blue, Prism Silver, Green, Fuchsia, Pink Fizz, Blue/Green Iridescent, Red/Green Iridescent.

SLIT DRAPE

Rosco's version of a slash curtain, made of overlapping ⅛" wide layers of durable, flame retardant vinyl picks up the bounces light in exciting new ways.

Width	Length	
36"	8', 16', 24'	Black/Diffraction, White/Diffraction, Silver/Diffraction, Iridescent, Black/Gold, Black/Silver, Solid Silver, Solid Black, Solid Gold, Silver/Iridescent/Gold, Silver/Gold/Diffraction, Red/White/Blue

Other Sources for Supplies

- **Gilshire Corporation**, 11-20 46th Road, Long Island City, NY 11101, Tel.: (718) 786-1381. This firm has Gray Bogus Scenery Liner to go under backdrops and scrims prior to preparation and painting. Gray Bogus paper comes 58 inches wide on a roll. Gilshire also has wax paper and Kraft paper.

- **Janovic/Plaza**, 30-35 Thomson Avenue, Long Island City, NY 11104, Tel.: (718) 786-4444. This company has numerous products for scenic painting, including graining brushes, fan-top grainers, overgrainers, fan blenders, rubber grainers, graining rollers, steel graining comb sets, scenic fitches, stencil brushes, sash brushes, stippling brushes, foam rollers, foam brushes, specialty rollers, design rollers, spray systems, aniline dyes, Hudson sprayers, casein paints, acrylic latex paints, latex paints, glues, and other products.

- **Mutual Hardware Corp.**, 5-45 49th Avenue, Long Island City, NY 11101-5686, Tel.: (718) 361-2480. Mutual is advertised as a complete service for the American television and theatrical industry. Its products include paints—Flo Paint (colors available in super vinyl flat and super vinyl gloss), vinyl acrylic latex paints, and casein paints; drapes, curtains, special effects, winches, fabrics for drops, velours, duvetynes, tools, casters, and other stage equipment.

This conversation with David Jenkins took place in his design studio and home on Riverside Drive in Manhattan. Born on July 30, 1937, in Hampton, Virginia, he was educated at Earlham College and the Yale School of Drama. His Broadway debut was designing the scenery for *The Changing Room* by David Storey in 1973. He has designed the settings for many productions at the Arena Stage, Long Wharf Theatre, Trinity Square Repertory Company, Goodman Theatre, Cincinnati Playhouse in the Park, McCarter Theatre, Mark Taper Forum, American Shakespeare Festival, Theatre of the Living Arts, Milwaukee Repertory Theatre, Hartford Stage Company, Circle Repertory Theatre, Manhattan Theatre Club, and San Diego Old Globe Theatre. He has been the production designer for numerous television and film assignments, and the resident set designer for the National Actors Theatre, founded by Tony Randall. David Jenkins is the recipient of the Drama Desk Award and the Dramalogue Award. He is married to scenic designer Leigh Rand. Among his scenic design credits are:

Broadway
Two Shakespearean Actors (1991)
Accomplice (1990)
Sherlock's Last Case (1987)
Stardust (1987)
Stepping Out (1986)
And a Nightingale Sang (1983)
   Newhouse Theatre
Total Abandon (1983)
The Queen and the Rebels (1982)
Special Occasions (1982)
Piaf (1981)
I Ought to Be in Pictures (1980)
The Elephant Man (1979)
Strangers (1979)
Checking Out (1976)

Rodgers & Hart (1975)
The Freedom of the City (1974)

Off Broadway
Other People's Money (1989)
No Way to Treat a Lady (1987)
Bunker Reveries (1987)
Talk Radio (1987)
The Common Pursuit (1986)
Angry Housewives (1986)
Short Eyes (1984)
Husbandry (1984)
Preppies (1983)
Quartermaine's Terms (1983)
Blue Plate Special (1983)

Lullabye and Goodnight (1982)
Poor Little Lambs (1982)
The Good Parts (1982)
Weekends Like Other People (1982)
Under Fire (1980)
The Art of Dining (1979)
Hamlet (1979)
Gorky (1975)

London
The Common Pursuit (1988)

New York City Opera
The Music Man (1988)
Song of Norway (1981)
The Student Prince (1980)

Model by David Jenkins
THE ELEPHANT MAN by Bernard Pomerance

Directed by Jack Hofsiss
Booth Theatre, New York (1979)

How did you become interested in designing for the theatre?

There was a series of happenings in my life that slowly brought everything into focus. I was first introduced to the theatre when I was in college. I'll never forget this. It was the spring of my junior year, and I was working in the art studio that was on the top floor of the same building that housed the theatre department. One day, the door flung open, and Arthur Little, the head of the drama department and to whom I owe a great debt, said, "Who in here is a painter? I need a painter." I piped up and said, "I am." He grabbed me by the arm and dragged me down five flights of stairs to the basement where they were painting scenery for *The Matchmaker*. He put a paint brush in my hand and said, "Start painting." I didn't know what I was doing. I didn't know anything about painting scenery at all. But I was working on large canvases, which was popular in the late fifties, and here was this large stretched canvas in front of me about 8 feet by 12 feet. It was terrific.

Were you a fine arts major?

I had tried to combine art and geology as an interdepartmental major. It was a stretch to make those two disciplines go together, but I loved mapmaking and was very good at it. However, I wasn't doing too well academically, and earlier in my junior year the head of the geology department advised me to find an alternative. And suddenly I had that experience of painting scenery for *The Matchmaker* just as I was having to find another interdepartmental major! It seemed more natural to combine theatre and art than geology and art, so I applied to the theatre department and they accepted me. Since this was towards the end of my junior year, I was behind in credits towards graduation. There was no way I could complete my studies in time without taking extra courses, which I did that summer at the University of Denver, where I took three theatre courses in design. Fortunately, I had strong training in drafting and some beginning work in architecture starting in high school. Ironically, the theatre courses I took at the University of Denver were with some of the faculty I would meet again at Yale.

You had no theatre experience prior to this?

No theatre at all. When I went back to Earlham College in the fall I took a blitz course in theatre and accumulated enough credits to graduate that spring. The theatre courses there were mostly theory and theatre literature, and there was very little play production. So I got introduced to theatre in a general way, not specifically in design. I had no idea then that I was going to be a scene designer.

When did you choose theatre design as a career?

Not for a while yet. I graduated from college still unsure of what I wanted to do. I was quite footloose. This was the era of Jack Kerouac and we were living lives of the beat poets. It was a very exciting time, and I had this idea that I wanted to travel. I had a little two-seater sports car and if I couldn't fit something into the car, then I decided that it wouldn't be a part of my life. And I drove around the country. In my travels I drove past the Hedgerow Theatre outside of Philadelphia, and I saw them building scenery out in the side yard, so I stopped and asked, "Can I help? Anything I can do here?" And they said, "Yes." And I started building and painting scenery there. Basically, it was a place to stay for a couple of months while I was driving around the country.

What year was this?

Roughly the spring of 1960. The Hedgerow wasn't a summer stock theatre. It was one of the few resident theatre companies that existed at that time. The regional theatre movement hadn't taken hold in America yet. When the season there ended someone from the company suggested that I come to New York, and then when I didn't have a job after I got here, someone else recommended me for a summer stock job at the Straight Wharf Theatre in Nantucket. I worked there for the summer of 1960 as a lighting designer, of all things. I knew nothing about what I was doing!

Had you had experience with theatre lighting?

Only whatever the broad-based college experience was. I drew from some of the work I had done at the University of Denver because I had taken a technical course there. Qualifications weren't needed a lot in those days. You could just talk your way into a job.

It was very hard work. I never thought that I would survive that summer! I started doing a little more scenic design because in groups like that someone either drops out or isn't interested in doing the work. So more and more I was getting cast in this role of being there when the job came along.

Did you go to New York after that?

After the season was over I planned to come to New York and look for work, but as I pulled up in front of the building, one of the people I was sharing an apartment with said, "There's a telephone number next to the telephone. Call it immediately." I made the call and it was this young, crazy, but fascinating person who was starting a theatre in Ohio. I literally didn't unpack the car and drove to Cincinnati, which was only sixty miles from my family home in Indiana.

When I got there, I discovered that the theatre existed only in the imagination of this young producer. But it was my first professional job in the theatre. The job was not so much designing as getting the theatre ready. We had no seats, for instance, and somebody heard that they were tearing down a movie house in Hamilton, Ohio. I bluffed my way again and said I could drive this huge truck to carry the seats from the movie house. They were disasters, but they were seats. We spent days getting them all in. I think there were 110, something like that. A lot of the people who recall the early days of the Cincinnati Playhouse in the Park miss that very first year because it's not recorded very accurately.

What shows did you design that season?

The first show we did there was *Compulsion*. It was the very first show in a shelter house in the middle of the park in Cincinnati. We also did *Our Town*, *Androcles and the Lion*, and *Death of a Salesman*. It was insane. But the theatre survived. That was the best part of all.

My vagabond days were over in the spring of 1961 when I was drafted into the army.

What kind of work did you do in the army?

I ended up as a clerk typist in the Signal Corps at Schofield Barracks in Hawaii. I decided that I was just going to forget about the theatre. But slowly and surely that changed. After about a year in the Signal Corps, I found out about an amateur theatre group on the post. I went down to see one of their productions, and asked around if there were something that I could do, and I started working with the group. I directed, painted, and acted. Eventually, I was transferred to the Special Services.

Then you were able to continue with theatre work while you were in the army.

Yes. We had a theatre group and we toured. We were also responsible for everything from the Harlem Globetrotters basketball team to USO shows. It was an interesting job, but I didn't learn much about professional theatre. But it certainly kept me a lot more pleasantly occupied than the Signal Corps.

After my discharge in 1963 I gravitated back to the Cincinnati Playhouse in the Park. By that time the leadership had changed hands, but I was offered a job as lighting and set designer. I shared the season with a couple of other designers. Two or three years had gone past and now the Cincinnati Playhouse was starting to become a reasonably well known regional theatre.

One of the designs that I did at the end of the season was an evening of two short Molière pieces—*The Forced Marriage* and *The Doctor in Spite of Himself*. Stephen Porter, a New York director, came out to do the production and he inherited me as the resident designer to design. I did some initial sketches for Stephen and he came out from New York to talk about it. In one of our meetings he said that he thought the idea of using Sebastian Serlio as a springboard for the design would be a great idea. And I said, "Who?" He said, "Serlio." I said, "I don't know who you're talking about." Then he asked, "Have you ever had any training in the theatre?" And I said, "Not really." Well, he marched me down to the Cincinnati Public Library and took out a book on the style of Sebastian Serlio to use as source material for the design. It was the first time in my life that I had been asked to tie in historical significance and theatre history with what I was currently designing. It had all been intuitive prior to that.

That experience made me realize that there was a vast void in my life that I needed to fill. At the opening night party of the Molière production, I asked Stephen, "Remember that conversation we had about Serlio and source material? I really don't know what to do next. I can't get much further as a designer with just intuition." And he said, "That's absolutely right, because you're not going to have that intuitive luck all the time, and you're going to have to fall back on something." I said, "Where do I get that kind of information?" He said, "The only place to go is the Yale School of Drama." Of course, I'd heard of Yale, but I wasn't aware that there was a school of drama there.

I went back to my undergraduate college and asked the head of the art department and the head of the theatre department, who has been quite instrumental in shaping my artistic life, "If I wanted to go back to school and study theatre design, where do I go?" And both of them said, "You go to the Yale School of Drama." That was the only place that people were recommending. So I applied. I drove to New Haven for my interview and I was accepted. In the fall of 1964, five years after I had gotten out of college, I went back to school.

But it was terrific. I knew for the first time in my life why I was in an academic situation and what I was there to study. It was very important to have that five years because I had found out a little more about myself and what I was interested in, so I was very fortunate. After I graduated in 1967, I came to New York.

What did you do when you got to New York?

I looked for work like everyone else. Coming to New York even now for the second time was a great shock, because Yale did not prepare us for the business of the professional theatre. Donald Oenslager prepared us for a great many things for which I will always be indebted. The Yale system got you ready and like the infant child they threw you out into the cold and said, "OK, sink or swim."

So I tried to swim and called someone I had known at Yale who was already working in New York and told him I needed a job. He made a couple of phone calls and I got a job at Feller Studios as a draftsperson. My job was to make technical drawings or shop drawings from the designer's sketches. Of course, I ran into Pete Feller, Sr., and a lot of people who had been in the business for a long time and I started picking up knowledgeable how-to there. Peter Larkin was also drafting in the room at the same time. That was a whole education. Working in the same room with Peter Larkin was invaluable.

My wife Leigh and I were married while I was working at Feller's. We met as students at Yale, and after graduation we both came to New York supposedly to go our separate ways. But it didn't quite work out that way. Leigh passed the union exam that spring but I didn't. I was just trying to do too many things at once and didn't finish the project. When the next spring came around I was determined to get in the union. From working at Pete Feller's I was also beginning to learn a bit more about the professional theatre. I worked there a little short of a year. After Feller's, I did an odd job here and there until Leigh and I decided to take a six-month tour of Europe. It was the best thing we could have done.

What did you do when you got back from Europe?

I started drifting into filming commercials. I was looking for work, and again it was a friend-of-a-friend kind of recommendation, where you fill in for a couple of days' work. I knew nothing about film design. I had not studied it. But I have a firm belief that if you understand theatre design, you have a great basis for branching out into television, feature films, commercials, or industrials. It's only a matter of vocabulary.

I started making commercials at Wylde Films, a commercial house down on Park Avenue South that cranked out one commercial after the other. Then there came a moment when Leigh and I had to stop and say, "Hold on a second. What are we doing? Where are we going?" It was one of those crossroads in life that one comes to now and then. I had a feeling that we could make a very comfortable living working in the commercial industry. But it wasn't quite satisfying enough and we could feel the danger lurking there—do we want to be financially comfortable and continue working in the commercial field or do we take the risk and do the work we both enjoy? So we decided to regroup and go back into theatre design, which I really preferred. And God knows, it was not lu-

Model by David Jenkins
THE CHANGING ROOM by David Storey
Directed by Michael Rudman
Morosco Theatre, New York (1973)
(Photograph by David Jenkins)

crative and it barely paid the bills. But at least my soul was in pretty good shape.

How did you go about it?

I decided that I had better start calling upon friends and some professional acquaintances I had met along the line who were working in the theatre. I wrote a letter to the Long Wharf Theatre in New Haven, which at that time was headed by Arvin Brown, whom I had known at Yale. It was another one of those coincidences because at the moment that my letter arrived, they were looking for a designer for *The Way of the World* by Congreve. I was hired to design that for them and got my foot in the door at the Long Wharf. And shortly thereafter—I think it was two or three productions later—I did a production that launched my career in New York. It was a play about rugby.

This was The Changing Room, *which was your first Broadway show, wasn't it?*

Yes. *The Changing Room* came from the Long Wharf and it was a big critical success in New York. It was one of the most important events for me in terms of designing because the cast, the di-

rector, the designers truly pulled together as one. It was a great experience. I felt very good about the design and I felt wonderful about the production.

Did you keep the Broadway production similar to what you had designed for the Long Wharf?

Yes. The key was we didn't try to change it at all. In fact, it was what I thought to be quite a bold move. We had a bench on the downstage edge of the three-quarter space at Long Wharf, which traditionally, one would think, should be removed in a proscenium setting as it would be a barrier that would keep the audience's attention from the upstage portion of the action. Well, we decided to leave the bench right where it was, and George Hearn, who was a very unknown actor at the time, sat on it with his back to the audience, blocking the view even more. But somehow it all worked. The design seemed to make the transition very well. It was a bit of a squash-and-push because we had to go from a set that was very, very deep to one that was shallow but wide. The Broadway design was built as a new set, but it was basically the same idea that we had on the thrust stage at the Long Wharf.

Did you get work as a result of the success of The Changing Room?

I was still a young brash designer and I thought, "Ah, I'm a Broadway designer. I'll just sit back and wait for the

phone to ring." Of course it didn't. It isn't like that. You have to keep proving yourself, and it was hard work and still is hard work. So twenty years later you still have to keep hustling for a job. I imagine that a few doors were opened that otherwise wouldn't have been because of *The Changing Room.*

That experience was such a positive one that it made me feel that I had made the right choice in leaving the TV commercial industry. In these twenty years I have designed for television and film, but I still think of myself as a theatre designer.

Why do you prefer theatre design to film design?

Film design on a large scale for a major studio doesn't interest me very much. The only kind of films I like working on are small films with a very small crew, and a dedicated group of people who are interested in the film and are not just interested in the job. I've found that so many people are just thinking that it doesn't matter how it turns out, it's just another job. And that isn't good enough for me. That's why I like working in the theatre.

Filmmaking is also such a long and multifaceted process that even the super production designer—that new role that's come into film design—may not recognize his work after the cinematographer, the director, and the editor and everybody have done their work. You lose control and you become just another member of a very large venture. I don't particularly enjoy to be a part of a big anonymous crowd that makes films. Theatre is gratifying because it's rather instant in comparison to the film process. You have a reasonably short period of time to put it on. You're still involved with it in the time the public starts to see it and the responses are there, good or bad, and you have that gratification much more immediately available to you. And then you go on to something else. That's the way I like to work.

How did The Elephant Man *come about?*

Well, my career is just full of accidents, coincidences, or whatever you might want to call it. John Conklin was asked to design *The Elephant Man* with a director other than the one who ended up directing it. John lives across the hall from us and he came over one evening and said, "Here's a great script. You know, you should read this." And so I read it, and said, "Yes, it's a great story." John was very enthusiastic about it. But the director that John was working with on the project was stricken with an illness and had to be hospitalized. The producer decided that he couldn't hold on to the project any longer without going ahead with it and he hired another director. The new director was Jack Hofsiss. He didn't know John but he knew me because we had worked together before, and so Jack asked if I would be interested in designing *The Elephant Man*. I told him that they already had a designer. And he said, "Well, that's not necessarily true because I'm replacing the original director."

This was a very delicate situation because not only is John our neighbor, but he is one of our best friends. I told John what had happened and he said that he was aware that they were changing directors, and John being such a gracious person that he is said, "Absolutely, there's no problem with this thing. In fact, here's the script. You can read it again." So I started working on it with Jack Hofsiss.

Was the set for The Elephant Man *changed much when it moved from the St. Peter's theatre in the Citicorp building to the Booth Theatre on Broadway?*

There were almost no changes. Interestingly enough, the depth of the theatre at St. Peter's is 30-some feet and the set was actually a little bit deeper there than what we ended up with at the Booth. So the depth was quite similar and the width was the same, give or take 6 inches. We had much more height at the Booth and there was a whole upper section to the Broadway production that wasn't in the original because the overhead height at the St. Peter's theatre was only about 10 feet.

Did you have any particular concept for the initial idea?

The design for that set was probably an accumulation of ideas over the years. It was very intuitive. Jack Hofsiss, the director, is so facile, quick, and easy to work with and very, very quick to come to a conclusion from a range of ideas. I really adore working with Jack. There is so much that we don't have to say to one another to reach a conclusion. Jack and I have a good working relationship in terms of a designer and a director. Who knows why? Sometimes it clicks and sometimes those combinations don't work. I think we kind of burst the balloon a little bit on the theory of design when we were on a panel together and were asked how long the creative gestation period for *The Elephant Man* was. Jack and I answered almost simultaneously, "About five minutes," which sounded shallow and insincere, but it did come very quickly. I mentioned earlier that a lot of my design at one point was intuitive. I don't think I've lost that entirely. A great deal goes into the design, but I don't spend much time trying to come up with a philosophical approach to design. I do spend a lot of time working out the details once the concept is in place.

If there's a criticism of my work, it's that there is too much attention to detail, it is too meticulous. Perhaps it loses some theatricality because of that. I think if I could single out a way that I'd like to work differently, I would like to give less attention to detail. Early on I did some film work and I did a lot of regional theatre work in which the audiences were very close. It wasn't like the proscenium arch on the New York stage.

The idea of detail has been concerning me because what I have been trying to do now is to get away from that identity. And curiously enough, if you look carefully at some of my work, you'll find that it isn't filled with detail. It's very abstract. And what I think I try to do as a designer is through the suggestion of detail or the abstraction or the essence you actually create more than what is physically there because then everyone's imagination or personal experience fills in the gaps. And a lot of this has to do, of course, with the lighting and the costumes. It all fits together as a cohesive production.

For instance, *The Elephant Man* is an extraordinarily simple set. It is just a plain raked board floor; some cast-iron columns holding up brick arches, walls, and windows. But there are no doors; there are no ceilings; there are no depths of reality, yet it is thought of as a very real set.

I'm often confused when people think of my work as being so naturalistic. I don't think it is at all. I think in the latter part of my career, if that can be said since I'm not a young designer any more, I'm trying to get away from this typecasting. It's what everyone tries to avoid, but perhaps I am typecast.

You have designed for the New York City Opera Company. How did your first production come about with them?

Jack Hofsiss asked me to design *The Student Prince*. I had never worked on that scale in my life, and I enjoyed it very much. There are a few things I would do differently now.

How much time did you spend designing it?

The Student Prince went a little faster than *The Song of Norway*, which I also did at City Opera. I would say *The Student Prince* six weeks, something like that. *The Song of Norway* was a little longer process. *The Music Man* at City Opera was forever in the making. It's a huge show. For *The Student Prince* and *The Song of Norway* you bring down the curtain between acts, and you change the scenery. *The Music Man* is a large-scale Broadway-type show in which there are many scenes, and the director, Artie Masella, chose to make the scene more contemporary-mannered with open scene changes. It was a good three-and-a-half-, maybe four-month project.

Comment on the space you worked in as far as proscenium width and height at the New York State Theatre.

The height is 26 feet and we went crazy with the width on *The Music*

Man. The normal opening there is about 44 to 46 feet wide. We chose to build out in front of the proscenium arch of the State Theatre. So on one side, on the apron in front of the proscenium, we had one house unit and on the other side we had the footbridge to the park. When you consider those two extensions, our stage picture was over 60 feet across. The width of the State Theatre is larger than a Broadway house, and the depth is about 50 feet.

What do you like least about the theatre?

I guess it's either the business or the politics of it. Economy dictates the decision, i.e., arguing with a producer that what you want to do is important and for them to tell you, "No, we can't do that because we can't afford it." I go crazy when I get an idea and I can't convince somebody that it is important enough to the show to spend the extra money, and I don't mean wildly extra money. I have trouble understanding why producers make decisions about scenery based on cost when I see expenditures made in other areas that seem reckless.

I'm very interested in the kind of materials that go into a set, and frankly some materials cost more than others. This is one of the reasons I like working in regional theatres. They really do care very much about how things look

Model by David Jenkins
ACCOMPLICE by Rupert Holmes
Directed by Art Wolff
Richard Rodgers Theatre, New York (1990)

and are done. This is not to say that New York isn't that way, but New York is always considering the financial ramifications of a decision before anything else. For instance, when *The Common Pursuit* was originally done at the Long Wharf, I said I wanted a real oak floor like we did for *Quartermaine's Terms.* Let's look into the idea of using real oak floor. The production carpenter in New Haven is a very good builder and he looked into and found what is called oak shorts. They're like oak pieces that are left over and none of them are longer than about 6 feet. They are used in flooring and can be bought in bundles at a cash-and-carry lumberyard. He said, "You know, I've made an interesting discovery. There is a curious relationship between the cost of the oak flooring shorts and the finishing of the floor versus the cost of pine plus the labor of having scenic artists paint it. We may be able to get the oak floor." The cost for both was close enough so that it became an aesthetic decision rather than a financial decision. So we put down the oak floor and the result was just tremendous. There's something about the way the oak floor sounds and the way oak wears. The best thing about an oak floor in a long run is that the longer it runs, the better it looks. It gets worn nicely and you see the patina where the shoes have gone up and down the stairs and where the continuous patterns of movement are. In fact, the floor really started looking wonderful right towards the end of the run.

An interesting thing about *The Common Pursuit* when it went to London was that they had to do the floor again because it didn't travel with the set in the container. I told them that I would really like it very much if they could use a real oak floor. Well, they looked at me like frogs were coming out of my mouth and they said, "We can do the same thing with paint. Don't worry, we've got a tremendous scenic artist here and you'll be very happy." The first thing I saw on the stage when I went over there was a great-looking floor. And I said, "I don't know how you did it, but this is really very good. How did you get it to look like oak?" And they said, "It is oak. We found these things called shorts. It cost us a little extra, but we knew you'd be much happier if we did it with the oak."

What do you like most about working in the theatre?

The thing I like most is the collaboration. I'm very much a collaborative artist and I prefer finding directors and other designers and stage managers and casts who all seem to be headed in the same direction on a piece. I think if I had been more of a painter or sculptor I wouldn't have gone into the theatre. I've always liked working with others.

If I were planning on a career in the theatre, what would you advise me to study in school to prepare myself to come to New York and design?

I would advise you to study accounting! As lofty as these conversations can

435

tend to get and all these ideas about artistry and craft, it is still a business. Unless you are prepared to make your way through the labyrinth of the business world, and you feel secure in that, you're going to be eaten alive. You can get representation to help you, which is probably very important in terms of contracts, but you have to have a good knowledge of the economics of the theatre, of business, and of making a living. Is it possible to muddle your way through a career and try to maintain some semblance of what you thought design in the theatre was all about? It's not easy.

Seriously, if I were coming into New York today as a graduate from a university, my first concern would be where do I live and how do I support myself? There are not very clear-cut ways to chart a career so that you can get to a point where you can make a living. How do you support yourself for five years as an assistant or working in low-paying jobs? It's complicated. If I lived alone with no responsibilities toward a family, I could probably think my way through the economic structure of the city.

Do you feel that it is important to get a lawyer to handle your business when you come to New York?

It's foolish to come here and the first thing you do is get an attorney. There is a time when you have to realize that you need representation, and that is when you are in a position to negotiate. There's no sense in getting someone to negotiate for you when they can't negotiate past the minimums you are going to be paid. Negotiation is only to get you above the basic minimums. I personally prefer a lawyer. But an agent will seek employment for you and an attorney only negotiates contracts for the work you have found.

But how many agents know how to read a portfolio and know how to get work that you want?

Well, that's a problem. How do you choose a dentist? Somehow it's got to be because they're doing the right thing for your teeth. So an agent has to be doing the right thing for your career. I think anybody who chooses an agent should be very careful not to choose one who already has a lot of designers in the stable, because you're going to be pretty well down on the pecking order.

I think you need to somehow develop a body of work before you invite an agent to see your work or go to an agent and say, "Here is my work," and they can say, "Oh yes, I remember seeing that last year at the Manhattan Theatre Club." I don't think a portfolio is going to get an agent's interest. The only thing that is going to get an agent's interest is that you are in the market of actually having done productions.

When I got a lucky break and came to New York with *The Changing Room* I didn't think I needed any kind of representation, but I should have gotten it right then. After I sat down with the general manager for that particular production I came out in shreds. It was like being thrown into the shark tank. I was humiliated as an artist. I was humiliated as a person, and how dare I come in and negotiate a contract? I found myself leaving that office totally demoralized. I'll never forget it. It was raining and I had no umbrella and no raincoat. I just walked for hours in the rain feeling just horrible about myself and how did I ever allow myself to get in this position. Later on when *The Elephant Man* came along, I had an attorney to negotiate with one of the most difficult managements in New York. And when the contract was all in place, the management was all smiles, hugs and kisses, and everything was fine. Had I gone through the negotiating personally, I could never have been able to turn my emotions around that quickly.

I think it's very important for potential designers to know that the theatre is not a terribly lucrative field. There are maybe a handful of stage designers who make what could be considered a decent income. It has a lot to do with talent, a lot to do with luck, and a lot to do with timing. The majority of designers who work exclusively in the theatre have a difficult time making it financially.

Is there any specific production you'd like to do in the theatre that you haven't done?

The only thing I would like to do is new scripts. I prefer to do work that hasn't been done before. For me, it's much more exciting than rethinking a script that has been designed many times over by so many different designers. Shakespeare is the exception.

Do you have favorites among the productions that you have designed?

What really counts is the satisfaction of time well spent, artistic goals met, the sense of a production being successful in that all the pieces fall together in a way that is memorable. It's a very rare event in the theatre, at least for me, when everything works as planned. If you have a dozen in a lifetime, that's quite remarkable. The common denominator in the work that I feel most identifiable with is a sense of a group of people getting together and somehow molding themselves into a single unit—designers, actors, directors, stage management. It's rare, but that's good. Wouldn't it be terrible if it were all so easy?

Model by David Jenkins
TWO SHAKESPEAREAN ACTORS by Richard Nelson
Directed by Jack O'Brien
Cort Theatre, New York (1991)

10

OPENWORK SCENERY, SURROUNDS, SUSPENDED SCENERY, AND FOLIAGE

OPENWORK SCENERY

Designing Openwork Scenery

Openwork scenery is always an interesting visual feature of a scenic design. An endless number of variations are possible in the design, the building, the materials, and the stage lighting of openwork scenery.

One reason why openwork scenery is so successful onstage is that a change in the lighting produces a variety of effects that can be judiciously used by the designer. Spectacular designs can be realized with sharp backlighting that brightly defines the network of silhouettes. Other theatrical effects, such as lighting the front of the actual cutouts and leaving the background in darkness or on a low light level, create another atmospheric extension of the same scenery. Openwork scenery is also extremely interesting when a combination of front and back lighting is used in the same production, giving the same set pieces an entirely different visual impact during the action of the play, opera, musical, or revue.

Openwork scenery is designed to be framed (hard) or unframed (soft). It is appropriate for almost any kind of setting, from interiors to exteriors to abstractions. These examples indicate something of the wide range of subject matter and materials possible with openwork scenery.

1. An opaque Gothic window design cut out of iron-on fabric that is adhered to a backdrop of linen scrim (for the window) and muslin (at the top and on each side).

2. A tall leaning open window cut out of ³/₄-inch plywood, backed with screen wire and positioned in a setting of solid walls for the artist's attic studio in *La Bohème*, Act 1.

3. A full-stage ballet design made by weaving rolls of narrow gauze bandages in and out of an open backdrop of standard 1-inch scenic netting.

4. A turn-of-the-century ornate open railing of ¹/₂-inch plywood that is almost waist height and is positioned parallel to and in front of a Magritte-style sky drop.

5. A full set in the style of Giotto consisting of fancy open arches, columns, railings, and finials, all made of ³/₄-inch plywood and placed in front of a dark red surround.

6. An average surround made of 18-inch-diameter circles cut out of ¹/₄-inch plywood, attached in an interlocking design with a black velour backdrop positioned upstage of it.

7. A full-stage setting of tall elaborate oriental screens with some of the openings backed with pieces of sharkstooth scrim and the rest left open and positioned upstage is a background of horizontal slatted panels.

8. A front portal for a musical made with large-scale tropical foliage cutouts, all backed with organza.

9. A large tilted ³/₄-inch plywood cutout Art Deco ceiling holding three-dimensional draped swags and jabots on the outer sides and upstage edges.

10. Seven panels of Spanish grillwork cut out of ¹/₂-inch plywood that are framed and hung vertically at random heights and positioned in front of metallic rain curtains.

11. Five Victorian lattice houses, dressed with leaves, vines, and Japanese lanterns, positioned in an asymmetrical ground plan in front of a dark blue sky.

Using Openwork Railings

Openwork railings are among the most popular pieces of cutout scenery. You see these railings on platforms, stairs, terraces, around parks, railroad stations, cemeteries, balconies, saloons, porches, on the tops of buildings, on ships, and other places. The shapes of the railings range from thin delicate swirling lines of metalwork detailing a Victorian design to a rustic and crude wooden pattern around a mountain chateau.

In a ground plan, the purpose of a railing may be to define a specific playing area in the stage space. It may also be a piece of scenery that joins one wall to another or one building to another, or be used alone in the stage space just to suggest a locale.

A Designer Doing Both Designing and Painting

Because a scenic designer outside a commercial situation (and union) not only designs but also paints scenery in addition to sometimes building part or all of it, the following discussion refers

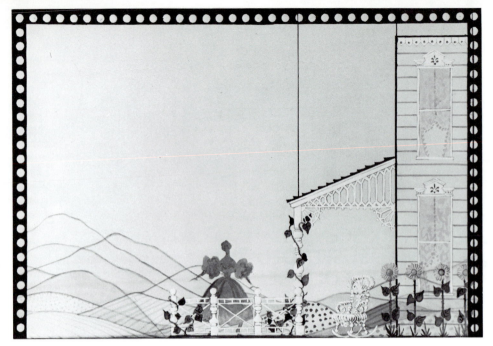

Stage design by William and Jean Eckart
THE GOLDEN APPLE—Helen's house
Written by John Latouche
Music by Jerome Moross
Directed by Norman Lloyd
Choreography and musical numbers staged by
    Hanya Holm
Phoenix and Alvin Theatres, New York (1954)

back and forth from the design studio to the scenic shop.

Openwork Scenery in Perspective

Openwork sets in perspective can be especially attractive as scenic designs, but additional time is usually required to draw and figure the proper vanishing points for building them. In the designer's studio this doesn't require a particularly large work area, but in the scenic shop a great deal of floor area may be needed that would take away from other things being worked on. For instance, if you are making a large full-scale drawing in perspective on the floor in the scenic studio, you need to have a large unobstructed space available even when working with only one vanishing point. The vanishing point is represented by a nail driven into the floor at one end of the space. A snapline

rubbed with charcoal is attached to the nail so lines can be snapped on the brown paper to make the perspective drawing. And frequently more than one vanishing point is needed in order to do a full-size perspective drawing.

A front elevation drawing of a single unit without any perspective can often be made by a building carpenter instead of a scenic artist. Another cost-saving aspect of designing a railing without perspective, for example, is that you can make one full-scale drawing and use it many times to repeat other sections of the same railing.

Drawing Openwork Scenery

When designing openwork scenery, draw accurate details both on the sheets of drafting and on the full-scale

Edward Gorey's show curtain design for DRACULA (1973), Nantucket, Massachusetts.

pounce in the shop. Specify dimensions of openings and repeats of the openwork design on the drafting. Always draw grids to serve as center lines when figuring out geometric designs. Standard grid lines may be horizontal, vertical, diagonal, or slanted (45 degrees and 30 to 60 degrees); circles also may work well as shapes for drawing certain objects.

Materials for Cutting Out Openwork Designs

Usually the most practical and available material for cutouts on flat surfaces is plywood in the thickness of ¾, ½, or ¼ inch. The proper thickness depends on the strength, visual, and budget requirements, but ¾-inch plywood is the one most often used.

Openwork scenery can also be created out of wallboard sheets, metal sheeting, and metal welding of round, square, and flat lengths. Upson board can be effective for lower-budget productions.

A list of materials to go behind openwork scenery may include such fabrics as sharkstooth scrim, linen scrim, organza, and chiffon. Screen wire, Plexiglas, and other acrylic sheets of various thicknesses (both clear and translucent) also are popular choices to go behind the basic cutout shapes.

Constructing Openwork Patterns

Sometimes in Off-Broadway or university theatres or stock you may have the opportunity to help build and paint the scenery. When so doing, use the following information to construct openwork patterns. Draw designs in full scale on brown Kraft paper, perforate the single outline of the design with a pounce wheel, then transfer the drawing onto the plywood surface with a bag of powdered charcoal and spray it with a fixative (Krylon or other). Mark areas to be cut out with an *X*. Drill appropriate holes in each area so the blade of the jigsaw can enter the plywood areas to be cut out.

Allow plenty of time to cut out neat patterns in plywood. Fill any holes and cracks with wood putty and sand the surfaces well. Usually plywood cutouts are not covered on the face because of the time and labor involved, unless some special effect like a metallic or mirror finish is desired.

Framing is needed around most typical flat cutout pieces. For support, the outer edges of screens and panels should be designed to have a standard straight 1 × 3-inch-thick wooden framing around the outer edges to hold the cutout patterns together. Or lengths of metal may be used as an outer support material, especially if a thinner width is desired.

Naturally, the outer framework of a cutout piece varies enormously. For example, an ornate cutout staircase railing unit could have the handrail support it at the top, the newel post support it at one end, a vertical stair member as support for the opposite end, and for the bottom support a cutout silhouette piece that matches the profile of the risers and treads of the steps.

Curved cutout pieces also need to have their outer edges supported, either with wood or metal or a combination of both. If you are doing a curved fence or stairway unit, you may want to use ⅛-inch (or ³⁄₃₂-inch) layers of plywood laminated together. Soak the plywood in water first, then glue each piece together until the desired thickness (¾ to 1 inch) is built up. When the piece is ready, use a pounce or draw or paint the cutout designs on the curved plywood piece so they can be cut out with a jigsaw. Plan how much wood you need to leave on the outer edges for support.

Remember, too, that the outer edges of cutout designs can vary a great deal. For instance, a hanging piece could work with only the horizontal top being the main support member.

Painting Openwork Scenery

Priming on openwork scenery may be done with vinyl, latex, or oil paints to get rid of the graining or imperfections in the wood. Overpainting may be done with the same paints and also with casein paints. To get all of the surfaces of the wooden edges, the paint should be applied by brush, then overpainting can be done by brush, spray, sponge, or paint roller.

Model by David Jenkins
OTHER PEOPLE'S MONEY by Jerry Sterner
Directed by Gloria Muzio
Minetta Lane Theatre, New York (1989)
(Photograph by David Jenkins)

Positioning Openwork Units Onstage

Openwork scenery may be positioned onstage as an independent piece, or it may work with another scenic unit. The cutout unit may be placed onstage in one or more of these ways:

1. Hinged freestanding with one or more other openwork units
2. Hung from the grid with hardware attached for flying in and out
3. Tracked on and off on a platform on the floor
4. Tracked on and off on a traveler track suspended from the grid
5. Hinged to fold onstage when it is part of another unit

Stage design by William and Jean Eckart
THE GOLDEN APPLE—the orchard
Phoenix and Alvin Theatres, New York (1954)

Designing Full-Stage Openwork Designs on Scenic Netting

There are enormous possibilities for designing full-stage openwork patterns to be cut out of pieces of fabric or materials such as ribbon on 1-inch scenic netting. In thinking about this, decide whether the full-stage scenery is to move or not during the show. Is it a design on scenic netting of which the outer edges are to be masked at the top and sides by a hard portal, by soft draperies, or other scenery? Or do you intend to have the edges show as part of the overall concept?

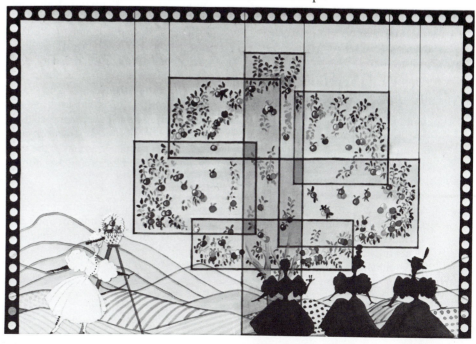

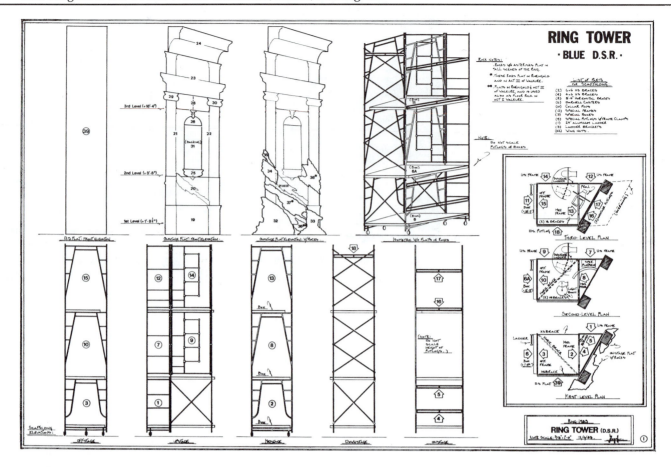

While resolving the latter question as a design project, keep in mind how many other pieces of various-sized scenery are to play with the full-scale large piece.

Checklist of Geometric Designs

Circles	Hexagons (and half
Arches	hexagons)
Diamonds	Octagons (and half
Squares	octagons)
Rectangles	Ellipses
Vertical and horizon-	Latticework
tal lines	Triangles

Designing and Constructing Framed Skeletonized Scenery

Cutout scenery may be designed to be cut from one piece of wood, such as ¾-inch plywood. Or it may be framed out of 1 × 3-inch wood with the cutouts attached inside and flush with the framing. Sometimes ¼-inch plywood cutouts are attached on the back of 1 × 3-inch framing. The point is to make the openwork scenery to appear neat and attractive when viewed from different angles, such as from the end,

from the back, or even through the front. The ¼-inch plywood corner blocks on the rear, and any similar pieces, should never be obvious, but should appear as if they are blocked in neatly. For example, on a large piece, you may need to block in strips of ¼-inch plywood in the vertical stiles and also the horizontal rails. On a very small piece, you might want to fill in the whole back, including the center cutout. This all depends on the desired effect. The entire back of it should be built up flush so it is in one plane. The idea is to make the openwork scenery look as if it is neatly cut out of one gigantic piece of illustration board.

One way to achieve this is to laminate two layers of wood together by gluing and nailing (or screwing) so that the breaks of the wood on the front and back are staggered. This makes the traditional corner blocks and keystones unnecessary.

Various combinations of layers for wood laminating pieces of scenery are possible. Listed are some common dimensions. Breaks in wood may be straight or for more strength, diagonal, V-shaped, or other.

¾″ on ¾″	¼″ on ¼″	¼″ on ⅜″
½″ on ½″	¼″ on ¾″	½″ on ¾″
⅜″ on ⅜″	¼″ on ⅜″	½″ on ⅜″

Using Screen Wire to Cover Open-Framed Scenery

Screen wire is an excellent material for covering open-framed scenery pieces when the idea is to have a see-through effect accentuated with various silhouettes and profiles. The stiffness of screen wire lends itself beautifully to creating irregular profiles within the open-framed scenery piece. Screen wire profiles readily retain their shape, often without additional support. If support is needed, thin flexible wire, which would be invisible to the audience, can be used. Texture is also easy to apply to screen wire.

Screening can be used to cover all sorts of open-framed pieces, such as flats, ground rows, and hanging portals. The wire is usually tacked or stapled onto wooden open frames or wired onto metal open frames. All sorts of shapes can be cut from another piece of screen wire and applied over the ba-

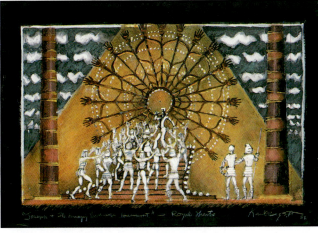

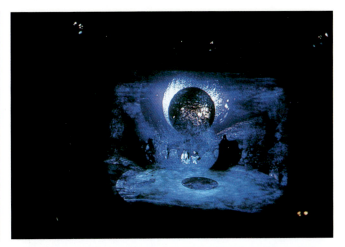

Above: Karl Eigsti: JOSEPH AND THE AMAZING TECHNICOLOR DREAMCOAT (1982); Tony Walton: FOUR BABOONS ADORING THE SUN (1992), Costumes: Willa Kim, Lighting: Richard Pilbrow, Projections: Wendall K. Harringon; James Stewart Morcom: MUSIC HALL FOLLIES (1960), Music Hall; Lynn Pecktal: AH, WILDERNESS! (1966), Lighting: Roger Morgan. *Below:* Adrianne Lobel: LULU (1981), Costumes: Rita Ryack, Lighting: Paul Gallo (Photographs by Adam Lobel); Randy Barcelo: BLOOD WEDDING (1979); Marjorie Bradley Kellogg: EXTREMITIES (1982).

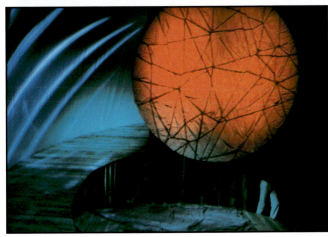

Carrie Robbins: HAMLET (1978)

William Ivey Long: FACE VALUE (1993)

Miles White: BLOOMER GIRL (1944)

Patricia Zipprodt: PIPPIN (1972)

Tony Walton: THE TRAVAILS OF SANCHO
PANZA (1969)

Patton Campbell: REGINA (1980)

John Scheffler: Mardi Gras (1988)

Robert Perdziola: THE PROTAGONIST (1993)

Randy Barcelo: STARMANIA (1979)

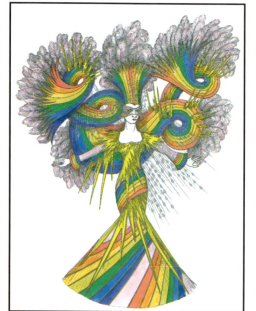

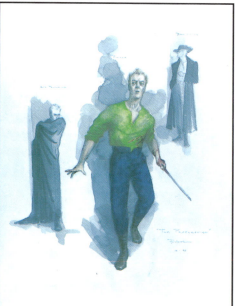

Varona: THE MERRY WIDOW (1979)

Alvin Colt: GUYS AND DOLLS (1950)

Robert Perdziola: THE MIDNIGHT ANGEL (1933)

 Barcelo: LES TROYENS (1976)

Gregg Barnes: PHANTOM (1993)

José Varona: ROMEO ET JULIETTE (1981)

do Sicangco: BABES IN TOYLAND (1991)

Eduardo Sicangco: THE ROYAL HUNT OF
THE SUN (1991)

Carrie Robbins: AGNES OF GOD (1982)

Robert D. Mitchell: UNDER THE SUN (1976) (Photographs by Patrick H. Horrigan)

  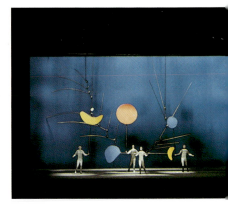

John Lee Beatty: FIFTH OF JULY (1980). *Left:* Act 1. *Right:* Act 2.

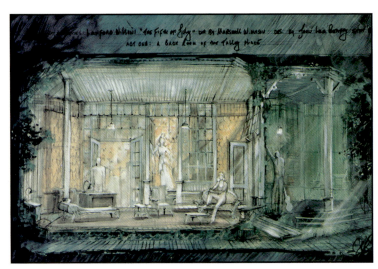 

Elmon Webb and Virginia Dancy: YOU NEVER CAN TELL (1978), Lighting: Bennet Averyt; Tony Walton: ANYTHING GOES (1987), Lighting: Paul Gallo; George Tsypin: LEON AND LENA AND LENZ (1987)

  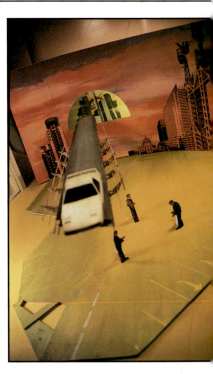

sic screen wire covering. These silhouettes may range in shape from curved to straight or zigzagged and may be positioned at random so that various parts overlap. Also, several layers of screen wire may be applied on one silhouette to give a more opaque effect. The additional pieces of wire can be attached to the basic covering by using short lengths of thin wire.

Instead of adding screen silhouettes, openings can be cut out of the basic wire covering to create more interest. However, if the openings are too numerous or too large, there is a danger of the positive area's losing its shape. Then thin wire must be used to support what is left of the basic wire covering. Profiles cut from screen wire can also be attached to open-framed scenery.

When screen wire is to be painted, it should be laid in with latex or acrylic paint so that overpainting can be done with the same paints, or with caseins, or dye. Also, scenic dope or other similar texture materials can be dragged over the screen wire surface to give more opaque and varied texturing.

A screen wire surface gives somewhat the same effect as sharkstooth scrim, and it takes both front and back lighting beautifully. Screen wire surfaces on profiled shapes are especially effective when silhouetted with careful lighting on a rear backdrop.

Using Plastic Screening for a See-Through Effect

Plastic screen can also be used for openwork scenery, but it does not retain its shape like screen wire. It can be too easily pulled and stretched out of shape. However, plastic screening is useful for a nice see-through effect behind windows and doors. It may also be used as a supplementary material for adding irregular layers onto screen wire.

Screen wire is usually tacked or stapled onto the wooden open frames, or if the open frames are metal, the screening is wired on. When desired, all sorts of shapes can be cut from the screen wire and applied in one or two layers over the basic screen covering. These can also be attached by thin wire, and additional layers of scenic dope or the like can be brushed and dragged over these appliqués give more opaque and varied texturing.

Creating Settings with Metal Scaffolding

Metal scaffolding units like those used in commercial construction work are striking scenic units for proscenium, black box theatre, and open stage productions. These metal units can be especially effective when designed with vertical and horizontal members and supported with diagonal and triangu-

Setting by John Scheffler
CARMEN by Georges Bizet
Directed by Patrick Bakman
Houston Grand Opera
Houston, Texas (1974)

"Industrial scaffolding was used as a basic set complete with interior staircases. All units were on wheels. Scenic pieces were added or deleted as the pieces were regrouped for the four various locations."

—John Scheffler

lar bracing. During performance, the units may remain stationary or may shift on heavy rubberized wheels or casters. The scaffolding units can be completely exposed or they can be disguised with partial or full scenery for the individual unit. The appearance of the scaffolding may be changed by the addition of planking, wire mesh, erosion cloth, canvas hangings, corrugated metal, and other materials. These units can also be brought together in a collage to form all sorts of interesting arrangements. Configurations may change during the course of action by opening hinged pieces that lift up, down, or swing around; by hoisting up draped curtains; or by lowering drop cloths over the units.

Sets of metal scaffolding may be created for a height of one story, two stories, or a half story in which both stairways and ladders may be utilized. Sets of metal scaffolding may be arranged in groups or as a single structure. These tall, square vertical units work beautifully for holding lighting instruments as well, and are ideal for black box theatres because of their practicality, versatility, and durability.

Creating Decorative Jacks That Are Seen from the Audience

Wooden jacks with a diagonal or triangular support have long been a standard way of bracing certain pieces of scenery from behind. But for cutout scenery designed to look as if it is standing without the aid of bracing, any number of plain or decorative supporting jacks may be designed to fit in with the rest of the cutout-type scenery. These jacks may be made of soft wood, plywood, or metal (flat, round, square), or a combination of all of these materials. Often jacks made of metal are created to be decorative because they are to be seen from the audience. Thin metal jacks are great for bracing ground rows, set pieces, or wings. These units may be completely open or may have cutout areas covered with gauze, scrim, or other see-through materials.

Use pin hinges to fasten decorative jacks to the scenery and attach a metal foot iron at the bottom. Hold the jack (with scenery) in place on the deck with a stage screw, pig iron, or sandbag, depending on the size and weight of the jack.

Openwork Designs for Windows, Standing Screens, Walls, and Hanging Panels

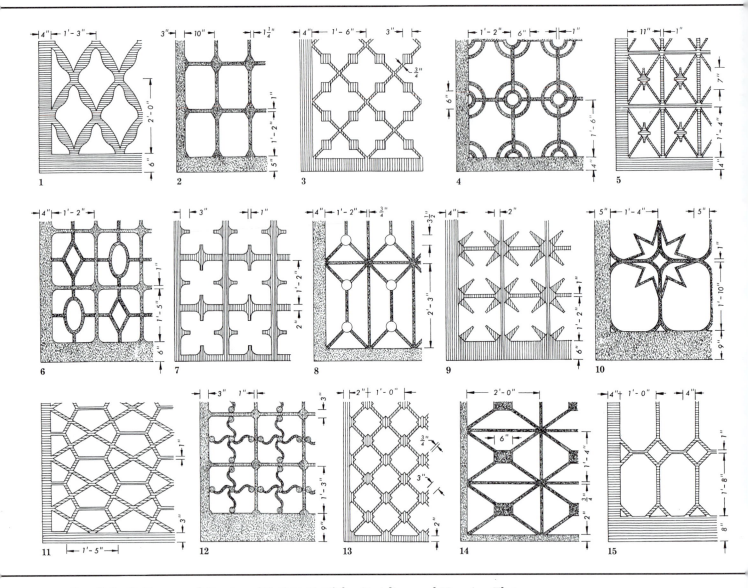

Small-Scale Openwork Designs (3'-4" × 2'-0") for Standing and Hanging Flats

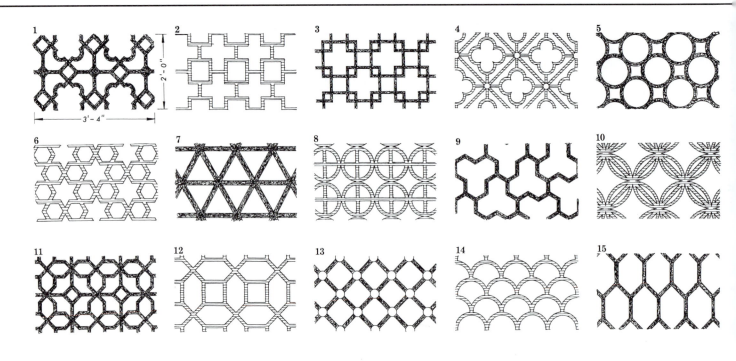

Using Gazebos Onstage

Gazebos are in the family of lovely openwork structures that includes bandstands, latticework hovels, and summer houses. These attractive scenic units always tend to create a feeling of romance, charm, and nostalgia. They work beautifully for exterior scenes in musicals, revues, operas, and ballets. They also make ideal settings for fashion shows, outdoor park concerts, tea dances, campus homecoming festivities, and garden parties. Gazebos are attractive units not only for the summer season, but also for spring, fall, and winter scenes.

While a stunning effect can be created by having a single large gazebo positioned in the center of the stage, another equally compelling design can be achieved by positioning a group of two, three, or four contrasting gazebo shapes together. This may seem lavish, but extremely exciting and highly theatrical variations can be obtained by using multiple gazebos in a handsome exterior setting.

Designing a Plan for a Gazebo

A gazebo is usually designed to be in full round and can be made in any number of shapes, including a square, a hexagon, an octagon, an oval, a circle, or a rectangle. When designing a gazebo, begin by working out the basic shape of the ground plan for it. For visual and practical purposes it works well to think of having a foundation platform unit on which to construct the walls and roof of the gazebo.

This platform base may be a 6-inch platform in the chosen geometric shape. If this shape is a square, an octagon, or a hexagon (or other), it may

have vertical flats (or walls) with widths approximately the same as the outer sides of these aforementioned platform shapes. For circular or oval platforms, of course, this would not be the same thing. Obviously then the side flats (or walls) would have to be broken up into arbitrary widths. In other words, the openwork walls of the gazebo may be built like individual flats and wrap around the sides of the basic bottom platform while at the same time the vertical outer edges would butt against each other. The vertical edges of the flats (joining each other) could also be cut on angles according to the shape of the bottom platform being used.

A second idea would be to have a higher platform, 1 foot high, with the bottom of the flats resting on top of the main geometric-shaped platform. In this case the flats would line up flush with the outer 1-foot-high face on the platform. Then, if preferred, a 6-inch-high step unit can be designed to go around the whole unit and rest on the stage floor.

Still a third method for designing the platform on which to position the gazebo would be to have a larger platform which extends past the outer walls and which is higher, too. The total height of this platform could be 2 to 3 feet, while the extension past the outer walls of the gazebo could be at least 2 feet 6 inches. This extension could

Settings by Rolf Beyer
THE COMEDY OF ERRORS by Shakespeare
Directed by Teddy Handfield
Lighting by Allen Lee Hughes
Catholic University
Washington, D.C. (1972)

GHOST SONATA by August Strindberg
Directed by Rod Alexander
Lighting by Alan Kibbe
Dartmouth College
Hanover, New Hampshire (1970)
(Photograph by Al Olson)

function as a nice walkway going around the entire outside structure of the actual gazebo. This platform unit could also have a handrail supported by simple posts. The sides of the actual platform unit could be designed with open panels of latticework, and step units going up to the walkway could alternate with the open side panels. There are numerous possibilities for creating interesting gazebos.

Designing the Gazebo Sides

For clarity, assume that the platform discussed in the first example is the one being built, and that it is a 6-inch high square platform. This means there would be four side flats. For a hexagon platform it would be six flats, eight for an octagon, and so on.

It is a good idea to keep the open flat design contained within each side of the gazebo. If there are four sides, there could be four open arches, or two arches and two latticed walls. With six sides there could be three and three of each, or two arches and four enclosed railings. The combinations go on and on.

How detailed each side gets, of course, depends on the basic design. However, for a neat job it is usually essential to block in the rear of each side. For instance, if you are building an outer shape of 1 × 3's to form the flat and overlapping with a ¼-inch latticework pattern on the back, where the lattice pattern is cut and ends on the back the area around the lattice should be filled in with the same thickness of wood to look finished. Or it could have a strip of molding running around the outside of the latticework to give it a neat-looking appearance.

The sides can then be held together with loose pin hinges on the inside, and also the sides can be attached (on

the inside) with pin hinges to the bottom platform.

Supporting the Tops of the Sides of a Gazebo

The tops of the flats should be supported by an openwork structure identical to the shape of the bottom platform. This may be a cutout geometric shape such as a square, hexagon, octagon, or other design. The bracing should be a pleasant visual structure that drops down in behind the top rails of the flats about an inch and is fastened by loose pin hinges or screws. For instance, this supporting openwork structure could be a 1×3-inch square shape with 1×3-inch lengths going diagonally to the corners and crossing in the center, or any number of shapes but with similar 1×3-inch members radiating from the center. This top member is a wonderful place to hang a chandelier.

Designing the Gazebo Top

Naturally, the finished top of the gazebo usually follows the shape of the bottom platform and also the supporting top structure holding the flats together. Some roof designs have a nice, wide overhang beyond the side flats, while others do not. Tops for gazebos vary considerably. They may have flat or curved surfaces or a mixture of both. They may appear solid with shingles or have an open structure at the very top which may also be finished off with identical shingles. Ornamentation on the top may be an enormous finial, a flagpole, or even a weathervane.

The Sizes of Gazebos

The overall size of a gazebo can be quite large if it is going on a proscenium stage that has an opening 38'-0" wide by 22'-0" high. It really depends on how the gazebo is to be used. For instance, an open structure designed to hold twenty musicians on chairs would have to be rather sizable, whereas a gazebo enclosing a table and chairs for six actors would most likely be smaller.

Lattice Strips

While the size and popularity of lattice strips vary with the place of purchase,

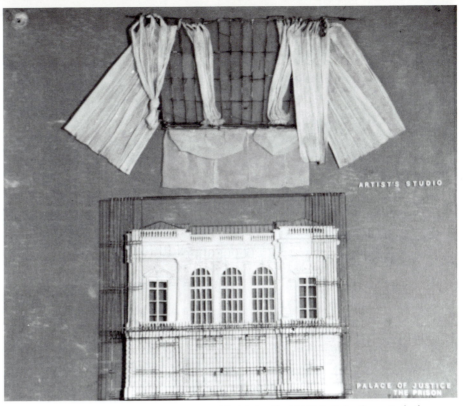

Models by David Mitchell for the revival of CAN-CAN (1981) at the Minskoff Theatre. (Photograph by David Mitchell)

"In the artist's studio the material was folded and rolled around the skylight window. As the window flew in and tilted to the audience, the material unfurled to the floor. The Palace of Justice hanger served as a courtroom background and with the addition of the jail bars became the prison." —David Mitchell

consider these basic sizes when creating openwork designs in settings:

$1/4'' \times 1/2''$	$1/4'' \times 1^3/8''$	$1/2'' \times 2^5/8''$
$1/4'' \times 3/4''$	$1/4'' \times 1^5/8''$	$1/4'' \times 3^5/8''$
$1/4'' \times 7/8''$	$1/4'' \times 2''$	$1/4'' \times 5^1/4''$
$1/4'' \times 1^1/8''$	$1/2'' \times 2^1/4''$	

Accessories for Gazebos

These items for dressing may be used on or in gazebos. A spectacular look can be obtained with the right selection and placement of objects. Accessories for a gazebo may include:

Chandeliers and sconces	Curtain panels
Hanging lamps	Paper lanterns
Tiny lights	Draped beads

FLOWERS AND PLANTS

Palm trees	Weeping willow
Vines	leaves
Spanish moss	Forsythia
Rhododendron	Geraniums and lilacs
leaves	Cherry blossoms
Hanging and sitting	Lilies
ferns	Sunflowers

FURNITURE

Wicker chairs and	Decorative metal
tables	chairs
Bentwood chairs	Tables with cloths
Ice-cream chairs	Ballroom chairs
Swings and benches	Built seats
Loveseats and settees	Stools

Checklist of Decorative Objects for Gardens, Terraces, and Exteriors

Shell and round birdbaths	Stone garden benches
Figures of the seasons	Sundials on pedestals
Classic boy and girl figures	Astrolabes
Italian terra-cotta pots	Cupid and cherub statues
Pine cone and pineapple finials	Deer and unicorn figures
Owl and peacock figures	Seahorses and dolphins
Stone fruit baskets	Fountains (one-, two-, or three-tier)
Fluted urns	Wall shells and carved heads
Fountain figures	Balustrade units
Metal tables and chairs	Wooden benches
Lanterns and lampposts	Trees and foliage
Flowers and blossoms	Latticework and trellises
Brick and stone walls	Metal and wooden fences
	Ornate bird houses

Painted Lattice Designs on a Muslin Cut Drop

Lattice House with Foliage Painted on Muslin, Cut Out and Glued on 1-inch Scenic Netting

Lattice Designs by Lynn Pecktal for THE MUSIC MAN (1979), Jones Beach Theatre, Wantagh, Long Island, New York; *below left:* Lattice Patterns for Other Shows

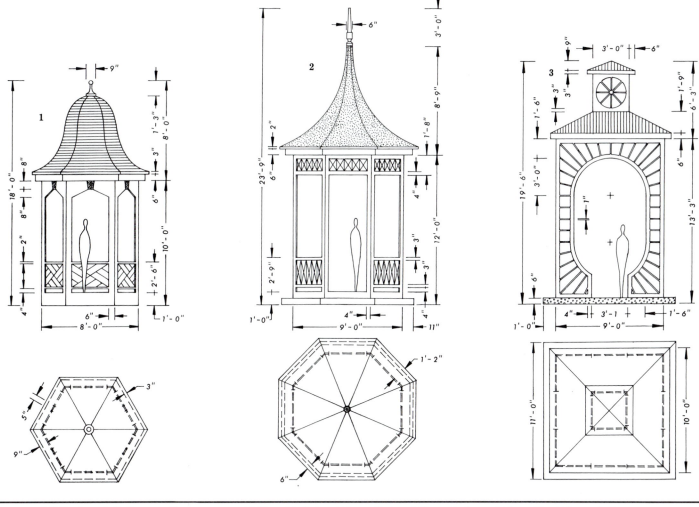

All Laths 1½"; Spaces Between: 1. 2½" × 2½"; 2. 4½" × 7"; 3. 4½" × 4½"; 4. 4½" × 7"; 4½" × 4½";
5. 4½" H × 2½" V; 2½" × 4½"; 6. 4½" × 4½"; 7. 7½" × 4½"; 8. 4½" × 7½"

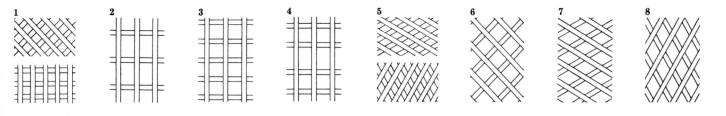

Arch Opening in Lattice Panels (5'-0" Wide by 3'-6" High)

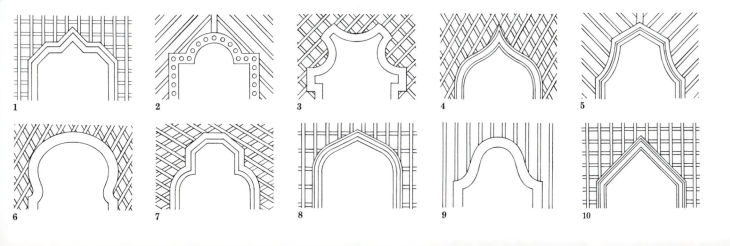

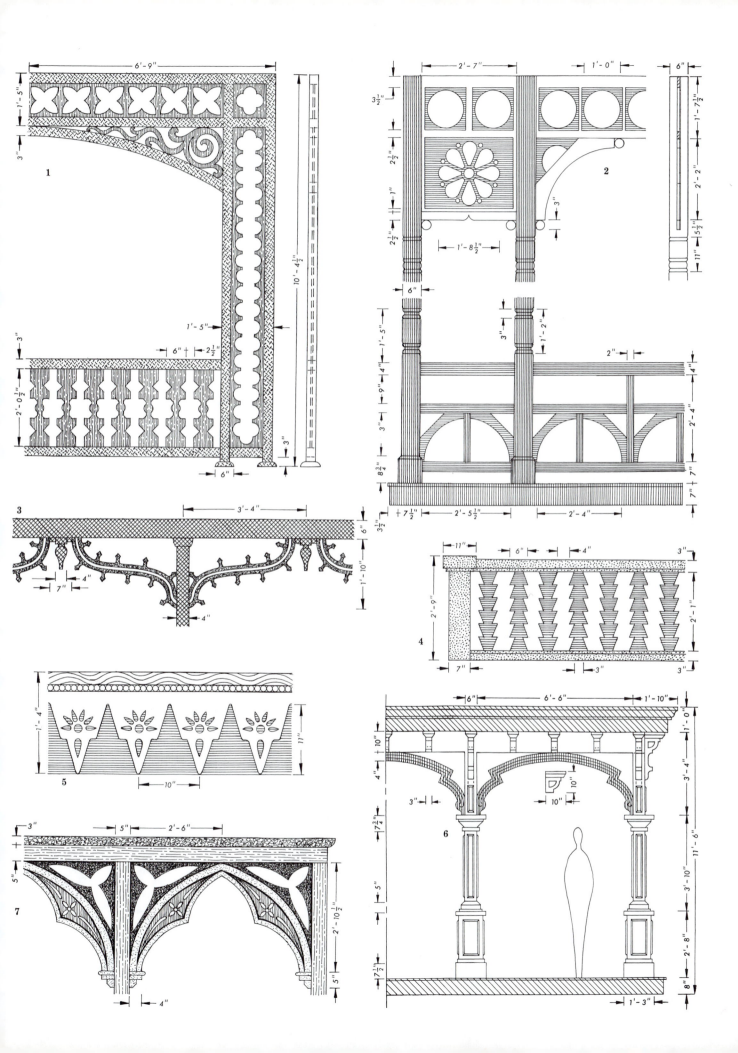

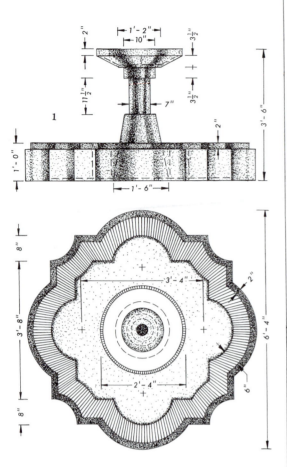

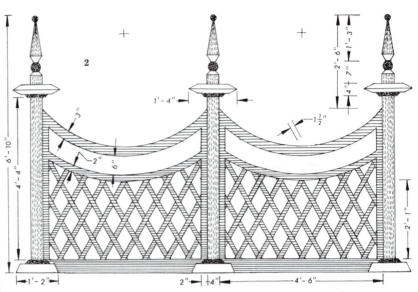

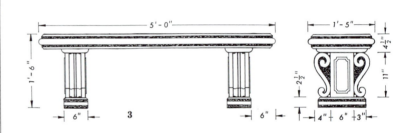

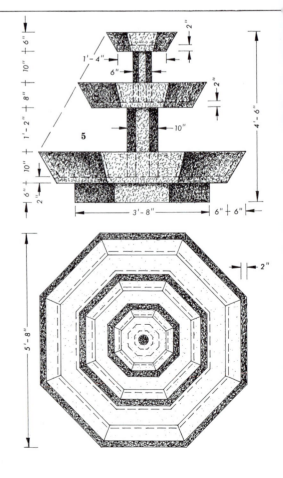

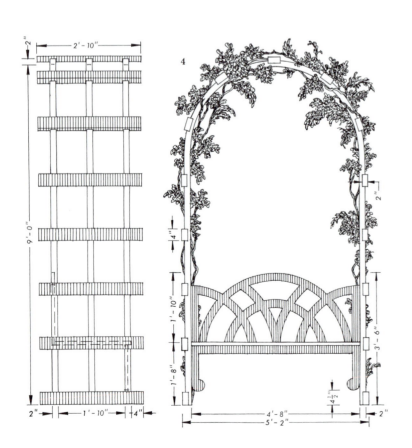

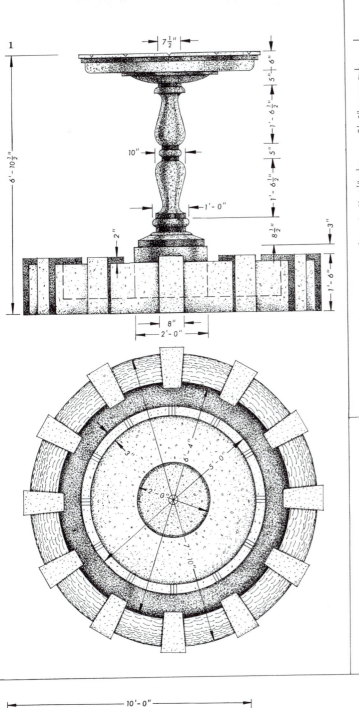

1

7 1/2"

6"
5 1/2"
6'-10 1/2"
1'-6 1/2"
5"
1'-6 1/2"
8 1/2"
3"
10"
1'-0"
2"
1'-6"

8"
2'-0"

6'-4"
5'-0"
2'-0"
1'-10"

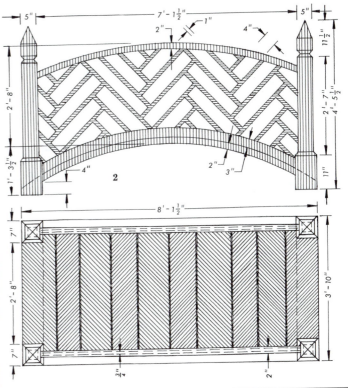

2

5"
7'-1 1/2"
1"
2"
4"
5"
11 1/2"
2'-8"
2'-7"
4'-5 1/2"
1'-3 1/2"
4"
11"
2"
3"

8'-1 1/2"
7"
2'-8"
7"
3'-10"
3/4"
2"

3

5'-2"
2"
1'-6"
2"
3"
11"
2'-4"
1'-3"

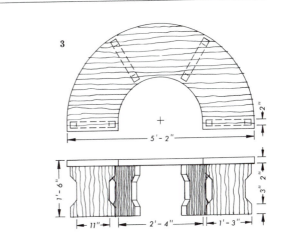

4

10'-0"
5'-0"
10'-6"
6"
2'-6"
6"
3'-0"
6"
6'-0"

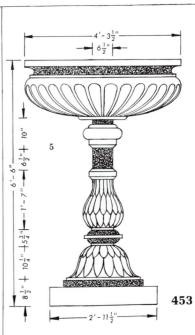

5

4'-3 1/2"
6 1/2"
10"
6 1/2"
1'-7"
6'-6"
5 3/4"
10 1/4"
8 1/2"
2'-11 1/2"

453

Model, setting, and lighting by Neil Peter
Jampolis
FIDELIO by Ludwig von Beethoven
Libretto by Josef Sonnleithner
Directed by Francesca Zambello
Houston Grand Opera
Jones Hall, Houston, Texas (1984)
(Photographs by Neil Peter Jampolis)

" 'Chain link' was plastic snow fence on PVC
frames. Translucent plastic backdrop. 'Bridges'
were suspended and flew in and out to a maximum 18 feet from the deck."
—Neil Peter Jampolis
Shown: ¼-inch model and Act 1 prisoners'
chorus.

FENCES

Using Openwork Fences Onstage

Fences for the stage are interesting to
design because they have such versatility and purpose in a setting. They
work beautifully for both proscenium
and open stages. Openwork fences are
often cut out of ¾-inch plywood or are
made of wood and combined with
metalwork. Except for very thin units,
complete fences are not ordinarily
made of all metal because of the excess
weight and expense. The style or kind
of fence dictates the materials to be
used for construction. Some simple
materials to use in making fences for
the stage are regular softwoods, rough
crafting wood, plywood, and metal.

Listed are some of the ways fences
may be used onstage.

1. To visually and practically tie one or
   more scenic units together, such as
   houses, sheds, barns, or other architectural pieces.
2. To define playing areas.
3. To be used for blocking the action, as
   a place for actors to sit on, climb over,
   or lean against.
4. To establish a certain historical period
   or locale.

5. To suggest seasons of the year according to whether the fence is covered
   with snow or vines and foliage.

SUSPENDED SCENERY

Designing Suspended Scenery

Whole or partial units of scenery are
often suspended in the stage space to
create lovely settings. The suspended
scenery may be one whole setting of
scenery or may be combined with
other scenic units, such as platforms,
wagons, backdrops, and various set
pieces positioned on the floor. In
this discussion, *suspended scenery*
refers to:

- Units not touching the stage floor.
- Units having outer profiled edges that
  are intended to be seen as part of the
  basic design.
- Units having openwork so that interesting lighting effects can be achieved by
  lighting from the front, back, and sides
  as well as using down lighting and up
  lighting.

Uses of Suspended Scenery on Proscenium Stages

Usually one or more portals are used
to frame a setting consisting of suspended scenery, but this depends
on the show. The suspended scenery
can be backed up by velour drops,
painted backdrops, cycloramas,
scrims, gauzes, or pieces of drapery.

Uses of Suspended Scenery on Open Stages

Suspended scenery is one of the most
effective kinds of scenery for the open
or arena stage because it can be hung

above the acting area and not interfere
with the sight lines of the audience. All
sides of the scenery can be seen, and
it is not always necessary to mask the
rigging.

Checklist of Suspended Scenery

Banners	Picture frames
Flags	Logos and monograms
Signs	Tilted panels
Cherubs	Sections or beams
Cartouches	Clusters of plastic tubes
Baffles	Overscale lace doilies
Chandeliers	Collage of various
Branches	materials
Flowers	Vertical and draped
Drapery pieces	beads
Plants	Architectural items
Ceiling pieces	An arrangement of lights
Draped garlands	Units of grillwork
Broken gridwork	Draped roping and
Window units	tassels

When designing suspended scenery,
also consider having electrified units
(partially or fully) whenever appropriate, as they always add a nice visual
punch to the sets. Examples are lighted
lamps or fixtures, a shadow box with
lights behind, outlines of lights bordering the outer edges of the unit, and
lights behind translucent materials.

Drafting Required for Suspended Scenery

1. *Front elevation.* Draw a straight-on
   view of the suspended scenery in position and indicate how it relates to the
   floor and portals, masking, or other
   scenery. Give overall dimensions and
   bottom trim of the suspended scenery.
2. *Hanging section drawing.* Draw a side
   view of the suspended scenery and indicate how it relates to the other scenery and the stage floor, proscenium

wall, upstage wall, and grid. Give overall dimensions and bottom trim. Specify whether the suspended scenery moves or not during performance and where it stores during the show.

SURROUNDS

Creating Surrounds

The family of scenic pieces that fill the large area in the upstage wall can be classified as *surrounds*. A surround may be made of any number of materials, ranging from a framed solid wall to a soft cyclorama, as well as a combination of various arranged soft hanging panels and framed set pieces resting on the upstage floor.

The Ground Plan of a Surround

The ground plan of a surround can take many shapes. A plan may be shown with a continuous solid line covering the entire upstage area, or with broken solid lines that denote spaces for actors to make entrances and exits and/or openings for lighting effects. The plan may be straight, curved, angular, zigzag, or free-form, and may have random panels or pieces. It may also be opaque, translucent, transparent, have open spaces, or be a combination of one or more of these.

Placement of the Surround on the Ground Plan

While the positioning of the surround on the master ground plan is determined generally by the physical stage and the type of production, in most cases it is pushed upstage as much as possible so there is maximum space in front of it, especially for multiset productions. Usually on the average stage as much depth as possible is desired. However, these factors should be considered.

1. Is a crossover needed upstage during the performance for both actors and stage crew? This is often the case even when there are crossovers under and above the stage because these crossovers demand more time to use. Allow a width of at least 30 inches of space behind the surround. This width permits two people to pass; if period costumes are involved, more space may be necessary.
2. Are there any structures, such as pipes, air-conditioning equipment, jogs, or columns, that extend out from the back wall of the theatre? These architectural and structural variations should always be checked out on site in the theatre.
3. Is it desirable to have lighting or special effects upstage of the surround during the performance? If so, can the space above the crossover walkway be used for lighting instruments, or will it be necessary to have instruments on the floor and the crossover space upstage of them?
4. Where do the last set of lines for hanging scenery in the stage house end? This varies with the individual theatre. If necessary, lines can be added upstage if time, space, and equipment are available.

To figure the width of the surround, assume that the ground plan of the surround is a long, straight line with wings on the end that return downstage. Draw a line upstage (running across stage) to indicate where you want the surround to be. Assume that three portals with the same size openings and legs are positioned downstage of the surround and that they are all spaced exactly 6 feet apart and the last portal is at least 6 feet from the upstage line of the surround. Also assume that these portals have 40'-0" openings (the same width as the proscenium opening) with legs that are 5'-6" wide. That would mean that the overall portal width is 51'-0". It is a good rule of thumb to make the surround at least this width, plus a few more feet. However, this is also determined by the sight lines, whether an entrance and exit is needed for actors or for scenery, the position of light instruments, and the overall design effect.

It is always helpful to extend four light guidelines (parallel to the center line) from the proscenium opening, extending upstage to the back wall and also on the outer edges of the portal as an aid to visually judge or to figure the overall width of the surround. For example, when indicating the size and placement of the surround on the ground plan when there are portals, it is usually helpful to draw light guidelines (parallel to the upstage and downstage center line) from downstage to upstage, first from the onstage

Stage designs by Neil Peter Jampolis
THE FLYING DUTCHMAN by Richard
    Wagner, Act 1 and Act 3
Directed by Bodo Igesz
Chapman Music Hall
Tulsa Opera Company
Tulsa, Oklahoma (1982)

"We had a permanent deck and a room with gauze walls and ceiling. Flying and projected elements appeared through the walls, and entrances were made through the picture frame up center."   —Neil Peter Jampolis

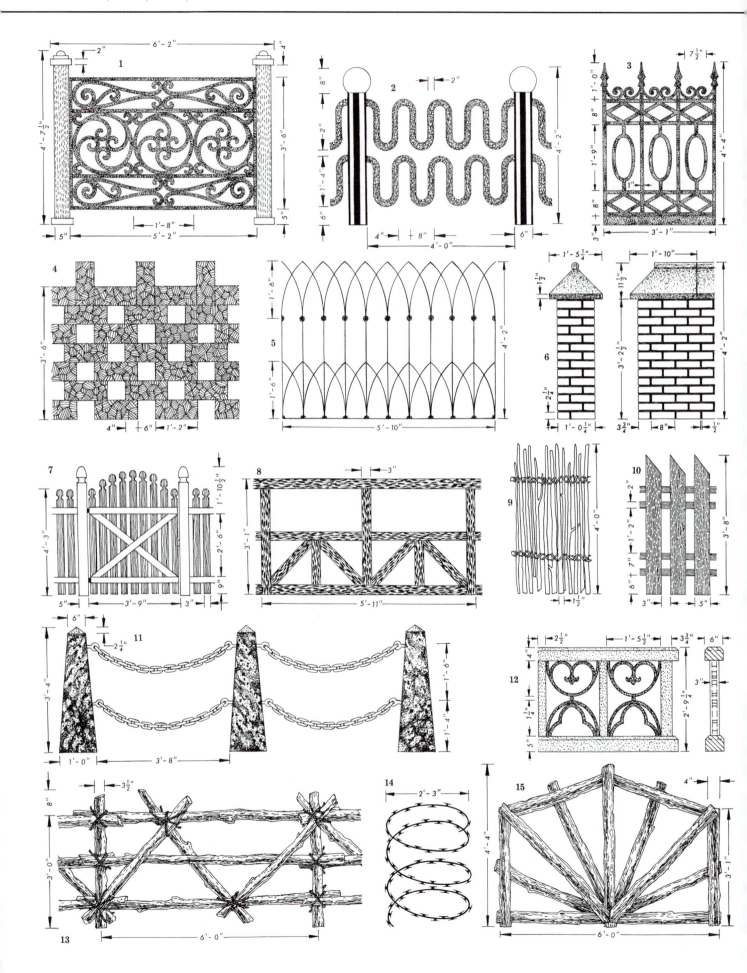

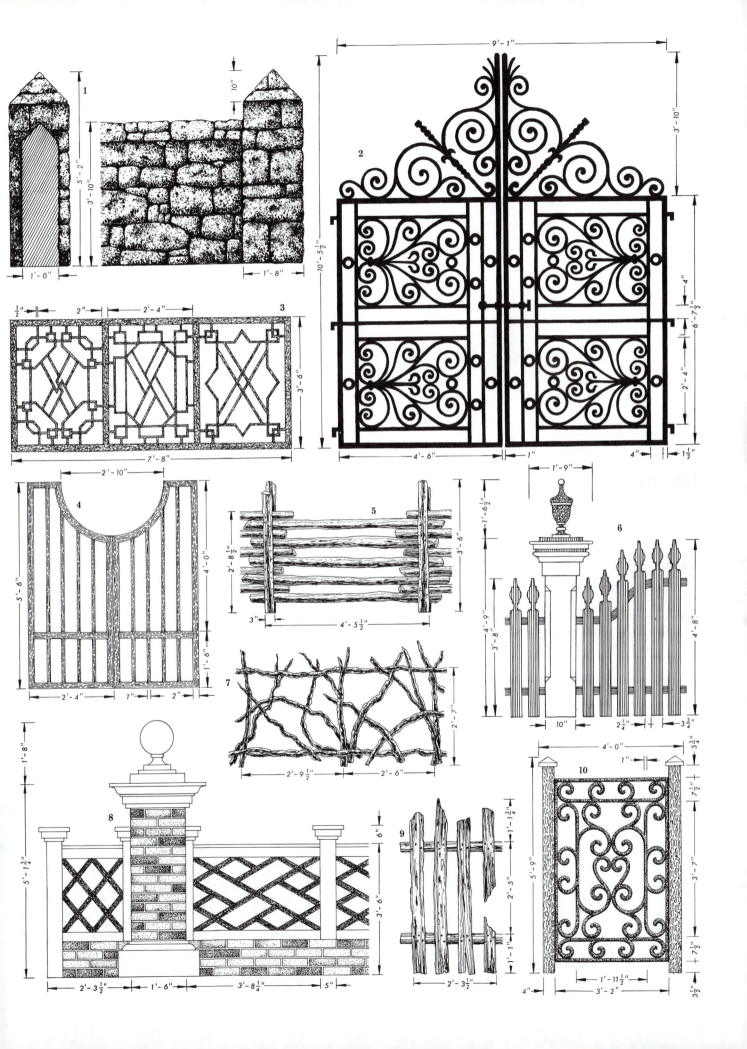

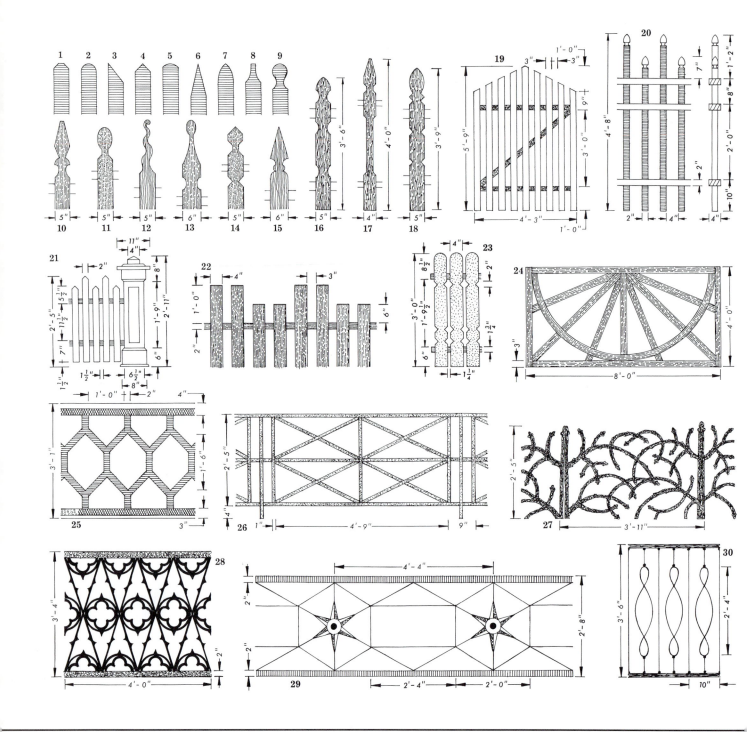

Farm Fence; Felix E. Cochren's Crating Lumber Fence for HOME (1980); Beach Fence
(Photographs by Lynn Pecktal)

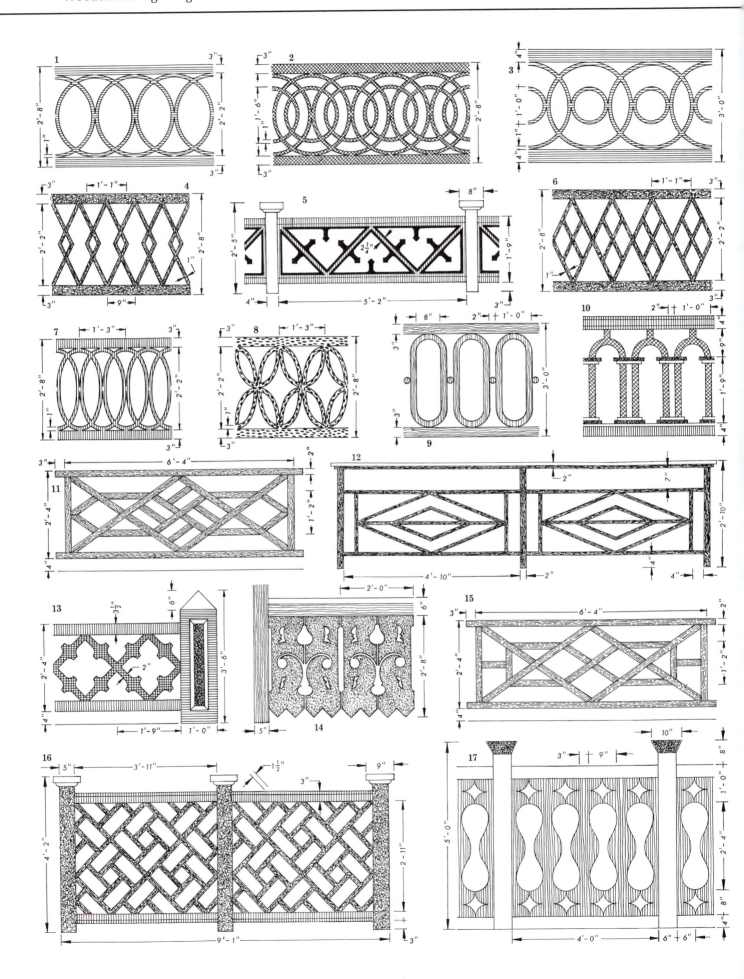

1 2¼" 1¾" 10" 5" 6" 1½" 2" 3'-2" 2'-0½" 2'-10½" 5" 2½" 10"

2 8" 6" 3'-10" 2'-9" 4" 3'-0" 1'-0" 8" 3"

3 7" 8" 3" 3" ¾" 2'-3" 3'-0" 1½"

4 8" 10" 5" 3½" 4" 2" 2'-4½" 1¼" 1½" 4" 5" 11½" 3½" 1½"

5 7'-4" 3'-2" 2'-7½" 4" 2½"

6 6" 2" 4" 1'-10½" ¾" 2'-8" 4" 3½" 7" 2"

7 7" 6" 3" 2½" ¾" 1'-11" 2'-8" 3" 3"

8 2'-2" 4" 3'-4" 2" 1'-4" 2'-10" 7'-0"

9 6" 10" 1¼" 3" 1½" 2'-6" 2'-0" 2" 8½" 3"

10 4½" 7" 6" 6" 4½" 3½" 1½" 2'-6" 2½" 1½" 3½" 8" 5"

11 4" 3'-6" 3" 8" 2'-0" 2"

12 6" 3" 4" 2" 4" 1" 1'-10½" 1'-8" 2'-8" 3" 2½" ¾" 2"

13 7" 2½" 7" 2" ¾" 2'-0" 2'-10" 1¾" 4½" 3"

14 2'-6" 2'-8" 2"

15 6" 5½" 5" 4" 2¼" 1'-4½" 1'-7½" 3'-4" ¾" 3½" 4" 3" 9"

16 4" 7" 2½" 2½" 1'-4" 2'-6" 2'-10½" 2" 9" 4" 8"

17 10" 1'-4" 1'-0" 3'-4" 2" 6"

18 1¼" 2'-5" 2½" 2" 5" 2'-5" 2½" 7" 3" 8" 6" 3½" 6" 9½"

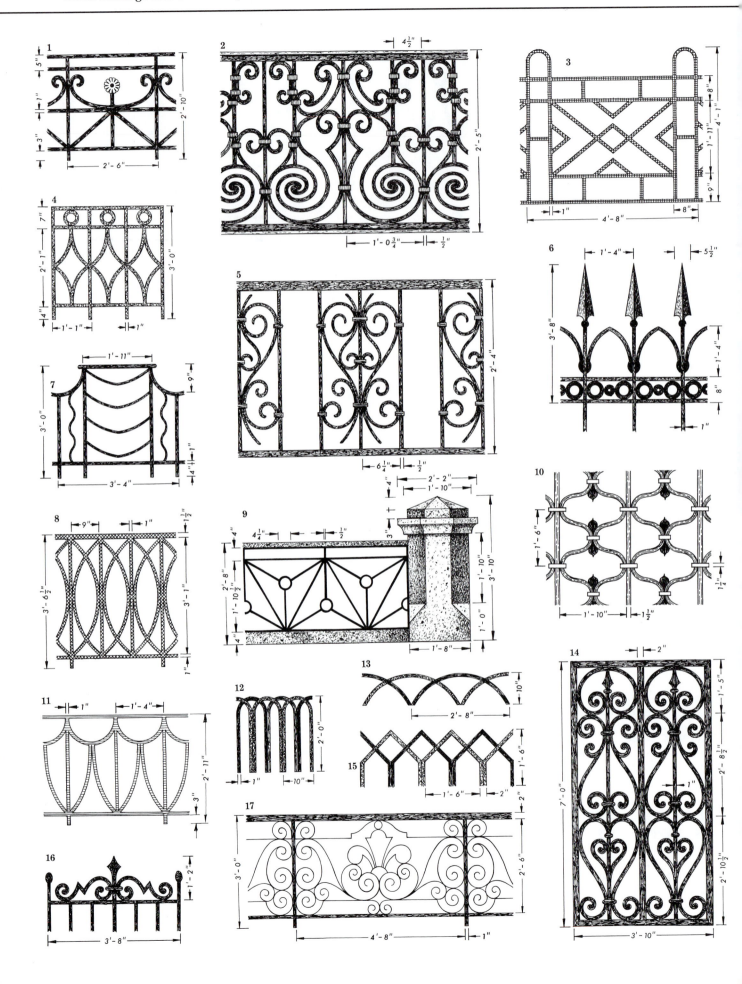

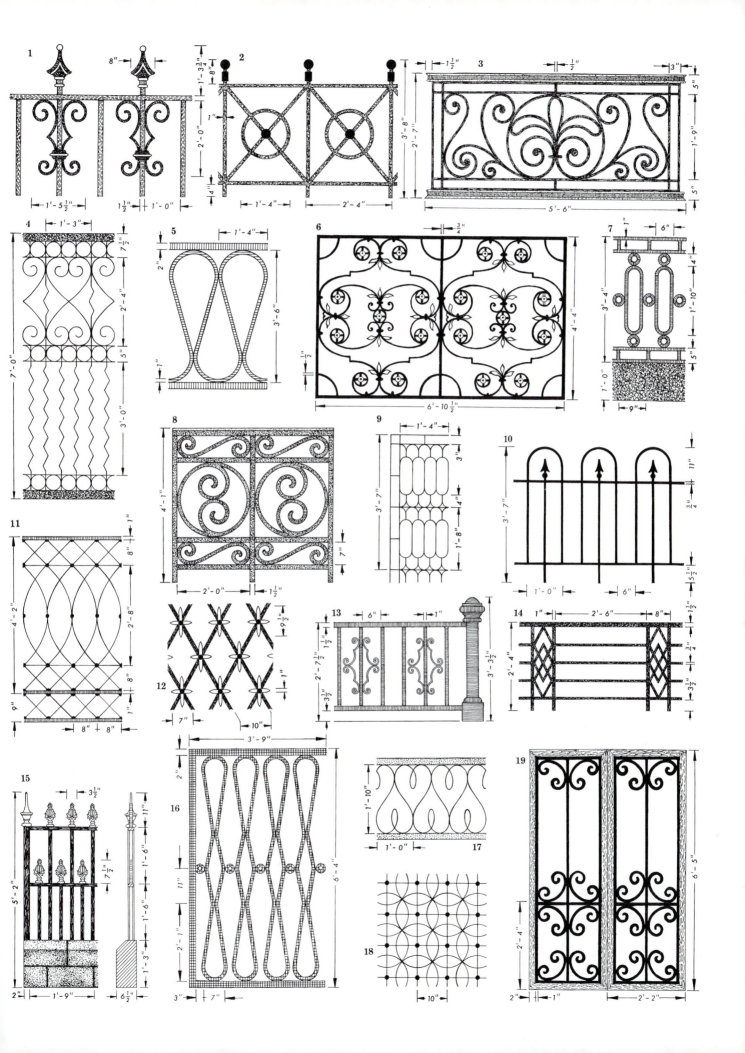

464 portal opening (total of two guidelines) and then from the offstage portal edges (total of two guidelines). These four light guidelines make it easier to see where the offstage edges of the surrounds should go and how much space is needed for the edges of the surround offstage so the audience cannot see where it ends.

Checklist of Items and Textures for Surrounds

Surrounds may be soft (unframed) or hard (framed) scenery pieces and may be designed with one or more of the following:

Brick or stone
Cinder block
Abstract patterns
Geometric patterns
Rough wood plank-
 ing
Fabric panels
Muslin cycloramas
Filled scrim cyclo-
 rama
Clusters of plastic
 tubes
Hanging rugs and
 carpets
Clear or opaque
 plastic panels

Overscale and stan-
 dard wire patterns
Straight and gath-
 ered arrangements
 of scenic netting
Erosion cloth panels
Scrim or opera net
 panels
Velour panels (flat
 or in fullness)
Wooden or bamboo
 slats
Groups of grillwork
Burlap hangings
Collages of synthetic
 materials

Using a Cyclorama

The cyclorama is perhaps the most familiar surround unit. It is usually positioned upstage and is made of muslin, filled scrim, or other material which is stretched out vertically on a set of curved metal pipes at the top and bottom and then also pulled out tight at the vertical sides (left and right). Occasionally in some regional and university theatres a permanent plaster dome is used in place of a cyclorama. A cyclorama may also be an arrangement of pleated draperies or curtains in fullness.

In ground plan the cyclorama may be drawn in various shapes. It may be completely curved or it may be straight in the main center area (parallel with the proscenium) and have curved sides, or other combinations.

The color of a cyclorama is usually a neutral tone such as gray or blue, depending on the effect desired. Or a cyclorama may be painted with horizontal washes of color to simulate a sky, or with a city skyline scene.

Using a Muslin Cyclorama

ADVANTAGES

1. It gives a nice surface for creating the effect of a sky or infinite space.
2. It may be used for projections.

DISADVANTAGES

1. It may be difficult to get rid of all the wrinkles in a muslin cyclorama.
2. It usually requires more fabric and thus is more expensive than a flat muslin backdrop.

Making Drawings for a Muslin Cyclorama

The necessary drawings for making a flat, stretched-out muslin cyclorama are usually three individual drawings in ½-inch scale: the ground plan, front elevation, and side elevation. When drawing the cyclorama, also (1) draw the same ground plan of the cyclorama on the master ground plan (½-inch scale) where it is to be positioned onstage, and (2) draw the side elevation or section view of the cyclorama on the hanging section drawing of the full set.

When you are drawing any of the three views (ground plan, front elevation, or side elevation) necessary for creating a muslin cyclorama, this information may be used as a guide.

GROUND PLAN

1. Draw the plan of the curved pipe showing how it rests on the stage floor. Make a note saying, "Duplicate same pipe above (suspended from the grid) for holding top of the cyclorama fabric."
2. Indicate upstage and downstage center line on the cyclorama pipe drawing.
3. Give dimensions of each curved cyclorama pipe (top and bottom) telling the overall width, depth, and radius. (When the pipes have an irregular curve, a separate drawing must be executed and the dimensions noted on that drawing as well as on the ground plan.)
4. Tell the diameter of the pipe (1¼-inch I.D.) and make notes on the drawing saying, "Top: provide hanging hardware. Bottom: provide floor hardware (clamps for holding pipe to floor)."
5. Put dimensions on the curved pipe drawing telling the overall width and overall depth.

FRONT ELEVATION

1. Draw the horizontal base line for the front view of the cyclorama.
2. Next, put in the vertical center line.
3. Project straight up from the ground plan of the cyclorama and draw the straight ends of the stretched cyclorama (left and right).
4. Put a dimension on the overall height telling the distance.
5. Since the elevation drawing of the cyclorama is usually a projected view, use the ground plan and, working with dividers, carefully measure the pipe where the fabric is to be attached and get a proper dimension from the overall stretched-out width. Make a note saying, "Actual size of the cyclorama is: (width by the height)."
6. State the material the cyclorama is made of: muslin, filled scrim, or other fabric. Tell if the fabric is to consist of widths sewn together with seams (running horizontally) or if it is to be without seams. Is it to be a combination of one large seamless piece of muslin at the bottom, then finished at the top with one or two widths running horizontally?

SIDE ELEVATION

1. Draw the base line.
2. Make a drawing of the side view of the cyclorama as it appears from one of the two sides (or ends). This side view should be put on the master hanging section view as it appears onstage. In this case, you should make the drawing a section view (through the center of the cyclorama).
3. Specify what is necessary at each vertical side of the cyclorama for attaching the sides of the fabric. One of these methods may be used:

- Vertical pipes at each side for attaching the sides of the fabric that have been presewn with webbing, to which grommets and tie lines have been attached.
- Vertical wooden sandwich battens at each side for stapling the sides of the fabric.
- Vertical steel cables that are stretched through side hems of the fabric and attached at the ends of the top and bottom pipes.
- A series of wooden clamps attached to the two vertical sides of the fabric and attached with lash lines tied to a vertical pipe or batten.

4. On the front or side elevation, make a note telling what specifications should be bid on for attaching the fabric cyclorama to the frame. For instance, indicate the following as it applies to your individual unit:

Top: Webbing, grommets, and tie lines. Provide curved pipe at top and equipment for hanging.

Bottom: Webbing, grommets, and tie lines. Provide curved pipe and hardware for attachment to floor.

Sides: Webbing, grommets, and tie lines for attaching to vertical pipe or batten. Provide whatever applies to your unit: 2½-inch hem in sides for running steel cable through and holding sides; or for stapling the two sides into two wooden sandwich battens; or for attaching wooden sandwich clamps and stretching fabric by tying it horizontally downstage to a vertically positioned pipe or batten.

Cyclorama sizes vary enormously. For *Harold and Maude* (1980) at the Martin Beck Theatre in New York, Tony Straiges designed a cyclorama to be made of filled scrim. In ground plan this cyclorama was 52'-0" wide by 12'-3" deep. (The portal openings in front of the cyclorama were 36'-0" wide by 26'-0" high.) The shape of the pipe was positioned in a straight line upstage with each end of the pipe curving downstage with a 9'-1" radius on each end (then continuing straight downstage with a length of 3'-2"). The actual true size of the filled scrim was 68'-4" wide by 42'-0" high.

The specifications for this cyclorama were:

Top: Webbing, grommets, and tie lines. Provide 1¼-inch I.D. curved cyc pipe (see plan).

Bottom: Webbing, grommets, and tie lines and 2½-inch skirt. Provide 1½-inch I.D. curved cyc pipe.

Ends: 2-inch hems. Provide wooden stiffeners on each end.

Making Drawings for a Cyclorama in Fullness

Sometimes a designer will want a curved cyclorama that has fabric in fullness. This may be made of any number of materials, such as velour, duvetyne, repp, or Granada cloth.

The reason for designing a cyclorama in fullness may be any of these:

1. The cyclorama must be pulled open and closed during the show to enable scenery or equipment to be changed and a cyclorama in fullness is faster to move than a stretched cyclorama.
2. To create visual effects such as vertical lines, textures, or colors.
3. As part of the action, it can be opened by actors to reveal scenery or mechanically to reveal an orchestra, chorus, or other groupings.
4. No other scenery and equipment may be available.

The design of the cyclorama in fullness and how it is to be used tell you what to put on the drawing. It never hurts to telephone the scenic shop and/or drapery house to clarify what you have in mind. You might want the cyclorama to be in one piece and to have 50 percent fullness, with webbing and grommets and tie lines at the top, attached to a curved pipe suspended from the grid, and a chain in a pocket at the bottom. Or you might want the cyclorama in fullness to be on a traveler track that opens in the center and has S-hooks at the top. It would also have a chain in the bottom. Always include these kinds of requirements when making a drawing for a cyclorama in fullness.

TREES AND FOLIAGE

Designing a Tree and Foliage Unit

When you are designing a flat tree and foliage unit that is to fly in upstage of a portal (or other masking), you must decide whether the unit is to be framed or unframed. Use these sample descriptions to help you make your selection and also as a guide in putting notes on the front elevation of the tree and foliage unit.

FRAMED HARD UNIT

Average total thickness: 4 to 5 inches.

Materials: Paints/dyes on canvas on ⅛- or ¼-inch ply on 1 × 3-inch wood with wooden stiffeners (1 × 3-inch or 1 × 4-inch) behind.

Tops: Provide hanging hardware.

Bottom: Provide dark rubber runner on bottom to deaden sound when flying in.

Edges: Paint all edges of 1 × 3-inch framing and ¼-inch ply profiles.

Breaks: Breaks are necessary for disassembling for travel and storage. Indicate where breaks are with heavy broken lines. Breaks in trees and foliage should flow with the shape of the trunks and limbs as opposed to being just straight cut edges.

Advantages: Smooth surface without wrinkles (plus stays as built and painted because of its hard mounting). Often proves most successful. Does not move and flap like soft scenery when brushed against or when there is a breeze.

Disadvantages: Much heavier than soft scenery. Takes up more hanging space with total thickness than a soft unit. Can be more expensive in cutout labor and materials.

UNFRAMED SOFT UNIT

Average total thickness: 1½ inches (pipe).

Materials: Paints/dyes on canvas (opaque on rear) glued on 1-inch square scenic netting, other netting, scrim, or gauzes.

Top: Webbing, grommets, and tie lines.

Bottom: 2-inch pocket for pipe or chain (with or without skirt in front).

Edges: Cut profile edges of netting according to drawing. Vertical and horizontal cutting tends to hang better. For other netting or gauzes, the cut may be straight, curved, or irregular, but any of these cuts should be made so the remaining material hangs properly (without undercuts).

Advantages: Very lightweight. Easy to fold and pack for storage and travel. Takes up less hanging space.

Disadvantages: When hung, ripples and wrinkles in canvas can show, especially under side and down lighting. Netting and gauzes in particular when supporting painted foliage can pick up light instead of being as invisible as one would want. Sometimes a designer will prefer to use framed scenery instead of having netting and gauzes support soft scenery.

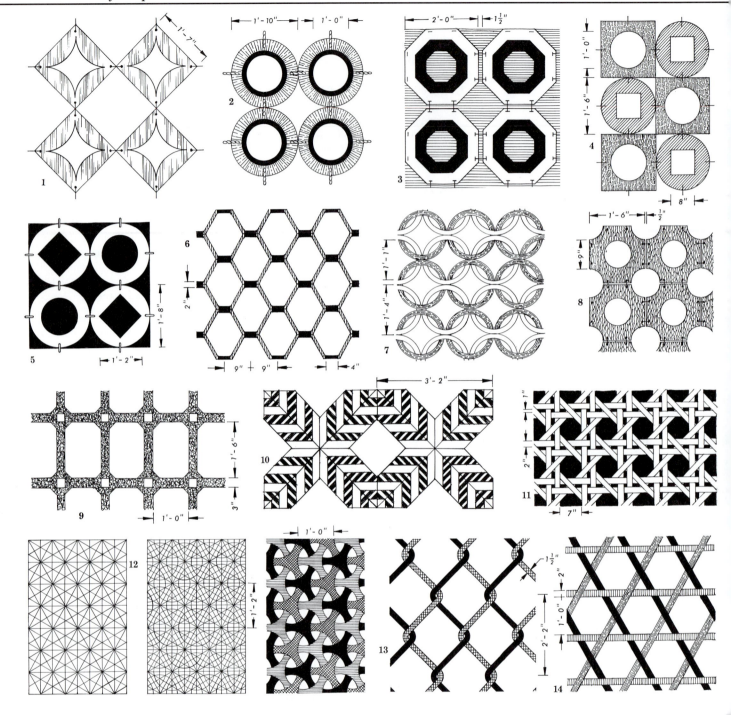

Basic Ground Plans for Unframed or Framed Surrounds

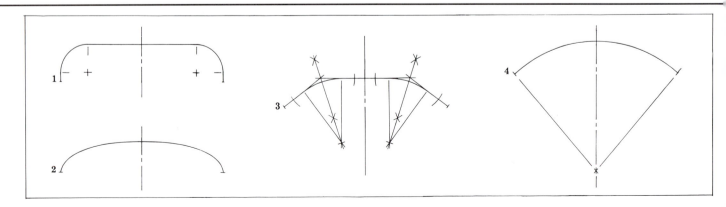

Drawings for Framed Surrounds with Profiled Cut-Down Tops

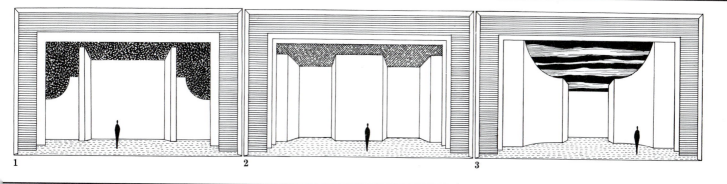

Irregular Surround Details: Cut Out and/or Painted on Flats and Backdrops

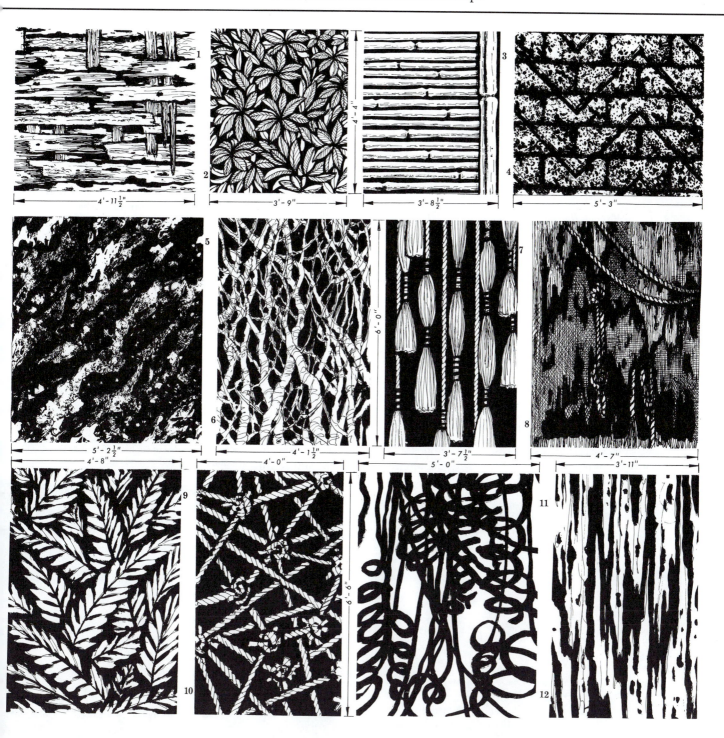

Making a Drawing for a Hanging Unit with Framed Flat Trees

Let us assume we are discussing two flat framed cutout tree units hanging on an overhead track that is 44'-0" long and that moves to the left and to the right for various scenes. The tree unit is designed to fly in and out, and also to move back and forth manually while suspended from the overhead track. At the top of the show the two framed pieces are positioned at the maximum length of the track (44'-0" overall). Both units are designed to have realistically painted tree trunks, foliage, and rocks at the base. The stage left unit has four profiled trees and is 11'-9" wide by 23'-0" high. The stage right unit has two trees and is 8'-0" wide by 23'-0" high.

When making drawings for framed tree units, use these steps.

FRONT ELEVATION

1. Draw the horizontal base line for the bottom of the framed tree units.
2. Draw the vertical center line which corresponds to the center line of the stage.
3. Draw the lines for the overall width and height of the units, and put the dimensions for each on the drawing.
4. Draw the details of the two individual units and label the bottom and top dimensions of each.

Stage design by John Scheffler
TERRA NOVA by Ted Tally
Directed by Katherine Long
Studio Arena Theatre
Buffalo, New York (1984)
(Photograph by Michael Piotrowski)

"The set was framed in metal; muslin was stretched around the frames for the basic shapes. 'Ice spikes' were cut from white foam rubber. The shapes were textured with muslin, cheesecloth, tissue paper, chancha, and joint compound, then glued to the stretched canvas and the units were painted."
—John Scheffler

5. Tell what materials are used to build the framed tree units: Painted muslin on 1/4-inch plywood cutouts on 3/4-inch wooden framing, or just painted muslin on 3/4-inch wooden framing with 1/4-inch plywood on the outer edges.
6. Tell where the units break vertically for travel and storage, or make a note saying, "Discuss all breaks of tree units before building."
7. Make a note on the drawing saying, "Provide wooden stiffeners where necessary," or "Add any necessary flat metal bracing on the rear."
8. Make a note to provide hardware at the top for hanging and for working on the overhead track.
9. Include a note to say, "Provide cable for hanging units."
10. Say if any openings are to get gauze glued on behind them.
11. Make a note saying, "Add a strip of rubber on the bottom of each unit to deaden noise when unit flies in and hits the stage floor."
12. Make a note saying, "Paint rear of all units and also all edges."
13. Make a note for adding any texture materials on tree trunks before painting. Heavy appliqués of textures are often discouraged because of the excess weight they add to already heavy hanging wooden units.

GROUND PLAN

1. Draw the plan of the two framed tree units directly under the front elevations.
2. Make each of the profile tree units 1 inch thick. Add another 4 inches behind the units for the 1 × 4-inch vertical stiffeners positioned on edge. Label the dimensions on the plan.
3. Tell what set of lines the units hang on, or if unknown, tell the distance from the back of the plaster line (on the upstage side of the proscenium

opening) on the stage to the face of the units.
4. Put the drawing of the plan of the framed units on the master ground plan where they play at the top of the show.

SIDE ELEVATION

1. Draw the side elevation of the tree units (on the left or the right of the front elevation) and show the 1-inch thickness of the framed trees and also the 1 × 4-inch vertical stiffeners on the rear.
2. Also put the side elevation on the hanging section drawing indicating where it plays at the top of the show.

Drawing a Three-Dimensional Tree with Soft Borders Overhead

Suppose you are making a drawing for a large three-dimensional tree trunk that is half-round and extends upward from the floor all the way up and in between two soft hanging foliage borders. The two borders are 25'-0" long and are 5'-0" apart. Branches extend upward from the trunk and go between the two soft foliage borders, and hang behind a portal with an opening that is 36'-0" wide by 20'-0" high. All the tree branches stay within the 5-foot span between the two borders. Some of the branches extending upward from the trunk are three-dimensional and other branches at the top go into 3/4-inch pro-

Stage design by Franco Colavecchia
TERRA NOVA by Ted Tally
Directed by Gene Lesser
Asolo Theatre
Sarasota, Florida (1981)
(Photograph by Phil Jones)

"I actually took Ted Tally's description of this set idea—the idea of Scott's ship sails becoming ship, snow, and ground cloth."
—Franco Colavecchia

Stage design by John Lee Beatty
REDWOOD CURTAIN by Lanford Wilson
Directed by Marshall W. Mason
Brooks Atkinson Theatre, New York (1993)

file. The main tree trunk has a bottom with casters on it if it needs to strike.

Sometimes you need to make two or more drawings of the same units to clarify relationships of pieces as well as to show complete shapes and sizes. For instance, one drawing of a front elevation could show everything in the playing order onstage. This could be the portal, the No. 1 foliage border, the dimensional tree unit, and the No. 2 foliage border. This drawing is fine for showing how the pieces appear together as a unit, but one or more other front elevations of the units may be needed to show the exact shapes and to put dimensions on them for construction and also for positioning them onstage. This is all determined by the individual design.

Use these steps when drawing a three-dimensional tree with borders suspended from above.

FRONT ELEVATION

1. Draw the portal with the given opening and also draw a center line which corresponds to the center line of the stage.

2. Draw the two foliage borders behind the portal in the position where they play.

3. Draw and position the tree unit between the two borders behind the portal.

4. Put dimensions on the drawing for the overall width and height of the front elevation of the tree and any other dimensions for the branches extending upward.

5. If any branches separate from the tree trunk and fly out on a batten, put dimensions and notes on the drawing to tell where.

6. Label any specific dimensions for points on the tree where there might be a special interest: a place where an actor may climb and sit, or a place to hang a prop or costume.

7. Say whether the casters under the bottom platform of the tree are swivel or fixed casters.

8. Describe the materials to make the tree: 3/4-inch plywood and cutout 3/4-inch plywood contoured shapes of the trunk at various points (averaging from 9 to 12 inches apart); chicken wire and forming wire covering the wooden armature; strips of canvas, muslin, burlap, or other materials glued on over the wire and textured with sawdust; shredded Styrofoam and pieces of erosion cloth

or simple carved Styrofoam covered with fabric and dope, then painted.

9. Mention if metal pipes or flat metal pieces are needed for extra strength and support.

10. Do separate drawings of each of the two foliage borders, and tell the overall width and height of each and put dimensions on the drawing.

11. Tell what materials to use to make the borders: painted canvas with cut edges (with or without scenic netting or other openwork materials behind for support). Are there applied leaves made of buckram, canvas, burlap, or muslin? When putting instructions on the drawing, make a note saying (if it applies), ''Top of borders: webbing, grommets, and tie lines.''

12. Show the borders together with the dimensional tree unit as all three play together onstage.

GROUND PLAN

1. Draw the plan of the portal with the center line. Then draw border No. 1 (with a broken line), the base of the tree, and border No. 2 (also with a broken line). Draw the trunk with the branches.

2. Put size dimensions for the overall width and depth of the tree.

3. Put position dimensions on the plan to indicate how to place the tree on-

Tree Drawing by Julia Rogoff for ORLANDO (1985), Designed by John Pascoe and Directed by John Copley for the San Francisco Opera

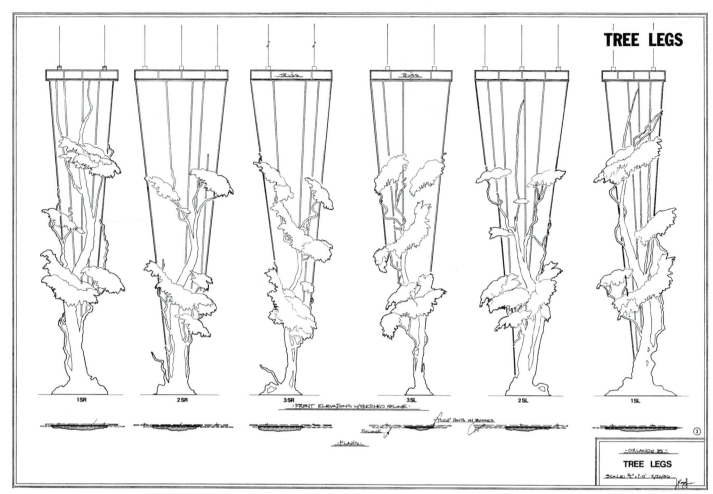

The trees consisted of vacuum-formed foliage pieces bolted onto aluminum frameworks. The trees tracked on and offstage to different preset positions at the beginning of various scenes.

Scenery by Lynn Pecktal and Robert Van Nutt for SHOT THRU THE HEART (1983), Birmingham Theatre, Birmingham, Michigan; *below:* Left and Right Apron Units

Below: Apron tree and rock units were painted on ¼-inch plywood on 1 × 3-inch framing.

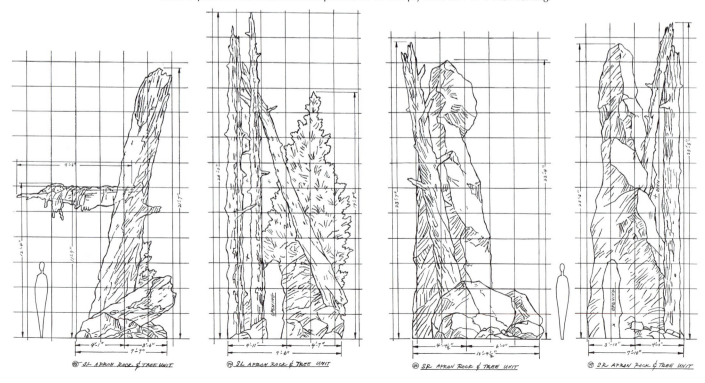

DSR Trees: Canvas on ¼-inch Plywood; Backdrop (Midstage): Canvas on 1-inch Netting

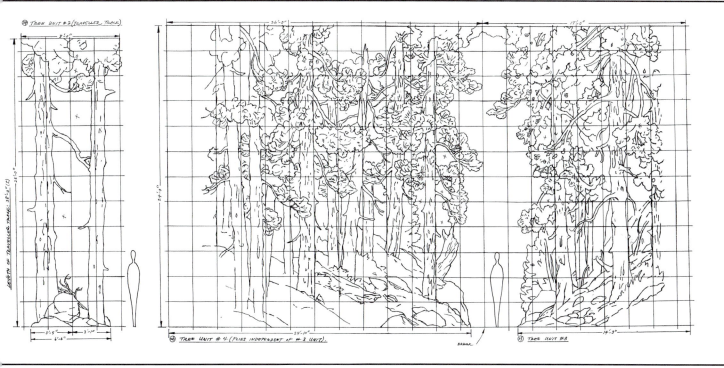

DSL Trees: Canvas on ¼-inch Plywood; Backdrop (Upstage): Canvas on 1-inch Netting

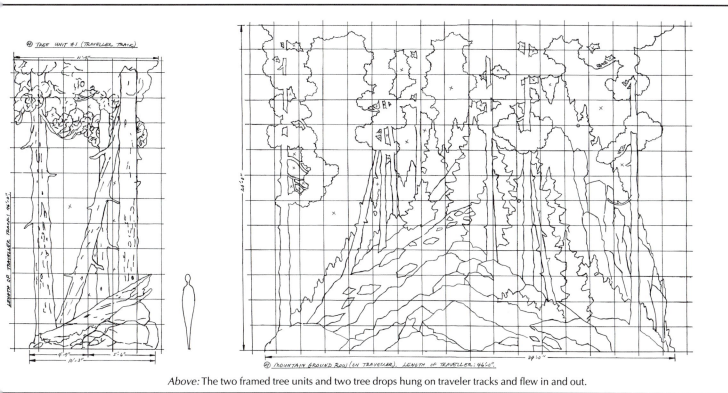

Above: The two framed tree units and two tree drops hung on traveler tracks and flew in and out.

Ground Row (Upstage): Canvas on 1 × 3-inch Framing with ¼-inch Plywood Profiles

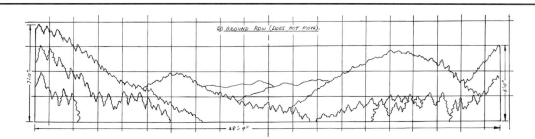

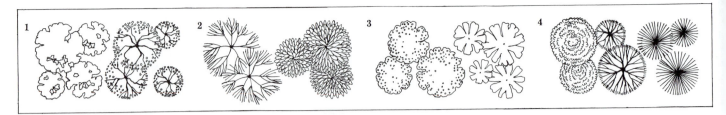

stage. This includes a dimension from the back of the smoke pocket to the face of the portal, and also a dimension from the face of the portal to the very back of the tree. Put a dimension going from the center line of the stage to the center line of the tree base.

4. Sometimes the upper portion of a dimensional tree unit is designed as a separate piece that flies in and out from above. If so, do a full elevation of this piece and give the overall width and height dimensions. Tell where it plays in relation to the dimensional tree trunk and limbs. For example: "2'-0" downstage of the top face of the front limbs." Also, tell what line it plays on to fly in and out. Describe the materials for making the foliage.

SIDE ELEVATION

1. Do a complete drawing of the dimensional tree from the side. The side chosen to be drawn usually is selected to indicate the features that are the most difficult to build, but that does not always apply.

2. Give the overall dimension for the total depth of the tree trunk, with limbs and foliage if the foliage is to be attached to the tree as opposed to hanging in front of it.

3. List the overall depth dimension (if the foliage is separate and hangs in front) of the front of the foliage to the rear of the dimensional tree.

4. Give the dimension of the base and three or four other dimensions in the depth (going from the bottom to the top).

5. Show any additional details on the individual tree.

6. Show metal handles for handling on the back of the dimensional tree. Put the side drawing of the tree on the hanging section drawing.

Creating Topiary Trees

Topiary trees have shapes that go from the simple to the fantastic. In real life both trees and hedges are carefully trimmed so that they grow and retain the preferred shape. But for stage purposes, topiary trees may be designed to appear as real and growing, or as decorative or fake. Topiary trees are found in both interior and exterior settings such as gardens, solariums, terraces, drawing rooms, foyers, balconies, libraries, and bedrooms. When making a topiary tree, draw it in full scale on brown paper. Then you can see the position of the trunk with the foliage and pot, and where the wooden supporting pieces should go.

Perhaps the most common topiary tree is the one with a round shape that seems to be growing from a large pot. This clipped tree may have one large ball shape or two or three. Usually, the largest ball is on the bottom with a few inches of space above it, then a me-

dium ball, another few inches of space above, and a small ball on the very top. All of these balls appear to be growing on one small tree trunk rising out of a large pot.

To make a tree like this, assume for discussion that it is 7'-1" high. The tapered pot at the bottom is 1'-8" in diameter (at the top). The pot is 1'-8" high and it has a trunk positioned in it. From the top of the pot to the large ball (1'-10" diameter) is 5 inches, with 3 inches of space above to the medium ball (1'-6" diameter), another 3 inches of space, and then the small ball (1'-2" diameter).

Select or carve a natural-looking tree trunk about 3 inches in diameter at the bottom and attach it in the pot. Cut out a circle of ¾-inch plywood to fit inside the bottom of the pot. Screw this wooden circle into the bottom of the trunk. Make another, larger, circle out of ¾-inch plywood to fit into the upper top of the pot about 2 inches down from the top edge. Cut out a hole in the center of this second plywood circle so that it slides down over the tree trunk and fits securely in the pot, holding the trunk vertically in place. Then, before actually attaching the second ¾-inch plywood circle on the tree trunk, cut out four 5-inch-diameter circles in it so a substance like sand, dirt, or pebbles can be put in the pot to give it a heavy weight.

Two Sets of Large-Scale Profile Trees: Painted Muslin on ¼-inch Plywood on 1 × 3-inch Framing (Larger or Smaller) with Stiffeners on the Rear

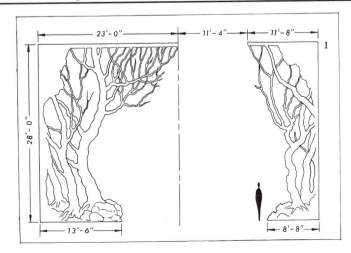

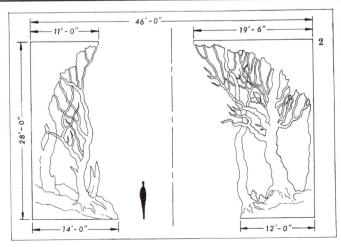

1. Plywood Foliage Portal; 2. Openings Cut in Plywood; 3. Covered with Muslin and Painted; 4. Soft Canvas Painted Foliage; 5. Same Foliage Cut Out and Glued on 1-inch Scenic Netting; 6. Muslin Cut Drop

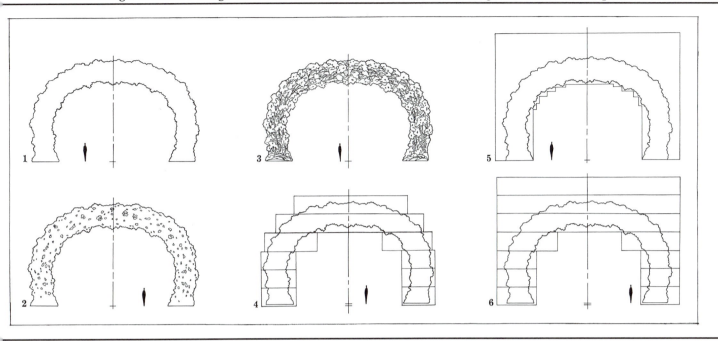

Peter Harvey's Unframed Forest Trees for A MIDSUMMER NIGHT'S DREAM Ballet (1979), Choreographed by George Balanchine, Zurich Opera House, Zurich, Switzerland

Notes on the tree drawing: Top—Webbing, grommets, and tie lines. *Bottom*—Pipe pocket. Scenery netting behind trees.

1. Stage right forest tree: Soft scenery tree cut out of muslin and mounted on scenic netting. Fern leaves and branch details made of scrim or gauze.

2. Center forest tree: Black velour (rubberbacked) for tree top. Body of tree on heavy black canvas. Surface texture built up with latex, and millinery leaves are applied to the surface as indicated.

3. Stage left forest tree: Main body of tree in muslin as customary but fern leaves and branches in muslin.

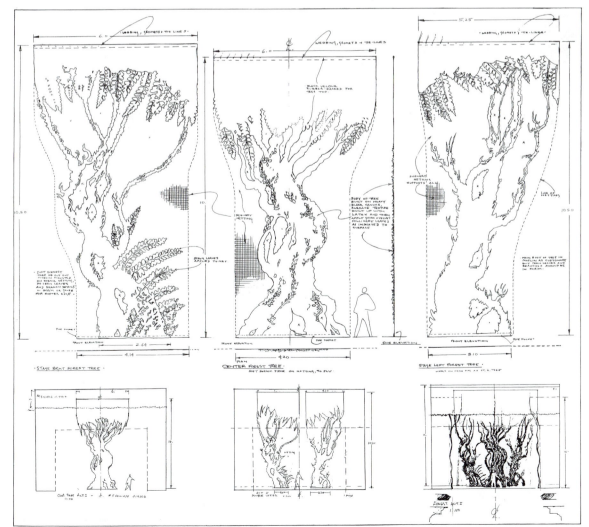

Patterns for Making Tree Leaves of Buckram, Felt, Heavy Paper, and Other Materials

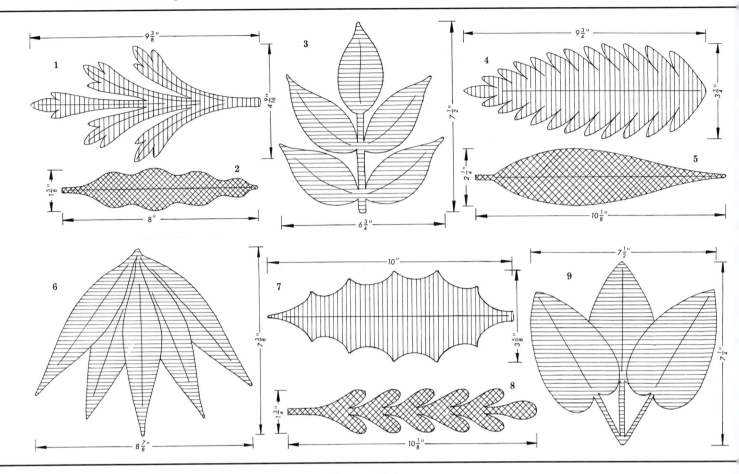

Wreaths, Trees, Hedges, and Other Objects (*Also at right*)

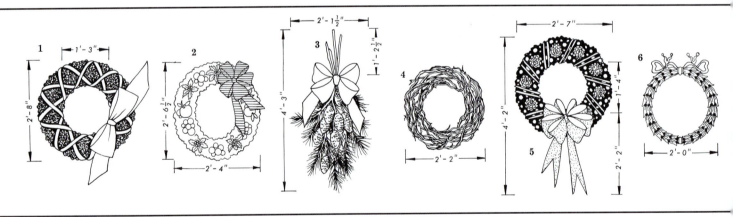

Various Tree Shapes

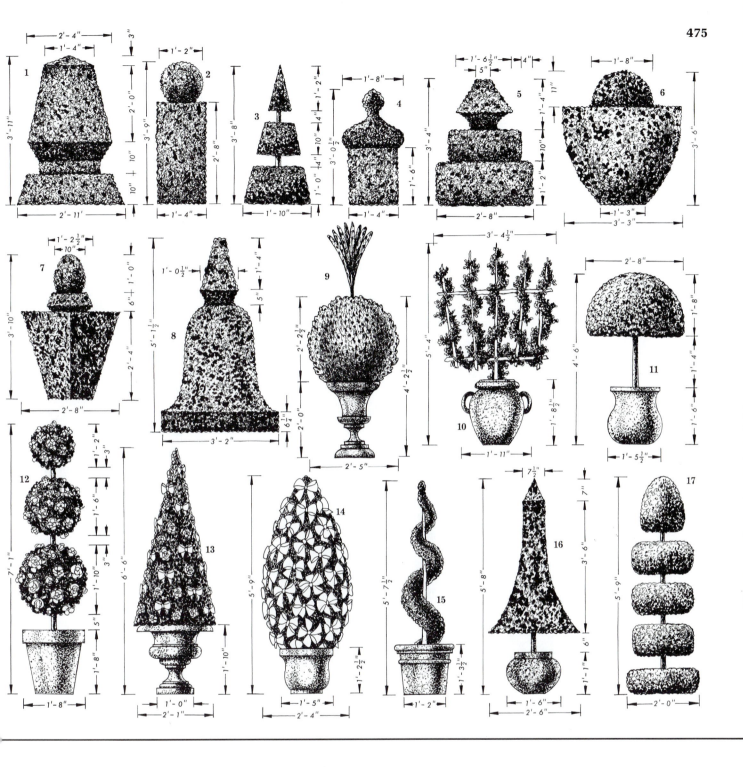

To construct the framework for the three balls of foliage, cut out three circles of ¾-inch plywood according to the diameters of the three balls. These circles are positioned horizontally and the trunk goes through each of them. Measure, mark, and cut out the three holes so the trunk can do that. Put the circles in place on the trunk and mark them. Remove them and cut out the extra weight of the ¾-inch plywood by leaving a 2-inch-wide circle around the openings for the trunk, a 2-inch-wide circle on the outer diameter, and a 2-inch-wide strip making a cross through the center like a wagon wheel with four 2-inch-wide spokes.

Put the three pieces of ¾-inch plywood back in place and attach them. Use heavy wire to create outer circle shapes on each of the three pieces. Fasten the heavy pieces of wire vertically around the horizontal plywood shapes with staples, spacing them equally apart to form the frameworks for the balls. Use pieces of chicken wire to cover over the wire shapes and fasten them with cut lengths of thin flexible wire. Finally, attach artificial leaves over the chicken-wire ball shapes until

---

Productions Designed with Trees and Foliage

Above:
Tree and stage design by John Scheffler
SUSANNAH by Carlisle Floyd
Directed by Patrick Bakman
Houston Grand Opera, Houston, Texas (1972)

Left:
Setting and lighting by Clarke Dunham
MORE FUN THAN BOWLING by Steven Dietz
Directed by Gregory Hurst
Pennsylvania Stage Company
Allentown, Pennsylvania (1987)
(Photograph by Clarke Dunham)

Below:
Stage designs by Charles E. McCarry
L'ORMINDO by Cavalli—Acts 1 and 2
Directed by Barbara Silverstein
Pennsylvania Opera Theatre
Philadelphia, Pennsylvania (1981)

they are completely covered with leaves.

Besides the topiary tree with three balls, other shapes abound—cones, pyramids, cubes, cylinders, and various combinations incorporating both trees and hedges. For whimsical ideas there are all sorts of wonderful trimmed shapes, such as birds, ducks, dogs, sheep, and other animals.

Materials for Topiary Trees and Hedges

The materials for making topiaries depend on whether you want to create trees or hedges, and also on whether the item is to appear realistically in a setting or to be a decorative item that could be used for a party or a Christmastime gala.

Suppose you are making a trimmed hedge unit that has two different shapes: a cylinder shape (2'-0" diameter by 4'-6" height) on the bottom and a cone shape (1'-6" diameter base by 2'-0" height) resting on top of the cylinder. To make the cylinder shape, cut four rings out of ¾-inch plywood. These should be 2'-0" diameter with an open center diameter 1'-6"

Right:
Setting, costumes, and lighting by Neil Peter Jampolis
A MIDSUMMER NIGHT'S DREAM by William Shakespeare
Directed by Colin Graham
Eric Harvie Theatre
Banff, Alberta, Canada (1984)
(Photograph by Neil Peter Jampolis)

"The central tree has an aluminum armature covered with plastic skin. Branches have the same construction. The tree and branches have 'grain of wheat' lamps beneath the skin. The tree revolves; branches all fly, travel, and trip. The floor is white fake fur. Vines are clear vinyl leaves on green sash cord."
—Neil Peter Jampolis

Above:
Stage designs by Charles E. McCarry
MERRILY WE ROLL ALONG
Beverly Hills Hotel
Franklin Shephard's Home
A project: Yale Drama School (1986)

Right:
Stage design by Desmond Heeley
SUOR ANGELICA by Giacomo Puccini
Directed by Lotfi Mansouri
San Francisco Opera
San Francisco, California (1988)

John Conklin lives and works in a spacious apartment on Riverside Drive overlooking the Hudson River. Born in 1938 in Farmington, Connecticut, he was educated at Yale College and the Yale Drama School. His first Broadway show was *Tambourines to Glory* in 1963. Since then he has designed sets and costumes for numerous productions at the Hartford Stage Company, Williamstown Theatre Festival, Long Wharf Theatre, Mark Taper Forum, American Shakespeare Festival, Guthrie Theatre, Arena Stage, Baltimore's Center Stage, Chicago's Goodman Theatre, Manhattan Theatre Club, McCarter Theatre Company, American Repertory Theatre, California Shakespeare Festival, Huntington Theatre Company, Louisville Actor's Theatre, Seattle Repertory Theatre, Studio Arena Theatre, New York Shakespeare Festival, Ahmanson Theatre, Portland Stage Company, and American Conservatory Theatre. John Conklin currently teaches design at the Tisch School of the Arts, New York University. Among his scenic and/or costume credits are:

Broadway
Measure for Measure (1989)
    Newhouse Theatre
The Philadelphia Story (1980)
    Beaumont Theatre
Bully (1977)
Rex (1976)
Lorelei (1974)
Cat on a Hot Tin Roof (1974)
Scratch (1971)

New York Shakespeare Festival
'Tis a Pity She's a Whore (1992)
Macbeth (1989)
The Leaf People (1975)
Richard III (1974) C only
    Newhouse Theatre

Pericles (1974) C only
    Delacorte Theatre
The Au Pair Man (1973)

Circle in the Square
A Streetcar Named Desire (1988)
Awake and Sing! (1984)
The Bacchae (1980)
Romeo and Juliet (1977) C only

Opera Companies
New York City Opera
Houston Grand Opera
Santa Fe Opera
Chicago Lyric Opera
Dallas Opera
Washington Opera Society
Metropolitan Opera

San Diego Opera
San Francisco Opera
Los Angeles Opera
Pittsburgh Opera
Netherlands Opera
Baltimore Civic Opera
Scottish Opera
Central City Opera
Minnesota Opera
Bayerischer Staatsoper

Ballet Companies
Boston Ballet
Royal Ballet
Pennsylvania Ballet
Hartford Ballet
Joffrey Ballet

Setting and costumes by John Conklin
HAMLET by William Shakespeare
Directed by Mark Lamos

Lighting by Pat Collins
Hartford Stage Company

Hartford, Connecticut (1987)
(Photograph by Jennifer Lester,
    courtesy of the Hartford Stage Company)

How did you start out designing for the theatre?

For some inexplicable reason I was always interested in being a designer. I started out as a seven-year-old doing puppet shows in the backyard with the neighborhood kids. I did sets in prep school, and at Yale as an undergraduate, and I went to the Yale Drama School and did sets. So I literally have been designing since I was six or seven years old. And it's very strange, because no one in my family has a theatre background. But my parents were very interested in music, and my grandparents were involved with the New England Conservatory in Boston so I went to operas when I was young, and I think that influenced me a lot.

You designed sets for the Dramat when you were an undergraduate at Yale.

Yes. Everything really focused when I was an undergraduate there. That was a very fertile time for the Dramat. That was the time of Dick Cavett, Sam Waterson, Austin Pendleton, Dick Maltby, Peter Hunt, and lots of people who have really gone on in the theatre. It was a group that was very oriented towards professional theatre, and I was lucky enough to be the only set designer. I just *had* to do the sets. I didn't have any training, but I really learned at that point. When I now look back on it, in some ways it was almost the best way to learn. I was just given the stage and told to do something, and I was allowed to do something. Nobody said, ''You couldn't do this or you shouldn't do that.'' So I sort of taught myself.

How many years did you design for the Dramat?

Basically for four years. I began designing for the Dramat when I was a freshman. Then the first year that I went to the drama school, I also did shows for the Dramat. So it was almost five years of work. We were doing things like *A View From the Bridge, Danton's Death,* and *Camino Real,* so it was good, strong, meaty stuff with a group of people who were very, very, serious about it.

And you used the university theatre at Yale?

We used the main stage. We had good crews, and, as I remember, a fair amount of money to do shows. You had

to paint it yourself, and also draft it yourself.

Did you design costumes for the Dramat?

I did some, yes. I never really learned how to sew and still do not know. I couldn't build a costume. I just had the design impulse and have always been very lucky and sought out good people to execute the work. I do less costumes now, partly, I think, because it takes so much time. It's infinitely more time-consuming than sets. And because of the amount of work that I do, I'm doing less and less costume work. But still, I will do both occasionally.

What about the time you had to work on productions at Yale?

I don't remember anything as specific as that. I just remember the general excitement. And that's when I really decided I wanted to or I would be able to go on with theatre design.

You stayed four years in the Dramat as an undergraduate. Did you go on to the drama school right away and stay for the graduate degree?

I went one year to the drama school, and I left. I went to New York for a couple of years and worked as an assistant with Will Armstrong. But I was able to take Mr. Oenslager's first-year graduate design course while I was still a senior at Yale, which I think that was the first time that anybody had been allowed to do that. So I almost finished my first year of drama school as an undergraduate. I did finally get a graduate degree. I can't remember quite why I did go back to finish, but it seemed a good idea at the time.

Did you come to New York again after you graduated from the drama school?

Yes. I've always been based in New York, but I have not worked a lot here. Because of the people I knew at Yale I started working in the regional theatres. I knew Jacques Cartier, who founded the Hartford Stage Company, and I started working there. And because of my connection with Nikos Psacharopoulos, the director of the Dramat, I worked at Williamstown. I've worked at Williamstown for over twenty-five years. And I started working at Long Wharf because I knew Arvin. I was interested in being able to do

plays like *Othello, The Balcony, Playboy of the Western World,* and those were the ones I did early on at those two places. And that continued. From the beginning regional theatre was, and still is, the main focus of my theatre work. I combine that with opera, which I also started doing fairly soon after getting my graduate degree from Yale. I went to Santa Fe early on and did a production there with Wes Balk, a director I had known at Yale.

Had you had opera experience prior to that?

Not really, no, not as a designer.

Was it because they knew your work?

I think it was mainly because of Wesley. He had been at the drama school as a director, and then he went to the Center Opera, which is now the Minnesota Opera in Minneapolis. So I worked a lot there. I had always been interested in opera, and as I said, from a fairly early age. I was anxious to do it. Opera and, I would say, classical work in the regional theatre has been my focus. I do very few new plays.

What is your usual method of doing sets and costumes for an opera production?

It's pretty much the same as it is with a theatre piece. In some ways I find opera easier to design, because there is the music that can give one such a strong emotional charge. The music gives one an impulse that's interestingly abstract or more abstract than the text of a play. I use a lot of instinctual drives and direct feelings about the piece, and combine that with the working out of a kind of intellectual structure for the piece.

One thing about opera that is perhaps different from theatre is that, in some cases, you are working on pieces so far ahead. Sometimes you're further along on the project than the director because if it's three or four projects ahead, he's perhaps tied up and hasn't really had time to think about it, or it may be an opera that he doesn't know or isn't familiar with. And so sometimes I go to the first meetings being more familiar with the piece than the director. Sometimes—and this is true in the theatre—sometimes you sense that a director wants you to kind of lead the way, or sometimes they have very definite ideas and you don't. I tend to

480 have very definite ideas, and I always try to figure out what's the best way to present them without threatening the director, without backing him into a place that stifles his feelings. And usually it works out well. One of the great things I find in my work is that I'm working now with a lot of directors that I have already worked with before.

Do you find that this makes a big difference in your way of working?

It makes a big difference. And it makes it easier in some ways, because you know who the other person is and how to get at their thinking or how to treat them. Although this year I worked with a lot of new directors for the first time—JoAnne Akalaitis, Irene Lewis, and Frank Galati. It was very stimulating and very rewarding to work with each of them. They were all directors who were not afraid of design.

All of these three directors and the other directors that I do work with are fascinated with visual things. And they love to use them, and they know how to use them, not just as decor, not as window dressing, and not as something to pump up or cover over weak actors or a poor script, but as something that's really integral to the piece. And they're willing to explore how the visual works, how it works emotionally, and how it can be as much a part of the effect on an audience as the text or the acting or the music. And that's what I find continually fascinating: how one gets an effect and what the effect really is.

You find some directors—and you find some designers—who are afraid of design. When I do a project I just like to do it as full-out as possible. And sometimes I feel, and certainly other people feel, the things I do are overdesigned or overly complicated. "Too operatic" is what some people use to describe my work even when I'm not working in opera. I try to see it as a compliment. But that's just the way I work.

I was giving a talk at a theatre conference in Atlanta not too long ago, and it suddenly occurred to me that designing is almost one of the least important things I do. I mean, I find that on a good production the designer is like a codirector, and a dramaturg, almost a therapist, and then sort of fourth on the list is actually designing it. The designing seems at times the least interesting and almost the least important.

Model and sketch by John Conklin
DIE GÖTTERDÄMMERUNG by Wagner—
    Act 2
Directed by Nicholas Lehnhoff
San Francisco Opera
San Francisco, California (1985)

Is that really the fourth on the list?

Well, in a way it is because it comes out of all the other things. But there is another very important function a designer has on a production. You see, I also think the designer is at a very wonderful place in a production, because from the beginning he or she has been close enough to it to understand it very deeply but at the same time is also slightly removed from it. The director and the actors, the actors particularly, are literally in the middle of it. And the producers and management are too far away. But the designer is the one who can, I think, help see what the production is really doing and what it needs. If the designer has a good relationship with the director, the designer can be the best critic that the director has.

People keep saying, "Why don't you become a director?" In the meeting with Jon Jory in Louisville on *Peter Pan*, I was describing ideas for the production and he said, "You should direct." (He didn't mean direct that production.) And I said, "Well, yeah I've thought about that, but I'm just doing the job that the designer *should* do." That is the job! The designer should be a kind of codirector.

We have not always been taught that.

No. Nor has it been taught that the directors should be the codesigner, and in the best situations they are. The best directors that I have worked with are, in a way, the most visual, but they are also the ones who want the most from me directorially. And I want them to give me very specific design ideas. It just seems an odd paradox because you think that that wouldn't be true, but it really is.

And then the work becomes very, very intense. My two favorite times on a production are at the beginning when you're just trying to get it going, and the tech and preview periods. Tech week, to me, is not just a time when you try to put together what you've done, although you are doing that, but it is the time when you can start creating the show. Even when the scenery, the costumes, and the lights are all there, that's just the beginning. Then

you see what you've got and you can change it and mold it.

Can you comment on a favorite opera production in which you did both sets and costumes?

Well, I think the one that was the best was the *Cosi Fan Tutte* that I did in St. Louis with Jonathan Miller directing. It was as close as I've come to being involved in what I thought was then an almost perfect production. It had a great cast and was brilliantly conducted by Calvin Simmons. It was a real synthesis of design and meaning.

Jonathan is, of course, a sort of an eighteenth-century man and so the production was very period-oriented. Usually the work that I do tends to not be so historically exact, because I feel that just doing things in "period" often is not doing true work; you're just doing a kind of archaeological work that doesn't connect the real meaning of the piece to modern sensibilities. But in this case Jonathan had such a deep understanding of the eighteenth century that he was able to lead me and the audience through this. And it was very simple, very direct. It is an extraordinarily difficult piece to find the correct emotional tone. It was half funny and half terribly serious. It was just a fascinating, fascinating production.

Did you do research for a long period of time?

Well, there was a lot of research on that. Jonathan is very knowledgeable about artifacts. I remember going to the first meeting more than slightly intimidated by Jonathan. I had not met him before, and I had gathered up some pieces of research and we were just going to meet and discuss. But I took a reproduction that's at the Metropolitan of David's painting of Lavoisier and his wife. It seemed to me to sum up the opera. And I remember showing it to him almost just as he pulled out the same painting! Well, it seemed as if this collaboration was going to work! And we used that specific painting a lot.

How did you come to select this particular painting?

I think it was because it was an evocation of an eighteenth-century scientist's enlightenment, and *Cosi* is a drama of enlightenment. The painting is a very observed, almost clinical object, and yet it has this subtle emotional relationship between a man and a woman, and a kind of elegance and cleanliness of vision. Since the painting is almost exactly contemporaneous with the writing of *Cosi*, we took specific objects from it. Jonathan wanted the physical things to be very accurate, not just approximations. All the clothes were taken from David paintings. The set, the furniture and the paneling and so on was taken from a real eighteenth-century French room. The first scene took place not in a café but in Don Alfonso's laboratory, so that he was indeed a scientist. So we did reproductions of the instruments that are in the Lavoisier painting.

I wouldn't do that with most directors. It worked in that case, but in general I don't feel that it usually does. I love research, and I do it a lot. But my attitude towards artifacts is to question how does this really work? Because I do feel that we are modern people with contemporary sensibilities, and that's it. You can't go back, you can't *be* an eighteenth-century person (except possibly for Jonathan Miller), no matter how much research, how much knowledge, how much you study it; you can't do it, really. So you have to get at the center of these pieces in another way.

What productions have you done with Mark Lamos?

I've done a lot with him. We did *Hamlet* in Hartford with Richard Thomas. There we searched around to find a way of doing the play, and we ended up basically doing it in a modern world. That was because everything we came up with using period seemed remote and unconnected.

We had done the play years before in Visalia, California at the California Shakespeare Festival. And there we had set it in a 1914 kind of middle-European kingdom that could have been Russia; it could have been Bucharest or Vienna. And that worked very well at that point, but we didn't want to do it again.

But in Hartford we played even there with the idea of the past. The set was a nineteenth-century theatre that was being torn down or restored, you didn't know which. But there were elements of the past and of a past theatre life. And the only thing that was costumed in period clothes was the play within the play, which was done Elizabethan.

What kind of set did you use?

Well, it was basically real and architectural; it was this kind of crumbling theatre. You saw part of the ruins of backstage with scaffolding and plastic. And then there were also paintings on moving racks and statues that were covered up with plastic. So there was a sense that it was also a museum or something that was in transition, some old world that was being packed up and taken away or being protected or being restored.

Comment on what the stage space is like at Hartford.

It's a big space, a thrust stage. It's a good space to work in. It's about 30 feet across, I guess 40 feet deep or more. It's good for me because I like a lot of scenery. I like to work with the crowding together of a lot of specific images.

The year before *Hamlet*, Mark and I did *Pericles* at the Hartford theatre. *Pericles* is a much stranger work. It is a scattered and fragmented play. And we also did it in a series of modern clothes. Some of them were thirties, some of them were contemporary. And the set was another combination of images— a broken Greek head, a series of yellow rocking chairs, a red curtain—all put together in a collage effect. In that case it was even deliberately surrealistic in a way.

I don't even really like to "design" anything per se. I like to take pieces of real things and try to reproduce them onstage and then put them in juxtaposition with other things that have been collected. Often I don't actually ever make any design decisions. I just collage and jam together images and see what happens.

Did you do a collage as opposed to a model for this?

Well, no, I did a model with just the design impulse of a collage behind it. I do fairly accurate models. If I'm going to do a nineteenth-century proscenium of a theatre I will find a real nineteenth-century proscenium and reproduce that in the model and on the stage. And

Stage design by John Conklin
DAS RHEINGOLD by Wagner—Scene 4
Directed by Nicholas Lehnhoff
San Francisco Opera
San Francisco, California (1985)

482 then if there's going to be a painting in it, I will, for instance, find a real Turner painting and that will be reproduced and if the original is in a gold frame, the reproduction is in a real gold frame.

You take these objects from the past, and you try to understand their inherent power or their possible inherent power, then you put them together on-stage. Most of my designs tend to be very chaotic, indeed messy. But I like mess. I think most good plays are messy. I mean, certainly *Hamlet* and God knows, *Pericles* are very messy plays. And they're deliberately so. Shakespeare was trying to suggest that life is not neat or even understandable. I don't think the great plays and great operas tend to neaten up situations. I think they tend to mirror in some way through artistic form the chaos of life. But they concentrate it and they set it out in front of you and then you have to decide, more so than you do in your chaotic life that goes on day by day—you have to decide what you feel about that, whether you think a resolution is possible or not possible. Most plays are full of tension, and I think that sometimes scenery design wants to unify things and tidy things up. I actually don't want to do that. I want to make it messy. I want to make it even confusing to the audience. I think most plays should be confusing.

All the great works of art, to me, are thought-provoking, but they also deal somehow with confusion. Their medium is confusion, and I think if you try to tidy up things visually, then the audiences will relax. I don't think audiences should relax. I think they

Models by John Conklin
THE RESISTIBLE RISE OF ARTURO UI by Bertolt Brecht
Directed by Peter Hunt
Williamstown Theatre Festival
Williamstown, Massachusetts (1972)

should be sitting on the edge of their seats, and they should be puzzling over it, and they should be stimulated or provoked or even irritated.

Are you talking about both plays and operas?

Yes, great plays, the great operas. And those are the kind of plays and operas that I want to do and try to do, because I find them so challenging and so stimulating. You have to sort of fight them in a strange way. They're very powerful, and in order to get at them, you have to struggle with them a bit. And I like doing that rather than just gliding through. Now that's not true of all pieces. That's why I tend to gravitate toward "classical" pieces.

I'm working now with Jon Jory on a production of *Peter Pan*, a play I've always liked. It will open the fall season at the Louisville Actor's Theatre. And people say, "Yeah, *Peter Pan*, a children's play." Well, I think it's a masterpiece because it's such an extraordinary exploration of Edwardian neuroses. We're approaching it that way. We're not approaching it as a children's play. We're not approaching it as a sort of "entertainment," although I think it will be entertaining. We are trying to really explore it. Because again, the play is a mess. James M. Barrie's psyche must have been a battlefield because it's so full of these unresolved neuroses. And we're just trying to do that onstage, not trying to clean it up, to make it "work."

I now don't worry about what the audience is going to think, because I don't know what that means. Everybody is always saying, "Is *the* audience going to understand this?" What does that mean?

You can't design a production with that kind of question.

You get six people in, and three people are stimulated and think it's wonderful and three people don't. Well, that's the audience, so what are you going to do? If things are reduced to a kind of common denominator or made simple, everybody will more or less understand it, yes, but then they're not stimulated by it, they just sort of sit there.

Pericles was, in a way, a sort of turning point in that because Mark and I were working with very personal images. We didn't discuss them a lot, and we didn't say, "Now what does this mean to the play?" We just sort of said, "Well, what about . . . ." And I said, "I just see yellow rocking chairs." And he said, "Fine." End of discussion. We never really sat down and figured out what yellow rocking chairs meant to the play; we just did it.

You didn't become analytical about it.

Not much. And we didn't say, "Well, is the audience going to understand what yellow rocking chairs mean?" There were yellow rocking chairs floating and there was a baby yellow rocking chair that rose up into the air at the end of Act 1. And we still to this day don't know exactly what they meant even to us.

In Hartford they would have discussions with the audience after the play. I remember one member of the audience asked the actors, "What did those rocking chairs mean?" And the actor said, "Well, what does it mean to you?" And so the entire audience erupted talking about rocking chairs. And they got quite passionate about it and said this and this and this. And the actors at the end said, "Well, *that's* what they meant." That's exactly it. There is no meaning and there is every meaning in it. I think that the problem is audiences

Model by John Conklin
MISS HAVISHAM'S FIRE by Domenick
  Argento
Directed by Wesley Balk
New York City Opera
New York State Theatre (1978)

think that scenery is a puzzle that the director and the designer know the answer to, and they (the audience) have to figure it out. They feel stupid if they can't get it, and that is wrong, but I don't know how you get around that.

But isn't our society geared to think that way?

Yes, you have to figure things out rather than feel them. You can't enjoy the emotion for what it is. And you feel that there *is* an answer and if you don't get it, then you're stupid.

How long do you like to have to work on an opera production?

Well it varies. I work very fast. I don't know whether I like to have a long time or a very short time. I tend to get at it very quickly. As soon as I read something or listen to it or—it was funny, just last night they called up from City Opera and said they were doing a new production of *Carmen*, an opera that I've done twice unsuccessfully, and an opera that I love, but I think is so difficult to do.

Why?

I don't know. Well, I think it's partly because it's a French opera about Spain, and you always design Spain. But it's not a Spanish opera; it's a French opera. The sensibility is very French; the music is very French, but more importantly the sensibility is not Spanish. I think the piece is just extraordinarily difficult to capture, not just visually. So I thought, "My God, do I really want to do this? And anyway I don't think I can do it because it conflicts with Santa Fe." Then all of a sudden I started thinking about designing it. My little mind was spinning around. And I suddenly came up with a whole idea of how to possibly do it. Now that was like half an hour after the phone conversation. So sometimes I work like that. I just start thinking about it instantly.

But then I also like it when I have more time and I have to modify things or work with a director or go through changes because you go away, you have time, you come back. So it varies. I tend to want to get at it quickly. So I

end up doing a lot of work because I can actually work very fast, and I like to. My mind just sort of snaps along. And sometimes I think that's bad. But I don't think there should be any rules. I think everybody works at totally different tempos. And I just like to work fast.

Do you do a painted sketch as well as a painted model for shows?

No, I hardly ever do sketches. I can't do them very well so I hate them. I also don't understand *why* you do them. I always work in painted models, mostly half inch. Sometimes I start with quarter-inch, because it's easier to carry around and quicker to do. It varies. I'm working on a project now for *Tancredi* for Chicago, a Rossini opera. We did a little quarter-inch model all painted, which is how I presented it to them. And now we're working on a half-inch model. This quarter-inch is all finished and painted and is good enough to see what the production is going to look like in a general sense, but it's not good enough to really build from or check on details. So what we're doing now is actually making a half-inch white paste-up model so that I can see it again. I'm starting to change proportions and things. Then we will build the finished model.

What is a good average budget for an opera today for sets and costumes?

It varies so. Well, in Chicago for this *Tancredi*, the budget is $100,000 (which is not enough for this way of doing *Tancredi*). Now the director and I knew that there was a lowish budget

for this, but we went ahead and did what we wanted to, keeping in mind that this production could not be an extravaganza, but that we still needed this, and this, and this. So when I went out with this quarter-inch model, which had all the pieces, we figured that it was going to come in for like $150,000, or if we were lucky, $120,000, or $125,000, and if we were hideously unlucky, $250,000. So we'll have to cut it.

I understand why people don't want to spend all that money. That's why I like working at regional theatres. An extravagant budget in regional theatre is well, let's say $15,000 just for materials, because the labor is in the overall seasonal budget. I've done shows where the budget is $8,000 or $7,000 for sets.

And how much for costumes?

The same, maybe, or less. It depends, of course, a lot on whether it's period or a big or a small cast. For $8,000 you can get a lot of scenery, but not in New York. I did *A Streetcar Named Desire* at Circle in the Square, which is a thrust stage, and there was a fair amount of scenery. The low bid was $80,000. The most expensive bid was something like $180,000. But I thought, this is obscene! How could you spend $80,000 for the scenery when in a regional theatre you might spend $15,000 for it? I mean fifteen, OK, that sounds about right, but eighty thousand!

For an opera you can spend $400,000 up on the scenery. It just seems so absurd, actually. There's something bothersome about it. It's the rules of the game, but it just seems wrong.

Budget very often does affect the way you would design a production, does it not?

It does. This *Tancredi* for instance. There are lots of scenes in *Tancredi*. I guess there are seven locations, as it were. I knew that we were never going to do seven full-stage sets. And since it is a period piece—it's an early nineteenth-century opera—it needs to have a certain kind of visual flavor of opulence to it, I think, and the director wanted that. So we're doing it in one set, which is a deserted nineteenth-century theatre. I think it's going to work very well for the piece. We're trying to do a kind of magic evocation of nineteenth-century theatre. Now the idea came at the same time as the budget, but because we're perhaps a third or half over budget at this point, I knew that we had to come up with some flexible scheme. There's this basic set, and there are lots of smaller pieces which you can then play with easily. If you can't have three drops, you could do it with one drop. It wouldn't be as interesting, but you could do it. So when we get it bid, we'll bid it with all the scenery, because the pieces are relatively easy to draft. We're not going to do the finished model until after we decide what the show really is. The bids will all be broken down. And then you add up the things and say, "Well, we can have this drop and we can have this throne." You add it up until it comes to about $100,000 and stop. I try to build a kind of flexibility into it so that you can get yourself out of trouble easier.

And there is a problem with expensive stagehands, too. In Chicago they kept saying, "You know, this is not going to take very many people to set up and to run." So they are going to save a lot of money there.

Sometimes they select their repertory by what is heavy and what is light.

When I did a *Traviata* in San Francisco, a lot of discussion was about how much is this going to cost to run, which had nothing to do with the set budget. But it was a strong consideration. And there was always that balance, because what might be cheaper to build would be more expensive to run and vice versa, or what might be easier to run would take up too much room to store. There were always questions like: Should this be on a wagon? How is this going to run? How are we going to store this? Is it going to take fifty or thirty-five men to run it?

La Traviata is going to be done a number of times in the season, and then it's going to be done maybe for the next ten years. They've got to have a production that goes together easily and that ships and stores easily, or no matter how economical it is to build it the first time or whatever, they will be losing money hand over fist. So one is very, very aware of these problems.

The design gets modified in all sorts of different directions budgetwise, but also in this matter of stagehands. That's even true at Hartford. For instance, they will say, "You know, we have three people to run the show. This is all we have!" And so you have to figure that if you're going to have a fly cue, you can't have something else going on or maybe the actors are going to have to do it.

How many productions have you done for the San Francisco Opera?

I did the *Ring* there, which either counts as one or four, as the case may be. And I've done maybe four others. I love working there. I think it's my favorite opera organization to work for, because they are big enough to be a producing company, but there's a real sense of an organization that is a family. I've done one thing at the Met, just costumes. But there I got almost no feeling of family.

Who directed the Ring *in San Francisco?*

The director on the *Ring* was Nikolaus Lehnhoff, a German director. We were brought together by Terry McEwen, the head of the organization. The whole *Ring* project was, in a way, an odd experience because from the time that I got the first phone call asking, "Do you want to design *The Ring*?" to the time that the curtain actually went up on the fourth opera, it was nine years! Oh my God, I hope I never work on another thing for nine years again! They couldn't find a director, and two and a half years went by in which I didn't do anything. But it was nine years! It was a monumental thing, but it was great, a wonderful experience. I feel very at home in San Francisco. And I think that's important. I feel that there are certain homes, theatre homes, that I have.

How many days would you be away for a production there at the San Francisco Opera Company?

For *Traviata*, for instance, I went out there maybe three times with designs that were rehashed and redone. It techs in the summer and you put the sets up and light them. And I was there for about a week in the summer for that. From that period when it loaded into the theatre and opened, it was about a week and a half. Maybe I only went once while they were building and painting. They've done so much work

Model by John Conklin
RAIN by John Colton and Clemence Randolph
Directed by Paul Weidner
Hartford Stage Company
Hartford, Connecticut (1978)

for me that they know the kind of painting that I like, so there's not so much checking up that I have to do there. I send the elevations and the model plus drafting. They know my style. It's great having the summer techs. Sometimes the shops get behind and the scenery isn't quite finished, which is not so good, but in this case it all worked because there was enough time to change things a little bit. The last-act set was really too green, and so they had a couple of months to repaint it before it opened in the fall. But with the summer tech you get to see the whole thing together and lit.

What do you like most about working in the theatre?

It's hard to describe. I guess it's creating something that you feel the audience is genuinely responding to in a way that it is never "just the scenery." It's as simple as that. The productions that I feel the most unhappy about are the ones where the scenery is OK, but then the production isn't. Then I don't feel as if I've failed. I feel so dissatisfied because nothing is happening. Then the scenery becomes a sort of technical exercise, and you have to summon your professional expertise to finish it and to get it done, and to get it looking right.

I do a lot of work. That also helps, because if some of it doesn't quite work, you always have something else. I sometimes do fifteen productions a year, and in two or three of them you have some real moments. And that's enough to keep you going.

But I always try to find something interesting and I usually always do find something interesting in a production, something to learn from it. And that I think is important. Maybe the thing I like best about the theatre is that it keeps teaching me things. It forces me to learn things or gets me interested in something else, and keeps me going. That's why I love teaching. I've been teaching many years at the Tisch School of the Arts at New York University, and that I find enormously stimulating.

When you designed the costumes for Khovanshchina *at the Met, how did your way of working there differ from working in a regional theatre?*

It didn't, really. It's just that there was more of it. There were something like 250 costumes. You see, I think it is

a fault to say that opera is bigger-scale and you should exaggerate the scale of everything. That didn't really come into it because there was no detail to exaggerate. I'm very suspicious about this theory that opera needs visual exaggeration. It is still predicated on a human figure, which doesn't get any bigger. Sure, there are ninety people playing in the orchestra down front and there are another seventy-five in the chorus, but that doesn't make it exaggerated, it just makes it more intense. The emotions are the same. The essential feelings are the basis of everything. That's why I don't think there is a big difference between the way I design for opera and the way I design for the theatre. It's exactly the same.

When I did this *Traviata* in San Francisco, which has a house almost as big as the Met, we did it almost like a movie set. They were very realistic rooms with most of the detail built. And everybody thought, "Now wait a minute. Is this ever going to read?" Here we are in this monstrous opera house—the front row is 20 feet away from the nearest piece of scenery and the last row is 200 feet away. David Walker, the English designer, did the costumes with all this little detail with lace about 2½ inches wide.

But when you got it all there with as much detail as there really is in a nine-

Settings and costumes by John Conklin
PERICLES by William Shakespeare
Directed by Mark Lamos
Lighting by Robert Wierzel
Hartford Stage Company
Hartford, Connecticut (1987)
(Photograph by Jennifer Lester, courtesy of the Hartford Stage Company)

teenth-century room, it felt absolutely real. It read! Something read. Now you couldn't actually see each little detail, but when the curtain went up, you knew exactly where you were. You knew exactly what this room was and you felt it almost rather than being able to see it. It was amazing! It would have been wrong to exaggerate the detail because it would have pushed it up out of the kind of reality that this had. And yet it didn't seem distant or small-scale. You could have taken a camera and panned around and it would have been as detailed as a movie. But the effect did come across.

After all the successes and the enjoyment that you've had with operas, would you be satisfied for the rest of your life if someone said that you couldn't design anything but plays from here on?

No, because I wouldn't want to do either just operas or just plays. I deliberately do half and half because they feed each other so that I don't go into a separate mode when I design for either opera or theatre. I use exactly the same principles. The square footage is different because opera takes place in theatres with huge auditoriums that are far too big for it. That's why I like working in St. Louis. The Opera Theatre of St. Louis plays in the Loretta Hilton Theatre, where the rep is housed. *Aïda* and *Götterdämmerung* should be done in theatres like that.

That is the depressing thing about working in opera in San Francisco or Chicago or Dallas or New York. The theatre auditoriums are too big. It's not that the stages are too big. It's just that

Model by John Conklin
CAMINO REAL by Tennessee Williams
Directed by Nikos Psacharopoulos
Williamstown Theatre Festival
Williamstown, Massachusetts (1979)

the audience should be close to it. The energy dissipates. You pump up all that energy onstage and there's just too much travel time. By the time it gets out there, it's gone. Most European opera houses are small, like Broadway musical houses. That's why doing musicals at Lincoln Center or City Opera is so crazy. They have to be done in small spaces so that all that energy doesn't dissipate. And you're too far away to see the faces and you're too far away to see the eyes of the performers. The energy is lost. I think that's why opera on television has been so successful, because you're close to it. You see that there are real people doing something.

You designed Rex *on Broadway. Can you comment on that?*

Rex I remember as being the sort of quintessential Broadway experience, and I thought, "OK, now I have done this and I'll never have to do this again." It was a great big musical with all these prestigious people connected with it and I thought it would be fun. It was a Richard Rodgers musical and Sheldon Harnick did the lyrics, and Ed Sherin directed and Nicol Williamson and Penny Fuller were in it. It was an amazing experience because it was so ultimately silly. It had all of those things that you think Broadway out-of-town tryout musicals have which everybody says is true hell when the show is not working. They were trying to make this very artsy entertainment out

of a piece that wasn't. So I've done a Broadway musical. That was fine. Actually, I had a great time. What made it tolerable for me was they decided not to pick on the scenery and costumes.

If you had a choice of a production that you would like to do in the future, what would it be?

Well, I think it would be almost any Verdi opera, and I would love to do a *King Lear*.

Where?

Anywhere. See, that's the thing. I would love to do a production of *King Lear* in a little tiny space with a $500 budget. I would also love to do another production of *Hamlet*, and I've already done it twice. I'd love to do *Aïda*, *Parsifal*—these kind of great difficult, big emotional pieces. Their emotion is so high. In some strange way, you get a little Verdi into you, get a little Shakespeare in you and suddenly you're a bigger person. You're energized by this extraordinary power of the piece. That's what I mean by doing battle with the play. By fighting them you get a little bit of their essence. I find that so energizing. I don't understand how people get bored by designing, bored by the theatre, because Shakespeare can't be boring. Just to do Shakespeare for the rest of my life would be fine.

You have worked in Europe?

I have worked in Europe a little bit and I've done only opera there, and not enough! I like European theatre and in some ways I'm more temperamentally drawn to the European way of doing theatre. They take more time and do more experimentation, or there's more

the ability to move out of the realistic naturalistic confines of a play and explore other things and take it a little more seriously. I think sometimes they take it too seriously and it can get ponderous. Theatre there is also much more related to painting and music and art—this whole contemporary art is all tied together and not an isolated thing.

Do you have any desire to work in films or television?

None at all. Because I think it's too controlled. It comes back to this mass syndrome. I love movies and I watch more movies than I do plays. But I find films and television too realistic, too naturalistic, and too focused. For instance, in the most sophisticated movies they use musical underscoring that would never occur to you even in your wildest imagination to use on the stage. It is so amazing to have music chosen by a director to tell you exactly what you should think, what you should feel. If you did that in the theatre—sometimes you do a bit of that in the theatre, but if you did it a lot it would be totally ludicrous. Isn't that strange? We just accept that in the movies without any compunction. I like the freedom that the theatre has and the kind of undisciplined, unfocused individuality of moment.

It goes back to what I was saying about chaos and mess. What I love about the theatre is that you present this thing and then—and I deliberately do this with the scenery—unfocus it sometimes. You don't tell the audience where to look. You don't tell them what's important. You present them with these series of facts, and that's it. Now you don't use "close-ups," you don't control it quite so much. I personally find that much more interesting than telling the audience what to look at or how important it is by how big it is.

I like the fact that in the theatre you have the curious situation of having a group of people sitting and looking at another group of people doing something. And then it gets thrown away when it's over. When the six weeks or the six months are over, you take all the scenery and you throw it away. You chop it up in little pieces and throw it away. It's great, it's over, done with, and the audience goes home and it doesn't exist. And it's over, and you do something new. And it's never the same.

11

PROPERTIES, SCENIC AND PROP DETAILS, AND MINIMAL SCENERY

PROPERTIES

Because props are an integral part of the overall visual picture, the scenic designer is always responsible for designing, selecting, and approving them. Props for a production may be bought, rented, borrowed, or built from scratch. At times the stage designer may find it necessary to do research on both set and hand props. Certain set props have to be checked out more than others for historical accuracy. A partial listing of these could include lamps, television sets, radios, record players and hi-fi equipment, telephones, typewriters, and electric fans.

Set props consist of draperies, pictures, mirrors, paintings, chandeliers, and other objects of set dressing, while hand props are items used by actors as part of their business in the staging of the play, musical comedy, opera, dance, or ballet. Hand props that may require special research are eyeglasses, umbrellas, hand fans, walking canes, compacts, smoke pipes, hat boxes, wrapped packages and gifts, magazines and newspapers, hand mirrors, brushes, combs, letters and scrolls, cups and saucers, decanters, and trays. Hand props may also be set props.

A stage designer and a properties person or an assistant may together or individually go to look for props. Either photographs of the found items along with their dimensions or the actual pieces are then shown to the director for final approval.

The Organization of Props in Storage

A good prop collection in an older resident company can be a great help to a stage designer. Over the years the theatre may have built up a collection of excellent choices of usable stage items.

The organization of props in storage is extremely important because it enables a designer to make selections quickly. When props are stored in good order finding items is a matter of walking through the aisles of a prop room with the property person and making choices. The best property persons take pride in their work and have items arranged according to a specific category. Usually the best approach is to have a file card for each item listing the name, number, description, and size. The same number can be placed on a tag attached to the item.

Normally, props as well as furniture must be kept under lock and key so they are not borrowed without permission. This means that when items are used in a show, they must be returned to their proper place. Appropriate storage means having appropriate crates for chandeliers, shelves for dishes, and wall hooks for pictures and paintings. Various assortments of boxes, cartons, and packing equipment are needed for storing small items and for transferring them from the prop room to the theatre to be used in the show and back to storage after the run. Of course, this procedure of taking care of the props is as important as taking care of the set itself.

The Organization of Props Offstage

While props to be used in a production may be positioned any number of places offstage, they must be well organized and placed on the spot where the actors can get them. This means that the property person running the props for a show must be very familiar with the production. Becoming familiar with props and how they are worked during the production is essential, and the prop master or prop mistress goes about it in several ways. The list below is typical.

1. Reads the script and goes over the list of props found at the back of the script, or for a new script goes through each act and makes a list.
2. Discusses at length with the director and designer what props are preferred by each.
3. Attends rehearsals and run-throughs to see how both real and practice props are working.
4. Attends technical and dress rehearsals and makes notes concerning any adjustments on new props that might be needed.

The property master or mistress may secure (find, borrow, or purchase) props for a production and run hand props during the performance, or someone else may be assigned to run the props during performance.

Usually, the property master has a table positioned offstage of any scenery

488 door or exit into the wings where actors bring on or take off props. This table may be similar in size and shape to a typical card table. Two or three tables may be needed for a large number of items.

Props are laid out neatly on the table in the order of their use. It is very effective to designate the individual space for each object by marking off the top of the table with strips of masking tape in a series of squares and rectangles. In this way, each prop can be easily seen and found by the actor. The space allotted a prop is labeled with the actor's name and the scene in which the prop plays. Typical examples of props brought on and off stage include drinks in cocktail glasses, a tray of hot food, a top hat, a chess set, or live goldfish in a bowl of water.

The most efficient property master knows the action in a scene and is standing in the wings waiting, for example, to take a cup of coffee from an actress who has to make a quick change of clothing, or to hand an umbrella to an actor dashing back onstage after a costume change.

Special and valuable items may be put in a storage cabinet positioned upstage in a hall or some other location with ample space. The cabinet is locked for safekeeping after each performance. Such items may be valuable both from a monetary and sentimental point of view as well as being vital to the performance. A vertical cabinet on casters with double doors that lock may be 4 feet wide by 6 feet high by 2 feet deep. The shelves inside can accommodate such objects as a Waterford crystal bowl, a sterling silver candelabra holding five candles, a large Spode platter, and two tall porcelain figurines. This cabinet is appropriate for both hand props and set props and such edible items as fruit, candy, or nuts.

Duties of the Property Person

Like good actors and good designers, good prop people are always in demand. When one hears of a property person with an excellent reputation for getting just the right props, one immediately wants to work with that person on the next show. The best property persons possess certain characteristics. Some of these include:

1. Possesses a knowledge of basic design, historical period furnishings, art objects, and paintings.
2. Is resourceful and imaginative, and can improvise.
3. Has a working knowledge of sources such as antique shops, auction houses, furniture houses, and individual collections that are available on loan.
4. Is prompt in having furniture and props picked up and returned; provides the owner with documentation of the production dates and any insurance that applies, and arranges for appropriate program credit; and cares for all props and furniture and sees that they are always in top condition.
5. Arranges for transportation and a Polaroid camera to take photos of found objects to show them to the scenic designer and director.

6. Can use a sewing machine, a hammer, and a paint brush.
7. Where applicable, knows which items are in a resident prop storage room or rooms and keeps them organized and cataloged.
8. Has a good sense of humor and is discreet, and never comes between the designer and the director on the choice of a prop.

Building Mirror Frames

Mirror frames can be designed and built for one production, stored in the prop room, and used over and over again for future shows. You may want a mirror frame for a fancy drawing room, or a gaudy mirror mosaic frame for a nightclub.

Often a frame for a mirror is built because an affordable mirror in the right scale and style cannot be found. Also, it is not practical to use a real mirror that may need to be sprayed down or have a piece of black bobbinet stretched over so it does not pop out too much onstage. It is usually better to use a plastic or simulated mirror rather than the real thing.

Wooden frames are very easy to construct. Once you have designed the mirror frame in a rough sketch, make a ½-inch scale (or larger) drawing on the drafting with dimensions and necessary instructions for building. Enlarge this drawing to make a full-scale drawing on brown paper with pencil or charcoal. Perforate the drawing with a pounce wheel so the design can be transferred onto the wooden surface by rubbing a bag of powdered charcoal over the tiny holes in the paper. Spray the charcoal pattern on the wood with a clear acrylic preservative from an aerosol can.

Use ¾-inch plywood to cut out the basic form in one piece. Once the design is cut out, either sand or rout the edges. A number of items and materials work well for adding details to the basic frame. Among these items are tiny wooden balls cut in half, sheet metal ornaments, lengths of pressed moldings and regular moldings, designs cut out of felt or other materials, patterns of heavy scenic dope squeezed from a waxed paper cone, and tiny pieces of cheesecloth dipped in scenic dope and shaped into semiflat ornaments, then pressed into place.

The thickness of the mirror frame varies with the overall size of the frame and the desired effect. Some frames

Stage design by Hugh Landwehr
MEASURE FOR MEASURE by Shakespeare
Directed by Douglas Hughes
Seattle Repertory Company (1989)

have enough interest so that the ¾-inch basic frame plus ¼-inch-thick applied ornament make the 1-inch thickness heavy enough in appearance. Others may have a thickness of 1½ inches, 2 inches, 3 inches, or more for Victorian frames, especially for floor-length, standing pier mirrors.

The final finish on mirror frames also varies. After the new wood and any ornament are basecoated, they may be sprayed with gold, silver, or other metallic paint. A mirror frame of natural wood free of glue stains may be painted with a coat of Minwax stain in walnut, mahogany, or oak. A mirror frame may be finished with gold leaf and antiqued. A mirror frame may also be painted with glossy black, Chinese, or Venetian red lacquer and have details applied with bright gold.

Mirrors to go inside frames may be cut from real glass or mirrored Plexiglas. In addition, there are products available that work nicely for simulated mirrors. The following are from Gerriets International, R. D. #1, 950 Hutchinson Road, Allentown, NJ, 08501, Tel.: (609) 758-9121.

Rigid Stage Mirror. This is safe, does not tarnish or shatter, is lightweight and easy to cut. This plastic sheet can be cut similarly to glass. Score along a line with a mat knife, place the plastic on the edge of a board or table, then sharply snap away from the scored line and the sheet will cleanly divide. This is available by the sheet, 39 × 98 inches.

Flexible Mosaic Mirror. This flexible material, cut in small ³⁄₁₆ or ⅜-inch squares, gives a mirror-ball effect. It can be bonded to any flat or curved smooth surface such as plastic, wood, Styrofoam, or tightly woven fabrics. When it is lighted, sparkling lights beam in many different directions. This material is available by the roll 19.5 inches wide by 98 inches long, in silver, gold, black, and bronze.

Making Frames for Paintings and Pictures

Like mirror frames, frames for paintings are sometimes hard to find for the stage for reasons of scale, period, cost, or availability. Usually wooden frames can be easily made for the stage. Examples of frames might be for a large full-length portrait positioned over a fireplace, or one created in perspective

Model designs by Randy Barcelo
OPUS McSHANN, ballet by Alvin Ailey
Choreographed by Alvin Ailey
City Center Theatre, New York (1988)

to go on a raked wall, or even one to hang at random in the open stage space.

The same procedure is used for making picture or painting frames as for mirrors. Decide what kind of frame you want to create. Draw a rough sketch, and when the design is set, decide what size it should be. Make a full-scale drawing of the frame on brown paper and perforate it. Then with powdered charcoal transfer the outline of the design onto a sheet of ¾-inch plywood. Plywood less than ¾ inch thick can also be used for smaller and more delicate frames. Edges may be sanded or routed. Dimensional cutouts may be made of softwoods, thin plywood, illustration board, felt, Foamcore board, and similar materials. The cutouts may be glued onto the basic frame. Frames may be textured with heavy scenic dope by brushing over the surface and then combing it with a steel comb. As with mirror frames, small fragments of cheesecloth may be dipped in scenic dope and shaped and put on already cutout details.

For individual details use beads, roping, metal discs, small blocks and diamonds, and other similar items. Frames may be painted in a tortoise-shell pattern, ebony, simulated gold leaf, terra-cotta, mustard, yellow, or

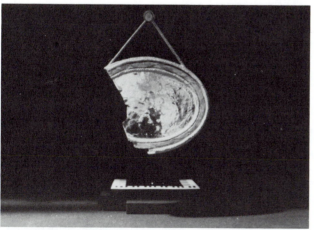

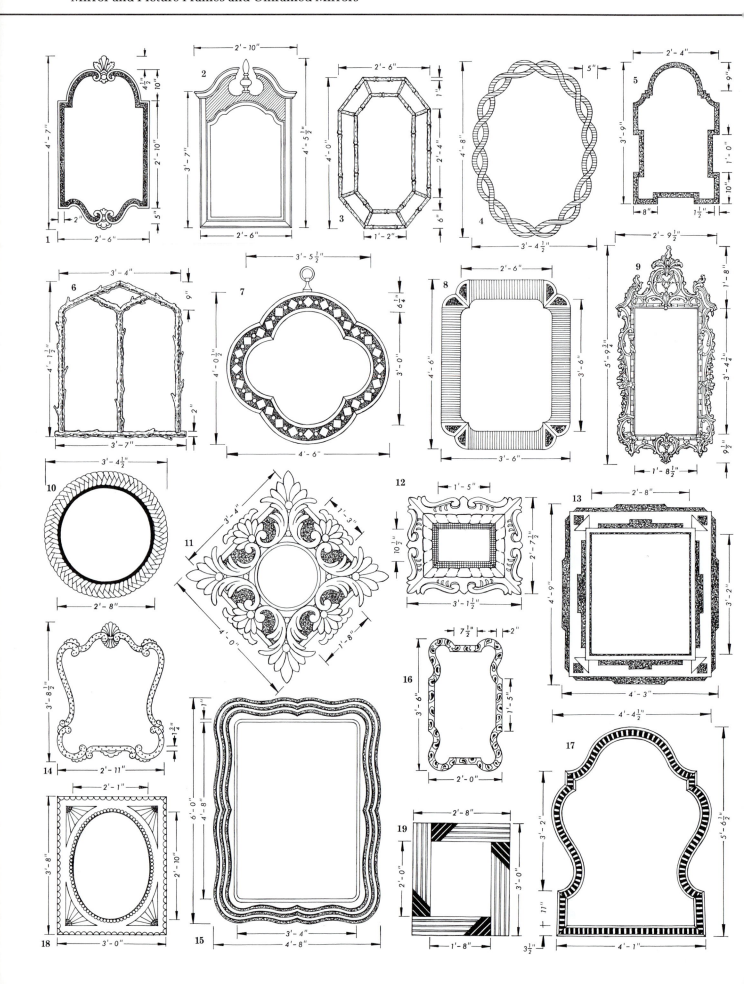

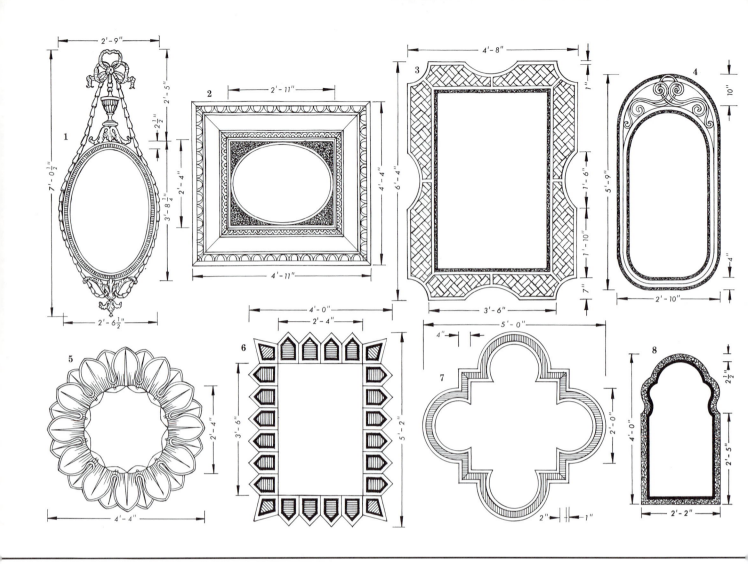

Ornamental Items Positioned as Support above Picture Frames and Mirrors

Making Picture Frames from Stock Molding   Full-Stage Picture Hanger

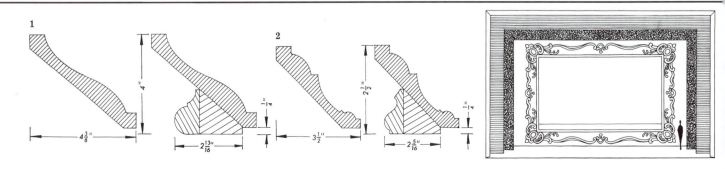

green. Picture glass may be simulated by cutting a piece out of a clear acrylic sheet.

STOCK SIZES OF PICTURE FRAMES (in inches)

8 × 10	14 × 18	24 × 30
9 × 12	16 × 20	24 × 36
11 × 14	18 × 24	30 × 40
12 × 16	20 × 24	

Repairing Damaged Picture Frames

Damaged picture frames can be found in junk shops, thrift shops, and antique shops. Many times the picture frames can be repaired without great difficulty and look beautiful onstage. These frames work to good advantage when they are large, not only because of the appropriate scale onstage, but also because they can be cut down to fit prints and paintings. The damaged areas are often on outer corners and can be cut away. To do this, mark the frame carefully and use a miter box and saw to make a 45-degree cut on each end of the frame. Then drill holes for the appropriate size nails to be hammered gently into the side corners of the frame. Do the drilling and nailing by holding the two pieces of frame against a large, thick 90-degree block that is attached firmly in place.

Because of their weight and size, very large picture frames sometimes need to be braced on the back. This can be done after any mitered corners are tightened by carefully hammering the corners with a small wooden block to keep from damaging the wood, and also at the same time by using a 90-degree square inside the corners to make sure they are in the proper positions. Regular plywood corner blocks can be glued onto the rear of the frame. These four corner blocks should be glued on, weighted, and clamped until the glue has dried. Then use small wooden blocks between the frame and the clamps so the face of the frame will not be damaged. When the glued blocks have completely set, drill holes through them and screw in appropriate size wood screws in strategic places to give a more solid bracing. This procedure is especially helpful for bracing very large and heavy frames.

Often, lovely old frames can be found with some of the ornamental detail missing. If the damage is not too severe, the detail can be copied from a part of the frame that is still intact and this can be used to restore the damaged area.

Materials for frame repair include small brushes, white Elmer's Glue-All, plaster of Paris, spackle, plastic wood, a mixture of fine sawdust and Duco Cement, small knives, scissors, razor blades, small pieces of cardboard, sandpaper, small strips of tissue paper, tiny pieces of cheesecloth, tracing paper, and a pencil.

Curlicue shapes on the corners of the frame can be traced with a pencil and tracing paper to make a pattern, and then the main shape can be cut out of cardboard. Next, the cardboard profile can be put in position and attached where it fits on the frame. Use white glue to attach it and masking tape to hold it in place while it is drying.

Mixed plaster of Paris can easily be brushed on and shaped to go under the cardboard profile. Later, after this has dried, the plaster of Paris can also be added on top of the cardboard to give a flat, concave, or convex surface, whichever is needed. Any other irregular shape can also be sculpted with the appropriate tools. Other smaller designs or missing parts can be replaced by applying spackle (or mixed plaster) with a small brush or tiny knife, then later sanding any of these added rough shapes with strips of sandpaper or emory boards. White glue should be brushed on the shapes to help hold them together with the rest of the frame.

Finally, when the desired shape has been carved, very small pieces of white tissue paper can be glued on to the new replacement to hold it to the frame and protect the added plaster or spackle shapes. Then the frame may be retouched, repainted, or given whatever finish is desired. For gold frames, a wax metallic finish such as Treasure Gold is ideal. It is available in gold, silver, and other metallic colors. It may be applied with a finger, small brush, or cloth and then polished with a soft cloth. Turpentine is used for cleaning up.

Creating Mats for Prints

For traditional interior dressing, scenic designers are always looking for new items to put on walls. Prints in color and black-and-white may be selected from a variety of subjects, including flowers, architecture, birds, hunting scenes, dogs, ornaments, pastoral scenes, coat of arms, seascapes, portraits, and many more. Prints tend to look more attractive when they have nice mats around them. Usually plain white is harsh onstage and stands out too much under stage lighting, but this also depends on the production. A print can become more interesting when double or triple mats are used and then finished off on the outer edges with a plain or detailed frame. Average frames can be black, silver, gold, or natural wood colors. Linen liners may also be a part of the frame.

The selection of the mat depends on the subject and how it goes with the colors in the print. Start by cutting the first mat that you wish to fit around the print. If a second mat is desired, make it ¼ inch wider than the first. (It may also be a bit wider than ¼ inch.) For example, if the first mat is a white one and is cut to be 14 × 18 inches, then the colored mat going on top of it would be 14½ × 18½ inches. Assume that you might want a third mat in still another color to go on top of the first two. It could be ½ inch wider and it would have an opening of 15½ × 19½ inches.

Bands or lines can also be added around the inner openings of the mats as an extra feature. These bands may be applied, painted, inked, or penciled directly on the mats. For example, bands can be cut out of metallic or other papers with a sharp razor blade or X-acto knife and glued around the inner edges of the top mat. These bands may be ⅛ inch, ³/₁₆ inch, or wider, and may be ¾ inches from the edges of the last cutout opening in the mat. One band can be used, or even two with a ¼-inch space between them.

While this kind of mat does take a bit of work, it is worth the effort when the mat turns out well, especially if the work is being done in a resident company where the mat can be used more than one time.

Mats can be bought in art supply shops or painted in the scenic studio. All sorts of colors can be used. These are some suggested combinations: cream, white, and gold; gray, silver, and garnet; off-white, yellow, gold, and green; white, mustard, and black; beige, gold, and terra-cotta. The thin bands and lines can be in similar or different colors. A sheet of nonreflective glass or Plexiglas can be substituted for the traditional glass.

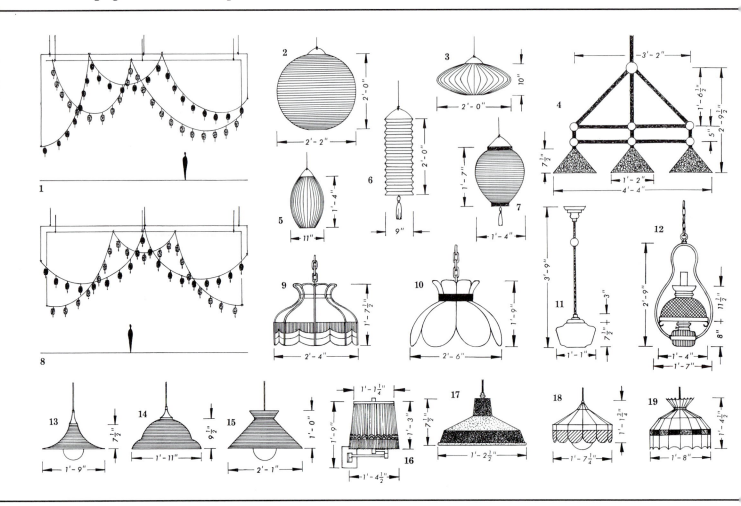

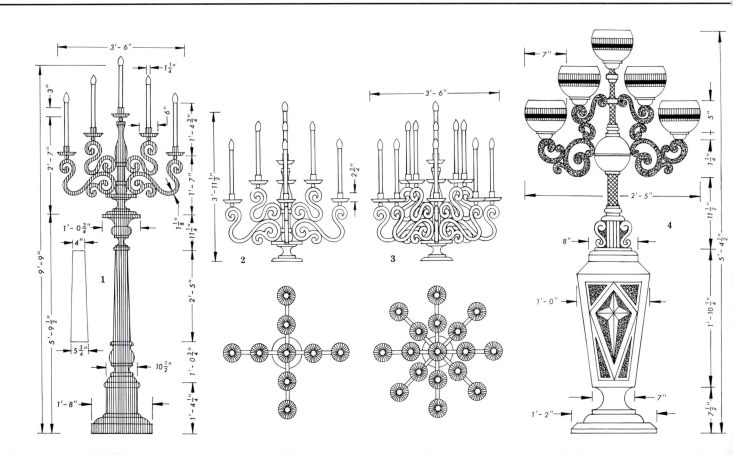

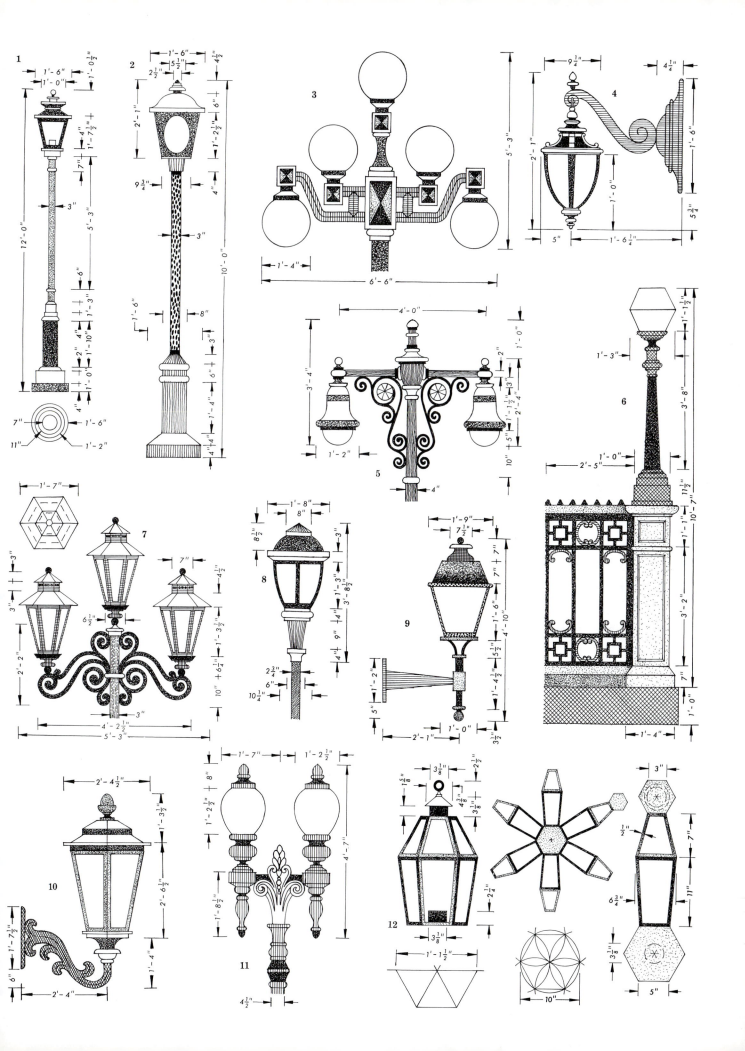

Table Lamps and Floor Lamps

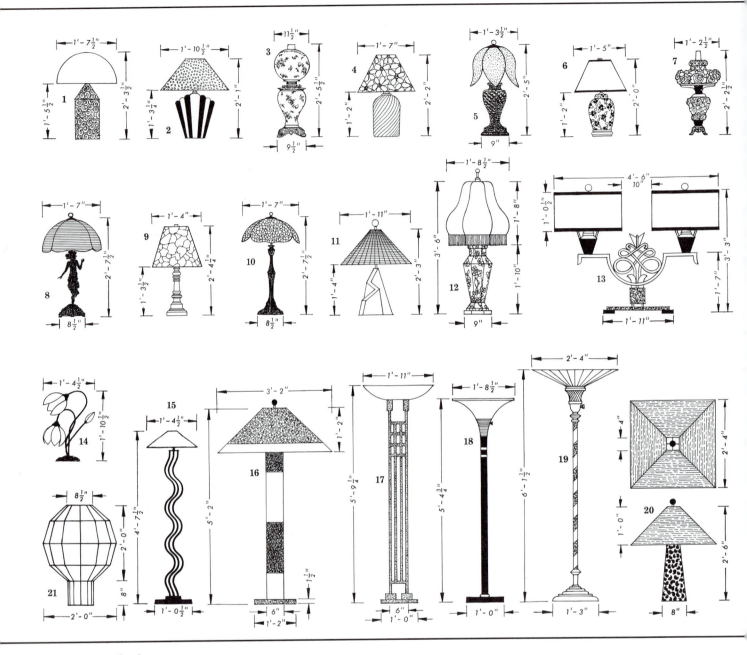

Lamp Shades

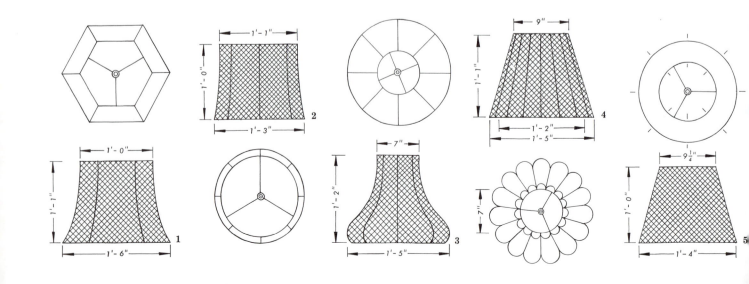

Setting and lighting by Neil Peter Jampolis
EUGENE ONEGIN by Peter Ilyich Tchaikovsky
Text by the composer and K. S. Shilovsky
Directed by Colin Graham
Costumes by Malabar
Banff Center
Eric Harvie Theatre
Banff, Alberta, Canada (1986)
(Photograph by Neil Peter Jampolis)

"The chandelier is all fabricated from plastic and weighs under 125 pounds. It is 8 feet wide, 12 feet tall, and 4 feet deep."

—Neil Peter Jampolis

Chandelier Crystals and Drops

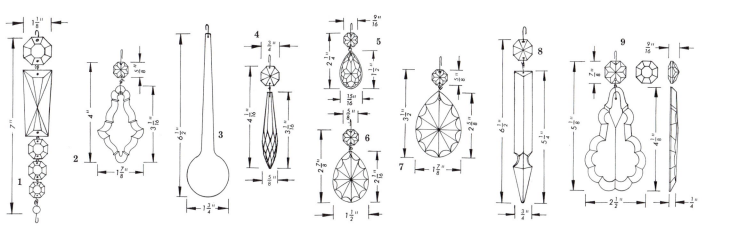

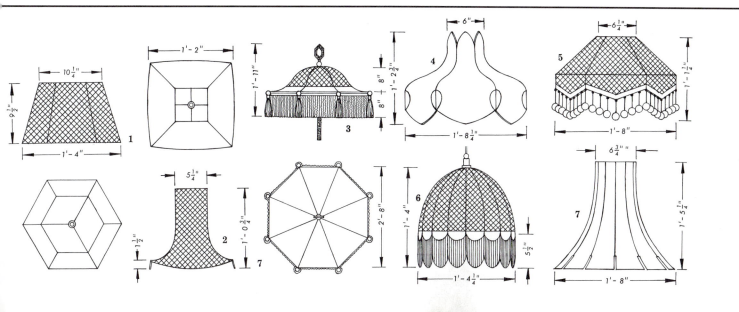

Sconces, Chandeliers, Wall Lamps, and Other Light Fixtures

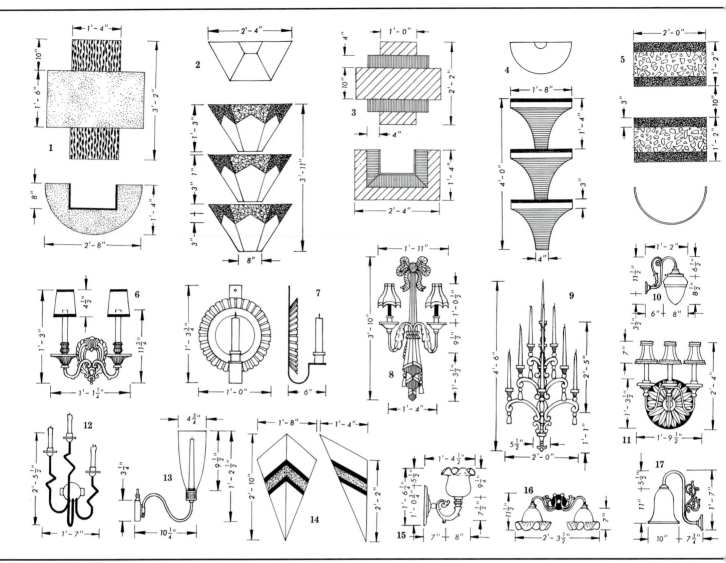

Overscale Candelabras (Decrease Sizes as Necessary)

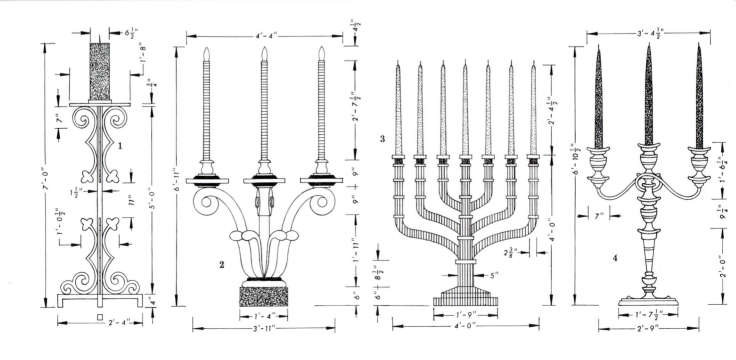

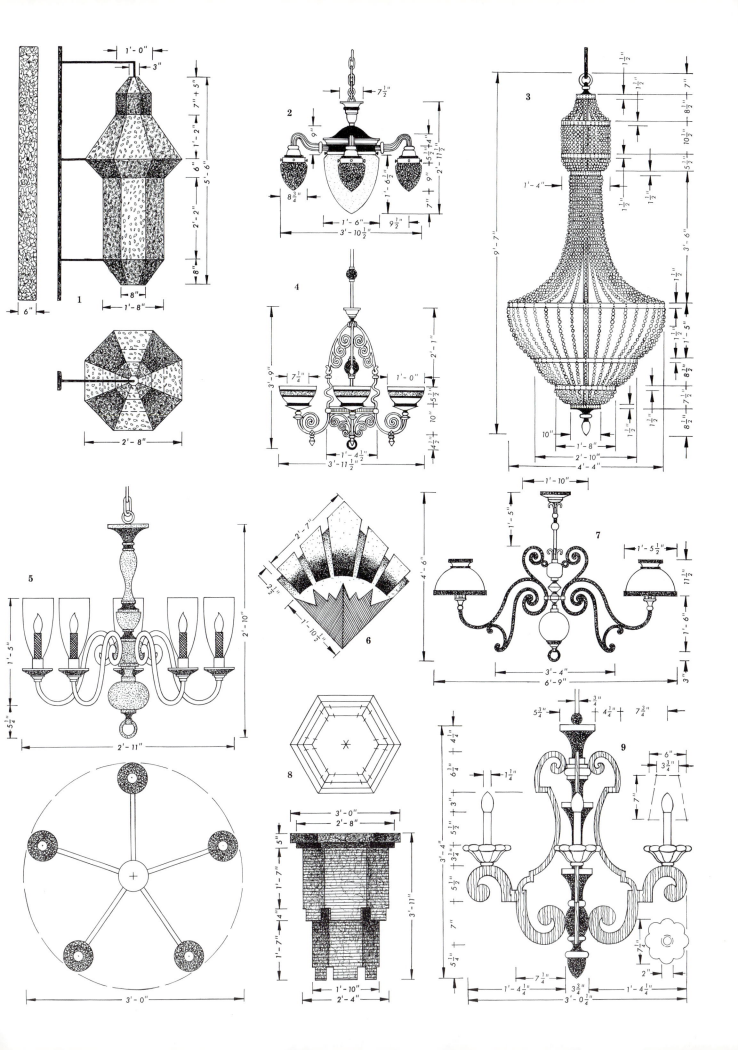

Designing Profile Chandeliers

There are several practical reasons for designing profile chandeliers rather than using three-dimensional light fixtures on the stage.

1. Profile chandeliers take up much less space (up- and downstage). One, two, or three chandeliers may be hung on one pipe.
2. Profile chandeliers are usually easier to pack and store than three-dimensional chandeliers.
3. Profile chandeliers can be duplicated simply and easily from a single full-scale drawing enlarged from the 1/2-inch scale elevation.
4. Profile chandeliers normally cost less to build than three-dimensional chandeliers.
5. Profile chandeliers can be built in larger scale than the three-dimensional chandeliers ordinarily found in a shop or rental house.

Drawing Three-Dimensional Chandeliers

If you feel that a three-dimensional chandelier is more appropriate than a profile chandelier, by all means use it. You may be lucky and find one that is perfect for the set. If not, then it may need to be built. This means that appropriate drawings must be made to show exactly how you want it to be built and hung in the theatre.

Custom building a chandelier for a show is a long-standing practice in the commercial theatre. A highly publicized example of a built chandelier in a show was the one designed by Maria Björnson for *The Phantom of the Opera* (1988). The massive chandelier, which was designed to collapse during the performance, was said to weigh a ton. It and several ornate candelabras were

part of Björnson's elaborate scenic scheme for *Phantom*.

Putting Chandeliers on the Drafting

Always give as much information as you feel is necessary when you are doing the drawings for a chandelier. For instance, mention whether the chandelier is to be purchased, rented, borrowed, or built. If it is to be built, quite possibly it will turn out to be very close to the actual design that is specified on the drawings. If it is to be selected, then the chandelier design may vary considerably.

For clarity, it is often necessary to repeat the same notes and dimensions on one or more drawings. These basic points may be used when drawing chandeliers on drafting.

FRONT ELEVATION (1/2-inch scale)

1. Specify by the drawing whether the chandelier is full-round, half-round, or profile.
2. Give the dimension for the low (bottom) trim of the chandelier.
3. Give the overall height and width of the chandelier.
4. Show the drawing of the chandelier in hanging position as it relates to the portal, main set, backdrop, cyc, draperies, or whatever.
5. Give sufficient dimensions and notes for building, or draw the chandelier in a larger scale if it is complex.
6. Specify bracing at the top of the chandelier, such as triangular pieces on each side of a vertical rod (or tube) so it does not turn during the show.
7. Label the paint treatment or other finish.
8. Describe any special effects if the chandelier is to be purchased and is to be altered or revamped in design (added or subtracted items, change in proportion, color or textures.)

9. State whether the chandelier flies in and out or remains in the same position.

GROUND PLAN (1/2-inch scale)

1. Give the location dimensions of where the chandelier is to be positioned onstage. Always start the dimension from the back of the smoke pocket (or upstage wall of the proscenium) to the center of the chandelier. This tells the production carpenter and the lighting designer exactly which hanging pipe (or deadtied line) the chandelier will hang on.
2. If the chandelier is to be positioned off-center (left or right), give the dimension to tell how far off-center.
3. Tell whether the chandelier flies in or out or if it remains stationary. This information lets the production carpenter know if he needs to plan for a stagehand to move the chandelier and also lets the lighting designer or electrician estimate how much cable is necessary to make the chandelier a practical (electrify).
4. Draw the extreme outer diameter of the chandelier on the plan. This shows how much space the overall chandelier occupies in the up- and downstage areas. Of course, a straight 3/4-inch profile chandelier takes up much less space up- and downstage than a round chandelier. Individual reference points must be used for arena or open stage productions when there is no proscenium wall to use as reference point for dimensions.

HANGING SECTION (1/2-inch scale)

1. Give the location in dimensions from back of smoke pocket to center of chandelier.
2. Give dimension for low (bottom) trim of the chandelier. This is the distance from the very bottom of the chandelier to the stage floor. It tells the production carpenter how much cable and what hardware is needed for hanging and lets the lighting designer or electrician know the exact position of the chandelier for focusing lights.
3. Show the side view of the chandelier on the drawing in solid lines in the scene(s) or act(s) where it plays. If the chandelier moves during performance, then show where it flies out of sight and stores above by using broken lines for the side profile of the chandelier.

MEASUREMENTS OF ROUND LAMPSHADES (in inches)			
HEIGHT	BOTTOM DIAMETER	TOP DIAMETER	OVERALL HEIGHT OF SHADE ON LAMP
11	13	12	29
11 3/4	15	9	28 1/2
12	16	9 1/4	28
13	18	10	35 1/4
13 3/4	17	16	35 1/2
14	15	14	34

MEASUREMENTS OF RECTANGULAR LAMPSHADES (in inches)			
BOTTOM	TOP	HEIGHT	OVERALL HEIGHT OF SHADE ON LAMP
12 × 8 1/2	10 1/4 × 6 3/4	8	25
16 × 10 1/2	16 × 10 1/2	11	30

4. Check to see if there is sufficient space downstage and upstage of the chandelier for clearance of other scenery. At least 6 inches in front and in back of the chandelier should be allowed.

Looking for Chandeliers

When a chandelier is to be purchased or rented, the scenic designer is expected to do a drawing in ½-inch scale (or larger) of the chandelier that he or she has in mind for the setting. Sometimes a complete description is given in the notes the prop person is to use as reference, but it is still best to make a drawing to show the prop house or particular antique shop exactly what you have in mind. The drawing not only shows the style and size, but also indicates how and where the chandelier is positioned in the set.

Depending on the size of the set and the stage, chandeliers usually need to be a bit larger than life to read well from the stage. In searching for the right chandelier it usually works best to have the prop person find several different chandeliers, take color Polaroid photos of them, and jot down the source, size, and price on the back of the picture.

Chandeliers may be rented, borrowed, or bought for a specific production. In the commercial theatre the rental price may be applied toward purchase if the show has a long run. Of course, it is great if the theatre has a permanent ongoing prop department and the chandelier can be purchased to add to the collection.

Measuring Lampshades

Finding the correct lampshade for a lamp base is almost an art in itself. Some people have an intuitive talent for making a good selection while others have to struggle with an appropriate decision.

When selecting a lampshade for a base, keep in mind that the height of the lamp base should always be a bit taller than the height of the lampshade. This is a good rule to follow, especially with contemporary and everyday lampshades. Use the chart of lampshade dimensions (left) to study the proportion of shade heights with lamp base heights.

Since round shades tend to be the most common shape, let us look at some basic sizes. There are three di-

mensions you need to get when measuring shades: overall height, bottom diameter, and top diameter.

Creating Lampshades

While new lampshades may be purchased, there are numerous ways to revamp contemporary lampshades and come up with nice creations for the stage. Do you want it to be an opaque or translucent lampshade? Should it be a heavy pleated paper or plastic? What about a covering of sheer fabric over an opaque cover?

IDEAS FOR CREATING NEW SHADES FROM OLD

1. Paint old paper lampshades by spraying them with paint from an aerosol can.
2. Use the metal framework of discarded lampshades that often can be found in attics, thrift shops, antique stores, and garage sales. Metal frameworks in various periods and several sizes are always excellent to have on hand because they can be re-covered, put on other lamps, and used in so many different stage sets. Clean off any old materials from the metal frames and spray them with paint if needed. Any fabric bands wrapped around the metal pieces may be left intact and used as a base for sewing or gluing on new material(s).
3. To cover the metal frames of the shades, choose from a variety of materials, such as all kinds of paper, fabrics, and plastic. If you are selecting papers to go on the metal frames, these may be painted light to heavy cardboard, marbleized paper adhered over heavy paper, or other printed paper glued onto heavy paper. If you want fabrics to go on the metal frames, these may be chintz, dotted Swiss, chiffon, burlap, satin or others. Depending on the style, fabrics can be stretched tight over the metal frame or gathered with fullness.

Designing Lampposts

The presence of a lamppost as a simple prop onstage tells the audience immediately that the scene is a street or a park. While it is important for the lamppost to fit the appropriate historical period, it is equally important for it to be made in the proper scale.

A lamppost should tower over a 6-foot actor to really read well. An av-

erage overall height for a lamppost is 10 to 12 feet. This height needs a well-designed base with sufficient weight so the lamppost is not top-heavy. Keep in mind, too, that as a scenic prop the lamppost must be movable off and on stage quickly and with ease. Swivel casters mounted and concealed in the base work ideally for this.

Bases for lampposts may be created in a variety of shapes—circular, hexagonal, octagonal, or square. A 12-foot high lamppost should have at least an 18- to 20-inch-diameter base. When casters are being used it makes good sense to mount the lamppost on a 4-inch-high base (allowing 1 inch for clearance). Assume that the base is circular and is 4 inches high. The top and bottom of the base should have the same shape and can be cut out of ¾-inch plywood, with blocks of wood positioned in between that measure 1½ inches wide by 2 inches deep by 1½ inches high. A hole can be cut out of the center of the base for the shaft of the lamppost, leaving a 2-inch width all around.

When designing the lamppost you may use wood, metal, or heavy cardboard for the main vertical (core) structure and then add more body and details onto it.

Detail of bed post and stringer by David Gropman, THE PRETENDERS
Directed by Alvin Epstein
Guthrie Theatre (1978)

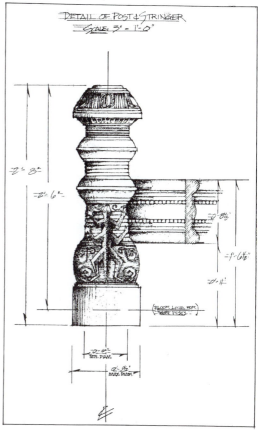

502

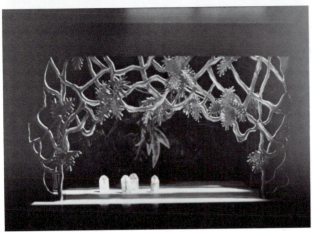

Model designs by Randy Barcelo
THE MAGIC OF KATHERINE DUNHAM
Choreographed by Katherine Dunham
City Center Theatre, New York (1987)
(Photographs by Randy Barcelo)

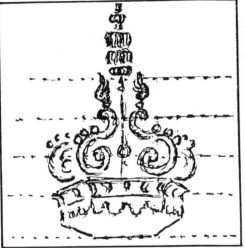

Canopy top sketch by Oliver Messel
THE SLEEPING BEAUTY (1976)
(Collection of Lynn Pecktal)
(Photograph by Lynn Pecktal)

Umbrellas by Tony Straiges
TIMBUKTU!
Directed and choreographed by Geoffrey
   Holder
Mark Hellinger Theatre, New York (1978)
(Photograph by Ney Tait Fraser)

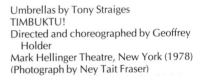

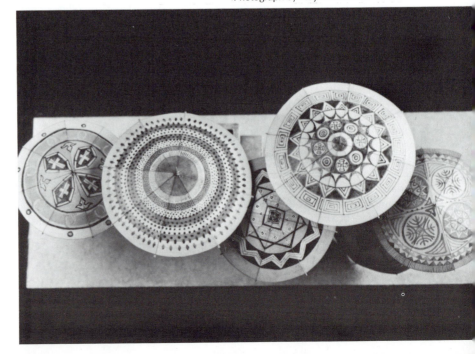

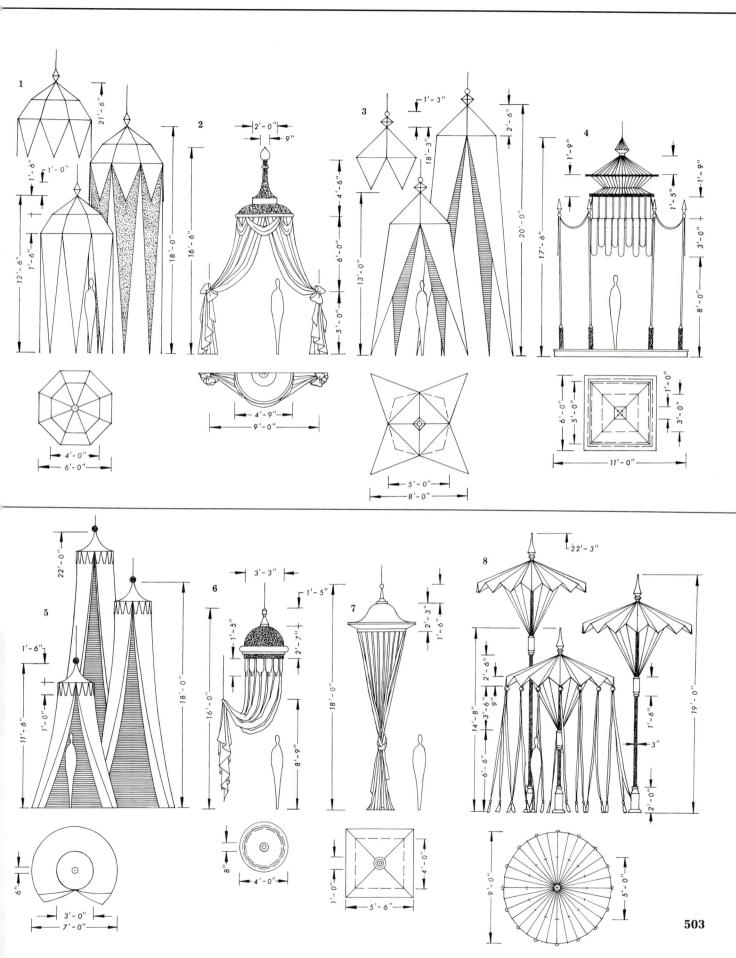

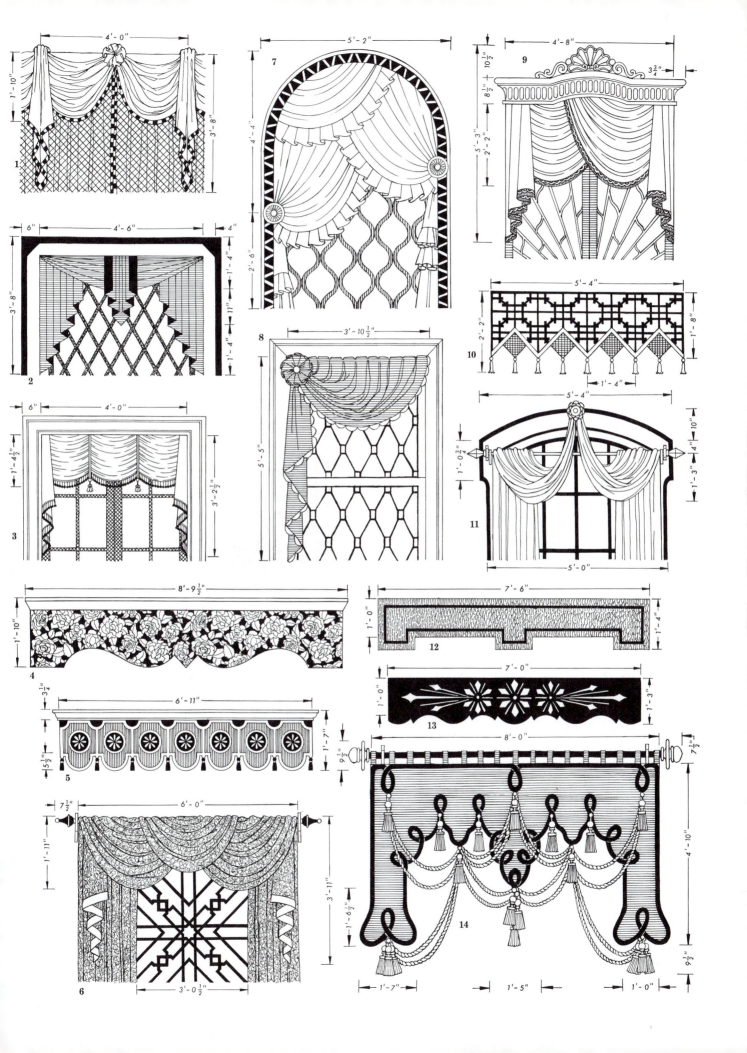

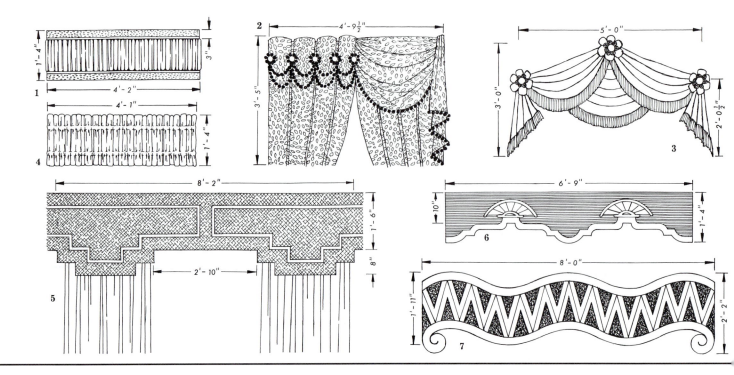

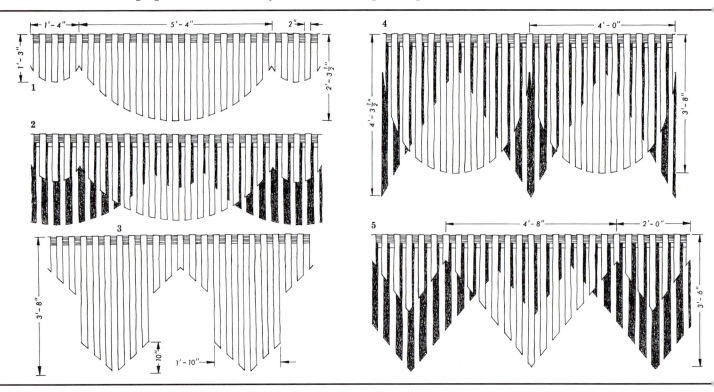

Decorative Hanging Patterns Formed by Cut Fabric or Paper Strips on Battens

Draped Garlands

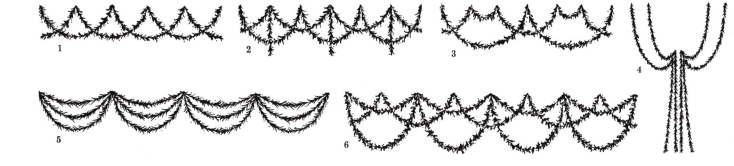

SCENIC AND PROP DETAILS

Canopies, Tents, and Umbrellas

Uses Three-dimensional canopies are wonderful structures for creating a highly theatrical effect for a number of objects. Canopies can be suspended over beds, tables, entrances, arches, fountains, windows, throne chairs, or exhibits. They can be used as tops of tents or just as decoration. These items may be attractive motifs for dance, operas, musicals, or plays.

Materials Frameworks may be wood, metal, or both, with shapes supported by forming cloth (woven wire that is not welded), chicken wire, or buckram. Fabrics vary a great deal, depending on the design and desired effect. Examples range from linen scrim, sharkstooth scrim, to organza, chiffon, duvetyne, muslin, to velour. The kind of ornamentation is also determined by the nature of the design. Examples include fringe, tassels, ribbons, streamers, roping, carved ornaments, cherubs, and flowers.

Canopies and tents may be used as an integral part of a setting or may be completely independent. Overscale and decorative umbrellas are designed to play on stage as a single prop or as a group.

Canopies and top ornaments may be constructed of thin metal rods, wood, carved Styrofoam, or a combination of these materials. The ornamental tops are often suspended on thin steel cables without requiring any bottom support. On other occasions canopies are designed to be attached to the flats with loose pin hinges.

Canopies may vary considerably in style, shape, and materials. Bed canopies range from a simple solid or ruffled lace canopy to a highly detailed baroque canopy with many swags and panels positioned over and around a sleigh bed. Canopies may have heavy or very simple ornamentation. Three-dimensional geometric shapes of thin metal covered with colorful fabric work extremely well as ornaments for canopies.

Tents also vary enormously. They range from a pup tent, wigwam, or camp tent to a large theatrical scrim tent which dancers perform in and around.

Large umbrellas may be effective for settings such as beaches, amusement parks, terraces, and gardens. Umbrellas range from the commercial type to the custom made. Umbrellas have to be built if they are designed to be in a very large scale or if they have a special style and shape.

Drapery Valances

Uses Drapery valances are ideal decorative features to go over draperies on windows, doors, arches, or bed alcoves. Valances used on window draperies tend to be the most common. Examples of typical window valances in a setting include a college dorm, a salon, a drawing room, a hotel banquet room, a beauty parlor, a boutique shop, a library, a bedroom, a hallway, and a foyer.

Materials Basic materials for a sturdy three-dimensional framework may be softwoods such as 1 × 2 inches and 1 × 3 inches, plywoods, and/or metalwork. Depending on the openness, curvature, and angles of the basic shape, chicken wire, forming wire, or buckram may be used. Muslin works well to serve as an undercover for other fabric to go on top. Fabrics for valances and window treatments may be damasks, velours, brocades, painted muslin and canvas, taffeta, and many others. Ornamentation includes all sorts of items, such as various fringes, roping, tassels, pom-poms, bands, braids, gimp, ribbons and bows, streamers, carved figures, and other ornaments.

Thicknesses of valance boxes average 4, 6, 8, or more inches according to the scale and kind of setting. The built valance box framework may have space and a rod for draperies and curtains, space for dramatic lighting equipment, and space and hardware for blinds or roll-up shades. They are usually attached to the flats with loose pin hinges. Like canopies, sturdy valance boxes may also be elaborately carved and have drapery or fabric attached in swags, jabots, or pulled-back panels.

Similar soft arrangements may be positioned over horizontal rods over windows or doors, in archways, or in bed alcoves. Other soft valance designs may be attached with Velcro, webbing, grommets and hooks, or other equipment.

Gravestones, Markers, and Monuments

Tombstones are found in a variety of sizes, shapes, and designs. The design and materials used can indicate the socioeconomic status of the person buried there. The simplest of grave markers may be designed to be made of wood or simulated to appear as such. It may be a flat vertical shape with the top cut straight across or a curved, vertical, pointed, or other profiled shape. Wooden crosses are also common. Materials for such grave markers may be actual rough wood or painted muslin glued on ¾-inch plywood. Simple wooden grave markers are sometimes built to lean slightly in any direction. In addition, they may have a small board or support block on the bottom so they can stand without bracing.

Gravestones may be designed and painted to appear as granite or marble or just as textured and aged stone. Let us assume we are discussing a gravestone that is 2'-0" wide by 2'-6" high by 9" deep. The basic framework may be made of 1 × 2-inch softwood framing covered with ¼-inch plywood. Depending on the desired effect, various materials are often added over the smooth ¼-inch plywood. These are among the various effects and finishes for gravestones.

1. For a general texturing and aging effect, heavily sand and grind down the edges, then brush on heavy scenic dope before painting.
2. For a heavily crumbling texture, glue a ½-inch-thick sheet of Styrofoam on the outer surfaces that are seen from the audience. Carve the shapes of the design, sand, and cover the finished shapes with pieces of linen scrim dipped in scenic dope; then paint. Lightweight baby flannel may also be used.
3. For ornamental designs such as leaves, flowers, scrolls, ribbons, and so on, use shapes cut out of felt or Styrofoam and glue them onto the surface. Cover with cheesecloth or linen scrim, texture with scenic dope, and paint.
4. For raised lettering, cut individual letters out of Foamcore board, glue them onto the textured surface of the gravestone and, if necessary, cover for protection, and then paint according to the desired effect.

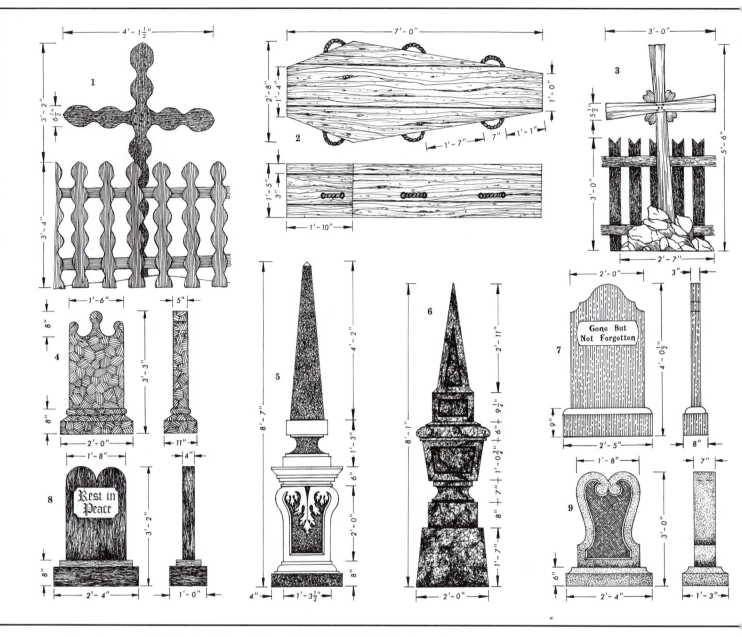

Drawings and Coffin for Edward Gorey's Set in DRACULA (1977)

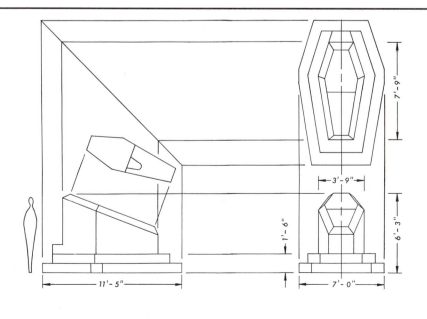

Drawings and Tomb for Eugene Berman's Scenery in PULCINELLA (1972)
(Drawings and photographs by Lynn Pecktal) (*Pictured at right:* Ben Kasazkow)

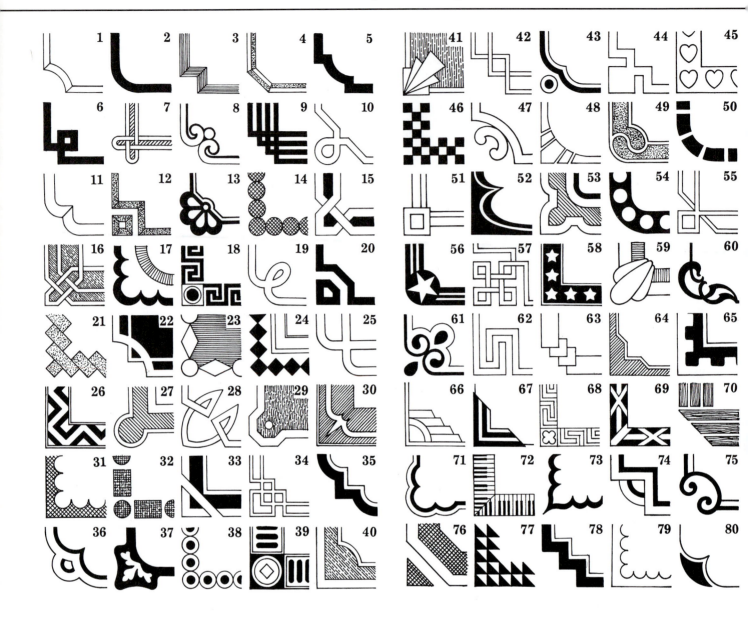

Flags and Signs (*Also on next two pages*)

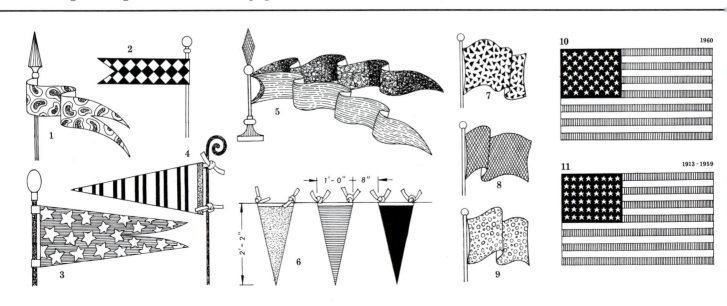

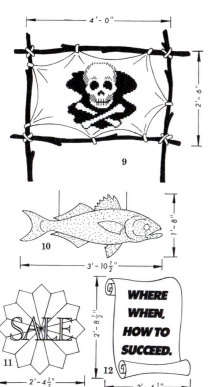

5. For carving letters into the surface of the gravestone, use Styrofoam to carve out the name or phrases, then cut out the ¼-inch plywood and attach the recessed Styrofoam lettering into the tombstone.

6. For carved designs, shape separately and attach them to the tombstone. These figures may be cherubs, angels, lambs, hearts, flowers, borders, or geometric designs. Small three-dimensional figures, such as simple cherubs, may have a flat center vertical support piece with a layer of Styrofoam glued on the front and back. After carving, cover with a thin fabric coated with scenic dope, and paint.

   Very large figures such as three-dimensional angels normally require an armature of wood and metal. Chicken wire or the like is usually needed to create the basic shape, and then details such as the face, hands, arms, and feet may be carved out of Styrofoam and covered with linen scrim. The rest of the large wire shape may be covered with muslin strips dipped in scenic dope. Any ornamentation may be cut out of layers of felt.

Designing Signs

Uses Everyone is familiar with signs. Signs serve many purposes and cover a vast range of subject matter. They tell us what to do, where to go, and identify buildings, firms, people, and places.

Materials Materials range from simple painted signs on flats and backdrops of canvas, muslin, and scrim to wood and metal signs, with and without lights. Painted signs may be created on Plexiglas or muslin with a light box built behind them.

Signs can be made in almost any size and shape and can be made of many materials. Both soft and framed signs can be designed to be stationary or to fly in or out. The many typefaces, logos, and ornamentation for signs are seemingly endless. Signs are painted on muslin banners, on simulated parchment scrolls that unroll, on the sides of buildings, on flags, on formal shapes, and on rustic boards. Letters are cut out and painted to form words hanging in space. Gigantic three-dimensional letters can be cut out and mounted on platforms to roll onstage.

Besides painting and using actual lights, the lettering on signs may be done with various materials, such as mirrored discs, sequins, bottle tops, wooden balls, Mylar designs, buttons, and assorted metal discs.

The idea in creating signs is always to try to come up with something new and clever. Signs have long been a decorative and telling feature onstage. John Keck and James Stewart Morcom have designed numerous varieties of painted and large-scale signs for the mammoth stage at Radio City Music Hall. They have created sign designs with tracer lights and stationary lights, neon and ultraviolet lights, plus all sorts of painted and cutout signs.

Show curtain design by Hugh Landwehr
JOHN BROWN'S BODY by Stephen Vincent Benet
Directed by Peter Hunt
Williamstown Theatre Festival (1989)

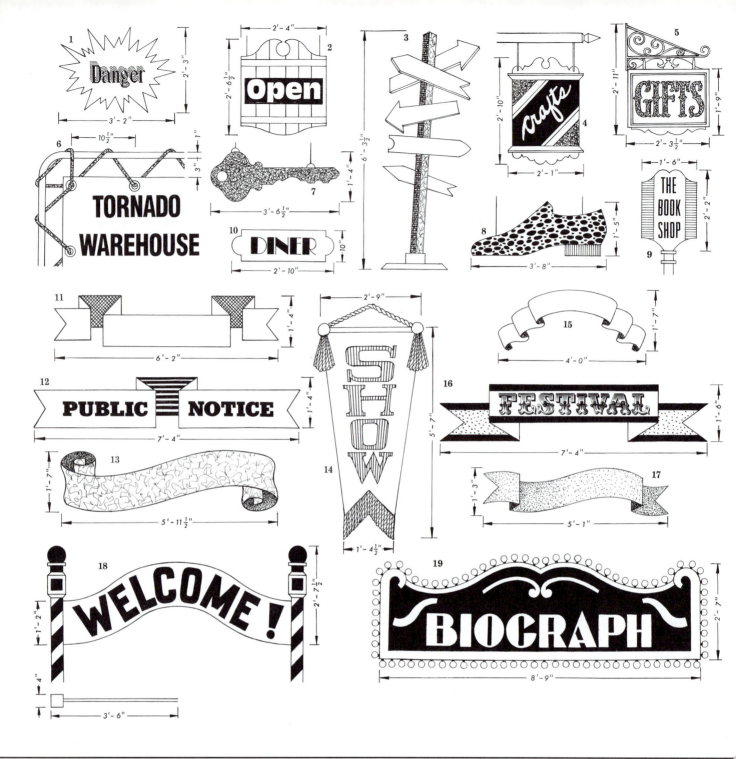

1 **Danger** 3'-2" 2'-3"

2 **open** 2'-4" 2'-6½" 3"

3 6'-3½"

4 **crafts** 2'-10" 2'-1"

5 **GIFTS** 2'-11" 1'-9" 2'-3½"

6 **TORNADO WAREHOUSE** 10½" 3"

7 3'-6½" 1'-4"

8 1'-5" 3'-8"

9 **THE BOOK SHOP** 1'-6" 2'-2"

10 **DINER** 10" 2'-10"

11 1'-4" 6'-2"

12 **PUBLIC NOTICE** 1'-4" 7'-4"

13 1'-7" 5'-11½"

14 **SHOW** 2'-9" 5'-7" 1'-4½"

15 1'-7" 4'-0"

16 **FESTIVAL** 1'-6" 7'-4"

17 1'-3" 5'-1"

18 **WELCOME !** 2'-7½" 1'-2" 4" 3'-6"

19 **BIOGRAPH** 2'-7" 8'-9"

Shapes for Tops of Individual Flats
and Also for Repeats of Flats

Shapes for Bottoms of Banners and Signs

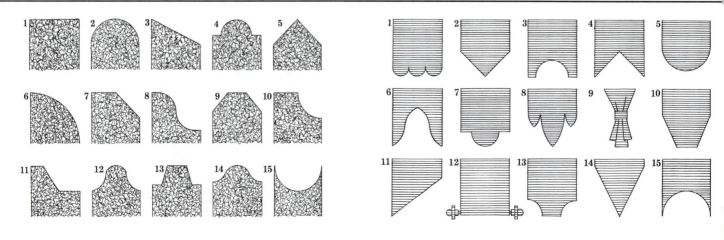

Pillows are wonderful for the stage because they serve a number of purposes. They are ideal for style, decoration, and comfort for the actors. All sorts of pillows can be arranged on sofas, chaises, beds, porch furniture, porch swings, hammocks, and on the floor. Pillow sizes range from petite throws arranged on a boudoir chaise to a stack of king-sized oriental pillows on the floor.

A change of pillows onstage may denote a passage of time or a change of season. Pillows may have reversible covers for a quick change. A lush, elegant feeling can be given with silk and satin pillows, or a simple, ordinary look with burlaps, Madras, aged cotton prints, and solid-colored fabrics.

Pillow Designs

Distinctive designs are created through the selection of size, shape, color, texture, and fabric. The possibilities for pillow designs are almost endless. A few are listed here.

Stripes	Bargellos
Checks	Fake furs
Plaids	Needlepoints
Florals	Animal patterns
Dots	Knitted covers
Damasks	Crewel works
Solids	Applied braidings
Monograms	Scenic views
Figures	Quilted patterns

Making Pillows

Various sizes and shapes of pillows can easily be made for the stage. Use regular sewing muslin to make a basic cover for the stuffing. The stuffing for pillows may be polyester or cotton. When the muslin cover is sewed and stuffed, make the outer cover just slightly larger than the stuffed muslin pillow.

Nice pillow covers are often made with piping covered in matching or contrasting fabric around the edges of the pillows. The openings for pillows may fasten with Velcro, zippers, or snaps.

Pillow Shapes

There is almost no limit to the shapes pillows may take. They can be square, rectangular, circular, triangular, octagonal, hexagonal, half-moon, oval, butterfly, and many other novelty shapes.

Bolsters are an excellent shape and style of pillow. They may be long and circular, long and square, long and rectangular, or have other shapes. Long and circular bolsters may have plain ends or ends gathered with a large covered button, a double ruffle, or a tassel on roping.

Fabrics for Pillows

Pillow fabrics can be as varied as pillow designs and shapes. Velvet, brocade, corduroy, chintz, sailcloth, moiré, terry cloth, sateen, taffeta, monk's cloth, tapestry, denim, and art needlework are a few of the most popular. Trims for the fabrics can be piping cord, fringe, ruffles, braid, tassels, buttons, bows, gimp, rickrack, and plain bands.

Pillow Sizes

The pillow sizes below may be used for the selection and making of pillows.

Standard bed pillow	20 × 26 in.
King	20 × 36 in.
Queen	20 × 30 in.
European	26 × 26 in.
Boudoir/Baby	12 × 16 in.
Neckroll	6 × 14 in.
Butterfly	26 in. long
Bolster	8 × 20 in.
Round	24 in. diameter
Round	18 in. diameter
Giant bolster	8 × 60 in.
Rectangular	12 × 16 in.
Standard pillow sham	20 × 26 in.
King-size pillow sham	20 × 36 in.

Bellpulls

The strip of cloth, handle, or cord that is pulled to ring a servant's bell in drawing room comedies and mystery plays is a very familiar and standard prop in many box sets.

Any number of patterns and designs can be used to create bellpulls. These may be classic motif (Greek frets, rosettes), geometrical designs (circles, squares, diamonds), nature subjects (flowers, leaves, vines), and the like. You may want to have a repeat pattern, an alternate repeat pattern, or a nonrepeating pattern.

Materials for Bellpulls

There are several different materials and ornaments that work well in creating bellpulls. These are a few suggestions.

1. Paint the design on muslin or canvas.
2. Choose a tapestry pattern as the actual material.
3. Partially paint over a textured fabric.
4. Make use of materials other than fabrics such as knitting yarn or crochet thread to simulate bargello or crewel patterns.
5. Finish off the pull with an ornament at the top. This may be a shield, wreath, shell, or the like, with a shiny metallic surface (gold, brass) or a plain subdued finish.
6. Add a bottom ornament also, to finish off the pull and to allow the actor to handle it. This ornament may be one or more tassels, pendants, a cluster of ribbon, an arrangement of small chains, a stuffed motif (animal or object), or various other designs.
7. To give some bounce to the bellpull when it is used by an actor, attach one end of a piece of elastic to the back of the top ornament, then attach the other end of the elastic to a piece of hardware which goes on the wall.
8. Hardware the bellpull at the top so it can be bolted, screwed, or clipped onto a flat.

Using Fake Blood for the Stage

Roscoblood, a product of Rosco Laboratories, is manufactured to appear as real blood onstage, and in film, tape, and video. It reads like blood, wet or dry, and is completely nontoxic, washable, and nonstaining. Roscoblood may be obtained from Rosco dealers. It is available in 2-ounce, 6-ounce, and 16-ounce containers.

Ordering Breakaway Bottles

Breakaway bottles are constantly in demand for all kinds of stage shows. The most important factor to consider is safety, and for this reason these bottles are made to shatter rather than break so that the actors will not be in danger of being cut by jagged edges.

A good source for bottles is Rosco Laboratories, Inc., at 38 Bush Avenue, Port Chester, NY 10573, Tel.: (914) 937-1300; or in Hollywood at 1135 North Highland Avenue, Hollywood, CA 90038, Tel.: (213) 462-2233; or at 69/71 Upper Ground, London, England SE 1 9PQ, Tel.: (01-633-9220).

Available breakaway bottles are beer bottles, whiskey bottles, and wine bottles.

MINIMAL SCENERY

Designing Sets with Minimal Scenery

Whether on a full proscenium stage or an experimental stage, in a black box theatre or an open stage in the round, some of the most exciting sets can be created with a great deal of imagination, a very small budget, and some materials that have been borrowed, rented, or salvaged from throwaway areas. Whenever you are designing sets with very little scenery, remember that the way the scenic items are arranged onstage and how they are lighted with stage lighting are both very important in creating an imaginative design.

Consider using some of the following items when you have a tight scenic budget. They may be used for both proscenium theatres and open stages. All are easy to store. These items may be positioned in front of a plain or brick wall, a cyclorama or drop, neutral or colorful curtains, or black velours.

Hanging Panels of Wooden Slats

Use rough crating lumber in 3- to 6-foot lengths and cut them 2 inches wide. Tie them together with heavy twine or thin clothesline or other flexible cord. For 3-foot panels, measure and come in 6 inches from each end and tie and knot the twine around the 2-inch slat. Leave 2 inches of space between the wooden slats. This may be varied according to the design. For 4-foot lengths, measure and come in 8 inches on each end; come in 10 inches for 5-foot lengths and 12 inches for 6-foot lengths. The height of the panels may be 15 to 20 feet or more; or it may be less, depending on the height available. While these are guidelines for basic panels, many variations can be used. For instance, you may want to have broken slats here and there and irregular spacing to provide interest. Slatted panels may be hung parallel to the proscenium or on angles. A combination of both parallel and angled hanging can create quite a pleasant design.

Stacked Arrangements of Cardboard Cartons

Cardboard cartons may be collected from a variety of stores over a period of time. Any number of sizes of cardboard boxes can be used to form a sculptured composition of walls. Random stacking of the boxes is also effective. It works well when you group boxes on small platforms on casters. These platforms may be 3 feet by 6 feet by 4 inches high. Boxes may be wired and glued together and painted with a roller, or used as they are. They may also be stacked in high arrangements (enlarging the base platform to accommodate the larger sizes) and moved around to show different compositions, textures, and colors on the opposite sides.

Rug Tubes and Other Cylinders

Rug tubes in small diameters and long lengths can be combined with clustered arrangements of cylinders emanating from the floor and extending upward 8 to 10 or 12 feet. Standing tubes can go from small to very large. Tubes may be created to have diameters of 1 foot, 1 foot 6 inches, or 2 feet 6 inches. The tubes may be painted in solid colors with metallic bands at the top, or they may be variegated with sprayed-on textures, have lights in them, or just be one color. These are effective and visually interesting not only when resting on the floor but also when suspended from the flies.

Pieces of Fabric

Both natural and synthetic fabrics can be worked into all sorts of lovely patterns to form creative stage designs. An imaginative craftsperson can work with pieces of fabric to make an inexpensive yet elegant and stunning unit onstage. Pieces of fabric can be inexpensive to buy or can be donated from the supplier's scrap collection. Often, fabrics ranging from 1 to 3 yards are suitable for making a crazy-quilt show curtain or collage backdrop of colorful patterns and textures.

To make a crazy-quilt drop, draw the full-scale design on gray bogus paper or brown paper that has been laid out flat on the floor and taped together. Then cut out each individual piece of fabric according to the shapes of the drawing, keeping in mind that the weave of the threads must run vertically or horizontally so that the fabric will hang properly. Allow at least ½ inch of fabric on the outer perimeter of each shape. Fasten the cutout fabric shapes together with straight pins before sewing them on a sewing machine. It works best to pin and sew several large groups of cutout pieces together and then join these large pieces to complete the drop. If the shapes are intricate, you may need to baste the fabric pieces together before sewing them on a machine.

The same method of drawing on the floor, pinning, and sewing can be used for making a backdrop of colorful patterns and textures. A collage of fabric can be used for any number of stage designs. It could be in the style of the painter Piet Mondrian, or some other abstract arrangements of patterns and/or textures.

Another way of using pieces of fabric is to hang various irregular lengths from the flies so that they extend down and stop well above the heads of the actors. In this case, the pieces of fabric can be attached to two or three wooden battens spaced 4 or 5 feet apart.

Vertically hung strips of fabric can be spaced so that they are completely asymmetrical. They can be gracefully arranged on wooden battens with diagonal folds and placed one in front of the other. The design can be further extended to create a three-dimensional effect by varying the shaping of the fabric on each of the three overhead wooden battens. Light instruments can be positioned between the battens of fabric to provide enormous contrast when the textures and patterns are lighted, and an even more extraordinary effect results when there is a variation in translucent, transparent, and opaque fabrics.

Long, 2-inch-wide lengths of fabric can be neatly cut with scissors and stapled onto a horizontal wooden batten and hung from the flies to form a colorful openwork backdrop. These vertically hung strips may be spaced 2 inches apart and may be as long as 20 feet. The fabric strips can all be one color or different colors, and patterns of color or fabric may be alternated. For example, there can be a series of eight red and eight yellow strips of fabric that is repeated all the way across the stage, or a series of ten red, ten white, and ten blue strips that are repeated as a color pattern.

To prevent long vertical streamers from becoming entangled with each other, they should be stapled to a wooden batten at the bottom. The bottom batten can be attached to the top

Minimal Scenery: Hanging Slats, Mobiles, Painted Flats and Fabric-Covered Hoops

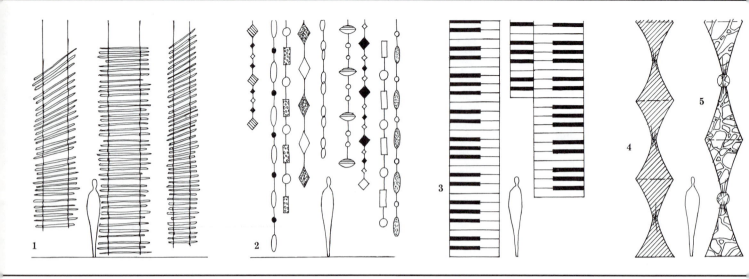

Patchwork Quilt Show Curtain

Overscale Styrofoam Chains

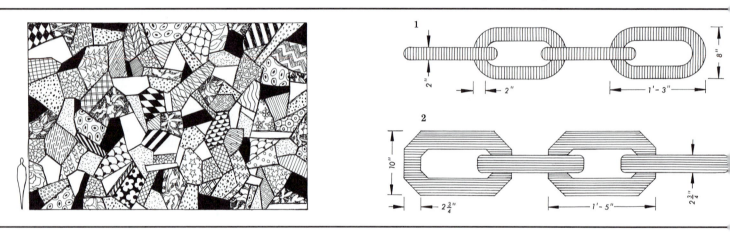

Overscale Snowflake Designs for Painting on Backdrops or for Hanging Cutouts

Creating Minimal Designs with Set Pieces Positioned Upstage of Basic Portals

1 2 3

4 5 6

7 8 9

10 11 12

Inner Proscenium Unit Sets with Openings for Scenic Pieces to Be Placed Behind

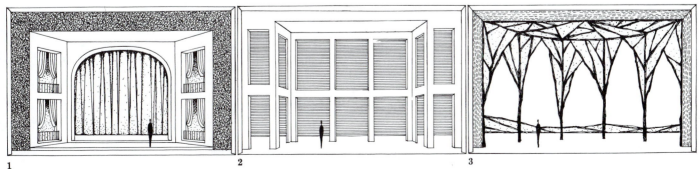

1 2 3

Scenery by Hugh Landwehr
CANDIDE by Len Jenkin
C. S. C. Rep
New York (1992)

batten with thin steel cables. The cables can be placed so that they are hidden by the 2-inch-wide strips.

The 2-inch-wide strips of fabric stapled onto a wooden batten can be cut at various heights or lengths to form dramatic patterns. The spacing should be 2 inches apart to create specific overhead shapes of swags and angled forms. Depending on the size of the stage, the overhead hanging lengths

Headboard of a bathtub and props designed by Nancy Winters for THE THREE MUSKETEERS (1984). (Courtesy of John Keck)

may range from 2 to 6 feet (see drawings). When fabric is not available for cutting out the 2-inch-wide strips, crepe paper could be used as a substitute.

Natural Tree Branches

A group of beautiful, natural tree branches is one of the most effective props for the stage. All sorts of shapes in an incredible range of formations can be found in nature.

Tree branches without foliage work best, because the natural leaves can wither and die during a long run. Although the foliage of evergreens such as pines and spruces hold up well, even these may have to be replaced in repertory situations. When foliage is needed, artificial leaves can easily be attached to selected naked tree branches.

Tree branches can be arranged very realistically onstage in a group rising up from grassy mounds of artificial grass that covers the supporting wooden base. Not only are real tree branches effective with attached artificial foliage, but for winter scenes white cotton batting or polyester upholstery stuffing can be used to give the appearance of fallen snow resting on the tree branches. It takes time and patience to apply these materials to create a subtle, natural-looking arrangement of fallen snow on the individual clusters of branches. In addition, Mica dust can be sparsely glued onto the synthetic snow, or pieces of polyester may be glued if the production plays in repertory.

The beauty of real tree branches is that they work nicely arranged in a group or as an individual tree standing alone on a full stage. They also make a pleasant visual statement when placed outside a box set to enhance a simple exterior backing unit. For a complete foliage setting that works wonders to give an outdoor feeling onstage, real branches may be put overhead on hanging battens. Then tall trees may be positioned stage left and right and very small trees scattered upstage in front of an exterior ground row masking the bottom of the drop.

Other lovely effects with natural tree branches are simple to achieve. Small twinkle lights may be strung randomly through the swinging branches. This is particularly effective and magical when used on an empty stage with nothing at all upstage, or perhaps positioned in front of a skydrop or even with black velour draperies.

Other effects may be obtained by spraying the tree branches all white or by applying metallics such as silver or gold paint.

Using Overscale Snowflakes as Designs

Giant patterns of snowflakes are ideal for winter scenes in musicals, revues, and children's shows. The diameter of these patterns may start at 15 inches and go to 18, 21, 24, 27, on up to 30 inches for large-scale productions. Usually a mixture of several diameters works best; these should be arranged in a pleasant random design.

Draw several individual pieces on brown paper so the drawings can be perforated with a pounce wheel and then transferred to the surface with powdered charcoal.

Snowflakes are usually drawn by constructing hexagons in which a design is created for one portion and then repeated five times. The overscale designs may be any of these:

1. *Snowflakes painted on a muslin backdrop.* Transfer the designs on a muslin backdrop with powdered charcoal and draw over the charcoal designs and the shapes with a pencil or a felt-tip pen. The snowflakes may be des-

For the production of FOR COLORED GIRLS WHO HAVE CONSIDERED SUICIDE/WHEN THE RAINBOW IS ENUF (1976), Ming Cho Lee designed a giant flower made of buckram with metal stems. (Photograph by Lynn Pecktal)

ignated to be translucent with an opaque background, or the whole drop may be opaque.

2. *Snowflakes cut out of fabric and glued on open material.* Draw the snow-flakes on pieces of muslin, canvas, or other fabric and then paint them and cut them out. Glue them on 1-inch scenic netting, sharkstooth scrim, or other openwork materials. In this case the snowflakes are usually opaque and are put on with white glue applied with a brush in small dots around the outermost edges. However, the white glue can be applied in small dots wherever needed. Lay the openwork drop flat on the floor over an equally large expanse of waxed paper, with the lengths of wax paper taped together so that they do not move. This taping is very necessary when putting the drop down over the paper.

A wax pencil can be used to mark the position of the snowflakes, provided the marks can be seen well through the openwork material.

Lay the openwork fabric drop (sharkstooth scrim, linen gauze, or 1-inch scenic netting) over the wax paper and staple on all four sides in the standard manner. Start at the center and bottom of the drop and make a grid of 3'-0" squares constructed over the drop with the same 3'-0" squares drawn on the ½-inch drafting so the painted and cutout snowflakes can be positioned according to the design. Metal weights should be placed on the fabric snowflakes to hold them in place while they are being glued to the fabric drop.

3. *Snowflakes cut out of rigid materials and suspended in space.* The snow-flakes may be cut out of pieces of ⅛- or ¼-inch plywood, Masonite, Foamcore board, illustration board, or other similar material. After the snowflakes are cut out and painted, small holes can be drilled in the outer edges so that thin lines or cables can be tied to them. These lines can be attached to one or more battens spaced a few feet apart overhead. Again, random placement with various sizes works well. One, two, or more snowflakes may be positioned on the same line. The movement of the snowflakes as they turn slightly can add interest to the overall scene. Materials such as glitter, mica, sequins, or small mirrored discs can add sparkle to the snowflakes. The same methods can be applied to large flowers and leaves, as well as to decorative ornaments. Examples of these include rosettes, medallions, and stars.

519

Drawings by Peter Harvey for Titania's Throne, A MIDSUMMER NIGHT'S DREAM Ballet (1979), Choreographed by George Balanchine, Zurich Opera House

---

Drawings of Titania's throne: Plan and top view front and rear elevations and cross section. *Also shown:* Titania's canopy (leaf), magic Eastern flower, and magic arrow.

NOTES: *Titania's throne (Venus shell):* Throne shell should be cast of fiberglass (very light and strong). The inside surface faced with foam rubber (1 cm.). This is covered in pink satin. The inside of the shell must be gleaming and lustrous like a real shell. Note that the cushion and horizontal part of the throne are asymmetrical to support a reclining figure (head toward stage right and legs stretched out diagonally).

The throne is structured rather like an office chair, for it swivels around as well as rolls any direction. If the rake of the stage is so steep that the throne rolls downstage on its own, then a foot pedal–type brake must be provided.

Giant rose: Petals shaped and wired out of large-weave buckram (like a hat) and then covered with an iridescent jersey gauze (stretchy and very light).

Leaves: Cut out of buckram or heavy organza with their veins of wire which will act as a support and make each leaf manageable. Basic look of rose, rosebud, and leaves is realistic.

Titania's canopy (leaf): Welded steel wire frame (veins) supports heavy organza leaf. Edge of leaf finished with horsehair ribbon and thin wire.

Magic Eastern flower: Note style of leaf is like that of scenery. Columbine (Aquilegia) style blossom with long spurs. Made of silk and buckram. Must separate from bush and be handled roughly by dancer. Leaves are scrimlike buckram on wire stems.

Magic arrow: Rig to slide down cable from offstage.

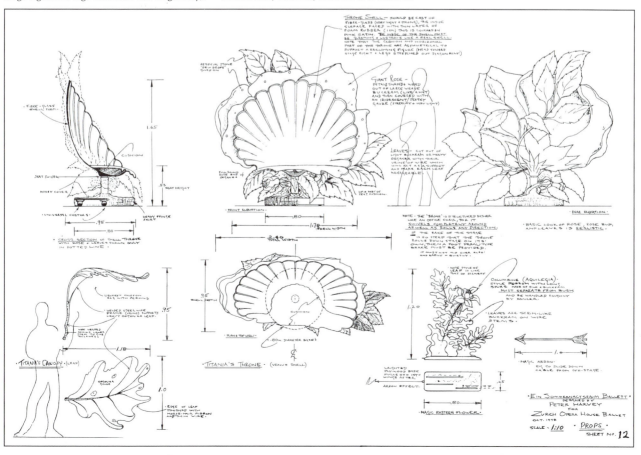

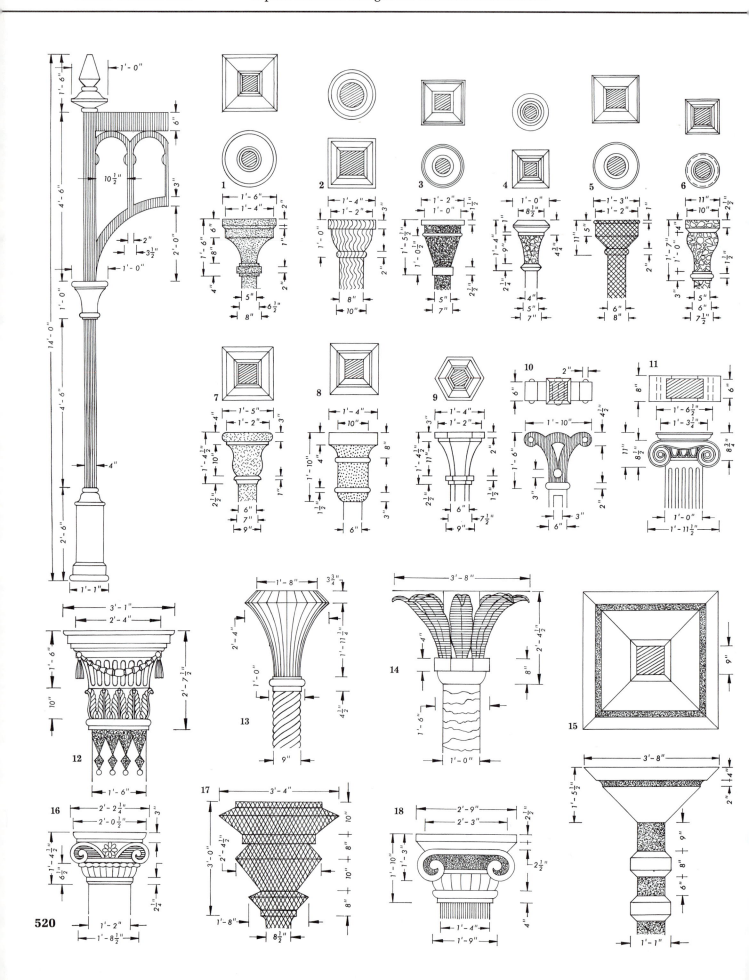

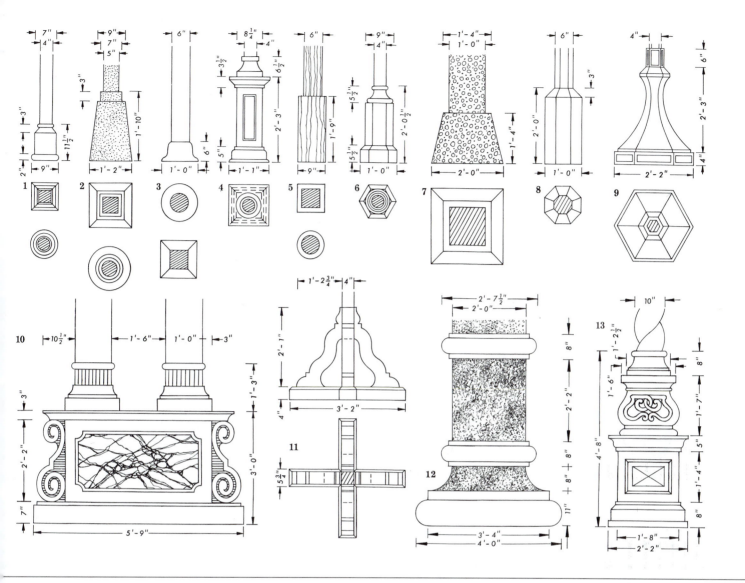

Suggestive Set Pieces Made of Rough Crating Lumber

Rough crating lumber is ideal for creating suggestive or fragmentary set pieces that can be used for either hanging or standing set pieces. These set pieces can work independently as hanging or standing units in the same set, or they may play as one structure that involves both hanging and standing pieces. For the best effects these wooden scenic pieces are usually rustic in appearance and have textures that are weather-beaten, with crumbling and peeling paint. The rough boards and lengths of aged wood can be most effective when there is from ½ to 1 inch of space between them to let light shine through from behind. These suggestive set pieces of rough lumber may form a side of a building, a gable below a roof, or a standing wall. While the rough boards are often po-

sitioned vertically, they may also work well when laid out horizontally.

If crating lumber is unavailable or if more strength and longer lengths are needed, then stock pieces of softwood such as 1 × 4 inches, 1 × 6 inches, or 1 × 8 inches can be substituted. These lengths of wood can easily be antiqued with heavy grinding and sanding on the edges, and the main surfaces can be nicely aged by randomly hitting them with pieces of metal chain.

The following scenery may be constructed as flat units and suspended by cable from the grid, or designed as three-dimensional pieces that come in and out on castered wagons. These scenic units may also be a mixture of both flat hanging pieces and three-dimensional units that work together as an overall stage set.

1. The top portion of a country church roof with belfry and random wooden

shingles, with a very irregular bottom-edge shape of jagged vertical boards.
2. A lean-to on the side of a barn with both horizontally and vertically positioned boards forming the design.
3. The vertical posts, roof, and ornate bric-a-brac of the front porch of an old Victorian farmhouse.
4. The run-down backyard fence of a tenement made up of vertical boards with an occasional one missing.

Painting the Rough Crating Lumber

The natural rough crating wood and the stock softwood may be painted with transparent aniline dye colors to let the grain show through, or with casein, vinyl, and latex paints. Heavy scenic dope may be dragged across the surface before painting to give a three-dimensional texturing. Sometimes it is not necessary to add texture.

Moving Props: Carabosse's Chariot and the Magic Barge Designed by Oliver Messel for THE SLEEPING BEAUTY (1976) for the American Ballet Theatre

Dimensions of chariot: 14'-0" long by 7'-8" high by 3'-9" wide. Overall height including vultures at top: 11'-0". Height of chariot floor: 1'-9". Vultures on metal support were designed to flap as chariot moved and snakes on front jiggled slightly. *Photographs:* 1. Wooden base with wheels and partial structure. 2. Metal frame constructed directly on paper pounce for each side. 3. Rear view of metal framework attached to wooden base and curved structure. 4. Side view of rear showing profiled wood with metalwork. 5. Forming wire attached to metal frame. Mask of papier-mâché and wire. 6. Framework is covered with ragging (muslin pieces and scenic dope). 7–9. Painted views of rear and side of chariot.

Right:
Dimensions of the magic barge: 10'-9" long by 10'-4" high by 3'-3" wide. Height of castered platform: 1'-4". *Photographs across:* 1. Papier-mâché mask created by Oliver Messel. 2. Rear view of magic barge with open wood framework and front and back profiled plywood pieces. 3. Ragging (muslin pieces dipped in scenic dope) is applied over the basic barge shape (forming wire over the open wooden framework). 4. Front view of barge with support for mask. 5. Side view showing three-dimensional and painted details. 6. Close-up of barge mask. (Photographed by Lynn Pecktal at Nolan Scenery Studios in Brooklyn, Arnold Abramson in charge)

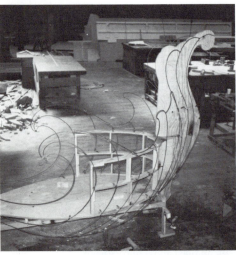

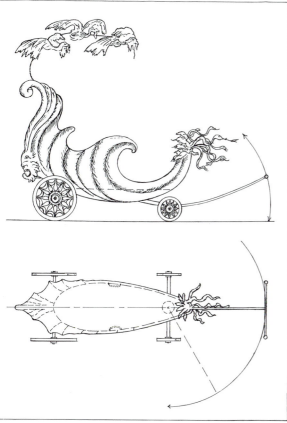

Drawings by Oliver Messel for the magic barge (*above*) and Carabosse's chariot (*left*) for THE SLEEPING BEAUTY.

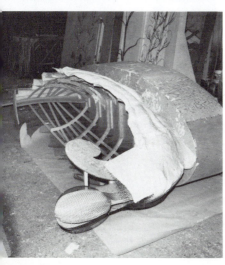

Brackets and Supports for Porches, Saloons, Halls, Alcoves, and under Platforms

Individual Corner Units

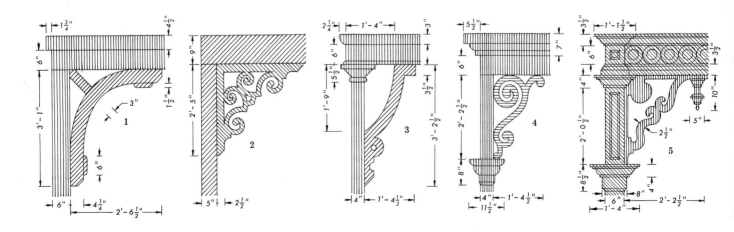

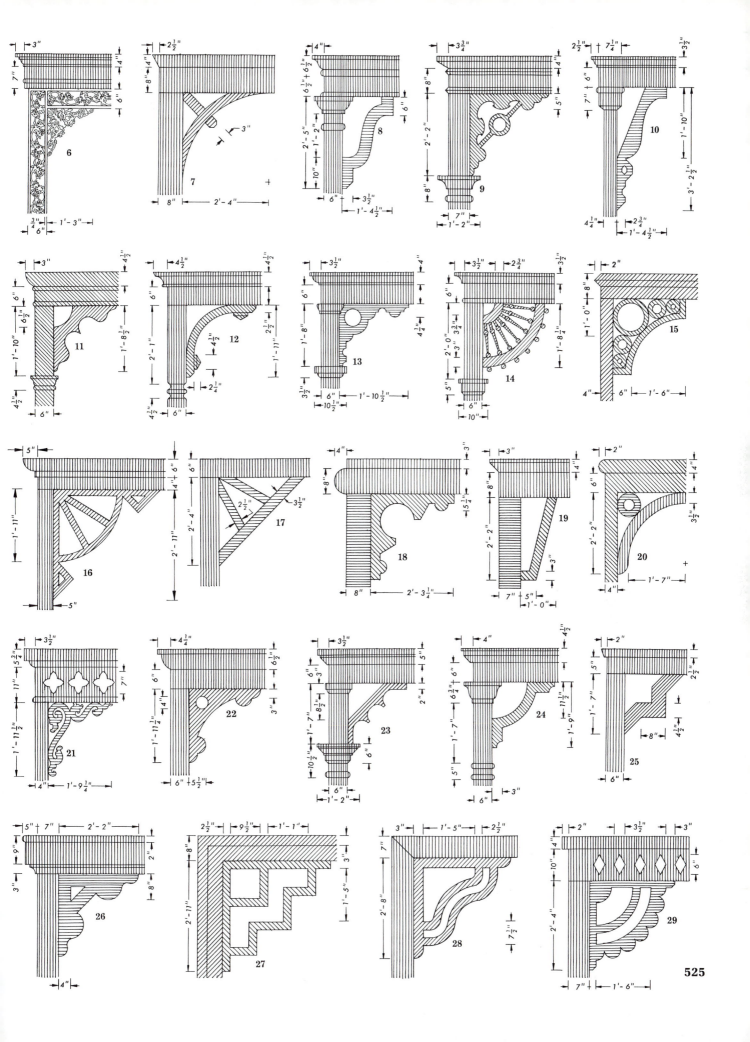

525

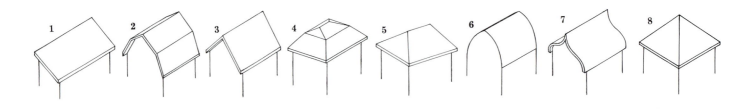

Individual Roof Shapes

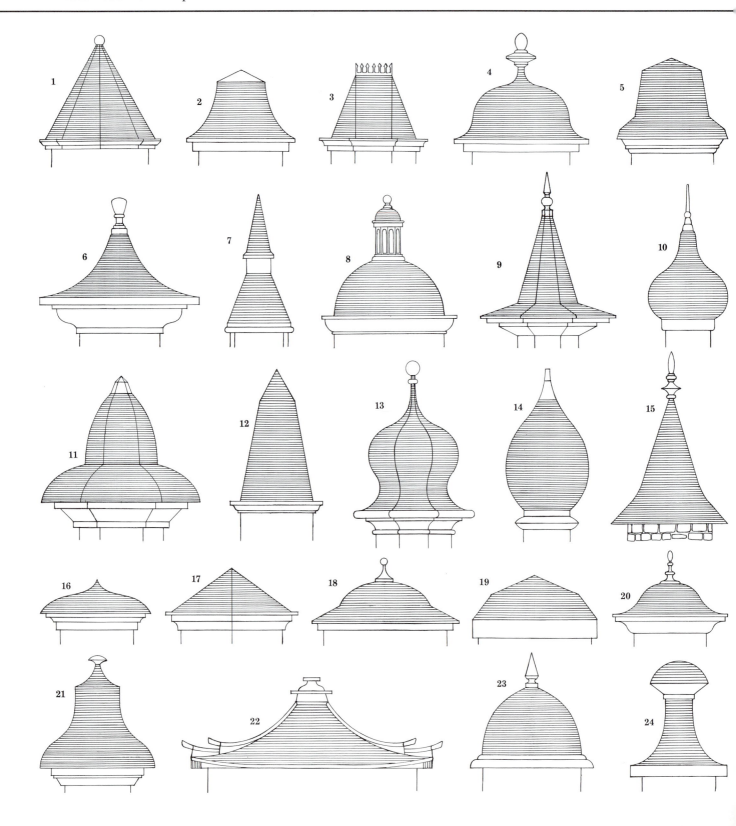

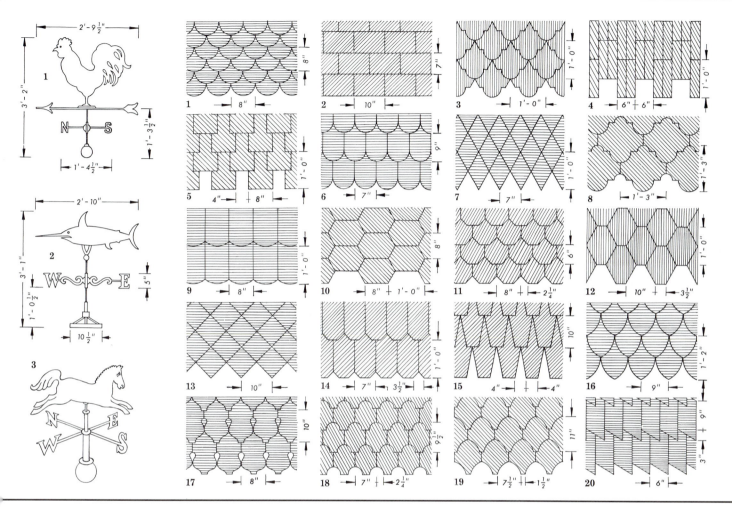

Belfreys and Cupolas

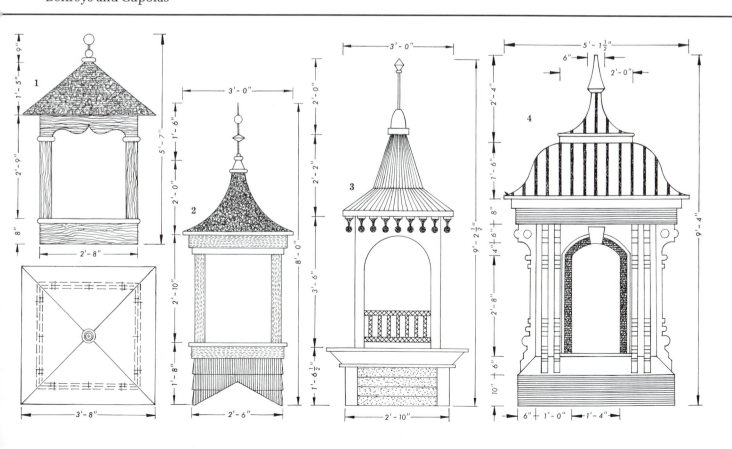

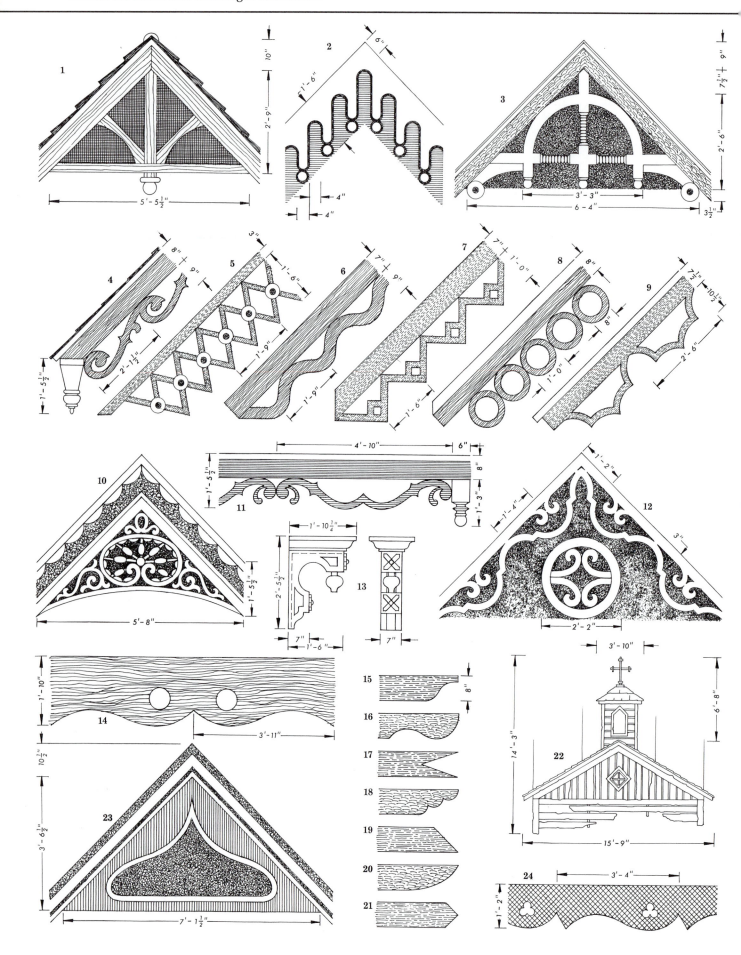

True shapes of roofs in full scale were created in the scenic studio for Jo Mielziner's scenery for THE BAKER'S WIFE. With the model and ½-inch scale drawings as references, the scenic artists at Nolan Scenery Studios used 1 × 2's, lash line, brown paper, and pieces of masking tape to make various roof pieces. The carpenters then worked with these paper patterns as a guide for building the actual roof scenery.

Shingles were cut out of outdoor carpet and put on the roof. They were textured with scenic dope and painted. (Photographs by Lynn Pecktal)

Chimneys and Smoke Exhausts

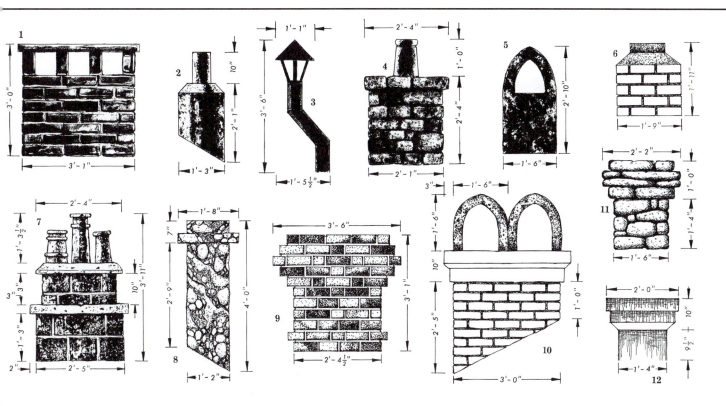

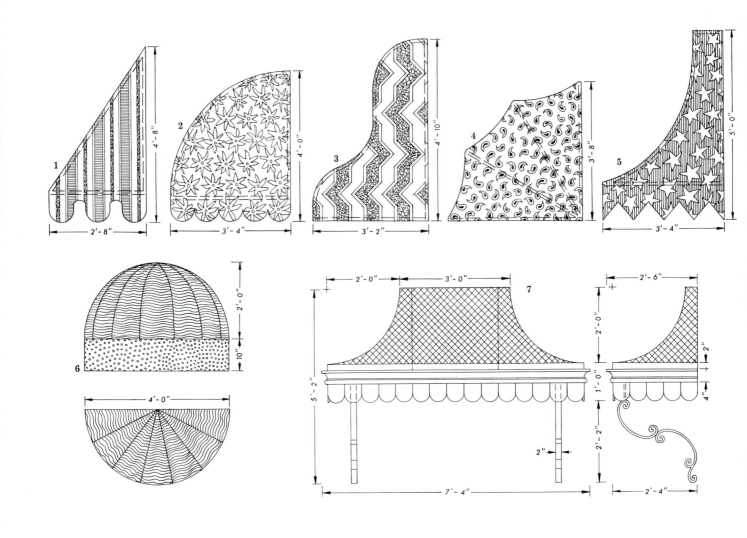

Canvas and Metal Porte-cochères and a Rooftop Skylight

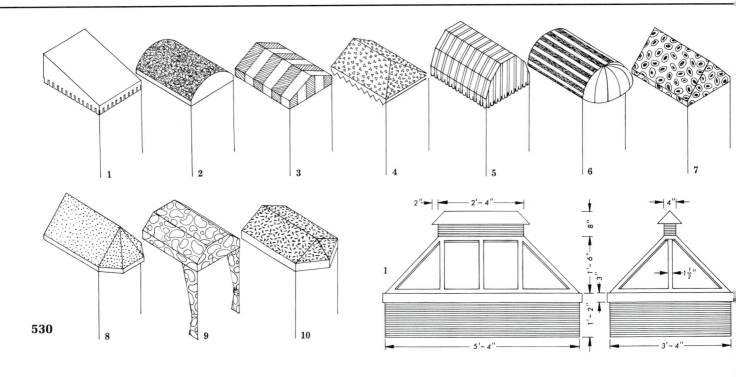

530

Spearheads for Weapons (and Pickets) and Finials for Simulating Cast-Iron Fences

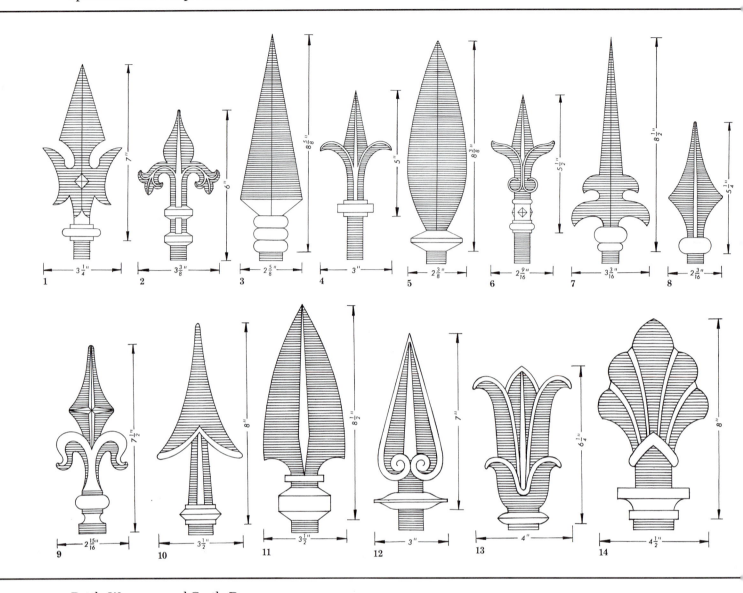

Battle Weapons and Castle Decor

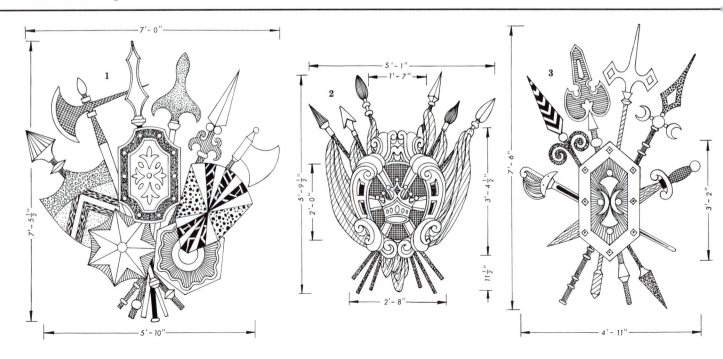

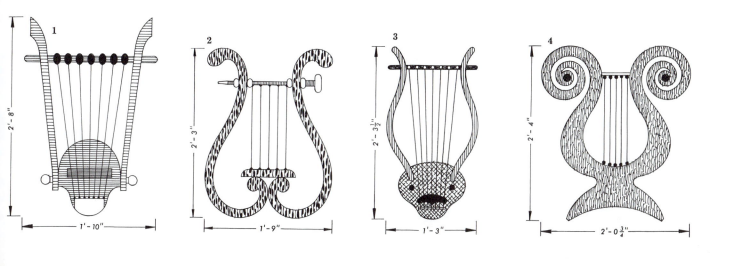

Lyres

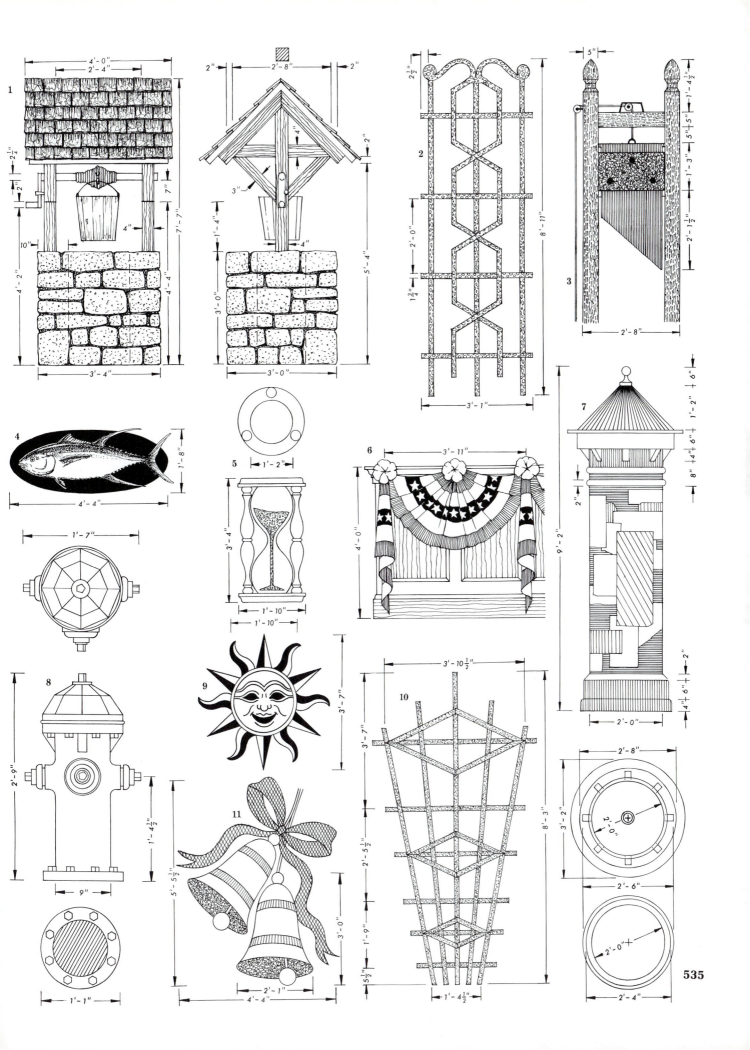

535

Trusses and Supports

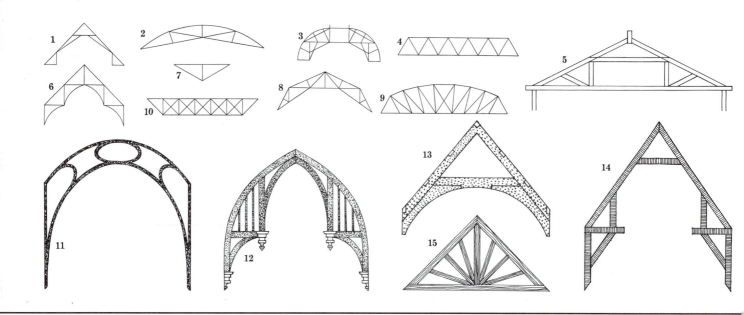

Bridges

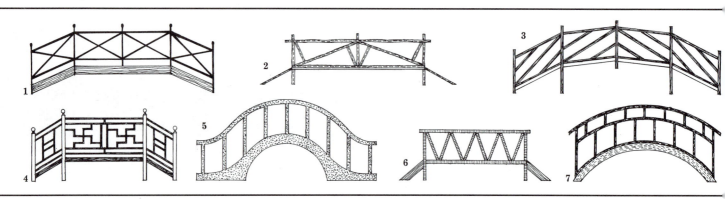

Booths and Refreshment Stands

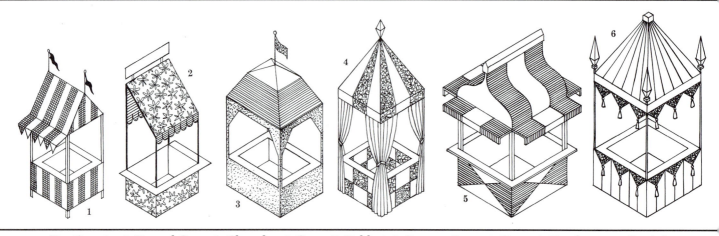

Routing: 1.–2. Round Over; 3. Chamfer; 4. Cove; 5. Rabbet; 6. Roman Ogee; 7. Ogee; 8. Bead; 9.–11. Straight; 12. V Groove; 13. Vein; 14. Core Box; 15. Dovetail

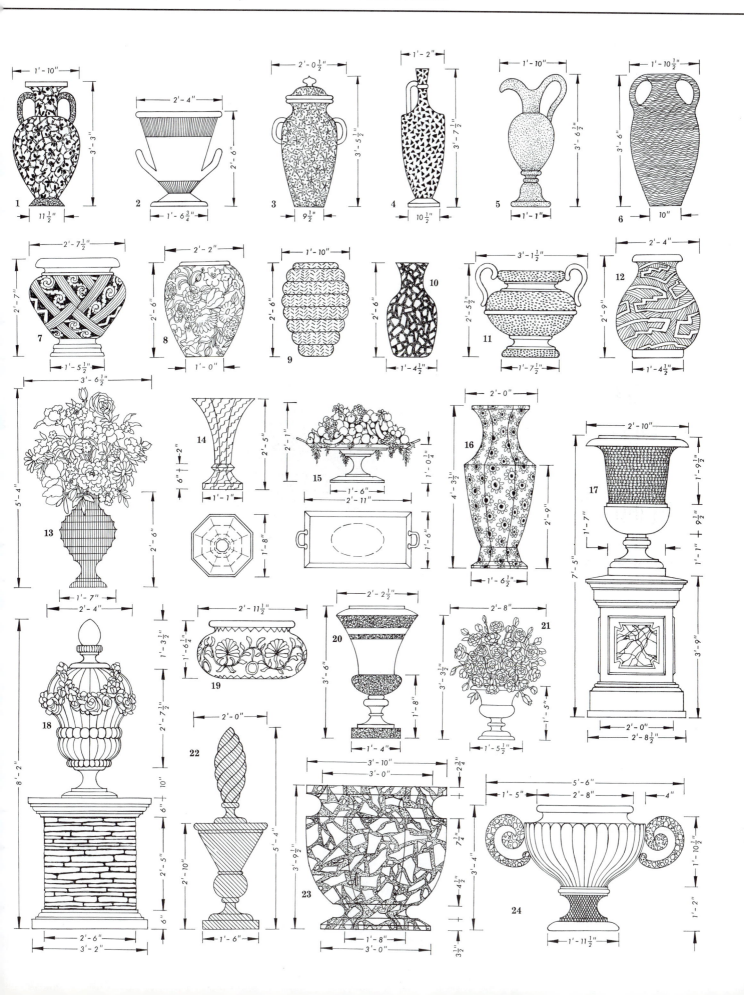

Photographs, above: Sculptured scenery designed by Jean-Pierre Ponnelle for IDOMENEO (1982), the Metropolitan Opera, New York. *Top left:* With the sketch of the large head at left, John Keck is shown carving details in Styrofoam. The Styrofoam was mounted on rigid framing and consisted of several long sections, averaging 3 feet deep in relief. Once details were carved, applied materials included scenic dope, burlap, erosion cloth, scenic netting, plastic foliage, and paints.

Photographs, right (top to bottom): Horse and figure for Franco Zeffirelli's LA BOHÈME

(1981). The almost life-size figure was 9 inches in relief. Carved on Styrofoam that was mounted on ¾-inch plywood backing, it was covered with pieces of velour dipped in scenic dope. The mane was pleated velour.

Center: Horse with figure designed by Pier Luigi Samaritani for ERNANI (1983). The full-round sculpture was positioned atop a tomb. The armature for the horse included sections of ¾-inch plywood and metal pipes. The horse was carved in Styrofoam and covered with velour applied with scenic dope. The entire sculpture was brushed over with scenic dope,

which was then combed while wet. This disguised the seams and gave a nice overall textured surface prior to painting. After the sculpture was laid in with paint, it was finished with metallic powders and Johnson's floor wax. (Photographs by Stanley Cappiello)

Bottom: Panel detail for a pair of bronze doors designed by Jean-Pierre Ponnelle for LA CLEMENZA DI TITO (1984). Full-scale drawings were made on brown paper. The designs were carved in 3-inch-thick pieces of Styrofoam, then mounted on backings of ½-inch plywood. (Photographs by Fred Berinato)

Left: Scenic sculpture for JOSEPH AND THE AMAZING TECHNICOLOR DREAMCOAT (1976), designed by Nadine Baylis. *Right:* Cherub drawing by John Keck for a production of HELLO DOLLY! (1965), designed by Oliver Smith. (Photographs by Lynn Pecktal)

Sculptured Props Executed by John Keck for Productions at the Metropolitan Opera, New York City
(Photographs courtesy of John Keck)

John Lee Beatty talked about theatre and design in the Upper West Side apartment in which he lives and maintains a studio. Born in Palo Alto, California on April 4, 1948, he graduated from Brown University and the Yale School of Drama. His Broadway debut was the 1976 production of *Knock, Knock* by Jules Feiffer. In addition to Broadway and Off Broadway, he has designed productions for the Circle Repertory Company, Manhattan Theatre Club, New York Shakespeare Festival, Mark Taper Forum, Seattle Repertory Company, Williamstown Theatre Festival, The Acting Company, Milwaukee Repertory Theatre, Indiana Repertory Theatre, Berkshire Theatre Festival, Goodman Theatre, Guthrie Theatre, Long Wharf Theatre, Yale Repertory Theatre, Brooklyn Academy of Music, Cincinnati Playhouse in the Park, Virginia Stage Company, South Coast Repertory Company, Folger Theatre, Ahmanson Theatre, Hartman Theatre, and Goodspeed Opera Company. He has also designed for opera and television. Among his awards are a Tony, an Obie, two Maharam Awards, two Drama Desk Awards, an Outer Circle Award, two Joseph Jefferson Awards, and three Los Angeles Drama Critics Awards. His scenic design credits include:

Broadway
The Sisters Rosensweig (1993)
Redwood Curtain (1993)
The Most Happy Fella (1992)
A Small Family Business (1992)
The Cemetery Club (1990)
Ain't Misbehavin' (1988)
Burn This (1987)
The Nerd (1987)
Penn and Teller (1987)
Loot (1986)
The Octette Bridge Club (1985)
Angels Fall (1983)
Baby (1983)
Monday After the Miracle (1982)
The Curse of an Aching Heart (1982)
Alice in Wonderland (1982)

Crimes of the Heart (1981)
Duet for One (1981)
Fools (1981)
Talley's Folly (1980)
Fifth of July (1980)
Hide and Seek (1980)
Whoopie! (1979)
Faith Healer (1979)
The Water Engine (1978)
Ain't Misbehavin' (1978)
The Innocents (1976)

Off Broadway
Lips Together, Teeth Apart (1991)
Song of Singapore (1991)
The Road to Mecca (1988)

The Mound Builders (1986)
Tomorrow's Monday (1985)
After the Fall (1984)
Miss Firecracker Contest (1984)
The Middle Ages (1983)
Livin' Dolls (1982)
A Tale Told (1981)
Catsplay (1978)
A Life in the Theatre (1977)
Ashes (1976)

Delacorte Theatre
The Taming of the Shrew (1990)

Newhouse Theatre
Mr. Gogol and Mr. Preen (1991)
Oh, Hell (1989)

Stage design by John Lee Beatty   Directed by Marshall W. Mason   Los Angeles
BURN THIS by Lanford Wilson   Mark Taper Forum   California (1987)

How did you become interested in scenic design and the theatre?

I'm one of those people who at an early age started doing what would eventually be chosen as a career. When I was in first grade I started designing my own scenery for *Peter Pan* after I had seen Mary Martin in a production of it in Los Angeles. And I continued to design just *Peter Pan* for about two more years. And then in third grade my parents took me to Europe and I saw plays at the Old Vic, operas at the Paris Opera and La Scala, and a spectacular Spanish zarzuela in Madrid. It was a popular operetta that had all that wonderful operetta scenery—the cut drops, the ground cloth that was changed for the different scenes, a raked deck for one scene, and doves that flew down from the balcony! Seeing the Shakespearean plays, operas, and musicals must have made me aware that there were other plays to design besides *Peter Pan*. After that I wrote, designed, directed, and acted in a play a year for the fourth, fifth, and sixth grades. I did my own little spectacles.

I made miniature models, and I built a miniature stage in the garage with a fly system and colored lights. And in early high school I had my own marionette troupe with hand and rod puppets as well, and I started to design both sets and costumes for the high school theatre productions. But basically, my interest was set design. I loved to do ground plans. My idea of fun used to be drawing ground plans and sketches while I watched an old movie on TV.

Did you plan to study stage design in college?

I don't think I thought about it. I don't ever remember saying, "Oh, I'm going to be a set designer," but I hardly remember not designing scenery. I had vague ideas that maybe I'd become an English professor like my father. I was an English major with an art minor, and that actually has turned out to be a better preparation for my work as a set designer than having studied scene design in undergraduate school would have been. I went to Brown University, which didn't even have a drama department at that time, but they had a drama club and I wrote, directed, and designed for that.

I also did summer stock, and I taught children's theatre during the summers while I was in college. I thought sum-

mer stock was great. You just did scenery all day and stayed up all night doing scenery and all you had to do was eat occasionally! That was my idea of heaven. It was excruciating work, but I loved it.

What made you decide to go to the Yale Drama School?

John Lucas, one of my teachers at Brown, had gone to Yale and he suggested that I apply. I had no plan really, and when I got in he was far more excited than I was. It wasn't until after the first couple of weeks in Ming Cho Lee's class at Yale that I realized I had always wanted to be a set designer, and now wanted to succeed at it.

One of the interesting things at Yale in terms of my English literature background was that I became a voracious reader on the side. I read an enormous amount of English and American novels and I also read through the theatrical biography section of the Yale drama library, which was really quite wonderful. And there were wonderful research books which I hadn't been exposed to before.

All this reading turned out to have an interesting effect on my career. When I've done period work especially, I oftentimes have known more about period theatre staging techniques than the people I have worked with—center door fancy, delayed entrances, framing lights off the star's entrance and popping them up when they come on, keeping everyone away from the star's entry door, how to key color off the star's coloring, and all those techniques. That was an important part of my training also.

What happened after you graduated from the drama school?

I came into New York and took the union scenic design and the scenic painting exams at the same time. I didn't know enough to be scared and I passed them. Then I went off again and did summer stock. I did two summers of classics and regular fare at the Wayside Theatre in Middletown, Virginia. But I wanted to design in regional theatre. I was still fairly naive about these things. Regional theatre was very strong then. I went around to a few of them and I thought I'd be asked to design in a regional theatre. But they didn't seem terribly interested and nothing was forthcoming. Then I overheard someone talking about how they

would probably rather hire people from New York. And since I'd gotten into the union as a painter as well as a designer I thought I could at least go to New York and maybe work as a scenic artist. So I came to New York with no job offering. I can't believe I did that!

Were you able to find a job in the theatre?

Actually, a classmate of mine from Yale who was assisting Doug Schmidt was leaving Doug to go into another line of work. He recommended me as his replacement so after Doug saw my portfolio, he hired me and I immediately started assisting him on a Broadway show. I was so amazed! I went out of town for the New Haven tryout, which was what I had been observing all those years as a graduate student at Yale. Unfortunately, that particular show, *Veronica's Room* by Ira Levin, didn't run long.

How did your own first show in New York come about?

While still assisting Doug I took a job at night designing a show at the Manhattan Theatre Club. At that time it was a small place on the East Side with only four people, one of whom, Susan Chase, I had gone to school with as an undergraduate at Brown. I made the costumes on the floor of my apartment. The drops for the set could only be the width of a bowling alley lane because that's what the space had been before the Manhattan Theatre Club took it over. So I made a series of little handkerchief drops painted in dyes on cheesecloth because we couldn't afford anything else. Everyone was impressed with what I did for so little money and that got me the job of designing one of their main stage shows. That show was a disaster, but because of it someone who was renting the theatre asked about someone to design, and I was recommended because I could do sets with so little money. Of course, I was doing carpentry and scenic artist work, whatever was needed. All this time I was assisting Doug during the day. Sometimes he would have a slow period, and I would cover that by going to Nolan's to paint scenery.

One show seemed to lead to another. I did a revival of *Come Back, Little Sheba* at the Queens Playhouse out in the old World's Fair ground with Marshall W. Mason. He was running Circle Repertory Company and I ended up do-

Stage design by John Lee Beatty
TOMORROW'S MONDAY by Paul Osborn
Directed by Kent Paul
Circle Repertory Company, New York (1985)

ing all five plays for the 1974 season at Circle Rep.

I was very lucky because I happened to come into New York just as both Manhattan Theatre Club and Circle Rep were starting to take off. I remember a quote in *The New York Times* saying "suddenly real plays about real people," or something like that. It was the rebirth of realism or naturalism or lyric realism, as they called it at Circle Rep. It was a return to what never really went away in the American tradition of acting and directing, and the design tradition of Mielziner or Robert Edmond Jones. I happened to be at the right place at the right time with the right disposition and the willingness to stay up all night killing myself working. But everybody pitched in, and it was a nice experience that way.

Also, it was that next big change in New York theatre that you saw with the Chelsea Theatre Company and the Shakespeare Festival, where theatre companies took the place of what had been the big Off-Broadway theatre scene. I only did a handful of Off-Broadway shows eventually, because the companies took over. The production of new plays by playwrights like Lanford Wilson, David Mamet, or Israel Horowitz basically shifted from the commercial Off-Broadway small productions done by independent managements to being done in a subscription season at the Manhattan Theatre Club, the Chelsea Theatre, Circle Rep, or the Shakespeare Festival where I ended up working.

When did you start to go out of town and work in regional theatre?

The regional theatres had starting reading my name in the New York papers and all of a sudden they called. And I finally got that dream call! At Yale my ambition in life wasn't to go to New York; it was to design at Arena Stage in Washington. That is what I thought I was supposed to do. That's what I was trained to do, because at Yale that was our idea of "class." Commercial theatre was wonderful and you did it, but doing a good revival of *The Three Sisters* someplace like Arena Stage was the Yale idea of heaven! I did *The Tot Family* there and while I was out of town with that and reading *Time* and *Newsweek* I learned that the Jules Feiffer play I had designed at Circle Repertory was moving to Broadway.

Your first Broadway show was one that moved from Off-Broadway?

Yes, in 1976, the same winter I was at Arena Stage. Jules Feiffer had been impressed by what was happening at Circle Rep and all of our work so he came to Circle with his play *Knock, Knock*. Basically we just did it again for Broadway. I realize now how deeply inexperienced I was in quite a few things. Even though I had assisted Doug Schmidt on Broadway shows, I wasn't aware of all the scenic things you need to know about designing for Broadway. For example, if you think you don't need a portal, think again, you probably do because it's going to save you a lot of masking problems and a lot of other things. I didn't know

enough to design a little bit more or to at least design something that could be cut for the bidding process so that you can be sure of ending up with the essentials.

Did you learn that through experience?

Yes. I had to end up cutting the masking because management couldn't afford it. The only way to do the set as well as we did it Off-Broadway was to cut all the masking so we would still have the set itself. But what I also started learning—since then I've done a lot of transfers from Off-Off-Broadway to Broadway—when you move a show, you have to reconceive. If you do the same thing that you did on a thrust stage or in a black box theatre, you don't get the same result in a bigger Broadway proscenium house.

Now when I move something to Broadway, the director and I talk about it again. I go back to my original sketch and see what the initial impulse was, and try to re-achieve that in the set for the Broadway house. Because I learned fast that you just can't strip the masking and expose the lights and pretend we're in an Off-Off-Broadway black box theatre. It doesn't work that way. And you end up with enormous problems with masking. I had cut the backdrop so there wasn't anything to hide the brick wall. The final Broadway set for *Knock, Knock* was still kind of neat-looking per se, but the way I put it into the theatre was kind of a disaster.

Did that show lead to other Broadway shows?

Once I'd done one Broadway show it seems that I was qualified to do another. Again, I had this reputation of being young, hardworking, and inexpensive. Actually the next Broadway producer, Arthur Cantor, said right to my face that he was looking for a poor man's Santo Loquasto. I thought that was funny, but when he told Jennifer Tipton that he was looking for a poor man's Tharon Musser she quit. I did two more Broadway shows right away for Arthur Cantor. One was with Harold Pinter directing and that was really interesting. Again the English literature background came up because it was *The Turn of the Screw, The Innocents*. Thank God I had read all that Henry James. There I was, twenty-seven years old, plopped down in a pub across from the British Museum with Harold Pinter and Claire Bloom talking about Henry James, and I had to keep up my end of the conversation. I was a bit intimidated by Harold Pinter, because who was I to tell Harold Pinter what to do? But he was a very nice man to work with. This production was also a precursor of how my career was to tilt, because I very soon was into doing plays that were literary-type events rather than commercial comedies and definitely away from musical comedy, which I had wanted to do.

How do you approach a design once you have decided to take the job?

The script arrives, and I read it first as a piece of literature. I decide whether I like it or not, which is a question one should always ask even under the most august circumstances. If I don't like it or if I don't approve of what is in the script, no matter who or how big a star, how big a budget, how wonderful a job opportunity, I can't do it. If it says something I would cringe to see onstage, I can't do it. I do a lot of work, so obviously I'm not impossible, but I have to like it. So that's the first thing.

And then I may look at a script to consider what I think the weaknesses are as a piece of literature. If it's a specific locale I may do some preliminary research. Right now I'm doing a play called *Road to Mecca* that takes place in South Africa. I must confess, I went to a bookstore and looked through a few books on South Africa just to make sure I had in my mind, at least clearly enough, what a little of it looked like. At this point I stay away from the specifics of the play.

But after that, I don't really deal with it as a design too much. I try to go to the first meeting with the director with a fairly clean slate. I haven't found that predesigning anything ever did much good. There are times when after reading a play a set does occur to me, at which point I often sketch it out. I believe one should always present oneself honestly to the director, and I can't pretend and say I don't have an idea. Then I would go into the first meeting with the director and say, "As I read the play an idea for the set

came to mind and I guess I need to get rid of this preconception before we go ahead." I believe it is dishonest to have this sort of secret. It's not going to help your relationship with the director.

But bringing a sketch to the first meeting also works, does it not?

Yes. Sometimes that's the taking-off point with the director. But if you haven't got anything in your mind or if it isn't clear, then it's very important to be free to have an open discussion with a director in the first meetings. You bring the raw materials with you to the meeting for discussion. At that first meeting you might discover that neither of you has a single idea, and then it's back for more homework. The first meeting with an intellectual director oftentimes becomes a discussion of why it's impossible to design the show, what the conundrums are, what the contradictions in the material are, and things like that. With a more intuitive director it's more of a wandering around in your brain finding things that remind you of elements in the play or having a discussion of how you're feeling about yourself right now.

The first meeting about a show is not necessarily always with the director. Sometimes you talk to a producer for ten minutes on the phone, and then you have the meeting with the director. I would roughly compare the preliminary work on a show to programming a computer. It's the time to put in all the information, and I don't think that's the time for me to be sending much information out until after I hear a lot of other people's conceptions of the play, too. Certainly directors come

with conceptions, and producers and costume designers have theirs.

You do a lot of original plays. Are they more exciting to work on than others?

Well, I find them more interesting just because they are constantly evolving, and also because you're doing the very first production of it. New plays don't always have set descriptions in them. It's open territory in terms of figuring out what it is you need to do, but it narrows down pretty fast once the parameters of the production are given, but you certainly aren't looking at anything printed in the back of Samuel French. You have to find your way through some of them. I've worked on new plays where you don't even know how many doors there are or whether it is an interior scene. It may have been written for seven doors but may end up being written for five, nine, seven, or no doors at all by the time you've worked it through.

There can be certain adjustments in other directions once the set is decided upon. The writing may adapt a bit to the design of the set. There is always a kind of reverberation going on when a group of people are putting something together. Directing things happen and lighting things happen, especially on the productions I've done with Marshall Mason directing, Lanford Wilson writing, and Dennis Parichy lighting.

Would you say that you, Marshall, and Dennis have more or less equal input in a collaboration on a production? Do you ever make suggestions to each other?

Stage design by John Lee Beatty
THE MISS FIRECRACKER CONTEST by Beth Henley
Directed by Stephen Tobolowsky
Manhattan Theatre Club
New York (1984)

As a designer I feel I have directed, and of course, all designers direct a bit just in terms of what our work forces actors and directors to do onstage. It is a big danger to think that you could direct a show better than the director. You may very well be able to direct it better, but that's really beside the point when you're the designer. My job as a designer is to design the scenery and to give a designer's point of view. When a director asks me for an opinion, I sometimes say, "Are you asking me as a designer or are you asking me as John, because I have a few other opinions as well, which you may or may not wish to hear." And you sort of have to clarify that for yourself and for the director. I think twice before I offer directing advice. But one measures it and one gives it out. The director is the leader in that he or she is directing in the purest sense of the word.

I sometimes feel my job, too, as a designer, is to ask the question that nobody else has asked the director, because the designer is also an observer and ends up knowing an awful lot about a production. In terms of collaborating and suggesting, Marshall, for example, will often have some pretty strong ideas and will tell me what he thinks the set should be, and that's fine with me. I love a director who has strong ideas. It's not the first or last show I will ever design, so I'm not terribly threatened by that. Indeed, if a director wants to bring in a ground plan, that's fine with me.

Does Marshall do that?

Sometimes he does. But he's also flexible. He might say, "You know, I always felt that it was this." If directors have a preconceived set in their heads, I think they need to tell the designers, and vice versa. It's not fair to the production for either person to hold it back. If a director has a picture of a set he or she wants, it doesn't bother me. That's because the next job is probably going to be working with someone who doesn't have a preconceived idea, so it's not terribly threatening to my creativity.

It's hard when you're starting out as a young designer in college situations where you have a student designer working with a teacher/director. They are not set up as equal collaborators. I follow a director's orders, but only as I would in a boating expedition with friends. One person has to be captain. I think we are all quite equal. At times it's my job to defer to the director and at other times it's my choice to defer to the director. It's hard for students or a very young designer to feel that.

I know when I was twenty-seven and doing a job with Michael Kidd and Feuer and Martin, I was thinking, "Who am I to tell Michael Kidd or Feuer and Martin that I don't like that idea? I'm the juvenile here!" And it's really not good to feel that way. I realize now that it's a career mistake. I felt that way too long, especially because I was so young on so many of my jobs. I think you are doing a disservice by being intimidated.

They want you to agree or disagree, and it really has nothing to do with age.

It has nothing to do with it. In fact, they probably hire a young person to bring in new ideas. The transaction involves you as what you have to offer as a designer. A lot of inexperienced directors see what you're offering as something of a criticism of them because they feel that they're supposed to think of everything themselves, which they're not.

In your observation, do you think younger directors are intimidated by older designers?

It depends. Some directors are intimidated by nothing, some are intimidated by everything. I would say even at my age it's harder and harder for me to get involved with younger directors because we're basically working in different spheres.

One thing that happened to me was I started working with people who were always twenty years older than me. All of a sudden I thought, "Hold it a second, I'm not working with anybody my own age or even a little younger. These people are going to stop working in another ten or twenty years and I'm going to be cast adrift because of being associated with one generation ahead of me." A lot of times I've met people for the first time who expected to see someone twenty years older than I am. After a certain point I consciously backed off and came back and did a lot more Off Broadway. Even so, I'm not plugged into really young directors anymore.

I think it's also sad because some of these older designers, and some who aren't with us anymore, are sensational. If I had the knowledge as a young director to know who they were and what their work was, I would be so into them. And I think there's a generational thing that happens in design that's really too bad.

Once you've read a script, and decided on doing a show, how long does it take you to do a sketch?

Well, it also depends upon how long I'm given to do a sketch. I think a lot of students have a funny idea that you have all the time you want to take. I give my students a week to design a set and they think it's unfair because that's not what the real world's like. Well, I've been given three and a half days to design a Broadway show! But time for the sketch isn't the hard part. Coming up with the design is what is hard. I normally do a ground plan and a rough

Stage design by John Lee Beatty
ANGELS FALL by Lanford Wilson
Directed by Marshall W. Mason
Longacre Theatre, New York (1983)

Stage design by John Lee Beatty
MR. GOGOL AND MR. PREEN by Elaine May
Directed by Gregory Mosher
Mitzi E. Newhouse Theatre
Lincoln Center, New York (1991)

sketch first. I work fairly large so it's mostly half-inch scale.

I usually show a fairly simple first sketch to a director. Again, I try not to follow any rules because every director is different and works differently from another. I try not to show a first sketch that will intimidate a director. If for some reason you have done a fabulous sketch the first time out, it's hard for a director to say, "I don't like that," because it looks as if you've done so much work already. Sometimes if I have done the color on a sketch for the first showing to the director, during the meeting I'll rip part of it off or use a magic marker on it or do something else to let the director know that it is not the Dead Sea Scrolls and he can mess around with it. We can take scissors to it, scribble a change right onto it and do anything we want. It's important to let the director know it's a work in progress.

I don't want a director to approve my first sketch. To approve a first sketch a director has to convince me that it's the right set. I'm not eager for the first thing to be approved because it means that the director is not participating in the design, and a director should examine it very closely before going forward.

I will tell the director that for the next meeting I'm going to bring in some sketches so we can start to agree or disagree on something tangible. This is just so we have a taking-off place, because if you just talk in generalities for more than one or two meetings, it's a waste of time. You really need to at least give them something to react to and push the components around.

I'm just doing *A Flea in Her Ear*, which is a really good example of this. I have done the show before and the director hasn't, so I said, "This is silly, but I'm just going to draw a box with the doors and windows where they're mentioned in the script just so we can see what the requirements are." It's one of those shows with enormous requirements in terms of doors and geographical layout. So I drew a nondesign, just a block drawing of lines like a child's drawing. "This is just so we know. This character runs out of this door, slams it, goes upstairs and comes out over here, and this room is the harem, and

this room. . . ." This exercise was just so we can get our bearings before we went anywhere in terms of look or meaning.

One place that you can never cut corners is the time it takes to have those meetings. With some directors it takes two meetings, and then with some directors it may take fifteen meetings, so there's no real rule in terms of time. You can't say, "Oh I don't have any more time to talk today." Well if you don't have any more time to talk that day, then you better find another time another day when you can, because that's not a time to cut corners. I would cut tech, I would cut rendering time, I would cut any time but I wouldn't cut the preparation time with the director. I've done a few shows with Marshall Mason with two meetings—one meeting to tell me what to do and one meeting with the finished colored sketches.

Marshall as a director is a technically gifted person who can read a ground plan and understand it. He is also someone who likes to be given new obstacles. In fact, sometimes the roles are reversed. I'll say, "You realize that there's a post down center? That means you're going to knock out a whole lot of sight lines." And he'll say, "Yes, I do, and it's OK. We've already seen their faces. We know what they look like. We can afford not to see them for a while." In real life we often speak to people we don't see. If we're driving in a car we tend to be looking forward. We don't always look at the person or we don't always see the person we're speaking to, so an audience doesn't always have to see everything. And Marshall will say something like, "Couldn't we have this furniture facing

upstage? It looks kind of artificial to have all of the furniture facing downstage." and he'll do something like have the desk chair face upstage. That's really exciting to me. This is a refreshing thing to hear from a director. The usual impulse is for a director to rearrange all of the furniture so the sight lines are better. But Marshall is a director who does the reverse. He's planning in his head to have the people sit on the back of the chair or spin it about, or he's thinking, "Wouldn't it be great if we didn't see this actor's face during that other person's speech? Wouldn't it be great if we were dying to know what that person was thinking and the only thing that told us was the actor tapping a pencil with his right hand during the whole speech. Wouldn't that add something to the scene?"

Not every director thinks that way.

No, and not every play should be directed that way. I find it really interesting when working with movie directors who direct in the theatre. They, oddly enough, can be the most conservative of directors. Now, a camera doesn't always show exactly everything. And onstage these directors tend to make everything very open and forward because a lot of the time they're imagining that the camera is moving and framing. So they don't add to a play the mystery that they get with camera work. They seem to forget that that has to be done by the stage director. The mystery has to be added by movement, or lighting or whatever.

After you have worked out the design with the director, what paints and materials do you use to do your sketches?

Stage design by John Lee Beatty
THE DIVINERS by Jim Leonard, Jr.
Directed by Tom Evans
Circle Repertory Company, New York (1981)

I do them on illustration board with a vellum finish. I try not to stay with the same medium for every sketch. Certain shows lend themselves to specific materials. I'm actually doing a show right now that is set in the late sixties which I did with colored magic markers. The basic "John Lee Beatty look" I guess is a lot of acrylic washes over a sub drawing of either pencil or ink. Every so often I'll work entirely in watercolor. I've done a few things in pastels, which I don't really like except for quick lighting effects. A couple of times I've actually done stenciling with spray paint, oddly enough. I think the medium should match the production. You just know from the first moment that a sketch is going to be done in a certain medium.

Also, oddly enough, I get an emotional reaction to what size the board or the watercolor paper should be. It's usually board, but again, there are no rules. My sketches are usually big. I use the full-size illustration board. And they're so big I have trouble taking them on the plane. The airlines don't like to take the portfolio and it gets to be a real threat just in terms of the portfolio not being lost and damaged. So I've learned to either ship them or to make them suitcase-size sketches. I also do a "regional theatre size" sketch, which is the size of the bottom of my suitcase! That is purely practical in terms of shipping to be sure that sets of sketches can be protected in travel rather than sending or taking a full-size portfolio on a plane.

I also draft a lot on pad-size paper because that's practical, too. It makes a neat, small size that will fit not only on my drafting table, but in a lot of situa-tions. Huge rolls of stuff begin to get in the way at a lot of meetings.

When you do a show in a regional theatre, how does it differ from the way you do a Broadway show?

Regional theatres are much more organized and have a resident staff of prop people and carpenters. In that respect I find it a relief to work there. They usually have stock scenery and props so you're not starting from zero the way you are on a Broadway show. Because space is so expensive, New York theatre companies can't store enough to make their stock viable as a really useful thing. So you're always starting close to scratch on a New York show.

At a regional theatre you might be able to do a show with a third of the materials from stock. There may also be someone from whom they borrow furniture and props. On the other hand, regional theatres have the problem of location. You can find everything in New York for a price. You can't find everything for a price in Cincinnati, Ohio, because what you need doesn't necessarily exist there. I often spend a lot of time buying upholstery and drapery fabric and small props here in New York and ship it to regional theatres.

Right now I'm doing a show that is set in New York and I'm doing it in Costa Mesa, California, which has no old furniture to speak of like New York. Costa Mesa doesn't have tin ceilings and it doesn't have anything that relates to New York; even the simplest thing like the phone book, the postcards, the stationery, even the potted plants are different. Just finding anything that resembles New York becomes a big chore and very time-consuming, with a lot of driving. Things out of town tend to be far away from each other so you end up driving around in vans or cars looking for props and furniture.

Propping a show in Los Angeles is different because of the movie studios. If you're lucky enough to have the money to rent from the motion picture studios, it's terrific because they have an incredible collection in very good condition, but it's very expensive. Otherwise, if you try to search props in Los Angeles you drive for days and days on end going from one little shop to another, to a different suburb, to a different county.

In New York, of course, we can't afford the furniture that's in the city anymore. It wasn't too long ago that you could, but now it usually involves renting a van and driving out into the country with the prop person and finding stuff. Certain things that are so easy anywhere else are next to impossible to find in New York. Dirt and rocks, which are free everywhere else, are not free in New York. Just to get a bucket of dirt involves getting a car, and going out to somewhere where it's legal to get it. A tree branch becomes very difficult to find in New York. But if you need eighty different colors of sequins, New York is fantastic. There is a huge selection and there's some guy in New York whose *life* is sequins.

How many days do you normally stay out of town on a regional theatre show?

It depends on the show, it depends on the theatre, and it depends on my schedule. I'd say two weeks, added up. It's very rare that you get away with less than three visits, and if you haven't seen the theatre, there's a fourth visit for doing that. Basically there's the time you bring the designs or send them ahead and you appear a day or two later. Then you go to see the progress of the set around the middle of the build or towards the end, there's the propping, and the major rehearsal period. The third visit, which is the big one, is the put-in and the adjustment and the tech to the first preview.

Usually in regional theatres, they let you leave after the first or second preview. They're oftentimes doing a revival, not a new show. They're not in that real killer commercial situation with a lot of changes to make. And of course, big complicated shows such as a big musical in a regional theatre take a lot of time. You really do have to take that into account when you accept a regional show, because you want to make sure that you do have the time to be there.

It's very frustrating that you can't work on a show for another theatre while you're at a regional theatre. In New York I can do three shows at once and visit one for an hour, visit another for three hours, and then spend the night in a tech rehearsal. When you're out of town there isn't much you can do on another show unless you want to draft in your room at night, which I don't like to do. The Goodman Theatre has a drafting board right off the stage, and I have been able to draft the next show sometimes during the lulls of a put-in. But on the whole, you're going to be pretty much tied up so you have to really take that into account when you accept the show.

Another thing to consider is that there are regional theatres that will only pay for three round-trips. If I have to be at one theatre for a week and I desperately have to go to another city for an afternoon meeting, or for a day to finish something, then I will pay for that trip myself. I wouldn't ask management to pay for something that they didn't know about from the start. That's not good business. It's not their fault if you're busy. So I will take a loss on that or I will explain to the other management that they, unfortunately, are going to have to pay for it. But you have to make that clear up front with everybody. You're not there to be indulged. Even if a company had all the money in the world, it might only be budgeted for three plane flights and it may not be a flexible budgeting situation for them.

What do you like least about working in the theatre?

What is it they say in *The Way of the World?* "I made a catalog of all her faults and fell in love with them one by one." Those same things that I dislike I must like. I must like all the criticism as well as dislike it.

What do you like most about working in the theatre?

In terms of my job what I like most is that no two days are ever the same. There's repetition of tasks but never in the same order and never quite the same way. Every production is different. And there are loves and hates in the theatre. It's terrible to have to say good-bye to people you like, but you do all the time. But if someone hates you and you hate them, it's all over in six weeks rather than this long-drawn-out relationship that happens in other professions. I see it in offices and in universities—this kind of slow-paced meanness. I like the swift meanness that we have in the theatre.

Working in the theatre is always very interesting because with every show I'm learning about something new. Right now I'm working on a show and I'm researching the late sixties and all the Pink Panther movies. And I'm trying to find shag carpet, which is impossible to find since it's not made now. And on another show I'm researching the Great Karoo, which is a desert in South Africa, and the lives of English-born, English-ancestry and the Afrikaners in South Africa and learning about that. And the third show I'm working on I've been learning about how police stake-outs work and how to present this on stage. And the fourth show I'm working on is about an Italian coffee shop going out of business in the Little Italy section in SoHo and I'm learning all about espresso machines, coffee grinding, and finding good substitutes for pressed tin and using a lot of anaglypta. I also get to meet a lot of interesting people in different places while doing this research. And that is another plus.

What would you advise a talented young person who wants to come to New York?

My first word of advice would be, don't fool yourself by thinking that you can ever get away with not doing your best job. Whatever job you do and wherever you do it, there is someone noticing how well you do it. You're going to have to try pretty hard most of the time. Right now I'm working with a director who was a classmate in college, and after all these years since graduation, this is the first time we have worked together professionally. You may think that you're not being seen, but you are all your life. Jobs come at you because you have accomplished yourself in some way from the very beginning.

And there is nothing that doesn't count. A quick job of gluing fringe on a lampshade may be the beginning of your career, because it may introduce you to somebody whom you weren't going to know otherwise. One of my assistants has been working with me since he came to the city because on one show we were desperate for someone to help finish upholstering a shirred window seat. The production manager called up this guy who really didn't want to do it, but he came in and he did a pretty good job and was very pleasant to work with. If he had not bothered with a job he really didn't want to do or if he had botched it up or had not been nice about it, he wouldn't have assisted me on five shows. Now he has gone on to get even better jobs. So there's nothing that doesn't count in terms of how well you do your job.

Stage design by John Lee Beatty
THREE MEN ON A HORSE by John Cecil Holm and George Abbott
Directed by John Hirsch
Royal Alexandra Theatre
Toronto, Ontario, Canada (1987)

One thing about coming to New York that I had to learn is when you don't have a job, you should tell all your friends that you're looking for something. I had been trained since childhood that if you didn't have a job that was something you didn't speak of because it's embarrassing. Once I got over that, things would come to me. But until then you're alone and you're not going to get any work if you don't at least let people know that you're available.

If you want to be a designer, a designer designs. If you really want to do it, you're going to have to do design somewhere and keep doing it for a while. Nobody's going to tap you on the shoulder after you've being living in a cocoon for a while and then all of a sudden you're designing. You're going to have to make your mistakes somewhere and continue to do it.

Is it important to get a degree or go to a drama school and study to design scenery?

I have mixed feelings about that. Some people obviously will become wonderful designers without going to school at all. But I'm one who did go to graduate school. School is the last place where you're allowed to experiment without any repercussions. I don't believe in undergraduate drama education, partly because of my own life experience. Liberal arts were so much more useful than learning about counterweight systems at that point. Graduate school is a different proposition in terms of preparing you. You have to have a degree of self-knowledge to know whether you're prepared

or not. I wasn't prepared after getting my undergraduate degree. I needed a little more time to develop. My level of work wasn't good enough and I knew it.

One of the good things about graduate school is that you emerge with a portfolio of work so that you can at least have something to show at a job interview. You and your portfolio are going to be fairly inseparable in terms of looking for work and introducing yourself to people.

I do think that a good training program in which you turn out a sketch a week, which I was trained to do at Yale, is an excellent preparation for exactly what you do professionally. I'm working at pretty much the rate that I was forced to work at in school. I do think that three years out of your life is a long time and maybe two and a half years would have been better for me. The degree has been helpful in other respects, such as credentials for teaching.

One thing you don't realize at the time is that a graduate school gives you a bedrock network of people who do what you do or at least related to what you do. Every school has a network of people who work together who help each other eventually. Classmates introduce you to other people and when they're working they bring you along or whatever so there's always that basic network established. A graduate program is much more focused than a college situation in that respect.

I've found from teaching that going through a graduate program gives you one more tool. If you've been through a graduate program in your field, you

might be able to re-create a graduate program for someone else sometime. I guess realistically speaking a lot of people become teachers. In the long run, the thing that I was most grateful for at Yale, besides excellent training from professional teachers, was that it was assumed from the beginning that we were going to work as designers. I don't think anybody should be taught this subject matter with the idea being the end product of graduate school is a teaching position. At that point I think you're in the wrong line of work, because a designer is a designer and that's the thing you have to achieve first and whatever happens after that, happens in life. I don't think there is any great mission in the world to send out more set design teachers anywhere, but I do think there is a mission in being a designer. To me, it's a relatively noble profession.

I think also in the graduate program it is important to develop the practical skills. The scene painting class I took has helped me as much in designing as the designing class helped, and the designing class helped a lot. What I learned about scene painting from Arnold Abramson was very useful in terms of doing sketches as well as painting scenery. I've remembered that he always said, "Make sure whatever you're painting that it's ready to be taken up off the floor at any time. Don't just start from the left and go to the right. Give it an overall of the basic colors and the basic washes and then keep refining, because you never know when it's going to be pulled out from under you and it's going to have to go out." The same thing is true with scene design sketches, and drafting as well— you never know when the phone is going to ring and you're going to have to go to a meeting with that sketch. You've got to find a way of doing that sketch so that sketch is always ready to be looked at no matter whether you've had three days or three hours to do it. It can be lifted up and put back down again and changed again. And the same thing with drafting in terms of the process. Learning a process that works for you is a good thing to learn at that time because erratic behavior is not going to be a real strong selling point in the professional world.

Stage design by John Lee Beatty
A LIFE IN THE THEATRE by David Mamet
Directed by Gerald Gutierrez
Theatre DeLys, New York (1977)

12

FURNITURE

FURNITURE FOR
THE STAGE

Designers working on commercial, regional, stock, university, or Off-Broadway productions are responsible for designing and supervising the set furniture. Depending on the kind of production and where they are working, designers not only create furniture on the drawing board, but also repair, paint, decorate, upholster, and in some cases build furniture. The discussions on set furniture in this chapter intentionally go back and forth from work done in the designer's studio to work done in the scenic studio in order to encompass the diversified working situations of theatre designers.

The many scaled drawings of furniture provided in this chapter can serve these purposes:

1. They can be copied and used on the stage as they are shown.
2. The basic shapes and dimensions can be used, but with some alterations in size and shape according to individual need.
3. They can be referred to for research when building furniture in scale models.
4. They can serve as inspiration for designers to develop their own ideas.

The materials for making full-size furniture and set dressing pieces from the drawings in this chapter are normally determined by the inherent qualities of each piece. In general, the basic materials for building theatrical furni-

ture and props include softwoods and plywoods, with a certain amount of metalwork for support, bracing, and ornamentation. Materials for carving three-dimensional items, covering, painting, and finishing are usually dictated by the individual piece and the intended effect. Designers usually know what materials are required for making furniture and props; when in doubt, good advice can be obtained from experienced carpenters and scenic artists.

Furniture for a completely new production in the commercial theatre is usually acquired for that production alone. The scenic designer and property master (or assistants) on a production search for appropriate furniture for the stage. The designer may go to antique shops and galleries to find furniture that is easily purchased outright or rented for the show. The designer and property master may also go to thrift shops, the Salvation Army, furniture outlets, and other similar places to select furniture.

Creating Three-Dimensional Furniture

Finding the kind of furniture that is needed is frequently a problem. A piece of furniture may be from the right historical period, but its scale may be wrong for a particular stage setting. When several identical pieces of furniture are needed in the same setting and only one or two can be found, the designer may have to make drawings for the furniture to be duplicated in the

scenic shop. In the noncommercial theatre (and sometimes in the commercial theatre) the most innovative property masters and stage carpenters usually enjoy building hard-to-find pieces of furniture. They take enormous pride in being able to make beautiful pieces for the stage when they are supplied with accurate drawings complete with dimensions and notations for execution.

When furniture is to be constructed by the scenic shop, property master, or stage carpenter, the designer would be wise to provide furniture designs that are not impossible to build.

It helps a great deal to keep extravagant turnings and highly curved surfaces to a minimum or eliminated completely in designing stage furniture that is to be built. This is not to say you should not use a curved surface that is easy to construct. For instance, you might want to build an Italian Dante chair using ¾-inch pieces of stock softwoods or ¾-inch plywood. The chair could be designed so that the legs, seat, arms, and the two vertical members of the back are made from this lumber, while the curved top part of the chair between the two vertical pieces could be created by using thin pieces of plywood glued and clamped together to make a nice curved wooden piece. After the glue has dried, the desired shape could be sawed from the piece, sanded, then mounted at the top of the Dante chair. Details such as small wooden buttons or rosettes can be applied around the edges of the curved piece, as well as finials on the top of the two

550 vertical members. A round three-dimensional design in the center of the chair back might be carved out of Styrofoam and covered with linen scrim or other thin material.

Many other examples of stage furniture can be built in the scenic studio. A Victorian armoire, a Chinese Chippendale cabinet, an eighteenth-century sofa, a Gothic throne chair, a trestle table, a stool for a Shakespearean production, or just a simple garden bench are items that are often built for the stage. You might even want to do a mock-up design in scale of a spinet piano.

Though it may seem like a big undertaking, an enormous selection of furniture can be built that will not have a homemade look to it. Not only is the building important, but so are the paint, stain, varnish, upholstery, trim, hardware, and any other accessories that are to be applied to the built furniture.

Making Drawings for Three-Dimensional Furniture

Once the idea for the design of a piece of furniture is set, the next step is to put it down on paper. This should always be done with care. Make drawings in ½-inch scale (or 1-inch, 1½-inch, or 3-inch, depending on the amount of detail). The following views are usually needed on the drafting: a ground plan (and/or a top view), a front elevation, and a side elevation. You may also find that you need to do a rear view, plus one or more section views, depending on the complexity of the piece of furniture. And, of course, it is always a smashing idea to do a painted model in scale. Notes may be put on the furniture drawings such as: "Turned wood," "Carve lion's head in Styrofoam, and then cover with linen scrim pieces dipped in scenic dope," or "Applied three-dimensional wood."

From these scaled drawings on the drafting, the artists in the scenic studio do full-scale drawings on brown paper for the building carpenter to use. In regional or university theatres or for Off-Broadway shows, full-scale drawings for building may be done by the designer, an assistant, or a scenic artist.

It is always a good idea to show the finished ½-inch scale drawings to the carpenter who will build the furniture and to discuss any questions about construction, materials, special finishes, or details. (While stage furniture is generally built of wood, it may include metal or other materials.) A superior carpenter will have thoughts about strength, weight, durability, and practicality, and may suggest adding more "body" or extra wood to a very thin piece. Also, the carpenter will discuss additional bracing or necessary hardware.

Perforating Full-Scale Furniture Drawings

As a designer, it is always good to know how full-scale drawings are made in the scenic studio from your ½-inch scale drawings. Then you will know to give as much information on the drafting as is necessary, as well as the number of required views to properly describe the piece of furniture that is to be built.

The full-scale drawings of furniture are normally made with a charcoal stick, regular pencil, or wax pencil on

Models by Loren Sherman
SLEIGHT OF HAND by John Pielmeier
Directed by Walton Jones
Cort Theatre
New York (1987)
(Photographs by Loren Sherman)

"A thriller about a magician and his dancer-girlfriend. Act 1 is set in a SoHo loft where they live and he builds and stores his magic tricks. It is one of those lofts where the elevator opens directly onto the space, making for sudden and surprising entrances. They sleep on a mattress up on the loft storage area, which is accessible by a rolling library ladder.

"Act 2 is set on the stage of a theatre where a musical about Edgar Allan Poe is in the process of loading in. There is a chase scene up a ladder and onto a catwalk. The bottoms of the flats fade to black so a helper in a black velvet suit remains unseen and can facilitate some of the magic tricks." —Loren Sherman

pieces of brown Kraft paper. While a carpenter can use the full-scale drawings to build from, or sometimes will build right on top of them, for certain items the outline must be perforated with tiny holes using a pounce wheel on a velour-covered tabletop. Then a charcoal bag can be rubbed over the holes to duplicate the shape of the drawings on the wood (or other materials) that is to be cut out in that particular shape. Artists in the scenic studio may perforate all of the designs for a chair, or just the stretcher at the bottom, or only the outer trim for a table top, or just the feet of an armoire, or whatever. Usually the building carpenter will say what or how much of the full-scale drawing needs to be perforated with the tiny pounce wheel.

Making Alterations on Furniture

A designer will often have furniture and props that are to undergo renovations delivered to the commercial scenic studio. Besides having to be partially or completely painted, furniture for the stage may be altered in several ways. Some examples are building up and cutting off legs of furniture to accommodate the slope of a raked stage, adding flat metal bracing to the rear of a side chair, cutting a width of wood out of the center of a table, building up the height of a pedestal, combining two medium-size bamboo tables to create a larger one, cutting off the back portion of a liquor cabinet to make the total depth less, and adding new upholstery and trim. Simple chairs and tables are sometimes duplicated, and on occasion very complex and involved furniture and props are built in the scenic studio.

Using Simple Furniture and Props

Designers working in regional, stock, or university theatres often know that the most reliable prop rooms in these theatres have many usable items. These include:

1. *Metal ice-cream chairs, stools, and tables.* Whether original or reproduction, this traditional furniture always looks great onstage because the simple, open metal lines read beautifully. Ice-cream parlor furniture may be painted black, white, or any color. These lightweight pieces of furniture can be easily moved off- and onstage by the actors.
2. *Bentwood chairs.* A variety of styles exist and reproductions can be found in many places. Bentwood chairs are used in restaurants, ballrooms, dressing rooms, dining rooms, kitchens, and other settings. These chairs may be stained wood or painted gold (especially for ballroom and dance hall settings) or given other appropriate finishes.
3. *Garden benches.* Classical garden benches are excellent for productions from Shakespeare to operettas. They are also ideal for park scenes. These benches are usually painted as concrete, stone, or a similar finish.
4. *Pedestals.* A formal mood can be created by using a random arrangement of pedestals, such as fluted columns that are 3, 4, or 5 feet high. Pedestals may hold containers of potted palms, urns of flowers, or crocks of ivy and fern. Four or five pedestals in a cluster

arrangement with plants look wonderful when positioned on one side of the stage with a group of gold ballroom chairs in a semicircle on the other side.
5. *Turned wood stools.* These are great for informal musical staging, for readings, or for solo performing. They look cheerful when painted white, off-white, pale ochre, or other light colors.
6. *Victorian wicker furniture.* A collection of chairs, settees, stools, and tables are available in Oriental import stores. Natural finish, white, or basic pastel shades work nicely onstage. Because these patterns of wicker are so ornate and graceful, they go beautifully with greenery in solariums, or in parlors, foyers, drawing and dining rooms, and in endless musical comedy locales.

Selecting Side Chairs and Armchairs

One of the most attractive and popular chairs for the stage is a Queen Anne side chair or armchair. The graceful lines and see-through back of a Queen Anne chair make it a big favorite for both simple or elegant interiors. Also, the fabric on the seat may be easily changed to give the chair a new look. Some resident and stock theatres have a basic set of four, six, or eight reproduction Queen Anne chairs as standard items in the prop room. They work extremely well in a number of different rooms onstage, including a drawing room, dining room, bedroom, library, foyer, hallway, or salon.

If you are making a model or drawing a floor plan or a front elevation of the stage setting and are using a side chair or armchair, accurate dimensions are essential. Dimensions of a classical mahogany reproduction Queen Anne side chair with an open back and a seat that has a curved front are: Outside 21½ inches wide, 21½ inches deep, and 39½ inches high. The seat is 19½ inches high.

Queen Anne chairs can be purchased in numerous furniture stores around the country, and many other styles of side and armchairs abound in reproductions of Regency, Hepplewhite, Sheraton, Chippendale, or other lovely styles.

Renovating Furniture and Props

For prop persons and for designers in regional, university, stock, and Off-Broadway productions who do their own props and painting as well as designing, there are certain pieces of furniture that can be repaired and altered according to need. Following are some descriptions of how to repair certain items of furniture for the stage.

Repairing a Straight-Back Wooden Chair

Quite often, broken furniture can be easily repaired for use on the stage. Simple repair jobs on chairs are easy to do. Of course, a chair with a completely broken leg should just be forgotten. But for damage due to wear over a long period of time, chairs usually need only to be reglued and given appropriate bracing. The legs of dining room side chairs often become loose at the dowel joints and need to be reglued as well as to be drilled and have screws added on the inside of the wooden corner blocks under the flat seat. The flat seat may need padding and upholstery. Sometimes the wooden dowels holding the legs with the seat frame have broken or come loose and need to be repaired or replaced.

If you are repairing a side chair such as the one just described, turn it upside down and remove the four screws holding the seat to the frame. Examine the different legs to see what is tight and what is loose. Perhaps one leg has to be dismantled from the rest of the chair, or possibly two or three legs have to be taken completely apart. Usually

some of the wooden dowels glued into the drilled holes either have come apart and need to be reglued or are broken and need to be replaced. While furniture dowels come in various sizes, small wooden dowels for this type of chair may be approximately ⅜ inch diameter by 1½ inches long or a bit longer. An old broken dowel can be removed by drilling it out with an electric drill. The diameter of the bit in the drill should be a size smaller than the old dowel. It may also require a bit of digging out with a punch, screwdriver, or other pointed tool. The idea is not to make the hole any larger. If that does happen accidentally, the hole can be filled in with plastic wood or a thick mixture of fine sawdust and Elmer's Glue-All. A mixture of fine sawdust and Duco Cement is also excellent.

In order to do this repair job, have all the replacements such as dowels or the four wooden corner blocks to be positioned diagonally under the seat ready so they can be assembled, screwed together, glued, and clamped tightly in a relatively short time. They must be glued quickly, then clamped tightly so that the chair parts with the dowels firmly lock together. Any new corner blocks should have the holes predrilled and the screws tried before the final put-together and gluing.

All the dowels, necessary chair parts, and four bracing blocks can be brushed with white glue, then clamped together. Small blocks of wood that are not part of the chair should be inserted to prevent clamp marks on the good wood of the chair. Once the white glue is applied, it is the very tight pressure of the clamps on strategic parts of the chair that makes a satisfactory repair job. After the clamps are removed, check to see if there are any small openings or cracks. If so, fill them with plastic wood or a thick mixture of sawdust and white glue.

Repairing Bentwood Chairs

Standard bentwood chairs without arms are often discarded because they are damaged. Usually one or two legs become loose because the screws or hardware have been lost or damaged. The seats of the bentwood chair may be made of caning or of thin wood that has worn out.

New wood screws (1½-inch to 1¾-inch) may be all that is needed. If the original screw holes have stretched, holes for the new screws may be drilled on a different angle in a new position. The seats on bentwood chairs may be already recessed, and a new seat may be cut out of ¼-inch plywood and placed down into that space. Damaged caned seats may also be replaced for the stage by cutting out a ¼-inch plywood seat shape just a bit larger than the outer caning of the seat and placing it on top of the framework where the caning was attached. For the stage, always drill holes for the plywood and use wood screws to fasten the top to the wooden framework. Make a paper pattern of the seat before cutting out the ¼-inch plywood.

If there is splintering on the very sharp curves in the bentwood where the curved shapes of the wood have opened up a bit, it can be repaired by brushing white glue in between the openings of the wood and applying pressure with metal clamps, always with small wooden blocks between the metal clamps and the wooden chair so the wood of the chair is not damaged.

Using Tables and Tablecloths

If chairs and stools tend to be the most frequently used stage furniture, the table is probably the second most popular piece of furniture. Tables have many uses. They are selected to go with or without chairs, and are positioned with sofas, beds, and other items of furniture. Tables are ideal for dining, for studying, for displaying and holding objects, for playing cards and other games, for doing work on, for serving food, for holding lamps and plants, and so on. In terms of their use onstage, tables can be grouped in three basic categories: uncovered, partially covered, and fully covered.

If a table is used *uncovered* its style, finish, period, and condition are usually appropriate and/or attractive. More importantly, its shape or silhouette may be interesting and lovely. For instance, the table might have an outstanding pedestal shape or Chinese fretwork around the top, or the table might just be a simple one with gorgeous Queen Anne legs.

A table *partially covered* may be appropriate when the covering points up the historical period, indicates the taste of the inhabitants, hides the flaws in the tabletop, is a tablecloth for dining, presents a decorative or dramatic change in the appearance of the table, shows different seasons of the year, suits a specific occasion such as a party, or helps signal a general change in circumstance, as when a down-and-out character rises in status or vice versa.

A *fully covered table* may be completely decorative, or it may enhance a look of a specific historical period with a long flowing cloth in fullness, or be a place to hide actors or props. Naturally, a full covering may also be used if the table is built as a basic crude table without any details. When designing a fully covered table, consider questions such as: Do you want the table built in three or four sections so it can be divided into seemingly smaller tables for another scene (with previously placed tablecloths placed underneath)? Do you want smaller sections to make the table easier and less cumbersome to shift? Does the table need special bracing for rough action in a scene, or does it have to be very sturdy for touring?

Three tablecloths can be effective when draped over each other. Have the first cloth go all the way to the floor, then place the second over the first so that it hangs two-thirds over the first cloth. The third cloth goes over the second and hangs one-third over it. This tiered arrangement works for both square and round tablecloths. Other combinations of draped cloths can be improvised.

Styles and fabrics for tablecloths include checks, stripes, paisleys, chintzes, lace, dots, and other figures. Velvet, velour, or duvetyne can also be used. The edge of a tablecloth is often straight, scalloped, ruffled, or fringed. Table decor over cloths includes garlands of leaves and flowers, roping, and other ornamental motifs.

Another approach to give the appearance of a tablecloth is to use vertical strips or streamers. Strips work wonderfully when they are 2 inches wide and attached directly and neatly to the top edge of the table with an overlap of 1 inch and continue all the way to the floor. Strips may be cut from paper, plastic, or fabric.

These vertical strips can be fashioned to form open swags, which are effective for tables with straight or curved edges. The three or four strips that form the swags should be twisted slightly. The swags should be correctly spaced before the strips are stapled at the end of each swag. An added touch is to make 6-inch diameter rosettes

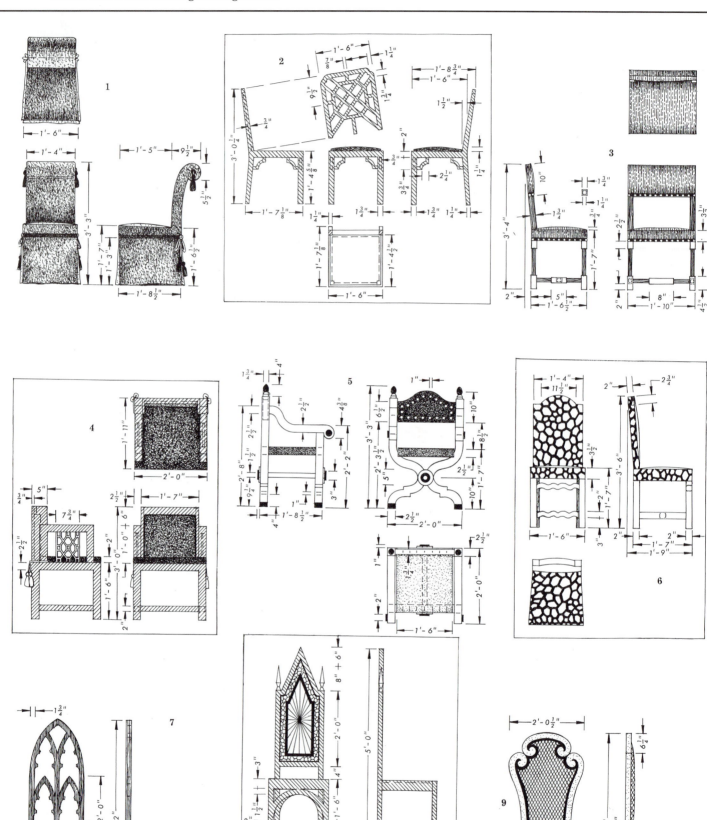

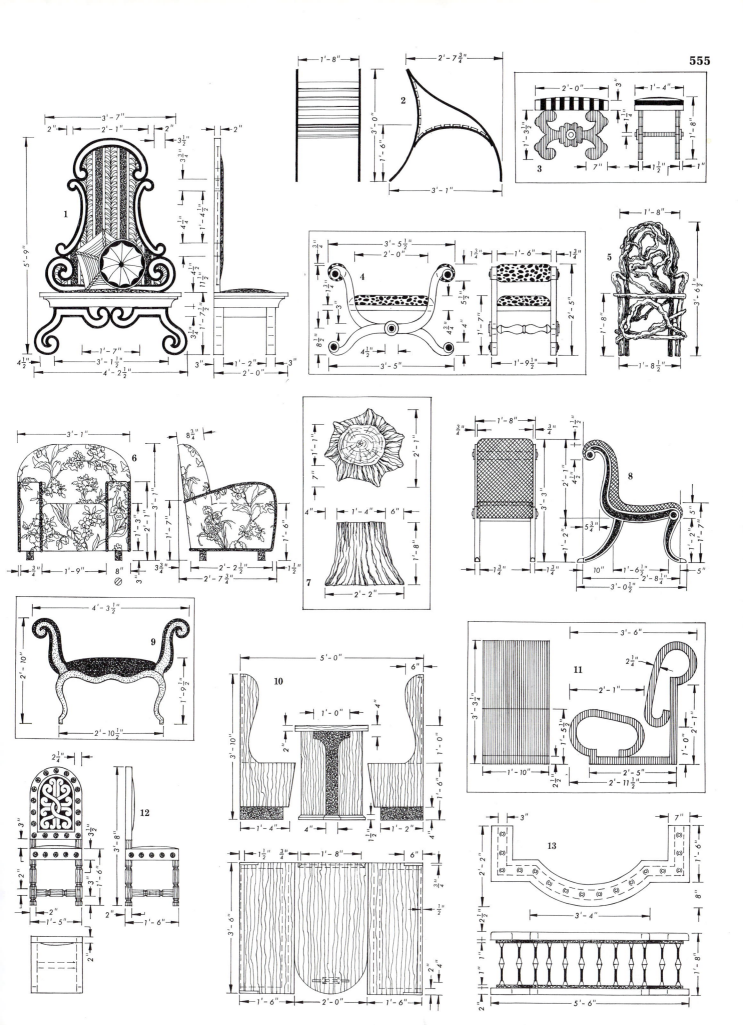

Cocktail and Coffee Tables

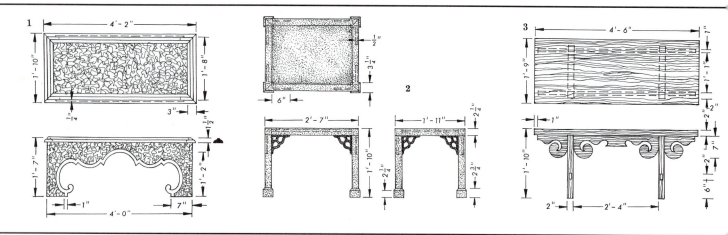

Dining Tables, Writing Tables, Occasional Tables, Console Tables, and Others

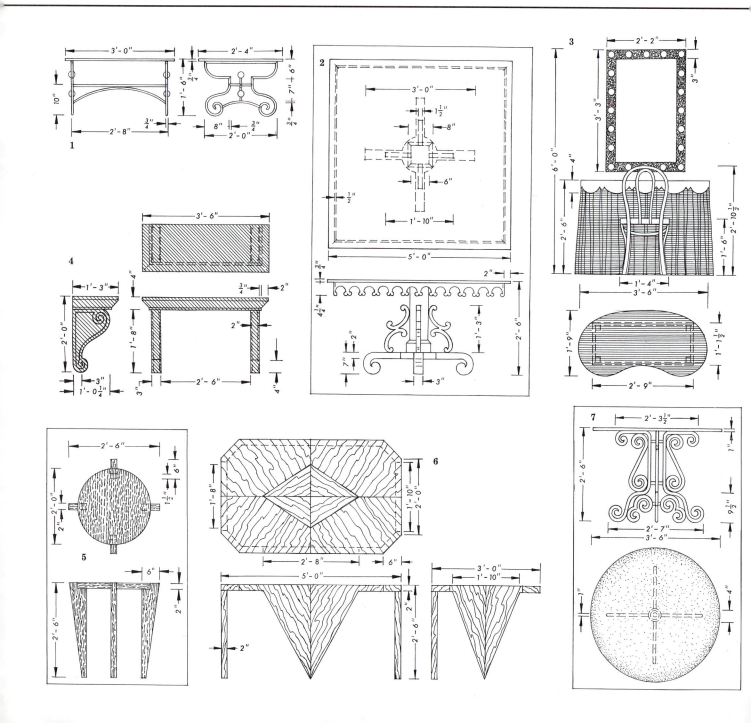

557

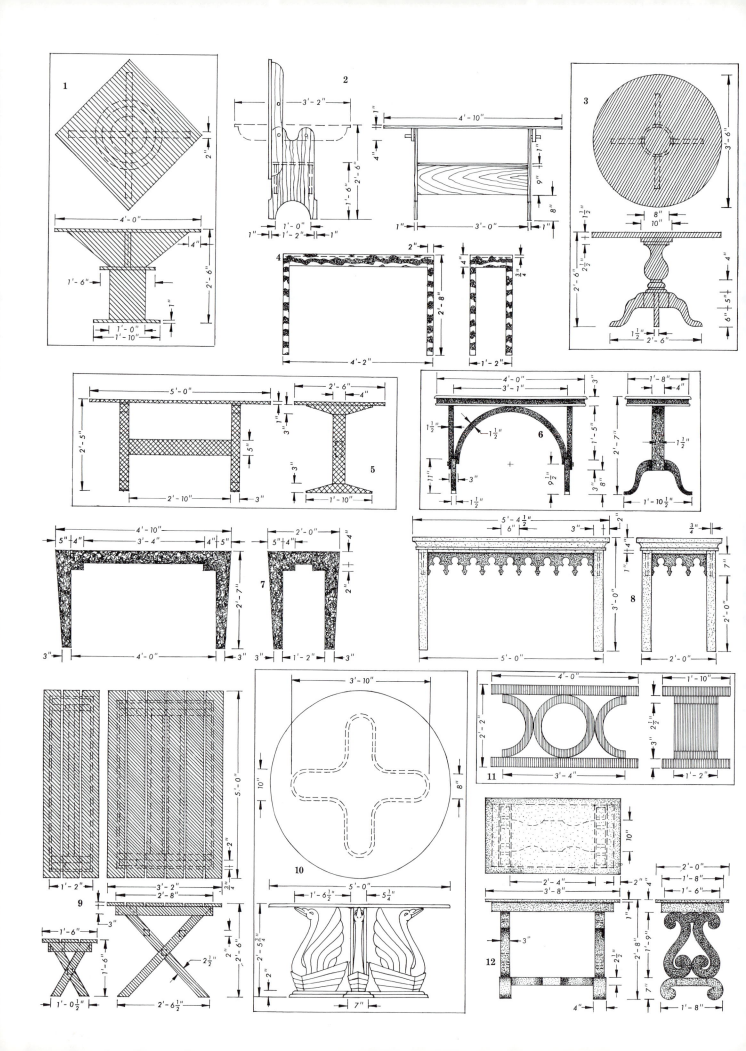

Drawings were made in 1-inch scale and also full-scale to duplicate the table desk for DRACULA. Several layers of plywood were utilized for the profile pieces forming the legs, which consisted of three-dimensional griffins. *Photographs, across:* 1. The original table desk purchased in an antique shop and painted gloss black. 2. Profile pieces forming the griffins (each ¼″ + ½″ + ¾″ + 1″ + ¾″ + ½″ + ¼″). 3. Two griffin legs made of the wooden pieces, glued and nailed together. 4. Two griffin legs (with wooden wings attached) have been heavily sanded and wooden balls have been added for the eyes. 5. Griffin legs fastened to the table base and top. 6. Wooden table on casters used for the first national company. 7. Painted table desk with three-dimensional details on the top, London production. (Photographs by Lynn Pecktal)

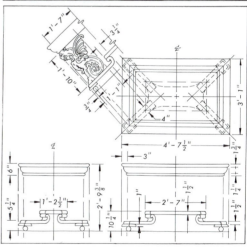

Table Dressing for Straight and Curved Tables

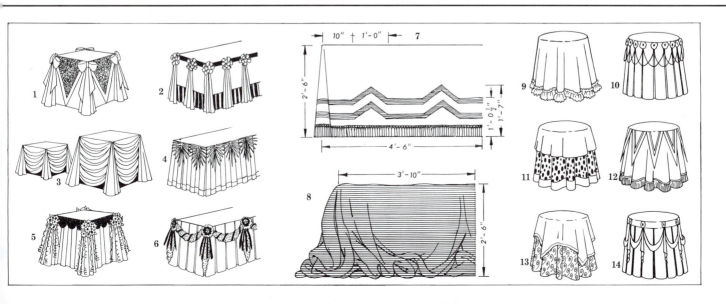

with the same 2-inch-wide strips and attach them at the ends of each swag. A cluster of bows also made from the strips is effective as an alternative for the rosettes.

Checklist of Types of Tables and Sizes of Tablecloths

BASIC TABLES

Drum tables	Square and rectangular dining tables
Gateleg tables	
Round pedestal tables	Console tables
	Tilt-top tables
Trestle tables	Drop-leaf tables
Butterfly tables	Tavern end tables
Hexagonal lamp tables	Writing tables
	Cigarette tables
Round and oval dining tables	Accent tables
	Candle stands
Octagonal pedestal tables	Console tables
	Nest of tables
Tables behind sofas	Square lamp tables
Pembroke drop-leaf tables	Tier tables
	Kitchen tables

COCKTAIL TABLES

Butler tray tables	Drop-leaf tables
Cobbler's benches	Oval tables
Trestle tables	Rectangular tables
Round tables	Square tables

Tablecloths

52″ × 52″ square	60″ × 102″ oblong/oval
52″ × 70″ oblong/oval	60″ × 104″
60″ × 84″ oblong/oval	60″ × 122″
60″ × 86″	72″ × 108″ oblong/oval
60″ × 88″	72″ × 126″ oblong/oval
60″ × 90″ oblong/oval	72″ × 144″ oblong
65″ round	70″ round
68″ round	72″ round

Napkins

18″ × 18″	20″ × 20″	24″ × 24″

Using Wicker Furniture

Whether old or new, wicker furniture works nicely onstage because of its lovely shapes and see-through qualities. The best-designed wicker furniture creates a quite gorgeous theatrical effect onstage. Prop collectors often find old wicker furniture that was made before or around the turn of the century in secondhand furniture stores. However, new and relatively inexpensive wicker can be found in various discount and Oriental shops.

Wicker furniture is used in both interior and exterior settings. It is appropriate in light and charming musicals such as *Tintypes* or in dramas like *Suddenly Last Summer* and *Long Day's Journey Into Night*. While wicker furniture is lightweight and easy to move, it is very fragile, especially if it is very old. Always remember that lightweight wicker furniture should not be used for heavy stage business.

Kinds of Wicker Furniture

There is a multitude of wicker pieces that can be suitable for the stage. The list includes settees, armchairs, side chairs, stools, folding screens, planters, and tables. Flower containers, mirror frames, and shelves are also available. Wicker furniture may be enhanced with solid or patterned cushions and pillows. According to the Gazebo wicker shop in New York City, and as reported in the *The New York Times*, wicker can be made of rattan, willow, rush or reed, and twisted paper. Rattan is a climbing palm with rough, slender stems, and rush and reed are both grasslike plants.

Repairing Wicker Furniture

Good wicker furniture has become increasingly expensive. A piece in good condition found in an antique store can cost from several hundred dollars up to a thousand dollars or more. In secondhand stores, sometimes a nice piece of wicker furniture can be found that is badly in need of repair. It is possible to repair wicker furniture and restore it to its original appearance.

A designer working in a regional, Off-Broadway, or university theatre may do the actual work of repairing wicker and other furniture. One of the most important things to keep in mind when repairing wicker is to match exactly the size of the various strands that need to be replaced. Collectors of wicker furniture can use badly damaged pieces to repair less damaged items. Various diameters and lengths of wicker and rattan are good to have on hand just for the purpose of repairing damaged furniture. Sometimes small sections must be woven in and out, and smaller diameters of wicker are needed to match original sizes.

Soak the lengths of wicker in warm water for a few minutes. Bend it gently to fit it into the curved area in need of repair. Use clear white Elmer's Glue-All to glue the new shape together. Thin wire, spring clothespins, pushpins, or metal screw C clamps can be used to hold the repaired area in place while the glue dries. When the glue has dried, neatly sand the area. Long, straight strands may also have to be completely replaced. If only a part of a long strand needs to be replaced, then splice in the new piece with diagonal cuts on each end, glue, and then paint.

Costume Design by Robert O'Hearn for DIE FRAU OHNE SCHATTEN (1966); Andrew B. Marlay for THE MUSIC MAN (1988); Zack Brown for ON YOUR TOES (1983).

Painting Wicker Furniture

Vinyl acrylic latex paint applied with a brush is good to use on old wicker furniture that needs to have a base coat. When brushed on, the paint helps fill cracks and cover repaired places well. Aerosol spray cans of paint in flat or gloss finish are especially good to use on wicker, because the intricate designs and turnings can be covered easier and faster than with a brush.

Removing Paint from Furniture

Found or purchased furniture for the stage often needs to have the paint or varnish removed just as furniture for the home does. The furniture may otherwise be in good shape except for a chipped or warped finish.

Every good prop person who keeps furniture in immaculate condition in the prop room knows how to take paint off furniture. It is really very easy. Let us say we are taking paint off a bentwood side chair. Materials needed are paint remover, a 16-ounce metal can and an old brush that will fit into the can, lots of rags, and protective work gloves. When working with paint remover, always have excellent ventilation or work outside. Never smoke or have flames around the work area.

There are several brand names of paint remover that work very well. Red Devil and Zip Strip are two good ones, and there are even more expensive brands available. Paint remover should be poured into a metal container (approximately 16-ounce) and the brush (an old one) dipped into the paint remover and then worked back

and forth over the surface where the paint or varnish is to be removed. It is simpler to work on small areas at one time.

After brushing on the paint remover, let it remain on the surface for a few minutes. Then use an absorbent rag and wipe vigorously over the area where the remover was applied. This process should be repeated until all the paint is removed. This method of applying the paint remover solution with a brush and then rubbing off the excess paint is far better, especially if the furniture is a good piece, than using scrapers, knives, and wire brushes, which can damage the wood.

Making a Furniture Polish

Once the surface of wooden furniture has been completely cleaned and has dried, the wood can be enhanced and protected with a nice furniture polish. A good furniture polish can be made with these ingredients:

$\frac{1}{3}$ cup boiled linseed oil
$\frac{1}{3}$ cup vinegar
$\frac{1}{3}$ cup turpentine

Mix these three ingredients together well and always shake thoroughly before using. Apply with a soft cloth and wipe the surface completely dry with another soft cloth.

Using Armoires

Armoires are tall units of furniture that function similarly to contemporary built-in closets. They are often used in the bedroom sets for operas or for plays such as *The Three Sisters* and *The*

Fourposter. Armoires can be modernized and used in more contemporary settings.

It is probably easier to build an armoire than to rent or borrow one, and certainly building is less expensive than purchasing. Also, the right size and appropriate period for an armoire may be difficult to find. Any armoire used for the stage should have swivel casters on the bottom so that it can move easily.

The way the space inside an armoire is divided depends on what it is to be used for. There may be only shelves or a combination of shelves, a hanging rod for clothes, and several drawers. Sometimes the panels in the doors on the front of armoires are removed and a decorative wire mesh or other very openwork material is substituted for the wooden doors. This open effect may be shown off to good advantage by arranging the objects in the armoire in an attractive manner and by putting small lights inside to shine on the displayed objects.

Armoires are ideal pieces for storing costume coats, dresses, trousers, hats, and other items of clothing used during the performance, as well as for holding props such as linens, blankets, and bedspreads. For a modern-day setting, armoires are an excellent place to put large television sets, stereos, record and tape collections, radios, and VCRs. Other prop items or set dressing could include art books, baskets of dried flowers, or collections of stone crocks, pottery, and the like. The doors of an armoire may be purposely left open in one scene to display the items inside, and then closed later for a following scene.

Costume Design by Peter Harvey for DAMES AT SEA (1985); Robert Perdziola for LA BOHÈME (1990); Gregg Barnes for THE WIZARD OF OZ (1992).

Armoires, Cabinets, Chest, Bookcase, and Other Objects

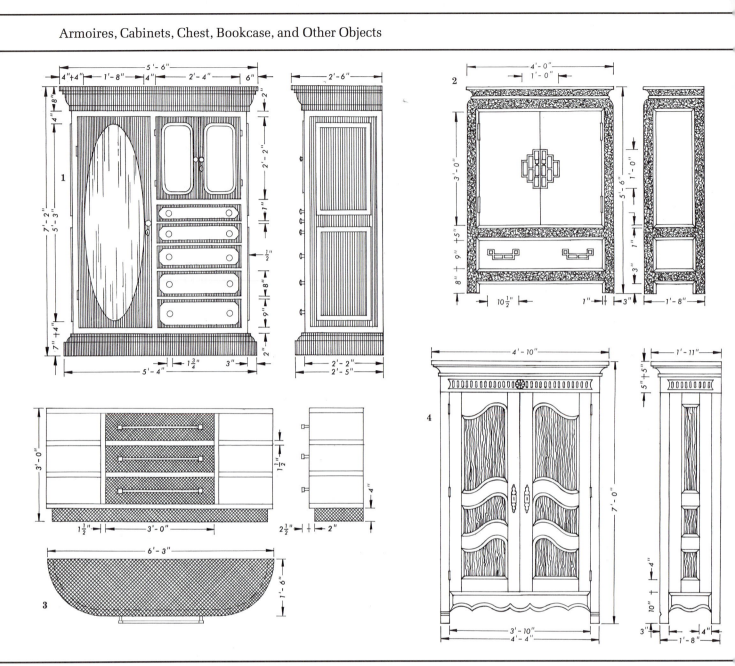

Piano and Musical Accessories

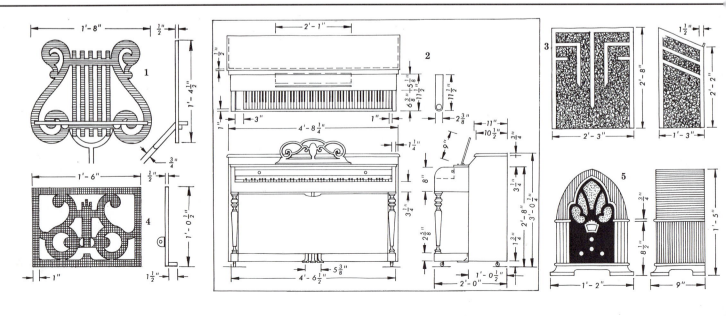

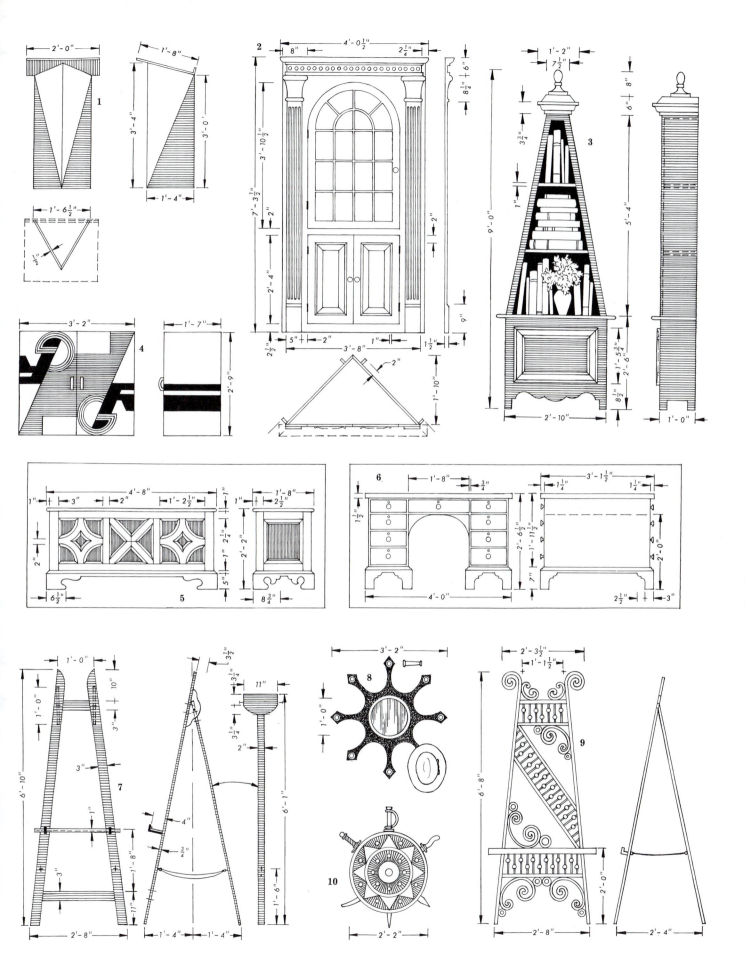

563

Benches

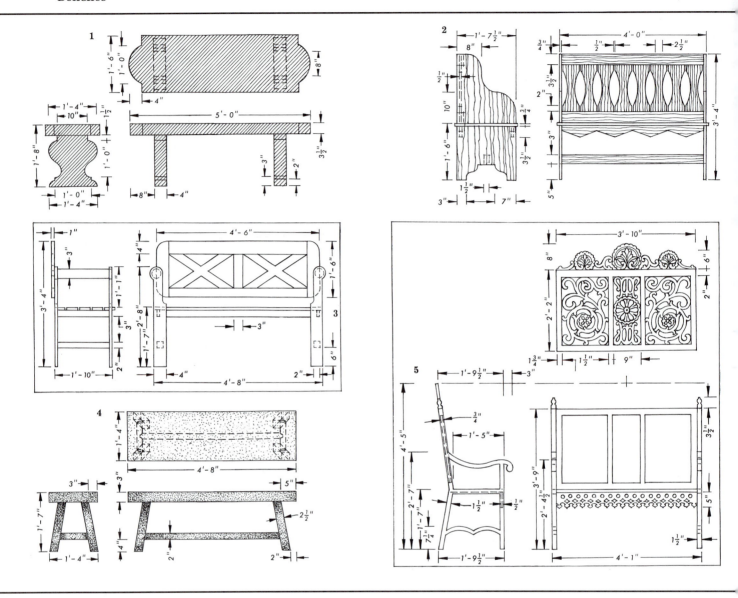

Stools

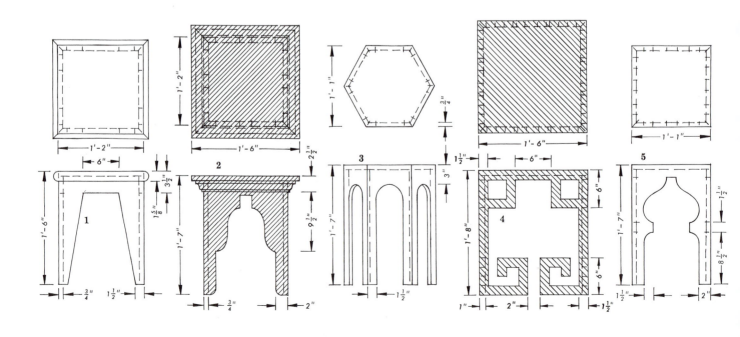

Window Seat

Bench Ends

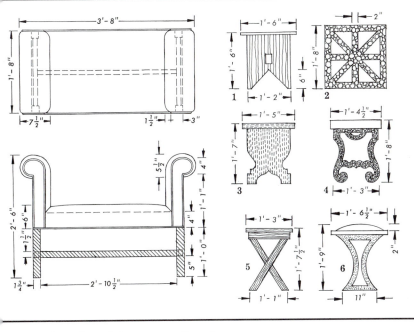

Church and Synagogue Benches

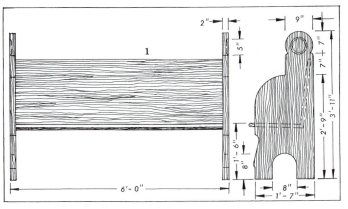

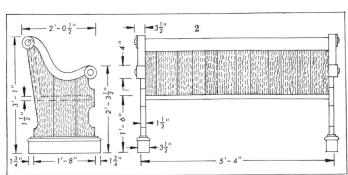

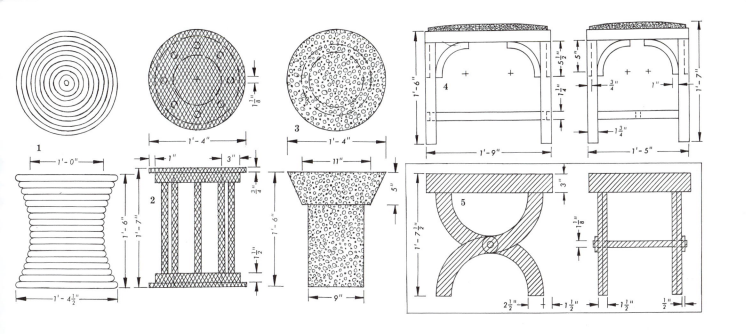

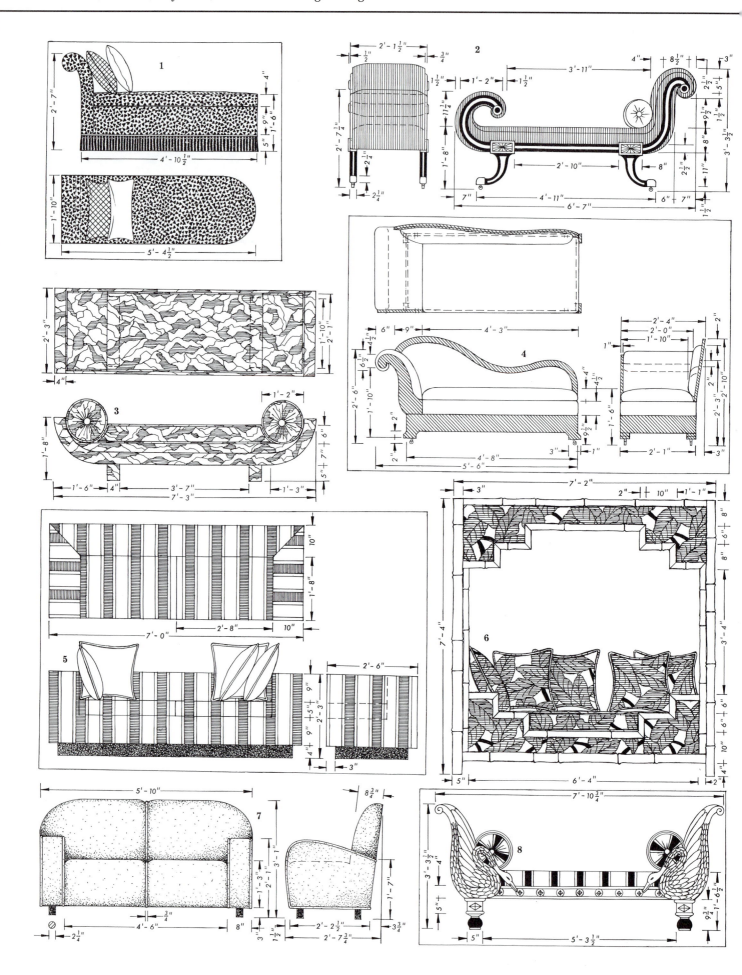

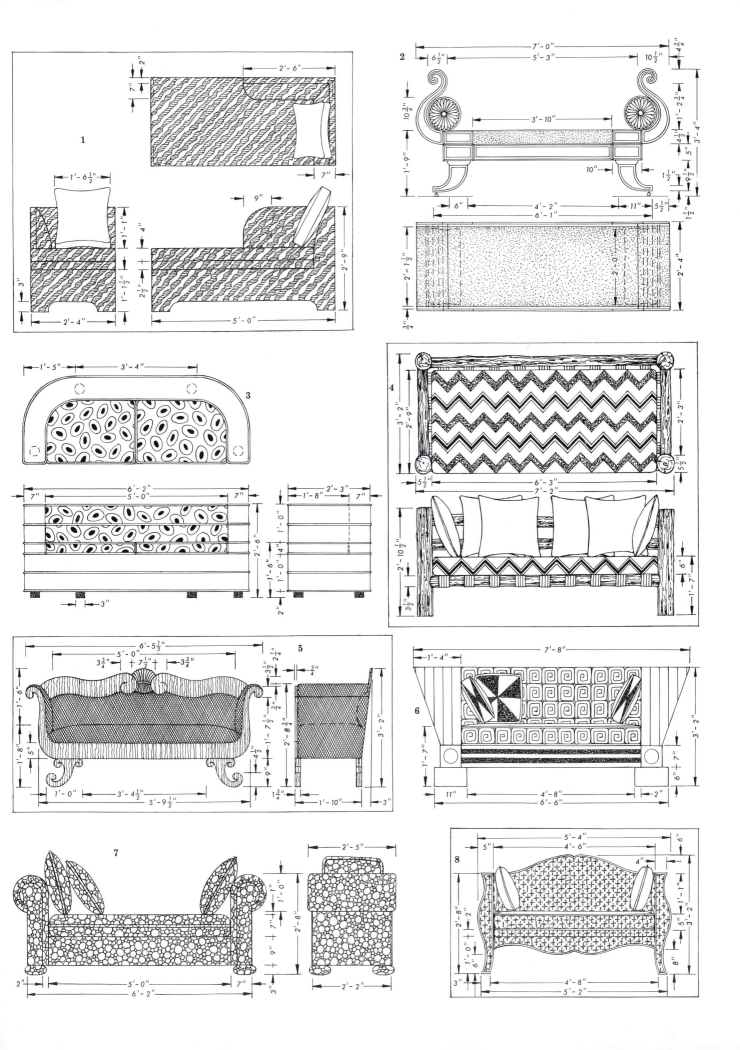

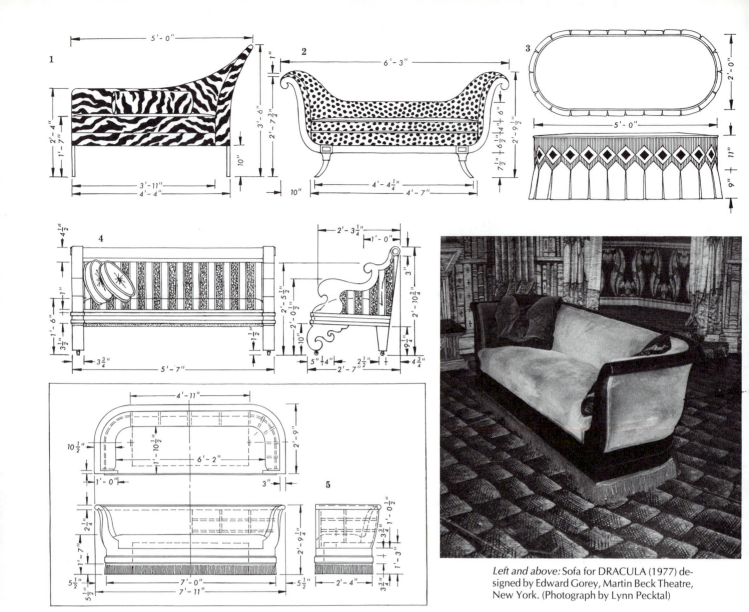

Left and above: Sofa for DRACULA (1977) designed by Edward Gorey, Martin Beck Theatre, New York. (Photograph by Lynn Pecktal)

Popular Overstuffed Sofas

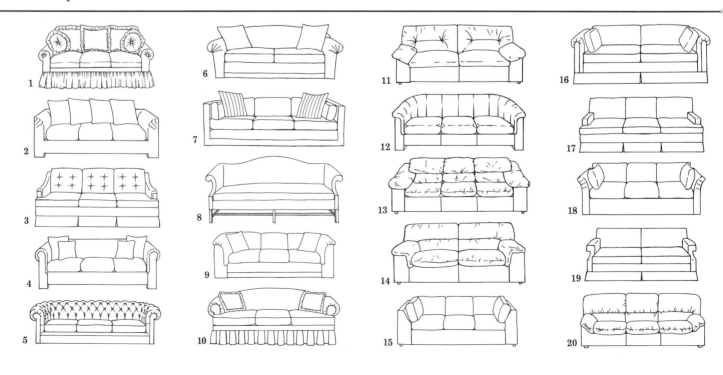

Seating Arrangements

Actors may use many different objects or areas for sitting during the course of a performance. Sometimes a highly creative director will prefer that a designer select or design items for sitting rather than using traditional furniture. A number of items are workable, including:

Chairs	Platforms	Rocks
Barrels	Crates	Blocks
Footstools	Pouffes	Kegs
Swings	Benches	Sofas
Stumps	Bleachers	Beds
Floors	Stools	Packages
Boxes	Ottomans	Beanbags

Selecting a Sofa

Finding the most appropriate sofa for a production should be fun, but sometimes difficulties arise because of the required size, style, or availability. Often it is wise to select the sofa early on, as a great deal of the furniture and set dressing has to work with it onstage.

While the stage director may leave certain aspects of the sofa selection, such as size, color(s), style, and shape, up to the designer, certain requirements still need to be thought out with the director. Some of these may be:

1. Is the sofa to have two or three cushions?
2. How many actors must be seated on the sofa at one time?
3. Must actors sit on the arms or back of the sofa?
4. Does the sofa have to be moved during scene changes?
5. Should the sofa be fully upholstered or should it be a settee with a see-through back?

The size of the sofa, particularly its length, may not be a problem on a 40-foot-wide proscenium opening, but it may very well be a problem on a smaller stage, such as one with a 24- to 25-foot-wide proscenium opening. For a small stage, a wise director will usually agree with the scenic designer and may go along with the idea of using a two-seater when it is appropriate for the production.

Repertory and resident theatres often have sofas in the prop room that are good scale for their stages and that have been used successfully several times over for different productions.

Changing the Appearance of a Sofa

If you need a basic sofa for an average interior set, it is usually a good idea to choose one that is covered with a fairly conservative fabric, especially considering its bulk and the fact that a sofa is usually positioned downstage and is going to be in bright lights. It is another matter when a flashy sofa is called for in a highly stylized production.

Designers working in a regional or university theatre may find that it is best to select solid or fairly dark colors for an upholstered sofa simply because the audience may remember a sofa with a prominent pattern and/or color that has been around more than once. For a sofa that is to be reused, a designer may want to select colors such as tobacco, wine, deep purple, gray, or navy blue.

These are some of the reasons for changing the appearance of a sofa.

1. To reuse and match the sofa with a new or different stage setting.
2. To indicate a passing of time in a play.
3. To use the same sofa in two different one-acts on the same bill.
4. To protect the cover on a borrowed sofa.

The fabric or pattern of the fabric on a sofa can be altered or completely changed with spray paints or a slipcover. When altering the current upholstery does not matter, fabric sprays and paints can be used to paint and/or age a sofa. The look of a sofa may also be altered with pillows and bolsters. Sometimes the basic silhouette (when looking straight on from the front) can be changed by adding a padded or stuffed profile shape onto the top of the back of the sofa, then covering it with the rest of the sofa.

When time permits, a sofa may be upholstered rather than slipcovered. Again, time, budget, and owner approval determine whether a piece is to be slipcovered or upholstered. While upholstering a sofa is often more time-consuming than making a slipcover, there may be a good reason to do it, such as using a fabric of cut velvet or brocade that would be unavailable in a slipcover fabric. Slipcovering mainly involves sewing; upholstering involves attaching the fabric to the sofa by tacking, but it may also involve quite a bit of sewing too.

Checklist of Patterns for Sofa Fabric

Stripes	Tapestries
Paisleys	Geometric patterns
Plaids	Floral
Damasks	Scenic patterns
Random textures	Brocades
Dots	Checks

Alternatives to Using a Sofa

Even though the historical period of the play and the concept may dictate the kind of furniture to be used, there are alternatives to selecting a sofa. Some of these may be:

1. Upholstered chairs on either side of a table
2. A settee or love seat with open legs and arms and sometimes openwork back
3. Two or three ottomans in a group arrangement
4. A daybed with bolsters
5. Benches
6. Module chairs and sofas

Corner Seats

Corner seats are simple, economical, and easy to construct. They work well because they can fit into corner areas where regular chairs or other furniture might seem inappropriate. Corner seats not only are great space savers, but can hold at least two actors at one time.

Corner seats are custom-made to fit the angle between the two walls where they are to be positioned. This may be the corner between regular flats, latticework units, or high platform facings. The angle of the corner seat is usually between 90 and 125 degrees.

Corner seats may or may not have backs. Area pillows can be made for comfort and visual interest. Medium-size tables (1 foot 6 inches to 2 feet in diameter) work nicely in front of corner seats.

The finish on corner seats may be fabric, wood, painted designs on muslin or canvas, Mylar or vinyl bands, or other materials. These seats may be covered like ottomans with a padding of 2-inch foam rubber under the muslin or other fabric. The front treatment of the seats may include box or pinched pleats, or the top of the seat may have an independent, sturdy box

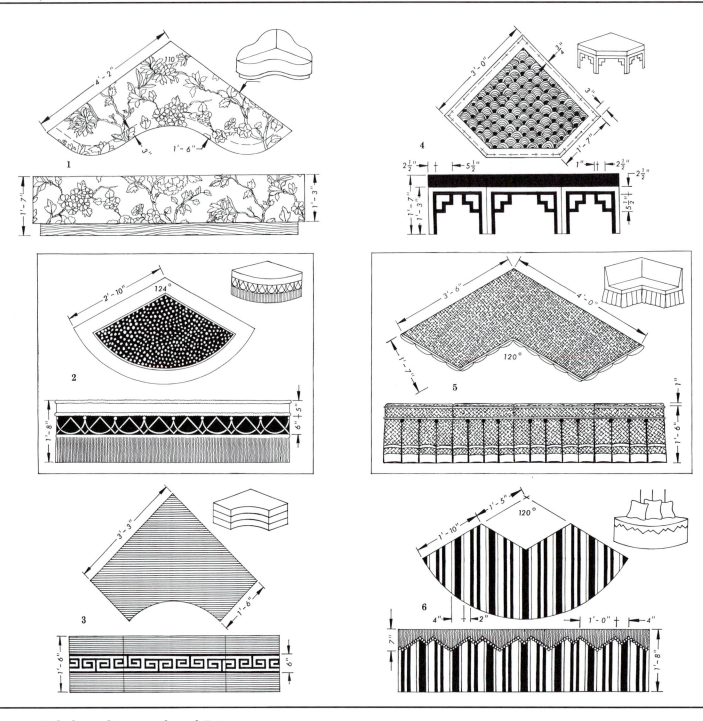

Upholstered Footstools and Ottomans

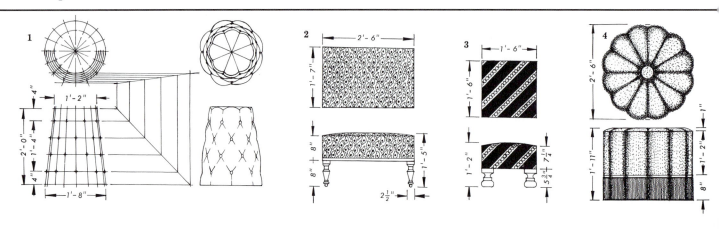

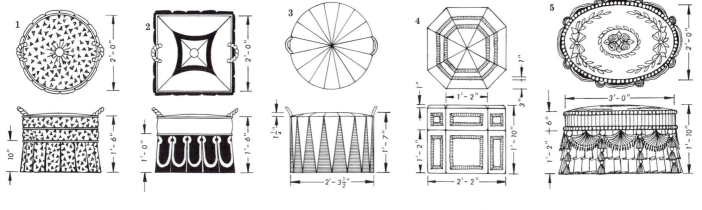

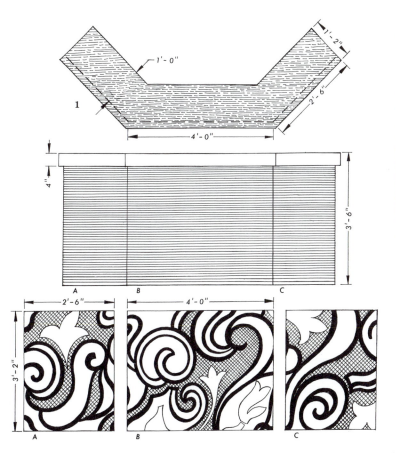

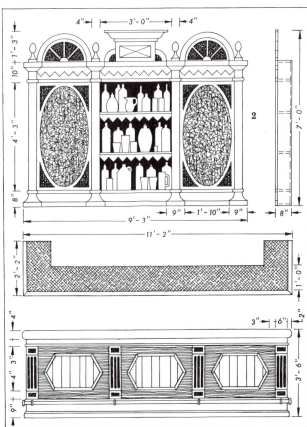

Finials for Furniture, Drapery Rods, Signs, Fences, and Grillwork

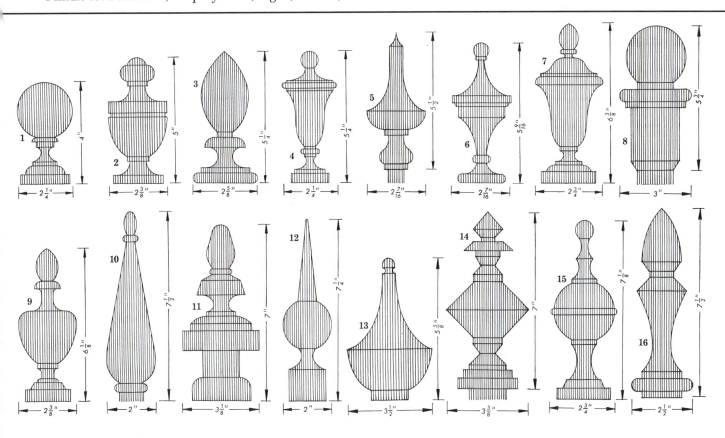

574 pillow with covered piping going around the top and bottom.

A wooden corner seat may have cut-out oriental designs on the front facings, or it may have panel moldings in rectangular shapes applied to a solid front. A curved front may be covered with fabric and given a Victorian flavor by using twisted roping in curved and zigzagged patterns at the top and long, thick fringe at the bottom.

When designing corner seats to be built in a shop, specify on the drafting to cut the top shape out of ½-inch plywood and mount it on lengths of 1 × 2-inch board. When pleated or gathered fabric covers the front, use 1½ × 1½-inch wood for the legs and use triangular bracing. Of course, the legs would be constructed differently when the front has a contoured facing that appears to be solid and hangs over a 4-inch base, or when the front has cut-out patterns in straight and curved shapes.

Making a Slipcover for an Overstuffed Chair

Slipcovers are wonderful for changing the appearance of a chair or a sofa. A chair may be used with upholstery on it in one scene and play in another scene with a slipcover over it. Not only can the colors and textures of the chair covering be changed with a slipcover, but the overall shape and appearance can be altered when the treatment at the bottom is designed with box or folded pleats or with ruffles or fringe. Pillows of contrasting materials can be a nice addition to indicate a time lapse for a later scene. The treatment at the bottom of the slipcovers may be made

Prop sketch by Oliver Messel for TRAVELLER WITHOUT LUGGAGE (1964), ANTA Theatre, New York. (Collection of Peter Harvey)

to cover the wooden legs and any bottom wooden trim, or it may be designed to leave the legs exposed. With a slipcover an old chair can be made fresh and cheerful. It may be redone in something like a patterned chintz, velvet, acrylic, fake fur, or antique taffeta.

The basic shape of an overstuffed chair dictates whether its shape, style, and size are suitable for a slipcover. Some chairs do not look right with slipcovers on them. An example of a chair that would not be suitable for a slipcover would be one designed with a combination of protruding woodwork and upholstery. The protruding wood under a slipcover would give a strange shape to such a chair.

Slipcovers are also an excellent way of protecting the fabric on a borrowed or rented chair, or of changing the appearance if the owner does not want the upholstery fabric changed.

There are several points to consider when creating a slipcover for a chair. Select a fabric with appropriate color(s), pattern, texture, and flexibility or stretch. Always purchase extra fabric so you can cut a new piece for an area in case there is a mishap. This is especially necessary when you have selected a large pattern and need to match repeats.

One of the most important aspects of making a slipcover (or upholstery, for that matter) is the process of pinning and cutting the fabric. While some beginners prefer to first make a cover out of muslin, others like to use a fabric with a particular pattern in order to practice working out the symmetrical patterns. Whatever the fabric, one should always plan on using a lot of pins.

A stage slipcover may be made in the same way as a home slipcover, or there may be shortcut variations in construction for the stage. For example, a slipcover for home use may be constructed in one piece (when it is all put together). It may also be done in two pieces if the pillow is separate. In the actual construction of the slipcovers, the basic parts of it may be put together by machine sewing the pieces of fabric together and working on the reverse side. While all of this may hold true for the stage too, it is not always done that way. For instance, it may be better to sew some of the large main areas on the sewing machine in the usual way and begin to put all the different areas of fabric together one by one directly on

the chair to see how everything fits, and then pin generously and hand baste with needle and thread. Then very carefully lift the basted cover off the chair and sew it on the sewing machine.

What really works well is to sew the pieces together on the face of the fabric without folding it over and working on the back side. This requires sewing on the cording (or piping) before the pieces are fitted on the chair and basted together, and machine sewing along the cording or piping which overlaps the adjoining piece. If there is no cording, then still machine sew along the folded-over edge of the fabric.

There are two simple reasons for following the above procedure when sewing a slipcover. First, it is relatively easy. Equally important, the slipcover usually fits better than when using more time-consuming and conventional methods, and therefore looks better. Machine sewing with matching or nylon thread on the face very close to the edge gives a very nice fit to the slipcover. Often the various parts of a slipcover have to be adjusted more than once before the proper fit is obtained.

A second approach to making a slipcover is to follow the same procedure as above, but instead of pinning and basting the different pieces of fabric together, just hand sew them directly on the chair. For this you will need curved upholstery needles to sew some of the areas. This is a quite practical way to cover a very large round overstuffed living room chair. The results are very workable for a three-week run in a resident company, but for touring and a long run the slipcover would need a sturdier construction.

While these procedures for making a slipcover may sound very time-consuming, there is the assurance of a good neat job, especially if a chair has a very bulky and difficult shape and a nice clinging cover is desired. This second technique of making a slipcover may be closer to being an upholstery job, but the result onstage is what appears to be a well-fitting slipcover.

Most slipcovers on chairs and sofas use covered cording or piping to add appropriate accent, point up divisions of areas, and give overall interest. Cording may be covered in the same fabric or in contrasting color. The same cording also goes around the bottom cushion and any matching pillows.

Upholstering an Overstuffed Chair

There is often a choice as to whether an overstuffed chair should be covered by upholstering or by slipcovering. Of course, upholstering a chair gives a more permanent cover than a slipcover. While the decision depends entirely on the individual piece of furniture being covered, you may find that some chairs are easy to upholster and for others it is simpler to make a slipcover.

The selection of upholstery fabric or material is determined by what is practical for the budget, how well the material will wear, and the amount of flexibility and stretch in the fabric. It is one thing to cover the flat and simple seats of Queen Anne side chairs, but something else again to upholster the many changing curves in the sides, back, and seat of a Victorian sofa.

A successful job of basic upholstering takes logical thinking. There is a logical order to follow in upholstering a piece of furniture, and in dealing with the covering material. The pattern and/or the nap of fabric must run up and down on the various shapes of a piece. Areas must be covered in a definite sequence. For instance, if you were upholstering a wing chair, the seat and the lower front portion would be done first, then the front of the back, next the inner arms, followed by the outer arms, the final vertical front pieces on the arms, the rear of the back, and so on.

Duplicating Furniture for National Companies

To maintain the ambience and style of the furniture in an original Broadway production, some pieces are often copied and built for the national touring companies. Because of special details in certain pieces of furniture, original ideas are sometimes needed regarding the construction. This was the case for the touring companies and the London production of *Dracula*, with scenery designed by Edward Gorey. Both the table desk and the sofa used in the library set had been purchased at antique galleries in Manhattan, and casters were added for easy moving.

Drawings in 1-inch scale were made for the construction of several pieces of furniture for the various *Dracula* productions. For example, the furniture that was built for the library set was the table desk, sofa, wine cabinet, and ra-

dio pedestal. All the bedroom furniture, except the bamboo chair, was also copied and built.

Full-scale drawings were created from the drafting (and some of the actual furniture) for the carpenters. While the sofa was duplicated by a traditional construction method, the table desk required simple basic construction, with special attention to resolving the duplication of the four three-dimensional legs of carved griffins.

While Styrofoam is an excellent material to use for carved detail such as that required to duplicate these table legs, it would not hold up well enough for touring (or for the run of the London production). A full-scale drawing was made of one of the legs, and it was decided that they should be made of wood. To duplicate the carved effect with this material, the idea was to combine several layers of profile plywood in various thicknesses that would be glued together to equal a 4-inch thickness. Each thickness of the four profile griffin pieces was worked out to be: $\frac{1}{4}'' + \frac{1}{2}'' + \frac{3}{4}'' + 1'' + \frac{3}{4}'' + \frac{1}{2}'' + \frac{1}{4}''$. For each $\frac{3}{4}$-inch-thick griffin wing (a total of eight wings), the two individual profile plywood pieces were figured to be $\frac{1}{2}'' + \frac{1}{4}''$. This made each leg, with the added wing, $5\frac{1}{2}$ inches thick. This created the effect of heavy wooden carved legs, and the wood as the material gave the strength needed. All the edges of the profile legs were well sanded to give the feeling of rounded surfaces. The overall table measured $4'\text{-}7\frac{1}{2}''$ long by $3'\text{-}1''$ wide by $2'\text{-}9\frac{3}{8}''$ high. In addition, the table was constructed so that it could be taken apart for easy travel for the touring companies. This not only saved space but protected the table's finish.

The sofa for *Dracula* was positioned to mask the upstage right trap door. The sofa was $7'\text{-}11''$ long by $2'\text{-}9\frac{1}{4}''$ high by $2'\text{-}9''$ deep. For the touring companies it was duplicated in the same size, but also included a cut-out open space underneath to mask the actor who played the character Dracula when a trap was unavailable.

For the production of *Home* (1980) by Samm-Art Williams at the Cort Theatre, New York, Felix E. Cochren designed several wooden boxes that were extremely versatile. The boxes were used separately and together for the many scenes ranging from locales in rural North Carolina to a very large city. The boxes with lids also doubled as storage for certain props.

Folding Screens

Folding screens are excellent stage props for any number of reasons. Not only are they useful in hospital and doctor's office scenes, but they can be part of the boudoir, the formal drawing room, and the actress's dressing room. Purposes of using the folding screen may include:

1. As decorative set dressing (to provide color, texture, line, and form)
2. To create an onstage area for actors to change costume
3. To create an area to conceal an actor
4. As an item to hang costumes on and over
5. To create an area to hold small hand props
6. To accent a certain area as a period prop or room divider

Materials for Folding Screens

While folding screens can be found in shops and used as they are, they can also be renovated with paints, fabrics, and trims. Or they can be made from scratch. The materials that can be used are listed in this table.

Framework	Covering Materials
Softwood	Canvas or muslin
Plywood	Fabrics behind and in
Metal	front of open frame
Wicker and rattan	Wood paneling
Bamboo	Painted mural
A combination of	Pressed wood
these materials	Plastic materials

Trims	
Decorative tacks	Appliqués
Gimps	Ribbons
Laces	Large sequins
Bands and braids	Discs

Screen design by Edward Gorey for GOREY STORIES (1978), Booth Theatre.

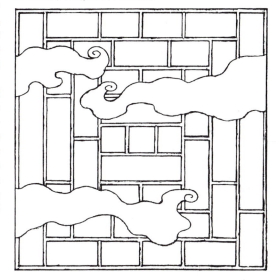

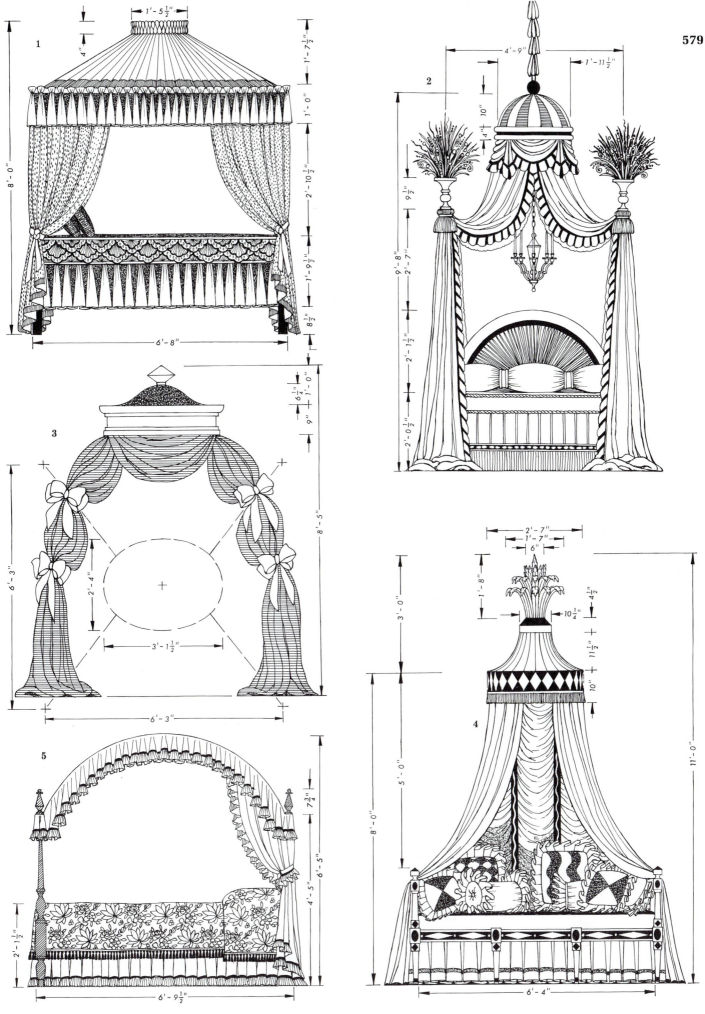

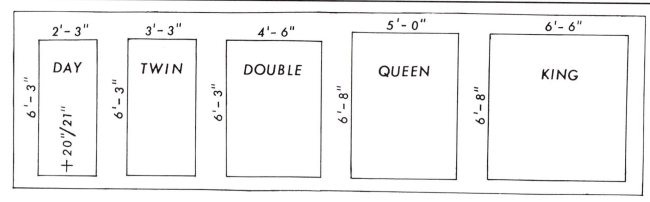

Day: 2'-3" × 6'-3" + 20"/21"
Twin: 3'-3" × 6'-3"
Double: 4'-6" × 6'-3"
Queen: 5'-0" × 6'-8"
King: 6'-6" × 6'-8"

Moving Folding Screens with Props

For a fast scene change with props hanging on a positioned folding screen, a small platform on casters may be attached from behind. The platform front can have the zigzagged profile shape of the folding screen in the same open position it plays onstage. This allows the screen to be moved by hand for a fast scene change, to carry costumes and hand props with it, and to always be in the same open position with no chance of falling over.

Bars and Counters

Like other scenic units, bars and counters for the stage vary tremendously in their design and function. You might create a chic portable bar with a mirrored front for a Park Avenue penthouse setting, and for another setting, such as the restaurant in Inge's *Bus Stop*, design a basic wood-paneled counter that is solidly braced for Elma to stand on as she recites from *Romeo and Juliet*. A bar or counter may be designed to have a simple canvas front with details painted on to make it appear three-dimensional; or, on the other hand, it may be designed to be built completely of wood with real panels and molding. It often works well to design bars and counters with a combination of both three-dimensional woodwork and painted details (using light, shade, and shadow) to make it appear three-dimensional. Depending on the script requirements, bars and counters can have shelves, drawers, and hooks to hold props of all sorts.

Kinds of Bars, Counters, and Materials

Bars and counters of various designs are appropriate in a number of different settings. These include:

1. A grass cloth–covered bar decorated with colorful paper streamers for serving soft drinks at a high school party

2. An oval-shaped Art Deco bar with a tufted vinyl front for a living room

3. A jewelry counter in a department store constructed with the upper two-thirds consisting of clear Plexiglas and the bottom third being of commercial prefinished paneling

4. A curved bar created with vertical lengths of bamboo for an outdoor terrace cocktail party in a tropical locale

5. A long wooden rectangular counter with matchstick paneling and turned wooden stools in a waterfront cafe

6. A hexagonal-shaped bar having open latticework sides with artificial ivy trailing in and out of the openings for a summer garden setting

7. A long straight counter with the face painted in bizarre abstract patterns for an open bar in a SoHo loft

8. A circular bar with horizontal strips of painted marble and vinyl in a sophisticated night spot in a large city

9. A large high table for drinks covered with red gathered fabric on which are attached garlands of holly with twinkle lights

Oliver Messel's Bed Sketches and Bed for THE SLEEPING BEAUTY (1976)

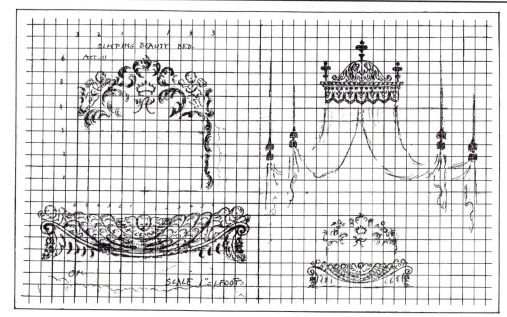

Oliver Messel's bed was created by gluing canvas profiled plywood and then painting it.

Creating Beds

Beds for the stage may be acquired from stores, antique and thrift shops; borrowed from homes, hotels, and other collections; or made from scratch. Like other stage furniture, beds must be carefully selected so that they are practical and appropriate for the scene. Among the productions where a bed is an important part of the stage setting and quite prominent in design are the plays *Cat on a Hot Tin Roof, Frankie and Johnny in the Clair de Lune, The Four Poster, I Do! I Do!, Dracula, Take Her, She's Mine, The Hasty Heart, Hamlet, Macbeth, Volpone, Sweet Bird of Youth, Bosoms and Neglect*; and the opera *La Traviata*.

Frequently, there are several reasons why it is better to build a stage bed from scratch. Among these may be:

1. A conventional size bed would not fit into the stage space designated for a bed.
2. The stage is on a rake or slope, or the intention is to design the bed on a rake for a regular flat stage.
3. Rather than a conventional size bed, a larger- or smaller-scale bed is needed for the particular stage setting.
4. The design of the bed must be compatible with the designer's concept.
5. A lavish headboard is needed and will be used without a footboard.
6. A firm support needs to be constructed under the mattress for the action of the scene.
7. A bed needs to be on casters or to be part of a rolling platform unit.

Bed headboards and footboards may be constructed of layers of plywood. All sorts of profiled designs may be cut out of ¾-inch plywood and then have the edges shaped with a router or by sanding. Posts, scrollwork, and other open designs may be made of metal. Sometimes cutout work needs flat metal pieces attached to the back to provide support for the cutout pieces.

Bed headboards may be made of wood but finished to simulate metal, bamboo, or various other materials. Headboards may be created in a wide variety of styles and types. They may be paneled wood with molding, tufted and upholstered with fabric, covered with vinyl or other plastic to simulate leather. According to type and style, headboards may also have painted scenic views, carved sculpture, or other details. Ornamentation may include carved Styrofoam or wooden finials and layers of designs cut out of ¼-inch plywood applied on the headboard surface.

When appropriate, canopies, tents, and bed curtains range from modest to lavish designs. Over-bed treatments of this kind are attached to the bed itself or to the wall in back of the bed. Sometimes canopies are also flown in to hang independently overhead. Draperies and curtains in a wide assortment of fabrics can be used to hang from the canopy. Scrim, chiffon, velour, damask, and brocades are popular fabrics to use for canopies and bed curtains. Ornamentation to be attached to the fabric can range from fringe, tassels, roping, and medallions, to tie-backs.

The framework for the fabric ranges from heavily ornate designs with statuary, urns, and carved elements to draped fabric swags and jabots to simple gathered pleated bands.

Checklist of Beds

Poster beds	Brass beds
Spindle beds	Tufted back beds
Bunk beds	Trundle beds
Spool beds	Tent beds
Bonnet beds	Murphy beds
Sleigh beds	Military beds
Dormitory beds	Painted iron beds
Bamboo beds	Wicker beds
Hospital beds	Ship bunks
Train berths	Alcove beds

Checklist of Sizes of Bed Coverings (in inches)

Bedsheets:
Twin flat: 70 × 100
Twin fitted: 39 × 75
Full flat: 80 × 100
Full fitted: 54 × 75
Queen flat: 90 × 104
Queen fitted:
60 × 80
King flat: 103 × 104
King fitted: 78 × 80
Cal. king flat:
114 × 120

Cal. king fitted:
72 × 84
*Standard pillow
sham:* 20 × 26
*King-size pillow
sham:* 20 × 36
Bedspreads:
Twin: 81 × 110
Full: 96 × 110
Queen: 100 × 118
King: 114 × 120

Using Pedestals

Pedestals are useful objects for set dressing in drawing rooms, libraries, bedrooms, salons, hallways, ballrooms, and foyers. Any number of items can be placed on pedestals. These include:

583

Edward Gorey's Rough Bed Sketch, Bed, and Bedside Table for DRACULA (1977)
The bed was made of metal and wood. (Photographs by Lynn Pecktal)

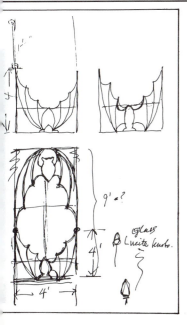

Statues	Candelabras
Urns	Flower arrangements
Vases	Busts
Potted plants	Stuffed animals
Lamps	Compotes of fruit

Not only do pedestals hold various objects, but they are a wonderful item to use when they are of a classical design and neutral enough to be used frequently in many different interior sets.

The ground plan of pedestals may be square, rectangular, round, pentagonal, hexagonal, or octagonal. Round and square-shaped pedestals tend to be the most common.

Building Pedestals

Round pedestals usually take longer to construct than square ones. However, a relatively simple manner of construction is to use a heavy rug tube for the basic shaft. A more elaborate manner of construction is to turn wood on a lathe to make the basic round shaft. Round shafts can also be created by using a vertical core of wood going through round horizontal discs of ¾-inch plywood. The discs can be spaced 9 inches apart. Then materials like sheet metal or illustration board can be wrapped around the horizontal sections of plywood and tacked to hold it in place.

Once the basic shaft is constructed, it can be covered with canvas or muslin before adding the base, top, and any molding detail. The base and top can be made of layers of ¾-inch softwood or other materials.

Lengths of flexible Ethafoam can be wrapped around the pedestal and attached with glue and small nails to create details on the round pedestal. Styrofoam and soft wood may also be shaped to form curved members.

Painting Pedestals

Pedestals may be painted with transparent or opaque colors to simulate wood, alabaster, all kinds of marble, and concrete or cement. The paint treatment may consist of application of colors by brush, roller, or spray. Paint from aerosol cans may be applied by spraying one color over the other to produce an interesting and variegated finish. Two, three, or four colors may be used.

Periods of History from *Elements of Design and Decoration* by Sherrill Whiton. Copyright 1951 by Sherrill Whiton. Reprinted by permission of HarperCollins Publishers.

EGYPTIAN HISTORY

1. Ancient Kingdom	Dynasties 1–8	4500–2445 B.C.
2. Middle Kingdom	Dynasties 9–17	2445–1580 B.C.
3. New Empire	Dynasties 18–25	1580–332 B.C.
4. Saitic & Persian Periods	Dynasties 26–31	663–332 B.C.
5. Greco-Roman Period		332 B.C.–A.D. 640
Alexander the Great & the Ptolemaic Period		332–30 B.C.
Roman Period		30 B.C.–A.D. 395
Byzantine or Coptic Period		A.D. 395–640
Arab domination		

GREEK ART

1. Primitive Period	2000–1000 B.C.
2. Archaic Period	1000–480 B.C.
3. Golden Age	480–400 B.C.
4. Fourth Century	400–336 B.C.
5. Alexandrian Age	336–323 B.C.
6. Hellenistic Age	323–30 B.C.

MIDDLE AGES

1. Byzantine	330–1453
2. Early Christian	330–800
3. Romanesque & Norman	800–1150
4. Gothic	1150–1500

ITALIAN RENAISSANCE

1. Quattrocento	1400–1500
2. Cinquecento (High Period)	1500–1600
3. Baroque	1506–1630
High Baroque	1630–1670
Rococo	1650–1750
4. Foreign Influence (French & English styles)	1650–1815

SPANISH & PORTUGUESE

1. Hispano-Mauresque or Hispano-Moorish	8th–15th C.
Mudejar or Morisco Art	13th–17th C.
Mozarabic	
2. Romanesque & Gothic	12th–early 16th C.
3. Plateresco	End of 15th–middle 16th C.
4. Renaissance & Desornamentado	16th–middle 17th C.

5. Churrigueresco or Baroque-Rococo	Early 17th–middle 18th C.
6. Foreign Influences (French, English, Indian, Chinese)	1700–1815

FRENCH

1. Early Renaissance	1484–1547
2. Middle Renaissance	1547–1589
3. Late Renaissance	1589–1643
4. Baroque Style	1643–1700
5. Regency Style	1700–1730
6. Rococo Style	1730–1760
7. Neo-Classical Style	1760–1789
8. Revolution & Directoire	1789–1804
9. Empire Style	1804–1820
10. Restoration Styles	1830–1870

ENGLISH

Early Renaissance (1500–1660)	
1. Tudor	1500–1558
2. Elizabethan	1558–1603
3. Jacobean	1603–1649
4. Cromwellian	1649–1660
Middle Renaissance (1660–1750)	
1. Restoration, Stuart, or Carolean Period	1660–1689
2. William and Mary	1689–1702
3. Queen Anne	1702–1714
4. Early Georgian	1714–1750
Late Renaissance (1750–1830)	
1. Middle Georgian	1750–1770
2. Late Georgian	1770–1810
3. Regency (Style goes to 1837)	1810–1820
4. Victorian	1830–1901

AMERICAN

1. Early American	1608–1720
Virginia	1608–1720
New England	1620–1720
2. Georgian Period	1720–1790
3. Post-Colonial or Federal Period	1790–1820
4. Greek Revival Period	1820–1860
5. Victorian Period	1840–1880
6. Eclectic Period	1870–1925
7. Contemporary Style	1925–to present day

Pedestals and Stands for Holding Statuary, Lamps, Urns, and Floral Arrangements

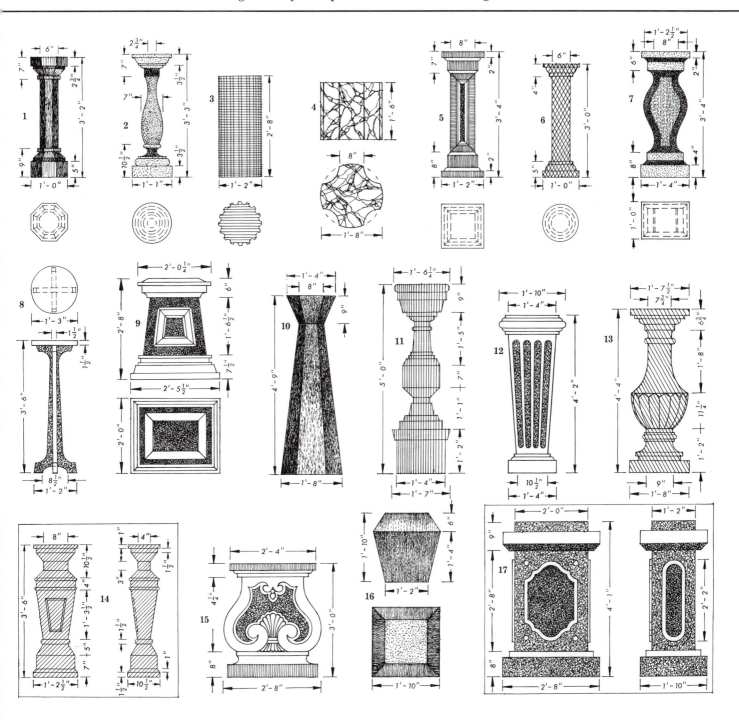

Telephones of Various Periods

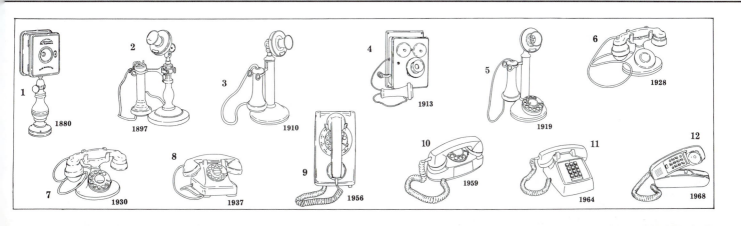

Settings, Models, and Designs
(*Photographs, clockwise from top left*)

Stage design by Hugh Landwehr
GLENGARRY GLEN ROSS by David Mamet
Directed by Gordon Edelstein
Capital Rep, Albany, New York (1989)

Setting by Loy Arcenas
SPRING'S AWAKENING by Frank Wedekind
Directed by Gerard Chapman; costumes by Catherine Zuber
Lighting by Beverly Emmons
Vassar College, Poughkeepsie, New York (1986)

Stage design by Thomas Lynch
ORPHEUS AND EURIDICE by Gluck
Directed by Stephen Wadsworth
Seattle Opera, Seattle, Washington (1988)

Setting by Clarke Dunham
MADAMA BUTTERFLY by Giacomo Puccini
Directed by Harold Prince; costumes by Florence Klotz
Lighting by Ken Billington
Lyric Opera of Chicago, Chicago, Illinois (1982)

Setting by Andrew Jackness
GENUISES by Jonathan Reynolds
Directed by Gerald Gutierrez
Lighting by James F. Ingalls
Playwrights Horizons and then to
   Douglas Fairbanks Theatre
New York (1982)

Setting by Loren Sherman
SHŌGUN: The Musical by James Clavell
Directed by Michael Smuin
Costumes by Patricia Zipprodt; lighting by Natasha Katz
Marquis Theatre, New York (1990)

Stage design by John Falabella
BLUES IN THE NIGHT
Conceived and directed by Sheldon Epps
Rialto Theatre, New York (1982)

Setting by Tony Walton
FOR ONE AND ALL, DIANA ROSS CONCERT
Directed by Steve Binder
Sheep Meadow, Central Park
New York (1983)

Model by Ben Edwards
DEATH OF A SALESMAN by Arthur Miller
Directed by Michael Rudman
Broadhurst Theatre, New York (1984)

Setting by David Jenkins
BETWEEN EAST AND WEST by Richard Nelson
Directed by Jack Hofsiss
Lighting by Beverly Emmons
McCarter Theatre
Princeton, New Jersey (1992)

Model by Tony Straiges
A LESSON FROM ALOES by Athol Fugard
Directed by Jackson Phippin
Center Stage, Baltimore, Maryland (1981)
(Photograph by Ney Tait Fraser)

Model by Charles E. McCarry
Project for a ballet, Yale Drama School
New Haven, Connecticut (1985)

I talked with John Napier about theatre and design in his hotel suite during a visit to New York City. Born in London on March 1, 1944, he was educated at the Hornsey College of Art (sculpture) and the Central School (theatre design). He made his Broadway debut designing the sets and costumes for *Equus* in 1974, followed by *Cats*, *Nicholas Nickleby*, *Starlight Express*, and *Les Misérables*. He has designed over 100 productions for all the major British companies and around the world. As an associate designer of the Royal Shakespeare Company, his work for them includes more than a dozen Shakespearean plays and also productions of *Peter Pan*, *Hedda Gabler*, and *Mother Courage*. In addition to the West End, he has designed for the Comédie Française in Paris and the Borg Theatre in Vienna, among others, as well as for opera, film, and television. Some of his sculpture was exhibited at Expo '70 in Tokyo. John Napier designed the ''Captain Eo'' video for Disney starring Michael Jackson, and *The Siegfried & Roy Show* in Las Vegas. Included in his numerous honors are four Tony Awards, four Drama Desk Awards, and two Olivier Awards (London). Among his scenic and costume design credits are:

Broadway
Miss Saigon (1991)
Les Misérables (1987)
Starlight Express (1987)
Cats (1982)
The Life and Adventures of
   Nicholas Nickleby (1981)
Equus (1974)

London
Sunset Boulevard (1993)
Miss Saigon (1989)
Time (1986)
Les Misérables (1985)
Starlight Express (1984)

Cats (1981)
The Life and Adventures of
   Nicholas Nickleby (1980)
Dr. Who (1974)
Knuckle (1974)
Equus (1973)
   National Theatre
The Party (1973)
   National Theatre
Big Wolf (1972)
Jump (1972)
Mister (1971)
Lear [Bond] (1971)
The Foursome (1971)

Cancer (1970)
The Ruling Class (1969)
Children's Day (1969)
La Turista (1969)
The Fun War (1969)
Fortune and Men's Eyes (1968)

Opera Companies
Royal Opera House
English National Opera
Glyndebourne Opera

Dance Companies
Sadler's Wells
Ballet Rambert

Designed by John Napier
STARLIGHT EXPRESS
Music by Andrew Lloyd Webber

Lyrics by Richard Stilgoe
Lighting by David Hersey
Choreography by Arlene Phillips

Directed by Trevor Nunn
Gershwin Theatre, New York (1987)
(Photograph © Martha Swope)

How did you first become interested in designing for the theatre?

It came out of several different experiences. I cannot say that I was an aficionado or a great theatre buff. I knew very little about the theatre in my youth. Theatre was a very elitist, distant thing to me. The occasional things that I was taken to see tended to be traditional English pantomime rather than straight theatre. I was primarily brought up queuing up at the local movie house.

I remember one incident when I was about fourteen years old. I was taken with a school party to see a film of Laurence Olivier playing Richard III. This entire cinema was filled with screaming adolescents who had been forced to see this film. The kids next to me had peashooters, and the girls were trying to get off with the boys, the usual mayhem like Saturday morning pictures. I was fully prepared to be one of the people involved in all of that. There was no halo around my head.

As this movie started, I suddenly got hooked on it. I recall watching something I didn't quite understand, but I was mesmerized by it. It wasn't what I would normally expect in the cinema. There was mayhem going on all around me, and yet I plugged away at that film. I recall the images to this day. So I would say that my first theatre experience, in some strange way, was at the movies. It was something to do with the essence of that kind of strange Machiavellian performance and the theatricality of it all.

Then, for reasons that I still do not understand, the tutor at the school where I was convinced my parents that I should go to art school. My parents are constantly recalling their conversations with that tutor, the ones that I wasn't privy to. He apparently said to them, "Look, I've had hundreds and hundreds of kids through my hands. John can draw, but what's more important than that, he has imagination. If his imagination continues in his adult life in the same way it has as a child, then he can expect to do something." Now I'm quoting my parents. They are not particularly artistic, so they were very concerned that studying art was either a dilettanted monied person's way of expressing himself or you had to be a pauper and live in a garret and spend all of your life in poverty in order to paint or sculpt or whatever. They had no understanding of that. But they

sent me to art school anyway, and they encouraged me, based on this man's appraisal of me.

I had no idea at that time of what I wanted to do, except that I had always been fascinated by using my hands in modeling things, by being tactile and developing things without there being a formula. I was never one to make model airplanes when I was a kid. I would always make something from string and chewing gum and Plasticene or whatever. I was fascinated by the whole idea of making something that wasn't already formulated. And to cut a very long story extremely short, I went off to art school.

Which school did you attend?

Hornsey College of Art in London, which was one of the top three art colleges in England. It was really during those years that I got an education. What I was given was a breathing space. I studied fine arts, primarily sculpture, the first five years.

There was a lady who taught pottery at the college who encouraged students to go to the theatre. Her husband was a theatre producer and a member of the Royal Court Theatre; subsequently one went to see things in the theatre through her good auspices. And through her continued encouragement as students, we'd get either cheap tickets or free tickets to other theatres. Something started to click, although it still hadn't entirely clicked. There was something going on that I felt I could be party to. There was a changing.

At the same time there was something happening, particularly in England, where theatre was becoming a much less elitist thing. There was experimenting with new forms, the growth of the Royal Shakespeare Company and the National Theatre and so on. I remember seeing a production of *The Rise and Fall of the City of Mahagonny* at Sadler's Wells which was designed by Ralph Koltai. I didn't know Ralph at that time, but I recall that production so vividly, because it was the first theatre production I had seen which seemed to be sculptural. It seemed to be using the stage as a space rather than using a series of backcloths.

I then finished my sculpture degree and I was asked to work for some theatre designers and some sculptors on a Shakespeare exhibition which was mounted in Stratford and subsequently in London. There were paint-

ers like Peter Blake and Sidney Nolan and theatre designers like Ralph Koltai and Tim O'Brien who were doing things for it. It was a marriage of fine artists and theatre designers putting together something about this great palette and this language.

Did that experience have a lot to do with your wanting to go into the theatre?

I completely got off on it. Here was something that was to do with the kind of things I wanted to do and with what I was good at doing, which was sort of playing with objects in space or thinking up ideas of how to make something come alive. I suddenly realized that I hadn't developed enough as an individual or experienced enough in life to continue to just do inanimate pieces of sculpture. And the things that I was doing were becoming inherently theatrical. They were asking for a reaction to them that was not one of an aesthetic of form, but an aesthetic of ideas and in some ways confrontational in those ideas. I was getting into a lot of conceptual ideas at that time.

You still hadn't decided to go into the theatre?

That triggered at exactly the same time the entire fringe and underground movement in theatre started to develop in England. It was like a sudden rush of adrenaline into the whole theatre system. Most of the major companies and the people that fed into that were the underground companies and the small fringe theatres. They didn't exist in that form before. In some ways, I took the easy route. I decided that I would continue my studies, but continue them now in theatre design, and while doing that, try to apply these ideas and the fine art training I'd had to find a new way of doing things. That sounds terribly arrogant, but at nineteen or twenty you are extremely arrogant and full of yourself in the arrogance of youth.

Where did you go next to study?

I went to the Central School, and I intended to leave after that first year. It was a very unhappy year, because it seemed to me that the teaching that was going on was far removed from what I was intending to do. It was partly because I had already had five years of art school, and I was leaps and bounds ahead of most of the other stu-

590 dents in terms of my relationship with the tutors. I wanted to ask questions, not just be told. I wasn't prepared to take stock formula. So I decided to leave at the end of that year. I had every intention of just forgetting about it and trying to make my way. And then Ralph Koltai took over the theatre course.

Did you decide to stay at the school then?

Ralph and I had a telephone conversation in which he asked me to come back to the school, because his intention was to do precisely what I was feeling I wasn't getting from the courses. I wanted to explore certain other territories, not just reiterate what had already been established. The sixties were a wild time, and any of us who survived it is pretty extraordinary, because there was some pretty strange thinking going on. It has all come full circle now. So Ralph convinced me to go back. And I had the most wonderful two years.

Was his approach to teaching theatre design a big influence on your career choice?

He was a huge, huge influence. We didn't always agree. We still don't always agree. But I think we certainly have mutual regard for each other. He's a delightful man and he was a wonderful inspiration. What Ralph instituted at the Central School was what really made it the best two years. He invited guest lecturers from outside who were in the throes of starting their careers or were established or whatever. But major people were coming in and giving their time for four and eight weeks. They were doing major projects with the students, so there was a reality about the situation. We weren't just doing an aspect. It wasn't just all theory. It was getting down and doing it. There was a thought process and there was at the end of it some kind of reality. You had created something that could work in theatre.

Were theatre productions also done at the school?

Yes. There were productions that were mounted in the theatre at the college. Ralph started this whole collaboration with people from Ballet Rambert and small opera companies, and there was much, much more. That has con-

tinued at the school until this day. So that's how I became involved in the theatre.

Have you ever regretted not going on with an art and sculpture career?

I think going into the theatre was the best thing I ever did, and not particularly because I have been successful at what I have been doing, but because I am still not sure to this day whether or not I really would have had anything to say as a sculptor. It's such a kind of introverted personalized thing. I still get terrible yearnings to do something that's completely private and that doesn't have to be compromised by having to fit into a situation. Maybe that's what I'll do as I get older. I'll start whittling at something.

How did your first show in London come about?

The first thing I ever did was for the Ballet Rambert. It was a very tiny piece choreographed by a delightful Japanese choreographer by the name of David Toguri. We just did this charming little piece. It was a very nice collaboration. Obviously, I was trying to do sculptural things and the dance thing at the same time. As I recall, it was just an aesthetic piece. It was done with ideas that I needed to just do.

The thing that happened after that is extremely bizarre. At the end of my second year at the college there was an exhibition of the work of the first-, second-, and third-year students. Unbeknown to me, a young director saw the exhibit and my work in it, and he subsequently invited me to become head of design for a provincial theatre. It was extremely scary. So at the end of that second year I had to make a decision about whether it would be possible to do this job and carry on with the schoolwork. I did fulfill my school obligations and took on this job. As head of design at the theatre I had to prepare scenery and other things for the season. Part of the work that I did for that period was my diploma show as well.

Was your diploma show like a thesis?

Yes. So it was like going to work and also getting some models together for the diploma show. Since then I've never stopped working. I can't explain it. I have no rationale for it. I don't even know how it works except by some

kind of osmosis or the grapevine or someone sees something you've done and you go on a roll.

Then what happened next?

I went to this provincial theatre and worked for about eighteen months, and then catastrophe! The theatre board didn't like the work that the director who employed me was doing. They found it too heavy going. They didn't want productions of Chekhov and Brecht or people like that. They wanted Agatha Christie and very lightweight comedies. It was a provincial theatre, but it had made its mark and was drawing good audiences. It was part of the upsurge of interest in the provinces and it gained a very good reputation. When the director resigned, it was obligatory that I resign. There was no way that I could do otherwise, since he had been so supportive and had given me the job in the first place. You have to stand up for what you believe in.

That very much meant that I had been out in the provinces on a limb for eighteen months, but I was doing something I loved doing. Within a week or two of that happening I was offered other things.

What were you offered?

I was offered some other provincial things, and I was also offered a play called *The Ruling Class* by Peter Barnes. It was the first play that I did in the provinces that came into the West End. It started at Nottingham and it was a big success in the sense that it was an extraordinary play and very bizarre and seemed to get a lot of attention.

Talk about your design for it.

It was a kind of multiset. It was meant to take place in a Gothic English country house in which this schizophrenic lord carries on. It goes from place to place in this country house and ends up in the House of Lords. There was a kind of nightmarish scene in the House of Lords in which there were banks of seats with encrusted figures, tiered up like grotesque sort of Gerald Scarf–type figures haunting this place. And I suppose what I did then, very unconsciously, somehow caught people's attention. At that time it was primarily from coming out of a sculptural situation.

Designed by John Napier
CATS—Music by Andrew Lloyd Webber
Based on *Old Possum's Book of Practical Cats*
   by T. S. Eliot
Lighting by David Hersey
Associate director and choreographer: Gillian
   Lynne
Directed by Trevor Nunn
Winter Garden Theatre, New York (1982)
(Photograph © Martha Swope)

Did that do things for your career once it played in the West End?

Without question. I was shocked at the time when it happened. When this transformation to the House of Lords happened onstage, people used to stand up and cheer. I mean they clapped and hooted, which was kind of shocking to me. It was embarrassing and also unexpected. I did it for one particular effect and it got another reaction. People enjoyed the way that it happened and what the final result was. There was an element of wit about it which people got off on. It was a very sixties piece.

One of your big successes was Equus. *How did that come about?*

Like most of these things, it came about primarily because I was working with John Dexter. We'd been working on some operas and on some things at the National Theatre, and *Equus* was one of the pieces that he was going to do. I suppose one of the reasons that he asked me to design it was that it was convenient since we were already working on an opera together. I sometimes have no illusion about that. But you know there is a certain element of fate or luck that goes with these things.

Equus was born out of very immediate thought processes. It was just those images that you know are going to work somehow, or they're what you have in your head and you either go with it or you don't. It didn't take very long to work out, which I think is self-evident when you look at it. The staging was quite complex.

Did you have a lot of discussion with John Dexter about how to approach that?

No, we didn't have a lot of discussion, but we talked about how is it that you could do something where you quite patently had to have an animal onstage, but it's not an animal. That's a theatrical device for which there have been many solutions in the past, but people always go on about the horse heads in *Equus*. To me, the horse heads weren't the key. To me, the key was actually the feet. It was the way in which those buskins only supported the front of the foot and the way that ran through the performers' spine up to their head. It forced the performers to stand and carry their bodies so that it gave the effect of the movement of a horse. I think if those horses' heads had been on the same actors with the same costume without the feet, it wouldn't have worked. And yet you could have performed it on the feet in the same costume without the head and still

have made it theatrically work, but not quite as electrically. It was something about the feet and the movement that did it. There was quite a battle to get people to go along with that. The choreographer wasn't very enamored of the idea when I explained it to her. I had to prove that it would work. So I cellotaped some baked bean cans to the soles of my shoes and stomped around the rehearsal room showing how I thought it would work.

You convinced him and that was what made it happen?

John said, "Well, well, we'll give it a try," meaning "All right, we'll pamper you for an hour, but it'll get dumped somewhere along the line." But it actually worked. Sometimes being persistent about things like that, being needling and not letting go, being a terrier at the ankle or something like that is what it's about.

You usually design both sets and costumes. Did art school have an influence on your doing both, or is it because it is the European tradition?

It is more the European tradition of doing both. Although these days I actually do tend to separate it more. At one point in my career, they were inseparable, they were one. They were the visualization of making paper come to life. You have to do your homework, but even if you aren't necessarily fully versed in cutting or in period what you have to be is someone who understands. If you're going to design an interior for someone, then you have to understand who those people are and what they look like as much as designing the interior. So designing the sets and costumes seemed to me to be a natural thing to do. It has certainly been part and parcel of my work. I've tried very much to do away with the idea of the separation of a scenic element with something stuck in front of it. It's rather the idea that what you're doing is creating a living and breathing environment, or world, in which something that has a sense of being is going to be performed. Sometimes it can work extremely well, especially when the people who come together to do it work very closely and understand each other.

You actually prefer doing sets and costumes when you have the time.

When I have the time. I will have to confess that I am personally less interested in costumes of a naturalistic period style. I think there are people who do it better than me. But I'm quite good at doing things that are eclectic like *Nickleby*, though it is a period piece. What you're after in that show is the bare bones of character and the way in which you can make people transform in seconds from one character to another, or in the case of *Cats* it is where you're actually conceptualizing a whole style in order for people to accept human beings playing cats. Obviously, there's a thread that runs through that to things like *Starlight*, which are just fun. They're just fun costumes. I like doing costumes when you've actually got to create a world for the performers to inhabit. I'm not so fond of doing just clothes. I've collaborated with a number of people over the years who are much better at doing that than I am. I'm not particularly

good at choosing buttons and collar shapes, and I get a bit irritable doing that. Some people enjoy it and love it and want to do it. It is much more strenuous to do costumes than to do sets. I'm much more at home in the physical world of moving objects around.

Tell me how you went about designing Nicholas Nickleby.

How something like that comes about is you get together a group of people who have worked together for approximately ten years, and you do it. You can rarely do a piece like that unless every cog in the wheel is being moved by another cog. What was so exhilarating and so extraordinary about doing that production was that each member of the team had complete faith in every other member of the team. Trevor Nunn directed it, David Hersey lighted it, I designed the sets and costumes, and a company of actors all of whom had been party to a season before and were, to a large extent, long-standing members of the Royal Shakespeare Company.

One of the great tragedies in American theatre is that that sort of ensemble hasn't happened here. If only there were something similar to a Royal Shakespeare Company or a national theatre institution in The United States. There are depths of talent and such exuberance here. There would be no problem in collaborators working together and developing ideas to the point where they are ready to be seen by a public rather than a group of people with money getting people together to push something onto the stage that has a name to make more money. *Nickleby* or some of the other shows that we've mentioned have come out of work of long-standing associations where there has been a sensibility among a group of people.

Nickleby in particular came at a point in RSC's history where the organization was going through very turbulent days in terms of monies and revenues and what we could do. We didn't have any money to put on anything. *Nickleby* was done on an extremely low budget, and it was written as the piece was being rehearsed. So when one is asked about how you design something like that, I would have to answer that you can only design something like that if you've done fifteen or twenty Shakespeare productions with

Trevor Nunn and David Hersey before. You have a kind of shorthand between each other and a kind of peculiar understanding of the space that you're dealing with, and how you ought to deploy things, and what the sniff of the evening is, what the small of the event is, what's the undertow of it, what's the theatricality of it, how do you present a novel that is three thousand pages long and tell it sometimes in minute detail and other times in huge bold sweeps? All those things were discovered during the rehearsal process.

When Trevor asked me to try to come up with something in which they could perform this event, it was using a combination of the experience of years and instinct until they started rehearsing. Then one applied theatrical ideas to that instinct. I mean, how are we going to do a stagecoach? Well, we can't do a literal stagecoach, and in theatre you don't want a literal stagecoach. But it could be done with people moving in period costume and the way in which it is lit says "a stagecoach." Over the hustle and bustle you can get five people actually building something onstage for these people to be then transported on that gives you much more of a sense of people actually preparing to travel, rather than having people walking on nicely with suitcases packed to get onto something that's already been put there. To that extent, it's just being inventive with the tools you have at hand.

Did you feel that Nickleby *was as successful on your part here as it was originally in London?*

Oh yes. I enjoyed doing it here very much. I thought it looked very good in the Plymouth. I was very disappointed with the subsequent television presentation that was made of it. It seemed to me that it was a purely theatrical event and to understand the logic of it you needed to be in a theatre. It didn't transpose to television very well and could look rather silly seeing a bunch of actors piling up cases onto a trolley. When you go into a theatre, once you pass those portals and you sit down, you have to go hand in hand with some kind of poetic imagination, because there is no possibility of being entirely literal or naturalistic.

That's the most wonderful thing about a theatre, isn't it? What you are doing is saying to an audience, "Come with me, come with me and we're going to investigate this. We're going to deploy these devices throughout the evening and you will believe that you are being transported somewhere." I suppose that's the single most important word in my vocabulary in terms of theatre designing, and that is believing. It doesn't matter if there is artificiality involved. It doesn't matter if it's fantastical. Even if it is fantastical, you have to believe in it. You are taking people into a magic place where anything is possible.

I'm becoming less and less convinced that the theatre is a place for dissecting minutely social problems in a documentary sense, in a naturalistic sense. It seems to me other media do that far better, because you can focus in, you can go into the eyeball, you can get to the retina, you can get into a twitch, you can get to the tiniest minute movement. In the theatre it always has to be broader than that and therefore by its very nature is nonnaturalistic.

I am becoming increasingly more interested and concerned that the theatre has a kind of flamboyant richness. I don't mean by that a decorative richness. I mean that it acknowledges that it doesn't have to compete with these other media. It is of itself and therefore able to have this linking of hands. This poetic imagination is its forte. You're not being fed domesticity.

Shakespeare, the greatest poet of all time, the greatest playwright of all time, can range from the fantastical to the domestic situations, but the poetic ideas, the verbal ideas always resonate. There are always counterpoints showing you one facet of a human being, then another, but in a way that it is bigger than talking about purely domestic issues. It has to do with the poetry of the soul.

That's really not my province. I'm not a director, I'm a designer. But my heart sinks sometimes as I wonder, Are we working with the phenomenon now where primarily most people who are working in it actually want to do movies or want to get on television? Do they understand the absolute fundamentals of it? Is it just a means by which you deploy your talents to become a mega–movie star or a big singing performer? And there are question marks about all of those things. Maybe I shouldn't concern myself with them, but I do.

Cats has been running on Broadway since 1982. Did you expect this kind of reception by the public?

I had no idea. People probably know me here because of three major megahits. But I am still the same person I have always been. It does change you in some respects, but basically I'm so naive. I have done hundreds of pieces of work in which I've poured my heart and soul that no one knows anything about. When I did *Cats* in London, I did it because Trevor Nunn asked me to do it, and it was a delightful idea, but everyone said it wouldn't work.

What was your main thought about the design?

The basic ingredient of *Cats* was that there is a danger of this becoming so twee and so pantomimic and so revue that we have to do something that is at odds with that. We decided it should be a bit tougher, a bit more street, a bit more punky. The cats should not be pantomime cats. They should be raunchy and yet streetwise and there should be something slinky and sexy about some of them, and stylish. So I as a designer got off on all of that. I don't think there was anyone more surprised than Trevor, David, Gillian, Andrew, and I when it was the hit it was in London. In those first previews or the dress rehearsals leading up to performance, we all thought, we have just about done it and that this is the end of our careers! If the truth were out, I think we were all in sheer turbulence, the same state that anyone else doing a musical gets into.

It was no different when we came to New York. There was more money. I enjoyed doing it. I got great service from everyone doing it, and made a lot of friends. We loved the general exuberance of the performance here and the talent that was many-layered, a great bunch. In London when they heard we were doing this show *Cats*, it was like "Give us a break!" I don't think *Cats* is the perfect show. I think it's a perfectly delightful evening. Its great success is the fact that it can appeal to anyone from three- to seventy-year-olds; therefore you have a huge audience for it. Some other shows are aimed at a particular group or a particular idea.

How would you describe what you did visually for Cats?

Well, it was really to create a place in which two things happened. One, that you could imagine that this would be somewhere where the cats would assemble—a piece of waste ground, very much taken from Eliot's poems, not the cat poems, but from the other poems. What I didn't want to do was rooftops and chimney tops and cats, but something that was a bit sort of funkier than that. I also wanted to scale it up and make an environment out of it so when those human beings dressed as cats came on, you were prepared to accept it because they stood next to objects that relatively reduced them in size. Also, if you're going to do a show in which there's no book, there's no idea except for about five songs, and you've got a cast and you've started to name who the cast might be, and a director says to you, "Design me a set," you say to yourself, "What are my options to be? If I design a junkyard come the day they want me to have Askimblishanks the railroad train, I'll have a train. I'll have bicycle wheels, I'll have old teapots, I'll have some dustbin lids, and I make a train." By creating a garbage dump that was fantastical, I was also giving myself the ability to improvise at whim, because anything could sit in that. So the humor and the wit would come out of when the cats have this thing called the Pekes and Pollices and the great battle. All the cats dress up and take the mickey out of dogs. They do that by making themselves look really stupid. They put sneakers on their heads with ties and things flopping down, and just kind of flop around, that kind of idea. Unlike *Nickleby*, I was giving a space in which a performance could take place, but I was also giving myself the option of improvising into that.

Almost exclusively, all of these shows we're talking about, and in particular *Nickleby*, *Cats*, and *Starlight Express*, there was no book. One did not know what the end result would be. There wasn't a piece of paper with stage directions written down or anything. There was a blank sheet of paper. You also had no idea of what the quality of the event would be at the end of the day. You just had to go in headfirst. You had to dive in and decide that you were going to do it and enjoy doing what you were doing. It's actually very rare that I've done things pictorial and once removed from the actual operation of rehearsal and what the directors are doing.

Comment on Starlight Express.

Starlight is a complete maverick. It's nonsensical, it's absurd, it's childish, it's banal. It seems to delight certain people and not others. It has several reasons for existing, a lot of which do not have to do with money, although I think that most people think it is to do with money. It was extremely risky when it was first attempted, and again, very naive. It's kind of an aberration. It has to be seen in context of doing fifteen years of extremely serious work. *Cats*, to a certain extent, is included in that. I mean work consisting of doing a lot of modern plays, new plays, and classics. There comes a time when you have to let your hair down; you have to be an absurdist. You have to do something that is risk-taking and not what people would expect of you, partly to just explore and to have fun. That was the initial reason for *Starlight* ever happening.

It was a workshop. It was a ludicrous idea that we could do this story about railway trains. It's patently absurd, but to me that's what's delightful about it. If you don't take off your adult cap, you say, "Oh well, you're never going to enjoy it," or "You're never going to get off on that."

Starlight was for me at the beginning purely an exercise in doing a music *event*, not doing a musical. This is often a mistaken thing, because I certainly didn't think we were doing a musical. I don't think Andrew thought we were doing a musical, nor did Trevor. What we were doing, we hoped, was a blending of a fantastical populist musical event that wasn't intended to move the musical theatre onward one iota. It was for all of us to have fun and be little boys again and stop having to be furrow-browed and intellectual and doing things that were "worthy." That's how it started.

My part of it was primarily a series of equations about how you could perform in a proscenium theatre on roller skates for two hours without just having to go round and round in circles all night. It's as simple as that. Then finding out the logistics of how you could do that. Subsequently that's how the bridge evolved, because to get from *A* to *B* without this continuing to go around in a spiral, you needed some way of crossing over.

Did you have to do a lot of research on the show?

None at all. It's absolutely out of the imagination. I looked at a few details of trains and then forgot about them. It was intended to be a lightweight spectacle, unabashed with no pretensions, and on roller skates, bizarre. To some extent it caught the popular public imagination and that's fine.

Would you say that your costume designs are more prominent than your set, or vice versa? Did you enjoy doing one more than the other?

Oh, I loved doing the costumes on *Starlight*. They were great fun. They were astronomically difficult to do technically when you imagine those people traveling around at enormous speeds. Modern choreographers always want people to be able to do everything in a conventional leotard, so they were all rehearsed for eight weeks in a leotard. And for *Starlight* you're trying to make characters larger than life. You're not dealing with a psychological human piece, you're dealing with spectacle and dynamics, and a plot of sorts. You're trying to make the characters big, and actually in some way give off the essence of what these characters are meant to be. The railway trains would be big and powerful, and the carriages would be sort of feminine and fun. The costumes were much more fun to do than the set.

The set was a nightmare because of the construction and technical part of it. *Starlight* was a maverick. It was out on a limb, it was a silly, peculiar idea, a dangerous idea because we could all have our legs chopped off. You can [go] on just being pompous and being artsy and being inward. Sometimes unless you just let it fly, you become dull. So it was a flyer like that and it took an enormous amount of energy, and years of my life. *Les Miz* was the one that came very easily.

You're saying that of the shows that we've talked about, that Les Miz *comes easy but* Starlight *took the most chunk out of your life?*

Oh yes, without question because it was to do primarily with the concern for how to design something in which people could perform safely. It had to be something that allowed them to go at a high speed all around the place. It was very difficult to do. And you see something like that and people react,

"Well, well, oh naturally you mean roller skates." Actually there are very few people living who could have done that show. I suspect that with *Les Miz* one or two other people could have done it, but not *Starlight*. It was a different kind of approach, a different kind of imagination, a different kind of ability.

One of the things that really irritates me about *Starlight* is that everyone who sees it or reviews it takes for granted the people who go around on roller skates. They have absolutely no idea of the dexterity of the actual physical things those kids do. They make you forget after ten minutes that they're actually performing on roller skates.

Was there ever a point on Starlight *where you or a member of your team thought that this may not work—not just physically but visually as well as aesthetically and artistically?*

Oh, of course. That has to be the case all our lives. You cannot ever do a show where you think, "I've cracked it." I go into pangs of self-criticism and loathing and all those emotions, and you wonder why you're doing things. We're just human beings doing things. On something like *Starlight* you have the added pressure of it being potentially dangerous. So that's your point of error and concern on something like that. As I said, in the case of almost all of these shows when we were doing the previews, I wanted to hide under the seats. And the same was true of *Equus*. Maybe because—I don't know. Maybe because it is totally untried and unproven.

Did you enjoy it more in London? Or did you enjoy it more here as far as the set was concerned?

I enjoyed it more the first time around in London. You don't really want to do two like that.

What you did in London as opposed to what you did here.

In London it was more complex and yet more simple. There were more tracks out in the audience because it was a theatre that you could do that with. There was less painting and less three-dimensional work on it. It was much, much more detailed in New York. What I did was in the spirit of the thing itself, which was crazy and nuts, and delighting in doing something that was over the top and childlike.

I suppose one gets terrible angst at certain things. When the Tony nominations came up for that year for the shows, ultimately you know what you've put into certain categories. It's all personal, and there's a huge amount of politics or whatever involved in those things. It sounds incredibly arrogant, but I was completely and utterly bemused as to why everyone else in the production team of *Starlight* was nominated, and I wasn't for the set. Even though I was nominated and won the Tony Award for the *Les Miz* set and the costumes for *Starlight*, it was slightly a thorn in my side, and I suppose it is just ego. I'm being absolutely blunt about this, because I don't give a damn who knows about it or whatever.

I've won quite a number of awards. I don't want to sound churlish, but the bizarre thing is if you paint something brown or you paint something black or you paint something gray, you'll win an award. If you put lights on it and sparkle it up, you won't win an award. I mean there seems to be a phenomenon of tastefulness which I find objectionable, and therefore I spoke up. I spoke my mind. I hadn't intended to, it just came blurting out on the award night. I was feeling quite a fool afterwards. Whatever happens in those things you intend to go along and be a good boy or whatever. It was in some

ways agitated by the fact that even some of the theatre reviews and critics had written articles the previous day mentioning the fact.

If you feel something, there's a question, Why do you do it? Why was that? Do you have to? And I say that simply because I do believe that there's a peril that lies down the road of this pigeon-holing what good scenic design is. I think there is something to be guarded against in the theatre which is what I call "Laura Ashley mentality." The designer is to beware of that, too. In some ways you should speak out. A lot of people don't actually have the guts or the confidence in themselves to actually ever do anything or vote for anything that might appear to be vulgar. There was vulgarity in Shakespearean theatre, and there should be vulgarity now. I don't approve of theatre that walks around only wearing one kind of hat subscribing to a particular kind of idea of a theatregoer being a forty-year-old university-educated male. I think theatre belongs to everyone.

I sometimes wondered why I've gotten an award for one thing and not for another. Then that plays out and you think well, it doesn't matter anyway because you are only going to believe in what you do, and it's of absolutely no consequence. It's rather charming and it's a delightful evening and everyone gets pissed and congratulates each

other and listens to these interminable stories, and it does the performers no end of good. If you are doing good work, you will continue to do good work. There are many great, great designers who have never had an award.

Good design is quite often about solving problems as well as what it looks like. The problems on *Starlight* were infinitely more complex than on *Les Miz*. I suppose this sounds pompous, and I don't want it to appear pompous, but a design for a show like *Les Miz* can come to you overnight. You have an image in your head and you go for it, and I knew I had an image and I said, "That's the way to do the barricades!"

There's one big problem in *Les Miz* and that is you have got to have the barricades, and they've got to be things that people can clamber over, they've got to be physically used. You can't use

Production designed by John Napier
MISS SAIGON by Alain Boublil and Claude-Michel Schönberg
Music by Claude-Michel Schönberg
Lyrics by Richard Maltby, Jr., and Alain Boublil
Lighting by David Hersey
Costumes by Andreane Neofitou and Suzy Benzinger
Musical staging by Bob Avian
Directed by Nicholas Hytner
Broadway Theatre, New York (1991)
(Photograph by Michael Le Poer Trench/Joan Marcus)

Designed by John Napier
LES MISÉRABLES by Alain Boublil and Claude-
  Michel Schönberg
Based on the novel by Victor Hugo
Music by Claude-Michel Schönberg
Lyrics by Herbert Kretzmer
Lighting by David Hersey
Costumes by Andreane Neofitou
Directed and adapted by Trever Nunn and John
  Caird
Broadway Theatre, New York (1987)
(Photograph by Joan Marcus)

an improvisational technique like *Nickleby*, because if you did the actors would be there for half an hour building the barricade before they get on with doing any acting. So I had to find a solution. The solution then in some respects led to the rest of the design. There are also images of Paris. I have been to Paris, and I had many books around just to refresh my memory about it. The use of the revolve is very much Trevor's idea, which I adapted insofar as how I wanted things to come on and go off. *Les Miz* was a show that was very very much in the history of the *Nickleby* RSC tradition in that all of us knew what we were doing. There was no question about that.

When you are preparing a show to go into the shop, what is your favorite way of working? Do you work in models or sketches or both?

Models. All the ideas are worked out as half-inch models. I rarely draw anything out. I get in extra help and have some assistants who draw things out. The models are usually as detailed as you can get. Sadly, none of them tend to exist after the productions have opened. I'm beginning to regret that now.

What happens? Do people cherish them and take them away?

I don't know. They get abused in the workshops. They get taken to pieces to get drawn up, and they disappear as various people work on them. Sometimes they get dropped in a bucket of white paint or something, all those things. One never has the time to reinstate them and rebuild and paint a second model.

Do you make all of your own sketches or do your assistants help?

What usually happens is that I work on the set models with assistants describing to them certain things that I want, and I will make some things myself. Then I will finish the detail. I do all my own costume drawings. I lock myself away to do them. I can't bear having anyone around, any interference, telephone, anyone over my shoulder, I hate it. I tend to work on costumes very late through the night.

What is the number of costume sketches you'd do for a show like Starlight?

Probably about seventy, partly because they're all individualized and highly detailed. It's not as many as some productions. For operas you tend to do the chorus in thumbprints.

How many productions, including road companies and foreign companies, have you had of Cats?

I couldn't tell you how many. There's only been three productions of *Starlight. Cats* must be in the fifties now, I should think. It's extraordinary. One has to take it all with a pinch of salt and one's not saying that these are the greatest pieces of work that were ever written or done, and quite clearly they are not. What is interesting about them is that they have resurrected a number of theatres around the world. Theatres have been reopened, theatres are being restored, new theatres are being built.

I suppose if I'm going to be on the defensive about things like *Starlight* and another production I did in London called *Time*, it is that these sort of hits actually are inhabiting theatres with huge auditoriums. You couldn't possibly do any production in those theatres that didn't have at its base root something of a spectacle nature, because they were primarily built for that. I'm talking about theatres that are over 1,600 seats and have always felt like caverns in which you are completely far removed from this postage-stamp stage once you get halfway back. They were always the venues for the producer who had a rerun of something that was cheap to put on and he would only go in there with a star, and he'd get a good turnover and he's off. The Dominion and the Apollo Victoria are theatres with no possibility of performing anything with a modicum of a naturalistic performance, or indeed anything that is remotely through any detail of sensibilities. So what I did with *Starlight* and *Time* was to make them into big events in deference to what people were doing thirty to forty years ago. That's all, but it's making people go to the theatre, and it's another generation of theatregoers.

Students always want to know how do you become well known and how do you become a successful designer and how do you make it work?

I've met people who've been so preoccupied with being successful that they've run out of steam. That preoccupation becomes obsessive and therefore that's all that motivates them. I think fundamentally the bottom line is it doesn't matter how clever you are, you've got to enjoy what you do. You've got to believe in what you do. And you've got to stick at it. You've got to be a trouper, you've got to be someone who doesn't give in easily. You've got to fight for what you believe in. And then things will take care of themselves. I think I have quite a strong constitution for just doing things and getting on with them, but knowing also that there are other things in the world.

Stage design by Carlo Galli Bibiena
(1728–1787)

COURTS OF DELIGHT
The Pierpont Morgan Library

New York, 1982.75:102
Gift of Mrs. Donald M. Oenslager

INDEX OF DESIGNERS, ARTISTS, AND OTHER COLLABORATORS

(Excluding captions and lists)

INDEX OF PHOTOGRAPHS

INDEX OF DRAWINGS

INDEX OF DIRECTORS, CHOREOGRAPHERS, AND OTHER COLLABORATORS

(Excluding captions and lists)